University Casebook Series

March, 1986

ACCOUNTING AND THE LAW, Fourth Edition (1978), with Problems Pamphlet (Successor to Dohr, Phillips, Thompson & Warren)

George C. Thompson, Professor, Columbia University Graduate School of Business.
Robert Whitman, Professor of Law, University of Connecticut.
Ellis L. Phillips, Jr., Member of the New York Bar.
William C. Warren, Professor of Law Emeritus, Columbia University.

ACCOUNTING FOR LAWYERS, MATERIALS ON (1980)

David R. Herwitz, Professor of Law, Harvard University.

ADMINISTRATIVE LAW, Seventh Edition (1979), with 1983 Problems Supplement (Supplement edited in association with Paul R. Verkuil, Dean and Professor of Law, Tulane University)

Walter Gellhorn, University Professor Emeritus, Columbia University.
Clark Byse, Professor of Law, Harvard University.
Peter L. Strauss, Professor of Law, Columbia University.

ADMIRALTY, Second Edition (1978), with Statute and Rule Supplement

Jo Desha Lucas, Professor of Law, University of Chicago.

ADVOCACY, see also Lawyering Process

AGENCY, see also Enterprise Organization

AGENCY—PARTNERSHIPS, Third Edition (1982)

Abridgement from Conard, Knauss & Siegel's Enterprise Organization, Third Edition.

ANTITRUST: FREE ENTERPRISE AND ECONOMIC ORGANIZATION, Sixth Edition (1983), with 1983 Problems in Antitrust Supplement and 1985 Case Supplement

Louis B. Schwartz, Professor of Law, University of Pennsylvania.
John J. Flynn, Professor of Law, University of Utah.
Harry First, Professor of Law, New York University.

BANKRUPTCY (1985)

Robert L. Jordan, Professor of Law, University of California, Los Angeles.
William D. Warren, Professor of Law, University of California, Los Angeles.

BUSINESS ORGANIZATION, see also Enterprise Organization

BUSINESS PLANNING, Temporary Second Edition (1984)

David R. Herwitz, Professor of Law, Harvard University.

BUSINESS TORTS (1972)

Milton Handler, Professor of Law Emeritus, Columbia University.

CHILDREN IN THE LEGAL SYSTEM (1983)

Walter Wadlington, Professor of Law, University of Virginia.
Charles H. Whitebread, Professor of Law, University of Southern California.
Samuel Davis, Professor of Law, University of Georgia.

CIVIL PROCEDURE, see Procedure

CLINIC, see also Lawyering Process

COMMERCIAL LAW (1983) with 1986 Bankruptcy Supplement

Robert L. Jordan, Professor of Law, University of California, Los Angeles.
William D. Warren, Professor of Law, University of California, Los Angeles.

COMMERCIAL LAW, CASES & MATERIALS ON, Fourth Edition (1985)

E. Allan Farnsworth, Professor of Law, Columbia University.
John Honnold, Professor of Law, University of Pennsylvania.

COMMERCIAL PAPER, Third Edition (1984)

E. Allan Farnsworth, Professor of Law, Columbia University.

COMMERCIAL PAPER (1983) (Reprinted from COMMERCIAL LAW)

Robert L. Jordan, Professor of Law, University of California, Los Angeles.
William D. Warren, Professor of Law, University of California, Los Angeles.

COMMERCIAL PAPER AND BANK DEPOSITS AND COLLECTIONS (1967), with Statutory Supplement

William D. Hawkland, Professor of Law, University of Illinois.

COMMERCIAL TRANSACTIONS—Principles and Policies (1982)

Alan Schwartz, Professor of Law, University of Southern California.
Robert E. Scott, Professor of Law, University of Virginia.

COMPARATIVE LAW, Fourth Edition (1980)

Rudolf B. Schlesinger, Professor of Law, Hastings College of the Law.

COMPETITIVE PROCESS, LEGAL REGULATION OF THE, Third Edition (1986), with Selected Statutes Supplement

Edmund W. Kitch, Professor of Law, University of Virginia.
Harvey S. Perlman, Dean of the Law School, University of Nebraska.

CONFLICT OF LAWS, Eighth Edition (1984)

Willis L. M. Reese, Professor of Law, Columbia University.
Maurice Rosenberg, Professor of Law, Columbia University.

CONSTITUTIONAL LAW, Seventh Edition (1985), with 1985 Supplement

Edward L. Barrett, Jr., Professor of Law, University of California, Davis.
William Cohen, Professor of Law, Stanford University.

CONSTITUTIONAL LAW, CIVIL LIBERTY AND INDIVIDUAL RIGHTS, Second Edition (1982), with 1985 Supplement

William Cohen, Professor of Law, Stanford University.
John Kaplan, Professor of Law, Stanford University.

CONSTITUTIONAL LAW, Eleventh Edition (1985), with 1985 Supplement (Supplement edited in association with Frederick F. Schauer, Professor of Law, University of Michigan)

Gerald Gunther, Professor of Law, Stanford University.

UNIVERSITY CASEBOOK SERIES—Continued

CONSTITUTIONAL LAW, INDIVIDUAL RIGHTS IN, Fourth Edition (1986), (Reprinted from CONSTITUTIONAL LAW, Eleventh Edition), with 1985 Supplement (Supplement edited in association with Frederick F. Schauer, Professor of Law, University of Michigan)

Gerald Gunther, Professor of Law, Stanford University.

CONSUMER TRANSACTIONS (1983), with Selected Statutes and Regulations Supplement

Michael M. Greenfield, Professor of Law, Washington University.

CONTRACT LAW AND ITS APPLICATION, Third Edition (1983)

The late Addison Mueller, Professor of Law, University of California, Los Angeles.
Arthur I. Rosett, Professor of Law, University of California, Los Angeles.
Gerald P. Lopez, Professor of Law, University of California, Los Angeles.

CONTRACT LAW, STUDIES IN, Third Edition (1984)

Edward J. Murphy, Professor of Law, University of Notre Dame.
Richard E. Speidel, Professor of Law, Northwestern University.

CONTRACTS, Fourth Edition (1982)

John P. Dawson, Professor of Law Emeritus, Harvard University.
William Burnett Harvey, Professor of Law and Political Science, Boston University.
Stanley D. Henderson, Professor of Law, University of Virginia.

CONTRACTS, Third Edition (1980), with Statutory Supplement

E. Allan Farnsworth, Professor of Law, Columbia University.
William F. Young, Professor of Law, Columbia University.

CONTRACTS, Second Edition (1978), with Statutory and Administrative Law Supplement (1978)

Ian R. Macneil, Professor of Law, Cornell University.

COPYRIGHT, PATENTS AND TRADEMARKS, see also Competitive Process; see also Selected Statutes and International Agreements

COPYRIGHT, PATENT, TRADEMARK AND RELATED STATE DOCTRINES, Second Edition (1981), with 1985 Case Supplement, 1986 Selected Statutes Supplement and 1981 Problem Supplement

Paul Goldstein, Professor of Law, Stanford University.

COPYRIGHT, Unfair Competition, and Other Topics Bearing on the Protection of Literary, Musical, and Artistic Works, Fourth Edition (1985), with 1985 Statutory Supplement

Ralph S. Brown, Jr., Professor of Law, Yale University.
Robert C. Denicola, Professor of Law, University of Nebraska.

CORPORATE ACQUISITIONS, The Law and Finance of (1986)

Ronald J. Gilson, Professor of Law, Stanford University.

CORPORATE FINANCE, Second Edition (1979), with 1984 Supplement

Victor Brudney, Professor of Law, Harvard University.
Marvin A. Chirelstein, Professor of Law, Columbia University.

CORPORATE READJUSTMENTS AND REORGANIZATIONS (1976)

Walter J. Blum, Professor of Law, University of Chicago.
Stanley A. Kaplan, Professor of Law, University of Chicago.

UNIVERSITY CASEBOOK SERIES—Continued

EQUITY, see also Remedies

EQUITY, RESTITUTION AND DAMAGES, Second Edition (1974)

Robert Childres, late Professor of Law, Northwestern University.
William F. Johnson, Jr., Professor of Law, New York University.

ESTATE PLANNING, Second Edition (1982), with 1985 Case, Text and Documentary Supplement

David Westfall, Professor of Law, Harvard University.

ETHICS, see Legal Profession, and Professional Responsibility

ETHICS AND PROFESSIONAL RESPONSIBILITY (1981) (Reprinted from THE LAWYERING PROCESS)

Gary Bellow, Professor of Law, Harvard University.
Bea Moulton, Legal Services Corporation.

EVIDENCE, Fifth Edition (1984)

John Kaplan, Professor of Law, Stanford University.
Jon R. Waltz, Professor of Law, Northwestern University.

EVIDENCE, Seventh Edition (1983) with Rules and Statute Supplement (1984)

Jack B. Weinstein, Chief Judge, United States District Court.
John H. Mansfield, Professor of Law, Harvard University.
Norman Abrams, Professor of Law, University of California, Los Angeles.
Margaret Berger, Professor of Law, Brooklyn Law School.

FAMILY LAW, see also Domestic Relations

FAMILY LAW Second Edition (1985)

Judith C. Areen, Professor of Law, Georgetown University.

FAMILY LAW AND CHILDREN IN THE LEGAL SYSTEM, STATUTORY MATERIALS (1981)

Walter Wadlington, Professor of Law, University of Virginia.

FEDERAL COURTS, Seventh Edition (1982), with 1985 Supplement

Charles T. McCormick, late Professor of Law, University of Texas.
James H. Chadbourn, late Professor of Law, Harvard University.
Charles Alan Wright, Professor of Law, University of Texas.

FEDERAL COURTS AND THE FEDERAL SYSTEM, Hart and Wechsler's Second Edition (1973), with 1981 Supplement

Paul M. Bator, Professor of Law, Harvard University.
Paul J. Mishkin, Professor of Law, University of California, Berkeley.
David L. Shapiro, Professor of Law, Harvard University.
Herbert Wechsler, Professor of Law, Columbia University.

FEDERAL PUBLIC LAND AND RESOURCES LAW (1981), with 1983 Case Supplement and 1984 Statutory Supplement

George C. Coggins, Professor of Law, University of Kansas.
Charles F. Wilkinson, Professor of Law, University of Oregon.

FEDERAL RULES OF CIVIL PROCEDURE, 1984 Edition

FEDERAL TAXATION, see Taxation

FOOD AND DRUG LAW (1980), with Statutory Supplement

Richard A. Merrill, Dean of the School of Law, University of Virginia.
Peter Barton Hutt, Esq.

UNIVERSITY CASEBOOK SERIES—Continued

FUTURE INTERESTS (1958)

Philip Mechem, late Professor of Law Emeritus, University of Pennsylvania.

FUTURE INTERESTS (1970)

Howard R. Williams, Professor of Law, Stanford University.

FUTURE INTERESTS AND ESTATE PLANNING (1961), with 1962 Supplement

W. Barton Leach, late Professor of Law, Harvard University.
James K. Logan, formerly Dean of the Law School, University of Kansas.

GOVERNMENT CONTRACTS, FEDERAL, Successor Edition (1985)

John W. Whelan, Professor of Law, Hastings College of the Law.

GOVERNMENT REGULATION: FREE ENTERPRISE AND ECONOMIC ORGANI-ZATION, Sixth Edition (1985)

Louis B. Schwartz, Professor of Law, University of Pennsylvania.
John J. Flynn, Professor of Law, University of Utah.
Harry First, Professor of Law, New York University.

HINCKLEY JOHN W., TRIAL OF: A Case Study of the Insanity Defense

Peter W. Low, Professor of Law, University of Virginia.
John C. Jeffries, Jr., Professor of Law, University of Virginia.
Richard C. Bonnie, Professor of Law, University of Virginia.

INJUNCTIONS, Second Edition (1984)

Owen M. Fiss, Professor of Law, Yale University.
Doug Rendleman, Professor of Law, College of William and Mary.

INSTITUTIONAL INVESTORS, 1978

David L. Ratner, Professor of Law, Cornell University.

INSURANCE, Second Edition (1985)

William F. Young, Professor of Law, Columbia University.
Eric M. Holmes, Professor of Law, University of Georgia.

INTERNATIONAL LAW, see also Transnational Legal Problems, Transnational Business Problems, and United Nations Law

INTERNATIONAL LAW IN CONTEMPORARY PERSPECTIVE (1981), with Essay Supplement

Myres S. McDougal, Professor of Law, Yale University.
W. Michael Reisman, Professor of Law, Yale University.

INTERNATIONAL LEGAL SYSTEM, Second Edition (1981), with Documentary Supplement

Joseph Modeste Sweeney, Professor of Law, Tulane University.
Covey T. Oliver, Professor of Law, University of Pennsylvania.
Noyes E. Leech, Professor of Law, University of Pennsylvania.

INTRODUCTION TO LAW, see also Legal Method, On Law in Courts, and Dynamics of American Law

INTRODUCTION TO THE STUDY OF LAW (1970)

E. Wayne Thode, late Professor of Law, University of Utah.
Leon Lebowitz, Professor of Law, University of Texas.
Lester J. Mazor, Professor of Law, University of Utah.

UNIVERSITY CASEBOOK SERIES—Continued

JUDICIAL CODE and Rules of Procedure in the Federal Courts with Excerpts from the Criminal Code, 1984 Edition

Henry M. Hart, Jr., late Professor of Law, Harvard University.
Herbert Wechsler, Professor of Law, Columbia University.

JURISPRUDENCE (Temporary Edition Hardbound) (1949)

Lon L. Fuller, Professor of Law Emeritus, Harvard University.

JUVENILE, see also Children

JUVENILE JUSTICE PROCESS, Third Edition (1985)

Frank W. Miller, Professor of Law, Washington University.
Robert O. Dawson, Professor of Law, University of Texas.
George E. Dix, Professor of Law, University of Texas.
Raymond I. Parnas, Professor of Law, University of California, Davis.

LABOR LAW, Tenth Edition (1986), with 1986 Statutory Supplement

Archibald Cox, Professor of Law, Harvard University.
Derek C. Bok, President, Harvard University.
Robert A. Gorman, Professor of Law, University of Pennsylvania.

LABOR LAW, Second Edition (1982), with Statutory Supplement

Clyde W. Summers, Professor of Law, University of Pennsylvania.
Harry H. Wellington, Dean of the Law School, Yale University.
Alan Hyde, Professor of Law, Rutgers University.

LAND FINANCING, Third Edition (1985)

The late Norman Penney, Professor of Law, Cornell University.
Richard F. Broude, Member of the California Bar.
Roger Cunningham, Professor of Law, University of Michigan.

LAW AND MEDICINE (1980)

Walter Wadlington, Professor of Law and Professor of Legal Medicine, University of Virginia.
Jon R. Waltz, Professor of Law, Northwestern University.
Roger B. Dworkin, Professor of Law, Indiana University, and Professor of Biomedical History, University of Washington.

LAW, LANGUAGE AND ETHICS (1972)

William R. Bishin, Professor of Law, University of Southern California.
Christopher D. Stone, Professor of Law, University of Southern California.

LAW, SCIENCE AND MEDICINE (1984)

Judith C. Areen, Professor of Law, Georgetown University.
Patricia A. King, Professor of Law, Georgetown University.
Steven P. Goldberg, Professor of Law, Georgetown University.
Alexander M. Capron, Professor of Law, Georgetown University.

LAWYERING PROCESS (1978), with Civil Problem Supplement and Criminal Problem Supplement

Gary Bellow, Professor of Law, Harvard University.
Bea Moulton, Professor of Law, Arizona State University.

LEGAL METHOD (1980)

Harry W. Jones, Professor of Law Emeritus, Columbia University.
John M. Kernochan, Professor of Law, Columbia University.
Arthur W. Murphy, Professor of Law, Columbia University.

UNIVERSITY CASEBOOK SERIES—Continued

LEGAL METHODS (1969)

> Robert N. Covington, Professor of Law, Vanderbilt University.
> E. Blythe Stason, late Professor of Law, Vanderbilt University.
> John W. Wade, Professor of Law, Vanderbilt University.
> Elliott E. Cheatham, late Professor of Law, Vanderbilt University.
> Theodore A. Smedley, Professor of Law, Vanderbilt University.

LEGAL PROFESSION, THE, Responsibility and Regulation (1985)

> Geoffrey C. Hazard, Jr., Professor of Law, Yale University.
> Deborah L. Rhode, Professor of Law, Stanford University.

LEGISLATION, Fourth Edition (1982) (by Fordham)

> Horace E. Read, late Vice President, Dalhousie University.
> John W. MacDonald, Professor of Law Emeritus, Cornell Law School.
> Jefferson B. Fordham, Professor of Law, University of Utah.
> William J. Pierce, Professor of Law, University of Michigan.

LEGISLATIVE AND ADMINISTRATIVE PROCESSES, Second Edition (1981)

> Hans A. Linde, Judge, Supreme Court of Oregon.
> George Bunn, Professor of Law, University of Wisconsin.
> Fredericka Paff, Professor of Law, University of Wisconsin.
> W. Lawrence Church, Professor of Law, University of Wisconsin.

LOCAL GOVERNMENT LAW, Second Revised Edition (1986)

> Jefferson B. Fordham, Professor of Law, University of Utah.

MASS MEDIA LAW, Second Edition (1982), with 1985 Supplement

> Marc A. Franklin, Professor of Law, Stanford University.

MENTAL HEALTH PROCESS, Second Edition (1976), with 1981 Supplement

> Frank W. Miller, Professor of Law, Washington University.
> Robert O. Dawson, Professor of Law, University of Texas.
> George E. Dix, Professor of Law, University of Texas.
> Raymond I. Parnas, Professor of Law, University of California, Davis.

MUNICIPAL CORPORATIONS, see Local Government Law

NEGOTIABLE INSTRUMENTS, see Commercial Paper

NEGOTIATION (1981) (Reprinted from THE LAWYERING PROCESS)

> Gary Bellow, Professor of Law, Harvard Law School.
> Bea Moulton, Legal Services Corporation.

NEW YORK PRACTICE, Fourth Edition (1978)

> Herbert Peterfreund, Professor of Law, New York University.
> Joseph M. McLaughlin, Dean of the Law School, Fordham University.

OIL AND GAS, Fourth Edition (1979)

> Howard R. Williams, Professor of Law, Stanford University.
> Richard C. Maxwell, Professor of Law, University of California, Los Angeles.
> Charles J. Meyers, Dean of the Law School, Stanford University.

ON LAW IN COURTS (1965)

> Paul J. Mishkin, Professor of Law, University of California, Berkeley.
> Clarence Morris, Professor of Law Emeritus, University of Pennsylvania.

UNIVERSITY CASEBOOK SERIES—Continued

PATENTS AND ANTITRUST (Pamphlet) (1983)

Milton Handler, Professor of Law Emeritus, Columbia University.
Harlan M. Blake, Professor of Law, Columbia University.
Robert Pitofsky, Professor of Law, Georgetown University.
Harvey J. Goldschmid, Professor of Law, Columbia University.

PERSPECTIVES ON THE LAWYER AS PLANNER (Reprint of Chapters One through Five of Planning by Lawyers) (1978)

Louis M. Brown, Professor of Law, University of Southern California.
Edward A. Dauer, Professor of Law, Yale University.

PLANNING BY LAWYERS, MATERIALS ON A NONADVERSARIAL LEGAL PROCESS (1978)

Louis M. Brown, Professor of Law, University of Southern California.
Edward A. Dauer, Professor of Law, Yale University.

PLEADING AND PROCEDURE, see Procedure, Civil

POLICE FUNCTION, Fourth Edition (1986)

Reprint of Chapters 1–10 of Miller, Dawson, Dix and Parnas's CRIMINAL JUSTICE ADMINISTRATION, Third Edition.

PREPARING AND PRESENTING THE CASE (1981) (Reprinted from THE LAWYERING PROCESS)

Gary Bellow, Professor of Law, Harvard Law School.
Bea Moulton, Legal Services Corporation.

PREVENTIVE LAW, see also Planning by Lawyers

PROCEDURE—CIVIL PROCEDURE, Second Edition (1974), with 1979 Supplement

The late James H. Chadbourn, Professor of Law, Harvard University.
A. Leo Levin, Professor of Law, University of Pennsylvania.
Philip Shuchman, Professor of Law, Cornell University.

PROCEDURE—CIVIL PROCEDURE, Fifth Edition (1984)

Richard H. Field, late Professor of Law, Harvard University.
Benjamin Kaplan, Professor of Law Emeritus, Harvard University.
Kevin M. Clermont, Professor of Law, Cornell University.

PROCEDURE—CIVIL PROCEDURE, Fourth Edition (1985)

Maurice Rosenberg, Professor of Law, Columbia University.
Hans Smit, Professor of Law, Columbia University.
Harold L. Korn, Professor of Law, Columbia University.

PROCEDURE—PLEADING AND PROCEDURE: State and Federal, Fifth Edition (1983), with 1985 Supplement

David W. Louisell, late Professor of Law, University of California, Berkeley.
Geoffrey C. Hazard, Jr., Professor of Law, Yale University.
Colin C. Tait, Professor of Law, University of Connecticut.

PROCEDURE—FEDERAL RULES OF CIVIL PROCEDURE, 1986 Edition

PRODUCTS LIABILITY (1980)

Marshall S. Shapo, Professor of Law, Northwestern University.

PRODUCTS LIABILITY AND SAFETY (1980), with 1985 Case and Documentary Supplement

W. Page Keeton, Professor of Law, University of Texas.
David G. Owen, Professor of Law, University of South Carolina.
John E. Montgomery, Professor of Law, University of South Carolina.

PROFESSIONAL RESPONSIBILITY, Third Edition (1984), with 1986 Selected National Standards Supplement

Thomas D. Morgan, Dean of the Law School, Emory University.
Ronald D. Rotunda, Professor of Law, University of Illinois.

PROPERTY, Fifth Edition (1984)

John E. Cribbet, Dean of the Law School, University of Illinois.
Corwin W. Johnson, Professor of Law, University of Texas.

PROPERTY—PERSONAL (1953)

S. Kenneth Skolfield, late Professor of Law Emeritus, Boston University.

PROPERTY—PERSONAL, Third Edition (1954)

Everett Fraser, late Dean of the Law School Emeritus, University of Minnesota.
Third Edition by Charles W. Taintor, late Professor of Law, University of Pittsburgh.

PROPERTY—INTRODUCTION, TO REAL PROPERTY, Third Edition (1954)

Everett Fraser, late Dean of the Law School Emeritus, University of Minnesota.

PROPERTY—REAL AND PERSONAL, Combined Edition (1954)

Everett Fraser, late Dean of the Law School Emeritus, University of Minnesota.
Third Edition of Personal Property by Charles W. Taintor, late Professor of Law, University of Pittsburgh.

PROPERTY—FUNDAMENTALS OF MODERN REAL PROPERTY, Second Edition (1982), with 1985 Supplement

Edward H. Rabin, Professor of Law, University of California, Davis.

PROPERTY—PROBLEMS IN REAL PROPERTY (Pamphlet) (1969)

Edward H. Rabin, Professor of Law, University of California, Davis.

PROPERTY, REAL (1984)

Paul Goldstein, Professor of Law, Stanford University.

PROSECUTION AND ADJUDICATION, Third Edition (1986)

Reprint of Chapters 11–26 of Miller, Dawson, Dix and Parnas's CRIMINAL JUSTICE ADMINISTRATION, Third Edition.

PSYCHIATRY AND LAW, see Mental Health, see also Hinckley, Trial of

PUBLIC REGULATION OF DANGEROUS PRODUCTS (paperback) (1980)

Marshall S. Shapo, Professor of Law, Northwestern University.

PUBLIC UTILITY LAW, see Free Enterprise, also Regulated Industries

REAL ESTATE PLANNING (1980), with 1980 Problems, Statutes and New Materials Supplement

Norton L. Steuben, Professor of Law, University of Colorado.

REAL ESTATE TRANSACTIONS, Second Edition (1985), with 1985 Statute, Form and Problem Supplement

Paul Goldstein, Professor of Law, Stanford University.

UNIVERSITY CASEBOOK SERIES—Continued

RECEIVERSHIP AND CORPORATE REORGANIZATION, see Creditors' Rights

REGULATED INDUSTRIES, Second Edition, 1976

William K. Jones, Professor of Law, Columbia University.

REMEDIES (1982), with 1984 Case Supplement

Edward D. Re, Chief Judge, U. S. Court of International Trade.

RESTITUTION, Second Edition (1966)

John W. Wade, Professor of Law, Vanderbilt University.

SALES, Second Edition (1986)

Marion W. Benfield, Jr., Professor of Law, University of Illinois.
William D. Hawkland, Chancellor, Louisiana State Law Center.

SALES AND SALES FINANCING, Fifth Edition (1984)

John Honnold, Professor of Law, University of Pennsylvania.

SALES LAW AND THE CONTRACTING PROCESS (1982)

Reprint of Chapters 1–10 of Schwartz and Scott's Commercial Transactions.

SECURED TRANSACTIONS IN PERSONAL PROPERTY (1983) (Reprinted from COMMERCIAL LAW)

Robert L. Jordan, Professor of Law, University of California, Los Angeles.
William D. Warren, Professor of Law, University of California, Los Angeles.

SECURITIES REGULATION, Fifth Edition (1982), with 1985 Cases and Releases Supplement and 1985 Selected Statutes, Rules and Forms Supplement

Richard W. Jennings, Professor of Law, University of California, Berkeley.
Harold Marsh, Jr., Member of California Bar.

SECURITIES REGULATION (1982), with 1985 Supplement

Larry D. Soderquist, Professor of Law, Vanderbilt University.

SECURITY INTERESTS IN PERSONAL PROPERTY (1984)

Douglas G. Baird, Professor of Law, University of Chicago.
Thomas H. Jackson, Professor of Law, Stanford University.

SECURITY INTERESTS IN PERSONAL PROPERTY (1985) (Reprinted from Sales and Sales Financing, Fifth Edition)

John Honnold, Professor of Law, University of Pennsylvania.

SENTENCING AND THE CORRECTIONAL PROCESS, Second Edition (1976)

Frank W. Miller, Professor of Law, Washington University.
Robert O. Dawson, Professor of Law, University of Texas.
George E. Dix, Professor of Law, University of Texas.
Raymond I. Parnas, Professor of Law, University of California, Davis.

SOCIAL SCIENCE IN LAW, Cases and Materials (1985)

John Monahan, Professor of Law, University of Virginia.
Laurens Walker, Professor of Law, University of Virginia.

SOCIAL WELFARE AND THE INDIVIDUAL (1971)

Robert J. Levy, Professor of Law, University of Minnesota.
Thomas P. Lewis, Dean of the College of Law, University of Kentucky.
Peter W. Martin, Professor of Law, Cornell University.

UNIVERSITY CASEBOOK SERIES—Continued

TAX, POLICY ANALYSIS OF THE FEDERAL INCOME (1976)

William A. Klein, Professor of Law, University of California, Los Angeles.

TAXATION, FEDERAL INCOME, Successor Edition (1985)

Michael J. Graetz, Professor of Law, Yale University.

TAXATION, FEDERAL INCOME, Fifth Edition (1985)

James J. Freeland, Professor of Law, University of Florida.
Stephen A. Lind, Professor of Law, University of Florida.
Richard B. Stephens, Professor of Law Emeritus, University of Florida.

TAXATION, FEDERAL INCOME, Volume I, Personal Income Taxation, Second Edition (1986), Volume II, Taxation of Partnerships and Corporations, Second Edition (1980), with 1985 Legislative Supplement

Stanley S. Surrey, late Professor of Law, Harvard University.
Paul R. McDaniel, Professor of Law, Boston College Law School.
Hugh J. Ault, Professor of Law, Boston College Law School.
Stanley A. Koppelman, Boston University

TAXATION, FEDERAL WEALTH TRANSFER, Second Edition (1982) with 1985 Legislative Supplement

Stanley S. Surrey, late Professor of Law, Harvard University.
William C. Warren, Professor of Law Emeritus, Columbia University.
Paul R. McDaniel, Professor of Law, Boston College Law School.
Harry L. Gutman, Instructor, Harvard Law School and Boston College Law School.

TAXATION, FUNDAMENTALS OF CORPORATE, Cases and Materials (1985)

Stephen A. Lind, Professor of Law, University of Florida.
Stephen Schwarz, Professor of Law, University of California, Hastings.
Daniel J. Lathrope, Professor of Law, University of California, Hastings.
Joshua Rosenberg, Professor of Law, University of San Francisco.

TAXATION, FUNDAMENTALS OF PARTNERSHIP, Cases and Materials (1985)

Stephen A. Lind, Professor of Law, University of California, Hastings.
Stephen Schwarz, Professor of Law, University of California, Hastings.
Daniel J. Lathrope, Professor of Law, University of California, Hastings.
Joshua Rosenberg, Professor of Law, University of San Francisco.

TAXATION, PROBLEMS IN THE FEDERAL INCOME TAXATION OF PARTNER-SHIPS AND CORPORATIONS, Second Edition (1986)

Norton L. Steuben, Professor of Law, University of Colorado.
William J. Turnier, Professor of Law, University of North Carolina.

TAXATION, PROBLEMS IN THE FUNDAMENTALS OF FEDERAL INCOME, Second Edition (1985)

Norton L. Steuben, Professor of Law, University of Colorado.
William J. Turnier, Professor of Law, University of North Carolina.

TAXES AND FINANCE—STATE AND LOCAL (1974)

Oliver Oldman, Professor of Law, Harvard University.
Ferdinand P. Schoettle, Professor of Law, University of Minnesota.

TORT LAW AND ALTERNATIVES, Third Edition (1983)

Marc A. Franklin, Professor of Law, Stanford University.
Robert L. Rabin, Professor of Law, Stanford University.

UNIVERSITY CASEBOOK SERIES—Continued

TORTS, Seventh Edition (1982)

William L. Prosser, late Professor of Law, University of California, Hastings College.
John W. Wade, Professor of Law, Vanderbilt University.
Victor E. Schwartz, Professor of Law, American University.

TORTS, Third Edition (1976)

Harry Shulman, late Dean of the Law School, Yale University.
Fleming James, Jr., Professor of Law Emeritus, Yale University.
Oscar S. Gray, Professor of Law, University of Maryland.

TRADE REGULATION, Second Edition (1983), with 1985 Supplement

Milton Handler, Professor of Law Emeritus, Columbia University.
Harlan M. Blake, Professor of Law, Columbia University.
Robert Pitofsky, Professor of Law, Georgetown University.
Harvey J. Goldschmid, Professor of Law, Columbia University.

TRADE REGULATION, see Antitrust

TRANSNATIONAL BUSINESS PROBLEMS (1986)

Detlev F. Vagts, Professor of Law, Harvard University.

TRANSNATIONAL LEGAL PROBLEMS, Third Edition (1986) with Documentary Supplement

Henry J. Steiner, Professor of Law, Harvard University.
Detlev F. Vagts, Professor of Law, Harvard University.

TRIAL, see also Evidence, Making the Record, Lawyering Process and Preparing and Presenting the Case

TRIAL ADVOCACY (1968)

A. Leo Levin, Professor of Law, University of Pennsylvania.
Harold Cramer, of the Pennsylvania Bar.
Maurice Rosenberg, Professor of Law, Columbia University, Consultant.

TRUSTS, Fifth Edition (1978)

George G. Bogert, late Professor of Law Emeritus, University of Chicago.
Dallin H. Oaks, President, Brigham Young University.

TRUSTS AND SUCCESSION (Palmer's), Fourth Edition (1983)

Richard V. Wellman, Professor of Law, University of Georgia.
Lawrence W. Waggoner, Professor of Law, University of Michigan.
Olin L. Browder, Jr., Professor of Law, University of Michigan.

UNFAIR COMPETITION, see Competitive Process and Business Torts

UNITED NATIONS LAW, Second Edition (1967), with Documentary Supplement (1968)

Louis B. Sohn, Professor of Law, Harvard University.

WATER RESOURCE MANAGEMENT, Second Edition (1980), with 1983 Supplement

Charles J. Meyers, Dean of the Law School, Stanford University.
A. Dan Tarlock, Professor of Law, Indiana University.

WILLS AND ADMINISTRATION, Fifth Edition (1961)

Philip Mechem, late Professor of Law, University of Pennsylvania.
Thomas E. Atkinson, late Professor of Law, New York University.

WORLD LAW, see United Nations Law

University Casebook Series

CASES AND MATERIALS

ON

THE INTERNATIONAL LEGAL SYSTEM

SECOND EDITION

By

JOSEPH MODESTE SWEENEY

Eberhard P. Deutsch Professor of
Public International Law
Tulane University

COVEY T. OLIVER

Ferdinand Wakeman Hubbell Professor of Law Emeritus
University of Pennsylvania

NOYES E. LEECH

Ferdinand Wakeman Hubbell Professor of Law
University of Pennsylvania

Mineola, New York
THE FOUNDATION PRESS, INC.
1981

Library of Congress Cataloging in Publication Data

Sweeney, Joseph M.
    Cases and materials on the international legal system.

    (University casebook series)
    Previous ed. published in 1973 as: Cases and materials
on the international legal system / by Noyes E. Leech,
Covey T. Oliver, Joseph Modeste Sweeney.
    Bibliography: p.
    Includes index.
    1. International law—Cases. 2. International and
municipal law—United States—Cases. I. Oliver,
Covey T., 1913-   . II. Leech, Noyes E. III. Leech,
Noyes E. Cases and materials on the international legal
system. IV. Title. V. Series.
JX68.S88   1981   341'.0268   81-3093
                                        AACR2

ISBN 0-88277-032-2

PREFACE TO THE FIRST EDITION

We have done our best to make this book a teaching tool. It may be useful also to practitioners and even to scholars—at least at some points. But what we have wanted most to do is to get the attention of today's law students, those men and women who, for better or worse, will have so much influence on how the world will go. We, like our brother and sister teachers in international legal studies, covet the attention of these students, largely because we know how much there is still to be done and how much new, trained minds are needed for operations—for actual decision-making in and about the system we call the "international legal system."

We try through the materials chosen and through the arrangement of them in the book to give to students bases for coming to perceive—with the guidance of their instructors—how the stuff that lawyers use (concepts, principles, norms, values, and interests) work, or are treated as if they worked. And beyond this understanding, we hope that individualized impressions will be formed as to how much is worthy of survival, how much ought to be pared away, what new applications are desirable for old principles, and how to formulate new rules within a paradigm of what is needed and what may be attainable. In a field that, for American lawyers at least, has seemed to be more than usually doctrinal and conceptualistic, we have tried to suggest functional ways of looking at problems and building new generalizations.

This book is intended for use in a core course in the international legal studies sector of a modern law school curriculum. The material does not slight the policy fundamentals of international public law in favor of bread and butter "international lawyering." But the book builds trails toward the various advanced courses in international transactions. It is also background for the further study of international organizations law and of transnational human rights law. With rearrangements that we shall suggest the book can be used outside law schools. For law schools that can include only one course in the sector, the coverage offered along specialty lines serves also the function of basic familiarization with them.

We have not wished to enlist in the old or current guerres des savants. These enliven but also often obfuscate the field. Nor do we see any point in beginning with the usual philosophic questions. We think that students ought to experience right from the start the reality that there are enough law-like materials and operations involved here to keep them occupied and concerned in professional ways. Our treatment of theory about international law, therefore, comes toward the end, when, we expect, students will be able to savor the implications and influences of legal philosophy in the context of the system they have observed in action. Some teachers may, of course, wish to alter our order of presentation, as to this or any other sequence.

We were all involved in the preparation of the Restatement of the Foreign Relations Law of the United States (1965), two of us as co-authors, the other as a substantive editor. We hope users and other readers will agree that we have achieved our objective not to make this a studybook companion to the Restatement. The Restatement was, as restatements are supposed to be, an evaluative and analytical presentation of lex lata, in this instance in a United States cross-section that included some (but not all) of the fundamentals of international public law, national law related to foreign affairs operations, and transnational conflict of laws. Here our task is a different one. The Restatement sometimes helps us, as when it seems to have helped the courts in this country. But, to use a phrase remembered with affection from the chief Reporter, Dean Adrian S. Fisher, "We are not fanatics about it."

We have been enthusiastic—if not fanatical—anti-parochialists in our selections of materials for this book. Wherever the same point could be made as well or better by a more recent decision, we have eliminated the old war-horses, but we have kept an "oldie" where our analysis showed that—to vary the metaphor—it is the only piano player the system has on the particular point. Wherever international law norms must be communicated through national decisions and other actions, we have tried to break away from Anglo-American sources into those of other legal systems. To us it seems that realistic conditioning to the international legal system requires this. And we have not forgotten the pioneering earlier efforts in this regard of, inter alia, Manley O. Hudson, Ernest G. Lorenzen, George W. Stumberg, and Hessel E. Yntema.

Recognizing that, unfortunately, the ratio of dross to pure gold is rather high in this field, we have pared sharply a lot of what we have included. We hope, however, that we know gold when we find it. The book should be comfortable to cover in a 60 classroom hour (3000 minute) course; manageable—with some variations in emphasis—in a 45 hour course; and impossibly tight in a 30 hour course. We should be happy to make individualized suggestions to such of our brethren and potential users who might have—but not for long, we hope—to suffer such a curricular indignity as 30 hours for international law.

This book comes on the scene at a time when the actual international legal system is very different from the projections that many of us and our colleagues in casebook architecture and in teaching had made, roughly from 1946 on. We have tried to grasp the differences. We cheerfully and unstintingly admit our ineluctable indebtednesses to our admired friends who have published studybooks since World

War II, particularly to that grand master and friend of us all, Professor William W. Bishop, Jr. The editions of Bishop, from the earliest mimeograph which one of us used first in 1949 on coming fresh to this field from government, to the latest edition, are quite literally parts of our professional beings. So is what we learned from Hudson's and Dickinson's casebooks as students. And from great and scholarly teachers, such as Philip C. Jessup.

————

Small type footnotes are minimal herein. If we bother to write a note, we want it to be perceived psychologically by students as being as important for development of analysis as the cases and other third source items we have selected for insertion. The footnotes we have included are of two varieties. Numbered footnotes are those we have retained from cases and other quoted material. We have eliminated most of such footnotes but have kept the original numbering of those we have retained. Our own footnotes are indicated alphabetically.

We have selected two closing dates, one for cases, the other for treaties. Cases have been Shepardized through October 1, 1972. In general, treaty information is given as of January 1, 1972, largely because we have relied on the United States Department of State publication (as of that date), Treaties in Force, for dates of entry into force for the United States and for lists of parties. We have not been rigid about this and thus have included treaty information as of later dates when it has come to our attention, such as a treaty's recent entry into force for the United States.

Aside from these two formal closing dates, the informational flow in this book is cut off at approximately March 1, 1973.

We have prepared a companion volume of primary source materials, a Documentary Supplement, referred to frequently throughout the book. It contains most of the multilateral conventions and United Nations declarations that comprise the modern body of "international legislation" in the general fields of public international law and international organizations.

————

This book has taken us a long time, largely because we have not been sufficiently free of other duties to do it quickly. We hope this has helped to make the result reasonably well-joined, but we know that a lot more sanding and polishing must come in later editions. We shall be most grateful for users' suggestions, whether from teachers, students, or others—including reviewers.

NOYES E. LEECH
COVEY T. OLIVER
JOSEPH MODESTE SWEENEY

June 1, 1973

PREFACE TO THE SECOND EDITION

We have been told by a good many of our users, both teachers and students, that the preface we wrote in 1973 is itself, as we had hoped, a useful guide. The view there expressed of what a teaching tool in this field ought to be, especially for students in law schools in the United States, seems to have received approval. Thus we have not changed it in this edition. What we have done, essentially, is to bring the casebook up to date. Occasionally we were compelled to modify the internal structure of a chapter in order to fit together older and newer materials. But on the whole, those who taught from the first edition will find themselves in familiar surroundings in the second.

Our major problem has been to keep the book from growing too big. We have had to make room—by removing some older material—for outpourings of relevant United States law, statutory and judge-made. In doing so we have had to draw difficult lines between fundamentals needed for a general course and more detailed treatment that falls to courses on international commercial and economic transactions, United Nations law, regional arrangements law, and the like. We have tried always not to cut back on our use of legal materials from other national systems. But there, too, much new *richesse* has had to be pared down.

The informational flow in this book is cut off at approximately December 1, 1980, though we were able to include, at the last minute, data—and questions—concerning the release of the American hostages in Teheran on January 19, 1981. Treaty information is given as of January 1, 1980 or December 31, 1979, largely because these are the cut-off dates for, respectively, the United States and the United Nations publications on which we rely for the information, but here again we have not been rigid and have included some of a later date whenever feasible and useful.

Much of the credit for bringing to completion the manuscript of the second edition belongs to Mrs. Francis J. Barry, Jr., a graduate of Tulane Law School and a practicing attorney before returning to an academic setting as an assistant to one of us. Janice Gonzales Barry totally dedicated her legal and many other talents to our enterprise. To its successful realization, her collaboration was essential and we gratefully acknowledge it.

We no longer feel that the tradition of specific dedication is too trite. Barbara, Barbara and Louise have always helped us greatly, with their patience, encouragement, and interest, the latter two at-

tributes not being, of course, the same thing. We dedicate this edition
to them especially, as well as to all others who seek to know in order
to quest for better order and more justice for a small planet.

JOSEPH MODESTE SWEENEY
COVEY T. OLIVER
NOYES E. LEECH

May 1, 1981

SUMMARY OF CONTENTS

TABLE OF CONTENTS

TABLE OF CONTENTS

TABLE OF CONTENTS

TABLE OF CONTENTS

PART II. LIMITATIONS ON THE
EXERCISE OF JURISDICTION

TABLE OF CONTENTS

xli

xliv

PART III. THE INDIVIDUAL IN THE INTERNATIONAL LEGAL SYSTEM

xlix

TABLE OF CONTENTS

PART IV. THE STRUCTURE OF THE
INTERNATIONAL SYSTEM

PART V. METHODS OF OPERATION IN THE INTERNATIONAL SYSTEM

TABLE OF CONTENTS

lxiv

TABLE OF CONTENTS

CHAPTER 19. THE USE OF FORCE BY STATES—Continued

*

A BIBLIOGRAPHY FOR COLLATERAL STUDY

The student who wishes to supplement his reading of the materials in this book will find this selected bibliography useful. Jacob Robinson's one volume work, International Law and Organization (A. W. Sijthoff-Leyden, 1967), a world-wide ranging bibliography, subtitled "General Sources of Information," remains a comprehensive reference.

Some of the works cited below are the sources of materials reproduced in this casebook; many are not.

General Texts on International Law

American Law Institute, Restatement of the Law, Second, Foreign Relations Law of the United States (1965)

American Law Institute, Restatement of the Law, Foreign Relations Law of the United States (Revised), T.D. No. 1 (1980), T.D. No. 2 (1981)

J. Brierly, The Law of Nations (7th ed. 1978)

I. Brownlie, Principles of Public International Law (3d ed. 1979)

R. Erickson, International Law and the Revolutionary State (1972)

K. Grzybowski, Soviet Public International Law (1970)

H. Kelsen, Principles of International Law (R. Tucker, 2d ed. 1966)

W. Levi, Contemporary International Law: A Concise Introduction (1979)

D. O'Connell, International Law (2d ed. 1970) (2 vols.)

L. Oppenheim, International Law (H. Lauterpacht, Vol. I, 8th ed. 1955; Vol. II, 7th ed. 1952, reprinted 1969)

C. Rousseau, Droit International Public (1970–80) (4 vols.)

G. Schwarzenberger, International Law as Applied by International Courts and Tribunals (Vol. I, 3d ed. 1957; Vol. II, 1968; Vol. III, 1976)

G. Schwarzenberger and E. Brown, A Manual of International Law (6th ed. 1976)

M. Sørensen, Manual of Public International Law (1968)

J. Starke, An Introduction to International Law (8th ed. 1977)

G. Tunkin, Theory of International Law (Butler trans., 1974)

A. Verdross and B. Simma, Universelles Völkerrecht. Theorie and Praxis (1976)

A. Verdross, Völkerrecht (5th ed. 1964)

S. Williams and A. deMestral, An Introduction to International Law (1979)

C. De Visscher, Theory and Reality in Public International Law (Corbett trans., rev. ed., 1968)

Texts on a Variety of Aspects of International Law and Organization

D. Bowett, Self-Defense in International Law (1958)

L. Buchheit, Secession. The Legitimacy of Self Determination (1978)

A. Chayes, The Cuban Missile Crisis (1974)

G. Clark and L. Sohn, World Peace Through World Law (3d ed. 1966)

T. Elias, The Modern Law of Treaties (1974)

R. Falk, ed., The Vietnam War and International Law (4 vols. 1968–1976)

R. Falk and S. Mendlovitz, eds., The Strategy of World Order (1966) (4 vols.)

L. Gross, ed., International Law in the Twentieth Century (1969)

L. Gross, ed., The Future of the International Court of Justice (1976) (2 vols.)

L. Henkin, Foreign Affairs and the Constitution (1972), reprinted 1973

L. Henkin, How Nations Behave (2d ed. 1979)

M. Hudson, The Permanent Court of International Justice, 1920–1942 (1943)

P. Jessup, A Modern Law of Nations (1948)

P. Jessup, Transnational Law (1956)

P. Jessup, The Use of International Law (1959)

O. Kahn-Freund, General Problems of Private International Law (1976)

M. McDougal and F. Feliciano, Law and Minimum World Public Order (1961)

M. McDougal, H. Lasswell and L. Chen, Human Rights and World Public Order (1980)

M. McDougal, H. Lasswell and J. Miller, The Interpretation of Agreements and World Public Order (1967)

Lord McNair, The Law of Treaties (1961)

H. Morgenthau, Politics Among Nations (5th ed. 1978)

D. O'Connell, State Succession in Municipal Law and International Law (1967) (2 vols.)

C. Okolie, International Law Perspectives of the Developing Countries (1978)

S. Rosenne, The World Court: What It Is and How It Works (3d rev. ed. 1973)

M. Tardu, Human Rights: The International Petition System (two loose-leaf binders as of 1980)

Texts on the United Nations

L. Goodrich, The United Nations in a Changing World (1974)

L. Goodrich, E. Hambro and A. Simons, Charter of the United Nations (3d ed. 1969)

R. Higgins, The Development of International Law Through the Political Organs of the United Nations (1963)

R. Higgins, United Nations Peacekeeping 1946–1967 (1969–80) (3 vols.)

P. Jacob, A. Atherton and A. Wallenstein, The Dynamics of International Organization (rev. ed. 1972)

H. Kelsen, The Law of the United Nations (2d ed. 1966)

E. Luard, The United Nations: How It Works and What It Does (1979)

H. Nicholas, The United Nations as a Political Institution (5th ed. 1975)

F. Seyersted, United Nations Forces in the Law of Peace and War (1966)

Digests

J. Cohen and H. Chiu, People's China and International Law: A Documentary Study (1974) (2 vols.)

G. Hackworth, Digest of International Law (1940–1944) (8 vols.), reprinted 1973

A. Kiss, Répertoire de la Pratique Francaise en Matière de Droit International Public (1962–1972) (7 vols.)

J. Moore, Digest of International Law (1906) (8 vols.), reprinted 1970

C. Parry, A British Digest of International Law (1965 on) (multi-volumed)

A. Rovine and others, Digest of United States Practice in International Law (1973 on) (multi-volumed)

United Nations, Repertory of Practice of United Nations Organs (5 vols. and Table of Contents and Subject Index, 1955–57), with Supplement no. 1 (2 vols. 1958), Supplement no. 2 (3 vols. 1963–64) and Supplement no. 3 (4 vols. 1971–72)

J. Verzijl, International Law in Historical Perspective (1968–79) (10 vols.)

M. Whiteman, Digest of International Law (15 vols. 1963–73)

Coursebooks and Case Collections

W. Bishop, Jr., International Law: Cases and Materials (3d ed. 1971)

A. Chayes, T. Ehrlich and A. Lowenfeld, International Legal Process (1968) (2 vols.) (with Document Supplement)

J.–G. Castel, International Law (3d ed. 1976)

F. Deak (and F. Ruddy), American International Law Cases (1971 on) (multi-volumed)

E. Dickinson, Cases and Materials on International Law (1950)

L. Green, International Law Through the Cases (4th ed. 1978)

D. Harris, Cases and Materials on International Law (2d ed. 1979)

L. Henkin, R. Pugh, O. Schachter and H. Smit, International Law Cases and Materials (1980)

M. Hudson, Cases and Other Materials on International Law (3d ed. 1951)

J. Jackson, Legal Problems of International Economic Relations. Cases, Materials and Text (1977) (with Documents Supplement)

F. Kirgis, Jr., International Organizations in their Legal Setting (1977)

R. Lillich and F. Newman, International Human Rights (1979)

A. Lowenfeld, International Economic Law (1975–79) (6 vols.)

C. Parry (and J. Hopkins), British International Law Cases (1964–1973) (multi-volumed)

C. Parry and J. Hopkins, Commonwealth International Law Cases (1974–1978) (multi-volumed)

L. Sohn, Cases on United Nations Law (2d ed., rev. 1967) (with Basic Documents Supplement)

H. Steiner and D. Vagts, Transnational Legal Problems (2d ed. 1976) (with Documentary Supplement)

B. Weston, R. Falk and A. D'Amato, International Law and World Order (1980) (with Basic Documents Supplement)

TABLE OF ABBREVIATIONS

The following are abbreviations that have been used by the editors in their citations to principal cases and major materials and in their notes.

A.B.A.J.	American Bar Association Journal
A.2d	Atlantic Reporter, Second Series
A.C.	Law Report series [British], House of Lords
A.D.2d	Appellate Division Reports, New York Supreme Court, Second Series
ADIZ	Air Defense Identification Zone
All E.R.	All England Law Reports [1936–date]
Am.J.Int'l L.	American Journal of International Law
A.M.C.	American Maritime Cases
Am.Soc.Int'l L.	American Society of International Law
ANCOM	Andean Common Market
Ann.Dig.	Annual Digest and Reports of International Law Cases [title of Int'l Law Reports prior to 1953]
Brit.Y.B.Int'l L.	British Yearbook of International Law
C.A.	Law Report series, Court of Appeal
CACM	Central American Common Market
C.F.R.	Code of Federal Regulations
Cal.2d	California Supreme Court Reports, Second Series
Cal.L.Rev.	California Law Review
CCH Trade Cases	Trade Regulation Reporter [Commerce Clearing House]
Ch.	Law Report series, Chancery [1891–date]
Cong.Rec.	Congressional Record, United States
C.M.A.	Court of Military Appeals Reports
C.–M.Rep.	Court-Martial Reports
Cr.Cas.Res.	Law Report series, Crown Cases Reserved [1865–1875]
Dalloz Rec.Heb.Jur.	Dalloz, Recueil Hebdomadaire de Jurisprudence en matière civile [France]
DEWIZ	Distant Early Warning Identification Zone
E.C.	European Community
ECOSOC Off.Rec.	United Nations Economic and Social Council, Official Records
EEC	European Economic Community
EFTA	European Free Trade Association
F.2d	Federal Reporter, Second Series [1924–date]
F.Supp.	Federal Supplement

Fed.Reg.	Federal Register
FCN	Friendship, Commerce and Navigation Treaties
FM	Department of the Army Field Manual
G.A.Res.	General Assembly Resolution
GATT	General Agreement on Tariffs and Trade
GNP	Gross national product
Harv.L.Rev.	Harvard Law Review
IATA	International Air Transport Association
ICI	Imperial Chemical Industries, Ltd.
I.C.A.O.	International Civil Aviation Organization
I.C.J.Rep.	International Court of Justice Reports
I.C.J.Y.B	International Court of Justice Yearbook
Ill.Rev.Stat.	Illinois Revised Statutes
I.L.C.	International Law Commission
I.L.O.Off.Bull.	International Labour Office, Official Bulletin
Int'l & Comp.L.Q.	International and Comparative Law Quarterly
I.L.M.	International Legal Materials
Int'l L.Rep.	International Law Reports
IMT	International Military Tribunal
IRA	Irish Republican Army
ITT	International Telephone and Telegraph Corp.
K.B.	Law Report series, Kings Bench
LAFTA	Latin American Free Trade Association
L.N.T.S.	League of Nations Treaty Series
MFN	Most favored nation
N.Y.Misc.	New York Miscellaneous [1892–1955]
N.Y.Misc.2d	New York Miscellaneous, Second Series [1955–date]
MNEs	Multinational enterprises
NATO	North Atlantic Treaty Organization
N.E.	North Eastern Reporter [1885–1936]
N.J.Super.	New Jersey Superior Court Reports
N.Y.	New York Reports
N.Y.S.	New York Supplement [1888–1937]
N.Y.S.2d	New York Supplement, Second Series [1937–date]
OPIC	Overseas Private Investment Coorporation
P.	Law Report series, Probate, Divorce and Admiralty
P.2d	Pacific Reporter, Second Series
P.C.I.J.	Permanent Court of International Justice
Pa.	Pennsylvania State Reports [1845–date]
Pub.L.	Public Law Number
S.Ct.	Supreme Court Reporter [U.S., 1882–date]
Sirey	Sirey, Recueil Général des Lois et des Arrêts [France]

So.2d .... Southern Reporter, Second Series [1941–date]

So.African L.Rep. ...... South African Law Reports

Stat. .... Statutes at Large, United States

T.I.A.S. .... Treaties and Other International Acts Series

T.L.R. .... Times Law Reports [England, 1884–1952]

U.N.Conf.Int'l Org. .... United Nations Conference on International Organization [San Francisco Conference]

UNCTAD .... United Nations Conference on Trade and Development

U.N.Doc. .... United Nations Document

U.N.Gen.Ass.Off.Rec. .. United Nations General Assembly, Official Records

U.N.Gen.Ass.Off.Rec.
  Supp. .... United Nations General Assembly Official Records, Supplement

U.N.Rep.Int'l Arb.
  Awards .... United Nations Reports of International Arbitration Awards

U.N.T.S. .... United Nations Treaty Series

U.Pa.L.Rev. .... University of Pennsylvania Law Review

U.S. .... United States Supreme Court Reports

U.S.A.I.D. .... United States Foreign Assistance Administration

U.S.App.D.C. .... United States Court of Appeals, District of Columbia Circuit Reports

U.S.C. .... United States Code

U.S.C.A. .... United States Code Annotated

U.S.Dep't State Bull. ... United States Department of State Bulletin

U.S.T. .... U. S. Treaties and Other International Agreements

Vand.L.Rev. .... Vanderbilt Law Review

W.L.R. .... Weekly Law Reports [England, 1953–date]

Western Weekly Rep. ... Western Weekly Reports, New Series [Canada]

Yale L.J. .... Yale Law Journal

*

TABLE OF SECONDARY SOURCES

We have listed below the major secondary sources from which we have excerpted material that appears in this book, as well as certain of those sources to which passing reference has been made or which have been briefly quoted.

TABLE OF SECONDARY SOURCES

ACKNOWLEDGMENTS

We wish to acknowledge our indebtedness to the following authors, publishers and organizations for giving us permission to reprint excerpts from the books, periodicals and other documents indicated in parentheses:

Academy of Sciences of the Soviet Union, Moscow (excerpts from International Law);

American Association for the International Commission of Jurists, New York (excerpts from Human Rights in United States and United Kingdom Foreign Policy);

American Bar Association, Chicago (excerpt from the American Bar Association Journal: Lippert, The Eichmann Case and the Nuremberg Trials);

American Law Institute, Philadelphia (excerpts from Restatement of Foreign Relations Law of the United States);

American Society of International Law, Washington, D. C. (excerpts from American Journal of International Law, Proceedings of the American Society of International Law, and International Legal Materials);

American University Law Review, Washington, D. C. (excerpts from Dillard, The World Court: Reflections of a Professor Turned Judge);

Asian-African Legal Consultative Committee, New Delhi (excerpts from the Reports of the Sessions);

Banco Nacional de Comercio Exterior, S. A., Mexico City (excerpts from Comercio Exterior);

Joseph W. Bishop, Jr. (excerpts from Justice Under Fire);

Burroughs & Co., Ltd., Calgary (excerpt from Western Weekly Reports);

Butterworth's, London (excerpts from All England Reports);

Carnegie Endowment for International Peace, New York (excerpts from Phillipson, Introduction to 2 Gentili, Classics of International Law, and Wolff, Classics of International Law);

Columbia University Press, New York (excerpts from Carlston, The Process of International Arbitration);

Commerce Clearing House, Chicago (excerpts from CCH Trade Cases);

Department of the Army (excerpts from Army Field Manual FM 27–10, The Law of Land Warfare, available from the Superintendent of Documents, United Government Printing Office, Washington, D.C. 20402);

The Dorsey Press, Inc., Homewood, Illinois (excerpts from Jacob and Atherton, The Dynamics of International Organization);

ACKNOWLEDGMENTS

Editions A. Pedone and Charles Rousseau, Paris (excerpts from Chronique des Faits Internationaux, Revue Générale de Droit International Public);

Editions du Centre National de la Recherche Scientifique, Paris (excerpts from Kiss, Répertoire de la Pratique Française en Matière de Droit International Public);

Editions Techniques, S.A., Paris (excerpts from Journal du Droit International);

Editoriale Scientifica, s.r.l., Naples (excerpts from the Italian Yearbook of International Law);

European Law Centre Limited, London (excerpts from Common Market Law Reports);

Export and Import Department of Social and Scientific Publications, Moscow (Soviet Yearbook of International Law);

Georgetown University and Stanley D. Metzger (excerpts from Metzger, International Law, Trade and Finance: Realities and Prospects);

Grotius Publications, Ltd. and Mr. Elihu Lauterpacht, Q. C., Cambridge, England (excerpts from International Law Reports);

The Hague Academy of International Law (excerpts from Recueil des Cours: Tunkin, Co-existence and International Law; Oliver, Contemporary Problems of Treaty Law; and McDougal, International Law, Power and Policy: A Contemporary Conception);

Harvard Law Review Association, Cambridge, Massachusetts (excerpts from Harvard Law Review);

Incorporated Council of Law Reporting for England and Wales, London (excerpts from Weekly Law Reports and Reports of Queen's Bench);

International Bureau of Fiscal Documents, Amsterdam (excerpts from European Taxation);

International Commission of Jurists, Chêñe-Bougeries/Geneva (excerpts from the Review of the International Commission of Jurists);

International Law Association of Japan, Tokyo (excerpts from Japanese Annual of International Law);

Juta & Co., Ltd., Kenwyn Cape, South Africa (excerpts from South African Law Reports);

Morton A. Kaplan (excerpts from Kaplan and Katzenbach, The Political Foundations of International Law);

The Lawyer's Co-operative Publishing Company, Rochester, New York (excerpts from United States Court of Military Appeals and Court-Martial Reports);

Longman Group Limited, Harlow, Essex, England (excerpt from Oppenheim, International Law);

ACKNOWLEDGMENTS

Max-Planck-Institut für ausländisches öffentliches Recht, Heidelberg, (Max Planck Institute for Comparative Public Law and International Law, International Symposium on Judicial Settlement of International Disputes);

Michigan Law Review (excerpts from Note, Punishment for War Crimes: Duty or Discretion?);

Macmillan Publishing Co., Inc., New York (excerpts from Schwartz, A Commentary on the Constitution of the United States; and Tuchmann, The Guns of August);

John Murray (Publishers) Ltd., London (excerpts from Austin, Jurisprudence);

The New York Times Company (excerpts from the New York Times);

Newsweek (excerpts from Newsweek);

Natural Resources Law Section of the American Bar Association (excerpts from the Natural Resources Lawyer);

Netherlands Yearbook of International Law, The Hague (excerpts from the Yearbook);

Martinus Nijhoff, The Hague (excerpts from Peaslee, Constitutions of Nations);

North-Holland Publishing Company, Amsterdam, *Richard W. Grant and Philip A. Loomis, Jr.* (excerpts from "The U. S. Securities and Exchange Commission, Financial Institutions outside the U. S. and Extraterritorial Application of the U. S. Securities Regulation," Journal of Comparative Corporate Law and Securities Regulation);

Oceana Publications, Inc., Dobbs Ferry, New York (excerpts from Anand, Studies in International Adjudications; and Metzger, International Law, Trade and Finance: Realities and Prospects);

Organization for Economic Co-operation and Development, Paris (excerpts from Draft Convention on the Protection of Foreign Property);

Oxford University Press, Inc., New York (excerpts from Lewy, America in Vietnam);

Princeton University Press (excerpts from De Visscher, translated by Corbett, Theory and Reality in Public International Law (rev. ed.); and Patterson, Discrimination in International Trade, The Policy Issues: 1945–1965);

Progress Publishers, Moscow (excerpts from Tunkin, Contemporary International Law);

Quadrangle Books, Inc., New York (excerpts from Taylor, Nuremberg and Vietnam);

ACKNOWLEDGMENTS

Random House-Alfred A. Knopf, Inc., New York (excerpts from Morgenthau, Politics Among Nations: The Struggle for Power and Peace);

The Royal Institute of International Affairs, London (excerpts from British Yearbook of International: Waldock, Decline of the Optional Clause; and Higgins, The Development of International Law through the Political Organs of the United Nations and United Nations Peacekeeping, 1946–1967, I. The Middle East);

St. Mary's Law Journal, San Antonio (excerpt from Oliver, The United States of America and Public International Law);

Schulthess Polygraphischer Verlag, Zurich (excerpts from Annuaire Suisse de Droit International);

M. E. Sharpe, Armonk, New York (excerpts from Chinese Law and Government);

Sijthoff and Noordhoff International Publishers b. v., Alphen aan den Rijn, The Netherlands (excerpts from Nederlands Tijdschrift Voor International Recht and Law in Eastern Europe);

Stockholm Institute for Scandinavian Studies and Carsten Smith, Stockholm (excerpts from Scandinavian Studies in International Law: Smith, International Law in Norwegian Courts);

Julius Stone (excerpts from Legal Controls of International Conflict);

Sweet & Maxwell, Ltd., London (excerpts from Law Quarterly Review: Kelsen, The Pure Theory of Law; The Law of the Air: McNair, From Theory to Treaty Law; Lauterpacht, The Development of International Law by the International Court; and O'Connell, Vols. 1 and 2 International Law (2d ed. 1970);

Thames & Hudson, London (excerpts from Luard (ed.), The International Protection of Human Rights);

The Times-Picayune Publishing Company, New Orleans (excerpts from the Times-Picayune);

U. S. News & World Report (excerpts);

University of Chicago Press, S. Houston Lay, and Howard J. Taubenfeld (excerpts from The Law Relating to the Activities of Man in Space, © 1970 by the American Bar Foundation);

University of Pennsylvania Law Review and Fred B. Rothman & Co., Littleton, Colorado (excerpts from University of Pennsylvania Law Review);

Virginia Journal of International Law (excerpts from the Journal: Krueger & Nordquist, The Evolution of the 200-Mile Exclusive Economic Zone: State Practice in the Pacific Basin and Kindt, The Effect of Claims by Developing Countries on LOS International Marine Pollution Negotiations);

ACKNOWLEDGMENTS

The Wall Street Journal, Chicapee, Massachusetts (excerpts from The Wall Street Journal);

The Washington Post (excerpts from Schwebel, "Cognition" and the Peking Visit, Is the Concept of Recognition Obsolete?);

Wayne Law Review (excerpts from Wilkes, The Use of World Resources Without Conflict: Myths about the Territorial Sea);

Yale University Press, New Haven (excerpts from Buchheit, Succession: The Legitimacy of Self-Determination).

*

TABLE OF CASES

The principal cases are in italic type. Cases cited or discussed are in roman type. References are to Pages.

*

THE INTERNATIONAL LEGAL SYSTEM

CASES AND MATERIALS

Chapter 1

APPLICATION OF THE LAW OF THE INTERNATIONAL SYSTEM

1. *The nature of international law.* This book begins with a sketch of the structure of the present legal order of the planet. Along with many others, we think there is such an order, albeit less intricate and possibly less assuredly applicable than internal law in those modern states where there is a reasonably high correlation between the rules and what happens.

We could have begun with such classic introductory devices as: (a) Is international law law? (b) What is law anyway? (c) Can there be law if there is no supranational authority to impose it? We believe, however, that the student will be better able to deal with these questions after some exposure to the subject matter that is the corpus juris of what is called international public law, transnational law, and foreign affairs law and dealt with as such by lawyers all over the world, whether in advocacy, consultative or decision making roles.

The more jurisprudential materials are in our Chapter 18. Some may prefer to take them earlier than this order suggests. Even so, we think Chapter 1 should be taken first.

The law we study is not adequate to the management of planetary affairs even now. A major purpose of a law school course in this area is to draw attention to the urgent need for the growth of order beyond the rules that have developed in the West, along with the national state system, over the past half millenium. In any case, it is imperative that men do the best they can with what is currently available.

Chapter 1 is analytically descriptive of the system. At the same time, it introduces some of the major operational challenges, viz: (a) universality, (b) effectiveness, (c) state dissent from binding effect, (d) limitations of the arbitral-adjudicatory process as a means of resolving conflicts.

2. *Sources of international law.* The subject is complex, but there is no attempt to treat it here in depth. It is presented merely in outline in the belief that its components can be discussed in detail wherever suitable in the book. The sole purpose of this note is to introduce the subject.

Article 38 of the Statute of the International Court of Justice provides:

1. The Court, whose function is to decide in accordance with international law such disputes as are submitted to it, shall apply:

a. international conventions, whether general or particular, establishing rules expressly recognized by the contesting states;

b. international custom, as evidence of a general practice accepted as law;

c. the general principles of law recognized by civilized nations;

d. subject to the provisions of Article 59, judicial decisions and the teachings of the most highly qualified publicists of the various nations, as subsidiary means for the determination of rules of law.

2. This provision shall not prejudice the power of the Court to decide a case ex aequo et bono, if the parties agree thereto.

The extent to which resolutions and declarations of the United Nations may be sources of international law is a matter of controversy. The position of the United States on that question was stated by Stephen M. Schwebel, Deputy Legal Adviser of the Department of State, as follows:

* * * As a broad statement of U.S. policy in this regard, I think it is fair to state that General Assembly resolutions are regarded as recommendations to Member States of the United Nations.

To the extent, which is exceptional, that such resolutions are meant to be declaratory of international law, are adopted with the support of all members, and are observed by the practice of states, such resolutions are evidence of customary international law on a particular subject matter. * * * McDowell, Digest of United States Practice in International Law 1975, at 85 (1976).

The position is questioned in the Third World as indicated by the following statement:

> The idea of attributing legislative force to resolutions of the General Assembly is of growing importance in the evolution of contemporary international law. It contrasts with the more traditional conception that all obligations in international law can be traced directly (via explicit agreements) or indirectly (via state practice) to the consent of sovereign states or to some system of natural rights and duties.
>
> *   *   *
>
> At several sessions of the Sixth Committee of the General Assembly, *   *   * representatives from Africa, Asia, South America, and joined by delegates from Poland and other eastern bloc countries, suggested that the resolutions of international organizations did in various ways contribute to [the] creation and operation of international law. The representative from Panama, for example, acknowledged as did several other delegates, that the principle of self determination had matured into a legal concept following successive United Nations Resolutions on the subject. Heliliah Bte. Yusof, The Impact on International Law and Relations of the "Legislative" Activity by the General Assembly, 1 Singapore Law Review 216 (1969).

States referring a dispute to an arbitral tribunal frequently specify in the compromis (the agreement to submit to arbitration) the governing rules to be applied. In drafting the compromis there is first the question whether the tribunal shall be instructed to decide in accordance with rules of international law or to be accorded a wider discretion to decide according to justice, equity or ex aequo et bono without regard to technical legal rights. At times the decision to direct one basis for decision rather than another has been thought by the states agreeing to arbitration to depend upon whether the dispute is of a non-legal nature. For a useful and extensive analysis of international practice, see Sohn, The Function of International Arbitration Today, [1963] I Académie de Droit International, Recueil des Cours 1, 41.

SECTION A.   APPLICATION WITHIN NATIONAL LEGAL SYSTEMS

---

1.   RULES OF CUSTOMARY INTERNATIONAL LAW NOT IN CONFLICT WITH DOMESTIC LAW

WEST RAND CENTRAL GOLD MINING CO. v. THE KING

England, King's Bench, 1905.
[1905] 2 K.B. 391.*

Lord ALVERSTONE, C. J.   In this case the Attorney-General, on behalf of the Crown, demurred to a petition of right presented in the month of June, 1904, by the West Rand Central Gold Mining Company, Limited.   The petition of right alleged that two parcels of gold, amounting in all to the value of 3804£, had been seized by officials of the South African Republic—1104£ on October 2 in course of transit from Johannesburg to Cape Town, and 2700£ on October 9, taken from the bank premises of the petitioners.   No further statement was made in the petition of the circumstances under which, or the right by which, the Government of the Transvaal Republic claimed to seize the gold; * * *.   The petition then alleged that a state of war commenced at 5 P.M. on October 11, 1899, that the forces of the late Queen conquered the Republic, and that by a Proclamation of September 1, 1900, the whole of the territories of the Republic were annexed to, and became part of, Her Majesty's dominions, and that the Government of the Republic ceased to exist.   The petition then averred that by reason of the conquest and annexation Her Majesty succeeded to the sovereignty of the Transvaal Republic, and became entitled to its property; and that the obligation which vested in the Government was binding upon His present Majesty the King.

* * *

* * * His main proposition was divided into three heads. First, that, by international law, the Sovereign of a conquering State is liable for the obligations of the conquered; secondly, that international law forms part of the law of England; and, thirdly, that rights and obligations, which were binding upon the conquered State, must be protected and can be enforced by the municipal Courts of the conquering State.

In support of his first proposition Lord Robert Cecil cited passages from various writers on international law.   In regard to this class of authority it is important to remember certain necessary limitations to its value.   There is an essential difference, as to certainty

---

* Reprinted by permission of the Incorporated Council of Law Reporting of England and Wales, London.

and definiteness, between municipal law and a system or body of rules in regard to international conduct, which, so far as it exists at all (and its existence is assumed by the phrase "international law"), rests upon a consensus of civilized States, not expressed in any code or pact, nor possessing, in case of dispute, any authorized or authoritative interpreter; and capable, indeed, of proof, in the absence of some express international agreement, only by evidence of usage to be obtained from the action of nations in similar cases in the course of their history. It is obvious that, in respect of many questions that may arise, there will be room for difference of opinion as to whether such a consensus could be shewn to exist. * * * The views expressed by learned writers on international law have done in the past, and will do in the future, valuable service in helping to create the opinion by which the range of the consensus of civilized nations is enlarged. But in many instances their pronouncements must be regarded rather as the embodiments of their views as to what ought to be, from an ethical standpoint, the conduct of nations inter se, than the enunciation of a rule or practice so universally approved or assented to as to be fairly termed, even in the qualified sense in which that word can be understood in reference to the relations between independent political communities, "law." * * *

Before, however, dealing with the specific passages in the writings of jurists upon which the suppliants rely, we desire to consider the proposition, that by international law the conquering country is bound to fulfil the obligations of the conquered, upon principle; and upon principle we think it cannot be sustained. When making peace the conquering Sovereign can make any conditions he thinks fit respecting the financial obligations of the conquered country, and it is entirely at his option to what extent he will adopt them. It is a case in which the only law is that of military force. This indeed, was not disputed by counsel for the suppliants; but it was suggested that although the Sovereign when making peace may limit the obligations to be taken over, if he does not do so they are all taken over, and no subsequent limitation can be put upon them. What possible reason can be assigned for such a distinction? * * * We can see no reason at all why silence should be supposed to be equivalent to a promise of universal novation of existing contracts with the Government of the conquered State. It was suggested that a distinction might be drawn between obligations incurred for the purpose of waging war with the conquering country and those incurred for general State expenditure. What municipal tribunal could determine, according to the laws of evidence to be observed by that tribunal, how particular sums had been expended, whether borrowed before or during the war? It was this and cognate difficulties which compelled Lord Robert Cecil ultimately to concede that he must contend that the obligation was absolute to take over all debts and contractual obligations incurred before war had been actually declared.

Turning now to the text-writers, we may observe that the proposition we have put forward that the conqueror may impose what terms he thinks fit in respect of the obligations of the conquered territory, and that he alone must be the judge in such a matter, is clearly recognised by Grotius: see "War and Peace," book iii. chap. 8, s. 4, and the Notes to Barbeyrac's edition of 1724, vol. ii. p. 632. For the assertion that a line is to be drawn at the moment of annexation, and that the conquering Sovereign has no right at any later stage to say what obligations he will or will not assume, we venture to think that there is no authority whatever. A doctrine was at one time urged by some of the older writers that to the extent of the assets taken over by the conqueror he ought to satisfy the debts of the conquered State. It is, in our opinion, a mere expression of the ethical views of the writers; but the proposition now contended for is a vast extension even of that doctrine. * * * But whatever may be the view taken of the opinions of these writers, they are, in our judgment, inconsistent with the law as recognised for many years in the English Courts * * *.

The second proposition urged by Lord Robert Cecil, that international law forms part of the law of England, requires a word of explanation and comment. It is quite true that whatever has received the common consent of civilized nations must have received the assent of our country, and that to which we have assented along with other nations in general may properly be called international law, and as such will be acknowledged and applied by our municipal tribunals when legitimate occasion arises for those tribunals to decide questions to which doctrines of international law may be relevant. But any doctrine so invoked must be one really accepted as binding between nations, and the international law sought to be applied must, like anything else, be proved by satisfactory evidence, which must shew either that the particular proposition put forward has been recognised and acted upon by our own country, or that it is of such a nature, and has been so widely and generally accepted, that it can hardly be supposed that any civilized State would repudiate it. The mere opinions of jurists, however eminent or learned, that it ought to be so recognised, are not in themselves sufficient. They must have received the express sanction of international agreement, or gradually have grown to be part of international law by their frequent practical recognition in dealings between various nations. We adopt the language used by Lord Russell of Killowen in his address at Saratoga in 1896 on the subject of international law and arbitration: "What, then, is international law? I know no better definition of it than that it is the sum of the rules or usages which civilized States have agreed shall be binding upon them in their dealings with one another." In our judgment, the second proposition for which Lord Robert Cecil contended in his argument before us ought to be treated as correct only if the term "international law" is understood in the sense, and subject to the limitations of application, which we have explained. * * * [T]he expressions used by Lord Mansfield when dealing with the particular and recognised rule of international law on this subject, that the law of nations forms part of the law of England, ought not to be construed so as to include as part of the law of England opinions of text-writers upon a question as to which there is no evidence that Great Britain has ever assented, and a fortiori if they are contrary to the principles of her laws as declared by her Courts. * * *

We pass now to consider the third proposition upon which the success of the suppliants in this case must depend—namely, that the claims of the suppliants based upon the alleged principle that the conquering State is bound by the obligations of the conquered can be enforced by petition of right. * * * Upon this part of the case there is a series of authorities from the year 1793 down to the present time holding that matters which fall properly to be determined by the Crown by treaty or as an act of State are not subject to the jurisdiction of the municipal Courts, and that rights supposed to be acquired thereunder cannot be enforced by such Courts. * * * We are of opinion, for the reasons given, that no right on the part of the suppliants is disclosed by the petition which can be enforced as against His Majesty in this or in any municipal Court; and we therefore allow the demurrer, with costs.

Judgment for the Crown.

THE PAQUETE HABANA
THE LOLA

Read this

United States Supreme Court, 1900.
175 U.S. 677, 20 S.Ct. 290.

Mr. Justice GRAY delivered the opinion of the court.

These are two appeals from decrees of the District Court of the United States for the Southern District of Florida, condemning two fishing vessels and their cargoes as prize of war.

Each vessel was a fishing smack, running in and out of Havana, and regularly engaged in fishing on the coast of Cuba; sailed under the Spanish flag; was owned by a Spanish subject of Cuban birth, living in the city of Havana; was commanded by a subject of Spain also residing in Havana; and her master and crew had no interest in the vessel, but were entitled to shares, amounting in all to two thirds, of her catch, the other third belonging to her owner. Her cargo consisted of fresh fish, caught by her crew from the sea, put on board as they were caught, and kept and sold alive. Until stopped by the blockading squadron, she had no knowledge of the existence of the war, or of any blockade. She had no arms or ammunition on board, and made no attempt to run the blockade after she knew of its existence, nor any resistance at the time of the capture.

* * *

Both the fishing vessels were brought by their captors into Key West. A libel for the condemnation of each vessel and her cargo as prize of war was there filed in April 27, 1898; a claim was interposed by her master, on behalf of himself and the other members of the crew, and of her owner; evidence was taken, showing the facts above stated; and on May 30, 1898, a final decree of condemnation and sale was entered, "the court not being satisfied that as a matter of law, without any ordinance, treaty or proclamation, fishing vessels of this class are exempt from seizure."

Each vessel was thereupon sold by auction; the Paquete Habana for the sum of $490; and the Lola for the sum of $800. * * *

* * *

We are then brought to the consideration of the question whether, upon the facts appearing in these records, the fishing smacks were subject to capture by the armed vessels of the United States during the recent war with Spain.

By an ancient usage among civilized nations, beginning centuries ago, and gradually ripening into a rule of international law, coast fishing vessels, pursuing their vocation of catching and bringing in fresh fish, have been recognized as exempt, with their cargoes and crews, from capture as prize of war.

This doctrine, however, has been earnestly contested at the bar; and no complete collection of the instances illustrating it is to be found, so far as we are aware, in a single published work, although many are referred to and discussed by the writers on international law, notably in 2 Ortolan, Règles Internationales et Diplomatie de la Mer, (4th ed.) lib. 3, c. 2, pp. 51–56; in 4 Calvo, Droit International, (5th ed.) §§ 2367–2373; in De Boeck, Propriété Privée Ennemie sous Pavillon Ennemi, §§ 191–196; and in Hall, International Law, (4th ed.) § 148. It is therefore worth the while to trace the history of the rule, from the earliest accessible sources, through the increasing recognition of it, with occasional setbacks, to what we may now justly consider as its final establishment in our own country and generally throughout the civilized world.

[The court then proceeds to trace the history of the rule through an extensive examination of state practice, beginning with the issuance of orders by Henry IV to his admirals in 1403 and 1406.]

Since the English orders in council of 1806 and 1810, before quoted, in favor of fishing vessels employed in catching and bringing to market fresh fish, no instance has been found in which the exemption from capture of private coast fishing vessels, honestly pursuing their peaceful industry, has been denied by England, or by any other nation. And the Empire of Japan, (the last State admitted into the rank of civilized nations,) by an ordinance promulgated at the beginning of its war with China in August, 1894, established prize courts, and ordained that "the following enemy's vessels are exempt from detention"—including in the exemption "boats engaged in coast fisheries," as well as "ships engaged exclusively on a voyage of scientific discovery, philanthropy or religious mission." Takahashi, International Law, 11, 178.

International law is part of our law, and must be ascertained and administered by the courts of justice of appropriate jurisdiction, as often as questions of right depending upon it are duly presented for their determination. For this purpose, where there is no treaty, and no controlling executive or legislative act or judicial decision, resort must be had to the customs and usages of civilized nations; and, as evidence of these, to the works of jurists and commentators, who by years of labor, research and experience, have made themselves peculiarly well acquainted with the subjects of which they treat. Such works are resorted to by judicial tribunals, not for the speculations of their authors concerning what the law ought to be, but for trustworthy evidence of what the law really is. Hilton v. Guyot, 159 U.S. 113, 163, 164, 214, 215.

*   *   *

This review of the precedents and authorities on the subject appears to us abundantly to demonstrate that at the present day, by the general consent of the civilized nations of the world, and independently of any express treaty or other public act, it is an established rule of international law, founded on considerations of humanity to a poor and industrious order of men, and of the mutual convenience of belligerent States, that coast fishing vessels, with their implements and supplies, cargoes and crews, unarmed, and honestly pursuing their peaceful calling of catching and bringing in fresh fish, are exempt from capture as prize of war.

The exemption, of course, does not apply to coast fishermen or their vessels, if employed for a warlike purpose, or in such a way as to give aid or information to the enemy; nor when military or naval operations create a necessity to which all private interests must give way.

Nor has the exemption been extended to ships or vessels employed on the high sea in taking whales or seals, or cod or other fish which are not brought fresh to market, but are salted or otherwise cured and made a regular article of commerce.

This rule of international law is one which prize courts, administering the law of nations, are bound to take judicial notice of, and to give effect to, in the absence of any treaty or other public act of their own government in relation to the matter.

*   *   *

The position taken by the United States during the recent war with Spain was quite in accord with the rule of international law, now generally recognized by civilized nations, in regard to coast fishing vessels.

On April 21, 1898, the Secretary of the Navy gave instructions to Admiral Sampson commanding the North Atlantic Squadron, to "immediately institute a blockade of the north coast of Cuba, extending from Cardenas on the east to Bahia Honda on the west." Bureau of Navigation Report of 1898, appx. 175. The blockade was immediately instituted accordingly. On April 22, the President issued a proclamation, declaring that the United States had instituted and would maintain that blockade, "in pursuance of the laws of the United States, and the law of nations applicable to such cases." 30 Stat. 1769. And by the act of Congress of April 25, 1898, c. 189, it was declared that the war between the United States and Spain existed on that day, and had existed since and including April 21. 30 Stat. 364.

On April 26, 1898, the President issued another proclamation, which, after reciting the existence of the war, as declared by Congress, contained this further recital: "It being desirable that such war should be conducted upon principles in harmony with the present views of nations and sanctioned by their recent practice." This recital was followed by specific declarations of certain rules for the conduct of the war by sea, making no mention of fishing vessels. 30 Stat. 1770. But the proclamation clearly manifests the general policy of the Government to conduct the war in accordance with the principles of international law sanctioned by the recent practice of nations.

* * *

Upon the facts proved in either case, it is the duty of this court, sitting as the highest prize court of the United States, and administering the law of nations, to declare and adjudge that the capture was unlawful, and without probable cause; and it is therefore, in each case,

Ordered, that the decree of the District Court be reversed, and the proceeds of the sale of the vessel, together with the proceeds of any sale of her cargo, be restored to the claimant, with damages and costs.

[Dissenting opinion of Mr. Chief Justice Fuller, with whom concurred Mr. Justice Harlan and Mr. Justice McKenna, omitted.]

Read
Class from
supplement

PRACTICES OF NATIONAL COURTS

It would be difficult, perhaps impossible, to find a national legal system the courts of which arbitrarily refused to apply rules of customary international law not in conflict with domestic law, and the two cases above are illustrative of the general practice of national courts. The main point at issue in this section is not whether courts in national legal systems give effect to such rules, but rather how they go about it.

1. *Where there is no constitutional or other legislative provision directing courts to apply rules of customary international law.* In states where the common law prevails, courts usually justify their application of such rules by stating that international law is part of the law of the land. The simplicity of the proposition is deceptive, however, for if it were accepted as literally true, courts would need only determine whether there was an applicable rule of customary international law and, so long as they found an applicable rule not in conflict with domestic law, apply it. Yet this is not quite the way the courts proceeded in the cases set forth above.

Even after determining there was no rule of customary international law applicable to the facts in issue, the English court went on to decide that in any event there was no applicable rule of domestic law under which the plaintiff could recover. In the American case, the court proceeded to determine there was an applicable rule of customary international law only after ascertaining there was no applicable rule of domestic law already established by previous executive or legislative act or judicial decision. If international law is part of the law of the land, why should it be necessary to determine whether there is an applicable rule of domestic law? Consider in this connection the following case.

In Triquet v. Bath, 3 Burr. 1478 (K.B.1764), Lord Mansfield delivered the opinion and in the course of it made the statements to which reference was made in the West Rand Central Gold Mining Company case. The defendant, an Englishman, was secretary to an ambassador from a foreign state. The issue was whether he was immune from arrest. Holding that he was, Lord Mansfield said:

> * * * This privilege of foreign ministers and their domestic servants depends upon the law of nations. The Act of Parliament of 7 Ann. c. 12, is declaratory of it. * * *
>
> * * *
>
> But the Act was not occasioned by any doubt "whether the law of nations, particularly the part relative to public ministers, was not part of the law of England; * * * nor intended to vary, an iota from it."
>
> I remember in a case before Lord Talbot, * * * the matter was very elaborately argued at the Bar; and a solemn deliberate opinion given by the Court. These questions arose and were discussed. * * * "What was the rule of decision: the Act of Parliament; or, the law of nations." Lord Talbot declared a clear opinion—"That the law of nations, in its full extent was part of the law of England."—"That the Act of Parliament was declaratory; and occasioned by a particular incident."—"That the law of nations was to be collected from the practice of different nations, and the authority of writers." Accordingly, he argued and determined from such instances, and the authority

of Grotius, Barbeyrac, Binkershoek, Wiquefort, &c. there being no English writer of eminence, upon the subject.

In states where the civil law or some other legal system prevails and there is no constitutional or other legislative provision directing them to apply rules of customary international law, the courts, just as those in states where the common law prevails, feel compelled to justify their application of such rules in some way. They do not necessarily resort to the proposition that international law is part of the law of the land, but in whatever way they determine a rule of customary international law is applicable, they often show the same proclivity as common law courts to find that there is in any event an applicable rule of domestic law. The following case is illustrative.

Immunity Case, Yugoslavia, Supreme Court of the People's Republic of Croatia, No. Gz–766–56 (1956), 86 Journal du Droit International 525 (1959). The plaintiff was injured by an automobile belonging to the military mission of a foreign embassy in Belgrade and sued the embassy for damages. The court held that the embassy could not be sued but ruled that the suit could be treated as one in effect against the state represented by the foreign embassy. In considering whether, and to what extent, the foreign state could be sued in the courts of Yugoslavia, the court said: [a]

> A practice exists in international relations under which a State enjoys before the Courts of another State a right which is known as "immunity from jurisdiction". This immunity means that the State which enjoys it cannot, without its own consent, be brought before the Courts of another State. This is considered to be a customary rule of public international law which ought to be respected.

> But there is also an internal legal provision on this subject. This is Article 19(2) of the Statute introducing the old Yugoslav Code of Criminal Procedure. This provision is still applicable under the terms of Article 4 of the Statute of 1946 * * * (see Official Gazette of the P.F.R. of Yugoslavia, No. 86/46). Under the terms of this provision the jurisdiction of the Yugoslav tribunals extends to all persons who, under the principles of international law, enjoy extra-territorial rights, on the condition always that they agree to submit to such jurisdiction, or that the case in which they are involved concerns their immovable property situated in Yugoslavia or a right in rem which they exercise over immovable property belonging to another person, but also situated in Yugoslavia. Although this provision is only designed to cover natural persons in their capacity as diplomatic representatives of a foreign State, it is beyond doubt that the foreign State itself cannot enjoy a lesser degree of immunity from juris-

a. English text in the Journal. Reprinted by permission of Editions Techniques, S.A., Paris.

diction * * * . In consequence it may be said that the immunity from jurisdiction enjoyed by foreign States before Yugoslav
tribunals is a rule of Yugoslav positive law.

* * *

In the light of the reasons just set out, the court of first instance acted in conformity with the law in rejecting the Plaintiff's action and asserting that the normal legal course was not
open to him in this case. * * *

Suppose that in the West Rand Central Gold Mining Company
case, the court had found there was a rule of customary international
law applicable to the facts in issue, though there was no applicable
rule of domestic law. Would it have applied the rule of customary
international law as the rule of decision? Did the Supreme Court of
the United States apply a rule of customary international law as the
rule of decision in The Paquete Habana? In the Yugoslav case, suppose the court had found there was no applicable rule of domestic
law, though there was an applicable rule of customary international
law. What would it have done? In those three cases, did the English, the American and the Yugoslav courts follow identical theories
concerning the relationship of customary international law to domestic law? In what way do their theories in the matter differ from the
theory implicit in the opinion of Lord Mansfield in Triquet v. Bath?

2. *Provisions in constitutions.* In national legal systems, constitutional provisions may provide a legal basis for the application by
the courts of rules of customary international law. Provisions expressing in broad terms the acceptance by the state of rules of international law are found in some national legal systems.

For example, Article 29(3) of the Constitution of Ireland provides: "Ireland accepts the generally recognized principles of international law as its rule of conduct in its relations with other states."
III (1) Peaslee, Constitutions of Nations 482 (3d ed. 1968). Article
211 of the Constitution of Burma declares: "The Union of Burma
* * * accepts the generally recognized principles of international
law as its rule of conduct in its relations with foreign states." II (1)
Peaslee, Constitutions of Nations 109 (3d ed. 1966). And Article 25
of the Constitution of the German Democratic Republic states: "The
generally accepted rules of international law are binding upon the
state power and upon every citizen." III (1) Peaslee, Constitutions of
Nations 386 (3d ed. 1968).

Whether a broadly worded constitutional provision is helpful to
courts in justifying their application of customary international law
may depend on their past practice. The French courts have traditionally given effect to such rules and for this reason some argue that
the preamble to the French Constitution of 1946 merely acknowledged
the fact in stating: "The French Republic, faithful to its tradition,
abides by the rules of international law." II Peaslee, Constitutions of
Nations 7 (2d ed. 1956). The provision was incorporated by refer-

ence in the 1958 Constitution of the Fifth French Republic but it has been contended by a French author that the provision is not only unnecessary but also dangerous, because it might put into question the inherent power of French courts to apply rules of international law. Rousseau, Droit International Public 14 (Précis Dalloz, 5th ed. 1970).

Some constitutions provide courts with a basis for applying rules of customary international law by declaring specifically that international law is part of the law of the land. Thus Article 2(3) of the Constitution of the Philippines states: "The Philippines * * * adopts the generally accepted principles of international law as part of the law of the Nation." II (2) Peaslee, Constitutions of Nations 1068 (3d ed. 1966). The Austrian Constitution states in Article 9: "The generally recognized rules of international law shall be considered as component parts of the Federal Law." III (1) Peaslee, Constitutions of Nations 25 (3d ed. 1968). And Article 25 of the Constitution of the German Federal Republic provides: "The general rules of public international law are an integral part of federal law." III (1) Peaslee, Constitutions of Nations 366 (3d ed. 1968).

A very few constitutions go further and contemplate not only the application of rules of customary international law by the courts but also the possibility of conflict between such rules and rules of domestic law and indicate the manner in which the conflict should be resolved. For the text of constitutional provisions of this type, see p. 21.

---

2. RULES OF DOMESTIC LAW IN CONFLICT WITH CUSTOMARY INTERNATIONAL LAW

THE OVER THE TOP
SCHROEDER v. BISSELL

United States District Court, D.Conn., 1925.
5 F.2d 838.

THOMAS, District Judge. * * *

[Three libels by the United States, one against the schooner Over the Top, and two against its cargo, with application by A. L. Schroeder, owner of the cargo, against Harvey Bissell, Collector, for return of cargo. Libels dismissed.]

From the evidence I find the following facts established: On August 27, 1924, the schooner Over the Top, carrying a cargo of whisky and operating under the British flag and under British registry, cleared for Cuba from St. Johns, New Brunswick. It arrived at a point off the coast of Block Island several weeks prior to October 19, 1924. * * *

On the 19th of October, 1924, at about 10 o'clock in the evening, the supercargo on board the schooner sold 25 cases of whisky for $550 to a special agent of the Internal Revenue Department. The sale was made in the presence of the captain, and thereupon the crew of the vessel, in the presence and under the direction of the captain, unloaded these cases of whisky and transferred the same to a sea sled employed in the government service. Both captain and supercargo knew that the whisky so transferred was to be transported to a point on the adjacent coast, but neither one of them knew that the sea sled or the men on it were in the government service. The transaction occurred at a point approximately 19 miles distant from the shore, or 115 degrees true from the southeast light of Block Island * * *.

On the following day, Over the Top was seized by officers of the United States coast guard, and the captain and crew were placed under arrest, and the ship and her cargo were towed into the Port of New London and turned over to the collector of customs and are now in his custody.

I further find that the schooner had been hovering for some time off the coast of the United States at the point where she was seized, and that those in command were engaged during that period in selling liquor and delivering the same to boats proceeding from the coast of the United States and returning thereto. The testimony seems to support the conclusion that business was slow.

Upon these facts, the United States demands judgment decreeing the forfeiture and sale of the ship and cargo. The owner of the ship and the owner of the cargo have appeared separately, but the trial of the three actions was consolidated, and, as will be seen in the sequel, the principles of law governing are applicable alike to both the schooner and cargo.

The government bases its claim of forfeiture upon the alleged violation of sections 447, 448, 450, 453, 585, 586, 593, and 594 of the Tariff Act of 1922 * * * as well as upon the provisions of the American-British Treaty which became effective May 22, 1924. The above sections of the Tariff Act provide as follows:

Sec. 447.   Unlading—Place.—It shall be unlawful to make entry of any vessel or to unlade the cargo or any part thereof of any vessel elsewhere than at a port of entry * * *.

* * *

Sec. 586.   Unlawful Unlading—Exception.—The master of any vessel from a foreign port or place who allows any merchandise (including sea stores) to be unladen from such vessel at any time after its arrival within four leagues of the coast of the United States and before such vessel has come to the proper place for the discharge of such merchandise, and before he has received a permit to unlade, shall be liable to a penalty equal to twice the value of the merchandise but not less than $1,000, and such vessel and the merchandise shall be subject to seizure and forfeiture * * *.

But before we proceed to discuss the above-quoted sections of the Tariff Act as well as the treaty, it may be well to dispose of one of the contentions made by counsel in behalf of the cargo and the schooner.

The proposition is advanced that, regardless of our municipal legislation, the acts complained of could not constitute offenses against the United States when committed by foreign nationals, on foreign bottoms, on the high seas at a point beyond the territorial jurisdiction of the country. Well-known principles of international practice are invoked in support of this contention accompanied with the citation of authority. Upon careful consideration, however, I am led to conclude that a misconception exists here as to the status, in a federal forum, of so-called international law when that law encounters a municipal enactment.

If we assume for the present that the national legislation has, by its terms, made the acts complained of a crime against the United States even when committed on the high seas by foreign nationals upon a ship of foreign registry, then there is no discretion vested in the federal court, once it obtains jurisdiction, to decline enforcement. International practice is law only in so far as we adopt it, and like all common or statute law it bends to the will of the Congress. It is not the function of courts to annul legislation; it is their duty to interpret and by their judicial decrees to enforce it—and even when an act of Congress is declared invalid, it is only because the basic law is being enforced in that declaration. There is one ground only upon which a federal court may refuse to enforce an act of Congress and that is when the act is held to be unconstitutional. The act may contravene recognized principles of international comity, but that affords no more basis for judicial disregard of it than it does for executive disregard of it. These libels, therefore, cannot be attacked upon the ground that the territorial jurisdiction of the United States cannot be extended beyond the three-mile sea zone under international law.

If, however, the court has no option to refuse the enforcement of legislation in contravention of principles of international law, it does not follow that in construing the terms and provisions of a statute it may not assume that such principles were on the national conscience and that the congressional act did not deliberately intend to infringe them. In other words, unless it unmistakably appears that a congressional act was intended to be in disregard of a principle of international comity, the presumption is that it was intended to be in conformity with it. It is with such a principle in mind that we now proceed to an examination of the legislation upon which the government relies.

Section 447 of the Tariff Act of 1922 * * * makes it unlawful for the vessel to make entry of or to unlade any part of its cargo elsewhere than at a port of entry. Part of the cargo of Over the Top was unloaded on the high seas, and the government contends that the statute was thereby violated. To me it seems that the statute was intended to prevent entry or unlading at a port or place in the country other than a port of entry. It had no reference to unlading on the seas even when done within the three-mile zone. But waiving that question, it is to be noted that the act is phrased in general language and that it bespeaks no suggestion of territorial limitation. The proposition has not heretofore been advanced that for that reason the act has attempted to extend the territorial jurisdiction of the United States over the whole earth. Almost all criminal statutes, or statutes prohibiting defined conduct, are phrased in general language without mention of territorial limitation. But they are all to be read in the light of the principle that jurisdiction is not extraterritorial and that the municipal legislation is not attempting to regulate or to punish conduct performed outside of the national domain. For example, the statutes of Connecticut do not forbid larceny in Connecticut —they forbid larceny. The statutes of the United States do not forbid counterfeiting in the United States—they forbid counterfeiting. That the Congress may, in disregard of the law of nations, prohibit acts by foreign nationals not committed within our domain, has already been conceded; but unless such intent clearly appears from the language of the statute such intent is not to be presumed.

* * *

The same considerations apply with equal force to the provisions of sections 448, 450, 453, 585, 593, and 594 of the Tariff Act of 1922. These enactments of the Congress are implicit with the proviso that the acts therein denounced be accomplished within the territory of the United States. No attempt is there discernible to extend the legislative jurisdiction of the United States beyond its boundaries. Of utmost significance, therefore, is the language of section 586 of the act providing that the master of any vessel from a foreign port, who allows any merchandise to be unladen from such vessel at any time after its arrival within four leagues of the coast of the United States, and before such vessel has come to the proper place for the discharge of such merchandise, and before permission has been given to unlade, shall be liable to a penalty, and the vessel and the merchandise shall be subject to seizure and forfeiture. It appears to me that this section has a most important, if not a determinative, bearing upon the point under discussion. This enactment has been part of our legislation for over a hundred years. Here we have a distinct extension of our sea jurisdiction to a point 12 miles from the coast—an assertion of authority which may perhaps clash with international practice, but which, whether challenged or not, is unmistakable, and which, therefore, it is the business of our courts to enforce. Had the master and supercargo of Over the Top been guilty of unlading the liquor at a point within this 12-mile zone, it may be that we would have had no difficulty in sustaining the libels.

* * *

My conclusion, then, is that as no statute embracing the subject-matter of sections 447, 448, 450, 453, 585, 586, 593, and 594 of the Tariff Act of 1922 has extended our territorial jurisdiction to a point on the high seas distant 19 miles from our coast, conduct which would have been in violation of these sections if performed within our territory cannot constitute an offense against the United States when performed at such a distance by foreign nationals on ships of foreign registry. If, for the purpose of our treasury, we can extend our sea jurisdiction to a point four leagues from the coast, I see no reason why we cannot extend it four leagues more. I merely observe that we have not done so yet.

* * *

[The court then examined the treaty and concluded it did not in fact enact new criminal legislation.]

The considerations as above expressed therefore impel the conclusion that there is no legal basis for these libels, and it follows that they must be and the same are dismissed. * * *

ATTORNEY–GENERAL OF ISRAEL v. EICHMANN

Israel, District Court of Jerusalem, 1961.
36 Int'l L.Rep. 5, 24 (1968).*

[Adolf Eichmann was tried in Israel under a law punishing Nazis and Nazi collaborators for crimes against the Jewish people committed in Germany in World War II.]

The first argument of counsel, that Israel law is in conflict with international law and that it therefore cannot vest jurisdiction in this Court, raises the preliminary question of the validity of international law in Israel and whether, in the event of conflict, it is to be preferred to the law of the land. The law in force in Israel resembles that in force in England in this regard. * * *

As regards Israel, the Deputy President, Justice Cheshin, said in Criminal Appeal 175/54 (10 Piske Din 5, 17):

As to the question of the incorporation of the principles of international law in the national law, we rely on Blackstone, Commentaries on the Laws of England (Book IV, Chap. 5):

In England * * * the law of nations * * * is * * * adopted in its full extent by the common law, and it is

* Reprinted by permission of E. Lauterpacht, ed., and Grotius Publications,
Ltd., Cambridge, England.

held to be a part of the law of the land * * * without which it must cease to be a part of the civilized world.

The same applies to other countries, such as the United States of America, France, Belgium and Switzerland, where the usages of international law have been recognized as part of the national law. * * *

With respect to statutory law, Justice Agranat said in High Court Case No. 279/51 (6 Piske Din 945, 966):

B. It is a well-known maxim that a municipal statute should—except where its contents require a different interpretation—be interpreted in accordance with the rules of public international law.

And in Criminal Appeal No. 5/51 (5 Piske Din 1061) Mr. Justice Sussman said (p. 1065):

It is a well-known rule that in interpreting a statute the Court will as far as possible try to avoid a conflict between the municipal law and the obligations incumbent on the State by virtue of international law. But this is only one of the canons of interpretation. That is to say, where we are dealing not with the Common Law but with a written statute which expresses the will of the legislator, then the Court must carry out the will of the legislator without considering if there exists a contradiction between the statute and international law * * *. Furthermore, the Courts here derive their jurisdiction from municipal law and not from international law.

Our jurisdiction to try this case is based on the Nazi and Nazi Collaborators (Punishment) Law, an enacted Law the provisions of which are unequivocal. The Court has to give effect to a law of the Knesset, and we cannot entertain the contention that this Law conflicts with the principles of international law. For this reason alone counsel's first submission must be rejected.

We have, however, also considered the sources of international law, including the numerous authorities cited by learned defence counsel in his basic written brief upon which he based his oral pleadings, and by the learned Attorney-General in his comprehensive oral pleadings, and have failed to find any foundation for the contention that Israel law is in conflict with the principles of international law. On the contrary, we have reached the conclusion that the Law in question conforms to the best traditions of the law of nations.[a]

* * *

a. For a discussion of this case as it relates to individual responsibility for war crimes, see Chapter 10.

THE NYUGAT

Netherlands, Supreme Court, 1959.
10 Nederlands Tijdschrift Voor International Recht 82 (1963).[a]

[The owners of The Nyugat, a merchant ship, sued the state of the Netherlands for damages suffered as a result of its capture by a Dutch warship in April 1941 and its eventual loss while it was under the control of the Dutch government in exile in London.

At the time of its capture, The Nyugat flew the Hungarian flag and since the Netherlands was not at war with Hungary, it would not have been subject to capture as a merchant ship flying an enemy flag under the Prize Rules for the Kingdom of the Netherlands in effect until 1941. Shortly before the capture, however, the Dutch government in exile had modified the Prize Rules by a series of decrees and under their provisions a ship sailing under the flag of a state not at war with the Netherlands would, under certain conditions, be treated as an enemy ship. In a previous ruling, the Supreme Court of the Netherlands had held that these conditions had been satisfied in the case of The Nyugat * * *. Hence the capture was valid under the prize law of the Netherlands and the shipowners were not entitled to damages.

On rehearing, the owners contended, inter alia, that the provisions for capture introduced by the decrees of 1941 were contrary to customary international law and argued the court had power to decide whether it was so by virtue of Article 66 of the Constitution of the Netherlands. The article empowered the Dutch courts to declare domestic legislation inapplicable if it were in conflict with certain international agreements entered into by the Netherlands. The plaintiffs argued that the court was implicitly empowered by the article to declare domestic legislation inapplicable if it were in conflict with customary international law.

While not conceding there was a conflict in the case, the court rejected the argument. A portion of its opinion appears below.]

It has been alleged that the régime as laid down by the Decrees * * * is contrary to customary and written international law and, for this reason, should not be applied. * * * According to the new Article 66 of the Constitution, legislation in force within the Kingdom shall, under certain circumstances, not apply if this application would be incompatible with provisions of [international] agreements * * * which have been entered into either before or after the enactment of such legislation. [The] shipowners are of the opinion that a principle of wider scope has been enunciated here. This

a. English text in the Tijdschrift. Reprinted from Netherlands International al Law Review with the permission of Sijthoff & Noordhoff, International Publishers b.v., P.O. Box 4, 2400 MA Alphen aan den Rijn, The Netherlands.

principle would, in a case of clear conflict * * * allow the national courts to review municipal law by rules of customary international law * * *. As appears from the history of the new Article 66, this provision specifically aimed to settle the difference of opinion as to how far a Netherlands court is entitled to judge Netherlands law by the standards of international law. The provision expressly * * * [intended] to restrict this review to the cases * * * of agreements mentioned by it. The Netherlands courts which until then were free to solve this question as they deemed fit, were, after its entry into force, bound by this provision of the Constitution, even where the facts of the case or the judgment challenged antedated the enactment of the new rule. The Supreme Court, therefore, is not entitled to enter into the question raised by [the] shipowners whether the Decrees are in conflict with customary international law * * *.

1. *Publicists' reaction to the Nyugat decision.* The decision of the Supreme Court of the Netherlands in The Nyugat was severely criticized. In the notes which follow the report of the case set forth above, Erades contends the courts of the Netherlands had previously given effect to rules of customary international law which deviated from domestic law and also maintains the Supreme Court of the Netherlands misconstrued the legislative history and meaning of the constitutional provision involved. Another author labels the decision "wrong in almost all respects." Verzijl, I International Law in Historical Perspective 97 (1968).

2. *Treatment of the problem in other national legal systems.* Article 10 of the Italian Constitution states: "Italy's legal system conforms with the generally recognized principles of international law." III (1) Peaslee, Constitutions of Nations 501 (3d ed. 1968). Conformity between the two means, according to the Supreme Court of Italy, that rules of municipal law which are contrary to customary internation law "must be eliminated." Re Martinez, Italy, Court of Cassation, 1959, 28 Int'l L.Rep. 170 (1963), the text of which appears at p. 191. Article 25 of the Constitution of the Federal Republic of Germany not only states that the general rules of public international law are an integral part of federal law, but goes on to provide: "They shall take precedence over the laws and shall directly create rights and duties for the inhabitants of the territory." III (1) Peaslee, Constitutions of Nations 366 (3d ed. 1968).

Article 28(1) of the Greek Constitution of 1975 declares that "the generally recognized rules of international law * * * are an integral part of Greek law and have an authority superior to any inconsistent legislative provision."[a] Roucounas, Le Droit International dans la Constitution de la Grèce du 9 Juin 1975, 29 Revue Héllénique de Droit International 63, 65 (1976).

a. Translation by the editors.

Absent such types of constitutional provisions, the courts of national legal systems frequently assert they would give effect to their domestic law if it were in clear conflict with customary international law. Yet should a national court resolve the conflict in such manner, the state to which it belongs would be in violation of international law. The rule on this point is clear and is stated in Section 3(2) of The Restatement of the Foreign Relations Law of the United States (1965) as follows: "The domestic law of a state is not a defense to a violation by the state of international law." Comment *i* to the section states: " * * * Thus a state cannot justify its violation of international law by invoking its own contrary domestic law even if embodied in its constitution."

Courts in national legal systems, however, are not often confronted with the necessity of resolving the conflict by giving precedence to their domestic law and their proclivity to say they would if necessary is seldom put to the test. For example, English courts usually make a point of stating that they would give effect to the will of the parliament if its legislation were in clear conflict with customary international law. But this is no more than "a deferential nod to Cerberus before by-passing him," according to an observer of English judicial practice. 1 O'Connell, International Law 57 (2d ed. 1970). He goes on to state that the "collision between international law and the will of Parliament is abstract and only on the rare occasion of the Second World War did it become actual." (at 57)

Smith, International Law in Norwegian Courts, 12 Scandinavian Studies in Law 1968, at 153, 160 (1968), discusses the question of conflict between domestic law and international law, whether customary or otherwise, and states:

> Legal writers have been especially concerned with the areas of conflict between international and national law. This is not, in my opinion, the most interesting aspect. In spite of everything the conflicts are the pathological cases. Besides, clear conflict situations are rare. Significantly enough, scarcely one has been brought before the Norwegian Supreme Court, and probably such cases will not be frequent in the future either. One will also acquire a somewhat distorted and a too negative view of the significance of international law in the municipal sphere by concentrating upon those situations.

> During the proceedings of the French-Norwegian gold clause case before the International Court of Justice at The Hague in 1957, Maurice Bourquin, the Belgian professor who represented the Norwegian Government, stated in the course of his oral argument that all the lacunae, all the obscurities, and all the uncertainties in the municipal law afford the Norwegian courts the opportunity to apply international law. It is here that one arrives at the more practically important fields. This statement may perhaps contain a certain element of over-emphasis.

But our courts have gone a long way in the direction of creating a harmonious relationship with international law.

TUNKIN, CO–EXISTENCE AND INTERNATIONAL LAW

[1958] III Académie de Droit International, Recueil des Cours, 1, 23.[a]

The concept that international custom constitutes a primary and the most important means of creating norms of international law was certainly correct for the 19th century, but * * * it no longer reflects the present day situation in international law. In contemporary conditions the principal means of creating norms of international law is a treaty. This is the point of view held by the great majority, if not by all, of the Soviet authors who have treated this subject.

LUKASHUK, SOURCES OF PRESENT–DAY INTERNATIONAL LAW

Contemporary International Law 164, 174 (Moscow 1969).

For historical reasons, custom predominated in the past. In the last century the situation has changed and it has been relegated to second place by the treaty. However, the rules of customary law continue to play a very big role in the practice of international law.

---

3. RULES OF DOMESTIC LAW IN CONFLICT WITH INTERNATIONAL AGREEMENTS

A conflict between domestic law and an international agreement may arise in either of two ways. First, the agreement may be in conflict with a rule of domestic law already in effect at the time the international agreement becomes binding. Second, a rule of domestic law may come into effect after the agreement has become binding and be in conflict with it. In either case, a state would be in violation of international law if it gave effect to the conflicting rule of domestic law, for it cannot invoke its contrary domestic law as justification for its failure to abide by the agreement any more than it can invoke it as a defense for its failure to abide by a rule of customary international law.

1. *International agreement in conflict with constitutional provision.* Should the provisions of an international agreement be in conflict with the constitution of the national legal system, and the constitution not expressly specify that it can be modified by an international agreement, such provisions usually would not become operative as domestic law. They would not be valid as the law of the United States. See Chapter 16. Neither would they be internally operative

a. English text in the Recueil.

in Mexico. In re Vera, Supreme Court, 1948, [1948] Ann.Dig. 328 (No. 114). The Court of Appeal for East Africa at Nairobi takes the same position. Criminal Appeal No. 156 of 1969, IX International Legal Materials 561 (1970). Article 324 of the Constitution of Nicaragua expressly provides that an international agreement in conflict with the constitution has no validity. IV (2) Peaslee, Constitutions of Nations 1006 (2d ed. 1970).

In recent years, however, the constitutions of some national systems have made provision for resolving conflicts between the constitution and an international agreement. Thus the Constitution of the Netherlands of 1815 was amended in 1953 to provide in Article 63: "If the development of the international legal order requires this, the contents of an agreement may deviate from certain provisions of the Constitution." The article goes on to provide that in such cases, the agreement must receive the approval of the legislature by a two-thirds majority of the votes cast. III (2) Peaslee, Constitutions of Nations 660 (3d ed. 1968).

In France, Article 54 of the Constitution of 1958 provides that if the Constitutional Council should declare that an international agreement contains a clause contrary to the constitution, the authorization of the legislature "to ratify or approve this commitment may be given only after amendment of the Constitution." III (1) Peaslee, Constitutions of Nations 323 (3d ed. 1968).

Upon becoming independent, former French overseas territories adopted similar provisions in their constitutions. Gabon, Article 53; Ivory Coast, Article 55; Mali, Article 39; Mauritania, Article 45; Senegal, Article 78; Togo, Article 68; Upper Volta, Article 55. A similar provision also appears in Article 11 of the Constitution of Congo-Kinshasa (now Zaire). I Peaslee, Constitutions of Nations 205, 249, 542, 555, 709, 901, 1019, 105 (3d ed. 1965).

2. *International agreement in conflict with legislation.* Where the conflict is between an international agreement and anterior legislation, courts have usually not found it difficult to resolve a conflict in favor of the international agreement, but in doing so courts usually do not take the position that the agreement is intrinsically superior to existing legislation. Instead, they treat it as equal in rank with the legislation and apply the rule of construction that as between anterior and posterior laws in conflict, the one later in time prevails.

In the United States, the equality in rank of treaties and acts of Congress is provided by Article VI, Clause 2, of the Constitution. Since neither is superior to the other, the one later in time is held to prevail. Hence a self-executing treaty, i. e. one whose provisions are directly applicable as rules of domestic law without the need of implementation by an act of Congress, supersedes the provisions of prior and inconsistent federal legislation. Should the treaty not be self-executing, its provisions, once enacted into rules of domestic law by act of Congress, also supersede, because they are later in time, the provisions of prior and inconsistent federal legislation. On these and other aspects of the internal effect of international agreements of the United States, see Chapter 16.

Article 133 of the Constitution of Mexico of January 31, 1917, is very similar to Article VI, Clause 2, of the Constitution of the United States and gives equal rank to a treaty and federal law. IV (2) Peaslee, Constitutions of Nations 951 (3d ed. 1970). So does Article 31 of the Constitution of Argentina of May 1, 1853. IV (1) Peaslee, Constitutions of Nations 12 (3d ed. 1970). The Supreme Court of Argentina has stated that since the article does not give precedence to either the treaty or federal law, a conflict between the two is resolved by giving effect to the one later in time. S. A. Martin & Cia. v. Nacion, 257 Fallos de la Corta Suprema 99 (1963).

National courts are presented with a more difficult issue when, absent an applicable constitutional provision, they must resolve a conflict between an international agreement and domestic legislation that becomes effective at a later date. The rule of construction that the law later in time prevails operates to deprive of internal effect the conflicting provisions of the prior agreement.

The position of the Supreme Court of the United States on the point is illustrative: "This Court has also repeatedly taken the position that an Act of Congress * * * is on a full parity with a treaty, and that when a statute which is subsequent in time is inconsistent with a treaty, the statute to the extent of conflict renders the treaty null." Reid v. Covert, 354 U.S. 1, 18, 77 S.Ct. 1222, 1231 (1957). The courts of many national legal systems frequently state they would apply the rule of construction should a conflict between an international agreement and subsequent domestic law arise and occasionally find themselves compelled to do just that. The Supreme Court of the United States in fact has given effect to a subsequent act of Congress in conflict with a prior treaty.

In recent years, however, the courts of some other national legal systems have shown a willingness to give more weight to international agreements in conflict with subsequent domestic law than might be expected under the doctrine of precedence for the one later in time. What rules for the resolution of this conflict are being applied by the courts in the next two cases?

LIBRAIRIE HACHETTE S.A. v. SOCIETE COOPERATIVE

Switzerland, Federal Tribunal, 1st Civil Court, 1967.
XXV Annuaire Suisse de Droit
International 239 (1968).[a]

A suit [for damages], brought before the Civil Court of Geneva and based on the law of cartels [of 1962], involved two Swiss corpo-

---

a. Translation by the editors. Reprinted with the permission of Schulthess Polygraphischer Verlag AG, Zurich.

rations, as plaintiffs, and four other corporations [as defendants] of which two were French [and two were Swiss]. The two French corporations [relying on the Franco-Swiss Convention of 1869] pleaded that the court had no jurisdiction. The court stated that the two [French] defendants, since they had no [business] establishment * * * in Switzerland, could in principle rely on the Franco-Swiss Convention on Jurisdiction and Execution of Judgments of June 15, 1869 * * *. The first article of that convention provides:

> In disputes involving claims in personam, whether civil or commercial, arising either between Swiss and French [nationals], or between French and Swiss [nationals], the plaintiff shall be required to bring his action before the natural judge [i. e. the courts in the state of nationality] of the defendant.

Holding however that the [Swiss] federal law on cartels and analogous arrangements of December 20, 1962, * * * was applicable to the case * * * and was not governed by the convention, the Civil Court of Geneva held it had jurisdiction. The two French corporations then appealed to the Federal Tribunal * * *. [A portion of the opinion by the Federal Tribunal appears below.]

That the convention controls as against [jurisdictional] rules of domestic law cannot be a matter of any doubt * * *. The case involves * * * a litigation between Swiss [nationals], domiciled in Switzerland and French [nationals], domiciled in France. The natural judge of the latter is the French judge * * *. [T]he French defendants are entitled to the benefit of the convention even though they are legal entities [rather than natural persons] * * *. The first article of the convention shall therefore be applicable if the claim asserted in the present case involves a claim in personam within the meaning of the article.

[The court went on to determine it did and hence the action would have to be brought in the courts of France.]

---

1. *Background in aid of analysis.* Though the Swiss court chose to give a broad construction to Article 1 of the 1869 Convention, there were weighty arguments for giving a strict construction to the article, declaring it inapplicable, and applying the Swiss law on cartels of 1962.

First, the reference of certain types of cases to the courts of the nationality of the defendant, though not unusual in some of the international agreements concluded in the 19th century, would be highly unusual today. National legal systems do not now normally relinquish the jurisdiction which is lawfully theirs under international law and there was no question in the case at hand that, aside from the convention, the Swiss courts had every right to proceed with the suit.

Second, national courts usually construe strictly rather than liberally derogations from rules of international law. French courts had held several times that Article 1 of the Convention of 1869, because it derogated from international law rules of jurisdiction, must be given a strict construction. In particular, they had held that since the article did not say anything about a plurality of defendants of different nationalities, some of them French and others Swiss, it was not applicable to that type of case and hence the plaintiff could sue either in France or in Switzerland.

Third, it was open to question whether a suit for damages arising from acts in restraint of trade should be assimilated to an ordinary suit in tort such as was contemplated by the convention. Though the Swiss law on cartels of 1962 was designed to protect both private economic interests and the public interest of Switzerland in its economy, there was no guarantee that the French courts would be willing to apply the law of cartels of Switzerland when the suit was brought before them.

Some of these arguments were made, but dimissed by the Swiss court, as explained in the comment on the decision by Lalive in Chronique de Jurisprudence Suisse, 97 Journal du Droit International 408, 434 (1970).

2. *Subsequent interpretation of treaty in France.* In 1975, a French plaintiff joined as defendants in the French courts two corporations, one from Switzerland and one from the United States. The Swiss corporation contended that jurisdiction belonged to the Swiss courts by virtue of Article 1 of the Convention of 1869. The lower court upheld its view. The court of appeals reversed on the ground the article had no application since it was silent about a plurality of defendants of different nationalities. The supreme court reversed the court of appeals, holding the plaintiffs could not sue in France when one of the defendants was a Swiss corporation domiciled in Switzerland and the other a foreign corporation domiciled in another foreign country. Ste Stauffer Chemical Europe & Ste Stauffer Chemical Company v. Ets Jean Lagarrigue, France, Court of Cassation, 1978, 105 Journal du Droit International 898 (1978).

MINISTER FOR ECONOMIC AFFAIRS v. S.A. FROMAGERIE FRANCO–SUISSE "LE SKI"

Belgium, Court of Cassation, 1971.
[1972] Common Market Law Reports 330.*

Facts

The S.A. Fromagerie Franco-Suisse "Le Ski," the respondent in the present proceedings and appellant before the Court of Appeal, is a successor in title to the S.A. Etablissements Detry * * *.

---

* Reprinted from Common Market Law Reports with the permission of the European Law Center, Ltd., London.

The original action was brought on 28 December 1965 against the State for repayment of 67,821,400 francs, which was reduced before the judge of first instance to 67,713,810 francs. This latter sum represents the special duties which * * * Detry paid from November 1958 to November 1964 on the import under licence of milk products. The portion of these duties relating to products imported from member-States of the European Communities amounted to 59,638,636 francs.

The duties were levied under an arrêté royal of 3 November 1958, * * * (subsequent arrêtés royaux replaced or amended this arrêté and fixed other maximum rates, while the rate in fact levied was determined by ministerial order). They were reduced to nil by ministerial order of 29 October 1964 and finally repealed by an arrêté royal of 23 October 1965.

On 13 November 1964, the European Court of Justice, in a case brought under Article 169(2) of the E.E.C. Treaty * * * held that Belgium, by establishing and applying after 1 January 1958 a special duty on the import of milk products, a tax of equivalent effect to that of customs duties, had failed to comply with Article 12 of the Treaty.

* * * [The arrêté royal of 3 November 1958 and some others] were retroactively ratified by the Law of 19 March 1968, which in addition provided as follows: "Sums paid in application of these arrêtés are irrecoverable. Their payment is irrevocable and may not give rise to dispute before any authority whatever. This ratification is effective as from the day of entry into force of the arrêtés".

The respondent * * * reduced the claim on appeal to 59,638,636 francs (relating to imports from E.E.C. countries only), basing its claim for money paid by mistake on the ground that by reason of Article 12 of the E.E.C. Treaty the duties in question did not apply to the products imported from member-States of the Community.

The Cour d'Appel of Brussels, reversing the lower court, held that the present respondent (then the appellant) was entitled to repayment of the sum claimed. The State appealed against this judgment to the Cour de Cassation.

Submissions of the Procureur Général

(M. Ganshof van der Meersch)

[The organization of the legal system of Belgium is somewhat different from that in the United States. Magistrates are civil servants under the control of the Ministry of Justice. Some of them are assigned to the bench while others are assigned to represent the public interest in civil and criminal cases in each of the courts in the system. At the apex of the pyramid of those assigned to represent the public interest is the procureur général, who is attached to the supreme court of Belgium.

In this case, the plaintiff is a corporation (technically a société anonyme, abbreviated as S.A.) and the defendant is the Belgian state represented by the Minister for Economic Affairs. Nevertheless the procureur général is arguing in effect on the side of the plaintiff because his duty is not necessarily to defend the position of the government, but rather to argue before the supreme court what he believes to be best for the public interest.

His argument is crucial to an understanding of the case and for that reason is usually published with the judgment. His argument runs to about 38 pages in the report while the judgment occupies less than three pages.]

The questions raised by this appeal deal with the very foundations of international law, in constant development today more than ever before, with its nature and with its effects on the exercise by the State of its powers. They also deal with the nature and the effects of Community law.

*   *   *

The Court of Appeal decided that in imposing and levying these special duties, the appellant had violated Article 12 of the Treaty and held that the respondent was justified in claiming refund of the special duties paid on the import of milk products from member-States of the Community.

The judgment justifies its decision to consider the Law of 19 March 1968 as ineffective so far as concerns the ratification of the decrees imposing a special duty on some milk products, on two grounds: firstly, rules established under international treaty law prevail over those of domestic law and therefore the Law of 19 March 1968 cannot override Article 12 of the Treaty of Rome [which came into force on January 1, 1958], and secondly, Article 12 of the Treaty, which is a directly applicable provision of Community Law, confers specific rights on individual persons, and therefore the Law of 19 March 1968 cannot override such rights.

*   *   *

The doctrine of the superiority of a rule of international law over that of domestic law, as formulated in the judgment, is correct. In the present case, this doctrine applies only so far as concerns a rule of international treaty law. It was within these limits that the question had been posed and decided in court. It is only within these limits that it should be considered here.

*   *   *

States have the duty of ensuring that a rule of domestic law which is incompatible with a rule of international treaty law stemming from the obligations into which they have entered, may not validly be set up against the latter rule. This duty, sanctioned by liability under international law, binds the legislator. It also binds the judge. In spite of the latter's statutory independence, "judicial decisions whose effects are contrary to international law do not free States from their liabilities vis-à-vis foreign countries."

The United Nations International Law Commission has included in its "Draft Declaration on the rights and duties of States" an Article asserting that every State, in its relations with other States, "has the duty of complying with international law and especially with the principle that international law overrides the sovereignty of States." Such a declaration would necessarily be of a declaratory nature.

The obligation of States not to create any rule of domestic law incompatible with a rule of international law must have as corollary the superiority of a norm of international treaty law over one of domestic law. If the rule of international law did not prevail, international law would be doomed, as it would constantly be threatened with obstacles preventing it from attaining or maintaining its general character.

Professor Virally has summed up in a striking phrase evidence of the superiority of international law over domestic law: "Every legal system confers on those subject to its rules legal rights and powers which they cannot claim without it" and "imposes on them obligations which bind them." By doing so, every legal system proclaims its superiority to those who are subject to it. "International law cannot be conceived other than superior to States, which are subject to it. To deny its superiority is to deny its existence."

The subjection of the State—and therefore of its laws—to international law in its international relations has its basis in the international legal system. This subjection implies the primacy of the rule of international law over that of domestic law.

* * *

The Court has not so far delivered an express ruling on the primacy of the rule of international law. Today, this question is formally posed.

The issue has been decided by the Cour supérieure de justice of the Grand-Duchy of Luxembourg, whose Constitution, like the Belgian Constitution, is silent so far as concerns the relationship between treaties and domestic laws. The Cour suprême of Luxembourg has expressly asserted the primacy of the rule of international treaty law, in a Cassation judgment, which has become a landmark.

* * *

Professor Pescatore has commented on this remarkable judgment as follows:

> A Treaty prevails over the statute, not only as a contractual act; it prevails also as an international act. What is involved is not only the primacy of the international order over the domestic order. * * * Serving the final aims of the international order, international law exceeds in value the particular legislative provisions which are in force in any national community. For that reason, the treaty is of a superior essence to the statute, in conformity with the judgment of the Court.

Also invoking the authority of the judgment and considering the matter from the point of view of the Belgian judiciary, Professor de Visscher says:

> * * * Many are those who believe today that the Cour de Cassation might, sooner or later, open the way to a development of case law along the lines of that which in Luxembourg has enabled judicial control to be exercised over the conformity of laws with treaties. To justify the hopes of this line of development in case law, it should not be forgotten that although the judiciary has for more than a century deferred to laws enacted in manifest violation of earlier treaties, this was not dictated by some formal provision of the Constitution.
> * * *

International law, as was pointed out recently, governs today to such a large extent the rights and obligations of mankind, that national courts, even more than international courts, in most of the countries in the world have to apply international law.

The ever-increasing number of normative treaties, the extension of the subject matter of these treaties and (as my predecessor * * * said recently in a statement which acquires its full significance in the case before you today) "the difficulty which the legislator himself has * * * [in noticing] any conflict between new legislation and treaties in force," do not permit you to escape taking a clear position over these conflicts which have not hitherto found any decisive answer in case-law and which a "conciliatory interpretation" cannot settle.

* * *

* * * [N]ot *every* treaty overrules all domestic laws; indubitably a treaty which binds the contracting parties only to enact legislation according to principles set out in the Treaty would not create any conflict, not even to that extent. On the other hand, any rule of international law directly applicable in the domestic system must prevail over the norm of domestic law.

This directly applicable provision of international law settles the conflict so far as concerns the domestic courts, which shall apply it notwithstanding any national law.

* * *

[The procureur général went on to discuss the second ground of the decision by the Court of Appeals of Brussels.]

Judgment

* * *

[1] Under Article 12 of the E.E.C. Treaty, the member-States undertake to refrain from introducing as between themselves any new customs duties on imports and exports or taxes of equivalent effect and from increasing those which they apply in their trade with one another.

[2] The special import duties, the refund of which has been claimed by the respondent, were levied by the applicant in pursuance of arrêtés royaux and ministerial orders, which were all adopted after 1 January 1958, the day on which the Treaty came into force.

*   *   *

[5] The arrêtés which imposed special duties on imports of some milk products after 1 January 1958, were contrary to Article 12 of the Treaty.

*   *   *

[7] Even if assent to a treaty, as required by Article 68 (2) of the Constitution, is given in the form of a statute, the legislative power, by giving this assent, is not carrying out a normative function. The conflict which exists between a legal norm established by an international treaty and a norm established by a subsequent statute, is not a conflict between two statutes.

[8] The rule that a statute repeals a previous statute in so far as there is a conflict between the two, does not apply in the case of a conflict between a treaty and a statute.

[9] In the event of a conflict between a norm of domestic law and a norm of international law which produces direct effects in the internal legal system, the rule established by the treaty shall prevail. The primacy of the treaty results from the very nature of international treaty law.

[10] This is a fortiori the case when a conflict exists, as in the present case, between a norm of internal law and a norm of Community law.

The reason is that the treaties which have created Community law have instituted a new legal system in whose favour the member-States have restricted the exercise of their sovereign powers in the areas determined by those treaties.

[11] Article 12 of the Treaty establishing the European Economic Community is immediately effective and confers on individual persons rights which national courts are bound to uphold.

[12] It follows from all these considerations that it was the duty of the judge to set aside the application of provisions of domestic law that are contrary to this Treaty provision.

*   *   *

The Court, for these reasons,

Dismisses this application and orders the applicant to pay costs.

*   *   *

---

1. *Primacy of international agreement over domestic law.* In addition to the High Court of Justice of Luxembourg, whose leading decision in point was discussed by the procureur général of Belgium in the principal case, the Federal Tribunal of Switzerland also holds that an international agreement prevails over subsequent and incon-

sistent domestic law.   Thareau v. Ministère Public Federal, 1974, XXXI Annuaire Suisse de Droit International, 204 (1975).

2. *Primacy of European Community law over domestic law.* The Court of Justice of the European Community (commonly called thus instead of the European Communities [a]) has held in several decisions that subsequent domestic legislation of the member states cannot prevail in case of inconsistency with the law—i. e. treaty and enactments deriving from it—of the Community.   In Simmenthal SpA v. Amministrazione delle Finanze dello Stato (no. 3), 1978, [1978] 3 Common Market Law Reports 670, the Court of Justice stressed that judges of the member states were under a duty not to give effect to such domestic legislation.

In that case, the courts of Italy were fighting a rear guard action against the doctrine of primacy of Community law.   The courts of the other five founding states (Belgium, France, Germany, Luxembourg and the Netherlands) had already accepted it.   Their decisions in point are reviewed in Raworth, Article 177 of the Treaty of Rome and the Evolution of the Doctrine of the Supremacy of Community Law, XV Canadian Yearbook of International Law 276 (1977). He points out that all the courts involved were very reluctant at first to depart from a tradition which commanded, at least in principle, giving effect to subsequent domestic law over a prior international agreement in case of inconsistency between the two.   (at 277–278)

The Simmenthal decision triggered in Great Britain a series of letters to the editor of The Times in which the correspondents debated whether British courts were also under a duty to declare Acts of Parliament without effect insofar as they conflicted with Community law.   Some of them were aghast at the idea.   The Times: April 18 (p. 17), April 21 (p. 19), April 27 (p. 19), May 3 (p. 17), May 11 (p. 17), 1978.

RE DRAFT ORDINANCE MODIFYING LAW 6/61 GOVERNING EXPROPRIATION

Gabon, Supreme Court, 1970.
48 Int'l L.Rep. 151 (1975).*

[The Supreme Court of Gabon was asked to give an opinion on the constitutionality of a draft ordinance amending legislation on expropriation for public utility purposes.   A portion of the opinion of the court appears below.]

* * *

The text of Article I introduces, so far as the right of property and respect for acquired rights are concerned, a discrimination between nationals, French citizens and the subjects (ressortissants) of

---

a. The European Communities are described at p. 892.

* Reprinted by permission of E. Lauterpacht, ed., and Grotius Publications, Ltd., Cambridge, England.

almost all the countries of O.C.A.M. (Organisation Commune Africaine et Malgache). This is in breach of the Convention on Establishment concluded on 17 August 1960 between the Republic of Gabon and the Republic of France and the Convention of 8 September 1961 relating to the status of individuals and the conditions of establishment of the subjects of the African and Malagasy States, including Gabon, which signed and ratified this Convention.

Furthermore, the same text, in that it does not provide for any compensation for the dispossessed owners, would, if it were applied, violate the rules of public policy enshrined in the Constitution of the Republic of Gabon of 21 February 1961. Indeed, the Constitution declares in Article I, paragraph 6 that

> No one may be arbitrarily deprived of his property, except if reasons of public necessity, legally established, require this and on condition that fair compensation is first paid.

Moreover, this rule applies implicitly to foreigners, and has even been formally extended to French nationals and to the subjects of the States signatory to the Convention of 8 September 1961 (Article 10, paragraph 3). These persons, by virtue of the afore-mentioned treaties, benefit from the same treatment as nationals in so far as the exercise of their civil rights and the protection of acquired rights are concerned.

     *   *   *

For these reasons:

Pronouncing, after having heard all parties, in the Council Chamber: [The Court] rejects the draft as unconstitutional and contrary to the provisions of international treaties duly ratified by Gabon and which, by virtue of Article 54 of the Constitution, have an authority superior to that of the Law.

Constitutions giving primacy to international agreements over domestic law. Article 54 of the Constitution of Gabon is modeled upon Article 55 of the French Constitution of 1958, according to which "treaties or agreements duly ratified or approved shall, upon their publication, have an authority superior to that of laws * * *." Though this provision does not specify that the term laws includes both anterior and posterior laws, French courts and scholars do not doubt it. They reason that once the international agreement is declared not equal in rank with domestic laws—but to have an "authority superior to laws," it makes no difference whether the laws are anterior or posterior to the agreement. The international agreement, in a literal sense, is supreme.

Like Gabon, other former French overseas territories adopted in their constitutions provisions similar to Article 55 in the French Constitution of 1958. Central African Republic, Article 35; Congo (Brazzaville), Article 62; Ivory Coast, Article 56; Mauritania, Article 46; Senegal, Article 79; Togo, Article 69; Upper Volta, Article 56. A similar provision also appears in Article 10 of the Constitution of Congo-Kinshasa (now Zaire) of May 30, 1964. I Peaslee, Constitutions of Nations, 59, 93, 206, 249, 555, 709, 901, 1019, 105 (3d ed. 1965).

According to Article 28(1) of the Greek Constitution of 1975, "international treaties * * * have an authority superior to any inconsistent legislative provision."[a] Roucounas, Le Droit International dans la Constitution de la Grèce du 9 Juin 1975, 29 Revue Hellénique du Droit International 63, 65 (1976). The author asserts that the article gives primacy to the treaty over both anterior and posterior domestic laws in conflict with it. (at 65)

In 1953, the Constitution of the Netherlands of 1815, was amended in order to provide in Article 66: "Legal regulations in force within the Kingdom shall not apply if this application should be incompatible with provisions * * * of agreements entered into either before or after the enactment of the regulations." III (2) Peaslee, Constitutions of Nations 660 (3d ed. 1968). In 1954 the Supreme Court of the Netherlands relied on this article in holding that provisions of a law of 1943 were inapplicable because they were in conflict with the 1868 Convention of Manheim on the Navigation of the Rhine. Public Prosecutor v. J. de B., 21 Int'l L.Rep. 3 (1957). In a note following the report the editor points out that before the constitutional enactment, the court had always found there was no conflict and reached the result by "interpreting either the law or the agreement in such a way as to obviate a conflict." (at 8)

---

4. DOMESTIC ARRANGEMENTS FOR INSURING NATIONAL ACTION IN CONFORMITY WITH INTERNATIONAL LAW

CREATION OF DEPARTMENT OF FOREIGN AFFAIRS

A first order of business for a new state is to create a department to conduct its foreign relations. In the case of the United States, it was created by the Act of July 27, 1789 for Establishing an Executive Department to be Denominated the Department of Foreign Affairs, 1 Stat. 28. The Act of September 15, 1789, 1 Stat. 68, directed that it be denominated the "Department of State." This early legislation was brief and general, consisting essentially of a broad delegation of powers from the President to the Secretary of State for conducting the foreign affairs of the United States. Since then, legislation concerning the Foreign Relations and Intercourse of the United States has grown voluminous and is collected in Title 22 of the United States Code.

During the early days, the legal work of the Department of State was often conducted personally by the Secretaries of State, who

a. Translation by the editors.

proved to be able lawyers. Eventually, the handling of legal affairs in the department became a specialized function and is now vested in the Office of the Legal Adviser.

___

LEGAL ADVISER TO DEPARTMENT OF FOREIGN AFFAIRS

ORGANIZATION OF LEGAL ADVISORY SERVICES ON INTERNATIONAL LAW

Asian-African Legal Consultative Committee.
Report of the Fourteenth Session 205 (1973).*

[The committee was created in 1956 by Asian states and named the Asian Legal Consultative Committee. In 1958, its name was changed to Asian-African Legal Consultative Committee to allow the participation of states on the African continent.

By the time the Fourteenth Session was convened in New Delhi in 1973, its membership was as follows:

Full members: Arab Republic of Egypt, Bangladesh, Democratic People's Republic of Korea, the Gambia, Ghana, India, Indonesia, Iran, Iraq, Japan, Jordan, Kenya, Kuwait, Malaysia, Nepal, Nigeria, Pakistan, Philippines, Republic of Korea, Sierra Leone, Singapore, Sri Lanka, Syrian Arab Republic, Tanzania and Thailand.

Associate members: Botswana and Mauritius.

As of July 4, 1980, the membership—as provided by a letter from the administration of the committee—had increased from 27 to 39. The states which had joined the committee since the Fourteenth Session were:

Full members: Libyan Arab Jamahiriya, Oman, Qatar, Somali Democratic Republic, Turkey, Uganda, United Arab Emirates, Yemen Arab Republic, Mongolia, Senegal.

Associate members: Ethiopia, Saudi Arabia.

The members of the committee had decided to exchange views on the organization of legal advisory services on international law in their respective countries. On the basis of this exchange and other information the committee prepared a report, a portion of which appears below.]

* * *

International law, in the modern sense, not only touches upon the political aspects of a State's relations with other States but embraces the field of trade and commerce, communications, transport etc. International conferences have become the order of the day at which governments have to be represented; there are in force volu-

* Reprinted by permission of the Asian–African Legal Consultative Committee, New Delhi.

minous treaties which are being multiplied every day to regulate the conduct of nations in different spheres which require to be interpreted and applied. In addition, there are the usual questions which frequently arise concerning the protection of the interests of the nationals of a State in other States, border disputes, refugee situations, utilisation of the resouces of the State, protection of a country's diplomatic and consular representatives abroad and many other problems which arise in the day-to-day functioning of a government. All this means that not only the Foreign Office but many other government departments also have to be kept abreast of the correct position and the most recent developments in international law relating to their sphere of activity. In modern time a government cannot function without competent legal advice on international law questions * * *.

I.   Organisation of Advisory Services

A brief survey of the practices obtaining in different countries of the world in the matter of organisation of legal advisory services on international law reveals three distinct patterns * * *. Some countries have a mixed system * * *.

(i) *Linking of the advisory services on international law with the general legal services of the government*

This pattern appears to be in vogue in some countries in Asia and several African countries which were formerly parts of the British Empire. The reason for this practice is not far to seek since even under the colonial rule these territories had fairly well organised government departments charged with the task of rendering legal advice to all government departments. * * * To begin with, the Legal Departments in the newly independent countries hardly had any person conversant with international law and consequently they had to rely heavily on outside sources. But gradually new officers with specialised knowledge and training in international law were recruited to deal specially with international law questions, even where the government had decided to retain the system of centralised Law Department to deal with all legal questions including questions on international law. * * *

[The report lists Asian-African states in which the system is followed—Botswana, Malaysia, Nepal, Nigeria, Uganda and Zambia—with a short description of the organization of the services in each state. In addition it discusses the advantages and disadvantages of the system.]

* * *

(ii) *Establishment of an International Law Division in the Foreign Office linked to the regular Foreign Service*

The second pattern which is gradually gaining ground in many countries is to have a department of international law within the

Foreign Office itself and to man the posts by officers of the Foreign Service who may be posted on a tour of duty in the International Law Division. In countries where this pattern is followed, regular members of the Foreign Service who have had a University degree or training in international law are eligible to be posted to the International Law Division. The head of the Division usually has the rank of an Ambassador or Minister Counsellor who is assisted by other Foreign Service officers of varying ranks depending on their number and the size of the Division. In addition to the diplomatic officers, a few lawyers are sometimes included on a permanent basis who are not liable to be transferred. The International Law Division which is directly responsible to the Minister for Foreign Affairs is often sub-divided in two or three sections to deal with international law advisory work, treaties, codification and development of international law which section is usually charged with the examination of drafts of international conventions and preparations for international legal conferences. In larger Foreign Offices individual officers of the International Law Division are assigned specific departments so that the officer concerned could act as the legal adviser of the department assigned to him subject to the overall supervision of the head of the Division.   *   *   *

[The report lists Asian-African states in which the system is followed—Arab Republic of Egypt, Dahomey, Indonesia, Iran, Japan, Jordan, Kuwait, The Philippines, Republic of Korea, Syrian Arab Republic and Togo—with a short description of the organization of services in each state. It also discusses the advantages and disadvantages of the system.]

        *   *   *

(iii) Establishment of a Specialist Division in the Foreign Office

The third method which has found favour in some countries is to have a specialist division within the Foreign Office to deal with all matters concerning international law and treaties and to man the Division with specialists who are not members of the regular Foreign Service. Britain adopted this system when she decided to have a regular set up in the Foreign Office for dealing with international legal problems. In the United States of America the pattern is very much similar.   *   *   *

[The report lists Asian-African states in which the system is followed—India, Pakistan and Sri Lanka—with a short description of the organization of the services of each. It also discusses the advantages and disadvantages of the system.]

        *   *   *

(iv) Mixed System

Some countries have a mixed system, that is to say, whilst maintaining a small international law section in the Foreign Office the ultimate responsibility for rendering advice on international legal questions is vested in the Attorney-General or the Principal Law Officer of the Government. This pattern is in vogue in Kenya and Malawi, subject to certain variations.

* * *

II. Nature of work in the International Law Division

(i) Advisory functions

The primary and most important function of an International Law Division is to render advice to the Government on issues affecting its foreign policy and other questions which involve some international law elements. In so far as the Foreign Office is concerned, a good deal of its work involving relations with other States often involves, directly or indirectly, questions of international law or practice, and consultations with the legal advisers become necessary before the Minister can decide upon the action that is to be taken in a particular case or cases. It has now become an almost invariable practice for the Minister to consult his legal advisers before making a policy statement, both in and outside the Parliament, and particularly so when it contains a reference to any acts or omissions on the part of some other State or States. Apart from purely routine communications between the Foreign Office and its diplomatic missions and consular posts abroad and the internal administration of the Foreign Service, there is hardly any matter which does not require consultation with the legal advisers. This is the reason why in larger Foreign Offices, such as in Britain or the United States, the Legal Adviser's Department is organised into branches corresponding to the organisation of the Foreign Office as a whole in various territorial and specialist divisions so that any problem arising in a particular division of the Foreign Office can be immediately referred to the Legal Adviser concerned. Beginning with questions relating to a country's frontiers, utilisation of its natural resources like the waters of an international river or the sea adjacent to its coast, treatment of foreign nationals in its territory, protection of its citizens abroad, examination of policies and practices of other States, the work of the Legal Adviser's Department extends even to such relatively minor matters as customs privileges of a diplomat and granting or refusal of passports. If a Government wishes to make a representation to a foreign Government or lodge a protest, the Foreign Office has to be satisfied that its stand is correct in accordance with the norms of international law and naturally the Legal Adviser has to be consulted before the Government takes any action.

* * *

Apart from the Foreign Office, as already stated, there are a large number of other departments whose work at some stage or the other involves questions of international law. Thus, for example, the Ministry of Interior is very much concerned with the question of the protection and treatment of aliens, granting of asylum, extradition of fugitive offenders, etc. whilst the Treasury or the Ministry of Finance would be directly responsible for questions relating to foreign aid, customs administration, taxation, and development programmes with foreign collaboration. The Ministries or Departments of Trade and Commerce are generally responsible for implementation of bilateral and multilateral trade agreements whilst the Ministries of Aviation, Transport and Communications would be concerned with matters relating to air transit agreements, shipping and other means of transportation, broadcasting, postal services, etc. The Ministry or the Department of Defence is also concerned with international law in the matter of use or deployment of the armed forces including passage of warships and aircraft.

[The report discusses the various ways in which departments other than the department for foreign affairs secures legal advice on international law questions.]

* * *

(ii) Treaty-making and interpretation

Another important branch of the work of the International Law Division is treaty-making and their interpretation. As a matter of fact, a good deal of advisory work not only in the Foreign Office but also in other Government Departments involves interpretation of treaties. Consequently, if the legal adviser is associated with the negotiation and conclusion of treaties, he is better suited to render advice on problems which may involve interpretation of that treaty. The practice in the Arab Republic of Egypt, Britain, Dahomey, India, Indonesia, Iran, Japan, Jordan, Kuwait, Pakistan, Philippines, Republic of Korea, Syria and Togo is usually to associate an officer of the Foreign Office legal department from the early stages of negotiations irrespective of the fact that the treaty may directly be related to the work of some other government department. Experience has shown that in matters of drafting as well as on substantive issues, the legal adviser's viewpoint should be set forth at the outset as it is often difficult to rectify a defect once the parties have come to an agreement after hard bargaining. It may be worthwhile to adopt this practice, especially in connection with the conclusion of political treaties and more important trade agreements.

Preparation of full powers and steps for ratification of treaties are generally taken practically in all countries in the Treaties Section of the Foreign Office. The Treaties Section is usually one of the wings of the Legal Adviser's Department where the Foreign Office maintains a legal department of its own.

(iii) Preparation of court cases

Although handling of litigation and preparation of court cases on behalf of the Government is generally the responsibility of a centralised department like the Treasury Solicitor in Britain or the Department of Justice in the United States and in the Attorney-General's Department or the Ministry of Justice in the case of Botswana, Kenya, Malaysia, Malawi, Nepal, Uganda, Zambia and most other countries, it is now generally accepted that the conduct of cases before the International Court of Justice or International Arbitral Tribunals should vest with the legal department of the Foreign Office. * * * Preparation of a case before the International Court of Justice or an international arbitral tribunal not only requires the collection of a good deal of factual data and legal material on the question at issue, but it also necessitates submission of detailed briefs containing arguments prior to the oral hearing. This is normally done in the International Law Section of the Foreign Office. * * * Cases involving international law before national courts and tribunals are usually handled by the department which is normally concerned with Government litigation, but here again the Foreign Office legal adviser is often associated with the preparation of the case.

   * * *

(iv) Codification and development of international law

One important aspect of the work of the International Law Division which has arisen in recent years relates to codification and development of international law. It is well known that since the establishment of the United Nations and the creation of the International Law Commission, a systematic attempt is being made to progressively develop rules of international law in order to suit modern conditions and in the context of an international community composed of independent nations all over the world. An attempt is also being made to codify and formulate principles of international law on some of the important topics in the form of law-making conventions so as to do away with nebulous and customary rules which may or may not be acceptable to all nations. This involves careful examination of formulations made by the International Law Commission as also preparatory work for participation in international conferences where the work of codification in the form of conventions normally takes place. In recent years, the Law of the Sea, Diplomatic and Consular Relations, the Law of Treaties are some of the subjects which have necessitated close attention of every Foreign Office and the task has naturally fallen on the legal adviser's department. Apart from the Sixth Committee of the United Nations and the International Law Commission, there are various other forums where international law is being codified or progressively developed, such as within the Organisation of African Unity, the Organisation of American States, the Council of Europe and various other forums. The United Nations Commission on International Trade Law and the United Nations Commission on Trade and Development are handling legal questions in the field of trade and commerce and the work of these bodies, though in the specialised field of trade, would need examination by the legal adviser's department in conjunction with the legal advisers of the departments which are directly involved.

III.   Status of the Legal Adviser and his role in policy making

The status of a legal adviser in practically every country all over the world has usually been kept at a high level so that by reason of his position in the Government, he is able to effectively participate in policy formulations.   *   *   *   Thus, in the United Kingdom, the first incumbent of the post of legal adviser in the Foreign Office was given the rank of an Under Secretary of State who directly dealt with the Secretary of State for Foreign Affairs. In the United States of America, the Legal Adviser of the Department of State also enjoys almost a similar status. In the Foreign Offices of the newly independent countries, the Legal Adviser is a person of the rank of an ambassador and at times that of a Minister Counsellor or a Secretary or a Joint Secretary.   *   *   *   It is desirable and necessary that the legal adviser should be in a position to offer independent and authoritative advice which should be given due weight by the policy-making departments of the Foreign Office and this can be so if the legal adviser is a person of high rank and directly responsible to the Minister.   *   *   *   [T]he influence which the legal adviser may be expected to bring to bear on the policy formulation would depend upon his own personality, his relationship with the policy making departments of the Foreign Office and his own experience and knowledge in the field of international law.

     *   *   *

EXPRESS LEGISLATIVE DIRECTIVE

RESTATEMENT OF THE FOREIGN RELATIONS LAW OF THE UNITED STATES

Reporters' Notes to Section 145 (1965).*

2.   The Internal Revenue Code.   Section 7852(d) of the Revenue Code of 1954 provides that "No provision of this title shall apply in any case where its application would be contrary to any treaty obligation of the United States in effect on the date of enactment of this title." Section 31 of the Revenue Act of 1962 provides that Section 7852(d) does not apply to the provisions of the 1962 Act.

The Treasury Department informed the Congress that in its view there would be no conflict between the Revenue Act of 1962 and provisions of tax treaties of the United States—"with one minor exception relating to the real estate clause of the Greek Estate Tax Treaty which the Treasury will seek to have renegotiated before July 1, 1964," the date upon which the conflicting provisions in the Revenue Act would become effective. H.R.Rep.No.2508, 87th Cong., 2d

Sess. 48. The treaty with Greece was renegotiated by protocol signed February 12, 1964. See S.Ex.A, 88th Cong., 2d Sess. (1964); Department of State Press Release No. 60, Feb. 13, 1964.

STANDING INSTRUCTIONS TO SERVICES

In the services of the Government of the United States such as the Armed Forces, the Coast Guard and the Foreign Service, standing instructions are issued to officers who, because of their position or mission, may have to handle situations susceptible of creating serious international repercussions for the United States.

The instructions may anticipate some specific situations and spell out procedures for meeting them which are in conformity with international law. For a flawless execution of procedures in a case of this type, see below the boarding and inspection by a U. S. naval vessel of a Soviet trawler suspected of damaging submarine cables. With respect to situations which cannot be specifically anticipated, the instructions provide for reference through channels to higher authority and eventually to the Department of State. For a situation where the system of reference broke down through human error, see below the case of the Soviet sailor who sought refuge aboard a Coast Guard vessel.

Of course, the issuance of standing instructions to services for insuring national action in conformity with international law is a practice followed in many national legal systems.

BOARDING AND INSPECTION BY UNITED STATES NAVAL VESSEL OF SOVIET TRAWLER SUSPECTED OF DAMAGING SUBMARINE CABLES: EXCHANGE OF NOTES BETWEEN THE UNITED STATES AND THE UNION OF SOVIET SOCIALIST REPUBLICS

53 United States Naval War College, International Law Studies
1959–1960, at 159 (1961).

[The boarding and inspection of the Soviet trawler were carried out on February 26, 1959. By an aide mémoire dated February 28, 1959, the embassy of the United States in Moscow informed the Minister of Foreign Affairs of the Soviet Union of the boarding and inspection. On March 4, 1959, the Minister of Foreign Affairs of the Soviet Union sent a note to the embassy in which it protested the "detention and inspection" of the Soviet fishing trawler. In a note dated March 23, 1959, the embassy of the United States conveyed the reply of the government of the United States. A portion of that note appears below.]

The Embassy of the United States of America refers to the Ministry's note No. 17/OSA, dated March 4, 1959 concerning recent breaks in certain transatlantic submarine tele-communication cables and the consequent visit to the Soviet trawler Novorossiisk by a boarding party of the U.S.S. Roy O. Hale, which was the subject of the Embassy's aide memoire of February 28, 1959.

* * *

For the reasons set out hereinafter the United States Government considers there is no basis for a protest in this case and the Soviet protest is therefore rejected. * * *

* * *

The Government of the United States, acting under the provisions of Article X of the Convention for the Protection of Submarine Cables, of 1884, to which both the United States and the Union of Soviet Socialist Republics adhere, and also in conformity with United States law (47 United States Code, Section 26), implementing the convention, on February 25, 1959, dispatched the United States radar picket escort U.S.S. Roy O. Hale to the area to investigate the reported breaks in the submarine cables. On February 26, 1959, about 11:55 a. m., eastern standard time, the Commander of the U.S.S. Roy O. Hale sent a party consisting of one officer and four enlisted men, without arms, aboard the Soviet trawler Novorossiisk. At the time of the visit the trawler was in position latitude 48° 26′N., longitude 49°10′W. There were no other ships in the immediate vicinity.

* * *

The boarding officer, communicating by means of French through an interpreter, duly informed and explained to the master of the trawler Novorossiisk the purpose of his visit and his authority to do so under the provisions of the convention of 1884. He examined, with the consent and acquiescence of the master, the papers of the trawler which appeared to be in order.

The boarding officer found that the latitude and longitude which the trawler Novorossiisk recorded in her journal for the previous days' positions also showed her to have been in the immediate vicinity of all five cable breaks. * * * On the basis of the foregoing evidence, the boarding officer concluded that an examination of the fishing gear and equipment was justified to determine whether the trawler was capable of causing the cable breaks.

The unarmed boarding officer, with the consent of the master of the trawler, observed without deep examination, on the upper deck of the trawler only, the trawling equipment and fishing gear. The boarding officer noted that the trawling equipment was of the type for deep sea fishing, and was in general fairly new, with the exception of the otter boards and net discs which were well worn and in poor condition. The trawling cable was estimated to be about 300 fathoms in length, sufficiently long enough to drag the gear on the bottom at the depth in the area—about 180 fathoms. Two broken sections of trawling cable each about 60 feet in length were observed wrapped around the hatch on deck. The four ends of these cables were shredded and frayed and appeared to have parted as a result of a sudden strain such as could have been caused by snagging the gear.

These sections are identical in type, age, and condition with the trawling cable. Some of the fish observed lying frozen on deck were of the bottom type.

The visit on board the trawler lasted about 70 minutes, and was completed at 1:05 p. m., eastern standard time.   *   *   *

A preliminary report emanating from the cable repair ship Lord Kelvin which has since repaired the first broken cable states that the eastern portion of the damaged cable had been badly scraped and scuffed for about a mile east of the break. The cable had been severed by cutting. The technical opinion is that such evidence indicates that a trawler had picked up the cable with its drag, then having pulled it on deck, had cut it to release the nets.

The protection of submarine telecommunications cables on the high seas constitutes an international obligation. The locations and presence of the transatlantic submarine cables that have been cut are widely known among world fishing and maritime circles. They are shown and marked on United States admiralty and navigation maps which are available to the general public.

The above-stated record of events shows that, contrary to the assertions and charges made in the above-mentioned note of the Union of Soviet Socialist Republics, the visit to the Soviet trawler Novorossiisk under the circumstances shown was entirely justified and was in every respect in accordance with international law and applicable treaty provisions.

     *   *   *

SOVIET SAILOR SEEKS U. S. HAVEN, BUT LOSES

U. S. News & World Report
December 14, 1970, at 30.*

An international controversy has boiled up around the case of a Soviet sailor who sought refuge in the U. S. and was turned back.[a]

     *   *   * The incident that set off all this uproar took place at sea off Martha's Vineyard, Mass., on November 23. The command ship for a Soviet fishing fleet and the U. S. Coast Guard cutter Vigilant were moored side by side while authorities discussed a new fishing agreement.

During the day, there were visits back and forth by crewmen of the two ships. One Soviet sailor, identified as a Lithuanian named Simas Kudirka, told U. S. sailors that he wished to defect and would leap into the water when the ships separated. The State Department and Coast Guard headquarters in Washington were notified.

---

a. The international law concerning asylum and refuge is treated in Chapter 9.

Later, Mr. Kudirka leaped directly onto the Vigilant. Russian crewmen were permitted to return him to the Soviet ship. Witnesses said they used force and the refugee was beaten.

Adm. Chester A. Bender, Coast Guard Commandant, said the decision to deny Mr. Kudirka sanctuary was that of the commander in the Boston area.

Said Admiral Bender:

While it is not yet clearly established whether or not he took the proper action, I believe it to be understood how he would make this decision on the existing circumstances.

I do not approve of the use of force on a Coast Guard ship by personnel of another nation, but do recognize that considerable force was required as the defector was resisting strongly.

Washington, the Admiral said, had not provided "specific advice * * * as to what action to take."

Well-founded fear. The U. N. agreement on defectors, which the U. S. has signed but Russia has not, defines a refugee this way:

Any person who, owing to well-founded fear of being persecuted for reasons of race, religion, nationality, membership of a particular social group, or political opinion, is outside the country of his nationality and is unable or, owing to such fear, is unwilling to avail himself of the protection of that country.

The obligation of a country which has signed the refugee agreement is also spelled out:

No contracting state shall expel or return a refugee in any manner whatsoever to the frontiers of territory where his life or freedom would be threatened on account of race, religion, nationality, membership of a particular social group, or political opinion.

Fugitives from criminal proceedings are not protected by the agreement. The Russians claimed Mr. Kudirka had stolen $2,000 from the ship's safe. The State Department later said the seaman's case "should have been handled through the U. S. judicial system."

Since 1945, nearly 1.5 million refugees have been admitted to the U. S. for political reasons. Cubans—totaling 538,000—make up the largest single nationality. East Europeans and ethnic Germans displaced from East Europe constitute the largest regional group.

White House action. In the wake of the incident, Mr. Nixon ordered a report from the State Department and the Department of Transportation, which controls the Coast Guard. After studying the report, said the White House, the President ordered "immediate remedial action to insure that there will never be a recurrence of a shocking incident of this kind."

Among actions taken:

The White House promulgated interim rules setting forth more specific policies on how to deal with would-be defectors and refugees.

Direct communication links were ordered between the Coast Guard and the State Department and White House.

Strict instructions were issued that the White House be immediately advised of similar incidents.

In Cambridge, Mass., the Coast Guard began a formal inquiry to determine if a court-martial is warranted.

The Voice of America told the world in 23 languages—including Lithuanian—that the denial of asylum was a bureaucratic bungle and that the United States had not changed its policy on refugees.

———

Happy ending four years later. Simas Kudirka was sentenced in the U.S.S.R. to ten years of prison on "treason charges". During the summer of 1974, the U.S. Department of State declared he could claim American citizenship because it had determined his mother was a natural born citizen of the United States. Shortly thereafter, he was ordered released by the Supreme Soviet and arrived in the United States on November 5. The Times-Picayune, November 6, 1974, sec. 1, p. 11, col. 2.

———

INTERVENTION BY HIGHEST AUTHORITY

NORWEGIAN STATE v. CARLILE

Norway, Supreme Court (Appeals Division), 1964.
96 Journal du Droit International 438 (1969).[a]

[Carlile, a British subject, was arrested and indicted for swindling. On several occasions, he had gone to hotels in Norway and simulated stumbling, falling and suffering injuries, and collected damages. He had done the same thing several times in Denmark and Sweden. The governments of Denmark and Sweden requested the Norwegian authorities also to indict Carlile for his acts in Denmark and Sweden. They did. Thereupon Carlile objected on the ground that Norway had no jurisdiction under international law to indict him for acts done in Denmark and Sweden.

On appeal, the Supreme Court held that even if international law prohibited the application of Norwegian penal law to acts committed in Denmark and Sweden, the prohibition did not apply at the stage of indictment for infractions punishable under the law of all three countries. Hence, it said, the objection was premature and would have to be ruled upon at trial. The British embassy in Oslo took up the matter with the Norwegian Ministry of Foreign Affairs and questioned the basis of jurisdiction of Norway with respect to the acts committed by Carlile in Denmark and Sweden. The outcome is explained in

a. Translation by the editors. Reprinted by permission of Editions Techniques, S.A., Paris.

a note which follows the report of the case. A portion of the note appears below.]

*   *   * At the request of the Public Prosecutor, the Ministry of Foreign Affairs requested an opinion from its Legal Adviser, Professor Castberg. He took the position that the grounds [relied upon by the Supreme Court] were highly questionable, despite the requests for prosecution made by Denmark and Sweden, so long as the United Kingdom did not consent to the exercise of jurisdiction over its national.

By decision of the Cabinet, a royal decree of April 17, 1964, voided the indictment to the extent it covered acts done in Denmark and Sweden.

*   *   *

NATIONAL APOLOGY

AFFAIRE MANTOVANI, ITALY–SWITZERLAND, 1965

Rousseau, Chronique des Faits Internationaux.
69 Revue Générale de Droit International Public 761, 834 (1965).[a]

On the 7th of March, at about one o'clock in the morning, three inspectors of the Italian police in civilian clothes and attached to the police of Milan, arrested an Italian national, a resident of Como already sentenced twice in Italy for contraband, one Bruno Giuseppe Mantovani, age thirty-five, when he was coming out of a restaurant in Lugano. After handcuffing him, they took him away in an Italian car which reached the Italian territory of Campione. Alerted by a passerby who had witnessed the scene, the *   *   * [local Swiss] police went into action immediately and the same day at about noontime Mantovani was brought back to Swiss territory. He said to the Swiss authorities that the Italian policemen had tried, while he was being interrogated at Campione, to make him sign a declaration to the effect that he had been arrested, not on Swiss territory, but on Italian territory, on the right bank of Lake Lugano. Again according to the *   *   * [local Swiss] police, Mantovani was being sought by the Italian police for contraband; but *   *   * the offense would not have been by itself a sufficient basis for a request of extradition to the Swiss authorities.

The 9th of March, the Federal Department of Justice and Police published a communique on the incident. [Its text follows.]

On Monday afternoon, the Attorney General of the Confederation granted audience at Berne, at their request, to *   *   * [high officials of the Italian Police from Milan and Rome], who came accompanied by the chief of the *   *   * [local Swiss] police.

a. Translation by the editors. Reprinted with permission of Charles Rousseau and Editions A. Pedone, Paris.

* * * According to the Italian officials, Mantovani was being
sought in Italy to make him serve certain prison terms to which he
had been sentenced, not only for acts of contraband, but also for
* * * other crimes.

On the basis of the statements by the * * * [local Swiss]
police and of the complementary explanations given by the two high
officials from Italy, it became clear that the frontier incident must be
attributed to the excess of zeal of a sergeant of the Italian police, who
was in charge of a patrol with the assignment of arresting Mantovani
at Campione (Italy) where he was expected to arrive.

The two high officials of the Italian police presented official
apologies for the violation of the territorial sovereignty of Switzerland by their subordinates and gave assurances that everything would
be done to avoid a repetition of such an incident, while measures
against the guilty subordinates, who acted without the knowledge of
their superiors, were being considered.

The federal authorities consider the case closed.

SECTION B.   APPLICATION IN DIPLOMATIC PRACTICE

CHARTER OF THE UNITED NATIONS

Article 33

1.   The parties to any dispute, the continuance of which is likely
to endanger the maintenance of international peace and security,
shall, first of all, seek a solution by negotiation, enquiry, mediation,
conciliation, arbitration, judicial settlement, resort to regional agencies or arrangements, or other peaceful means of their own choice.

Diplomatic practice. The primary means of resolving claims asserted under international law by one state against another is diplomatic correspondence. It is the everyday working method of the international system for settling legal disputes and its effectiveness is
attested to by centuries of practice. Hence correspondence recording
the diplomatic negotiations of states in settling their legal claims is a
vast and valuable repository of information on the application of the
law of the international system.

A note of caution is in order, however, concerning the use of this
correspondence.

The assertion of a claim under international law by one state
against another is a contentious statement and in the diplomatic presentation of its claim a state is often stating a partisan position, a
one-sided view of the facts and the law applicable to them. In some
cases, of course, the claim may be exactly stated and incontrovertible

on both facts and law and, hence, may be accepted as valid by the other. In many more cases, however, the defending state questions either or both. Not until they have achieved mutual agreement as to both can it be said they have recognized a particular rule of international law as applicable to the particular case.

Thus the totality of the relevant diplomatic exchanges has to be considered before any conclusion can be reached regarding the rule of international law applied to the resolution of a claim. Moreover, it must be kept in mind that the resolution of a claim by diplomatic negotiation may turn in the end, not solely on considerations of international law, but partly on political, economic and other empirical factors.

Digests of International Law published in the United States contain, inter alia, a great deal of diplomatic correspondence on issues of international law. The digest of Moore of 1906 was followed by that of Hackworth in 1940, and since 1963 fifteen volumes of Whiteman's Digest of International Law have been published. The volumes of the Foreign Relations of the United States, usually published from 20 to 25 years after the events, frequently throw light on legal issues involved in originally highly classified documents.

Information on diplomatic practice relating to international law is also becoming increasingly available in other states. It may be provided by specialized publications such as the British Digest of International Law, the Répertoire de la Pratique Française en Matière de Droit International Public and the Prassi Italiana di Diritto Internazionale. More often a national journal of international law will reserve a section for periodic reports on national diplomatic practice. Journals so doing include: the American Journal of International Law; the Annuaire Français de Droit International; the Annuaire Suisse de Droit International; the Australian Yearbook of International Law; the Canadian Yearbook of International Law; the Italian Yearbook of International Law; the Japanese Annual of International Law; the Netherlands Yearbook of International law; the Revue Belge de Droit International; the Malaya Law Review.

THE RED CRUSADER

Commission of Enquiry, (Denmark-United Kingdom), 1962.
35 Int'l L.Rep. 485 (1967).*

* * * On May 29, 1961, the British trawler Red Crusader was arrested by the Danish authorities off the coast of the Faroe Islands. A Commission of Enquiry was set up by an Exchange of Notes of November 15, 1961, between the Governments of Denmark

* Reprinted by permission of E. Lauterpacht, ed., and Grotius Publications,
Ltd., Cambridge, England.

and the United Kingdom to investigate certain incidents relating to this arrest and to subsequent events.

The Exchange of Notes requested the Commission to investigate and report to the two Governments:

(1) the facts leading up to the arrest of the British trawler, Red Crusader, on the night of the 29th of May, 1961, including the question whether the Red Crusader was fishing, or with her fishing gear not stowed, inside the blue line on the map annexed to the Agreement between the two Governments concerning the Regulation of Fishing around the Faroe Islands constituted by the Exchange of Notes of the 27th of April, 1959;

(2) the circumstances of the arrest; and

(3) the facts and incidents that occurred thereafter before the Red Crusader reached Aberdeen.

The Commission was constituted on November 21, 1961, in The Hague, with Professor Charles De Visscher as President, and Professor André Gros and Captain C. Moolenburgh as Members.

*   *   *

The Commission heard the Danish witnesses and experts at the meetings held on March 5–9.   After examination by the Danish Agent the witnesses were cross-examined by British Counsel and, in some cases, re-examined.   From March 10, the British witnesses and one expert were heard by the Commission.   After examination by the British Counsel the witnesses and the expert were cross-examined by the Danish Agent and, in some cases, re-examined.   From March 14–16 the Commission heard the oral statements and replies.

[There follows the text of the commission's report with findings concerning the facts leading up to the arrest of the Red Crusader, the circumstances of the arrest, the attempted escape of the Red Crusader after the arrest, the use of gunfire by the Danish naval vessel to stop the escape and the actions of British naval vessels which had come on the scene.]

*   *   *   On April 4, 1962, the Lord Privy Seal, a Minister in the British Government, said in the House of Commons:

In accordance with the Agreement for reference to the Commission, Her Majesty's Government accept its findings as final. House of Commons Debates, Vol. 657, Written Answers, col. 43.

On January 23, 1963, the Joint Under-Secretary of State for Foreign Affairs made the following statement in the House of Commons:

Her Majesty's Government and the Danish Government have now completed their consultation about the Report of the Commission of Enquiry into the incidents affecting the Scottish trawler Red Crusader at the end of May 1961.   In their desire to remove a source of disagreement between them, the two Governments have decided that the incident should be settled by a mutual waiver of all claims and charges arising out of the incident. These waivers enter into effect forthwith. The owners of the trawler have concurred in this settlement.

As a result Skipper Wood and the Red Crusader are free to enter Danish waters without fear of arrest in relation to the events of May 1961, and the owners' claim for compensation has been dropped. The two Governments consider that the incident can now be considered closed, though without prejudice to the view on points of law maintained by each Government. House of Commons Debates, Vol. 670, Written Answers, cols. 77–78.

Use of commissions of inquiry. Stuyt, Survey of International Arbitrations 1794–1970, Appendix I C, 508–512 (1972), lists a total of five bilateral commissions of inquiry for the period covered by his book. During the same period the applications of international law in diplomatic negotiations were innumerable.

UNION OF SOVIET SOCIALIST REPUBLICS—UNITED STATES: REPORT OF THE U.S.—U.S.S.R. FISHERIES CLAIMS BOARD FOR THE YEAR 1974

January 1, 1975.
XIV International Legal Materials 447 (1975).*

[On February 21, 1973, the United States and USSR signed an Agreement Relating to the Consideration of Claims Resulting from Damage to Fishing Vessels or Gear and Measures to Prevent Fishing Conflicts and on June 21, 1973, a Protocol to the agreement. 24(1) U.S.T. 669, 24(2) U.S.T. 1588.

The agreement provides for the establishment of two boards, one in Washington and one in Moscow. Article I(1). Each consists of four members, two appointed by the United States and two by the Soviet Union. Article II(2). The function of the boards is to consider claims advanced by a national of one country against a national of the other regarding financial loss resulting from damage to or loss of the national's fishing vessel or fishing gear. Article II(1).

Article III(1) specifies: "A Board shall establish its procedures for conciliation in accordance with this Agreement." Article III(7) states: "The Board shall act as an intermediary between the claimant and the respondent and, at any stage of its consideration of a claim, may approach the claimant and the respondent to try to bring about a conciliation." Under Article IV(1) "the Board shall prepare a report" on each claim, including "the amount which should be paid" in its opinion as compensation. In Article IV(5), the two govern-

* Reprinted with the permission of the
American Society of International
Law.

ments undertake to encourage the settlement of claims and facilitate the payments.

The Washington Board began to operate in April 1974. One of its reports appears below.]

Decision Report—10 July 1974

Case 71–5—Sea Dog.

The claimant, Western Ocean Resources, Inc., of Gloucester, Massachusetts, owner of the American lobster vessel Sea Dog, alleged the Soviet vessel Imant Sudmalis (PB-0246) caused damage to their fixed gear at position 40°28.5′N. and 67°51′W. It was alleged that gear losses were $7,789.00 and the financial loss of catch was $12,000.00.

Based upon the report (30 April 1971) of the Commanding Officer USCGC Vigilant (WMEC 617) at the scene, the affidavit (7 May 1971) of Steven W. Goodwin, master of the Sea Dog, and the statement of damage costs submitted to the Board, the Board unanimously recommends that the claimant be paid in full for the alleged gear damage ($7,789.00). The Board considers that the documentation submitted to it to support the $12,000.00 claim of financial loss supports a claim only for the value of the lobster in a landing prior to the gear loss; this amount is $494.00 for 450 pounds of lobster. The Board recommends that the claimant be paid $494.00 for financial loss. Accordingly, the Board unanimously recommends that the claimant be paid $7,789.95 for gear replacement and $494.00 for financial loss—a total of $8,283.95.

U. S. Members:	U.S.S.R. Members:
C. J. Blondin Chairman	Y. A. Znamenskiy Vice-Chairman
C. J. Maguire	A. G. Afanasyev

———

Use of commissions for conciliation. A feature of recently proposed international conventions (not all of which are in force) has been the provision of commissions for conciliation to which parties can resort for an amicable solution of their disputes, either in place of or prior to submission of the dispute to arbitration or to adjudication. Among the conventions in the Documentary Supplement see, e. g., the following: Article 42 of the International Covenant on Civil and Political Rights, Article 12 of the International Convention on the Elimination of all Forms of Racial Discrimination, Article 66 of the Vienna Convention on the Law of Treaties, Article III of the Optional Protocol to the Vienna Convention on Diplomatic Relations, Article IV of the Optional Protocol to the Conventions on the Law of the Sea.

Historically, few disputes have been brought before conciliation commissions. Stuyt, Survey of International Arbitrations 1794–1970, Appendix I B, 491–507 (1972), lists a total of 17, the first taking place in 1924 and the last in 1956. One involved claims of the United States under the Italian Peace Treaty in 1947.

SECTION C.   APPLICATION IN INTERNATIONAL TRIBUNALS

----

1.   THE INTERNATIONAL COURT OF JUSTICE

The first world court. In 1920 the Council of the League of Nations appointed an Advisory Committee of Jurists to prepare a draft for the establishment of the Permanent Court of International Justice contemplated in Article 14 of the Covenant. Though the United States had refused to become a member of the League, Elihu Root, American lawyer and statesman, was one of the ten jurists chosen for the task, with James Brown Scott, a widely recognized authority on international law, serving as his adviser. The names of both were closely associated with the efforts made by the United States at the Second Hague Peace Conference of 1907, albeit just as unsuccessfully as at the First Hague Peace Conference of 1899, to create such a court.

THE ORIGINAL DREAM

Permanent Court of International Justice, Advisory Committee of Jurists, Procès-Verbaux of the Proceedings of the Committee, June 16– July 24, 1920, at 2, 3, 5, 7, 11, 693, 727 (1920).

Speech delivered by M. le Jonkheer van Karnebeek.

[After reviewing the accomplishments and the failures of the two Hague Peace Conferences, the speaker made this statement.]

Gentlemen, events have not been able to arrest the onward march of ideas. The League of Nations has taken up again the thread which for a long time seemed abandoned, and has entrusted to you the task of assisting it, by your advice, to formulate the important decisions to be taken in the near future. The grandeur of this task is apparent when, above the conflict of interests and passions of mankind, is seen the guiding star of the noble idea of governing the future by the laws of justice. In a world which has passed through one of the greatest trials which history has ever known, in an international society shaken to its foundations, and almost at the end of its resources, the work of justice which is to be carried on in this Palace appears like an awakening, like a promise of moral reconstruction, like the message of a better future worthy of the League of Nations.

Speech delivered by M. Léon Bourgeois

* * *

I have come here, Gentlemen, in the name of the Council of the League of Nations. * * * A Memorandum by the Secretary-General has set out for you * * * the principal questions which you will have to resolve. * * *

* * *

From the start, however, some points will appear to you to be already certainly obtained. The Court of Justice must be a true Permanent Court. It is not simply a question of arbitrators chosen on a particular occasion, in the case of conflict, by the interested parties; it is a small number of judges sitting constantly and receiving a mandate the duration of which will enable the establishment of a real jurisprudence, who will administer justice. This permanence is a symbol. It will be a seat raised in the midst of the nations, where judges are always present, to whom can always be brought the appeal of the weak and to whom protests against the violation of right can be addressed. Chosen not by reason of the State of which they are citizens, but by reason of their personal authority, of their past career, of the respect which attaches to their names known over the whole world, these judges will represent a truly international spirit
* * *.

* * *

You are about, Gentlemen, to give life to the judicial power of humanity. * * *

Report

* * *

Article 34 consequently lays down that the Court may hear and determine, without any special convention, disputes between States which are Members of the League of Nations if such disputes are of a legal nature * * *. There is no question of binding States to submit to arbitration without their consent. The competence of arbitral jurisdiction is dependent upon the existence of a convention. In this case the convention establishing compulsory arbitration is the constituent Statute of the Court.

* * *

THE OPTIONAL CLAUSE

James Brown Scott, Editorial Comment, The Permanent Court of International Justice, 15 American Journal of International Law 260, 264–266 (1921).*

[In a previous editorial in the journal concerning the amendments made by the Assembly of the League to the draft prepared by the Advisory Committee of Jurists, James Brown Scott had said: "We should not criticize the defects of the plan [as amended]. We should rather fall upon our knees and thank God the hope of the ages is in process of realization." 15 Am.J.Int'l L. 52, 55 (1921). In the excerpt which follows, he is commenting on the adoption by the Council of the League of the optional clause—i. e. the option for states voluntarily to accept the compulsory jurisdiction of the court in an instrument separate from the statute creating it.]

*   *   *

Chapter 2, on the competence of the court, which was to register the advance of 1920 over 1907, had hard luck, to put it mildly, with the Council and with the Assembly. *   *   * The Advisory Committee *   *   * [proceeded] on the theory that the court should have some definite jurisdiction and a certain category of cases in which nation sues nation as man sues man in national courts. *   *   * This theory is correct and can not be gainsaid, but neither the Council nor the Assembly was willing to accept and to give effect to the recommendation. No nation is to be forced to appear before the tribunal as defendant and judgment taken in the case presented by the plaintiff in the defendant's absence, should the State invited fail to attend. *   *   *

But a happy compromise was reached. It was suggested, and the suggestion found favor, that the general rule could be varied by the parties. Those who wished the procedure characteristic of a court of arbitration, which was the rule adopted by the Assembly, were satisfied. Those nations, on the other hand, which wished to vest the court with jurisdiction within the categories of disputes mentioned in *   *   * the Covenant might do so, and among them judicial instead of arbitral procedure would prevail. All they needed to do was to accept the procedure which becomes a court at signing or ratifying a protocol to this effect, to be annexed to the constitution of the court, or to declare at some later time their adherence to this method; and in the protocol they might accept unconditionally or upon condition of reciprocity. This is a very wise provision. *   *   *

*   *   *

*   *   * The future will decide which method is to prevail.

———

1. *The use of the Permanent Court of International Justice.* The obstacle to the use of the court turned out to be less the lack of

* Reprinted with the permission of the American Society of International Law.

compulsory jurisdiction in the statute creating it than the reluctance of states to settle their disputes by judicial means.

Between 1920 and 1939, some 41 states accepted at one time or another the compulsory jurisdiction of the court through the optional clause. This was a large number, being as it were about four-fifths of the 52 states which became members of the League of Nations in 1920. Yet the court gave judgments disposing of the dispute before it in only 18 instances according to André Gros, French judge on the International Court of Justice. Twice it held itself without jurisdiction and in nine instances the cases were discontinued. A Propos de Cinquante Années de Justice Internationale, 76 Revue Générale de Droit International Public 5, 6 (1972). If rulings prior to judgment, such as rulings on preliminary objections and requests for interim measures of protection, are counted as separate cases, the number of disputes handled by the court will appear larger.

During the same period, however, the court gave 27 advisory opinions, all at the request of the Council of the League. Opponents of the court in the United States were very much concerned that it should be empowered to give such opinions. When the Senate considered giving its advice and consent to the United States becoming a party to the statute of the court, a resolution the Senate discussed, but did not pass, contained a reservation virtually ensuring to the United States a veto power over the whole advisory jurisdiction of the court.

The United States did not become a party to the statute. Opposition to the court in the Senate could not be surmounted from 1920 to 1935, when the final negative vote on giving advice and consent took place.

2. *Dissolution of the first court and creation of its successor.* After winding up some unfinished business in the fall of 1945, the surviving members of the court submitted their resignation to the Secretary General of the League of Nations on January 1, 1946. The Assembly of the League thereupon resolved that the Permanent Court of International Justice was for all purposes to be regarded as dissolved. See Rosenne, Documents on the International Court of Justice 491–493 (1979).

Its successor, the International Court of Justice, was brought into being by the Charter of the United Nations, signed at San Francisco on June 26, 1945. The Statute of the Court, which is essentially the same as the statute of its predecessor, is in the Documentary Supplement.

On 31 July 1979 the composition of the court was as follows:

Order of Precedence	Country	Date of Expiry of Term of Office
President Sir Humphrey Waldock	United Kingdom	5 February 1982
Vice-President T. O. Elias	Nigeria	5 February 1985
Judges I. Forster	Senegal	5 February 1982
A. Gros	France	5 February 1982
M. Lachs	Poland	5 February 1985
P. D. Morozov	USSR	5 February 1988
Nagendra Singh	India	5 February 1982
J. M. Ruda	Argentina	5 February 1982
H. Mosler	Federal Republic of Germany	5 February 1985
S. Tarazi [Deceased, 1980]	Syria	5 February 1985
S. Oda	Japan	5 February 1985
R. Ago	Italy	5 February 1988
A. El-Erian	Egypt	5 February 1988
J. Sette-Camara	Brazil	5 February 1988
R. R. Baxter [Deceased, 1980]	United States	5 February 1988

International Court of Justice, Yearbook 1978–1979, at 6 (1979).

3. *Acceptance of the compulsory jurisdiction of the International Court of Justice.* On July 31, 1979, only 45 states were subject to the compulsory jurisdiction of the International Court of Justice, by virtue of a declaration of acceptance. This is less than one-third of the 149 states which were members of the United Nations on the same date. International Court of Justice, Yearbook 1978–1979, at 56 (1979).

EXAMPLES OF DECLARATIONS UNDER ARTICLE 36(2) OF THE STATUTE OF THE INTERNATIONAL COURT OF JUSTICE

International Court of Justice, Yearbook 1978–1979, at 56 (1979).

FINLAND

[Translation from the French]

On behalf of the Finnish Government, I hereby declare that I recognize as compulsory ipso facto and without special agreement, in relation to any other State accepting the same obligation, that is to say, on condition of reciprocity, the jurisdiction of the International Court of Justice, in accordance with Article 36, paragraph 2, of the Statute of the Court, for a period of five years from 25 June 1958. This declaration shall be renewed by tacit agreement for further periods of the same duration, unless it is denounced not later than six months before the expiry of any such period. This declaration shall apply only to disputes arising in regard to situations or facts subsequent to 25 June 1958.

New York, 25 June 1958.

(Signed) G. A. GRIPENBERG,
Permanent Representative of Finland
to the United Nations.

NICARAGUA

[Translation from the French]

On behalf of the Republic of Nicaragua I recognize as compulsory unconditionally the jurisdiction of the Permanent Court of International Justice.[a]

Geneva, 24 September 1929.

(Signed) T. F. MEDINA.

SWITZERLAND

[Translation from the French]

The Swiss Federal Council, duly authorized for that purpose by a Federal decree which was adopted on 12 March 1948 by the Federal Assembly of the Swiss Confederation and became operative on 17 June 1948.

Hereby declares that the Swiss Confederation recognizes as compulsory ipso facto and without special agreement, in relation to any other State accepting the same obligation, the jurisdiction of the International Court of Justice in all legal disputes concerning:

(a) the interpretation of a treaty;

(b) any question of international law;

(c) the existence of any fact which, if established, would constitute a breach of an international obligation;

(d) the nature or extent of the reparation to be made for the breach of an international obligation.

This declaration, which is made under Article 36 of the Statute of the International Court of Justice, shall take effect from the date on which the Swiss Confederation becomes a party to that Statute

a. Under Article 36(5) of the Statute of the International Court of Justice, declarations of states accepting the jurisdiction of the Permanent Court of International Justice, which have not lapsed or been withdrawn, are deemed to be acceptances of the compulsory jurisdiction of the present court. "There are now eight such declarations." International Court of Justice, Yearbook 1978–1979, at 56 (1979).

and shall have effect as long as it has not been abrogated subject to one year's notice.

Done at Berne, 6 July 1948.

> On behalf of the Swiss Federal Council:
> (Signed) CELIO,
> The President of the Confederation.
> (Signed) LEIMGRUBER,
> The Chancellor of the Confederation.

UNITED STATES OF AMERICA

I, Harry S. Truman, President of the United States of America, declare on behalf of the United States of America, under Article 36, paragraph 2, of the Statute of the International Court of Justice, and in accordance with the Resolution of 2 August 1946 of the Senate of the United States of America (two-thirds of the Senators present concurring therein), that the United States of America recognizes as compulsory ipso facto and without special agreement, in relation to any other State accepting the same obligation, the jurisdiction of the International Court of Justice in all legal disputes hereafter arising concerning

(a) the interpretation of a treaty;

(b) any question of international law;

(c) the existence of any fact which, if established, would constitute a breach of an international obligation;

(d) the nature or extent of the reparation to be made for the breach of an international obligation;

Provided, that this declaration shall not apply to

(a) disputes the solution of which the parties shall entrust to other tribunals by virtue of agreements already in existence or which may be concluded in the future; or

(b) disputes with regard to matters which are essentially within the domestic jurisdiction of the United States of America as determined by the United States of America; or

(c) disputes arising under a multilateral treaty, unless (1) all parties to the treaty affected by the decision are also parties to the case before the Court, or (2) the United States of America specially agrees to jurisdiction; and

Provided further, that this declaration shall remain in force for a period of five years and thereafter until the expiration of six months after notice may be given to terminate this declaration.

Done at Washington this fourteenth day of August 1946.

> (Signed) HARRY S. TRUMAN.

The self-judging reservation. Of the 45 states subject on July 31, 1979, to the compulsory jurisdiction of the court by virtue of a declaration of acceptance, more than half attached to it reservations substantially limiting the scope of the jurisdiction accepted. While the reservations cover a wide variety of matters, 18 of them exclude from the declaration of acceptance matters or disputes within the domestic jurisdiction of the signatory but do so in differing terms. In some cases, the reservations exclude matters which, by international law, are essentially within its domestic jurisdiction. But in six cases —see for example supra the reservation devised by the United States —the signatory reserves to itself the power to determine what is a matter or dispute within its domestic jurisdiction.

CASE OF CERTAIN NORWEGIAN LOANS
(FRANCE v. NORWAY)

International Court of Justice, 1957.
[1957] I.C.J.Rep. 9.

[Legislation in Norway permitted payment of Norwegian loans in Bank of Norway notes instead of gold. The French government espoused the claims of French nationals who held the Norwegian bonds and desired payment in gold. The French government asserted to the Norwegian government "that it would not seem that a unilateral decision can be relied upon as against foreign creditors." The Norwegian government rejected French proposals to submit the matter to a mixed commission of economic and financial experts, to arbitration or to the International Court of Justice, maintaining that the claims of bondholders involved solely the interpretation and application of Norwegian law and that the bondholders should sue in the Norwegian courts.

The French government referred the matter to the International Court of Justice.]

*   *   *

The Application [of France] expressly refers to Article 36, paragraph 2, of the Statute of the Court and to the acceptance of the compulsory jurisdiction of the Court by Norway on November 16th, 1946, and by France on March 1st, 1949. The Norwegian Declaration reads:

> I declare on behalf of the Norwegian Government that Norway recognizes as compulsory ipso facto and without special agreement, in relation to any other State accepting the same obligation, that is to say, on condition of reciprocity, the jurisdiction of the International Court of Justice in conformity with Article 36, paragraph 2, of the Statute of the Court, for a period of ten years as from 3rd October 1946.

The French Declaration reads:

> On behalf of the Government of the French Republic, and subject to ratification, I declare that I recognize as compulsory

ipso facto and without special agreement, in relation to any other State accepting the same obligation, that is on condition of reciprocity, the jurisdiction of the International Court of Justice, in conformity with Article 36, paragraph 2, of the Statute of the said Court, for all disputes which may arise in respect of facts or situations subsequent to the ratification of the present declaration, with the exception of those with regard to which the parties may have agreed or may agree to have recourse to another method of peaceful settlement.

> This declaration does not apply to differences relating to matters which are essentially within the national jurisdiction as understood by the Government of the French Republic.

* * *

After presenting the first ground of its first Preliminary Objection on the basis that the loan contracts are governed by municipal law, the Norwegian Government continues in its Preliminary Objections:

> There can be no possible doubt on this point. If, however, there should still be some doubt, the Norwegian Government would rely upon the reservations made by the French Government in its Declaration of March 1st, 1949. By virtue of the principle of reciprocity, which is embodied in Article 36, paragraph 2, of the Statute of the Court and which has been clearly expressed in the Norwegian Declaration of November 16th, 1946, the Norwegian Government cannot be bound, vis-à-vis the French Government, by undertakings which are either broader or stricter than those given by the latter Government.

* * *

It will be recalled that the French Declaration accepting the compulsory jurisdiction of the Court contains the following reservation:

> This declaration does not apply to differences relating to matters which are essentially within the national jurisdiction as understood by the Government of the French Republic.

In the Preliminary Objections filed by the Norwegian Government it is stated:

> The Norwegian Government did not insert any such reservation in its own Declaration. But it has the right to rely upon the restrictions placed by France upon her own undertakings.

> Convinced that the dispute which has been brought before the Court by the Application of July 6th, 1955, is within the domestic jurisdiction, the Norwegian Government considers itself fully entitled to rely on this right. Accordingly, it requests the Court to decline, on grounds that it lacks jurisdiction, the function which the French Government would have it assume.

In considering this ground of the Objection the Court notes in the first place that the present case has been brought before it on the basis of Article 36, paragraph 2, of the Statute and of the corresponding Declarations of acceptance of compulsory jurisdiction; that in the present case the jurisdiction of the Court depends upon the Declarations made by the Parties in accordance with Article 36, paragraph 2, of the Statute on condition of reciprocity; and that, since two unilateral declarations are involved, such jurisdiction is conferred upon the Court only to the extent to which the Declarations coincide in conferring it. A comparison between the two Declarations shows that the French Declaration accepts the Court's jurisdiction within narrower limits than the Norwegian Declaration; consequently, the common will of the Parties, which is the basis of the Court's jurisdiction, exists within these narrower limits indicated by the French reservation. * * *

France has limited her acceptance of the compulsory jurisdiction of the Court by excluding beforehand disputes "relating to matters which are essentially within the national jurisdiction as understood by the Government of the French Republic". In accordance with the condition of reciprocity to which acceptance of the compulsory jurisdiction is made subject in both Declarations and which is provided for in Article 36, paragraph 3, of the Statute, Norway, equally with France, is entitled to except from the compulsory jurisdiction of the Court disputes understood by Norway to be essentially within its national jurisdiction. *even though its declaration did not contain such a clause*

* * *

The Court does not consider that it should examine whether the French reservation is consistent with the undertaking of a legal obligation and is compatible with Article 36, paragraph 6, of the Statute which provides:

> In the event of a dispute as to whether the Court has jurisdiction, the matter shall be settled by the decision of the Court.

The validity of the reservation has not been questioned by the Parties. It is clear that France fully maintains its Declaration, including the reservation, and that Norway relies upon the reservation.

* * *

For these reasons,

The COURT, by twelve votes to three, finds that it is without jurisdiction to adjudicate upon the dispute which has been brought before it by the Application of the government of the French Republic of July 6th, 1955.

* * *

Separate Opinion of Judge Sir HERSCH LAUTERPACHT

* * * I consider that as the French Declaration of Acceptance excludes from the jurisdiction of the Court "matters which are essentially within the national jurisdiction as understood by the Government of the French Republic"—the emphasis being here on the words "as understood by the Government of the French Republic"—it is for the reason of that latter qualification an instrument incapable

of producing legal effects before this Court and of establishing its jurisdiction. * * *

* * * [T]he first reason for that view is that that particular part of the acceptance of the Optional Clause on the part of the French Republic is contrary to the Statute of the Court. In the reservation in question the Government of France says in effect: If a Government brings an application before the Court in reliance on the French acceptance of the jurisdiction of the Court and if the Government of France maintains that the Court has no jurisdiction on the ground that the subject-matter of the dispute is essentially within the domestic jurisdiction of France, then the Court has no power to decide upon that particular allegation; it must accept as binding the French understanding of the legal position on the subject.

If that type of reservation is valid, then the Court is not in the position to exercise the power conferred upon it—in fact, the duty imposed upon it—under paragraph 6 of Article 36 of its Statute. That paragraph provides that "in the event of a dispute as to whether the Court has jurisdiction, the matter shall be settled by a decision of the Court". The French reservation lays down that if, with regard to that particular question, there is a dispute between the Parties as to whether the Court has jurisdiction, the matter shall be settled by a decision of the French Government. The French reservation is thus not only contrary to one of the most fundamental principles of international—and national—jurisprudence according to which it is within the inherent power of a tribunal to interpret the text establishing its jurisdiction. It is also contrary to a clear specific provision of the Statute of the Court as well as to the general Articles 1 and 92 of the Statute and of the Charter, respectively, which require the Court to function in accordance with its Statute.

Now what is the result of the fact that a reservation or part of it is contrary to the provisions of the Statute of the Court? The result is that that reservation or that part of it is invalid. * * *

* * *

My conclusion is therefore that, having regard to the reservation relating to matters which are essentially within domestic jurisdiction as understood by the French Republic, the French Declaration of Acceptance is invalid for the reason:

(1) That it is contrary to the Statute of the Court;

(2) That it is incapable of giving rise to a legal obligation inasmuch as it claims, and effectively secures, the right of unilateral determination of the extent and of the existence of the obligation of judicial settlement with regard to a comprehensive and indefinite category of disputes covering potentially most disputes which may come before the Court;

(3) That the particular qualification of the reservation in question forms an essential part of the Acceptance and that it is not pos-

sible to treat it as invalid and at the same time to maintain the validity of the reservation to which it is attached or of the Acceptance as a whole.

Accordingly, in my view the entire French Declaration of Acceptance must be treated as devoid of legal effect and as incapable of providing a basis for the jurisdiction of the Court. It is for that reason that, in my view, the Court has no jurisdiction over the dispute. The majority of the Court has reached the same result by acting upon the "automatic reservation" and the French Declaration of Acceptance—both of which I consider to be invalid. However, as the Court has expressly stated that, having regard to the circumstances before it, its Judgment does not pre-judge the major issue involved, I feel that a Separate Opinion—as distinguished from a Dissenting Opinion —meets the requirement of the case.

[A declaration, a separate opinion and dissenting opinions omitted.]

---

1. *Problems.*

a. Suppose the Norwegian declaration had been made unconditionally rather than in terms of reciprocity. Would the court have reached a different result? Consider paragraph (3) of Article 36 of the statute of the court and the following commentary in Waldock, Decline of the Optional Clause, 32 Brit. Y.B. Int'l L. 1955–6, at 244, 255 (1957):

> Paragraph 3 of Article 36 * * * provides that a declaration may be made "unconditionally or on condition of reciprocity on the part of several or certain States or for a certain time". This paragraph does not relate to "reciprocity". It simply authorizes States to accept compulsory jurisdiction under the Optional Clause for limited periods, and to make their liability to jurisdiction conditional on compulsory jurisdiction having been also accepted by a particular number of other States or by particular named States. The reference in paragraph 3 to a "condition of reciprocity on the part of several or certain States" is, indeed, a legacy from a special preoccupation of the Brazilian delegate, M. Fernandez, in the 1920 Committee of Jurists. Brazil considered it impolitic to venture on a unilateral acceptance of compulsory jurisdiction unless some at least of the Great Powers did likewise. Accordingly, M. Fernandez proposed the following formula for the Optional Clause:

>> They may adhere unconditionally or conditionally to the Article providing for compulsory jurisdiction *a possible condition* being reciprocity on the part of a certain number of Members or, again, of a number of Members including such and such specified Members.

> Although M. Fernandez's version of the Optional Clause itself was dropped in favour of the one which now appears in the Stat-

ute, the "condition of reciprocity" on the part of several or certain States was included in paragraph 3 in order to satisfy him. Afterwards Brazil did in fact make her declaration subject to a condition of reciprocity on the part of two, at least, of the Great Powers, but she is the only State to have resorted to this form of condition. Such a condition, as will be appreciated, is not really a "condition of reciprocity" but rather a condition that the declaration is not to be in force unless and until a certain number of States or certain named States have accepted compulsory jurisdiction under the Optional Clause.

b. If France were a respondent and pleaded its reservation in an effort to oust the court of jurisdiction, what result? What if the matter before the court involved a question of treaty interpretation and the applicant state (plaintiff) argued that the French government could not lawfully understand the matter to be "essentially within the national jurisdiction" of France? (What was the position of the parties in the Norwegian Loans case as to the validity of the French reservation?)

c. The so-called Nuclear Test Ban Treaty contains the following provision:

> Each Party shall in exercising its national sovereignty have the right to withdraw from the Treaty if it decides that extraordinary events, related to the subject matter of this Treaty, have jeopardized the supreme interests of its country.

What effect does this clause have on the jurisdiction of the International Court of Justice to decide what is meant by the words "extraordinary events"? The Nuclear Test Ban Treaty appears in the Documentary Supplement.

2. *The United States reservation in the International Court.* In the Interhandel case (Switzerland v. United States), [1959] I.C.J. Rep. 6, Switzerland asked the court to declare that the United States was under an obligation to restore assets of the Interhandel Company, a Swiss company. Interhandel owned most of the shares of General Aniline and Film Corporation (GAF); almost all of these shares had been vested by the United States during World War II under the Trading With the Enemy Act, on the ground that General Aniline's shares in reality belonged to I. G. Farben, a German company, or that GAF was controlled by that company. Among the preliminary objections raised by the United States was that the court was "without jurisdiction to entertain the Application of the Swiss Government, for that reason that the sale or disposition by the Government of the United States of the shares of the GAF which have been vested as enemy property 'has been determined by the United States of America, pursuant to paragraph (b) of the Conditions attached to this country's acceptance of this Court's jurisdiction, to be a matter essentially within the domestic jurisdiction of this country.' " (at 25)

The court did not rule upon this objection, but upheld a different preliminary objection and thereby held that the Application of the Swiss Government was inadmissible because Switzerland had not exhausted the local remedies available to it in the United States courts.

Judge Sir Hersch Lauterpacht filed a separate opinion in which he reiterated the views he had expressed about the self judging reservation in the Case of Certain Norwegian Loans.

---

1. *The use of the International Court of Justice.* The Yearbook of the International Court of Justice supplies a list of contentious cases filed with the court. In the Yearbook for 1978–1979, at 3 (1979), the list shows that as of July 31, 1979, 45 cases had been filed. Of those, 44 had been acted upon by the court and one was pending. The 44 may be broken down as follows.[a]

a. The cases on the list in the Yearbook have been assigned numbers.

Title	Dates
1. Corfu Channel (United Kingdom v. Albania)	1947–1949
2. Fisheries (United Kingdom v. Norway)	1949–1951
3. Protection of French Nationals and Protected Persons in Egypt (France v. Egypt)	1949–1950
4. Asylum (Colombia/Peru)	1949–1950
5. Rights of Nationals of the United States of America in Morocco (France v. United States)	1950–1952
6. Request for Interpretation of the Judgment of 20 November 1950 in the Asylum case (Colombia v. Peru)	1950
7. Haya de la Torre (Colombia v. Peru)	1950–1951
8. Ambatielos (Greece v. United Kingdom)	1951–1953
9. Anglo-Iranian Oil Co. (United Kingdom v. Iran)	1951–1952
10. Minquiers and Ecrehos (France/United Kingdom)	1951–1953
11. Nottebohm (Liechtenstein v. Guatemala)	1951–1955
12. Monetary Gold Removed from Rome in 1943 (Italy v. France, United Kingdom and United States)	1953–1954
13. Electricité de Beyrouth Company (France v. Lebanon)	1953–1954
14. Treatment in Hungary of Aircraft and Crew of United States of America (United States v. Hungary)	1954
15. Treatment in Hungary of Aircraft and Crew of United States of America (United States v. USSR)	1954
16. Aerial Incident of 10 March 1953 (United States v. Czechoslovakia)	1955–1956
17. Antarctica (United Kingdom v. Argentina)	1955–1956
18. Antarctica (United Kingdom v. Chile)	1955–1956
19. Aerial Incident of 7 October 1952 (United States v. USSR)	1955–1956
20. Certain Norwegian Loans (France v. Norway)	1955–1957
21. Right of Passage over Indian Territory (Portugal v. India)	1955–1960
22. Application of the Convention of 1902 Governing the Guardianship of Infants (Netherlands v. Sweden)	1957–1958
23. Interhandel (Switzerland v. United States)	1957–1959
24. Aerial Incident of 27 July 1955 (Israel v. Bulgaria)	1957–1959
25. Aerial Incident of 27 July 1955 (United States v. Bulgaria)	1957–1960
26. Aerial Incident of 27 July 1955 (United Kingdom v. Bulgaria)	1957–1959
27. Sovereignty over Certain Frontier Land (Belgium/Netherlands)	1957–1959
28. Arbitral Award Made by the King of Spain on 23 December 1906 (Honduras v. Nicaragua)	1958–1960
29. Aerial Incident of 4 September 1954 (United States v. USSR)	1958
30. Barcelona Traction, Light and Power Company, Limited (Belgium v. Spain)	1958–1961

In 16 cases, the court issued a judgment on the merits. In eight cases, the court held it could not consider the merits for lack of jurisdiction or some other reason such as failure of the applicant to exhaust domestic remedies. In three cases, it ruled that the state instituting the proceedings had no standing to raise the legal issue involved. In two cases it ruled that the issue had become moot. In seven instances the court ordered the cases removed from the list at the request of the parties. In eight instances, the cases were removed from the list on the initiative of the court because the states against whom the proceedings were initiated were not subject to its jurisdiction.

The total of 44 is artificially enlarged, however, by including as separate cases parallel proceedings resulting from an identical dispute between two states and another, and by counting as three separate cases a judgment in a dispute between two states and their two subsequent requests for elaboration of that judgment. When these factors are taken into account, the total number of cases comes to 38. On the other hand, the total will be larger than 44 if it includes as

---

a. The cases on the list in the Yearbook have been assigned numbers.—Continued.

	Title	Dates
31.	Compagnie du Port, des Quais et des Entrepôts de Beyrouth and Société Radio-Orient (France v. Lebanon)	1959–1960
32.	Aerial Incident of 7 November 1954 (United States v. USSR)	1959
33.	Temple of Preah Vihear (Cambodia v. Thailand)	1959–1962
34.	South West Africa (Ethiopia v. South Africa; Liberia v. South Africa)	1960–1966
35.	Northern Cameroons (Cameroon v. United Kingdom)	1961–1963
36.	Barcelona Traction, Light and Power Company, Limited (New Application: 1962) (Belgium v. Spain)	1962–1970
37.	North Sea Continental Shelf (Federal Republic of Germany/Denmark; Federal Republic of Germany/Netherlands)	1967–1969
38.	Appeal Relating to the Jurisdiction of the ICAO Council (India v. Pakistan)	1971–1972
39.	Fisheries Jurisdiction (United Kingdom v. Iceland)	1972–1974
40.	Fisheries Jurisdiction (Federal Republic of Germany v. Iceland)	1972–1974
41.	Nuclear Tests (Australia v. France)	1973–1974
42.	Nuclear Tests (New Zealand v. France)	1973–1974
43.	Trial of Pakistani Prisoners of War (Pakistan v. India)	1973
44.	Aegean Sea Continental Shelf (Greece v. Turkey)	1976–1978
	Continental Shelf (Tunisia/Libyan Arab Jamahiriya)	1978–

Using the numbers for identification, the breakdown of the cases is as follows:

Judgments on the merits: Cases 1, 2, 4–7, 5, 8, 10, 21, 22, 27, 28, 33, 37, 38, 39–40. Total 16, or 14 if 4–7 and 39–40 are counted as 2 cases.

Judgments that the merits cannot be considered: Cases 6, 9, 12, 20, 23, 24, 35, 44. Total 8, or 7 if 6 is taken with 4 and 7 as constituting one case.

Judgments that the state plaintiff lacks standing: Cases 11, 34, 36. Total 3.

Judgments that the case is moot: Cases 41–42. Total 2 or 1 if they are not treated as separate cases.

Orders removing cases from list at the request of the parties: Cases 3, 13, 25–26, 30, 31, 43. Total 7, or 6 if 25 and 26 are treated as one case.

Orders removing cases from list at the court's initiative: Cases 14, 15, 16, 17–18, 19, 29, 32. Total 8, or 7 if 17 and 18 are treated as one case.

Overall totals: $16 + 8 + 3 + 2 + 7 + 8 = 44$.
or $14 + 7 + 3 + 1 + 6 + 7 = 38$.

separate items rulings given prior to judgment such as rulings on preliminary objections and requests for interim measures of protection.

One case was decided by the court in 1980: Case Concerning United States Diplomatic and Consular Staff in Teheran. The text of the judgment is in XIX International Legal Materials 553 (1980).

During the 33 years of its existence, the court also gave 16 advisory opinions, a substantially smaller number than the 27 advisory opinions the Permanent Court of International Justice gave during the 19 years it sat at The Hague.

2. *Third World complaints.* States of the Asian-African Legal Consultative Committee expressed displeasure with the court over its decision in the South West Africa case of which an excerpt appears infra at p. 621. Some states in Latin America complained of the court's decision in the Asylum case. G.E. do Nascimento e Silva, of Brazil, put it thus:

> The two sentences of the International Court of Justice on the asylum granted by the Colombian Embassy in Lima to Haya de la Torre are the outstanding examples of diplomatic asylum. The sentences received wide publicity and were the object of various learned papers; those written in Spain and Latin America were, with rare exception, highly critical of the stand taken by the International Court of Justice. The sentence passed in 20 November, 1950 was most unsatisfactory * * *. From a Latin American point of view, it contains certain affirmations which simply went to prove that the Court was not qualified to pass judgment since it had examined a typical Latin American juridical institution exclusively from a European and biased point of view. * * *
>
>   * * *
>
> Just as the sentences of the International Court of Justice on the question of the international status of South-West Africa made most Afro-Asian States distrust the court, the Haya de la Torre case alienated most Latin American States, thus contributing to the atmosphere of ill-will which characterizes the relations of most States with the principal judicial organ of the United Nations. Diplomacy in International Law 104–106 (1972).

A jurist from Africa, commenting some years later on the advisory opinion of the court in the Western Sahara case (1975), again charged the court with a European bias, "europecentrisme" as he called it. Ndiaye, Avis de la C.I.J. sur le Sahara Occidental 16 October 1975, 19 Revue Sénégalaise de Droit 31 (1976).

3. *Refusal of respondent states to appear.* From 1920 to 1971, France was party plaintiff and party defendant in more proceedings before the Permanent Court of International Justice and the International Court of Justice than any other state. See Gros, A Propos de Cinquante Années de Justice Internationale, 76 Revue Générale de Droit International Public 5, 6 (1972). Nevertheless, it

refused to appoint an agent and become a party to parallel proceedings brought against it in the Nuclear Test Case by Australia and New Zealand, International Court of Justice, 1974, [1974] I.C.J. Rep. 253 and 457.

India also refused to appoint an agent and become a party to the proceedings brought against it in the Trial of Pakistani Prisoners of War Case, [1973] I.C.J. Rep. 328, 347. So did Iceland in parallel proceedings brought against it by the United Kingdom and the Federal Republic of Germany in the Fisheries Jurisdiction Case, International Court of Justice, [1974] I.C.J. Rep. 3 and 175. So did Turkey when Greece instituted proceedings against it in the Aegean Sea Continental Shelf Case, [1978] I.C.J. Rep. 1. And so did Iran when the United States instituted proceedings against it for the release of American hostages in Teheran.

Moreover, France withdrew its declaration of acceptance of the compulsory jurisdiction of the court before judgment in the Nuclear Test Case was rendered. For statements by the French government in explanation of its position in the matter, see Charpentier, Pratique Française du Droit International, XX Annuaire Français de Droit International 1027, 1053 (1974).

4. *The future of the court.* There were only six cases brought before the court between 1972 and 1980, and at that five of them were those in which the states named as parties defendant refused to appear. The unwillingness of states to resolve their disputes by referring them to the court has caused concern about its future.

Thus on November 24, 1974, the General Assembly of the United Nations adopted Resolution 3232, 29 U.N. GAOR, Supp. (No. 31) (Agenda Item 93) 141 (1974), in which it called upon states to use the court more often. Among the various considerations upon which it based the resolution, the General Assembly cited the revision by the court, in 1972, of its own rules and the resulting simplification of its procedures and the reduction in undue delays and costs.

Some observers also blame the lack of business of the world court upon defects in its organization and operation. See, for example, Some Thoughts on the Future of the International Court of Justice by Petren, Swedish judge on the court from 1957 to 1976, in VI Netherlands Yearbook of International Law 59 (1975). The United States Department of State study, on Widening Access to the International Court of Justice, by Willis, recommends permitting national courts to request from the international court advisory opinions on issues being litigated before them, thereby providing indirect access to the world court by individuals and corporations. McDowell, Digest of United States Practice in International Law 1976, at 650 (1977).

5. *Other international courts.* The function of the Court of Justice of the European Community is to serve, not world-wide, but the special purposes of the constituent communities (i. e., the European Economic Community, the European Coal and Steel Community, and the European Atomic Energy Community), the members of which are

Belgium, Denmark, France, Ireland, Italy, Luxembourg, the Netherlands, the United Kingdom and West Germany.[a] Whereas parties to cases before the International Court of Justice are limited to states, parties before the court of the communities, in proper cases, can consist of individuals and firms as well as member states or institutions of the communities. For a brief description of the jurisdiction of the court, see Marsh, Foreword to 1 Common Market Law Reports (1962). An analysis of the structure of the European Community is made in Chapter 14.

Another international court serving the purposes of a regional group of states (the Council of Europe) is the European Court of Human Rights, established by the European Convention for the Protection of Human Rights and Fundamental Freedoms. Its jurisdiction is limited to cases referred to it by the European Commission of Human Rights or by a state party to the convention (i. e., not by individuals). See Chapter 9 for a fuller description of the work of the court.

Similarly serving a regional organization (in this case the Organization of American States) is the Inter-American Court of Human Rights. This court was created by the American Convention on Human Rights, of which the United States was a signatory but not a party as of January 1, 1981. Like its older, European counterpart, its jurisdiction does not permit access by individuals, since only states parties to the convention or the Inter-American Commission on Human Rights can submit cases to the court. For the text of the convention, see the Documentary Supplement. For the statute of the court, see XIX International Legal Materials 634 (1980).

See Chapter 9 for a fuller description of both of these human rights courts.

See Hudson, The Central American Court of Justice, 26 Am.J. Int'l L. 759 (1932), for an account of the creation, jurisprudence and demise of "the first international court in modern history to be endowed with continuing functions." The court sat from 1908 to 1918; its jurisdiction included cases between individuals and governments other than those of the individuals' own country.

a. Greece became a member on January 1, 1981.

2. INTERNATIONAL ARBITRATION

MAX PLANCK INSTITUTE FOR COMPARATIVE PUBLIC LAW AND INTERNATIONAL LAW, INTERNATIONAL SYMPOSIUM ON JUDICIAL SETTLEMENT OF INTERNATIONAL DISPUTES

417, 463–468, 470–471 (1974) *

Arbitration and Conciliation
by Hans von Mangoldt

I. Arbitration

1. A comprehensive arbitration practice within a particular subject area has only been achieved in one special sphere of international arbitration: namely in the area of the mixed claims commissions established in considerable numbers between the United States and some European States on the one side, and the Latin American States on the other, the mixed arbitral tribunals created after the First World War, the "conciliation commissions" established between some of the victorious and defeated States after the Second World War, and finally the Arbitral Commission on Property, Rights and Interests in Germany. These arbitral tribunals were established after events akin to civil war, and sometimes only after the application of direct force against the opponent State, * * * or they were established through peace treaties or kindred treaties. They were therefore primarily, and in some cases exclusively, entrusted with the settling of claims arising out of measures undertaken by the defeated party in the course of war, or of claims due to injury to foreign nationals in events akin to civil war * * *.

* * *

Leaving aside the awards of the mixed claims commissions, the remaining picture of the international arbitration practice does not seem to live up to the great expectations often placed in settlement of disputes by arbitration, especially at the time of conclusion of general arbitration treaties. * * *

2. First of all, since the Hague Conferences [of 1897 and 1907] relatively few States have been parties to arbitration proceedings, leaving the special area of postal disputes aside for the time being. These States have also been concentrated in particular geographical regions; States in Asia, even the older ones, have hardly ever been involved, and nor have African States or States in Australia/Oceania. But even within the two Americas and Europe, instances of arbitration are unequally distributed. The USA, Great Britain, France and Italy have been parties in a relatively large number of arbitration proceedings, i. e. States which were great powers at least at certain times within this historical period. In these proceedings the predominant questions concerned diplomatic protection * * *.

* Reprinted by permission of the Max Planck Institute for Comparative   Public Law and International Law, Heidelberg.

3. The relatively limited number of subject matters brought before arbitration tribunals is also striking. Along with the already-mentioned questions concerning treatment of another State's nationals in breach of international law, and especially the violation of their acquired rights, the following subjects have been the main ones with which arbitration tribunals have repeatedly been concerned: territorial and border disputes, questions of international law concerning neighbourly relations, disputes between warring parties and neutral States based upon discriminatory measures taken against the latter as part of the conduct of the wars or based upon questions of internment, disputes involving the law of the sea, settlement of debts, and postal disputes. It is also interesting to note that treaty disputes are by no means of primary importance in arbitration practice. Although the interpretation of treaties applicable between the parties has played a role in a large number of cases, disputes concerning only the interpretation and/or application of a treaty have occurred relatively seldom as compared with the total number of matters brought before arbitration tribunals. * * *

4. A further prominent characteristic of past arbitration practice lies in the fact that very few cases have been brought before an arbitration tribunal as a result of the application of a general arbitration treaty or compromissory clause and that—almost without exception—a dispute has only been submitted to an arbitral tribunal after the parties have reached a basic agreement to that effect. This has been the case even when it would have been possible according to the treaties existing between these parties to bring a matter before the arbitral tribunal without cooperation of the other party. * * *

   * * *

5. A further characteristic of the history of international arbitration so far is the fact that it has been less and less often used since the First World War. Whereas a large number of arbitral tribunals were entrusted with the settling of disputes between States before and during the First World War, the number of arbitral tribunals that actually handled disputes decreased considerably between the two world wars and has reached its all-time low in the past 26 years since the end of the Second World War.

   * * *

---

1. *Arbitration practice of the United States.* In Stuyt, Survey of International Arbitrations 1794–1970 (1972), the United States is listed as participating in 26 arbitrations between 1922 and 1939; during the period 1945–1970, it is listed as participating in seven. (Index 1, at 543, 553–554). Out of those, four involved World War II claims (No. 415, 417, 418 and 419). Still, seven is nearly one-third of the 25 arbitrations which took place world-wide from 1945 to 1970 (No. 410–435).

2. *Arbitration of disputes between states and persons.* For a recent development in the field of international arbitration, see the discussion of the International Centre for Investment Disputes in Chapter 17. This new institution provides for access to an arbitral board by individuals, and firms, who have certain disputes with states other than those of their own nationality.

3. *Provisions for arbitration in the agreement for the release of American hostages in Teheran.* The agreement, dated January 19, 1981, consists of two "Declarations" by the government of Algeria. In each it sets forth the commitments entered into by the United States and Iran. The agreement is in the Documentary Supplement.

In paragraph 11 of the second Declaration, the parties agree to arbitration of the claims of their nationals arising out of debts, contracts, and expropriation or other measures affecting property rights, subject to certain exceptions.

-----

3. COMPLIANCE WITH DECISIONS OF INTERNATIONAL TRIBUNALS

JUDGMENTS OF THE WORLD COURT

Anand, Studies in International Adjudications 274–275 (1969).*

* * * [T]he history of international adjudication since 1945 * * * clearly demonstrates that the execution of international judicial awards is not an altogether negligible problem. There have been several cases, if not of open defiance, at least of disregard of the decisions of an international court. In the present tension-ridden, polarized world society, where even a small dispute can develop into a nuclear catastrophe, it may not be as prudent to use force to compel a State—even a small and weak State—to adhere to such a judgment as it was, perhaps, in earlier times. Albania can disregard the judgment in the *Corfu Channel* case with impunity. Haya de la Torre had to remain a virtual prisoner in the Colombian Embassy for almost three years after the Court's final decision. Thailand took upon itself to declare, though for a brief period, that it would not abide by an adverse decision; and it ultimately accepted the decision only under protest and with a reservation attached to its acceptance. Also it must not be forgotten that none of these cases involved the vital interests of a nation. In any event, these cases do demonstrate that countries do not always accept an adverse decision.

Moreover, advisory opinions of the International Court of Justice also have been disregarded at times. * * * It is important to note that in practice the United Nations General Assembly, as well as other international organs which have requested advisory opinions, always have approved the opinions of the Court and have tried to

* Anand, Studies in International Adjudication. Reprinted by permission   of Oceana Publications, Dobbs Ferry, New York.

adapt their future actions to accord with the advice given.   Despite
this formal approval of the opinions, however, several opinions of the
Court have remained absolutely ineffective.   Thus the Court's opinions in the *Conditions of Admission of a State to Membership in the
United Nations*, the *Interpretation of Peace Treaties (First Phase)*,
and the *International Status of South-West Africa* case were conveniently disregarded by the States concerned.   Non-acceptance of the
opinion in the *Certain Expenses* case led to a crisis in the United Nations.   Also, the order made by the Court in the *Anglo-Iranian Oil
Company* case, indicating certain provisional measures for the preservation of the rights of the parties, was never accepted by Iran.

      *   *   *

---

   1.   *Judgment concerning the release of American hostages in
Teheran.*   The decision, which is referred to supra p. 69 ordered
Iran to release the hostages immediately and make reparation to the
United States in a form and amount to be settled, if necessary, by a
subsequent procedure before the court.   It was dated May 24, 1980.

   The release of the hostages was eventually secured by the Declarations of January 19, 1981, which are briefly discussed above.   In
paragraph 11 of the first Declaration, the United States agreed to
withdraw promptly "all claims now pending before the International
Court of Justice."   See the Documentary Supplement.

   2.   *Role of the United Nations.*   Article 94 of the United Nations Charter provides:

      1.   Each Member of the United Nations undertakes to com-
ply with the decision of the International Court of Justice in any
case to which it is a party.

      2.   If any party to a case fails to perform the obligations
incumbent upon it under a judgment rendered by the Court, the
other party may have recourse to the Security Council, which
may, if it deems necessary, make recommendations or decide
upon measures to be taken to give effect to the judgment.

   The Security Council of the United Nations has never decided upon measures to be taken "to give effect to the judgment."   Questions as
yet undecided include the following: Does the Security Council have
power under the Charter to order a state to comply with a judgment?
Can the Security Council direct or authorize the use of force to enforce such an order?   Is the council limited, in its use of force to "enforce" a judgment of the court, to those situations in which non-performance of an order of the court can be considered a threat to the
peace, breach of the peace, or act of aggression under Article 39 of the
Charter of the United Nations?

   3.   *Awards of arbitral tribunals.*   The effectiveness of the
awards of international arbitral tribunals depends upon the willingness of states to abide by their agreements to be bound by such
awards.   "It is a striking fact that states have seldom refused to car-

ry out or abide by the decisions of international tribunals. * * * In the vast majority of instances in which positive action has been required, execution has followed as a matter of course." Hudson, International Tribunals 129 (1944). The statement is still generally valid today.

In some instances, however, disputes over the award have delayed final compliance or settlement for years.

THE CHAMIZAL BOUNDARY DISPUTE

49 United States Department of State Bulletin 199 (1963).

Department Statement, July 18

The Presidents of the United States and Mexico announced today their agreement to conclude a convention for the settlement of the Chamizal boundary dispute. The recommended terms of settlement which the Presidents have approved were submitted to them in identical memoranda by the Department of State and the Mexican Ministry of Foreign Relations. According to the terms of the recommended settlement, the United States would transfer to Mexico 437 acres in the vicinity of El Paso, Texas. Conclusion of the convention will be a final step in the resolution of this controversy, which has been earnestly sought by every United States administration since 1910.

An international arbitral commission awarded to Mexico in 1911 an undeterminable part of the Chamizal zone in El Paso, Texas. The area of the zone then totaled approximately 598 acres. The Mexican claim was based on a shift in the channel of the Rio Grande. The United States Government, which had disputed the claim, rejected the award on several grounds,[a] but in the understanding that the Govern-

---

a. Carlston, The Process of International Arbitration 153 (1946):

The validity of the award in attempting to divide the Chamizal tract was vigorously attacked by the American commissioner in a dissenting opinion upon the following bases: (1) It clearly departed from the terms of reference in deciding a question not submitted by the parties. Article I of the convention of 1910 bounded the tract with technical accuracy; Article III provided that the commission was to decide solely whether the title to the tract was in the United States or in Mexico. Neither government, in its diplomatic correspondence or in its arguments before the tribunal, took any other position than that the question was as to the ownership of the tract in its entirety. (2) It departed from

the terms of submission by failing to apply the rules of the convention of 1884. In the language of the Hague Court in the Orinoco Steamship Company Case, " 'excessive exercise of power may consist * * * in misinterpreting the express provisions of the agreement in respect of the way in which they are to reach their decisions, notably with regard to the legislation or the principles of law to be applied.' " That convention classed all changes either as slow and gradual erosion and accretion or the cutting of a new bed. The decision imported into the treaty a rule unknown to it as well as to international law—rapid and violent erosion. (3) It was "equivocal and uncertain in its terms and impossible of accomplishment." It would

ments of the two countries could proceed at once to settle their differences through diplomatic channels. Since 1911 the controversy has been a major problem in relations between the two countries. Every United States administration beginning with that of President Taft has attempted to resolve it in a mutually satisfactory manner. Proposals for a settlement have varied, and every practical means of settling the matter is believed to have been explored by the Governments at one time or another. In June 1962 President López Mateos urged that a further attempt be made, and President Kennedy agreed. The two Presidents instructed their respective executive agencies to recommend a complete solution which, without prejudice to the juridical positions of the two Governments, would take into account the entire history of the tract. They recognized that any mutually acceptable settlement would affect many people in the city of El Paso and agreed that respect for the rights and interests of the people affected on both sides of the border should be a principal consideration in reaching a solution. The recommended settlement follows generally the solution set forth in the international arbitral award of 1911.

*   *   *

SECTION D.   APPLICATION IN THE UNITED NATIONS

THE CASE OF AN ATTACK ON A SENEGALESE POST BY PORTUGAL

IX U.N. Monthly Chronicle, Oct. 1972, p. 3.

The Security Council met on 19, 20 and 23 October [1972] at the request of Senegal. The request was contained in a letter dated 16 October, addressed to the President. In its letter, Senegal stated that on 12 October at about 5 p. m., a unit of the regular Portuguese army, including five armoured cars, had attacked a Senegalese post in the department of Velingara, in the region of Casamance. One Senegalese soldier was killed, another wounded and a civilian working in his fields was killed by a Portuguese tank. The letter said the Senegalese army had intervened and forced the enemy troops to withdraw to their base at Pirada, three kilometres from the Senegalese border.

The letter further recalled that the Council had adopted several resolutions condemning Portugal for systematic acts of aggression and provocation against Senegal, but that the latest incident, although not the first that had occurred on the border between Senegal and Guinea (Bissau), must be considered the most serious and significant, because a deliberately planned act of war had been involved. Senegal said that Portugal's main aim in its constant aggressive conduct to-

be impossible to locate the channel
of 1864. Reprinted by permission
of the Columbia University Press.

wards various African countries was to show that the United Nations was powerless and to make its highest decision-making body appear ridiculous.

* * *

In a letter dated 18 October, addressed to the President of the Council, Portugal replied to the aforementioned letter from Senegal. In its letter Portugal said, referring to the incident of 12 October, that the Commander Headquarters of the Portuguese armed forces in Portuguese Guinea had published a communiqué, on 13 October, stating:

> "On the 12th of the current month, at about 1800 hours, a unit of the Portuguese army, composed of three armoured cars, violated the frontier of Senegal in the region of Pirada, causing one dead and one wounded in a detachment of the Senegalese army, and also one civilian dead of Portuguese nationality. The Command-in-Chief laments deeply this occurrence and has ordered that criminal proceedings be begun against the commander of the unit in question, so that he may be submitted to trial by court martial. It is presumed that this was a case of mental agitation on the part of the unit commander, seeing that he operated outside the zone to which he was assigned and in violation of all superior orders.

> "This Commander Headquarters immediately entered into contact with the Senegalese authorities in order to present to them its apologies and to express its readiness immediately to pay all the compensation that justice should dictate."

The Portuguese letter further stated that the Portuguese Government in Lisbon had summoned the Ambassador of Switzerland, whose country represented Portuguese interests in Senegal, to inform him of the details of the incident and to request that he transmit to the Government of Dakar the willingness of the Portuguese Government to pay compensation and to give all necessary guarantees to the Senegalese Government.

The Portuguese letter said that Portugal was unable to understand the purpose of the meeting of the Council convened at the request of Senegal, since no other conclusions could be drawn from the facts of the incident in question beyond those detailed in the communiqué of the Commander Headquarters of the Portuguese armed forces in Portuguese Guinea and transmitted to the Senegalese Government through the Swiss Ambassador. In those circumstances the Council meetings were one more step in the campaign against Portugal being carried on by certain interests hostile to it in the United Nations, with a view to serving predetermined policies to which those interests were dedicated.

With the consent of the Council, the President invited the representatives of Algeria, Mali, Mauritania and Senegal to participate in the discussion without the right to vote.

* * *

[Members of the Security Council debated whether to adopt a draft resolution sponsored by Guinea, Somalia and the Sudan. Among the arguments presented in this debate were the following:]

Coumba N'Doffene DIOUF, Minister for Foreign Affairs (Senegal), said that on 12 October at about 1700 hours, Portuguese military forces, including five armoured cars, attacked the Senegalese post of Nianao in the district of Kourane. The attack caused the death of a Senegalese lieutenant and a civilian worker in the fields, and seriously wounded a peaceful farmer. It was not the first time the Council had had to be seized of such provocations committed by Portuguese troops in violation of the sovereignty and territorial integrity of Senegal.

Since the first month of its independence Senegal had had to confront on its southern frontier acts of deliberate aggression by Portugal, which maintained in Guinea (Bissau) an unfortunate African Territory, and a colonial war which the Council had unequivocally condemned. In resolution 178 (1963) the Council had requested "the Government of Portugal, in accordance with its declared intentions, to take whatever action may be necessary to prevent any violation of Senegal's sovereignty and territorial integrity". That resolution had never been complied with.

Incursions into Senegal's territory by Portugal had been frequent, and while Senegal maintained its faith in the Security Council, the time had come for Senegal to defend by all measures within its means its population and territory against repeated actions of the Portuguese troops. At the same time, it was for the Council to take up the challenge Portugal had launched against the world community and prevent it from pursuing with impunity an anachronistic colonial war in Africa.

Portugal had made a public declaration concerning its most recent incursion, which recognized physical facts, and even offered apologies to the Senegalese Government and compensation for the victims of the attack. Portugal announced that the chief of the military district responsible for the horrible crime would eventually be court-martialled. Senegal wished to protest against such a subtle and immoral manoeuvre which suggested there might be justice with regard to what had happened at Pirada. It was inaccurate for Portugal to say its military commander had at any time lost his mental faculties. He knew exactly what he was doing. He was able to travel in his car with the lights off and to slow down in order to carry out his surprise attack. Senegal categorically rejected the proposal for compensation which Portugal hastened to present.

By what means had a country with such limited material and technical capacity as Portugal, not only faced the restraints imposed on it because of 10 years of colonial wars, but even thought unceasingly of enlarging the circle of its enemies? It was because of the impunity guaranteed by countries that had withdrawn from all open colonial actions—members of NATO, which at the time of certain votes did not hesitate practically to approve the attitude of defiance permanently observed by Portugal for the international community.

Imperialism and colonialism were doomed. Portugal must realize that. It must create immediate conditions of peace in Guinea (Bissau) by negotiating with PAIGC on the basis of the three-stage peace plan presented by Senegal in March 1969. The first phase would consist of a cease-fire followed by negotiations without any pre-condition. The second phase would start, as a result of the negotiation, by a period of internal automony for Guinea (Bissau). The modalities and time-limits would be discussed freely between the representatives of the Portuguese Government and the representatives of the various political movements of Guinea (Bissau). In the last stage, independence would be granted after negotiations, within the framework of a Portuguese-African community, which was not to be excluded a priori.

* * *

Lazar MOJSOV (Yugoslavia) said it was in the context of Portugal's long-established, systematic and carefully planned policy of aggression against African States, and of its unremitting colonial wars, that the Council must consider and finally reject the Portuguese apology and explanation for its most recent incursion into Senegalese territory. That act was not, as Portugal maintained, the result of the madness of one man but of a policy that thought it could stop the winds of change in what it called "its corner of Africa". The Portuguese "apology" was an apology until the next aggression.

The Portuguese policy of trying to keep its colonial possessions and of attacking and threatening the sovereignty and territorial integrity of African States was all part of the same policy. One needed the other, one fed the other, and without the removal of both, both would persist. Without the removal of major political, economic and military assistance and support by the allies of Portugal and South Africa, those two colonial and racist régimes, together with the illegal régime of Ian Smith in Southern Rhodesia, would not cease to conduct co-ordinated and mutually essential policies of subjugating southern Africa and threatening the rest of it. Juxtaposed with those grave realities, bland apologies could not be seriously considered.

* * *

Edouard LONGERSTAEY (Belgium) said the text of the revised draft resolution was out of proportion to its object. However regrettable the incursion into Senegalese territory on 12 October by a detachment of the Portuguese army, it was not comparable to the acts of violence and destruction that had been going on since 1963. Instead of the condemnation that appeared in operative paragraph 2, the Council should have merely deplored the recent incident, as well as the resulting threats to the territorial integrity and sovereignty of Senegal and the loss of human lives entailed.

The revised draft should not have missed the opportunity, how-ever tenuous and fragile, to lessen tension in the area by taking note of the assurances Portugal was prepared to give to Senegal and by requesting it to take appropriate measures to prevent the repetition of frontier incidents with Senegal. Belgium would abstain from vot-ing. Portugal should not be condemned on the basis of background alone, without taking into account its intentions, regrets and prom-ises to pay compensation.

* * *

Christopher PHILLIPS (United States) said the United States retained its conviction that the people of Portuguese Guinea had an inalienable right to self-determination. The United States had ab-stained because of the one-sided nature of the resolution. That reso-lution, while taking note of the letter from the representative of Por-tugal, did not reflect adequately its contents as they bore on the com-plaint before the Council. The Foreign Minister of Senegal had em-phasized the need to look for some form of peaceful settlement by the parties concerned in the conflict. Regrettably, nothing of that spirit of conciliation had been included in the resolution.

Last November the United States had suggested establishing a commission "acceptable to all parties, which might be in a position to investigate border incidents, and to report periodically to the Security Council on such questions as progress towards self-determination in Guinea (Bissau) and other elements which could lead to a satisfac-tory settlement in the region". The Council should point its activities in that direction in dealing with the difficult problem before it.

* * *

[The following] resolution was adopted by a vote of 12 in favour (Argentina, China, France, Guinea, India, Italy, Japan, Panama, So-malia, Sudan, USSR, Yugoslavia) to none against, with 3 abstentions (Belgium, United Kingdom, United States).

* * *

Text of Resolution 321 (1972)

THE SECURITY COUNCIL,

Considering the complaint of the Republic of Senegal against Portugal contained in document S/10807,

Having heard the Minister for Foreign Affairs of Senegal,

Taking note of the letter of the representative of Portugal con-tained in document S/10810,

Considering its resolutions 178 (1963) of 24 April 1963, 204 (1965) of 19 May 1965, 273 (1969) of 9 December 1969, 302 (1971) of 24 November 1971 and the report of 2 February 1971 (E/CN.-4/1050) of the Working Group of Experts of the Commission on Hu-man Rights concerning Portuguese acts of violence in Senegalese ter-ritory,

Deeply disturbed by the attitude of Portugal, which persistently refuses to comply with the relevant Security Council resolutions,

Deeply concerned about the multiplication of incidents which entail the risk of a threat to international peace and security,

Reaffirming that only complete respect for the sovereignty and territorial integrity of Senegal and all the African States bordering the territories of Guinea (Bissau), Angola and Mozambique, and for the principle of self-determination and independence defined in particular in General Assembly resolution 1514 (XV), will make it possible to eliminate the causes of tension in those regions of the African continent and create a climate of confidence, peace and security,

1.   Condemns the frontier violation and attack on the Senegalese post at Nianao committed by regular forces of the Portuguese army on 12 October 1972;

2.   Recalls its resolution 294 (1971) condemning the acts of violence and destruction committed by the Portuguese forces against the people and villages of Senegal since 1963;

3.   Demands that the Government of Portugal should stop immediately and definitively any acts of violence and destruction directed against Senegalese territory and scrupulously respect the sovereignty, territorial integrity and security of that State and all other independent African States;

4.   Calls upon the Government of Portugal to respect the principle of self-determination and independence defined in particular in General Assembly resolution 1514 (XV) and to take immediately all necessary steps to apply that principle;

5.   Declares that if Portugal does not comply with the provisions of the present resolution the Security Council will meet to consider other steps;

6.   Decides to remain seized of the question.

---

1.   *Questions.*   Did the Security Council of the United Nations apply any rules of law in the case of the attack on a Senegalese post by Portugal?   Did it find Portugal in violation of Article 2(4) of the charter?   Could it have so found?   What constitutional basis did the Security Council have for its adoption of the resolution?   Did it act under Chapter VI of the charter, or under Chapter VII?   Or did it act unlawfully?

Suppose that Portugal does not comply with the provisions of the resolution.   In paragraph 5 of the resolution, the council declares that it will meet to consider other steps.   What steps can it take to bring Portugal into compliance with its legal obligations?   Further attention is given to these problems in Chapter 20 of this casebook.

2.   *Law-making by the political organs of the United Nations.* In its resolution in the Senegalese case the Security Council refers to

General Assembly resolution 1514 (XV). That resolution is entitled Declaration on the Granting of Independence to Colonial Countries and Peoples. (Its text is set forth in the Documentary Supplement.) Does the council imply that Portugal is legally bound by the terms of that resolution? By what process, if any, can a resolution of the General Assembly become law so that its provisions can subsequently be applied by other organs of the United Nations?

SECTION E. WHEN SUPREME INTERESTS ARE JEOPARDIZED

TUCHMAN, THE GUNS OF AUGUST 127 (1962) *

Berlin, August 4, 1914:

At three o'clock members reconvened in the Reichstag to hear an address by the Chancellor and to perform the remainder of their duty which consisted first of voting war credits and then adjournment. The Social Democrats agreed to make the vote unanimous, and spent their last hours of parliamentary responsibility in anxious consultation whether to join in a "Hoch!" for the Kaiser which they satisfactorily resolved by making it a Hoch for "Kaiser, People, and Country."

Everyone, as Bethmann rose to speak, waited in painful expectancy for what he had to say about Belgium. A year ago Foreign Minister Jagow had assured a secret session of the Reichstag steering committee that Germany would never violate Belgium, and General von Heeringen, then War Minister, had promised that the Supreme Command in the event of war would respect Belgium's neutrality as long as Germany's enemies did. On August 4 deputies did not know that their armies had invaded Belgium that morning. They knew of the ultimatum but nothing of the Belgian reply because the German government, wishing to give the impression that Belgium had acquiesced and that her armed resistance was therefore illegal, never published it.

"Our troops," Bethmann informed the tense audience, "have occupied Luxembourg and perhaps"—the "perhaps" was posthumous by eight hours—"are already in Belgium." (Great commotion.) True, France had given Belgium a pledge to respect her neutrality, but "We knew that France was standing ready to invade Belgium" and "we could not wait." It was, he said inevitably, a case of military necessity, and "necessity knows no law."

So far he had his hearers, both the right which despised him and the left which mistrusted him, in thrall. His next sentence created a sensation. "Our invasion of Belgium is contrary to international law

* Reprinted with permission of Macmillan Publishing Co., Inc. from The Guns of August by Barbara Tuchman. © 1962.

but the wrong—I speak openly—that we are committing we will make good as soon as our military goal has been reached." Admiral Tirpitz considered this the greatest blunder ever spoken by a German statesman; Conrad Haussman, a leader of the Liberal party, considered it the finest part of the speech. The act having been confessed in a public mea culpa, he and his fellow deputies of the left felt purged of guilt and saluted the Chancellor with a loud "Sehr richtig!" In a final striking phrase—and before his day of memorable maxims was over he was to add one more that would make him immortal—Bethmann said that whoever was as badly threatened as were the Germans could think only of how to "hack his way through."

A war credit of five billion marks was voted unanimously, after which the Reichstag voted itself out of session for four months or for what was generally expected to be the duration. Bethmann closed the proceedings with an assurance that carried overtones of the gladiators' salute: "Whatever our lot may be, August 4, 1914, will remain for all eternity one of Germany's greatest days!"

SECTION F. REPRISE: NATURE OF INTERNATIONAL LAW

The heading of this section is a conventional way to begin a casebook on international law. We have begun this one somewhat differently for the reasons stated in the Preface and the first note in the chapter. Nonetheless, by this time you will think you have identified some rules of international law and will be wanting to get an overall concept of the nature of the beast you are supposed to be studying. This is a backward and forward cross reference to help you form your own concept—by the time you finish the course.

In the excerpt from The Guns of August, what was the international law that (Bethmann volunteered) Imperial Germany had violated? Was it imposed upon Germany as a state among states? If so, by what authority? In Part VI we ask you to consider the influence of jurisprudence (in the sense of conceptualizing and philosophizing about law and legal processes) in the international law sector of total law. Was the law that Bethmann said Germany had broken a general principle of morality, a doctrine of German foreign policy, a broad rule of law, or a very specific rule of law? How does international law differ from international relations? That is, is law a prediction of what will (must?) happen? Or, is it something else? If so, what?

Thus, where did the international law (whose mention by Bethmann disturbed Admiral Tirpitz) come from? Review the sources of international law enumerated in the Statute of the International Court of Justice. In 1914 there was no such court. Were the sources then the same as now? Was there then a rule against use of force by states to get what they wanted? Is there today? (See Chapter 19 as to the last two questions.)

Assume that all Bethmann meant was that Germany by invading Belgium (to facilitate a hinge sweep across France) had violated a treaty providing for the neutrality (neutralization) of Belgium. Is (was) an international agreement law as to its specific stipulations? Or was (is) there in play a law (principle, broad rule, specific norm) that states parties to treaties are legally obligated to perform them? If so, how is that law stated? Where does it come from?

NOTE TO PARTS I, II AND III

Every state in the international system has capacity to administer a national legal system. In one way or another, all the rules in the system serve to regulate the conduct of people. An obvious illustration is supplied by rules of criminal law. But the regulation of the conduct of people by rules of domestic law goes far beyond the regulation of criminal activity. It embraces the totality of their lives and actions. Rules of domestic law determine, for example, the status of a person—i. e. whether the person is married or a minor and so on—as well as the kind of interest—i. e. ownership, possession and the like—the person may have in a thing such as a piece of land. But the freedom of a state to administer a national legal system is restricted by rules of international law.

It is restricted, in the first place, by international law rules of jurisdiction which determine the categories of persons, events and places that a state may subject to rules of domestic law. Thus a state may not regulate everyday affairs within the territory of another.

In the second place, there are rules of international law which determine whether or not a state—even though it has capacity to subject persons, events and places to its rules of domestic law—may exercise such capacity. Thus a state may not apply its rules of domestic law to certain persons such as diplomatic representatives.

In the third place, rules of international law regulate the manner in which a state may exercise its capacity to subject persons, events and places to its domestic law. They require a state to administer its rules of domestic law in accordance with international standards of fairness and justice, which may be different from domestic standards of fairness and justice.

Whenever a state violates any of these three sets of international law rules, it gives another state a basis for claim to redress. Conceivably a state might violate more than one of the sets of international law rules involved and thus give another state several bases for claims to redress. Whichever the case, the claim or claims would require settlement through one or more of the international procedures covered in the Introductory Chapter.

Part I of this book deals with the restrictions imposed by international law upon the capacity of a state to subject persons, events and places to its rules of domestic law. Part II deals with the limitations imposed by international law upon the exercise of this capacity. Part III deals, inter alia, with the standards of fairness and justice a state must observe when it is using its capacity to administer a national legal system.

Part I

ALLOCATION OF JURISDICTION IN THE INTERNATIONAL SYSTEM

1. *Meaning of jurisdiction in national legal systems.* The term jurisdiction, or its equivalent in other languages, expresses a concept which is common to national legal systems.

In the United States, for example, we speak of federal jurisdiction as opposed to the jurisdiction of the states of the Union. We do so because under our domestic law—the Constitution in this instance —certain categories of persons, events or places are subject to federal law and others to the law of the several states. Whenever we say a matter is one of federal jurisdiction, we mean that the federal government is empowered under the domestic law of the United States to act—by way of legislation, judicial decision or executive action—with respect to the particular category of persons, events or places involved in the matter at hand. And we have the same concept in mind when we speak of the jurisdiction of the states.

The concept of jurisdiction is also commonly used in national legal systems to allocate the judicial function to different courts. In many states of the world, domestic law places limits upon the categories of persons, events or places with which particular courts may deal. Thus we may find certain courts have jurisdiction over civil matters and others over criminal matters. In certain states the civil courts are specialized, each having jurisdiction over certain civil matters but not others. In some, the jurisdiction of different criminal courts is determined by the level of gravity of the offense. There are states where jurisdiction over litigation between individuals and the government is vested in a system of administrative courts, separate and distinct from the other civil courts.

2. *Meaning of jurisdiction in the international legal system.* In the international legal system, the term jurisdiction expresses a concept similar to the concept it expresses in national legal systems. When we speak of the jurisdiction of a state in the international system, we mean the state is entitled under international law to subject certain categories of persons, events or places to its rules of law. It does not follow, however, that the rules of international law determining whether a state has jurisdiction over a particular person, event or place, are the same as those used in a national legal system in determining, for example, whether this court or that court has jurisdiction over a particular person, event or place.

In the international legal system, jurisdiction refers to the jurisdiction of the state as a whole and not of its constituent units or political subdivisions. The United States is a federation and France, for example, is not. Whether in the United States an alien is tried by a court of New York State or a federal court, or whether in France he is tried by a court in Paris or Marseilles, does not create an international issue of jurisdiction. The jurisdictional question in the international system is whether the United States in the one case, or France in the other, is entitled to try the alien, and not where or by what court in the United States or France he is being tried.

Furthermore, the international legal system is not concerned with the allocation by a state of its jurisdiction among its branches of government. In a national legal system, the making of legal rules might be vested in a legislature and their enforcement vested in the executive or judicial branch. But this division of functions is not always so clear cut. The House of Lords in the United Kingdom has legislative functions and also functions as a law court. In turn a court of law in a national legal system may not have been instructed by its legislature to apply a particular rule and may have to articulate one of its own devising before it can proceed to give it effect. Or the executive may be empowered to make legal rules. International law does not determine which branch of government should do what.

Accordingly it is advisable, if not indeed necessary, to discuss the jurisdiction of states under international law in terms which are neutral so far as the organs of government exercising the jurisdiction are concerned.

Chapter 2

BASES OF JURISDICTION

1. *Jurisdiction to prescribe and jurisdiction to enforce.* The term jurisdiction is all too often used imprecisely. A sharp distinction between rule-making and rule-enforcing jurisdiction is essential to effective analysis. First, the state prescribes a rule, which is to say that either by act of the legislature, decree of the executive, administrative regulation, or decision of a court, it declares a principle or legal norm. Second, the state enforces the rule. That is, it arrests, subpoenas witnesses and documents, tries and punishes for violation of the rule, or enters a judgment in vindication of the rule. Any one of these actions—and of course all of them together—is enforcement. Hence we discuss jurisdiction in terms of the jurisdiction of a state to prescribe rules of domestic law and its jurisdiction to enforce them.

A state normally has jurisdiction to prescribe rules of domestic law governing conduct taking place physically within its territory. At the other extreme no state has jurisdiction to prescribe rules of domestic law governing the conduct of everyone everywhere in the world. A state normally also has jurisdiction to enforce within its own territory the rules of law it has properly prescribed. Yet at the other extreme, a state may not normally send its police and courts outside its borders to arrest and punish people even for murders committed within its territory.

Between these extremes lies the international law of jurisdiction. This chapter examines some of the factual bases which are accepted in the international legal system as adequate foundations for a state's prescription and enforcement of rules of domestic law. The materials in this chapter are introductory only; jurisdictional issues will be presented in greater complexity in subsequent chapters.

2. *The legal consequences of lack of jurisdiction.* Under the domestic law of states these consequences are frequently different from those in the international legal system. Thus, should a court purport to convict an alien of a crime when it lacks jurisdiction to do so under the domestic law of a state, the consequence usually will be the release of that person from imprisonment. Yet should the trial be in violation of international law rules of jurisdiction, there may be no legal consequence under the domestic law of the state involved, i. e. the person may remain in prison. The legal consequence under international law, however, would be the accrual to the state of nationality of the alien of a claim against the offending state.

3. *Jurisdiction, vel non, not always dispositive.* One must be careful not to read too much into the term jurisdiction. To say that a state has acted outside its jurisdiction suggests an immediate legal consequence. But to say that it has acted within its jurisdiction may be only the first step in analysis. As will be seen, a state is considered to owe special obligations of fair treatment to aliens who are within the state. For example, the United States is required by international law to give a fair trial to an alien arrested here for a murder committed here. If the United States tries the alien unfairly, the state of his nationality has a claim against the United States, even though the United States, in trying the alien at all, acted within its rights under international rules of jurisdiction.

SECTION A. JURISDICTION TO PRESCRIBE RULES OF LAW

---

1. CONDUCT WITHIN THE TERRITORY

J. H. G. v. PUBLIC PROSECUTOR

Netherlands, Court of Appeal of Arnhem, 1958.
26 Int'l L.Rep. 158 (1963).*

The Facts.—The driving license of J. H. G. had been withdrawn by an order of a Netherlands Court. According to Article 32, paragraph I, of the Netherlands Road Traffic Act, it is an offence to drive a car when one's driving licence has been withdrawn by a court. J. H. G., who had been a passenger in a car while it was being driven in the Netherlands, took over the driving after the car had passed the Netherlands-German frontier and drove the car further into Germany. Subsequently, he was charged with an offence under Article 32, paragraph I, and the lower Court imposed a fine.

Held: that the prosecutor's case should be dismissed. [A portion of the opinion of the court appears below.]

* * * One of the elements of the offence defined by Article 32, paragraph I, of the Act on Road Traffic is the driving of a car on a road. Article I of this Act defines "road" as a road open to public traffic, whether motorized or otherwise. According to the preamble of this Act, it purports to lay down rules for traffic on the roads. As a rule, the Netherlands Legislature can only legislate for its own territory, i. e., the territory of the Realm in Europe. This is quite certainly the case when the matter involved is of such a typically territorial character as road traffic. A "road" as mentioned in Article 32, paragraph I, can only be understood to mean a road in that territory.

* Reprinted by permission of E. Lauterpacht, ed., and Grotius Publications, Ltd., Cambridge, England.

This provision is not applicable to roads outside the Realm in Europe. The appellant, therefore, did not commit an offence.

RE PENATI

Italy, Court of Cassation, 1946.
[1946] Ann.Dig. 74 (No. 30).*

The Facts.—The appellant, a Swiss subject resident in Italy, was convicted on the ground that he had given aid to the enemy, namely, the German occupation authorities in Italy. Upon appeal, he contended that, being an alien, he was not subject to the Italian rules of criminal law relating to treason and similar crimes.

* * *

Held: that the appeal must be dismissed. * * * [A portion of the opinion of the court appears below.]

Contrary to the contention of the appellant, the crime of favouring the political designs of the enemy can also be committed by an alien. According to Article 3 of the Penal Code, Italian criminal law binds all those who, whether they are Italian nationals or aliens, reside in Italy, subject to the exceptions provided by Italian public law or by international law. There is no rule of Italian public law or of international law which exempts from punishment an alien who commits an act in Italy which constitutes a crime against the existence of the State, against its military defence, and against the duty of loyalty of the citizens towards the State which he attempts to undermine. Not only does no rule of this kind exist, but it is legally inconceivable, for no State can allow aliens who enjoy its hospitality to carry out activities which are contrary to its vital interests in the military and political sphere. The prohibition of such activities does not only exist, but it must be enforced with special rigour in time of war. * * * The crime of which the appellant has been found guilty, is not less a crime because the appellant is a Swiss national * * *.

ARMENGOL v. MUTUALITÉ SOCIALE AGRICOLE DE L'HÉRAULT

France, Court of Cassation, 1966.
47 Int'l L.Rep. 135 (1974).*

* * *

* * * According to the decision under appeal, which was of final effect, Armengol, a national of Andorra domiciled at Massana (Andorra) and the owner of flocks of sheep which he moves between winter and summer pastures, has these sheep driven into France and looked after by his Andorran and Spanish shepherds. He pays a rent for grazing rights.

* Reprinted by permission of E. Lauterpacht, ed., and Grotius Publications,
Ltd., Cambridge, England.

The decision is criticized for adjudging that this activity rendered Armengol liable in France to make contributions in respect of family allowances, although, however, neither he nor his shepherds could enjoy the corresponding benefits since there was no treaty of reciprocity between France and the Principality of Andorra. According to Articles 1060, 1061 and 1144 of the Rural Code, however, the scheme of family benefits is applicable to stock-rearing operations and to whosoever employs labour for work in agriculture. Since these provisions are couched in general terms, they are applicable to everyone who performs such an activity on French territory. To exempt aliens from their scope would require the addition to the text of an exception for which it does not provide.

* * *

For these reasons, the Court dismisses the appeal brought against the decision rendered on 27 February 1963 by the Commission of first instance of Hérault.

———

1. *Meaning of conduct.* The last case indicates that conduct within the territory encompasses many forms of human behavior, not just criminal behavior. Employment within the territory is conduct which a state has jurisdiction to control by prescribing that it shall be taxed. In addition a state has jurisdiction to regulate conduct within its territory that results in marriage, the acquisition of property, the disposition of wealth, the conclusion of contracts, the commission of torts, and other consequences or relationships of a private nature.

2. *Conduct having effect outside the territory.* In many instances conduct within the territory has its effect exclusively therein. This is not always the case, however; there are situations where the effect of conduct within the territory takes place outside of it. Whether the effect be within or without the territory, the state where the conduct occurs has jurisdiction to prescribe rules of law dealing with it. It is true that if the effect is outside the territory, the state in whose territory it takes place also has jurisdiction to prescribe rules of law dealing with the conduct. The jurisdiction of that state is considered at p. 95, but does not affect the jurisdiction of the state where the conduct occurs. The following case is illustrative.

Public Prosecutor v. D. S., Netherlands, Supreme Court, 1958, 26 Int'l L.Rep. 209 (1963). A Dutch merchant sent a defamatory letter from the Netherlands to an acquaintance in London where the letter was received and read by the addressee. He contended that the offense had taken place in England. The court said:

> The contention of the accused that if a person is insulted by another person by means of a letter sent to him by post, the offence is committed exclusively at the place where the letter reaches, and is read by, the person insulted, is incorrect. The offence, in such circumstances is committed at the place where the

offender posted the letter. It is therefore unnecessary to decide whether the place where the letter came into the hands of the addressee can likewise be considered as the locus delicti.

The state in which the conduct takes place may treat its effect outside its territory as criminal, even though it is not deemed criminal in the state in whose territory it takes effect. Act Committed, but not Punishable in West Germany, by an Austrian, Austria, Supreme Court 1972, 101 Journal du Droit International 632 (1974). Two Austrians caused an illustrated book to be published by a West German publishing house. They were charged in Austria with pornography. They argued that charges of pornography against them in West Germany had been dismissed and their illustrations were accepted there as modern art. The court rejected the argument and, though predicating jurisdiction on the ground they were Austrians, indicated that their conduct in Austria, i. e., assembling and arranging the components of the book, was also a basis for making their conduct criminal even though it was not punishable in West Germany.

3. *Conduct partly within and partly without the territory.* In some situations, the conduct may consist of a series of acts, some taking place within the territory and some outside of it. This was the case in Denunciation to the Enemy, Netherlands, Court of Cassation, 1958, 88 Journal du Droit International 893 (1961).[a] The reporter summarized the case as follows:

> Benders, an employee of the Twentsche Bank, revealed to the German authorities in 1936 that the Spier brothers, Jews of German nationality, had, contrary to the legislation then in force in Germany, placed a considerable fortune in safety in the Twentsche Bank in the Netherlands. By * * * imprisoning one of the Spier brothers and the wife of the other the German authorities were able to constrain them to return the fortune to Germany, after which, naturally under a cloak of legitimacy, it was almost entirely confiscated. The heirs now sued Benders and the Bank.

> What is the law governing Benders' unlawful act? In order to carry out his * * * design, he went just beyond the Netherlands frontier, to make contact in Germany with Oberzollrat Kinzel of Dusseldorf. The interview consummating this betrayal, which netted 10,000 deniers for Benders, therefore took place in Germany. Was Germany therefore the locus delicti and German law for that reason applicable? The Court of Appeal of Amsterdam rightly thought that this was a little too easy. The execution of the design, the Court said, began by the compilation of documents in the offices of the Bank in the Netherlands; the infamous act was directed against a fortune in the Netherlands,

a. English text in the Journal. Reprinted by permission of Editions Techniques, S.A., Paris.

while it was at the same time calculated to injure the Bank in the Netherlands. "In the light of all these facts" goes on the Court, "Benders' act took place to such an extent in the Netherlands that the Tribunal was fully justified in subjecting it to Netherlands law."

* * * [The decision below was upheld by the supreme court.]

4. *Conduct in the territory involving events outside of it.* Even though the conduct takes place entirely in the territory, it may be made criminal because of prior events which took place outside of it. This was the situation in R. v. Nel, South Africa, Supreme Court, Appellate Division, 1953, 20 Int'l L.Rep. 192 (1957), which is reported in part as follows:

The facts. Nel was convicted in a South African Magistrate's Court on nine counts of contravening s. 2 of the Stock Theft Act. The relevant provisions read:

A person who in any manner, otherwise than at a public sale, acquires or receives into his possession from any other person stolen stock or stolen produce without having reasonable cause, proof of which shall be on such first mentioned person, for believing at the time of such acquisition or receipt, that such stock or produce was the property of the person from whom he received it or that such person was duly authorized by the owner thereof to deal with or dispose of it shall be guilty of an offence.

He appealed against his conviction to the Transvaal Provincial Division of the Supreme Court on the ground, inter alia, that the cattle had been stolen in Rhodesia, beyond the borders of the Union, and therefore the Act invoked had no application to the present circumstances, as the criminal jurisdiction of a State is strictly territorial in its operation. The appeal was dismissed, but leave was granted to take the case to the Appellate Division of the Supreme Court. Nel again put forward the same argument. [A portion of the opinion of the court appears below.]

It was clear from the evidence and was admitted by the appellant that in each of the counts (a) the cattle concerned were acquired by him otherwise than at a public sale, (b) that these cattle had been stolen. * * * But counsel contended that the Act applied only to stock stolen in the Union, that consequently the words "stolen stock" in the section meant stock so stolen and that the appellant's acts, therefore, did not fall within the section because the evidence showed it had been stolen in Rhodesia. The argument was based on the general submission that, at any rate in the absence of express provision, the Courts of any State have no jurisdiction in regard to crimes committed outside the borders of such State and that the provisions of the Stock Theft Act showed that it was not intended to apply in any respect to stock stolen outside the Union. Counsel conceded that if stock is so stolen by an accused person and brought into the Union by that person, he falls within the provisions of the Act because theft is a continuous offence (R. v. von Elling, 1945, A.D. 234) and the accused in such a case would be stealing within the Union; but counsel contended that this doctrine would not apply in this case where the only transaction proved against the appellant was that he had bought the cattle in the Union. I am prepared to assume that the general submission put forward by counsel is well-founded, but this in itself would not avail the appellant as the act, viz., the purchase of the cattle, on which his conviction was founded, took place within the Union * * *. There is no warrant for holding that the words "stolen stock" mean stock stolen in the Union or that they mean anything more than stock which, according to our law, is stolen stock * * *. The appellant * * * was therefore rightly convicted. (at 193)

5. *Problem.* Suppose something more complicated than cattle theft had been involved, say, securities fraud, with different standards of fraud in the two states. Would the result be the same, (a) in a criminal case, (b) in a civil case?

---

2.   CONDUCT OUTSIDE THE TERRITORY CAUSING EFFECT WITHIN

THE CUTTING CASE
LETTER, SECRETARY OF STATE TO UNITED STATES AMBASSADOR TO MEXICO

[1887] Foreign Relations of the United States 751 (1888).
Department of State, Washington, November 1, 1887.

SIR: On the 19th of July, 1886, the minister of the United States at the City of Mexico was instructed to demand of the Mexican Government the release of A. K. Cutting, a citizen of the United States, then imprisoned at Paso del Norte, where he had been incarcerated since the 23d of the preceding month on a charge of libel alleged to have been published by him in Texas.

The case was first brought to the notice of the Department by Mr. Brigham, consul of the United States at Paso del Norte, who, in a dispatch dated the 1st July, 1886, reported that Mr. Cutting had been arrested and imprisoned for the publication in Texas, in the United States, of an alleged libel against a citizen of Mexico. Accompanying the consul's dispatch were affidavits substantiating his statements. * * *

* * * It is sufficient here to state, as was set forth at the time of the demand, that the ground upon which Mr. Cutting's release was demanded was that the judicial tribunals of Mexico were not competent under the rules of international law to try a citizen of the United States for an offense committed and consummated in his

own country, merely because the person offended happened to be a Mexican. * * *

* * * Not only was this claim, which is defined in Article 186 of the Mexican penal code, defended and enforced by Judge Zubia, before whom the case of Mr. Cutting was tried, and whose decision was affirmed by the supreme court of Chihuahua * * *, but the claim was defended and justified by the Mexican Government in communications to this Department, emanating both from the Mexican minister at this capital and from the department of foreign affairs in the City of Mexico.

The statement of the consul at Paso del Norte that Mr. Cutting was arrested on the charge of the publication in Texas of an alleged libel against a Mexican is fully sustained by the opinion of Judge Zubia. Under the head of "It appears 6," in that decision, it is stated that on the 22d of June, 1886, "the plaintiff enlarged the accusation, stating that although the newspaper, the El Paso Sunday Herald, is published in Texas, Mr. Cutting had had circulated a great number in this town (Paso del Norte) and in the interior of the Republic, it having been read by more than three persons, for which reason an order had been issued to seize the copies which were still in the office of the said Cutting." The conclusive inference from this statement is that the charge upon which the warrant of arrest was issued was the publication of the alleged libel in Texas. * * * It appears, however, under "Considering 6," in Judge Zubia's decision, that the claim made in Article 186 of the Mexican penal code was actually enforced in the case in question as a distinct and original ground of prosecution. The decision of Judge Zubia was framed in the alternative, and it was held that, even supposing the defamation arose solely from the publication of the alleged libel in the El Paso (Texas) Sunday Herald, Article 186 of the Mexican penal code provided for punishment in that case; Judge Zubia saying that it did not belong to the judge to examine the principle laid down in that article but to apply it fully, it being the law in force in the State of Chihuahua. It nowhere appears that the Texas publication was ever circulated in Mexico so as to constitute the crime of defamation under the Mexican law. As has been seen, this was not a part of the original charge on which the warrant for Mr. Cutting's arrest was issued; and while it is stated in Judge Zubia's decision that an order was issued for the seizure of copies of the Texas paper which might be found in the office of Mr. Cutting in Paso del Norte, it nowhere appears from that decision that any copies were actually found in that place or elsewhere in Mexico.

But, however this may be, this Government is still compelled to deny what it denied on the 19th of July, 1886, and what the Mexican Government has since executively and judicially maintained, that a citizen of the United States can be held under the rules of international law to answer in Mexico for an offense committed in the United States, simply because the object of that offense happens to be a citizen of Mexico. * * *

* * *

As to the question of international law, I am unable to discover any principle upon which the assumption of jurisdiction made in Article 186 of the Mexican penal code can be justified. There is no principle better settled than that the penal laws of a country have no extraterritorial force. Each state may, it is true, provide for the punishment of its own citizens for acts committed by them outside of its territory; but this makes the penal law a personal statute, and while it may give rise to inconvenience and injustice in many cases, it is a matter in which no other Government has the right to interfere. To say, however, that the penal laws of a country can bind foreigners and regulate their conduct, either in their own or any other foreign country, is to assert a jurisdiction over such countries and to impair their independence. Such is the consensus of opinion of the leading authorities on international law at the present day * * *. There being then no principle of international law which justifies such a pretension, any assertion of it must rest, as an exception to the rule, either upon the general concurrence of nations or upon express conventions. Such a concurrence in respect to the claim made in Article 186 of the Mexican penal code can not be found in the legislation of the present day. Though formerly asserted by a number of minor states, it has now been generally abandoned, and may be regarded as almost obsolete.

* * *

It has constantly been laid down in the United States as a rule of action, that citizens of the United States can not be held answerable in foreign countries for offenses which were wholly committed and consummated either in their own country or in other countries not subject to the jurisdiction of the punishing state. When a citizen of the United States commits in his own country a violation of its laws, it is his right to be tried under and in accordance with those laws, and in accordance with the fundamental guaranties of the Federal Constitution in respect to criminal trials in every part of the United States.

To say that he may be tried in another country for his offense, simply because its object happens to be a citizen of that country, would be to assert that foreigners coming to the United States bring hither the penal laws of the country from which they come, and thus subject citizens of the United States in their own country to an indefinite criminal responsibility. Such a pretension can never be admitted by this Government.

* * *

You are therefore instructed to say to the Mexican Government, not only that an indemnity should be paid to Mr. Cutting for his arrest and detention in Mexico on the charge of publishing a libel in the United States against a Mexican, but also, in the interests of good

neighborhood and future amity, that the statute proposing to confer such extraterritorial jurisdiction should, as containing a claim invasive of the independent sovereignty of a neighboring and friendly state, be repealed. * * *
    * * *

I am, etc.

T. F. BAYARD.

GOSTELRADIO SSSR v. WHITNEY AND PIPER

Levitsky, Copyright, Defamation and Privacy
in Soviet Civil Law, 22 (I) Law in Eastern Europe 151 (1979).*

[In May 1978, Zviad Gamsakhurdia, a dissident from Georgia, was brought to trial for anti-Soviet agitation and propaganda, and sentenced to three years in prison, to be followed by two years of banishment. In a nationally televised interview after the trial, he admitted he was guilty and expressed repentance. Two American newsmen—Whitney of The New York Times and Piper of the Baltimore Sun—went to Georgia and spoke to friends of the dissident and his wife. In the despatches which were printed in their newspapers on May 25, they reported that friends of the dissident, or sources close to him, considered the televised confession "fabricated," or "false."

Whitney and Piper were sued for libel by Gostelradio SSSR—a juridical person—under Section 7 of the Soviet Civil Code. The action was civil, not criminal. The code provides:

Section 7. Defence of honour and dignity

    A citizen or an organisation is entitled to demand of the court the refutation of statements which reflect upon his/its honour and dignity unless the person publishing such statements proves that they are true.

    If the statements referred to are published in the press and are untrue they must be retracted in the press. * * *

    If the judgment of the court is not carried out, the court may impose on the offender a fine recoverable by the State. * * * The Civil Code of the RSFSR, 11 Law in Eastern Europe 15 (1966).

After a three hour proceeding in which they refused to participate and a finding of libel, they were ordered to publish retractions and pay costs—roughly $1,700 dollars each. They had ten days to appeal. Whitney returned to Moscow and was summoned to court for his failure to comply with the order for retraction. After a hearing on August 3, he was fined—about 75 dollars—for contempt of court in not complying with the order. On August 4, he paid under protest the costs and the fine for himself and for Piper, who, though

* Reprinted with the permission of Sijthoff & Noordhoff, International Publishers b.v., P.O. Box 4, 2400 MA Alphen aan den Rijn, The Netherlands.

still in the United States, had also been fined for contempt. A short time thereafter Gostelradio SSSR discontinued the suit.

Levitsky points out that circulation of the newspaper was essential to the case and discusses the matter as follows.]

The third element of the corpus delicti to be established in a civil libel suit under Section 7 is circulation of the untrue, defamatory statements. * * *

"What I cannot understand," Whitney told Newsweek, "is how a Soviet court can have jurisdiction over material that is not disseminated in the Soviet Union." Piper made a similar comment * * *. The publisher of The Sun, Donald H. Patterson, Sr., wondered: " * * * philosophically, why should we allow our correspondent to be subjected to a court trial for something which wasn't published in Russian?" A somewhat questionable philosophy, considering that "a rose, by any other name * * *," and that some Russians do read English.

At the trial, * * * V. Liubovtsey, who had signed the original complaint, testified that the articles written by Whitney and Piper had, in fact, been disseminated in the Soviet Union. He claimed that "It is possible to buy The New York Times at hotels or at Intourist offices, at the airport and at kiosks," adding that there were subscribers to the Baltimore Sun in the Soviet Union. Procurator Skaredov supplied the statement that an account of Whitney's and Piper's articles had also been disseminated in a Russian broadcast by the Voice of America. Judge Almazov read into the record pertinent portions of this broadcast.

This having been said, one must point out that in order to prove "circulation" within the meaning of Section 7, communication of the defamatory statement even to one person other than the plaintiff would have been sufficient. It was therefore without significance whether The New York Times was, or was not, on sale in Moscow's kiosks, as long as one government bureaucrat in Moscow had seen it. (at 159–160)

Questions. Many newspapers in the United States and elsewhere, including some of the best, widely created the impression that the case was a criminal trial by reporting in headlines the "conviction" of the reporters, translating the words "court costs" as fines, and reporting the fine for contempt as a "fine for libelling" the Russian State.

The United States made no protest in this case. Suppose the trial had been a criminal trial and a fine imposed consisting precisely of the amount of the court costs in the civil case. Would the Department of State have protested as it did in the Cutting Case? Should it have? Why did it not protest in this case, for example, on the ground of lack of jurisdiction? Was it because it was a civil case?

THE S. S. "LOTUS" (FRANCE v. TURKEY)

Permanent Court of International Justice, 1927.
P.C.I.J., Ser. A, No. 10.

* * *

By a special agreement signed at Geneva on October 12th, 1926, between the Governments of the French and Turkish Republics * * *, [France and Turkey] have submitted to the Permanent Court of International Justice the question of jurisdiction which has arisen between them following upon the collision which occurred on August 2nd, 1926, between the steamships Boz-Kourt and Lotus.

According to the special agreement, the Court has to decide the following questions:

(1) Has Turkey, contrary to Article 15 of the Convention of Lausanne of July 24th, 1923, respecting conditions of residence and business and jurisdiction, acted in conflict with the principles of international law—and if so, what principles—by instituting, following the collision which occurred on August 2nd, 1926, on the high seas between the French steamer Lotus and the Turkish steamer Boz-Kourt and upon the arrival of the French steamer at Constantinople—as well as against the captain of the Turkish steamship—joint criminal proceedings in pursuance of Turkish law against M. Demons, officer of the watch on board the Lotus at the time of the collision, in consequence of the loss of the Boz-Kourt having involved the death of eight Turkish sailors and passengers?

(2) Should the reply be in the affirmative, what pecuniary reparation is due to M. Demons, provided, according to the principles of international law, reparation should be made in similar cases?

* * *

On August 2nd, 1926, just before midnight, a collision occurred between the French mail steamer Lotus, proceeding to Constantinople, and the Turkish collier Boz-Kourt, between five and six nautical miles to the north of Cape Sigri (Mitylene). The Boz-Kourt, which was cut in two, sank, and eight Turkish nationals who were on board perished. After having done everything possible to succour the shipwrecked persons, of whom ten were able to be saved, the Lotus continued on its course to Constantinople, where it arrived on August 3rd.

At the time of the collision, the officer of the watch on board the Lotus was Monsieur Demons, a French citizen, lieutenant in the merchant service and first officer of the ship, whilst the movements of the Boz-Kourt were directed by its captain, Hassan Bey, who was one of those saved from the wreck.

* * *

On August 5th, Lieutenant Demons was requested by the Turkish authorities to go ashore to give evidence. The examination, the length of which incidentally resulted in delaying the departure of the Lotus, led to the placing under arrest of Lieutenant Demons—without previous notice being given to the French Consul-General—and Hassan Bey, amongst others. This arrest, which has been characterized by the Turkish Agent as arrest pending trial (arrestation préventive), was effected in order to ensure that the criminal prosecution instituted against the two officers, on a charge of manslaughter, by the Public Prosecutor of Stamboul, on the complaint of the families of the victims of the collision, should follow its normal course.

The case was first heard by the Criminal Court of Stamboul on August 28th. On that occasion, Lieutenant Demons submitted that the Turkish Courts had no jurisdiction; the Court, however, overruled his objection. When the proceedings were resumed on September 11th, Lieutenant Demons demanded his release on bail: this request was complied with * * *.

On September 15th, the Criminal Court delivered its judgment, the terms of which have not been communicated to the Court by the Parties. It is, however, common ground, that it sentenced Lieutenant Demons to eighty days' imprisonment and a fine of twenty-two pounds, Hassan Bey being sentenced to a slightly more severe penalty.

       *   *   *

The action of the Turkish judicial authorities with regard to Lieutenant Demons at once gave rise to many diplomatic representations and other steps on the part of the French Government or its representatives in Turkey, either protesting against the arrest of Lieutenant Demons or demanding his release, or with a view to obtaining the transfer of the case from the Turkish Courts to the French Courts.

As a result of these representations, the Government of the Turkish Republic declared on September 2nd, 1926, that "it would have no objection to the reference of the conflict of jurisdiction to the Court at The Hague". The French Government having, on the 6th of the same month, given "its full consent to the proposed solution", the two Governments appointed their plenipotentiaries with a view to the drawing up of the special agreement to be submitted to the Court; this special agreement was signed at Geneva on October 12th, 1926, * * * and the ratifications were deposited on December 27th, 1926.

       *   *   *

I

Before approaching the consideration of the principles of international law contrary to which Turkey is alleged to have acted—thereby infringing the terms of Article 15 of the Convention of Lau-

sanne of July 24th, 1923, respecting conditions of residence and business and jurisdiction—, it is necessary to define, in the light of the
written and oral proceedings, the position resulting from the special
agreement. * * *

1.   The collision which occurred on August 2nd, 1926, between
the S.S. Lotus, flying the French flag, and the S.S. Boz-Kourt, flying
the Turkish flag, took place on the high seas: the territorial jurisdiction of any State other than France and Turkey therefore does not
enter into account.

2.   The violation, if any, of the principles of international law
would have consisted in the taking of criminal proceedings against
Lieutenant Demons. It is not therefore a question relating to any
particular step in these proceedings—such as his being put to trial,
his arrest, his detention pending trial or the judgment given by the
Criminal Court of Stamboul—but of the very fact of the Turkish
Courts exercising criminal jurisdiction. That is why the arguments
put forward by the Parties in both phases of the proceedings relate
exclusively to the question whether Turkey has or has not, according
to the principles of international law, jurisdiction to prosecute in this
case.

The Parties agree that the Court has not to consider whether the
prosecution was in conformity with Turkish law; it need not therefore consider whether, apart from the actual question of jurisdiction,
the provisions of Turkish law cited by Turkish authorities were really applicable in this case, or whether the manner in which the proceedings against Lieutenant Demons were conducted might constitute
a denial of justice, and accordingly, a violation of international law.
The discussions have borne exclusively upon the question whether
criminal jurisdiction does or does not exist in this case.

3.   The prosecution was instituted because the loss of the Boz-
Kourt involved the death of eight Turkish sailors and passengers.
* * *   [N]o criminal intention has been imputed to either of the
officers responsible for navigating the two vessels; it is therefore a
case of prosecution for involuntary manslaughter. * * *   Moreover, the exact conditions in which these persons perished do not appear from the documents submitted to the Court; nevertheless, there
is no doubt that their death may be regarded as the direct outcome of
the collision, and the French Government has not contended that this
relation of cause and effect cannot exist.

* * *

5.   The prosecution was instituted in pursuance of Turkish legislation. The special agreement does not indicate what clause or
clauses of that legislation apply. No document has been submitted to
the Court indicating on what article of the Turkish Penal Code the
prosecution was based; the French Government however declares
that the Criminal Court claimed jurisdiction under Article 6 of the
Turkish Penal Code, and far from denying this statement, Turkey, in
the submissions of her Counter-Case, contends that that article is in

conformity with the principles of international law. It does not appear from the proceedings whether the prosecution was instituted solely on the basis of that article.

Article 6 of the Turkish Penal Code, * * * runs as follows:

[Translation] Any foreigner who, apart from the cases contemplated by Article 4, commits an offence abroad to the prejudice of Turkey or of a Turkish subject, for which offence Turkish law prescribes a penalty involving loss of freedom for a minimum period of not less than one year, shall be punished in accordance with the Turkish Penal Code provided that he is arrested in Turkey. * * *

* * *

Even if the Court must hold that the Turkish authorities had seen fit to base the prosecution of Lieutenant Demons upon the above-mentioned Article 6, the question submitted to the Court is not whether that article is compatible with the principles of international law; it is more general. The Court is asked to state whether or not the principles of international law prevent Turkey from instituting criminal proceedings against Lieutenant Demons under Turkish law. Neither the conformity of Article 6 in itself with the principles of international law nor the application of that article by the Turkish authorities constitutes the point at issue; it is the very fact of the institution of proceedings which is held by France to be contrary to those principles. * * *

II

Having determined the position resulting from the terms of the special agreement, the Court must now ascertain which were the principles of international law that the prosecution of Lieutenant Demons could conceivably be said to contravene.

It is Article 15 of the Convention of Lausanne of July 24th, 1923, respecting conditions of residence and business and jurisdiction, which refers the contracting Parties to the principles of international law as regards the delimitation of their respective jurisdiction.

This clause is as follows:

Subject to the provisions of Article 16, all questions of jurisdiction shall, as between Turkey and the other contracting Powers, be decided in accordance with the principles of international law.

* * * In these circumstances it is impossible—except in pursuance of a definite stipulation—to construe the expression "principles of international law" otherwise than as meaning the principles which are in force between all independent nations and which therefore apply equally to all the contracting Parties.

* * *

III

* * * The French Government contends that the Turkish Courts, in order to have jurisdiction, should be able to point to some title to jurisdiction recognized by international law in favour of Turkey. On the other hand, the Turkish Government takes the view that Article 15 allows Turkey jurisdiction whenever such jurisdiction does not come into conflict with a principle of international law.

* * *

International law governs relations between independent States. The rules of law binding upon States therefore emanate from their own free will as expressed in conventions or by usages generally accepted as expressing principles of law and established in order to regulate the relations between these co-existing independent communities or with a view to the achievement of common aims. Restrictions upon the independence of States cannot therefore be presumed.

Now the first and foremost restriction imposed by international law upon a State is that—failing the existence of a permissive rule to the contrary—it may not exercise its power in any form in the territory of another State. In this sense jurisdiction is certainly territorial; it cannot be exercised by a State outside its territory except by virtue of a permissive rule derived from international custom or from a convention.

It does not, however, follow that international law prohibits a State from exercising jurisdiction in its own territory, in respect of any case which relates to acts which have taken place abroad, and in which it cannot rely on some permissive rule of international law. Such a view would only be tenable if international law contained a general prohibition to States to extend the application of their laws and the jurisdiction of their courts to persons, property and acts outside their territory, and if, as an exception to this general prohibition, it allowed States to do so in certain specific cases. But this is certainly not the case under international law as it stands at present. Far from laying down a general prohibition to the effect that States may not extend the application of their laws and the jurisdiction of their courts to persons, property and acts outside their territory, it leaves them in this respect a wide measure of discretion which is only limited in certain cases by prohibitive rules; as regards other cases, every State remains free to adopt the principles which it regards as best and most suitable.

This discretion left to States by international law explains the great variety of rules which they have been able to adopt without objections or complaints on the part of other States; it is in order to remedy the difficulties resulting from such variety that efforts have been made for many years past, both in Europe and America, to prepare conventions the effect of which would be precisely to limit the discretion at present left to States in this respect by international law, thus making good the existing lacunae in respect of jurisdiction or removing the conflicting jurisdictions arising from the diversity of the principles adopted by the various States.

In these circumstances, all that can be required of a State is that it should not overstep the limits which international law places upon its jurisdiction; within these limits, its title to exercise jurisdiction rests in its sovereignty.

It follows from the foregoing that the contention of the French Government to the effect that Turkey must in each case be able to cite a rule of international law authorizing her to exercise jurisdiction, is opposed to the generally accepted international law to which Article 15 of the Convention of Lausanne refers. *   *   *

*   *   *

The Court therefore must, in any event, ascertain whether or not there exists a rule of international law limiting the freedom of States to extend the criminal jurisdiction of their courts to a situation uniting the circumstances of the present case.

IV

The Court will now proceed to ascertain whether general international law, to which Article 15 of the Convention of Lausanne refers, contains a rule prohibiting Turkey from prosecuting Lieutenant Demons.

For this purpose, it will in the first place examine the value of the arguments advanced by the French Government, without however omitting to take into account other possible aspects of the problem, which might show the existence of a restrictive rule applicable in this case.

The arguments advanced by the French Government [include the following]:

(1) International law does not allow a State to take proceedings with regard to offences committed by foreigners abroad, simply by reason of the nationality of the victim; and such is the situation in the present case because the offence must be regarded as having been committed on board the French vessel.

*   *   *

As regards the first argument, the Court feels obliged in the first place to recall that its examination is strictly confined to the specific situation in the present case, for it is only in regard to this situation that its decision is asked for.

As has already been observed, the characteristic features of the situation of fact are as follows: there has been a collision on the high seas between two vessels flying different flags, on one of which was one of the persons alleged to be guilty of the offence, whilst the victims were on board the other.

This being so, the Court does not think it necessary to consider the contention that a State cannot punish offences committed abroad by a foreigner simply by reason of the nationality of the victim. For this contention only relates to the case where the nationality of the victim is the only criterion on which the criminal jurisdiction of the State is based. Even if that argument were correct generally speaking—and in regard to this the Court reserves its opinion—it could only be used in the present case if international law forbade Turkey to take into consideration the fact that the offence produced its effects on the Turkish vessel and consequently in a place assimilated to Turkish territory in which the application of Turkish criminal law cannot be challenged, even in regard to offences committed there by foreigners. But no such rule of international law exists. No argument has come to the knowledge of the Court from which it could be deduced that States recognize themselves to be under an obligation towards each other only to have regard to the place where the author of the offence happens to be at the time of the offence. On the contrary, it is certain that the courts of many countries, even of countries which have given their criminal legislation a strictly territorial character, interpret criminal law in the sense that offences, the authors of which at the moment of commission are in the territory of another State, are nevertheless to be regarded as having been committed in the national territory, if one of the constituent elements of the offence, and more especially its effects, have taken place there. French courts have, in regard to a variety of situations, given decisions sanctioning this way of interpreting the territorial principle. Again, the Court does not know of any cases in which governments have protested against the fact that the criminal law of some country contained a rule to this effect or that the courts of a country construed their criminal law in this sense. Consequently, once it is admitted that the effects of the offence were produced on the Turkish vessel, it becomes impossible to hold that there is a rule of international law which prohibits Turkey from prosecuting Lieutenant Demons because of the fact that the author of the offence was on board the French ship. Since, as has already been observed, the special agreement does not deal with the provision of Turkish law under which the prosecution was instituted, but only with the question whether the prosecution should be regarded as contrary to the principles of international law, there is no reason preventing the Court from confining itself to observing that, in this case, a prosecution may also be justified from the point of view of the so-called territorial principle.

* * * The fact that the judicial authorities may have committed an error in their choice of the legal provision applicable to the particular case and compatible with international law only concerns municipal law and can only affect international law in so far as a treaty provision enters into account, or the possibility of a denial of justice arises.

* * *

The offence for which Lieutenant Demons appears to have been prosecuted was an act—of negligence or imprudence—having its origin on board the Lotus, whilst its effects made themselves felt on board the Boz-Kourt. These two elements are, legally, entirely inseparable, so much so that their separation renders the offence nonexistent. Neither the exclusive jurisdiction of either State, nor the limitations of the jurisdiction of each to the occurrences which took place on the respective ships would appear calculated to satisfy the requirements of justice and effectively to protect the interests of the two States. It is only natural that each should be able to exercise jurisdiction and to do so in respect of the incident as a whole. It is therefore a case of concurrent jurisdiction.

* * *

For These Reasons, the COURT, having heard both Parties, gives, by the President's casting vote [a]—the votes being equally divided—, judgment to the effect

(1) that, following the collision which occurred on August 2nd, 1926, on the high seas between the French steamship Lotus and the Turkish steamship Boz-Kcurt, and upon the arrival of the French ship at Stamboul, and in consequence of the loss of the Boz-Kourt having involved the death of eight Turkish nationals, Turkey, by instituting criminal proceedings in pursuance of Turkish law against Lieutenant Demons, officer of the watch on board the Lotus at the time of the collision, has not acted in conflict with the principles of international law, contrary to Article 15 of the Convention of Lausanne of July 24th, 1923, respecting conditions of residence and business and jurisdiction;

(2) that, consequently, there is no occasion to give judgment on the question of the pecuniary reparation which might have been due to Lieutenant Demons if Turkey, by prosecuting him as above stated, had acted in a manner contrary to the principles of international law.

* * *

[Separate and dissenting opinions omitted.]

---

1. *Question.* Does the decision in the Lotus case state (a) a rule of jurisdiction in international law or (b) the legal consequences of the lack of a rule of international law on the issue?

2. *Present rule as to prosecution for high seas collision.* The Convention on the High Seas,[b] the text of which appears in the Documentary Supplement, provides in Article 11:

> In the event of a collision or of any other incident of navigation concerning a ship on the high seas, involving the penal or disciplinary responsibility of the master or of any person in the service of the ship, no penal or disciplinary proceedings may be

---

a. Article 55 of the Statute of the International Court of Justice provides: "1. All questions shall be decided by a majority of the judges present. 2. In the event of an equality of votes, the President or the judge who sits in his place shall have a casting vote." The text of the statute is in the Documentary Supplement.

b. 56 states were parties to this convention on January 1, 1980.

instituted against such persons except before the judicial or administrative authorities either of the flag state or of the state of which such person is a national.

An identical provision appears in Article 97 of the United Nations Draft Convention on the Law of the Sea.

The text of the draft is in the Documentary Supplement.

In Case "U" No. 1243 of 1974, Japan, High Court of Osaka, 1976, 22 Japanese Annual of International Law 131 (1978), a Liberian vessel collided with a Japanese vessel and members of the crew of the Japanese vessel suffered burns and other injuries. The first mate and the third mate of the Liberian vessel were prosecuted in Japan for their negligence in causing the collision and the resulting injuries. In upholding the convictions, the court said that even if the waters in which the collision took place were not territory of Japan, Japanese jurisdiction existed because the criminal conduct took effect on a Japanese vessel. The opinion made no reference to Article 11 of the Convention on the High Seas or the nationality of the defendants, though, if the names are any indication, they may well have been Japanese.

3. *Present rule as to prosecution based on nationality of victim.* The court in the Lotus case did not decide whether France was correct in contending that international law does not allow a state to bring proceedings with regard to offenses committed by foreigners abroad simply by reason of the nationality of the victim.

What then of the French and Israeli laws involved in the case which follows?

AFFAIRE ABU DAOUD

France, Court of Appeal of Paris, 1977.
104 Journal du Droit International 843 (1977).[a] *

[Abu Daoud was suspected of having participated in the taking of Israeli athletes as hostages, and in their subsequent murder, at the Olympic Games held in Munich in 1972. He came to Paris in January 1977 as a member of an official delegation of the Palestine Liberation Organization attending the funeral of one of its members assassinated a few days earlier. He was detained by the French police on January 8 at the request of the German authorities pending their request for extradition. The Israeli authorities also requested his detention pending request for extradition. He was released by order of the French court on January 11. A portion of the opinion of the court appears below.]

Raju Ben Yousef Ben Hanna, born on June 16, 1937, in Baghdad, is the object of a request for provisional arrest for purpose of ex-

a. Translation by the editors. Reprinted by permission of Editions Techniques, S.A., Paris.

tradition by the Israeli authorities pursuant to a warrant issued by Judge Shalgi of the Court of Jerusalem on January 10, 1977, for murder, involuntary homicide, conspiracy to commit a crime, kidnapping, * * * illegal acts of violence, assault and battery * * * and complicity and conspiracy to commit these offenses, the identity of the person being given as Muhamad Daoud Uda Eith Halidi El Silwani, known as Abu Daoud, born in Jerusalem in 1937.

Article 3 of the [French] law of March 10, 1927, provides that extradition may be granted only if the crime has been committed: either on the territory of the requesting state by a national * * * or an alien; or outside its territory by a national * * *; or outside its territory by an alien * * * whenever the crime is among those whose prosecution in France is authorized by French law even when committed abroad by an alien.

It appears from the request * * * made by telegram by the Israeli authorities, that the criminal acts with which this person is charged were committed in September 1972 on the territory of the German Federal Republic.

Raji Yousef Ben Hanna asserts that he is of Iraqi nationality, presenting identification papers and a passport attesting to this nationality, while the Israeli authorities making the request neither indicate nor claim that he is of Israeli nationality.

Though the law of July 11, 1975, gives jurisdiction to French courts over any foreigner guilty in a foreign country of a crime when the victim of the crime is of French nationality, * * * this cannot justify the application of the last proviso in Article 3 of the law of March 10, 1927, referred to above, although most of the victims were of Israeli nationality; for the law of July 11, 1975, cannot have a retroactive effect and thus may not be applied to acts committed in September 1972 * * *.

There being consequently no reason to examine the crimes despite their exceptional gravity, or the political nature which might be attributed to them, the extradition of Raji Yousef Ben Hanna cannot be granted * * *.

It is proper, therefore, to order the release of Raji Yousef Ben Hanna.

Use by Israel of passive personality principle. In March of 1972, Israel amended its criminal laws to provide:

2B. (a) The courts of Israel shall be competent to try in Israel under Israeli law a person who has committed abroad an act which would be an offense if it had been committed in Israel and which harmed or was intended to harm the life, person, health, freedom or property of a national or resident of Israel. Penal Law Amendment (Offences Committed Abroad) (Amendment No. 4) Law, 5732–1972, Laws of the State of Israel No. 26 (1971–1972).

Suppose Abu Daoud was clearly of Iraqi nationality and the French court had approved his extradition to Israel. Would Iraq have a basis under international law for objecting to his trial? Did it have a basis under international law for objecting to his extradition from France?

RIVARD v. UNITED STATES

United States Court of Appeals, Fifth Circuit, 1967.
375 F.2d 882.[a]

[Four Canadian nationals were indicted for conspiracy to smuggle heroin into the United States. They were extradited from Canada, tried and convicted in a United States District Court in Texas. The defendants were at all times prior to their extradition outside of the United States.]

* * *

Under international law a state does not have jurisdiction to enforce a rule of law prescribed by it, unless it had jurisdiction to prescribe the rule. Restatement, Second, Foreign Relations Law of the United States § 7(2).

It is for this reason that the mere physical presence of the four alien appellants before the court did not give the District Court jurisdiction. The question remains whether their conduct without the United States had such a deleterious effect within the United States to justify this country in prohibiting the conduct. Restatement, Second, supra § 18.

* * * All nations utilize the territorial principle, and it is under this principle that the District Court had jurisdiction over appellants. There are, however two views as to the scope of the territorial principle. Under the subjective view, jurisdiction extends over all persons in the state and there violating its laws. Under the objective view, jurisdiction extends over all acts which take effect within the sovereign even though the author is elsewhere. * * *

* * *

The first question we are called upon to decide is whether the District Court had jurisdiction to try an alien for a conspiracy to commit a crime against the United States, formed without the United States, several of the overt acts having been committed in furtherance of the conspiracy within the United States by a co-conspirator.

* * *

* * * Rivard twice sent co-conspirator Caron across the Canadian border to deliver caches of heroin brought back from Europe

a. Cert. denied 389 U.S. 884, 88 S.Ct.
   151 (1967).

by Massey and Jones to another co-conspirator, Miller, in Connecticut. Caron also travelled by automobile from Quebec to Mexico through the United States and was on his way back through the United States with yet another load of heroin to be delivered in Connecticut when he was apprehended in Texas. There is thus no doubt that the object of the conspiracy was to violate the narcotics laws of the United States; that the conspiracy was carried on partly in and partly out of this country; and that overt acts were committed within the United States by co-conspirators. *   *   *

———

1. *Conduct outside the territory producing intangible effects within the territory.* Under customary international law are the following cases distinguishable as to the legitimacy of the application of its law by State B?

In State A, X and Y conspire to and do send poisoned chocolates into State B with the intention that Z, the addressee, eat them and die. This happens. State B has X and Y before its courts on indictment for murder. X and Y are nationals of State A, and State A objects on the ground that international law does not authorize State B to apply its law.

The same states and the same parties, except that in State A, X and Y conspire to and do perpetrate a stock fraud by mail on Z in State B. State B has X and Y before its courts on indictment for embezzlement. X and Y are nationals of State A. State A objects on the ground that international law does not authorize State B to apply its law of fraudulent stock offers to X and Y.

The same states and the same parties, except that in State A, X and Y agree to divide world markets, allocate and restrict production, and fix prices for commodities as to which, between them, they have a dominant world position. In State B this agreement is assumed to have the effect of reducing State B's exports of the commodity and of increasing its imports, at higher prices, thus reducing its favorable balance of trade. State B has X and Y before its courts on indictment under its antitrust law. State A objects on these grounds: (a) same as in cases 1 and 2; (b) that economic effects cannot be likened to shooting bullets or sending poisoned chocolates across frontiers; (c) that no measurement of adverse effect is possible; (d) that A and B did not intend any injury to State B or its nationals but only to achieve their profit maximization objectives.

Would it make any difference as to any of State A's arguments if the suit in State B had been private litigation by B nationals in the same commodity trade who claim injury and seek recovery under a treble damages provision in the antitrust law of State B?

The above hypothetical cases pose the major variables in a continuing debate on the role and rule of customary international law as to the extent to which a state may prescribe the legal consequences of economic conduct outside the territory by non-nationals that is objec-

tionable to the state. Detailed consideration of the reach of antitrust laws of the United States is in Chapter 7.

2.   *Illustrations of the effects doctrine in national courts.*

German cartel law.   On July 27, 1957, the Federal Republic of
Germany enacted an Act against Restraints of Competition, Gesetz
gegen Wettbewerbsbeschränkungen, usually cited as GWB. An English translation of it appears in 1 Guide to Legislation on Restrictive
Business Practices, Germany 1.0, 1 (1964), published by the Organization for Economic Cooperation and Development (OECD). As
translated, Section 98(2) of the cartel law provides:

> This Act shall apply to all restraints of competition which have
> effect in the area in which this Act applies, even if they result
> from acts done outside such area. (at 42)

Ali Ahmed v. The State of Bombay, India, Supreme Court, 1957,
24 Int'l L.Rep. 156 (1961). The defendant, a Pakistani, is before the
courts of India, and is convicted of "cheating", an offense under §
420 of the Indian Penal Code. The accused, while in Karachi, Pakistan, fraudulently induced an Indian in Bombay to part with a substantial sum of money. The supreme court affirmed the conviction,
as against the defendant's contention that he " * * * is a Pakistani national who during the entire period of the [alleged] commission
of the offense never stepped into India * * * and cannot be tried
by an Indian Court." The supreme court cited the Lotus in support
of the objective territorial principle.

Missisi v. Republic, Kenya, High Court, 1969, 48 Int'l L.Rep. 90
(1975). The defendant, an employee of the Kenya government, went
to study in Uganda. He sent from there, through the post, two
forged invoices for purchases of books, which were detected on arrival in Nairobi. He was convicted of attempting to obtain the money
through false pretenses on the ground that it was in Nairobi he
sought to induce the Kenya government to act upon his invoices.

Regina v. Baxter, United Kingdom, Court of Appeal, 1971,
[1972] 1 Q.B. 1, 8. The defendant was charged with attempting to
obtain property by deception. He had posted from Northern Ireland
to football promoters in England false claims that he had correctly
forecast the outcome of games on a certain day and was entitled to
payment. His false representations were detected when the letters
arrived in England. The court held the attempt to obtain money by
deception occurred at the moment of discovery, i. e. when the letters
arrived in England. The court noted its decision was in accord with
an early American case, Simpson v. State, 92 Ga. 41, 17 S.E. 984
(1893), in which a bullet having been fired from South Carolina and
having missed the man at whom it was aimed in Georgia, the Supreme
Court of Georgia held it had jurisdiction over the attempt.

Beausir, France, Court of Cassation, 1977, 82 Revue Générale de
Droit International Public 1171 (1978). A Belgian industrialist in
Belgium polluted by chemical discharges a river flowing from Bel-

gium to France. He was charged under a provision of French law prohibiting the discharge in waterways of any substance which destroys fish or adversely affects its food supply, its reproduction or its quality for eating. It was enough, said the court, that the effect upon the biological milieu required for the life of the fish had taken place in France. In reporting the case, the editor of the Revue referred to several previous French cases upholding jurisdiction on the basis of the effect doctrine in diverse matters.

3. *Illustration of the effects doctrine in an international court.* Handelswekerij G. J. Bier and Stiching Reinwater (The Reinwater Foundation) v. Mines de Potasse d'Alsace S.A., Court of Justice of the European Communities, 1976, [1977] 1 Common Market Law Reports 284. The plaintiff, in the business of nursery gardening in the Netherlands, used for irrigation water coming mostly from the Rhine. It had a high salinity content and required expensive treatment before it could be used for irrigation. The Reinwater Foundation, created to improve the quality of the water of the Rhine, joined Bier in a suit in tort against a French company whose works in Alsace discharged large quantities of industrial wastes in the Rhine, thus considerably augmenting its salinity.

The lower Dutch court held that it had no jurisdiction because the event causing the damage had taken place in France and therefore was not covered by Article 3 of the European Convention of September 27, 1968, on Jurisdiction and Enforcement of Judgments which provided that jurisdiction belongs to "the place where the harmful event occurred." The court of appeal asked for an interpretation by the Court of Justice of the European Community of the operative words in the convention.

The Advocate General, advising the court, reviewed the judicial practice of the several members of the community whose legislation contained similar or identical provisions, including the practice of the Federal Republic of Germany, France, Italy, Belgium, the United Kingdom and Denmark. The Advocate General concluded that the practice suggested two possible interpretations: the place where the act was committed or the place where the damage occurred. Upon his recommendation, the court ruled that "place where the harmful event occurred" in the convention was intended to cover both. Hence the plaintiff could sue either in the courts of the place where the damage occurred or in the courts of the place where the event giving rise to the damage took place.

Thereupon the Dutch court of appeal held that the court below had jurisdiction over the suit for pollution originating in France and causing damage in the Netherlands. 81 Revue Générale de Droit International Public 1186 (1977).

AMERICAN GETS STIFF SENTENCE IN CZECHOSLOVAKIA

The Times-Picayune of New Orleans, Louisiana.
December 19, 1970, at 5, col. 1.*

Prague, Czechoslovakia (AP)—A young American who once worked as a researcher and broadcast monitor for Radio Free Europe in West Germany in order to finance his college studies was convicted Friday of subversion against Czechoslovakia and sentenced to four years in prison.

Fred H. Eidlin, 28, of Rochester, N. Y., had eight days to appeal the sentence, and he is expected to do so.

A U. S. Embassy spokesman said the embassy was "surprised at the severity of the sentence but is withholding any further comment until we know the nature of any further legal steps planned on Eidlin's behalf."

Eidlin's Czech lawyer, Waclav Petracek, argued for an acquittal, reminding the five-man panel of municipal court judges that all his client had done was to work "as an American in an American agency in the territory of a state where this is not prohibited."

He described Eidlin as "a progressive boy who has his own ideas and who did not come with hostile attitudes to our country." But the court found in its verdict delivered after a seven-hour trial, that Eidlin's job with the U.S.-financed anti-Communist station was in itself subversion against Czechoslovakia.

Eidlin, who learned Czech before going to work for Radio Free Europe, made an eloquent personal defense.

"I am not a Communist," he told the court. "I don't agree with many things that are done in your country. But this is not my home so I never intervened in your affairs."

Eidlin said he had always tried to convince his friends that they should visit Communist nations for themselves because "if tension is to be relaxed there must be travel without fear." That is why he never dreamed he would be arrested on the two occasions he traveled into Czechoslovakia, he added. He was arrested in Prague last July 26 and has been in prison since.

Eidlin testified he worked as a "policy assistant" for RFE from August 1968 until November 1969. He said his work was about 95 per cent research and scientific and 5 per cent listening to Czech language broadcasts over the propaganda station to make sure they were not too rabidly anti-communist. He said he helped in "slowing down the immigrants * * *. When I heard negative polemics or cold war criticism, I would report it to the director." Eidlin said he worked at the station so he could resume his studies at the University of Toronto, in Canada.

RESTATEMENT OF THE FOREIGN RELATIONS LAW OF THE UNITED STATES (1965) *

§ 18. Jurisdiction to Prescribe with Respect to Effect within Territory

A state has jurisdiction to prescribe a rule of law attaching legal consequences to conduct that occurs outside its territory and causes an effect within its territory, if either

(a) the conduct and its effect are generally recognized as constituent elements of a crime or tort under the law of states that have reasonably developed legal systems, or

(b) (i) the conduct and its effect are constituent elements of activity to which the rule applies; (ii) the effect within the territory is substantial; (iii) it occurs as a direct and foreseeable result of the conduct outside the territory; and (iv) the rule is not inconsistent with the principles of justice generally recognized by states that have reasonably developed legal systems.

---

3. CONDUCT AFFECTING GOVERNMENTAL INTERESTS

UNITED STATES v. PIZZARUSSO

United States Court of Appeals, Second Circuit, 1968.
388 F.2d 8.[a]

MEDINA, Circuit Judge. This case is of interest because it brings before this Court for the first time the question of the jurisdiction of the District Court to indict and convict a foreign citizen of the crime of knowingly making a false statement under oath in a visa application to an American consular official located in a foreign country, in violation of 18 U.S.C. Section 1546.[1] Supreme Court cases give some guidance but none of them passes on this question directly.[2] A Ninth Circuit decision, Rocha v. United States, 288 F.2d

---

a. Cert. denied 392 U.S. 936, 88 S.Ct. 2306 (1968).

1. Fraud and misuse of visas, permits and other entry documents. * * *

Whoever knowingly makes under oath any false statement with respect to a material fact in any application, affidavit, or other document required by the immigration laws or regulations prescribed thereunder, or know-ingly presents any such application, affidavit, or other document containing any such false statement—

Shall be fined not more than $2,000 or imprisoned not more than five years, or both.

2. United States v. Bowman, 260 U.S. 94, 43 S.Ct. 39, 67 L.Ed. 149 (1922), cited by appellee as authority for upholding jurisdiction in the instant case is distinguishable as that case involved imposition of criminal liability on United States citizens for acts committed abroad.

545 (9th Cir.), cert. denied 366 U.S. 948, 81 S.Ct. 1902, 6 L.Ed.2d 1241 (1961), is in point but we sustain jurisdiction on the basis of somewhat different reasons.

The indictment charges that on March 4, 1965 Jean Philomena Pizzarusso wilfully made under oath a number of false statements in her "Application for Immigrant Visa And Alien Registration" at the American Consulate, Montreal, Canada. * * * Although at all times pertinent to this case she was a citizen of Canada, she was taken into custody in the Southern District of New York on April 18, 1966.

Upon the issuance of the visa and by its use Mrs. Pizzarusso immediately entered the territory of the United States, but this fact is not alleged in the indictment nor required by the terms of the statute, nor is it material, as we find the crime was complete when the false statements were made to an American consular official in Montreal. We shall return later to this feature of the case.

The evidence to sustain the charge is so overwhelming that we shall not pause to discuss it. Indeed, the only contention made on this appeal is that the District Court lacked jurisdiction to indict appellant and convict her of the crime alleged.[3] As we find no lack of jurisdiction, we affirm the judgment. Our reasons follow.

    *   *   *

International law has recognized, in varying degrees, five bases of jurisdiction with respect to the enforcement of the criminal law. See Harvard Research In International Law, Jurisdiction with Respect to Crime, 29 Am.J. Int'l L. Spec. Supp. 435, 445 (1935) (hereinafter cited as Harvard Research). Thus both the territoriality and nationality principles, under which jurisdiction is determined by either the situs of the crime or the nationality of the accused, are universally accepted. The third basis, the protective principle, covers the instant case. By virtue of this theory a state "has jurisdiction to prescribe a rule of law attaching legal consequences to conduct outside its territory that threatens its security as a state or the operation of its governmental functions, provided the conduct is generally recognized as a crime under the law of states that have reasonably developed legal systems." Restatement (Second), Foreign Relations, Section 33. See also Harvard Research Section 7.[5]

Traditionally, the United States has relied primarily upon the territoriality and nationality principles, * * * and judges have often been reluctant to ascribe extraterritorial effect to statutes. * * * Nonetheless, our courts have developed what has come to be termed the objective territorial principle as a means of expanding the power to control activities detrimental to the state. This principle has been aptly defined by Mr. Justice Holmes in Strassheim v. Daily,

---

3. Appellant received a one-year suspended sentence and was placed on probation for two years.

5. The other two principles are universality, where jurisdiction is determined by the custody of the person committing the offense and passive personality where jurisdiction is determined by reference to the nationality of the person injured. Harvard Research at p. 445.

221 U.S. 280, 285, 31 S.Ct. 558, 560, 55 L.Ed. 735 (1911). "Acts done outside a jurisdiction, but intended to produce and producing detrimental effects within it, justify a state in punishing the cause of the harm as if he had been present at the effect * * *." * * * Underlying this principle is the theory that the "detrimental effects" constitute an element of the offense and since they occur within the country, jurisdiction is properly invoked under the territorial principle. * * *

However, the objective territorial principle is quite distinct from the protective theory. Under the latter, all the elements of the crime occur in the foreign country and jurisdiction exists because these actions have a "potentially adverse effect" upon security or governmental functions, Restatement (Second) Foreign Relations Law, Comment to Section 33 at p. 93, and there need not be any actual effect in the country as would be required under the objective territorial principle. Courts have often failed to perceive this distinction. Thus, the Ninth Circuit,[6] in upholding a conviction under a factual situation similar to the one in the instant case, relied on the protective theory, but still felt constrained to say that jurisdiction rested partially on the adverse effect produced as a result of the alien's entry into the United States. The Ninth Circuit also cited Strassheim and Aluminum Company of America as support for its decision. With all due deference to our brothers of the Ninth Circuit, however, we think this reliance is unwarranted. A violation of 18 U.S.C.A. Section 1546 is complete at the time the alien perjures himself in the foreign country. It may be possible that the particular criminal sanctions of Section 1546 will never be enforced unless the defendant enters the country, but entry is not an element of the statutory offense. Were the statute re-drafted and entry made a part of the crime we would then be presented with a clear case of jurisdiction under the objective territorial principle.

Statutes imposing criminal liability on aliens for committing perjury in United States Consulates in foreign countries have been in existence for over one hundred years * * *. Only one court has ever held that the United States did not have jurisdiction to proceed against an alien under the legislation governing this case. United States v. Baker, 136 F.Supp. 546 (S.D.N.Y.1955). In Baker it was conceded that there was authority for deporting an alien for making perjurious statements to a United States Consul, United States ex rel. Majka v. Palmer, 67 F.2d 146 (7th Cir. 1933), but the court thought the imposition of criminal sanctions was "far different" from deportation and dismissed the indictment. We would have sustained jurisdiction in Baker had the case been before us, and in this view we are apparently joined by the judge who decided Baker, since he presided over the instant case in the court below.

Affirmed.

6. Rocha v. United States, 288 F.2d 545 (9th Cir.), cert. denied 366 U.S. 948, 81 S.Ct. 1902, 6 L.Ed.2d 1241 (1961).

1. *Distinction between the territorial and protective principles.*
In United States v. Rodriguez, 182 F.Supp. 479 (S.D.Cal.1960),[a] the
defendant aliens were charged with making false statements in immigration applications while they were outside the United States. The
court discussed the territorial and the protective principles in the following terms:

> Acts committed outside the territorial limits of the State but
> intended to produce, or producing, effects within the boundaries
> of the State are subject to penal sanctions; * * * Where the
> effect is felt by private persons within the State, penal sanctions
> rest on the "objective," or "subjective," territorial principle
> * * *. Where the effect of the acts committed outside the
> United States is felt by the government, the protective theory af-
> fords the basis by which the state is empowered to punish all
> those offenses which impinge upon its sovereignty, wherever
> these actions take place and by whomever they may be commit-
> ted. The results of such a theory are, in many ways, similar to
> those reached in the Strassheim case * * * where the court
> directed its attention to the objective results of the criminal act
> and the location of its effect. Any act which would offend the
> sovereignty of a nation must, of necessity, have some effect
> within the territorial limits of that state or there would be no
> adverse effect upon the government justifying a penal sanction.
> (at 488–489)

2. *Expansion of protective principle in the United States.* Both
the Court of Appeals for the second circuit in Pizzarusso and the District Court in Rodriguez predicate the jurisdiction of the United
States on the protective principle. It is true they phrase it somewhat
differently. The court in Pizzarusso holds the principle to be applicable because the conduct of the aliens abroad had a "potentially adverse effect" upon the governmental function. The court in Rodriguez holds the principle applicable because the conduct of the aliens
abroad of necessity had "some effect" upon the governmental function in the United States. It may be that the difference between the
two formulations is metaphysical.

The alternative in both cases would have been to hold that an effect in the territory had taken place when the aliens entered the
United States. Had the courts involved adopted this position, they
would have reflected a traditional attitude towards the protective
principle, for little use has been made of it in the United States in the
past. A manifestation of this traditional attitude can be found in
legislation concerning counterfeiting: it is a federal offense to counterfeit foreign currency in the United States, but not a federal offense to counterfeit United States currency abroad.

a. Affirmed sub nom. Rocha v. United States, 288 F.2d 545 (9th Cir. 1961), with respect to the substantive counts of the indictment, reversed as to conspiracy counts not at issue in Rodriguez; cert. denied 366 U.S. 948, 81 S.Ct. 1902 (1961).

The wider use of the protective principle reflected in the two cases is consistent with an international practice of long standing. The Restatement of the Foreign Relations Law of the United States (1965) reflects this international practice in its formulation of the protective principle. Section 33 provides: "A state has jurisdiction to prescribe a rule of law attaching legal consequences to conduct outside its territory that threatens its security as a state or the operation of its governmental functions * * *." The section adds the qualification that the conduct must be generally recognized as a crime.

3. *Dangers inherent in the protective principle.* It is beyond doubt that the protective principle applies to crimes such as the counterfeiting of state seals, currency, stamps, passports or other public documents. Most states punish these offenses wheresoever and by whomever committed. The danger, however, is that the principle can be abused because it is susceptible of practically unlimited expansion.

In United States v. Daniszewski, 380 F.Supp. 113 (E.D.N.Y. 1974), the defendant was a citizen of the United States prosecuted for distributing heroin in Thailand with intent to have it imported into the United States. While predicating jurisdiction on nationality, the court indicated it would be prepared to rely on the protective principle by giving it a broader scope than Section 33 of the Restatement:

> There is artificiality of limitation in treating jurisdiction based on the Protective Principle as confined to those species of conduct abroad that threaten certain narrowly defined interests in the security of the enacting state and in the integrity of its governmental operations (e. g. visa fraud, counterfeiting) and in excluding those acts abroad which threaten the peace of the enacting state as that peace lies in the security of its citizens from criminal intrusion. (at 115–116)

See also United States v. Keller, 451 F.Supp. 631 (D.P.R.1978), involving the arrest on the high seas of citizens of the United States charged, inter alia, with conspiracy to import marijuana into the United States and attempt to import it, where the court said: "The planned invasion of the customs territory of the United States is sufficient basis for invocation of jurisdiction under the protective theory * * *. This is equally applicable to the charges * * * dealing with attempted importation into the United States." (at 635)

The danger is particularly great when the principle is formulated in broad terms, as it often is, and made to cover any crime against the security, territorial integrity or political independence of the state. Consider the instance which follows.

A CASE FOR MERCY

The New York Times, June 11, 1978, Sec. IV, p. 20, col. 1.*

[In March of 1972, Israel amended its criminal law to provide:

2(a).   The courts in Israel are competent to try under Israeli
law a person who has committed abroad an act which
would be an offence if it had been committed in Israel
and which harmed or was intended to harm the State of
Israel, its security, property or economy or its transport
or communication links with other countries. Penal Law
Amendment (Offences Committed Abroad) (Amendment
No. 4) Law, 5732–1972, Laws of the State of Israel No.
26 (1971–1972).]

The Tel Aviv court that last Wednesday convicted a Brooklyn-
born American of Arab descent because of his membership in a proscribed organization was undoubtedly conforming to Israeli law, even
though all of Sami Esmail's association with the People's Front for
the Liberation of Palestine took place outside Israel. But we hope
that the judges who pass sentence on him tomorrow will nevertheless
free him to return to his engineering studies at Michigan State University.

Mr. Esmail was arrested and jailed when he arrived in Israel
last December to visit his dying father. Israeli authorities concede
that they have no evidence he intended harm while in the country.
But they argue that since the P.F.L.P. is committed to Israel's destruction, and since Mr. Esmail received training in guerrilla warfare
during a month's visit to Libya in 1976, his associations are ample
ground for conviction.

*   *   *   The Israeli prosecutor has asked for a jail term to discourage other foreigners from joining groups like the P.F.L.P., which
recruited Mr. Esmail at Michigan State. But would-be terrorists
should need no persuasion that they will be sternly dealt with if they
attempt violence in Israel.

*   *   *

---

4.   JURISDICTION BASED ON UNIVERSAL INTEREST

1. *Crimes of universal interest.* The essential characteristic of
crimes of universal interest is that a state may participate in their
repression even though they were not committed in its territory, were
not committed by one of its nationals, or were not otherwise within
its jurisdiction to prescribe and enforce.

The most ancient crime of universal interest is piracy, which is
considered in Chapter 3, infra p. 201. It became a universal crime

under customary international law because it was in the common interest of all states to preserve freedom of navigation for vessels on the high seas. Since its development, several other crimes have also become recognized as being of universal interest. Such recognition may have begun in customary international law for some of these crimes, but it is now usually embodied in international agreements. These agreements must be consulted to determine under what circumstances and to what extent a state may participate in the repression of the particular crime. Some of the crimes involved are:

Acts of violence against diplomats, see Chapter 13.

Genocide, see Chapter 9.

Hijacking, see Chapter 4.

Sabotage of civil aircraft, see Chapter 4.

Slave trade, see in the Documentary Supplement Articles 13 and 22 of the 1958 Convention on the High Seas and Articles 99 and 110 of the Draft Convention on the Law of the Sea.

War crimes, see Chapter 10.

2. *Is terrorism a crime of universal interest?* Despite the increase in the number of acts of terrorism in recent years, it is still a matter of controversy whether it is a crime of universal interest.

The General Assembly of the United Nations adopted a resolution concerning terrorism in 1973. G.A.Res. 3034 (XXVII), U.N. doc. A/RES/3034 (1973). The United States voted against it because it did not contain concrete proposals for strong international legal action against acts of terror and violence. 68 U.S. Dept. of State Bull. 81 (1973). Much of the difficulty lies in the willingness of a number of states to tolerate terrorism as a means of furthering political objectives to which they are sympathetic. The General Assembly, however, adopted and opened for signature in December 1979 an International Convention Against the Taking of Hostages. XVIII International Legal Materials 1456 (1979). The penultimate paragraph of the preamble to the convention indicates that its purpose is the adoption of effective measures for the prosecution and punishment of all acts of taking of hostages "as manifestations of international terrorism."

The Council of Ministers of the Council of Europe adopted on November 10, 1976, the European Convention on the Suppression of Terrorism. XV International Legal Materials 1272 (1976). It entered into force August 4, 1978. XIX International Legal Materials 325 (1980). The United States is a party to the convention on terrorism of the Organization of American States of February 2, 1971. 27 U.S.T. 3949. It went into effect for the United States on October 20, 1976.

The growth of acts of terrorism revived interest in the creation of an International Criminal Court which would have jurisdiction over a long list of international crimes. See Blishchenko and

Shdanov,[a] The Problem of International Criminal Jurisdiction, XIV Canadian Yearbook of International Law 283 (1976).

SECTION B. JURISDICTION TO ENFORCE RULES OF LAW

---

1. DEPENDENCE OF JURISDICTION TO ENFORCE UPON JURISDICTION TO PRESCRIBE

ARRET FORNAGE

France, Court of Cassation, 1873.
84 Journal du Palais 229 (1873).[b]

[The accused was prosecuted for grand larceny committed in Switzerland. In accordance with French procedure, the indictment was presented to a court whose function was to decide whether the evidence was sufficient to support prosecution and which criminal court had jurisdiction to try the case. It found sufficient evidence for prosecution and decided the case should be tried by the Court of Assizes. From this decision, the accused could have appealed to the Court of Cassation, i. e. the supreme court, but failed to do so.

At trial, he objected he could not be prosecuted in the French courts for a crime committed in a foreign country. Previously, the supreme court had held several times that decisions of the indicting court as to which criminal court had jurisdiction to try a case must be appealed directly and the Court of Assizes, once seized of the case, could not entertain jurisdictional attacks. Accordingly, the Court of Assizes ruled it could not hear the objection. From the ruling, the accused appealed to the Court of Cassation.

The appeal was heard by the Criminal Section of the Court of Cassation and decided in accord with the arguments presented by a conseiller rapporteur, i. e. a member of the court appointed to make recommendations, and those presented by the avocat general, i. e. simultaneously the prosecutor for the state and representative of the general public interest.

The conseiller rapporteur conceded the ruling of the Court of Assizes was in accord with the precedents established by the Court of Cassation, but went on to make the argument which appears below.]

Is it not possible also to say that, in the case presented to you, there are considerations of a superior nature justifying an exception to the general rule? The only basis for the right to punish is sovereignty, which dies at the border. If French law allows the prosecution of French nationals for crimes or offenses committed in a foreign country, it is because criminal law applies both on a territorial and personal basis. A French national, even abroad, still remains a

---

a. Both of the Institute of International-   b. Translation by the editors.
al Relations, Moscow.

citizen of his country and as such remains subject to French law, which has power over him as soon as he comes back to France. But the law itself cannot give French courts the power to try foreign nationals for crimes or offenses committed outside French territory; such exorbitant jurisdiction, whose basis could neither be territorial nor personal, would constitute a violation of international law, a breach of the sovereignty of other states. There is only one exception to this rule of international law. When a foreign national has committed, even abroad, a crime against the security of the state, he can be prosecuted, tried and punished in France. But apart from this exception, which is based on the right of self-defense, foreign nationals can only be prosecuted by the courts of their own country for acts committed outside the territory. * * * The Court of Assizes, by punishing this act, would commit an abuse of power; it would usurp a right of sovereignty belonging to a foreign power. Would it not be contrary to all principles of justice to force the judges into knowingly becoming guilty of an arbitrary act, a violation of international law? * * * [The Court of Assizes] must examine the evidence presented by the accused in support of his claims and declare itself without jurisdiction if it finds that he is an alien and the act of which he is accused has been committed outside French territory.

[The avocat general argued the precedents did not control the case and could be distinguished because of the nature of the objection raised. His conclusion appears immediately below.]

Indeed, French justice has jurisdiction only to try French nationals for crimes committed by them outside the territory * * *; it has no jurisdiction over aliens; so the question of nationality must be decided beforehand; for the right of jurisdiction depends upon the resolution of the question. The ruling which is challenged appears to me to have overlooked those fundamental principles.

[The opinion of the court appears below.]

* * * [I]t is a general principle that if the judgment * * * which sends an accused to the Court of Assizes is not appealed within the time provided by Art. 296 of the Code of Criminal Instruction, the court may not declare itself without jurisdiction * * *; but this jurisdiction, however broad it may be, cannot extend to crimes committed outside the territory by aliens who, in respect to those acts, are not punishable in French courts. * * * [T]his lack of jurisdiction in this regard is absolute, permanent; it can be cured neither by the silence nor by the consent of the accused; it continues to exist at all levels * * * [and the indicting court] cannot give the Court of Assizes a right it does not itself possess, to try acts which do not come under the jurisdiction of French law. * * * [R]aymond Fornage was sent to the Court of Assizes of Haute-Savoie and accused of having committed grand larceny in the Canton of Valais (Switzerland); before the trial began, he presented arguments to the effect that the court was without jurisdiction, because he was born in France of foreign parents, did not claim French

nationality and consequently did not come under the jurisdiction of
French courts for an act committed in a foreign country. *   *   *
[T]he claim, which challenged the very legality of the prosecution
and the jurisdiction of the Court of Assizes *' *   * had to be decided by the court before hearing the merits; *   *   * the accused
could not be deprived of the right to present this peremptory argument either by his silence during the investigation or by his failure to
appeal the judgment of *   *   *   [the indicting court]. *   *   *
[I]n ruling the accused could not present his motion for lack of jurisdiction *   *   * the Court of Assizes wrongly applied *   *   *
[the law]; and by ordering the trial to proceed without deciding the
motion based on nationality *   *   * disregarded the rights of the
defendant.

RESIDENTS OF OKINAWA

Japan, Osaka District Court, 1967.
15 Japanese Annual of International Law 113 (1971).*

The accused, having their permanent domiciles in Okinawa and
having lived in Okinawa since their births or their infancies, committed murders and other ordinary crimes and fled to mainland Japan.
The accused were arrested in mainland Japan and prosecuted in the
Osaka District Court, for crimes committed in Okinawa.

The accused made a motion demanding that the suit be dismissed. In connection with the jurisdiction over the present case, the
Osaka District Court, in the text of judgment, stated as follows:

It is clear in view of both international law and domestic
law that residents of Okinawa have Japanese nationality. It is
an established principle of international law that the State reserves its personal sovereignty over people who have its nationality, regardless of the places of their residence. Taking this principle into consideration in the present case, it is recognized that,
since the residents of Okinawa have Japanese nationality, the
State of Japan, from which their nationality derives, can exercise its personal sovereignty over the residents. *   *   *

      *   *   *

In cases where residents of Okinawa are living in the Ryukyu
Islands, it should be considered that, while the Japanese laws and
regulations based on the territorial principle are precluded from
application, [Okinawa was at the time under U. S. administra-
tion] those based on the personal principle are still applicable to
them.

For these reasons, the Court recognized jurisdiction over the accused in this case.

---

* Original in Japanese. Translation into
  English by the editorial staff of The
  Japanese Annual of International
  Law. Reprinted with the permission
  of the International Law Association
  of Japan.

1. *Enforcement of rules prescribed on the basis of nationality of the individual.* States exercise their jurisdiction to prescribe rules governing the conduct of their nationals in various degrees. They often exercise it to punish treasonable acts by their nationals wherever committed. The United States does. 18 U.S.C. § 2381. It does not use extensively its prescriptive jurisdiction based on nationality, however. More generally, the use of this prescriptive jurisdiction is the exception rather than the rule in common law states. Civil law states usually make more use of it, sometimes going so far as to provide that all, or nearly all, offenses committed by their nationals abroad are punishable if they are found in the national territory, but in some cases conditioning the application of national law upon certain restrictive factors. Some illustrative cases follow.

In the case of In re Guttierez, the defendant was a Mexican national charged with stealing a truck in Texas. The Mexican court dismissed his challenge to its jurisdiction on the broad ground, apparently, that a crime committed abroad by a Mexican national is punishable in Mexico. Supreme Court, 1957, 24 Int'l L.Rep. 265 (1961). A Dutch national "is liable to prosecution in Holland for an offense committed abroad, which is punishable under Netherlands law and which is also punishable under the law of the country where the offense was committed." Public Prosecutor v. Y., Supreme Court, 1957, 24 Int'l L.Rep. 264, 265 (1961).

In the case of In re Roquain, Belgium, Court of Cassation, 1958, 26 Int'l L.Rep. 209 (1963), the defendant, while lawfully married, committed adultery in Paris. The court held the defendant could not be prosecuted because under "the law governing criminal proceedings in respect of offenses committed outside Belgian territory," the offense of adultery may be prosecuted only if it was committed against a Belgian national. As to offenses generally, Spain apparently will not prosecute a Spanish national for an offense committed abroad unless the victim is also of Spanish nationality. Forgery Committed in Venezuela by a Spaniard, Supreme Court, 1960, 89 Journal du Droit International 189 (1962).

In X. v. Prosecutor, Netherlands, District Court of Middelburg, 1952, Court of Appeal of the Hague, 1952, 19 Int'l L.Rep. 226 (1957), the defendant was a national of the Netherlands. She lost her nationality by marriage, then committed outside the Netherlands a criminal offense for which she was prosecuted and convicted in the state where it was committed. Upon the dissolution of her marriage, she recovered her former Dutch nationality. She was then prosecuted for the same offense in the Netherlands. It was held that the previous prosecution abroad did not preclude a new prosecution in Holland, though it might mitigate the punishment, and moreover she could not object to the prosecution on the ground that she had lost her nationality at the time the offense was committed. Any alien committing an offense abroad could be prosecuted if and when such person subsequently became a citizen of the Netherlands.

The Supreme Court of India, on the other hand, takes the view that a person cannot be prosecuted in India for an offense committed abroad if he was not a national of India at the time of commission of the offense. Central Bank of India v. Ram Narain, 1954, 21 Int'l L. Rep. 95 (1957). Moreover, a number of states will not prosecute their nationals again if they were previously prosecuted for an offense committed outside the territory. Harvard Research in International Law, Jurisdiction with Respect to Crime, 29 Am.J.Int'l L.Supp. 435, 606 (1935).

Prescriptive jurisdiction based on the nationality of individuals is also applicable to corporations or other legal entities which are nationals of the state. Suppose a corporation organized in a foreign state and doing all its business there is owned by United States nationals. May the United States use its prescriptive jurisdiction to compel its nationals to conduct the business of the corporation in violation of the law of the foreign state?

2. *Enforcement of rules prescribed on the basis of the nationality of vessels, aircraft and military services.* Whereas the prescriptive jurisdiction of a state based upon the nationality of individuals is limited in its effectiveness because the rules prescribed on this basis can be enforced only by action taken in the territory, prescriptive jurisdiction based on the nationality of vessels, aircraft and military services does not suffer from the same limitation. Jurisdiction to enforce rules prescribed on this basis accompanies the vessels, aircraft or military services wherever they go, although the exercise of the enforcement jurisdiction is limited by rules of international law when the vessels, aircraft or military services are in the territory of another state. See Chapters 3, 4 and 7.

Jurisdiction based on the nationality of vessels, aircraft and military services extends, moreover, to persons aboard the vessels or aircraft, as well as to members of the military services, regardless of the nationality of the individuals involved. In The Queen v. Anderson, [1868] L.R. 1 Cr.Cas.Res. 161, an American seaman was convicted of manslaughter on a British vessel which was in the Garonne river in France, some 45 miles upstream from the sea. While France had concurrent jurisdiction on the basis of territory, it did not claim to exercise it. The court held that the defendant was subject to British law and hence the conviction was valid.

3. *Enforcement of rules prescribed on other bases.* In the chapters which follow, other bases of jurisdiction to prescribe are considered as well as the scope of enforcement jurisdiction of rules prescribed on such bases.

As to prescriptive and enforcement jurisdiction based on proximity to territory (contiguous zone, hot pursuit and continental shelf), see Chapter 3.

As to prescriptive and enforcement jurisdiction based on the protection of universal interests (piracy, collision and salvage on the high seas, and fisheries conservation), see Chapter 3.

HARRY WINSTON INC. v. TUDURI

Spain, Supreme Court, 1961.
34 Int'l L.Rep. 49 (1967).*

The Facts.—On June 15, 1951, Tuduri, a citizen of Mexico domiciled in Barcelona, Spain, bought from Harry Winston Inc. of New York City a diamond necklace valued at $115,000, for which he never paid. The American corporation brought an action before the Court of first instance of Barcelona against Tuduri, demanding payment of the sum due or, alternatively, the return of the necklace. The defendant challenged the jurisdiction of Spanish courts to decide the case on the ground that both the plaintiff and the defendant were foreigners, averring that the case could only be tried before either Mexican or American courts. The Court of first instance of Barcelona affirmed its jurisdiction to decide the case. On appeal, the superior Court reversed the decision. The case was then brought before the Supreme Court.

Held: that the appeal must be dismissed. Spanish courts had jurisdiction in all civil law questions that might be raised in Spanish territory.

The Court said: "It is an undeniable principle derived from the sovereignty inherent in every State that its courts have absolute and undisputed jurisdiction in all civil law questions, whatever their nature, that may be raised within its territory, be they between nationals or between foreigners. This has been accepted by Article 51 of our Law of Civil Procedure, which states that ordinary jurisdiction is the only one competent in all civil law questions that may be raised in Spanish territory between Spanish nationals, between foreigners and between nationals and foreigners. It follows that, in accordance with the said article and with Article 70 of the same Law, the rules on jurisdiction laid down in Sections 1 and 2 of Title II apply to foreigners whenever they appear either as plaintiffs or as defendants before Spanish courts, and such jurisdiction as derives from national sovereignty cannot be set aside by such courts nor can they renounce it in favour of another sovereignty without a previous validating treaty, as has repeatedly been declared by this Chamber.

Consequently, the decision of the superior Court, in so far as it gave rise to the exception of lack of jurisdiction, is declared null and void."

———

1. *Enforcement of rules of conflict of laws.* Though the decision does not expressly say so, it suggests, and we will assume for our purpose, that Tuduri bought the diamond necklace in New York City.

* Reprinted by permission of E. Lauterpacht, ed., and Grotius Publications, Ltd., Cambridge, England.

Clearly the courts in New York have jurisdiction to prescribe a rule of law governing a transaction that took place in its territory and the courts of Mexico have jurisdiction to prescribe based upon the nationality of Tuduri.   What then is the basis of Spain's jurisdiction to prescribe justifying the exercise by its courts of jurisdiction to enforce?

The answer is that a state may prescribe rules of law *for the settlement of claims* between persons—nationals or aliens—present in the territory or for the resolution of claims asserted against property located in the territory, even though it otherwise has no jurisdiction to prescribe substantive rules of law with respect to the persons involved or the property in issue.   The prescription of rules for disposing of such claims is governed by what is called in the United States conflict of laws and everywhere else private international law.

Such rules will guide the Spanish court in choosing between the three sets of laws that it could conceivably enforce, i. e. the law of New York, Mexican law, or possibly the Spanish law.   Of course, the problem of choice of law is immensely more complex than its presentation here indicates.   The subject is dealt with fully in books and courses on private international law.   For an instance in which public international law and private international law intersect, see Chapter 6.

2.   *Treatment of subject in Restatement.*   Section 19 of the Restatement of the Foreign Relations Law of the United States (1965), provides:

Jurisdiction to Prescribe Rules for Adjudication or Other Determination of Claims

(1) Subject to the limitation of Subsection (2), a state has jurisdiction to prescribe a rule as to choice of the law governing the substantive adjudication or other determination of a claim asserted in its territory against a person, or with respect to a thing, located there, or another interest localized there, even though the state does not otherwise have a basis of jurisdiction under § 10 to prescribe a rule of law with respect to the conduct giving rise to the claim.

(2) In prescribing a rule of choice of law as indicated in Subsection (1), a state is acting within its jurisdiction if it gives effect either

(a) to a rule of law applicable to the conduct giving rise to the claim, prescribed by a state having jurisdiction to prescribe with respect to that conduct, or

(b) to a rule of its own law that would have been applicable to the conduct giving rise to the claim if the state had had jurisdiction to prescribe with respect to that conduct.   However, the rule of choice of law prescribed under Subsection (1) must be a conflict of laws rule designed primarily for the adjudication or other determination of claims of a private nature rather than a rule designed to control conduct not within the state's jurisdiction to prescribe.

3. *Treatment of subject in revision of Restatement.* A revision of the Restatement of the Foreign Relations Law of the United States (1965) was begun in 1979. The constitutive elements of jurisdiction under the definition in Section 6 of the Restatement are jurisdiction to prescribe and jurisdiction to enforce. Under the approach proposed in the revision, jurisdiction would have three constitutive elements: jurisdiction to prescribe, jurisdiction to enforce and jurisdiction to adjudicate. This third component would cover, inter alia, what is discussed here under the rubric of enforcement of rules of conflict of laws. See Sections 401 and 441 of Tentative Draft No. 2 (1981) of the Restatement of the Foreign Relations Law of the United States (Revised).

---

2.   TERRITORIAL CHARACTER OF JURISDICTION TO ENFORCE

THE SCHOONER EXCHANGE v. McFADDON

United States Supreme Court, 1812.
7 Cranch 116, 136.

MARSHALL, C. J.   *   *   *

*   *   *

The jurisdiction of the nation within its own territory is necessarily exclusive and absolute. It is susceptible of no limitation not imposed by itself. Any restriction upon it, deriving validity from an external source, would imply a diminution of its sovereignty to the extent of the restriction, and an investment of that sovereignty to the same extent in that power which could impose such restriction.

*   *   *

UNITED STATES v. LIRA

United States Court of Appeals, Second Circuit, 1975.
515 F.2d 68.

MANSFIELD, Circuit Judge:

Rafael Lira, whose true name is Rafael Mellafe, appeals from a narcotics conviction entered against him in the Southern District of New York after a jury trial before Judge Charles E. Stewart. Prior to the trial defendant moved to dismiss the indictment against him, alleging that, since he had been illegally abducted from Chile and tortured by agents of the United States Government, dismissal was mandated by our decision in United States v. Toscanino, 500 F.2d 267 (2d Cir. 1974). After an evidentiary hearing of the type prescribed by us in *Toscanino*, Judge Stewart denied the motion. We agree that "the *Toscanino* case does not control this matter," and affirm.

At the evidentiary hearing Mellafe testified that on March 7, 1974, he was arrested at the home of his common law wife in Santiago by Chilean police officers who took him to a local police station. According to his testimony he was blindfolded by the Chilean police, beaten, strapped nude to a box spring, tortured with electric shocks, and questioned about the whereabouts of one Christian Alvear, who had been named as a co-conspirator with Mellafe in the indictment forming the basis of the proceedings below. During this process, Mellafe testified, he heard English being spoken in a low tone, but he neither knew nor was told the identity of the English-speaking persons. He stated that after being held at the local police station for four days he was transferred to the Chilean Naval Prison at Valparaiso where he was held for about three weeks, during which period he was beaten and tortured.

Mellafe further testified that he was thereafter taken before the Chilean Naval Prosecutor where he was questioned again about Christian Alvear and about illegal firearms transactions. On May 3, 1974, he was forced to sign a decree expelling him from Chile and was photographed, being told that some Americans were waiting for his photograph. At this time Mellafe says he saw in a hallway outside the Chilean Prosecutor's office two men who were identified to him by Jorge Dabed, a fellow prisoner, as Special Agents Charles Cecil and George Frangulis of the U.S. Drug Enforcement Administration ("DEA"). Mellafe testified that finally he was taken to Pudahuel Airport and examined by a person thought by him to be an American physician, who gave him some pills. On May 4, 1974, he was placed aboard a plane, on which were Cecil, Frangulis and eight Chilean policemen. All but Frangulis then made the flight to New York, where Mellafe was arrested on arrival.

     *   *   *

In general a court's power to bring a person to trial upon criminal charges is not impaired by the forcible abduction of the defendant into the jurisdiction. Ker v. Illinois, 119 U.S. 436, 7 S.Ct. 225, 30 L. Ed. 421 (1888); Frisbie v. Collins, 342 U.S. 519, 72 S.Ct. 509, 96 L. Ed. 541 (1952). However, in United States v. Toscanino, supra, we held that this general rule, sometimes referred to as the "Ker-Frisbie doctrine," is subject to the overriding principle that where the Government itself secures the defendant's presence in the jurisdiction through use of cruel and inhuman conduct amounting to a patent violation of due process principles, it may not take advantage of its own denial of the defendant's constitutional rights. * * * More recently in United States ex rel. Lujan v. Gengler, 510 F.2d 62 (2d Cir. 1975), we reaffirmed the principle that the Ker-Frisbie doctrine does not bar judicial scrutiny of "conduct of the most outrageous and reprehensible kind by United States government agents," which results in denial of due process, 510 F.2d at 65, although we there found that the Government conduct did not reach the level proscribed by *Toscanino.*

Essential to a holding that *Toscanino* applies is a finding that the gross mistreatment leading to the forcible abduction of the defendant was perpetrated by representatives of the United States Government. In *Toscanino*, for instance, we stated that upon remand the defendant would be required to establish "that the action was taken by or at the direction of United States officials," 500 F.2d at 281. In the present case a suspicion of United States involvement in the Chilean police actions might arise from the fact that the Chilean officials appear to have been most cooperative in honoring the DEA's requests, even going so far as to provide a sizeable Chilean escort on the plane to the United States. But the evidentiary hearing produced no proof that representatives of the United States participated or acquiesced in the alleged misconduct of the Chilean officials. While we would have preferred a finding on this key issue by the district judge, the record fails to reveal any substantial evidence that Chilean police were acting as agents of the United States in arresting or mistreating Mellafe or that United States representatives were aware of such misconduct.

The only suggestion of possible involvement on the part of United States officials comes from Mellafe's testimony that he heard English spoken during the time of his torture in Santiago, that he saw the Special Agents at the Naval Prosecutor's office, and that he was told that his photograph was "for the Americans." However there was no evidence that American agents were present at or privy to his interrogation or that the persons overheard to speak English were Americans, much less Government agents. Agent Cecil, furthermore, testified that he was not at the prosecutor's office or aware of the activities of the Chilean police, and that he did not see Mellafe until he boarded the plane on May 4, 1974. Thus on this record there was no direct evidence of any misconduct on the part of the United States Government.

*   *   *

Affirmed.

OAKES, Circuit Judge (concurring):

While I concur in the result, I find the case more troublesome perhaps than does the majority. Having sat on both United States v. Toscanino * * * and United States ex rel. Lujan v. Gengler * * * and now on this case, I agree that this case falls just barely on the *Lujan* rather than the *Toscanino* side of the line. But since this is the third case in our court of DEA abduction from abroad, and we were told on argument that there were six more likely to come before us, one is led to wonder whether, by giving further countenance to this kind of conduct by law enforcement agents, we are forgetting the admonitions, albeit in Fourth Amendment contexts, of the judicial lions of the past—Mr. Justice Brandeis's ringing phrases in dissent in Olmstead v. United States; * * * Judge Learned Hand's remark in United States v. Kirschenblatt; * * * Mr. Justice Frankfurter's essay also in dissent in Harris v. United States * * *.

I recognize that only the other day, citing Ker v. Illinois, * * * and Frisbie v. Collins, 342 U.S. 519, 72 S.Ct. 509, 96 L.Ed. 541 (1952), the Supreme Court said "Nor do we retreat from the established rule that illegal arrest or detention does not void a subsequent conviction." Gerstein v. Pugh, 420 U.S. 103, 95 S.Ct. 854, 43 L.Ed.2d 54 (1975). We are, of course, bound by Supreme Court decisions as evidenced by *Lujan* supra. In addition to what Judge Mansfield said in *Toscanino*, 500 F.2d at 277–79, it is well to point out, however, that there is a very strong policy which would be operative if the abduction here were from an objecting country (as was allegedly the case in *Toscanino*) or in violation of a treaty. * * * That policy is of course respect for the law of nations, the requirements of world society, and the integrity and independence of other nations, not only under formal charters like those of the United Nations (art. 2, para. 4) and the Organization of American States (art. 17), but as unwritten obligations of international law. * * * That respect for the sovereign integrity of other nations is, in addition to conforming to high moral principles, a self-serving pragmatic viewpoint for the United States to take; we can better demand in the international court of public opinion similar respect for our sovereign integrity if we extend such respect to others. Nothing in *Lujan* is to the contrary.

Finally it should be said that, regardless of the abstract doctrine *Ker* and *Frisbie* are said to stand for, we can reach a time when in the interest "of establishing and maintaining civilized standards of procedure and evidence," we may wish to bar jurisdiction in an abduction case as a matter not of constitutional law but in the exercise of our supervisory power * * *. As we pointed out in *Toscanino*, supra, that "supervisory power is not limited to the admission or exclusion of evidence, but may be exercised in any manner necessary to remedy abuses of a district court's process." 500 F.2d at 276. To my mind the Government in the laudable interest of stopping the international drug traffic is by these repeated abductions inviting exercise of that supervisory power in the interests of the greater good of preserving respect for law.

---

1. *Standing to object to unlawful arrest.* Ker v. Illinois, 119 U.S. 436, 7 S.Ct. 225 (1886). The defendant had been kidnapped in Peru by officials from Illinois, but the court held the mode of his arrest was not constitutional ground for objection to his trial. The defendant appeared to be a national of the United States, but the court did not discuss the bearing, if any, of the nationality of the defendant in holding he had no standing to object to his unlawful arrest. In

Frisbie v. Collins, 342 U.S. 519, 72 S.Ct. 509 (1952), tne court relied on its decision in Ker v. Illinois in holding that a defendant arrested in Illinois by officers from Michigan similarly had no constitutional ground for objecting to his trial.

Re Argoud, France, Court of Cassation, 1964, 45 Int'l L.Rep. 90 (1972). Colonel Argoud, a French national notorious for his opposition to General de Gaulle's policies of independence for Algeria, was being sought for prosecution by the French authorities but found refuge in West Germany. He was kidnapped there by persons unknown and found tied up in a truck in Paris after an anonymous phone call. The court ruled that, in the absence of an objection by the Federal Republic of Germany, no international law issue was before it. In argument before the court, and in the prior proceedings, much was made by the prosecution of applicable precedents in Anglo-Saxon countries.

Attorney General of Israel v. Eichmann, supra, Chapter 1, p. 18. The kidnapping of the accused on Argentine territory by Israeli agents did raise an international law issue, in contrast to the Argoud case, but Eichmann was not given standing to raise it in the Israeli courts. The issue was treated as a matter only between Israel and Argentina and was disposed of by the agreement between the two states to consider the incident closed.

2.　*Law enforcement efforts outside the territory.* In many cases, the violation of a state's sovereignty in its territory arises from overzealous behavior at or near the border on the part of law enforcement authorities of a low echelon. Instead of becoming causes célèbres as the Eichmann and Argoud cases did, they are usually resolved more quietly by bureaucratic action. Illustrative instances follow.

A Belgian national had crossed over the border to visit in a café in France and had returned to Belgium. Suspecting him of theft, the proprietor of the café called two French policemen who crossed into Belgium, arrested him and brought him back to France where he was indicted. The Belgian government lodged an official protest with the French government through diplomatic channels. The court ordered the release of the defendant. In Re Jolis, France, Tribunal Correctionel d'Avesnes, 1933, [1933–1934] Ann.Dig. 191 (No. 77). For a similar case involving Italy and Switzerland, see the Mantovani Affair, 1965, supra, Chapter 1, p. 48.

Ronald Anderson, an American citizen and a conscientious objector during the hostilities in Vietnam, was living in British Columbia. While attemping to cross the border in order to visit his mother in the state of Washington, he was seized by American customs officers. A number of witnesses, and a photograph by a reporter, established that he had been seized by the American customs officers on the Canadian side. Following a protest by the Canadian Ministry for Foreign Affairs, the U. S. military authorities returned him to Canada. 79 Revue Générale de Droit International Public 462 (1975).

A Swiss, implicated in charges of drug traffic, crossed into France when her fiancé was arrested. The clerk of the Swiss judge in charge of the case went to her residence in France and convinced her to return to Geneva, where she was promptly arrested. In reporting her release in his Chronique des Faits Internationaux, Rousseau asserts that the same acts by a French clerk, and a French judge, had he known of the clerk's action, would have been severely punished in France. 78 Revue Générale de Droit International Public 1158 (1974).

3. *Other acts.* An inspector from the Spanish police was arrested in 1975 upon entering the French territory near Hendaye and found to be carrying a hand gun. He stated he had come to do some shopping and had forgotten to leave the gun home. He was given a suspended sentence of two months in prison. 80 Revue Générale de Droit International Public 248 (1976).

An Italian inspector was working in 1973 with the French police in seeking the arrest on French territory of an Italian accused of having killed two Italian policemen in Italy. At the moment the arrest by the French police took place, the Italian inspector, believing his life was in danger, pulled his gun and wounded the suspect. He was immediately indicted on a number of criminal charges. 79 Revue Générale de Droit International Public 1159 (1975).

In 1973, an Italian inspector of finances was making in Switzerland, across the border from Italy, inquiries about the movement of contraband towards Italian territory. He was arrested for violation of Article 271 of the Swiss Penal Code which provides: "Whoever, without being so authorized, engages on Swiss territory on behalf of a foreign state in acts [the exercise of which] appertains to the [Swiss] public authorities shall be punished by imprisonment." 78 Revue Générale de Droit International Public 851 (1974).[a]

States may differ, though, on whether certain acts should be treated as manifestations of foreign public authority violative as such of a state's rights under international law. Consider the materials that follow.

DEPARTMENT OF JUSTICE INSTRUCTIONS TO U. S. MARSHALS FOR PROCESSING REQUESTS FOR SERVING AMERICAN JUDICIAL DOCUMENTS ABROAD

XVI International Legal Materials 1331, 1338 (1978).*

* * *

C. Service of American Subpoenas Abroad

1. U.S. Marshals are not authorized to travel to foreign countries to deliver subpoenas in either criminal or civil cases. Marshals

---

a. Translation by the editors.   * Reprinted with the permission of the American Society of International Law.

may, however, mail subpoenas to an American national or resident who is in a foreign country in an appropriate case * * *. If a federal court issues an order requiring a U.S. Marshal to serve a subpoena abroad, the Marshal should immediately consult with the General Counsel, U.S. Marshals Service, Washington, D.C. * * *

U.S. Marshals are cautioned not to attempt personally to serve subpoenas in foreign countries without obtaining express approval from, and guidance by, the Director, U.S. Marshals Service.

[A footnote to this paragraph states:

10. Ignorance or disregard of this salutary rule has led to a damage suit abroad for malicious trespass against an Assistant U.S. Attorney who served a subpoena at a private residence in the Bahamas, and to a criminal indictment of an SEC staff attorney who served an administrative subpoena in France.]

2. The United States Consular Regulations provide in pertinent part as follows (22 C.F.R. 92.86 (1975)):

When directed by the Department of State, officers of the Foreign Service will serve a subpoena issued by a court of the United States on a national or resident of the United States who is in a foreign country unless such action is prohibited by the law of the foreign country.

SERVICE OF SUMMONS IN CRIMINAL PROCEEDINGS CASE

Austria, Supreme Court, 1961.
38 Int'l L.Rep. 133 (1969).*

The Facts.—A German citizen was tried in Austria in absentia and convicted of a criminal offence. The question arose whether the trial and the subsequent verdict were valid, having regard to the fact that the summons to attend the trial was served by the Austrian trial court on the accused in Germany by ordinary post. It was contended before the Supreme Court that an Austrian court was not entitled to serve a summons by post on a foreign citizen in a foreign country, and that proceedings before an Austrian court in pursuance of a summons so served were null and void.

Held: (i) that a summons in criminal proceedings can be served abroad only in accordance with the procedure laid down in treaties between Austria and the foreign country concerned; (ii) that as the relevant provisions of the treaty between Austria and the Federal Republic of Germany did not provide for service of a summons by post, the summons in the present case had not been validly served. The proceedings and the subsequent verdict were therefore null and void

* Reprinted by permission of E. Lauterpacht, ed., and Grotius Publications,
Ltd., Cambridge, England.

and must be set aside. [A portion of the opinion of the court appears below.]

* * *

According to the generally recognized rules of international law, which by Article 9 of the Constitution form part of Austrian federal law, the exercise of sovereign authority in foreign territory is permissible in Continental Europe only in so far as it has been generally recognized in international law * * * or is in accordance with general international usage * * * or, as the case may be, has been expressly provided for in treaties * * *. Where these conditions are not present and where the conduct of criminal proceedings in individual cases requires the performance of official acts of a sovereign character in the territory of a foreign State—even though it may only be service of a document—the court conducting the proceedings must invoke the assistance of the competent foreign authority for the purpose. The assistance which is feasible and required in individual cases is laid down in treaties and in municipal statutes enacted in pursuance of such treaties.

It follows that in the present case the District Court of R. was not entitled to summon the accused, who was then in his home State, i. e. the Federal Republic of Germany, to attend the trial, by sending the summons to him through the post and enclosing an international reply coupon. The District Court should have summoned the accused in accordance with the Decree for Judicial Assistance in Criminal Matters (of 13 July 1959) by invoking the assistance of the competent court of the Federal Republic of Germany. In accordance with this Decree it could have entered into direct contact with the competent German court, but on no account was it permitted to effect postal service on the accused who was in a foreign country. * * *

Accordingly, there has been no "proper" summons within the meaning of section 459 of the Code of Criminal Procedure because a proper summons is one served in accordance with the procedural provisions laid down by law. * * * The direct service of the judgment and the dispatch of an international reply coupon were in violation of the law, and service so effected could not produce any legal effect. Accordingly there was no basis for the request to pay the fine and the costs of the proceedings, nor was there any basis for the threat to impose imprisonment in lieu of a fine or any of the other orders of the District Court of R., which all rested on the assumption that a judgment in absentia had been validly given.

SECURITIES AND EXCHANGE COMMISSION v. BRIGGS

United States District Court, N.D.Ohio, 1964.
234 F.Supp. 618.

[The S.E.C. sought to enjoin defendant from violating the antifraud provisions of the Securities Act of 1933. The defendant was physically located in Canada at the time of suit.]

On the filing of the complaint a temporary restraining order was granted, and an order was entered pursuant to Rule 4(i) of the Federal Rules of Civil Procedure providing for service upon the defendant Briggs by any one or more of four methods: Service by registered mail, personal service by the sheriff of Vancouver County, British Columbia or any of his designated agents, service by said sheriff in accordance with the local rules of British Columbia, or service upon her by the United States Marshal. Pursuant to that order the defendant Briggs was served by registered mail on September 10, 1964. (Cf. Affidavit of Harry M. Jones) On September 17, 1964 the defendant Briggs was personally served by a Deputy Sheriff of British Columbia, Canada. (Cf. Affidavit of Alfred J. Tuttle) On September 18, 1964 counsel for the defendant Jessie Briggs appeared specially in open court and, by oral motion under Rule 12(b) of the Federal Rules of Civil Procedure, objected to this Court's assertion of jurisdiction over the defendant Briggs and moved to dismiss the complaint.

* * *

The defendant next contends that we cannot exercise that power lest we offend the sovereignty of our neighbor Canada, where the defendant was found and served. The defendant suggests that our right to exercise jurisdiction must be conditioned upon approval by Canada through a treaty. We seriously doubt that the defendant, admittedly a citizen of the United States, has standing to complain of an affront to a sovereign which is foreign to her. We need not reach that issue, however, because we perceive of no such invasion of Canada's sovereignty. In Blackmer v. United States, 284 U.S. 421, 52 S. Ct. 252 * * * the Supreme Court stated:

> * * * The mere giving of such a notice to the citizen in the foreign country of the requirement of his government that he shall return is in no sense an invasion of any right of the foreign government * * *.

Therefore, we find no principle of comity between nations which precludes this Court from the exercise of jurisdiction over Mrs. Briggs.

---

1. *Problem.* Suppose that the Briggs case had been a suit for damages for securities fraud and the defendant had not appeared. Would a default judgment for the plaintiff give Canada a claim against the United States under international law: (a) if the defendant were a citizen of the United States; (b) if he were a Canadian?

Suppose the defendant were French and the Canadian government did not complain. Would France have a claim against the United States?

2. *Distinction between service of notice and service of compulsory process.* In Federal Trade Commission v. Compagnie de Saint-Gobain-Pont-à-Mousson, 636 F.2d 1300 (D.C.Cir. 1980), the commission sent to the defendant in France by registered mail an investiga-

tory subpoena ordering the production of documents under threat of penalties. The court found that the service was improper under the Federal Trade Commission Act, "as construed　＊　＊　＊　in conformity with general principles of international law." The court drew a distinction between service of notice and service of a subpoena, stating the first was informational in nature and thus relatively benign, while the second, especially when served upon a foreign subject on foreign soil, was an exercise of sovereignty in another nation's territory and as such a violation of international law.

3. *Position of Switzerland.* This country has consistently taken the position that the service of judicial documents on persons residing in Switzerland is a governmental function.

Hence it stated in an aide-mémoire delivered to the U.S. Department of State on November 16, 1961, that "service of such documents by mail constitutes an infringement of Switzerland sovereign powers." The Department replied it had informed the competent United States authorities of the Swiss position and regretted the inadvertent violation of Swiss law by United States authorities. 56 Am.J.Int'l L. 794 (1962).

Switzerland took the same position in 1977 when it objected to a notice of suit by registered mail issued by the European Community Commission. It asserted that the mailing of this notice was a violation of Swiss law and sovereignty. XXXIII Annuaire Suisse de Droit International 203–205 (1977).

SECTION C. EXTRADITION

A summary of extradition law. If an individual goes from State Z to State A, there is no rule of international law that requires State A to return that individual to State Z. This is true even though State Z claims the individual as its national and, indeed, even though the individual admits that he is State Z's national. This is true also even though the individual has committed a crime in State Z, no matter what the nature of that crime may be.

The practice of extradition has been developed to moderate the absolute inability of a state to procure the return of a person who has committed or been convicted of a crime in its territory and thereafter fled to another state. Under extradition practice, State A will honor State Z's request to return an individual claimed by State Z to have committed (or to have been convicted of) a crime in Z. Under United States law, such a request will not be honored unless the United States has entered into a treaty with the requesting state. Valentine v. United States ex rel. Neidecker, 299 U.S. 5, 57 S.Ct. 100 (1936). The United States has many bilateral extradition treaties in force. The extradition treaty between the United States and Japan which entered into force on March 26, 1980, is set forth in full in the Documentary Supplement. An extradition treaty entered into by the United States typically contains a list of offenses; the states agree that they will extradite to each other persons charged with or convicted of those offenses committed in the territory of the requesting state. See, for example, the schedule of offenses covered by the United States-Japan treaty.

At times, treaties will provide for an exception from obligatory extradition of a person who is a national of the requested state; that exception is provided for in the treaty with Japan. The United States will surrender its own national unless the treaty provides otherwise. Charlton v. Kelly, 229 U.S. 447, 33 S.Ct. 945 (1913). A major exception in extradition treaties is for crimes of a political character, which creates problems in the event that extradition is sought for an act of killing which formally fits the schedule of extraditable crimes (such as murder) but was committed with a political motive. The cases that follow illustrate different approaches to the definition of political offenses.

THE STATE v. SCHUMANN

Ghana, Court of Appeal of Accra, 1966.
39 Int'l L.Rep. 433 (1970).*

[The Government of the Federal Republic of Germany requested the Government of Ghana to extradite Dr. Horst Schumann on a charge of murder.

The specific acts for the charge were the killing from 1939 to 1941 of more than 30,000 patients in mental establishments within two concentration camps in Germany and the killing from 1942 to 1944 of a large number of Jews at Auschwitz in the course of experiments with mass sterilization.

At the time the request for extradition was made, Schumann was employed by the government as a medical officer. A portion of the opinion follows.]

AKUFO-ADDO, C.J.:

* * *

Counsel for the State submitted that the principles relating to an offence of a political character have been examined and enunciated in the English cases of Re Meunier [1894] 2 Q.B.D. 415, Re Castioni [1891] 1 Q.B.D. 149; and R. v. Governor of Brixton Prison, Ex parte Kolczynski [1955] 1 All E.R. 35, and that none of the facts stated in the appellant's evidence fell within these principles. In the cases of Re Meunier and Re Castioni, the principle is stated that to constitute an offence of a political nature there must be some political disturb-

* Reprinted by permission of E. Lauterpacht, ed., and Grotius Publications, Ltd., Cambridge, England.

ance or upheaval or there must be some physical struggle between two opposing political parties for the mastery of the government of the country, and that the crime in question must have been committed in furtherance of that disturbance or struggle. The principle was extended in the *Kolczynski* case to cover "offences committed in association with a political object (e. g., anti-Communism) or with a view to avoiding political persecution or prosecution for political defaults" * * *.

It is clear beyond argument that the appellant's case is not covered by these principles. It is not his case that the poor helpless lunatics at the Munsungen Asylum or the Jews at Auschwitz had rebelled against the Nazi ideology and had thereby created some form of political disturbance which needed quelling, nor indeed does he claim to have committed the offence charged with a view to avoiding political persecution or prosecution. [at 437]

[CRABBE, J.A., amplified somewhat the holding in Kolczynski as follows.]

* * * It seems to have been established by *Kolczynski's* case that an act committed solely on the ground of fear of prosecution for a political offence or of political persecution will be sufficient to give the crime a political colouring, if such fear led immediately or directly to the commission of the crime for which extradition is sought. There must exist a direct connexion of the criminal act with a political object. [at 448]

[LASSEY, J.A., conceded the killings were done "in circumstances which were not entirely without political significance" and went on to state what follows.]

The crucial question here is this: In those circumstances is it necessary to widen the scope or meaning of these magic words, "of a political character", if only for reasons of humanity? I desire to answer this by saying that in order to determine the political character of the particular offence so as to make it not extraditable there must necessarily be present at the time of the commission of the particular crime some element of organized or violent opposition or resistance to the execution of the planned policy of the ruling political party and the offence must be committed in the conflict which might result between the opposing parties. In this context any such offence committed either by the agents of the ruling political party seeking to carry out their principal's orders or by the agents of those who dislike or resist the carrying into effect of the particular political policy may be brought under the category of an offence "of a political nature or character" and therefore excusable in extradition proceedings. * * *

* * *

In my view neither the helpless lunatics in the mental institution at "Munsungen" nor the Jews in "Auschwitz" appeared to have of-

fered any organized resistance to the Nazi Party in Germany
* * *. [at 451–452]

PUBLIC PROSECUTOR v. ZIND

Italy, Court of Cassation, 1961.
40 Int'l L.Rep. 214 (1961).*

The Facts.—During a discussion in a beer hall in West Germany
the respondent Zind expressed approval of the anti-Jewish measures
of the Nazis. On the basis of these comments he was charged with
the offence of insulting and profaning the memory of the dead. He
was convicted by the Court of Offenburg and on 11 April 1958 was
sentenced to one year's imprisonment. However, he escaped to Italy.
On 2 August 1960 the Ministry of Justice of the Federal Republic of
Germany requested Zind's extradition. On 23 August the Public
Prosecutor of the Offenburg Court advanced further grounds supporting the request for extradition, namely, that Zind was charged
with incitement to aid in the commission of an offence, the illegal use
of an identity document, and violation of the laws on passports. Zind
was arrested in Italy but objected to extradition on the ground that
the offence with which he had been charged in Germany was political
in nature, and Article 8 of the Italian Penal Code and Article 4 of the
Extradition Treaty between Italy and Germany provide that there
shall be no extradition for political offences. The case came before
the Naples Court of Appeal, which held that Zind's offence was political in nature. The Public Prosecutor appealed to the Court of
Cassation.

Held: that the appeal must be dismissed. [A portion of the
opinion follows.]

In Italian law the expression "political offence" includes an ordinary offence committed wholly or in part for political motives. As is
well known, the political motivation is a factor to be considered along
with the ordinary criminal aspects of the act. The two notions are
parallel, and in examining the political aspects particular importance
is given to the motives for committing the offence, whatever may be
the legal right or interest offended against. A subjectively political
offence is therefore characterized by the nature of the motive, appearing from the offender's purpose in committing the crime, which
must go beyond the personal interests of the offender and be concerned wholly or in part with wider interests connected with the
carrying into effect of different political ideals or theories. It is precisely in considering this particular characteristic of motive that
when a court is assessing the political nature of the crime it should
put aside any moral or social judgement and its own opinions as to

* Reprinted by permission of E. Lauterpacht, ed., and Grotius Publications,
Ltd., Cambridge, England.

the nobility and aims of the offender, for they may also be distasteful to those who belong to different political parties or social classes or who support other social principles. *   *   *

In fact, when a man professes a particular political ideology he cannot always be in harmony—indeed, he is almost always at variance—with the principles of moral order and social doctrine held by the majority of those who live in his society. *   *   * From this follows the current definition of a political offence, according to which a crime is said to be subjectively political whenever the accused has acted to promote aims which are in opposition to the general order of the society in which he lives by means of fomenting ideas or carrying out activities whose object is to uphold or impose particular solutions of a political or socio-economic kind. This is independent of the moral aspects of the objects which the wrongdoer hoped to achieve.

*   *   * The facts show that the first subject touched on in the conversation between Zind and a group of students in a beer hall was the subject of university studies. From comparisons between the present state of institutions for higher studies and the situation in his youth, Zind went on to speak of the politics of the National-Socialist régime, on which he made certain comments. The conversation continued even after the intervention of the Jewish student Linser, touching on more specifically political matters. It was then that Zind came out with opinions and comments supporting the anti-Jewish measures of Nazi times and the methods used for the so-called "final solution of the Jewish problem." Zind's remarks were therefore intended to oppose the contrary Jewish ideology. They included an expression of full support for the policies unfortunately followed in this matter by the National-Socialist régime under Hitler. Thus Zind's remarks were basically motivated not by some personal object but by one which involved, as was said in the German judgment, opinions of a political and ideological nature.

*   *   *

*   *   * This Court therefore rejects the Public Prosecutor's appeal.

RE BRESSANO

Argentina, Camara Federal de la Capital, 1965.
40 Int'l L.Rep. 219 (1975).*

The Facts.—Peru requested the extradition of Hugo M. Bressano on charges of bank robbery and assault committed in the Miraflores branch of the Credit Bank of Peru. *   *   * The Court of first instance refused extradition on the ground that the offences constituted

* Reprinted by permission of E. Lauterpacht, ed., and Grotius Publications,
Ltd., Cambridge, England.

common crimes connected with a political offence and hence were not extraditable * * *. On appeal to the Federal Court of the Capital (Buenos Aires).

Held: that extradition must be granted * * *. [A portion of the opinion appears below.]

Even if we accept the contention that the motive for the principal offence was to provide funds for the support of a programme of training of groups in guerrilla warfare to be directed against the existing political, social and economic order in Peru, and with the ultimate objective of directing this subversive activity against other Latin-American States, we cannot agree that this argument affords a valid reason for treating the offence in question as a political offence, thereby enabling the perpetrators to enjoy protection in any country in which they might seek asylum. As Carrara notes, there can be no doubt that the characterization of an offence as "political" is a relative matter, for the definition depends upon the relationship between the circumstances surrounding the commission of the act in question and the institutional organization of the country in a particular historical epoch. Furthermore, the definition of political offence, whether in terms of objective criteria or from the subjective point of view, must take into account the fact that the term is applied to those acts designed for altruistic reasons to bring about a change in a tyrannical and despotic political system where the only available means of action is resort to rebellion.

[The court went on to hold that, even if it were not established as positive law that the doctrine of political offense presupposed the existence of a democratic state, offenses as preparation for guerrilla warfare on an international scale did not qualify as political in any case.]

---

1. *Refusal to extradite.* A court ruling favorable to extradition does not necessarily mean the executive will extradite the person involved.

Moise Tshombe ran copper-rich Katanga as a secessionist state in the early 1960's and became premier of the Congo for a while. Forced out by a coup, he went into exile in Spain, whence he was kidnapped on a private plane to Algeria. The Congolese government immediately requested his extradition. The Algerian court ruled in favor of it. Procureur Général v. Kapenda Tshombe Moise, Supreme Court, 1967, 1 Revue Algérienne des Sciences Juridiques, Economiques et Politiques 592 (1968). Nevertheless the president of Algeria never did proceed with the extradition and Tshombe eventually died in Algiers.

The converse, i. e. a court ruling against extradition, usually means that the executive will not proceed with it. In the United States, the executive cannot extradite unless a federal court has found a prima facie case for extradition and, as indicated supra p. 138, such a court cannot make this finding unless the request for ex-tradition comes within an extradition treaty.

When the late Shah of Iran came to New York for medical treat-ment in the fall of 1979, there was no extradition treaty between the United States and Iran. The regime of the Ayatollah Khomeini de-manded the return of the Shah, but never sought an extradition pro-ceeding. The demand, which the United States denied, led to the sei-zure of hostages at the American Embassy in Teheran on November 4, 1979. For further references to this incident, see supra Chapter 1, pp. 74 and 75, and infra Chapter 13, p. 856.

When the Supreme Court of Chile ruled against the extradition of Chileans and others accused of murdering in the United States Or-lando Letelier, a Chilean official in exile, the executive in the United States criticized the decision and denied Chile certain economic assist-ance.

2. *Questions.* Suppose Iran had sought an extradition proceed-ing for the return of the Shah and the Supreme Court of the United States had ruled against it. Would the ruling justify measures of re-taliation by Iran?

Suppose there had been a treaty of extradition between Iran and the United States and it contained an exception for political offenses. Do you think the Shah, assuming he were held for extradition at the request of Iran, would have a good defense if he argued the crimes with which he was charged were political?

3. *Increased importance of extradition.* With the world wide increases of terrorism and hijacking of planes, extradition has be-come of crucial importance in their repression. See Chapter 2 for the former and Chapter 4 for the latter.

Chapter 3

LAW OF THE SEA

1. *Codification of the law of the sea.* Navigation, fishing and extraction of minerals take place on or under the sea. For centuries, there has been an ongoing struggle over whether these activities can be engaged in freely by all almost anywhere in the sea or whether states can carve out areas of the sea for their exclusive use and control.

Attempts at resolving the issue by codification of the law of the sea began as early as 1930 at a conference of some 40 states held at The Hague under the auspices of the League of Nations, but it was not successful.

More than 80 states participated in the 1958 Geneva Conference on the law of the sea and produced four conventions codifying portions of the customary law and creating new law in some cases. Three are set forth in the Documentary Supplement. They are:

1. Convention on the Territorial Sea and the Contiguous Zone, which entered into force on September 10, 1964; as of January 1, 1980, 44 states were parties to this convention;

2. Convention on the High Seas, which entered into force on September 30, 1962; as of January 1, 1980, 56 states were parties to this convention; and

3. Convention on the Continental Shelf, which entered into force on June 10, 1964; as of January 1, 1980, 53 states were parties to this convention.

The fourth, Convention on Fishing and Conservation of the Living Resources of the High Seas, is not included. The text of this convention is in 17 U.S.T. 138, 559 U.N.T.S. 285.

After a second conference on the law of the sea failed to agree on the breadth of the territorial sea, the General Assembly of the United Nations decided to convene a third conference on the law of the sea, with mandate to prepare a comprehensive codification of it. The conference settled procedural and administrative matters at its first session in 1973 and met on matters of substance at its second session in 1974. By 1980, some 150 states were attending its ninth session. The conference is commonly referred to as UNCLOS III.

2. *United Nations Draft Convention on the Law of the Sea.* At the outset UNCLOS III decided not to adopt texts by voting on them. Rather it reached a gentleman's agreement to proceed on the basis of consensus as far as possible. The chairmen of Committees I, II and III of the conference were given the task of preparing texts reflect-

ing the result of the negotiations in a form which might be expected to win a consensus.

At the close of the third session in 1975, the three chairmen produced a Single Negotiating Text and the end of the fourth session in 1976, they prepared a Revised Single Negotiating Text. At the sixth session in 1977, the conference directed its president to undertake, with the chairmen of the three committees, the preparation of an Informal Composite Negotiating Text. At the conclusion of the first part of the eighth session, March 19–April 27, 1979, the same persons plus the chairman of the drafting committee and the rapporteur-general were directed to make certain revisions in the Informal Composite Negotiating Text and directed further to revise it at the close of the first part of the Ninth Session, March 3–April 4, 1980. At the close of the second part of the Ninth Session, July 28–August 29, 1980, the document, as modified, was labelled *Draft Convention on the Law of the Sea (Informal Text)*. This text is in the Documentary Supplement.

SECTION A.   CONTROL OF NATIONAL VESSELS

---

1.   NATIONALITY OF VESSELS

PUBLIC MINISTRY v. MOGENS GLISTRUP

Denmark, Maritime and Commercial Court, 1967.
95 Journal du Droit International 979 (1968).*

A vessel belonging to a Danish corporation and registered in Denmark and flying the Danish flag, was bareboat chartered[a] to an American company which used it in Nigerian waters. While the vessel was under charter, it had a crew which did not meet the conditions of the Danish Act on the Manning of Ships of 1965. According to paragraph 1, the act applies to all Danish vessels. The director of the American corporation had interpreted this provision as applying only to vessels under actual Danish control.

The court held however that the act applied to all Danish vessels even when bareboat chartered. The law of the flag controls. Otherwise, said the court, a vessel flying the Danish flag could escape all legislation or public control [of Denmark].

Even though Denmark has not ratified the Geneva Convention on the High Seas, the rule in Article 5 of the convention which makes the nationality of vessels depend upon the existence of a genuine link between the state and vessels flying its flag, must be considered without any question to be a part of public international law. The decision [therefore] seems to be perfectly in accord with the principle ex-

---

* Translation by the editors. Reprinted   a. Leased without provision of officers
  by permission of Editions Techniques,   or crew by the owner.
  S.A., Paris.

pressed in that article: genuine link means that the state effectively exercises its jurisdiction and its control * * *.

---

1. *Article 5 of the Geneva Convention on the High Seas.* The article provides, in Paragraph 1:

> Each state shall fix the conditions for the grant of its nationality to ships, for the registration of ships in its territory, and for the right to fly its flag. Ships have the nationality of the state whose flag they are entitled to fly. There must exist a genuine link between the state and the ship; in particular, the state must effectively exercise its jurisdiction and control in administrative, technical and social matters over ships flying its flag.

What is the function of the genuine link? Consider in connection with this question the statement made before the United States Senate Committee on Foreign Relations by Mr. Arthur H. Dean, the head of the delegation of the United States at the 1958 Geneva Conference. He said:

> The International Law Commission did not decide upon a definition of the term "genuine link." This article as originally drafted by the Commission would have authorized other states to determine whether there was a "genuine link" between a ship and the flag state for purposes of recognition of the nationality of the ship.

> It was felt by some states attending the Conference on the Law of the Sea that the term "genuine link" could, depending upon how it were defined, limit the discretion of a state to decide which ships it would permit to fly its flag. Some states, which felt their flag vessels were at a competitive disadvantage with vessels sailing under the flags of other states, such as Panama and Liberia, were anxious to adopt a definition which states like Panama and Liberia could not meet.

> By a vote of 30 states, including the United States, against 15 states for, and 17 states abstaining, the provision was eliminated which would have enabled states other than the flag state to withhold recognition of the national character of a ship if they considered that there was no "genuine link" between the state and the ship.

> Thus, under the Convention on the High Seas, it is for each state to determine how it shall exercise jurisdiction and control in administrative, technical and social matters over ships flying its flag. The "genuine link" requirement need not have any effect upon the practice of registering American built or owned vessels in such countries as Panama or Liberia. The existence of a "genuine link" between the state and the ship is not a condition of recognition of the nationality of a ship; that is, no state can

claim the right to determine unilaterally that no genuine link exists between a ship and the flag state. * * * Excerpt from Executive Report No. 5—Law of the Sea Conventions, 106 Cong. Rec. 11189, 11190 (1960).

2. *Measures of control over flag vessels mandated by Article 94 of U.N. Draft Convention.* The text of Article 5 in the Geneva Convention on the High Seas is reproduced verbatim in Article 91 of the United Nations Draft Convention on the Law of the Sea, except for the last clause of the second sentence. That clause is incorporated in Article 94 of the draft as follows:

1. Every state shall effectively exercise its jurisdiction and control in administrative, technical and social matters over ships flying its flag.

In sharp contrast to the Geneva Convention, however, the Draft Convention specifies in detail what the duties of the flag state are if it is going effectively to exercise its jurisdiction and control over its flag vessels. Thus, Article 94 of the draft provides in Sections 3, 4 and 5:

3. Every State shall take such measures for ships flying its flag as are necessary to ensure safety at sea with regard, inter alia, to:

    (a) The construction, equipment and seaworthiness of ships;

    (b) The manning of ships, labour conditions and the training of crews, taking into account the applicable international instruments;

    (c) The use of signals, the maintenance of communications and the prevention of collisions.

4. Such measures shall include those necessary to ensure:

    (a) That each ship, before registration and thereafter at appropriate intervals, is surveyed by a qualified surveyor of ships, and has on board such charts, nautical publications and navigational equipment and instruments as are appropriate for the safe navigation of the ship;

    (b) That each ship is in the charge of a master and officers who possess appropriate qualifications, in particular in seamanship, navigation, communications, and marine engineering, and that the crew is appropriate in qualification and numbers for the type, size, machinery and equipment of the ship;

    (c) That the master, officers and, to the extent appropriate, the crew are fully conversant with and required to observe the applicable international regulations concerning the safety of life at sea, the prevention of collisions, the prevention, reduction and control of marine pollution, and the maintenance of communications by radio.

5. In taking the measures called for in paragraphs 3 and 4 each State is required to conform to generally accepted international regulations, procedures and practices and to take any steps which may be necessary to secure their observance.

Nevertheless, the Draft Convention does not go so far as to strip from a vessel the nationality of the flag state in the event that the flag state fails to exercise its jurisdiction and control effectively. Section 6 of Article 94 of the draft provides:

6. A State which has clear grounds to believe that proper jurisdiction and control with respect to a ship have not been exercised may report the facts to the flag State. Upon receiving such a report, the flag State shall investigate the matter and, if appropriate, take any action necessary to remedy the situation.

For the full text of Article 94, see the Documentary Supplement.

3. *Oil spills and flags of convenience.* The term flags of convenience refers, broadly speaking, to vessels operating under the flags of states that do not require the owners to be nationals or long term residents. The practice, also called open registry, means that such states are seldom directly concerned with the management of the vessels and, in some cases, show little interest in regulating their operation. The opportunity is thereby created for less scrupulous owners to run substandard vessels with inadequate equipment or incompetent crews.

The regulations mandated by Article 94 of the draft reflect the increased concern of the international community with the improper management of vessels flying flags of convenience. Of course it is well known that substandard vessels and incompetent crews can also be found in fleets from certain states with closed registries. Nevertheless, much of the pressure for the adoption of the regulations was generated in recent years by spectacular oil spills from wrecked or sinking tankers flying flags of convenience and the publicity given thereafter to the lack of competence of the crew, the inadequacy of the equipment aboard and the faulty design of the vessel.

Quite aside from the publicity given the matter by the press and other means of communication, some learned journals also dealt with it. Thus after the Amoco-Cadiz, under Liberian flag, sank off the coast of Brittany in 1978 and poured out some 230,000 tons of oil, Rousseau published an account of the disaster and its aftermath, ending with a bitter denunciation of flags of convenience. 82 Revue Générale de Droit International Public 1125 (1978). Some of the instances of incompetence of crews and unseaworthiness of the vessels reported there are scarcely believable.

4. *Growth and use of flags of convenience.* According to Rousseau, flags of convenience which constituted 5% of the world's commercial fleet in 1950 now constitute 50% of it, including 40% of the tankers (at 1148). Even if the estimate is on the high side, there can be no doubt about the growth of their numbers.

Liberia is, reportedly, the state with the largest fleet in tonnage of flags of convenience, followed by Panama, Singapore, Cyprus, Bermuda and the Bahamas (at 1148). The beneficiaries, i. e. the states deriving the main financial benefits from flags of convenience, are, according to the article, the United States, followed by Greece, Hong Kong and Japan (at 1148).

In February of 1977, the People's Republic of China was reported as having placed some 80 of its merchant vessels under the Panamanian flag, thereby following the example of the USSR which long before that had placed about one hundred of its merchant vessels under the same flag. 81 Revue Générale de Droit International Public 1120 (1977).

What benefits do you suppose are derived by the People's Republic of China and the USSR from the use of flags of convenience? Is such use consistent with earlier vigorous attacks by the USSR and other socialist states upon the employment of flags of convenience as economic colonialism?

Another aspect of the problems created by flags of convenience is considered infra, p. 155.

---

2. JURISDICTION OVER VESSELS

THE PEOPLE v. ROBERT J. THOMAS

Eire, Supreme Court, 1954.
22 Int'l L.Rep. 295 (1958).*

The Facts. The accused was convicted of the manslaughter of one Humphries. The accused and Humphries were travelling together on the Irish ship Munster, from Liverpool to Dublin. They had both been drinking, when, some 15 miles out from the Welsh coast, about midnight, there was a fight in which Humphries went overboard and was lost. Thomas was not an Irish citizen.

There was an appeal on the ground, first, of alleged lack of evidence, and secondly on the ground that the Court had no jurisdiction to try an offence of manslaughter on an Irish ship where the death did not occur on board the ship, or within the jurisdiction.

Held (affirming the Court of Criminal Appeal): that the appeal failed on both grounds. [A portion of the opinion of the court appears below.]

* * * The next ground of appeal is that there was no jurisdiction in the Central Criminal Court to try the appellant for manslaughter as the death did not occur on board the ship and so was not within the jurisdiction of the Court. It is clear that the Central

* Reprinted by permission of E. Lauterpacht, ed., and Grotius Publications,
Ltd., Cambridge, England.

Criminal Court has all the jurisdiction formerly exercised by the Admiral and later exercised by the Commissioners of Oyer and Terminer appointed to exercise the Admiralty jurisdiction in criminal cases (11, 12, 13 Jac. 1, c. 2 (Ir.)). This was not contested. Mr. Bell [counsel for the accused] contended that the jurisdiction was confined to the trial of persons committing offences on board an Irish ship on the high seas where such offences were committed and completed on the ship. Manslaughter, Mr. Bell says, is a complex crime consisting of two essential ingredients. The first is some unlawful act or culpable neglect, which causes the death, and the second is the fact of death itself. The death admittedly did not take place on the ship. The crime, therefore, according to the argument, not being completed on board the ship was not committed within the jurisdiction. Mr. Bell referred at length to the case of The Queen v. Keyn, 2 Ex.D. 63. Keyn, a foreigner, was in command of a foreign ship which ran into a British ship within three miles of the English shore and sank her. A passenger on board the English ship was drowned. The facts were such as would in English law amount to manslaughter. On his being indicted for that offence in the Central Criminal Court the jury found Keyn guilty. Counsel for the prisoner objected that the Court had no jurisdiction. Pollock B., the trial Judge, stated a case on the point for the opinion of the Court for Crown Cases Reserved. The majority of the Court held that as the offence was not committed on a British ship there was no jurisdiction to try the prisoner, even though the ship at the time of the occurrence was within what has become known as the "three-mile limit."

        *   *   *

Applying these observations to the present case, the contention on behalf of the appellant is that since the death took place, if at all, in the water, the crime was not complete upon the Irish ship and therefore no crime in fact or in law took place on the ship, and it follows that the jurisdiction of the Central Criminal Court which is confined in its admiralty jurisdiction to trying cases of crimes committed in Irish ships is not brought into operation. If the argument is correct it would appear that there is no jurisdiction in any Court of this country to try either a citizen or foreigner on an Irish ship who by culpable negligence or design throws another overboard with the result that death occurs in the water.

        *   *   *

It will be convenient in discussing the matter of the Admiral's jurisdiction to consider it from two aspects. First, what jurisdiction the Admiral had as regards the place where the crime was committed, and, secondly, in respect of what persons that jurisdiction operated.

        *   *   *

The other aspect of the jurisdiction now requires consideration. It is not necessary for the purposes of this case to enumerate all persons over whom the jurisdiction may extend. It is sufficient to say that it is clear law that the jurisdiction extends to a foreigner on an Irish ship.

It being undoubted that crimes committed by foreigners on board British or Irish ships are cognizable by British or Irish Courts, as the case may be, without any statute, is there anything in the origins or the legal theory giving rise to this rule of law to indicate that whatever jurisdiction attaches is limited to the punishment of a crime begun and completed on board the ship, as distinct from a crime completed by the death taking place in the water surrounding the ship?

The basis of the jurisdiction is the right of the country to which the ships belong to control the conduct of those on board from the point of good order and the prevention of crime by virtue of the protection afforded to such persons while sailing in such ship. In The Queen v. Anderson, 1 Cr.Cas.Res. 161, Blackburn, J., at p. 169 says: "There are a vast number of cases which decide that when a ship is sailing on the high seas and bearing the flag of a particular nation, the ship forms a part of that nation's country, and all persons on board of her may be considered as within the jurisdiction of that nation whose flag is flying on the ship, in the same manner as if they were within the territory of that nation." Coke says: "Protectio trahit subjectionem et subjectio protectionem." Lord Coleridge in The Queen v. Carr, 10 Q.B.D. 76, says, at p. 85: "The true principle is, that a person who comes on board a British ship where English law is reigning, places himself under the protection of the British flag, and as a correlative, if he thus becomes entitled to our law's protection, he becomes amenable to its jurisdiction, and liable to the punishment it inflicts upon those who there infringe its requirements." He adds that there is no distinction to be drawn between a member of the crew and a passenger.

     * * *

The verdict of manslaughter in this case involved a finding of fact that Humphries is dead. The evidence points only to a death by drowning on the high seas. The other ingredient of the crime, the act or omission causing the death, occurred on board the M.V. "Munster", an Irish ship. Thus the event leading to the death also took place upon the high seas. The two elements necessary to give jurisdiction were thus both present. The crime was committed on the high seas and the appellant was at the time of its commission on an Irish ship. The appellant was, therefore, properly triable in the Central Criminal Court.

The appeal in so far as it was based on want of jurisdiction also fails.

This Court does not see any reason for interfering with the sentence.

———————

Question. Consider the discussion by the court of The Queen v. Keyn in which it was held that "as the offense was not committed on a British ship there was no jurisdiction to try the prisoner, even though the ship at the time of the occurrence was within what has become known as the three-mile limit." Was this a statement of a rule of international law? See infra, p. 186.

RE BIANCHI

Argentina, Cámara Nacional Especial, 1957.
24 Int'l L.Rep. 173 (1961).*

The Facts. The appellant, Gerónimo C. Bianchi, a member of the crew of the R. T., a ship of Argentine registry, was charged with the commission of a theft on board the ship while it was anchored in the harbour of Río de Janeiro, Brazil. In the absence of any action in the matter by Brazilian authorities, charges were brought against Bianchi in Argentina. It was unsuccessfully argued for the defendant that the Argentine court lacked jurisdiction over an offence which had been committed in foreign territorial waters. On appeal,

Held: that the judgment appealed from must be affirmed. Where local authorities did not take jurisdiction over an offence committed on board a ship anchored in foreign territorial waters, jurisdiction reverted to the courts of the State of registry of the ship.

[A portion of the opinion of the court appears below.]

* * * According to the record of proceedings in the trial Court, an inquiry was made into a theft which was allegedly committed on board the R. T., a ship of Argentine registry, while it was at anchor in the port of Río de Janeiro. Article 1, para. 1, of the Penal Code provides that this Code is applicable (inter alia) to offences committed in places subject to the national jurisdiction. According to the rules of public international law, which have not been reproduced for obvious reasons in the said Article but which are none the less binding upon Argentine courts, offences committed on board a private ship fall within the jurisdiction of the courts of the flag State if the ship is on the high seas, and fall within the jurisdiction of a foreign State only in the event that such offences have been committed while the ship is in the territorial waters of that other State.

This latter principle is not an absolute rule, however, for if the foreign State does not choose to exercise its right to institute proceedings because it considers that the act has not affected the community at large or the peace of the port (as maintained in French and Italian doctrine), the flag State may then assert full authority over the ship for the purpose of restoring order and discipline on board or protecting the rights of the passengers (Herrera, La Reforma Penal, p. 134). We may reasonably conclude with regard to the case before us, given the fact that the preliminary hearing was apparently held

* Reprinted by permission of E. Lauterpacht, ed., and Grotius Publications, Ltd., Cambridge, England.

"en route", that the Brazilian authorities had relinquished jurisdiction over the alleged offence, so that this offence then became subject to the jurisdiction of the Argentine courts. As this reasoning accords with the judgment of the trial Court and with the opinion of the Fiscal of this Court regarding the case, the judgment under appeal · is affirmed.

SPECIAL MARITIME AND TERRITORIAL JURISDICTION OF THE UNITED STATES

18 U.S.C. § 7.

The term "special maritime and territorial jurisdiction of the United States", as used in this title, includes:

(1) The high seas, any other waters within the admiralty and maritime jurisdiction of the United States and out of the jurisdiction of any particular State, and any vessel belonging in whole or in part to the United States or any citizen thereof, or to any corporation created by or under the laws of the United States, or of any State, Territory, District, or possession thereof, when such vessel is within the admiralty and maritime jurisdiction of the United States and out of the jurisdiction of any particular State.

(2) Any vessel registered, licensed, or enrolled under the laws of the United States, and being on a voyage upon the waters of any of the Great Lakes, or any of the waters connecting them, or upon the Saint Lawrence River where the same constitutes the International Boundary Line.

* * *

---

1. *Crimes included in special maritime jurisdiction of the United States.* Title 18 of the United States Code defines as criminal a number of acts that are performed within the special maritime jurisdiction of the United States: Sections 113, assaults; 114, maiming; 661, theft; 662, receiving stolen goods; 1111, murder; 1112, manslaughter; 1113, attempt to commit murder or manslaughter; 2031, rape; 2032, statutory rape; 2111, robbery. (See, also Title 49, Section 1472(k), dealing with these same crimes when committed within the "special aircraft jurisdiction of the United States." This jurisdiction is discussed in Chapter 4.)

2. *Vessels included in special maritime jurisdiction of the United States.* In civil matters involving vessels on the high seas such as collision and salvage, the United States as well as other states apply the rules of maritime law to foreign flag vessels as well as to vessels sailing under their national flag. The general law maritime is not itself a part of international law. Rather, it is a body of rules reflecting the universal interest of states in achieving a substantial degree of uniformity in the handling of civil claims arising on the high seas.

In the application of such rules, each state may use its own understanding or domestic version of the rules without subjecting itself thereby to a claim under international law by another state.

But would it be valid under international law for the United States to apply rules of criminal law under Section 7 of Title 18 to vessels owned by United States citizens or corporations if the vessels were registered under a foreign flag?

McCULLOCH, CHAIRMAN, NATIONAL LABOR RELATIONS BOARD v. SOCIEDAD NACIONAL de MARINEROS de HONDURAS

United States Supreme Court, 1963.
372 U.S. 10, 83 S,Ct. 671, 9 L.Ed.2d 547.

Mr. Justice CLARK delivered the opinion of the Court.

These companion cases, involving the same facts, question the coverage of the National Labor Relations Act, as amended, 61 Stat. 136, 73 Stat. 541, 29 U.S.C.A. § 151 et seq. A corporation organized and doing business in the United States beneficially owns seagoing vessels which make regular sailings between United States, Latin American and other ports transporting the corporation's products and other supplies; each of the vessels is legally owned by a foreign subsidiary of the American corporation, flies the flag of a foreign nation, carries a foreign crew and has other contacts with the nation of its flag. The question arising is whether the Act extends to the crews engaged in such a maritime operation. The National Labor Relations Board in a representation proceeding on the application of the National Maritime Union held that it does and ordered an election. 134 N.L.R.B. 287. The vessels' foreign owner sought to enjoin the Board's Regional Director from holding the election, but the District Court for the Southern District of New York denied the requested relief. 200 F.Supp. 484. The Court of Appeals for the Second Circuit reversed, holding that the Act did not apply to the maritime operations here and thus the Board had no power to direct the election. 300 F.2d 222. The N. M. U. had intervened in the proceeding, and it petitioned for a writ of certiorari (No. 93), as did the Regional Director (No. 91). Meanwhile, the United States District Court for the District of Columbia, on application of the foreign bargaining agent of the vessels' crewmen, enjoined the Board members in No. 107. 201 F.Supp. 82. We granted each of the three petitions for certiorari, 370 U.S. 915, 82 S.Ct. 1559, and consolidated the cases for argument.

We have concluded that the jurisdictional provisions of the Act do not extend to maritime operations of foreign-flag ships employing alien seamen.

I.

The National Maritime Union of America, AFL-CIO, filed a petition in 1959 with the National Labor Relations Board seeking certification under § 9(c) of the Act, 29 U.S.C.A. § 159(c), as the representative of the unlicensed seamen employed upon certain Honduran-flag vessels owned by Empresa Hondurena de Vapores, S.A., a Honduran corporation. The petition was filed against United Fruit Company, a New Jersey corporation which was alleged to be the owner of the majority of Empresa's stock. Empresa intervened and on hearing it was shown that United Fruit owns all of its stock and elects its directors, though no officer or director of Empresa is an officer or director of United Fruit and all are residents of Honduras. In turn the proof was that United Fruit is owned by citizens of the United States and maintains its principal office at Boston. Its business was shown to be the cultivation, gathering, transporting and sale of bananas, sugar, cacao and other tropical produce raised in Central and South American countries and sold in the United States.

United Fruit maintains a fleet of cargo vessels which it utilizes in this trade. A portion of the fleet consists of 13 Honduran-registered vessels operated[2] by Empresa and time chartered to United Fruit, which vessels were included in National Maritime Union's representation proceeding. The crews on these vessels are recruited by Empresa in Honduras. They are Honduran citizens (save one Jamaican) and claim that country as their residence and home port. The crew are required to sign Honduran shipping articles, and their wages, terms and condition of employment, discipline, etc., are controlled by a bargaining agreement between Empresa and a Honduran union, Sociedad Nacional de Marineros de Honduras. Under the Honduran Labor Code only a union whose "juridic personality" is recognized by Honduras and which is composed of at least 90% of Honduran citizens can represent the seamen on Honduran-registered ships. The N. M. U. fulfils neither requirement. Further, under Honduran law recognition of Sociedad as the bargaining agent compels Empresa to deal exclusively with it on all matters covered by the contract. The current agreement in addition to recognition of Sociedad provides for a union shop, with a no-strike-or-lockout provision, and sets up wage scales, special allowances, maintenance and cure provisions, hours of work, vacation time, holidays, overtime, accident prevention, and other details of employment as well.

United Fruit, however, determines the ports of call of the vessels, their cargoes and sailings, integrating the same into its fleet organization. While the voyages are for the most part between Central and South American ports and those of the United States, the vessels

2. Ten of the 13 vessels are owned and operated by Empresa. Three are owned by Balboa Shipping Co., Inc., a Panamanian subsidiary of United Fruit. Empresa acts as an agent for Balboa in the management of the latter vessels.

each call at regular intervals at Honduran ports for the purpose of taking on and discharging cargo and, where necessary, renewing the ship's articles.

II.

The Board concluded from these facts that United Fruit operated a single, integrated maritime operation within which were the Empresa vessels, reasoning that United Fruit was a joint employer with Empresa of the seamen covered by N. M. U.'s petition. Citing its own West India Fruit & Steamship Co. opinion, 130 N.L.R.B. 343 (1961), it concluded that the maritime operations involved substantial United States contacts, outweighing the numerous foreign contacts present. The Board held that Empresa was engaged in "commerce" within the meaning of § 2(6) of the Act [3] and that the maritime operations "affected commerce" within § 2(7),[4] meeting the jurisdictional requirement of § 9(c)(1).[5] It therefore ordered an election to be held among the seamen signed on Empresa's vessels to determine whether they wished N. M. U., Sindicato Maritimo Nacional de Honduras, or no union to represent them.

*   *   *

III.

Since the parties all agree that the Congress has constitutional power to apply the National Labor Relations Act to the crews working foreign-flag ships, at least while they are in American waters, The Exchange, 7 Cranch 116, 143 (1812); Wildenhus's Case, 120 U. S. 1, 11, 7 S.Ct. 385 (1887); Benz v. Compania Naviera Hidalgo, 353 U.S. 138, 142, 7 S.Ct. 699 (1957), we go directly to the question whether Congress exercised that power. Our decision on this point being dispositive of the case, we do not reach the other questions raised by the parties and the amici curiae.

3. 29 U.S.C.A. § 152(6):
"The term 'commerce' means trade, traffic, commerce, transportation, or communication among the several States, or between the District of Columbia or any Territory of the United States and any State or other Territory, or between any foreign country and any State, Territory, or the District of Columbia, or within the District of Columbia or any Territory, or between points in the same State but through any other State or any Territory or the District of Columbia or any foreign country."

4. 29 U.S.C.A. § 152(7):
"The term 'affecting commerce' means in commerce, or burdening or obstructing commerce or the free flow of commerce, or having led or tending to lead to a labor dispute burdening or obstructing commerce or the free flow of commerce."

5. 29 U.S.C.A. § 159(c)(1):
"Whenever a petition shall have been filed * * * the Board shall investigate such petition and if it has reasonable cause to believe that a question of representation affecting commerce exists shall provide for an appropriate hearing * * *."
Section 10(a) of the Act, 29 U.S.C.A. § 160(a), imposes the same requirement, empowering the Board to "prevent any person from engaging in any unfair labor practice * * * affecting commerce."

The question of application of the laws of the United States to foreign-flag ships and their crews has arisen often and in various contexts. As to the application of the National Labor Relations Act and its amendments, the Board has evolved a test relying on the relative weight of a ship's foreign as compared with its American contacts. That test led the Board to conclude here, as in West India Fruit & Steamship Co., supra, that the foreign-flag ships' activities affected "commerce" and brought them within the coverage of the Act. Where the balancing of the vessel's contacts has resulted in a contrary finding, the Board has concluded that the Act does not apply.

Six years ago this Court considered the question of the application of the Taft-Hartley amendments to the Act in a suit for damages "resulting from the picketing of a foreign ship operated entirely by foreign seamen under foreign articles while the vessel [was] temporarily in an American port." Benz v. Compania Naviera Hidalgo, supra, 353 U.S., at 139, 77 S.Ct., at 700. We held that the Act did not apply, searching the language and the legislative history and concluding that the latter "inescapably describes the boundaries of the Act as including only the workingmen of our own country and its possessions." Id., at 144, 77 S.Ct., at 702, 703. *   *   *

It is contended that this case is nonetheless distinguishable from Benz in two respects. First, here there is a fleet of vessels not temporarily in United States waters but operating in a regular course of trade between foreign ports and those of the United States; and, second, the foreign owner of the ships is in turn owned by an American corporation. We note that both of these points rely on additional American contacts and therefore necessarily presume the validity of the "balancing of contacts" theory of the Board. But to follow such a suggested procedure to the ultimate might require that the Board inquire into the internal discipline and order of all foreign vessels calling at American ports. Such activity would raise considerable disturbance not only in the field of maritime law but in our international relations as well. In addition, enforcement of Board orders would project the courts into application of the sanctions of the Act to foreign-flag ships on a purely ad hoc weighing of contacts basis.[9] This would inevitably lead to embarrassment in foreign affairs and be entirely infeasible in actual practice. The question, therefore, appears to us more basic; namely, whether the Act as written was in-

9. Our conclusion does not foreclose such a procedure in different contexts, such as the Jones Act, 46 U.S. C.A. § 688, where the pervasive regulation of the internal order of a ship may not be present. As regards application of the Jones Act to maritime torts on foreign ships, however, the Court has stated that "[p]erhaps the most venerable and universal rule of maritime law relevant to our problem is that which gives cardinal importance to the law of the flag." Lauritzen v. Larsen, 345 U.S. 571, 584, 73 S.Ct. 921 (1953); see Romero v. International Terminal Operating Co., 358 U.S. 354, 381–384, 79 S.Ct. 468 (1959); Boczek, op. cit., supra, note 7, at 178–180.

tended to have any application to foreign registered vessels employing alien seamen.

Petitioners say that the language of the Act may be read literally as including foreign-flag vessels within its coverage. But, as in Benz, they have been unable to point to any specific language in the Act itself or in its extensive legislative history that reflects such a congressional intent. Indeed, the opposite is true as we found in Benz, where we pointed to the language of Chairman Hartley characterizing the Act as "a bill of rights both for American workingmen and for their employers." 353 U.S., at 144, 77 S.Ct., at 702. We continue to believe that if the sponsors of the original Act or of its amendments conceived of the application now sought by the Board they failed to translate such thoughts into describing the boundaries of the Act as including foreign-flag vessels manned by alien crews. Therefore, we find no basis for a construction which would exert United States jurisdiction over and apply its laws to the internal management and affairs of the vessels here flying the Honduran flag, contrary to the recognition long afforded them not only by our State Department [11] but also by the Congress.[12] In addition, our attention is called to the well-established rule of international law that the law of the flag state ordinarily governs the internal affairs of a ship. See Wildenhus's Case, supra, 120 U.S., at 12, 7 S.Ct., at 387; Colombos, The International Law of the Sea (3d rev. ed. 1954), 222–223. The possibility of international discord cannot therefore be gainsaid. Especially is this true on account of the concurrent application of the Act and the Honduran Labor Code that would result with our approval of jurisdiction. Sociedad, currently the exclusive bargaining agent of Empresa under Honduran law, would have a head-on collision with N. M. U. should it become the exclusive bargaining agent under the Act. This would be aggravated by the fact that under Honduran law N. M. U. is prohibited from representing the seamen on Honduran-flag ships even in the absence of a recognized bargaining agent. Thus even though Sociedad withdrew from such an intramural labor fight—a highly unlikely circumstance—questions of such international import would remain as to invite retaliatory action from other nations as well as Honduras.

The presence of such highly charged international circumstances brings to mind the admonition of Mr. Chief Justice Marshall in The Charming Betsy, 2 Cranch 64, 118 (1804), that "an act of congress ought never to be construed to violate the law of nations if any, other possible construction remains * * *." We therefore conclude, as

---

11. State Department regulations provide that a foreign vessel includes "any vessel regardless of ownership, which is documented under the laws of a foreign country." 22 CFR § 81.-1(f).

12. Article X of the Treaty of Friendship, Commerce and Consular Rights between Honduras and the United States, 45 Stat. 2618 (1927), provides that merchant vessels flying the flags and having the papers of either country "shall, both within the territorial waters of the other High Contracting Party and on the high seas, be deemed to be the vessels of the Party whose flag is flown."

we did in Benz, that for us to sanction the exercise of local sovereignty under such conditions in this "delicate field of international relations there must be present the affirmative intention of the Congress clearly expressed." 353 U.S., at 147, 77 S.Ct., at 704. Since neither we nor the parties are able to find any such clear expression, we hold that the Board was without jurisdiction to order the election. This is not to imply, however, "any impairment of our own sovereignty, or limitation of the power of Congress" in this field. Lauritzen v. Larsen, 345 U.S. 571, 578, 73 S.Ct. 921 (1953). In fact, just as we directed the parties in Benz to the Congress, which "alone has the facilities necessary to make fairly such an important policy decision," 353 U.S., at 147, we conclude here that the arguments should be directed to the Congress rather than to us. Cf. Lauritzen v. Larsen, supra, 345 U.S., at 593, 73 S.Ct., at 933, 934.

The judgment of the District Court is therefore affirmed in No. 107. The judgment of the Court of Appeals in Nos. 91 and 93 is vacated and the cases are remanded to that court, with instructions that it remand to the District Court for dismissal of the complaint in light of our decision in No. 107. It is so ordered.

Mr. Justice DOUGLAS, concurring. * * * The practical effect of our decision is to shift from all the taxpayers to seamen alone the main burden of financing an executive policy of assuring the availability of an adequate American-owned merchant fleet for federal use during national emergencies. * * *

Question. Suppose the Congress of the United States had specifically provided that the National Labor Relations Act applied to flag of convenience vessels. Would the application of the act be consistent with international law? See p. 443 dealing with the extraterritorial reach of the antitrust laws of the United States.

SECTION B.   WATERS WITHIN THE TERRITORY

---

1.   BASELINE SEPARATING INTERNAL WATERS
FROM TERRITORIAL SEA

1. *Significance of baseline.* The baseline separates internal waters from the territorial sea; the breadth of the territorial sea is measured from that line. The manner in which the baseline is drawn is important because this can be done in such a way as to thrust it far away from the coast with two resulting consequences: first, expansion of the area of inland waters lying between the coast and the baseline; second, placing the outer limit of the territorial sea, which is measured from the baseline, at great distances from the coast.

Suppose, by way of exaggerated example, that the baseline on the eastern coast of the United States were drawn by means of a straight line running from Maine to the tip of Florida. A huge area of the sea inside the baseline would become internal waters, i. e. assimilated to land territory so far as concerns the jurisdiction of the United States. Moreover the outer limit of the territorial sea of the United States would at some points be so many miles from the coast as to make arguments about the breadth of the territorial sea entirely meaningless.

2. *The Fisheries case in the International Court of Justice.* Both the Geneva Convention on the Territorial Sea and the Contiguous Zone and the United Nations Draft Convention on the Law of the Sea contain provisions on the delineation of the baseline. Prior to these formulations, the International Court of Justice had dealt with the delineation of the baseline in the Fisheries Case (United Kingdom v. Norway), [1951] I.C.J.Rep. 116.

The case involved a portion of the coastline of Norway with a very distinctive configuration, i. e., a mountainous coast on the mainland constantly opening into indentations penetrating great distances inland (fjords) and in front of it a "skjærgaard", or rock rampart, made up of large and small islands mountainous in character, islets, rocks and reefs, all in effect an extension of the mainland. Of this coastline the court said: "The coast of the mainland does not constitute, as it does in practically all other countries, a clear dividing line between land and sea. What matters, what really constitutes the Norwegian coastline, is the outerline of the "skjærgaard." (at 127)

Norway delineated its baseline in this region by drawing straight lines connecting fixed points on the islands, islets, rocks, and reefs of the skjærgaard, thus claiming as inland waters the rich and extensive fishing grounds landward of the baseline. The court held that the straight baselines method used by Norway, and the straight baselines drawn by Norway in application of this method, were not contrary to international law.

3. *Baseline under Geneva Convention and U.N. Draft Convention.* The Geneva Convention on the Territorial Sea and the Contiguous Zone deals in detail with the drawing of the baseline in Articles 3–5 and 7–13. The United Nations Draft Convention on the Law of the Sea essentially reproduces those provisions, with a few additions, in Articles 4 through 16. For both, see the Documentary Supplement.

Article 4 of the first and 7 of the second deal specifically with the use of the straight baselines method.

Article 5 of the Geneva text and Article 8(2) of the draft make provision for a right of innocent passage, under certain conditions, through inland waters created by the use of the straight baselines method. Why? *b/c might not be apparent*

4. *Archipelagic baselines.* Totally new in the draft is the provision made by Article 47 for the drawing of straight archipelagic baselines.

The drawing of such baselines, limited in length to 100–125 miles between the islands of an archipelago, obviously is susceptible of enclosing vast areas of waters previously considered as high seas and used for international navigation. Article 49 stipulates for them a new status, archipelagic waters, over which the archipelagic state has sovereignty except for the regime of sea lanes.

The sea lanes which the archipelagic state may establish in its archipelagic waters are intended to provide continuous and expeditious passage of foreign ships (and aircraft), and all ships (and aircraft) enjoy the right of archipelagic sea lane passage in such sea lanes. See the elaborate provisions in point in Article 53. Apparently, the right of innocent passage can be restricted by the coastal state by compelling the use of sea lanes.

Within archipelagic waters, the archipelagic state may draw closing lines for the delineation of internal waters. Article 50.

———

ILLUSTRATIONS FROM PEARCY,[a] MEASUREMENT OF THE U. S. TERRITORIAL SEA

40 United States Department of State Bulletin 963 (1959).

[The illustrations below show how the baseline is drawn when the coastline does not present the special geographic features of the Norwegian coastline in the Fisheries case or those of an archipelago.]

a. Geographer of the U. S. Department of State.

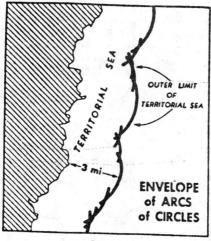

Figure 1

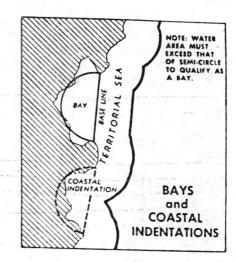

Figure 2

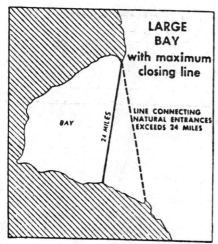

Figure 3

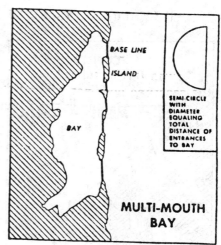

Figure 4

[C3007]

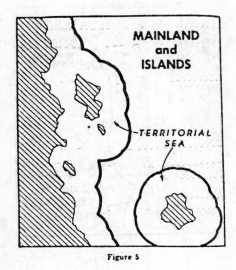

Figure 5

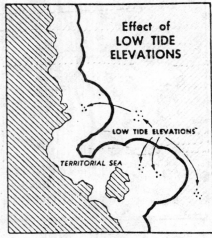

Figure 6

Figure 7

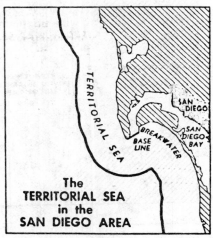

Figure 8

[C3008]

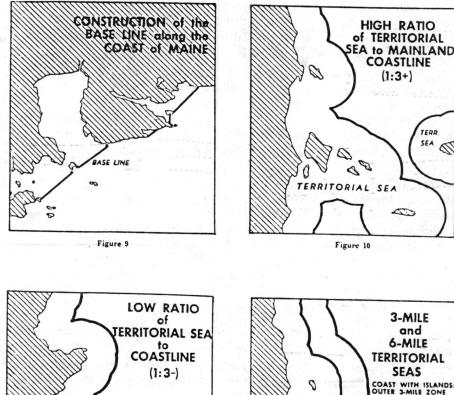

Figure 9

Figure 10

Figure 11

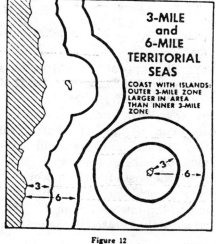

Figure 12

[C3009]

2. FOREIGN VESSELS IN INTERNAL WATERS

Consent to entry into internal waters. Foreign vessels enter the internal waters of a coastal state only with its consent. As to merchant vessels, the consent is usually implied. Prohibiting the entry of foreign merchant vessels is the exception rather than the rule in practice. The entry, however, may be conditioned upon the giving of notice. In September 1980, the merchant vessels of the People's Republic of China received permission to enter 55 ports in the United

States on four-day notice and other ports on a longer notice, while merchant vessels of the United States were given access to 20 Chinese ports on seven-day notice. Editorial, The Times-Picayune/The States-Item, September 20, 1980, Sec. 1, p. 12.

As to naval vessels, formal notification of their intended visit is customary. Unless the coastal state expressly prohibits the visit, naval vessels are deemed to have received the necessary consent. Some states, nevertheless, insist on issuing a prior authorization before allowing a foreign naval vessel to enter its internal waters. Algeria is such a state and permits entry following notification alone only if the foreign naval vessel is compelled to come in by bad weather or by some other force majeure. Bendeddouche, Note sur la Réglementation Algérienne du Passage et du Séjour des Navires de Guerre Etrangers dans les Eaux Territoriales et Intérieures de l'Algérie (Décret du 5 Octobre 1972), XI Revue Algérienne des Sciences Juridiques Economiques et Politiques 461, 469 (1974).

[handwritten margin notes: Held: - imprisonment of Belgian national by NJ authorities for murder was proper and did not contravene Treaty between U.S. + Belgium were nature of the crime was such that it disturbed the peace + tranquility of the port, thus NJ authorities had power to enforce local law in this case]

WILDENHUS'S CASE

United States Supreme Court, 1887.
120 U.S. 1, 7 S.Ct. 385.

This appeal brought up an application made to the Circuit Court of the United States for the District of New Jersey, by Charles Mali, the "Consul of His Majesty the King of the Belgians, for the States of New York and New Jersey, in the United States," for himself as such consul, "and in behalf of one Joseph Wildenhus, one Gionviennie Gobnbosich, and one John J. Ostenmeyer," for the release, upon a writ of habeas corpus, of Wildenhus, Gobnbosich, and Ostenmeyer from the custody of the keeper of the common jail of Hudson County, New Jersey, and their delivery to the consul, "to be dealt with according to the law of Belgium." The facts on which the application rested were thus stated in the petition for the writ:

Second. That on or about the sixth day of October, 1886, on board the Belgian steamship Noordland, there occurred an affray between the said Joseph Wildenhus and one Fijens, wherein and whereby it is charged that the said Wildenhus stabbed with a knife and inflicted upon the said Fijens a mortal wound, of which he afterwards died.

Third. That the said Wildenhus is a subject of the Kingdom of Belgium and has his domicil therein, and is one of the crew of the said steamship Noordland, and was such when the said affray occurred.

Fourth. That the said Fijens was also a subject of Belgium and had his domicil and residence therein, and at the time of the said affray, as well as at the time of his subsequent death, was one of the crew of the said steamship.

Fifth. That at the time said affray occurred the said steamship Noordland was lying moored at the dock of the port of Jersey City, in said state of New Jersey.

Sixth. That the said affray occurred and ended wholly below the deck of the said steamship, and that the tranquillity of the said port of Jersey City was in nowise disturbed or endangered thereby.

Seventh. That said affray occurred in the presence of several witnesses all of whom were and still are of the crew of the said vessel, and that no other person or persons except those of the crew of said vessel were present or near by.

Eighth. Your petitioner therefore respectfully shows unto this honorable court that the said affray occurred outside of the jurisdiction of the said state of New Jersey.

Ninth. But, notwithstanding the foregoing facts, your petitioner respectfully further shows that the police authorities of Jersey City, in said state of New Jersey, have arrested the said Joseph Wildenhus, and also the said Gionviennie Gobnbosich and John J. Ostenmeyer, of the crew of the said vessel (one of whom is a quartermaster thereof), and that said Joseph Wildenhus has been committed by a police magistrate, acting under the authority of the said state, to the common jail of the county of Hudson, on a charge of an indictable offence under the laws of the said state of New Jersey, and is now held in confinement by the keeper of the said jail, and that the others of the said crew arrested as aforesaid are also detained in custody and confinement as witnesses to testify in such proceedings as may hereafter be had against the said Wildenhus.

* * *

Article XI of a Convention between the United States and Belgium "concerning the rights, privileges, and immunities of consular officers," concluded March 9, 1880, and proclaimed by the President of the United States, March 1, 1881, 21 Stat. 776, 781, is as follows:

The respective consuls-general, consuls, vice-consuls, and consular agents shall have exclusive charge of the internal order of the merchant vessels of their nation, and shall alone take cognizance of all differences which may arise, either at sea or in port, between the captains, officers, and crews, without exception, particularly with reference to the adjustment of wages and the execution of contracts. The local authorities shall not interfere, except when the disorder that has arisen is of such a nature as to disturb tranquillity and public order on shore, or in the port, or when a person of the country or not belonging to the crew, shall be concerned therein.

In all other cases, the aforesaid authorities shall confine themselves to lending aid to the consuls and vice-consuls or consular agents, if they are requested by them to do so, in causing the arrest and imprisonment of any person whose name is inscribed on the crew list, whenever, for any cause, the said officers shall think proper.

The claim of the consul was, that, by the law of nations, and the provisions of this treaty, the offence with which Wildenhus was charged is "solely cognizable by the authority of the laws of the Kingdom of Belgium," and that the State of New Jersey was without jurisdiction in the premises. The Circuit Court refused to deliver the prisoners to the consul and remanded them to the custody of the jailer. 28 Fed.Rep. 924. To reverse that decision this appeal was taken.

* * *

Mr. Chief Justice WAITE, after stating the case as above reported, delivered the opinion of the court.

By §§ 751 and 753 of the Revised Statutes the courts of the United States have power to issue writs of habeas corpus which shall extend to prisoners in jail when they are in "custody in violation of the Constitution or a law or treaty of the United States," and the question we have to consider is, whether these prisoners are held in violation of the provisions of the existing treaty between the United States and Belgium.

It is part of the law of civilized nations that when a merchant vessel of one country enters the ports of another for the purposes of trade, it subjects itself to the law of the place to which it goes, unless by treaty or otherwise the two countries have come to some different understanding or agreement; for, as was said by Chief Justice Marshall in The Exchange, 7 Cranch, 116, 144, "it would be obviously inconvenient and dangerous to society, and would subject the laws to continual infraction, and the government to degradation, if such * * * merchants did not owe temporary and local allegiance, and were not amenable to the jurisdiction of the country." * * * And the English judges have uniformly recognized the rights of the courts of the country of which the port is part to punish crimes committed by one foreigner on another in a foreign merchant ship. * * * As the owner has voluntarily taken his vessel for his own private purposes to a place within the dominion of a government other than his own, and from which he seeks protection during his stay, he owes that government such allegiance for the time being as is due for the protection to which he becomes entitled.

From experience, however, it was found long ago that it would be beneficial to commerce if the local government would abstain from interfering with the internal discipline of the ship, and the general regulation of the rights and duties of the officers and crew towards the vessel or among themselves. And so by comity it came to be generally understood among civilized nations that all matters of discipline and all things done on board which affected only the vessel or those belonging to her, and did not involve the peace or dignity of the country, or the tranquillity of the port, should be left by the local government to be dealt with by the authorities of the nation to which the vessel belonged as the laws of that nation or the interests of its commerce should require. But if crimes are committed on board of a character to disturb the peace and tranquillity of the country to which the vessel has been brought, the offenders have never by comity or usage been entitled to any exemption from the operation of the local laws for their punishment, if the local tribunals see fit to assert their authority. Such being the general public law on this subject, treaties and conventions have been entered into by nations having commercial intercourse, the purpose of which was to settle and define the rights and duties of the contracting parties with respect to each other in these particulars, and thus prevent the inconvenience that might arise from attempts to exercise conflicting jurisdictions.

     *   *   *

Next came a form of convention which in terms gave the consuls authority to cause proper order to be maintained on board and to decide disputes between the officers and crew, but allowed the local authorities to interfere if the disorders taking place on board were of such a nature as to disturb the public tranquillity, and that is substantially all there is in the convention with Belgium which we have now to consider. This treaty is the law which now governs the conduct of the United States and Belgium towards each other in this particular. Each nation has granted to the other such local jurisdiction within its own dominion as may be necessary to maintain order on board a merchant vessel, but has reserved to itself the right to interfere if the disorder on board is of a nature to disturb the public tranquillity.

The treaty is part of the supreme law of the United States, and has the same force and effect in New Jersey that it is entitled to elsewhere. If it gives the consul of Belgium exclusive jurisdiction over the offence which it is alleged has been committed within the territory of New Jersey, we see no reason why he may not enforce his rights under the treaty by writ of habeas corpus in any proper court of the United States. This being the case, the only important question left for our determination is whether the thing which has been done—the disorder that has arisen—on board this vessel is of a nature to disturb the public peace, or, as some writers term it, the "public repose" of the people who look to the state of New Jersey for their protection. If the thing done—"the disorder," as it is called in the treaty—is of a character to affect those on shore or in the port when it becomes known, the fact that only those on the ship saw it when it was done is a matter of no moment. Those who are not on the vessel pay no special attention to the mere disputes or quarrels of the seamen while on board, whether they occur under deck or above. Neither do they as a rule care for anything done on board which relates only to the discipline of the ship, or to the preservation of order and authority. Not so, however, with crimes which from their gravity awaken a public interest as soon as they become known, and especially those of a character which every civilized nation considers itself bound to provide a severe punishment for when committed within its own jurisdiction. In such cases inquiry is certain to be instituted at once to ascertain how or why the thing was done, and the popular excitement rises or falls as the news spreads and the facts become known. It is not alone the publicity of the act, or the noise and clamor which attends it, that fixes the nature of the crime, but the act itself. If that is of a character to awaken public interest when it becomes known, it is a "disorder" the nature of which is to affect the community at large, and consequently to invoke the power of the local government whose people have been disturbed by what was done. The very nature of such an act is to disturb the quiet of a peaceful community, and to create, in the language of the treaty, a "disorder" which will "disturb tranquillity and public order on shore or in the port." The principle which governs the whole matter is this: Disorders which disturb only the peace of the ship or those on board are to be dealt with exclusively by the sovereignty of the home of the ship, but those which disturb the public peace may be suppressed, and, if need be, the offenders punished by the proper authorities of the local jurisdiction. It may not be easy at all times to determine to which of the two jurisdictions a particular act of disorder belongs. Much will undoubtedly depend on the attending circumstances of the particular case, but all must concede that felonious homicide is a subject for the local jurisdiction, and that if the proper authorities are proceeding with the case in a regular way, the consul has no right to interfere to prevent it. That, according to the petition for the habeas corpus, is this case.

> * * *

The judgment of the Circuit Court is affirmed.

---

1. *Peace of the port doctrine in customary international law.* Is a treaty necessary for the application of the doctrine enunciated by the court, or is it a rule of international law arising from custom and practice?

According to Section 83.8b of Title 22 of the U.S. Code of Federal Regulations, an offense which does not involve the peace of the port "is usually left" by local governments to be adjusted by officers of the vessel. The jurisdiction of U.S. vessels in foreign ports in such a class of cases, the section indicates, is insured in many places by a treaty of friendship, commerce and navigation or by a consular convention. Even in the absence of a treaty, the section specifies, the local foreign government "will usually refrain" from intervening.

The State v. Jannopulos, Italy, Court of Naples, 1974, I Italian Yearbook of International Law 268 (1975) *, involved a Greek sailor on a Cypriot vessel in the port of Naples. He was charged with pos-

* Reprinted by permission of Scientifica
s.r.l., Naples.

session of drugs when a considerable quantity of marijuana was found in his cabin. There was no applicable treaty between Italy and Cyprus. The court acquitted the defendant on the ground that the mere possession of drugs aboard a foreign vessel, without a showing of an intent to sell the drugs in Italy, was what the court called an internal matter. The decision stated in part:

> * * * Modern writers on international law and international state practice * * * recognise the existence of an international custom whereby a foreign ship retains its separate identity as long as it does not interfere in local life by acts which cause or are likely to cause a breach of the peace on shore. Only such an interference would create a link between the shore and the ship, so that in that case the coastal State would be entitled to intervene because of its interest in the peaceful course of life in its own community on shore.
>
> That means that all so-called internal matters on board the ship are outside the criminal jurisdiction of the coastal State, unless they infringe the interest of that State in the peaceful course of life in its own community on shore.
>
> * * *
>
> In the case before us the defendant was in possession of drugs in his cabin on board a Cypriot ship, and there is no evidence at all that he intended to sell it in Italy (and in particular within the jurisdiction of the Court of Naples). We must suppose that he intended to sell it in some other port on the ship's route. There is therefore no link at all between this purely "internal" fact, on board, and the community on shore, whose safety and peaceful course of life and activity were not affected in the slightest by the simple fact of possession. Since the fact occurred in a place which cannot be considered subject to Italian sovereignty because of an exception under international law, we declare that the Italian legal authorities have no jurisdiction and that the case falls under the criminal jurisdiction of the Republic of Cyprus. (at 269–270)

Compare the language used by the Argentinian court in Re Bianchi, supra p. 153, which identifies peace of the port as Italian doctrine.

The doctrine, so far as it applies to passage through the territorial sea, is labelled "peace of the country" in Article 19, 1(b) of the 1958 Convention on the Territorial Sea and Contiguous Zone. See the Documentary Supplement and this chapter, p. 187.

2. *Foreign naval vessels in port.* In the Schooner Exchange v. McFaddon, 7 Cranch 116 (U.S. 1812), Chief Justice Marshall said: "[T]he Exchange being a public armed ship, in the service of a foreign sovereign, with whom the government of the United States is at peace, and having entered an American port open for her reception, on the terms on which ships of war are generally permitted to enter the ports of a friendly power, must be considered as having come into the

American territory, under an implied promise that   *   *   *   she should be exempt from the jurisdiction of the country."   (at 147)

In 1975, two sailors from the HMS Hermes, a British aircraft carrier, were arrested and held in jail in Quebec for breaking into the apartment of a Canadian, beating him up and causing considerable damage to the premises. Thereupon a Canadian federal court enjoined the vessel from departing. It left, without the two sailors, in defiance of the injunction. The British consulate in Quebec issued a communiqué justifying the departure on the ground that the order of a federal court in Canada could not be enforced against a vessel of the sovereign forces of Her Majesty. Rousseau, in reporting the incident in his Chronique des Faits Internationaux, approved. 80 Revue Générale de Droit International Public 233 (1976).

3. *Note.* Neither the Geneva Convention on the Territorial Sea and the Contiguous Zone, nor the United Nations Draft Convention, deals with the jurisdictional issues raised by the presence in port of foreign merchant or naval vessels.

HOFF, ADMINISTRATRIX
(UNITED STATES v. UNITED MEXICAN STATES)

General Claims Commission, 1929.
IV U.N.Rep.Int'l Arb. Awards 444.

Commissioner NIELSEN, for the Commission:

Claim in the amount of $10,000.00 with interest is made in this case by the United States of America in behalf of Kate Allison Hoff, Administratrix of the estate of Samuel B. Allison. The latter was the owner of a small American schooner called the Rebecca, which together with its cargo was seized by Mexican authorities at Tampico in 1884. Allegations with respect to the occurrences on which the claim is predicated are made in the Memorial in substance as follows:

The Rebecca was built in the United States and registered at Galveston, Texas. Its approximate value was $5,000.00. In the month of January, 1884, Gilbert F. Dujay, the master of the vessel, loaded it at a small port called Patersonville, nine miles above Morgan City, in the State of Louisiana, with a cargo consisting of six cases of merchandise destined for Brazos Santiago, Texas, and of a consignment of lumber for Tampico, Mexico. The vessel cleared at Brashear City, now known as Morgan City, on the 30th day of January, 1884, bound for Santiago, Texas. When it reached a point off this port the wind and the tide were so high that it was unsafe to enter. While lying off Brazos Santiago, on the 13th of February, waiting for a favorable opportunity to enter the port, an adverse wind from the north became so strong and the sea so rough, that the vessel was driven to the southward before a furious wind and sea, and when the wind abated it was found that the vessel was in a disabled and unsafe condition off the port of Tampico. The master, realizing the dangerous condition of his vessel, entered the port of Tampico as the nearest place of safety for the vessel, cargo and crew. The crew concurred in and advised such action. When the Rebecca entered the port she was leaking badly. Her standing rigging had been torn away. The cabin windows were broken. The cooking stove was so badly broken it could not be used. While at sea the vessel began to leak so that the water reached the cases of merchandise, and the crew was compelled to break open the packages and store them so that they would not be ruined by the water.

When the Rebecca entered the port the master presented to the Mexican customs official a manifest for the goods destined for Tampico and a so-called "master's manifest" for the consignment for Brazos Santiago, Texas, which met the requirements of the law of the United States. As soon as the vessel reached Tampico, which was on Sunday afternoon, February 17th, it was anchored off the custom house and a protest of distress was immediately entered with A. J. Cassard, the American Consul at that port.

On the day following the arrival at Tampico, February 18, 1884, the Mexican custom house officials demanded from the master of the Rebecca the packages of merchandise on board the vessel. The demand was refused and thereupon the packages were taken by force and no receipt or other evidence of possession by the custom house authorities was given.

On the 21st of February the master was arrested on a charge of attempt to smuggle, was placed in the barracks with armed soldiers guarding him, was not permitted to speak to anyone, and was kept in close confinement until the day following, a period of 28 hours, when he was brought before the Judge of the District Court at Tampico, and without the privilege of having counsel, was tried and was acquitted and released. On the 23rd of February the master was again arrested by the Mexican authorities and was required to give bond for his appearance before the Criminal Court at Tampico to answer a charge of bringing goods into a Mexican port without proper papers. While awaiting trial he remained under bond, but without permission to leave Mexico, until the 24th day of April, a period of over two months. On that date a decree was entered by the court which released the master from bail but assessed treble damages against the merchandise seized, and charged the master with the cost of revenue stamps used in the proceedings. Because of the refusal and inability of the master to pay the penalties thus assessed, the Rebecca and its cargo were sold by order of court, and the proceeds were applied to the Federal Treasury, a balance being distributed among certain customs employees.

*   *   *

It is of course well established that, when a merchant vessel belonging to one nation enters the territorial waters of another nation, it becomes amenable to the jurisdiction of the latter and is subject to its laws, except in so far as treaty stipulations may relieve the vessel from the operation of local laws. On the other hand, there appears to be general recognition among the nations of the world of what may doubtless be considered to be an exception, or perhaps it may be said two exceptions, to this general, fundamental rule of subjection to local jurisdiction over vessels in foreign ports.

Recognition has been given to the so-called right of "innocent passage" for vessels through the maritime belt in so far as it forms a part of the high seas for international traffic. Similarly, recognition has also been given—perhaps it may be said in a more concrete and emphatic manner—to the immunity of a ship whose presence in territorial waters is due to a superior force. The principles with respect to the status of a vessel in "distress" find recognition both in domestic laws and in international law. * * *

* * *

While recognizing the general principle of immunity of vessels in distress, domestic courts and international courts have frequently given consideration to the question as to the degree of necessity prompting vessels to seek refuge. It has been said that the necessity must be urgent. It seems possible to formulate certain reasonably concrete criteria applicable and controlling in the instant case. Assuredly a ship floundering in distress, resulting either from the weather or from other causes affecting management of the vessel, need not be in such a condition that it is dashed helplessly on the shore or against rocks before a claim of distress can properly be invoked in its behalf. The fact that it may be able to come into port under its own power can obviously not be cited as conclusive evidence that the plea is unjustifiable. If a captain delayed seeking refuge until his ship was wrecked, obviously he would not be using his best judgment with a view to the preservation of the ship, the cargo and the lives of people on board. Clearly an important consideration may be the determination of the question whether there is any evidence in a given case of a fraudulent attempt to circumvent local laws. And even in the absence of any such attempt, it can probably be correctly said that a mere matter of convenience in making repairs or in avoiding a measure of difficulty in navigation can not justify a disregard of local laws.

The Rebecca did sail into Tampico, as observed by the judge who condemned the vessel, under its own power. However, it did not enter the port until after it had for three days, in a crippled condition, been contending with a storm in an attempt to enter the port at Brazos Santiago, Texas. It is therefore certain that the vessel did not by choice abandon its attempt to make port at that place, but only because according to the best judgment of the captain and his crew absolute necessity so required. In such a case a captain's judgment would scarcely seem subject to question. It may also be concluded from the evidence in the case that a well grounded apprehension of the loss of the vessel and cargo and persons on board prompted the captain to turn south towards Tampico. It was argued in behalf of the United States that under the conditions of the weather it could be assumed that no other port of refuge was available. And even if such were not the case, there would seem to be no reason why refuge should not have been sought at Tampico. The fact that the ship had cargo for that place in addition to that consigned to Brazos Santiago, did not make the former any less available as the port of refuge. It may be concluded from the evidence that the captain had no intent to perpetrate a fraud on Mexican customs laws. Indeed his acquittal on the criminal charge preferred against him appears to be conclusive on that point, even if there were no other evidence bearing on the matter which there is. It may also be concluded that the captain had no intent merely as a matter of convenience to flout Mexican laws. This very small vessel had been driven before a strong north wind; its cabin had been damaged; its pumps had been broken and repaired; the cooking stove on the vessel had been rendered useless; there were one and a half to two feet of water in the vessel; and it had been leaking.

* * * The ship entered the port of Tampico in distress, and the seizure of both the vessel and cargo was wrongful.

* * *

Decision

The United Mexican States shall pay to the United States of America on behalf of Kate A. Hoff the sum of $5,000.00, with interest at the rate of six per centum per annum from April 24, 1884, to the date on which the last award is rendered by the Commission.

---

1. *Basis of decision.* The compromise establishing the USA/Mexican General Claims Commission provided that the claims to be submitted to the commission should be decided "in accordance with the principles of international law, justice and equity." IV U.N.Rep.Int'l Arb.Awards 11, 12.

2. *Nuclear vessels.* A Convention on the Liability of Operators of Nuclear Ships was signed at Brussels, May 25, 1962. Its text appears at 57 Am.J.Int'l L. 268 (1963). Article 17 provides:

Nothing in this Convention shall affect any right which a Contracting State may have under international law to deny access to its waters and harbours to nuclear ships licensed by another Contracting State, even when it has formally complied with all the provisions of this Convention.

Does a contracting state have a right under international law to deny access to a nuclear ship entering in distress? What if the distress is a leaking nuclear reactor? See the Restatement of the Foreign Relations Law of the United States, Reporters' Note to Section 48 (1965).

3. *Note.* Neither the Geneva Convention on the Territorial Sea and the Contiguous Zone, nor the United Nations Draft Convention

on the Law of the Sea, deals with the jurisdictional issues raised by the entry in distress into internal waters of a foreign vessel.

---

3.   BREADTH OF THE TERRITORIAL SEA

THE ORIGIN OF THE THREE–MILE LIMIT

Wilkes, The Use of World Resources Without
Conflict: Myths About the Territorial Sea.
14 Wayne Law Review 441 (1968).*

MYTH #1

"The concept of the territorial sea originated from the distance a cannon could shoot from land. Thus, with increased capabilities of military control, we should have an increased territorial sea."

FACT

The concept of a narrow belt of territorial sea beyond which the seas would be open to vessels of all nations did not originate with late eighteenth century references to a "cannon shot." This concept may be traced to Hugo de Groot's Mare Liberum, first published in 1609, when he excepted the belt of sea "visible from shore" from the compelling arguments by which he established the doctrine of "Freedom of the Seas."

It is true that de Groot based this doctrine on the two-pronged argument that (1) the sea was not reducible to possession because of its limitlessness, and (2) the sea must remain free and open to all for navigation, trade and fishing because it is self-evidently adapted for the use of all. Yet he never limited his concept of the territorial belt to any supposed "zone of effective control," nor did he ever permit the "use" argument to become dependent on the "possession" argument. Indeed, in something akin to a prevision of the approach which was to be taken with regard to "Texas towers" under the Convention on the Continental Shelf, Hugo de Groot dealt with the question of attempts to appropriate the sea through piles that could be driven into it. He recognized that piles could be driven into the sea, and that the man who drove them would own them. Nevertheless, the freedom of the seas was paramount and could neither be diminished nor interfered with by this type of possession.

It is vital to appreciate the context in which de Groot's doctrine contested Spanish, Portuguese and Venetian claims to be able to appropriate the seas by establishing effective military control over them, a contest that was not fully won until the nineteenth century. After the Treaty of Tordesillas of 1494, Spain and Portugal set about establishing dominion over the seas and lands divided between them along a line close to that assigned them by Pope Pius VI. By the time of de Groot's Mare Liberum, Spain had been enforcing "control by arms" over the Pacific Ocean and the Gulf of Mexico while Portugal had dominated the whole Atlantic south of Morocco and the Indian Ocean.

Over the next two centuries, these claims were disputed and were finally laid to rest in favor of a narrow belt of territorial sea beyond which all was open and free. The way in which the doctrine of this narrow belt was described differed from country to country and from time to time. For instance, the eighteenth century Dutch writer Bynkershoek, in a dissertation reaffirming the freedom of the seas doctrine in 1702, said that the power of the coastal state went only so far as the reach of its arms. In fact, for a very brief period a few nations actually made agreements between themselves to recognize sovereignty within cannon shot range of the coastal state.

However, it was not the "cannon shot" rule that gained the widest acceptance. The marine league, which had the virtues of being fixed and of guaranteeing the narrowness of the coastal state's encroachment on the free seas, became the most widely accepted. It is true that some early writers referred to the new three-mile rule as also matching the farthest range of a cannonball. However, it is not because British and American cannon shot three miles, Norwegian, Swedish and Danish cannon shot four miles and Spanish cannon shot nine miles that different rules emerged. The fact is that the British, American and continental marine league was three miles, the Scandinavian marine league was four miles, and the old Spanish marine league was nine miles. Indeed, six years after Jefferson obtained English agreement on a three-mile limit, the British rejected an American proposal to make the limit two leagues instead of one on the ground of increased ability of shore batteries to effect control. The rejection, accepted by the United States, was based in part on the British Law Officer's concern that "[i]f the right of territory is to extend to two Leagues, may not demand be set up to extend it to twenty or two hundred?"

We have lived to see such a 200-mile claim made in the Santiago Declaration on the Maritime Zone by Chile, Ecuador and Peru. The claim for such increased extension was made solely on the ground of fish and marine conservation. Ecuador, on the other hand, had just raised its territorial sea claim some twenty-one months before to a twelve-mile limit on the ground that military considerations had led nations to extend their territorial waters.

In each case of a claimed extension by Chile, Ecuador and Peru, we have seen reasons advanced for an assertion of total sovereignty that went beyond the circumstance upon which it was grounded. An attempt has been made to enlarge the small intrusion originally made into the open seas. In each case, there were two tacit assumptions made by the claimants: (1) that the self-interest of the coastal state overrides the interests of the 100-odd other nations of the planet;

and (2) that this self-interest is served, not by preserving freedom of the seas, but by narrowing the open area in some way.

The basic fallacy in both of these assumptions is that, with increased mobility, each nation will often be "the other nation" in someone else's claimed private preserve carved from the open seas. Any fair examination of the first assumption—that of the overriding interest—reveals that this rule is more likely to increase potential conflict rather than reduce it. Further, precisely because the chance of conflict is raised, the second assumption—that extension serves national interests—proves false as well.

The freedom of the seas doctrine is in every nation's self-interest for two reasons. First, it preserves access to seas away from its shore. Second, it reduces the possibility of military conflict with its risks of escalation. Thus the military necessity arguments advanced by Ecuador and some other Latin American states to justify initial extensions from the three-mile limit prove ill-conceived. One's real military necessity in this enlightened age is to foster climates that reduce conflict and pave the way for cooperation.

_____

Evolution of the position of the United States. From the time of Jefferson until 1958, the United States consistently supported a three-mile limit as the appropriate breadth of the territorial sea. At the First Geneva Conference on the Law of the Sea in 1958, the United States first maintained its support of the three-mile limit, but eventually shifted its support to a compromise proposal providing for a six-mile limit of territorial sea and, subject to certain qualifications, a six-mile fishing zone beyond it. The proposal was not adopted. It supported a similar proposal at the Second Geneva Conference on the Law of the Sea in 1960 and again the proposal failed. Since then the position of the United States has continued to evolve some more, as shown by the materials which follow.

_____

STATEMENT BY THE LEGAL ADVISER OF THE U. S. DEPARTMENT OF STATE CONCERNING A TWELVE–MILE LIMIT, AUGUST 3, 1971

66 American Journal of International Law 133 (1972).*

[Before UNCLOS III was convened, the United Nations had assigned the task of preparing draft articles for the conference to its Committee on the Peaceful Uses of the Seabed and the Ocean Floor Beyond the Limits of National Jurisdiction. The Committee met in Geneva from July 19 to August 27, 1971. John R. Stevenson, Legal Adviser of the Department of State and U.S. Representative to the

* Reprinted by permission of the American Society of International Law.

Committee, submitted on August 3 draft articles to Subcommittee II and made a statement, an excerpt of which follows.]

The first article presented by my Government would establish a maximum breadth of 12 miles for the territorial sea. The prime distinguishing characteristic of the territorial sea is that the coastal state exercises jurisdiction over navigation and overflight, subject to a limited right of innocent passage for vessels. We believe agreement must be reached on a narrow territorial sea. While my Government adheres to the traditional 3-mile limit, it is prepared to take into account the views of others and to agree to a treaty fixing the maximum breadth of the territorial sea at 12 nautical miles, if there is an adequate agreement concerning international straits—to which I shall refer shortly. We use the 12-mile figure because it represents the best—probably the only—possibility for reaching agreement. It is apparent that the overwhelming majority of states are prepared to accept the 12-mile limit. In most cases where broader jurisdictional claims have been made, the reasons for those claims were resource-oriented. We believe that the real concerns of those few states that have claimed broader limits for the territorial sea can be accommodated in the course of the work of this and the other subcommittees.

THE TWELVE–MILE LIMIT AT UNCLOS III

Stevenson and Oxman, the Third United Nations Conference on the Law of the Sea: The 1974 Caracas Session, 69 American Journal of International Law 1, 13–14, (1975).*

[John R. Stevenson, author of the preceding statement, had become Ambassador and Special Representative of the President of the United States for the Law of the Sea Conference, by the time he wrote the article.]

Agreement on a 12-mile territorial sea is so widespread that there were virtually no references to any other limit in the public debate, although other alternatives are presented in the working paper. Major conditions for acceptance of 12 miles as a maximum limit were agreement on unimpeded transit of straits and acceptance of a 200-mile exclusive economic zone.   *   *   *

* Reprinted by permission of the American Society of International Law.

Start here on Wed 2/11/87

4. FOREIGN VESSELS IN THE TERRITORIAL SEA

CORFU CHANNEL CASE (UNITED KINGDOM v. ALBANIA)

International Court of Justice, 1949.
[1949] I.C.J.Rep. 4.

[On May 5, 1946, British cruisers were fired upon by an Albanian battery while passing through the Corfu Channel, which, on that date, was clear of minefields.

The government of the United Kingdom protested on the ground that innocent passage through straits was a right recognized by international law. The government of Albania answered that neither foreign naval vessels, nor foreign merchant vessels, had a right under international law to pass through Albanian territorial waters without prior notification to, and permission of, the Albanian authorities.

On October 22, 1946, a squadron of British naval vessels proceeded through the Corfu Channel without the permission of the Albanian authorities and in the passage two destroyers were heavily damaged by mines, with loss of life.

By special agreement, the parties submitted questions to the International Court of Justice, one of which was whether the acts of the Royal Navy on October 22, 1946, violated the sovereignty of Albania.

The court dealt with the question as follows.]

The Court will now consider the Albanian contention that the United Kingdom Government violated Albanian sovereignty by sending the warships through this Strait without the previous authorization of the Albanian Government.

It is, in the opinion of the Court, generally recognized and in accordance with international custom that States in time of peace have a right to send their warships through straits used for international navigation between two parts of the high seas without the previous authorization of a coastal State, provided that the passage is innocent. Unless otherwise prescribed in an international convention, there is no right for a coastal State to prohibit such passage through straits in time of peace.

The Albanian Government does not dispute that the North Corfu Channel is a strait in the geographical sense; but it denies that this Channel belongs to the class of international highways through which a right of passage exists, on the grounds that it is only of secondary importance and not even a necessary route between two parts of the high seas, and that it is used almost exclusively for local traffic to and from the ports of Corfu and Saranda.

It may be asked whether the test is to be found in the volume of traffic passing through the Strait or in its greater or lesser importance for international navigation. But in the opinion of the Court

the decisive criterion is rather its geographical situation as connecting two parts of the high seas and the fact of its being used for international navigation. Nor can it be decisive that this Strait is not a necessary route between two parts of the high seas, but only an alternative passage between the Aegean and the Adriatic Seas. It has nevertheless been a useful route for international maritime traffic.
* * *

   * * *

Having regard to these various considerations, the Court has arrived at the conclusion that the North Corfu Channel should be considered as belonging to the class of international highways through which passage cannot be prohibited by a coastal State in time of peace.

On the other hand, it is a fact that the two coastal States did not maintain normal relations, that Greece had made territorial claims precisely with regard to a part of Albanian territory bordering on the Channel, that Greece had declared that she considered herself technically in a state of war with Albania, and that Albania, invoking the danger of Greek incursions, had considered it necessary to take certain measures of vigilance in this region. The Court is of opinion that Albania, in view of these exceptional circumstances, would have been justified in issuing regulations in respect of the passage of warships through the Strait, but not in prohibiting such passage or in subjecting it to the requirement of special authorization.

For these reasons the Court is unable to accept the Albanian contention that the Government of the United Kingdom has violated Albanian sovereignty by sending the warships through the Strait without having obtained the previous authorization of the Albanian Government.

In these circumstances, it is unnecessary to consider the more general question, much debated by the Parties, whether States under international law have a right to send warships in time of peace through territorial waters not included in a strait.
   * * *

Having thus examined the various contentions of the Albanian Government in so far as they appear to be relevant, the Court has arrived at the conclusion that the United Kingdom did not violate the sovereignty of Albania by reason of the acts of the British Navy in Albanian waters on October 22nd, 1946.
   * * *

---

1. *Innocent passage under Geneva Convention and U.N. Draft Convention.* The Geneva Convention on the Territorial Sea and the Contiguous Zone deals with the right of innocent passage in Articles 14–20. The United Nations Draft Convention on the Law of the Sea deals with it in Articles 17–32. For both texts, see the Documentary Supplement.

Some of the articles in the Draft Convention deal with matters not covered in the Geneva text. Article 21, for example, is new in providing a list of the matters with respect to which a coastal state may enact laws and regulations applicable to foreign vessels in innocent passage. So is Article 22, which specifies a coastal state may establish sea lanes and traffic separation schemes in the territorial sea and lists the factors it must take into account in so doing. Article 23 is also new in dealing with foreign nuclear-powered vessels and vessels carrying nuclear or other dangerous substances.

Other articles in the draft incorporate principles already in the Geneva text, but expand them by elaborating their meaning or application in great detail. Such is the case with Article 19 of the draft. It repeats paragraph 4 of Article 14 in the Geneva text: "Passage is innocent so long as it is not prejudicial to the peace, good order or security of the coastal state." Then it goes on to give a list of 12 activities which will render the passage prejudicial if engaged in by a foreign vessel in the territorial sea.

The net effect of such additions and expansions in the draft may be to give coastal states more control over foreign vessels in innocent passage than granted in the Geneva Convention. Whether the draft thus provides opportunities for coastal states to restrict innocent passage unduly is the issue raised by the problem which follows.

2. *Problem.* In 72 Revue Générale de Droit International Public 383 (1968), there appears an account of a minor naval incident which arose in 1967 between the United States and Algeria. It involved the claim of Algeria to 12 miles of territorial waters and the passage through them, about seven miles from the coast and during the night, of three minesweepers of the United States Navy. According to the Algerian communiqué, they were detected by radar but refused to identify themselves when summoned to do so by Algerian naval units, though they eventually made for the high seas.

In a diplomatic note to the United States, Algeria protested the passage as a violation of international law and the sovereignty of Algeria. In rejecting the protest, the United States pointed out, inter alia, that it did not recognize Algeria's claim to 12 miles of territorial waters and went on to state that, even if the minesweepers were in Algerian territorial waters, they were in innocent passage and, in view of their minimal defensive armament, could not constitute a threat to anyone.

Under paragraph 4 of Article 14 in the Geneva Convention, the United States could assert that the passage of the minesweepers was innocent because it could not have been "prejudicial to the peace, good order or security" of Algeria. Suppose Article 19 of the draft had been in effect instead of Article 14(4) of the Geneva text and further suppose the United States had recognized the claim of Algeria to 12 miles of territorial waters. Moreover, assume the United States naval units were carrying military material to Israel and keep in mind that the Security Council of the United Nations called upon

Israel in several resolutions to withdraw its armed forces from the Arab territories it occupied during the Six Day War.

Paragraph 2 of Article 19 in the Draft Convention provides: "Passage of a foreign ship shall be considered to be prejudicial to the peace, good order of security of the coastal state, if in the territorial sea it engages in * * * any threat or use of force against the sovereignty, territorial integrity or political independence of the coastal state, or in any other manner in violation of the principles of international law embodied in the Charter of the United Nations." Would Algeria's position be justified under this provision?

For arguments supporting an affirmative answer, see Reisman, The Regime of Straits and National Security: An Appraisal of International Lawmaking, 74 Am.J. Int'l L. 48 (1980). For arguments supporting a negative answer, see Moore, The Regime of Straits and the Third United National Conference on the Law of the Sea, 74 Am. J. Int'l L. 77 (1980). Both writings are based upon Articles 17–26 in the Informal Composite Negotiating Text as revised at the conclusion of the first part of the eighth session, March 19–April 27, 1979, of UNCLOS III. The articles remained unchanged in the Draft Convention.

3. *The new right of transit passage.* There are at least 120 straits in the world 24 miles in width, or less. Thus the universal adoption of 12 miles as the breadth of the territorial sea would place the waters in all such straits under the national jurisdiction of bordering states, subject only to a right of innocent passage. Transit through many of these straits is not important for international traffic, but transit through certain of them is essential for international maritime commerce and crucial for global deployment of naval power.

In preparation for the 1958 Geneva Conference on the Law of the Sea, the Secretariat of the United Nations made a study of straits constituting routes for international traffic which would be affected should 12 miles become the breadth of the territorial sea. The study listed 33. I United Nations Conference on the Law of the Sea 114 (1958).

The Office of the Geographer of the United States Department of State has issued a chart entitled World Straits Affected by a 12 Mile Territorial Sea on which there appears the notation: "Capitalization used to denote major straits from other and minor straits." From this notation, Pirtle infers that the straits whose names are in capitals are of strategic significance to the security of the United States. Transit Rights and U.S. Security Interests in International Straits: The "Straits Debate" Revisited, 5 Ocean Development and International Law 477, 488 (1978). These straits include some straits not listed in the United Nations study.[a]

a. The United Nations study lists the following straits: Bab el Mandeb, Gibraltar, Zanzibar Channel, The Serpent's Mouth, The Dragon's Mouth, St. Lucia Channel, Strait between St. Lucia and St. Vincent, Dominica Channel, Straits between Dominica and Guadeloupe, Magellan, Juan de Fuca, Chosen, Hainan, Palk, Malacca, Ombae, Soenda, San Bernardino, Su-

From the moment the United States announced that it was willing to support 12 miles as the breadth of the territorial sea, it made its acceptance of the limit conditional upon the recognition by the community of nations of a new right of free transit through international straits.   Thus, John R. Stevenson, whose statement supporting the 12 mile limit appears supra at p. 179, proposed at the same time a draft article providing in part: "In straits used for international navigation between one part of the high seas and another part of the high seas or the territorial sea of a foreign state, all ships and aircraft in transit shall enjoy the same freedom of navigation and overflight, for the purpose of transit through and over such straits, as they have on the high seas."   66 Am.J.Int'l L. 133, 135 (1972).

At UNCLOS III, a right of free transit was sharply opposed at first, partly because it availed warships and submerged submarines. "Many observers tend to believe that the right of free transit for warships and submarines involves such a drastic change in the extant legal practice that even its most ardent supporters, the superpowers, cannot realistically expect it to be accepted, and that it is merely a negotiating position."   Shyam, International Straits and Ocean Law, 15 Indian Journal of International Law 17, 33 (1975).   Eventually a compromise was reached and a right of transit passage included in Part III, Straits Used for International Navigation—Articles 34–44—of the Draft Convention.

For conflicting interpretations of these articles as to the scope and effectiveness of the right of transit passage provided therein, especially as concerns submerged submarines, see the writings of Reisman and Moore cited supra p. 183.   Both writings are based upon Articles 34–44 in the Informal Composite Negotiating Text as revised at the conclusion of the first part of the eighth session, March 19–April 27, 1979, of UNCLOS III.   The articles remained unchanged in the Draft Convention, except for the replacement of the word "juridical" by the word "legal" in the title of Article 34.   For a comprehensive analysis of the right of transit passage, see Kuribayashi, the Basic Structure of the New Regime of Passage Through International Straits, 21 Japanese Annual of International Law 29 (1977).

Note that foreign aircraft, as well as vessels, enjoy the right of transit passage through straits used for international navigation. See Article 38 of the Draft Convention in the Documentary Supplement.   In contrast foreign aircraft do not enjoy a right of innocent passage through the territorial sea of a state.   See Article 17 of the Draft Convention and Article 14 of the Geneva Convention on the

rigao, Hormuz, St. George's Channel (Bismarck Archipelago), Cook, Foveaux, Kaiwi Channel, Dover, Canal de Menorca, Messina, Bonifacio, The Dardanelles, Sea of Marmara and the Bosphorus, Kithera, Carphatos, The Sound and Singapore Strait.

Pirtle lists the 16 straits of strategic importance to the United States as follows: West Korean, Malacca, Sunca, Lombok, Ombai, West Bering, Juan de Fuca, Old Bahamas Channel, Dominica Channel, Martinique Channel, St. Lucia Channel, St. Vincent Passage, Gibraltar, Bab el Mandeb, Hormuz.

Territorial Sea and the Contiguous Zone in the Documentary Supplement.

4. *The Straits of Malacca and UNCLOS III.* Indonesia and Malaysia have taken the position that the Straits of Malacca are not international straits in which free transit passage would prevail. Rather they recognize that the straits may be used by international shipping in accordance with the principle of innocent passage. For a defense of their position and an argument that they need to regulate passage in the straits because of problems of navigational safety and oil pollution by huge numbers of tankers—mostly Japanese—see Logaraj, Navigational Safety, Oil Pollution and Passage in the Straits of Malacca, 20 Malaya Law Review 287 (1978).

Part XII of the United Nations Draft Convention on the Law of the Sea deals with the protection and preservation of the marine environment. Articles 192–237. The subject is considered infra, this chapter, p. 210. Article 233 deals specifically with pollution in straits. It provides:

> Nothing in　 *　 *　 *　 [these sections on the protection of the marine environment] affects the legal regime of straits used for international navigation. However, if a ship other than　 *　 *　 *　 [one entitled to sovereign immunity] has committed a violation of the laws and regulations [on navigation and pollution] referred to in article 42, paragraphs 1(a) and (b), causing or threatening major damage to the marine environment of the straits, the States bordering the straits may take appropriate enforcement measures　 *　 *　 *.

According to Moore, "the current version of Article 233 was worked out in 1977 after the adoption of the straits chapter as part of a concession on commercial vessels made to Malaysia." The Regime of Straits and the Third United Nations Conference on the Law of the Sea, 74 Am.J. Int'l L. 77, 109 (1980).

5. *The Straits of Denmark.* Lassen in Passage Through Straits, 47 Nordisk Tidsskrift for International Ret 93 (1978), discusses the need for Denmark to regulate navigation through its straits to protect itself from the risks of oil pollution from the wreck of oil tankers and concludes the provisions proposed by UNCLOS III do not satisfy the need.

6. *The Strait of Dover.* Compulsory traffic separation routes, i. e. a one way southbound corridor and a one way northbound corridor, were established in the Strait of Dover in 1967 by joint action of France and the United Kingdom, with the approval of the International Maritime Consultative Committee. 71 Revue Générale de Droit International Public 1091 (1967). The intensity of the traffic made the regulations necessary. They were revised and made more stringent in 1977. At that time some 400 ships crossed the strait daily. 81 Revue Générale de Droit International Public 1158 (1977).

PUBLIC PROSECUTOR v. KAIRISMAA

Sweden, Court of Appeal of Svea, 1960.
Supreme Court, 1960.
32 Int'l L.Rep. 117 (1966).*

The Facts. Kairismaa, a Finnish citizen, was charged before the City Court of Stockholm with, inter alia, obtaining a loan of 1,000 Swedish crowns from another Finnish citizen, Stjernvall, superintendent on the Finnish ship the Bore II, by fraudulently alleging that he needed the money immediately for a business transaction concerning an automobile and that he would repay it later the same day. The Public Prosecutor alleged that the crime had been committed within Swedish territorial waters. The City Court having found the defendant guilty, he appealed. Referring to the fact that the ship was Finnish, that both he himself and Stjernvall were Finnish citizens, and claiming that the transaction had taken place while the Bore II was outside Swedish territorial waters, the defendant urged the Appeal Court to reject the present part of the charge.

Held (by the Court of Appeal of Svea): that the appeal must fail and the judgment of the Court below must be confirmed. [The Court said:]

* * * It has been made clear [however], chiefly by the evidence given by Stjernvall before the City Court, that the transaction had taken place after the ship's entry into the Stockholm archipelago. As the Bore II—which plies in regular passenger traffic between Stockholm and Helsinki—thus at the time when the act was committed was in Swedish territorial waters, the Court of Appeal finds that the act shall be deemed to have taken place within the country. Under Chapter 1, Article 2, paragraph 1, of the Penal Code, a Swedish Court is consequently competent to consider the present part of the charge.

Kairismaa applied for permission to appeal to the Supreme Court and urged that Court to reject the charge. * * *

* * *

Kairismaa also contended that it was not clear from the reasons given by the Court of Appeal for its judgment whether the present charge could be brought in Sweden on the sole ground that, at the time when the crime was committed, the ship was in Swedish territorial waters, or whether a second condition was required, namely, that the ship be plying in regular traffic between a Swedish and a foreign port. * * * It was true that the principle applied by the Court of Appeal had been expressed earlier, in cases concerning crimes by Swedish citizens. * * * It was much more natural, however, to consider a crime committed against an alien on a foreign ship within

* Reprinted by permission of E. Lauterpacht, ed., and Grotius Publications, Ltd., Cambridge, England.

Swedish territorial waters as a matter of Swedish concern when committed by a Swede than when it was committed by an alien.　* * *

Held (by the Supreme Court): that the application for permission to appeal must be rejected.

The Court found no reason to alter the decision of the City Court. Accordingly, the judgment of the Court of Appeal must be affirmed.

---

1. *Amendment of Swedish law subsequent to decision.* The decision appears to have been the cause of an amendment to the Swedish code of criminal law which went into effect on January 1, 1965. Under this amendment, special permission from the executive is required before prosecution is initiated for an offense committed by an alien aboard a foreign vessel in Swedish territory and affecting another alien or alien interests. The amendment is reported in a note at the end of a comment on the case by Eek, Chronique de Jurisprudence Suédoise Relative au Droit International Privé 1960–1964, 93 Journal du Droit International 410 (1965–1966).

2. *Jurisdiction over merchant vessels in innocent passage under Geneva Convention and U.N. Draft Convention.* As to criminal jurisdiction, see in the Documentary Supplement Article 19 of the Geneva Convention on the Territorial Sea and the Contiguous Zone and Article 27 of the United Nations Draft Convention or the Law of the Sea. As to civil jurisdiction, see Article 20 of the former and Article 28 of the latter.

SECTION C.　WATERS BEYOND THE TERRITORIAL SEA

1.　FREEDOM OF NAVIGATION

THE PRINCIPLE

EUROPEAN AGREEMENT FOR THE PREVENTION OF BROADCASTS TRANSMITTED FROM STATIONS OUTSIDE NATIONAL TERRITORIES OF JANUARY 22, 1965 [a]

634 U.N.T.S. 239.

The member states of the Council of Europe signatory hereto,

Considering that the aim of the Council of Europe is to achieve a greater unity between its Members;

Considering that the Radio Regulations annexed to the International Telecommunication Convention prohibit the establishment and

a.　Entered into force Oct. 19, 1967.

use of broadcasting stations on board ships, aircraft or any other floating or airborne objects outside national territories;

Considering also the desirability of providing for the possibility of preventing the establishment and use of broadcasting stations on objects affixed to or supported by the bed of the sea outside national territories;

Considering the desirability of European collaboration in this matter,

Have agreed as follows:

Article 1

This Agreement is concerned with broadcasting stations which are installed or maintained on board ships, aircraft, or any other floating or airborne objects and which, outside national territories, transmit broadcasts intended for reception or capable of being received, wholly or in part, within the territory of any Contracting Party, or which cause harmful interference to any radio-communication service operating under the authority of a Contracting Party in accordance with the Radio Regulations.

Article 2

1.   Each Contracting Party undertakes to take appropriate steps to make punishable as offences, in accordance with its domestic law, the establishment or operation of broadcasting stations referred to in Article 1, as well as acts of collaboration knowingly performed.

2.   The following shall, in relation to broadcasting stations referred to in Article 1, be acts of collaboration:

(a) the provision, maintenance or repairing of equipment;

(b) the provision of supplies;

(c) the provision of transport for, or the transporting of, persons, equipment or supplies;

(d) the ordering or production of material of any kind, including advertisements, to be broadcast;

(e) the provision of services concerning advertising for the benefit of the stations.

Article 3

Each Contracting Party shall, in accordance with its domestic law, apply the provisions of this Agreement in regard to:

(a) its nationals who have committed any act referred to in Article 2 on its territory, ships, or aircraft, or outside national territories on any ships, aircraft or any other floating or airborne object;

(b) non-nationals who, on its territory, ships or aircraft, or on board any floating or airborne object under its jurisdiction have committed any act referred to in Article 2.

Article 4

Nothing in this Agreement shall be deemed to prevent a Contracting Party:

(a) from also treating as punishable offences acts other than those referred to in Article 2 and also applying the provisions concerned to persons other than those referred to in Article 3;

(b) from also applying the provisions of this Agreement to broadcasting stations installed or maintained on objects affixed to or supported by the bed of the sea.

Article 5

The Contracting Parties may elect not to apply the provisions of this Agreement in respect of the services of performers which have been provided elsewhere than on the stations referred to in Article 1.

Article 6

The provisions of Article 2 shall not apply to any acts performed for the purpose of giving assistance to a ship or aircraft or any other floating or airborne object in distress or of protecting human life.

Article 7

No reservation may be made to the provisions of this Agreement.

*   *   *

---

1. *Pirate broadcasting from tower affixed to the seabed outside the territorial sea.* The facts of the situation are reported in Rousseau, Chronique des Faits Internationaux, 69 Revue Générale de Droit International Public 436, 517 (1965).

Under Dutch law, radio (and television) broadcasting in the territory is a state monopoly and no privately owned radio station may be built and operated without the prior authorization of the government. A radio broadcasting station was established on a tower outside the territorial sea of the Netherlands. The builders did not seek authorization from the Dutch government. The tower was built in an Irish factory belonging to a Dutch financier. The broadcasting equipment was purchased in the United States, despite attempts by the Dutch government to prevent the sale. The tower and the broadcasting equipment were owned by persons who were not Dutch nationals.

The station was operated by a Dutch corporation and began broadcasting in July of 1964. Its income came from advertising and it is probable—though Rousseau does not say so in his report—that the owners of the station escaped such taxation as the Dutch government would levy if the station were located in its territory. On December 11, 1964, Dutch legislation was enacted which authorized the government to take action against broadcasting stations outside the territorial sea of the Netherlands, even if owned by aliens. The day the legislation became effective, ownership of the station was transferred to a Panamanian corporation and the operation of the facilities was contracted to an English corporation.

On December 17, 1964, police brought in by helicopters of the Dutch navy took possession of the platform, without resistance from the personnel of the station, and closed down the facilities. Was the action of the Dutch government valid under international law? Under the European Agreement for the Prevention of Broadcasts Transmitted from Stations Outside National Territories?

2. *Pirate broadcasting from foreign vessel anchored outside the territorial sea.* Is the situation different if the broadcasting facilities are located outside the territorial sea but on a foreign vessel at anchor instead of an object affixed to or supported by the seabed?

In issuing a warrant for the arrest of persons aboard a foreign vessel carrying a pirate broadcasting station, a court in Great Britain specified the arrest could be carried out only in the territorial waters of Great Britain. The Times, December 12, 1975, p. 4, col. 2. Why? Another case involved two pirate broadcasting stations operating from vessels with foreign flags stationed outside the territorial sea of the Netherlands. The director of one gave money to equip and recruit a crew for a raid against his competitor. The raiders seized the vessel of the competitor and forced the master to sail into the territorial sea of the Netherlands. The director was convicted of being an accessory to the crime of piracy. Public Prosecutor v. N.C.J., Netherlands, District Court of The Hague, 1971, V Netherlands Yearbook of International Law 331 (1974). The crime of piracy is considered infra p. 201.

See Article 6 of the Geneva Convention on the High Seas and Article 92 of the Draft Convention. Does Article 24 of the Geneva Convention on the Territorial Sea and the Contiguous Zone contribute to the solution of the problem?

3. *Solution to pirate broadcasting proposed in Article 109 of U.N. Draft Convention.* The article provides:

Unauthorized broadcasting from the high seas

1.   All States shall co-operate in the suppression of unauthorized broadcasting from the high seas.

2.   Any person engaged in unauthorized broadcasting from the high seas may be prosecuted before the court of the flag State of the vessel, the place of registry of the installation, the State of which the person is a national, any place where the transmissions can be received or any State where authorized radio communication is suffering interference.

3.   On the high seas, a State having jurisdiction in accordance with paragraph 2 may, in conformity with article 110, ar-

rest any person or ship engaged in unauthorized broadcasting and seize the broadcasting apparatus.

4. For the purposes of this Convention, "unauthorized broadcasting" means the transmission of sound radio or television broadcasts from a ship or installation on the high seas intended for reception by the general public contrary to international regulations, but excluding the transmission of distress calls.

Under Article 110 of the draft, a reasonable suspicion of unauthorized broadcasting by a vessel on the high seas justifies her stopping and boarding by a naval vessel of different nationality. Under Article 22 of the Geneva Convention on the High Seas, this "right of visit" of a foreign vessel extends to only two other crimes: piracy and slave trade. For the text of Article 110 of the draft, see the Documentary Supplement.

THE CONTIGUOUS ZONE

RE MARTINEZ

Italy, Court of Cassation, 1959.
28 Int'l L.Rep. 170 (1963).*

The Facts. Article 2 of the Italian Maritime Code fixes the limit of territorial waters at six miles from the coast. Article 33 of the Customs Law of September 25, 1940, on the other hand, provides that Italy shall be entitled to exercise jurisdiction over a further six-mile zone for the purpose of preventing and punishing smuggling along the Italian coast. This latter zone is referred to as the "zone of vigilance" (contiguous zone). The appellants, who were foreign nationals, were convicted of smuggling in the following circumstances: while their vessel was at a distance of nine miles from the coast, warning shots were fired, and upon these shots being ignored the vessel was pursued and ultimately captured at a distance of 54 miles from the coast. The appellants appealed against their conviction and contended that Article 24 of the Geneva Convention of 1958 on the Territorial Sea and the Contiguous Zone was declaratory of existing customary international law and accordingly a coastal State, while entitled to prevent customs offences from being committed in the contiguous zone, was not entitled to exercise jurisdiction and inflict punishment in respect of such offences; that jurisdiction could only be exercised if an offence had actually been committed within the territorial sea, and therefore Article 33 of the Customs Law was contrary to Article 10 of the Italian Constitution, which provided that Italian law must be consistent with international law. They therefore contended that their conviction should be quashed.

* Reprinted by permission of E. Lauterpacht, ed., and Grotius Publications, Ltd., Cambridge, England.

Held: that the appeal must be dismissed.   *   *   *   [A portion of the opinion of the court appears below.]

  *   *   *   It is contended that Article 33 of the Customs Law, which extends the territorial sea beyond the limit of six nautical miles laid down in Article 2 of the Maritime Code, and confers on the coastal State sovereignty and jurisdiction over a stretch of sea between six and twelve miles, is contrary to Article 10 of the Italian Constitution which provides that Italian law shall be in conformity with the generally recognized rules of international law. By a rule of customary international law recognized and laid down in Article 24 of the "Convention on the Territorial Sea and the Contiguous Zone", which was adopted at the Geneva Conference on February 24 and April 27, 1958, the sovereignty and jursidiction of the coastal State —it is said—cannot extend beyond six miles, and sovereignty and jurisdiction over a belt extending between six and twelve miles from the coast, this belt being defined as the contiguous zone, are not recognized except in specially defined cases. According to the argument put forward on behalf of the appellants, the coastal State can exercise the requisite control for the purpose of preventing and punishing offences against its customs, tax and sanitary laws over a portion of the high seas contiguous to the territorial sea, on condition only that the offences have been committed in the territorial sea within six miles from the coast. It follows—so it is said—that the coastal State can exercise its jurisdiction over the contiguous zone only in respect of offences committed in its territorial sea, the contiguous zone being the intermediate zone between the territorial sea and the high seas. This, it is said, would be contrary to Article 33 of the Customs Law which, in delimiting the zone of customs vigilance as being twelve miles from the coast, includes in the latter the territorial sea as laid down in Article 2 of the Maritime Code and the zone of vigilance, which latter it makes coincide with the territorial sea.

The contention that Article 33 of the Customs Law is contrary to the Constitution is misconceived and has been rejected by the judgment under appeal. It is undoubtedly true that the rule laid down in Article 10 of the Constitution, according to which Italian law must comply with generally recognized rules of international law, ensures the compatibility of Italian municipal law with international law, viz., with the duties imposed upon the State by international law, so that rules of municipal law which are contrary to international law must be eliminated. However, in order for this to be so, it is necessary for the rules of international law to be generally recognized, and it is admitted on behalf of the defendants that the Geneva Convention, which has been signed by Italy, is not yet in force.

It is not true that Article 24 of the Convention constitutes a customary rule of international law governing the delimitation of the territorial sea in the sense that the sovereignty of the coastal State is limited to the territorial sea itself, without being capable of being extended over the contiguous zone when smuggling has occurred in the latter and not in the territorial sea. No such rule can be said to have been generally accepted in international law. In substance custom is a manifestation of social life which hardens by means of constant and uniform repetition of certain acts on the part of States or individuals, extending over a period of time, to which municipal law attributes legal relevance. In the international field this presupposes the existence of a substantive element, namely, the constant repetition of certain rules of conduct between States, and a psychological element, namely, the conviction that such conduct is obligatory for everybody, so that others can insist upon it, and which does not depend on purely subjective judgment. Only then can custom be a source of law equal to municipal law.

As far as the present case is concerned, not all maritime States have accepted such a rule in practice. The International Law Commission, in its draft code prepared at the session held between April and July 1956, recognized (in Article 3) "that international practice is not uniform as far as the delimitation of the territorial sea is concerned". The comment on Article 66 of the draft code relating to the contiguous zone states that smuggling could not be dealt with adequately, having regard to the fact that Article 66 provided only for offences committed "within the territory or in the territorial sea". The Italian delegation [sic] observed that "having regard to the geographical position of the country and the configuration of its coasts, the limitation of the powers conferred on the coastal State in the contiguous zone would render preventive and punitive measures against smuggling ineffective, especially in parts of the sea adjacent to the Italian coast where smuggling was particularly active and aggressive".

At the Geneva Conference, which opened on February 24, 1958, there was no change. The Italian delegation proposed an amendment aiming at the omission of the words "in the territorial sea", in order to be able to prevent and punish offences committed in the contiguous zone and not only on State territory and in the territorial sea. This proposal was not accepted in plenary session, nor was any other put forward by way of compromise by other delegations, on the extension of the territorial sea. A solution of the problem could not be found.

It is contended on behalf of the defendants that the [International Law] Commission was set up for the progressive development and codification of international law, and that when preparing the report on which the Convention is based it investigated substantially the rules of customary international law. This, it is argued, shows that these rules existed prior to codification, which was merely intended to lay down in codified form what was already custom. Hence the wording of the rule contained in Article 24 of the Convention, which is said to be a faithful reproduction of a pre-existing customary rule which as such is generally recognized and must be considered, by virtue of Article 10 of the Constitution, as having been automatically incorporated in Italian law, and which must not be contrary to the rule laid down in that article.

It must be remembered, however, that this rule cannot be said to be a generally recognized rule of customary international law because the rule relating to the width of the territorial sea is still under discussion between States. States apply different rules according to their respective municipal laws, which fact in itself precludes recognition of any pre-existing custom in the matter. In fact, although the Conference on the Law of the Sea was successful in defining a number of rules governing the matter under discussion, if left unsolved the problem of the width of the territorial sea, as can be seen from the preparatory work of the Conference. The disagreement was due to different contrasting views put forward by participating States, one group being in favour of the three-mile limit for territorial waters, as in the past, another holding the opposite view and applying various criteria to the actual width of the territorial sea, without affirming a right to twelve miles. Although various proposals were put forward to reconcile the opposing wishes of States, no positive solution was found. Accordingly, it cannot be said that the rule contained in Article 24 of the Convention existed previously as a generally recognized customary rule when the conditions surrounding the delimitation of the territorial sea and the contiguous zone were very different from those contained in that article and when agreement could not be reached. * * *

In fact, not all States have accepted the three-mile limit, which in the past represented a compromise between States: Norway and Sweden have fixed the limit of their territorial sea at four miles; Spain, Portugal, Yugoslavia, Italy and other countries at six, while Bulgaria, the Soviet Union, Communist China, Egypt, Ethiopia, Rumania and Guatemala have fixed it at twelve miles, and Chile and other countries at two hundred. Italy, on the other hand, as we have already stated, has not accepted the limit of the contiguous zone in the form in which it is expressed in Article 24. The rules of municipal law of coastal States have therefore remained in force. In Italy it is the rule laid down in Article 33 of the Customs Law, which cannot be said to be contrary to Article 10 of the Constitution. It follows that the offence of smuggling committed in the zone of vigilance, the so-called contiguous zone, is punishable in Italy, and that the arrest of a foreign national is lawful by Article 137 of the Customs Law. Equally lawful is the pursuit of a foreign vessel. * * *

The appellants contend that as Article 2 of the Maritime Code fixes the limit of the territorial sea at six miles from the coast and provides that this is without prejudice to various legal provisions which are to apply in specific cases, the only purpose of the Code was to lay down a six-mile limit for the territorial sea, reserving the right to extend the limit for specific purposes other than sovereignty, and less extensive than the latter. Accordingly, the zone of vigilance provided for by Article 33 of the Customs Law as being between six and twelve miles is not the territorial sea but merely an area of the sea which is subject to control for the purpose of prevention only and not punishment. Although in theory it may seem as if in the contiguous zone only police and preventive measures may be taken, because this zone forms part of the open sea rather than the territorial sea, a different view must be taken when one considers that the draft code of the Institute of International Law on the contiguous zone clearly recognizes the right to exercise jurisdiction. The International Law Commission, in its report on the session held in 1953, was decidedly in favour of acknowledging the right to exercise jurisdiction, while in its 1951 draft it merely referred to preventive measures.

          *   *   *

1. *Contraband outside the customs zone.* A British vessel transferred contraband goods to an Italian vessel outside the 12 miles customs zone of Italy. An Italian coast guard cutter boarded the British vessel and arrested its crew while it was still on the high seas. The Supreme Court of Italy ordered the release of the crew on the ground that a state cannot exercise its jurisdiction over foreign vessels on the high seas, save in the exceptional case of hot pursuit. Re McSporran et al.; s.s. Sito, Court of Cassation, 1957, 89 Journal du Droit International 229 (1962).

2. *Contiguous zone under Geneva Convention and U.N. Draft Convention.* Article 33 of the draft reproduces verbatim Article 24 of the Geneva Convention on the Territorial Sea and the Contiguous Zone, except that it would extend the breadth of the contiguous zone to 24 miles from the baseline, instead of the 12 miles provided in the Geneva Convention.

―――――――

HOT PURSUIT

RE PULOS AND OTHERS

Italy, Tribunal of Naples, 1976.
III Italian Yearbook of International Law 282, 286 (1977).*

    *   *   *   On 11 November 1976 the vessel "Olimpios Hermes", flying the Greek flag, left the port of Antwerp carrying 25,000 cartons of cigarettes. *   *   *   The voyage was regular until the Straits of Gibraltar were navigated after which, from 16 November there is no further entry in the log-book or the radio-telephone journal: the vessel was surprised on the morning of 29 November 1976 off the coast of the island of Ischia, 27 miles at 220 degrees from Punta Imperatore (this is clear from the file), that is on the high seas, surrounded by some 20 motor-boats whilst another 12 motor-boats were further away and nearer the land which was some 15 miles distant.

* Reprinted by permission of Editoriale
Scientifica, s.r.l., Naples.

* * * It must be held established that one of the said motor-boats was carrying from the "Olimpios Hermes" 80 cartons of cigarettes (it should have taken 100 cartons but evidently the arrival of the Guardia di Finanza interrupted the operation).

* * * It is also clear from the file that after the motor-boat had taken on board the said cigarettes it fled despite the orders of the servicemen to stop; however, pursued without interruption first by helicopters and then by coastguards and the patrol boat of the Guardia di Finanza, it sailed initially towards the coast, returning, however, amongst the other motor-boats which were still in the vicinity of the vessel, and endeavoured, by reckless manoeuvres entailing a risk of collision, to hinder the pursuing craft and finally turned again towards the coast; it was captured in territorial waters (10 miles at 220 degrees from Punta Imperatore, Ischia) after the discharge of 70 rounds from light machine guns, some of which damaged the driving gear of the two 350 HP engines of the motor-boat. Thereafter the naval unit notified the capture of the motor-boat in territorial waters to the coastguard vessels Guglielmi and Di Sessa which were lying near the "Olimpios Hermes"; the latter was slowly moving away in a south-south-west direction and the coastguards called upon it to stop by visual and auditory signals and ultimately by hailing; when this proved fruitless the "Olimpios Hermes" was boarded 28 miles at 220 degrees from Punta Imperatore, that is on the high seas, the remainder of the cargo of cigarettes was seized and the persons on board the vessel were arrested. It was subsequently established that the contraband cigarettes carried by the "Olimpios Hermes", part of which had already been unloaded and part of which was about to be unloaded whilst on the high seas to the motor-boats for transshipment to the coast, had been sold in advance in Naples by a person or persons unknown to the prosecution.

* * * To that extent, since it is clear from the file that the police operation against the motor-boat which was captured, concerned an Italian-registered craft, with Italian nationals on board and moreover ended in Italian territorial waters following the said commission of the crime of smuggling 800 kg of foreign cigarettes, it merely remains to consider the lawfulness of that operation since the defence for the accused contests this point because, so far as the "Olimpios Hermes" is concerned, it constitutes the seizure of a foreign vessel on the high seas.

Italian criminal legislation covers all persons, apart from exceptions concerning so-called immunity, whether nationals or foreign, who are on the territory of the state (Art. 3, para. 1, c.p.), that is the territory of the Republic of Italy and accordingly all other places subject to the sovereignty thereof, including Italian vessels or aircraft wherever they may be, apart from exceptions created by international law (Art. 4, para. 2, c.p.). The sovereign right of the State covers the territorial waters up to 12 miles from the coast * * *.

Beyond the territorial waters lies the open sea or high seas. It is precisely the absence of State sovereignty over the area of sea lying beyond the territorial waters which creates the principle of the freedom of such seas which, as it is expressed in Article 2 of the Geneva Convention of 29 April 1958 on the High Seas, are open "to all nations" * * * and are guaranteed for the use of all States (for navigation, use of the resources and any other freedom acknowledged by the general principles of international law).

Upon this is based the further principle of international law, whether customary or conventional—Art. 6 of the said Geneva Convention—, which has also been adopted in municipal legislation (in the case of Italy in Art. 4 c.p. and Art. 4 c. nav.) whereby ships sailing on high seas come under the exclusive jurisdiction of the State whose flag they fly, save in exceptional cases expressly provided for in international law. Naturally the principle of freedom of the high seas is not without its limits since it is subject to derogations and restrictions on the basis of international customary law and international agreements. * * *

[The court said one limit was the right of a state to repress smuggling and the mother ship had engaged in smuggling through the use of small boats to take the cigarettes ashore.]

The other (specific) limit to the principle in question is that concerning the right of pursuit whereby the coastal State may pursue and seize on the high seas foreign civil vessels which are guilty of infringements of its legislation on internal waters or territorial waters. It must be held that this right is established first of all on the basis of international customary law, as is clear from its usual application in international disputes (in which the disputes were chiefly settled on the basis of the conduct of the State concerned in the exercise of that right) or in the replies given in this connexion by States in the course of the travaux préparatoires for the Hague Codification Conference of 1930; these States, by providing unanimously an affirmative answer to the questions drawn up by the League of Nations and arriving easily at agreement on the wording of Art. II of Appendix No. I to the Report of the second Commission which was systematizing the right, merely noted the existence of that custom for the purpose of establishing its details, prescribing limits to prevent abuses of it.

The same conclusions were reached in substance by the Geneva Conference on the High Seas which repeated at Art. 23 the old principles whilst extending their scope (by providing in the contiguous zone for pursuit by aircraft, that the ship or aircraft need not also be in territorial waters, that the ship or aircraft undertaking the arrest need not be that which initiated the pursuit where boats are operating as a team). In sum it may be stated that with regard to the right of pursuit, Art. 23 of the Geneva Convention, whilst going beyond the scope of the Codification Conference of 1930, is nevertheless narrower than the rules of the relevant customary international law where no specific limits are laid down, which indicates that States are tending to return to a broad conception of the right in order to provide better protection for their national interests which are increasingly threatened by well-trained and highly organised groups of criminals.

The said Art. 23 in fact lays down that foreign civil vessels may be arrested on the high seas if the following conditions are met:

(1) The laws and regulations of the coastal state were infringed;

(2) The vessel itself, or one of its boats, or other craft working as a team and using the said vessel as a mother ship was within the internal waters, territorial waters or the contiguous zone;

(3) Pursuit, begun in territorial waters or the contiguous zone and continued on the high seas, was uninterrupted, although the pursuing craft may have changed;

(4) Visual or auditory signals, which can be seen or heard, conveying an order to halt were given;

(5) Pursuit was given by warships or military aircraft, or other ships or aircraft on government service especially authorized to that effect.

With regard to the first condition it has been established above that there was an infringement of the customs legislation of the coastal State, Italy. The foreign vessel stationed itself near the boundary of the Italian territorial waters, following the sale in advance in Naples of the entire cargo of foreign cigarettes with which it was laden, and supplied those cigarettes to the numerous motorboats which came from the coast to which they transshipped the cigarettes, in breach of customs legislation, until the arrival of the Guardia di Finanza cut short the unloading.

With regard to the second condition it is established that the vessel was supplying from its cargo the said motor-boats which, drawn up in a queue and in groups alongside the vessel (as is clear from the photographs taken from the helicopters), transshipped, or intended to transship, to the shore to the purchasers. The foreign vessel accordingly acted as the mother ship to those boats by furnishing the latter with the relevant materials, that is the cigarettes, which the boats took to the destination and then returned for more until the vessel was completely unloaded. * * * It may be inferred from the foregoing that those boats operated as a team with the vessel. The whole unloading and subsequent transshipment to the coast, organised by a buyer and sellers unknown, by their agents and by the person in charge of the vessel, with the assistance of the skippers of the motor-boats shows clearly that all those persons acted in concert for the same purpose namely to convey the cigarettes to the shore in breach of Italian customs legislation. This constitutes working as a team and in pursuance of the rule in question the situation is the same as if the vessel itself had entered the territory of the State in order to unload the cigarettes. * * *

With regard to the third condition it has already been shown that after the pursuit of the motor-boat, which carried over into and terminated in the territorial waters, the other craft of the Guardia di Finanza immediately began continuous pursuit of the foreign vessel which soon terminated in the seizure of the vessel on the high seas through which it had been slowly proceeding. It is quite clear that no relevance in the present case can attach to the fact that pursuit of the motor-boat began on the high seas (it nevertheless continued in the territorial waters where it also terminated) in that, since the boat in question was Italian, pursuit and any capture which took place on the high seas was entirely lawful. Accordingly, commencement of pursuit in the territorial waters constituted the precise circumstance permitting the pursuers to hold that they had obtained fulfilment of the condition for "extending" the right of pursuit to the foreign vessel on the high seas.

With regard to the fourth and fifth conditions it has been shown that they were fully complied with since visual and auditory signals were given to halt and the pursuit was carried out by the military craft of the Guardia di Finanza. * * *

---

1. *Hot pursuit under Geneva Convention and U.N. Draft Convention.* The provisions of Article 23 of the Geneva Convention on the High Seas are extended mutatis mutandis by Article 111 of the draft to violations in the exclusive economic zone or on the continental shelf. As to that zone, and the shelf, see infra pp. 203 and 212 respectively.

2. *Use of force in hot pursuit.* In 1977 a local union in Nantes, France, opposed the departure of a merchant vessel flying the Panamanian flag in a dispute over the wages paid the crew. It sailed down the estuary of the Loire river and to sea without taking a pilot aboard as required by law. The pursuit was begun by a small boat of the customs service and taken up by a submarine chaser. After ordering it to stop and firing warning shots, the submarine chaser fired machine gun bursts in the hull above the water, which were ignored. Thereupon the submarine chaser "deeming the infraction not serious enough to risk sinking the vessel," gave up the pursuit and the vessel escaped to the high seas. 81 Revue Générale de Droit International Public 1161–1162 (1977).

Compare the case of the I'm Alone, infra 246.

RIGHT OF APPROACH AND VISIT

RIGHT OF APPROACH

4 Whiteman, Digest of International Law 667 (1965).

The right of any ship to fly a particular flag must obviously be subject to verification by proper authority, and from this it follows that warships have a general right to verify the nationality of any merchant ship which they may meet on the high seas. This "right of approach" (*vérification du pavillon* or *reconnaissance*) is the only qualification under customary law of the general principle which forbids any interference in time of peace with ships of another nationality upon the high seas. Any other act of interference (apart from the repression of piracy) must be justified under powers conferred by treaty. Provided that the merchant vessel responds by showing her flag the captain of the warship is not justified in boarding her or taking any further action, unless there is reasonable ground for suspecting that she is engaged in piracy or some other improper activity. In the absence of good cause for suspicion his government may have to accept substantial responsibility for any interference. If the vessel approached shows a foreign flag even suspicious conduct will not justify active interference except in those cases, such as slave trading, where it is authorized by treaty. Otherwise the captain should merely report the incident to superior authority so that further action, if deemed necessary, may be taken through diplomatic channels.

In the past the question of the right of approach has been the subject of some controversy and has occasionally given rise to friction. Under modern conditions the general use of wireless and other developments have made the matter one of very small importance. Smith, The Law and Custom of the Sea (1959) 64– 65.

On December 20, 1960, the Soviet Ministry of Foreign Affairs addressed the following note to the American Embassy at Moscow:

[The note alleged that an American destroyer had engaged in provocative and dangerous maneuvers toward a Soviet merchant vessel in the Mediterranean Sea.]

After a careful investigation of the facts concerning the alleged incident, the Department of State, on January 4, 1961, addressed the following reply to the Soviet Government:

The Department of State refers the Embassy of the Union of Soviet Socialist Republics to the note 138/OSA of December 20, 1960 from the Ministry of Foreign Affairs of the Union of Soviet Socialist Republics to the Embassy of the United States of America in Moscow alleging that an American destroyer carried out maneuvers in the Mediterranean Sea on November 4, 1960 which seriously endangered the Soviet ship *Faleshty*, and wishes to state the following.

A careful investigation of the facts has clearly established that the American ship which passed the *Faleshty* on November 4 did not carry out any provocative maneuvers. No alerts were sounded for a mock attack, as alleged in the Ministry's note, nor did the American ship ever approach the *Faleshty* in such a way as to endanger the Soviet ship.

It is common practice for ships moving in international waters to establish mutual identification. This, the investigation clearly showed, was the full extent of the American vessel's action.

Under the circumstances, the Government of the United States rejects the Soviet Government's charges.

* * *

1. *Right of visit under Geneva Convention and U.N. Draft Convention.* See in the Documentary Supplement Article 22 of the Geneva Convention on the High Seas and Article 110 of the United Nations Draft Convention on the Law of the Sea.

2. *Right of visit under an international agreement.* See Chapter 1, p. 43, for a case of boarding by a U. S. naval vessel of a Soviet trawler suspected of damaging submarine cables, pursuant to the Convention for the Protection of Submarine Cables of March 14, 1884. Both the Soviet Union and the United States are parties to the convention.

PIRACY

ROBBERY ON THE HIGH SEAS

6 Whiteman, Digest of International Law 348 (1968).

[The author quotes from Smith, The End of the Consular Courts, 37 Foreign Service Journal (Jan. 1960) 44, 47–48.]

* * * In November 1952 there occurred on the high seas between Tangier and Malaga, Spain, one of the most audacious crimes in modern legal history. Two American citizens, Elliot Forrest and Sidney Paley, were suspected of highjacking a Dutch ship, the Combinatie, and relieving it of its cargo of American cigarettes, valued at more than $100,000, under circumstances reminiscent of the days of Captain Kidd. Men wearing hoods, and armed with machine guns, were alleged to have boarded the Combinatie on the High Seas, in the early morning hours, and to have handcuffed the Master and members of the crew and locked them in their quarters. The piratical crew was said to have sailed the Combinatie to a point off Marseille, where they unloaded part of the cargo onto small fishing boats and then proceeded to Corsica to unload the remainder of the cargo before returning the vessel to its rightful masters. Paley was arrested in Madrid and returned to the Consular Court at Tangier for trial. *   *   *

Paley was not present at the actual robbery and was charged with aiding and abetting robbery on the high seas and with conspiring to commit the crime of robbery on the high seas. The judge of the United States Consular Court [a] at Tangier found him guilty on both counts "and sentenced him to three years imprisonment on both counts, the sentences to run concurrently. The judge's associates [assessors] in the case, however, found Paley not guilty and, in accordance with the existing laws, the case was referred to the Ministerial Court for final decision."

" *   *   * Forrest, the other American involved, later was arrested and tried in France, where he was found guilty and given a very heavy fine in addition to a five-year sentence." Forrest had participated in the actual robbery.

*   *   *

After [a] rehearing, the Ministerial Court again sustained "the conviction as found by the Consul on both Counts of the Information". The Court, however, was of the opinion that "under the power of adjudication conferred by Section 152, Title 22, United States Code, this Court is not bound by the judgment and sentence of the Consular Court and that in the present case the ends of justice would be best served by the imposition of less rigorous punishment". The case was, therefore, remanded to the Consular Court with instructions to affirm the finding of guilty on the first count and the sentence of imprisonment but to suspend such sentence on condition that the appellant be placed on probation in the United States for 3 years. The finding of guilty and the sentence of imprisonment on the second count were also to be affirmed but the sentence was suspended on condition that the appellant pay a fine of $6,500.

---

1. *Piracy under international law.* In a British case, In re Piracy Jure Gentium, [1934] A.C. 586, His Majesty in Council referred to the Judicial Committee a question concerning piracy under international law. The answer stated in part:

With regard to crimes as defined by international law, that law has no means of trying or punishing them. The recognition

a. On the basis of treaties concluded with Morocco as early as 1787, the United States, like a number of other states, had rights of "extraterritorial jurisdiction" in Moroccan territory. By virtue of this jurisdiction, American nationals who committed crimes in Morocco were tried, not by the Moroccan courts and under Moroccan law, but rather by the consul of the United States and under American law. Appeals from the consular court were taken to the court of the American minister in Tangier. The United States exercised this jurisdiction until 1956, when the protectorate of France over Morocco was terminated.

of them as constituting crimes, and the trial and punishment of the criminals, are left to the municipal law of each country. But whereas according to international law the criminal jurisdiction of municipal law is ordinarily restricted to crimes committed on its terra firma or territorial waters or its own ships, and to crimes by its own nationals wherever committed, it is also recognized as extending to piracy committed on the high seas by any nationals on any ship, because a person guilty of such piracy has placed himself beyond the protection of any state. He is no longer a national, but hostis humani generis and as such he is justiciable by any state anywhere: Grotius (1583–1645) De Jure Belli ac Pacis, vol. 2, cap. 20, § 40. * * *

2. *Piracy under Geneva Convention and U.N. Draft Convention.* The first deals with it in Articles 14 through 21 and the second in Articles 100–107. See in particular the definitions in Articles 15 and 101.

Piracy is still a prevalent crime in some parts of the world. It is common in the waters off Southeast Asia, as became widely known during the flight from Vietnam of the "boat people" and other Indochinese refugees. See in connection with these, Chapter 9 infra, p. 639.

3. *Problem.* Suppose that a group of political dissidents in a small motor launch board a cruise vessel flying their country's flag and sailing on the high seas. They seize control of the ship, confine the officers and set sail for a foreign port. They broadcast their exploit, explaining that it is to publicize to the world the "intolerable state of affairs in our beloved homeland and the ruthless and oppressive nature of the illegitimate regime that governs her." Are they pirates under Article 15 of the convention?

---

2. THE EXCLUSIVE ECONOMIC ZONE

THE CONCEPT OF THE EXCLUSIVE ECONOMIC ZONE

Krueger and Norquist, The Evolution of the 200-Mile Exclusive Economic Zone: State Practice in the Pacific Basin

19 Virginia Journal of International Law 321 (1979).*

I. INTRODUCTION

The establishment of the 200-mile exclusive economic zone (EEZ) is the most significant development in oceans law since the articulation of the doctrine of the freedom of the high seas. * * *

While the concept is not complicated, its implications are astounding. Two hundred-mile EEZ's off the U.S. and Australian coasts alone cover four million square nautical miles. If asserted by all coastal States, 200-mile claims would embrace 105 million square

* Reprinted by permission of the Virginia Journal of International Law.

nautical miles, or thirty-six percent of the earth's ocean surface. Within these waters, fishermen take over ninety percent of the world's fish catch and eighty-seven percent of the globe's known submarine oil deposits is found. Also, certain bodies of water which are now only semi-enclosed, such as the Persian Gulf, the Gulf of Mexico, the Bay of Bengal, and the Norwegian and Ockhotask Seas, are becoming zone-locked by such jurisdictional claims. Even the North Pole, long the symbol of international scientific cooperation, is being hemmed in by 200-mile zones around the Canadian Arctic archipelago, Greenland, Svalbard, and Franz Josefland and other Soviet island groups.

     *   *   *

II. THE EXCLUSIVE ECONOMIC ZONE CONCEPT

A. *Historical Background*

     *   *   *

The concept of a resource-oriented zone extending beyond the territorial sea, like the concept of continental shelf jurisdiction, first developed in Latin America. Colombia in 1919 claimed the exclusive right to exploit hydrocarbons beneath the territorial sea, and in 1923 enacted legislation extending its territorial sea jurisdiction from three to twelve nautical miles for the purposes of exploiting hydrocarbons and fisheries. Panama and Venezuela, in 1921 and 1935 respectively, enacted laws claiming jurisdiction over pearl fisheries beyond the limits of their territorial seas. Later Venezuela claimed the fishery resources of the continental shelf and epicontinental sea, and Argentina made a similar geographical assertion over "mineral reserves." *   *   *

On September 28, 1945, President Truman legitimated the nationalization of ocean space by issuing proclamations asserting jurisdiction over continental shelf and fisheries resources in and under the high seas contiguous to the United States. U.S. jurisdiction over the continental shelf was claimed to be legally justified because

> the effectiveness of measures to utilize or conserve these resources would be contingent upon cooperation and protection from the shore, since the continental shelf may be regarded as an extension of the landmass of the coastal nation and thus naturally appurtenant to it, since these resources frequently form a seaward extension of a pool or deposit lying within the territory, and since self-protection compels the coastal nation to keep close watch over activities off its shores which are of the nature necessary for utilization of these resources. *   *   *

The United States was careful, however, to preserve the high seas character of the waters above the continental shelf and the right of free and unimpeded navigation therein. The Truman Proclamation specified no outer limits to jurisdiction, but an accompanying press release referred to the 100-fathom or 600-foot depth line.

* * *

The maritime claims following the Truman Proclamation were not always limited to continental shelf resource jurisdiction. Some developing countries that claimed full sovereignty over the waters above the shelf did not share the interest of the maritime powers in freedom of navigation. Again, Latin American countries spearheaded the movement. In 1945 Mexico proclaimed jurisdiction over the continental shelf and established a fishery conservation zone. In 1946, Argentina claimed not only the shelf and its resources, but also the superjacent waters, while Panama made a similar claim. The following year, Chile and Peru took steps toward establishing an EEZ by claiming national sovereignty 200 miles seaward for the purposes of preserving and exploiting their "patrimonial" resources. These claims were not limited to minerals, as were prior continental shelf claims; nor were they aimed at protecting and conserving local or regional fisheries. Instead, the claims asserted exclusive jurisdiction over all resources of the adjacent coastal waters, both living and non-living. Five years later Chile and Peru joined Ecuador in the Santiago Declaration, which proclaimed the three States' sole sovereignty and jurisdiction 200 miles seaward, although preserving innocent passage.

In 1970, several Latin American countries issued the Declaration of Montevideo on the Law of the Sea and the Declaration of Latin American States on the Law of the Sea. These declarations proclaimed the right to establish zones of sovereignty and jurisdiction over marine resources, without specifying a limit. The Santo Domingo Declaration, issued in 1972 at the Specialized Conference of the Caribbean States on Problems of the Law of the Sea, refined this position in the concept of the "patrimonial sea." This declaration provided for a 12-mile territorial sea and a 200-mile patrimonial sea within which the coastal State has sovereign rights over all resources and jurisdiction over scientific research and marine pollution. The zone retained the freedoms of navigation, overflight, and the laying of submarine cables and pipelines.

The African States also considered the idea of an exclusive economic zone. At a 1971 meeting, the Council of Ministers of the Organization of African Unity (OAU) issued a resolution on fisheries and a resolution on the sovereignty of African countries over their natural resources. Through these measures, the council urged all African States to "extend their sovereignty over the natural resources of the high seas adjacent to their territorial waters and up to the limits of their continental shelves."

The African States' Regional Seminar on the Law of the Sea, held in 1972, recommended an EEZ of unspecified width but including "at least the continental shelf." In this EEZ the coastal State would have "exclusive jurisdiction for the purpose of control, regulation, and national exploitation" of both the living and non-living resources, although the freedoms of navigation, overflight, and cable and pipeline laying would be preserved. * * *

The OAU Council of Ministers adopted the EEZ * * * in its Declaration on the Issues of the Law of the Sea of May 1973. The OAU position thus was essentially the same as that of the Latin American countries at Santo Domingo, with the important addition of a provision allowing landlocked States access to the living resources of the EEZ. * * *

By June of 1974, when the first substantive session of UNCLOS III opened in Caracas, the concept of a 200-mile EEZ had gained substantial support from two important regional groups, the Latin Americans and the Africans, and was recognized as a "common aim of the Group of 77," the largest bloc of developing countries. At Caracas, both in the Plenary and in the Second Committee, over 100 States spoke in favor of some version of an EEZ. * * * Part V of the Informal Composite Negotiating Text (ICNT) comprises the current version of the EEZ. * * *

B. *The Informal Composite Negotiating Text.*[a]

While the concept of extended resource jurisdiction originated early in the twentieth century, the 200-mile EEZ owes its rapid acceptance in international practice to the global educational effects of the negotiations at UNCLOS III. * * *

Article 55 of the ICNT defines the EEZ as "an area beyond and adjacent to the territorial sea, subject to the specific legal regime established in this Part." Article 57 fixes the maximum breadth of the EEZ at 200 nautical miles. Article 56 sets out the rights and duties of the coastal State in its EEZ. These are described as "sovereign rights" for the exploration, exploitation, conservation and management of all natural resources and other economic activities in the EEZ, such as energy production. The coastal State also has jurisdiction regarding artificial islands and structures, scientific research, and the preservation of the marine environment. The coastal State must exercise these rights and duties with due regard to the rights and duties of other States and in conformity with the law of the sea convention. * * *

Article 60 concerns artificial islands, installations, and structures in the zone: the coastal State has exclusive rights regarding their construction, operation and use, and exclusive jurisdiction over them, with the obligation to give due notice that such structures exist. The coastal State may establish reasonable safety zones, general-

a. The articles discussed here did not   U. N. Draft Convention on the Law of
    undergo substantial change in the   the Sea.

ly not to exceed 500 meters, around such structures, taking into account applicable international standards. No artifical islands, structures, or safety zones may be established where they would interfere with "the use of recognized sea lanes essential to international navigation." Such structures do not affect the delimitation of the territorial sea, the EEZ, or the continental shelf.

Articles 61 and 62 provide for the conservation and utilization of the living resources in the EEZ. The coastal State has considerable discretion; it has the right to determine not only the allowable catch but also its own capacity to harvest the living resources. The obligations of the coastal State are to establish proper conservation and management measures to prevent overexploitation, to promote optimum utilization of the living resources, and to grant other States access to the surplus allowable catch. The coastal State may establish detailed regulations, with which foreign fishermen must comply, for conservation and utilization purposes. Article 63 directs the coastal States to seek agreement on the conservation and utilization of stocks which are found within the EEZ's of two or more coastal States or which are both within and beyond the EEZ.

     *   *   *

Article 73 provides coastal States with various enforcement mechanisms. Boarding, inspection, arrest, and judicial proceedings, but not imprisonment or corporal punishment, are permissible measures. The coastal State has a duty to notify the flag State promptly of any arrest or detention of the flag State's vessels and to release vessels and crews on the posting of security.

Article 74 supplies procedures for the delimitation of the EEZ between adjacent and opposite States. Such delimitation shall be by agreement "in accordance with equitable principles," using an equidistance line where appropriate. States which do not conclude an agreement within a reasonable time must resort to the dispute settlement procedures in Part XV of the ICNT. Finally, article 75 provides for the drawing of charts and lists of geographical coordinates defining the limits and boundaries of the EEZ. The affected coastal State has the obligation to publicize such charts and lists.

     *   *   *

[Appendix A, giving a list of 200 mile claims as of November 1978, accompanied the article.   This list follows.]

200-MILE CLAIMS AS OF NOVEMBER 1978

Territorial Sea	Fishery Zone	Exclusive Economic Zone
Argentina [1]	Angola	Bangladesh
Benin	Australia [2]	Barbados
Brazil	Bahamas	Burma
Congo	Belgium [10]	Cape Verde
Ecuador	Bermuda [3]	Colombia
El Salvador	Canada	Comores Islands
Ghana	Cayman Islands [3]	Cook Islands [3, 7]
Guinea	Chile	Costa Rica
Liberia	Denmark [10]	Cuba
Panama	Germany, Dem. Rep.	Dem. Kampuchea
Peru	Germany, Fed. Rep.	Dominican Republic
Sierra Leone	Gilbert Islands [3]	Fiji [8]
Somalia	Iceland	France [11]
Uruguay	Ireland [4, 10]	French Pacific Is. Terr. [3]
	Italy	Grenada
	Japan [5]	Guatemala
	Korea, Rep. of [6]	Guinea-Bissau
	Micronesia [3]	Guyana
	Netherlands [10]	Haiti
	Nicaragua	India
	Northern Marianas	Ivory Coast
	Oman	Korea, Dem. Rep.
	Poland	Malagasy Republic [9]
	Sao Tome & Principe	Maldive Islands [8]
	Solomon Islands	Mauritania
	South Africa	Mauritius
	Sweden	Mexico
	Tuvalu	Mozambique
	U.S.S.R.	New Zealand [11]
	Ukranian S.S.R.	Nigeria
	United Kingdom [10]	Norway [11]
	U.S.A. [5]	Pakistan
		Papua New Guinea [8]
		Portugal
		Senegal
		Seychelles Island
		Spain
		Sri Lanka
		Surinam
		Togo
		Tokelau [8]
		Venezuela
		Vietnam
		Yemen (Aden)
		Honduras
		Niue (New Zealand assoc.)
		Western Samoa

1. Does not affect rights of navigation or overflight.
2. Pending proclamation of the 200-mile provisions of Fisheries Amendment Act, 1978.
3. Territory not yet independent.
4. 50-mile exclusive fishery zone.
5. Excludes highly migratory species.
6. 20 to 200-mile zone.
7. Subject to preemption by UNCLOS treaty.
8. Modified archipelago.
9. 150-mile exclusive economic zone.
10. Member of European Economic Community, which voted to extend the fishing limits of members to 200 miles.
11. Has passed EEZ legislation but currently enforces only fishery jurisdiction.

1. *Relationship to the continental shelf concept.* Article 56 of the Draft Convention gives the coastal state exclusive control of the natural resources of the seabed and subsoil and the superjacent waters. The seabed includes the continental shelf.

The resources of the continental shelf and those of the superjacent waters were kept distinct and treated differently at the Geneva Conference of 1958. The Convention on the Continental Shelf recognized to coastal states the exclusive right to exploit the resources of the shelf and its subsoil and expressly stated these rights did not affect the legal status of the superjacent waters as high seas. At the same time, the Convention on Fishing and Conservation of the Living Resources of the High Seas expressly recognized the right of all states for their nationals to engage in fishing on the high seas, though subject to the provisions in the convention for conservation.

Inasmuch as the exclusive economic zone concept gives coastal states control of the resources in both the shelf and the superjacent waters, the continental shelf concept is not relevant in situations where the shelf does not extend beyond 200 miles. But it becomes relevant whenever the shelf extends beyond that limit. The continental shelf concept is considered infra p. 212.

2. *U.S. Fishery Conservation and Management Act of 1976.* It is codified at 16 U.S.C. §§ 1801–1882. The United States already exercised exclusive jurisdiction over the resources of the continental shelf off its coast. See infra, p. 212. The act, accordingly, dealt with fishing only, claiming under Section 1811 exclusive jurisdiction over the activity within a conservation zone of 200 miles from the baseline. The result of the coupling of the two jurisdictions is a legal regime very much like the legal regime of the exclusive economic zone in the draft, though some differences exist.

Under Section 1812, the United States exercises "exclusive fishery management authority" over all fish within the fishery conservation zone, all continental shelf fishery resources beyond the zone, and all anadromous species throughout their migratory range except when they are within any foreign territorial sea or conservation zone recognized by the United States. Foreign fishing may be conducted in the zone only after the conclusion of an international agreement and the issuance of a permit by the Secretary of Commerce, according to Sections 1821(a), (b), (c) and 1824. Sections 1858–1861 provide for arrest, boarding, and seizure, and for civil and criminal penalties, in case of violation of the act.

3. *Problem.* Section 1813 of the act states that the exclusive fishery management authority of the United States does not extend to highly migratory species of fish. Albacore tuna is such a species.

Suppose that fishing vessels flying the American flag followed albacore tuna in the 200-mile Canadian fishing zone, where Canada exercises exclusive jurisdiction over all species of fish, and the vessels were seized and heavy fines levied following judicial proceedings. Should the United States assert that the arrest and penalty are violations of international law, would the claim be valid? Note, inter alia, the provisions in Articles 64 and 73 of the draft.

———

3. PROTECTION AND PRESERVATION OF THE MARINE ENVIRONMENT

1. *Protection and preservation of the marine environment in the U. N. Draft Convention.* The subject is covered in Articles 192–237. Under Article 194(1), states have the duty of taking all the measures necessary to prevent, reduce and control pollution of the marine environment from any source. The sources of pollution to which the duty applies include land-based sources, seabed activities, dumping and vessels. Article 194(3).

a. *Vessels in general.* Under Article 211(1), states shall establish, through an international organization or a diplomatic conference, international standards for the control of pollution from vessels and under Article 211(2) they are to adopt for vessels flying their flags national rules conforming to the international standards. Article 217(1) requires states to ensure compliance by their flag vessels with the applicable international standards and the national rules they adopt in accordance with the convention. It specifies they must provide effective enforcement of the standards and rules wherever their violation occurs.

b. *Vessels in the territorial sea.* Under Article 211(4), a coastal state may adopt national rules for the control of pollution from vessels in the territorial sea, including vessels in innocent passage, provided that in accordance with Section 3 of Part II of the convention, the rules do not hamper the innocent passage of foreign vessels. Article 21 in that section provides, inter alia, that the coastal state may make laws and regulations for the control of pollution by foreign vessels in innocent passage, but specifies: "Such laws and regulations shall not apply to the design, construction, manning or equipment of foreign ships unless they are giving effect to generally accepted international rules or standards."

Enforcement of applicable international standards and national rules in the territorial sea is provided for in Article 220(2). Where there are "clear grounds" for believing that a vessel navigating in the territorial sea violated such standards or rules, the coastal state may make a physical inspection of the vessel and, subject to the safeguards in Articles 223–233, institute proceedings which may include detention.

c. *Vessels in the exclusive economic zone.* In the exclusive economic zone, a coastal state may establish national rules giving effect to international standards for the control of pollution from vessels. Article 211(5). Should a vessel violate in the zone such standards or rules, the coastal state may take action, while the vessel is navigating in the exclusive economic zone or in the territorial sea, as follows.

Where there are "clear grounds" for believing the vessel violated the standard or rules, the coastal state may require the vessel to give information concerning its identification and other information needed to establish whether a violation has occurred. Article 220(3). If the violation resulted in a "substantial discharge" causing or threatening "significant" pollution of the environment and the vessel refused to give the information or the information was not satisfactory, the coastal state may make a physical inspection of the vessel. Article 220(5).

Where there is "clear objective evidence" the vessel violated the standards or rules and the violation resulted in a discharge causing or threatening "major damage" to the coastline or any resources of the territorial sea or economic zone, the coastal state may, subject to the safeguards in Articles 223–233, institute proceedings, which may include detention. Article 220(6). But if appropriate procedures have been established for bonding, it must let the vessel proceed. Article 220(7).

d. *Vessels in internal waters.* A vessel may be voluntarily in the port, or at the off-shore terminal, of a state and have violated in the territorial sea or exclusive economic zone of the state, its applicable national rules or international standards for the control of pollution. In such a case the state may, subject to the safeguards in Articles 223–233, institute proceedings. Article 220(1).

e. *Vessels in "port states."* A vessel may be voluntarily in the port, or at the off-shore terminal, of a state and have caused a discharge in violation of international standards to occur in the internal waters, territorial sea, or exclusive economic zone of another state, or in the high seas. The port state is permitted by Article 218(1) to conduct an investigation and, subject to the safeguards in Articles 223–233, to institute proceedings as follows.

It may institute them if, and only if, requested to by the state in whose internal waters, or territorial sea, or exclusive economic zone, the violation took place; or by the flag state; or by a state threatened or damaged by the discharge violation. It may also institute the proceedings, however, if the violation has caused or is likely to cause pollution of its own internal waters, territorial sea or exclusive economic zone. Article 218(2).

Under Article 218(4), the state in whose internal waters, territorial sea, or exclusive economic zone the violation took place may preclude the continuation of the proceedings in the port state by requesting the transfer of the evidence and records.

f. *Safeguards.* Among the safeguards provided with respect to the exercise of enforcement powers, Article 228 permits the flag state to preclude, under certain conditions, the continuation of proceedings by a coastal state for a violation beyond its territorial sea of international standards for the control of pollution.

Under Article 230, only monetary penalties may be imposed for violations beyond the territorial sea of a state of applicable international standards or national rules. With respect to violations in the territorial sea, only monetary penalties are permitted except in the case of a willful and serious act of pollution.

g. *Ice-covered areas.* Article 234 provides:

Coastal States have the right to adopt and enforce non-discriminatory laws and regulations for the prevention, reduction and control of marine pollution from vessels in ice-covered areas within the limits of the exclusive economic zone, where particularly severe climatic conditions and the presence of ice covering such areas for most of the year create obstructions or exceptional hazards to navigation, and pollution of the marine environment could cause major harm to or irreversible disturbance of the ecological balance. Such laws and regulations shall have due regard to navigation and the protection and preservation of the marine environment based on the best available scientific evidence.

2. *Canadian action concerning pollution of Arctic waters.* In the Arctic Waters Pollution Prevention Act of June 17, 1970, Canada asserted jurisdiction to regulate all shipping in zones up to 100 nautical miles off its Arctic coasts in order to guard against pollution of the region's coastal and marine resources. Though protested against by the United States as a unilateral action it could not recognize, the act was claimed by Canada to be a positive contribution to the development of rules of international law for the protection of the marine environment. For an article supporting the Canadian view, see Akinsanya, Canadian and British Approaches to International Environmental Law: An Overview, 17 Indian Journal of International Law 335 (1977).

SECTION D.   ALLOCATION OF THE RESOURCES OF THE SEABED

---

1.   THE CONTINENTAL SHELF

1. *Evolution of the doctrine of the continental shelf.* President Truman proclaimed on September 28, 1945, that "the natural resources of the subsoil and sea bed of the continental shelf beneath the high seas but contiguous to the coast of the United States" were regarded by the United States as appertaining to it and "subject to its jurisdiction and control." Presidential Proclamation No. 2667, 59 Stat. 884. Thereafter, claims to the resources of the continental shelf were made by a large number of other states.

Only thirteen years after the presidential proclamation, the Convention on the Continental Shelf was signed. As of January 1, 1980, 53 states were parties to it. The ready acceptance of the new basis of jurisdiction illustrates the capacity of international law to adapt and change very rapidly when the international community so demands.

2. *Division of the resources of the continental shelf between the States and the federal government.* In the Submerged Lands Act of May 22, 1953, 67 Stat. 29, the States of the United States were granted rights to the lands which are part of the continental shelf of the United States up to three nautical miles from the coast on the Atlantic and Pacific Oceans, and up to nine nautical miles in the Gulf of Mexico if the states involved could establish an historical claim to such distance. Beyond those limits, the federal government controls the resources of the continental shelf. Outer Continental Shelf Lands Act of August 7, 1953, 67 Stat. 462. The division of the resources does not create an issue of international law, however. The issue is one of domestic law. The Outer Continental Shelf Lands Act conforms to the Convention on the Continental Shelf.

CONVENTION ON THE CONTINENTAL SHELF
OF APRIL 29, 1958

15 U.S.T. 471, 499 U.N.T.S. 311.

Article 1

For the purpose of these articles, the term "continental shelf" is used as referring (a) to the seabed and subsoil of the submarine areas adjacent to the coast but outside the area of the territorial sea, to a depth of 200 metres or, beyond that limit, to where the depth of the superjacent waters admits of the exploitation of the natural resources of the said areas; (b) to the seabed and subsoil of similar submarine areas adjacent to the coasts of islands.

UNITED STATES v. RAY

United States Court of Appeals, Fifth Circuit, 1970.
423 F.2d 16.

AINSWORTH, Circuit Judge. Triumph and Long Reefs are two coral reefs which lie in international waters about four and one-half miles off the southeast coast of Florida, near Miami, and are the subject of this interesting and fantastic controversy between two rival private claimants and the United States. To the District Court (Judge Charles B. Fulton), the case was reminiscent of a fairy tale.[1] To the defendants, the reefs were to become an island nation to be known as Grand Capri Republic; to intervenor, a new sovereign country would be established on the reefs, to be named Atlantis, Isle of Gold. Defendants would organize some semblance of a defense but

---

1. Judge Fulton quoted the following as appropriate to his remark:

"They thought I was crazy when I bought the island. I said it was a bargain * * *.

They thought it was anarchy to fly my own personal flag * * * ."

Donleavy, J. P.; "At Longitude and Latitude," in Meet My Maker the Mad Molecule, pp. 26–28; Delacorte Press, N. Y. (1960); United States v. Ray, S.D.Fla., 1969, 294 F.Supp. 532.

have no intention of attacking the Coast Guard or Navy. Intervenor envisioned the reefs as a property worth one billion dollars, where a post office, building offices, stamp department and foreign office would be built, as well as a government palace and congress.

The fairy tale has an unhappy ending, with the granting by the District Court of the petition of the United States for a permanent injunction against the activities of defendants and intervenor on these reefs, and by the action which we take here in affirming in part and reversing in part the judgment of the trial court. The dreams of the separate groups for a new nation must perish, like the lost continent "Atlantis," beneath the waves and waters of the sea which constantly submerge the reefs.

The United States brought this action for injunctive relief against Louis M. Ray and Acme General Contractors, Inc. alleging interference with the rights of the United States on coral reefs located on its Continental Shelf on two grounds. In the first count the Government alleged that the activities of these defendants in building caissons on the reefs, dredging material from the seabed and depositing that material within the caissons was causing irreparable injury to the reefs which are subject to the control of the United States, and that these activities constituted trespass. The second count alleged that these activities were being unlawfully conducted without the required authorization of the Secretary of the Army. See 33 U.S.C. § 403; 43 U.S.C. § 1333(f). A preliminary injunction was granted against defendants. Thereafter Atlantis Development Corporation, Ltd., which was also contemplating commercial development of the reefs, was allowed by this Court to intervene in the proceedings. Intervenor filed a cross claim, alleging its superior title to the property by virtue of discovery of the reefs by its predecessor. After an extensive nonjury trial, at which numerous witnesses, lay and expert, testified and at which voluminous exhibits were introduced, the District Court adopted all of the facts stipulated by the parties and further found:

1. Triumph and Long Reefs are a part of the Continental Shelf extending seaward from the East Coast of Florida, and all waters overlying the reefs do not exceed one hundred fathoms in depth.

2. Triumph and Long Reefs are completely submerged at all times, except when their highest projections are fleetingly visible while awash at mean low water. Accordingly, Triumph and Long Reefs are part of the "seabed" and "subsoil" of the Outer Continental Shelf within the Outer Continental Shelf Lands Act of 1953, 43 U.S.C. § 1331, et seq.

3. These reefs, together with the organisms attached thereto, are "natural resources" within the Outer Continental Shelf Lands Act, and the Geneva Convention on the Continental Shelf.

4.   The caissons positioned by Ray and the jack platform construction or "boathouses" built on pilings proposed by Atlantis constitute "artificial islands and fixed structures * * * erected * * * for the purpose of * * * developing" the reefs, within the Outer Continental Shelf Lands Act.

The District Court denied all claims of defendants and intervenor, granted the claim of the Government under its second count, but denied the Government's claim of trespass under the first count. In so doing, the District Court recognized the sovereign rights of the United States, but concluded that those rights are limited as the claimed interest of the United States is something less than a property right, consisting of neither ownership nor possession, and consequently not supporting a common law action for trespass quare clausum fregit.

All parties have appealed. The Government's appeal is limited to the Court's denial of an injunction on count one of the amended complaint. We affirm the District Court's factual findings and its grant of injunctive relief under the Government's second count. However, we reverse the Court's denial of injunctive relief on the first count of the Government's amended complaint.

LACK OF STATUTORY PERMIT ISSUE:

The District Court correctly concluded that the past and proposed activities of defendants and intervenor were unlawful in the absence of a statutory permit from the Secretary of the Army. Section 10 of the Rivers and Harbors Act, 33 U.S.C. § 403, prohibits construction in navigable waters of the United States unless the work has been "recommended by the Chief of Engineers and authorized by the Secretary of the Army." The authority of the Secretary of the Army is extended to the Outer Continental Shelf by Section 1333(f) of the Outer Continental Shelf Lands Act, 43 U.S.C. § 1331 et seq.:

The authority of the Secretary of the Army to prevent obstruction to navigation in the navigable waters of the United States is extended to artificial islands and fixed structures located on the outer Continental Shelf.

It is undisputed that defendants and intervenor did not obtain permission or authority for their activities on the reefs. The argument is made that the area is not navigable and therefore not governed by Section 1333(f) of the Outer Continental Shelf Lands Act. Apparently the Court did not, nor do we, deem it necessary to predicate the injunction on navigability of waters covering the reefs, although a specific finding of navigability was made. The quoted section extends the authority of the Secretary to "fixed structures located on the outer Continental Shelf" without regard to the navigability of the particular area involved. If it were necessary to find navigability, however, the evidence amply supports such a finding, and fully establishes that the structures herein involved interfere with the exclusive rights of the United States under the Convention to explore the Continental Shelf and exploit its natural resources. Under the circumstances we do not decide what the result would be if the structures did not interfere with the rights of the United States as recognized by the Convention, our decision being limited to the particular facts of this case.

THE TRESPASS ISSUE:

It is clear that the reefs in question are within the area designated as the Continental Shelf by both national (Outer Continental Shelf Lands Act, supra) and international (Geneva Convention on the Continental Shelf, 15 U.S.T. 473, executed in 1958 and effective in 1964) law.

The Outer Continental Shelf Lands Act, 43 U.S.C. § 1331(a), in pertinent part provides:

> The term "outer Continental Shelf" means all submerged lands lying seaward and outside of the area of lands beneath navigable waters as defined in section 1301 of this title, and of which the subsoil and seabed appertain to the United States and are subject to its jurisdiction and control.

Article 1 of the international Convention on the Continental Shelf similarly reads:

> For the purpose of these articles, the term "continental shelf" is used as referring (a) to the seabed and subsoil of the submarine areas adjacent to the coast but outside the area of the territorial sea, to a depth of 200 metres or, beyond that limit, to where the depth of the superjacent waters admits of the exploitation of the natural resources of the said areas; * * * 15 U.S.T. 473.

The evidence shows that the reefs are completely submerged at mean high water, and as the Court specifically found, "at all times, except when their highest projections are fleetingly visible while awash at mean low water." Thus the reefs are contemplated within the definition of the Outer Continental Shelf Lands Act and the Geneva Convention on the Continental Shelf, if they meet the definition of "seabed" or "subsoil" contained therein. Webster defines "seabed" as "lands underlying the sea." The evidence establishes that the term "seabed" is commonly understood to be any terrain below the high water line. The federal and common law comports with this understanding in defining the "bed" of a body of water as lands below the ordinary high water mark. * * * The record shows that on the death of the coral, which has a natural predilection for cementing itself onto preexisting rocky structures, its skeletal remains become part of the seabed of the Continental Shelf. The District Court's finding that the reefs are part of the "seabed" of the Shelf is fully supported by substantial evidence of record.

The same national and international laws (The Outer Continental Shelf Lands Act and the Geneva Convention on the Continental

Shelf) explicitly recognize the sovereign rights of the United States and the exclusiveness of those rights to explore the Shelf and exploit its natural resources.

The Outer Continental Shelf Lands Act (43 U.S.C. § 1332(a)) states:

> It is declared to be the policy of the United States that the subsoil and seabed of the outer Continental Shelf appertain to the United States and are subject to its jurisdiction, control, and power of disposition as provided in this subchapter.

To the extent that any of the terms of the Act are inconsistent with the later adopted Geneva Convention on the Continental Shelf they should be considered superseded. See Cook v. United States, 288 U.S. 102, 118–119, 53 S.Ct. 305, 77 L.Ed. 641 (1933). But there is nothing in the pertinent language of the Geneva Convention on the Continental Shelf which detracts from or is inconsistent with the Outer Continental Shelf Lands Act. To the contrary, the Geneva Convention confirms and crystallizes the exclusiveness of those rights, particularly with reference to the natural resources of the Shelf.

Article 2 of the Geneva Convention on the Continental Shelf provides:

1. The coastal State exercises over the continental shelf sovereign rights for the purpose of exploring it and exploiting its natural resources.

2. The rights referred to in paragraph 1 of this article are exclusive in the sense that if the coastal State does not explore the continental shelf or exploit its natural resources, no one may undertake these activities, or make a claim to the continental shelf, without the express consent of the coastal State.

3. The rights of the coastal State over the continental shelf do not depend on occupation, effective or notional, or on any express proclamation.

4. The natural resources referred to in these articles consist of the mineral and other non-living resources of the seabed and subsoil together with living organisms belonging to sedentary species, that is to say, organisms which, at the harvestable stage, either are immobile on or under the seabed or are unable to move except in constant physical contact with the seabed or the subsoil.

It is unnecessary for us to decide whether the Outer Continental Shelf Lands Act, Section 1332(a), supra (which does not limit the nation's "jurisdiction, control, and power of disposition" to the natural resources of the Shelf), alone confers rights sufficient to authorize the injunctive relief sought. The right of the United States to control those resources is implicit in Article 2, paragraphs 1, 2 and 3, supra, of the Geneva Convention on the Continental Shelf, and explicitly recognized in the Submerged Lands Act, 43 U.S.C. § 1301 et seq. This Act further provides (43 U.S.C. § 1302) the definition of "natural resources" of the Continental Shelf:

> Nothing in this chapter shall be deemed to affect in any wise the rights of the United States to the natural resources of that portion of the subsoil and seabed of the Continental Shelf lying seaward and outside of the area of lands beneath navigable waters, as defined in Section 1301 of this title, all of which natural resources appertain to the United States, and the jurisdiction and control of which by the United States is confirmed.

Section 1301, referred to within the above-quoted section, defines "natural resources" as including, *without limiting the generality thereof,* oil, gas, and all other minerals, and *fish,* shrimp, oysters, clams, crabs, lobsters, sponges, kelp, *and other marine animal* and plant *life * * *."* (Emphasis supplied.)   43 U.S.C. § 1301(e).

Article 2, paragraph 4, of the Geneva Convention on the Continental Shelf includes in its definition of "natural resources" both living and non-living resources, for it defines the term as consisting of "* * * mineral and other non-living resources of the seabed and subsoil together with living organisms belonging to sedentary species. * * *"

Having thus concluded that the United States has the exclusive right for purposes of exploration and exploitation of the reefs, there remains only the question of whether injunctive relief was improperly denied to the Government on its first count which alleged trespass.

Although the complaint is inaccurately framed in terms of trespass in count one, the Government repeatedly stresses that it is not claiming ownership of the reefs. We do not question the District Court's conclusion that the Government's interest, being something less than fee simple, cannot support a common law action for trespass quare clausum fregit. But we do not understand that claim to seek such a remedy, despite the language in which the petition is couched. Damages, an inseparable element in the common law action for trespass, are not sought here, and the only relief requested is restraint from interference with rights to an area which appertains to the United States and which under national and international law is subject not only to its jurisdiction but its control as well. It is in this light that we consider the allegations of amended count one.

Neither ownership nor possession is, however, a necessary requisite for the granting of injunctive relief. This principle is implicit in the companion decisions of the Supreme Court, United States v. State of Louisiana, 339 U.S. 699, 70 S.Ct. 914, 94 L.Ed. 1216 (1950); United States v. State of Texas, 339 U.S. 707, 70 S.Ct. 918, 94 L.Ed. 1221 (1950), in which injunctive relief was granted to protect "paramount rights" of the United States beyond the territorial limits of Louisiana and Texas, to distances farther out in international waters than that involved here and at a time when those rights had not yet been statutorily established.

*   *   *

The evidence overwhelmingly shows that the Government has a vital interest, from a practical as well as an aesthetic viewpoint, in preserving the reefs for public use and enjoyment. The protective underwater crannies of the reefs serve as a haven and spawning ground for myriad species of tropical and game fish. The unique and spectacular formations of the submerged coral deposits attract scores of water sports enthusiasts, skin divers, nature students, and marine researchers. Certain organisms living on the reefs contain substances useful in pharmacology. The reefs protect the inland waters from the heavy wave action of the open sea, thus making the area conducive to boating and other water sports. Congress, intent on conserving the value and natural beauty of the area, recently enacted the Biscayne National Monument Bill establishing the area, which includes both Triumph and Long Reefs, as a national monument. The reefs are a part of the series of coral reefs which dot the coastal and international waters extending out from southeastern Florida. Slightly to the south and west of the Triumph and Long Reefs and straddling the three-mile dividing line between federal and state waters, is the huge federal-approved John Pennekamp Coral Reef State Park, also known as Key Largo Coral Reef Preserve. The fact that the area is worthy of preservation is abundantly demonstrated by the evidence. But more importantly, the evidence shows that protective action by the Government to prevent despoliation of these unique natural resources is of tantamount importance. There was convincing evidence that the activities of defendants in dredging and filling the reefs has and would continue to kill the sensitive corals by smothering them; that the construction would constitute a navigational hazard to pleasure craft, and would destroy a very productive marine area and other natural resources. Obviously the United States has an important interest to protect in preventing the establishment of a new sovereign nation within four and one-half miles of the Florida Coast, whether it be Grand Capri Republic or Atlantis, Isle of Gold.

The rights of the United States in and to the reefs and the vital interest which the Government has in preserving the area require full and permanent injunctive relief against any interference with those rights by defendants and intervenor.

*   *   *

Affirmed in part, reversed in part.

DRAFT CONVENTION ON THE LAW OF THE SEA
(INFORMAL TEXT)

United Nations, Third Conference on the Law of the Sea.
A/CONF. 62/WP. 10/Rev. 3, 22 September 1980.

Article 76

Definition of the continental shelf

1.   The continental shelf of a coastal State comprises the sea-bed and subsoil of the submarine areas that extend beyond its territorial sea throughout the natural prolongation of its land territory to the outer edge of the continental margin, or to a distance of 200 nautical miles from the baselines from which the breadth of the territorial sea is measured where the outer edge of the continental margin does not extend up to that distance.

2.   The continental shelf of a coastal State shall not extend beyond the limits provided for in paragraphs 4 to 6.

3.   The continental margin comprises the submerged prolongation of the land mass of the coastal State, and consists of the sea-bed and subsoil of the shelf, the slope and the rise. It does not include the deep ocean floor with its oceanic ridges or the subsoil thereof.

4.   (a) For the purposes of this Convention, the coastal State shall establish the outer edge of the continental margin wherever the margin extends beyond 200 nautical miles from the baselines from which the breadth of the territorial sea is measured, by either:

(i) A line delineated in accordance with paragraph 7 by reference to the outermost fixed points at each of which the thickness of sedimentary rocks is at least 1 per cent of the shortest distance from such point to the foot of the continental slope; or

(ii) A line delineated in accordance with paragraph 7 by reference to fixed points not more than 60 nautical miles from the foot of the continental slope.

(b) In the absence of evidence to the contrary, the foot of the continental slope shall be determined as the point of maximum change in the gradient at its base.

5.   The fixed points comprising the line of the outer limits of the continental shelf on the sea-bed, drawn in accordance with paragraph 4(a)(i) and (ii), either shall not exceed 350 nautical miles from the baselines from which the breadth of the territorial sea is measured or shall not exceed 100 nautical miles from the 2,500 metre isobath, which is a line connecting the depth of 2,500 metres.

6.   Notwithstanding the provisions of paragraph 5, on submarine ridges, the outer limit of the continental shelf shall not exceed 350 nautical miles from the baselines from which the breadth of the territorial sea is measured. This paragraph does not apply to subma-

rine elevations that are natural components of the continental margin, such as its plateaux, rises, caps, banks and spurs.

7.   The coastal State shall delineate the seaward boundary of its continental shelf where that shelf extends beyond 200 nautical miles from the baselines from which the breadth of the territorial sea is measured by straight lines not exceeding 60 nautical miles in length, connecting fixed points, such points to be defined by co-ordinates of latitude and longitude.

8.   Information on the limits of the continental shelf beyond the 200 nautical mile exclusive economic zone shall be submitted by the coastal State to the Commission on the Limits of the Continental Shelf set up under annex II on the basis of equitable geographical representation.   The Commission shall make recommendations to coastal States on matters related to the establishment of the outer limits of their continental shelf.   The limits of the shelf established by a coastal State on the basis of these recommendations shall be final and binding.

9.   The coastal State shall deposit with the Secretary-General of the United Nations charts and relevant information, including geodetic data, permanently describing the outer limits of its continental shelf.   The Secretary-General shall give due publicity thereto.

10.   The provisions of this article are without prejudice to the question of delimitation of the continental shelf between adjacent or opposite States.

Article 82

Payments and contributions with respect to the exploitation of the continental shelf beyond 200 nautical miles

1.   The coastal State shall make payments or contributions in kind in respect of the exploitation of the non-living resources of the continental shelf beyond 200 nautical miles from the baselines from which the breadth of the territorial sea is measured.

2.   The payments and contributions shall be made annually with respect to all production at a site after the first five years of production at that site.   For the sixth year, the rate of payment or contribution shall be 1 per cent of the value or volume of production at the site.   The rate shall increase by 1 per cent for each subsequent year until the twelfth year and shall remain at 7 per cent thereafter.   Production does not include resources used in connexion with exploitation.

3.   A developing State which is a net importer of a mineral resource produced from its continental shelf is exempt from making such payments or contributions in respect of that mineral resource.

4.   The payments or contributions shall be made through the Authority, which shall distribute them to States Parties to this Convention, on the basis of equitable sharing criteria, taking into account

the interests and needs of developing States, particularly the least developed and the land-locked amongst them.

---

2. MINERAL RESOURCES BEYOND NATIONAL JURISDICTION

1. *Technological advances induce quest for law as to mineral resources under the high seas.* For most of the modern era, conflicts of national interest did not arise as to the extraction of substances from the waters, bed, and subsoil of what once were called the high seas but now must be more exactly characterized as areas beyond national jurisdiction. By analogy to high seas fishing, anyone could take natural materials from these waters; and even the fixing of installations by mooring and otherwise was considered not to be illegal per se.

By the 1960s, technologies for the drilling for oil and gas in very deep water and collection and lifting from the seabed of polymetallic nodules became feasible. These technological developments coincided in a general way with increasing need everywhere for liquid hydrocarbons and deficiencies in national production by some states, particularly highly industrialized states such as the United States, of highly strategic alloy metals contained in the seabed nodules, viz., manganese, cobalt, and nickle. Copper and iron (usually in highly attractive ferromanganese compounds) are also found in nodular form. Nodules vary in metallic composition and content from place to place. The quantities are immense, and the areas of concentration are vast.

It was the developed states, particularly the United States in its private sector, that brought about the improvements in technology that have made extraction of the substances referred to feasible. These states also have capabilities for mobilizing the capital such operations will require. The less well developed states, faced with disappointments as to expectations for rapid growth and in an environment of a widening gap—rather than a narrowing one—between rich countries and poor countries, viewed with apprehension the prospect that the planet's last source of natural wealth not already appropriated would be denied to them through preemption by states able to take the lead in exploitation.

In the developed states, the profit motive in the private sector (reflected, of course, in national politics) and a security interest in the public sector created pressures for action to use the new technology on an individual state basis. But in these same states, a prudent concern for national image, the verdict of history, and the broader national interest in world stability supported the search for means to achieve equitable sharing of the new resources on the basis of respective needs and national contributions.

In 1968 a private international consortium, without leave of any state, claimed exclusive rights to the extraction of seabed brine from a large area in the Red Sea, asserting that no licensing authority existed anywhere. See Nanda, Some Legal Questions on the Peaceful Uses of Ocean Space, 9 Va.J.Int'l L. 343, 384 (1969). Other plans to act unilaterally were announced and received publicity. The basic issues came rapidly to the attention of various segments of the United Nations, the Senate Committee on Foreign Relations, and legal writers.

Collins, Mineral Exploitation of the Seabed: Problems, Progress, and Alternatives, XII Natural Resources Lawyer 599, at 636 (1979) *, describes what has come to be recognized as a key development:

* * * August 17, 1967, was the date on which the seabed question was born. On that date Malta's United Nations ambassador, Arvid Pardo, proposed that an item entitled "Declaration and Treaty Concerning the Reservation Exclusively for Peaceful Purposes of the Seabed and of the Ocean Floor Underlying the Seas Beyond the Limits of Present National Jurisdiction and the Use of their Resources in the Interests of Mankind" be added to the agenda of the General Assembly. It was Dr. Pardo's subsequent speech to the General Assembly that set off the explosion of international interest in the formation of a regime to exploit the seabed not then under national jurisdiction. Pardo * * * mesmerized many United Nations delegations from developing countries with his assertions that the vast, readily exploitable mineral wealth of the seabed could quickly redress the inequities of economic development * * *

The Pardo proposal contained the following essential points:

—that the ocean floor and its resources * * * are to be considered the common property of mankind;

—that they are not subject to national appropriation;

—that they must be used for peaceful purposes only;

—that the resources should be developed cooperatively, not competitively, and particularly for the benefit of developing nations; and

—that an international regime should be created, within the framework of the United Nations or emanating from the United Nations, to guarantee these principles and plan for the development of common ocean resources.

The initiative just described set in train a long process of negotiations at UNCLOS III. On the one hand the less well developed states made determined efforts to vest exclusive rights of exploitation of seabed resources beyond national jurisdiction in an international authority so organized they could dominate it by taking full advantage of their number. On the other hand the developed states, while

* Reprinted by permission of the Section on Natural Resources Law of the American Bar Association.

willing to accommodate to the principles stated above, resisted the creation of an international authority not responsive to their interests even though the successful operation of the authority would depend on technology and risk capital they alone could provide.

In some quarters in developed states, the free enterprise system as to mining is seen as imperiled by the insistence of the developing states that structured international controls be provided for all significant activities in the seabed area beyond national jurisdiction. Concern about national security in relation to supplies of scarce substances is also prominent in developed states. Some states, mainly developing ones, are producers on land of vital metals also found on the ocean floor in nodules. These fear damage to markets and price structure from additional production of these metals from the new source and wish to have such production controllable in support of their interests, or, alternatively, guaranteed commodity price support systems for their production of the metals concerned.

The seabed beyond national jurisdiction is named "The Area" in the Draft Convention on the Law of the Sea and Articles 133–191 of Part XI of the draft are devoted to organizing the exploitation of its resources which are declared in Article 136 to be "the common heritage of mankind."

The Authority set up to function in the Area consists of an Assembly, Articles 159–160, a Council which is the executive body of the seabed authority, Articles 161–165, a Secretariat, Articles 166–169, and an Enterprise, Article 170, which is to carry out the activities in the Area, including the transportation, processing and marketing of minerals recovered from the Area. In this Authority, however, the conflicting state interests sketched above are not yet fully harmonized. Structurally, and in the statements of principle, the draft favors, as have previous drafts, the views of the developing states. But through complex weighted voting formulas for the Council in Article 161, and otherwise, some assurances are or ought to be provided the developed countries. Compare, however, the composition and voting provisions for the Assembly in Article 159 which is declared to be " * * * the supreme organ of the Authority to which the other principal organs shall be accountable as specifically provided for in this Convention. * * * "

2. *Initial United States compromise proposal.* The item that follows is the original United States effort to compromise with the developing countries. Why did it not satisfy them, in the light of the sketch of basic conflicts of interest, above?

SUMMARY OF PROVISIONS OF DRAFT PROPOSED BY THE UNITED STATES FOR A "UNITED NATIONS CONVENTION ON THE INTERNATIONAL SEABED AREA," AUGUST 3, 1970

65 American Journal of International Law 179 (1971).*

[The United Nations Committee on the Peaceful Uses of the Seabed and the Ocean Floor Beyond the Limits of National Jurisdiction met in Geneva during the month of August, 1970. On August 3, the United States Delegation tabled, as a working paper, a Draft United Nations Convention on the International Seabed Area. The following summary of the provisions of that draft was prepared by John R. Stevenson, The Legal Adviser of the Department of State.]

On May 23, 1970, President Nixon announced a new oceans policy for the United States and stated that the United States would make specific proposals at the U.N. Seabeds Committee in August with regard to the proposed regime for the seabeds beyond national jurisdiction which he set forth in broad outline in his announcement. The submission of a draft "United Nations Convention on the International Seabed Area" to the Seabeds Committee as a working paper for discussion within that committee as well as with other governments and within the United States, implements the President's announcement. The draft convention and its appendices raise a number of questions with respect to which further detailed study is clearly necessary and do not necessarily represent the definitive views of the United States Government.

The basic structure of the convention reflects the President's proposals that states should by international agreement renounce their sovereign rights in the seabed under the high seas beyond a water depth of 200 meters; establish an international regime for the area beyond with certain basic principles and general rules applicable throughout this area; authorize coastal states as Trustees for the international community to carry out the major administrative role in licensing the exploration and exploitation of natural resources from the limit of coastal state national jurisdiction to the edge of the continental margin, and to share in the international revenues from the Trusteeship Area which they administered; and establish international machinery to perform similar functions in the area beyond the continental margin.

Basic Principles

Among the basic principles which would become applicable to the entire International Seabed Area (including the International Trusteeship Area) under the convention would be the following:

The International Seabed Area would be the common heritage of mankind and no state could exercise sovereignty or sovereign rights

---

* Reprinted by permission of the American Society of International Law.

over this area or its resources or, except as provided in the convention, acquire any right or interest therein.

The International Seabed Area would be open to use by all states without discrimination, except as otherwise provided in the convention, and would be reserved exclusively for peaceful purposes.

Provision would be made for the collection of revenues from mineral production in the Area to be used for international community purposes including economic advancement of developing countries and for promotion of the safe, efficient and economic exploitation of the mineral resources of the seabed.

Exploration and exploitation of the natural resources of the Area must not result in unjustified interference with other activities in the marine environment, and all activities in the Area must be conducted with adequate safeguards against pollution and for the protection of human life and the marine environment.

A contracting party would be responsible for insuring that those authorized by it (as Trustee in the Trusteeship Area) or sponsored by it (in the area beyond) complied with the convention. Contracting parties would also be responsible for any damage caused by those authorized or sponsored by them.

The general rules would be as follows:

Mineral Resources

All exploration and exploitation of the mineral deposits in the Area would be licensed by the appropriate Trustee in the Trusteeship Area and by the International Seabed Resource Authority in the area beyond, subject to general provisions relating to the terms of licenses included in appendices forming part of the convention, a number of which allow greater discretion to the Trustee State in the case of the Trusteeship Area. The contracting parties would have primary responsibility for inspecting activities licensed or sponsored by them. The International Seabed Resource Authority would also have authority to inspect and determine if a licensed operation violates the convention. Licenses would be revoked only for cause and in accordance with the convention. Expropriation of investments made, or unjustifiable interference with operations conducted pursuant to a license, would be prohibited.

Living Resources of the Seabed

All contracting parties would have the right to explore and exploit these resources (e. g., king crab) subject to necessary conservation measures and the right of the Trustee in the Trusteeship Area to decide whether and by whom such resources should be exploited.

Protection of the Marine Environment, Life, and Property

The International Seabed Resource Authority would be authorized to prescribe rules to protect against pollution of the marine environment and injury to persons and resources resulting from exploration and exploitation and to prevent unjustifiable interference with other activities in the marine environment.

Scientific Research

Each party would agree to encourage, and to obviate interference with, scientific research and to promote international cooperation in scientific research.

International Trusteeship Area

The provisions of the convention relating to the International Trusteeship Area would define the outer limit of this area as a line beyond the base of the continental slope where the downward inclination of the seabed reaches a specified gradient. Such gradient would be determined by technical experts who would take into account, among other factors, ease of determination, the need to avoid dual administration of single resource deposits, and the avoidance of including excessively large areas in the Trusteeship Area. Other provisions would limit the Trustee's rights to those set forth in the convention. These rights of the Trustee State would include the issuing, suspending and revoking of mineral exploration and exploitation licenses subject to the rules set forth in the convention and its appendices, full discretion to decide whether a license should be issued and to whom a license should be issued, exercise of criminal and civil jurisdiction over its licensees, and retention of a portion (a figure between 33⅓ percent and 50 percent is suggested for consideration) of the fees and payments required under the convention for activities in the Area. The Trustee State would also be able to collect and retain additional license and rental fees to defray its administrative expenses and to collect other additional payments, retaining the same portion as indicated above of such other additional payments.

International Seabed Resource Authority

The principal organs of the proposed International Seabed Resource Authority would be an Assembly of all contracting parties; a Council of 24 members, including the six most industrially advanced contracting states, at least 12 developing countries and at least two landlocked or shelf-locked states; and a Tribunal of from five to nine judges elected by the Council.

The Assembly, which would meet at least once every 3 years, would elect members of the Council, approve budgets proposed by the Council, approve proposals of the Council for changes in allocation of net income within the limits prescribed in an appendix to the convention, and make recommendations.

The Council, which would make decisions only with the approval of a majority of both the six most industrially advanced contracting states, and of the 18 other contracting states, would appoint the commissions provided for in the convention, submit to the Assembly budgets and proposals for changes in the allocation of net income within the limits prescribed in an appendix, and could issue emergency orders at the request of a contracting party to prevent serious harm to the marine environment.

The Tribunal would decide all disputes and advise on all questions relating to the interpretation and application of the convention. It would have compulsory jurisdiction in respect of any complaint brought by a contracting party against another contracting party for failure to fulfill its obligations under the convention, or whenever the Operations Commission, on its own initiative or at the request of any licensee, considered that a contracting party or licensee had failed to fulfill its obligations under the convention. If the Tribunal found the contracting party or licensee in default, such party or licensee would be obligated to take the measures required to implement the Tribunal's judgment. The Tribunal would have the power to impose fines of not more than $1,000 for each day of an offense as well as to award damages to the other party concerned. Where the Tribunal determined that a licensee had committed a gross and persistent violation of the provisions of the convention and within a reasonable time had not brought its operations into compliance, the Council could either revoke the license or request the Trustee Party to do so. Where a contracting party failed to perform the obligations incumbent on it under a judgment of the Tribunal, the Council, on application of the other party to the case, could decide upon measures to give effect to the judgment, including, when appropriate, temporary suspension of the rights of the defaulting party under the convention (the extent of such suspension to be related to the extent and seriousness of the violation). In addition, any contracting party, and any person directly affected, could bring before the Tribunal the question of the legality of any measure taken by the Council, or one of its commissions, on the ground of violation of the convention, lack of jurisdiction, infringement of important procedural rules, unreasonableness, or misuse of powers; and the Tribunal could declare such measure null and void.

The convention also provides for the establishment of three commissions, each of from five to nine members. The Rules and Recommended Practices Commission would consider and recommend to the Council adoption of annexes as described below. The Operations Commission would issue licenses for mineral exploration and exploitation in the area beyond the International Trusteeship Area and supervise the operations of licensees in cooperation with the Trustee or sponsoring party, but not itself engage in exploration or exploitation. The International Seabed Boundary Review Commission would review the delineation of boundaries submitted by the contracting parties for approval in accordance with the convention, negotiate differences among the parties and if the differences were not resolved initiate appropriate proceedings before the Tribunal, and render advice to contracting parties on boundary questions.

The members of the Rules and Recommended Practices Commission and the International Seabed Boundary Review Commission would not be full-time employees of the Authority.

The Secretariat of the Authority would consist of a Secretary General appointed by the Council and a staff appointed by the Secretary General under the general guidelines established by the Council.

Any amendment of the convention or the appendices would require the approval of the Council and a two-thirds vote of the Assembly and would come into force only when ratified by two-thirds of the contracting parties, including each of the six most industrially advanced contracting states.

Appendices, which are integral parts of the convention, are included in the draft convention by way of example only, as they require extensive consideration of the questions involved by technically qualified experts.

* * *

The moratorium resolution and the United States Deep Seabed Hard Mineral Resources Act. General Assembly Resolution 2574 (XXIV) of December 15, 1969, was voted by the developing country bloc (the so-called Group of 77 that is actually many more) to seek to freeze any unilateral national action toward exploitation of the resources of the areas in question prior to the establishment of an international regime. The United States did not accord legal effect to this action, but the executive repeatedly urged the Congress to postpone action on national legislation to license and control activities by the United States concerns in the area, pending efforts to reach agreement on a treaty. Private interests actively supported such national legislation, and the Congress increasingly became impatient or dubious as the Third Law of the Sea Conference dragged on. Before 1980, legislation designed to provide an interim federal regime, pending the coming into effect for the United States of a seabed treaty, was considered several times in Congress. See 96th Cong., 1st Sess., House Report, Deep Seabed Hard Mineral Resources Act, Hearings and Markup on H.R. 2759, July 11, November 1, December 19, 1979; April 30, 1980. An act of the above name became law on June 28, 1980; P.L. 96–283, 94 Stat. 553, 96th Cong., 1st Sess., 30 U.S.C. § 1401. Sections 1441 and 1442, dealing with the relationship between rights acquired under this statute and any subsequent international agreement on the same subject matter, are of considerable interest from policy and interpretation standpoints.

Chapter 4

LAW OF AIRSPACE, SPACE AND CELESTIAL BODIES

When the 20th Century began, the techniques of air flight and space exploration were almost all in the future. Little in the way of positive law existed for the regulation of the technology that exploded in the first decade of the century and that has periodically advanced with astonishingly new and unforeseen capacities. It is instructive to observe the ways in which international law has been created by a process that either anticipated changes or reacted to events that had not been foreseen.

SECTION A. ACTIVITIES IN AIRSPACE

1. AERIAL TRANSIT

DRAFT CONVENTION, REGIME OF AEROSTATS AND WIRELESS TELEGRAPHY (1906)

21 Annuaire de l'Institut de Droit International 293, 327 (1907).[a]

Mr. Fauchille, rapporteur, * * * summarizes the main conclusions in his report.

* * *

The fundamental difficulty * * * concerns the nature of airspace and the rights of states in the atmosphere. How can this question be solved? First of all, it must be defined. The atmosphere can be divided in three zones. Above 5000 meters [there is] a zone where breathing is impossible and where balloons cannot penetrate. Close to earth, [there is] a zone [which is] subject to appropriation through building up to, at present, a height of 330 meters since the highest construction today, the Eiffel Tower, is 300 meters high and the highest telegraphic masts reach 30 meters. But even in that situation, one cannot say that airspace is subject to appropriation by the state. What is state property is not airspace but the constructions in the airspace. Thus, it is only in that airspace from the ground up, where there are no constructions, and up to 5000 meters, that there exists a [third] zone whose [legal] regime must be determined.

Two absolute theories have been advanced.

In the one * * * airspace is completely free in all its zones, be it for aerial navigation or for radio telegraphy. In the other, the

a. Translation by the editors. The text in the Annuaire is a summary minute of what the rapporteur said rather than the verbatim transcript of his statement.

230

subjacent state has a right of property or sovereignty in airspace within a limit, according to one view, * * * [equivalent] to the range of a cannon, or according to another view, * * * within limits to be determined by an international agreement similar to the one proposed by the Netherlands in 1895 for territorial waters.

Mr. Fauchille objects that the first system does not take into account the dangers for states in the matter of espionage, especially, and the operation of radio telegraphy, [which would result] from the passage of aerostats at low altitude. To the second system * * * he objects that [since] the range of a cannon varies widely and may attain, it is said, a range of 4800 meters, it would follow that aerial navigation would in fact become impossible. * * * [To the extent] the second system involves determining the rights of the subjacent state by international agreement, he objects that the determination, not having any rational basis, would be arbitrary. To both aspects of this second system, he replies with a single observation: airspace, *by its very nature,* is not susceptible of appropriation or subjection to sovereignty.

The rapporteur proposes, accordingly, a combination of two uncontested principles: (1) airspace is not susceptible of appropriation or subjection to sovereignty, and therefore is free; (2) a state has a right of self-preservation and of self-defense to guaranty the essential elements of its existence, both in a material sense and as a legal person. Hence this formula: airspace is free, subject to the right of self-preservation and self-defense of the subjacent state.

Two consequences follow from the proposal:

(1) What is the most serious danger from aerostats? Espionage. What form does this danger take? Photography. But useful photography of a country's fortifications can be made only at an altitude of less than 1500 meters. Thus, under 1500 meters, the navigation of aerostats should be forbidden.

(2) What is today the most serious problem for wireless telegraphy? It is the possibility of interference with telephone communications and ordinary telegraphy. (at 293)

* * *

[The following article was adopted by the Institute.]

Article 1. Airspace is free. States have in it, in time of peace or in time of war, only the rights necessary for their self-preservation. (at 327)

FROM THEORY TO TREATY LAW

McNair, The Law of the Air 4 (Kerr & Evans, 3d ed. 1964).*

* * * Until after the war of 1914–18 the only aspects of aerial navigation which had engaged the serious attention of English law-

* Reprinted with the permission of
Stevens & Sons, Ltd., London.

yers, and, indeed, of the lawyers of almost any country, were the rules of public international law and of the Conflict of Laws which ought to govern it. * * *

Over the high seas it was generally admitted that the airspace was free. * * *

(1) *That the airspace is free, subject only to the rights of states required in the interests of their self-preservation.* This theory, which will always be associated with the name of its champion, Fauchille, was adopted by the Institute of International Law in 1906. * * *

(2) The second theory was that *upon the analogy of the maritime belt or territorial waters there is over the land and waters of each state a lower zone of territorial airspace, and a higher, and unlimited, zone of free airspace.*

(3) The third theory was *that a state has complete sovereignty in its superincumbent airspace to an unlimited height,* thus applying the *cujus est solum* maxim in its crude form.

(4) The fourth theory was the third *with the addition of a servitude of innocent passage for foreign non-military aircraft,* akin to the right of innocent passage of merchant ships through territorial waters.

The war of 1914–18 brought about a realisation of the importance of aerial navigation and of its potential danger to the subjacent state and its inhabitants. It is therefore not surprising to find now the almost universal adoption by international treaty and by national legislation of the theory of complete sovereignty (No. (3) above), subject to a mutual, carefully safeguarded, and easily determinable treaty right of free entry and passage for the non-military aircraft of foreign countries.

Thus the first Article of the Paris Convention of 1919 [a] was as follows:

> The High Contracting Parties recognise that every Power has complete and exclusive sovereignty over the air space above its territory.

> For the purpose of the present Convention the territory of a State shall be understood as including the national territory, both that of the Mother Country and of the Colonies, and the territorial waters adjacent thereto.

GOEDHUIS, CIVIL AVIATION AFTER THE WAR

36 American Journal of International Law 596, 605 (1942).[*]

The unprecedentedly accelerated speed of change in the last thirty years has been such that, politically, air navigation has already

a. 11 L.N.T.S. 174.   * Reprinted with the permission of the American Society of International Law.

passed through many of the phases which it took sea navigation centuries to span.

As to air navigation, it may be observed that in 1910 the states were preoccupied only with guaranteeing the safety of their territory; the necessity of permitting other states to navigate freely to and over their territory was recognized to the fullest extent where this freedom did not affect the security of the state. The period 1910–1919 can thus be compared with that period in the history of shipping in which the adjacent seas were appropriated primarily to secure the land from invasion.

In 1919 the first consideration was still the security of the states, but the study of the minutes of the meetings held by the Aëronautical Commission of the Peace Conference reveals the fact that some small clouds were already appearing on the horizon of the free sky. In the minds of some of the delegates the idea took shape to use the power of the state over the air to protect its own air navigation against foreign competition. As in shipping, the pretensions to the appropriation of the sea and the power to restrict foreign sea commerce grew in proportion to the increase of the direct profits to be expected from them, so in aviation the pretensions to unrestricted sovereignty—not in doctrine but in practice—grew in proportion to the development of aviation during the period from 1919 to 1929.

THE CHICAGO CONVENTION (THE CONVENTION ON INTERNATIONAL CIVIL AVIATION OF DECEMBER 7, 1944): THE HISTORY

[1944] 2 Foreign Relations of the United States 599 (1967).

The Chairman of the American Delegation to the International Civil Aviation Conference (Berle) to President Roosevelt

[Chicago,] December 7, 1944

My Dear Mr. President: I have the honor to report the results of the International Civil Aviation Conference, held at Chicago from November 1 to December 7, 1944.

* * *

(a) International Organization

The first problem discussed was that of the power of an international organization. We stated very bluntly that we simply could not cede dispositive power over United States air traffic to any international body in the present state of affairs. For one thing, there was no method or project of creating an impartial regulatory body: instead, the memberships in that body were to be apportioned among states and would represent political interests. Under these circumstances, any international body had to be in the position of applying exact defined rules agreed to by all hands. The fundamental problem was therefore drafting of the rules.

We said we could agree to an international body primarily to stimulate consultation and to make recommendations; and that if recommendations were not satisfactory, the international body might get together the interested parties and cause them to work out their difficulties. The enforcing power would have to remain in the several countries,—an international body at this stage of the game would have neither the machinery nor the prestige to enforce orders. The British finally acceded to this position, agreeing that obligations taken by treaty or agreement were quite adequate to meet the situation. Accordingly, agreement was reached on an international Council responsible to an international Assembly, the Council to have recommendatory powers; and failure to agree to recommendation would give rise to a prompt process of diplomatic consultation.

(b) Avoidance of Rate Wars

The second problem related to rates. There was general agreement that some method ought to be found of avoiding rate wars and other violences of competition which have disfigured transportation history. Substantial agreement was finally reached on a clause to the general effect that rates should be agreed upon by conferences of air operators analogous to ship operators conferences—a procedure which is specifically authorized by the Civil Aeronautics Act of 1938, and to which the United States can therefore agree. We were fortified in this by an opinion of the Attorney General to the general effect that such agreements were legal provided they were approved by the Civil Aeronautics Board. Since under the recommendatory procedure these agreements would come back to the various countries for acceptance, the procedure would be to have such operators agreements referred to the Civil Aeronautics Board. While the Civil Aeronautics Board does not have general power of enforcement, it could make it plain to any United States operator who violated an agreement that he would thereby forfeit diplomatic protection for his landing and transit rights abroad. It was the opinion of our operating advisers that no airline would violate an agreement thus made. By consequence, we felt that we had an adequate machinery.

* * *

(c) Rights of Commercial Entry

Third, we then got down to the main problem of commercial air rights. The British wanted agreements which would severely limit international rights in air transport. They were prepared to concede the so-called "freedoms of the air", namely:

(1) Freedom of innocent transit;

(2) Freedom of technical stop;

(3) Freedom to take traffic from the homeland out to other countries;

(4) Freedom to take traffic from other countries back to the homeland—and possibly, to a limited extent,

(5) Freedom to pick up and discharge traffic between points en route—

if, but only if, their operations were severely limited, traffic routes parceled out, and so forth, by an international body, or conceivably by rules appearing in a convention.

*   *   *

*   *   * [A]fter ten days of extremely difficult negotiation, we reported out to the Conference the points on which we had been able to agree; and also our alternative plans. The British plan was one of limitation, as above described; ours was a plan by which each country, having established its transport lines, might increase capacity as rapidly as its planes filled up.

There followed the tensest debate at the Conference. Lord Swinton presented the British view, urging the necessity of protecting small nations from competition. I presented the United States view which was for freedom of the air, with competition, and without cartel or other similar agreements, and without limitation except for the proposed arrangement against rate wars, and the "full plane" clause.

(The debate was in fact a modern version of the old controversy when Grotius argued for the freedom of the seas, and Selden argued for the closed seas; a debate which went on in the 17th century until it was finally settled by the British adopting the freedom of the seas. Another almost exact historical analogy is the debate which went on in this country when Livingston in New York tried to argue for limitation and allocation of steamship transportation as against Fulton and Daniel Webster who argued for open transportation and freedom of development of steamships.)

*   *   *

The close of the debate was dramatic and somewhat unexpected. Fifteen small countries in quick succession got up and protested against the British position. They said it meant strangulation and, far from protecting them, it virtually excluded them from the air. This position, which was supported by all the expert opinion of the Conference, was most ably argued by the Netherlands *   *   *. At the close of it, the British position was smashed flat, even the Canadians deserting the British and the New Zealanders declining to support their position.

The following day, after consultation, the United States Delegation proposed that all matters which had been agreed upon be embodied in a convention; and that a side agreement consisting of the mutual grant of the "five freedoms" be drawn, open to those countries which wished the exchange as between themselves. This was done after consultation with the Chinese, who urged it; with the delegates of the 19 other American republics, who asked that this be done; and with the delegates of the Scandinavian bloc, which was very firm for some such arrangement. The Netherlanders, Turks, and Spaniards likewise urged some such arrangement.

We accordingly drafted and put in a document along this line.
* * *

* * * [T]he British stated that they were prepared to accept agreement covering the "two freedoms"—right of transit and technical stop. This in turn surprised us, because Swinton had steadily and bitterly opposed any such agreement throughout the entire Conference—saying that they could not touch freedom of transit and technical stop except as a part of an agreement including the "controls" on which we had been unable to agree.ª Thereupon, taking the United States document proposing mutual exchange of the "five freedoms", the British drafted an almost exactly similar document containing mutual exchange of the "two freedoms" among the countries signatory to it. This, as a second side agreement, was proposed and approved by the Conference.

For the United States, this was a real gain.

The countries which agreed to exchange between themselves the "five freedoms" were isolated blocs in various parts of the world—and the blocs could not interconnect. But with freedom of transit and technical stop these countries could interconnect and thereby enable commerce to be carried on.
* * *

In result, we have:

(1) A permanent convention providing for permanent international organization * * *;
* * *

(3) A document by which the signatories thereto mutually exchange rights of freedom of transit and freedom of non-traffic stop (document of the "two freedoms") * * *;

(4) A document by which the signatories reciprocally grant to each other the "five freedoms" (commonly known as the "five freedoms" or United States document) * * *; and

(5) A set of completed or partially completed negotiations for bilateral agreements between the United States and a considerable number of countries in various parts of the world.

a. In a footnote to his report, Mr. Berle stated:

I think that part of the reason for this was that everyone by this time knew exactly the real interests involved. Freedom of transit and technical stop meant on the British part grant of stop at Newfoundland, which makes transit possible across the Atlantic. At the moment, there is no commercial route across the Atlantic which does not involve the transit of Newfoundland and a stop at a Newfoundland point—this being the nearest North American landing both to Iceland and to the Azores. On our side, freedom of transit means permitting a stop at Hawaii or the Aleutians, thereby making it possible to connect Australia and New Zealand with Canada, an old and entirely legitimate ambition. Had the British opposed publicly the "two freedoms," they would have been in a position of keeping Australia and Canada disconnected, and at the same time of endeavoring to prevent American commercial crossings in the Atlantic—a position which would have been hard to justify before the public opinion both of the United States and of the British Commonwealth.

So far as the strictly American interest is concerned, the combination of bilateral agreements, right of transit and technical stop, and "five freedoms" agreements vastly enlarged possibilities presently available to American aviation. The full benefits for American aviation cannot be completely ascertained until the negotiations for bilateral agreements are concluded; but the commitments obtained are such as to make it plain that these, if properly handled, can be brought to prompt fruition.

On the international side, the great issue of air transport has been faced and met; the positions are fully understood; an international organization capable of administering the agreements made has been established, and the same organization is charged with the duty of carrying forward further study in those respects on which agreement was not reached.

    *   *   *

Finally, a substantial beginning has been made towards opening the air to commerce. It is not too much to say that we entered the Conference in the law and atmosphere of the 17th century; and we came out with a fair prospect of obtaining 20th century conditions.

THE CHICAGO CONVENTION: EXCERPTS

61 Stat. 1180, 15 U.N.T.S. 295.

[The Convention is applicable only to civil (not state) aircraft.]

Article 1

Sovereignty

The contracting States recognize that every State has complete and exclusive sovereignty over the airspace above its territory.

Article 2

Territory

For the purposes of this Convention the territory of a State shall be deemed to be the land areas and territorial waters adjacent thereto under the sovereignty, suzerainty, protection or mandate of such State.

Article 5

Right of non-scheduled flight

Each contracting State agrees that all aircraft of the other contracting States, being aircraft not engaged in scheduled international air services shall have the right, subject to the observance of the terms of this Convention, to make flights into or in transit non-stop across its territory and to make stops for non-traffic purposes without the necessity of obtaining prior permission and subject to the right of the State flown over to require landing. Each contracting

State nevertheless reserves the right, for reasons of safety of flight, to require aircraft desiring to proceed over regions which are inaccessible or without adequate air navigation facilities to follow prescribed routes, or to obtain special permission for such flights.

Such aircraft, if engaged in the carriage of passengers, cargo, or mail for remuneration or hire on other than scheduled international air services, shall also, subject to the provisions of Article 7, have the privilege of taking on or discharging passengers, cargo, or mail, subject to the right of any State where such embarkation or discharge takes place to impose such regulations, conditions or limitations as it may consider desirable.

Article 6

Scheduled air services

No scheduled international air service may be operated over or into the territory of a contracting State, except with the special permission or other authorization of that State, and in accordance with the terms of such permission or authorization.

Article 17

Nationality of aircraft

Aircraft have the nationality of the State in which they are registered.

---

1. *I.C.A.O.* The convention creates the International Civil Aviation Organization, an intergovernmental organization the objectives of which are to "develop the principles and techniques of international air navigation and to foster the planning and development of international air transport."

The convention entered into force for the United States on April 4, 1947. As of January 1, 1980, 146 states were parties to the convention, including the United States and the USSR.

2. *Subsequent treaty developments.* In 1945 the United States became a party to the International Air Services Transit Agreement, 59 Stat. 1693; 84 U.N.T.S. 389. Article 1, Section 1, provides the so-called "two freedoms" for scheduled air services:

Each contracting State grants to the other contracting States the following freedoms of the air in respect of scheduled international air services:

(1) The privilege to fly across its territory without landing;

(2) The privilege to land for non-traffic purposes.

The privileges of this section shall not be applicable with respect to airports utilized for military purposes to the exclusion of any scheduled international air services. In areas of active hostilities or of military occupation, and in time of war along the supply routes leading to such areas, the exercise of such privileges shall be subject to the approval of the competent military authorities.

As of January 1, 1980, 95 states were parties to the Transit Agreement.

3. *The International Air Transport Agreement.* The United States became a party to it in 1945. 59 Stat. 1701. So few states became parties to this agreement that the United States withdrew as a party in 1947. Article 1, Section 1, provides the so-called "five freedoms" for scheduled air service:

Each contracting State grants to the other contracting States the following freedoms of the air in respect of scheduled international air services:

(1) The privilege to fly across its territory without landing;

(2) The privilege to land for non-traffic purposes;

(3) The privilege to put down passengers, mail and cargo taken on in the territory of the State whose nationality the aircraft posseses;

(4) The privilege to take on passengers, mail and cargo destined for the territory of the State whose nationality the aircraft possesses;

(5) The privilege to take on passengers, mail and cargo destined for the territory of any other contracting State and the privilege to put down passengers, mail and cargo coming from any such territory.

With respect to the privileges specified under paragraphs (3), (4) and (5) of this Section, the undertaking of each contracting State relates only to through services on a route constituting a reasonably direct line out from and back to the homeland of the State whose nationality the aircraft possesses.

* * *

4. *Scheduled air services.* The package of agreements emanating from the Chicago conference thus did not include a multilateral agreement of wide acceptance sufficient to deal with the question of scheduled air service. To provide the authorizations and permissions foreshadowed in Article 6 of the Chicago Convention, states entered into a vast network (or cobweb) of bilateral agreements, covering routes, types of traffic and volume of traffic (capacity), as well as a variety of administrative and legal matters of concern to the airline industry. See Lissitzyn, Bilateral Agreements on Air Transport, 30 J. of Air L. & Commerce 248 (1964); Gertler, Bilateral Air Transport Agreements: Non-Bermuda Reflections, 42 J. of Air L. & Commerce 779 (1976); Hill, Bermuda II: The British Revolution of 1976, 44 J. of Air L. & Commerce 111 (1978). Following the Chicago conference rates were set for many years by conference machinery set

up by the International Air Transport Association (IATA), a private association of airlines, sometimes referred to as a cartel. See Schwartz and Flynn, Antitrust and Regulatory Alternatives 580–610 (1977). Recent developments in the United States to deregulate the airline industry and to create a less protectionist environment through negotiation of new bilateral agreements looking toward more competition and lower fares are described in Klem and Leister, The Struggle for a Competitive Market Structure in International Aviation: the Benelux Protocols Take United States Policies a Step Forward, 11 L. & Policy in Int'l Bus. 557 (1979).

POWERS CASE

Union of Soviet Socialist Republics, Supreme Court
Military Collegium, 1960.
30 Int'l L.Rep. 69 (1966).*

* * * On May 1, 1960, at 5 hours 36 minutes, Moscow time, a military unit of the Soviet anti-aircraft defence in the area of the city of Kirovabad, the Tajik S.S.R., at an altitude of 20,000 metres, unattainable for planes of the civil air fleet, spotted an unknown aircraft violating the State frontier of the U.S.S.R.

The military units of the Soviet anti-aircraft defence vigilantly followed the behaviour of the plane as it flew over major industrial centres and important objectives, and only when the intruder plane had penetrated 2,000 kilometres into Soviet territory and the evil purpose of the flight, fraught with disastrous consequences for world peace in an age of thermonuclear weapons, become absolutely obvious, a battery of ground-to-air missiles brought the aggressor plane down in the area of Sverdlovsk at 8 hours 53 minutes as ordered by the Soviet Government.

The pilot of the plane bailed out and was apprehended upon landing. On interrogation, he gave his name as Francis Gary Powers, citizen of the United States of America. Examination of the wreckage of the plane which had been brought down showed that it was of American make, specially designed for high altitude flights and fitted with various equipment for espionage reconnaissance tasks.

In view of this, the pilot Powers was arrested and committed for trial on charges of espionage against the Soviet Union.

During the court hearings, the defendant Powers testified in detail about his espionage activity and the circumstances connected with the violation of Soviet air space on May 1, 1960.

In 1950 Powers volunteered for the American army, completed his training at an Air Force school, and served as pilot at various United States Air Force bases with the rank of Senior Lieutenant.

* Reprinted by permission of E. Lauterpacht, ed., and Grotius Publications, Ltd., Cambridge, England.

In April 1956, Powers was recruited by the Central Intelligence Agency of the United States for special intelligence missions in high-altitude aircraft.

After he had concluded a secret contract with the United States Central Intelligence Agency for a term of two years, Powers was allotted a high salary of 2,500 dollars a month for espionage activity. He underwent special training and was assigned to the intelligence air detachment under the code name of "Ten-Ten", stationed at the American-Turkish war base of Incirlik, near the town of Adana, in Turkey.

The Court has established that the detachment "Ten-Ten" is a special combination of the United States military and civilian intelligence designed for espionage against the Soviet Union with the help of reconnaissance planes sent into Soviet air space.

Starting with 1956 Powers systematically flew on espionage missions along the Soviet Union's frontiers with Turkey, Iran and Afghanistan, on orders from the "Ten-Ten" detachment's commander. In May 1958, Powers renewed his secret contract with the Central Intelligence Agency of the United States for a term of two years, and in January 1960 for yet another year.

The Materials of the case and the testimony of defendant Powers have established that the criminal intrusion into the air space of the Soviet Union, committed by him on May 1, 1960, was carefully prepared long before it took place.

On April 27, 1960, Powers, together with the commander of the detachment "Ten-Ten", the American Colonel Shelton and a group of technical personnel intended for preparing the U–2 plane for its flight, were brought in a United States Air Force transport aircraft from the Incirlik base to the Peshawar airport in Pakistan.

Another pilot ferried the U–2 plane in which Powers was to violate the air space of the Soviet Union to this same airfield from Turkey on April 30 of this year.

On the night of April 30, 1960, Colonel Shelton gave Powers the assignment to fly over the territory of the Soviet Union at an altitude of 20,000 metres along the following course: Peshawar, the Aral Sea, Sverdlovsk, Kirov, Archangel, Murmansk, and to land in Norway, at Bodoe airport, with which Powers familiarized himself back in 1958.

Flying over Soviet territory, Powers, on Shelton's orders, was to switch on at definite points his special equipment for aerial photography and the registration of the operation of Soviet anti-aircraft defence radar stations. Powers was to give special attention to two spots—in one of them American intelligence suspected the presence of missile launching ramps and in the other a particularly important defence objective.

The material evidence of the case and his testimony has established that Powers fulfilled the criminal mission given him.

Having taken off from Peshawar airport in Pakistan, Powers flew over the territory of Afghanistan and for more than 2,000 kilometres over the Soviet Union in accordance with the established course. Besides Powers' testimony, this is confirmed by the American flight map discovered in the debris of the U–2 plane and submitted to the Court, bearing the route plotted out by Major Dulak, navigator of the detachment "Ten-Ten", and also notes and signs made by Powers, who marked down on this map several important defence objectives of the Soviet Union he had spotted from the plane.

Throughout the flight, to the very moment the plane was shot down, Powers switched on his special intelligence equipment, photographed important defence objectives and recorded signals of the country's anti-aircraft radar installations. The development of the rescued aerial photography films established that defendant Powers photographed from the U–2 plane industrial and military objectives of the Soviet Union—plants, depots, oil storage facilities, communication routes, railway bridges and stations, electric transmission lines, aerodromes, the location of troops and military equipment.

The numerous photos of the Soviet Union's territory, taken by defendant Powers from an altitude of 20,000 metres, in possession of the Military Collegium of the U.S.S.R. Supreme Court, make it possible to determine the nature of industrial establishments, the design of railway bridges, the number and type of aircraft on the airfields, the nature and purpose of military material.

Powers tape-recorded impulses of certain radar stations of the Soviet Union with a view to detecting the country's anti-aircraft defence system.

According to the conclusion of experts, the information collected by defendant Powers during his flight in Soviet air space on May 1, 1960, constitutes a State and military secret of the Soviet Union, which is specially guarded by law.

Powers testified to the Court that the U–2 plane was provided with demolition devices, intended for the destruction of the plane in case of a forced landing on Soviet territory, and that before the flight on May 1, 1960, Colonel Shelton impressed upon him the necessity of committing suicide in case he were to fall into the hands of Soviet authorities and were tortured. It was precisely for this purpose that Colonel Shelton gave him a special poison needle.

Besides the poison needle, the following objects were confiscated from Powers during his apprehension: a noiseless pistol with cartridges, a dagger, fishing gear, a pneumatic boat, topographical maps of the Soviet Union, means for making camp fires, signal boxes, an electric torchlight, compasses, a saw, food concentrates, drugs, 7,500 roubles in Soviet currency, and valuables (gold coins, rings, wrist watches) which, as Powers testified, were intended for bribing Soviet people in case of a forced landing of the U–2 in Soviet territory.

The Military Collegium of the U.S.S.R. Supreme Court has also examined other evidence confirming that a Soviet rocket unit brought down on May 1, 1960, an aircraft belonging to the United States Air Force.

Despite the fact that the plane which was brought down lacked identification marks, the experts have determined through the examination of the wreckage of the plane and the equipment on board that it was a subsonic U–2 reconnaissance aircraft of the American Lockheed company with one turbo-jet engine.

The equipment and parts of the plane had trade-marks of various American companies, which show, in particular, that the turbo-jet engine was manufactured by the Pratt-Whitney company, and the starting and electrical supply equipment by the Hamilton-Standard and General Electric companies. Furthermore, the equipment had markings indicating that it belonged to the United States military establishment.

The material evidence put before defendant Powers was recognized by him as belonging to the U–2 aircraft in which he violated the air space of the Soviet Union on May 1 of this year.

The identification card AFI 288,068 found on Powers and included in the materials of the case, carried the emblem of the United States Defence Department and the inscription: "Defence Department. United States of America."

Thus, the court hearings have established definitely that the Lockheed U–2 reconnaissance aircraft belonged to the United States Air Force and that defendant Powers was a secret agent of the Central Intelligence Agency of the United States of America.

Powers was an obedient executor of the perfidious designs of the Central Intelligence Agency of the United States of America, carried out with the consent of the American Government.

Powers himself admitted that he realized when intruding into the air space of the Soviet Union that he was violating the national sovereignty of the U.S.S.R. and flying over its territory on an espionage mission, whose main purpose consisted of detecting and marking down missile launching sites.

Examined by the court, witnesses V. P. Surin and A. F. Cheremisin, L. A. Chuzhakin, and P. E. Asabin testified that they witnessed the falling of the plane in the area of Sverdlosvk and the landing of the parachutist, whom they apprehended and disarmed.

The detained person proved to be Powers.

* * *

Article 2 [of the Law on Criminal Responsibility for State Crimes] provides:

Espionage

The giving away, theft or collection with the intention of conveying to a foreign Power, a foreign organization, or their agents, of information constituting a State or military secret, as well as the giving away or collection on the instructions of foreign intelligence agencies of other information to be used against the interests of the U.S.S.R., if the espionage is committed by a foreigner or by a stateless person—is punishable by deprivation of liberty for a period of from seven to fifteen years with confiscation of property, or by death and confiscation of property.

* * * In considering the Powers case, the Military Collegium of the U.S.S.R. Supreme Court takes into account that the intrusion of the American military intelligence plane constitutes a criminal breach of a generally recognized principle of international law, which establishes the exclusive sovereignty of every State over the air space above its territory. This principle, laid down by the Paris Convention of October 13, 1919, for the regulation of aerial navigation, and several other subsequent international agreements, is proclaimed in the national legislations of different States, including the Soviet Union and the United States of America.

Violation of this sacred and immutable principle of international relations creates in the present conditions a direct menace to universal peace and international security.

At the present level of military technology, when certain States possess atomic and hydrogen weapons, as well as the means of delivering them quickly to targets, the flight of a military intelligence plane over Soviet territory could have directly preceded a military attack. This danger is the more possible in conditions when the United States of America, as stated by American generals, constantly keeps bomber patrols in the air, always ready to drop bombs on earlier marked-out targets of the Soviet Union.

Under these conditions the aggressive act of the United States of America, carried out on May 1 of this year by defendant Powers, created a threat to universal peace.

Material evidence at the disposal of the Military Collegium of the Supreme Court leaves no doubt that, by his aggressive intrusion into the air space of the Soviet Union, defendant Powers implemented far-reaching plans of reactionary quarters of the United States of, America, calculated to aggravate international tension.

After the head of the Soviet Government, N. S. Khrushchov, announced at the session of the Supreme Soviet of the U.S.S.R. on May 5 of the current year that an American plane had been shot down over the territory of the Soviet Union, the State Department of the United States of America, having recognized as "fully possible" the fact of the violation of the Soviet frontier by an American plane, tried to mislead world public opinion.

Such was the purpose of the fabricated statements by the United States National Aeronautics and Space Administration and the State Department about the U-2 plane accidentally straying off course while allegedly conducting scientific research.

In his winding-up speech at the session of the Supreme Soviet of the U.S.S.R. on May 7, Comrade N. S. Khrushchov exposed the falsity of these allegations.

After that the American leaders—President Eisenhower, Vice-President Nixon and State Secretary Herter—admitted that spying flights over Soviet territory by American planes constitute part of the "calculated policy of the United States of America".

Thus, the leaders of the United States of America proclaimed the violation of the sovereignty of other States and espionage against them as the official State policy of America.

The subsequent events confirmed that the aggressive intrusion of the U–2 intelligence plane into the air space of the Soviet Union on May 1 was deliberately prepared by reactionary quarters of the United States of America in order to torpedo the Paris Summit meeting, to prevent the easing of international tension, to breathe new life into the senile cold war policy which is hated by all the peoples.

The Military Collegium of the Supreme Court of the Soviet Union has established that Powers could not have carried out the spy missions assigned to him without the use by the United States of America, for aggressive purposes, of the war bases and aerodromes on the territories of the States neighbouring on the Soviet Union, including the territories of Turkey, Iran, Pakistan and Norway.

Powers' flight has proved that the Government of the United States of America, having bound Turkey, Iran, Pakistan, Norway and other States by bilateral military agreements, has established war bases and aerodromes on their territories for dangerous provocative actions, making these States accomplices in the aggression against the Soviet Union.

Having examined the materials of the case, material and other evidence and expert findings, and having heard the testimony of the defendant and the witnesses, the speeches of the State Prosecutor and of the Defence Counsel, and also the last plea of the defendant, the Military Collegium of the U.S.S.R. Supreme Court holds established that defendant Powers was for a long time an active secret agent of the United States Central Intelligence Agency, directly fulfilling espionage missions of this agency against the Soviet Union; and that on May 1, 1960, with the knowledge of the Government of the United States of America, in a specially equipped U–2 intelligence plane, he intruded into Soviet air space and with the help of special radio-technical and photographic equipment collected information of strategical importance, which constitutes a State and Military secret of the Soviet State, thereby committing a grave crime covered by Article 2 of the Soviet Union's Law "On Criminal Responsibility for State Crimes".

At the same time, weighing all the circumstances of the given case in the deep conviction that they are inter-related, taking into account Powers' sincere confession of his guilt and his sincere repentance, proceeding from the principles of socialist humaneness, and guided by Articles 319 and 320 of the Code of Criminal Procedure of the Russian Federation, the Military Collegium of the U.S.S.R. Supreme Court

Sentences

Francis Gary Powers, on the strength of Article 2 of the U.S.S. R. Law "On Criminal Responsibility for State Crimes", to ten years' confinement with the first three years to be served in prison.

The term of punishment, including the preliminary detention, shall be counted as from May 1, 1960.

The material evidence is to be kept with the file of the case. The money and valuables taken from Powers shall be forfeited to the State treasury.

In conformity with Article 44 of the "Fundamental Principles of the Criminal Procedure of the Soviet Union and the Union Republics", the sentence is final and not subject to appeal or cassation.

———

1. *Sanctions against aircraft entering airspace.* Does the fact that a state has jurisdiction to prescribe law governing an event mean that it has freedom of choice in the methods used to exercise that jurisdiction? Does a state have a right to shoot down any plane that enters its airspace? In 1955, an El Al Israel Airlines Ltd. commercial airplane, with passengers aboard, entered the airspace of Bulgaria for some unknown reason. Bulgarian fighter aircraft fired at the plane; it exploded in flight and crashed in Bulgarian territory. All 58 persons aboard were killed, including American and British passengers. Proceedings were instituted against Bulgaria in the International Court of Justice by Israel, the United States and the United Kingdom, protesting the inhuman and excessive use of force by the Bulgarians, the lack of adequate warning, the failure of Bulgaria to recognize the right of entry in distress. The cases did not proceed to the merits because of Bulgaria's having failed to consent to the jurisdiction of the Court. 9 Whiteman, Digest of International Law 326–340 (1963).

2. *Excessive use of force: analogies from the law of the sea.* The I'm Alone, 1935, III U.N. Rep. Int'l Arb. Awards 1609 involved a dispute between Canada and the United States arising out of the sinking of a Canadian rum-running vessel. A convention between the United States and Great Britain permitted search and seizure by the United States of British vessels suspected of liquor smuggling if the vessels were found close to, though outside, United States territorial waters. The hot pursuit of the I'm Alone ended 200 miles away from the Louisiana coast in the Gulf of Mexico. The commanding officer of the pursuing American coast guard cutter ordered the I'm Alone to stop and informed the commander of the I'm Alone that it would be sunk unless it stopped. After warning shots were fired, the

United States vessel put enough shots into the hull of the I'm Alone to sink her. Commissioners appointed to report on this event stated:

The question is whether, in the circumstances, the Government of the United States was legally justified in sinking the I'm Alone.

The answer given to this question is as follows:—

On the assumptions stated in the question, the United States might, consistently with the Convention, use necessary and reasonable force for the purpose of effecting the objects of boarding, searching, seizing and bringing into port the suspected vessel; and if sinking should occur incidentally, as a result of the exercise of necessary and reasonable force for such purpose, the pursuing vessel might be entirely blameless. But the Commissioners think that, in the circumstances stated in paragraph eight of the Answer, the admittedly intentional sinking of the suspected vessel was not justified by anything in the Convention.

        *   *   *

It will be recalled that the I'm Alone was sunk on the 22nd day of March, 1929, on the high seas, in the Gulf of Mexico, by the United States revenue cutter Dexter. By their interim report the Commissioners found that the sinking of the vessel was not justified by anything in the Convention. The Commissioners now add that it could not be justified by any principle of international law. (at 1617)

Are there special risks associated with aircraft that require peremptory use of destructive force?

3. *Beyond trespass: espionage as a state offense.* Issues other than technical trespass of Soviet airspace were involved in the U–2 incident. The criminal charge against Powers in the Soviet Union was of espionage as defined in the domestic law of that state. In the tradition of the international spy, fictional and real, the espionage agent is "out in the cold" all by himself. He expects to be disowned if caught. And the conventional practice of states is not overtly to charge another state with espionage but to counter-attack in kind, in what Dean Acheson once called "the underworld of international relations." In the U–2 case, however, although Powers was caught and prosecuted under Soviet law, the USSR openly charged the United States with responsibility, calling for condemnation by the Security Council of the United Nations of the aggressive acts of the United States. President Eisenhower responded with the unprecedented admission that the United States was responsible for Powers' flight, justifying it " 'to obtain information now concealed behind the iron curtain' in order to lessen the danger of surprise attack on the free world * * *." Wright, Legal Aspects of the U–2 Incident, 54 Am.J.Int'l L. 836, 838 (1960).

Are there, therefore, issues of espionage at the international level? That is, is the law of espionage purely domestic, directed at the individual only, or is there state responsibility to the state spied upon? In view of the practices of states over centuries, it is not possible to find a consentio juris that spying per se is an offense under customary law. Has it become so under the United Nations Charter, either as to (a) conventional espionage through the penetration of the state's ground frontier, or (b) aerial espionage through the penetration of airspace? See Article 2(4).

---

2. OFFENSES ABOARD AIRCRAFT

GENERAL OFFENSES

SILBERWACHT v. ATTORNEY–GENERAL

Israel, District Court of Tel-Aviv, 1953.
20 Int'l L.Rep. 153 (1957).*

The Facts. This was an appeal from a decision of the Magistrate's Court convicting the appellant of smuggling and of being in possession of smuggled goods. The appellant was employed at Lydda Airport where there existed a clandestine organization for purchasing tinned food from South African airmen and bringing it on to the market without customs examination and payment of customs duty. By s. 2 of the Customs Ordinance smuggling is defined as:

> Any importation, exportation, carriage coastwise or over the land frontiers, or attempted importation, exportation, carriage coastwise or over the land frontiers, of goods, with intent to defraud the revenue or to evade any prohibition of, restriction on, or regulations as to, the importation, exportation, carriage coastwise or over the land frontiers of any goods; and "smuggle" and "smuggled goods" have corresponding meanings.

One of the grounds of appeal was that when the tins were removed from the aircraft by the aircrew they had already been smuggled by the South African crew and were therefore smuggled goods, so that the appellant could not be convicted of smuggling.

Held: that the appeal must be admitted and the conviction dismissed. [A portion of the opinion of the court appears below.]

* * * This ground of appeal raises several important questions of public international law * * *. The question whether the removal of the goods from the aircraft (which, it seems, was a South African aircraft, although it is not clear whether it was privately owned or a State aircraft) constitutes their importation into Israel, or whether the goods entered Israel at the moment when the aircraft entered Israel, is connected with the question whether an aircraft has to be regarded as foreign territory. Although the rule is nowhere explicitly laid down, it seems that the law of Israel presupposes that the

* Reprinted by permission of E. Lauterpacht, ed., and Grotius Publications, Ltd., Cambridge, England.

law governing territorial sovereignty (from the point of view of jurisdiction) is similar to the concept of ownership of land, and includes authority not only over the surface of the land but also down to its depth and also in the skies above jusque ad coelum. The general opinion in public international law is similar. See Article I of the Chicago Air Agreement of 1944. * * *

* * *

* * * [E]ven if South Africa has jurisdiction over acts performed in her aircraft in accordance with South African laws regarding the air and regarding jurisdiction (assuming that the existence of extraterritorial laws of that character is not contrary to international law and the public policy of Israel)—nevertheless the foreign aircraft is not foreign territory. The result, therefore, is that the act of smuggling came to an end when the pilot imported the tins into Israel with the intention of defrauding the customs. The act of smuggling did not commence at the moment when the tins were removed from the aircraft since they were already within Israel. * * *

Judge Avissar, dissenting, said: "As to the smuggling, it seems to me to make no difference to the appellant whether the pilot who landed at Lydda airport with the tinned goods on board and intending to smuggle them was guilty of an offence or not. * * * When the appellant received the goods from the aircraft and removed them from Lydda Airport without paying customs—as has been proved to have occurred—he committed the offence. The position of a person who receives goods from an aircraft at an airport cannot be any different from the position of a person who receives goods from a ship within the territorial waters of the country and imports them by smuggling. At all events, such a person is to be considered as an importer in the sense of the definition of smuggling contained in section 2 of the Customs Ordinance; and why should any discrimination be made in favour of the man who commits the smuggling by receiving the goods from an aircraft which has landed at an airport? * * *"

Problem. A South African commercial aircraft is making a non-stop transit through the airspace of Israel on a flight to Turkey at an altitude of 30,000 feet. No Israeli nationals are on board the plane. A passenger in the plane assaults a stewardess. Both are South African nationals. If the passenger subsequently travels to Tel Aviv, and is arrested and tried there for assault, does South Africa have any basis for complaint under international law?

UNITED STATES v. CORDOVA

United States District Court, E.D. New York, 1950.
89 F.Supp. 298.

KENNEDY, District Judge. On March 30, 1949, an information was filed against the defendant Cordova, along with one Santano, the charge consisting of four counts: 1) that on August 2, 1948 Cordova assaulted one Machada, pilot of an airplane owned by Flying Tigers, Inc., an American corporation, while the plane was flying over the high seas from San Juan, Puerto Rico, to New York; (2) that at the same time and place Cordova assaulted one Santiago, stewardess of the air carrier; 3) that at the same time and place Cordova assaulted the codefendant Santano; and 4) that at the same time and place Santano assaulted Cordova.

The statutory bases for jurisdiction alleged in the information are respectively (a) the act forbidding striking, wounding and beating and simple assault within the admiralty and maritime jurisdiction of the United States, 18 U.S.C.A. § 455, now 18 U.S.C.A. § 113(d) and (e), (b) the act defining the admiralty and maritime jurisdiction, 18 U.S.C.A. § 451, now 18 U.S.C.A. § 7, and (c) the venue statute for the prosecution of crimes within the admiralty and maritime jurisdiction, 28 U.S.C.A. § 102, now 18 U.S.C.A. § 3238. The pertinent portions of these statutes, as they existed on August 2, 1948, the date of the alleged offenses, are given in the margin: [1]

As will appear shortly, after the facts have been outlined, the revision of the criminal code has no bearing on the case: the relevant statutes are substantially the same now as they were at the time of the offenses set forth in the information.

When the trial commenced, the government moved to dismiss the fourth count of the information (which charges the codefendant Santano with assault upon the defendant Cordova), a jury was waived, and the cause was tried to the court. Motions appropriate to challenge the jurisdiction of the court over the offenses charged were made at every stage of the case. * * *

1. Title 18 U.S.C.A. § 451, reads in part:

"Places and waters applicable; on board American vessel on high seas or Great Lakes; on land under exclusive control of United States; guano islands. The crimes and offenses defined in this chapter shall be punished as herein prescribed: "First. When committed upon the high seas, or on any other waters within the admiralty and maritime jurisdiction of the United States and out of the jurisdiction of any particular State, or when committed within the admiralty and maritime jurisdiction of the United States and out of the jurisdiction of any particular State on board any vessel belonging in whole or in part to the United States or any citizen thereof, or to any corporation created by or under the laws of the United States, or of any State, Territory, or District thereof."

Title 18 U.S.C.A. § 455 (part of the same chapter) is entitled "Felonious assaults; to murder or rape; other felony; with weapons; beating; simple assault," and reads in part:

"Whoever shall unlawfully strike, beat, or wound another, shall be fined not more than $500, or imprisoned not more than six months or both. Whoever shall unlawfully assault another, shall be fined not more than $300, or imprisoned not more than three months, or both."

Title 28 U.S.C.A. § 102 is entitled "Offenses on the high seas," and reads: "The trial of all offenses committed upon the high seas, or elsewhere out of the jurisdiction of any particular State or district, shall be in the district where the offender is found, or into which he is first brought."

The facts are simple and clear. At 6:42 P.M., New York time, the carrier plane DC–4 No. NC–90911 took off from San Juan Airfield in Puerto Rico, bound for New York. The plane is the property of Flying Tigers, Inc., an American corporation, and at the time of the flight was under charter to Air America, Inc., another American corporation, organized under the laws of California. On board when the flight began were 60 passengers and 6 crew members. Of the passengers 43 were adults, 11 were children under 2 years of age, and 6 were children over that age.

At 8:15 P.M. on August 2, 1948 the plane, travelling at an air speed of 180 m. p. h., was over the Atlantic Ocean on a course 324 degrees true bound for Charleston, S. C., having been on her course for 1½ hours. This means that the plane was to the northward of the Bahama Islands at a point approximately 270 miles northwest of San Juan, Puerto Rico. The plane's altitude was 8,500 feet. At that time (8:15 P.M., August 2, 1948) the plane became tail heavy, and her indicated air speed fell from 180 miles per hour to 150 miles per hour. The nose was rising so fast that the automatic pilot could not make corrections which would keep the ship on an even keel, and it became necessary to adjust the instrument. At this juncture the steward notified the pilot Machada that there was a fight going on in the passenger compartment. Machada turned the controls over to his First Officer and went aft. What he found was a brawl in progress between the passengers Cordova and Santano, which the steward and the stewardess (one Santiago) had been attempting to stop in vain. The passengers had crowded aft to watch the flight; it was because of this fact that the plane had become tail heavy.

Machada intervened, with the result that the defendant Cordova bit him on the shoulder, and during this portion of the fracas Cordova struck not only his adversary Santano, but also the stewardess Santiago.

The story of the origin of the fight is an old one. Apparently when these planes leave from San Juan, the relatives and friends of the passengers participate in a bon voyage celebration, the principal attraction being Puerto Rican rum in large quantities. And to fortify themselves for the flight, on this particular occasion many of the passengers, including Cordova and Santano, had boarded the plane with bottles of rum in paper shopping bags, which they took to their seats. Cordova and Santano had been toasting each other effusively for the first part of the flight, but soon a dispute arose over a missing bottle. Cordova seems literally to have gone berserk: while the main object of his viciousness was Santano, anyone else who crossed his path, including the captain of the plane, was in danger. The efforts of Machada (the captain) to subdue Cordova were reasonable. He began by attempting to hold Cordova's arms. At that time the weather being warm, Machada was wearing no flight jacket, and Cordova, attempting to free himself, bit Machada in the shoulder, drawing blood and necessitating first aid treatment. Eventually Cordova was locked up in a compartment.

The plane landed at La Guardia Field at 4:45 A.M. on August 3, 1948. Cordova and Santano were immediately apprehended in this District and charged with assault. It thus appears that the venue requirements of the statute, 28 U.S.C.A. § 102, heretofore quoted in the margin, are satisfied if a crime within the jurisdiction of the United States Courts was committed. It is also plain that Cordova did in fact, and without just cause or excuse strike and bite Machada (count 1), Santiago (count 2), and Santano (count 3). The case under the third count is weaker than the others, because Santano was at least in the beginning himself an active participant in the fight. Later, however, he attempted to retreat when the pilot of the plane and the stewardess intervened and the striking or biting which were then committed by Cordova on all three victims clearly violated the terms of the specific substantive statute, 18 U.S.C.A. § 455, heretofore quoted in the margin.

But the statute condemning striking, wounding and beating, and simple assault, within the admiralty and maritime jurisdiction of the United States does not become operative unless the acts complained of meet one of two tests, 18 U.S.C.A. § 451: (1) Where those acts committed on the high seas, or on any other waters within the admiralty and maritime jurisdiction of the United States and out of the jurisdiction of any particular State? or (2) Were those acts committed within the admiralty and maritime jurisdiction of the United States and out of the jurisdiction of any particular State on board any vessel belonging in whole or in part to the United States or any citizen thereof or any corporation created by or under the laws of the United States, or of any State, Territory or District thereof?

The second question gives less difficulty than the other, and perhaps should be dealt with first. The answer that ought to be made turns on the question whether an airplane is a vessel, within the meaning of the statute, and obviously the answer should be in the negative.

* * *

* * * [W]hen, 18 U.S.C.A. § 451, Congress speaks of a "vessel" within the admiralty and maritime jurisdiction of the United States, it evokes in the common mind a picture of a ship, not of a plane.

* * *

It now becomes necessary to return to the first branch of the statute, which denounces certain crimes committed on the high seas or other waters within the admiralty and maritime jurisdiction of the United States and out of the jurisdiction of any particular state, 18 U.S.C.A. § 451. Beyond any doubt, Cordova's misconduct took place over the high seas. Is it proper, then, in a criminal case, to extend federal criminal jurisdiction to a plane in flight over the high seas under a statute which speaks of crimes committed upon the high seas or on any other waters within the admiralty and maritime jurisdiction of the United States? * * *

It is perhaps irrelevant, but I have little doubt that had it wished to do so Congress could, under its police power, have extended federal criminal jurisdiction to acts committed on board an airplane owned by an American national, even though such acts had no effect upon national security.[2] In U. S. v. Flores, 1933, 289 U.S. 137, 53 S.Ct. 580, 77 L.Ed. 1086, the Supreme Court of the United States went the extreme length of holding that the criminal jurisdiction of the United States, under this very statute, 18 U.S.C.A. § 451, was broad enough to include acts committed on an American flag vessel, even though she was within the territorial waters of another sovereign. The Court has even suggested that a State of the union may make a regulation valid and effective to rule conduct on the high seas, so long as the federal government has not occupied the field. Skiriotes v. Florida, 1941, 313 U.S. 69, 61 S.Ct. 924, 85 L.Ed. 1193. And on occasion the Supreme Court has not been over technical to ascertain whether the crime was committed on the ship itself or in adjacent waters. United States v. Holmes, 1820, 5 Wheat. 412, 5 L.Ed. 122. For such a case the expression "high seas" was held to have a general meaning, and a similar result was reached when the Court was dealing with the question whether the term "high seas" was applicable to the Great Lakes. United States v. Rodgers, 1893, 150 U.S. 249, 14 S.Ct. 109, 37 L.Ed. 1071.

But none of these cases, nor the principles on which they rest, would justify the extension of the words "high seas" to the air space over them. It is at this point that the case at bar, I think, becomes one of first impression. * * *

The acts for which Cordova stands charged were vicious in the extreme. He jeopardized the lives of others on the plane, including a considerable number of infants. But it seems to me clear that those acts have not been denounced by a statute which forbids them when committed on board an American "vessel", or when committed on the "high seas".

The situation may call for correction. There has been for some years discussion by experts in the field of aeronautic law of how the problem can be solved. For example, the so-called de Wisscher Draft Convention of 1937 suggests that crimes of this character ought to be punishable under the laws of the state of which the victim is a na-

---

2. The reason I mention "national security" is this. It seems clear that Congress can denounce as crimes acts affecting the well-being of the government, and committed by American nationals, even when those acts take place on land within the jurisdiction of a foreign sovereign. U. S. v. Bowman, 1922, 260 U.S. 94, 43 S. Ct. 39, 67 L.Ed. 149; United States v. Chandler, D.C.Mass.1947, 72 F.Supp. 230, affirmed 1 Cir., 1949, 171 F.2d 921, certiorari denied 1949, 336 U.S. 918, 69 S.Ct. 640, rehearing denied 1949, 336 U.S. 947, 69 S.Ct. 809. But Congressional power over vessels on the high seas, or in admiralty waters outside the jurisdiction of any state, is even wider. It can be exercised to punish acts (such as assault) which have no relationship to national security. A different theory of jurisdiction comes into play, namely, that the American flag vessel is itself territory of the United States. There are no international complications, as there might be for land crimes against a person.

tional, or of which the accused is a national, or of the state where the airplane arrives, if, in the latter case, what was done affects its security interests. The British Air Navigation Act of 1920 provides that any offense committed on a British aircraft shall be deemed committed in any place where the offender may for the time be. It is my understanding that French criminal law applies to French aircraft in flight any place in the world. Air Nav. Law 1924, Title V, Art. 20. Italian law, I have been told, also applies to Italian planes in flight anywhere, although this may be merely a civil code.

What I gather is that there is little likelihood, if any, of an international agreement involving, as it necessarily would, difficult and delicate questions of sovereignty. However that may be, as the law now stands, acts like those committed by Cordova will go unpunished, unless the law of the domicile of the corporation can be considered to cover them.

I, therefore, find Cordova guilty of the acts charged. But I must arrest judgment of conviction since there is no federal jurisdiction to punish those acts.

I feel very strongly that the government should have the opportunity to review this decision. And I draw the attention of the United States Attorney to the procedure followed in U. S. v. Flores, supra, and also to the criminal appeals statute in its present form, 18 U.S.C.A. § 3731, which seems to give ample protection against appeal to the wrong court. For what it may be worth, I certify that my decision turns on no issue of fact, but merely the determination of a question of law, namely, the construction of 18 U.S.C.A. § 451 and § 455.[4]

---

1. *Special maritime and territorial jurisdiction of the United States.* As discussed on p. 154, the special maritime and territorial jurisdiction of the United States is defined in Title 18, Section 7 of the United States Code. Shortly after the Cordova decision was rendered, the definition was amended to include:

> (5) Any aircraft belonging in whole or in part to the United States, or any citizen thereof, or to any corporation created by or under the laws of the United States, or any State, Territory, district, or possession thereof, while such aircraft is in flight over the high seas, or over any other waters within the admiralty and maritime jurisdiction of the United States and out of the jurisdiction of any particular State.

4. It is true that I have found the facts against Cordova, including intent, wilfullness, and lack of excuse. But I have construed the statute on the basis of what the information says concerning the place of the offenses, and this is a fact not in dispute nor capable of debate. It may seem odd that fact-finding and a verdict of guilty are combined with an order in arrest of judgment because of want of jurisdiction. But I thought this procedure wise because, in the event my decision is wrong, I can proceed to sentence under the mandate, and save another trial.

Title 18 defines as criminal a number of acts that are performed within the special maritime and territorial jurisdiction. For a list of such acts, see Chapter 3, p. 154. Title 49, Section 1472(k) of the United States Code deals with these same crimes when committed within the "special aircraft jurisdiction of the United States." For the definition of this jurisdiction, see Section 1301(38) of Title 49.

2. *Problem.* All the facts are the same as in the Cordova case, except that the aircraft is privately owned by an American citizen and is registered in State X. The United States prosecution is based upon Title 18, Section 113, of the United States Code (assaults within the special maritime and territorial jurisdiction) and Title 18, Section 7(5), of the United States Code, (above).

a. Are the events in the case covered by the statute?

b. Would they be covered if the defendant were not a national of the United States? Section 113 provides: "Whoever, within the special maritime and territorial jurisdiction of the United States, is guilty of an assault shall be punished as follows: *   *   *."

c. If the defendant convicted and punished were not a United States national, would State X have a basis for complaint against the United States under international law? See Article 17 of the Chicago Convention, p. 238.

3. *Identification zones.* The United States has established air defense identification zones (ADIZ) and a distant early warning identification zone (DEWIZ) in areas of the airspace over the high seas adjacent to its coasts. Similar zones have been established by some other states. Aircraft operating in or penetrating such zones are subject to requirements with respect to filing flight plans; pilots of aircraft entering the United States through an ADIZ or a DEWIZ are required to report positions. 14 C.F.R., Part 99. Since these zones extend seaward several hundreds of miles, do they entail a violation of international law respecting the jurisdiction of the United States over airspace? Can the United States lawfully prescribe rules regulating activity in these zones on the ground that obedience to the rules is a condition to entry into the territory of the United States? See Restatement of the Foreign Relations Law of the United States, Comment *d* to Section 17 and Comment *e* to Section 21 (1965).

HIJACKING

A passenger in a commercial airplane threatens to explode a bomb which, he asserts, is in a handbag he is carrying. The pilot diverts the flight of the plane to a destination demanded by the passenger. The passenger leaves the plane at that destination and the plane is flown to its original destination.

Even in this simple example there may be a number of problems of domestic and international law. The plane may be registered in the United States or in some other country. The passenger may hijack the plane on the ground in New York, or while it is over the Atlantic on its way to London, or while it is on the ground in London. The hijacker may be a United States national, or the national of another state. He may or may not eventually return to the United States and thus be subject to its enforcement jurisdiction. The United States may ask the government of the foreign state in which the hijacker is located to return him to the United States by extradition proceedings. The government of a state to which the hijacker has fled may decide to try him even though that state has had no connection with the event other than having become a place of refuge.

---

1. International Conventions.

The Tokyo Convention (Convention on Offenses and Certain Other Acts Committed on Board Aircraft, 20 U.S.T. 2941; Documentary Supplement) was drafted under the auspices of the International Civil Aviation Organization and signed in 1963. It entered into force for the United States on December 4, 1969. 104 states were parties to the convention on January 1, 1980.

The convention is concerned broadly with the question of crimes on board aircraft in flight, on the surface of the high seas or any other area outside the jurisdiction of a nation state. A special purpose of the convention is to provide that there be no lapse of jurisdiction with respect to such crimes. To that end Article 3(1) provides that at least one state shall have jurisdiction: "The State of registration of the aircraft is competent to exercise jurisdiction over offenses and acts committed on board." This jurisdiction is not exclusive, however. The convention deals in detail with the powers of the aircraft commander to "off-load" and to restrain offenders or suspected offenders. Article 11 deals specifically with hijacking:

1. When a person on board has unlawfully committed by force or threat thereof an act of interference, seizure, or other wrongful exercise of control of an aircraft in flight or when such an act is about to be committed, Contracting States shall take all appropriate measures to restore control of the aircraft to its lawful commander or to preserve his control of the aircraft.

2. In the cases contemplated in the preceding paragraph, the Contracting State in which the aircraft lands shall permit its passengers and crew to continue their journey as soon as practicable, and shall return the aircraft and its cargo to the persons lawfully entitled to possession.

The provision on extradition (Article 16) is relatively weak:

1. Offences committed on aircraft registered in a Contracting State shall be treated, for the purpose of extradition, as if they had been committed not only in the place in which they have occurred but also in the territory of the State of registration of the aircraft.

2. Without prejudice to the provisions of the preceding paragraph, nothing in this Convention shall be deemed to create an obligation to grant extradition.

The Hague Convention (Convention for the Suppression of Unlawful Seizure of Aircraft, 22 U.S.T. 1641, Documentary Supplement) was also the product of the work of the ICAO. It was approved at a diplomatic conference at The Hague in 1970 and entered into force for the United States on October 14, 1971. 108 states were parties to the Convention on January 1, 1980. In contrast to the Tokyo Convention, the Hague Convention is directed narrowly to the question of hijacking. Its major provisions create universal jurisdiction for the prosecution of hijackers and impose an obligation on the states either to prosecute the hijacker or to extradite him:

Article 1

Any person who on board an aircraft in flight:

(a) unlawfully, by force or threat thereof, or by any other form of intimidation, seizes, or exercises control of, that aircraft, or attempts to perform any such act, or

(b) is an accomplice of a person who performs or attempts to perform any such act

commits an offence (hereinafter referred to as "the offence").

Article 4

1. Each Contracting State shall take such measures as may be necessary to establish its jurisdiction over the offence and any other act of violence against passengers or crew committed by the alleged offender in connection with the offence, in the following cases:

(a) when the offence is committed on board an aircraft registered in that State;

(b) when the aircraft on board which the offence is committed lands in its territory with the alleged offender still on board;

(c) when the offence is committed on board an aircraft leased without crew to a lessee who has his principal place of business or, if the lessee has no such place of business, his permanent residence, in that State.

2. Each Contracting State shall likewise take such measures as may be necessary to establish its jurisdiction over the offence in the case where the alleged offender is present in its territory and it does not extradite him pursuant to Article 8 to any of the States mentioned in paragraph 1 of this Article.

3. This Convention does not exclude any criminal jurisdiction exercised in accordance with national law.

Article 7

The Contracting State in the territory of which the alleged offender is found shall, if it does not extradite him, be obliged, without exception whatsoever and whether or not the offence was committed in its territory, to submit the case to its competent authorities for the purpose of prosecution.

Those authorities shall take their decision in the same manner as in the case of any ordinary offence of a serious nature under the law of that State.

Article 8

1. The offence shall be deemed to be included as an extraditable offence in any extradition treaty existing between Contracting States. Contracting States undertake to include the offence as an extraditable offence in every extradition treaty to be concluded between them.

2. If a Contracting State which makes extradition conditional on the existence of a treaty receives a request for extradition from another Contracting State with which it has no extradition treaty, it may at its option consider this Convention as the legal basis for extradition in respect of the offence. Extradition shall be subject to the other conditions provided by the law of the requested State.

3. Contracting States which do not make extradition conditional on the existence of a treaty shall recognize the offence as an extraditable offence between themselves subject to the conditions provided by the law of the requested State.

4. The offence shall be treated, for the purpose of extradition between Contracting States, as if it had been committed not only in the place in which it occurred but also in the territories of the States required to establish their jurisdiction in accordance with Article 4, paragraph 1.

2. *French legislation.* France deposited its ratification to the Hague Convention on September 18, 1972. The following legislation, Law 72–623,[a] was enacted July 5, 1972:

Art. L. 121–7. French courts have jurisdiction over any infraction committed aboard an airplane registered in France. They have jurisdiction as well over any crime or tort committed against such plane outside of the French territory.

Art. L. 121–8. French courts have jurisdiction with respect to a crime or a tort committed aboard a plane which is not registered in France when the author or the victim has French nationality, when the plane lands in France after the commission of the crime or tort, or when the infraction was committed aboard a plane which is rented

---

a. Translation by the editors.

without crew to a person who has his principal place of establishment or, if there be none, his permanent residence in France.

Moreover, in case a plane is forced off its course [i. e. hijacked] which is not registered in France, French courts have jurisdiction over the infraction and over every other act of violence against the passengers or the crew done by the person alleged to have forced the plane off its course in the commission of [literally, in direct relationship to] the offense, when the person is found in France. 92 Gazette du Palais (Legislation) 360 (1972).

3. *United States legislation.* Even before the United States became a party to the Hague Convention, it was a crime to commit aircraft piracy (i. e., "any seizure or exercise of control, by force or violence or threat of force or violence and with wrongful intent, of an aircraft within the special aircraft jurisdiction of the United States"), Title 49, Section 1472 of the United States Code. After becoming a party to the convention, the United States enacted legislation to broaden its definition of special aircraft jurisdiction to take account particularly of Subsections (b) and (c) of Section 1 of Article 4 of the convention. Title 49, Section 1301(38) of the United States Code.

In implementation of Section 2 of Article 4 of the convention, the following provision was added to Title 49, Section 1472 of the United States Code:

(n)(1) Whoever aboard an aircraft in flight outside the special aircraft jurisdiction of the United States commits "an offense", as defined in the Convention for the Suppression of Unlawful Seizure of Aircraft and is afterward found in the United States shall be punished—

(A) by imprisonment for not less than 20 years; or

(B) if the death of another person results from the commission or attempted commission of the offense, by death or by imprisonment for life.

(2) A person commits "an offense", as defined in the Convention for the Suppression of Unlawful Seizure of Aircraft when, while aboard an aircraft in flight, he—

(A) unlawfully, by force or threat thereof, or by any other form of intimidation, seizes, or exercises control of, that aircraft, or attempts to perform any such act; or

(B) is an accomplice of a person who performs or attempts to perform any such act. * * *

4. *Problem.* A hijacker is found in the United States and is prosecuted under Subsection (n), above. The aircraft was outside the special aircraft jurisdiction of the United States and is registered in State X; the hijacker is a national of State Y. But State Y is not a party to the Hague Convention. Has the United States violated the rights of State Y? Could the United States justify its assertion of jurisdiction by claiming that the provisions of Subsection (n) are an implementation not only of the Hague Convention's grant of jurisdic-

tion but also of the jurisdiction that is recognized by the general international law of piracy? See Jacobson, From Piracy on the High Seas to Piracy in the High Skies: a Study of Aircraft Hijacking, 5 Cornell Int'l L.J. 161 (1972), for a discussion of the doctrinal controversies of the past with regard to the question whether piracy requires action by one ship against another. (I. e., when a ship is seized by persons already on board, has piracy been committed?)

Prosecution of such a hijacker under Title 18, Section 1651 of the United States Code would not only involve the foregoing one ship/two ship problem but would also involve the problem raised by the case of United States v. Cordova, above:

> Whoever, on the high seas, commits the crime of piracy as defined by the law of nations, and is afterwards brought into or found in the United States, shall be imprisoned for life.

SABOTAGE

The Sabotage Convention—Convention for the Suppression of Unlawful Acts Against the Safety of Civil Aviation—was adopted by a Conference on International Air Law at Montreal in 1971. 24 U.S. T. 564. The text is in the Documentary Supplement. It entered into force as to the United States on January 26, 1973. On January 1, 1980, 106 states were parties to the convention. The scope of the convention was described by the head of the United States delegation as follows:

> Although this convention is similar to the Hijacking Convention in many respects, it is significantly distinct: It does not, basically, require states to define any new offenses—it covers acts which already are common crimes; it does not, for the most part, establish new crimes to fall within the extradition process —most of the acts already are extraditable crimes. These were important elements of the Hijacking Convention. It might be said that states could punish offenders or extradite them without this convention.

> What this convention does is to impose an obligation on states *requiring* them to prosecute or extradite offenders. It serves as a warning to any person who contemplates such acts that the international community has responded with unanimity to condemn such acts. In this respect it is like the Hijacking Convention.

> And in an important respect this convention does more than the Hijacking Convention. It covers acts against aircraft in a state's domestic service, even when the acts take place wholly within that same state, if the offender escapes to another state. While this element is not critical for the Hijacking Convention, it is crucial for the effectiveness of the convention we have concluded, because of the possibility that offenders may escape be-

fore they are discovered. This convention declares that no one who sabotages a civil aircraft—whether in domestic or international service—no one who places a bomb on board such an aircraft, no evildoer who commits violence aboard such an aircraft in flight, no criminal of this character shall ever find sanctuary anywhere in the world, no matter how deviously he may seek to evade retribution for his deeds. The parties to this convention have declared that this despicable criminal shall be pursued without respite. 65 U.S. Dept. State Bull. 464 (1971).

EXTRADITION AND AIRCRAFT OFFENSES

Extradition under the Hague Convention. Article 8(1) of the Hague Convention provides, in effect, for the automatic amendment of extradition treaties to add hijacking to the list of extraditable crimes. What, then, of the individual who seeks to escape from a country which refuses to allow him to emigrate by hijacking a plane in the domestic air service of that country and requiring the pilot to fly the plane to a country of refuge? If the underlying extradition treaty provides for the usual exception for crimes of a political character, can the requested state consider that hijacking under those circumstances is such a crime? If it does so consider it and refuses to extradite, the obligation to prosecute, under Article 7 of the Hague Convention, comes into play.

A CASE OF REFUSAL OF EXTRADITION

McDowell, Digest of United States Practice
in International Law 1975, at 168 (1976).

On April 14, 1975, the Chambre d'accusation of the Cour d'appel of Paris refused a request of the United States for extradition of Willie Roger Holder and Mary Katherine Kerkow for trial in the United States on aircraft hijacking charges. The refusal was on the basis of the fugitives' allegations of political motive. They had been indicted in June 1972 in both New York and California in connection with the 1972 hijacking of a flight between Los Angeles and Seattle, followed by a forced landing in San Francisco, a stop for refueling in New York, and a forced flight to Algeria.

In support of its request for extradition, the United States had submitted to the French Foreign Ministry and to the Justice Ministry the following memorandum of law, dated April 3, 1975:

Memorandum of Law

The fugitives, William Roger Holder and Mary Katherine Kerkow, have been indicted for the crimes of aircraft piracy, kidnapping and extortion, which are extraditable offenses under Article II of the Extradition Treaty between the United States and France, of January 6, 1909, as amended by the supplementary convention of February 12, 1970. Thus, France has a treaty obligation to surrender these fugitives for prosecution in the United States, unless the case comes within the terms of the exemption established in Article VI for political offenses. Article VI provides:

Extradition shall not be granted in any of the following circumstances:

* * *

4. If the offense for which the individual's extradition is requested is of a political character, or if he proves that the requisition for his surrender has, in fact, been made with a view to try or punish him for an offense of a political character. If any question arises as to whether a case comes within the provisions of this subparagraph, the authorities of the government on which the requisition is made shall decide.

* * *

Under this provision the requested state determines whether a crime is of a political character. However, the determination does not involve an exercise of discretion. It is a legal determination as to whether a treaty obligation exists on the facts of the particular case. No allegation has been made in this case, nor could it be sustained, that the United States requests the surrender of these fugitives in order to punish them for any offense other than the common crimes for which extradition is requested. Therefore, the sole question for the court is whether the crimes charged constitute offenses of a "political character" in the legal sense of Article VI.

Although the treaty does not prescribe a specific definition of offenses of a "political character" there is considerable jurisprudence and international extradition practice which establish the parameters of this concept. Offenses "of a political character" include traditional political crimes such as sedition and treason. The concept may also include common crimes which are clearly connected with offenses of a political character under special circumstances which have been defined by the tribunals of states and international practice.

There are numerous decisions holding that ordinary common crimes cannot be considered offenses of a political character unless they occur in the context of a civil war, rebellion or similar political disturbance. * * * [For cases involving this question, see pp. 139–143, supra.]

Although political offenses have been found by tribunals in some other circumstances—usually involving compelling human considerations—it is well established that political motive alone does not give a common crime the character of a political offense. * * *

* * *

In this case the fugitives were not engaged in any attempt to overthrow the Government of the United States or in any other political offense with which their crime could be connected. There is no evidence and no allegation that they belonged to any political group or had engaged in any political activities in the past. There is no allegation that the fugitives were subject to political persecution or harassment of any kind. The defense bases its claim of political offense exclusively on the alleged motive of the defendants to have the hijacked aircraft fly to Hanoi. The only evidence on this point is that the defendant Holder asked that the first plane fly to Hanoi and did not persist in that request when he was provided a second aircraft with the capacity to do so. His references to Angela Davis at the outset of the flight and to Eldridge Cleaver near the destination at Algiers evidence a confused mixture of vague and ill-defined motives. There is no precedent and no basis for construing the criminal activity of these fugitives as an offense of a political character.

Aircraft piracy is a serious, common crime which threatens the lives of innocent persons, disrupts international civil aviation, and causes tensions in international relations. It is an offense against the human rights of passengers and crew, and against the public order of all states. As such, it has been repeatedly condemned by the Security Council, the United Nations General Assembly and the International Civil Aviation Organization in solemn resolutions supported by France and the United States. The General Assembly resolution of November 25, 1970, "condemns, without exception whatsoever, all acts of aircraft hijacking" and "calls upon states to take all appropriate measures to deter, prevent or suppress such acts within their jurisdiction * * *." The Hague Convention for the Suppression of Unlawful Seizure of Aircraft, signed December 16, 1970, to which France and the United States are party, provides for the extradition or prosecution of the perpetrators of such crimes.

While there are cases in years past in which states held a particular hijacking to be a political offense where the persons involved were fleeing from tyranny and faced severe political persecution if they were returned, the danger inherent in the increasing incidence of aircraft hijacking in more recent years has alarmed the entire international community and given grounds for a presumption that aircraft hijacking is a most serious common crime regardless of the circumstances. Moreover, there is wide recognition in the international community that cases of aircraft hijacking involving extortion or actual injury to passengers or crew represent an aggravated form of the offense which requires punishment as a common crime.
* * *

In this case there is no suggestion that the fugitives were subject to any political persecution or needed the transportation to leave the country; they did threaten the lives of passengers and crew to extort $500,000 from the airline. This extortion contradicts any notion of idealism or of "political character" in this case.

It is recognized that extradition is the most effective deterrent to the crime of aircraft hijacking. Surrender of these fugitives for prosecution in the United States will contribute to such deterrence and thus protect lives and the interests of France as well as those of the United States. Refusal of extradition on the specious grounds that this crime is an offense of a political character would appear to condone hijacking and could contribute to repetition of such crimes to the danger of the entire international community.

[End of Memorandum of Law.]

On July 7, 1975, the United States Embassy at Paris delivered to the Acting Legal Adviser in the French Foreign Ministry a note with respect to the French refusal of extradition and the applicability of the U.S.-French extradition convention, as supplemented (TS 561; TIAS 7075; 37 Stat. 1526; 22 UST 407). The substantive portion of the note follows:

* * *

The Embassy notes that the decision of the Chambre d'accusation regarding the question of extradition is final and that in accordance with the Convention for the Suppression of Unlawful Seizure of Aircraft, signed at The Hague on December 16, 1970, a case has been opened against the accused at the Parquet de Paris on charges of the illegal seizure of an aircraft and restraint of hostages under threat. The Embassy trusts that these proceedings will result, in the event the accused are found guilty, in the application of the penalty which is proportionate to the seriousness of the crime and which will further the purposes of the Hague Convention to deter aircraft hijacking.

The interested officials of the United States Government have now had the opportunity to review the decision of the Chambre d'accusation on the request for extradition made by the United States, and this Embassy has been instructed to bring to the attention of the Foreign Ministry the serious concern of the United States Government over the rejection of its extradition request.

In the view of the United States Government the decision of the French Government in this case to deny extradition on the sole grounds of an alleged political motivation for the crime is inconsistent with France's obligations under the Treaty of Extradition between the United States of America and the Republic of France of January 6, 1909, as amended by the supplementary convention signed at Paris on February 12, 1970.

Although the treaty does not prescribe a specific definition of an offense of a "political character," and international practice is somewhat varied, the considerable jurisprudence and numerous cases in this field clearly establish that mere political motive is not sufficient to characterize a serious common crime as a political offense. * * *

A strong case can be made that serious crimes such as aircraft hijacking are so dangerous to human life and so inimical to international order that they should not be regarded as "political offenses" regardless of the circumstances. Even if it is assumed that there are special circumstances in which an act of hijacking may be considered to have a political character, it is an extreme position to argue that the mere plea of political motive is sufficient to establish the political nature of the offense. * * *

The effect of the decision by the Cour d'appel is to construe hijacking as a "political offense" in any case in which a political motive is alleged, even where large sums of money are extorted under the threat of murder of the passengers and crew. The effect of the decision in this case, if it were followed by other states, would be virtually to eliminate extradition as a remedy in hijacking cases, and by suppressing the most effective deterrent to aircraft hijacking, would encourage the commission of more such crimes in the future.
*   *   *

1. *Subsequent conviction.* "On June 13, 1980, Willie Holder received a suspended five-year prison sentence for the hijacking. His companion, Mary Kerkov, left France earlier and was to be tried in absentia." The New York Times, June 15, 1980, Sec. A, p. 8, col. 1.

2. *Question.* There are quite a few cases involving hijackers from states behind the Iron Curtain, such as Poland and Czechoslovakia, in which the authorities of the state where they landed—Denmark, Austria, Western Germany—denied the requests for extradition and gave these hijackers light sentences when they tried them. See the Revue Générale de Droit International Public, Vol. 76 at 484 and 509 (1972) and Vol. 82 at 1082 (1978). Would the Department of State protest these denials of extradition on the ground that mere political motive is not sufficient to characterize hijacking as a political offense? Should it? And if, as the Department of State says, a strong case can be made that hijacking is so dangerous to human life it should not be regarded as a political offense regardless of the circumstances, how do you explain its immediate denial of extradition when two persons from Eastern Germany hijacked a Polish plane and forced it to land at Tempelhof airport, in the American zone of Berlin? 83 Revue Générale de Droit International Public 480 (1979).

3. *Deterrence.* Speaking to the United Nations General Assembly in 1977 in support of a resolution calling upon states not only to adopt the anti-hijacking conventions but also to take steps to improve security arrangements at airports and by airlines, the United States Representative, Congressman Lester L. Wolff, made the following observation:

> One might ask whether the sorts of actions which this resolution envisages will really have much impact on hijacking. In our view, the answer to any such questions can only be an emphatic yes. I would cite in this connection the experience of the United States in its successful effort against hijacking domestically. In 1969, prior to the establishment of security measures, designed to prevent incidents of this type, there were 40 attempts to hijack U. S. civilian aircraft, 33 of which were successful. In 1973, the first full year after stringent security procedures were made mandatory for all U. S. airports, the number of

such incidents fell to two. In 1976 as well, there were only two incidents. These figures speak for themselves.

Looking at the current situation on a worldwide basis, we find that the number of hijacking incidents is once again on the rise and that lax security procedures at airports have been responsible for most of them. The figures are striking. Of the 28 airline hijackings thus far this year—as opposed to 16 during all of 1976—20 can be attributed to failures in passenger screening procedures. Since 1973 there have been no hijackings in the United States which resulted from a failure to detect guns and other weapons during the screening process. I might point out that the United States has been and continues to be willing to share its experience in this area with other interested countries. For instance, the United States has offered to share its screening procedures, equipment, and testing measures with other countries, and thus far 36 countries have taken advantage of this offer.

In calling upon the competent specialized U.N. agency, ICAO, to develop additional measures to increase international civil aviation security, the resolution we have adopted clears the way for new initiatives in that respected and impartial Organization. Among the steps which we believe ICAO should take are the following:

(1) Strengthening of the current ICAO standard on passenger screening to require specifically the screening of all passengers and all carry-on baggage for all airline flights, both foreign and domestic;

(2) Elevation of certain ICAO recommended practices dealing with security to the status of standards, including: (a) provision of law enforcement support for aviation security and (b) provision of security for aircraft under hijacking or sabotage threat; and

(3) Continuing emphasis by ICAO on universal adherence to and ratification of The Hague (hijacking) and Montreal (sabotage) conventions. Such action would effectively eliminate safe havens for aviation criminals. U. S. Dept. of State Bull., January 1978, p. 54.

4. *Self help.* The Israeli rescue of hijacked passengers at Entebbe Airport is considered in Chapter 19.

3. POLLUTION OF AIRSPACE

TRAIL SMELTER CASE (UNITED STATES v. CANADA)

Arbitral Tribunal, 1941.
III U.N.Rep. Int'l Arb. Awards 1905, 1907 (1949).

CONVENTION FOR SETTLEMENT OF DIFFICULTIES ARISING FROM
OPERATION OF SMELTER AT TRAIL, B.C.

* * *

ARTICLE III.

The Tribunal shall finally decide the questions, hereinafter referred to as "the Questions", set forth hereunder, namely:

(1) Whether damage caused by the Trail Smelter in the State of Washington has occurred since the first day of January, 1932, and, if so, what indemnity should be paid therefor?

(2) In the event of the answer to the first part of the preceding Question being in the affirmative, whether the Trail Smelter should be required to refrain from causing damage in the State of Washington in the future, and if so, to what extent?

(3) In the light of the answer to the preceding Question, what measures or régime, if any, should be adopted or maintained by the Trail Smelter?

(4) What indemnity or compensation, if any, should be paid on account of any decision or decisions rendered by the Tribunal pursuant to the next two preceding Questions?

ARTICLE IV.

The Tribunal shall apply the law and practice followed in dealing with cognate questions in the United States of America as well as international law and practice, and shall give consideration to the desire of the high contracting parties to reach a solution just to all parties concerned.

* * *

DECISION

REPORTED ON MARCH 11, 1944, TO THE GOVERNMENT OF THE UNITED STATES OF AMERICA AND TO THE GOVERNMENT OF THE DOMINION OF CANADA, UNDER THE CONVENTION SIGNED APRIL 15, 1935.

* * *

On April 16, 1938, the Tribunal reported its "final decision" on Question No. 1, as well as its temporary decisions on Questions No. 2 and No. 3, and provided for a temporary régime thereunder. The decision reported on April 16, 1938, will be referred to hereinafter as the "previous decision". * * *

In conclusion (end of Part Two of the previous decision), the Tribunal answered Question No. 1 as follows:

Damage caused by the Trail Smelter in the State of Washington has occurred since the first day of January, 1932, and up to October 1, 1937, and the indemnity to be paid therefor is seventy-eight thousand dollars ($78,000), and is to be complete and final indemnity and compensation for all damage which occurred between such dates. Interest at the rate of six per centum per year will be allowed on the above sum of seventy-eight thousand dollars ($78,000) from the date of the filing of this report and decision until date of payment. This decision is not subject to alteration or modification by the Tribunal hereafter. The fact of existence of damage, if any occurring after October 1, 1937, and the indemnity to be paid therefor, if any, the Tribunal will determine in its final decision.

* * *

In 1896, a smelter was started under American auspices near the locality known as Trail, B.C. In 1906, the Consolidated Mining and Smelting Company of Canada, Limited, obtained a charter of incorporation from the Canadian authorities, and that company acquired the smelter plant at Trail as it then existed. Since that time, the Canadian company, without interruption, has operated the Smelter, and from to time has greatly added to the plant until it has become one of the best and largest equipped smelting plants on the American continent. In 1925 and 1927, two stacks of the plant were erected to 409 feet in height and the Smelter greatly increased its daily smelting of zinc and lead ores. This increased production resulted in more sulphur dioxide fumes and higher concentrations being emitted into the air. In 1916, about 5,000 tons of sulphur per month were emitted; in 1924, about 4,700 tons; in 1926, about 9,000 tons—an amount which rose near to 10,000 tons per month in 1930. In other words, about 300–350 tons of sulphur were being emitted daily in 1930. (It is to be noted that one ton of sulphur is substantially the equivalent of two tons of sulphur dioxide or SO_2.)

From 1925, at least, to 1937, damage occurred in the State of Washington, resulting from the sulphur dioxide emitted from the Trail Smelter as stated in the previous decision. * * *

The second question under Article III of the Convention is as follows:

In the event of the answer to the first part of the preceding question being in the affirmative, whether the Trail Smelter should be required to refrain from causing damage in the State of Washington in the future and, if so, to what extent?

Damage has occurred since January 1, 1932, as fully set forth in the previous decision. To that extent, the first part of the preceding question has thus been answered in the affirmative. * * *

The first problem which arises is whether the question should be answered on the basis of the law followed in the United States or on the basis of international law. The Tribunal, however, finds that this problem need not be solved here as the law followed in the United States in dealing with the quasi-sovereign rights of the States of the Union, in the matter of air pollution, whilst more definite, is in conformity with the general rules of international law.

Particularly in reaching its conclusions as regards this question as well as the next, the Tribunal has given consideration to the desire of the high contracting parties "to reach a solution just to all parties concerned".

As Professor Eagleton puts in (Responsibility of States in International Law, 1928, p. 80): "A State owes at all times a duty to protect other States against injurious acts by individuals from within its jurisdiction." A great number of such general pronouncements by leading authorities concerning the duty of a State to respect other States and their territory have been presented to the Tribunal. These and many others have been carefully examined. International decisions, in various matters, from the Alabama case onward, and also earlier ones, are based on the same general principle, and, indeed, this principle, as such, has not been questioned by Canada. But the real difficulty often arises rather when it comes to determine what, pro subjecta materie, is deemed to constitute an injurious act.

A case concerning, as the present one does, territorial relations, decided by the Federal Court of Switzerland between the Cantons of Soleure and Argovia, may serve to illustrate the relativity of the rule. Soleure brought a suit against her sister State to enjoin use of a shooting establishment which endangered her territory. The court, in granting the injunction, said: "This right (sovereignty) excludes * * * not only the usurpation and exercise of sovereign rights (of another State) * * * but also an actual encroachment which might prejudice the natural use of the territory and the free movement of its inhabitants." As a result of the decision, Argovia made plans for the improvement of the existing installations. These, however, were considered as insufficient protection by Soleure. The Canton of Argovia then moved the Federal Court to decree that the shooting be again permitted after completion of the projected improvements. This motion was granted. "The demand of the Government of Soleure", said the court, "that all endangerment be absolutely abolished apparently goes too far." The court found that all risk whatever had not been eliminated, as the region was flat and absolutely safe shooting ranges were only found in mountain valleys; that there was a federal duty for the communes to provide facilities for military target practice and that "no more precautions may be demanded for shooting ranges near the boundaries of two Cantons than are required for shooting ranges in the interior of a Canton". (R.O. 26, I, pp. 450, 451; R.O. 41, I, p. 137; see D. Schindler, "The Administration of Justice in the Swiss Federal Court in Intercantonal Disputes", American Journal of International Law, Vol. 15 (1921), pp. 172–174).

No case of air pollution dealt with by an international tribunal has been brought to the attention of the Tribunal nor does the Tribunal know of any such case. The nearest analogy is that of water pollution. But, here also, no decision of an international tribunal has been cited or has been found.

There are, however, as regards both air pollution and water pollution, certain decisions of the Supreme Court of the United States which may legitimately be taken as a guide in this field of international law, for it is reasonable to follow by analogy, in international cases, precedents established by that court in dealing with controversies between States of the Union or with other controversies concerning the quasi-sovereign rights of such States, where no contrary rule prevails in international law and no reason for rejecting such precedents can be adduced from the limitations of sovereignty inherent in the Constitution of the United States.

In the suit of the State of Missouri v. the State of Illinois (200 U.S. 496, 521) concerning the pollution, within the boundaries of Illinois, of the Illinois River, an affluent of the Mississippi flowing into the latter where it forms the boundary between that State and Missouri, an injunction was refused. "Before this court ought to intervene", said the court, "the case should be of serious magnitude, clearly and fully proved, and the principle to be applied should be one which the court is prepared deliberately to maintain against all considerations on the other side. (See Kansas v. Colorado, 185 U.S. 125.)" The court found that the practice complained of was general along the shores of the Mississippi River at that time, that it was followed by Missouri itself and that thus a standard was set up by the defendant which the claimant was entitled to invoke.

As the claims of public health became more exacting and methods for removing impurities from the water were perfected, complaints ceased. It is significant that Missouri sided with Illinois when the other riparians of the Great Lakes' system sought to enjoin it to desist from diverting the waters of that system into that of the Illinois and Mississippi for the very purpose of disposing of the Chicago sewage.

In the more recent suit of the State of New York against the State of New Jersey (256 U.S. 296, 309), concerning the pollution of New York Bay, the injunction was also refused for lack of proof, some experts believing that the plans which were in dispute would result in the presence of "offensive odors and unsightly deposits", other equally reliable experts testifying that they were confidently of the opinion that the waters would be sufficiently purified. The court, referring to Missouri v. Illinois, said: "* * * the burden upon the State of New York of sustaining the allegations of its bill is much greater than that imposed upon a complainant in an ordinary suit between private parties. Before this court can be moved to exercise its extraordinary power under the Constitution to control the conduct of one State at the suit of another, the threatened invasion of rights must be of serious magnitude and it must be established by clear and convincing evidence."

What the Supreme Court says there of its power under the Constitution equally applies to the extraordinary power granted this Tribunal under the Convention. What is true between States of the Union is, at least, equally true concerning the relations between the United States and the Dominion of Canada.

In another recent case concerning water pollution (283 U.S. 473), the complainant was successful. The City of New York was enjoined, at the request of the State of New Jersey, to desist, within a reasonable time limit, from the practice of disposing of sewage by dumping it into the sea, a practice which was injurious to the coastal waters of New Jersey in the vicinity of her bathing resorts.

In the matter of air pollution itself, the leading decisions are those of the Supreme Court in the State of Georgia v. Tennessee Copper Company and Ducktown Sulphur, Copper and Iron Company, Limited. Although dealing with a suit against private companies, the decisions were on questions cognate to those here at issue. Georgia stated that it had in vain sought relief from the State of Tennessee, on whose territory the smelters were located, and the court defined the nature of the suit by saying: "This is a suit by a State for an injury to it in its capacity of quasi-sovereign. In that capacity, the State has an interest independent of and behind the titles of its citizens, in all the earth and air within its domain."

On the question whether an injunction should be granted or not, the court said (206 U.S. 230):

It (the State) has the last word as to whether its mountains shall be stripped of their forests and its inhabitants shall breathe pure air. * * * It is not lightly to be presumed to give up quasi-sovereign rights for pay and * * * if that be its choice, it may insist that an infraction of them shall be stopped. This court has not quite the same freedom to balance the harm that will be done by an injunction against that of which the plaintiff complains, that it would have in deciding between two subjects of a single political power. Without excluding the considerations that equity always takes into account * * * it is a fair and reasonable demand on the part of a sovereign that the air over its territory should not be polluted on a great scale by sulphurous acid gas, that the forests on its mountains, be they better or worse, and whatever domestic destruction they may have suffered, should not be further destroyed or threatened by the act of persons beyond its control, that the crops and orchards on its hills should not be endangered from the same source. * * * Whether Georgia, by insisting upon this claim, is doing more harm than good to her own citizens, is for her to determine. The possible disaster to those outside the State must be accepted as a consequence of her standing upon her extreme rights.

Later on, however, when the court actually framed an injunction, in the case of the Ducktown Company (237 U.S. 474, 477) (an agreement on the basis of an annual compensation was reached with the most important of the two smelters, the Tennessee Copper Company), they did not go beyond a decree "adequate to diminish materially the present probability of damage to its (Georgia's) citizens".

Great progress in the control of fumes has been made by science in the last few years and this progress should be taken into account.

The Tribunal, therefore, finds that the above decisions, taken as a whole, constitute an adequate basis for its conclusions, namely, that, under the principles of international law, as well as of the law of the United States, no State has the right to use or permit the use of its territory in such a manner as to cause injury by fumes in or to the territory of another or the properties or persons therein, when the case is of serious consequence and the injury is established by clear and convincing evidence.

The decisions of the Supreme Court of the United States which are the basis of these conclusions are decisions in equity and a solution inspired by them, together with the régime hereinafter prescribed, will, in the opinion of the Tribunal, be "just to all parties concerned", as long, at least, as the present conditions in the Columbia River Valley continue to prevail.

Considering the circumstances of the case, the Tribunal holds that the Dominion of Canada is responsible in international law for the conduct of the Trail Smelter. Apart from the undertakings in the Convention, it is, therefore, the duty of the Government of the Dominion of Canada to see to it that this conduct should be in conformity with the obligation of the Dominion under international law as herein determined.

The Tribunal, therefore, answers Question No. 2 as follows: (2) So long as the present conditions in the Columbia River Valley prevail, the Trail Smelter shall be required to refrain from causing any damage through fumes in the State of Washington; the damage herein referred to and its extent being such as would be recoverable under the decisions of the courts of the United States in suits between private individuals. The indemnity for such damage should be fixed in such manner as the Governments, acting under Article XI of the Convention should agree upon.

The third question under Article III of the Convention is as follows: "In the light of the answer to the preceding question, what measures or régime, if any, should be adopted and maintained by the Trail Smelter?"

Answering this question in the light of the preceding one, since the Tribunal has, in its previous decision, found that damage caused by the Trail Smelter has occurred in the State of Washington since January 1, 1932, and since the Tribunal is of opinion that damage may occur in the future unless the operations of the Smelter shall be subject to some control, in order to avoid damage occurring, the Tribunal now decides that a régime or measure of control shall be applied to the operations of the Smelter and shall remain in full force unless and until modified in accordance with the provisions hereinafter set forth.   *   *   *

1. *Jurisdiction to legislate with respect to air pollution.* Does either the State of Washington or the United States have jurisdiction to prescribe laws regulating the pollution of Washington or United States airspace by Canadian polluters?

2. *Applicable law.* Heretofore in this chapter the law governing events occurring in airspace has been domestic law and the inquiry has been whether or not a state has jurisdiction to prescribe the relevant rule. In what respect does the Trail Smelter case present a different problem? What is the source of the governing rule?

Why is Canada held responsible in this case? By what standard is its conduct measured? Does international law impose an obligation on Canada only after a showing of historical injury, or would a showing of potential injury be sufficient? For a discussion of the implications of the Trail Smelter case for situations in which modern technological developments threaten the environment (e. g., weather modification), see Kirgis, Technological Challenge to the Shared Environment: United States Practice, 66 Am. J. Int'l L. 290 (1972).

3. *International negotiations.* Forty years after the decision just reported, the United States and Canada were still negotiating an air quality agreement. New York Times, Oct. 21, 1979, Sec. 1, p. 19, col. 1. According to the report, a joint United States-Canada Research Consultation Group on the Long-Range Transport of Air Pollutants found cross frontier deposits in each country of acid rain, through precipitation of sulfur dioxide, believed to be causing damage to aquatic life in lakes and rivers as well as to crops and forests. The "largest single sulfur dioxide emission source in North America" is reported to be a company in Canada with "one of the highest smokestacks in the world. The smokestack enables the company to blow its pollutants away from Sudbury and into large areas of Southern Ontario, Quebec and northern New York, where in the Adirondacks 100 lakes above the altitude of 2000 feet have lost their fish." While noting that the greater part of each country's domestic sulfur deposits was caused by its own emissions, the Group reported that more acid rain was being sent to Canada by the United States than vice versa. On the same point, see Acid Rain, Sierra— The Sierra Club Bulletin, May/June 1980, pp. 38, 41.

Can liability be predicated on a violation of a state's sovereignty by the "mere fact of   *   *   *   transfrontier crossing" by pollutants, by a "moral injury" alone? See Handl, Territorial Sovereignty and the Problem of Transnational Pollution, 69 Am. J. Int'l. L. 50, 75 (1975).

4. *Nuclear test ban treaty.* The Treaty Banning Nuclear Weapon Tests in the Atmosphere, in Outer Space and Under Water, 4 U.S.T. 1313, 480 U.N.T.S. 43, Documentary Supplement, entered into force for the United States on October 10, 1963. The preamble to the Treaty recites that the parties desired "to put an end to the contamination of man's environment by radioactive substances." There were 110 parties to the treaty on January 1, 1980.

NUCLEAR TESTS (AUSTRALIA v. FRANCE), INTERIM PROTECTION, ORDER OF 22 JUNE 1973

International Court of Justice, 1973.
[1973] I.C.J. Reports 99.[a]

The International Court of Justice,　*　*　*

Having regard to the Application by Australia filed in the Registry of the Court on 9 May 1973, instituting proceedings against France in respect of a dispute concerning the holding of atmospheric tests of nuclear weapons by the French Government in the Pacific Ocean, and asking the Court to adjudge and declare that the carrying out of further atmospheric nuclear weapon tests in the South Pacific Ocean is not consistent with applicable rules of international law, and to order that the French Republic shall not carry out any further such tests,

Makes the following Order:

1. Having regard to the request dated 9 May 1973 and filed in the Registry the same day, whereby the Government of Australia, relying on Article 33 of the General Act of 1928 for the Pacific Settlement of International Disputes and on Article 41 of the Statute and Article 66 of the Rules of Court, asks the Court to indicate, pending the final decision in the case brought before it by the Application of the same date, the following interim measures of protection:

> The provisional measures should be that the French Government should desist from any further atmospheric nuclear tests pending the judgment of the Court in this case;

*　*　*

6. Whereas by a letter dated 16 May 1973 from the Ambassador of France to the Netherlands, handed by him to the Registrar the same day, the French Government stated that it considered that the Court was manifestly not competent in the case and that it could not accept the Court's jurisdiction, and that accordingly the French Government did not intend to appoint an agent, and requested the Court to remove the case from its list;

*　*　*

---

a. Parallel proceedings were instituted by New Zealand. [1973] I.C.J. Reports 135.

13.   Whereas on a request for provisional measures the Court need not, before indicating them, finally satisfy itself that it has jurisdiction on the merits of the case, and yet ought not to indicate such measures unless the provisions invoked by the Applicant appear, prima facie, to afford a basis on which the jurisdiction of the Court might be founded;

*   *   *

17.   Whereas the material submitted to the Court leads it to the conclusion, at the present stage of the proceedings, that the provisions invoked by the Applicant appear, prima facie, to afford a basis on which the jurisdiction of the Court might be founded; and whereas the Court will accordingly proceed to examine the Applicant's request for the indication of interim measures of protection   *   *   *.

*   *   *

22.   Whereas the claims formulated by the Government of Australia in its Application are as follows:

(i)   The right of Australia and its people, in common with other States and their peoples, to be free from atmospheric nuclear weapon tests by any country is and will be violated;

(ii)   The deposit of radio-active fall-out on the territory of Australia and its dispersion in Australia's airspace without Australia's consent:

(a) violates Australian sovereignty over its territory;

(b) impairs Australia's independent right to determine what acts shall take place within its territory and in particular whether Australia and its people shall be exposed to radiation from artificial sources;

(iii)   the interference with ships and aircraft on the high seas and in the superjacent airspace, and the pollution of the high seas by radioactive fall-out, constitute infringements of the freedom of the high seas;

23.   Whereas it cannot be assumed a priori that such claims fall completely outside the purview of the Court's jurisdiction, or that the Government of Australia may not be able to establish a legal interest in respect of these claims entitling the Court to admit the Application;

24.   Whereas by the terms of Article 41 of the Statute the Court may indicate interim measures of protection only when it considers that circumstances so require in order to preserve the rights of either party;

25.   Whereas the Government of Australia alleges, inter alia, that a series of atmospheric nuclear tests have been carried out by the French Government in the Pacific during the period from 1966 to 1972, including the explosion of several hydrogen bombs and a number of devices of high and medium power; that during recent months there has been a growing body of reports, not denied by the French

Government, to the effect that the French Government is planning to carry out a further series of atmospheric nuclear tests in the Pacific in 1973; that this series of tests may extend to 1975 and even beyond that date; that in diplomatic correspondence and in discussions earlier in the present year the French Government would not agree to cease nuclear testing in the atmosphere in the Pacific and would not supply Australia with any information as to the dates of its proposed tests or the expected size and yield of its explosions; and that in a statement made in the French Parliament on 2 May 1973 the French Government indicated that, regardless of the protests made by Australia and other countries, it did not envisage any cancellation or modification of the programme of nuclear testing as originally planned;

26. Whereas these allegations give substance to the Australian Government's contention that there is an immediate possibility of a further atmospheric nuclear test being carried out by France in the Pacific;

27. Whereas the Government of Australia also alleges that the atmospheric nuclear explosions carried out by France in the Pacific have caused wide-spread radio-active fall-out on Australian territory and elsewhere in the southern hemisphere, have given rise to measurable concentrations of radio-nuclides in foodstuffs and in man, and have resulted in additional radiation doses to persons living in that hemisphere and in Australia in particular; that any radio-active material deposited on Australian territory will be potentially dangerous to Australia and its people and any injury caused thereby would be irreparable; that the conduct of French nuclear tests in the atmosphere creates anxiety and concern among the Australian people; that any effects of the French nuclear tests upon the resources of the sea or the conditions of the environment can never be undone and would be irremediable by any payment of damages; and any infringement by France of the rights of Australia and her people to freedom of movement over the high seas and superjacent airspace cannot be undone;

28. Whereas the French Government, in a diplomatic Note dated 7 February 1973 and addressed to the Government of Australia, the text of which was annexed to the Application in the present case, called attention to Reports of the Australian National Radiation Advisory Committee from 1967 to 1972, which all concluded that the fall-out from the French tests did not constitute a danger to the health of the Australian population; whereas in the said Note the French Government further expressed its conviction that in the absence of ascertained damage attributable to its nuclear experiments, they did not violate any rule of international law, and that, if the infraction of the law was alleged to consist in a violation of a legal norm concerning the threshold of atomic pollution which should not be crossed, it was hard to see what was the precise rule on which Australia relied;

29.   Whereas for the purpose of the present proceedings it suffices to observe that the information submitted to the Court, including Reports of the United Nations Scientific Committee on the Effects of Atomic Radiation between 1958 and 1972, does not exclude the possibility that damage to Australia might be shown to be caused by the deposit on Australian territory of radio-active fall-out resulting from such tests and to be irreparable;

30.   Whereas in the light of the foregoing considerations the Court is satisfied that it should indicate interim measures of protection in order to preserve the right claimed by Australia in the present litigation in respect of the deposit of radio-active fall-out on her territory;

31.   Whereas the circumstances of the case do not appear to require the indication of interim measures of protection in respect of other rights claimed by Australia in the Application;

32.   Whereas the foregoing considerations do not permit the Court to accede at the present stage of the proceedings to the request made by the French Government in its letter dated 16 May 1973 that the case be removed from the list;

33.   Whereas the decision given in the present proceedings in no way prejudges the question of the jurisdiction of the Court to deal with the merits of the case, or any questions relating to the admissibility of the Application, or relating to the merits themselves, and leaves unaffected the right of the French Government to submit arguments in respect of those questions;

34.   Having regard to the position taken by the French Government in its letter dated 16 May 1973 that the Court was manifestly not competent in the case and to the fact that it was not represented at the hearings held between 21 May and 25 May on the question of the indication of interim measures of protection;

35.   Whereas, in these circumstances, it is necessary to resolve as soon as possible the questions of the Court's jurisdiction and of the admissibility of the Application;

Accordingly,

The COURT

Indicates, by 8 votes to 6, pending its final decision in the proceedings instituted on 9 May 1973 by Australia against France, the following provisional measures:

The Governments of Australia and France should each of them ensure that no action of any kind is taken which might aggravate or extend the dispute submitted to the Court or prejudice the rights of the other Party in respect of the carrying out of whatever decision the Court may render in the case; and, in particular, the French Government should avoid nuclear tests causing the deposit of radio-active fall-out on Australian territory;

Decides that the written proceedings shall first be addressed to the questions of the jurisdiction of the Court to entertain the dispute, and of the admissibility of the Application * * *.

[Declarations and dissenting opinions omitted.]

Subsequent proceedings in the Nuclear Tests Cases. Despite the court's order for interim measures of protection, France continued to conduct tests during the summer months of 1973 and 1974. The court held hearings on the question of its jurisdiction, France not participating, see supra, Chapter 1, p. 69. Thereafter the court took note of a number of public declarations by the French government, including a communique issued by the President of France stating that "in view of the stage reached in carrying out the French nuclear defence programme France will be in a position to pass on to the stage of underground explosions as soon as the series of tests planned for this summer is completed." The court read these unilateral acts as creating a legally binding obligation on the part of France to cease testing in the atmosphere in the South Pacific. Since the court concluded that Australia's objective in this proceeding was to obtain termination of French atmospheric nuclear tests in the South Pacific, it found, by a vote of nine to six "that the claim of Australia no longer has any object and that the court is therefore not called upon to give a decision thereon." [1974] I.C.J. Reports 253. The same result was reached in the New Zealand proceedings. Id. at 457.

SECTION B. ACTIVITIES IN SPACE

LAY AND TAUBENFELD, THE LAW RELATING TO ACTIVITIES OF MAN IN SPACE, 39 (1970) *

The Upward Extent of Sovereignty

Since it is by now clear that every national state claims and, to the extent it can do so, exercises complete sovereignty in superjacent airspace, and since airspace remains legally undefined for most purposes with no generally accepted limit to its extent, we come directly to a multifaceted dilemma. Of course, the term "airspace" or "atmospheric space" is found in most treaties, but it is only in the last decade that man has been able to send objects and humans beyond what all could readily agree is "airspace." * * * Where then does "airspace" end? And is this a critical question for pursuit at this time?
* * *

Government Views: The United States

It is clear from the outset that, despite the suggestions of many commentators, the states, at least the major powers, have been quite unready to set specific limits by altitude to their claims to sovereign rights. Unlike the case of lower reaches of airspace, it appears to be the security problem almost exclusively, rather than a mixture of economic and security issues, which has led to this result.

But in the early post-Sputnik period, at least a few states took the position that an airspace boundary should be set and set soon. Sweden, for example, urged a decision as to "the altitude where this [outer] space * * * begins." At different times, representatives of Spain, Canada, France, Chile, and Italy have all suggested a formal limitation by altitude on the extent of national sovereignty in space.

Formal statements of the United States' position on the outward extent of its sovereignty in space indicate a notable shift in the course of the first space decade. In the earlier years, official policy called for a slow, step-by-step approach to space problems with the "utmost flexibility and freedom of action with regard to future events" retained for the United States. It was acknowledged that the Chicago Convention left it unclear where "airspace" and national sovereignty ended and that since traces of the atmosphere might be found up to 10,000 miles, "it follows that it would be perfectly rational for us to maintain that under the Chicago Convention the sovereignty of the United States extends 10,000 miles from the surface of the earth." * * *

* * *

In more recent years, although the United States has continued to note its right to defend itself wherever an apprehended source of danger might be located, there has been a shift away from the notion that this might call for an extension of "sovereignty" outward. The boundary line between airspace and outer space is still undetermined, but it is taken as a fact that all satellites orbited to date operate in "outer space" and that, hence, "airspace" must be at least limited below the orbital height of satellites. As we shall see, the United States now persistently relies in many contexts on this concept that orbiting satellites are now in "free" outer space and are not within any state's "territory" nor subject to any state's "territorial" jurisdiction. Thus, while the United States has given little support to the notion of drawing any single "line" and certainly to a very close-in line, there is evidence of tacit support for the principle that outer space begins (and "sovereign" airspace at a maximum must consequently end) at some point equal to or more probably somewhere below that at which an unpowered satellite can be maintained in orbit. * * *

Government Views: The Soviet View

Soviet writers have suggested a wide variety of approaches to the question of the upward extent of sovereignty. The Soviet claim to complete sovereignty in airspace is the basis for all discussions and received thorough airings both in connection with the alleged appearance of United States weather balloons in Soviet airspace in the mid-1950's and with the U–2 incident. Throughout the mid-1950's a commonly expressed view was that there was no limit to the upward extent of national sovereignty.

If all nations made unlimited claims upward, the flight of Sputniks would of course have violated the sovereign rights of every subjacent state and Soviet writers were quick to shift their approach. In 1958 and thereafter, there were suggestions of a limit based on aerodynamic lift, on "effective control," and on "national security." Although this last is hardly a limiting definition, it does avoid the dangers to national security found by Soviet writers in the other two.

In their quest for security, Soviet authors have rejected a search for traces of the atmosphere or the "density of the gas cloud at one or another distance from the earth" and all other alleged physical criteria. Soviet writers in general, however, have not made claims to the infinite; they seem to agree that at some point in space, out "far enough" from earth, a nation would be sufficiently secure to permit the "free" use of these reaches by all for activities beyond that point. For most activities, the "peaceful" ones, this might be the area where satellite orbits begin, thus again protecting the Sputnik flights as "legal" and according with more recent United States views.

Recently, the emphasis has been, as in the United States, on the nature of the activity, not on the altitude at which it takes place. Thus, to Soviet spokesmen, "espionage," as they define it, whether by land, by sea, by U–2, or by reconnaissance satellite, is "illegal" in international law. In their words, high-altitude nuclear tests by the United States, even before the Test Ban Treaty of 1963, are "illegal" as is the scattering of copper needles by the United States (Project West Ford); private "monopoly" enterprise in outer space is "piratical" and incompatible with the concept of "free" space.

Certainly, however, the Communist writers have been as consistent as those in the West in urging that, at least at some point, outer space and the celestial bodies are free for the peaceful activities of all men. As the Polish scholar Machowski put it: "The * * * question, whether state sovereignty extends into outer space, has already been tacitly answered negatively by practice and lack of protests on the part of any states in connection with the orbiting of space objects over their respective territories." Thus, the official view of the United States and that of the Soviet Union, as far as it can be determined, are similar on most points. Both agree that national sovereignty ends at some point "out," but each retains its right to counter deleterious acts, wherever they occur. Neither encourages the formal drawing of a line delimiting sovereign claims based on a territorial concept, but both agree that satellites fly in nonsovereign outer space, although there is no overall agreement on all issues concerning legally permissible activities. The views of other powers conform, in general, to the position of the major space powers.

The Writers

The literature concerning the desirability of establishing a precise overall boundary to the outward extent of national sovereignty is vast and its beginnings predate the flight of Sputnik I. While it seems clear that the nations are not likely to adopt any single line or division for all purposes, a brief review of the suggestions proposed on various bases by writers around the world is still useful since the argument is a continuing one.   *   *   *

Granting that nations are sovereign in superjacent airspace, a vast number of scholars have for these and other reasons proposed limiting the extent of this iron control by limiting the definition of airspace itself. Of course the definition varies depending on the criteria used for calculation. Scientists themselves agree generally that "atmosphere" itself has no single scientific meaning, and indeed the various sciences disagree since they look to different characteristics. Recall, too, that the Chicago Convention of 1944 itself nowhere defines airspace.

To proceed logically (if naively from the political point of view), it is possible to suggest a "scientific" limitation in airspace as the height at which a human can live without artificial breathing apparatus, conceivably as high as ten miles. With perhaps more operational meaning, the maximum height to which aircraft can ascend has been offered as a definition, at least within the outlook of the civil aviation conventions, for airspace or "atmospheric" space. This would place it, given present technology, at about twelve miles for conventional aircraft or perhaps twenty to twenty-five for the ram jet. Several years ago, for example, Cooper wrote: "After many years of careful research, I am convinced that the term airspace, as used in the Paris Convention in 1919, was there meant to include only those parts of the atmosphere above the surface of the earth where gaseous air is sufficiently dense to support balloons and airplanes, the only types of aircraft then in existence."

Focusing more directly upon the somewhat elliptical terminology of the conventions has not in itself led to uniformity. Thus airspace or atmospheric space might be limited, for purposes of sovereignty and jurisdiction, to what scientists tell us is the "geophysical limit of the atmosphere"; or it is "infinite, at least in theory" or "without limit or height"; or it is all regions "accessible to man"; or it is the outside limit of the earth's atmosphere, perhaps 60,000 miles, etc.

Actually, it is reasonably clear that those who drafted the Chicago Convention, and certainly those who created the Paris Convention, simply never considered the problem of vehicles moving above what would be considered by all to be airspace.   *   *   *

One special problem of the use of the concept of aerodynamic lift and "aircraft," whether considered under the terms of the civil air-law conventions or not, is that, due to technological change, it no longer has an operationally clear justification. Thus, "hybrid" craft, the American X–15, and others noted earlier in chapter 2, possess the characteristics of both aircraft and spacecraft; the X–15 has already flown at heights over 65 miles above the earth. Its performance does not fit neatly within the proposed definitions and limitations, and several of its pilots have won American astronaut wings by piloting it at or above an altitude of 50 miles, the altitude administratively established by military regulation as the basis for qualifying a pilot for such award.

Other "scientific" definitions of "airspace," not necessarily tied to the conventions, have also been offered to support altitudes greater than those at which conventional aircraft can fly. Ambrosini has suggested a height of about 100 kilometers as supported by "physical" considerations. Reintanz, of East Germany, has also supported this height of about 62 miles as "the upper limit of national airspace." Professor Cheng at one time found the limit of airspace at the base of the exosphere, perhaps "300–500 miles above the surface of the earth," and offered this as "the upper limit of national airspace." Others, thinking in terms of "air" or "atmosphere" also reach distances of 10,000 miles or more, since at least oxygen particles can be found a great distance from the earth. At such distances, the "line" then becomes functionally meaningless; most important, close-in space activities will take place within the area bounded by such a line and such regions will be difficult to police, or at least it would be too expensive, given the foreseeable risks.

Other suggestions for fixing a "natural" or "scientific" or "logical" boundary have called for combinations of physical factors including velocity, gravitation, centrifugal force, and the like. One of the more vigorously asserted proposals is that espoused by Haley and others and called generally the Von Karman line. As noted in The Law of Outer Space: [a]

> [I]t accepts the basic concept of aerodynamic lift but argues that such lift need not be the only "support" and that present law could be interpreted as extending sovereignty up to the point where any aerodynamic lift is available. For an object traveling at 25,000 feet per second, that line is said to be about 275,000 feet from the earth's surface. While this line is thought to have more stability than the proposal first put forward, it would also vary with atmospheric conditions and with design changes and other factors affecting the flight of objects.

Others have suggested about the same height for similar or related reasons. Moreover, the International Astronautical Federation now classifies all flight above 62 miles (100 km) as "space flight." It should also be noted that the David Davies Memorial Institute in

---

a. The reference is to Lipson and Katzenbach, The Law of Outer Space, 12–13 (1961).

both its Draft Code of Rules on the Exploration and Uses of Outer Space and in its Draft Rules Concerning Changes in the Environment of the Earth defines airspace as "the volume of space between the surface of the earth at sea level and an altitude of 80,000 meters above it." This would place the upper line at about the distance of the Von Karman line.

One other suggestion deserves special mention. It was perhaps first advanced in recent times by Kelsen in commenting, in 1944, on the Paris Convention and suggests that claims to sovereignty reach as far out as a state can exercise effective control. There would thus be several boundaries, since some states are more technologically advanced than others. The diversity question could be eliminated by placing the line at maximum height which any state could exercise control. This same problem was extensively debated at the time of the U–2 incident. The instability of any such boundary or set of boundaries has been often remarked and the proposal is infrequently heard today.

Limits based on technology, whether it is the technology of flight characteristics or of the ability of a ground state to interdict the flight, have the great defects of instability and uncertainty. New materials, new techniques, new military developments might alter the line significantly, eliminating the alleged certainty which proponents offer as the basic utility of having a known, "scientifically" sound line. * * *

A few writers have also suggested the use of more than one line, a division into zones. There might be, for example, a fairly low area of complete national control, an intermediate zone free for nonmilitary transit or other internationally agreed uses, and "outer space," free for the peaceful use of all. Haley, for example, also, suggested at one time that states should continue supreme in airspace (up to about 37.3 miles), and in the area of the "astronautic regime," starting about 3,728 miles (except for earth satellites which are in it at any altitude), states should have a limited competence, and that the "escape corridor" between the two altitudes needs further study and consideration. Despite the possible lure of these proposals as analogous to known patterns on the seas, they have thus far attracted little national support.

* * *

---

1. *International conventions.* Several international conventions address the legal problems of space.

The Outer Space Treaty (Treaty on Principles Governing the Activities of States in the Exploration and Use of Outer Space, Including the Moon and Other Celestial Bodies), 18 U.S.T. 2410, 610 U. N.T.S. 205—see the Documentary Supplement—entered into force for the United States on October 10, 1967. 79 states were parties on

January 1, 1980. The following articles are suggestive of the generality of its provisions:

Article I

The exploration and use of outer space, including the moon and other celestial bodies, shall be carried out for the benefit and in the interests of all countries, irrespective of their degree of economic or scientific development, and shall be the province of all mankind.

Outer space, including the moon and other celestial bodies, shall be free for exploration and use by all States without discrimination of any kind, on a basis of equality and in accordance with international law, and there shall be free access to all areas of celestial bodies.

There shall be freedom of scientific investigation in outer space, including the moon and other celestial bodies, and States shall facilitate and encourage international co-operation in such investigation.

Article III

States Parties to the Treaty shall carry on activities in the exploration and use of outer space, including the moon and other celestial bodies, in accordance with international law, including the Charter of the United Nations, in the interest of maintaining international peace and security and promoting international co-operation and understanding.

In analyzing this treaty, which purports to set general principles, the following questions should be addressed:

i. Has the treaty made any change in the law that would be applicable without the treaty? Another way of putting this question is: is a non-party to the treaty freer than a party to do as it wishes in space and, if so, in what respects?

ii. Are enough facts known about space to justify a state's committing itself at this stage of technological development to the principles enunciated in the treaty? How can a state protect its interests if startling new facts are discovered about space in the future?

The Agreement on the Rescue of Astronauts, the Return of Astronauts, and the Return of Objects Launched Into Outer Space, 19 U.S.T. 7570, entered into force for the United States on December 3, 1968. 76 states were parties on January 1, 1980.

The Convention on International Liability for Damage Caused by Space Objects—see the Documentary Supplement—entered into force for the United States on October 9, 1973. 59 states were parties on January 1, 1980. The convention provides that the launching state shall be liable for damage caused by its space object absolutely in some cases, or for its fault in others. A claims procedure involves a Claims

Commission, whose decision shall be binding if the parties have so agreed or whose award shall be recommendatory "which the parties shall consider in good faith." (Article XIX). The legal principles to be applied in determining compensation are particularly interesting:

Article XII

The compensation which the launching State shall be liable to pay for damage under this Convention shall be determined in accordance with international law and the principles of justice and equity, in order to provide such reparation in respect of the damage as will restore the person, natural or juridical, State or international organization on whose behalf the claim is presented to the condition which would have existed if the damage had not occurred.

Convention on Registration of Objects Launched into Outer Space. As of January 1, 1980, 27 states were parties. It entered into force for the United States on September 15, 1976. 28 U.S.T. 695.

2. *Work on new conventions at the United Nations.* The Committee on the Peaceful Uses of Outer Space has for several years worked on the drafting of agreements relating to remote sensing of the environment of the earth from outer space, and the definition and/or delimitation of outer space and outer space activities (including questions relating to the geostationary orbit). Issues involved in the effort to reach agreement on these subjects are whether the state to which direct broadcasts are made from satellites must give its consent, whether data collected by remote sensing devices may be freely communicated throughout the world or can be communicated only with the approval of the state observed and, as to the geostationary orbit, whether a geostationary orbit which is fixed over land is within the jurisdiction of the relevant state. The progress of the United Nation's Outer Space Committee is reported from time to time in the U.N. Monthly Chronicle (e. g., XVI U.N. Monthly Chronicle July–October 1979, p. 36). The United States' position on remote sensing is set forth in 72 U.S. Dept. of State Bull. 419 (1975). For its position on the geostationary orbit, see Boyd, Digest of U.S. Practice in International Law 1977, at 658 (1978). See also Gorove, The Geostationary Orbit: Issues of Law and Policy, 73 Am. J. Int'l L. 444 (1979).

SECTION C. CELESTIAL BODIES

---

1. *The Outer Space Treaty.* Article II of the treaty provides:

Outer space, including the moon and other celestial bodies, is not subject to national appropriation by claim of sovereignty, by means of use or occupation, or by any other means.

Suppose that a state discovers a particularly rare and valuable mineral on the moon, which it is able to mine cheaply with manned or unmanned equipment. Does the treaty prohibit that state from exploiting the moon's resources for its own exclusive benefit? Can the state set up a base over which it has exclusive control so as to prevent another state from exploiting resources within that base? See Article XII.

What law governs the state, not a party to the treaty (or one that has withdrawn pursuant to Article XVI) that wishes to claim a portion of the moon as its territory? Do the principles relating to the acquisition of territory on the surface of the earth apply? If so, what facts would support a claim that a state has lawfully acquired a portion of the moon as its territory?[a]

2. *The Moon Treaty.* In December, 1979, the United Nations General Assembly approved a draft Agreement Governing the Activities of States on the Moon and Other Celestial Bodies. The treaty was signed in early 1980 by Chile, France, Romania, the Philippines and Austria. The text is set forth in the Documentary Supplement. The treaty reiterates, in Article 11(2), the prohibition against national appropriation set forth in the Outer Space Treaty. In addition to provisions dealing with notice of activities undertaken on the moon (and other celestial bodies), freedom of scientific investigation, and protection of the moon's environmental balance, the agreement looks ahead to an eventual partial internationalization of the moon. Article 11 provides:

> States Parties to this Agreement hereby undertake to establish an international regime, including appropriate procedures, to govern the exploitation of the natural resources of the moon as such exploitation is about to become feasible.

One of the main purposes of such an international regime is described as follows:

> An equitable sharing by all States Parties in the benefits derived from those resources, whereby the interests and needs of the developing countries, as well as the efforts of those countries which have contributed either directly or indirectly to the exploration of the moon, shall be given special consideration.

To what extent does the treaty inhibit commercial exploitation of the moon's resources by a state party? Does the agreement provide for a moratorium on such exploitation prior to the establishment of the projected international regime? There is debate in the United States on these issues. See the Committee Print on the Agreement

---

a. Of some utility in the analysis of the legal problems of celestial bodies is a study of Antarctica. See the Antarctic Treaty, 12 U.S.T. 794, 402 U.N.T.S. 71, which entered into force for the United States on June 23, 1961; 22 states were parties as of January 1, 1980. The treaty is briefly discussed in Chapter 11. The text of the treaty and bibliographic references are also in Lay and Taubenfeld, The Law Relating to Activities of Man in Space 59–62 (1970).

prepared for the Committee on Commerce, Science, and Transportation, United States Senate, 96th Cong., 2d Sess., Parts 1 and 2 (May 1980), p. 57, and Part 3 (Aug. 1980), pp. 311, 331.

Compare the efforts in the Third Law of the Sea Conference to internationalize the exploitation of the resources of the sea in areas beyond national jurisdiction, Chapter 3, supra.

Part II

LIMITATIONS ON THE EXERCISE OF JURISDICTION

Chapter 5

THE IMMUNITY OF STATES

SECTION A. EXTENT OF THE IMMUNITY OF THE STATE

SWEENEY, THE INTERNATIONAL LAW OF SOVEREIGN IMMUNITY

20–21

United States Department of State Publication 1963.

The international law of sovereign immunity has undergone considerable change during the last sixty years. * * *

Until about 1900, the immunity of a state from the judicial process of another—or immunity from jurisdiction as it is frequently called for convenience—was broad, but not without limitations. It was not granted when the litigation involved ownership or other interests in immovables in the territory or when it involved an interest in an estate locally administered. Even though these limitations were well recognized, the immunity was usually stated in terms giving it an absolute character.

In Spanish Government v. Lambège et Pujol, decided in 1849, the Supreme Court of France stated the rule thus:

The reciprocal independence of states is one of the most universally respected principles of international law, and it follows as a result therefrom that a government cannot be subjected to the jurisdiction of another against its will, and that the right of jurisdiction of one government over litigation arising from its own acts is a right inherent to its sovereignty that another government cannot seize without impairing their mutual relations. [1849] D, 1, 5, 9.

The British courts expressed the rule in equally broad terms. In The Parlement Belge, decided in 1880, the court stated:

As a consequence of the absolute independence of every sovereign authority, and of the international comity which induces every sovereign state to respect the independence and dignity of

288

every other sovereign state, each and every one declines to exercise by means of its courts any of its territorial jurisdiction over the person of any sovereign *   *   *. (1880) 5 P.D. 197, 217.

About 1900, a judicial practice developed in some states of denying immunity from jurisdiction to a foreign state when it was made a respondent with respect to an act of a commercial or so-called private nature. The courts involved reasoned that the traditional rule of immunity from jurisdiction covered only litigation arising from public acts of a foreign state and did not extend to litigation arising from other types of acts. The courts of other states did not draw this distinction and extended immunity from jurisdiction to a foreign state irrespective of the nature of the act involved.

In Société Anonyme des Chemins de Fer Liègeois Luxembourgeois v. the Netherlands, decided in 1903, the Supreme Court of Belgium stated the distinction between public and commercial or private acts as follows:

> Sovereignty is involved only when political acts are accomplished by the state; *   *   *. However, the state is not bound to confine itself to a political role, and can, for the needs of the collectivity, buy, own, contract, become creditor or debtor, and engage in commerce *   *   *. In the discharge of these functions, the state is not acting as public power, but does what private persons do, and as such, is acting in a civil and private capacity. When after bargaining on a footing of equality with a person or incurring a responsibility in no way connected with the political order, the state is drawn in litigation, the litigation concerns a civil right, within the sole jurisdiction of the courts, by article 92 of the Constitution, and the foreign state as civil person is like any other foreign person amenable to the Belgian courts. [1903] Pas. 1, 294, 301.

>   *   *   *

Thus two concepts of sovereign immunity from jurisdiction came to coexist by the late 1930's: the one termed "absolute" because of its broader scope, and the other termed "restrictive" because of its narrower scope. *   *   *

1. ABSOLUTE AND RESTRICTIVE THEORIES: HISTORICAL PERSPECTIVE

ABSOLUTE THEORY OF IMMUNITY

ALDONA S. v. UNITED KINGDOM

Poland, Supreme Court, 1948.
90 Journal du Droit International 191 (1963).[a]

The facts. The Plaintiff Aldona S. was engaged as typist in the editorial office of the weekly "Voice of England" published in Cracow by the British Foreign Office. On January 31st 1947 she was suddenly dismissed without being paid the rest of her salary due to her, amounting to 52,500 zl. She filed a claim with the District Court of Cracow against the * * * United Kingdom for payment of the mentioned amount as compensation for work performed.

This was an appeal against the decision of the Court of Appeal of Cracow which confirmed the judgment of the District Court rejecting the claim of the plaintiff as being inadmissible in view of the defendant being a foreign state * * *. In her appeal the plaintiff alleged that the dispute in question concerned relations with regard to a contract of employment of a private person by a weekly magazine which, as an organized commercial entity, constitutes an enterprise which is juridically private property of the Treasury of the United Kingdom of Great Britain. The Court of Appeal enquired with the Ministry of Justice whether a custom exists in Great Britain by virtue of which it is not admissible to sue a foreign state before an English court. The Ministry of Justice, in its statement of March 4, 1948 * * * expressed the opinion that foreign countries may not be summoned * * *, whereupon the Court of Appeal, on March 10, 1948, approved the appealed decision, concurring completely with the reasons of that decision. It stated in addition that * * * the weekly magazine "Voice of England" is not an enterprise in the sense of article 5, paragraph 2 of Code of Civil Procedure. In the appeal against that decision, Aldona S. demanded its rejection on the ground that it infringes substantive law and violates the basic rules of procedure. In particular the plaintiff opposed the view of the Court of Appeal considering it as being in conflict with previous judgments of the Supreme Court and with Polish case law. She suggested that a magazine published by a foreign state on Polish territory, is not part of diplomatic but of economic activity. The refusal of legal protection in such cases would render the obligations of a magazine publisher incomplete, and not binding, and, therefore, meaningless. * * * [The activities involved, she argued, were those] of the treasury of a

---

a. English text in the Journal. Reprinted by permission of Editions Techniques, S.A., Paris.

foreign state, based on a private law labour contract, and does not concern the activity of the foreign state itself.

[A portion of the opinion of the court appears below.]

* * * [O]n examining questions concerning immunity from jurisdiction of foreign states, one has to base oneself directly on general principles universally adopted in international relations. The most essential of these principles is the principle of reciprocity among states which results from the fundamental principle of their equality * * *. The principle of reciprocity is based on recognition or non-recognition of the immunity from jurisdiction by one state of another in the same measure as the latter recognizes or refuses to recognize immunity from jurisdiction of other states. Absence of reciprocity may simply stem from clear provisions of the law, but it may also be the result of a continuous and well established practice of the courts of a foreign state. In case of doubt, therefore, in this respect, it is necessary to obtain the opinion of the Ministry of Justice which renders it in agreement with the Ministry of Foreign Affairs.

Passing from the above considerations to the present case directed against the Treasury of the United Kingdom of Great Britain, the Supreme Court states the generally known fact that English Courts have been consistently and rigorously safeguarding the immunity from jurisdiction of foreign States for a long time (Phillimore, p. 153). Thus in the present case, in view of the well established * * * [case law] of English Courts recognizing immunity from jurisdiction of foreign states, i. e., potentially also the Polish State, Polish Courts were unable, given the principle of reciprocity, to accept for deliberation the claim submitted by Aldona S., even if it concerned a commercial enterprise on behalf of the British authorities. However, such is really not the case, for the Court of Appeal held that the publishing house of "Voice of England" is not a commercial enterprise. The objection of the plaintiff that this does not concern diplomatic but economic activity cannot be admitted as valid, for although the activity may not be diplomatic, it is political by its content, and economic only by its form as a result of the laws and regulations of the country (payment of taxes, purchase of registration cards, etc.).

Finally, the last objection of the plaintiff, that refusal of legal protection would render the obligations of the British Foreign Office as a publisher of a magazine in the territory of our State incomplete and unreal, is also unfounded, for, if the plaintiff does not wish to seek justice before English courts, she may take advantage of general international usage in connection with immunity from jurisdiction, and approach the Ministry of Foreign Affairs, which is obliged to take up the matter with the Ministry of Foreign Affairs of a foreign country with a view to obtain satisfaction for a just claim * * *. This approach frequently produces speedier results than court procedure.

In view of the principles explained above, the Supreme Court considering the contentions of the plaintiff against the judgment of the Court of Appeal as unfounded and * * * finding no basis for them in the views of the majority Polish jurisprudence, has dismissed the appeal.

Position of socialist states. Socialist states are committed to the absolute theory of sovereign immunity and claim international law requires that it be granted even in cases where the litigation arises from commercial activities. In many states in western Europe and elsewhere, however, the courts apply the restrictive theory and deny immunity to socialist states—and other states—in litigation arising from such activities. Socialist states look upon the denial of immunity in these cases as unwarranted interference with the conduct of their trade abroad through state monopolies. In requiring proof of reciprocal treatment as a condition for granting immunity to the United Kingdom, the Polish decision reflects the opposition of socialist states to the restrictive theory and their attempt to induce general acceptance of the absolute theory.

KRAJINA v. THE TASS AGENCY

England, Court of Appeal, 1949.
[1949] 2 All E.R. 274.*

[This was a suit for alleged libel in a news sheet published by Tass.]

COHEN, L. J.   This appeal is against an order of BIRKETT, J., dated Dec. 10, 1948, whereby he affirmed an order of Master Simner dated Nov. 29, 1948, by which it was ordered that the writ herein and service of it on the Tass Agency of Moscow be set aside. The writ was issued by the plaintiff on June 2, 1948, the defendants being described as "The Tass Agency (of Moscow) (trading as a firm or corporation at No. 72/78, Fleet Street in the city of London)" * * *. On June 10, 1948, a conditional appearance was entered on behalf of the * * * defendants, to whom I shall refer hereafter as Tass, and on June 23, 1948, Tass issued a summons asking for the order which they ultimately obtained from Master Simner. * * *

In support of the application Tass filed an affirmation by a Mr. Andrienko, who is described as the legal adviser of the trade delegation of the Union of Soviet Socialist Republics in the United Kingdom. The affirmation contains a summary of some of the provisions of the statute concerning Tass, which was published on Jan. 15, 1935, and there was exhibited to it an extract from the statute, which contained the first of its sixteen clauses. In his affirmation Mr. An-

* Reprinted with the permission of Butterworth's, London.

drienko described Tass as "the central information organ of the Union of Soviet Socialist Republics" and as "coming under the Council of Ministers of the Union of Soviet Socialist Republics." He did not make any definite statement as to the legal position of Tass, and the only other evidence before the master at the first hearing was an extract under the heading "Tass Agency" from the register kept under the Registration of Business Names Act, 1916. The master rightly did not consider this evidence sufficient to enable him to reach a decision on the matter, and he adjourned the summons for further evidence. On Nov. 20 an affidavit by Percy Charles Smith was filed, to which was exhibited a certificate from the Soviet Ambassador, the material portion of which was in the following terms:

> I, Georgi Nikolaevich Zaroubin, ambassador of the Union of Soviet Socialist Republics in Great Britain, hereby certify that the telegraph agency of the Union of Soviet Socialist Republics, commonly known as Tass, or the Tass Agency, constitutes a department of the Soviet State, i. e., the Union of Soviet Socialist Republics, exercising the rights of a legal entity.

On this evidence the master made the order for which Tass asked and that order was confirmed by BIRKETT, J. * * *

    * * *

When the present appeal came before us, counsel for the plaintiff asked leave (which was granted) to put in further evidence which consisted of the full text of the statute establishing the Tass agency, and a translation thereof. Clause 1 is in these terms:

> The telegraphic agency of the Union of Soviet Socialist Republics (TASS) is the central information organ of the U.S.S.R. and is attached to the Soviet of People's Commissars of the U.S.S.R.

It will be observed that this translation does not entirely agree with that in the exhibit to Mr. Andrienko's affirmation, the words, "and comes under the Council" in that exhibit being replaced by "is attached to the Soviet", but I do not think that anything turns on that discrepancy. It seems clear that, in the light of the ambassador's certificate, we are bound to come to the conclusion that the Tass Agency is a department of the Soviet State, but whether that State has given this department a separate juridical existence is another matter which I shall consider later. * * *

    * * *

* * * Counsel for the plaintiff said that, reading the statute as a whole, the effect is that Tass not only has the right of a legal entity, but is also a legal entity * * *. If that is established, certain consequences, it is argued, follow—in particular, the doctrine of sovereign immunity is not applicable, since Tass has a separate juridical existence from that of the sovereign, the U.S.S.R. Counsel for the plaintiff also argued that, even if the Tass agency was a department of the U.S.S.R. without separate legal existence, the nature of its activities was such as to deprive it of sovereign immunity. He ad-

mitted that he could not succeed on that point before us in view of
the decision of this court in the United States Shipping Board case
and the decision in The Porto Alexandre, but he said that the correctness of these decisions had been doubted by Lord MAUGHAM in
Compania Naviera Vascongado v. Cristina S.S. For the plaintiff it
was also argued that the evidence before the court as to the status of
the Tass agency was ambiguous and self-contradictory, and that, as
the onus of establishing their right to immunity was on the defendants, their application must fail.

It is obvious that the first question we have to decide is whether
or not the evidence makes out a prima facie case that Tass was a separate legal entity, for, if it was not, it seems quite plain that the evidence does establish that Tass was a department of the Soviet State,
and, unless counsel for the plaintiff can establish it to be a separate
legal entity, it is not disputed that this appeal, in this court at any
rate, must fail. * * *

     * * *

     * * * It seems to me that the evidence as to the nature of
Tass must depend on its constitution and must be a question of Russian law, and that we must look at the Russian statutes and to any
relevant evidence that is adduced as to Russian law (and for all practical purposes in this case, that is nil) to determine whether or not
Tass is a separate legal entity. * * *

     * * *

     * * * Our attention has been called to nothing which can be
said to amount to a declaration that Tass is a corporation sole. It is
said in the translation of the statute and by the ambassador that it
has the rights of a juridical or legal entity, but it seems to me that
the evidence falls far short of that which would be necessary to establish that Tass is a legal entity and that the Union of Soviet Socialist
Republics, by procuring its incorporation, has deprived that particular department of the immunity which normally attaches to a department of a sovereign State in accordance with the principles of comity
established by international law and recognized by this country.

That is really sufficient to dispose of the case and to lead to the
dismissal of the appeal, but, as the case may go higher, I think I
ought to say just a few words on what the position would be had I
come to the opposite conclusion and been of opinion that the evidence
did establish that Tass was given the status of a separate juridical
entity. It does not seem to me necessary to follow that it would
thereby have been deprived of its immunity. The history of the legislation in this country as regards the departments of State seems to
me to show that it is quite possible that a State may for certain purposes under its own legislation give some department of State the status and the rights of a juridical entity without depriving the department of its general immunity from suit, and it seems to me that it
would be impossible to say—no doubt, our government would not
wish to say—that the Crown had thereby deprived itself of the right

to rely on that immunity if an attempt were made to sue it in a foreign country. One must look in every case at the facts to reach a conclusion whether the Crown has intended to give up its immunity generally or only for limited and defined purposes.

       *   *   *

I desire to say one word more on the last point in the argument of counsel for the plaintiff that the evidence was ambiguous and self-contradictory, and that, as the onus of establishing their right to immunity is on the defendants, their application must fail. I think that turns upon what I have already said, that, in my view, the defendants do establish that Tass was, and in essence is, a department of State to the necessary extent to shift the onus of proving that they were a separate legal entity to the plaintiff. That onus, in my opinion, he has failed to discharge. For these reasons I think that the decision of BIRKETT, J., was right and ought to be affirmed.

     [Other opinions omitted.]

---

     1. *The position of English courts on sovereign immunity.* In The Porto Alexandre, [1920] P. 30 (C.A.), the immunity of foreign states, previously established with respect to litigation arising from an activity which was not commercial, was granted in litigation involving a ship owned by a foreign state and used for trading. In The Cristina, [1938] A.C. 485, several of the Law Lords indicated they doubted the immunity should have been granted with respect to a commercial activity in The Porto Alexandre, and suggested the extension of immunity in the case was not required by the previous decision in point. But the facts in The Cristina did not afford them the opportunity of passing anew on the issue. The precedents established in the United Kingdom with respect to sovereign immunity were followed generally by courts in the British Commonwealth.

     In Trendtex Trading Corporation v. Central Bank of Nigeria, [1977] 1 Q.B. 529, however, the Court of Appeals of England held that the restrictive theory of sovereign immunity had become the rule of international law and, by "incorporation" into the law of England, the new rule of English law to be applied by the courts without waiting for the House of Lords to say so. In a highly interesting opinion, Lord Denning relied, inter alia, upon the language used by Lord Mansfield in Triquet v. Bath, supra Chapter 1, p. 11. For subsequent legislation adopting the restrictive theory, see infra p. 311.

     2. *Applicability of the immunity of the state.* A basic issue in cases involving state immunity is whether the claimant is a part of the government.

     In civil law states as discussed infra, p. 299, an agency which is a part of the government, such as a department or ministry, is entitled to the immunity, but not, as a rule, one created as a separate legal entity. In common law states, an agency created as a separate legal entity would not necessarily be denied immunity. The issue, not reached in Krajina, would be whether the relationship between the agency and the state was such as to make it in fact a part of the governmental process. A similar reasoning applies with respect to a corporation owned or controlled by the state. In civil law states, such a corporation is not usually entitled to immunity inasmuch as it is a separate legal entity, while in common law states it may be entitled to immunity if it acts on behalf of the government in the same manner as an agency of the foreign state. In addition public officials such as the head of government, foreign ministers or any other public minister, are entitled to the immunity of the state for acts done in their official capacity if the suit is in effect a suit against the state. On all of this see Sweeney, The International Law of Sovereign Immunity 52–55 (U.S. Dept. of State Publication 1963).

FUNDAMENTALS OF CIVIL LEGISLATION OF THE UNION OF SOVIET SOCIALIST REPUBLICS, APPROVED BY THE SUPREME SOVIET, DECEMBER 8, 1961, SOVIET LEGISLATION SERIES (MOSCOW, 1961)

Article 11. Juridical Persons

Juridical persons are such organizations as possess separate property, and may in their own name acquire property and non-property rights and assume duties, and appear as plaintiffs and defendants in a court of law, or before an arbitration or mediation board.

   *   *   *

Article 12. Legal Capacity of Juridical Persons

Juridical persons shall have civil legal capacity in accordance with the established purposes of their activity.

   *   *   *

Article 13. Liability of Juridical Persons for Their Obligations

Juridical persons shall be liable for their obligations in the property they own (and state organisations, in the property assigned to them) which, in accordance with the legislation of the U.S.S.R. and Union Republics, is subject to attachment.

The state shall not be liable for the obligations of state organisations which are juridical persons, nor shall these organisations be liable for the obligations of the state.

   *   *   *

ACADEMY OF SCIENCES OF THE U.S.S.R., INSTITUTE OF STATE AND LAW, INTERNATIONAL LAW 305 (MOSCOW, 1961)

Legal Status of Trade Missions. The main definitive act governing the legal status of trade missions abroad and their rights and duties is the Statute on Trade Missions and Agencies of the U.S.S.R. Abroad adopted by the Central Executive Committee and the Council of People's Commissars of the U.S.S.R. on September 13, 1933.

Under the terms of this Statute, trade missions are an integral part of the diplomatic missions of the U.S.S.R. abroad and enjoy the same privileges as the latter. Trade missions fulfil three main functions:

(a) the representation of the interests of the U.S.S.R. in the field of foreign trade and the promotion of the commercial and other economic relations between the U.S.S.R. and the country in which the mission is resident;

(b) the regulation of the trade between the U.S.S.R. and the country in which they are resident;

(c) the implementation of the trade between the U.S.S.R. and the country in which they are resident.

Trade missions function on behalf of the Government of the U.S.S.R. and are organs of the Soviet State abroad. As a result, they enjoy the rights and privileges of diplomatic missions. It is generally recognised that the trade representative of the U.S.S.R. and his deputies enjoy complete diplomatic immunity. They have the right of inviolability of person. They are safeguarded against threats and coercive measures and are exempt from local jurisdiction.

The premises of the trade mission and the property therein are inviolable. Searches and the removal of property from these premises can take place only with the permission of the trade representative. The trade mission has the right to use ciphers. Its correspondence enjoys complete inviolability.

A trade mission enjoys legal immunity in the country in which it is resident. Even in cases when the Soviet State voluntarily limits its legal immunity and consents to submission to local jurisdiction, local courts have no right to take measures to enforce a suit, to arrest property, to execute judgments by force, to summon the trade representative or his deputy to court, or to take administrative action against the trade mission, since such action constitutes a violation of the sovereign rights of the U.S.S.R.

*   *   *

Trade missions enjoy all the powers necessary for the fulfilment of these functions. They can conclude all kinds of agreements and contracts on behalf of the U.S.S.R., enter into commitments, including through the issue of promissory notes, give guarantees, conclude agreements regarding the submission of disputes to arbitration courts and in general undertake all legal actions necessary to carry out the responsibilities with which they are vested, including appearing in foreign courts as a plaintiff. Trade missions can be defendants only in cases arising out of contracts concluded or guaranteed by them in the country concerned, and only in countries in relation to which the Government of the U.S.S.R. has by means of an international treaty or unilateral declaration clearly and precisely expressed its consent to the trade mission being subject to local courts in disputes of the character concerned.

A trade mission is not a legal person. The treasury of the U.S. S.R. is liable for its commitments, since the Soviet State is the subject of foreign trade transactions which it concludes.

* * *

Attempts to Restrict the Rights of Trade Missions. The foreign trade links of the Soviet State based on the foreign trade monopoly have a long history, telling of the Soviet State's constant struggle for its rights in the world market, for equality between the two systems of property ownership, and for normal commercial relations between all States, both large and small.

This struggle was especially bitter during the early years of the Soviet State, when foreign capital made desperate attempts to wreck the monopoly of foreign trade and to subject the Soviet economy to the economies of the capitalist States.

The capitalist countries as a rule did not conclude commercial transactions on the territory of the U.S.S.R. The overwhelming majority of such transactions were concluded abroad.

The work of Soviet trade missions abroad was constantly subjected to every kind of obstacle, from police raids on premises they occupied to the violation of their elementary rights as state organs of the U.S.S.R.

There were cases of the infringement of the rights and privileges of the trade missions: attacks upon trade representatives, nonrecognition of their diplomatic immunity and violation of the immunity of premises occupied by trade delegations. Their legal immunity was ignored and their property made the object of illegal action, etc.

In attempts to justify these illegal measures, bourgeois jurists put forward the theory of the "trading State", in accordance with which a trade mission was considered as a "merchant", as an ordinary legal person, allegedly having none of the rights characteristic of a diplomatic mission.

In accordance with these theories, bourgeois courts permitted suits against Soviet Trade Missions, confiscated their property and did not recognise their rights to legal immunity.

The consistent and resolute policy of the Soviet Government led to the defeat of all the attacks upon the foreign trade monopoly and upon the organs carrying it out. The rights of the Soviet State in exercising its monopoly of foreign trade are now recognised by the absolute majority of States.

* * *

Juridical persons and trade missions of the USSR. According to Fundamentals of Civil Legislation of the USSR, a juridical person is one which possesses separate property, can sue and be sued and is liable, rather than the state, for its own obligations. The law of the USSR has its foundation, in part, in the civil law system. In states where that system prevails, the term juridical person is a term of art and usually means, prima facie, that the entity involved is separate and distinct from the government.

In the Tass Agency case the evidence showed only that the agency exercised the rights of a juridical person. Hence it was open to argument whether it exercised such rights because it was in fact a juridical person, or whether it was given the rights of a juridical person though it was not one in fact. This last possibility would be regarded as anomalous in many civil law states.

According to the Soviet textbook on International Law, a Trade Mission of the USSR is not a legal person, is an integral part of a Soviet diplomatic mission, and the treasury, of the USSR is liable for its commitments. Apparently, the foreign trade missions of other socialist states are sometimes given juridical personality. A Czech author writes: "Under the Acts [of 1948 and 1949] establishing *   *   * [them], foreign trade undertakings [of Czechoslovakia] are autonomous units endowed with juridical personality. They have a separate budget and their property is liable to answer for the obligations assumed by them. Foreign trade undertakings are not answerable for such claims as one may have against the state [and] its organs *   *   * ." Zourek, Some Comments on the Difficulties Encountered in the Judicial Settlement of Disputes Arising from Trade Between Countries with Different Economic and Social Structures, 86 Journal du Droit International 639, 665 (1959).

The author goes on to note that, as a necessary consequence of being endowed with juridical personality, the foreign trade missions of Czechoslovakia are not entitled to immunity in the courts of other states. (at 665)

In the Soviet textbook on International Law, quoted above, the restrictive theory of sovereign immunity is presented as a device invented by bourgeois states for the specific purpose of wrecking the monopoly over foreign trade of the USSR and subjecting the Soviet economy to the economies of the capitalist states.

The statement should be taken with caution. The restrictive theory appeared in western continental Europe in the latter part of the 19th century and was steadily gaining ground by the time the USSR began to engage in trade with European and other nations. It is true, however, that litigation arising from the commercial transactions of the trade missions of the USSR probably gave impetus to the growth of the restrictive theory.

BERIZZI BROS. CO. v. THE PESARO

United States Supreme Court, 1926.
271 U.S. 562, 46 S.Ct. 611, 70 L.Ed. 1088.

[In The Schooner Exchange v. McFaddon, see supra p. 171, Chief Justice Marshall held that a war vessel was immune from the jurisdiction of the United States. When The Pesaro, a merchant vessel operated by the Italian government and engaged in the carriage of merchandise, was threatened with a libel for damages to a shipment, the Italian government requested the Department of State to take steps to prevent its arrest. The answer was:

> The Department is of the opinion that vessels owned by a state and engaged in commerce are not entitled * * * to the immunity accorded vessels of war * * *.

2 Hackworth, Digest of International Law 437 (1941).

After litigation on a preliminary issue concerning the proper procedure for a suggestion of immunity, the case came before Judge Mack who denied immunity. The Pesaro, 277 F. 473 (S.D.N.Y. 1921). He pointed out, inter alia, that upon making an inquiry from the Department of State, he had received the following statement:

> It is the view of the Department of State that government-owned merchant vessels * * * should not be regarded as entitled to the immunities accorded public vessels of war * * *. (note 3, at 479–480)

The order of Judge Mack was vacated, however, because of a decision by the Supreme Court in an unrelated case concerning the proper procedure for claiming immunity. The case went to another district court judge who ruled that the Italian government was entitled to immunity and the Supreme Court upheld the decision below, making, inter alia, the statement which follows.]

We think the principles [of immunity] are applicable alike to all ships held and used by a government for a public purpose, and that when, for the purpose of advancing the trade of its people or providing revenue for its treasury, a government acquires, mans and operates ships in the carrying trade, they are public ships in the same sense that war ships are. We know of no international usage which regards the maintenance and advancement of the economic welfare of a people in time of peace as any less a public purpose than the maintenance and training of a naval force. (at 574)

Deference to suggestions of immunity. As a result of two later decisions by the Supreme Court, Ex parte Republic of Peru, 318 U.S. 578, 63 S.Ct. 793 (1943), and Republic of Mexico v. Hoffman, 324 U. S. 30, 65 S.Ct. 530 (1945), courts in the United States came to defer automatically to a suggestion of immunity made by the Department of State through the Department of Justice.

The practice of the courts in the United States to let the Department of State control the grant of immunity was unique in the international system. In no other state in the world, so far as can be ascertained, was a suggestion of immunity considered binding by the courts.

RESTRICTIVE THEORY OF IMMUNITY

Evolution of the restrictive theory. As indicated supra, p. 289, the Supreme Court of Belgium adopted the restrictive theory in 1903. Société Anonyme de Chemins de Fer Liègeois Luxembourgeois v. the Netherlands, [1903] Pasicrisie I, 294. In Egypt, the Court of Appeals of the Mixed Courts—then the highest court with jurisdiction over sovereign immunity cases—sanctioned in 1920 the restrictive theory in a litigation involving the United Kingdom. Captain Hall v. Captain Zacarias Bengoa, 33 Bulletin de Législation et Jurisprudence Egyptiennes 25 (1920–1921). The court had already made clear in a decision of 1912 it would apply the restrictive theory. Dame Marigo Kildani v. The Ministry of Finance of Greece, 24 Bulletin de Législation et Jurisprudence Egyptiennes 330 (1911–1912).

By 1918, the Supreme Court of Switzerland was applying the restrictive theory. Ministry of Finance of Austria v. Dreyfus, [1918] Journal des Tribunaux 594. The restrictive theory was formulated as early as 1886 by the lower courts of Italy. The Supreme Court of Italy adopted it in 1925 when a trade mission of the USSR became involved in litigation before the Italian courts which arose from its commercial activities. Trade Delegation of the USSR v. Ditta Tesini e Malvezzi, [1925] Giurisprudencia Italiana I, 204.

By 1928 the lower courts in Greece were declining to grant immunity to the USSR in a suit involving a commercial act. X v. USSR, [1927–1928] Ann.Dig. 172 (No. 109). The Supreme Court of France sanctioned in 1929 the restrictive theory, previously declared and applied in the lower courts, when a trade mission of the USSR was sued in connection with its commercial activities in France. USSR v. Association France-Export, [1929] Dalloz Recueil Hebdomadaire 161.

In 1921, the Supreme Court of Germany declined to apply the restrictive theory on the ground that it had not yet acquired sufficient support to justify its application. Selling v. United States Shipping Board (The Ice King), 1921, 26 Am. J. Int'l L. Supp. 620 (1932). Since then the courts of the German Federal Republic have become committed to the restrictive theory. Decision of the Federal Constitutional Court, Second Chamber, 1963, 59 Am. J. Int'l L. 654 (1965).

In the Netherlands, the restrictive theory was applied by the lower courts as early as 1916. Thereafter an ambiguous decision of the Supreme Court in date of 1922 left the issue in a state of confusion and divided the lower courts for a long time. De Booij Case, 48 Journal du Droit International 274 (1921), 26 Am. J. Int'l L. Supp.

538 (1932). A similar situation prevailed in Austria where the restrictive theory became a controversial issue as early as 1918. Its supreme court has since become a leading exponent of the restrictive theory. Dralle v. Republic of Czechoslovakia, 17 Int'l L. Rep. 155 (1956).

As a result, apparently, of the development of the restrictive theory and the repeated denial of immunity to its trade missions by European courts in the years following World War I, the USSR adopted a policy of entering into international agreements whereby its trade missions submit in advance to local jurisdiction with respect to disputes arising from their commercial transactions.

UNITED STATES: LETTER FROM THE ACTING LEGAL ADVISER OF THE DEPARTMENT OF STATE TO THE DEPARTMENT OF JUSTICE, MAY 19, 1952

26 United States Department of State Bulletin 984 (1952).

MY DEAR MR. ATTORNEY GENERAL:

The Department of State has for some time had under consideration the question whether the practice of the Government in granting immunity from suit to foreign governments made parties defendant in the courts of the United States without their consent should not be changed. The Department has now reached the conclusion that such immunity should no longer be granted in certain types of cases. In view of the obvious interest of your Department in this matter I should like to point out briefly some of the facts which influenced the Department's decision.

A study of the law of sovereign immunity reveals the existence of two conflicting concepts of sovereign immunity, each widely held and firmly established. According to the classical or absolute theory of sovereign immunity, a sovereign cannot, without his consent, be made a respondent in the courts of another sovereign. According to the newer or restrictive theory of sovereign immunity, the immunity of the sovereign is recognized with regard to sovereign or public acts (jure imperii) of a state, but not with respect to private acts (jure gestionis). There is agreement by proponents of both theories, supported by practice, that sovereign immunity should not be claimed or granted in actions with respect to real property (diplomatic and perhaps consular property excepted) or with respect to the disposition of the property of a deceased person even though a foreign sovereign is the beneficiary.

The classical or virtually absolute theory of sovereign immunity has generally been followed by the courts of the United States, the British Commonwealth, Czechoslovakia, Estonia, and probably Poland.

The decisions of the courts of Brazil, Chile, China, Hungary, Japan, Luxembourg, Norway, and Portugal may be deemed to support the classical theory of immunity if one or at most two old decisions anterior to the development of the restrictive theory may be considered sufficient on which to base a conclusion.

The position of the Netherlands, Sweden, and Argentina is less clear since although immunity has been granted in recent cases coming before the courts of those countries, the facts were such that immunity would have been granted under either the absolute or restrictive theory. However, constant references by the courts of these three countries to the distinction between public and private acts of the state, even though the distinction was not involved in the result of the case, may indicate an intention to leave the way open for a possible application of the restrictive theory of immunity if and when the occasion presents itself.

A trend to the restrictive theory is already evident in the Netherlands where the lower courts have started to apply that theory following a Supreme Court decision to the effect that immunity would have been applicable in the case under consideration under either theory.

The German courts, after a period of hesitation at the end of the nineteenth century have held to the classical theory, but it should be noted that the refusal of the Supreme Court in 1921 to yield to pressure by the lower courts for the newer theory was based on the view that that theory had not yet developed sufficiently to justify a change. In view of the growth of the restrictive theory since that time the German courts might take a different view today.

The newer or restrictive theory of sovereign immunity has always been supported by the courts of Belgium and Italy. It was adopted in turn by the courts of Egypt and of Switzerland. In addition, the courts of France, Austria, and Greece, which were traditionally supporters of the classical theory, reversed their position in the 20's to embrace the restrictive theory. Rumania, Peru, and possibly Denmark also appear to follow this theory.

Furthermore, it should be observed that in most of the countries still following the classical theory there is a school of influential writers favoring the restrictive theory and the views of writers, at least in civil law countries, are a major factor in the development of the law. Moreover, the leanings of the lower courts in civil law countries are more significant in shaping the law than they are in common law countries where the rule of precedent prevails and the trend in these lower courts is to the restrictive theory.

Of related interest to this question is the fact that ten of the thirteen countries which have been classified above as supporters of the classical theory have ratified the Brussels Convention of 1926 under which immunity for government owned merchant vessels is waived. In addition the United States, which is not a party to the Convention, some years ago announced and has since followed, a policy of not claiming immunity for its public owned or operated merchant vessels. Keeping in mind the importance played by cases involving public vessels in the field of sovereign immunity, it is thus noteworthy that these ten countries (Brazil, Chile, Estonia, Germany, Hungary, Netherlands, Norway, Poland, Portugal, Sweden) and the United States have already relinquished by treaty or in practice an important part of the immunity which they claim under the classical theory.

It is thus evident that with the possible exception of the United Kingdom little support has been found except on the part of the Soviet Union and its satellites for continued full acceptance of the absolute theory of sovereign immunity. There are evidences that British authorities are aware of its deficiencies and ready for a change. The reasons which obviously motivate state trading countries in adhering to the theory with perhaps increasing rigidity are most persuasive that the United States should change its policy. Furthermore, the granting of sovereign immunity to foreign governments in the courts of the United States is most inconsistent with the action of the Government of the United States in subjecting itself to suit in these same courts in both contract and tort and with its long established policy of not claiming immunity in foreign jurisdictions for its merchant vessels. Finally, the Department feels that the widespread and increasing practice on the part of governments of engaging in commercial activities makes necessary a practice which will enable persons doing business with them to have their rights determined in the courts. For these reasons it will hereafter be the Department's policy to follow the restrictive theory of sovereign immunity in the consideration of requests of foreign governments for a grant of sovereign immunity.

It is realized that a shift in policy by the executive cannot control the courts but it is felt that the courts are less likely to allow a plea of sovereign immunity where the executive has declined to do so. There have been indications that at least some Justices of the Supreme Court feel that in this matter courts should follow the branch of the Government charged with responsibility for the conduct of foreign relations.

In order that your Department, which is charged with representing the interests of the Government before the courts, may be adequately informed it will be the Department's practice to advise you of all requests by foreign governments for the grant of immunity from suit and of the Department's action thereon.

     Sincerely yours,

     For the Secretary of State:

JACK B. TATE
Acting Legal Adviser

CHOU KENG–SHENG, NEW TRENDS IN CONTEMPORARY ANGLO–AMERICAN THEORY OF INTERNATIONAL LAW (SHIH–CHIEH CHIH–SHIH CU'U–PAN–SHE, PEKING 1963)

III(1) Chinese Law and Government 20, 78–80 (1970).*

* * * [The Tate Letter] revealed the new policy of the State Department toward the question of the jurisdictional immunities of foreign states, and it apparently had a great impact on the theoretical underpinnings of international law. Although the Tate Letter was sent by the acting legal adviser of the State Department on behalf of the Secretary of State to the Acting Attorney General, it was tantamount to a directive from the U. S. government to its judiciary. Thus the letter itself was replete with great political significance, and immediately attracted wide attention among jurists. * * *

[The writer then gave a summary of the letter, which ended as follows.] Thus, with the exception of the Soviet Union and other states in the socialist camp * * * [The Letter] added, very few states now supported absolute immunity. In all candor, the letter pointed out that in the face of the insistence on absolute immunity by states that engaged in state trading, it was all the more necessary for the United States to change its policy. * * *

* * *

The United States is a country that subscribes to the so-called "separation of powers," under which the judiciary is supposed to be independent. What effect does a statement of policy from the Department of State have on American courts? * * * In fact, American courts are, more often than not, obliged to defer to the policy of the government on questions of the immunity of foreign states or their assets. More recently, United States courts have increasingly paid attention to the foreign relations aspect of such questions and have openly admitted that they must respect the opinion of the Department of State. * * *

The above directive from the U. S. Department of State was a glaring manifestation and summation of an attempt, over the years, by the U. S. government to limit the jurisdictional immunity of foreign states. Its principal purpose was obviously to counter the growing external economic activities of the socialist states. * * *

* * *

Departure from the Tate letter. In time, the Department of State departed from the announced policy of the Tate letter and made suggestions of immunity, which were accepted as binding by courts, in cases where they were not justified by the distinction between public acts and private acts. An illustration follows.

* Excerpted from Chinese Law and Government, Vol. III, No. 1, Spring 1970, pp. 20, 78–80, by permission of publisher, M. E. Sharpe, Inc., Armonk NY 10504.

ISBRANDTSEN TANKERS, INC. v. PRESIDENT OF INDIA

United States Court of Appeals, Second Circuit, 1971.
446 F.2d 1198.[a]

J. JOSEPH SMITH, Circuit Judge: Appellant shipowner instituted suit in the United States District Court for the Southern District of New York against the defendant-appellee, seeking damages resulting from alleged delays of its vessels during October and November of 1966 near the port of Calcutta. The District Court * * * dismissed one of the three causes of action alleged in appellant's second amended complaint, and the shipowner appeals. We find no error and affirm the dismissal.

The dismissal * * * was premised upon a formal written suggestion of immunity by the United States Department of State, transmitted through the office of the United States Attorney General, after hearings and the filing of briefs with the State Department.

Appellant shipowner and appellee entered into a charter party in July of 1966 for the transportation of grain to India. The shipment was part of a massive effort on the part of the Indian government to end a food shortage, resulting from an extreme drought in 1965 and 1966. The cause of action which is the subject of this appeal sought damages for improper and unreasonable detention of appellant's vessels, preventing discharge of their cargo and causing substantial loss of time and money. Appellant contends that notwithstanding the advisory letter from the State Department recommending immunity, the District Court has jurisdiction in this matter because of the existence of a waiver of immunity by appellee, said to be contained in paragraph 34 of the contract charter between the parties.[3] Additionally, appellant argues that the appearance by appellee by means of serving and filing answering papers constitutes a waiver of any sovereign immunity that may have previously existed.

Whether or not these arguments possess logical force, in cases involving the governments of foreign powers the judiciary has candidly admitted that there exist interests beyond those of purely legal concern. A judicial decision against the government of a foreign nation could conceivably cause severe international repercussions, the full consequences of which the courts are in no position to predict. As this court noted in Victory Transport, Inc. v. Comisaria General, 336 F.2d 354, 358 (2d Cir. 1964), cert. denied, 381 U.S. 934, 85 S.Ct. 1763, 14 L.Ed.2d 698 (1965), "[i]n delineating the scope of a doctrine designed to avert possible embarrassment to the conduct of

---

a. Cert. denied 404 U.S. 985, 92 S.Ct. 452 (1971).

3. Paragraph 34 of the charter party provides:

Any and all differences and disputes arising under this Charter Party are to be determined by the U.S. Courts for the Southern District of New York, but this does not preclude a party from pursuing any in rem proceedings in another jurisdiction or from submission by mutual agreement of any differences or disputes to arbitration.

our foreign relations, the courts have quite naturally deferred to the policy pronouncements of the State Department." * * *

Appellant emphasizes that traditionally, sovereign immunity has been afforded to foreign governments only in regard to actions of a public, as opposed to a private/commercial, nature. Here, it is contended, the actions of the Indian government were wholly concerned with a commercial purchase of grain, and therefore do not concern matters of public policy or governmental discretion. This argument is premised upon the famed letter of Jack B. Tate, Acting Legal Advisor to the State Department, to Philip B. Perlman, Acting Attorney General, dated May 19, 1952 [appearing in 26 State Dept. Bull. 984 (1952)], indicating that it was the policy of our government to adopt the restrictive theory of sovereign immunity, i. e. to grant immunity to acts of a public nature, and to deny it to those of a private nature.

This proposed distinction between acts which are jure imperii (which are to be afforded immunity) and those which are jure gestionis (which are not), has never been adequately defined, and in fact has been viewed as unworkable by many commentators. In Victory Transport, this court adopted the view that acts which are jure imperii would be limited to the following:

(1) internal administrative acts, such as expulsion of an alien;

(2) legislative acts, such as nationalization;

(3) acts concerning the armed forces;

(4) acts concerning diplomatic activity;

(5) public loans. 336 F.2d at 360.

Were we required to apply this distinction, as defined, to the facts of the present case, we might well find that the actions of the Indian government were, as appellant contends, purely private commercial decisions.

It is true that the mere fact that a contract with a private commercial interest is involved does not automatically render the acts of the foreign government private and commercial. As this court recently noted:

> The view that all contracts, regardless of their purpose, should be deemed "private" or "commercial" acts would lead to the conclusion that a contract by a foreign government for the purchase of bullets for its army or for the erection of fortifications do not constitute sovereign acts—a result we viewed as "rather astonishing" in Victory Transport, 336 F.2d at 359. * * *

In Victory Transport, the contract was, as here, for the carriage of grain, and in the absence of State Department action, jurisdiction was upheld. * * *

In situations where the State Department has given a formal recommendation, however, the courts need not reach questions of this type. The State Department is to make this determination, in light of the potential consequences to our own international position.

Hence once the State Department has ruled in a matter of this nature, the judiciary will not interfere. * * *

   * * *

The potential harm or embarrassment resulting to our government from a judicial finding of jurisdiction, in the face of an Executive recommendation to the contrary, may be just as severe where the foreign sovereign had initially contracted to waive its claim of sovereign immunity as where it had not done so. Though we sympathize with appellant because of the difficult position in which such a holding places it, we have no alternative but to accept the recommendation of the State Department.

The order of the District Court dismissing appellant's second cause of action is affirmed.

TESTIMONY OF THE LEGAL ADVISER OF THE DEPARTMENT OF STATE OF THE UNITED STATES ON THE FOREIGN SOVEREIGN IMMUNITIES ACT OF 1976

Hearings on H.R. 11315 before the Subcommittee on Administrative Law and Governmental Relations of the Committee on the Judiciary, House of Representatives, 94th Cong., 2d Sess. 24, 26–27 (1976).

[Monroe Leigh, The Legal Adviser, gave the testimony, an excerpt of which follows.]

The first objective is to vest sovereign immunity decisions exclusively in the courts. The bill would accomplish this by prescribing the standards the courts are to apply in deciding questions of sovereign immunity.

Under our current system, after a foreign-state defendant raises the defense of sovereign immunity, it has an option: either the foreign state can litigate this legal defense entirely in court, or, as is more usually the case, it can make a formal diplomatic request to have the State Department decide the issue.

If it does the latter, and if the State Department believes that immunity is appropriate, the State Department asks the Department of Justice to file a "suggestion of immunity" with the court hearing the case. Under the Supreme Court's decision in *Ex Parte Peru*, which was decided in 1943, U.S. courts automatically defer to such suggestions of immunity from the executive branch.

In response to various developments in international law, the State Department in 1952 adopted its so-called Tate letter. Prior to the Tate letter, the Department of State, when called on to decide questions of immunity, followed the so-called absolute rule of sovereign immunity: a state was immune from suit irrespective of whether it was engaged in a government or a commercial act.

Under the Tate letter, the Department undertook to decide future sovereign immunity questions in accordance with the international legal principle which I have mentioned and which is known as the "restrictive theory"—namely, that a foreign state's immunity is "restricted" to cases based on its public acts, and does not extend to cases based on its commercial or private acts. The Tate letter was based on a realization that the prior absolute rule of sovereign immunity was no longer consistent with modern international law.

The Tate letter, however, has not been a satisfactory answer. From a legal standpoint, it poses a devil's choice. If the Department follows the Tate letter in a given case, it is in the incongruous position of a political institution trying to apply a legal standard to litigation already before the courts.

On the other hand, if forced to disregard the Tate letter in a given case, the Department is in the self-defeating position of abandoning the very international law principle it elsewhere espouses.

From a diplomatic standpoint, the Tate letter has continued to leave the diplomatic initiative to the foreign state. The foreign state chooses which case it will bring to the State Department and in which case it will try to raise diplomatic considerations.

Leaving the diplomatic initiative in such cases to the foreign state places the United States at a disadvantage. This is particularly true since the United States cannot itself obtain similar advantages in other countries. In virtually every other country in the world, sovereign immunity is a question of international law decided exclusively by the courts and not by institutions concerned with foreign affairs.

For this reason, when we and other foreign states are sued abroad, we realize that international law principles will be applied by the courts and that diplomatic relations will not be called into play.

Moreover, from the standpoint of the private citizen, the current system generates considerable commercial uncertainty. A private party who deals with a foreign government entity cannot be certain of having his day in court to resolve an ordinary legal dispute. He cannot be entirely certain that the ordinary legal dispute will not be artificially raised to the level of a diplomatic problem through the government's intercession with the State Department.

The purpose of sovereign immunity in modern international law is not to protect the sensitivities of 19th-century monarchs or the prerogatives of the 20th-century state. Rather, it is to promote the functioning of all governments by protecting a state from the burden of defending law suits abroad which are based on its public acts.

However, when the foreign state enters the marketplace or when it acts as a private party, there is no justification in modern international law for allowing the foreign state to avoid the economic costs of the agreements which it may breach or the accidents which it may cause.

The law should not permit the foreign state to shift these everyday burdens of the marketplace onto the shoulders of private parties.

[The Legal Adviser went on to analyze the provisions of the proposed bill.]

---

1. *Foreign Sovereign Immunities Act of 1976.* The act went into effect in January 1977. The text is in the Documentary Supplement. Generally speaking it incorporates the restrictive theory. As the Legal Adviser put it in the course of his testimony in the hearings: "Under international law today, a foreign state is entitled to sovereign immunity only in the cases based on its 'public' acts. However, where a law suit is based on a commercial transaction or some other 'private' act of the foreign state, the foreign state is not entitled to sovereign immunity. The specific applications of this principle of international law are codified in * * * the proposed bill." (at 25)

2. *Immunity of political subdivisions under the act.* In one respect, the act departs from its intended purpose of restricting the immunity of the state. It does this by broadening the definition of a state in Section 1603(a): "A foreign state * * * includes a political subdivision of a foreign state * * *." Thus all governmental units beneath the central government are entitled to claim the immunity of the state.

While there is a divergence in the case law in the matter, the majority view is that a constituent unit or political subdivision of a state is not entitled to the immunity. See Section 69 of the Restatement of the Foreign Relations Law of the United States (1963) and the Reporters' Notes which follow it. Article 28 of the European Convention on State Immunity is in accord. 66 Am. J. Int'l L. 923, 933 (1972). The reasoning is that the immunity does not avail entities which have no independent existence in the conduct of foreign relations. For an analysis of the status under international law of the Land of Hesse in West Germany, which had the power to conclude some international agreements taking effect within the Land alone, and a ruling it was not entitled to immunity, see Neger v. Etat de Hesse, France, Tribunal de Grande Instance of Paris, 1969, 52 Int'l L. Rep. 329 (1979).

3. *Immunity of agency or instrumentality under the act.* In this respect the act also departs from its intended purpose of restricting the scope of the immunity. It does so by incorporating into the definition of a state under Section 1603(a): "an agency or instrumentality of a state" and in turn defining these terms in Section 1603(b) as follows:

> An agency or instrumentality of a foreign state means any entity—
>> (1) which is a separate legal person, corporate or otherwise, and
>> (2) which is an organ of a foreign state or political subdivision thereof, or a majority of whose shares or other owner-

ship interest is owned by a foreign state or political subdivision thereof, and

> (3) which is neither a citizen of a State of the United States as defined in section 1332(c) and (d) of this title, nor created under the laws of any third country.

Thus such agencies and instrumentalities are entitled to the immunity of the state under Section 1604, subject to the exceptions in Section 1607 to 1609, even though the result is not required by international law and does not obtain in many states. See supra, p. 295.

In contrast, the European Convention on State Immunity eliminates from its definition of a state "any legal entity of a Contracting State which is distinct therefrom and is capable of suing or being sued, even if that entity has been entrusted with public functions." Article 27, 1, 66 Am. J. Int'l L. 923, 933 (1972). Under paragraph 2 of the article, such an entity may be sued in the same manner as a private person except in cases where the acts involved were "in the exercise of sovereign authority (acta jure imperii)."

4. *United Kingdom: State Immunity Act of 1978.* The act gives effect to the European Convention on State Immunity of May 16, 1972, which entered into force on June 11, 1976. For the text of the act, see XVII International Legal Materials 1123 (1978). For all practical purposes, the convention codifies the restrictive theory of state immunity. For the text of the convention, see 66 Am. J. Int'l L. 923 (1972).

---

2. THE DISTINCTION BETWEEN PUBLIC AND PRIVATE ACTS

1. *Relevance of French administrative law concepts.*[a] A short excursus in the concepts of administrative law developed in France during the 19th century can be of help in understanding the distinction between public and private acts which characterizes the restrictive theory in civil law states.

After the Revolution of 1789, there were established in France two parallel systems of courts, one judicial and the other administrative. For all practical purposes, they are equal in rank and neither is subordinate to the other. As a roughly valid proposition, we may say the judicial system was given jurisdiction over disputes between private parties, while the administrative system was given jurisdiction over disputes between private parties and the state. Thereupon the administrative courts proceeded to develop—on a case by case basis —a body of administrative law which has no exact counterpart in England or the United States, but has become the basis of adminis-

---

a. In the preparation of this portion of the materials, the editors consulted primarily A. de Laubadère, Traité, Elémentaire de Droit Administratif (4th ed. 1968) and L. Brown and J. Garner, French Administrative Law (1967).

trative law in much of continental Europe and has influenced the administrative law of a number of states elsewhere.

It cannot be entirely an accident that states whose courts led the development of the restrictive theory, or eventually adopted it, are also, in the main, those where French administrative law was followed or acquired influence. For in a French type of administrative law, a fundamental distinction is drawn between situations where the state exercises its public power, and hence litigation concerning such situations belongs to the administrative courts, and situations where the state acts in its private capacity, and hence litigation concerning them is left to the judicial system of courts. The distinction is elementary to civil law lawyers, even though it is subject in its application to exceptions, qualifications and refinements as complex as those surrounding the application of the concept of due process in American courts.

In the administrative law of France, for example, the property of the state is divided in two categories: the public domain and the private domain. The first is owned by the state in its public capacity and includes such things as the territorial sea, the sea shore, navigable waters and public roads. This public domain is governed by rules of administrative law which are not found in private law and, generally speaking, litigation concerning it belongs to the administrative courts. The private domain includes land and structures which are managed and exploited by the state for a commercial or industrial purpose. The state owns such domain in its private capacity and legal questions concerning it are governed, as a general proposition, by rules of private law and adjudicated in the judicial courts.

2. *Reflection in the restrictive theory of civilian concepts of administrative law.* Because of their experience with concepts of administrative law of the French type, the courts of a number of civil law states were intellectually conditioned by the turn of the century to engage in a critical analysis of the doctrine of sovereign immunity and not take it for granted that all acts of a foreign state needed to be treated as acts of sovereignty. The theory they worked out to delimit acts of sovereignty entitled to immunity, and separate them from other acts not entitled to immunity, borrows the differentiation from administrative law of the French type and uses it as the basis for determining immunity vel non.

Suppose, for example, a state purchases land in the territory of another. In France, the French state may acquire land by exercising its power of eminent domain, an act of sovereignty or public power basically governed by administrative law and within the jurisdiction of the administrative courts. But the French state may also acquire land through an ordinary contract of sale, a private act governed by private law and under the jurisdiction of the judicial courts. Should litigation arise concerning the interest acquired by the foreign state through its purchase of land, is it entitled to immunity?

The answer, in France and other states where French concepts of administrative law have influence, is "no," for the act clearly was not one of sovereignty and could not be considered an exercise of public power even if the purpose of the purchase was to build an embassy upon the land. The courts of such states normally classify the purchase as a private act not entitled to immunity in litigation connected with it. It was so classified by the Supreme Court of Chile as early as 1912. Inscripción de Bienes Raíces del Gobierno de Bolivia, [1912] 2 Gaceta de los Tribunales (No. 1170).

UNITED STATES OF AMERICA (DIRECTOR OF THE UNITED STATES FOREIGN SERVICE) v. PERIGNON AND OTHERS

France, Court of Appeal of Paris, 1962.
44 Int'l L.Rep. 76 (1972).*

This is a decision on the appeal brought by the Enterprise Perignon, and by Omnes, Lallemont and Ferrari acting in the capacity of judicial co-administrators of that company, from a judgment of the Tribunal de grande instance of the Seine given on 10 April 1957.

The appellant, by a writ dated 19 October 1956, sued the United States of America in the person of their Ambassador in Paris and the Regional Director of the Foreign Buildings Operation Department for payment of the sum of 141,700,059 Francs on account of work carried out for the building of apartments, and for damages.

The Court noted the failure of the United States to enter an appearance and declared that it lacked jurisdiction on account of the principle of the sovereignty and independence of foreign States.

The building company stated before this Court that it had concluded with the defendant, on 1 and 5 December 1952, two contracts for the construction, at Boulogne-Billancourt and at Neuilly-sur-Seine, of buildings for the accommodation of American citizens, who, whether or not they were officials, did not enjoy diplomatic immunity. According to the company, these contracts, which were governed by the general conditions drawn up by the American body, did not involve, either in respect of their subject matter or their terms, either a public service or the public power, and they included no provision alien to ordinary private law.

The appellant adds that there is no relevant treaty permitting the Government of the United States to exercise prerogatives pertaining to the public power on French territory, and that it should be deemed in the present case to have been fulfilling private interests and performing a commercial act. Although Article 8 of the contracts in question gives to the contracting "officer", and then to the American Secretary of State, competence to settle any disputes which

* Reprinted by permission of E. Lauterpacht, ed., and Grotius Publications, Ltd., Cambridge, England.

might arise, that clause must be regarded as absolutely void under French *ordre public*, since those two persons clearly combined the capacities of both judge and party to the dispute.

After thus asserting the jurisdiction of the French courts, the appellant company asks for judgment on the merits on the basis of its submissions at first instance and, subsidiarily, requests the appointment of an expert with the task, in particular, of verifying the grounds of the reasons given by the United States for cancelling the contracts in question, of determining the party to whom responsibility for the delays which occurred in the work must be imputed, of drawing up accounts, and assessing the damage suffered.

The United States and the Foreign Service [Foreign Buildings Operation Department] entered an appearance through counsel at the appeal and pleaded the jurisdictional immunity of foreign States; they also claim that the Court lacks jurisdiction because of the provisions of the contract providing for the settlement of disputes arising between the parties.

It is not contested that the contracts in dispute are the work of a State entity, contracting by the order or on behalf of a foreign Government. It appears from the official documents which have been produced that the buildings at Boulogne-Billancourt and Neuilly-sur-Seine were intended for the accommodation of American officials administering in France the Treaty on European Economic Co-operation, known as the "Marshall Plan", which was signed on 16 April 1948 by the Governments of the United States of America and sixteen European States. Moreover, these works were financed by funds emanating from the opening of credits granted to France by the United States for that purpose. The contracts were exempted from all French taxes, by virtue of the "Instruction of the General-Directorate of Taxes" of 9 May 1949, which granted certain privileges and immunities for the purpose of facilitating the functioning of international organizations.

Furthermore, the "general conditions" of the contracts of 1 and 5 December 1952 provide in Article 8 for the settlement of disputes by special proceedings before the "contracting officer" and the Secretary of State, and Articles 21 and 22 give the foreign authority itself the right to execute the work if the company does not observe the time-limits or if the work is not executed; finally, Articles 23 and 24 confer on the United States the power of unilateral cancellation at the discretion of the Government.

The contracts in dispute therefore contain provisions alien to private law and pertaining to the prerogatives of the public power of the United States, which was undoubtedly acting in fulfilment of a public interest. Consequently, the Court below was correct in declaring itself without jurisdiction, and its decision must be confirmed.

　　*　*　*

[The decision of the Court of Appeal was upheld by the Supreme Court of France in 1964. 45 Int'l L. Rep. 82 (1972).]

Question. Would the case be decided the same way if the distinction were not between public and private acts, but rather between public and commercial acts? See the note on the characterization of commercial acts, infra, p. 324.

ETAT ESPAGNOL v. SOCIETE ANONYME DE L'HOTEL GEORGE V

France, Tribunal de Grande Instance of Paris, 1970.
52 Int'l L.Rep. 317 (1979).*

*   *   *

The facts are as follows. According to a document dated at Paris on 1 December 1955, the Hotel George V company leased to the Direccion General del Turismo, the headquarters of which is in Madrid, but which has offices in Paris (16 Rue de la Chausée-d' Antin), under the name "Office Espagnol du Tourisme", and is represented by M. Roman de la Prasella, the Spanish Consul-General (domiciled in Paris at 165 Boulevard Malesherbes), certain premises forming part of a building situated in Paris at 29 Avenue George V and 45 Avenue Pierre 1er de Serbie.

*   *   *

The agreement further contains all the stipulations usual in this type of contract, including, in particular, the facility of triennial revision of the rent by arbitration, and a cancellation clause. In Clause 7 it is stated that the lessee is obliged "not to use the premises leased except as a tourist agency and for any activities concerning air transport and railways, publicity concerning handicrafts and, in general, all commercial publicity activities relating to tourism in Spain, including a banking counter".

According to a document dated at Paris on 29 January 1959 the premises leased were limited to the ground floor.

On 16 December 1965 the Hotel George V company gave to the Direccion General del Turismo notice to quit, expiring on 31 December 1968. This notice was repeated on 24 June 1966; renewal of the lease was refused and no compensation for eviction offered *   *   *.

*   *   *

The Spanish State declares that the office named "Office National Espagnol du Tourisme" has no legal personality. It is merely one of the offices opened in foreign countries by the Direccion General del Turismo, which itself lacks legal personality and is one of the departments of the Spanish State. That department, it is contended, is designated by a Law of 8 August 1939, it was at one time connected with the Spanish Ministry of the Interior and now, since the Decree of 19 July 1951, with the Ministry of Information and Tourism. Finally, the Spanish State contends, a Decree of 31 October 1962 united under the single title "Spanish National Tourist Office" the various names under which the officers of the Ministry of Information and Tourism operated abroad. It is further contended that the employees of the Office are all appointed by the Spanish Minister of Information and Tourism and are remunerated through the Spanish Embassy in Paris. The Spanish State observes that the lease of 1 December 1950 was signed in its name by the Spanish Consul-General in Paris, who was authorised to this effect, after the rent for the premises had been approved by the Council of Ministers, meeting at La Corona, on 8 September 1950.

The Spanish State considers that in "contracting for its administrative departments through an agent accredited to the French Government [it] acted within the plentitude of its sovereignty; and [that] the signature of the lease on 1 December 1950 constitutes an act of public authority which is outside the jurisdiction of the French courts".

* * * The plaintiff contends that the Direccion General del Turismo and the Spanish State which has intervened in its place, cannot in this case claim jurisdictional immunity in the French courts. According to the Hotel George V, it is accepted both in theory and judicial precedent "that commercial activities performed by a foreign State, or by one of its departments, are not acts of sovereignty and may be examined by the courts without their interfering in the administration of that State". In the present case, the company continues, it is indisputable that the conclusion of a commercial lease, expressly governed by the legislation on commercial property, and the premises forming the subject matter of which are intended for commercial use (sale of air-tickets, railway-tickets, operation of a banking branch), is a commercial activity, concluded and performed according to the formalities prescribed by commercial private law. Therefore, by so acting, and in accordance with the stipulations of the lease, the Direccion General del Turismo, even if it is a department of the Spanish State, has behaved as a private law entity and is justiciable by the French courts. * * * Applying what it regards as the principles extracted from recent judicial decisions, the company examines whether or not the Spanish State acted in this case in the same way as an individual, and finds proof of this in some clauses in the lease which, according to the company, constitute a waiver of jurisdictional immunity.

In a document dated 4 December 1969, the Spanish State gave its reply. It contends that, according to the approach adopted by the courts, it is necessary to consider the purpose of the act, including whether it is intended to satisfy the needs of a government department, whatever be the legal procedure used for the purpose. According to the Spanish State, it is then necessary to decide that jurisdictional immunity must be accorded. In the present case, since the Direccion General del Turismo is a department of the Spanish State, the lease of 1 December 1950 has the purpose of performing a public service and the principle of jurisdictional immunity must therefore be applied.

                         *   *   *

It is proved by the legislation and regulations submitted in evidence by the Spanish State that the Direccion General del Turismo is a department of the Spanish State connected with the Ministry of Information and Tourism. It is found, moreover, that the employees of that office are appointed by the Ministry of Information and Tourism and that their salaries are paid through the Spanish Embassy in Paris, and the director of the office has the status of an attaché at the Embassy.

The lease of 1 December 1950 was signed by the Spanish Consul-General in Paris, and the rent for the premises approved by the Spanish Council of Ministers.

The lease of 1 December 1950 was therefore concluded by an entity of the Spanish State; but this fact does not mean that the claim to jurisdictional immunity is well-founded. The lease itself, including both its form and its content, must be examined.

The agreement includes all the usual provisions. First of all, there is express reference to the dispositions of the Law of 30 June 1926 and to subsequent legislation concerning commercial property; and there are all the normal clauses, concerning in particular, upkeep of the premises, repairs, payment of rent, insurance, sub-letting, inspection of the premises by the company's architect, triennial revision of the rent by arbitration, choice of domicile in the premises leased, together with a cancellation clause in case of non-payment of rent or non-performance of one of the conditions of the lease.

The use of the premises is stated in Clause 7: the Direccion General del Turismo contracted the obligation "not to use the premises leased other than as a tourist agency, and for all operations connected with air and rail transport, publicity for handicrafts, and in general for all commercial and publicity activities relating to tourism in Spain, including a banking branch".

That is the purpose to which the premises were to be put according to the agreement; it indisputably and explicitly refers to commercial activities, at least in part. Such activities are, according to the French view, completely alien to the principle of State sovereignty. It has been found that the premises at 29 Avenue George V were used for many years for some of the services of Iberia Airways and air-tickets were sold there.

We conclude from these facts that the lease, far from containing clauses which are not of a private law character, re-affirms, on the contrary, all the usual stipulations. Therefore the Direccion General del Turismo contracted with the Hotel George V company in the form, in the manner and in accordance with private law, as if it had been an individual. It acted in performance of an activity which is at least in part commercial, and without recourse to the exercise of any public authority. There is no fact indicating that in so acting the department performed an act involving the sovereignty of the Spanish State.

The Court must therefore dismiss the plea of jurisdictional immunity and order the trial of the merits of the case *   *   *.

[The Court of Appeal of Paris reversed in 1971, holding that the conclusion of the lease was a public act, but the Court of Cassation quashed the decision of the Court of Appeal in 1973 on the ground that the conclusion of the lease was not a public act. XX Annuaire Français de Droit International 1019–1020 (1974).]

COLLISION WITH FOREIGN GOVERNMENT OWNED MOTOR CAR

Austria, Supreme Court, 1961.
40 Int'l L.Rep. 73 (1970).*

The Facts: The plaintiff, an Austrian citizen, alleged that his motor car had been damaged by the negligent driving of a car owned by the Government of the United States of America. He brought an action for damages for negligence against the United States Government. The latter raised a plea to the jurisdiction of the Austrian courts and contended that since at the time of the alleged collision their motor car was carrying mail intended for the United States Embassy, the Austrian courts were not entitled to exercise jurisdiction. The carriage of mail for and on behalf of the United States Embassy constituted the performance of a "sovereign act" by the United States Government.

*   *   *

[A portion of the opinion of the court appears below.]

In its appeal the defendant contends that the means whereby a State exercises its sovereign rights are irrelevant because all means at its disposal belong to the sphere of private law, and that the decisive factor is the act performed by the State with the aid of those means. It is contended that in this case the motor car was the means whereby the sovereign act (the collection of mail for the embassy) was carried out, and that the case must be judged in accordance with this act. This Court is unable to accept this contention. The distinction between private and sovereign acts is easily understood if one considers the following: Eminent writers, e. g. Schnitzler (Private International Law, at pp. 833 et seq.) point out that an act must be deemed to be a private act where the State acts through its agencies in the same way as a private individual can act. An act must be deemed to be a sovereign act where the State performs an act of legislation or administration (makes a binding decision). Sovereign

* Reprinted by permission of E. Lauterpacht, ed., and Grotius Publications,
Ltd., Cambridge, England.

acts are those in respect of which equality between the parties is lacking, and where the place of equality is taken by subordination of one party to the other. Spruth (Jurisdiction over Foreign States) defined this distinction as follows: "To act as a sovereign State means to act in the performance of sovereign rights. To enter into private transactions means to put oneself on the basis of equality with private individuals." * * *

Thus, we must always look at the act itself which is performed by State organs, and not at its motive or purpose. We must always investigate the act of the State from which the claim is derived. Whether an act is of a private or sovereign nature must always be deduced from the nature of the legal transaction, viz. the nature of the action taken or the legal relationship arising. * * *

* * *

If we apply the basic principles here outlined to the case before us, we must conclude that the act from which the plaintiff derives his claim for damages against the defendant is not the collection of mail but the operation of a motor car by the defendant and the latter's action as a road user. By operating a motor car and using the public roads the defendant moves in spheres in which private individuals also move. In these spheres the parties face one another on a basis of equality, and there is no indication here of any supremacy and subordination. It follows that, so far as liability for damage is concerned, the foreign State must be treated like a private individual. * * *

* * *

The Court is therefore of opinion that this action has been properly brought in the Austrian courts. * * *

LETELIER v. REPUBLIC OF CHILE

United States District Court, District of Columbia, 1980.
488 F.Supp. 665.

JOYCE HENS GREEN, District Judge.

* * *

Filed in August 1978 by Isabel, Christian, Jose, Francisco, and Juan Pablo Letelier, and Michael Maggio, respectively the widow, sons, and personal representative of Orlando Letelier, as well as by Michael Moffitt and Murray and Hilda Karpen, respectively the widower-personal representative and parents of Ronni Karpen Moffitt, the complaint herein, as amended, seeks recompense for tortious injuries connected with the deaths of both former Chilean ambassador and foreign minister Orlando Letelier and Ronni Moffitt in the District of Columbia on September 21, 1976, when Letelier's car, in which they were riding to work with Michael Moffitt, was destroyed by an explosive device. Plaintiffs allege that the bomb was constructed, planted, and detonated by defendants Michael Vernon Townley, Alvin

Ross Diaz, Virgilio Paz Romero, Jose Dionisio Suarez Esquivel, Guillermo Novo Sampol, and Ignacio Novo Sampol, acting in concert and purportedly at the direction and with the aid of defendants Republic of Chile, its intelligence organ the Centro Nacional de Intelligencia (CNI) (formerly Direccion de Intelligencia Nacional, a/k/a DINA), and supposed CNI–DINA agents and officers Pedro Espinoza Bravo, Juan Manuel Contreras Sepulveda, and Armando Fernandez Larios. In accord with their allegations and acting pursuant to the provisions of the District of Columbia Code governing survival of actions, D.C. Code § 12–101 (1973), and wrongful death, id. § 16–2701 (Supp. V 1978), plaintiffs have set forth   *   *   *   five causes of action that they contend give rise to civil liability on the part of the defendants * * *.

     *   *   *

     As to the Republic of Chile and CNI, pursuant to the terms of the Foreign Sovereign Immunities Act of 1976, 28 U.S.C. § 1608(a)(4), two copies of the summons and amended complaint were dispatched by the Clerk of the Court to the United States Department of State on October 24, 1978. One of these copies, along with an explanatory diplomatic note, was delivered by the State Department to the Ministry of Foreign Affairs of the Republic of Chile in Santiago on November 17, 1978. On February 9, 1979, the Clerk of the Court was notified by letter from the Department of State that the Chilean Foreign Affairs Ministry, by a diplomatic note dated January 16, 1979, had requested that the copy of the summons and amended complaint be returned to the Court. In the note, the Ministry of Foreign Affairs made it clear that CNI was not a separate legal entity but only an organ of the Chilean government and that the Republic of Chile would not acquiesce in the jurisdiction of this Court over the subject matter of this suit.

     On May 2, 1979, following the plaintiffs' filing that same day of a motion, with supporting memorandum of law, seeking the entry of a default against the Republic of Chile, the Honorable John H. Pratt held a hearing on that request. The next day an order was filed entering a default against the Republic of Chile.

     *   *   *

     *   *   * Although Judge Pratt's entry of a default could be considered an implicit recognition that the courts of the United States do have subject matter jurisdiction over the Republic of Chile in this action, the nature of this litigation, it apparently being the first instance in which redress for tortious injuries such as are alleged here has been sought under the Foreign Sovereign Immunities Act, as well as the potential diplomatic impact of any action by the Court, make it necessary that the question of jurisdiction be fully and sensitively explored on the record.

     Turning then to that task, it is necessary to focus upon the provisions of the Foreign Sovereign Immunities Act, which, like all other statutory enactments regulating the subject matter jurisdiction of the federal district courts, delimits the boundaries within which the jurisdictional power of this Court can be exercised.   *   *   *

    *   *   *

As is made clear both in the Act and in its legislative history, one of its principal purposes was to reduce the foreign policy implications of sovereign immunity determinations and assure litigants that such crucial decisions are made on purely legal grounds, an aim that was to be accomplished by transferring responsibility for such a decision from the executive branch to the judiciary.   *   *   *   In addition, the Act itself is designed to codify the restrictive principle of sovereign immunity that makes a foreign state amenable to suit for the consequences of its commercial or private, as opposed to public, acts.   Id.

In considering the related questions of jurisdiction and sovereign immunity under the Act, one court has observed:

> The Act's central feature is its specification of categories of actions for which foreign states are not entitled to claim the sovereign immunity from American court jurisdiction otherwise granted to such states.   These exceptions are contained not in the sections of the Act which describe the grounds on which jurisdiction may be obtained, however, but are phrased as substantive acts for which foreign states may be found liable by American courts.   This effects an identity between substance and procedure in the Act which means that a court faced with a claim of immunity from jurisdiction must engage ultimately in a close examination of the underlying cause of action in order to decide whether the plaintiff may obtain jurisdiction over the defendant.

Yessenin-Volpin v. Novosti Press Agency, 443 F.Supp. 849, 851 (S. D.N.Y.1978).   In the instant action, relying on section 1605(a)(5) as their basis for combatting any assertion of sovereign immunity, plaintiffs have set forth several tortious causes of action arising under international law, the common law, the Constitution, and legislative enactments, pp. 666–667 supra, all of which are alleged to spring from the deaths of Orlando Letelier and Ronni Moffitt.   The Republic of Chile, while vigorously contending that it was in no way involved in the events that resulted in the two deaths, further asserts that, even if it were, the Court has no subject matter jurisdiction in that it is entitled to immunity under the Act, *which does not cover political assassinations because of their public, governmental character.*   [Emphasis supplied.]

As supportive of its conclusion that political, tortious acts of a government are to be excluded, the Republic of Chile makes reference to the reports of the House and the Senate Judiciary Committees with regard to the Act, in which it was stated:

> Section 1605(a)(5) is directed primarily at the problem of traffic accidents but is cast in general terms as applying to all tort actions for money damages.   *   *   *

    *   *   *

The purpose of section 1605(a)(5) is to permit the victim of a traffic accident or other noncommercial tort to maintain an action against a foreign state to the extent otherwise provided by law.

H.R.Rep.No.94–1487, supra at 20–21; S.Rep.No.94–1310, supra at 20–21. It is clear from these passages, the Chilean government asserts, that the intent of Congress was to include only private torts like automobile accidents within the exclusion from immunity embodied in section 1605(a)(5).

Prominently absent from defendant's analysis, however, is the initial step in any endeavor at statutory interpretation: a consideration of the words of the statute. * * * Subject to the exclusion of these discretionary acts defined in subsection (A) and the specific causes of action enumerated in subsection (B), neither of which have been invoked by the Republic of Chile, by the plain language of section 1605(a)(5) a foreign state is not entitled to immunity from an action seeking money damages "for personal injury or death * * * caused by the tortious act or omission of that foreign state" or its officials or employees. Nowhere is there an indication that the tortious acts to which the Act makes reference are to only be those formerly classified as "private," thereby engrafting onto the statute, as the Republic of Chile would have the Court do, the requirement that the character of a given tortious act be judicially analyzed to determine whether it was of the type heretofore denoted as jure gestionis or should be classified as jure imperii. Indeed, the other provisions of the Act mandate that the Court not do so, for it is made clear that the Act and the principles it sets forth in its specific provisions are henceforth to govern all claims of sovereign immunity by foreign states. 28 U.S.C. §§ 1602, 1604 (1976).

Although the unambiguous language of the Act makes inquiry almost unnecessary, further examination reveals nothing in its legislative history that contradicts or qualifies its plain meaning. The relative frequency of automobile accidents and their potentially grave financial impact may have placed that problem foremost in the minds of Congress, but the applicability of the Act was not so limited, for the committees made it quite clear that the Act "is cast *in general terms* as applying to *all tort actions* for money damages" so as to provide recompense for "the victim of a traffic accident or *other noncommercial tort.*" H.R.Rep.No.94–1487, supra at 20–21 (emphasis supplied); S.Rep.No.94–1310, supra at 20–21 (same). Further, any notion that the Congress wished the courts to go outside the scheme promulgated by legislative action to determine the extent to which the defense of sovereign immunity could be invoked is foreclosed by the committee reports that not only state that "[t]his bill * * * sets forth the *sole and exclusive* standard to be used in resolving questions of sovereign immunity raised by foreign states before Federal and State courts in the United States," H.R.Rep.No.94–1487, supra at 12 (emphasis supplied); S.Rep.No.94–1310, supra at 11 (same), but also provide that the burden of proof shall be upon the foreign state to present evidence "that the plaintiff's claim relates to a *public act* of the foreign state—that is, *an act not within the exceptions in section 1605–1607*," H.R.Rep.No.94–1487, supra at 17 (emphasis supplied); S.Rep.No.94–1310, supra at 17 (same). Thus, it is apparent that the terms of section 1605(a)(5) set the sole standard under which any claim of sovereign immunity must be examined.

Examining then the specific terms of section 1605(a)(5), despite the Chilean failure to have addressed the issue, the Court is called upon to consider whether either of the exceptions to liabiilty for tortious acts found in section 1605(a)(5) applies in this instance. It is readily apparent, however, that the claims herein did not arise "out of malicious prosecution, abuse of process, libel, slander, misrepresentation, deceit, or interference with contract rights," 28 U.S.C. § 1605(a)(5)(B) (1976), and therefore only the exemption for claims "based upon the exercise or performance or the failure to exercise or perform a discretionary function regardless of whether the discretion be abused," id. § 1605(a)(5)(A), can be applicable.

As its language and the legislative history make apparent, the discretionary act exemption of subsection (A) corresponds to the discretionary act exception found in the Federal Tort Claims Act. * * * As defined by the United States Supreme Court in interpreting the Federal Tort Claims Act, an act that is discretionary is one in which "there is room for policy judgment and decision." * * * Applying this definition to the instant action, the question becomes, would the alleged determination of the Chilean Republic to set into motion and assist in the precipitation of those events that culminated in the deaths of Orlando Letelier and Ronni Moffitt be of the kind in which there is "room for policy judgment and decision."

While it seems apparent that a decision calculated to result in injury or death to a particular individual or individuals, made for whatever reason, would be one most assuredly involving policy judgment and decision and thus exempt as a discretionary act under section 1605(a)(5)(A), that exception is not applicable to bar this suit. As it has been recognized, there is no discretion to commit, or to have one's officers or agents commit, an illegal act. Cruikshank v. United States, 431 F.Supp. 1355, 1359 (D.Hawaii 1977); see Hatahley v. United States, 351 U.S. 173, 181, 76 S.Ct. 745, 751, 100 L.Ed. 1065 (1956). Whatever policy options may exist for a foreign country, it has no "discretion" to perpetrate conduct designed to result in the assassination of an individual or individuals, action that is clearly contrary to the precepts of humanity as recognized in both national and international law. Accordingly there would be no "discretion" within the meaning of section 1605(a)(5)(A) to order or to aid in an assassination and were it to be demonstrated that a foreign state has undertaken any such act in this country, that foreign state could not be accorded sovereign immunity under subsection (A) for any tort claims resulting from its conduct. As a consequence, the Republic of

Chile cannot claim sovereign immunity under the Foreign Sovereign Immunities Act for its alleged involvement in the deaths of Orlando Letelier and Ronni Moffitt.

* * *

[The court awarded damages to the plaintiffs in the amount of nearly five million dollars for wrongful death, pain and suffering and punitive damages. The New York Times, Nov. 6, 1980, p. A14, col. 3.]

---

3.   THE DISTINCTION BETWEEN PUBLIC ACTS AND COMMERCIAL ACTS

Characterization of commercial acts. The restrictive theory developed by courts in civilian jurisdictions is not grounded on a distinction between commercial and other acts of state. Commercial acts are part of the larger category of acts which civilians denominate private. In the Tate letter, the Department of State committed itself to the civil law distinction between the public acts and the private acts of a state. Nevertheless, the Department of State tended at times to construe the Tate letter as if it set forth a distinction between public and commercial acts. Thus in 1969, a Deputy Legal Adviser to the Department of State said: " * * * [T]he Tate letter tried to draw a distinction between governmental and commercial activities." Belman, New Departures in the Law of Sovereign Immunity, 1969 Proceedings of the American Society of International Law 182, 183–184.

There are, literally, hundreds of decisions dealing with sovereign immunity. Of those, many are decisions by courts in civil law states where immunity was denied because the activity of the foreign state giving rise to the litigation was commercial and hence classified as a private act not entitled to immunity. In a large number of these cases, common law courts would also characterize the activity involved as commercial in nature and it would not make much difference if they did not approach the issue in terms of public versus private acts.

Difficulties arise, however, when the test of public versus private acts does not yield the same result as the test of public versus commercial acts. Consider for example, the case of Trutta v. State of Rumania decided by the Supreme Court of Italy in 1926, 26 Am.J. Int'l L.Supp. 629 (1932). The contract was for the supply of leather to the army of Rumania. If the purpose of the transaction were looked upon as controlling, the contract could be regarded as involving a public purpose rather than a commercial one and hence as covered by sovereign immunity. The Supreme Court of Italy, however, did not approach the issue in these terms. Instead it ruled that the contract was not of the kind which only a state, in the exercise of its public power, could conclude and hence Rumania was not entitled to immunity in litigation on the contract.

The illustration indicates the basic cleavage between the two tests involved. A public purpose and an act of public power are not, in the view of courts from civil law states, the same thing. They would agree that a state always acts for a public purpose, but say that the relevant question is whether or not it accomplishes its public purpose by an act of public power. When, however, the purpose of the act is made the criterion, the issue becomes whether the act of the foreign state has only a public purpose or, if it has also a commercial purpose, whether the one should be considered as more controlling than the other.

When the issue is framed in terms of the purpose of the act, inconsistent determinations often follow. Thus Belman, the Deputy Legal Adviser of the Department of State whose interpretation of the Tate Letter has just been discussed above, would take the view that a contract for the supply of leather to an army is a commercial act. 1969 Proceedings 183. Yet the United States Court of Appeals for the Second Circuit declared in 1964 it was astonishing that immunity should be denied by some European courts in purchases of bullets or shoes for the army and repeated its remark in the Isbrandtsen case, supra, p. 306.

Section 1603(d) of the Foreign Sovereign Immunities Act of 1976 provides in part: "The commercial character of an activity shall be determined by reference to the nature of the course of conduct or particular transaction or act, *rather than by reference to its purpose.*" [Emphasis supplied.]

SUGARMAN v. AEROMEXICO

United States Court of Appeals, Third Circuit, 1980.
626 F.2d 270.

LOUIS H. POLLAK, District Judge.

The question posed by this appeal is whether Aeromexico, Inc.— the national airline of Mexico, and a common carrier of passengers between Mexico and the United States—is shielded by the Foreign Sovereign Immunities Act of 1976, 28 U.S.C. §§ 1602 et seq., from responding in a court in the United States to claims of the sort here pressed against Aeromexico by a United States citizen. The essence of Alan Sugarman's claim against Aeromexico is that, in the last twenty-four hours of a trip to Mexico and return, he suffered manifold hardships—injurious to his serenity, health and pocketbook—by reason of an extended, unanticipated, and unexplained delay at the Acapulco airport before the departure of his Aeromexico flight back home.

Assuming proper service and venue, such a claim would fall within the subject matter jurisdiction of most nisi prius courts, state or federal, in the United States, if Aeromexico were a private enterprise.[2] The critical question in this case is whether Aeromexico's public status precludes a court in the United States—in this instance a federal district court—from exercising the subject matter jurisdiction it would possess if Aeromexico were not a national airline.

I.

The question arises in the following way:

In November of 1978, plaintiff Sugarman filed a complaint in a federal district court in New Jersey. As to jurisdiction, Sugarman alleged that he was a citizen of New Jersey and that Aeromexico was a New York corporation. As to the merits, Sugarman alleged that "[d]efendant entered into a [c]ontract with the [p]laintiff * * * to carry plaintiff as a passenger from Mexico to Newark, New Jersey on January 2nd 1977": that "defendant failed to exercise that degree of care [required by the contract of carriage] in that it caused the plaintiff to wait for 15 hours under extremely brutal conditions"; that "defendant * * * negligently failed to alleviate same and continually caused plaintiff to wait in the airport * * * without any facilities or adequate food"; and that "[a]s a result of being exposed to these conditions, plaintiff suffered cardiac insufficiency, angina and arrhythmia," causing him "physical pain and mental anguish," injury to his health, and loss of "time and wages."

Aeromexico, asserting by way of affidavit that it was a Mexican corporation wholly-owned by the Mexican government, moved for summary judgment on grounds of sovereign immunity. Aeromexico pointed out (1) that 28 U.S.C. § 1604, subject to certain exceptions discussed below, lays down the general principle that "a foreign state shall be immune from the jurisdiction of the courts of the United States and of the States"; and (2) that 28 U.S.C. § 1603(a), defines

---

2. Very likely such a claim could also be entertained in many Mexican courts. Whether tried in a Mexican court or a court in the United States, such a claim would be tried subject to substantive rules of decision—drawn from the law of Mexico, or from the law of one or another state of the United States, or from "federal" United States law, or from some admixture thereof—the selection of which, pursuant to conventional choice-of-law doctrines, would depend on the court's perception of the operative facts underlying the claim's component parts. In most choice-of-law contexts, by virtue of the variety of assertedly relevant operative facts and the flexibility of assertedly applicable choice-of-law doctrines, the choice-of-law question is unlikely to yield one immutable answer or group of answers which any court seized of the case would necessarily adopt.

There are, however, occasional controversies in which the connections with a particular country are of such preemptive significance that a court in the United States would be obliged, as a matter of substantive due process, to look to that country's substantive law for the rules of decision. But, since courts in the United States are competent to apply foreign law, a determination that a court in the United States would be bound as a matter of substantive due process to look to the substantive law of Mexico rather than to the substantive law of a state of the United States (see, e. g., Home Insurance Co. v. Dick, 281 U.S. 397, 50 S.Ct. 338, 74 L.Ed. 926 [1930]), would not mean that there was any procedural due process impediment to the exercise by a court in the United States of in personam jurisdiction otherwise validly attained.

"foreign state" to include an "agency or instrumentality of a foreign state"; and (3) that 28 U.S.C. § 1603(b), in turn defines an "agency or instrumentality of a foreign state" to include a corporation "a majority of whose shares or other ownership interest is owned by a foreign state," (provided that the corporation is not incorporated in, and hence for diversity purposes is not a citizen of, a state of the United States). Wherefore, so Aeromexico contended, it was immune from the jurisdiction of any court in the United States.

* * *

First, the court concluded, as it was bound to do, that Aeromexico was an "agency or instrumentality of a foreign state."

Next, the district court considered Sugarman's submission that, notwithstanding Aeromexico's status as an "agency or instrumentality, of the Republic of Mexico, Aeromexico was not in this instance immune from suit for the reason that Sugarman's claim against Aeromexico was embraced by at least one of the exceptions to immunity contained in 28 U.S.C. § 1605(a)(2). That section provides as follows:

(a) A foreign state shall not be immune from the jurisdiction of courts of the United States or of the States in any case—

* * *

(2) in which the action is based upon a commercial activity carried on in the United States by the foreign state; or upon an act performed in the United States in connection with a commercial activity of the foreign state elsewhere; or upon an act outside the territory of the United States in connection with a commercial activity of the foreign state elsewhere and that act causes a direct effect in the United States;

Reading section 1605(a)(2) against the meager factual recitals in Sugarman's complaint, the district court concluded that none of the three clauses, had application:

Clauses one and two of § 1605(a)(2) cannot qualify as the exceptions upon which jurisdiction over Aeromexico is obtained. The action is not based on commercial activity, but rather a tortious [sic] act that did not take place in the United States. The first half of clause three of § 1605(a)(2) is met, but what of the final criterion of clause three—the act must cause a direct effect in the United States.

I conclude that causing injury to American citizens abroad is simply not a direct enough effect.

Opinion of July 19, 1979 at p. 3; reproduced in Appendix for Appellant, p. 36a.

II.

A.

We agree with the district court that clauses two and three of section 1605(a)(2) afford no basis for piercing the immunity which, prima facie, Aeromexico derives from its sovereign parent. And, if we felt confined by the recitals in the complaint, standing alone, we would acknowledge that the complaint does not provide very sturdy underpinning for a finding that Sugarman's claim is "based upon a commercial activity carried on in the United States," as called for by the first clause of section 1605(a)(2). To be sure, the first paragraph of the complaint alleges Aeromexico operations in New York which plainly constitute "commercial activity carried on in the United States," but the balance of the complaint leaves somewhat opaque the respects in which Sugarman's claim is allegedly "based upon" Aeromexico's operations in New York or any other state.

In any event, the complaint is not the only source of information which may be consulted in ruling on a motion for summary judgment. The record contains other information which tends to show a nexus between Sugarman's grievance and Aeromexico's "commercial activity carried on in the United States": The delayed flight from Acapulco—Aeromexico's flight No. 404—was bound for New York City. Flight 404 was Sugarman's "return trip"—i. e., the homeward portion of a round-trip flight from the United States to Mexico and return. Moreover, Sugarman's tickets were purchased at a travel agency in Eatontown, New Jersey. Accordingly, we conclude that Sugarman's claim was "based upon a commercial activity carried on [by Aeromexico] in the United States." 28 U.S.C. § 1605(a)(2) (clause 1). At a time when Aeromexico was conducting airline operations in the United States as a common carrier, Sugarman in his home state purchased Aeromexico tickets to Mexico and return. The events complained of were alleged to have transpired at the mid-point of the round-trip passage, and the claimed injury is said to have caused continuing suffering and economic loss to Sugarman after he got back home. The only way in which the first clause of 28 U.S.C. § 1605(a)(2) could be read not to comprehend Sugarman's claim against Aeromexico is to construe the phrase "in which the action is based upon a commercial activity carried on in the United States" to be a requirement that the particular misconduct complained of take place "in the United States." But so limiting a construction is belied by the very next clause, which excepts from immunity an action "based * * * upon an act performed in the United States in connection with a commercial activity of the foreign state elsewhere." When Congress intended to limit the acts subjected to liability to acts carried out (or, as in the third clause, having direct effects) in the United States, the statute makes that limitation clear. It is a limitation that would be expected—perhaps even required by due process considerations—when, as in the situations addressed in the second and third clauses, the underlying "commercial activity of the foreign state" takes place not in the United States but "elsewhere." Compare Upton v. Empire of Iran, 459 F.Supp. 264 (D.D.C.1978); Yessenin-Volpin v. Novosti Press Agency, 443 F.Supp. 849 (S.D.N.Y. 1978). It is a limitation not to be expected—and surely not required by due process considerations—when the acts complained of, although themselves extraterritorial, grow out of "a regular course of commercial conduct," 28 U.S.C. § 1603(d), which was "carried on in the United States." 28 U.S.C. § 1605(a)(2) (clause 1). See Outboard Marine Corp. v. Pezetel, 461 F.Supp. 384 (D.Del.1978).

B.

The construction of the Foreign Sovereign Immunities Act required by its syntax is confirmed by its legislative history. That legislative history began twenty-four years before the Act—in 1952, when the celebrated "Tate Letter" signalled a fundamental change in the official position of the United States on the venerable international law doctrine of sovereign immunity.

The Tate Letter takes its name from the official who dispatched it—Jack B. Tate, Acting Legal Adviser of the State Department. The Letter's addressee was Acting Attorney General Philip B. Perlman. The core of the letter was in the following paragraphs:

[The court quoted the pertinent paragraphs and supplied footnote 8, which appears below.]

The Foreign Sovereign Immunities Act was not a departure from the Tate Letter. The Act was a codification of the Letter, writing into statutory law the "principle [that] the immunity of a foreign state is 'restricted' to suits involving a foreign state's public acts (jure imperii) and does not extend to suits based on its commercial or private acts (jure gestionis)." H.Rep.No.94–1487, 94th Cong., 2nd Sess. (1976), 5 U.S.Code Cong. & Admin.News, p. 6605.

A principal purpose of [codification was] to transfer the determination of sovereign immunity from the executive branch to the judicial branch, thereby reducing the foreign policy implications of immunity determinations and assuring litigants that these often crucial decisions are made on purely legal grounds and under procedures that insure due process.

Id. 6606.

---

8. Dept. of State Bull. 984 (1952).

On June 10, 1980, during initial floor consideration by the members of the American Law Institute of the draft revised Restatement of the Foreign Relations Law of the United States, Monroe Leigh, Esq.—himself a former Legal Adviser of the State Department— expressed dubiety at Reporter Louis Henkin's view that the development of United States doctrines of international law owes less to the judiciary than to the executive. Mr. Leigh suggested that no Legal Adviser's exposition of international law was as consequential as Chief Justice Marshall's discussion of sovereign immunity in The Schooner Exchange vs. M'Faddon and Others, 7 Cranch 116, 3 L.Ed. 287 (1812). Professor Henkin responded that the Tate Letter was a doctrinal development of comparable magnitude.

Although Mr. Tate achieved some measure of doctrinal immortality because of the letter he wrote, it may fairly be said that his larger contribution to the law came later, after he left government service: For many years, until his untimely death, he served as Associate Dean and Professor of Law at Yale, befriending hundreds upon hundreds of law students whose subsequent careers bear the imprint of his mind and heart.

III.

We hold, pursuant to the Foreign Sovereign Immunities Act, that Aeromexico is not immune from suit in the court below for the wrongs allegedly suffered by passenger Sugarman in Acapulco Airport as he was awaiting his delayed homeward flight. In so holding, we intimate no view on what jurisdiction's substantive law should serve as the rule of decision with respect to any of the issues posed by this suit.

IV.

The judgment of the District Court will be reversed.

_____

YESSENIN–VOLPIN v. NOVOSTI PRESS AGENCY

United States District Court, S.D. New York, 1978.
443 F.Supp. 849.

TENNEY, District Judge.

Plaintiff Alexander S. Yessenin-Volpin, "a persistent defender of the civil and human liberties of the Russian people," Complaint ¶ 5, commenced this action in New York State Supreme Court seeking damages for libel against defendants Tass Agency (Tass), Novosti Press Agency ("Novosti") and The Daily World, a newspaper of the Communist Party of the United States. By petition filed February 9, 1977, Tass removed the action to this Court. Defendants Tass and Novosti now move for the dismissal of this action on the grounds: (1) that they are immune from the jurisdiction of this Court with respect to the acts alleged in the complaint under the Foreign Sovereign Immunities Act of 1976 ("Immunities Act"), 28 U.S.C. §§ 1602–11; (2) that the Court lacks personal jurisdiction over the defendants; and (3) that the complaint fails to state a cause of action against these defendants. For the reasons set forth below, the Court concludes that Tass and Novosti are entitled to claim sovereign immunity with respect to the claims against them in this action and that the case against them must therefore be dismissed for want of jurisdiction.

Immunities Act

The Immunities Act establishes a comprehensive procedure whereby a plaintiff may bring a foreign state or one of its political subdivisions, agencies or instrumentalities before an American court, either federal or state, obtain a ruling on the sovereign immunity of that entity, and, if immunity is found not to exist, secure an adjudication and satisfaction of its claims. The Act's central feature is its specification of categories of actions for which foreign states are not entitled to claim the sovereign immunity from American court jurisdiction otherwise granted to such states. These exceptions are contained not in the sections of the Act which describe the grounds on which jurisdiction may be obtained, however, but are phrased as substantive acts for which foreign states may be found liable by American courts. This effects an identity between substance and procedure in the Act which means that a court faced with a claim of immunity from jurisdiction must engage ultimately in a close examination of the underlying cause of action in order to decide whether the plaintiff may obtain jurisdiction over the defendant.

The Court's attention must first focus, however, on whether the entity sued may be classified as a "foreign state" within the meaning of 28 U.S.C. § 1603 and thus invoke in any set of circumstances the protection of the Immunities Act. In this case both Tass and Novosti have claimed such protection.

Status as a Foreign State

[The court found that both Tass and Novosti were foreign states within the meaning of the act.]

Immunity

The validity of a claim of immunity is predicated, as was discussed above, upon the Court's classification of the cause of action alleged: if it comes within one of the exceptions to immunity set out in 28 U.S.C. § 1605, then immunity is not appropriate and the action must proceed. In the instant action, the plaintiff has alleged four acts of libel, two against Novosti and two against Tass. Specifically, Novosti is charged in the first and second causes of action with having written articles which allegedly defamed the plaintiff and with having caused those articles to be published in February 1976 in two periodicals, Sowjetunion Heute and Krasnaya Zvezda, both of which are alleged to be distributed in the United States. Similarly, Tass is said to have written two allegedly defamatory articles and caused them to be published in June 1976 in two other publications, Izvestia and Sovietskaya Russiya, likewise alleged to be circulated to the public in the United States.

Two provisions of section 1605 could be construed to apply to these causes of action. The first, subsection (a)(5), was intended to cover noncommercial torts which were not covered by the other subsection, (a)(2). H.R.Rep.No.94–1487, 94th Cong., 2d Sess. 20–21, reprinted in [1976] U.S.Code Cong. & Admin.News pp. 6604, 6619 ("House Report"). Application of these provisions would be immediately fatal to the plaintiff's assertion of jurisdiction, however, for it specifically excludes (i. e., reinstates a grant of immunity for) "any claim arising out of * * * libel." 28 U.S.C. § 1605(a)(5)(B). Thus, immunity must be granted to Tass and Novosti unless the Court finds that the acts alleged are within the scope of subsection (a)(2).

That subsection states that a foreign state shall not be immune in any case

> in which the action is based upon a commercial activity carried on in the United States by the foreign state; or upon an

act performed in the United States in connection with a commercial activity of the foreign state elsewhere; or upon an act outside the territory of the United States in connection with a commercial activity of the foreign state elsewhere and that act causes a direct effect in the United States   *   *   *.

The plaintiff seems to rely on the third of these three possible bases of jurisdiction—an act committed outside the United States which has a direct effect inside the United States. Memorandum 8. Indeed, that provision seems to be the only relevant basis. With respect to the first possible ground, this action is not based on any commercial activity carried on *inside* the United States by Novosti or Tass since the allegedly offending articles were published outside the country and sent into the United States by means wholly outside the control of either Tass or Novosti. Similarly, the second ground is inapposite since the "acts" alleged—the writing and publication of the articles—were not performed in the United States. The language of the third provision seems to track that of the complaint: acts performed outside the United States (here, writing and publication of the articles) which caused a direct effect in the United States (e. g., injury to the good name and reputation of the plaintiff).

One essential requirement remains to be established however: the act must be "in connection with a commercial activity of the foreign state." 28 U.S.C. § 1605(a)(2). In attempting to demonstrate that this requirement has been fulfilled, the plaintiff cites section I(2) of the Novosti Statute, as exhaustively listing Novosti's commercial activies. Thus, the plaintiff's argument in this regard seems to be based on the unstated premise that an entity which engages in commercial activity is a commercial *entity* and thus is not entitled to claim sovereign immunity. The Immunities Act does not embody such a principle, however. Rather, it clearly contemplates that a given entity may at some time engage in commercial activities, on which it would not be immune, and at other times take actions "whose essential nature is public or governmental," on which it would be immune. See House Report 16. For example, a foreign government, otherwise clearly entitled to immunity, would lose that immunity with respect to its sale of a product to an American citizen. See id. Thus, the inquiry under subsection (a)(2) must focus on the specific activity at issue and determine whether it may be characterized as "commercial."

     *   *   *

There is no doubt that Novosti does engage in commercial activity. For example, it sells articles to foreign media. The relevant issue in this case, however, is not whether Novosti or Tass engage in commercial activities but whether their alleged libels were "in connection with a commercial activity." The Court concludes that they were not.

The four publications in which the alleged libels appeared are all publications of the U.S.S.R. itself. The masthead of Sowjetunion

Heute identifies its publisher as "Press Department of the Embassy of the U.S.S.R. [in West Germany] in collaboration with the press agency Nowosti." Popper Affidavit Exh. A (as translated). Krasnaya Zvezda is identified as the "Central Organ of the Ministry of Defense of the USSR." Id. Exh. B (as translated). Izvestia, somewhat better known in the West, is identified as the "Organ of the Soviets of Working People's Deputies," published by "The Presidium of the Supreme Soviet of the USSR." Id. Exh. C (as translated). Finally, Sovetskaya Rossiya (or Russiya) describes itself as the "Organ of the Central Committee of the Communist Party of the Soviet Union, The Supreme Soviet of the Russian Federative Socialist Republic [RSFSR] and the Council of Ministers of the RSFSR." Id. Exh. D (as translated). Thus, by collaborating in the publication of stories in these journals, Novosti, as well as Tass, was engaged not in "commercial activity" but in acts of intra-governmental cooperation of a type which apparently constitutes much of Novosti's (and presumably more of Tass's) activity. See Novosti Statute § I(2)(c). Such action was not in connection with a contract or other arrangement with a nongovernmental or foreign party, which activity would be found commercial under most circumstances. Rather, it was one instance of a cooperative arrangement with a governmental agency and thus cannot be characterized either as "a regular course of commercial conduct" or as "a particular commercial transaction or act." 28 U. S.C. § 1603(d).

Furthermore, the net result of this cooperative relationship was the publication of articles which, under the circumstances, must be regarded as official commentary of the Soviet government. Whether or not the Court admires the tone of such commentary, it cannot be gainsaid that it constitutes "an activity whose essential nature is public or governmental." To reach around the various organs of the Soviet government which actually published the alleged libels and subject to this Court's jurisdiction a news agency whose ownership by and identification with the Soviet state has been demonstrated, as in the case of Novosti, or admitted, as with Tass, would contravene the spirit of sovereign immunity as well as the letter of the Immunities Act.

The Court therefore concludes that Novosti and Tass are immune under the Immunities Act from this Court's jurisdiction on the claims alleged against them by the plaintiff in this action. Accordingly, the complaint is dismissed as against Novosti and Tass.

So ordered.

EAST EUROPE DOMESTIC INTERNATIONAL SALES CORP. v. TERRA

United States District Court, S.D. New York 1979.
467 F.Supp. 383.

IRVING BEN COOPER, District Judge.

In this action brought by a New York corporation against a Romanian trading company, jurisdiction is alleged under the Foreign Sovereign Immunities Act of 1976, Pub.L.No.94–583, 90 Stat. 2891 (1976), codified as 28 U.S.C. §§ 1330, 1601–1611 and amending 28 U.S.C. §§ 1391, 1441. Plaintiff seeks to recover compensatory and punitive damages allegedly caused by defendant's interference with a contract between plaintiff and a third-party and by defendant's alleged wrongful interference with plaintiff's trade and business.

Plaintiff has moved for partial summary judgment on the issue of liability, an expedited trial if summary judgment is denied and for permission to withdraw its demand for a jury trial since juries are forbidden under section 1330(a). Defendant, which initially appeared pro se, asked leave to file an amended answer and cross-moved for summary judgment on the grounds that this Court lacks jurisdiction in personam and, in the event that this Court has jurisdiction, that this dispute should be submitted to arbitration.

Plaintiff's motion to withdraw its jury demand heretofore has been granted. Mem.Dec. March 28, 1978. On June 20, 1978, we directed the parties to "delve further into the threshold issue of personal jurisdiction." We now find that this Court lacks personal jurisdiction over the defendant and order that plaintiff's complaint be dismissed.

Facts Relating to the Transaction at Issue

* * *

Plaintiff East Europe Domestic International Sales Corp. ("East Europe") is a "domestic international sales corporation" pursuant to the special provisions of section 992 et seq. of the Internal Revenue Code. It is a New York corporation and maintains its corporate headquarters and sole office in New York City.

On or about March 1, 1977, plaintiff entered into a contract with Vitrocim, a Romanian company, to purchase 20,000 metric tons ("mtons") of Portland cement at a price of $25.00/mton. The contract was negotiated by plaintiff's President, Robert Ross, while on a trip to Bucharest, Romania during the winter of 1977. As the date for delivery under the contract preceded the date of its execution, various changes in the contract were anticipated and needed. Plaintiff negotiated these changes with Vitrocim through the Office of the Economic Counselor of the Embassy of Romania in New York City and by telex communication. Vitrocim requested that the contract should be amended to include, inter alia, the requirement that a letter of credit "has to be received by Vitrocim not later than April 10,

1977," (Easter Sunday). * * * By telex of March 17th, East Europe accepted this amendment. * * *

Throughout March and early April, 1977, plaintiff asserts, the world price of cement was rising. By telex dated March 24, 1977, plaintiff had its first contact with Terra. The Telex reads:

Kind Att Mr. Robert Ross

We have been informed that you bought 20,000 mtons Romanian cement * * * from Messrs. Vitrocim, delivery in April 1977. We are ready to take over this quantity from you in same conditions as yours with Messrs Vitrocim at price of US Doll 26.-10/Mton.

Pls act very fast.

Regards Terra 2C

* * *

Plaintiff replied by return telex expressing its willingness to enter into a deal with Terra, at a price of $27.00/mton, provided that Terra established an irrevocable, confirmed and transferable letter of credit in favor of Vitrocim by March 28, 1977, the letter of credit to be confirmed by Vitrocim. Terra was required to pay plaintiff the $2.00/mton difference in price from the price under the Vitrocim contract by cabling $44,000.00 to a John Foster at Chase Manhattan Bank in New York City. Tlx Nr. 15536, id., Exh. 10.

After negotiating by telex over the next several days, plaintiff, Vitrocim and Terra agreed on a price of $26.25/mton, with 40 cents of plaintiff's $1.25 profit going to Vitrocim as commission. The three-way deal, however, ultimately fell through. Although Terra represented, on at least two separate occasions, that it had established a letter of credit in favor of Vitrocim, * * * and plaintiff repeatedly requested confirmation of this fact from Vitrocim, * * * Vitrocim failed to answer until April 7th.

On April 7th, Vitrocim responded to an East Europe telex sent on April 5th: " * * * we did not receive the Elcee [letter of credit] and we think we would not receive it as far as matters were still not clarified." * * * Plaintiff unsuccessfully protested to Vitrocim by return telex that it had waited since March 31st for confirmation of the opening of a letter of credit and asked for additional time to open one. * * * Plaintiff also telexed Terra, stating that it would hold Terra responsible for all damages "occurred by your failure to open your letter of credit as you had advised us you had done." * * *

On April 8th (Good Friday) Terra responded to plaintiff:

* * * Messrs Vitrocim Bucharest advised us that you requested from them 40,000 mtons cement instead of 20,000 mtons. Due this is not possible and you already engaged 20,000 mtons with another partner, and in order to avoid troubles with your

partner to whom you already sold cement, we renounce to this deal and on this line we already cancelled formalities for letter of credit in favor of Messrs. Vitrocim Bucharest

Regards

Terra 2C

* * * Plaintiff attempted to save the deal, but was unable to alter Terra's position. * * *

The April 8th telex from Terra was plaintiff's last contact with Terra until commencement of the instant litigation. Plaintiff and Vitrocim continued to trade telexes through April 13th but were unable to resolve their differences and their contract was cancelled.

On August 24, 1977, plaintiff filed its complaint naming Terra as the sole defendant. Plaintiff seeks compensatory and punitive damages primarily on the theory that Terra and Vitrocim conspired to thwart performance of plaintiff's contract to enable both companies to take advantage of the rising world price of cement. As we find that this Court lacks personal jurisdiction over Terra, we do not address ourselves to plaintiff's motion for summary judgment on the issue of liability.

Personal Jurisdiction Under the Foreign Sovereign Immunities Act of 1976

Plaintiff alleges that this Court has jurisdiction under the Foreign Sovereign Immunities Act of 1976 ("the Act"), effective January 19, 1977. Pub.L. No. 94–583, 90 Stat. 2891 (1976), 28 U.S.C. §§ 1330, 1601–1611 and amending 28 U.S.C. §§ 1391, 1441. The Act codifies the principle of "restrictive" sovereign immunity in that, under international law, foreign states are immune from suits based on their public acts, but not on their commercial or private acts. Prior to the Act, the decision on whether an action was public or commercial was made by the executive branch. The Act now specifically enumerates those actions which may be termed commercial and grants the United States District Courts original jurisdiction over disputes involving them. * * *

Section 1605(a)(2) explicitly applies to the case before us:

(a) A foreign state shall not be immune from the jurisdiction of courts of the United States or of the States in any case—

(2) in which the action is based upon a commercial activity carried on in the United States by the foreign state; or upon an act performed in the United States in connection with a commercial activity of the foreign state elsewhere; or upon an act outside the territory of the United States in connection with a commercial activity of the foreign state elsewhere and that act causes a direct effect in the United States.

A "foreign state" is defined to include "an agency or instrumentality of a foreign state." 28 U.S.C. § 1603(a). An "agency or instrumentality" includes "any entity" which:

> is an organ of a foreign state or political subdivision thereof, or a majority of whose shares or other ownership interest is owned by a foreign state or political subdivision thereof.

Id., § 1603(b)(2). Terra concedes that, for purposes of the Act, it is a foreign state. Def's Mem. of Law in Opposition to Plaintiff's Motion for Summary Judgment on the Issue of Liability, p. 3.

The Act is intended to be a longarm statute. Modelled after the District of Columbia long arm statute, it is designed to embody the "requirements of minimum jurisdictional contacts and adequate notice." H.R.Rep.No.94–1487 at p. 13, reprinted in [1976] U.S.Code Cong. & Adm.News at p. 6612, citing International Shoe Co. v. Washington, 326 U.S. 310, 66 S.Ct. 154, 90 L.Ed. 95 (1945) and McGee v. International Life Insurance Co., 355 U.S. 220, 223, 78 S.Ct. 199, 2 L.Ed.2d 223 (1957). Section 1605's itemization of non-immune transactions is a prescription of "the necessary contacts which must exist before our courts can exercise personal jurisdiction." H. R.Rep.No.94–1487 at p. 13. To find personal jurisdiction over Terra we must be satisfied that the due process requirements incorporated in section 1605(a)(2) have been met.

Terra's Contacts with the United States

Personal jurisdiction over Terra under section 1605(a)(2) will be present if we find that Terra either (1) conducts commercial activity in the United States; or (2) performed an act in the United States in connection with its commercial activity elsewhere or (3) acted outside the United States in connection with its commercial activity and that act caused a "direct effect in the United States."

Commercial activity is defined as a *"regular course of commercial conduct or a particular commercial transaction or act.* The commercial character of an activity shall be determined by reference to the nature of the course of conduct or particular transaction or act, rather than by reference to its purpose." 28 U.S.C. § 1603(d) [emphasis supplied]. "[C]ommercial activity carried on in the United States" means "commercial activity carried on by such state [the foreign state] and having *substantial contact* with the United States." Id. § 1603(e) [emphasis supplied].

We will deal with each of the three possible jurisdictional bases in turn.

1. Does Terra carry on commercial activity in the United States? Terra is a Romanian state-owned trading corporation. Its principal activities are export, import and re-export. Founded in 1970 on an experimental basis, Terra achieved permanent status in 1971. In examining Terra's activities in the United States since 1970, we must determine whether they are sufficiently "continuous and systematic" to satisfy the demands of due process. International

Shoe Co. v. Washington, 326 U.S. 310, 317–19, 66 S.Ct. 154, 90 L.Ed. 95 (1945).

Prior to the instant dispute, Terra had dealt with other companies in the United States, but only at arms-length and usually by telex. Nicolae Gheorghiu, a Department Chief of Terra, states that since Terra's inception its "sales to the United States accounted for less than 1% of Terra's total business with foreign nations." Reply Affidavit, dated April 28, 1978, ¶ 7. When questioned about the one percent figure, Dipl. Ing. Gr. Logafatu, Chief of Terra's Export, Import and Re-Exportation Department explained that the "percentage is too big * * *—the actual percentage is negligible. * * *" Deposition of Terra by Logafatu, Sept. 26, 1978, p. 13, lns. 20–22 ("Terra Dep.").

Apart from very few and scattered contacts, there is no evidence of systematic or continuous activity in the United States by Terra. The proof adduced by the parties shows that until August, 1977, when this suit was commenced, Terra had never: maintained an office in the United States; sent representatives or salesmen to the United States; entered into any contracts with United States companies either for the purchase or sale of goods; or engaged in any organized publicity in the United States.

We cannot find that Terra has "purposely availed itself of the privilege of conducting business in the United States." See Hanson v. Denckla, 357 U.S. 235, 253, 78 S.Ct. 1228, 1240, 2 L.Ed.2d 1283 (1958); International Shoe Co. v. Washington, supra.

2. Has Terra performed an act in the United States in connection with its commercial activity elsewhere? This portion of section 1605(a)(2) "looks to conduct of the foreign state in the United States which relates either to a regular course of commercial conduct elsewhere or to a particular commercial transaction concluded or carried out in part elsewhere." H.R.Rep.No.94–1487, p. 19, reprinted in [1976] U.S.Code Cong. & Admin.News at p. 6617. We find on the facts heretofore discussed that Terra has not performed an act in the United States in connection with its commercial activity abroad. We find no presence of Terra in the United States and, hence, no jurisdiction over Terra under this part of the clause.

3. Has Terra acted outside the United States in connection with its commercial activity and has that action caused a "direct effect in the United States"? This phrase in section 1605(a)(2) requires us to examine defendant's contacts with the United States in connection with the specific transaction at issue. Cases construing the District of Columbia long-arm statute, on which section 1605 is based, have held that negotiations without more are insufficient for an assertion of in personam jurisdiction. See, e. g., Textile Museum v. F. Eberstadt & Co., Inc., 440 F.Supp. 30 (D.D.C.1977), Bueno v. La Compania Peruana de Radio-Difusion, 375 A.2d 6 (D.C.Ct.App.1977). The court "should undertake an analysis of the quality and nature of an activity in relation to a forum state" to determine if the defendant

has "projected itself" into the United States. Textile Museum v. F. Eberstadt & Co., Inc., 440 F.Supp. at 32.

In a recent case decided under the Act, the Court of Appeals for the Second Circuit applied an "entering the marketplace" test in finding no personal jurisdiction over the country of Libya and a Libyan company. Carey v. National Oil Corporation, 592 F.2d 673 (2d Cir. 1979) (per curiam). The company had entered into a contract with a Bahamian subsidiary of a New York corporation for the delivery of oil. In an action by the parent company and an assignee of the bahamian subsidiary based on defendant's alleged failure to deliver the oil, the court found no "direct effect in the United States" under section 1605(a)(2). Even if the Libyan government was aware that the oil would be channeled into the United States, the court found insufficient "minimum contacts" and stated that "there was no real entering of the marketplace in the United States." At 676–677.

As has been described, the entire course of dealing between East Europe and Terra was by telex. It is undisputed that Terra initiated the transaction with its telex of March 24th. Had the deal materialized, Terra would have paid East Europe by cabling funds to Plaintiff's New York bank. The rest of the transaction is located in Romania. The cement was never supposed to leave Romania. Under plaintiff's contract with Vitrocim, the letter of credit to be established in favor of Vitrocim, was to be payable in Bucharest. Ross affidavit, Exh. 1. Plaintiff claims, however, that evidence of Terra's purposeful activity in the United States can be derived from other contacts which relate to the instant dispute.

In March, 1978, after this litigation had been commenced, Terra sent company representatives to the United States. Its dual goal, apparently, was to try to settle this matter and to obtain additional business. Terra emerged from the trip without a settlement, but with a contract with another American company, Amicale. Defendant represents that this trip was the first ever made by a Terra representative to the United States. The contract with Amicale was Terra's first with an American company. We decline to base personal jurisdiction on defendant's contacts with the United States after formal litigation over the instant dispute has been commenced and, in fact, after the instant motion for summary judgment was made. Cf. Lehigh Valley Industries, Inc. v. Birenbaum, 527 F.2d 87 (2d Cir. 1975) (Settlement negotiations cannot be the basis for jurisdiction where unrelated to the subject matter of the litigation or where they result in a release of claims between the parties. Settlement negotiations occurred prior to commencement of the action.)

Plaintiff claims that Terra was represented in New York by the Office of the Economic Counselor and that this principal-agent relationship was a sufficient contact for this Court to have in personam jurisdiction over defendant. Plaintiff claims that it negotiated with Terra and Vitrocim through the Economic Counselor's office. It is clear that plaintiff negotiated with Vitrocim through Mr. Sapotoru, the Assistant Economic Counselor. Once Terra became involved, Robert Ross, plaintiff's president, communicated with Sapotoru almost daily. Ross testified that he hoped Sapotoru would pressure Terra into further confirmation of its opening of the letter of credit. When the contract negotiations broke off, Ross complained about Terra to Sapotoru, Napolen Fodor, the Economic Counselor, as well as to the Romanian ambassador. Dep. of plaintiff, by Robert Ross, dated July 5, 1978.

Defendant refutes the agency theory by submitting a letter from Fodor, the Economic Counselor himself, denying any such representative capacity. Dated April 21, 1978, on Romanian Embassy stationery, and addressed to defendant's attorneys, Arutt, Nachamie & Benjamin P. C., it reads, in pertinent part:

> We hereby confirm what we have told you verbaly [sic] and namely that the activity of this Office is as per art. IX of the Agreement on Trade Relations between the Socialist Republic of Romania and the United States of America, signed in Bucharest on April 2, 1975 and ratified on August 3 the same year.

> In fact the activity of this Office and its members (including my assistant Mr. Constantin Sapotoru, you referred to) is to promote trade relation between Romanian and U.S. companies, to provide assistance to Romania and U.S. companies and economic organizations in carrying out their trade.

> As a consequence we are not participating directly in the negotiation, execution or fulfillment of any trade transactions. [sic]

As cited by defendant, Article IX, ¶ 2 states:

The governmental commercial offices, the members and the personnel of these offices, as far as they have been granted diplomatic immunity, will not participate directly in the negotiations, execution or fulfilling of the commercial transactions, or to do any other commercial acts. [sic]

Spizz, Affidavit in Opposition, dated April 21, 1978, ¶ 6. In addition, Terra denies ever asking the Office of the Economic Counselor to assist in the negotiations with East Europe. Terra Dep. p. 28.

While the activities of an agent may be attributed to the principal for jurisdictional purposes, * * * we do not find an agency relationship between the Office of the Economic Counselor and Terra. The Office of the Economic Counselor, at most, acted to facilitate the transaction. It was not Terra's authorized representative.

We find that Terra's sole contacts with the United States in the course of the transaction in dispute are the telexes which comprise the negotiations between it and plaintiff. Although Terra made the initial communication, we find that the March 24th telex does not constitute activity having a "direct effect" in the marketplace of the United States; it is an insufficient factor upon which to confer jurisdiction.

East Europe claims that its injury in tort consists of damages occasioned by Terra's interference with its trade or business. Had Terra not represented that it had established the letter of credit, plaintiff asserts, the contract with Vitrocim would have been performed and plaintiff would have sold the cement to another customer. The alleged tortious activity took place outside the United States. The purported injury took place in the United States only because the plaintiff is domiciled or doing business here. This, too, is an insufficient contact for due process purposes. See, Lehigh Valley Industries, Inc. v. Birenbaum, 527 F.2d 87, 94 (2d Cir. 1975) (construing the New York long-arm statute's section on jurisdiction when tortious activity occurs outside the state, CPLR § 302(a)(3), and finding no jurisdiction on this basis.)

Defendant has no other contacts with the United States besides negotiations. Plaintiff's reliance on National American Corporation v. Federal Republic of Nigeria, 448 F.Supp. 622 (S.D.N.Y.1978), is misplaced. The facts here do not include the formal letter of credit "having a New York beneficiary, advised by and payable through New York banks" which Judge Goettel found sufficient, in dicta, to satisfy the requirements of section 1605(a)(2). Id. at 639. Here we are forced to analyze a series of telexes relating to a transaction which, for one reason or another, was never consummated to decide if there is minimal contact with the United States sufficient to satisfy due process.

Disposition

For the foregoing reasons, plaintiff's motion for summary judgment to the extent not previously decided is denied. Defendant's cross-motion for summary judgment is granted. Plaintiff's complaint is dismissed.

Settle order on notice.

---

4. WAIVER OF THE IMMUNITY

IPITRADE INTERNATIONAL v. FEDERAL REPUBLIC OF NIGERIA

United States District Court, District of Columbia, 1978.
465 F.Supp. 824.

MEMORANDUM

On June 6, 1978, Petitioner Ipitrade International, S.A. (Ipitrade) filed a Petition to Confirm Arbitration Award under the provisions of the Convention on the Recognition and Enforcement of Foreign Arbitral Awards, 9 U.S.C. § 201 et seq. Jurisdiction against Respondent, the Federal Republic of Nigeria, is based upon the Foreign Sovereign Immunities Act, 28 U.S.C. § 1330(a), and venue lies in the District of Columbia under 9 U.S.C. § 204 and 28 U.S.C. § 1391(f)(4).

On March 17, 1975 Nigeria and Ipitrade entered into a written commercial contract for the purchase and sale of cement. By entering into the contract, Nigeria expressly agreed that the construction, validity, and performance of the contract would be governed by the laws of Switzerland and that any disputes arising under the contract would be submitted to arbitration by the International Chamber of Commerce, Paris, France. During 1975 and 1976 various disputes arose with respect to the contract and on May 12, 1976, Petitioner filed a demand for arbitration with the Secretariat of the Court of Arbitration of the International Chamber of Commerce. Thereafter, an arbitration proceeding was conducted in which the Federal Republic of Nigeria refused to participate, relying on the legal defense of sovereign immunity. The arbitrator, Dr. Max Brunner of Basel, Switzerland, found that under Swiss law Respondent was bound by the obligations it voluntarily entered into and proceeded with the arbitration. On April 25, 1978, the arbitrator issued his written decision (the Award), granting some of Petitioner's claims but rejecting others. Under Swiss law the Award of April 25, 1978 is final and binding on Respondent. Petitioner has made demand upon Respondent for payment pursuant to the terms of the Award but Respondent has not made such payment.

The Award is subject to the United Nations Convention on the Recognition and Enforcement of Foreign Arbitral Awards to which the United States, France, Nigeria, and Switzerland are each signatories. Article V of the Convention specifies the only grounds on which recognition and enforcement of a foreign arbitration award may be refused. 9 U.S.C. § 201. None of the enumerated grounds exists in the instant case. The Foreign Sovereign Immunities Act, which codifies existing law with respect to suits against foreign states in United States courts, gives federal district courts original jurisdiction against a foreign state as to "any claim for relief in personam with respect to which the foreign state is not entitled to immunity under sections 1605–1607 of this title or any applicable international agreement." 28 U.S.C. § 1330. The Act specifies that there is no immunity in any case "in which the foreign state has waived its immunity either explicitly or by implication, notwithstanding any withdrawal of the waiver which the foreign state may purport to effect except in accordance with the terms of the waiver." 28 U.S.C. § 1605(a)(1). The legislative history of this section expressly states that an agreement to arbitrate or to submit to the laws of another country constitutes an implicit waiver. H.Rep.No.94–1487, 94th Cong., 2d Sess., reprinted in [1976] U.S.Code Cong. & Admin.News, at 6604, 6617. Consequently, Respondent's agreement to adjudicate all disputes arising under the contract in accordance with Swiss law and by arbitration under International Chamber of Commerce Rules constitutes a waiver of sovereign immunity under the Act. This waiver cannot be revoked by a unilateral withdrawal.

Service of the Petition to Confirm Arbitration Award was made pursuant to the Foreign Sovereign Immunities Act, 28 U.S.C. §

1608(a), and by Order of this Court dated June 7, 1978. That Court Order fixed August 23, 1978 as the date by which Respondent was directed to appear, plead, answer or otherwise move with respect to the petition, or in default thereof, have the foreign arbitral award confirmed. There has been return receipt from the service on the Embassy of the Federal Republic of Nigeria, 2201 M Street, N.W., Washington, D. C., made pursuant to this Court's Order of June 7, 1978, but no return receipt from the service made upon the Honorable Commissioner of External Affairs, Federal Republic of Nigeria, Lagos, Nigeria. According to the affidavit of Carl F. Salans, filed with the Court, Respondent has actual notice of the pendency of this proceeding.

No judgment by default shall be entered by a federal district court against a foreign state unless the claimant establishes his right to relief by evidence satisfactory to the Court. 28 U.S.C. § 1608(e). In the instant case, Petitioner is entitled to such relief because the provisions of the Convention on the Recognition and Enforcement of Foreign Arbitral Awards and of the Foreign Sovereign Immunities Act are satisfied.

[The court ordered a judgment to be entered against the Federal Republic of Nigeria for the amounts claimed by the plaintiff.]

NATIONAL CITY BANK OF NEW YORK v. REPUBLIC OF CHINA

United States Supreme Court, 1955.
348 U.S. 356, 75 S.Ct. 423, 99 L.Ed. 389.

Mr. Justice FRANKFURTER delivered the opinion of the Court.

The Shanghai-Nanking Railway Administration, an official agency of respondent Republic of China, established a $200,000 deposit account in 1948 with the New York head office of petitioner National City Bank of New York. Subsequently, respondent sought to withdraw the funds, but petitioner refused to pay, and respondent brought suit in Federal District Court under 48 Stat. 184, as amended, 12 U.S.C.A. § 632.

In addition to various defenses, petitioner interposed two counterclaims seeking an affirmative judgment for $1,634,432 on defaulted Treasury Notes of respondent owned by petitioner. After a plea of sovereign immunity, the District Court dismissed the counterclaims, 108 F.Supp. 766, and entered judgment on them pursuant to Rule 54(b), Federal Rules of Civil Procedure. Petitioner appealed, and while the appeal was pending sought leave from the District Court to amend the counterclaims by denominating them setoffs and including additional data. The District Court denied leave. 14 F.R. D. 186. The Court of Appeals for the Second Circuit affirmed the dismissal and the denial on the ground that the counterclaims were not based on the subject matter of respondent's suit (whether they be treated as requests for affirmative relief or as setoffs) and, therefore, it would be an invasion of respondent's sovereign immunity for our courts to permit them to be pursued. 208 F.2d 627. Because of the importance of the question and its first appearance in this Court, we granted certiorari. 347 U.S. 951.

The status of the Republic of China in our courts is a matter for determination by the Executive and is outside the competence of this Court. Accordingly, we start with the fact that the Republic and its governmental agencies enjoy a foreign sovereign's immunities to the same extent as any other country duly recognized by the United States. See Guaranty Trust Co. v. United States, 304 U.S. 126, 137–138.

The freedom of a foreign sovereign from being haled into court as a defendant has impressive title-deeds. Very early in our history this immunity was recognized, De Moitez v. The South Carolina, Bee 422, 17 Fed.Cas. 574, No. 9,697 (Admiralty Court of Pa., 1781, Francis Hopkinson, J.), and it has since become part of the fabric of our law. It has become such solely through adjudications of this Court. Unlike the special position accorded our States as party defendants by the Eleventh Amendment, the privileged position of a foreign state is not an explicit command of the Constitution. It rests on considerations of policy given legal sanction by this Court. *   *   *

*   *   *

And so we come to the immediate situation before us. The short of the matter is that we are not dealing with an attempt to bring a recognized foreign government into one of our courts as a defendant and subject it to the rule of law to which nongovernmental obligors must bow. We have a foreign government invoking our law but resisting a claim against it which fairly would curtail its recovery. It wants our law, like any other litigant, but its wants our law free from the claims of justice. *   *   * As expounded in The Schooner Exchange, the doctrine is one of implied consent by the territorial sovereign to exempt the foreign sovereign from its "exclusive and absolute" jurisdiction, the implication deriving from standards of public morality, fair dealing, reciprocal self-interest, and respect for the "power and dignity" of the foreign sovereign.

*   *   *

(c) Respondent urges that fiscal management falls within the category of immune operations of a foreign government as defined by the State Department's 1952 pronouncement. This is not to be denied, but it is beside the point. A sovereign has freely come as a suitor into our courts; our State Department neither has been asked nor has it given the slightest intimation that in its judgment allowance of counterclaims in such a situation would embarrass friendly relations with the Republic of China.

(d) It is recognized that a counterclaim based on the subject matter of a sovereign's suit is allowed to cut into the doctrine of immunity. This is proof positive that the doctrine is not absolute, and that considerations of fair play must be taken into account in its application. But the limitation of "based on the subject matter" is too indeterminate, indeed too capricious, to mark the bounds of the limitations on the doctrine of sovereign immunity. There is great diversity among courts on what is and what is not a claim "based on the subject matter of the suit" or "growing out of the same transaction." * * * No doubt the present counterclaims cannot fairly be deemed to be related to the Railway Agency's deposit of funds except insofar as the transactions between the Republic of China and the petitioner may be regarded as aspects of a continuous business relationship. The point is that the ultimate thrust of the consideration of fair dealing which allows a setoff or counterclaim based on the same subject matter reaches the present situation. The considerations found controlling in The Schooner Exchange are not here present, and no consent to immunity can properly be implied. * * *

The judgment of the Court of Appeals must be reversed and the case remanded to the District Court with directions to reinstate the counterclaims and for further proceedings not inconsistent with this opinion.

Reversed.

[Mr. Justice Douglas did not participate in the consideration or decision of the case. Dissenting opinions omitted.]

Foreign Sovereign Immunities Act of 1976. Section 1607 deals with counterclaims; paragraph (c) of the section incorporates the rule in this case. See the Documentary Supplement.

SECTION B. IMMUNITY OF THE PROPERTY OF THE STATE

---

1. PROCEEDINGS INVOLVING INTERESTS OF THE STATE IN PROPERTY

THE GOVERNMENT OF ADEN AND THE GOVERNMENT OF THE FEDERATION OF SOUTH ARABIA v. THE EAST AFRICAN CURRENCY BOARD AND THE WESTMINSTER BANK LIMITED

England, High Court of Justice, Chancery Division, 1967.
43 Int'l L.Rep. 154 (1971).*

[The East African Currency Board consisted of the Permanent Secretary to the Treasury of the Republic of Kenya, the Secretary of the Treasury of the Republic of Uganda, the Governor of the Bank of

---

* The text of the decision was not published in the English reports. Reprinted by permission of E. Lauter- pacht, ed., and Grotius Publications, Ltd., Cambridge, England.

Tanzania and the Financial Secretary of the Government of Aden, plus a Chairman and Technical Member appointed by the four governments. The function of the board was to control the East African currency circulating in the states concerned by exchanging it against sterling and vice versa. When these states became independent and introduced their own currencies, the board's operations consisted mostly of withdrawing its own currency against payment in the new currencies and of managing its assets, some 30 million pounds sterling held largely in the United Kingdom.

The board having proposed to distribute surplus income to the constituent states, the Government of Aden objected and with South Arabia sought to restrain the Westminster bank from parting with assets of the board until disputes over the proper percentage of the distributions could be settled. The Governments of Kenya, Uganda and Tanzania applied for a stay of the proceedings on the ground that they were directed against foreign sovereigns entitled to immunity in the English courts.

A portion of the opinion appears below.]

In this matter, in which I intend to deliver an extempore judgment now, primarily for the benefit of learned Counsel, Mr. Stable initially moves to continue an injunction granted on 16 August ex parte to restrain the Westminster Bank, the second defendants, and the East African Currency Board, the first defendants, from— * * *—dealing with the assets held by the Westminster Bank to the order of the East African Currency Board.

     * * *

The main point, as I have already indicated, is contained in the second part of the application made by Mr. MacCrindle. That is that the

> Writ of Summons in this action be set aside, or alternatively that all further proceedings in this action be stayed on the following grounds or one or other of them, that is to say: (*a*) That the said action impleads the said Republics and each of them being Sovereign States and not subject to the jurisdiction of this Court. (*b*) That the said action relates to and seeks to enforce an international agreement made between the plaintiffs or one or other of them and the said Republics and each of them such agreement not being subject to the jurisdiction of or enforceable in this Court, and (*c*) that the said action and the relief sought therein relates to the property or an interest in property of the said Republics and each of them being Sovereign States.

     * * *

[Mr. MacCrindle] says that the East African Currency Board is simply an agent of the four Governments whose currency it now deals with or did in the past deal with. He says further that it is on that basis not a matter which a municipal Court of this country should entertain for this reason. He says that the Board, acting as agents of the Governments concerned, is dealing with money which is the property of the constituent Governments, and he says that if the Board is dealing simply as an agent in their States with that money, then that money is property under the control of the Sovereign States, and accordingly not the subject of an action in these Courts.

In support of that argument he cites various cases. The first case was the Dollfus Mieg case, reported in 1952 Appeal Cases at p. 582. The headnote reads as follows:

> The Bank of England held, as bailee for the Governments of the United States, France and the United Kingdom, 64 numbered gold bars claimed to be the property of a French company. The bars had been wrongfully seized by the German authorities during the Second World War and taken to Germany. After their recovery by Allied forces they were lodged with the Bank by the Governments for safe custody pending their ultimate disposal. The Bank sold 13 of the bars by mistake, retaining 51. The company brought an action against the Bank claiming delivery of the bars, an injunction restraining the Bank from parting with possession of them, and, alternatively, damages:—Held, (1) that the action must be allowed to proceed as regarded the 13 bars, since the Bank had by its own act terminated the bailment, but (2) that the action must be stayed as regarded the remaining bars since the doctrine of the immunity of a foreign soverign applied to the case of a claim to recover property in the hands of a bailee for a foreign sovereign, and, further, there was no jurisdiction to order the bailee to pay damages for conversion, since the bailee would thereby acquire the title to the property so as to be able to set it up against the bailor, the foreign sovereign.

That case is applicable to the circumstances of the present case, with one important distinction, because there the House was concerned with an action concerning physical objects, namely gold bars in the hands of a third party. But in the present case, as I have indicated, the matters we are concerned with here are funds held by the second defendants, the Westminster Bank, in the name of the East African Currency Board, and are consequently choses in action rather than choses in possession like gold bars. In order to cover that point, the case of Rahimtoola v. Nizam of Hyderabad was cited to me. That case was reported in [1958] A.C. at p. 379. The facts from the headnote were these:

> In 1948, when Indian troops were invading Hyderabad, money standing in the account of the Nizam and his Government at an English bank was transferred without authority by M. (one of the persons entitled to operate the account) into the name of R. (then High Commissioner for Pakistan in the United Kingdom), who received it on the instructions of the Foreign Minister of Pakistan. The Nizam and his Government brought an action against R. and the bank, claiming the money as money had and received to their use. R. asked that the writ in the action be set aside as against him and that the proceedings be

stayed as against the bank on the ground that the action sought
to implead a foreign sovereign, Pakistan, or sought to interfere
with the right or interest of the Government of Pakistan in the
money. It was conceded that R. had not established any equitable title to the money and the claim to immunity was based on
the fact that the legal title to the debt was vested in him as High
Commissioner for Pakistan:—Held, that the writs should be set
aside against R. and the proceedings stayed against the bank
notwithstanding that the money was paid to R. wrongfully or by
a mistake of fact, for R. was the agent of the Sovereign State of
Pakistan which had the legal title to the subject-matter of the action and the right to sue the bank for it.

On p. 402 in the Opinion of Lord Reid the following passage occurs:

> The point at issue in this case, he says, can now be stated in
> a simple form. The State of Pakistan has a right to sue the re-
> spondent bank but Pakistan claims no beneficial right to the
> money owed by the bank. Does that entitle Pakistan to have this
> action stayed (1) in so far as it is directed against the appellant,
> and (2) in so far as it is directed against the respondent bank?
> I do not see any reason why the right of that state to claim sov-
> ereign immunity should depend on whether the bank account
> stands in the name of the State itself or stands in the name of its
> servant, agent or nominee. It was not disputed that, if the bank
> account had stood in the name of the State itself, the State could
> not have been made a party to this action against its will. It ap-
> pears to me to follow that the State is entitled to object to its
> agent being made a party; the agent would merely be defending
> the action on behalf of his principal. I am therefore of opinion
> that the action must be stayed in so far as it is directed against
> the appellant, and I proceed to consider whether it can continue
> against the bank alone.

* * *

Bearing in mind that this is an interlocutory application, and
moreover an interlocutory application made in the vacation, those are
nevertheless the principles by which I must endeavour to be guided.

The matter is set out in Dicey and Morris on The Conflict of
Laws (Eighth Edition), at p. 123 and following, in this way:

> Subject to the exception hereinafter mentioned, and to cer-
> tain other qualifications, the court has no jurisdiction to enter-
> tain an action or other proceeding against: (1) any foreign
> State or the head or Government or any department of the Gov-
> ernment of any foreign State.

The exception which is relevant to this particular circumstance
is to be found on p. 128 and reads as follows:

> The Court of Chancery has in a number of unreported cases
> distributed a trust fund among the beneficiaries, even though a

foreign sovereign may have been entitled to an interest therein. And on the same principle, the Chancery Division of the High Court will not refuse to make an order for the winding up of a company, even though a foreign sovereign may be interested in any surplus assets.

The upshot of that passage from The Conflict of Laws and from the two cases from which I have cited extracts, seems to be this: if the Board was acting as the agent of the foreign Sovereign States, then this Court should not allow the action to proceed. If, on the other hand, the function of the Board was to act as trustee of the funds in its hands or in the hands of the Westminster Bank in its name, then the action should be allowed to proceed. It seems to me that this is a circumstance which really does not fall happily either in the category of agency or in the category of trusteeship. What exactly it is I do not propose to inquire. But the overriding rule seems to me to be this, that in general the Courts of this country will not entertain actions the subject matter of which is the property of a foreign Sovereign State, and in order to take the case out of that category the person seeking so to do must show, at least for the purposes of this interlocutory application, a prima facie case of trusteeship.

In order to examine that matter, one has to look at the Regulations with which I have been supplied, because apparently there have been numbers of Amendments to them, Regulations which deal with the powers and duties, and define the constitution of the East African Currency Board. Those are exhibited to an Affidavit of Mr. Ockba, who is Secretary of Finance of the Government of Aden. They are the Regulations of 1955 and 1961. * * *

           *   *   *

The importance of those Regulations is obvious. The Secretary of State, in so far as the Independent Territories are concerned, has now been replaced by the governments of the Independent Territories; accordingly if the board at the stage when these regulations were made, or more accurately when it was originally set up, was acting as agent of the Secretary of State, then it would now be acting as the agent of the Independent Territories, and consequently, if that were to be the case, it would be administering these funds as agent, and accordingly they would be the funds of the Independent Governments and would be caught by the Rule of Law that these Courts will not entertain actions in respect of such funds.

Sir John Hobson, on behalf of the Westminster Bank Limited, submits that that series of Regulations is totally inconsistent with agency. In his argument he suggests that it is wholly inconsistent with any concept of agency that the words in, for example, paragraph 19 should be found. Those words are:

> The Board may with the approval of the Secretary of State, pay any sum which it thinks proper out of its income by way of contribution to the revenues of the Constituent Territories.

Sir John said that had this been agency, such a provision would have been quite unnecessary, and indeed out of place, because the principal would have had power to direct his agent to do what he liked, and such power to direct would have been contained in this instrument.

The answer to that argument put forward by Mr. MacCrindle on behalf of the Independent Republics is this: that it was quite unnecessary for the Secretary of State to set out expressly what his powers were. These Regulations were simply permissive Regulations showing what the Board was entitled to do. He says that that state of affairs is well illustrated by the fact that the Board was at one stage dismissed by the Secretary of State, and that a new Board was appointed. Such a circumstance, he says with some force, is only consistent with an agency; it is not only consistent with an agency but it is entirely inconsistent with the idea of this Board being set up as trustees. Had that been the case, he says, it would have been quite impossible for the person setting up the Board, summarily to dismiss the trustees and to appoint new ones.

The upshot of the matter is this: in my judgment the arguments of Mr. MacCrindle are correct. There is no basis here to suggest in my view that a trusteeship such as is suggested by Sir John on behalf of the Bank existed; indeed, from what I have said and from the authorities which I have read, and more particularly from the history of this Board and the Regulations under which it was set up, it is clear to me that no trusteeship ever existed. Whether what did exist was an agency or something else does not seem to me to matter, because trusteeship is the only way that this affair can properly be dealt with by the Court.

* * *

[The court stayed the action.]

LIMBIN HTEIK TIN LAT v. UNION OF BURMA

Japan, District Court of Tokyo, 1954.
32 Int'l L.Rep. 124.*

* * * The claimant filed with the Court an application for provisional disposition to determine the provisional status of a piece of land to which he claimed title. The land in question, situated next to the premises of the Burmese Consulate-General in Tokyo, was actually purchased in 1944 by A. (third party in the present case), father-in-law of the claimant and the then Burmese Ambassador to Japan. The claimant purchased the land in question in 1953 from the wife and daughter of A., who were his joint legal successors under Burmese law. He came to Japan, obtained delivery of the land then in the possession of the administrator, and completed the registration of the transfer on the ground of purchase.

The respondent, the Government of the Union of Burma, was of the view that the purchase of the land in question was made by A. in his capacity as agent of the respondent, so that the title to the land belonged to the latter. The respondent sought a provisional disposition for striking out of the registration, which the Court granted. The claimant thereupon filed with the Court the present application for provisional disposition in order to prevent disturbance to his title and possession of the land.

The point at issue before the Court was whether a Japanese court had jurisdiction in a case in which the respondent was a foreign State. [A portion of the opinion of the court appears below.]

A State is not subject to the exercise of power by another State, and therefore is not subject to the jurisdiction of another State in the matter of civil proceedings. This is to be admitted as a principle of international law recognised in general. * * * However, it need hardly be added that in cases where a foreign State has consented by agreement to submit to the jurisdiction of another State, or where a State has waived as against another State its privilege, based on this principle, to submit to the jurisdiction of the latter, a foreign State may be subject to the jurisdiction of another State. Again, in an action concerning immovables, it is widely admitted that jurisdiction belongs exclusively to the State of the situs, and consequently it must be said that a foreign State may be subject to the jurisdiction of another State.

* * * [T]here is no denying the fact that an immovable is an object par excellence of territorial sovereignty of the State of its situs * * *; hence it has come to be recognised for a long time that an action directly concerning immovables comes within the exclusive jurisdiction of the State of the situs. It has to be admitted, therefore, that, judging from its motive and its history, this principle has been recognised as applicable in actions in which a foreign State is a party, as well as where a private person is a party.

Accordingly * * * it has to be concluded that Japan has jurisdiction and the present Court has competence, over the present proceedings in which the Union of Burma is designated as respondent.

* * *

_____

1. *Interests in immovables and estates.* As the case indicates, it is law of old standing that the immunity does not extend to actions for the determination of an interest in immovable—or real—property. It was so held as early as 1882. Ziemer v. Rumanian State, Germany, Court of Conflicts of Berlin, 26 Am.J.Int'l L. 588 (1932).

The U.S. Foreign Sovereign Immunities Act of 1976 provides for this exception to immunity in Section 1605(a)(4). See the Documentary Supplement. The European Convention on State Immunity provides for it in Article 9, 66 Am.J.Int'l L. 923, 926 (1972).

Those provisions also specify that the immunity does not extend to cases in which the state has an interest in an estate locally administered.

2. *Problem.* In Mahe v. Agent Judiciaire du Trésor Français, Madagascar (Malagasy Republic), Court of Appeal, 1965, 40 Int'l L. Rep. 80 (1970), the French Permanent Mission of Aid and Cooperation built a parking lot next to the house of the Chief of Mission which widely encroached on the property of the plaintiff. He sued for the value of the land and damages and was denied recovery apparently on the ground, inter alia, of diplomatic immunity.

Suppose the court involved still applied the absolute theory of immunity and the owner was not a diplomat. Would the result be different? Should the plaintiff select a different remedy?

---

2. EXTENT OF IMMUNITY OF STATE PROPERTY FROM ATTACHMENT OR EXECUTION

WEILAMANN v. CHASE MANHATTAN BANK

United States, New York Supreme Court, 1959.
21 Misc.2d 1086, 192 N.Y.S.2d 469.

[An action in aid of a warrant of attachment was issued against property of the USSR (accounts in defendant bank). The USSR made a claim, through the United States Department of State, that its property in the bank was immune from seizure under the warrant of attachment. A portion of the Court's opinion appears below.]

  *   *   *

  *   *   *   The Department of State has recognized this claim of the USSR; and, through the U. S. Attorney for Southern District of New York, has filed in this action a suggestion of interest of the United States to the effect that property of the USSR in the United States is immune "from execution or other action analogous to execution" and that, "this court should proceed forthwith to release any property of the State of the Union of Soviet Socialist Republics hitherto attached in this proceeding and to deny any pending motion for execution or action analogous to execution."

  *   *   *

It is true that the suggestion of interest indicating the position of the Department of State would not deprive this court of determining any question left open by such Department for decision by this court.   *   *   *   In this connection, the plaintiffs contend that the Department of State has heretofore recognized a distinction between "immunity from jurisdiction" and "immunity from execution"; that, consequently, it has been its position not to extend the doctrine of immunity so as to bar an attachment of property of a foreign nation for purpose of obtaining jurisdiction, but that its policy was merely directed to opposing the execution of a judgment against the property of a foreign nation. In this connection, the plaintiffs point out that the suggestion of interest filed herein is stated to be based upon a position of the State Department that the property of the USSR should be "immune from execution or other action analogous to execution." Thus, the plaintiffs argue that this court should retain jurisdiction to determine whether or not this action is to be regarded as a proceeding looking toward the execution of a judgment in favor of the plaintiff Weilamann. In this connection, the plaintiffs contend that this action, being one in aid of an attachment, is merely a step in the court toward the perfecting of the attachment for the purpose of vesting the court with jurisdiction, and, therefore, may not be said to constitute action looking toward the execution of a judgment against the USSR.

Now, it does appear that the former action of the plaintiff Weilamann against the USSR, on default of appearance of the latter, has proceeded to judgment in plaintiff's favor for the sum of $77,154.66. Under these circumstances, a recovery by the said plaintiff and the sheriff in the action now brought by them in aid of the attachment would result in the application of the funds from the attached bank accounts to the satisfaction of the judgment. See, Civil Practice Act, § 943 and § 922, subd. 3. Thus, the proceeding with this action here is, in effect, the taking of action for the purpose of the execution of a judgment.

In any event, it is clear that we should not be concerned here with classifying this particular action for the purpose of determining whether or not, technically speaking, under the law of this state, it is in the nature of "action analogous to execution on the property" of the USSR. We are to be concerned solely with the position which is taken by the State Department; and its position with respect to the immunity of the particular bank accounts must be honored by this court. The court may not proceed contrary thereto in this or any similar case and thereby jeopardize international relations. Here, the State Department's position, as indicated by the suggestion of interest and the letter of March 9, 1959, is clearly to the effect that this court should deny to plaintiffs the relief sought in this action.

The complaint is dismissed without costs. * * *

RESTATEMENT OF THE FOREIGN RELATIONS LAW OF THE UNITED STATES

Reporters' Notes to Section 69 (1965).*

2. *Immunity from execution.*

* * *

The view indicated by the State Department in the Weilamann case, that execution by levy upon the attached property is precluded by international law, appears to be inconsistent with the views expressed in a number of cases in foreign states. In these states, a distinction is made between property of the state connected with its public acts (or political acts or acts jure imperii) and its private acts (or acts of a civil nature or acts jure gestionis, which include commercial acts). Property of the state connected with its public acts is entitled to immunity from execution. Property of the state connected with its private acts is not.

Cases supporting execution upon property of a state that is connected with its private acts include: Soviet Distillery in Austria Case, Administrative Court, Austria, Jan. 13, 1954, 9 VwGH (F) 5 (1954), 83 Clunet 86 (1956), [1954] Int'l L.Rep. 101; Socobelge v. Greek State, Civil Tribunal of Brussels, Belgium, April 30, 1951, 79 Clunet 244, [1951] Int'l L.Rep. 3 (No. 2), 47 Am.J.Int'l L. 508 (1953); Decision of the Supreme Court, Czechoslovakia, Decision No. R.I. 305/28, May 8, 1928, 64 Clunet 394 (1937), 26 Am.J.Int'l L.Supp. 585 (1932); Jacovidis v. Monopoly of Tobacco in Turkey, Court of Appeals (M.C.), Egypt, Jan. 22, 1930, 42 Bulletin de Legislation et de Jurisprudence Egyptiennes 212 (1929–1930); Egyptian Delta Rice Mills Co. v. Comisaria General de Abastecimientos y Transportes de Madrid, Commercial Tribunal of Alexandria (M.C.), Egypt, March 29, 1943, 55 Bulletin de Legislation et de Jurisprudence Egyptiennes 114 (1942–1943), [1943–1945] Ann.Dig. 103 (No. 27); Procureur Général près la Cour de Cassation v. Vestwig, Cour de Cassation, France, Feb. 5, 1946, [1947] Sirey I. 137, 73–76 Clunet 1 (1946–1949), [1946] Ann.Dig. 78 (No. 32); State of Yugoslavia v. S. A. Sogerfin, Supreme Court, Switzerland, Oct. 7, 1938, [1939] S.J. 327; U. A. R. v. Dame X., Supreme Court, Switzerland, Feb. 10, 1960, 55 Am.J.Int'l L. 167 (1961), 88 Clunet 459 (1961); see also Kingdom of Greece v. Banque Julius Bar, Tribunal Federal, Switzerland, June 6, 1956, 82 R.O. 75 (1956).

It does not appear that states whose property involved with private acts has been executed upon have as a rule protested against the execution as being a violation of international law. See Lauterpacht, The Problem of Jurisdictional Immunities of Foreign States, 28 Brit. Yb.Int'l L. 220, 242–243 (1951). From an examination of the cases in point, a number of writers have concluded that there is no rule of international law prohibiting execution upon property of a state connected with its private acts. See Lalive, L'Immunité de Juridiction des Etats et des Organisations Internationales, 84 Rec. des Cours, 205, 274–75 (1953); Garcia Mora, Sovereign Immunity of Foreign States and its Recent Modifications, 42 Va.L.Rev. 335, 359 (1956); Sorensen, Principes de Droit International Public, 101 Rec. des Cours 1, 172 (1960).

In certain situations the United States approves the subjecting to execution of state-owned property that is connected with its commercial activities. Indications to this effect are to be found in international agreements to which it is a party. Between 1948 and 1958, the United States concluded treaties with fourteen states, each of which provides that state enterprises engaged in business activities in the territory of the other cannot claim immunity from execution upon their property. See, for example, Article XVIII(3) of the Treaty of Friendship, Commerce and Navigation with Israel of August 23, 1951, [1954] 1 U.S.T. & O.I.A. 550, T.I.A.S. No. 2948, 219 U.N.T.S. 237. The United States has also ratified the Convention on the Territorial Sea and the Contiguous Zone of April 27, 1958, and under Article 21 of the Convention, measures of enforcement may be taken against government vessels operated for commercial purposes while they are exercising the right of innocent passage, to the same extent that they may be taken against private vessels. U.N.Doc.A/Conf. 13/L.38, 38 Dep't State Bull. 1111 (1958), 52 Am.J.Int'l L. 834 (1958).

JET LINE SERVICES, INC. v. M/V MARSA EL HARIGA

United States District Court, District of Maryland, 1978.
1979 A.M.C. 543*

JOSEPH H. YOUNG, District Judge.

I. The Facts

On January 17, 1978, Jet Line Services, Inc. ("Jet Line") intervened in a pending in rem action before this Court, Promet Marine Services Corp. v. Elrakwa, Civil No. Y–78–62, to recover $11,283.29 for services rendered from October 8 to October 10, 1977 in connection with the cleanup of an oil spill from the M/V Elrakwa. Also, on or about January 17, 1978, Jet Line filed its own complaint in this Court against the M/V Elrakwa in rem. This suit was for breach of contract arising out of the alleged failure to pay for the services rendered the M/V Elrakwa in August, 1977. Subsequently, the claims by Promet and Jet Line against the M/V Elrakwa were settled, and, accordingly, the arrest of the M/V Elrakwa in Civil Action No. Y–78–62 was released and that case is now moot.

On or about January 17, 1978, Jet Line filed a suit in this Court against the M/V Marsa el Hariga, in rem, and National Oil Company of Libya, erroneously referred to in the Complaint as the alleged

---

* At a crucial point, the text of the opinion in the Federal Supplement is ambiguous, if not misleading. The text in American Maritime Cases does not present any problem and, for that reason, was chosen by the editors.

owner of the M/V Marsa el Hariga. The Complaint sought to recover $91,310.00 for services allegedly performed with regard to the discharge of the M/V Marsa el Hariga in Sandwich, Massachusetts in August, 1977. When the suit was instituted, Jet Line prayed that the M/V Elrakwa, which was still present within the District of Maryland and under arrest by virtue of the previous suit, Civil Action No. Y–78–62, be attached by issuance of process of maritime attachment and garnishment against the defendant, National Oil Company of Libya, and that the interest of the National Oil Company of Libya in the M/V Elrakwa be attached. Accordingly, the United States Marshal attached the M/V Elrakwa.

Upon discovering that the National Oil Company of Libya did not in fact own the M/V Elrakwa, plaintiff moved to amend its complaint to name the General National Maritime Transportation Company ("GNMTC") as the proper owner of the M/V Elrakwa. This motion was granted by Judge Harvey on January 19, 1978.

Shortly after the attachment of the M/V Elrakwa by the Marshal, defendant GNMTC, through special appearance before this Court, moved to vacate the attachment of the vessel on the grounds that it is a corporation organized and created under the laws of The Socialist People's Libyan Arab Jamahiriya ("Libya"), and, under the Foreign Sovereign Immunities Act, 28 U.S.C. §§ 1330, 1332, 1602–1611 (the "Immunities Act"), any arrest or attachment of the vessel was improper and void. Attached to the original motion to vacate was the statement of Shaban F. Gashut, Chargé d'Affaires of the Libyan Embassy in Washington, D.C., to the effect that GNMTC was a corporation organized under the laws of the Libyan government and has owned the M/V Elrakwa and M/V Marsa el Hariga continuously from 1977 to the present.

On January 20, 1978, Judge Harvey conducted a hearing on the motion to vacate, at which time he denied the motion because, inter alia, Mr. Gashut's statement was not in proper affidavit form, lacked proper authentication, and did not specifically state that GNMTC was an "organ" of the Libyan government. Judge Harvey also ruled that the motion could be renewed once these deficiencies were cured.

On May 15, 1978, GNMTC, appearing specially before this Court in accordance with Rule E(8) of the Supplemental Rules of Federal Civil Procedure for Certain Admiralty and Maritime Claims, moved this Court to vacate and release the security posted pursuant to the Immunities Act, supra. The M/V Elrakwa had already been released from attachment on the basis of a Letter of Undertaking to Jet Line signed by The West of England Ship Owners Mutual Protection and Indemnity Association (Luxembourg) ("West of England"), defendant's indemnitor, in which West of England agreed to appear on behalf of the owner of the M/V Elrakwa in connection with this case and to pay and satisfy any final judgment entered in favor of Jet Line up to and not exceeding $102,600.00. GNMTC also advanced a separate ground for contesting the arrest and attachment, namely, that the procedure was defective and void in that it violated the due process clause of the Fifth Amendment and was not in accord with recent decisions of the U. S. Supreme Court dealing with prejudgment arrest and attachment of property. To support its claim of immunity under the Immunities Act, GNMTC again submitted a statement from Mr. Shaban F. Gashut certifying and attesting to the effect that GNMTC: (1) is an entity of the Socialist People's Libyan Arab Jamahiriya, (2) is a corporation organized and created under the laws of Libya, is a separate legal person, and has offices located in Tripoli, (3) is an "organ" of Libya's government, (4) is not a citizen of the United States and was not created under the laws of any third country, and (5) is the sole owner of the M/V Elrakwa and M/V Marsa el Hariga, and owned said vessels continuously during 1977 and up to the present. Accompanying this statement were certified statements from Stuart W. Rockwell, Deputy Chief of Protocol at the Department of State, indicating that Mr. Gashut's signature on his statement is, to the best of his knowledge, the same signature appearing on the official form submitted by the Libyan Embassy notifying the State Department of his appointment as a foreign diplomatic officer. Mr. Rockwell also stated that according to official State Department records, Mr. Gashut has been duly notified to the Department of State since September 25, 1975, as Counselor, Chargé d'Affaires ad interim at the Libyan Embassy, and in that capacity he acts provisionally as head of the mission.

*   *   *

II. Discussion

Sovereign immunity is a doctrine of international law under which domestic courts, given the proper circumstances, will relinquish jurisdiction over a foreign state. See generally N. E. Leech, C. T. Oliver, J. M. Sweeney, The International Legal System 306–91 (1973). [The court proceeded to discuss the Foreign Sovereign Immunities Act of 1976.]

Under the terms of the Immunities Act, this Court must determine without reference to political considerations the claims of sovereign immunity advanced by GNMTC. See Edlow International Co. v. Nuklearna Elektrarna Krsko, 441 F.Supp. 827 (D.C.D.C.1977). *   *   * [The court examined the documents submitted and concluded as follows.] In terms of meeting the statutory requirements of Section 1603(b), GNMTC has demonstrated with regard to its being an "agency or instrumentality of a foreign state" that it is a separate legal person which functions as an organ of a foreign state or political subdivision thereof, and that it is not a citizen of the United States nor created under the laws of any third country.

While GNMTC would *   *   * fit within the prerequisites for receiving sovereign immunity, section 1605(b) codifies a general exception to sovereign immunity in cases involving maritime liens:

"(b) a foreign state shall not be immune from the jurisdiction of the courts of the United States in any case in which a suit in admiralty is brought to enforce a maritime lien against a vessel or cargo of the foreign state, which maritime lien is based upon a commercial activity of the foreign state: Provided, That—

(1) notice of the suit is given by delivery of a copy of the summons and of the complaint to the person, or his agent, having possession of the vessel or cargo against which the maritime lien is asserted; but such notice shall not be deemed to have been delivered, nor may it thereafter be delivered, if the vessel or cargo is arrested pursuant to process obtained on behalf of the party bringing the suit—unless the party was unaware that the vessel or cargo of a foreign state was involved, in which event the service of process of arrest shall be deemed to constitute valid delivery of such notice; and

(2) notice to the foreign state of the commencement of suit as provided in section 1608 of this title is initiated within ten days either of the delivery of notice as provided in subsection (b)(1) of this section or, in the case of a party who was unaware that the vessel or cargo of a foreign state was involved, of the date such party determined the existence of the foreign state's interest.

Whenever notice is delivered under subsection (b)(1) of this section, the maritime lien shall thereafter be deemed to be an in personam claim against the foreign state which at that time owns the vessel or cargo involved: Provided, That a court may not award judgment against the foreign state in an amount greater than the value of the vessel or cargo upon which the maritime lien arose, such value to be determined as of the time notice is served under subsection (b)(1) of this section."

The legislative history is once more instructive on the meaning of this exception:

(b) Maritime liens.—Section 1605(b) denies immunity to a foreign state in cases where (i) a suit in admiralty is brought to enforce a maritime lien against a vessel or cargo of that foreign state, (ii) the maritime lien is based upon a commercial activity of the foreign state, and (iii) the conditions in paragraphs (1) and (2) of section 1605(b) have been complied with.

"The purpose of this subsection is to permit a plaintiff to bring suit in a U.S. district court arising out of a maritime lien involving a vessel or cargo of a foreign sovereign without arresting the vessel, by instituting an in personam action against the foreign state in a manner analogous to bringing such a suit against the United States. Cf. 46 U.S.C. 741, et seq. In view of section 1609 of the bill, section 1605(b) is designed to avoid arrests of vessels or cargo of a foreign state to commence a suit. Instead, as provided in paragraph (1), a copy of the summons and complaint must be delivered to the master or other person having possession of the vessel or cargo (such as the second in command of the ship). [1976] U.S.Code Cong. & Admin.News, p. 6620.

As noted above, Jet Line arrested and attached the M/V Elrakwa only to discover shortly thereafter that the ship belonged to GNMTC rather than the National Oil Company. Jet Line then released the ship on the basis of a Letter of Undertaking signed by West of England. This Letter was submitted to this Court by letter dated January 23, 1978 from plaintiff's Baltimore counsel and said in part:

> Pursuant to the terms of the agreement reached between counsel, the letter of undertaking would be substituted as collateral for the vessel, the owner of the vessel, General National Maritime Transport Company, will enter its appearance and no longer object to the jurisdiction of this Count [sic] and the two cases will then be tried on their respective merits.

Plaintiff, however, ignores the actual wording of the Letter of Undertaking, the last paragraph of which reads:

> This letter of undertaking shall apply vessel lost or not lost and is given entirely without prejudice to any rights or defenses which may be available to the M/V Elrakwa, and/or her claimant, and/or General under any statutes or rules in effect, none of which are regarded to be waived. This letter is not to be considered to be binding on John H. West, III or the law firm of Ober, Grimes & Shriver but is to be binding only on The West of England Ship Owners Mutual Protection and Indemnity Association (Luxemborg).

Although GNMTC may now have entered its appearance, such entry cannot be equated with a waiver or forfeiture of its sovereign immunity claims. Final resolution of this case depends, in fact, upon the relationship between plaintiff's arrest and attachment of the M/V Elrakwa and the exception to jurisdictional immunity for maritime liens codified in Section 1605(b).

One of the goals of the Immunities Act was to end the inconvenience associated with arresting and attaching property of a foreign state in order to obtain jurisdiction:

> Such attachments can also give rise to serious friction in United States' foreign relations. In some cases, plaintiffs obtain numerous attachments over a variety of foreign government assets found in various parts of the United States. This shotgun approach has caused significant irritation to many foreign governments.

> At the same time, one of the fundamental purposes of this bill is to provide a long-arm statute that makes attachment for jurisdictional purposes unnecessary in cases where there is a nexus between the claim and the United States. Claimants will clearly benefit from the expanded methods under the bill for service on a foreign state (sec. 1608), as well as from the certainty that section 1330(b) of the bill confers personal jurisdiction over a foreign state in Federal and State courts as to every claim for which the foreign state is not entitled to immunity. The elimination of attachment as a vehicle for commencing a lawsuit will ease the conduct of foreign relations by the United

States and help eliminate the necessity for determinations of claims of sovereign immunity by the State Department. [1976] U.S.Code Cong. & Admin.News, p. 6626.

The appropriate new procedures for obtaining such jurisdiction are explained in Section 1605(b)(1) and (2) and preclude attachment as a means for initiating a lawsuit.[3] Accordingly, when the foreign state reveals its interest in a ship or its cargo which has been mistakenly arrested, the arrest or attachment must be dissolved immediately. The Letter of Undertaking between West of England and Jet Line was "[i]n consideration of [Jet Line] releasing the M/V Elrakwa, which vessel was arrested on or about January 16, 1978, and from refraining from arresting or attaching any other vessels, funds or property belonging to General National Maritime Transport Co. * * *." Oddly enough, West of England must not have been aware of the provisions of the Immunities Act. No agreement such as that contained in the Letter of Undertaking would have been necessary since the arrest of the M/V Elrakwa was improper in the first place. The attachment would have had to be dissolved under 28 U.S.C. § 1609 as soon as Libya made known its interest in the vessel. The only other explanation for the Letter of Undertaking was as a means to expedite the release of the ship so that it could continue on its commercial voyage.

According to the legislative history of the Immunities Act, "[i]f * * * the vessel or its cargo is arrested or attached, the plaintiff will lose his in personam remedy and the foreign state will be entitled to immunity—except in the case where the plaintiff was unaware that the vessel or cargo of a foreign state was involved." [1976] U. S.Code Cong. & Admin.News, p. 6620. The legislative history furthermore explains that instances in which a party would be unaware of the involvement of a foreign sovereign would be rare:

> This would be a rare case because the flag of the vessel, the circumstances giving rise to the maritime lien, or the information contained in ship registries kept in ports throughout the United States should make known the ownership of the vessel in question, if not the cargo. By contrast, evidence that a party had relied on a standard registry of ships, which did not reveal a foreign state's interest in a vessel, would be prima facie evidence of the party's unawareness that a vessel of a foreign state was involved. More generally, a party could seek to establish its lack of awareness of the foreign state's ownership by submitting affidavits from itself and from its counsel. If, however, the vessel or cargo is mistakenly arrested, such arrest or attachment must, under section 1609, be immediately dissolved when the foreign

---

3. Under the holding in Weilamann v. Chase Manhattan Bank, 21 Misc.2d 1086, 192 N.Y.S.2d 469 (Sup.Ct.N.Y. 1959), it was recognized that one could attach the property of a foreign government for jurisdictional reasons where under international law a foreign government is not immune from suit, and where the property located in the United States was of a commercial nature. While such attachment could serve to obtain jurisdiction, it could not, however, be retained to satisfy a judgment as property of a foreign sovereign is traditionally immune from execution.

state brings to the court's attention its interest in the vessel or cargo and, hence, its right to immunity from arrest. [1976] U.S.Code Cong. & Admin.News, pp. 6620–21.

In its own initial unamended complaint, plaintiff describes itself as being "in the business among other things of furnishing services to merchant vessels." Presumably, since plaintiff furnishes such services on a professional basis, it was undoubtedly aware of the possible complications which can arise when its customers are foreign-owned rather than U.S.-owned vessels. Although plaintiff did mistakenly name the wrong party as a defendant, this error is not indicative of plaintiff's not knowing that a foreign state might be involved as both the National Oil Company and GNMTC are organs of the Libyan government.

Mindful of the legislative history behind the Immunities Act stating that a plaintiff will lose his in personam remedy if he wrongfully arrests or attaches a ship belonging to a foreign state "except * * * where the plaintiff was unaware that the vessel or cargo of a foreign state was involved," this Court directed the parties to this litigation to submit memoranda and any additional supporting materials addressing in detail the extent to which plaintiff knew, or should have known, that the seized vessel was the property of a foreign subject. 28 U.S.C. § 1605(b)(1). Plaintiff responded with an affidavit from its President, Robert Dee, who, inter alia, stated that "[w]hen Jet Line does work for a foreign flag vessel, it relies on the vessel's agent for information concerning ownership, not the vessel's flag." Consequently, Dee maintains that Jet Line had no reason to know of the M/V Elrakwa's claim of sovereign immunity. Remarking that "Jet Line is not particularly concerned with the flag the vessel is flying, or the registered name of the owner," Dee further observed that the ship's agent never advised Jet Line that the ships belonged to a foreign sovereign.[4] Finally, Dee unequivocally states that he was wholly unfamiliar with the existence of the Immunities Act and its requirements:

> Jet Line has no in house legal counsel and neither I nor any of the officers of Jet Line had ever heard of the Foreign Sovereign Immunities Act prior to this litigation.

> I have no reason to investigate who actually owns the vessels Jet Line works on as long as I am convinced that the vessel has a reputable agent, appropriate insurance and I hear nothing from the agent to indicate that the vessel will not be able to pay for the services rendered.

It has frequently been stated that all persons are presumed to know the law of the land, regardless of whether the law involved is

4. To support his claim of ignorance as to the ships' ownership, Dee refers to the following factors: the M/V Elrakwa's captain was not a Libyan; the ship's officer and crew did not wear military uniforms; the vessels were not painted gray and lacked guns; and wives and children were on board. While these factors together may have misled plaintiff as to the true ownership of the ship in question, the Immunities Act does not provide that these factors may be taken into account.

state or federal.   *   *   *   Perhaps one of the most commonly recognized truisms of American legal jurisprudence is that ignorance of the law does not constitute a proper defense.   *   *   *   More importantly, parties engaging in business or commercial transactions are conclusively presumed to know the law.   *   *   *   The legislative history behind the Immunities Act recognizes that where a party attaching a ship could not have known that the ship's owner was a foreign sovereign, that party's in personam jurisdiction over the sovereign will not be lost. Such cases, however, are clearly recognized to be "rare."

Responding to the Court's request for more information as to the actual knowledge plaintiff had or should have had as to the identity of the owner of the M/V Elrakwa and the M/V Marsa el Hariga, defendant has moved to dismiss plaintiff's action pursuant to section 1605(b)(1) of the Immunities Act. In support of its motion, defendant points to several publications, readily available to interested parties throughout the shipping trade, which indicate that plaintiff should have known that a sovereign entity's vessel was involved. For example, a recent excerpt from Lloyd's Shipping Index states that the owner of the M/V Marsa el Hariga and M/V Elrakwa is "G.N.M.T.C." which stands for General National Maritime Transport Co. of Tripoli, Libya. Both vessels are shown to fly the Libyan flag. Furthermore, an excerpt from the Lloyd's Register of Shipping List of Shipowners for 1977–78 says with reference to G.N.M.T.C., "See government of Libya." Finally, an excerpt from Lloyd's Register of Ships, 1976–1977, published yearly, identifies GNMTC as the M/V Marsa el Hariga's owner. With regard to the M/V Elrakwa, defendant explains that no such similar entry exists since the M/V Elrakwa was not built until 1977. Moreover, defendant notes that plaintiff has already conceded the presence of common ownership between the two ships. As defendant argues, these entries would appear to constitute "the information contained in ship registries kept in ports throughout the United States [which] should make known the ownership of the vessel in question." [1976] U.S.Code Cong. & Admin.News, p. 6620.

To the extent that plaintiff expects to prevail upon whatever maritime liens which it might claim in the future, it will now have reason to investigate who actually owns a maritime vessel before it takes action to arrest or attach a ship. While it is perhaps unfortunate that plaintiff should lose on an apparent technicality, such a "technicality" is firmly rooted in the sound public policy as to foreign sovereign immunities. To allow plaintiff to prevail despite its self-proclaimed ignorance of the law would be to encourage a policy of "attach first, ask later," and such an attitude would be in flagrant derogation of the policies behind the Immunities Act. Notice of the "new" U.S. immunities policy was contained in a letter from Monroe Leigh, Legal Adviser to the Department of State, to the Attorney General, Dep't of State Public Notice No. 507 (November 10, 1976), and reprinted in the 1976 compilation of American Maritime Cases at page 2362. The Immunities Act had been effective since January 19,

1977, almost exactly one year to the day before the events in this suit began. This Court cannot excuse plaintiff's failure to comply with codified U.S. law, and as a consequence, plaintiff must lose its in personam remedy in accordance with the provisions of the Immunities Act.

*   *   *

The requirements of Section 1605 are precisely and clearly written so as to give effect to the restrictive theory of sovereign immunity. The exception provided for maritime liens in that section is itself premised upon the *"commercial activity* of a foreign state." In the present case, plaintiff could easily have obtained in personam jurisdiction to maintain the suit by mailing a copy of the summons and complaint to a representative of GNMTC or the Libyan government pursuant to Section 1605(b)(1). While attachment of a vessel worth some $24,000,000 might have provided plaintiff with a sense of comfort in terms of realizing on its claim of $91,310.00, it was precisely this type of precipitous behavior which the Immunities Act was intended to discourage.

Accordingly, it is this 27th day of November, 1978, by the United States District Court for the District of Maryland, ordered:

    1. That defendant's motion to dismiss be, and the same is, hereby granted; and

    2. That defendant's motion to vacate and release Security be, and the same is, hereby granted.

UNITED STATES, FOREIGN SOVEREIGN IMMUNITIES ACT OF 1976, EXCEPTIONS TO IMMUNITY FROM ATTACHMENT OR EXECUTION

28 U.S.C. 1610.

(a) The property in the United States of a foreign state, as defined in section 1603(a) of this chapter, used for a commercial activity in the United States, shall not be immune from attachment in aid of execution, or from execution, upon a judgment entered by a court of the United States or of a State after the effective date of this Act, if—

    (1) the foreign state has waived its immunity from attachment in aid of execution or from execution either explicitly or by implication, notwithstanding any withdrawal of the waiver the foreign state may purport to effect except in accordance with the terms of the waiver, or

    (2) the property is or was used for the commercial activity upon which the claim is based, or

    (3) the execution relates to a judgment establishing rights in property which has been taken in violation of international law or which has been exchanged for property taken in violation of international law, or

(4) the execution relates to a judgment establishing rights in property—

    (A) which is acquired by succession or gift, or

    (B) which is immovable and situated in the United States: *Provided*, That such property is not used for purposes of maintaining a diplomatic or consular mission or the residence of the Chief of such mission, or

(5) the property consists of any contractual obligation or any proceeds from such a contractual obligation to indemnify or hold harmless the foreign state or its employees under a policy of automobile or other liability or casualty insurance covering the claim which merged into the judgment.

(b) In addition to subsection (a), any property in the United States of an agency or instrumentality of a foreign state engaged in commercial activity in the United States shall not be immune from attachment in aid of execution, or from execution, upon a judgment entered by a court of the United States or of a State after the effective date of this Act, if—

(1) the agency or instrumentality has waived its immunity from attachment in aid of execution or from execution either explicitly or implicitly, notwithstanding any withdrawal of the waiver the agency or instrumentality may purport to effect except in accordance with the terms of the waiver, or

(2) the judgment relates to a claim for which the agency or instrumentality is not immune by virtue of section 1605(a)(2), (3), or (5), or 1605(b) of this chapter, regardless of whether the property is or was used for the activity upon which the claim is based.

(c) No attachment or execution referred to in subsections (a) and (b) of this section shall be permitted until the court has ordered such attachment and execution after having determined that a reasonable period of time has elapsed following the entry of judgment and the giving of any notice required under section 1608(e) of this chapter.

(d) The property of a foreign state, as defined in section 1603(a) of this chapter, used for a commercial activity in the United States, shall not be immune from attachment prior to the entry of judgment in any action brought in a court of the United States or of a State, or prior to the elapse of the period of time provided in subsection (c) of this section, if—

(1) the foreign state has explicitly waived its immunity from attachment prior to judgment, notwithstanding any withdrawal of the waiver the foreign state may purport to effect except in accordance with the terms of the waiver, and

(2) the purpose of the attachment is to secure satisfaction of a judgment that has been or may ultimately be entered against the foreign state, and not to obtain jurisdiction.

Chapter 6

THE ACT OF STATE DOCTRINE

Judicial disinclination to pass on the legitimacy of an otherwise determinative rule of foreign law. Courts in one state are sometimes faced with this problem: a private party claims against another private party, and the defendant says that plaintiff has no case under the legal rule of another state that should apply to the issue. Plaintiff rejoins that the foreign rule is invalid and therefore should not be applied. The plaintiff may make this contention in a normal conflict of laws context, i. e. that the foreign rule, although a part of the everyday legal system of the other state, is so deeply shocking to fundamental values as seen at the forum as to require rejection as against the public policy of the forum. But, if circumstances warrant, the plaintiff may contend that the foreign rule is unconstitutional in the foreign legal system or that the rule violates international law.

If the plaintiff contends along the first line, the issue is joined in an entirely private law context; and the forum court will not ordinarily be apprehensive that its decision will be taken as intrusive or insulting in the foreign state.

But if the foreign rule stems from an exercise of sovereignty by the foreign state, such as an act of governance, and the plaintiff is seeking to attack the fundamental validity of that conduct by the foreign state, the forum judge will become more cautious. When that happens, the problems considered in this chapter arise.

In the Anglo-American legal world a legal consequence deriving from high-level state action—a legal result outside the ordinary field of private law—is given the rather awesome label, *act of state*. In Great Britain the term is usually, but not exclusively, used to refer to the principle that an Officer of the Crown when personally sued for an act committed abroad against a foreigner may defend that he acted at the Crown's command. (He is not allowed this defense as against an assertion of personal responsibility as to acts committed within British territory.) As to the use by courts in Britain of the principle of non-examination of the acts of a foreign state, see the United States Supreme Court's note 21 to its opinion in Banco Nacional de Cuba v. Sabbatino, p. 378. The United States Supreme Court also makes brief reference in this note to the manner in which tribunals in civil law systems use the principle against examination of the legitimacy of an otherwise applicable foreign legal rule. The term act of state, however, is rarely used in these systems.

Yet another problem of semantics arises, because the civil law systems will not apply an otherwise applicable foreign rule that is violative of the public order of the forum state, and this notion of public order is not the same as that of a common law court when, in a routine conflict of laws case it has to decide whether the foreign law should not be chosen to apply, because against the public policy of the forum. The civilian doctrine of *ordre public* concerns itself only with exceptional or highly significant manifestations of the foreign sovereign will and with whether in certain situations it clashes with an equally highly held principle of proper governance and national interest in the forum state.

An unresolved question exists whether the widely shared disinclination to declare invalid an act of governance of another state is, internationally, a principle of international relations or a rule of international law. Even if not required by international law, act of state is nonetheless significant in the international legal system.

In the United States the earlier cases on the act of state doctrine were of the classic sort mentioned at the outset, where the plaintiff and the defendant are both private parties and the plaintiff mounts the attack. The major cases in recent years, however, have involved a foreign state as plaintiff, and the defendant has attacked the legitimacy of the foreign law on which the plaintiff relies. In the older cases the immunity of a state was not involved at all. In the later cases, with the foreign state as plaintiff, there may arise the question whether this is a relationship between the doctrine of act of state and the doctrine of immunity of a state sued on a counterclaim. In the most recent development a private party is suing a state engaged in trade for an alleged invalid act of nationalization (nationalization is almost always deemed an act of state), and before the act of state (or ordre public) issue is reached, an issue of immunity from suit has to be resolved. See Chapter 17.

SECTION A. THE BASIC COURT–MADE DOCTRINE IN THE UNITED STATES

The American act of state doctrine and political crises in foreign relations. The American act of state doctrine is closely linked to situations abroad involving political crises in the course of which officials of a foreign government take actions harmful or outrageous to a person who, later, seeks redress by bringing a suit in the United States.

In the agreement for the release of American hostages in Teheran of January 19, 1981, the United States undertook to bar the hostages from prosecuting claims against Iran for their seizure and detention. See in the Documentary Supplement paragraph 11 of the first Declaration by the government of Algeria. Suppose, however, it had not done so and some of hostages were able to find and serve in the United States former officials of the government in control in Iran at the time it so grossly violated the diplomatic immunity, and human dignity, of the plaintiffs. The defendants would plead that under the law of the United States governing its foreign relations, their conduct was an Iranian act of state and as such beyond cognizance by American courts.

The link to political crises abroad is apparent, startlingly so in retrospect, in the extensive history of the doctrine given in the majority opinion of the Supreme Court in the Sabbatino case, infra p. 372. The first case it cites, Underhill v. Hernandez, involved an insurgent general in Venezuela in the 1890's who mounted a successful coup, and was recognized as the head of government, but later fell from power and came to the United States, only to find himself sued for mistreating the plaintiff in Venezuela during the insurgency. The chronology of the cases after Underhill v. Hernandez takes the doctrine through the Mexican revolution of 1910–21, the outrages of the Nazi government of Germany, the crisis between the United States and Castro's Cuba, a relatively recent dictatorship in Venezuela and the overthrow of the King of Libya by the military regime of Colonel Qaddafi.

A troublesome aspect of the doctrine is that it tends to keep the courts from serving justice. The point is dramatically made in two suits brought by a former German Jew whose ships, while he was still a German citizen, were seized by the Nazi government and sold for value to purchasers with notice. In the first one, Judge Learned Hand applied the act of state doctrine and threw the case out of court. In the second suit, the Legal Adviser of the Department of State informed the court by letter that it would be contrary to the policy of the United States towards occupied Germany to recognize as valid the title to ships acquired by the purchaser under the notorious racial laws of Hitlerian Germany. The court gave effect to this view and did not apply the act of state doctrine.

As a result of the second case, the way was open for efforts, through congressional legislation and executive action, to get the act of state doctrine turned around so it does not apply unless the Department of State says it should. The justification for side-tracking the doctrine is that the courts should be allowed to do justice for plaintiffs who are victims of governmental acts of foreign states done in their own territory. But are we to assume that the courts, if left alone by Congress and the executive branch, would continue to apply the doctrine, no matter how brutal or uncivilized the acts of state involved?

JIMENEZ v. ARISTEGUIETA

United States Court of Appeals, Fifth Circuit, 1962.
311 F.2d 547.[a]

ESTES, District Judge. This is an appeal from the judgment of the United States District Court for the Southern District of Florida, Judge Wm. A. McRae, Jr., dated August 23, 1961, dismissing the original and amended petitions for habeas corpus filed by appellant, Marcos Perez Jimenez, and discharging the original and amended orders to show cause issued on the petitions for habeas corpus. The petitions for habeas corpus incorporate by reference the entire file in an international extradition proceeding under 18 U.S.C. § 3184 et seq., filed in the United States District Court for the Southern District of Florida, Miami Division, on August 24, 1959, by Manuel Aristeguieta, Consul General of the Republic of Venezuela, on behalf of appellee, the Republic of Venezuela (Venezuela), in which the return to Venezuela of appellant, a former president of Venezuela, now in Miami, Florida, is sought under the Treaty of Extradition between the United States and Venezuela (43 Stat. 1698).

＊ ＊ ＊

The extradition proceeding was concluded by orders entered by Judge Whitehurst, under 18 U.S.C. § 3184, finding that the proof did not establish probable cause on the charges of murder and participation in murder. He further found that probable cause had been shown as to each of the financial crimes which were separately and independently alleged in plaintiff's Second Amended Complaint and that the acts charged constituted crimes named in the specified provisions of the Treaty of Extradition, and he committed the appellant to the custody of the appellee United States Marshal to await the action of the Secretary of State under 18 U.S.C. § 3186. The order of commitment was entered by Judge Whitehurst on June 16, 1961. His findings and order of certification to the Secretary of State, entered June 23, 1961, attach a copy of the Second Amended Complaint in the extradition proceeding, to which certain sections of the certification order specifically refer.

Venezuela's Second Amended Complaint, upon which the extradition proceeding and orders under attack were based, charged appellant, chief executive of Venezuela (first as a member of a three-man junta, then as provisional President, and later as President, having legal responsibility for the administration of the funds and contracting authority of Venezuela), with two distinct groups of crimes committed in Venezuela during the years 1948–1958, the first group composed of four charges of murder and participation in murder as an accessory before the fact, the second group comprised financial crimes for his own private personal gain. The financial crimes are separately and

a. Cert. denied sub nom. Jimenez v. Hixon, 373 U.S. 914, 83 S.Ct. 1302 (1963).

independently charged in the complaint and are based on certain alleged transactions briefly summarized as follows:

1. The appellant secured commissions or kickbacks in ten specific instances on Venezuelan Government contracts, some of which the appellant himself had executed.

2. Through a "front" or alter ego the appellant secured a portion of the compensation paid by the Venezuelan Government for two tracts of land expropriated by decrees promulgated by him.

3. By his twenty per cent ownership of EVICSA, a construction company, the appellant secured a portion of the compensation paid by the Venezuelan Government on construction contracts with the appellant's Ministry of Development, with the connivance of two of his ministers, one of whom was head of that ministry.

4. The appellant secured improvements on and maintenance of his private, personal estate at public expense at specified times.

The charges of financial crimes allege that the transactions numbered 1 through 4 above make appellant guilty of embezzlement or criminal malversation by a public officer as provided in paragraph 14 of Article II of the Treaty, guilty of fraud or breach of trust as provided in paragraph 20 of Article II of the Treaty, and that the transactions numbered 1 through 3 above make him guilty of receiving money or valuable securities knowing the same to have been unlawfully obtained as provided in paragraph 18 of Article II of the Treaty.

The same charges are pending in the Supreme Court of Justice (formerly the Federal Court), the highest court of Venezuela, upon petition of the Attorney General of Venezuela with a substantial quantity of supporting evidence. The Supreme Court of Justice determined that if the charges are proved they would constitute violations of the penal code of Venezuela and that such charges are crimes specified in the Treaty of Extradition Article II, paragraphs 14, 18 and 20; found that good cause had been shown for prosecution and issued its warrant of arrest. The proceedings before the Supreme Court of Justice, with a substantial amount of evidence from its record—all documentary—were transmitted to the United States through appropriate diplomatic channels. Venezuela invokes these Treaty provisions in its complaint and requisition for surrender of appellant.

Appellant contends that Judge McRae erred in not discharging appellant from custody on the grounds that: (1) Judge Whitehurst did not have jurisdiction to conduct the extradition proceeding, (2) appellant was not accorded due process of law in the proceeding before Judge Whitehurst, sitting as extradition magistrate, (3) the acts for which appellant's extradition is sought are acts in the exercise of sovereign authority or acts of state the legality of which the judicial authorities of the United States have no authority to determine, (4) failure of the extradition magistrate to determine whether the claim for extradition was for any crime or offense of a political character or for acts connected with such crimes or offenses, (5) the decision of Judge Whitehurst was not based on legal, competent and adequate evidence, (6) the alleged financial crimes were not within the Treaty of Extradition, and (7) the extradition magistrate was without jurisdiction by virtue of Article XII of the Treaty of Extradition, inasmuch as the Venezuelan government had failed to lay legal evidence of criminality before the extradition magistrate within the two months prescribed by the Treaty.

* * *

Appellant contends that the acts with which he is charged are "acts done in the exercise of or in color of his sovereign authority and by virtue of the law of nations as stated in Underhill v. Hernandez, 168 U.S. 250, 18 S.Ct. 83, 42 L.Ed. 456, [he] was entitled to be discharged from custody inasmuch as the judicial authorities cannot review the acts done by a sovereign in his own territory to determine illegality".[6]

Seizing upon Venezuela's characterization of appellant as a "dictator" he argues that as a "dictator" he himself would be the sovereign—the government of Venezuela—and that all his acts constituting the financial crimes with which he is charged and as to which probable cause of guilt has been found are acts of state or sovereign acts, the legality of which the Act of State Doctrine precludes an extradition judge or magistrate from adjudicating.

Essentially the Act of State Doctrine is "the principle that the conduct of one independent government cannot be successfully questioned in the courts of another * * *." Oetjen v. Central Leather Co., 246 U.S. 297, 303, 38 S.Ct. 309, 311, 62 L.Ed. 726 (1918).

Even though characterized as a dictator, appellant was not himself the sovereign—government—of Venezuela within the Act of

---

6. Appellant relies on Subdivision (c)(4) of 28 U.S.C. § 2241 the habeas corpus statute, which provides that the writ shall extend to citizens and domiciliaries of a foreign state "in custody for an act done or omitted under any alleged right, title, authority, privilege, protection, or exemption claimed under the commission, order or sanction of any foreign state, or under color thereof, the validity and effect of which depend upon the law of nations."

This is only a jurisdictional provision conferring no substantive right on appellant to discharge from custody merely upon allegation of jurisdictional facts. See Horn v. Mitchell, 223 F. 549, affirmed 232 F. 819 (1 Cir. 1916), appeal dismissed 243 U.S. 247, 37 S.Ct. 293, 61 L.Ed. 700.

"The Act of State Doctrine, briefly stated, holds that American courts will not pass on the validity of the acts of foreign governments performed in their capacities as sovereigns within their own territories. * * * This doctrine is one of the conflict of laws rules applied by American courts; it is not itself a rule of International Law." Banco Nacional de Cuba v. Sabbatino, 2 Cir., 307 F.2d 845, p. 855.

"International law is derived indeed from the customs and usages of civilized nations, but its concepts are subject to generally accepted principles of morality whether most men live by these principles or not." Id., p. 860.

State Doctrine. He was chief executive, a public officer, of the sovereign nation of Venezuela. It is only when officials having sovereign authority act in an official capacity that the Act of State Doctrine applies. Bernstein v. Van Heyghen Freres, S. A., 163 F.2d 246, 249 (2d Cir. 1947), cert. den. 332 U.S. 772, 68 S.Ct. 88, 92 L.Ed. 357 (1947); Banco de Espana v. Federal Reserve Bank, 114 F.2d 438, 444 (2d Cir. 1940).

Appellant's acts constituting the financial crimes of embezzlement or malversation, fraud or breach of trust, and receiving money or valuable securities knowing them to have been unlawfully obtained as to which probable cause of guilt had been shown were not acts of Venezuela sovereignty. Judge Whitehurst found that each of these acts was "for the private financial benefit" of the appellant. They constituted common crimes committed by the Chief of State done in violation of his position and not in pursuance of it. They are as far from being an act of state as rape which appellant concedes would not be an "Act of State".

A policy underlying the Act of State Doctrine is that to adjudicate the validity of an act of a foreign government under its own law in the courts of the United States would "imperil the amicable relations between governments and vex the peace of nations." Oetjen v. Central Leather Co., supra.

The judiciary abstains from decision in the ordinary Act of State case in deference to the executive, the branch of government charged with international relations. In a comprehensive and discriminating opinion on the Act of State Doctrine by Judge Waterman of the Second Circuit, in Banco Nacional de Cuba v. Sabbatino, it was held that

> * * * when the executive branch of our Government announces that it does not oppose inquiry by American courts into the legality of foreign acts, an exception to the judicial abnegation required by the act of state doctrine has arisen.

In this extradition case the executive branch, through its representation of the appellee United States Marshal, has manifested its desire that the judiciary act and decide this case on its merits.

Underhill v. Hernandez does not support appellant's claim of sovereign immunity. In that case a citizen of the United States brought an action in United States courts for damages for unlawful detention and assault in Venezuela by soldiers in the revolutionary forces in Venezuela under the command of Hernandez. The Supreme Court held that Hernandez, as a military commander representing a de facto government in the prosecution of a war, was not civilly responsible for those acts; pointed out that Hernandez was not "actuated by malice or any personal or private motives;" and made it clear that its decision would have been otherwise had defendant's action been differently motivated, as is the case here. Judge Whitehurst expressly found that the acts of appellant establishing probable cause of guilt of the financial crimes were "for the private financial benefit of the defendant".

The very reason for this extradition case is that the United States has agreed with Venezuela for the extradition of persons charged with crimes enumerated in the Treaty. This Treaty deals expressly in paragraph 14 of Article II with embezzlement or criminal malversation by public officers. Appellant notes that a public officer is one who exercises "in part sovereign power". The two governments intended the tribunals to act when the accused is a public officer charged with crimes enumerated in the Treaty. The acts constituting crimes charged for which the extradition of appellant is sought are not "acts of Venezuela" as in Hernandez, and the Act of State Doctrine is no bar to this extradition proceeding or justification for the discharge from custody of appellant.

* * *

The record contains no reversible error and the judgment of the District Court dismissing the appellant's petition for habeas corpus and discharging the orders to show cause issued thereon is hereby Affirmed. The mandate of the Court will issue forthwith.

BANCO NACIONAL DE CUBA v. SABBATINO, RECEIVER

United States Supreme Court, 1964.
376 U.S. 398, 84 S.Ct. 923, 11 L.Ed.2d 804.[a]

Mr. Justice HARLAN delivered the opinion of the Court.

The question which brought this case here, and is now found to be the dispositive issue, is whether the so-called act of state doctrine serves to sustain petitioner's claims in this litigation. Such claims are ultimately founded on a decree of the Government of Cuba expropriating certain property, the right to the proceeds of which is here in controversy. The act of state doctrine in its traditional formulation precludes the courts of this country from inquiring into the validity of the public acts a recognized foreign sovereign power committed within its own territory.

I.

In February and July of 1960, respondent Farr, Whitlock & Co., an American commodity broker, contracted to purchase Cuban sugar, free alongside the steamer, from a wholly owned subsidiary of Compania Azucarera Vertientes-Camaguey de Cuba (C. A. V.), a corporation organized under Cuban law whose capital stock was owned principally by United States residents. Farr, Whitlock agreed to pay for the sugar in New York upon presentation of the shipping documents and a sight draft.

On July 6, 1960, the Congress of the United States amended the Sugar Act of 1948 to permit a presidentially directed reduction of the sugar quota for Cuba. On the same day President Eisenhower exer-

---

a. See Chapter 12, Section A, for that part of the opinion which declares irrelevant the fact that the United States had severed diplomatic relations with Cuba.

cised the granted power. The day of the congressional enactment, the Cuban Council of Ministers adopted "Law No. 851," which characterized this reduction in the Cuban sugar quota as an act of "agression, for political purposes" on the part of the United States, justifying the taking of countermeasures by Cuba. The law gave the Cuban President and Prime Minister discretionary power to nationalize by forced expropriation property or enterprises in which American nationals had an interest. Although a system of compensation was formally provided, the possibility of payment under it may well be deemed illusory. Our State Department has described the Cuban law as "manifestly in violation of those principles of international law which have long been accepted by the free countries of the West. It is in its essence discriminatory, arbitrary and confiscatory."

Between August 6 and August 9, 1960, the sugar covered by the contract between Farr, Whitlock and C. A. V. was loaded, destined for Morocco, onto the S. S. Hornfels, which was standing offshore at the Cuban port of Jucaro (Santa Maria). On the day loading commenced, the Cuban President and Prime Minister, acting pursuant to Law No. 851, issued Executive Power Resolution No. 1. It provided for the compulsory expropriation of all property and enterprises, and of rights and interests arising therefrom, of certain listed companies, including C. A. V., wholly or principally owned by American nationals. The preamble reiterated the alleged injustice of the American reduction of the Cuban sugar quota and emphasized the importance of Cuba's serving as an example for other countries to follow "in their struggle to free themselves from the brutal claws of Imperialism." In consequence of the resolution, the consent of the Cuban Government was necessary before a ship carrying sugar of a named company could leave Cuban waters. In order to obtain this consent, Farr, Whitlock, on August 11, entered into contracts, identical to those it had made with C. A. V., with the Banco Para el Comercio Exterior de Cuba, an instrumentality of the Cuban Government. The S. S. Hornfels sailed for Morocco on August 12.

Banco Exterior assigned the bills of lading to petitioner, also an instrumentality of the Cuban Government which instructed its agent in New York, Societe Generale, to deliver the bills and a sight draft in the sum of $175,250.69 to Farr, Whitlock in return for payment. Societe Generale's initial tender of the documents was refused by Farr, Whitlock, which on the same day was notified of C. A. V.'s claim that as rightful owner of the sugar it was entitled to the proceeds. In return for a promise not to turn the funds over to petitioner or its agent, C. A. V. agreed to indemnify Farr, Whitlock for any loss. Farr, Whitlock subsequently accepted the shipping documents, negotiated the bills of lading to its customer, and received payment for the sugar. It refused, however, to hand over the proceeds to Societe Generale. Shortly thereafter, Farr, Whitlock was served with an order of the New York Supreme Court, which had appointed Sabbatino as Temporary Receiver of C. A. V.'s New York assets, enjoining it from taking any action in regard to the money claimed by C. A.

V. that might result in its removal from the State. Following this, Farr, Whitlock, pursuant to court order, transferred the funds to Sabbatino, to abide the event of a judicial determination as to their ownership.

Petitioner then instituted this action in the Federal District Court for the Southern District of New York. Alleging conversion of the bills of lading, it sought to recover the proceeds thereof from Farr, Whitlock and to enjoin the receiver from exercising any dominion over such proceeds. Upon motions to dismiss and for summary judgment, the District Court, 193 F.Supp. 375, sustained federal in personam jurisdiction despite state control of the funds. It found that the sugar was located within Cuban territory at the time of expropriation and determined that under merchant law common to civilized countries Farr, Whitlock could not have asserted ownership of the sugar against C. A. V. before making payment. It concluded that C. A. V. had a property interest in the sugar subject to the territorial jurisdiction of Cuba. The court then dealt with the question of Cuba's title to the sugar, on which rested petitioner's claim of conversion. While acknowledging the continuing vitality of the act of state doctrine, the court believed it inapplicable when the questioned foreign act is in violation of international law. Proceeding on the basis that a taking invalid under international law does not convey good title, the District Court found the Cuban expropriation decree to violate such law in three separate respects: it was motivated by a retaliatory and not a public purpose; it discriminated against American nationals; and it failed to provide adequate compensation. Summary judgment against petitioner was accordingly granted.

The Court of Appeals, 307 F.2d 845, affirming the decision on similar grounds, relied on two letters (not before the District Court) written by State Department officers which it took as evidence that the Executive Branch had no objection to a judicial testing of the Cuban decree's validity. The court was unwilling to declare that any one of the infirmities found by the District Court rendered the taking invalid under international law, but was satisfied that in combination they had that effect. We granted certiorari because the issues involved bear importantly on the conduct of the country's foreign relations and more particularly on the proper role of the Judicial Branch in this sensitive area. 372 U.S. 905, 83 S.Ct. 717. For reasons to follow we decide that the judgment below must be reversed.

     *   *   *

IV.

The classic American statement of the act of state doctrine, which appears to have taken root in England as early as 1674, Blad v. Bamfield, 3 Swans. 604, 36 Eng.Rep. 992, and began to emerge in the jurisprudence of this country in the late eighteenth and early nineteenth centuries, see e. g., Ware v. Hylton, 3 Dall. 199, 230; Hudson v. Guestier, 4 Cranch 293, 294; The Schooner Exchange v. M'Faddon, 7 Cranch 116, 135, 136; L'Invincible, 1 Wheat. 238, 253;

The Santissima Trinidad, 7 Wheat. 283, 336, is found in Underhill v. Hernandez, 168 U.S. 250, p. 252, 18 S.Ct. 83, at p. 84, where Chief Justice Fuller said for a unanimous Court:

> Every sovereign State is bound to respect the independence of every other sovereign State, and the courts of one country will not sit in judgment on the acts of the government of another done within its own territory. Redress of grievances by reason of such acts must be obtained through the means open to be availed of by sovereign powers as between themselves.

Following this precept the Court in that case refused to inquire into acts of Hernandez, a revolutionary Venezuelan military commander whose government had been later recognized by the United States, which were made the basis of a damage action in this country by Underhill, an American citizen, who claimed that he had been unlawfully assaulted, coerced, and detained in Venezuela by Hernandez.

None of this Court's subsequent cases in which the act of state doctrine was directly or peripherally involved manifest any retreat from Underhill. See American Banana Co. v. United Fruit Co., 213 U.S. 347, 29 S.Ct. 511; Oetjen v. Central Leather Co., 246 U.S. 297, 38 S.Ct. 309; Ricaud v. American Metal Co., 246 U.S. 304; Shapleigh v. Mier, 299 U.S. 468, 57 S.Ct. 261; United States v. Belmont, 301 U.S. 324, 57 S.Ct. 758; United States v. Pink, 315 U.S. 203, 62 S.Ct. 552. On the contrary in two of these cases, Oetjen and Ricaud, the doctrine as announced in Underhill was reaffirmed in unequivocal terms.

Oetjen involved a seizure of hides from a Mexican citizen as a military levy by General Villa, acting for the forces of General Carranza, whose government was recognized by this country subsequent to the trial but prior to decision by this Court. The hides were sold to a Texas corporation which shipped them to the United States and assigned them to defendant. As assignee of the original owner, plaintiff replevied the hides, claiming that they had been seized in violation of the Hague Conventions. In affirming a judgment for defendant, the Court suggested that the rules of the Conventions did not apply to civil war and that, even if they did, the relevant seizure was not in violation of them. 246 U.S., at 301–302, 38 S.Ct. at 310. Nevertheless, it chose to rest its decision on other grounds. It described the designation of the sovereign as a political question to be determined by the legislative and executive departments rather than the judicial department, invoked the established rule that such recognition operates retroactively to validate past acts, and found the basic tenet of Underhill to be applicable to the case before it.

> The principle that the conduct of one independent government cannot be successfully questioned in the courts of another is as applicable to a case involving the title to property brought within the custody of a court, such as we have here, as it was held to be to the cases cited, in which claims for damages were based upon acts done in a foreign country, for it rests at last

upon the highest considerations of international comity and expediency. To permit the validity of the acts of one sovereign State to be reexamined and perhaps condemned by the courts of another would very certainly "imperil the amicable relations between governments and vex the peace of nations." Id., 246 U.S. at 303-304, 38 S.Ct. at 311.

In Ricaud the facts were similar—another general of the Carranza forces seized lead bullion as a military levy—except that the property taken belonged to an American citizen. The Court found Underhill, American Banana, and Oetjen controlling. Commenting on the nature of the principle established by those cases, the opinion stated that the rule

> does not deprive the courts of jurisdiction once acquired over a case. It requires only that, when it is made to appear that the foreign government has acted in a given way on the subject-matter of the litigation, the details of such action or the merit of the result cannot be questioned but must be accepted by our courts as a rule for their decision. To accept a ruling authority and to decide accordingly is not a surrender or abandonment of jurisdiction but is an exercise of it. It results that the title to the property in this case must be determined by the result of the action taken by the military authorities of Mexico * * *. 246 U.S., at 309, 38 S.Ct. at 314.

To the same effect is the language of Mr. Justice Cardozo in the Shapleigh case, supra, where, in commenting on the validity of a Mexican land expropriation, he said (299 U.S., at 471, 57 S.Ct. at 262): "The question is not here whether the proceeding was so conducted as to be a wrong to our nationals under the doctrines of international law, though valid under the law of the situs of the land. For wrongs of that order the remedy to be followed is along the channels of diplomacy."

In deciding the present case the Court of Appeals relied in part upon an exception to the unqualified teachings of Underhill, Oetjen, and Ricaud which that court had earlier indicated. In Bernstein v. Van Heyghen Freres Societe Anonyme, 2 Cir., 163 F.2d 246, suit was brought to recover from an assignee property allegedly taken, in effect, by the Nazi Government because plaintiff was Jewish. Recognizing the odious nature of this act of state, the court, through Judge Learned Hand, nonetheless refused to consider it invalid on that ground. Rather, it looked to see if the Executive had acted in any manner that would indicate that United States Courts should refuse to give effect to such a foreign decree. Finding no such evidence, the court sustained dismissal of the complaint. In a later case involving similar facts the same court again assumed examination of the German acts improper, Bernstein v. N. V. Nederlandsche-Amerikaansche Stoomvaart-Maatschappij, 2 Cir., 173 F.2d 71, but, quite evidently following the implications of Judge Hand's opinion in the earlier case, amended its mandate to permit evidence of alleged invalidity, 210 F.

2d 375, subsequent to receipt by plaintiff's attorney of a letter from the Acting Legal Adviser to the State Department written for the purpose of relieving the court from any constraint upon the exercise of its jurisdiction to pass on that question.[18]

This Court has never had occasion to pass upon the so-called Bernstein exception, nor need it do so now. For whatever ambiguity may be thought to exist in the two letters from State Department officials on which the Court of Appeals relied,[19] 307 F.2d, at 858, is now removed by the position which the Executive has taken in this Court on the act of state claim; respondents do not indeed contest the view that these letters were intended to reflect no more than the Department's then wish not to make any statement bearing on this litigation.

The outcome of this case, therefore, turns upon whether any of the contentions urged by respondents against the application of the act of state doctrine in the premises is acceptable: (1) that the doctrine does not apply to acts of state which violate international law, as is claimed to be the case here; (2) that the doctrine is inapplicable unless the Executive specifically interposes it in a particular case; and (3) that, in any event, the doctrine may not be invoked by a foreign government plaintiff in our courts.

V.

Preliminarily, we discuss the foundations on which we deem the act of state doctrine to rest, and more particularly the question of

18. The letter stated:

1. This government has consistently opposed the forcible acts of dispossession of a discriminatory and confiscatory nature practiced by the Germans on the countries or peoples subject to their controls.

* * *

3. The policy of the Executive, with respect to claims asserted in the United States for the restitution of identifiable property (or compensation in lieu thereof) lost through force, coercion, or duress as a result of Nazi persecution in Germany, is to relieve American courts from any restraint upon the exercise of their jurisdiction to pass upon the validity of the acts of Nazi officials. State Department Press Release, April 27, 1949, 20 Dept. State Bull. 592.

19. Abram Chayes, the Legal Advisor to the State Department, wrote on October 18, 1961, in answer to an inquiry regarding the position of the Department by Mr. John Laylin, attorney for amici:

The Department of State has not, in the Bahia de Nipe case or elsewhere, done anything inconsistent with the position taken on the Cuban nationalizations by Secretary Herter. Whether or not these nationalizations will in the future be given effect in the United States is, of course, for the courts to determine. Since the Sabbatino case and other similar cases are at present before the courts, any comments on this question by the Department of State would be out of place at this time. As you yourself point out, statements by the executive branch are highly susceptible of misconstruction.

A letter dated November 14, 1961, from George Ball, Under Secretary for Economic Affairs, responded to a similar inquiry by the same attorney:

I have carefully considered your letter and have discussed it with the Legal Adviser. Our conclusion, in which the Secretary concurs, is that the Department should not comment on matters pending before the courts.

whether state or federal law governs its application in a federal diversity case.[20]

We do not believe that this doctrine is compelled either by the inherent nature of sovereign authority, as some of the earlier decisions seem to imply, see Underhill, supra; American Banana, supra; Oetjen, supra, 246 U.S. at 303, 38 S.Ct. at 311, or by some principle of international law. If a transaction takes place in one jurisdiction and the forum is in another, the forum does not by dismissing an action or by applying its own law purport to divest the first jurisdiction of its territorial sovereignty; it merely declines to adjudicate or makes applicable its own law to parties or property before it. The refusal of one country to enforce the penal laws of another (supra, pp. 932–933) is a typical example of an instance when a court will not entertain a cause of action arising in another jurisdiction. While historic notions of sovereign authority do bear upon the wisdom of employing the act of state doctrine, they do not dictate its existence.

That international law does not require application of the doctrine is evidenced by the practice of nations. Most of the countries rendering decisions on the subject fail to follow the rule rigidly.[21] No international arbitral or judicial decision discovered suggests that international law prescribes recognition of sovereign acts of foreign governments, see 1 Oppenheim's International Law, § 115aa (Lauterpacht, 8th ed. 1955), and apparently no claim has ever been raised before an international tribunal that failure to apply the act of state doctrine constitutes a breach of international obligation. If international law does not prescribe use of the doctrine, neither does it for-

20. Although the complaint in this case alleged both diversity and federal question jurisdiction, the Court of Appeals reached jurisdiction only on the former ground, 307 F.2d at 852. We need not decide, for reasons appearing hereafter, whether federal question jurisdiction also existed.

21. In English jurisprudence, in the classic case of Luther v. James Sagor & Co., [1921] 3 K.B. 532, the act of state doctrine is articulated in terms not unlike those of the United States cases. See Princess Paley Olga v. Weisz, [1929] 1 K.B. 718. But see Anglo-Iranian Oil Co. v. Jaffrate, [1953] 1 Weekly L.R. 246, [1953] Int'l L.Rep. 316 (Aden Sup.Ct.) (exception to doctrine if foreign act violates international law). Civil law countries, however, which apply the rule make exceptions for acts contrary to their sense of public order. See, e. g., Ropit case, Cour de Cassation (France), [1929] Recueil Général Des Lois et Des Arrêts (Sirey) Part I, 217; 55 Journal De Droit International (Clunet) 674 (1928), [1927–1928] Ann.Dig., No. 43; Graue, Germany: Recogni-

tion of Foreign Expropriations, 3 Am.J.Comp.L. 93 (1954); Domke, Indonesian Nationalization Measures Before Foreign Courts, 54 Am.J.Int'l L. 305 (1960) (discussion of and excerpts from opinions of the District Court in Bremen and the Hanseatic Court of Appeals in N. V. Verenigde Deli-Maatschapijen v. Deutsch-Indonesische Tabak-Handelsgesellschaft m. b. H., and of the Amsterdam District Court and Appellate Court in Senembah Maatschappij N. V. v. Republiek Indonesie Bank Indonesia); Massouridis, The Effects of Confiscation, Expropriation, and Requisition by a Foreign Authority, 3 Revue Hellénique De Droit International 62, 68 (1950) (recounting a decision of the court of the first instance of Piraeus); Anglo-Iranian Oil Co. v. S. U. P. O. R. Co., [1955] Int'l L.Rep. 19 (Ct. of Venice), 78 Il Foro Italiano Part I, 719; 40 Blätter für Zürcherische Rechtsprechung No. 65, 172–173 (Switzerland). See also Anglo-Iranian Oil Co. v. Idemitsu Kosan Kabushiki Kaisha, [1953] Int'l L.Rep. 312 (High Ct. of Tokyo).

bid application of the rule even if it is claimed that the act of state in question violated international law. The traditional view of international law is that it establishes substantive principles for determining whether one country has wronged another. Because of its peculiar nation-to-nation character the usual method for an individual to seek relief is to exhaust local remedies and then repair to the executive authorities of his own state to persuade them to champion his claim in diplomacy or before an international tribunal. See United States v. Diekelman, 92 U.S. 520, 524. Although it is, of course, true that United States courts apply international law as a part of our own in appropriate circumstances, Ware v. Hylton, 3 Dall. 199, 281; The Nereide, 9 Cranch 388, 423; The Paquete Habana, 175 U.S. 677, 700, 20 S.Ct. 290, the public law of nations can hardly dictate to a country which is in theory wronged how to treat that wrong within its domestic borders.

Despite the broad statement in Oetjen that "The conduct of the foreign relations of our Government is committed by the Constitution to the Executive and Legislative * * * Departments," 246 U.S., at 302, 38 S.Ct. at 311, it cannot of course be thought that "every case or controversy which touches foreign relations lies beyond judicial cognizance." Baker v. Carr, 369 U.S. 186, 211, 82 S.Ct. 691. The text of the Constitution does not require the act of state doctrine; it does not irrevocably remove from the judiciary the capacity to review the validity of foreign acts of state.

The act of state doctrine does, however, have "constitutional" underpinnings. It arises out of the basic relationships between branches of government in a system of separation of powers. It concerns the competency of dissimilar institutions to make and implement particular kinds of decisions in the area of international relations. The doctrine as formulated in past decisions expresses the strong sense of the Judicial Branch that its engagement in the task of passing on the validity of foreign acts of state may hinder rather than further this country's pursuit of goals both for itself and for the community of nations as a whole in the international sphere. Many commentators disagree with this view; [22] they have striven by means of distinguishing and limiting past decisions and by advancing various considerations of policy to stimulate a narrowing of the apparent scope of the rule. Whatever considerations are thought to predominate, it is plain that the problems involved are uniquely federal in nature. If federal authority, in this instance this Court, orders the field of judicial competence in this area for the federal courts, and

---

22. See, e. g., Association of the Bar of the City of New York, Committee on International Law, A Reconsideration of the Act of State Doctrine in Unites States Courts (1959); Domke, supra, note 21; Mann, International Delinquencies Before Municipal Courts, 70 L.Q.Rev. 181 (1954); Zander, The Act of State Doctrine, 53 Am.J.Int'l L. 826 (1959). But see, e. g., Falk, Toward a Theory of the Participation of Domestic Courts in the International Legal Order: A Critique of Banco Nacional de Cuba v. Sabbatino, 16 Rutgers L.Rev. 1 (1961); Reeves, Act of State Doctrine and the Rule of Law—A Reply, 54 Am.J.Int'l L. 141 (1960).

the state courts are left free to formulate their own rules, the purposes behind the doctrine could be as effectively undermined as if there had been no federal pronouncement on the subject.

We could perhaps in this diversity action avoid the question of deciding whether federal or state law is applicable to this aspect of the litigation. New York has enunciated the act of state doctrine in terms that echo those of federal decisions decided during the reign of Swift v. Tyson, 16 Pet. 1. In Hatch v. Baez, 7 Hun 596, 599 (N.Y. Sup.Ct.), Underhill was foreshadowed by the words, "the courts of one country are bound to abstain from sitting in judgment on the acts of another government done within its own territory." More recently, the Court of Appeals in Salimoff & Co. v. Standard Oil Co., 262 N.Y. 220, 224, 186 N.E. 679, 681, has declared, "The courts of one independent government will not sit in judgment upon the validity of the acts of another done within its own territory, even when such government seizes and sells the property of an American citizen within its boundaries." Cf. Dougherty v. Equitable Life Assurance Society, 266 N.Y. 71, 193 N.E. 897; Holzer v. Deutsche Reichsbahn-Gesellschaft, 277 N.Y. 474, 14 N.E.2d 798. But cf. Frenkel & Co. v. L'Urbaine Fire Ins. Co., 251 N.Y. 243, 167 N.E. 430. Thus our conclusions might well be the same whether we dealt with this problem as one of state law, see Erie R. Co. v. Tompkins, 304 U.S. 64, 58 S.Ct. 817; Klaxon Co. v. Stentor Elec. Mfg. Co., 313 U.S. 487, 61 S.Ct. 1020; Griffin v. McCoach, 313 U.S. 498, 61 S.Ct. 1023, or federal law.

However, we are constrained to make it clear that an issue concerned with a basic choice regarding the competence and function of the Judiciary and the National Executive in ordering our relationships with other members of the international community must be treated exclusively as an aspect of federal law.[23] It seems fair to assume that the Court did not have rules like the act of state doctrine in mind when it decided Erie R. Co. v. Tompkins. Soon thereafter, Professor Philip C. Jessup, now a judge of the International Court of Justice, recognized the potential dangers were Erie extended to legal problems affecting international relations.[24] He cautioned that rules of international law should not be left to divergent and perhaps parochial state interpretations. His basic rationale is equally applicable to the act of state doctrine.

The Court in the pre-Erie act of state cases, although not burdened by the problem of the source of applicable law, used language sufficiently strong and broad-sweeping to suggest that state courts were not left free to develop their own doctrines (as they would have been had this Court merely been interpreting common law under

23. At least this is true when the Court limits the scope of judicial inquiry. We need not now consider whether a state court might, in certain circumstances, adhere to a more restrictive view concerning the scope of examination of foreign acts than that required by this Court.

24. The Doctrine of Erie Railroad v. Tompkins Applied to International Law, 33 Am.J.Int'l L. 740 (1939).

Swift v. Tyson, supra). The Court of Appeals in the first Bernstein case, supra, a diversity suit, plainly considered the decisions of this Court, despite the intervention of Erie, to be controlling in regard to the act of state question, at the same time indicating that New York law governed other aspects of the case. We are not without other precedent for a determination that federal law governs; there are enclaves of federal judge-made law which bind the States. A national body of federal-court-built law has been held to have been contemplated by § 301 of the Labor Management Relations Act, Textile Workers v. Lincoln Mills, 353 U.S. 448, 77 S.Ct. 912. Principles formulated by federal judicial law have been thought by this Court to be necessary to protect uniquely federal interests, D'Oench, Duhme & Co. v. Federal Deposit Ins. Corp., 315 U.S. 447, 62 S.Ct. 676; Clearfield Trust Co. v. United States, 318 U.S. 363, 63 S.Ct. 573. Of course the federal interest guarded in all these cases is one the ultimate statement of which is derived from a federal statute. * * *

* * * We conclude that the scope of the act of state doctrine must be determined according to federal law.[25]

VI.

If the act of state doctrine is a principle of decision binding on federal and state courts alike but compelled by neither international law nor the Constitution, its continuing vitality depends on its capacity to reflect the proper distribution of functions between the judicial and political branches of the Government on matters bearing upon foreign affairs. It should be apparent that the greater the degree of codification or consensus concerning a particular area of international law, the more appropriate it is for the judiciary to render decisions regarding it, since the courts can then focus on the application of an agreed principle to circumstances of fact rather than on the sensitive task of establishing a principle not inconsistent with the national interest or with international justice. It is also evident that some aspects of international law touch much more sharply on national nerves than do others; the less important the implications of an issue are for our foreign relations, the weaker the justification for exclusivity in the political branches. The balance of relevant considerations may also be shifted if the government which perpetrated the challenged act of state is no longer in existence, as in the Bernstein case, for the political interest of this country may, as a result, be measurably altered. Therefore, rather than laying down or reaffirming an inflexible and all-encompassing rule in this case, we decide

---

25. Various constitutional and statutory provisions indirectly support this determination, see U.S.Const., Art. I, § 8, cls. 3, 10; Art. II, §§ 2, 3; Art. III, § 2; 28 U.S.C. §§ 1251(a)(2), (b)(1), (b)(3), 1332(a)(2), 1333, 1350–1351, by reflecting a concern for uniformity in this country's dealings with foreign nations and indicating a desire to give matters of international significance to the jurisdiction of federal institutions. See Comment, The Act of State Doctrine—Its Relation to Private and Public International Law, 62 Col.L.Rev., 1278, 1297, n. 123; cf. United States v. Belmont, supra; United States v. Pink, supra.

only that the Judicial Branch will not examine the validity of a taking of property within its own territory by a foreign sovereign government, extant and recognized by this country at the time of suit, in the absence of a treaty or other unambiguous agreement regarding controlling legal principles, even if the complaint alleges that the taking violates customary international law.

There are few if any issues in international law today on which opinion seems to be so divided as the limitations on a state's power to expropriate the property of aliens.[26] There is, of course, authority, in international judicial [27] and arbitral [28] decisions, in the expressions of national governments,[29] and among commentators [30] for the view that a taking is improper under international law if it is not for a public purpose, is discriminatory, or is without provision for prompt, adequate, and effective compensation. However, Communist countries, although they have in fact provided a degree of compensation after diplomatic efforts, commonly recognize no obligation on the part of the taking country.[31] Certain representatives of the newly independent and underdeveloped countries have questioned whether rules of state responsibility toward aliens can bind nations that have not consented to them [32] and it is argued that the traditionally articulated standards governing expropriation of property reflect "imperi-

---

26. Compare, e. g., Friedman, Expropriation in International Law 206–211 (1953); Dawson and Weston, "Prompt, Adequate and Effective": A Universal Standard of Compensation? 30 Fordham L.Rev. 727 (1962), with Note from Secretary of State Hull to Mexican Ambassador, August 22, 1938, V Foreign Relations of the United States 685 (1938); Doman, Postwar Nationalization of Foreign Property in Europe, 48 Col.L.Rev. 1125, 1127 (1948). We do not, of course, mean to say that there is no international standard in this area; we conclude only that the matter is not meet for adjudication by domestic tribunals.

27. See Oscar Chinn Case, P.C.I.J., ser. A/B, No. 63, at 87 (1934); Chorzow Factory Case, P.C.I.J., ser. A., No. 17, at 46, 47 (1928).

28. See, e. g., Norwegian Shipowners' Case (Norway/United States) (Perm. Ct.Arb.) (1922), 1 U.N.Rep.Int'l Arb. Awards 307, 334, 339 (1948), Hague Court Reports, 2d Series, 39, 69, 74 (1932); Marguerite de Joly de Sabla, American and Panamanian General Claims Arbitration 379, 447, 6 U.N. Rep.Int'l Arb. Awards 358, 336 (1955).

29. See, e. g., Dispatch from Lord Palmerston to British Envoy at Athens,

Aug. 7, 1846, 39 British and Foreign State Papers 1849–1850, 431–432. Note from Secretary of State Hull to Mexican Ambassador, July 21, 1938, V Foreign Relations of the United States 674 (1938); Note to the Cuban Government, July 16, 1960, 43 Dept. State Bull. 171 (1960).

30. See, e. g., McNair, The Seizure of Property and Enterprises in Indonesia, 6 Netherlands Int'l L.Rev. 218, 243–253 (1959); Restatement, Foreign Relations Law of the United States (Proposed Official Draft 1962), §§ 190–195.

31. See Doman, supra, note 26, at 1143–1158; Fleming, States, Contracts and Progress, 62–63 (1960); Bystricky, Notes on Certain International Legal Problems Relating to Socialist Nationalisation, in International Assn. of Democratic Lawyers, Proceedings of the Commission on Private International Law, Sixth Congress (1956), 15.

32. See Anand, Role of the "New" Asian-African Countries in the Present International Legal Order, 56 Am.J.Int'l L. 383 (1962); Roy, Is the Law of Responsibility of States for Injuries to Aliens a Part of Universal International Law? 55 Am.J.Int'l L. 863 (1961).

alist" interests and are inappropriate to the circumstances of emergent states.[33]

The disagreement as to relevant international law standards reflects an even more basic divergence between the national interests of capital importing and capital exporting nations and between the social ideologies of those countries that favor state control of a considerable portion of the means of production and those that adhere to a free enterprise system. It is difficult to imagine the courts of this country embarking on adjudication in an area which touches more sensitively the practical and ideological goals of the various members of the community of nations.[34]

When we consider the prospect of the courts characterizing foreign expropriations, however justifiably, as invalid under international law and ineffective to pass title, the wisdom of the precedents is confirmed. While each of the leading cases in this Court may be argued to be distinguishable on its facts from this one—Underhill because sovereign immunity provided an independent ground and Oetjen Ricaud, and Shapleigh because there was actually no violation of international law—the plain implication of all these opinions, and the import of express statements in Oetjen, 246 U.S., at 304, 38 S.Ct. at 311, and Shapleigh, 299 U.S., at 471, 57 S.Ct. at 262, is that the act of state doctrine is applicable even if international law has been violated. In Ricaud, the one case of the three most plausibly involving an international law violation, the possibility of an exception to the act of state doctrine was not discussed. Some commentators have concluded that it was not brought to the Court's attention,[35] but Justice Clarke delivered both the Oetjen and Ricaud opinions, on the same day, so we can assume that principles stated in the former were applicable to the latter case.

The possible adverse consequences of a conclusion to the contrary of that implicit in these cases is highlighted by contrasting the practices of the political branch with the limitations of the judicial process in matters of this kind. Following an expropriation of any significance, the Executive engages in diplomacy aimed to assure that United States citizens who are harmed are compensated fairly. Representing all claimants of this country, it will often be able, either by bilateral or multilateral talks, by submission to the United Nations, or by the employment of economic and political sanctions, to achieve some degree of general redress. Judicial determinations of invalidity of title can, on the other hand, have only an occasional impact, since

33. See 1957 Yb.U.N.Int'l L. Comm'n (Vol. 1) 155, 158 (statements of Mr. Padilla Nervo (Mexico) and Mr. Pal (India)).

34. There are, of course, areas of international law in which consensus as to standards is greater and which do not represent a battleground for conflicting ideologies. This decision in no way intimates that the courts of this country are broadly foreclosed from considering questions of international law.

35. See Restatement, Foreign Relations Law of the United States, Reporters' Notes (Proposed Official Draft 1962), § 43, Note 3.

they depend on the fortuitous circumstance of the property in question being brought into this country.[36] Such decisions would, if the acts involved were declared invalid, often be likely to give offense to the expropriating country; since the concept of territorial sovereignty is so deep seated, any state may resent the refusal of the courts of another sovereign to accord validity to acts within its territorial borders. Piecemeal dispositions of this sort involving the probability of affront to another state could seriously interfere with negotiations being carried on by the Executive Branch and might prevent or render less favorable the terms of an agreement that could otherwise be reached. Relations with third countries which have engaged in similar expropriations would not be immune from effect.

The dangers of such adjudication are present regardless of whether the State Department has, as it did in this case, asserted that the relevant act violated international law. If the Executive Branch has undertaken negotiations with an expropriating country, but has refrained from claims of violation of the law of nations, a determination to that effect by a court might be regarded as a serious insult, while a finding of compliance with international law, would greatly strengthen the bargaining hand of the other state with consequent detriment to American interests.

Even if the State Department has proclaimed the impropriety of the expropriation, the stamp of approval of its view by a judicial tribunal, however impartial, might increase any affront and the judicial decision might occur at a time, almost always well after the taking, when such an impact would be contrary to our national interest. Considerably more serious and far-reaching consequences would flow from a judicial finding that international law standards had been met if that determination flew in the face of a State Department proclamation to the contrary. When articulating principles of international law in its relations with other states, the Executive Branch speaks not only as an interpreter of generally accepted and traditional rules, as would the courts, but also as an advocate of standards it believes desirable for the community of nations and protective of national concerns. In short, whatever way the matter is cut, the possibility of conflict between the Judicial and Executive Branches could hardly be avoided.

Respondents contend that, even if there is not agreement regarding general standards for determining the validity of expropriations, the alleged combination of retaliation, discrimination, and inadequate compensation makes it patently clear that this particular expropriation was in violation of international law. If this view is accurate, it would still be unwise for the courts so to determine. Such a decision now would require the drawing of more difficult lines in subsequent cases and these would involve the possibility of conflict with the Executive view. Even if the courts avoided this course, either by pre-

---

36. It is, of course, true that such determinations might influence others not to bring expropriated property into the country, * * * so their indirect impact might extend beyond the actual invalidations of title.

suming the validity of an act of state whenever the international law standard was thought unclear or by following the State Department declaration in such a situation, the very expression of judicial uncertainty might provide embarrassment to the Executive Branch.

Another serious consequence of the exception pressed by respondents would be to render uncertain titles in foreign commerce, with the possible consequence of altering the flow of international trade. If the attitude of the United States courts were unclear, one buying expropriated goods would not know if he could safely import them into this country. Even were takings known to be invalid, one would have difficulty determining after goods had changed hands several times whether the particular articles in question were the product of an ineffective state act.

Against the force of such considerations, we find respondents' countervailing arguments quite unpersuasive. Their basic contention is that United States courts could make a significant contribution to the growth of international law, a contribution whose importance, it is said, would be magnified by the relative paucity of decisional law by international bodies. But given the fluidity of present world conditions, the effectiveness of such a patchwork approach toward the formulation of an acceptable body of law concerning state responsibility for expropriations, is, to say the least, highly conjectural. Moreover, it rests upon the sanguine presupposition that the decisions of the courts of the world's major capital exporting country and principal exponent of the free enterprise system would be accepted as disinterested expressions of sound legal principle by those adhering to widely different ideologies.

It is contended that regardless of the fortuitous circumstances necessary for United States jurisdiction over a case involving a foreign act of state and the resultant isolated application to any expropriation program taken as a whole, it is the function of the courts to justly decide individual disputes before them. Perhaps the most typical act of state case involves the original owner or his assignee suing one not in association with the expropriating state who has had "title" transferred to him. But it is difficult to regard the claim of the original owner, who otherwise may be recompensed through diplomatic channels, as more demanding of judicial cognizance than the claim of title by the innocent third party purchaser, who, if the property is taken from him, is without any remedy.

Respondents claim that the economic pressure resulting from the proposed exception to the act of state doctrine will materially add to the protection of United States investors. We are not convinced, even assuming the relevance of this contention. Expropriations take place for a variety of reasons, political and ideological as well as economic. When one considers the variety of means possessed by this country to make secure foreign investment, the persuasive or coercive effect of judicial invalidation of acts of expropriation dwindles in comparison. The newly independent states are in need of continuing foreign investment; the creation of a climate unfavorable to such investment by wholesale confiscations may well work to their long-run economic disadvantage. Foreign aid given to many of these countries provides a powerful lever in the hands of the political branches to ensure fair treatment of United States nationals. Ultimately the sanctions of economic embargo and the freezing of assets in this country may be employed. Any country willing to brave any or all of these consequences is unlikely to be deterred by sporadic judicial decisions directly affecting only property brought to our shores. If the political branches are unwilling to exercise their ample powers to effect compensation, this reflects a judgment of the national interest which the judiciary would be ill-advised to undermine indirectly.

It is suggested that if the act of state doctrine is applicable to violations of international law, it should only be so when the Executive Branch expressly stipulates that it does not wish the courts to pass on the question of validity. See Association of the Bar of the City of New York, Committee on International Law, A Reconsideration of the Act of State Doctrine in United States Courts (1959). We should be slow to reject the representations of the Government that such a reversal of the Bernstein principle would work serious inroads on the maximum effectiveness of United States diplomacy. Often the State Department will wish to refrain from taking an official position particularly at a moment that would be dictated by the developing of private litigation but might be inopportune diplomatically. Adverse domestic consequences might flow from an official stand which could be assuaged, if at all, only by revealing matters best kept secret. Of course, a relevant consideration for the State Department would be the position contemplated in the court to hear the case. It is highly questionable whether the examination of validity by the judiciary should depend on an educated guess by the Executive as to probable result and, at any rate, should a prediction be wrong, the Executive might be embarrassed in its dealings with other countries. We do not now pass on the Bernstein exception, but even if it were deemed valid, its suggested extension is unwarranted.

However offensive to the public policy of this country and its constituent States an expropriation of this kind may be, we conclude that both the national interest and progress toward the goal of establishing the rule of law among nations are best served by maintaining intact the act of state doctrine in this realm of its application.

 *   *   *

The judgment of the Court of Appeals is reversed and the case is remanded to the District Court for proceedings consistent with this opinion.

It is so ordered.

Mr. Justice WHITE dissenting.

I am dismayed that the Court has, with one broad stroke, declared the ascertainment and application of international law beyond the competence of the courts of the United States in a large and important category of cases. I am also disappointed in the Court's declaration that the acts of a sovereign state with regard to the property of aliens within its borders are beyond the reach of international law in the courts of this country. However clearly established that law may be, a sovereign may violate it with impunity, except insofar as the political branches of the government may provide a remedy. This backward-looking doctrine, never before declared in this Court, is carried a disconcerting step further: not only are the courts powerless to question acts of state proscribed by international law but they are likewise powerless to refuse to adjudicate the claim founded upon a foreign law; they must render judgment and thereby validate the lawless act. Since the Court expressly extends its ruling to all acts of state expropriating property, however clearly inconsistent with the international community, all discriminatory expropriations of the property of aliens, as for example the taking of properties of persons belonging to certain races, religions or nationalities, are entitled to automatic validation in the courts of the United States. No other civilized country has found such a rigid rule necessary for the survival of the executive branch of its government; the executive of no other government seems to require such insulation from international law adjudications in its courts; and no other judiciary is apparently so incompetent to ascertain and apply international law.[1]

1. The courts of the following countries, among others, and their territories have examined a fully "executed" foreign act of state expropriating property:

England: Anglo-Iranian Oil Co. v. Jaffrate, [1953] Int'l L.Rep. 316 (Aden Sup.Ct.); N. V. de Bataafsche Petroleum Maatschappij v. The War Damage Comm'n, [1956] Int'l L.Rep. 810 (Singapore Ct.App.).

Netherlands: Senembah Maatschappij N. V. v. Republiek Indonesie Bank Indonesia, Nederlandse Jurisprudentie 1959, No. 73, p. 218 (Amsterdam Ct. App.), excerpts reprinted in Domke, Indonesian Nationalization Measures Before Foreign Courts, 54 Am.J.Int'l L. 305, 307–315 (1960).

Germany: N. V. Verenigde Deli-Maatschapijen v. Deutsch-Indonesische Tabak-Handelsgesellschaft m. b. H. (Bremen Ct.App.), excerpts reprinted in Domke, supra, at 313–314 (1960); Confiscation of Property of Sudeten Germans Case, [1948] Ann.Dig. 24, 25 (No. 12) (Amtsgericht of Dingolfing).

Japan: Anglo-Iranian Oil Co. v. Idemitsu Kosan Kabushiki Kaisha, [1953] Int'l L.Rep. 305 (Dist.Ct. of Tokyo), aff'd, [1953] Int'l L.Rep. 312 (High Ct. of Tokyo).

Italy: Anglo-Iranian Oil Co. v. S. U. P. O. R. Co., [1955] Int'l L.Rep. 19 (Ct. of Venice); Anglo-Iranian Oil Co. v. S. U. P. O. R. Co., [1955] Int'l L.Rep. 23 (Civ.Ct. of Rome).

France: Volatron v. Moulin, [1938–1940] Ann.Dig. 24 (Ct. of App. of Aix); Société Potasas Ibericas v. Nathan Bloch, [1938–1940] Ann.Dig. 150 (Ct. of Cassation).

The Court does not refer to any country which has applied the act of state doctrine in a case where a substantial international law issue is sought to be raised by an alien whose property has been expropriated. This country and this Court stand alone among the civilized nations of the world in ruling that such an issue is not cognizable in a court of law.

The Court notes that the courts of both New York and Great Britain have articulated the act of state doctrine in broad language similar to that used by this Court in Underhill v. Hernandez, 168 U.S. 250, 18 S.Ct. 83, and from this it infers that these courts recognize no international law exception to the act of state doctrine. The cases relied on by the Court involved no international law issue. For in these cases the party objecting to the validity of the foreign act was a citizen of the foreign state. It is significant that courts of both New York and Great Britain, in apparently the first cases in which an international

I do not believe that the act of state doctrine as judicially fashioned in this Court, and the reasons underlying it, require American courts to decide cases in disregard of international law and of the rights of litigants to a full determination on the merits.

[The remaining text of Mr. Justice WHITE's extensive dissenting opinion is omitted.]

How much of United States foreign affairs law is conclusively determinable only by the United States Supreme Court, despite the doctrine of Erie R. R. Co. v. Tomkins? Students of federal courts law, admiralty, and conflict of laws will recognize the possibilities inherent in the breadth of the court's statement covering its holding that the act of state doctrine falls, even in diversity of citizenship cases, within the penumbra of federal interest, i. e. where the federal courts find or make law: " * * * [W]e are constrained to make clear that an issue concerned with a basic choice regarding the competence and function of the judiciary and the National Executive in ordering our relationships with other members of the international community *must* be treated *exclusively* as an aspect of federal law." [Emphasis supplied.] This statement is certainly sufficient to cover all the concerns about the Erie decision that Jessup had in mind in his 1939 article, cited in the court's note 24. Additionally it could serve to expand the authority of the federal courts to declare the rules governing private rights and duties in a variety of international transactions situations. The trend, as is well known, has been for the Supreme Court to enlarge the sectors of federal interest in which, even in diversity cases, the federal courts make or find rules where there is no specific federal statutory norm, as is slowly the continual development of the general law maritime, which governs even in state court proceedings.

law issue was squarely posed, ruled that the act of state doctrine was no bar to examination of the validity of the foreign act. Anglo-Iranian Oil Co. v. Jaffrate, [1953] Int'l L.Rep. 316 (Aden Sup.Ct.): "[T]he Iranian Laws of 1951 were invalid by international law, for, by them, the property of the company was expropriated without any compensation." Sulyok v. Penzintezeti Kozpont Budapest, 279 App.Div. 528, 111 N.Y.S.2d 75, aff'd, 304 N.Y. 704, 107 N.E.2d 604 (foreign expropriation of intangible property denied effect as contrary to New York public policy).

SECTION B. LEGISLATIVE AND EXECUTIVE INFLUENCES ON JUDICIAL APPLICATION OR NON–APPLICATION OF THE DOCTRINE IN THE UNITED STATES

UNITED STATES: THE "HICKENLOOPER AMENDMENTS" TO THE FOREIGN ASSISTANCE ACT

22 U.S.C. § 2370.

Prohibitions against furnishing assistance

*   *   *

(e)(1) The President shall suspend assistance to the government of any country to which assistance is provided under this chapter or any other Act when the government of such country or any government agency or subdivision within such country on or after January 1, 1962—

(A) has nationalized or expropriated or seized ownership or control of property owned by any United States citizen or by any corporation, partnership, or association not less than 50 per centum beneficially owned by United States citizens, or

(B) has taken steps to repudiate or nullify existing contracts or agreements with any United States citizen or any corporation, partnership, or association not less than 50 per centum beneficially owned by United States citizens, or

(C) has imposed or enforced discriminatory taxes or other exactions, or restrictive maintenance or operational conditions, or has taken other actions, which have the effect of nationalizing, expropriating, or otherwise seizing ownership or control of property so owned,

and such country, government agency, or government subdivision fails within a reasonable time (not more than six months after such action, or, in the event of a referral to the Foreign Claims Settlement Commission of the United States within such period as provided herein, not more than twenty days after the report of the Commission is received) to take appropriate steps, which may include arbitration, to discharge its obligations under international law toward such citizen or entity, including speedy compensation for such property in convertible foreign exchange, equivalent to the full value thereof, as required by international law, or fails to take steps designed to provide relief from such taxes, exactions, or conditions, as the case may be; and such suspension shall continue until the President is satisfied that appropriate steps are being taken *   *   *.

Upon request of the President (within seventy days after such action referred to in subparagraphs (A), (B), or (C) of this paragraph), the Foreign Claims Settlement Commission of the United States (established pursuant to Reorganization Plan No. 1 of 1954, 68 Stat. 1279) is hereby authorized to evaluate expropriated property, determining the full value of any property nationalized, expropriated, or seized, or subjected to discriminatory or other actions as aforesaid, for purposes of this subsection and to render an advisory report to the President within ninety days after such request. Unless authorized by the President, the Commission shall not publish its advisory report except to the citizen or entity owning such property. There is hereby authorized to be appropriated such amount, to remain available until expended, as may be necessary from time to time to enable the Commission to carry out expeditiously its functions under this subsection.

(2) Notwithstanding any other provision of law, no court in the United States shall decline on the ground of the federal act of state doctrine to make a determination on the merits giving effect to the principles of international law in a case in which a claim of title or other right to property is asserted by any party including a foreign state (or a party claiming through such state) based upon (or traced through) a confiscation or other taking after January 1, 1959, by an act of that state in violation of the principles of international law, *including the principles of compensation and the other standards set out in this subsection: Provided,* That this subparagraph shall not be applicable (1) in any case in which an act of a foreign state is not contrary to international law or with respect to a claim of title or other right to property acquired pursuant to an irrevocable letter of credit of not more than 180 days duration issued in good faith prior to the time of the confiscation or other taking, or (2) in any case with respect to which the President determines that application of the act of state doctrine is required in that particular case by the foreign policy interests of the United States and a suggestion to this effect is filed on his behalf in that case with the court. [Emphasis supplied.]

                    *   *   *

_____

1. *The second Hickenlooper amendment, 22 USC § 2370(e)(2), held not to violate separation of powers or other constitutional requirements.* The Supreme Court let stand the decision of the Court of Appeals for the Second Circuit to the above effect in Banco Nacional de Cuba v. Farr, Whitlock & Co., 383 F.2d 166 (1967). In deciding the Farr, Whitlock case the court of appeals reiterated its earlier holding in the Sabbatino case that the taking by Cuba had violated customary international law, an issue that the Supreme Court did not reach in the Sabbatino case, because of its holding that the act of state doctrine precluded decision on the merits. As a result, the denial of certiorari in Farr, Whitlock also let stand the consequence of the court of appeals decision in the Sabbatino case, that the violation of international law by the act of nationalization authorized the remedy of invalidation of title to the property (and its produce) sought to have been nationalized. Also, in Farr, Whitlock (which is the Sabbatino case again with a slight change in a nominal

party) after the remand from the Supreme Court to the District Court: " * * * for proceedings consistent with this [the Sabbatino] opinion * * *," the court of appeals found nothing constitutionally wrong with the application to the same real parties and the same cause of action of the intervening second Hickenlooper amendment, which was enacted after the Supreme Court remanded the Sabbatino case and which was explained in a Senate report as being legislation designed " * * * to reverse in part the recent decision of the Supreme Court * * *" in the Sabbatino case. In fact, the court of appeals quoted this report in support of its decision in the Farr, Whitlock case. In the United Kingdom an act of Parliament has been held to overrule the final judgment of the highest court in the land. Is this possible also under the Constitution of the United States? Normally it certainly is not. Should the issue of valid or invalid retroactive application of the second Hickenlooper amendment turn on the legal effect of the Supreme Court's remand order? Did the successful parties in the Sabbatino case have a vested right in the decision in their favor on the act of state doctrine? Or, did the remand leave the case open as if not previously decided, so as to be validly reachable by the later enacted second Hickenlooper amendment?

2. *The Hickenlooper amendments and international law and practice as to nationalization.* The first Hickenlooper amendment to the Foreign Assistance Act, Section 2370(e)(1), lays down a set of standards as to what Congress evidently assumed customary international law requires of a state that nationalizes or otherwise impairs the economic interests of an American citizen or corporation. These standards should be reviewed as to their correctness as international law, as a later note will suggest, after the material in Chapter 17, Section B, has been studied. The same standards are, of course, the basis for the directive to the courts in the second Hickenlooper amendment, Section 2370(e)(2).

Section 2370(e)(1) requires appropriate affirmative action, under international law (as interpreted by the standards in the legislation), within not more than six months after the act of taking, or, in the event that referral is made to the Foreign Claims Settlement Commission of the United States, within 20 days after that body has passed on the validity of the claim or claims submitted to it. As the alternative of referral to the commission has not been used so far in recent instances of nationalization, the effective deadline is usually six months. Within that period the statute requires that nationalizing state " * * * to take appropriate steps, which may include arbitration, to discharge its obligations * * *" to the satisfaction of the President of the United States. This is a far shorter time span than the usual period required for reaching an assured solution to a nationalization problem by diplomatic means, including an agreement to arbitrate or to refer the case to adjudication. Moreover, a number of developing countries that have nationalized adamantly refuse to accept arbitration or external adjudication.

3. *Presidential discretion as to the application of 22 USC §
2370(e)(1)*. The code section cited contains a series of congressional
prohibitions on foreign assistance that as subsections exhaust the al-
phabet, although three of these lettered sub-sections have been repealed. The first Hickenlooper amendment in (e)(1) was, until a few
years ago, unusual among these prohibitions in that it did not allow
presidential waiver on foreign policy grounds, as the other sub-sections
did, although on the basis of a requirement that the President report
such waivers to Congress, with reasons. The refusal to extend waiver to (e)(1) in part reflected the intensity of feeling of those who
supported—and lobbied for—denial of foreign assistance as an inducement against nationalizations not strictly conforming to congressional notions of what international law requires as to such host state
conduct. An *in terrorem* effect was firmly believed in by a self-
styled rule of law group of lawyers representing American business
investments abroad. Also involved was mounting congressional determination to influence foreign affairs operations directly.

Nonetheless, experience with several post-enactment nationalization crises showed that developing countries were not being deterred
by the threat of suspension of foreign assistance. When in 1968 a
military junta that first deposed the president of Peru for having settled a nationalization case involving the International Petroleum Company (acquired from Canadian interests by the then Standard Oil
Company of New Jersey) and then nationalized International without
compensation, the first Hickenlooper amendment was not applied,
even though well after six months no signs of willingness on the part
of the junta to settle on Congress's terms had become evident. Instead, the President's representatives sought out key congressional
figures to explain why it would be undesirable to apply the amendment. The reason given and accepted was that so public a use of the
American power to deny foreign assistance in a tense nationalization
situation would induce wholesale nationalizations of American investments in other Latin American countries.

Subsection (e)(1), actually, has been used only once, against Sri
Lanka, with no discernible results. In all other cases quiet diplomacy
has been the vehicle of settlement.

4. *The second Hickenlooper amendment and the six months period*. In the decisions that follow we shall see that the courts have
not been prone to apply Sub-section (e)(2) any more widely than exactly as written. It remains to be seen whether the problems mentioned above as to the running of time for Sub-section (e)(1) will be
taken into account by courts in Sub-section (e)(2) cases. Suppose,
for example, that oil now in the United States is identifiable as having been refined in the nationalizing state and a private purchaser is
sued in the United States for conversion during a period of informal
suspension of Sub-section (e)(1). What effect will be given by a
court to Sub-section (e)(2) if the Department of State chooses not to
express a position to the court? What if the Department of State

suggests that Sub-section (e) (2) should be applied by the court, even though the executive branch has not applied Sub-section (e) (1)?

FIRST NATIONAL CITY BANK v. BANCO NACIONAL DE CUBA

United States Supreme Court, 1972.
406 U.S. 759, 92 S.Ct. 1808.

Mr. Justice REHNQUIST announced the judgment of the Court, and delivered an opinion in which The Chief Justice and Mr. Justice WHITE, join.

In July 1958, petitioner loaned the sum of $15 million to a predecessor of respondent. The loan was secured by a pledge of United States Government bonds. The loan was renewed the following year, and in 1960 $5 million was repaid, the $10 million balance was renewed for one year, and collateral equal to the value of the portion repaid was released by petitioner.

Meanwhile, on January 1, 1959, the Castro government came to power in Cuba. On September 16, 1960, the Cuban militia, allegedly pursuant to decrees of the Castro government, seized all of the branches of petitioner located in Cuba. A week later the bank retaliated by selling the collateral securing the loan, and applying the proceeds of the sale to repayment of the principal and unpaid interest. Petitioner concedes that an excess of at least $1.8 million over and above principal and unpaid interest was realized from the sale of the collateral. Respondent sued petitioner in the Federal District Court to recover this excess, and petitioner, by way of set-off and counterclaim asserted the right to recover damages as a result of the expropriation of its property in Cuba.

The District Court recognized that our decision in Banco Nacional de Cuba v. Sabbatino, 376 U.S. 398, 84 S.Ct. 923, 11 L.Ed.2d 804 (1964), holding that generally the courts of one nation will not sit in judgment on the acts of another nation within its own territory would bar the assertion of the counterclaim, but it further held that congressional enactments since the decision in Sabbatino had "for all practical purposes" overruled that case. Following summary judgment in favor of the petitioner in the District Court on all issues except the amount by which the proceeds of the sale of collateral exceeded the amount which could properly be applied to the loan by petitioner, the parties stipulated that in any event this difference was less than the damages which petitioner could prove in support of its expropriation claim if that claim were allowed. Petitioner then waived any recovery on its counterclaim over and above the amount recoverable by respondent on its complaint, and the District Court then rendered judgment dismissing respondent's complaint on the merits.

On appeal, the Court of Appeals for the Second Circuit held that the congressional enactments relied upon by the District Court did not govern this case, and that our decision in Sabbatino barred the assertion of petitioner's counterclaim. We granted certiorari and vacated the judgment of the Court of Appeals for consideration of the views of the Department of State which had been furnished to us following the filing of the petition for certiorari. 400 U.S. 1019, 91 S. Ct. 581, 27 L.Ed.2d 630 (1971). Upon reconsideration, the Court of Appeals by a divided vote adhered to its earlier decision. We again granted certiorari, First National City Bank v. Banco Nacional de Cuba, 404 U.S. 820, 92 S.Ct. 79, 30 L.Ed.2d 48.

We must here decide whether, in view of the substantial difference between the position taken in this case by the Executive Branch and that which it took in Sabbatino, the act of state doctrine prevents petitioner from litigating its counterclaim on the merits. We hold that it does not.

* * *

In Sabbatino, the Executive Branch of this Government, speaking through the Department of State, advised attorneys for amici in a vein which the Court described as being "intended to reflect no more than the Department's then wish not to make any statement bearing on this litigation." 376 U.S., at 420, 84 S.Ct., at 936. The United States argued before this Court in Sabbatino that the Court should not "hold for the first time that Executive silence regarding the act of state doctrine is equivalent to executive approval of judicial inquiry into the foreign act."

In the case now before us, the Executive Branch has taken a quite different position. The Legal Adviser of the Department of State advised this Court on November 17, 1970,[a] that as a matter of principle where the Executive publicly advises the Court that the act of state doctrine need not be applied, the Court should proceed to examine the legal issues raised by the act of a foreign sovereign within its own territory as it would any other legal question before it. His letter refers to the decision of the Court below in Bernstein v. N. V. Nederlandsche Amerikaansche, etc., 210 F.2d 375 (CA 2 1954), as representing a judicial recognition of such a principle, and suggests that the applicability of the principle was not limited to the *Bernstein* case. The Legal Adviser's letter then goes on to state:

> The Department of State believes that the act of state doctrine should not be applied to bar consideration of a defendant's counterclaim or set off against the government of Cuba in this or like cases.

a. The letter from the Legal Adviser is discussed and reproduced in part on p. 398.

The question which we must now decide is whether the so-called *Bernstein* exception to the act of state doctrine should be recognized in the context of the facts before the Court. In Sabbatino, the Court said:

> This Court has never had occasion to pass upon the so-called *Bernstein* exception, nor need it do so now. 276 U.S., at 420, 84 S.Ct., at 936.

* * *

The line of cases from this Court establishing the act of state doctrine justify its existence primarily on the basis that juridical review of acts of state of a foreign power could embarrass the conduct of foreign relations by the political branches of the government.

* * *

United States v. Belmont, 301 U.S. 324, 57 S.Ct. 758, 81 L.Ed. 1134, is another case that emphasized the exclusive competence of the executive branch in the field of foreign affairs. A year earlier, the Court in United States v. Curtiss-Wright Corp., 299 U.S. 304, 319, 57 S.Ct. 216, 220, 81 L.Ed. 255, had quoted with approval the statement of John Marshall when he was a member of the House of Representatives dealing with this same subject:

> The President is the sole organ of the nation in its external relations, and its sole representative with foreign nations.

* * *

We think that the examination of the foregoing cases indicates that this Court has recognized the primacy of the Executive in the conduct of foreign relations quite as emphatically as it has recognized the act of state doctrine. The Court in Sabbatino throughout its opinion emphasized the lead role of the executive in foreign policy, particularly in seeking redress for American nationals who had been the victims of foreign expropriation, and concluded that any exception to the act of state doctrine based on a mere silence or neutrality on the part of the executive might well lead to a conflict between the executive and judicial branches. Here, however, the Executive Branch has expressly stated that an inflexible application of the act of state doctrine by this Court would not serve the interests of American foreign policy.

The act of state doctrine is grounded on judicial concern that application of customary principles of law to judge the acts of a foreign sovereign might frustrate the conduct of foreign relations by the political branches of the government. We conclude that where the Executive Branch, charged as it is with primary responsibility for the conduct of foreign affairs, expressly represents to the Court that the act of state doctrine would not advance the interests of American foreign policy, that doctrine should not be applied by the courts. In so doing, we of course adopt and approve the so-called *Bernstein* exception to the act of state doctrine. We believe this to be no more than an application of the classical common-law maxim that "the reason of the law ceasing, the law itself also ceases" (Black's Law Dictionary, p. 288).

Our holding is in no sense an abdication of the judicial function to the Executive Branch. The judicial power of the United States extends to this case, and the jurisdictional standards established by Congress for adjudication by the federal courts have been met by the parties. The only reason for not deciding the case by use of otherwise applicable legal principles would be the fear that legal interpretation by the judiciary of the act of a foreign sovereign within its own territory might frustrate the conduct of this country's foreign relations. But the branch of the government responsible for the conduct of those foreign relations has advised us that such a consequence need not be feared in this case. The judiciary is therefore free to decide the case free from the limitations that would otherwise be imposed upon it by the judicially created act of state doctrine.

* * *

The act of state doctrine, as reflected in the cases culminating in Sabbatino, is a judicially accepted limitation on the normal adjudicative processes of the courts, springing from the thoroughly sound principle that on occasion individual litigants may have to forego decision on the merits of their claims because the involvement of the courts in such a decision might frustrate the conduct of the Nation's foreign policy. It would be wholly illogical to insist that such a rule, fashioned because of fear that adjudication would interfere with the conduct of foreign relations, be applied in the face of an assurance from that branch of the Federal Government which conducts foreign relations that such a result would not obtain. Our holding confines the courts to adjudication of the case before them, and leaves to the Executive Branch the conduct of foreign relations. In so doing, it is both faithful to the principle of separation of powers and consistent with earlier cases applying the act of state doctrine where we lacked the sort of representation from the Executive Branch which we have in this case.

We therefore reverse the judgment of the Court of Appeals, and remand the case to it for consideration of respondent's alternative bases of attack on the judgment of the District Court.

Reversed.

Mr. Justice DOUGLAS, concurring in the result.

Banco Nacional de Cuba v. Sabbatino, 376 U.S. 398, 84 S.Ct. 923, 11 L.Ed.2d 804, does not control the central issue in the present case. Rather, it is governed by National City Bank v. Republic of China, 348 U.S. 356, 75 S.Ct. 423, 99 L.Ed. 389.

* * *

It would offend the sensibilities of nations if one country, not at war with us, had our courthouse door closed to it. It would also offend our sensibilities if Cuba could collect the amount owed on liquidation of the collateral for the loan and not be required to account for any setoff. To allow recovery without more would permit Cuba to have her cake and eat it too. Fair dealing requires allowance of the setoff to the amount of the claim on which this suit is brought—a precept that should satisfy any so-called rational decision.

* * *

Mr. Justice POWELL, concurring in the judgment.

Although I concur in the judgment of reversal and remand, my reasons differ from those expressed by Mr. Justice REHNQUIST and Mr. Justice DOUGLAS. While Banco Nacional de Cuba v. Sabbatino, 376 U.S. 398, 419–420, 84 S.Ct. 923, 935–936, 11 L.Ed.2d 804 (1964), technically reserves the question of the validity of the *Bernstein* exception, as Mr. Justice BRENNAN notes in his dissenting opinion, the reasoning of Sabbatino implicitly rejects that exception. Moreover, I would be uncomfortable with a doctrine which would require the judiciary to receive the executive's permission before invoking its jurisdiction. Such a notion, in the name of the doctrine of separation of powers, seems to me to conflict with that very doctrine.

* * *

I nevertheless concur in the judgment of the Court because I believe that the broad holding of Sabbatino was not compelled by the principles, as expressed therein, which underlie the act of state doctrine. As Mr. Justice Harlan stated in Sabbatino, the act of state doctrine is not dictated either by "international law [or] the Constitution," but is based on a judgment as to "the proper distribution of functions between the judicial and the political branches of the Government on matters bearing upon foreign affairs." 376 U.S., at 427–428, 84 S.Ct., at 940. Moreover, as noted in Sabbatino, there was no intention of "laying down or reaffirming an inflexible and all-encompassing rule. * * *" Id., at 428, 84 S.Ct., at 940.

I do not disagree with these principles, only with the broad way in which Sabbatino applied them. Had I been a member of the Sabbatino Court, I probably would have joined the dissenting opinion of Mr. Justice White. The balancing of interests, recognized as appropriate by Sabbatino, requires a careful examination of the facts in each case and of the position, if any, taken by the political branches of government, I do not agree, however, that balancing the functions of the judiciary and those of the political branches compels the judiciary to eschew acting in all cases in which the underlying issue is the validity of expropriation under customary international law. Such a result would be an abdication of the judiciary's responsibility to persons who seek to resolve their grievances by the judicial process.

Nor do I think the doctrine of separation of powers dictates such an abdication. To so argue is to assume that there is no such thing as international law but only international political disputes that can be resolved only by the exercise of power. Admittedly, international legal disputes are not as separable from politics as are domestic legal disputes, but I am not prepared to say that international law may never be determined and applied by the judiciary where there has been an "act of state." Until international tribunals command a wider constituency, the courts of various countries afford the best means for the development of a respected body of international law. There is less hope for progress in this long neglected area if the resolution of all disputes involving "an act of state" is relegated to political rather than judicial processes.

Unless it appears that an exercise of jurisdiction would interfere with delicate foreign relations conducted by the political branches, I conclude that federal courts have an obligation to hear cases such as this. This view is not inconsistent with the basic notion of the act of state doctrine which requires a balancing of the rules of the judiciary and the political branches. When it is shown that a conflict in those roles exists, I believe that the judiciary should defer because, as the Court suggested in Sabbatino, the resolution of one dispute by the judiciary may be outweighed by the potential resolution of multiple disputes by the political branches.

In this case where no such conflict has been shown, I think the courts have a duty to determine and apply the applicable international law. I therefore join in the Court's decision to remand the case for further proceedings.

Mr. Justice BRENNAN, with whom Mr. Justice STEWART, Mr. Justice MARSHALL, and Mr. Justice BLACKMUN join, dissenting.

The Court today reverses the judgment of the Court of Appeals for the Second Circuit that declined to engraft the so-called "*Bernstein*" exception upon the act of state doctrine as expounded in Banco Nacional de Cuba v. Sabbatino, 376 U.S. 398, 84 S.Ct. 923, 11 L.Ed.2d 804 (1964). The Court nevertheless, affirms the Court of Appeals' rejection of the *Bernstein* exception. Four of us in this opinion unequivocally take that step, as do Mr. Justice Douglas and Mr. Justice Powell in their separate concurring opinions.

The anomalous remand for further proceedings results because three colleagues, Mr. Justice Rehnquist, joined by The Chief Justice and Mr. Justice White, adopt the contrary position, while Mr. Justice Douglas finds National City Bank v. Republic of China, 348 U.S. 356, 75 S.Ct. 423, 99 L.Ed. 389 (1955), dispositive in the circumstances of this case and Mr. Justice Powell rejects the specific holding in Sabbatino, believing it was not required by the principles underlying the act of state doctrine. [Remainder of dissenting opinion omitted.]

---

1. *Excerpts from the letter of the Legal Adviser, Department of State.* The full text of the latest executive branch viewpoint on the act of state doctrine (referred to by the Supreme Court in the text of its opinion at footnote a, p. 394) is carried as an appendix to the second consideration of this case by the Court of Appeals for the Second Circuit, 442 F.2d 530, 536 (1971). The Legal Adviser of the Department of State referred to the first decision by the court of ap-

peals in the First National City Bank case (i. e. Section 2370(e)(2) of Title 22 of the United States Code did not apply to the claim and hence the act of state doctrine as laid down by the Supreme Court in the Sabbatino case did apply) [a] and stated that the decision involved matters of importance of the foreign policy of the United States, called attention to the Bernstein exception, disagreed with the non-application of it in the first opinion by the court of appeals, and continued as follows:

> While the Department of State in the past has generally supported the applicability of the act of state doctrine, it has never argued or implied that there should be no exceptions to the doctrine. In its Sabbatino brief, for example, it did not argue for or against the Bernstein principle; rather it assumed that judicial consideration of an act of state would be permissible when the Executive so indicated, and argued simply that the exchange of letters relied on by the lower courts in Sabbatino constituted "no such expression in this case." Brief of the United States, page 11.

> Recent events, in our view, make appropriate a determination by the Department of State that the act of state doctrine need not be applied when it is raised to bar adjudication of a counterclaim or setoff when (a) the foreign state's claim arises from a relationship between the parties existing when the act of state occurred; (b) the amount of the relief to be granted is limited to the amount of the foreign state's claim; and (c) the foreign policy interests of the United States do not require application of the doctrine.

> The 1960's have seen a great increase in expropriations by foreign governments of property belonging to United States citizens. Many corporations whose properties are expropriated, financial institutions for example, are vulnerable to suits in our courts by foreign governments as plaintiff, for the purpose of recovering deposits or sums owed them in the United States without taking into account the institutions' counterclaims for their assets expropriated in the foreign country.

> The basic considerations of fairness and equity suggesting that the act of state doctrine not be applied in this class of cases, unless the foreign policy interests of the United States so require in a particular case, were reflected in National City Bank [of New York] v. Republic of China, 348 U.S. 356 [75 S.Ct 423, 99 L. Ed. 389] (1956), in which the Supreme Court held that the pro-

---

a. Because the property at issue in the case (the excess of collateral over debt) was not the property (banks in Cuba) actually taken by Castro. The court said:

* * * [W]e can find no basis for holding that the present case is one "in which a claim of title or other right to property is asserted by [First National City] * * * based upon (or traced through) a confiscation or other taking * * * " 22 U.S.C. § 2370(e)(2). To do so would stand the statute on end. * * * 431 F.2d 394, 402 (1970).

tection of sovereign immunity is waived when a foreign sovereign enters a U. S. court as plaintiff. While the Court did not deal with the act of state doctrine, the basic premise of that case—that a sovereign entering court as plaintiff opens itself to counterclaims, up to the amount of the original claim, which could be brought against it by that defendant were the sovereign an ordinary plaintiff—is applicable by analogy to the situation presented in the present case.

In this case, the Cuban government's claim arose from a banking relationship with the defendant existing at the time the act of state—expropriation of defendant's Cuban property—occurred, and defendant's counterclaim is limited to the amount of the Cuban government's claim. We find, moreover, that the foreign policy interests of the United States do not require the application of the act of state doctrine to bar adjudication of the validity of a defendant's counterclaim or set-off against the Government of Cuba in these circumstances.

The Department of State believes that the act of state doctrine should not be applied to bar consideration of a defendant's counterclaim or set-off against the Government of Cuba in this or like cases.

2. *Some questions suggested by the First National City Bank case.*

A. Why did the Department of State change its general attitude about the weight that should be given to executive branch viewpoints as to the applicability or not of the act of state doctrine in nationalization cases? This was a Cuban nationalization case. What do you guess the Department of State would advise the court as to act of state in the hypothetical case at p. 392? What procedure, as to notice, hearing, and the like, if any, do you think the Department of State should provide—or be required to provide—as a prelude to its taking of a position very likely to control the outcome of the case?

b. This case was remanded " * * * for the consideration of respondent's alternative bases of attack on the judgment of the District Court * * *." What law, federal or state, will govern as to issues on remand not covered by federal statutes? See p. 388.

c. What do you think of Justice Douglas' treatment of the case as one of immunity in regard to a counterclaim against a foreign state when it has sued as plaintiff? See p. 343.

d. What does Justice Powell's opinion suggest as to the future of the act of state doctrine?

e. Considering the second Hickenlooper amendment and the decision of the Supreme Court in the instant case, do you think that the courts have any assured independence of the Congress or the executive with respect to the application of the act of state doctrine?

f. If your answer is no, does the doctrine have any remaining utility in the foreign affairs law of the United States?

g.   If your answer is yes, what is the probable future of the doctrine in this country?

h.   What would be your impartial professional attitude as to a federal statute to simplify the present situation by striking the present second Hickenlooper amendment and substituting the following:

> The so-called Act of State doctrine shall never be available as a bar to consideration of any case on the merits in any court in the United States with jurisdiction over the parties and the subject matter, unless the President, through his authorized representative, shall state to the court that he has no objection to the application of the said doctrine to bar the suit.

The policy and legal issues raised by the present status of the act of state doctrine in the United States are examined in Lowenfeld, Act of State and Department of State: First National City Bank v. Banco Nacional de Cuba, 66 Am.J.Int'l Law 795 (1972).

WHAT TYPES OF INTERESTS AND CAUSES OF ACTION BENEFIT FROM SECOND HICKENLOOPER?

HUNT v. COASTAL STATES GAS PRODUCING CO.

United States, Supreme Court of Texas, 1979.
583 S.W.2d 322 (1979).[a]

BARROW, Justice.

This suit was instituted by Nelson Bunker Hunt, Herbert Hunt and Lamar Hunt (Hunt) seeking damages against Coastal States Gas Producing Company and Coastal States Marketing, Inc. (Coastal States) for the alleged conversion of oil to which Hunt was entitled by virtue of a concession agreement with Libya. Coastal States counterclaimed for damages for Hunt's allegedly tortious interference with the contract and business opportunities of Coastal States. Both parties moved for summary judgment on the issue of liability after extensive development of the case. The trial court denied relief on all claims and the court of civil appeals affirmed. 570 S.W.2d 503. We affirm the judgment of the court of civil appeals.

In 1957 the Government of Libya granted Hunt a concession which gave him the right, for fifty years, to explore, drill and extract oil in an area now identified as the Sarir field. Hunt assigned a one-half undivided interest in this concession to British Petroleum Exploration Company, Ltd. (British Petroleum) in 1960. Oil was discovered in the concession area in 1961 and, by 1967, it was produced in marketable quantities. In September 1969, Colonel Mu'ammar al-Qadhafi assumed power in Libya under a new government, the Revolutionary Command Council, and commenced making changes in the

a.   Rehearing denied, July 18, 1979; application for certiorari denied 100 S.Ct. 523, 62 L.Ed.2d 421 (1979).

existing contractual relations with the various oil producers holding concession agreements with Libya. In 1971, the Libyan Government nationalized the operations and interest of British Petroleum in the Sarir field and transferred its rights to the Arabian Gulf Exploration Company (AGECO). AGECO is a corporation whose entire capital stock is owned by the Libyan Government.

On June 20, 1973, by Libyan Law No. 42 of 1973, the Libyan Government nationalized all the rights and assets of Hunt in the concession agreement and assigned these rights to AGECO. Although Libya agreed to pay compensation, the amount was to be determined by a committee designated by the State. In response to this action, Hunt published notices in newspapers throughout the world claiming that the Libyan nationalization violated international law and threatened suit against anyone who came into possession of Sarir oil. In May 1973, Coastal States entered into a contract with AGECO to purchase oil from the Sarir field and it continued to purchase oil under this contract despite Hunt's claims against Libya and threatened suits. This oil was transported by Coastal States to a refinery in Italy where it was processed and sold to third parties. It was stipulated that a portion of the products derived from this oil was subsequently taken to the United States, although it was not stipulated that Coastal States transported or caused any of such products to be brought here. Nevertheless, Coastal States is domiciled in the United States and, at least, the net proceeds derived from the Sarir oil were brought here and are the basis of Hunt's suit for conversion.

British Petroleum was a party to the controversy with Coastal States at one time, but it subsequently entered into a full settlement with the Libyan Government after arbitration of its claim and it does not now assert any claim against Coastal States.[1] In May 1975 Hunt entered into a settlement agreement with the Libyan Government whereby, for the sum of approximately $19,000,000, it released any and all claims against the Libyan Government arising out of the nationalization of the Sarir field. Coastal States was not a party to this agreement and Hunt now seeks to recover the proceeds realized by Coastal States from oil allegedly purchased from AGECO prior to the May 1975 settlement.

Both the trial court and the court of civil appeals concluded that the trial court was foreclosed from inquiring into the validity of the Libyan nationalization of Hunt's interest in the Sarir field by the Act of State Doctrine. These courts further concluded that as a matter of law, Hunt's actions in giving notice of his claim to oil from the Sarir field did not violate either state or federal law and would not support Coastal States' claim for damages for tortious interference. Hunt and Coastal States both filed applications for writ of error and complain of the take-nothing judgment entered on the claim of each.

---

1. The arbitrator held that Hunt did not acquire title to the oil in the strata.

Appeal by Hunt

Hunt's claim against Coastal States is necessarily based upon the assertion that Libya's expropriation was invalid so that Coastal States acquired no title from AGECO. The critical question involved in Hunt's appeal is the applicability of the Act of State Doctrine and more precisely, whether Hunt's suit comes within the exception to the doctrine created by the Hickenlooper Amendment, 22 U.S.C. § 2370(e)(2). The lower courts have held that the doctrine bars inquiry by a Texas court into the validity of acts done by a foreign sovereign.

The Act of State Doctrine is a judicially created doctrine of restraint. The landmark case of Banco Nacional de Cuba v. Sabbatino, 376 U.S. 398, 84 S.Ct. 923, 11 L.Ed.2d 804 (1964) reaffirmed the doctrine as originally articulated in Underhill v. Hernandez, 168 U.S. 250, 18 S.Ct. 83, 42 L.Ed. 456 (1897) in the following language:

> Every sovereign State is bound to respect the independence of every other sovereign State, and the courts of one country will not sit in judgment on the acts of the government of another, done within its own territory. Redress of grievances by reason of such acts must be obtained through the means open to be availed of by sovereign powers as between themselves.

In *Sabbatino* it was stated that the doctrine "arises out of the basic relationships between branches of government in a system of separation" and the court's prior recognition of the doctrine "expresses the strong sense of the Judicial Branch that its engagement in the task of passing on the validity of foreign acts of state may hinder rather than further this country's pursuit of goals both for itself and for the community of nations as a whole in the international sphere."

In Hunt v. Mobil Oil Corp., 550 F.2d 68 (2d Cir. 1977), cert. denied, 434 U.S. 984, 98 S.Ct. 608, 54 L.Ed.2d 477, the Act of State Doctrine was held to bar Hunt's inquiry into the validity of Libya's nationalization of Hunt's concession. In holding that the trial court properly dismissed Hunt's claim against seven major oil producers in the Persian Gulf area for damages under the anti-trust statute, the circuit court said:

> We conclude that the political act complained of here was clearly within the act of state doctrine and that since the disputed pleadings inevitably call for a judgment on the sovereign acts of Libya the claim is non-justiciable.

This final judgment against Hunt in that case controls his present suit for conversion unless it comes within the exception to the Act of State Doctrine created by the Hickenlooper Amendment. Benson v. Wanda Petroleum Company, 468 S.W.2d 361 (Tex.1971).

The Hickenlooper Amendment was enacted by Congress in 1964 shortly after the Sabbatino holding and in obvious reaction to it. It provides in part:

[N]o court in the United States shall decline on the ground of the federal act of state doctrine to make a determination on the merits giving effect to the principles of international law in a case in which a *claim of title or other right to property* is asserted by any party including a foreign state * * * based upon (or traced through) a confiscation or other taking * * * by an act of that state in violation of the principles of international law * * *. (Emphasis Added)

22 U.S.C. § 2370(e)(2). It must be recognized at the outset that this exception which was adopted over the objections of the Executive Department of the United States has been narrowly construed by our courts. Occidental of Umm Al Qay., Inc. v. Cities Serv. Oil Co., 396 F.Supp. 461 (D.C.La.), aff'd in part, 577 F.2d 1196 (5th Cir. 1978), petition for cert. filed, 440 U.S. 934, 99 S.Ct. 1276, 59 L.Ed.2d 491 (1978); Occidental Petroleum Corp. v. Buttes Gas & Oil Co., 331 F. Supp. 92 (D.C.Cal.) aff'd, 461 F.2d 1261 (9th Cir. 1972), cert. denied, 409 U.S. 950, 93 S.Ct. 272, 34 L.Ed.2d 221; United Mexican States v. Ashley, 556 S.W.2d 784 (Tex.1977).

The statute enumerates three requirements which must exist in order to avoid the Act of State Doctrine under the Hickenlooper Amendment. 1. Expropriated property must come within the territorial jurisdiction of the United States. 2. The act of the expropriating nation must be in violation of international law. 3. The asserted claim must be a claim of title or other right to property. 22 U.S.C. § 2370(e)(2). The court of civil appeals concluded, without consideration of the first two requirements, that the Hickenlooper Amendment is not applicable to this case because Hunt acquired only a contract right by the agreement with Libya. We agree with this conclusion and therefore limit our consideration to the third requirement stated above.

Since Libya is both the place of the contract's execution and performance as well as the location of the subject matter, Libyan substantive law governs the interpretation and construction of the rights conferred to Hunt by the Concession Agreement. Cantu v. Bennett, 39 Tex. 304 (1873).

The Concession Agreement expressly provides that the applicable law is the Libyan Petroleum Law No. 25 of 1955 and this law provides in part:

> (1) All petroleum in Libya in its natural state in strata is the property of the Libyan State.

> (2) No person shall explore or prospect for, mine or produce petroleum in any part of Libya, unless authorized by a permit or concession issued under this Law.

The expressed intent of the Concession Agreement was to grant Hunt the *right* to search for and to extract oil within the defined area for the stated term. It did not grant Hunt title to the oil in the strata. Under Libyan law title to the oil passed at the wellhead. In

1966 Hunt and Libya voluntarily amended the 1957 Concession Agreement. Clause 16 of the amended agreement states:

> (1) The Government of Libya will take all the steps necessary to ensure that the Company enjoys all the rights conferred by the Concession. The *contractual rights* expressly created by this concession shall not be altered except by mutual consent of the parties.

> (2) This Concession shall throughout the period of its validity be construed in accordance with the Petroleum Law and the Regulations in force on the date of the execution of the agreement of amendment by which this paragraph (2) was incorporated into this concession agreement. Any amendment to or repeal of such Regulations shall not affect the *contractual rights* of the Company without its consent. (Emphasis added)

This language is significant in that it not only refers to Hunt's rights as "contractual," but it also recognizes Libya's ownership of the oil. We conclude that Hunt obtained only a contractual right under the Concession Agreement.

The Hickenlooper Amendment by its express terms applies only to a claim of title or other right to property. This construction was made abundantly clear in 1965 when Congress added the words "to property" following the phrase "claim of title or other right." Thus this exception to the Act of State Doctrine has no application here where only a contractual right was expropriated from Hunt. See Occidental of Umm Al Qay., Inc. v. Cities Serv. Oil Co., supra; French v. Banco Nacional de Cuba, 23 N.Y.2d 46, 295 N.Y.S.2d 433, 242 N. E.2d 704 (1968); Menendez v. Saks and Company, 485 F.2d 1355 (2nd Cir. 1973), cert. denied, 425 U.S. 991, 96 S.Ct. 2201, 48 L.Ed.2d 815 (1976); Present v. U. S. Life Ins. Co., 96 N.J.Super. 285, 232 A. 2d 863, aff'd, 51 N.J. 407, 241 A.2d 237 (1968). We have been cited to no case, and have discovered no case, holding to the contrary.

The trial court and the court of civil appeals did not err in concluding that the Act of State Doctrine bars judicial inquiry into the validity of Libya's actions.

Appeal by Coastal States

We agree with the holding of the court of civil appeals that Hunt's motion for summary judgment was properly granted on Coastal States' claim of tortious interference with business contracts and business relations. Hunt's contractual rights in the Sarir field were expropriated by Libya and Hunt was fully justified in apprising the international community of his intent to file suit if they dealt with oil from this field.

The judgment of the court of civil appeals is affirmed.

[Dissenting opinion by Justice STEAKLEY omitted.]

1. *The Hunts' legal actions involving oil from Libya.* The revolutionary regime that deposed the king of Libya cancelled the Hunt brothers' concessions from the latter. The efforts of the brothers to reach all parties possibly involved against their interests in oil from Libya have become litigation legend in their own time. Here you observe a post-nationalization hot oil suit against a purchaser of oil from the Hunts' concessions that were taken over by the revolutionary regime. In Chapter 17, you will consider two arbitral awards dealing with the Hunts' claims that the revolutionary regime must respect the concession rights granted them by the king. In other litigation the Hunt brothers have sued certain major American oil companies on theories of conspiracies with the revolutionary regime that, as to the majors, were claimed to violate the plaintiffs' rights under the antitrust laws of the United States.

2. *Questions.* Can you discern from the opinion in the Texas decision whether the Department of State expressed to the Texas courts its viewpoints as to the applicability of (a) the second Hickenlooper amendment or (b) the principle of the second Bernstein case?

If there had been diversity of citizenship between all plaintiffs and all defendants this case could have been brought in or removed to the federal district court. Without diversity do you think it could have been brought in federal court as a federal question case, as to (a) the applicability of the second Hickenlooper amendment or (b) the second Bernstein case doctrine, (i) with a statement in favor of the doctrine from the Department of State, (ii) without such a statement?

ARANGO v. GUZMAN TRAVEL ADVISORS CORP.

United States Court of Appeals, Fifth Circuit, 1980.
621 F.2d 1371.

REAVLEY, Circuit Judge.

Plaintiffs-appellants, Ramiro Arango and his family, attack the district court's dismissal of their tort and breach of contract claims against appellee, Compania Dominicana de Aviacion ("Dominicana"), the national airline of the Dominican Republic. Dominicana, one of four defendants against whom suit had originally been filed in a Florida state court, had removed the claims to federal district court pursuant to 28 U.S.C. § 1441(d). We conclude that § 1441(d) operated to remove the claims against the remaining state court defendants, as well, and, consequently, that the order dismissing Dominicana, alone, did not constitute a final judgment appealable under 28 U.S.C. § 1291 because it failed to adjudicate the rights and liabilities of all parties properly before the court. Fed.R.Civ.P. 54(b). Therefore, we dismiss the appeal.

The Arangos' claims arose from the events of an abortive package vacation tour from Miami, Florida to the Dominican Republic.

The Arangos' jaunt terminated abruptly and prematurely when Dominican immigration officials denied them entry into that country upon their arrival at the airport in Santo Domingo, apparently because of their inclusion on an official list of "undesirable aliens." The officials then compelled the Arangos' immediate, "involuntary re-routing" back to the United States via Dominicana, the air carrier on which they had arrived. Because of the unavailability of immediate return flights directly to Miami, the requirement that the Arangos leave the country resulted in their being shunted first to San Juan, Puerto Rico, and the next day to Port-au-Prince, Haiti, where they apparently were left to arrange and pay for their own return to Miami, which they finally were able to accomplish four days later.

*   *   *

Because some of the theories upon which the district court may have predicated its dismissal of Dominicana may also bear upon the disposition of claims against the other defendants and because rule 54(b) explicitly renders even the order dismissing Dominicana still subject to revision by the district court, we shall, in the interest of expediency, proceed to offer that court some guidance in its further handling of these issues.

[The court first discussed sovereign immunity.]

The second theory proffered to the district court as grounds for dismissal was the act of state doctrine. "The act of state doctrine in its traditional formulation precludes the courts of this country from inquiring into the validity [or legality] of the public acts a recognized foreign sovereign power [has] committed within its own territory." Banco Nacional de Cuba v. Sabbatino, 376 U.S. 398, 401, 84 S. Ct. 923, 926, 11 L.Ed.2d 804 (1964). Relegating grievances from acts of this sort to executive channels of international diplomacy, the rule is an embodiment of the deference to be accorded the sovereignty of other nations; it averts potential diplomatic embarrassment from the courts of one sovereign sitting in judgment over the public acts of another. Alfred Dunhill of London, Inc. v. Republic of Cuba, 425 U. S. 682, 697, 96 S.Ct. 1854, 1862, 48 L.Ed.2d 301 (1975); Underhill v. Hernandez, 168 U.S. 250, 252, 18 S.Ct. 83, 85, 42 L.Ed. 456 (1897).

Unlike foreign sovereign immunity, the act of state doctrine affects the viability of the Arangos' claims against all the defendants. It does not simply relieve the foreign government of liability for its acts, but operates as an issue preclusion device, foreclosing judicial inquiry into the validity or propriety of such acts in litigation between any set of parties. National American Corp. v. Federal Republic of Nigeria, 448 F.Supp. at 640; see, e. g., Hunt v. Mobil Oil Corp., 550 F.2d 68 (2d Cir.), cert. denied, 434 U.S. 984, 98 S.Ct. 608, 54 L.Ed.2d 477 (1977) (foreclosing antitrust conspiracy suit against private oil companies that would have required inquiry into alleged untoward motives behind Libya's nationalization of its oil industry). Consequently, the Arangos' battery and false imprisonment claims would be foreclosed under this doctrine, as well as under the FSIA, since they would, by definition, require an adjudication of the propriety and legality of the acts of the Dominican immigration authorities —and, more specifically, of Dominicana employees while effectively deployed as agents of that government under the orders of these authorities—in the performance of their official governmental duties in denying the Arangos' entry into the Dominican Republic and effecting their removal. See Underhill v. Hernandez, 168 U.S. 250, 18 S.Ct. 83, 42 L.Ed. 456 (1897) (foreclosing suit under act of state doctrine against foreign agent who detained American citizen); United States v. Henry, 604 F.2d 908, 912 (5th Cir. 1979) (characterizing exclusion of aliens as a sovereign governmental act).

Dominicana urges that, beyond this, since the Arangos' expulsion by Dominican authorities was the precipitating factor for all plaintiffs' claims, all should be foreclosed by the act of state doctrine. This contention accords that doctrine too great a breadth. The act of state doctrine only precludes judicial inquiry into the legality, validity, and propriety of the acts and motivations of foreign sovereigns acting in their governmental roles within their own boundaries, it does not preclude judicial resolution of all commercial consequences stemming from the occurrence of such public acts. See National American Corp. v. Federal Republic of Nigeria, 448 F.Supp. at 639– 40. The Arangos' contract and negligence claims require only a determination of the respective rights and duties of the parties in the wake of the sovereign acts of the Dominican immigration authorities. The claims raise the questions of who bears the risk of loss following such an incident and whether there existed a duty on the part of any defendant to protect the Arangos from, or to warn of, the possibility of its occurrence. They do not necessitate a consideration or evaluation of the legitimacy of those "acts of state", themselves. Consequently, the act of state doctrine * * * should not have required dismissal with respect to the Arangos' contract and negligence claims.

 * * *

SECTION C. THE SCOPE OF THE ACT OF STATE DOCTRINE IN THE INTERNATIONAL SYSTEM

1. PROPERTY LOCALIZED OUTSIDE THE NATIONALIZING STATE

REPUBLIC OF IRAQ v. FIRST NATIONAL CITY BANK

United States Court of Appeals, Second Circuit, 1965.
353 F.2d 47.[a]

FRIENDLY, Circuit Judge. King Faisal II of Iraq was killed on July 14, 1958, in the midst of a revolution in that country which

a. Cert. denied 382 U.S. 1027, 86 S.Ct. 648 (1966).

led to the establishment of a republic, recognized by the United States in August. On July 19, 1958, the new government issued Ordinance No. 23 which decreed that "all property [of the dynasty] * * * whether moveable or immoveable * * * should be confiscated." At the time of his death King Faisal had a balance of $55,925 and 4,008 shares of Canada General Fund, Ltd., a Canadian investment trust, in deposit and custody accounts with Irving Trust Company in New York. In October 1958, the Surrogate's Court for New York County issued to the defendant letters of administration with respect to King Faisal's New York assets. During that month the Consul General of the Republic of Iraq notified Irving Trust that the Republic claimed all assets of King Faisal by virtue of Ordinance No. 23. Notwithstanding the notice, Irving Trust subsequently transferred to the administrator the balance in the account and certificates for the shares, which were later sold.

In March 1962, the Republic brought this action against the administrator in the District Court for the Southern District of New York to recover the bank balance and the proceeds of the shares. From a judgment dismissing the complaint, 241 F.Supp. 567 (1965), the Republic appeals. We affirm.

The District Court properly held that it had jurisdiction of the action. Under 28 U.S.C. § 1332(a) the district courts are vested with original jurisdiction of all civil actions "where the matter in controversy exceeds the sum or value of $10,000, exclusive of interest and costs, and is between * * * (2) citizens of a State, and foreign states or citizens or subjects thereof." Although this general language does not grant jurisdiction to probate a will or administer an estate, it has been established by a long series of decisions "that federal courts of equity have jurisdiction to entertain suits 'in favor of creditors, legatees and heirs' and other claimants against a decedent's estate 'to establish their claims' so long as the federal court does not interfere with the probate proceedings or assume general jurisdiction of the probate or control of the property in the custody of the state court." Markham v. Allen, 326 U.S. 490, 494, 66 S.Ct. 296, 298, 90 L.Ed. 256 (1946), citing Waterman v. Canal-Louisiana Bank & Trust Co., 215 U.S. 33, 43, 30 S.Ct. 10, 54 L.Ed. 80 (1909), and other cases.

The principal questions raised in this appeal are the proper definition of the act of state doctrine and its application to foreign confiscation decrees purporting to affect property within the United States. Although difficulty is sometimes encountered in drawing the line between an "act of state" and more conventional foreign decrees or statutes claimed to be entitled to respect by the forum, the Ordinance involved in this case is nowhere near the boundary. A confiscation decree, which is precisely what Ordinance No. 23, purported to be, is the very archetype of an act of state. See ALI, Restatement of Foreign Relations Law of the United States § 41c (Proposed Official Draft, 1962) [hereinafter cited as Restatement].

The Supreme Court has declared that a question concerning the effect of an act of state "must be treated exclusively as an aspect of federal law." Banco Nacional de Cuba v. Sabbatino, 376 U.S. 398, 423–427, 84 S.Ct. 923, 939, 11 L.Ed.2d 804 (1964). We deem that ruling to be applicable here even though, as we conclude below, this is not a case in which the courts of the forum are bound to respect the act of the foreign state. Like the traditional application of the act of state doctrine to preclude judgment with respect to another government's acts concerning property within its own territory at the time, see Underhill v. Hernandez, 168 U.S. 250, 18 S.Ct. 83, 42 L.Ed. 456 (1897); Oetjen v. Central Leather Co., 246 U.S. 297, 38 S.Ct. 309, 62 L.Ed. 726 (1918); Ricaud v. American Metal Co., 246 U.S. 304, 38 S. Ct. 312, 62 L.Ed. 733 (1918), the exercise of discretion whether or not to respect a foreign act of state affecting property in the United States is closely tied to our foreign affairs, with consequent need for nationwide uniformity. It is fundamental to our constitutional scheme that in dealing with other nations the country must speak with a united voice. See United States v. Belmont, 301 U.S. 324, 331, 57 S.Ct. 758, 81 L.Ed. 1134 (1937); United States v. Pink, 315 U.S. 203, 233–234, 62 S.Ct. 552, 86 L.Ed. 796 (1942). It would be baffling if a foreign act of state intended to affect property in the United States were ignored on one side of the Hudson but respected on the other; any such diversity between states would needlessly complicate the handling of the foreign relations of the United States. The required uniformity can be secured only by recognizing the expansive reach of the principle, announced by Mr. Justice Harlan in Sabbatino, that all questions relating to an act of state are questions of federal law, to be determined ultimately, if need be, by the Supreme Court of the United States.

Under the traditional application of the act of state doctrine, the principle of judicial refusal of examination applies only to a taking by a foreign sovereign of property within its own territory, see Ehrenzweig, Conflict of Laws § 48 at 172 (1962); cf. Banco Nacional de Cuba v. Sabbatino, supra, 376 U.S. at 401, 428, 432, 84 S.Ct. 923; when property confiscated is within the United States at the time of the attempted confiscation, our courts will give effect to acts of state "only if they are consistent with the policy and law of the United States." Restatement § 46.

In this case, neither the bank account nor the shares in the Canadian investment trust can realistically be considered as being within Iraq simply because King Faisal resided and was physically present there at the time of his death; in the absence of any showing that Irving Trust had an office in Iraq or would be in any way answerable to its courts, we need not consider whether the conclusion would differ if it did. Cf. United States v. First Nat'l City Bank, 379 U.S. 378, 85 S.Ct. 528, 13 L.Ed.2d 365 (1965). So far as appears on this record, only a court in the United States could compel the bank to pay the balance in the account or to deliver the certificates it held in custody. The property here at issue thus was within the United

States. Although the nationality of King Faisal provided a jurisdictional basis for the Republic of Iraq to prescribe a rule relating to his property outside Iraq, Restatement § 30(1)(b), this simply gives the confiscation decree a claim to consideration by the forum which, in the absence of such jurisdiction, it would not possess—not a basis for insisting on the absolute respect which, subject to the qualifications of Sabbatino, 376 U.S. at 428, 84 S.Ct. 923, the decree would enjoy as to property within Iraq at the time.

Extra-territorial enforcement of the Iraqi ordinance as to property within the United States at the date of its promulgation turns on whether the decree is consistent with our policy and laws. We perceive no basis for thinking it to be. Confiscation of the assets of a corporation has been said to be "contrary to our public policy and shocking to our sense of justice," Vladikavkazsky Ry. Co. v. New York Trust Co., 263 N.Y. 369, 378, 189 N.E. 456, 460, 91 A.L.R. 1426 (1934); see also Zwack v. Kraus Bros. & Co., 237 F.2d 255, 259 (2 Cir. 1956) (partnership); Plesch v. Banque Nationale de la République d'Haiti, 273 App.Div. 224, 77 N.Y.S.2d 43 (1st Dept.), aff'd, 298 N.Y. 573, 81 N.E.2d 106 (1948). Confiscation of the assets of an individual is no less so, even if he wears a crown. Compare Banco de Vizcaya v. Don Alfonso de Borbon y Austria, [1935] 1 K.B. 140. Our Constitution sets itself against confiscations such as that decreed by Ordinance No. 23 not only by the general guarantees of due process in the Fifth and Fourteenth Amendments but by the specific prohibitions of bills of attainder in Article I. See United States v. Brown, 381 U.S. 437, 85 S.Ct. 1707, 14 L.Ed.2d 484 (1965), and cases cited therein. It is true that since these provisions are addressed to action by the United States or a state, they might not prevent a court of the United States from giving effect to a confiscatory act of a foreign state with respect to property in the United States. But at least they show that, from its earliest days under the Constitution, this nation has had scant liking for legislative proscription of members of a defeated faction, although—or perhaps because—many states, in their dealings with property of the loyalists immediately after the Revolution, had practiced exactly that. See United States v. Brown, supra, 381 U.S. at 441–446, 85 S.Ct. 1707. Foreigners entrusting their property to custodians in this country are entitled to expect this historic policy to be followed save when the weightiest reasons call for a departure. In saying this we are not guilty of disrespect to the recitals in the preamble of Ordinance No. 23, see fn. 1; subject to the narrow exception discussed below, the policy of the United States is that there is no such thing as a "good" confiscation by legislative or executive decree.

The only cases cited to us that might seem to suggest a deviation from this view are United States v. Belmont, 301 U.S. 324, 57 S.Ct. 758 (1937), and United States v. Pink, 315 U.S. 203, 62 S.Ct. 552 (1942). Language in the latter opinion did indeed lead "some commentators to protest that the Court had laid down the revolutionary doctrine that recognition requires the recognizing state to give extra-

territorial effect to all acts of state of the recognized government."
Stevenson, Effect of Recognition on the Application of Private International Law Norms, 51 Colum.L.Rev. 710, 720 & n. 54 (1951); see
Borchard, Extraterritorial Confiscations, 36 Am.J.Int'l L. 275 (1942);
Jessup, The Litvinov Assignment and the Pink case, id. at 282. The
facts of the cases, however, required no such overturn of established
principles. By the Litvinov agreement our Government had procured, as an incident to recognition, an assignment of the Soviet Union's claims to American assets of nationalized Russian companies,
for the benefit of United States nationals whose property in the Soviet Union had been confiscated. Such action of the Chief Executive,
taken under his power to conduct the foreign relations of the United
States, was considered to make the Soviet confiscation decrees consistent with the law and policy of the United States from that time
forward, and, as we now know from Sabbatino, federal law controls.
See Restatement § 46, comment (c) and the discussion of United
States v. Pink. In this case, by contrast, nothing remotely resembling the Litvinov agreement is present; on the contrary, the Department of State has disclaimed any interest of the executive department
in the outcome of the litigation.[5]

Appellant insists that, however this may be, a New York court
would give effect to Ordinance No. 23 because of the New York Decedent Estate Law, McKinney's Consol.Laws, c. 13, § 47, which provides:

> Except where special provision is otherwise made by law,
> the validity and effect of a testamentary disposition of any other
> property [i. e. other than real estate] situated within the state,
> and the ownership and disposition of such property, where it is
> not disposed of by will, are regulated by the laws of the state or
> country, of which the decedent was a resident, at the time of his
> death.

As already indicated, we read Sabbatino to mean that New York
could not, by application of its choice of law rules, give a foreign act
of state an effect, whether less or greater, differing from that dictated by federal law. But appellant's position would be baseless in any
event. Not only does § 47 refer to the law existing at the time of decedent's death, but no state has been stronger in its opposition to foreign confiscation decrees than New York, see, e. g., Vladikavkazsky
Ry. Co. v. New York Trust Co., supra; Plesch v. Banque Nationale de

---

5. The Deputy Legal Adviser to the
Department of State said in a letter
dated January 15, 1965, to defendant's counsel:

   While the recognition of and
maintenance of diplomatic relations
with a foreign government are political matters within the province
of the executive department of the
Federal Government, questions regarding the administration of estates and the determination of
rights and interests in property in
the United States ordinarily are
matters for determination by the
courts of competent jurisdiction.
Accordingly, the Department considers that the legal effect of Ordinance No. 23 as it may pertain to
title to property in the United
States of King Faisal II is a question for determination by the competent United States court.

la République d'Haiti, supra. Indeed, it was this opposition that required the Supreme Court's intervention in the Pink case. We are thus confident that the courts of New York would not strain to read the general language of the Decedent Estate Law to include what on its face is a confiscation decree.

Since the district judge properly concluded the complaint to be lacking in merit, we do not reach the question whether dismissal would have been required in any event on the ground that a prior decree of the Surrogate's Court distributing the assets of the estate operated as res judicata despite the sovereign character of the Republic of Iraq and the pendency of this suit. See Restatement § 71, comment (e).

Affirmed.

The problem of jurisdiction to nationalize. A number of decisions in other countries also hold that a state's purported act of state in seeking to take into public ownership assets not localized within its territory will not be recognized. These decisions hold either that the act of state doctrine does not apply to such situations, that such takings are clearly against ordre public, or that the state has no jurisdiction to nationalize property that is within the jurisdiction to nationalize of the forum state or some third state. Problems of extraterritorial nationalization, then should be distinguished from the act of state doctrine, and decisions denying recognition of extraterritorial nationalization should not be counted as decisions rejecting the act of state doctrine where the extraterritorial issue is not present. See Reeves, The Sabbatino Case and the Sabbatino Amendment: Comedy—or Tragedy—of Errors, 20 Vand.L.Rev. 429 (1966–1967), especially Appendix II. But see paragraphs 12–16 of the first Declaration of the government of Algeria in the agreement for the release of the American hostages in Teheran of January 19, 1981. The text of the agreement is in the Documentary Supplement.

As in conflict of laws, there is a problem as to the localization— or ascribed situs—of intangibles, in a range from unliquidated claims against a debtor to negotiable securities. Most nationalization cases, however, involve either land or movables that are capable of having an actual physical location. Illustration: when Egyptian President Nasser nationalized the assets of the Universal Suez Canal Corporation, he got the canal, but the big investment portfolio of the company kept in Paris remained beyond his grasp.

---

2. INVALIDATION OF TITLE AND RESTITUTION AS REMEDIES FOR NATIONALIZATION

Introductory comments. In the Sabbatino case, the lower federal courts demonstrated a somewhat remarkable determination to correct nationalization injustices in national tribunals by judicial dead-reckoning. Both the district court and the court of appeals decided that the Supreme Court's prior creation, the act of state doctrine, did not bar judicial examination of the legitimacy under customary international law of a taking in Cuba. In this they were held in error in Sabbatino.

In its first Sabbatino decision, the court of appeals also addressed the remedy issue squarely: if the act of state doctrine is no bar to examination and if examination shows that the taking by Cuba did violate customary international law, what is the remedy? The court's answer, in no uncertain terms, was that the old owner still has title to his property. The act of nationalization is a legal nullity. This is corroborated by the disposition of the case: the Banco Nacional had sued the sugar broker for conversion of the proceeds of the sale of the sugar from the nationalized sugar mill. The district judge granted the defendant's motion for summary judgment, and the court of appeals affirmed—i. e. no conversion; the proceeds were defendant's.

In this decision, 307 F.2d 845 (2d Cir. 1962), the court of appeals said:

> * * * We need not at present go into the question whether the granting of this type of remedy is a feature of international law or of domestic law. But we do suggest that the failure of an international tribunal to give a remedy of this type results from the inability of that kind of court to enforce its awards and is not a result of the dictates of substantive international law principles * * *.

To this statement the court added in a note that it did not hope to resolve a chicken-and-egg issue on rights and remedies, and continued:

> * * * If one believes legal rights exist separate from and prior to the existence of legal remedies, he may interpret our holding to mean that we have recognized an international wrong and have fashioned an appropriate remedy. If, on the other hand, the reader believes legal rights cannot exist in the absence of legal remedies, he is free to interpret our words as meaning that since municipal courts can grant a remedy which divests an international title, the appellant's title is invalid.

This decision led to a great debate in the literature; but, as has been seen, the Supreme Court did not reach the issue, because it held that act of state barred further inquiry. Then, the second Hickenlooper amendment was passed, and its specific retroactive application to the Supreme Court's order in the Sabbatino case was upheld by the court of appeals in the Farr case. There also the court of appeals ruled that its prior decision on the international law issue had not been affected by the Supreme Court decision, which had reversed on act of state alone. But in Farr the remedies issue in relationship to international law was not separated for re-examination from the issue of validity of taking under international law. The parties disputed the remedies issue in the certiorari pleadings, and the petitioner

(Banco Nacional de Cuba) also advanced the viewpoint that in this case, which involved only the proceeds of the sale of the sugar, damages and restitution are identical. However, the United States Supreme Court denied certiorari without any indication of viewpoint on the international law issues, including the remedies issue as distinct from the issue of violation in the taking.

Thus, there is some authority in the United States that, where the act of state doctrine does not apply and the taking violates international law, the remedy of invalidation of title or of specific restitution is available.

The cases that follow are representative of decisions in other states on the subject matter of this chapter. What do they hold on remedies?

ANGLO–IRANIAN OIL CO., LTD. v. JAFFRATE
(THE ROSE MARY)

Aden, Supreme Court, 1953.
20 Int'l L.Rep. 316 (1957).*

The Facts: On June 17, 1952, the Rose Mary, flying the flag of Honduras, arrived in Aden harbour with a cargo of crude oil which had been loaded at Bundar Mashur in Southern Iran. The Anglo-Iranian Oil Company Limited brought this action in the Supreme Court of the Colony of Aden in detinue, claiming delivery up to them of this oil or, alternatively, a declaration that it was their property. The action was brought against Captain Guiseppe Jaffrate, the then master, the Compania de Navegacion Teresita S.A. of Panama City, Panama, the owners, and Bubenberg A.G. of Spiez, Switzerland, the charterers, of the Rose Mary.

The plaintiffs claimed the property in, or the immediate right to possession of, the oil by virtue of the Convention between them and the Imperial Government of Persia concluded on April 29, 1933, by which they were granted the exclusive right within the territory of a specified concession to search for and extract petroleum for a period ending on December 31, 1993. The agreement provided, by Article 21, that it should not be altered by legislation and, by Article 22, that in the event of any disputes they were to be referred to arbitration— a procedure which Iran now declined to adopt. The oil in question, the plaintiffs alleged, was produced by plants established by them in the concession in Southern Iran, and this was admitted by all the defendants.

The owners of the Rose Mary refused to give possession of the cargo to the plaintiffs on the ground that the title to it was in dispute, but stated that it was loaded against their instructions. The master pleaded that the Rose Mary entered Aden harbour under du-

* Reprinted by permission of E. Lauterpacht, ed., and Grotius Publications, Ltd., Cambridge, England.

ress, and that, accordingly, the Aden Court had no jurisdiction in the matter. He also claimed that the cargo belonged to the charterers. The charterers also alleged duress, and, alternatively, relied on the Iranian Laws of March and May 1951, which purported to nationalize and expropriate as from May 1, 1951, all property vested in the plaintiffs by the concession of 1933.

Held: that the Company were entitled to the oil, which had remained their property and to which the Government of Iran had acquired no title, since (1) "the Iranian Laws of 1951 were invalid by international law, for, by them, the property of the company was expropriated without any compensation;" and (2) "British courts treated international law as incorporated into their domestic law so far as it was not inconsistent with their own rules (per Lord Atkin in Chung Chi Cheung v. Rex (1939) A.C. 160, 168; 55 T.L.R. 184; [1938] All E.R. 786)". It was further held that "the principle in Aksionairnoye Obschestvo A. M. Luther Co. v. James Sagor and Co. [1921] 3 K.B. 532; 37 T.L.R. 777, and Princess Paley Olga v. Weisz [1929] 1 K.B. 718; 45 T.L.R. 365, that a court would not inquire into the legality of acts done by a foreign government in respect of property situate in that government's territory applied only where the property was that of the government's own subjects; and * * * accordingly, following international law as incorporated in the domestic law of Aden, the court must refuse validity to the Iranian Laws of 1951." Judgment was, therefore, given for the plaintiffs.

    * * *

ANGLO–IRANIAN OIL CO. LTD. v. S.U.P.O.R. CO.

Italy, Court of Venice, 1953.
22 Int'l L.Rep. 19 (1958).*

The Facts: The respondent Company had purchased in Persia certain oil which was shipped in the Miriella from Abadan and lay in store in Venice. The Anglo-Iranian Oil Company (A.I.O.C.) claimed the oil on the ground that the Persian Law of May 1, 1951, nationalizing the petroleum industry had not affected the ownership of A.I.O.C. in this particular cargo of oil and that in any event the Oil Nationalization Law could not properly be enforced by an Italian court as it violated the principles of Italian "public order". The A.I.O.C. applied for "judicial sequestration" [an order for interim custody] of the oil pending the hearing of their claim. S.U.P.O.R. objected on the ground that for the Court to grant such an order would amount to prejudging the substantive claim and so to "annulling" the law of a foreign sovereign State, namely, the Persian Oil Nationalization Law.

* Reprinted by permission of E. Lauterpacht, ed., and Grotius Publications,
Ltd., Cambridge, England.

Held: that the application must fail. Although the respondents were in error in contending that the Court had no power to examine, and if necessary to refuse to apply, the law of a foreign State, on the merits of the substantive claim the Court found that the Persian Oil Nationalization Law was not contrary to Italian "public order"; the applicant Company therefore had no claim to the ownership of the oil in question. [A portion of the opinion of the court appears below.]

If, however, the question is tested by examining the Nationalization Law in regard to public order, which has been referred to at some length in the contentions put forward on behalf of A.I.O.C., the claim of ownership appears unjustified, which supports the rejection of the request for sequestration.

*   *   *

It can be seen   *   *   *   that the Nationalization Law does not exclude the payment of compensation to A.I.O.C.; moreover, it unequivocally recognizes the right to claim such compensation. In fact, whilst Article 2 envisages a deposit to meet the claims of the Company, Article 3 contains the solemn undertaking on the part of the Persian Government to examine, in addition to its own claims, those of the Company; these claims, which are not specified in Article 2 but which are "likely" ("probable" in the English text produced by A.I.O.C.), are in Article 3 defined as being "rightful", and the argument maintained by A.I.O.C. that among these legitimate claims the Law does not include the claim for compensation—which is the most likely and most legitimate, though not the only one—must be regarded as being an entirely arbitrary view.

Little importance, from a legal point of view, can be attached to the argument of A.I.O.C. that the Law does not fix the measure of compensation nor require promptness in payment. Even considering the exceptional nature of the question, which—it must be recognized—as compared with the normal application of a foreign Law almost touches the limits contemplated by Article 31 of the Preliminary Rules, the Persian Law can be examined only with a view to establishing whether it fails to provide for the payment of any compensation, so as to be contrary to our Constitution, the provisions of which present the principle of public order and which admits expropriation "provided that compensation is paid". And other questions, such as the measure of compensation, its form, and promptness in payment, do not concern the public order: these are accessory elements which should be agreed upon on the basis of present historical, political, social and economic conditions, which should be proportionate to the nature and importance of the property in question, and which do not enter the sphere of public order provided that they do not in practice annul the compensation and make it illusory.

*   *   *

DECISION ON EXPROPRIATION

Federal Republic of Germany, Oberlandesgericht, Bremen, 1959.
90 Journal du Droit International 1127 (1963).[a]

During the period under review, as in previous years, the German courts have had to devote a great part of their attention to the question how far they are bound to respect the expropriation of subjective rights by foreign States where such rights are the subject of an internal dispute.

In a judgment of 21 August 1959 the High Court of Bremen adjudicated on a case of breach of public international law by measures of foreign expropriation (AWD 1959, 207 JIR 984 et seq., reproducing a slightly different extract). Application was made to the Court for measures of conservation against a German-Indonesian trading company which had shipped to Bremen tobacco grown on the plantations of two Netherlands firms expropriated by the Indonesian State. The Court began by finding that the Plaintiffs had not established their ownership of the 1958 crop of tobacco (prior to expropriation) because they had no genuine right of usufruct over the land cultivated by them. Even if they had become the owners of the tobacco, continued the Court, they would have lost the ownership by virtue of the acts of expropriation; in effect, even assuming that these measures were contrary to the jus gentium, there is nothing to establish the existence of an international rule requiring the German courts automatically to treat expropriation effected contrary to the jus gentium as being null and void. The judgment concludes that, since the controversy on this question leaves the Court full discretion to recognize either the confiscation contrary to the jus gentium or the claims of the former owners, it takes the former course, mainly in the light of "the positive effect of the principle of territoriality" which is, moreover, in keeping with the interests of universal peace and world trade. Furthermore, the Court questioned whether the Indonesian expropriation law was contrary to the jus gentium from the angle of discrimination according to nationality, or as a means of political pressure. It considered that, in any event, the law was not contrary to German public policy, even though there was a sufficiently close link with the German courts.

The expropriation of things in action raises a more delicate problem than that of immovable property. Some decisions continue to be based on the idea that a claim is "located" solely in the debtor's country of domicile, even where the debtor owns property in other countries. * * *

---

a. English text in the Journal. The text is a summary of the decision rather than a translation of it. Reprinted by permission of Editions Techniques, S. A., Paris.

The decisions of French courts.

Union des Républiques Socialistes Soviétiques v. Intendant Général Bourgeois ès qual. et Soc. La Ropit, Court of Cassation, 1928, [1927–1928] Ann.Dig. 67 (No. 43). The ships of the Russian company La Ropit were nationalized by decree while they were in Odessa. Odessa at the time was not yet under the control of the Soviet revolutionary government and a number of the ships escaped to Marseilles. After being recognized by France, the government of the USSR sued in the French courts claiming title to the ships. The supreme court rejected the claim because giving effect in France to foreign legislation expropriating property without compensation would conflict with French established order (i. e. ordre public).

Société Potasas Ibericas v. Bloch, Court of Cassation, [1939] Dalloz Rec.Heb. 257. The plaintiff was a corporation whose mines and other facilities in Spain had been nationalized. Bloch was the consignee of a shipment of chemical products from the Spanish state company which had taken over the facilities. The plaintiff claimed title to the shipment. A first decree of nationalization had been issued on August 8, 1936, against industries belonging to absent owners, but without specific mention of the plaintiff and without provision for compensation. The shipment arrived in France before the issuance of a second decree which specifically took the property of the plaintiff and provided for compensation. The court held that the second decree could not take effect retroactively in France with respect to a shipment already there and hence the consignee could not justify his possession of it.

Société Hardmuth, Court of Appeal of Paris, 1950, 44 Revue Critique de Droit International Privé 501 (1955). Hardmuth, a corporation in Czechoslovakia, was nationalized. Its new directors claimed the property of the corporation in France as against the former owners. The court rejected the claim insofar as concerned the tangible property in France, such as buildings, because measures of nationalization without compensation could not be given effect in France. But it recognized the claim so far as concerns the trademarks. Their nationalization was effective in Czechoslovakia and their protection in France was required by a convention on industrial property to which France and Czechoslovakia were parties.

Martin v. Bank of Spain, Court of Cassation, 1952, 42 Revue Critique de Droit International Privé 425 (1953). Spanish law required bills of Spanish currency, especially those coming in from France, to be embossed with a special seal in order to be legal tender. The plaintiff acquired in France bills of Spanish currency which were not so embossed and presented them for exchange against valid ones at the Spanish customs. They were given a receipt, but no money. Their invalid bills were turned over to the Bank of Spain. They sued the bank for payment in valid currency of the amount of their receipt. The court said that, even if the principle of immunity were disregarded, the refusal to pay the plaintiffs in valid currency "constituted acts of authority outside the control of the French courts."

De Keller v. Maison de la Pensée Française, Tribunal Civil de la Seine (référés) 1954, 44 Revue Critique de Droit International Privé 502 (1955). The plaintiff invoked an emergency and summary procedure by which the court was requested to take temporary custody of 37 out of 49 paintings by Pablo Picasso exhibited by the defendant, a nonprofit organization. The defendant had the 37 Picassos on loan from the Russian state art galleries in Leningrad and Moscow. The plaintiffs alleged that the paintings in issue belonged to their deceased father, whose private art gallery the Russian state had confiscated in 1918, and contended they would establish their title to them in further proceedings. The court denied the request. It would have to determine whether the presence in France of paintings acquired by a foreign state in its own territory, and by a method legally valid there, violated to such a degree the French juridical order that it was imperative to end the situation. Such a determination raised difficult questions which could not be resolved in the instant procedure without prejudging the merits as well as the jurisdiction of the French courts in the matter.

The Algerian nationalization cases. The nationalizations in Algeria gave rise in France to a great deal of litigation. On April 23, 1969, the supreme court decided a series of cases involving nationalizations. For a list of them, see Lachaume, Chronique de Jurisprudence Française Relative au Droit International Public 1969, Annuaire Français de Droit International 1970, at 874, 898 (1971).

Chapter 7

RESOLUTION OF JURISDICTIONAL CONFLICTS

As demonstrated heretofore, particularly in Chapter 2, international law recognizes a number of bases of jurisdiction under which a state may apply its own public law, essentially regulatory law, to a defendant properly before its judicial or administrative authorities. No one base excludes another. In The Queen v. Anderson, p. 126, an American citizen committed a murder on board a British vessel within the territorial waters of France. International law recognizes that all three states have jurisdiction to prescribe a rule of law governing that event. Thus if the man were in the custody of any one of the states, that state could properly try him for a violation of its own law of homicide. It could, therefore, make a real difference to the accused to be tried in one state rather than another; a defense of insanity or of intoxication might be treated much more favorably in one of these states than in either of the other two.

In the fields of income and death taxation, multiple bases of jurisdiction to tax create serious problems as to burdens on international transactions and about fiscal fairness. To illustrate: it is universally recognized that states may tax income at its source, and most income tax systems do so. But it is also permissible to tax income to its recipients upon the basis of nationality or even alien resident status. Some developing countries, particularly in Latin America, object on policy and interest grounds—but not on legal grounds—to United States income taxation on the nationality basis of business income having its source in their territories. Resolution of jurisdictional conflicts in the taxation fields is usually by treaties for the elimination or reduction of double (it could even be triple or quadruple in some cases) taxation. These treaties commonly provide, item by item and situation by situation, which of two states, each with valid jurisdiction to tax, shall actually tax. Some of the older consular and FCN (Friendship, Commerce and Navigation) treaties between the United States and another country still govern as to the death taxation of assets within a particular state owned at death by a national of another. Generally, see Wilson, United States Commercial Treaties and International Law, Ch. VI (1960).

In at least one instance, that of visiting naval vessels, a general practice of states has given the international legal system an accommodation (without treaty) that allocates to one of the two states having jurisdiction exclusive authority as to its exercise. It would be difficult to deny any jurisdiction to a territorial state whose ports are visited by an aircraft carrier or a cruiser of another state; but "it just isn't done" that the territorial host state, uninvited, should, for example, send a squad on board to make an arrest. Another device, for the resolution of the territory-nationality conflict as to non-naval vessels, is the peace of the port doctrine, exemplified in Wildenhus's case, p. 166. Here, for vessels other than public vessels in naval service, the principle of customary international law evolved from a few earlier bilateral treaties.

Jurisdictional conflicts may result from the presence within the territory of a state of a visiting foreign military force, which as an organized unit, naturally, has its own internal system of law and discipline. The problems and the lines of resolution (or reduction) of conflicts in the exercise of jurisdiction over military personnel in a visiting foreign force are suggested by the cases and materials in Section B of this chapter.

Until comparatively recent times the United States was practically the only country in the world with a well-developed antitrust law to enforce and with a strong interest in applying it to transnational economic activities. Between 1946 and 1966, or so, much debate took place as to whether international law authorized the exercise of prescriptive jurisdiction, as to a defendant fairly and properly before the courts here, on the basis that economic activity outside the United States had effects on the economy of the United States. Today a number of law-making authorities, such as the Federal German Republic and the European Community, join with the United States in affirming that the state where economic consequences are felt may apply its law on that basis alone. But multinational economic activity may have economic effects in many countries, and the problems of resolving conflicts of jurisdiction in this field have to be faced. A number of writers, and some states, still contend, however, that the problem ought to be solved by the outlawry of the economic effects doctrine, which is denounced as contrary to territorialistic limitations on prescriptive jurisdiction. In this situation, therefore, the resolution or reduction of conflicts is more involved—as well as frequently highly charged with nationalism and other emotions.

The greater part of this chapter is directed toward an exploration of ways in which the conflicts thus generated are being or may be resolved. One way, obviously, is to reduce or eliminate the differences in the rules that would govern the outcomes of decisions, e. g., by the development in the international legal system of uniform rules for stating the legal consequences of particular types of conduct. Another is to accept, for the time being at least, the reality of divisiveness as to the governing rules and to develop within the international legal system rules or methods, or both, for the resolution of conflicts. An effort along this line was Section 40 of the Restatement of the Foreign Relations Law of the United States (1965).

SECTION A. MULTINATIONAL TAXATION

TAX DECISION

Federal German Republic, Supreme Tax Court, 1971.
12 European Taxation II/36.*

I. The Facts

Since the taxpayer, to be known as A, in this case was deceased, his heirs were a party to the proceedings. A was a United States citizen who was domiciled in Italy and who had neither a domicile (Wohnsitz) nor a residence (gewöhnliche Aufenthalt) in Germany.

He had concluded, with a Panamanian company to be known as X, a contract under which X could offer A's services to other companies, in particular movie companies. On May 5, 1958, X concluded a contract with a German company to be known as Y under which A would make a movie for Y. Both companies would be entitled to copies of the film and the right to rent those films to movie theaters. Y paid to X an amount of $200,000 (approximately DM 840,000) as a fee plus granted X a right to a percentage of the movie rentals. The work was performed by A both in Germany and in Italy and it was established that 28/82 and 54/82 of the work was performed in each country respectively.

In 1959 Y paid DM 536,491 to X of which amount the latter kept DM 82,026 and the remainder of DM 454,465 was paid to A.

The German tax administration assumed that the DM 536,491 was income from employment derived by A through X and imposed income tax (wage tax) in the following manner:

$$
\begin{array}{llr}
15\% \text{ on } {}^{28}\!/_{82} \text{ of DM } 536,491.60 = & \text{DM } 27,478.81 \\
25\% \text{ on } {}^{54}\!/_{82} \text{ of DM } 536,491.60 = & \text{DM } 88,324.76 \\
\hline
& \text{DM } 115,803.57 \\
\hline
\end{array}
$$

II. The Law

Section 49(4) of the Individual Income Tax Law (Einkommensteuergesetz) provides that nonresident individuals receiving income from employment which is either carried out in Germany or "utilized" in Germany (this term denotes that the economic effect of the work performed abroad is of direct benefit to the German economy) are subject to German individual income tax with respect to such employment income.

Section 50a(2) of the Individual Income Tax Law provides that in the case of an artist—such as a movie star like A—the rate of the

* Reprinted with the permission of the
International Bureau of Fiscal Documentation, Amsterdam.

income tax is 15% for that part of the income derived for work performed in Germany and 25% for that part which is performed abroad, but utilized in Germany. Article 7 of the German-Italian Tax Treaty of October 21, 1925 (which is still in force), provides that "impersonal" taxes are levied only on income from labor by the State where the personal activity from which the income is derived is carried on. Article 1 defines the term "impersonal" tax as, inter alia, the German individual income tax (Einkommensteuer) insofar as it is levied without regard to the nationality, domicile or residence of the taxpayer, i. e., the individual income tax as it was levied in the present case would be considered an "impersonal" tax.

Article XI of the Friendship, Trade and Shipping Treaty of October 29, 1954, between Germany and the United States provides that citizens of one of the two contracting States who are resident in the other contracting State may not be subjected to any taxation which is more burdensome than the taxation to which citizens of the other State in the same circumstances are or may be subjected.

III. The Issue

The issue was whether A was subject to German individual income tax with respect to the work performed abroad.

It was contended for the taxpayer that only part of this work could be deemed to be "utilized" in Germany, since although all the films were shown in Germany, these domestic showings accounted for only 15% of total usage of the films. Consequently only a minor part of the salary for the work performed abroad could be subject to income tax in Germany.

The tax administration, on the other hand, contended that A had assisted in producing a German movie and consequently the work performed abroad was fully "utilized" in Germany, whether the films were shown in Germany or abroad. The taxpayer therefore was fully taxable with respect to his salary.

IV. The Decision of the Lower Tax Court (Finanzgericht) of Munich of October 23, 1967

The Lower Tax Court of Munich supported the taxpayer's opinion and ruled that only 15% of the work performed abroad could be considered as "utilized" in Germany. It also ruled that A was employed by X so that the salary he received was DM 536,491.60 less DM 82,026 (i. e., the amount which was actually paid by X to A).

* * *

V. The Decision of the Supreme Tax Court (Bundesfinanzhof) of September 15, 1971

The Supreme Tax Court held that the Lower Tax Court of Munich had not sufficiently examined the facts and referred the case back to the same Court.

The Supreme Tax Court made the following important statements.

*   *   *

2. The Supreme Tax Court agreed that either the amount of DM 454,465 or DM 536,491 (depending on whether A would be considered an employee of X or of Y respectively) was at least $\frac{29}{32}$ subject to the 15% rate of individual income tax. However, the Supreme Tax Court rejected the Lower Tax Court's opinion that $\frac{54}{32}$ of the above amounts should only be partially subject to individual income tax in Germany, holding instead that the work performed by A abroad was fully "utilized" in Germany. The crucial point is where the work is utilized and not—as in the Lower Tax Court's opinion— where the result of the work is utilized. The fact that the films were also shown abroad is therefore for this case immaterial. Thus the Supreme Tax Court found that in this case the work performed abroad (i. e., in Italy) was indeed fully utilized in Germany, since (i) the movie as such was produced in Germany, and (ii) the copyrights were initially acquired by a German company (Y) (although they were to a large extent later transferred to X).

3. The Supreme Tax Court also rejected the view that Germany would be denied the right to impose individual income tax on the work performed in Italy and utilized in Germany, by virtue of the German-Italian Tax Treaty of October 21, 1925. According to the Court's view, this Treaty exclusively applies to citizens of Germany and Italy and since A was a United States citizen he cannot benefit from any of its provisions. It is true that the Treaty does not expressly provide that its provisions only apply to income derived by German and Italian citizens, but the Supreme Tax Court formed its opinion from some of the Treaty provisions themselves in connection with the historical development of the Treaty.

4. The Supreme Tax Court also rejected the view that the article XI of the Friendship, Trade and Shipping Treaty of October 29, 1954, would apply since the provisions of this Treaty apply only to residents of Germany and the United States. As A was a resident of Italy, neither he nor his heirs can benefit thereof.

ILLUSTRATIVE ARTICLES OF A MODERN TAX TREATY

Cyprus-United Kingdom (Income) Tax Arrangement
Supplementary Service to European Taxation
No. 3, March, 1970, § C.*

Article 3

(1) The industrial or commercial profits of a United Kingdom enterprise shall not be subject to Cyprus tax unless the enterprise is

* Reprinted with the permission of the
International Bureau of Fiscal Documentation, Amsterdam.

engaged in trade or business in Cyprus through a permanent establishment situated therein. If it is so engaged, tax may be imposed on those profits by Cyprus but only on so much of them as is attributable to that permanent establishment.

(2) [Reciprocally for Cyprus enterprise in the United Kingdom]

(3) Where an enterprise of one of the territories is engaged in trade or business in the other territory through a permanent establishment situated therein, there shall be attributed to that permanent establishment the industrial or commercial profits which it might be expected to derive from its activities in that other territory if it were an independent enterprise engaged in the same or similar activities under the same or similar conditions and dealing at arm's length with the enterprise of which it is a permanent establishment.

(4) No portion of any profits arising from the sale of goods or merchandise by an enterprise of one of the territories shall be attributed to a permanent establishment situated in the other territory by reason of the mere purchase of the goods or merchandise within that other territory.

Article 5

Notwithstanding the provisions of paragraphs 3 and 4, profits which a resident of one of the territories derives from operating ships or aircraft shall be exempt from tax in the other territory.

Article 6

(1) Dividends paid by a company resident in one of the territories to a resident of the other territory who is subject to tax in that other territory in respect thereof and not engaged in trade or business in the first-mentioned territory through a permanent establishment situated therein, shall be exempt from any tax in that first-mentioned territory which is chargeable on dividends in addition to the tax chargeable in respect of the profits or income of the company.

(2) Where a company which is a resident of one of the territories derives profits or income from sources within the other territory, the Government of that other territory shall not impose any form of taxation on dividends paid by the company to persons not resident in that other territory, or any tax in the nature of an undistributed profits tax on undistributed profits of the company, by reason of the fact that those dividends or undistributed profits represent, in whole or in part, profits or income so derived.

(3) If the recipient of a dividend is a company which owns 10 per cent. or more of the class of shares in respect of which the dividend is paid then sub-paragraph (1) shall not apply to the dividend to the extent that it can have been paid only out of profits which the company paying the dividend earned or other income which it received in a period ending twelve months or more before the relevant date. For the purposes of this sub-paragraph the term "relevant date" means the date on which the beneficial owner of the dividend became

the owner of 10 per cent. or more of the class of shares in question.
Provided, that this sub-paragraph shall not apply if the beneficial
owner of the dividend shows that the shares were acquired for bona
fide commercial reasons and not primarily for the purpose of securing the benefit of this paragraph.

Article 9

(1) An individual who is a resident of the United Kingdom shall
be exempt from Cyprus tax on profits or remuneration in respect of
personal (including professional) services performed within Cyprus
in any year of assessment if—

    (a) he is present within Cyprus for a period or periods not ex-
ceeding in the aggregate 183 days during that year, and

    (b) the services are performed for or on behalf of a person
resident in the United Kingdom, and

    (c) the profits or remuneration are subject to United Kingdom
tax.

(2) An individual who is a resident of Cyprus shall be exempt
from United Kingdom tax on profits or remuneration in respect of
personal (including professional) services performed within the United Kingdom in any year of assessment if—

    (a) he is present within the United Kingdom for a period or
periods not exceeding in the aggregate 183 days during that
year, and

    (b) the services are performed for or on behalf of a person resi-
dent in Cyprus and

    (c) the profits or remuneration are subject to Cyprus tax.

(3) The provisions of this paragraph shall not apply to the profits or remuneration of public entertainers such as stage, motion picture or radio artists, musicians and athletes.

Article 11

The remuneration derived by a professor or teacher who is ordinarily resident in one of the territories, for teaching, during a period
of temporary residence not exceeding two years, at a university, college, school or other educational institution in the other territory,
shall be exempt from tax in that other territory.

Article 12

A student or business apprentice from one of the territories who
is receiving full-time education or training in the other territory shall
be exempt from tax in that other territory on payments made to him
by persons in the first-mentioned territory for the purposes of his
maintenance, education or training.

Article 14

(1) The taxation authorities of the United Kingdom and Cyprus shall exchange such information (being information available under their respective taxation laws) as is necessary for carrying out the provisions of this Arrangement or for the prevention of fraud or the administration of statutory provisions against legal avoidance in relation to the taxes which are the subject of this Arrangement. Any information so exchanged shall be treated as secret and shall not be disclosed to any persons other than those concerned with the assessment and collection of the taxes which are the subject of this Arrangement. No information shall be exchanged which would disclose any trade secret or trade process.

(2) As used in this paragraph, the term "taxation authorities" means the Commissioners of Inland Revenue or their authorised representative in the case of the United Kingdom and the Commissioner of Income Tax or his authorised representative in the case of Cyprus.

IMPERIAL TOBACCO CO. OF INDIA, LTD. v. COMMISSIONER OF INCOME TAX

Pakistan, Supreme Court, 1958.
27 Int'l L.Rep. 103 (1963).*

The Facts: The appellant, the Imperial Tobacco Company of India, Ltd., was assessed to income-tax as a "resident" by an Income-tax Officer in Pakistan. The assessment was for the year 1948–49, for which the previous year was the financial year 1947–48. The registered office of the Company and the control and management of its affairs throughout the previous year was in Calcutta, India, though the Company carried on some business in Pakistan in that year. The Income-tax Officer, the Appellate Assistant Commissioner, the Appellate Tribunal and the High Court of West Pakistan at Karachi all held that the Company was rightly taxed as a "resident" under the Pakistan Income-Tax Law, with the result that the Company's profits which accrued to it in India and not in Pakistan during the previous year were taxed. The Company appealed to the Supreme Court.

Held: that the appeal must be allowed. It was a rule of international law that a State was entitled to tax foreigners only if they earned or received income within the territory of that State, and municipal legislation must not be construed as abrogating international law unless its language clearly had that result. [A portion of the opinion of the court appears below.]

* * * To appreciate the question involved, it is necessary to refer to the provisions of our Income-Tax Law which deal with the

* Reprinted by permission of E. Lauter-pacht, ed., and Grotius Publications, Ltd., Cambridge, England.

taxability of income. * * * The principle underlying these provisions is that income may be taxed on two bases: (1) receipt of income and (2) accrual of income. If a person is not resident in Pakistan all that can be taxed is the income that he receives in Pakistan or that accrues to him in Pakistan during the previous year. But if he is resident in Pakistan the income is taxable if it is received by him in Pakistan or if it accrues to him in Pakistan or outside Pakistan during the previous year. On this principle the appellant Company's profits in India during the previous year could be taxed only if the Company were held to be resident in Pakistan during the previous year. The simple issue therefore is whether the Company having its registered office outside Pakistan throughout the previous year could be held to be resident in Pakistan. * * *

* * * [T]he definition of "resident" * * * is:

A company is resident in British India in any year (a) if the control and management of its affairs is situated wholly in British India in that year. * * *

* * * Under the Pakistan Income-Tax Law the taxable territory can only be Pakistan, and if this definition were to be applied today a company would be resident in any year in Pakistan only if the control and management of its affairs were situated wholly in Pakistan in that year. On this definition, it was conceded by the learned advocate for the Commissioner of Income-Tax that the Department would have no authority to tax the company as a resident company. * * * This interpretation is in accordance with, and gives full effect to, the principle that statutes are not to be construed as abrogating international law unless their language clearly leads to that result, and that extraterritorial operation of a statute over foreigners is not to be presumed as having been intended unless it is expressly so stated. * * *

Thus, the Pakistan authorities' power to tax the foreign income of a company, the registered office of which has throughout the previous year been in Calcutta, is not to be easily inferred and unless the words of the statute unmistakably lend themselves to a contrary result, full effect must be given to the principle recognized by our own Income-Tax Law, that if a foreigner earns or receives income in Pakistan, that income alone is liable to income-tax and not the income earned by him in the country of his origin or elsewhere * * *. This construction is consistent with the words and the sense of the definition of "British India" as well as with the principle observed in Section 4 of the Income-Tax Act, and the rule of international law that a legislature has authority to tax its citizens wherever they be, and to tax foreigners only if they earn or receive income in the country for which that legislature has the authority to make laws. The interpretation adopted by the Departmental authorities and by the High Court is opposed to these principles and leads to this absurdity, that the Pakistan income-tax authorities may tax the foreign income of a company even if that company had its registered office for only a day during the previous year in Pakistan.

For the reasons given above, we allow this appeal and hold that the assessee Company was not resident within the meaning of Section 4–A(c) of the Income-Tax Act so as to be taxed by the Pakistan income-tax authorities under Section 4(1)(b)(ii). The Department must pay the appellant's costs.

---

1. *Mutual state interests as to taxation.* As has been observed more than once, taxation is an intensely practical matter. If any one of the states having jurisdiction to tax acts unreasonably in making its claim, or in refusing to take into account in some way, through some channel or other, the tax expectations of another state with jurisdiction to tax, the tax source itself is apt to be affected to the common fiscal detriment of the states concerned. Hence through networks of international agreements (although the German-Italian-United States agreements did not help the American actor in the case at p. 423) or the granting of credits against the national tax for foreign taxes of the same sort paid to another state having jurisdiction, multiple taxation of the same increment of economic power is reduced or eliminated.

2. *Parallel problem within the United States.* It is a curious fact, that, as between the states of the Union, the interstate compact approach to the reduction or avoidance of multistate death and income taxation has been so little used in the United States. Some degree of uniformity of treatment of resident and nonresident income exists in the various state income tax laws, and there is a practice of informal consultation between state taxing authorities as to both death and income taxes. The threat of multistate taxation within the United States became greater when the United States Supreme Court abandoned the view that substantive due process of law limited jurisdiction to tax in particular instances to a single state among a number of states having tax contacts. The problem of multistate tax claims tends to become more serious in the state income field as rates rise above the one to four percent that once characterized state income taxation.

SECTION B. VISITING FOREIGN FORCES

Persons in the armed services may fail in the performance of their military duties, and they may make mistakes or misbehave when off duty and amidst the civilian community. Or they may deviate from the performance of their official duty while on a mission off post, with resultant injury to someone who is not a member of the military. In general, the problems of conflicts of jurisdiction that arise when a state receives within its territory an organized military unit of a friendly state, usually an ally, are like those that arise between the military and civilian authorities in the environs of any domestic military installation. For some types of conduct, all agree that the military person should be responsible only to the law of his military unit. At the opposite extreme, all agree that in other instances he should be treated like anyone else within the civilian jurisdiction in which he has acted. As experience with friendly foreign forces present at the invitation of the territorial state has accumulated, principles have been worked out for the allocation of "primary" jurisdiction to one or the other of the states concerned. As the following cases show, applications of the rules of allocation may present problems inherently more difficult than the concoction of the rules themselves. Behind the problem there may be one involving a protected human right against double jeopardy or denial of the defenses of prior acquittal or prior conviction.

WHITLEY v. AITCHISON

France, Court of Cassation, 1958.
26 Int'l L.Rep. 196 (1963).*

The Facts: Article VII(3)(b) of the N.A.T.O. Status of Forces Agreement of June 19, 1951, provides that in the case of offences not arising out of acts done in the performance of the official duty of a member of a visiting force, "the authorities of the receiving State shall have the primary right to exercise jurisdiction". Subparagraph (c) of the same paragraph provides that "if the State having the primary right decides not to exercise jurisdiction, it shall notify the authorities of the other State as soon as practicable * * *." Article VII(8) of the Agreement provides:

Where an accused has been tried by the authorities of one Contracting Party and has been acquitted, or has been convicted and is serving, or has served, his sentence or has been pardoned, he may not be tried again for the same offence within the same territory by the authorities of another Contracting Party.

On November 25, 1953, the appellant, a major of the United States Air Force stationed in France under the provisions of the North Atlantic Treaty, was driving his car at high speed along a road within the judicial district of the French town of Corbeil. He was carrying as a passenger one Aitchison, an officer in the Royal Canadian Air Force. As subsequently found, the applicant drove negligently and as a result of his driving the car crashed and Aitchison was killed. It was also found that when driving the car the appellant was not acting in the performance of his official duty; and in accordance with Article VII(3)(b) of the Agreement of June 19, 1951, the primary right of jurisdiction was vested in the French courts. The United States military authorities requested the French authorities to waive their primary right of jurisdiction, and this request was ap-

* Reprinted by permission of E. Lauterpacht, ed., and Grotius Publications, Ltd., Cambridge, England.

Sweeny, O. & L. Cs.Inter.Leg.Sys.2d Ed. UCB—12

proved by the French Ministry of Justice and the Prosecutor of the Court of Corbeil. The French authorities duly notified the United States military authorities in accordance with Article VII(3)(c) of the Agreement that they had decided not to exercise jurisdiction.

Notwithstanding the waiver of their primary right of jurisdiction by the French authorities, however, the widow of Aitchison (the respondent herein) instituted proceedings against the appellant for damages as *partie civile*, as is customary under French law in connection with criminal proceedings arising out of the same set of facts. At that time the United States military authorities had not yet made any decision as to the manner in which they intended to proceed against the appellant in the exercise of the right of jurisdiction granted to them by the French authorities, but subsequently they decided not to take any action against the appellant.

The appellant objected to the jurisdiction of the French court on the ground that the waiver by the French authorities of their primary right of jurisdiction was irrevocable, and that the right once waived could not be revived by the decision of the United States authorities not to prosecute. The Court of Corbeil overruled the objection and held itself competent to adjudicate upon the respondent's claim for damages, and the Court of Appeal of Paris dismissed the appellant's appeal against that decision.[1]

On further appeal to the Court of Cassation,

Held: (i) that the appeal must be allowed. Once the French authorities had waived their right to primary jurisdiction and notified the United States military authorities of the waiver, their right to exercise jurisdiction was incapable of being revived, notwithstanding that the United States military authorities had decided not to prosecute the appellant.

(ii) Even though under French municipal law a prosecutor cannot definitively waive the right to prosecute, the Agreement, in accordance with Article 26 of the French Constitution of October 27, 1946, must take precedence and as, according to the Agreement, a right of primary jurisdiction once waived cannot be revived, the French courts were no longer competent. [A portion of the opinion of the court appears below.]

* * * The notice of appeal alleges, in addition to the matters raised before the Courts below, a violation of Articles VII(3)(c) and XX(3) of the N.A.T.O. Status of Forces Agreement of June 19, 1951, promulgated by Decree dated October 13, 1952; a violation of Articles 26 et seq. of the Constitution of October 27, 1946; of Articles 3 and 182 of the Code of Criminal Procedure; and of Article 7 of the Law of April 20, 1810. It is contended that the judgment under appeal, notwithstanding the waiver of the right of primary jurisdiction by

1. The judgment of the Court of Appeal of Paris is reported in International Law Reports, 1956, p. 255.

the Minister of Justice as well as by the Prosecutor of the Court of Corbeil, in favour of .the United States authorities, wrongly considered the Magistrates' Court of Corbeil entitled to deal with the civil action and the criminal prosecution. The Court of Corbeil, it is said, took this view on the ground that a waiver by the authorities of the country entitled to the right of primary jurisdiction is neither irrevocable nor unconditional, and that in order to be final and irrevocable and generally binding, a waiver must be subject to the requirement of the existence of a judgment against the accused. As long as such a judgment has not come into existence the victim, according to the view expressed by the lower courts, cannot be deprived of his right to bring proceedings in the criminal courts with a view to obtaining damages for the injury sustained. Neither the Minister of Justice nor the Public Prosecutor, according to this view, is in full control of the criminal proceedings, and they cannot waive these because such waiver would have no legal effect and could not, in any event, deprive the claimant (*partie civile*) of his own rights which the law confers on him.

If the host State which has the right of primary jurisdiction decides to waive this right, there arises a genuine lack of competence for the benefit of the other State which is not entitled to the right of primary jurisdiction. The State which has waived its right can no longer exercise jurisdiction unless the State which benefits from the waiver decides not to exercise jurisdiction and notifies the State which has waived its right. International conventions have the force of law even if they conflict with municipal law, and they must be applied instead of the latter where occasion demands. The provisions of the North Atlantic Treaty necessarily imply that it is the Public Prosecutor's department which is entitled to waive the right of primary jurisdiction, and that when the right has been waived the French courts are no longer competent, notwithstanding that according to French municipal law the Public Prosecutor cannot waive the right to institute criminal proceedings. The victim of the criminal offence, who can always bring his claim before the civil courts, cannot question a renunciation of competence which has been made for reasons of international courtesy.

Article VII(3)(c) of the Agreement of June 19, 1951, between the Parties to the North Atlantic Treaty, as published in the Decree dated October 11, 1952, provides as follows:

If the State having the primary right decides not to exercise jurisdiction, it shall notify the authorities of the other State as soon as practicable. The authorities of the State having the primary right shall give sympathetic consideration to a request from the authorities of the other State for a waiver of its right in cases where that other State considers such waiver to be of particular importance.

Where, in accordance with this provision, the authorities of the State which has the right of primary jurisdiction have, at the request of the other State, waived that right, their decision is final, and the criminal courts of the State concerned can no longer exercise jurisdiction over facts in respect of which there has been a waiver. There is no need to enquire whether the State in whose favour the right has been waived has exercised jurisdiction through its own courts. The only exception to this would be the case where the State which has been granted the right to exercise jurisdiction by the State in which the primary right was vested, expressly informs the latter that it does not wish to exercise jurisdiction and leaves the matter to the judicial authorities of the other Contracting Party.

According to Article 26 of the Constitution of October 27, 1946, international treaties duly ratified and published have the force of law even if they conflict with French municipal law. After the death of Aitchison, the latter's widow instituted proceedings against Whitley before the criminal court of Corbeil-Essonnes in whose district the accident had occurred, alleging involuntary homicide committed against her husband while Whitley was not acting in the performance of his official duties. That Court, in arriving at a finding that the subsidiary civil action (action de la partie civile) was subject to the jurisdiction, held that if before the institution of these proceedings the Minister of Justice and the Public Prosecutor of Corbeil-Essonnes agreed, at the request of the United States authorities and in accordance with the [N.A.T.O. Status of Forces] Agreement, to waive the right of primary jurisdiction, this did not imply a waiver of the right subsequently to exercise jurisdiction if, as in this case, the alleged offender has not been tried by the judicial authorities of his home State, because the Agreement itself contemplates the case of an accused who has not been tried in the home State and of an accused who, though convicted, has not served his sentence—unless there has been an amnesty.

The judgment under appeal has misinterpreted the provisions of the Agreement of June 19, 1951, and violated the provisions referred to in the notice of appeal, because it arrived at its finding notwithstanding the absence of any express declaration by the home State that it waived its right to exercise jurisdiction, which jurisdiction had been recognized by France when that country agreed not to exercise its primary right of jurisdiction. The judgment of the Court of Appeal of Paris is therefore reversed, and there is no need for the case to be sent back.

* * *

WILSON, SECRETARY OF DEFENSE v. GIRARD

United States Supreme Court, 1957.
354 U.S. 524, 77 S.Ct. 1409.

PER CURIAM. Japan and the United States became involved in a controversy whether the respondent Girard should be tried by a Japanese court for causing the death of a Japanese woman. * * *

Girard, a Specialist Third Class in the United States Army, was engaged on January 30, 1957, with members of his cavalry regiment in a small unit exercise at Camp Weir range area, Japan. Japanese civilians were present in the area, retrieving expended cartridge cases. Girard and another Specialist Third Class were ordered to guard a machine gun and some items of clothing that had been left nearby. Girard had a grenade launcher on his rifle. He placed an expended 30-caliber cartridge case in the grenade launcher and projected it by firing a blank. The expended cartridge case penetrated the back of a Japanese woman gathering expended cartridge cases and caused her death.

The United States ultimately notified Japan that Girard would be delivered to the Japanese authorities for trial. Thereafter, Japan indicted him for causing death by wounding. Girard sought a writ of habeas corpus in the United States District Court for the District of Columbia. The writ was denied, but Girard was granted declaratory relief and an injunction against his delivery to the Japanese authorities. 152 F.Supp. 21. The petitioners appealed to the Court of Appeals for the District of Columbia, and, without awaiting action by that court on the appeal, invoked the jurisdiction of this Court under 28 U.S.C.A. § 1254(1). Girard filed a cross-petition for certiorari to review the denial of the writ of habeas corpus. We granted both petitions. U. S. Supreme Court Rule 20; 354 U.S. 928, 77 S.Ct. 1390.

A Security Treaty between Japan and the United States, signed September 8, 1951, was ratified by the Senate on March 20, 1952, and proclaimed by the President effective April 28, 1952. Article III of the Treaty authorized the making of Administrative Agreements between the two Governments concerning "[t]he conditions which shall govern the disposition of armed forces of the United States of America in and about Japan * * *." Expressly acting under this provision, the two Nations, on February 28, 1952, signed an Administrative Agreement covering, among other matters, the jurisdiction of the United States over offenses committed in Japan by members of the United States armed forces, and providing that jurisdiction in any case might be waived by the United States. This Agreement became effective on the same date as the Security Treaty (April 28, 1952) and was considered by the Senate before consent was given to the Treaty.

Article XVII, paragraph 1, of the Administrative Agreement provided that upon the coming into effect of the "Agreement between the Parties to the North Atlantic Treaty regarding the Status of their Forces," signed June 19, 1951, the United States would conclude with Japan an agreement on criminal jurisdiction similar to the corresponding provisions of the NATO Agreement. The NATO Agreement became effective August 23, 1953, and the United States and Japan signed on September 29, 1953, effective October 29, 1953, a Protocol Agreement pursuant to the covenant in paragraph 1 of Article XVII.

Paragraph 3 of Article XVII, as amended by the Protocol, dealt with criminal offenses in violation of the laws of both Nations and provided:

3.   In cases where the right to exercise jurisdiction is concurrent the following rules shall apply:

(a) The military authorities of the United States shall have the primary right to exercise jurisdiction over members of the United States armed forces or the civilian component in relation to

(i) offenses solely against the property or security of the United States, or offenses solely against the person or property of another member of the United States armed forces or the civilian component or of a dependent;

(ii) offenses arising out of any act or omission done in the performance of official duty.

(b) In the case of any other offense the authorities of Japan shall have the primary right to exercise jurisdiction.

(c) If the State having the primary right decides not to exercise jurisdiction, it shall notify the authorities of the other State as soon as practicable. The authorities of the State having the primary right shall give sympathetic consideration to a request from the authorities of the other State for a waiver of its right in cases where that other State considers such waiver to be of particular importance.

Article XXVI of the Administrative Agreement established a Joint Committee of representatives of the United States and Japan to consult on all matters requiring mutual consultation regarding the implementation of the Agreement; and provided that if the Committee " *   *   * is unable to resolve any matter, it shall refer that matter to the respective Governments for further consideration through appropriate channels."

In the light of the Senate's ratification of the Security Treaty after consideration of the Administrative Agreement, which had already been signed, and its subsequent ratification of the NATO Agreement, with knowledge of the commitment to Japan under the Administrative Agreement, we are satisfied that the approval of Article III of the Security Treaty authorized the making of the Administrative Agreement and the subsequent Protocol embodying the NATO Agreement provisions governing jurisdiction to try criminal offenses.

The United States claimed the right to try Girard upon the ground that his act, as certified by his commanding officer, was "done in the performance of official duty" and therefore the United States had primary jurisdiction. Japan insisted that it had proof that Girard's action was without the scope of his official duty and therefore that Japan had the primary right to try him.

The Joint Committee, after prolonged deliberations, was unable to agree. The issue was referred to higher authority, which authorized the United States representatives on the Joint Committee to notify the appropriate Japanese authorities, in accordance with paragraph 3(c) of the Protocol, that the United States had decided not to exercise, but to waive, whatever jurisdiction it might have in the case. The Secretary of State and the Secretary of Defense decided that this determination should be carried out. The President confirmed their joint conclusion.

A sovereign nation has exclusive jurisdiction to punish offenses against its laws committed within its borders, unless it expressly or impliedly consents to surrender its jurisdiction. The Schooner Exchange v. M'Faddon, 7 Cranch 116, 136. Japan's cession to the United States of jurisdiction to try American military personnel for conduct constituting an offense against the laws of both countries was conditioned by the covenant of Article XVII, section 3, paragraph (c) of the Protocol that

> *   *   *   The authorities of the State having the primary right shall give sympathetic consideration to a request from the authorities of the other State for a waiver of its right in cases where that other State considers such waiver to be of particular importance.

The issue for our decision is therefore narrowed to the question whether, upon the record before us, the Constitution or legislation subsequent to the Security Treaty prohibited the carrying out of this provision authorized by the Treaty for waiver of the qualified jurisdiction granted by Japan. We find no constitutional or statutory barrier to the provision as applied here. In the absence of such encroachments, the wisdom of the arrangement is exclusively for the determination of the Executive and Legislative Branches.

The judgment of the District Court in No. 1103 is reversed, and its judgment in No. 1108 is affirmed.

[Mr. Justice DOUGLAS took no part in the consideration or decision of this case.]

Background facts for appraisal. In a Joint Statement of the Secretaries of State and Defense appended to the opinion as Appendix B, at 545, the following account is given of the facts of this case:

> The incident occurred in a maneuver area provided by the Japanese Government for part-time use of United States forces. The Japanese Defense Force uses the same area about 40% of the time. When the area is not in use by either the United States or Japanese armed forces, Japanese civilians are permitted to farm or otherwise use the area.

> Efforts to keep civilians away from the area during such military exercises have not proved effective. In this particular

case, red boundary flags were, as customary, erected as a warning to civilians to keep off, and local authorities were notified of the proposed exercises. But, as was frequently the case, a number of Japanese civilians were in the area gathering empty brass cartridge cases at the time of the incident. These civilians had created such a risk of injury to themselves in the morning exercises when live ammunition was used that the American officer in charge withdrew live ammunition from the troops prior to the afternoon exercises. In the interval between two simulated attacks during the afternoon, Girard and another soldier, Specialist 3rd Class Victor M. Nickel, were ordered by their platoon leader, a Lieutenant, to guard a machine gun and several field jackets at the top of a hill. Girard and Nickel were not issued live ammunition for this duty.

It was while these soldiers were performing this duty that the incident occurred. Mrs. Naka Sakai, a Japanese civilian, died a few moments after being hit in the back by an empty brass rifle shell case fired by Girard from his rifle grenade launcher. She was not over 30 yards from Girard and was going away from him when he fired the rifle. Girard had previously fired similarly in the vicinity of a Japanese man, who was not hit.

Girard's action in firing empty shell cases from the rifle grenade launcher was not authorized. He asserted that he fired from the waist, intending only to frighten the Japanese civilians. Others stated, but Girard denied, that empty shell cases were thrown out to entice the Japanese to approach.

JAPAN v. GIRARD

Japan, District Court of Maebashi, 1957.
26 Int'l L.Rep. 203 (1963).*

The Facts: The accused, William S. Girard, was charged with the offence of bodily injury resulting in death. The accused was a member of the United States Army stationed in Japan in accordance with the Administrative Agreement under Article 3 of the Security Treaty concluded between Japan and the United States in 1952. At the time of the offence he was a driver with the rank of Specialist Third Class in a cavalry regiment.

On January 30, 1957, the accused took part as a rifleman in an exercise in a manoeuvre area near a Japanese village. Japanese and American authorities had previously set up "no admittance" signs at strategic points surrounding the manoeuvre area and, in addition, whenever exercises were to be held, the residents in the area were notified in advance through the offices concerned. On the actual day of

* Reprinted by permission of E. Lauterpacht, ed., and Grotius Publications, Ltd., Cambridge, England.

the manoeuvre, red flags were flown at easily visible and specific points around the area. Warnings were issued prohibiting entry into the area because of danger, and local Japanese police authorities undertook various measures to keep out the public. The Japanese and American authorities concerned held frequent discussion meetings and planned counter measures to make these precautions effective. But effective control could not be achieved as originally intended for various reasons, including the fact that the scrap metal from rifle cartridge casings and fragments from artillery shells could be sold at a high price. As a result, many of the local residents entered the manoeuvre area to collect scrap, and eventually they came to ignore the warnings and entered the area even during exercises.

On the day in question, some sixty or seventy brass pickers entered the manoeuvre area and their activities were such that the lives of both soldiers and brass pickers were endangered. The live ammunition exercise was halted and only blank ammunition was used for the afternoon exercise. The accused and another private, Nickel, were ordered to guard a light machine gun and other items on a piece of high ground. Many brass pickers were gathered on the slopes below them. The two men threw some empty cartridge casings down the slopes and the accused called out to one of them, a woman, and pointed to a foxhole indicating that there were cartridge cases there. The woman, Naka Sakai, approached the foxhole, whereupon the accused, having placed an empty cartridge case into the mouth of the grenade launcher attached to his rifle, suddenly turned toward the woman and chased after her, shouting at her. He fired a blank shell from his rifle and the gas pressure from this caused the cartridge casing to be ejected from the launcher. The woman was hit, and died from her injuries.

It was argued for the defense that the accused's act was a crime resulting from an act done in the course of official duty as stipulated in Article 17, paragraph 3(a)(ii), of the Administrative Agreement under Article 3 of the Security Treaty between Japan and the United States. On this basis, the defense contended that the military authorities of the United States had the primary right to exercise jurisdiction. It was further contended that although the United States had notified Japan that they would not exercise jurisdiction in this instance, this notification differed from the case in which the primary right of jurisdiction was waived at the request of the Japanese authorities. Consequently, the notification could not be regarded as meaning that Japan automatically obtained the right of secondary jurisdiction. Alternatively, it was contended that Japan did not have jurisdiction because the provisions of paragraph 6(a) of Article 17 of the Administrative Agreement had not been fulfilled in that the Japanese authorities did not show to the military authorities certain statements made to the Japanese procurators, and that, therefore, the proceedings had been instituted in breach of the stipulations of mutual assistance concerning the collection and production of evidence and the investigation of a crime by the authorities of both countries.

Held: on the submissions regarding jurisdiction, that Japan had jurisdiction in this case. It was a case of concurrent jurisdiction within Article 17, paragraph 1(a) and (b), of the Administrative Agreement. The notification by the United States authorities had the same effect as a waiver so far as the loss of jurisdiction by the United States military authorities, in Japan was concerned. The Court also held that there had been no breach of the provisions of paragraph 6(a) of Article 17. These provisions did not demand that the authorities of either country submit to the authorities of the other all the evidential material of the case concerned. [A portion of the opinion of the court appears below.]

* * * The defense, in viewing the offense in this case, have regarded it as a crime resulting from an act done in the course of official duty as stipulated in Article 17, paragraph 3(a)(ii), of the Administrative Agreement, based on Article 3 of the Security Treaty between the United States and Japan, and, on this premise, the defense have advocated that the military authorities of the United States have the primary right to exercise jurisdiction in this case. The defense further have contended that although the United States of America has notified Japan that they will not exercise jurisdiction in this case, this notification differs from the case in which the primary right of jurisdiction is waived at the request of the Japanese authorities.

Thus, the above notification cannot be regarded as meaning that Japan automatically has obtained the right of secondary jurisdiction.

However, in the present case, regardless of whether the crime resulted from an act done in the course of the performance of official duty or not, this is a case based on Article 17, paragraph 1(a) and (b), where both Japan and the military authorities of the United States have concurrent jurisdiction. Thus, in this case of concurrent jurisdiction, the provision of paragraph 3 of the above Article applies. Since the military authorities of the United States notified Japan in a letter dated May 17, 1957, in accordance with (c) of paragraph 3 of the above Article, to the effect that they would not exercise criminal jurisdiction in this case, it stands to reason that this should be interpreted as meaning that the United States military authorities have lost jurisdiction in Japan over this case.

Further, the above notification of non-exercise of jurisdiction differs, as advocated by the defense, from the case of waiving jurisdiction at the request of the authorities of the other State. In other words, it differs from the case stipulated in the latter part of (c) of paragraph 3 of the above Article. However, it must be said that in either of the above cases it is absolutely the same so far as the loss of jurisdiction by the United States military authorities in Japan is concerned. Consequently, there is no doubt that a Japanese court has jurisdiction in this case, in accordance with the terms of Article 17, paragraph 1(b) of the Administrative Agreement.

So the question of whether Japanese authorities or whether the United States military authorities have the primary right to exercise jurisdiction in this case is already a matter of the past, and there is no advantage in dilating further on this point. Thus, from an absolute point of view, there is no need to determine whether this is a case of a crime committed in the course of the performance of official duty or not. However, in another sense, since the Court recognizes that this is an important point of contention, it will dwell further on this point as follows:

Although the Court is able to recognize that this offense took place while the accused was on official duty and that it occurred at the place of duty, the act has no direct connection whatsoever with the execution of the duty of guarding a light machine gun, etc., as ordered by a senior officer. Thus, it is self-evident from the facts found by this Court that the act was not committed in the process of carrying out one's official duty. Moreover, as is clear from the various points of evidence listed above, the Court does not recognize the existence of any concrete anxieties with respect to the light machine guns and field jackets being either damaged or stolen by brass pickers. Rather, the brass pickers were only intent on collecting expended cartridges.

It is for this reason that Specialist Third Class Nickel, who, together with the accused, was ordered to guard duty, was resting at a place toward the eastern part of the saddle a little distance removed from the location of the light machine gun. And, as indicated in the Court findings, Nickel is to be regarded as having thrown a number of empty cartridges a number of times without any specific meaning or, in other words, just to pass the time away. Further, the fact that the accused fired at brass pickers is not limited to the case of Naka Sakai alone, as indicated in the findings of the Court. Just prior to this, there is the case of Eiji Onozeki. Onozeki, one of the brass pickers mentioned in the Court findings, was descending the east slope of the West Peak, when the accused ran towards him. The said brass picker was surprised at this, and began running away. The accused then, aiming towards Onozeki's immediate vicinity from behind, fired an empty cartridge. This has been indicated in the Court findings. Such actions as inviting brass pickers to approach and then of chasing them away, cannot in any sense be regarded as necessary to the performance of official duty. Furthermore, the firing of a blank cartridge by inserting an empty cartridge in a grenade launcher and thereby projecting the casing is a practice that is not permitted by the United States military authorities because it damages the weapons. In addition, the firing of blank cartridges at close distance towards any person without cause is also forbidden. In this case before the Court, the act can only be regarded as excessive mischief, completely irrelevant to the performance of the duty of guarding light machine guns and other items and as having no subjective or objective relationship, an action simply carried out for the sole purpose of satisfying the momentary caprice of the accused him-

self.   Thus, this behaviour cannot be accepted, as contended by the
defense, as corresponding to a justifiable action as stipulated in Article 35 of the Criminal Code.

     *   *   *

SECTION C.   CONTROL OF ECONOMIC ACTIVITY

---

    1.   *Multiple state interests.*   On a small planet the economic ac-
tivities of significant persons and business associations can involve
the governmental interests of several different states and of at least
one new association of states, the European Community.   If it is accepted that international law permits the exercise of prescriptive jurisdiction on the basis of economic effects within the territory of a
state, and hence that several states have jurisdiction to regulate the
same economic activity, actual regulation by all states that have jurisdiction would be chaotic, as well as unjust.   What state then, under
what circumstances, and in what way and by what means, should
yield the exercise of its jurisdiction to another?

    Where economic or social conduct is involved, the question is dif-
ficult, because the easy-to-formulate allocation devices considered in
the preceding sections are not relevant.   Ideally, what is needed is
some way of quantifying state regulatory interests and of leaving the
whole regulatory job to the law-making authority with the highly
preponderant interest.   But how are such interests to be determined
and what is the authority of the law-appliers in one state to disregard
its own law?

    Clearly in the situation of transnational business activity tres-
passing on the interests of two or more national states, just as in the
case of everyday conflicting police power interests of two states of
the Union, neither law as rules nor law as method has yet given
clear cut and reliable solutions.   Perhaps such methods for the partial resolution of conflicts as we shall consider below might be
thought to yield the conclusion that the reciprocal judicial deference,
moderation, equity and comity approaches are not reliable enough
and that conflict must be reduced by the adoption of new rules.
What rules?   Rules to narrow the bases of national jurisdiction?   Or
new universal regulatory rules that would replace the welter of national regulatory laws?

    2.   *Areas of economic activity involved.*   The problems of con-
flicts involving regulatory policy in the field of anticompetitive practices (restrictive business practices and practices tending toward
market domination and monopoly) are the ones that have been the
most fully considered.   Thus, in the cases to follow you will study,
first, in an antitrust context, the problems of reach of law including
both those related to investigative preliminaries and those related to
actual imposition of a particular law.   Then we direct your attention

to various approaches to resolutions of those problems through one moderative device or another. We follow the antitrust presentation with one involving the reach of national regulation of securities transactions. This area seems to be developing conflicts of jurisdiction problems but at the same time seems, so far as American judicial decisions go, to be focusing more at the outset than was true as to antitrust on elements of moderation—or even, possibly, limitation of the effects doctrine as a matter of jurisdiction, either under national or international law.

------

1. JURISDICTIONAL CONFLICTS AS TO UNITED STATES ANTITRUST

Hypothetical case to illustrate the differences between antitrust laws. Assume that all the law enforcement authorities involved in the hypothetical case below know and can prove that the producers of 95% of the world supply of a certain basic hard mineral, some thirty corporations that are nationals of ten countries, conform to a pattern in which each national market is left to the companies organized there and total production by all the companies is adjusted to total demand in such a way as to keep prices stable and relatively high. However, it is not possible to prove that the thirty companies have made any contractual arrangement to these ends. (This is a simple and classic antitrust problem, that of concerted action to allocate markets and control price by restricting production of a single product.)

The Facts:

a. In some of the ten countries even a contractual cartel arrangement would not violate any law; and, indeed, a breach of such a contract would be actionable.

b. In the United States the concerted action would violate the Sherman Act, even if it did not result in market dominance, i. e., a per se violation. Moreover, the sanctions would include invalidation of the contract, criminal prosecution, equitable enforcement by imprisonment or fines for civil contempt, or treble damages to injured competitors outside the cartel arrangement.

c. In the Federal German Republic the supreme court has held that the cartel law, see p. 112, does not reach concerted actions where there is no contract.

d. In the United States and in the Federal German Republic an antitrust violation under national law, if otherwise actionable, exists if the companies' conduct, wherever it took place, has economic effects within the territories of these states.

e. But in Germany, unlike the United States, criminal and civil contempt sanctions would not lie; the fine is the major sanction.

f. In Great Britain, prior to its entry into the European Community [a] the cartel arrangement would have to be considered by one or the other of two commissions, the Restrictive Practices Commission or the Monopolies Commission, most likely the former, before any sanction whatsoever might be applied. Also, if certain British scholarly voices should be heeded by the relevant commission and/or the courts on judicial review, customary international law would limit British regulation to conduct within Great Britain having its effects within Great Britain.

g. In Great Britain, now that it has entered the European Community, the Community antitrust law, as elaborated by the Court of the Community, will be directly applicable to British (or any other Community) nationals involved in the cartel. The Community Court has decided that, although not explicit in the Treaty of Rome, concerted action without contract as to allocation of markets and the control of production and prices violates Article 85–1 of the Treaty of Rome. It has also held that the Rome Treaty rule will apply to any such conduct carried on within the Community by an out-of-Community corporation through its controlled subsidiaries within the Community.

h. But the Community rule does not preempt and render nugatory the various national antitrust laws (if any) of member states. Thus, subject to a superior, valid demand from the Commission of the Community (e. g., on the authority of the decision of the Court of the Community), France may continue to deal with the cartel on the basis that its actions interfere with the French price controls laws.

i. The Community antitrust law uses fines as the sanction and permits tentative immunity to companies that have registered their anti-competitive agreements and have not been told that they are deemed violations. In any event, it—Treaty of Rome, Art. 85–3—authorizes the commission to except certain otherwise anti-competitive arrangements if found to contribute to the improvement of the production or distribution of goods or to the promotion of technological or economic progress while reserving to consumers an equitable share in the profit resulting therefrom, and which neither impose on the enterprises concerned any restrictions not indispensable to the attainment of the above objectives, nor enable such enterprises to eliminate competition in respect of a substantial proportion of the goods concerned.

Such variances from liability are unknown in United States antitrust practice, but there is no rule specifying when the Department of Justice must prosecute an antitrust case or that the Federal Trade Commission must begin an administrative proceeding.

a. The European Community is described, as to its three constituent communities created by different treaties, at p. 892. The Treaty of Rome, 1958, created the community involved in this problem, the European Economic Community (EEC), informally known as the Common Market.

Questions.

Now, suppose that by coincidence antitrust proceedings are brought in all legal systems except those in category (a). In the United States proceeding, to the shock of the Europeans, there is a criminal count against the executives of the companies in the cartel, only a few of which can be personally served. Also, in the United States, foreign corporations that cannot otherwise be served with process in the proceedings against the corporations are served through companies organized in the United States as subsidiaries of the foreign companies but which, the United States claims, are really the parent companies and control the foreign companies. The United States also demands of the corporations so served that they produce for an American grand jury the books and records kept abroad by the ostensible foreign parent company.

What results if:

a.   A state in category (a) objects under customary international law to every aspect of the United States proceeding, insofar as its citizens and companies organized under its law are concerned. What do you think the legal counts in a diplomatic protest would be, and the proper legal response of the Department of State?

b.   The ambassador of the United States to the European Community, acting on the instruction of his government, asks the commission not to proceed with its case against the cartel, as the matter is being prepared for trial in the United States, the world's largest consumer of the mineral involved. What is a proper response of the commission to the ambassador?

c.   The Commission of the Community grants an exception under Article 85-3 of the Treaty of Rome, the United States thereafter proceeds to final judgment against all members of the cartel that can be served in the United States, and the commission protests to the American ambassador. What is a proper legal and policy response from him?

d.   Is there any better way to deal with these conflicts of regulatory law? What is it?

CCH, Common Market Reporter, is a useful source in English of the antitrust laws—or the lack of them—in European states. There is extensive discussion of the divergencies between national legal systems in this regard, and of the problems these create, in the Report of the International Law Association, Fifty-first Conference, Tokyo 1964, at 304–592 (1965), with summaries of national laws beginning at 417.

THE SHERMAN ACT [a]

15 U.S.C. §§ 1–2.

Sec. 1. Every contract, combination in the form of trust or otherwise, or conspiracy, in restraint of trade or commerce among the several States, or with foreign nations, is [hereby] declared to be illegal * * *.

Sec. 2. Every person who shall monopolize, or attempt to monopolize, or combine or conspire with any other person or persons, to monopolize any part of the trade or commerce among the several States, or with foreign nations shall be deemed guilty of a misdemeanor * * *.

[To the declarations of invalidity and the criminal penalties provided above, the United States antitrust laws contain as sanctions the use of injunctions, with the corresponding power to punish for civil contempt, and treble damages for injured private parties. European antitrust laws in many instances provide only for fines; such is the case with the provisions against restraints of trade (Article 85) and monopoly power misused (Article 86) of the Treaty of Rome, which establishes the European Economic Community.]

AMERICAN BANANA CO. v. UNITED FRUIT CO.

United States Supreme Court, 1909.
213 U.S. 347, 354, 29 S.Ct. 511, 53 L.Ed. 826.

[This was a private suit for treble damages brought under the Sherman Act. The court summarized the complaint of the plaintiff as follows.]

* * * The plaintiff is an Alabama corporation, organized in 1904. The defendant is a New Jersey corporation, organized in 1899. Long before the plaintiff was formed, the defendant, with intent to prevent competition and to control and monopolize the banana trade, bought the property and business of several of its previous competitors, with provision against their resuming the trade, made contracts with others, including a majority of the most important, regulating the quantity to be purchased and the price to be paid, and acquired a controlling amount of stock in still others. For the same purpose it organized a selling company, of which it held the stock, that by agreement sold at fixed prices all the bananas of the combining parties. By this and other means it did monopolize and restrain the trade and maintained unreasonable prices. The defendant being in this ominous attitude, one McConnell in 1903 started a banana plantation in Panama, then part of the United States of Colombia, and began to build a railway (which would afford his only means of export), both

------

a. The original and still basic federal antitrust law, now supplemented by legislation such as the Clayton Act and the Federal Trade Commission Act.

in accordance with the laws of the United States of Colombia. He was notified by the defendant that he must either combine or stop. Two months later, it is believed at the defendant's instigation, the governor of Panama recommended to his national government that Costa Rica be allowed to administer the territory through which the railroad was to run, and this although that territory had been awarded to Colombia under an arbitration agreed to by treaty. The defendant, and afterwards, in September, the government of Costa Rica, it is believed by the inducement of the defendant, interfered with McConnell. In November, 1903, Panama revolted and became an independent republic, declaring its boundary to be that settled by the award. In June, 1904, the plaintiff bought out McConnell and went on with the work, as it had a right to do under the laws of Panama. But in July, Costa Rican soldiers and officials, instigated by the defendant, seized a part of the plantation and a cargo of supplies and have held them ever since, and stopped the construction and operation of the plantation and railway. In August one Astua, by ex parte proceedings, got a judgment from a Costa Rican court, declaring the plantation to be his, although, it is alleged, the proceedings were not within the jurisdiction of Costa Rica, and were contrary to its laws and void. Agents of the defendant then bought the lands from Astua. The plaintiff has tried to induce the government of Costa Rica to withdraw its soldiers and also has tried to persuade the United States to interfere, but has been thwarted in both by the defendant and has failed. The government of Costa Rica remained in possession down to the bringing of the suit.

As a result of the defendant's acts the plaintiff has been deprived of the use of the plantation, and the railway, the plantation and supplies have been injured. The defendant also, by outbidding, has driven purchasers out of the market and has compelled producers to come to its terms, and it has prevented the plaintiff from buying for export and sale. This is the substantial damage alleged. There is thrown in a further allegation that the defendant has "sought to injure" the plaintiff's business by offering positions to its employés and by discharging and threatening to discharge persons in its own employ who were stockholders of the plaintiff. But no particular point is made of this. It is contended, however, that, even if the main argument fails and the defendant is held not to be answerable for acts depending on the coöperation of the government of Costa Rica for their effect, a wrongful conspiracy resulting in driving the plaintiff out of business is to be gathered from the complaint and that it was entitled to go to trial upon that.

[The court affirmed the dismissal of the complaint as not setting forth a cause of action. Justice Holmes stated in the opinion of the Court.]

It is obvious that, however stated, the plaintiff's case depends on several rather startling propositions. In the first place the acts causing the damage were done, so far as appears, outside the jurisdiction of the United States and within that of other states. It is surprising to hear it argued that they were governed by the act of Congress.

* * * [T]he general and almost universal rule is that the character of an act as lawful or unlawful must be determined wholly by the law of the country where the act is done. * * * For another jurisdiction, if it should happen to lay hold of the actor, to treat him according to its own notions rather than those of the place where he did the acts, not only would be unjust, but would be an interference with the authority of another sovereign, contrary to the comity of nations, which the other state concerned justly might resent. * * *

* * *

The foregoing considerations would lead in case of doubt to a construction of any statute as intended to be confined in its operation and effect to the territorial limits over which the lawmaker has general and legitimate power. "All legislation is prima facie territorial." Ex parte Blain, In re Sawers, 12 Ch.Div. 522, 528; State v. Carter, 27 N.J. (3 Dutcher) 499; People v. Merrill, 2 Parker, Crim.Rep. 590, 596. Words having universal scope, such as "Every contract in restraint of trade," "Every person who shall monopolize," etc., will be taken as a matter of course to mean only every one subject to such legislation, not all that the legislator subsequently may be able to catch. In the case of the present statute the improbability of the United States attempting to make acts done in Panama or Costa Rica criminal is obvious, yet the law begins by making criminal the acts for which it gives a right to sue. We think it entirely plain that what the defendant did in Panama or Costa Rica is not within the scope of the statute so far as the present suit is concerned. Other objections of a serious nature are urged but need not be discussed.

For again, not only were the acts of the defendant in Panama or Costa Rica not within the Sherman Act, but they were not torts by the law of the place and therefore were not torts at all, however contrary to the ethical and economic postulates of that statute. The substance of the complaint is that, the plantation being within the de facto jurisdiction of Costa Rica, that state took and keeps possession of it by virtue of its sovereign power. But a seizure by a state is not a thing that can be complained of elsewhere in the courts. Underhill v. Hernandez, 168 U.S. 250. The fact, if it be one, that de jure the estate is in Panama does not matter in the least; sovereignty is pure fact. The fact has been recognized by the United States, and by the implications of the bill is assented to by Panama.

* * *

* * * Giving to this complaint every reasonable latitude of interpretation we are of opinion that it alleges no case under the act of Congress and discloses nothing that we can suppose to have been a tort where it was done. A conspiracy in this country to do acts in

another jurisdiction does not draw to itself those acts and make them unlawful, if they are permitted by the local law.

    *   *   *

Questions. To what extent does the court's ruling depend upon the act of state doctrine? Upon the fact that the "acts of the defendant in Panama or Costa Rica * * * were not torts by the law of the place"? How would the court have ruled if the Costa Rican government had not been involved in the oppression of the Banana Company?

UNITED STATES v. ALUMINUM CO. OF AMERICA

United States Court of Appeals, Second Circuit, 1945.
148 F.2d 416, 442.

[This was a prosecution for violation of the Sherman Act. One of the defendants was Aluminum Limited, a Canadian corporation formed to take over properties of the Aluminum Company of America outside the United States. (Not quite half of each company's shares were owned by the same group of individuals.) The court was concerned about the participation of each company in a foreign cartel, called the Alliance. The court concluded that the American company, Alcoa, was not a party to the Alliance and "did not join in any violation of § 1 of the Act, so far as concerned foreign commerce." Judge Learned Hand's opinion continued:]

Whether "Limited" itself violated that section depends upon the character of the "Alliance." It was a Swiss corporation, created in pursuance of an agreement entered into on July 3, 1931, the signatories to which were a French corporation, two German, one Swiss, a British, and "Limited." The original agreement, or "cartel," provided for the formation of a corporation in Switzerland which should issue shares, to be taken up by the signatories. This corporation was from time to time to fix a quota of production for each share, and each shareholder was to be limited to the quantity measured by the number of shares it held, but was free to sell at any price it chose. The corporation fixed a price every year at which it would take off any shareholder's hands any part of its quota which it did not sell. No shareholder was to "buy, borrow, fabricate or sell" aluminum produced by anyone not a shareholder except with the consent of the board of governors, but that must not be "unreasonably withheld."
    *   *   *

The agreement of 1936 abandoned the system of unconditional quotas, and substituted a system of royalties. Each shareholder was to have a fixed free quota for every share it held, but as its production exceeded the sum of its quotas, it was to pay a royalty, graduated progressively in proportion to the excess; and these royalties the "Alliance" divided among the shareholders in proportion to their shares. This agreement—unlike the first—did not contain an express promise that the "Alliance" would buy any undisposed of stocks at a fixed price, although perhaps § 3 of Subdivision A, of Part X may have impliedly recognized such an obligation. Probably, during the two years in which the shareholders operated under this agreement, that question did not arise for the demand for aluminum was very active. Nevertheless, we understand from "Limited's" answer to an interrogatory that the last price fixed under the agreement of 1931 was understood to remain in force. Although this agreement, like its predecessor, was silent as to imports into the United States, when that question arose during its preparation, as it did, all the shareholders agreed that such imports should be included in the quotas. The German companies were exempted from royalties—for obvious reasons—and that, it would seem, for practical purposes put them out of the "cartel" for the future, for it was scarcely possible that a German producer would be unable to dispose of all its production, at least within any future period that would be provided for. The shareholders continued this agreement unchanged until the end of March, 1938, by which time it had become plain that, at least for the time being, it was no longer of service to anyone. Nothing was, however, done to end it, although the German shareholders of course became enemies of the French, British and Canadian shareholders in 1939. The "Alliance" itself has apparently never been dissolved; and indeed it appeared on the "Proclaimed List of Blocked Nationals" of September 13, 1944.

Did either the agreement of 1931 or that of 1936 violate § 1 of the Act? The answer does not depend upon whether we shall recognize as a source of liability a liability imposed by another state. On the contrary we are concerned only with whether Congress chose to attach liability to the conduct outside the United States of persons not in allegiance to it. That being so, the only question open is whether Congress intended to impose the liability, and whether our own Constitution permitted it to do so: as a court of the United States, we cannot look beyond our own law. Nevertheless, it is quite true that we are not to read general words, such as those in this Act, without regard to the limitations customarily observed by nations upon the exercise of their powers; limitations which generally correspond to those fixed by the "Conflict of Laws." We should not impute to Congress an intent to punish all whom its courts can catch, for conduct which has no consequences within the United States. American Banana Co. v. United Fruit Co., 213 U.S. 347, 357, 29 S.Ct. 511, 53 L.Ed. 826, 16 Ann.Cas. 1047; United States v. Bowman, 260 U.S. 94, 98, 43 S.Ct. 39, 67 L.Ed. 149; Blackmer v. United States, 284 U.S. 421, 437, 52 S.Ct. 252, 76 L.Ed. 375. On the other hand, *it is settled law*—as "Limited" itself agrees—*that any state may impose liabilities, even upon persons not within its allegiance, for conduct outside its borders that has consequences within its borders which the state reprehends;*[a] and these liabilities other states will ordinarily

a. Emphasis supplied by the editors.

recognize. Strassheim v. Daily, 221 U.S. 280, 284, 285, 31 S.Ct. 558, 55 L.Ed. 735; Lamar v. United States, 240 U.S. 60, 65, 66, 36 S.Ct. 255, 60 L.Ed. 526; Ford v. United States, 273 U.S. 593, 620, 621, 47 S.Ct. 531, 71 L.Ed. 793; Restatement of Conflict of Laws § 65. It may be argued that this Act extends further. Two situations are possible. There may be agreements made beyond our borders not intended to affect imports, which do affect them, or which affect exports. Almost any limitation of the supply of goods in Europe, for example, or in South America, may have repercussions in the United States if there is trade between the two. Yet when one considers the international complications likely to arise from an effort in this country to treat such agreements as unlawful, it is safe to assume that Congress certainly did not intend the Act to cover them. Such agreements may on the other hand intend to include imports into the United States, and yet it may appear that they have had no effect upon them. That situation might be thought to fall within the doctrine that intent may be a substitute for performance in the case of a contract made within the United States; or it might be thought to fall within the doctrine that a statute should not be interpreted to cover acts abroad which have no consequence here. We shall not choose between these alternatives; but for argument we shall assume that the Act does not cover agreements, even though intended to affect imports or exports, unless its performance is shown actually to have had some effect upon them. Where both conditions are satisfied, the situation certainly falls within such decisions as United States v. Pacific & Artic R. & Navigation Co., 228 U.S. 87, 33 S.Ct. 443, 57 L.Ed. 742; Thomsen v. Cayser, 243 U.S. 66, 37 S.Ct. 353, 61 L.Ed. 597, Ann.Cas. 1917D, 322 and United States v. Sisal Sales Corporation, 274 U.S. 268, 47 S.Ct. 592, 71 L.Ed. 1042. (United States v. Nord Deutcher Lloyd, 223 U.S. 512, 32 S.Ct. 244, 56 L.Ed. 531, illustrates the same conception in another field.) * * *

Both agreements would clearly have been unlawful, had they been made within the United States; and it follows from what we have just said that both were unlawful, though made abroad, if they were intended to affect imports and did affect them. Since the shareholders almost at once agreed that the agreement of 1931 should not cover imports, we may ignore it and confine our discussion to that of 1936: indeed that we should have to do anyway, since it superseded the earlier agreement. The judge found that it was not the purpose of the agreement to "suppress or restrain the exportation of aluminum to the United States for sale in competition with Alcoa." By that we understand that he meant that the agreement was not specifically directed to "Alcoa," because it only applied generally to the production of the shareholders. If he meant that it was not expected that the general restriction upon production would have an effect upon imports, we cannot agree, for the change made in 1936 was deliberate and was expressly made to accomplish just that. It would have been an idle gesture, unless the shareholders had supposed that it would, or at least might, have that effect. The first of the conditions which we mentioned was therefore satisfied; the intent was to set up a quota system for imports.

The judge also found that the 1936 agreement did not "materially affect the * * * foreign trade or commerce of the United States"; apparently because the imported ingot was greater in 1936 and 1937 than in earlier years. We cannot accept this finding, based as it was upon the fact that, in 1936, 1937 and the first quarter of 1938, the gross imports of ingot increased. It by no means follows from such an increase that the agreement did not restrict imports; and incidentally it so happens that in those years such inference as is possible at all, leads to the opposite conclusion. It is true that the average imports—including "Alcoa's"—for the years 1932–1935 inclusive were about 15 million pounds, and that for 1936, 1937 and one-fourth of 1938 they were about 33 million pounds; but the average domestic ingot manufacture in the first period was about 96 million and in the second about 262 million; so that the proportion of imports to domestic ingot was about 15.6 per cent for the first period and about 12.6 per cent for the second. We do not mean to infer from this that the quota system of 1936 did in fact restrain imports, as these figures might suggest; but we do mean that nothing is to be inferred from the gross increase of imports. We shall dispose of the matter therefore upon the assumption that, although the shareholders intended to restrict imports, it does not appear whether in fact they did so. Upon our hypothesis the plaintiff would therefore fail, if it carried the burden of proof upon this issue as upon others. We think, however, that, after the intent to affect imports was proved, the burden of proof shifted to "Limited." In the first place a depressant upon production which applies generally may be assumed, ceteris paribus, to distribute its effect evenly upon all markets. Again, when the parties took the trouble specifically to make the depressant apply to a given market, there is reason to suppose that they expected that it would have some effect, which it could have only by lessening what would otherwise have been imported. If the motive they introduced was over-balanced in all instances by motives which induced the shareholders to import, if the United States market became so attractive that the royalties did not count at all and their expectations were in fact defeated, they to whom the facts were more accessible than to the plaintiff ought to prove it, for a prima facie case had been made. Moreover, there is an especial propriety in demanding this of "Limited," because it was "Limited" which procured the inclusion in the agreement of 1936 of imports in the quotas.

There remains only the question whether this assumed restriction had any influence upon prices * * *. To that Socony-Vacuum Oil Co. v. United States, supra, 310 U.S. 150, 60 S.Ct. 811, 84 L. Ed. 1129, is an entire answer. * * * The underlying doctrine was that all factors which contribute to determine prices, must be kept free to operate unhampered by agreements. For these reasons we think that the agreement of 1936 violated § 1 of the Act.

* * *

Why a circuit court case for this important ruling on effects? This case has the theoretical standing of a Supreme Court decision, because it was decided on certification and transfer from the Supreme Court for lack of a quorum of qualified justices. The Supreme Court has decided other antitrust cases along similar lines, post American Banana: United States v. Sisal Sales Corp., 274 U.S. 268, 47 S.Ct. 592, 71 L.Ed. 1042 (1927); United States v. Holophane Co., 352 U.S. 903, 77 S.Ct. 144, 1 L.Ed.2d 114 (1956) (per curiam affirmance of lower court order under the Sherman Act requiring the defendants to compete actively in foreign markets); Continental Ore Co. v. Union Carbide & Carbon Corp., 370 U.S. 690, 82 S.Ct. 1404, 8 L.Ed.2d 777 (1962). In the 1911 dissolution of the American Tobacco Trust in United States v. American Tobacco Co., 221 U.S. 106, 31 S.Ct. 632, 55 L.Ed. 663 (1910), the decree ran to the British-American Tobacco Company, a United Kingdom company.

The ICI-DuPont-Nylon Spinners Cases: basic facts for three cases. DuPont invented nylon and, as is customary, patented its invention in all—or certainly all industrial—countries, including the United Kingdom. The patent for exploitation of the British market was transferred to Imperial Chemicals Industries (ICI). The United States Department of Justice charged that this transfer was one item in an arrangement whereby the large United States chemical company and the very big British one had pooled their patents and divided the world between them as to markets for products deriving from all the patents in the pool. ICI was properly served in the United States and unsuccessfully contended before the United States court that British law and patent policy favored such territorial divisions in patent cases. The trial judge ordered the dissolution of the pool and directed ICI by an affirmative decree in equity to open the British nylon patent to all wishing to use the patent on payment of standard royalties.

ICI accepted its defeat in the United States with apparent good grace, only to be met, doubtless to its surprise, with a suit for specific performance in a British court. The plaintiff was British Nylon Spinners, Ltd. It had not been served in the United States case and claimed an exclusive assignment by ICI to it of the British nylon patent before the litigation in the United States had begun. The United States was not represented in the British proceeding, and the question of affiliation between the British plaintiffs and defendants was not put in issue in the British suit in equity.

UNITED STATES v. IMPERIAL CHEMICAL INDUSTRIES, LTD.

United States District Court, S.D. of New York, 1951.
100 F.Supp. 504.

RYAN, District Judge.

* * *

The complaint was filed under   *   *   *   the Sherman Anti-Trust Act—to restrain and prevent alleged continuing violations of Section 1 of the Act.

In essence, the complaint charges a conspiracy among the defendants, having as its purpose a division of world markets and the elimination of competition among themselves and between them and third parties in the trade and commerce of chemical products, sporting arms and ammunition. The complaint alleges the achievement of this purpose by the execution of unlawful contracts, agreements, arrangements and understandings and the establishment and maintenance of jointly-owned foreign companies; and the continued existence and accomplishment of this conspiracy and its purposes despite various temporary arrangements necessitated by the war. By reason of this, it is alleged that judicial remedy is necessary to restore competition among the defendants and between them and third parties. The complaint prays that the combination and conspiracy and the practices alleged be decreed unlawful and that defendants be perpetually enjoined from continuing, reviving or renewing any of the said violations.

Generally, the several answers of the defendants consist of a denial that any of them violated the anti-trust laws.

* * *

[The bulk of a very long opinion is omitted.]

We have found that the various patents and processes agreements were made in furtherance of the conspiracy alleged. These agreements, irrespective of their per se legality, were instruments designed and intended to accomplish the world-wide allocation of markets; their object was to achieve an unlawful purpose—an illegal restraint of trade prohibited by Section 1 of the Sherman Act. The agreements are unlawful because they provided a means for the accomplishment of this purpose and objective. We have also found that these agreements did, in operation, result in restraints of United States trade.

We have found that the jointly-owned companies were means designed and used by duPont and ICI to avoid and prevent competition between themselves and with others in the non-exclusive territories. They were a means used for the accomplishment of the basic understanding for the division of world-wide territories. We have found that not only were they intended to affect the export and import trade of the United States but that the limitations placed on duPont and other American companies on the exports to these jointly-owned companies and the restrictions placed on these companies with respect to sales and exports by them to the United States did achieve the purpose and end for which they were organized. Cf. United States v. Aluminum Co. of America, 2 Cir., 1945, 148 F.2d 416, 443–444. The operations of these jointly-owned companies were in violation of the law. United States v. National Lead Co., D.C.S.D.N.Y. 1945, 63 F.Supp. 513, 524. * * *

After an exhaustive examination of the voluminous evidence presented in this case, we conclude that the Government has proved its case: the defendants had entered into a conspiracy to divide markets, and the agreements considered in this opinion were instruments of that conspiracy.

In the face of this finding, the law is crystal clear: a conspiracy to divide territories, which affects American commerce, violates the Sherman Act. United States v. Timken Roller Bearing Co., D.C., 83 F.Supp. 284, affirmed 341 U.S. 593, 71 S.Ct. 971; United States v. National Lead Co., D.C., 63 F.Supp. 513, affirmed 332 U.S. 319, 67 S.Ct. 1634, 91 L.Ed. 2077; United States v. General Electric Co., D. C., 80 F.Supp. 989. So settled is the law on this that in the National Lead case, supra, Judge Rifkind wrote: "No citation of authority is any longer necessary to support the proposition that a combination of competitors, which by agreement divides the world into exclusive trade areas, and suppresses all competition among the members of the combination, offends the Sherman Act." 63 F.Supp., at page 523.

* * *

Proposed decrees may be filed within thirty days from the date of the filing of this opinion and thereafter all will be heard on due notice.

UNITED STATES v. IMPERIAL CHEMICAL INDUSTRIES, LTD.

United States, Federal District Court, S.D. New York, 1952.
105 F.Supp. 215.

RYAN, District Judge. We now approach the task of formulating a final decree designed to prevent and restrain the violations of law which we have found. 15 U.S.C.A. § 4.

Our objective is to fashion, in the terms of a decree, means by which the agreement found to exist is terminated, its revival prevented and its effects destroyed by the reestablishment of competitive conditions insofar as they pertain to United States exports and imports. * * *

Where competition has been eliminated, it must be restored. Only those provisions reasonably necessary to accomplish correction and adjustment of a dislocated competitive situation may be applied.

The essence of the violation found was the unlawful agreement to divide world territories. It was this enduring and basic understanding which was fundamental to all of the dealings of the conspirators.   It was to accomplish this purpose and end that the various means were adopted.

The decree will contain injunctions prohibiting agreements and arrangements between the defendants dividing territory and allocating customers and markets so as to unlawfully limit the commerce of the United States.   *   *   *

*   *   *   The decree, however, must contain additional provisions to implement these injunctive directions, so that they are made probable of observance.   The jointly-owned companies and the patents, processes, and technologies of the defendants must be brought within the scope of the judgment.   *   *   *

The restraints sought to be accomplished were achieved also in part by the patents and processes agreements.   *   *   *

*   *   *

We decree compulsory licensing because the patent rights which were granted the defendants were misused.   The failure to export products manufactured under the patents resulted from the agreement to divide territories.   What might have been done lawfully by one, acting as a result of his own decision, became unlawful because it was brought about by common agreement.   The failure to export, which might have been legal in itself, also became unlawful because of the purpose and end it was employed to accomplish.   One of the means employed was the patents and processes agreements.   The needs and requirements of local markets from which the patentee was excluded by the underlying agreement were met by patent grants to fellow conspirators.   Thus, the patents themselves and the right to grant licenses under them were used to implement and carry out the allotment of territories.   The use of these existing patents must be regulated because of their past abuse.

*   *   *

The Government does not seek a decree directing ICI to grant compulsory licenses of its British patents.   The Government requests that ICI be required to grant immunity under its foreign patents which correspond to the United States patents which we have made subject to compulsory licensing.   *   *   *   We have had testimony offered on behalf of ICI by an expert in British law that a provision for granting immunities is contrary to British public policy and that a British court will not enforce such a provision in the judgment of a court of a foreign jurisdiction.   As to this, we observe that, acting on the basis of our jurisdiction in personam, we are merely directing ICI to refrain from asserting rights which it may have in Britain, since the enforcement of those rights will serve to continue the effects of wrongful acts it has committed within the United States affecting the foreign trade of the United States.

We are not unmindful that under British law there are restrictions upon exports from the United States by reason of the existence of the British patents owned by ICI.   The exclusion of unlicensed imports and the prohibition of unlicensed sales is enforceable because of the legal rights which attach to a British patent.

* * *

While it is true that these rights exist independent of any provision in the patents and processes agreements, they were granted to ICI by the disclosure or assignment of inventions by duPont pursuant to the terms of these agreements. Inventions were also licensed by ICI to duPont for its exclusive use and exploitation in the United States in accordance with the agreements. In the first instance the patents were employed to restrain duPont's exports to Great Britain, in plain violation of American anti-trust laws; in the second instance, the patents were used as a means to prevent ICI exports to the United States and placed a restraint upon the foreign trade of Great Britain, in violation of her declared policy, if not her laws. It does not seem presumptuous for this court to make a direction to a foreign defendant corporation over which it has jurisdiction to take steps to remedy and correct a situation, which is unlawful both here and in the foreign jurisdiction in which it is domiciled. Two evils have resulted from the one understanding of ICI and duPont—restraints upon the foreign trade and commerce of the United States as well as on that of Great Britain. It is not an intrusion on the authority of a foreign sovereign for this court to direct that steps be taken to remove the harmful effects on the trade of the United States.

We recognize that substantial legal questions may be raised with respect to our power to decree as to duPont's foreign patents as well as those issued to ICI. Here, we deal with the regulation of the exercise of rights granted by a foreign sovereign to a domestic corporate defendant and to a foreign corporate defendant. Our power so to regulate is limited and depends upon jurisdiction in personam; the effectiveness of the exercise of that power depends upon the recognition which will be given to our judgment as a matter of comity by the courts of the foreign sovereign which has granted the patents in question.

* * *

The history of the basic British nylon patents reveals a studied and continued purpose on the part of ICI and duPont to remove these patents from within the scope of any decree which might ultimately be made by this court (Op. pp. 115, 116, 197, 198). These British patents were issued to duPont. By the agreement of March 30, 1939, ICI received an exclusive license under them; in January, 1940, ICI granted irrevocable and exclusive rights to make nylon yarn from nylon polymer (which is manufactured by ICI) to British Nylon Spinners, Ltd. (BNS). ICI has a stock interest of 50% in BNS, the remaining 50% is held by Courtaulds, Inc. BNS is in the business of manufacturing and distributing nylon yarn. Not content with this arrangement and with the deliberate purpose to "materially reduce the risk of any loss of rights" as a result of this suit (Ex. 708, p. 2705), duPont pursuant to the nylon agreement of 1946 assigned the basic British nylon patents to ICI. It is now urged that we may not decree with reference to these British patents so as to direct ICI to remove restrictions on imports into Great Britain of nylon polymer or nylon yarn from the United States. It is argued that the sum total of all these agreements is not to create by itself any restrictions against American imports, and that those which exist arise from the right to be free from competition which is inherent in the British patents and cannot possibly be repugnant to the American anti-trust laws.

BNS is not before this court; although they were knowing participants in acts designed to thwart the granting of full relief, we may not direct our decree to them. The lack of majority stock ownership in ICI likewise prevents control of the future acts of BNS by this means; however, we are not without some remedy still available.

Objection is raised by ICI that we are without power to decree that the British nylon patents may not be asserted to prevent the importation of nylon polymer and nylon yarn into Great Britain because BNS has rights which exist independent of those processed by ICI. This overlooks the circumstances under which BNS acquired its rights to these patents by licenses from ICI.

* * *

* * * Throughout all these negotiations it appears that BNS was advised of the dealings between ICI and duPont concerning the British nylon patents. Both ICI and duPont are parties to the instant suit; they were advised in fact and realized that the further use and control of the rights pertaining to the British nylon patents were subject to a decree of this court to be entered in this suit. * * *

We do not hesitate therefore to decree that the British nylon patents may not be asserted by ICI to prevent the importation of nylon polymer and of nylon yarn into Great Britain. What credit may be given to such an injunctive provision by the courts of Great Britain in a suit brought by BNS to restrain such importations we do not venture to predict. We feel that the possibility that the English courts in an equity suit will not give effect to such a provision in our decree should not deter us from including it.

In any event it appears that BNS would have the right under Section 63 of the Patents Act of 1949, as the exclusive licensee to bring suit for infringement against an importer of yarn and staple fiber. There would then be a speedy determination of the effectiveness of the immunity provision of the decree with reference to these products. If the British courts were not to give credit to this provision, no injury would have been done; if the holding of the British courts were to the contrary, a remedy available would not have been needlessly abandoned.

* * *

BRITISH NYLON SPINNERS LTD. v. IMPERIAL CHEMICAL INDUSTRIES LTD.

England, Court of Appeal, 1952.
[1953] Ch. 19.*

Interlocutory appeal from UPJOHN J.

By an agreement made on December 31, 1946, the defendants, Imperial Chemical Industries Ltd. and an American corporation, du Pont de Nemours & Co. Inc., the latter agreed to assign to the defendants certain patents and applications for patents scheduled to the agreement, such assigned patents to be registered as British patents in the United Kingdom.

On March 5, 1947, the defendants entered into a contract in England with the plaintiffs, British Nylon Spinners Ltd., an English corporation. The plaintiffs claimed that under this contract they had a licence or the right to be granted a licence to exercise and practise within a defined field all the inventions covered by the patents and applications for patents in the schedule to the agreement of December 31, 1946, between the defendants and the American corporation.

In June, 1952, the plaintiffs asked the defendants' solicitors to execute formal licences under the assigned patents to enable the plaintiffs to register them, and were informed that, owing to the existence of legal proceedings in the United States, the defendants could not execute any documents relating to the patents in question.

On July 30, 1952, in the United States District Court of New York, his Honour Sylvester J. Ryan delivered a final judgment in an action brought by the United States of America against the defendants, du Pont de Nemours & Co. Inc., and others under the anti-trust law known as the Sherman Act: United States of America v. Imperial Chemical Industries Ld. and Others. The plaintiffs were not parties to those proceedings.

By a clause in that judgment the United States court ordered that the agreement of December 31, 1946, between the defendants and du Pont de Nemours & Co. Inc. be cancelled, and that the defendants should reconvey within 90 days all the patent rights assigned to them under that agreement.

Other clauses in the judgment forbade any disposition of foreign patents by the defendants unless they obtained from the grantee an undertaking in writing to hold licences subject to the right of American manufacturers to import goods manufactured in accordance with the patents freely into any foreign country.

The plaintiffs thereupon issued a writ claiming declarations as to their rights to licences, and asking for an order that the defendants should execute formal grants of those licences, and for specific

* Reprinted by permission of the Incorporated Council of Law Reporting of England and Wales, London.

performance of the contract of March 5, 1947. They also asked for an injunction to restrain the defendants from assigning or dealing with or parting with any of the patent rights in question in obedience to the order of the United States court.

On August 13, 1952, Upjohn J. granted an interlocutory injunction to restrain the defendants from assigning the patents until judgment or further order.

The defendants appealed.

* * *

EVERSHED M. R. stated the facts and continued:—This is an interlocutory matter, and, therefore, it is inappropriate for the court to say more about the case, or the merits of the case, than is necessary to make clear the grounds of the conclusion which it reaches. It is plain that there is here a question of the comity which subsists between civilized nations. In other words, it involves the extent to which the courts of one country will pay regard and give effect to the decisions and orders of the courts of another country. I certainly should be the last to indicate any lack of respect for any decision of the district courts of the United States. But I think that in this case there is raised a somewhat serious question, whether the order, in the form that it takes, does not assert an extraterritorial jurisdiction which the courts of this country cannot recognize, notwithstanding any such comity. Applied conversely, I conceive that the American courts would likewise be slow (to say the least) to recognize an assertion on the part of the British courts of jurisdiction extending (in effect) to the business affairs of persons and corporations in the United States.

Having said that much, I must make one reference to a passage in the second of the opinions which his Honour delivered, dated May, 1952. It is plain that the judge considered this matter most carefully, and indeed, as Upjohn J. pointed out, expressed his own doubts whether, in giving effect, as he felt it his duty to do, to the implications of the Sherman Act, he might not be going beyond the normally recognized limits of territorial jurisdiction. He said: "It is not an intrusion on the authority of a foreign sovereign for this court to direct that steps be taken to remove the harmful effects on the trade of the United States." If by that passage the judge intended to say (as it seems to me that he did) that it was not an intrusion on the authority of a foreign sovereign to make directions addressed to that foreign sovereign or to its courts or to nationals of that foreign Power effective to remove (as he said) "harmful effects on the trade of the United States," I am bound to say that, as at present advised, I find myself unable to agree with it.

Questions affecting the trade of one country may well be matters proper to be considered by the government of another country. Tariffs are sometimes imposed by one country which obviously affect the trade of another country, and the imposition of such tariffs is a matter for the government of the particular country which imposes them.

And if that observation of the judge were conversely applied to directions designed to remove harmful effects on the trade, say, of Great Britain or British nationals in America, I should myself be surprised to find that it was accepted as not being an intrusion on the rights and sovereign authority of the United States.

On the other hand, there is no doubt that it is competent for the court of a particular country, in a suit between persons who are either nationals or subjects of that country or are otherwise subject to its jurisdiction, to make orders in personam against one such party —directing it, for example, to do something or to refrain from doing something in another country affecting the other party to the action. As a general proposition, that would not be open to doubt. But the plaintiffs in this case (unlike Imperial Chemical Industries) are neither subjects nor nationals of the United States, nor were they parties to the proceedings before his Honour, nor are they otherwise subject to his jurisdiction.

What the precise relationship, commercially or otherwise, is between the plaintiffs and the defendants we have not at this stage of the proceedings considered at all, and I proceed on the assumption (and I am not to be taken as hinting that the contrary is the fact) that the plaintiffs are an independent trade corporation and entitled to be treated as independent of Imperial Chemical Industries Ld. Being so independent, they have beyond question, according to the laws of England, certain rights, certain choses in action, by virtue of the contract of 1947, which the courts of this country, in pursuance of the laws which the courts of this country claim to be entitled to administer, will in this country protect and enforce. Broadly, the right which they have may be described as their right under the contract, being an English contract made between English nationals and to be performed in England, to have it performed and, if necessary, to have an order made by the courts of this country for its specific performance. That is a right—it might be said, a species of property, seeing particularly that it is related to patents—which is English in character and is subject to the jurisdiction of the English courts; and it seems to me that the plaintiffs have at least established a prima facie case for saying that it is not competent for the courts of the United States or of any other country to interfere with those rights or to make orders, observance of which by our courts would require that our courts should not exercise the jurisdiction which they have and which it is their duty to exercise in regard to those rights.

But I think that the matter goes somewhat further. The subject-matter of the contract of December, 1946, is a number of English and Commonwealth patents. An English patent is a species of English property of the nature of a chose in action and peculiar in character. By English law it confers certain monopoly rights, exercisable in England, on its proprietor. A person who has an enforceable right to a licence under an English patent appears therefore to have at least some kind of proprietary interest which it is the duty of our courts to protect. And, certainly so far as the English patents are concerned, it seems to me, with all deference to his Honour's judgment, to be an assertion of an extraterritorial jurisdiction which we do not recognize for the American courts to make orders which would destroy or qualify those statutory rights belonging to an English national who is not subject to the jurisdiction of the American courts.

* * *

I think it undesirable that I should say more, except to reaffirm the proposition that the courts of this country will, in the natural course, pay great respect and attention to the superior courts of the United States of America; but I conceive that it is none the less the proper province of these courts, when their jurisdiction is invoked, not to refrain from exercising that jurisdiction if they think that it is their duty so to do for the protection of rights which are peculiarly subject to the protection of the English courts. In so saying, I do not conceive that I am offending in any way against the principles of comity which apply between the two countries; and like Upjohn J., I take some comfort from the doubts which Judge Sylvester Ryan himself entertained about the extent to which this order might, if carried to its logical conclusion, go.

* * *

DENNING L. J. I agree. It would be a serious matter if there were a conflict between the orders of the courts of the United States and the orders of these courts. The writ of the United States does not run in this country, and, if due regard is had to the comity of nations, it will not seek to run here. But, as I read this judgment of the United States court, there is a saving clause which prevents any conflict, because although Imperial Chemical Industries has been ordered to do certain acts by the United States court, nevertheless there is a provision which says that nothing in the judgment shall operate against the company for action taken in complying with the law of any foreign government or instrumentality thereof to which the company is for the time being subject. With that saving clause, I hope that there will be no conflict between the orders.

ROMER L. J. I also agree, and there is nothing that I wish to add.

Appeal dismissed.

BRITISH NYLON SPINNERS, LTD. v. IMPERIAL CHEMICAL INDUSTRIES LTD.

England, Court of Chancery, 1954.
[1955] Ch. 37.*

July 9.　DANCKWERTS, J., read the following judgment:
* * *

The view thus asserted by the Master of the Rolls seems to me to be entirely in accordance with the decision of the Court of Appeal in Kleinwort, Sons & Co. v. Ungarische Baumwolle Industrie Akt. & Hungarian General Creditbank (2), in which Du Parcq, L. J., said ([1939] 3 All E.R. 44):

> One starts with the rule that English law is the law which governs the performance of this contract. An elementary principle of English law is that people should keep their contracts and carry them out.

It was argued on behalf of the defendant company that this court would not enforce a contract which involved the deliberate violation of the laws of a friendly country, and I was referred to Dicey's Conflict of Laws, 6th ed., p. 607, and to Foster v. Driscoll (3), which was a case of a contract, the object of which was the illegal importation of whisky into the United States of America. There is no evidence before me that the object of the contract of Mar. 5, 1947, was to do anything contrary to the law of the United States of America and no evidence that the plaintiff company was party to or had knowledge of any conspiracy contrary to the law of the United States when that contract was entered into. It is impossible for me to accept the conclusions of the United States court as findings of fact binding in this action against the plaintiff company which was not a party to the American proceedings.　*　*　*

There are, however, further considerations which also lead to the same result. I had the advantage of the evidence of Mr. Marshall Konopak Skadden, a member of the Bar of the State of New York, practising in the relevant United States courts. His evidence was that the British court would be accepted under the law of the United States as an appropriate court having jurisdiction for the enforcement of the contract under consideration in the present case. Further, his evidence was that, if the defendant company, though prohibited from doing so by a judgment of a court in the United States, complied with an order of a British court and executed a license, this would not be treated by an American court as a contempt of court. Mr. Skadden referred to a number of decisions of American courts in support of those propositions. This evidence indicates to me that the American courts would not regard a judgment of this court in the present circumstances enforcing against the defendant company the

---

* Reprinted by permission of the Incorporated Council of Law Reporting of England and Wales, London.

contract of Mar. 5, 1947, as in any way inappropriate, and there does not appear, therefore, to be any difficulty in regard to comity between the courts of the two countries in this case.

Furthermore, it would appear that the judgments of His Honour Judge Sylvester Ryan recognised this principle and were intended to provide for and limit his own judgment in this very respect. This appears to be the intention of art. IV, para. 3, of the judgment of July 30, 1952:

> No provision of this judgment shall operate against [the defendant company] for action taken in compliance with any law of the United States Government, or of any foreign government or instrumentality thereof, to which [the defendant company] is at the time being subject, and concerning matters over which, under the law of the United States, such foreign government or instrumentality thereof has jurisdiction.

"Instrumentality" of a government is an inaccurate, and, indeed, repellent, description of an English court; but it appears, none the less, that the learned judge was using the word in this manner from his observations on the occasions of further applications which were made to him. On Oct. 27, 1952, His Honour said:

> The court understands that and expects [the defendant company] to obey all orders and regulations that I have enumerated, of all government agencies and of the courts having jurisdiction over the matter on which they seek a ruling * * *. And that is provided for in another section of the decree, I forget which one.

On counsel referring him to art. IV, para. 3, he added: "I think that provision covers this situation". On the same occasion His Honour said:

> Suppose they did, it was a suit in the nature of a declaratory action and I would not see anything contemptuous about such an act. Both [the defendant company] and [the plaintiff company], I think, are well within their rights to have it judicially determined by the courts of Great Britain and as to just what effect will be given to the provisions of the decree of this court which affect the British patents. I do not find anything wrong with that at all.

A further instance is, I think, to be found in the limitation contained in art. IX, para. 4 [of the judgment of July 30, 1952], in which, "until June 30, 1977, to the extent they have the legal right to do so," the American company and the defendant company are directed to make certain grants of immunities. It was argued by counsel for the defendant company that this limitation of the order could not apply to the plaintiff company's rights under the agreement of Mar. 5, 1947, because these rights were only equitable and not legal. I do not, however, read the language of the judgment in that way. I regard the words "to the extent they have the legal right to do so" as equivalent to "so far as they may lawfully do so", that is, not in breach of their obligations, including the equitable as well as the legal rights of other persons, as long as such rights are enforceable in a court of appropriate jurisdiction. Consequently, the prohibition, in art. IX, para. 13(b) [of the judgment of July 30, 1952] of dispositions of foreign patents or rights thereunder, which deprive them of the power or authority to issue the grants of immunity required by the judgment, is similarly limited, as the judgment does not require the issue of grants of immunity which du Pont and the defendant company may not lawfully grant.

These passages indicate to me that His Honour Judge Sylvester Ryan has been careful so to limit his judgment that neither his judgment, nor any judgment of mine which the law of England requires me to give, will disturb the comity which the courts of the United States and the courts of England are so anxious and careful to observe. I would only add that counsel for the defendant company fully carried out to the best of his ability, in somewhat difficult circumstances, the desire expressed by His Honour that the considerations which led the American court to reach the conclusions and make the order that it did should be before this court.

In the result, my conclusion is that, notwithstanding the judgment of the United States court of July 30, 1952, the defendant company is bound by English law to carry out the agreement of Mar. 5, 1947, and I ought to make the declaration which is asked by the amended statement of claim, and grant specific performance of the contract.

Judgment for the plaintiffs.

———

Questions. Suppose the United States had thereafter moved before Judge Ryan to adjudge ICI guilty of civil contempt. What judicial response? Do you suppose the Department of Justice would have made any such request? Why or why not?

Having considered the United States and the United Kingdom set of opinions, what seems to you to be the utility of judicial deference in the resolution of conflicts of jurisdiction?

———

UNITED STATES v. THE WATCHMAKERS OF SWITZERLAND INFORMATION CENTER, INC.

United States District Court, S.D. New York, 1965.
1965 CCH Trade Cases ¶ 71,352.*

[In the original proceeding in the United States antitrust case that follows, the contention was strongly made by the defendants, charged as being corporate and trade association members of a nongovernmental Swiss effort to control and monopolize the watch-mak-

* Reproduced by permission from CCH Trade Cases 1965, published and copyrighted in 1966 by Commerce Clearing House, Inc., 4025 W. Peterson Ave., Chicago, Ill., 60646.

ing industry through control of the export of watch-making machinery, that it was illicit for the United States to apply its antitrust laws to ventures having their roots and principal places of activity in Switzerland, particularly when these activities were entirely compatible with Swiss law and policy. The trial judge reserved jurisdiction to modify his decree upon any showing that defendants might under it be required to act contrary to Swiss law. The order below illustrates one way in which conflicts can be reconciled, viz. making it clear that a person will not be subject to contempt proceedings in the United States for acting as required by the law of his nationality.]

Memorandum

CASHIN, District Judge: On January 22, 1964 this court entered a Final Judgment in the captioned action. Under Section XIII(A) of that Judgment I retained jurisdiction for the purpose of enabling the parties to apply for modifications of any of the provisions thereof. Plaintiff, United States of America, now moves to modify the Judgment as follows:—

     *   *   *

Revision of Section XI

[The decree will not restrain]

(E) * * * any defendant, FH member or any other person from:

(1) Performing any act in Switzerland which is required of it under the law of Switzerland;

(2) Refraining from any act in Switzerland which is illegal under the law of Switzerland;

(3) Taking any joint or individual action, consistent with the applicable law of the nation where the party taking such action is domiciled, to comply with conditions for the export of watch parts from Switzerland established by valid ordinances, or rules and regulations promulgated thereunder, of the Swiss Government;

(4) Taking any joint or individual action required by the scheme of regulation of the Swiss watch industry based on Article 31 bis of the Swiss Constitution, with respect to imports of watch parts into Switzerland other than from U. S. companies;

(5) Advocating the enactment of laws, decrees or regulations or urging upon any Swiss governmental body, department, agency or official the taking of any official action;

(6) Furnishing to the Swiss Government or any body, department, agency or official thereof, its independent advice or opinion when requested to do so.

Revision of Section XII

(A)(3) Upon receipt of such a written request for books, ledgers, accounts, correspondence, memoranda, and other records and documents in the possession or under the control of defendants FH, Ebauches, Eterna A. G., Gruen S. A., and Wittnauer-Geneva, particularized or identified in the request to the extent reasonably practicable, and relating to any of the matters as to which such defendants are enjoined or directed to take action pursuant to any of the terms of this Final Judgment, reasonable access during office hours to duly authenticated copies thereof at any office in the City of New York designated by such defendant, provided, however, that no such defendant shall be obligated to bring to the United States any books or other records, or any copies thereof, except upon order of this Court specifically so providing; and provided further that no defendant shall be required to bring to the United States any books or other records, or any copies thereof, when such action is prohibited by the law of Switzerland and such defendant has exercised good faith efforts to obtain the permission of the appropriate authorities but such permission has not been secured.

* * *

Several grounds have been advanced in support of the requested modifications. They are as follows:

(1) Since the entry of the judgment, the Swiss Confederation has issued official regulations with respect to the issuance of export permits for parts from Switzerland;

(2) The United States Department of State has indicated to the Justice Department that a resolution of this litigation on a basis consistent with United States antitrust laws and the basic objectives of the judgment would be advantageous from the standpoint of American foreign policy;

(3) The termination of the litigation, without any appeal, would give immediate relief in restoring free and open competition in the United States production, import, export and sale of watches, watch parts and watchmaking machinery. In this connection it should be pointed out that more than ten years have elapsed since the complaint herein was filed in October 1954, and if appeals were taken an additional number of years would inevitably be consumed before final relief could be granted. On the other hand, if the proposed modifications are made, the defendants have agreed that they will not appeal the Final Judgment herein, subject to the withdrawal of the appeals by the other defendants.

It is the Court's opinion that the modifications requested do not affect the crucial objectives sought to be achieved in the Final Judgment heretofore filed, and that the above circumstances in their totality justify the granting of the motion. Moreover, these modifications will prevent any situation from arising such as has occurred in other litigation in the past when there was believed to be a possible conflict between a decree of a United States court and the sovereignty of a foreign nation. See United States v. Imperial Chemicals, 105 F. Supp. 215 (S.D.N.Y.1952), and British Nylon Spinners Limited v. Imperial Chemical Industries, Limited, 1 Ch. 19 (1953). In the main the modifications relate to peripheral areas of the judgment which might have been construed to have bearing upon the sovereignty of the Swiss Confederation.

The defendants in this action have filed stipulations with the court consenting to a dismissal of their joint appeal from the Final Judgment if this court sees fit to grant the modifications of that Judgment requested by the plaintiff. (Rule 14(1) of the Revised Rules of the Supreme Court of the United States.) They have also stipulated, along with the plaintiff, to waive any right to appeal from said Final Judgment as so modified.

The motion of the plaintiff, United States of America, is granted on the condition that one of the parties enter an order dismissing the joint appeal as provided for in the stipulations. The plaintiff shall submit an order incorporating the modifications granted.

The cross-motion of defendants, Gruen Watch Manufacturing Company, S. A. and Wittnauer et Cie., S. A., that section XII(D) of the Final Judgment be further modified, is denied as premature.

It is so ordered.

THE PRINCIPLE OF SECTION 40 OF THE RESTATEMENT OF FOREIGN RELATIONS LAW OF THE UNITED STATES

UNITED STATES OF AMERICA v. FIRST NATIONAL CITY BANK

United States Court of Appeals, Second Circuit, 1968.
396 F.2d 897.

KAUFMAN, Circuit Judge. The issue presented on this appeal is of considerable importance to American banks with branches or offices in foreign jurisdictions. We are called upon to decide whether a domestic bank may refuse to comply with a valid Grand Jury subpoena duces tecum requiring the production of documents in the possession of a foreign branch of the bank on the ground that compliance would subject it to civil liability under the law of the foreign state.

* * *

On March 7, 1968, First National City Bank of New York [Citibank] was served with a subpoena duces tecum in connection with a federal Grand Jury investigation of certain alleged violations of the antitrust laws by several of its customers. The subpoena required the production of documents located in the bank's offices in New York City and Frankfurt, Germany, relating to any transaction in the name of (or for the benefit of) its customers C. F. Boehringer & Soehme, G.m.b.H., a German corporation, and Boehringer Mannheim Corporation, a New York corporation [referred to jointly hereinafter as "Boehringer"]. Citibank complied with the subpoena insofar as it called for the production of material located in New York but failed to produce or divulge any documents reposited in Frankfurt. Indeed, the bank even refused to inquire or determine whether any relevant papers were overseas. Instead, William T. Loveland, Citibank's vice-president responsible for the decision to defy the subpoena, appeared before the Grand Jury and asserted that the bank's action was justified because compliance would subject Citibank to civil liability and economic loss in Germany.

On May 8, 1968, Judge Pollack conducted an initial hearing at which the sole witness was Dr. Martin Domke, an expert in German law. He testified on behalf of Citibank that under the "bank secrecy law" of Germany, a bank—including a foreign bank (such as Citibank) licensed to do business in Germany—cannot divulge information relating to the affairs of its customers even in response to the process of a court of the United States. To do so, he claimed, would amount to a breach of the bank's "self evident" contractual obligation which flows from the business relationship between bank and customer. Domke made it clear that bank secrecy was not part of the statutory law of Germany; rather, it was in the nature of a privilege that could be waived by the customer but not the bank. He insisted that a violation of bank secrecy could subject the bank to liability in contract or tort but not to criminal sanctions or their equivalent. But, he made it plain, that it was a simple matter for a bank customer to obtain an ex parte restraining order enjoining a bank from disclosing privileged material and that a violation of such an injunction would be punished under a general provision of the criminal law governing violations of court orders. As a result of this testimony, the district judge appropriately decided to adjourn this hearing in order to afford an opportunity to Citibank to ascertain whether its customers would obtain such an injunction and which would have the effect of subjecting the bank to criminal penalties if it complied with the subpoena. This did not prove fruitful however, for the very next day, the court was advised by Citibank's counsel that Boehringer did not intend to take advantage of the readily available injunctive procedures under German law. Instead, the judge was told that Boehringer had informed Citibank that it would have to "suffer the consequences" if it obeyed the subpoena. It was suggested that Boehringer would sue the bank for breach of contract and would also use its influence within German industrial circles to cause Citibank to suffer business losses.

In any event, Citibank remained adamant in its refusal to produce the documents located in Frankfurt and on May 21, 1968, a second hearing was held, this time on the government's order to show cause why the bank and Loveland should not be held in civil contempt. Domke testified once again as did a government expert, Dr. Magdalena Schoch. Both witnesses discussed with great particularity the precise nature of German bank secrecy and Citibank's prospective liability under German law if it were sued for disclosing privileged information. Domke made the point that compulsion by an American court would not be accepted as an excuse for violating bank secrecy and that in a civil suit under German law the court would determine "in its free discretion" the amount of damages, if any. Schoch insisted, however, that Citibank would have a number of valid defenses in the event Boehringer ever sued. Moreover, Schoch's testimony made clear that in a criminal proceeding in Germany bank secrecy does not provide a basis for refusing to obey a court order to provide evidence.

In a reasoned opinion, Judge Pollack concluded that Citibank had failed to present a legally sufficient reason for its failure to comply with the subpoena. He determined that it was manifest that Citibank would not be subject to criminal sanctions or their equivalent under German law, that it had not acted in good faith, and that there was only a "remote and speculative" possibility that it would not have a valid defense if it were sued for civil damages. Accordingly, he adjudged the bank and Loveland to be in civil contempt and fined the bank $2,000 per day for its failure to act; he sentenced Loveland to 60 days' imprisonment. For the reasons stated below, we conclude that Judge Pollack's order was justified and affirm.

The basic legal question confronting us is not a total stranger to this Court. With the growing interdependence of world trade and the increased mobility of persons and companies, the need arises not infrequently, whether related to civil or criminal proceedings, for the production of evidence located in foreign jurisdictions. It is no longer open to doubt that a federal court has the power to require the production of documents located in foreign countries if the court has in personam jurisdiction of the person in possession or control of the material. See, e. g., First National City Bank of New York v. Internal Revenue Service etc., 271 F.2d 616 (2d Cir. 1959), cert. denied, 361 U.S. 948, 80 S.Ct. 402, 4 L.Ed.2d 381 (1960). Thus, the task before us, as Citibank concedes, is not one of defining power but of developing rules governing the proper exercise of power. The difficulty arises, of course, when the country in which the documents are located has its own rules and policies dealing with the production and disclosure of business information—a circumstance not uncommon. This problem is particularly acute where the documents are sought by an arm of a foreign government. The complexities of the world being what they are, it is not surprising to discover nations having diametrically opposed positions with respect to the disclosure of a wide range of information. It is not too difficult, therefore, to empathize with the party or witness subject to the jurisdiction of two sovereigns and confronted with conflicting commands. For an example of a comparable dilemma resulting from the application of the antitrust laws, see British Nylon Spinners Ltd. v. Imperial Chemical Industries, Ltd., [1953] 1 Ch. 19. See also Note, Limitations on the Federal Judicial Power to Compel Acts Violating Foreign Law, 63 Colum.L.Rev. 1441 (1963); Note, Subpoena of Documents Located in Foreign Jurisdictions, 37 N.Y.U.L.Rev. 295 (1962).

In any event, under the principles of international law, "A state having jurisdiction to prescribe or enforce a rule of law is not precluded from exercising its jurisdiction *solely* because such exercise requires a person to engage in conduct subjecting him to liability under the law of another state having jurisdiction with respect to that conduct." Restatement (2d), Foreign Relations Law of the United States, § 39(1) (1965) (emphasis supplied). It is not asking too much however, to expect that each nation should make an effort to minimize the potential conflict flowing from their joint concern with the prescribed behavior. Id. at § 39(2). Compare Report of Oral Argument, 25 U.S.L.W. 3141 (Nov. 13, 1956), Holophane Co. v. United States, 352 U.S. 903, 77 S.Ct. 144, 1 L.Ed.2d 114 (1956). Where, as here, the burden of resolution ultimately falls upon the federal courts, the difficulties are manifold because the courts must take care not to impinge upon the prerogatives and responsibilities of the political branches of the government in the extremely sensitive and delicate area of foreign affairs. See, e. g., Chicago & Southern Air Lines v. Waterman S. S. Corp., 333 U.S. 103, 111, 68 S.Ct. 431, 92 L.Ed. 568 (1948). Mechanical or overbroad rules of thumb are of little value; what is required is a careful balancing of the interests involved and a precise understanding of the facts and circumstances of the particular case.

With these principles in mind, we turn to the specific issues presented by this appeal. Citibank concedes, as it must, that compliance with the subpoena does not require the violation of the criminal law of a foreign power, as in Societe Internationale etc. v. Rogers, 357 U.S. 197, 78 S.Ct. 1087, 2 L.Ed.2d 1255 (1958) (discovery under the Federal Rules of Civil Procedure); Ings v. Ferguson, 282 F.2d 149, 152, 82 A.L.R.2d 1397 (2d Cir. 1960), or risk the imposition of sanctions that are the substantial equivalent of criminal penalties, as in Application of Chase Manhattan Bank, 297 F.2d 611, 613 (2d Cir. 1962), or even conflict with the public policy of a foreign state as expressed in legislation, compare Restatement, supra, § 39, Reporters' Notes at p. 113. Instead, all that remains, as we see it, is a possible prospective civil liability flowing from an implied contractual obligation between Citibank and its customers that, we are informed, is considered implicit in the bank's license to do business in Germany.

But, the government urges vigorously, that to be excused from compliance with an order of a federal court, a witness, such as Citibank must show that following compliance it will suffer criminal liability in the foreign country. We would be reluctant to hold, however, that the mere absence of criminal sanctions abroad necessarily mandates obedience to a subpoena. Such a rule would show scant respect for international comity; and, if this principle is valid, a court of one country should make an effort to minimize possible conflict between its orders and the law of a foreign state affected by its decision. Cf. Restatement, supra, § 39(2); Ings v. Ferguson, supra, 282 F.2d at 152. The vital national interests of a foreign nation, especially in matters relating to economic affairs, can be expressed in ways other than through the criminal law. For example, it could not be questioned that, insofar as a court of the United States is concerned, a statement or directive by the Bundesbank (the central bank of Germany) or some other organ of government, expresses the public policy of Germany and should be given appropriate weight. Equally important is the fact that a sharp dichotomy between criminal and civil penalties is an imprecise means of measuring the hardship for requiring compliance with a subpoena. * * * It would be a gross fiction to contend that if the Bundesbank were to revoke the license of Citibank for a violation of bank secrecy the impact would be less catastrophic than having to pay an insignificant fine because the revocation is theoretically not "equivalent to a misdemeanor" or criminal sanction. We are not required to decide whether penalties must be under the "criminal law" to provide a legally sufficient reason for noncompliance with a subpoena; but, it would seem unreal to let all hang on whether the label "criminal" were attached to the sanction and to disregard all other factors. In any event, even were we to assume arguendo that in appropriate circumstances civil penalties or liabilities would suffice, we hold that Citibank has failed to provide an adequate justification for its disobedience of the subpoena.

In evaluating Citibank's contention that compliance should be excused because of the alleged conflict between the order of the court below and German law, we are aided materially by the rationale of the recent Restatement (2d), Foreign Relations Law of the United States, § 40 (1965):

Where two states have jurisdiction to prescribe and enforce rules of law and the rules they may prescribe require inconsistent conduct upon the part of a person, each state is required by international law to consider, in good faith, moderating the exercise of its enforcement jurisdiction, in the light of such factors as

(a) vital national interests of each of the states,

(b) the extent and the nature of the hardship that inconsistent enforcement actions would impose upon the person,

(c) the extent to which the required conduct is to take place in the territory of the other state,

(d) the nationality of the person, and

(e) the extent to which enforcement by action of either state can reasonably be expected to achieve compliance with the rule prescribed by that state.

In the instant case, the obvious, albeit troublesome, requirement for us is to balance the national interests of the United States and Germany and to give appropriate weight to the hardship, if any, Citibank will suffer.

The important interest of the United States in the enforcement of the subpoena warrants little discussion. The federal Grand Jury before which Citibank was summoned is conducting a criminal investigation of alleged violations of the antitrust laws. These laws have long been considered cornerstones of this nation's economic policies, have been vigorously enforced and the subject of frequent interpretation by our Supreme Court. We would have great reluctance, therefore, to countenance any device that would place relevant information beyond the reach of this duly impaneled Grand Jury or impede or delay its proceedings. * * *

We examine the importance of bank secrecy within the framework of German public policy with full recognition that it is often a subtle and difficult undertaking to determine the nature and scope of the law of a foreign jurisdiction. There is little merit, however, in Citibank's suggestion that the mere existence of a bank secrecy doctrine requires us to accept on its face the bank's assertion that compliance with the subpoena would violate an important public policy of Germany. * * * While we certainly do not intend to deprecate the importance of bank secrecy in the German scheme of things, neither can we blind ourselves to the doctrine's severe limitations as disclosed by the expert testimony. We have already made the assumption that the absence of criminal sanctions is not the whole answer to or finally determinative of the problem. But, it is surely of considerable significance that Germany considers bank secrecy simply a privilege that can be waived by the customer and is content to leave the matter of enforcement to the vagaries of private litigation. Indeed, bank secrecy is not even required by statute. See Restatement, supra, § 40, comment (c): "A state will be less likely to refrain from exercising its jurisdiction when the consequence of obedience to its order will be a civil liability abroad." See also Restatement, supra, § 39, Reporters' Notes at p. 113.

Moreover, Section 300 of the Criminal Code of Germany provides that:

> Anybody who without authority discloses the secrets of another, shall be punished by imprisonment for a term not to exceed six months or by a fine, if the secret was intrusted or became known to him in his capacity as a
>
> (1) Physician, dentist, pharmacist [and similar professions]
>
> (2) Attorneys, patent attorney, notary public, defense counsel, auditor, Certified Public Accountant, or tax consultant.

It is not of little significance that a German court has noted, "The fact that bank secrecy has not been included in the penal protection of Section 300 of the Criminal Code must lead to the conclusion that the legislature did not value the public interest in bank secrecy as highly as it did the duty of secrecy of doctors and attorneys." District Court of Frankfurt (1953). Further, Section 53 of the German Code of Criminal Procedure grants the right of refusal to testify to a number of persons, ranging from clergymen and mid-wives to publishers and printers; again, reference to bankers is conspicuously absent. It would be anomalous if Citibank, deprived of any right to assert bank secrecy in a criminal investigation conducted in Germany, could—in the absence of statutes imposing greater limitations upon foreign governments, cf. First National City Bank of New York v. Internal Revenue Service etc., supra, 271 F.2d at 619–620—benefit from German bank secrecy in a criminal investigation in the United States.

In addition, it is noteworthy that neither the Department of State nor the German Government has expressed any view on this case or indicated that, under the circumstances present here, enforcement of the subpoena would violate German public policy or embarrass German-American relations. * * * We are fully aware that when foreign governments, including Germany, have considered their vital national interests threatened, they have not hesitated to make known their objections to the enforcement of a subpoena to the issuing court. See, e. g., In re Grand Jury Investigation of the Shipping Industry, 186 F.Supp. 298, 318 (D.C.1960). So far as appears, both the United States and German governments have voiced no opposition to Citibank's production of the subpoenaed records.

We turn now to the nature and extent of the alleged hardships to which Citibank would be subjected if it complied with the subpoena. It advances two grounds on which it will suffer injury. First, it states that it will be subjected to economic reprisals by Boehringer and will lose foreign business that will harm it and the economic interests of the United States. It paints a dismal picture of foreign companies boycotting American banks for fear that their business records will be subject to the scrutiny of our courts. A partial answer is that the protection of the foreign economic interests of the United States must be left to the appropriate departments of our government, especially since the government is the moving litigant in these proceedings. Cf. United States v. First National City Bank, supra. Moreover, and not without importance, is the fact that the alleged economic reprisals are of doubtful legal relevance in light of the Supreme Court's rejection of a similar argument in First National City Bank (Omar), see 379 U.S. at 402, 85 S.Ct. 528 (dissenting opinion of Justice Harlan), and this Court's decision in First National Bank of New York v. Internal Revenue Service, etc., supra, 271 F.2d at 619, n. 2; and the factual underpinning for this claim is quite feeble considering Citibank's overseas growth following the decision in First National City Bank (Omar), supra.

Second, Citibank complains that it will be subjected to civil liability in a suit by Boehringer. The importance of the possible financial loss Citibank might suffer as a result of such a suit must be viewed in light of Loveland's statement that: "[W]e were not concerned with this isolated case and what one individual might do. The importance [sic], I believe, is the effect that it would have on our operations all over the world * * *." We have already rejected the contention that Citibank's alleged loss of business abroad is a sound justification for disobedience of the subpoena. In any event, Judge Pollack concluded that risk of civil damages was slight and speculative, and we agree. The chance that Boehringer will suffer compensable damages is quite remote and Citibank appears to have a number of valid defenses if it is sued, both under the terms of the contract and principles of German civil law. In addition, as we have noted, German courts are given wide latitude in determining whether to award any damages even in the face of liability. In the unlikely event that Boehringer were to sue Citibank, we cannot believe that Boehringer's adamant refusal to apply for a readily available injunction will pass unnoticed by the Court.

Finally, additional factors support our conclusion that the district judge was correct in citing Citibank and Loveland for civil contempt. As noted above, Citibank has failed to produce or segregate documents or records which reflect the bank's own work product. And, the expert testimony indicated that disclosure of such material would not violate any policy of bank secrecy. Moreover, one of the companies being investigated by the Grand Jury—Boehringer Mannheim Corporation—is incorporated in New York. Whatever one may think of requiring disclosure of records of a German corporation reposited in a bank in Germany, surely an American corporation cannot insulate itself from a federal Grand Jury investigation by entering into a contract with an American bank abroad requiring bank secrecy. Compare Restatement, supra, § 40, Comment (c). If indeed Citibank might suffer civil liability under German law in such circumstances, it must confront the choice mentioned in First National City Bank of New York v. Internal Revenue Service etc., supra, 271 F.2d at 620—the need to "surrender to one sovereign or the other the privileges received therefrom" or, alternatively a willingness to accept the consequences.

Since the life of the Grand Jury is rapidly drawing to a close, we direct that the mandate issue forthwith but that it be stayed for a period of seven days from the date of the filing of this opinion to permit Citibank, if it so chooses, to apply to the Supreme Court or a Justice thereof for a further stay or other relief.

Affirmed.

Interest analysis in conflict of laws and Section 40 of the Restatement of Foreign Relations Law as a requirement of international public law. In the early 1960's, Section 40 was presented to and approved by the American Law Institute as an emerging principle of customary international law that ought to be recognized. The section provides as a requirement of international public law that courts, administrative tribunals and similar agencies within a state should under certain circumstances recognize that international law requires a good faith effort to accommodate the different laws of one or more states as to a transnational economic problem, even though nothing in the national law of the forum authorizes specifically any moderation of the impact of the forum rule that otherwise would apply.

Interest analysis, originally developed by the late Brainerd Currie as a process for choosing the applicable rule of law in a private law case involving the law of two (or more) law-making entities, directed a court always to apply the rule of the forum state if that state had any governmental interest in the outcome of the case, even if there were a true conflict in the sense that another state also had a governmental interest in the application of its rule to produce a different outcome. The effect of this position was that true conflicts could never be resolved by a single principle applicable regardless of where the case was brought. Forum shopping would thus clearly be encouraged. In time the interest analysis approach was modified by Professor Currie to provide that the court responsible for the choice of law operation should act, as to foreign law, in a restrained and enlightened manner. By the end of the decade the interest analysis approach to choice of law in private international law had evolved in America toward the position taken as to public law by Section 40 of the Restatement of the Foreign Relations Law of the United States.

Although the American Law Institute was formulating a new restatement of Conflict of Laws in the same decade, this work did not follow the interest analysis approach in either its original or its modified versions. See, however, Restatement, Second, Conflict of Laws, § 6.

------

2. PROBLEM AS TO THE REACH OF UNITED STATES SECURITIES REGULATION

LOOMIS AND GRANT, THE U. S. SECURITIES AND EXCHANGE COMMISSION, FINANCIAL INSTITUTIONS OUTSIDE THE U. S. AND EXTRATERRITORIAL APPLICATION OF THE U. S. SECURITIES LAWS

1 Journal of Comparative Corporate Law and Securities Regulation 3 (1978).*

* * *

The extent of extraterritorial application of U. S. laws, and of U. S. securities laws in particular, has been discussed many times, and this article will not attempt an exhaustive treatment of that subject. Nevertheless, some analysis of the leading cases will be necessary as background and to set forth general guiding principles, particularly because three recent cases, Bersch v. Drexel Firestone, Inc.,[4] IIT v. Vencap, Ltd.,[5] and S.E.C. v. Kasser,[6] have not yet received extensive analysis or interpretation. Consequently, the first part of this article will treat some of the major principles concerning the application of U. S. securities laws to transactions having international aspects and will summarize the statutory bases for Commission jurisdiction. The second part of the article will look at the types of cases in which the Commission has asserted jurisdiction to proceed against

------

* Reprinted with the permission of P. Loomis and R. Grant and the North-Holland Publishing Company.

4. 519 F.2d 974 (2d Cir. 1975).

5. 519 F.2d 1001 (2d Cir. 1975).

6. 548 F.2d 109 (3d Cir. 1977).

non-U. S. financial institutions and will attempt to formulate some conclusions as to the proper role of the Commission in those cases.

2. Pertinent provisions of the securities laws

Before getting into the substance of the discussion, it seems appropriate to summarize those provisions of the U. S. securities laws which prescribe the Commission's authority to bring suit and which define the jurisdictional elements of a violation. Unfortunately, the U. S. securities laws are not explicit about whether and to what extent they are to be applied extraterritorially. Nevertheless, the concern of Congress with the problem of transnational securities dealings is expressed in the very title of the Securities Exchange Act of 1934 ("Exchange Act") :

> An act to provide for the regulation of securities exchanges and of over-the-counter markets operating in interstate and foreign commerce and through the mails, to prevent inequitable and unfair practices on such exchanges and markets, and for other purposes.

*   *   *

The substantive provisions of the securities laws are many and complex; however, the preponderance of extraterritoriality cases have involved a relatively small number of key sections. A substantial majority of the cases have involved Section 10(b) of the Exchange Act and Rule 10b–5 thereunder. As indicated earlier, Section 10(b) is the basic antifraud provision of the Exchange Act. It proscribes the use of "any manipulative or deceptive device or contrivance" in connection with the purchase or sale of any security by use of any means or instrumentality of interstate commerce or of the mails, or any facility of any national securities exchange. It is a very broadly worded section, and, as will be seen, the Commission has consistently argued that it should be applied broadly in cases of international fraud.

Another fundamental provision of the U. S. securities laws which has been involved in some of these cases is Section 5 of the Securities Act of 1933. Section 5 is the heart of the Securities Act and requires public offerings of securities to be registered with the Commission and sold pursuant to a prospectus containing proper disclosure. Like Section 10(b) of the Exchange Act, Section 5 makes it unlawful for any person to use the mails or any means of interstate commerce to accomplish various aspects of the offer and sale of securities without complying with the substantive provisions of the Section.

Two other provisions which have frequently been involved in international cases are Sections 13(d) and 16 of the Exchange Act. These provisions are of the type alluded to earlier which apply when a registered security is involved. Section 13(d) imposes reporting requirements on certain beneficial owners of more than five percent of a class of stock that is registered under Section 12. Section 16 imposes reporting requirements and trading restrictions on certain 10 percent beneficial owners, officers, and directors. These sections apply to "any person" or "every person" in the designated class, and Section 13(d) defines "person" to include a group of persons acting together. These provisions have frequently come into play in international cases because persons seeking to evade the law have attempted to use non-U. S. financial institutions as a shield. The Commission has aggressively sought to prevent such evasion.

3.   **Summary of extraterritorial application of the securities laws in decided cases**

Since the U. S. securities laws, like most U. S. statutes, are not explicit about extraterritoriality, the U. S. courts have sought to ascertain Congressional intent, recognizing that the only limitation on the exercise of Congressional power is the U. S. Constitution. As the court said in Leasco Data Processing Equipment Corp. v. Maxwell ("Leasco"):

> [I]f Congress has expressly prescribed a rule with respect to conduct outside the United States, even one going beyond the scope recognized by foreign relations laws, a United States court would be bound to follow the Congressional direction unless this would violate the due process clause of the Fifth Amendment.

However, since the legislative history behind the securities laws does not provide any significant guidance as to extraterritoriality, the courts have been unwilling to " * * * assume that the legislature always means to go to the full extent permitted".[29] In attempting to define appropriate limitations on the extraterritorial application of the securities laws, the courts have referred extensively to principles of international law. Moreover, the courts seem uniformly to have considered the Restatement (Second) of Foreign Relations Law of the United States (1965) (hereinafter referred to as the Restatement) to be an authoritative statement of international law.

However, the cases have not simply adopted the Restatement principles as rigorous guides to the extraterritorial application of the securities laws. Indeed, the courts have engaged in extensive speculation as to the intent of Congress of the "what would Congress have wanted, if it had ever thought of this problem" type.

Nonetheless, the courts (as well as academic commentators) have frequently used the Restatement principles as a framework for the analysis of the issue, making it convenient to do so for the purposes of this discussion as well. In particular, the discussion of extraterritoriality has turned on two provisions of the Restatement: Section 17 and Section 18. Section 17 describes what is generally referred to as the "subjective territorial principle", which is, in substance, that a state has jurisdiction over acts which occur within its territory even

29. Leasco Data Processing Equipment
Co. v. Maxwell, 468 F.2d 1326, 1334
(2d Cir. 1972).

when the effects of such acts are felt only outside the state's territory. Jurisdiction based on this principle is also described as conduct-based jurisdiction. Section 18 describes the so-called "objective territorial principle", which provides that a nation may regulate conduct which occurs outside its territory and produces an effect within its territory. Jurisdiction based on this principle is sometimes called effects-based or impact-based jurisdiction. Accordingly, determinations as to whether jurisdiction should lie in particular cases have tended to be based on an analysis of whether there was sufficient conduct in the United States and/or whether transactions performed entirely outside the United States nevertheless had a direct, foreseeable, and substantial impact on U. S. investors or securities markets.

*   *   *

5.   Objective territorial principle

Generally speaking, it would be permissible under Restatement Section 18 to assert jurisdiction with respect to foreign violative conduct having a substantial, direct and foreseeable domestic effect. There has been substantial controversy and uncertainty as to whether the U. S. cases support assertion of jurisdiction to the full extent permitted by international law. *   *   * It now appears that jurisdiction may exist under the decided cases on the basis of harmful effects alone.

*   *   *

*   *   * *Bersch* appears to have resolved the problem. As indicated earlier, the *Bersch* court viewed its determination as to jurisdiction with respect to U. S. resident members of the plaintiff class as involving an application of the objective territorial principle and permitted suit against two defendants whom it found responsible for "dispatch[ing] from abroad misleading statements to United States residents", characterizing the case as being of the type contemplated by Restatement Section 18. The specific holding was:

*   *   * The anti-fraud provisions of the federal securities laws:

Apply to losses from sales of securities to Americans resident in the United States whether or not acts (or culpable failures to act) of material importance occurred in this country.

The court went on to uphold jurisdiction over an accountant for IOS which had certified the financial statements used in the offering, stating that "*   *   * action in the United States is not necessary when subject matter jurisdiction is predicated on a direct effect here *   *   *". Accordingly, *Bersch* made it explicit that jurisdiction may be based on adverse domestic effects alone.

Other U. S. Courts of Appeal appear to agree. In Travis v. Anthes,[79] the Eighth Circuit court stated:

We are also persuaded that Section 10(b) and Rule 10b–5 are applicable to defendants' self-dealing, even if it is assumed that all

---

79.   473 F.2d 515 (8th Cir. 1973).

such dealings took place in Canada. "It is settled law * * * that any state may impose liabilities, even upon persons not within its allegiance, for conduct outside its borders that has consequences within its borders which the state reprehends * * * ".[80]

The Ninth Circuit said recently in Des Brisay v. The Goldfield Corporation:[81]

* * * In short, in view of Congress's intention to protect the integrity of domestic securities markets in a particular stock, the fact that an allegedly improper transaction occurred outside the United States or involved parties other than United States citizens has been held not to defeat subject matter jurisdiction where the securities involved in the transaction were registered and listed on a national exchange and the effect of the foreign transaction adversely affected buyers, sellers and holders of those securities.[82]

Of course, the Restatement requires that those effects be substantial, direct, and foreseeable. The cases have not fully defined these concepts, but they do suggest some important characteristics. For one thing, it is not sufficient to allege that foreign acts have had "an adverse effect on the American economy or American investors generally". Nor is a U. S. investor protected from a securities fraud committed entirely abroad because the harm such an investor suffered abroad was felt at home. Moreover, it has been held that any impairment of the value of U. S. investments must result from the securities fraud itself and not from subsequent unrelated transactions, and that real estate investments in the U. S. by a foreign issuer did not create the necessary impact. In short, it appears clear that, in order for there to be jurisdiction over foreign acts constituting a substantive violation of the U. S. securities laws, those acts must in and of themselves result in substantial damage to an interest protected by the U. S. securities laws. In a fraud case, that would mean that the violations would have to affect investors "in whom the United States has an interest", presumably U. S. investors who were the victims of fraud that had some U. S. nexus, or that the fraud would have to have a direct effect on the market for a domestically traded security (i. e., a foreign-based manipulation of such a security). In the case of provisions like Section 13(d) and Section 16 of the Exchange Act —which require disclosure of certain securities transactions by large stockholders and corporate officers—the protected interest would be defined by the Congressional purpose behind them. Accordingly, if Congress's intent that certain beneficial ownership interests be dis-

---

80. Id. at 527–528.

81. 549 F.2d at 133 (9th Cir. 1977).

82. Id. at 135. The California Court of Appeals recently took the same position in UFITEC, S.A. v. Carter, CCH Fed.Sec.L.Rep. ¶ 95,874 (Ct.App. Cal.1977), a contract suit in a state court. The question arose because the defendant claimed the contract was void pursuant to Section 29 of the Exchange Act [15 U.S.C. 78cc (1970)].

closed, for example, is thwarted by acts occurring abroad, it would appear that a sufficient impact would have occurred.

On the other hand, it does not appear to be necessary that the securities be registered or exchange-listed (except in the case of provisions which only apply if registered or listed securities are involved) or that the issuer of the securities be a U. S. company. Nor does the nationality of the defendant appear to be crucial. Again, the salient factor appears to be impact on a U. S. interest which the courts believe Congress meant to protect.

* * *

8. U. S. requirements that may violate foreign law

At times, one party in a U. S. law suit seeks documents which the other party claims may not lawfully be produced under applicable foreign law. The court in such a case must decide whether or not to order production of the documents in the face of the claim that to do so would violate foreign law and, if it orders their production, what sanctions may be imposed for noncompliance with the order.

Recently, the Tenth Circuit had occasion to consider these problems in a case under the U. S. securities laws: Arthur Andersen & Co. v. Finesilver.[110] In that case, Arthur Andersen & Co. objected to the production of certain documents on the ground that their production would violate the Swiss secrecy laws. The district court had overruled the objections, which had led to appeals and a petition for a writ of mandamus. The Court of Appeals relied heavily on the U. S. Supreme Court's decision in Société Internationale v. Rogers [111] and concluded that consideration of foreign law in a discovery context is required in dealing with sanctions to be imposed for disobedience and not in deciding whether the discovery order should issue. The court criticized certain Second Circuit cases which suggest that a district court should not order production if the order would cause a party to violate foreign law. According to the Tenth Circuit court, these decisions fail to recognize the distinction between the power to compel discovery and the imposition of sanctions for noncompliance with an order for production.[112]

---

110. 546 F.2d 338 (10th Cir. 1976).

111. In Société Internationale v. Rogers, 357 U.S. 197, 78 S.Ct. 1087, 2 L.Ed.2d 1255 (1958), the U.S. Supreme Court confronted this problem in a case under the Trading with the Enemy Act. The claimant in that case asserted that it was unable to produce certain relevant documents because to do so would involve disclosure of banking records in violation of Swiss laws. The district court had ordered production and had dismissed the case for noncompliance. The Court of Appeals affirmed. The Supreme Court found that the district

court was justified in issuing the production order but determined that dismissal was not an appropriate sanction for failure to comply when it had been established that such failure was due to inability and not to willfulness, bad faith, or any fault of the petitioner. However, the court went on to imply strongly that the inability of the petitioner to produce the documents might prove a serious handicap in its efforts to prove its case.

112. 546 F.2d at 341. For a different approach, see United States v. First

The Tenth Circuit court stated that the dilemma it confronted was that of accommodation of the principles of the law of the forum with concepts of due process and international comity. The court stated that it was not impressed by Arthur Andersen's contention that international comity prevents a U. S. court from ordering actions which violate foreign law. The court stated that foreign law may not control local law.[113] The court then determined that the district court's discovery order was not a final decision and was not appealable. Consequently, the appeals were dismissed. The petition for mandamus was also denied.

These cases do not make it clear exactly what the consequences would be of the failure of a defendant in a Commission enforcement action to produce documents on the ground that to do so would violate foreign law. However, in S. E. C. v. American Institute Counsellors, Inc., the district court judge, at the Commission's request, ordered the transfer of certain assets held by Swiss Credit Bank from Switzerland to the U. S., recognizing that such a transfer would violate Swiss law. The judge declined to defer to Swiss banking law and customs because of Swiss Credit Bank's participation in the alleged violations and because control of the assets in question was necessary for the proper protection of investors. An agreement which satisfied the Commission was reached without appeal.

Clearly, there remain unresolved problems in this area, which could make it difficult for the Commission to obtain relief in future cases.

* * *

11.   International cooperation

As indicated, the Commission has disagreed with those who express concern that a broad assertion of jurisdiction will damage international relations or international business. Indeed, international cooperation has been extensive and extremely valuable in two of the Commission's most significant international cases: S. E. C. v. Vesco and S. E. C. v. American Institute Counsellors, Inc. The *Vesco* case has been one of the Commission's most complicated and far-reaching enforcement actions. The Commission named 42 corporate and individual defendants and alleged violation of the antifraud, filing, and

Nat'l City Bank ("Citibank"), 396 F. 2d 897 (2d Cir. 1968), one of the cases criticized by the *Finesilver* court. The Second Circuit affirmed a finding of contempt against Citibank for failure to produce documents in the possession of its branch in West Germany. The court found that production would apparently not violate West German criminal law and would at most expose Citibank to civil liability. However, the court rested its determination not so much on its conclusions as to whether or not production would violate the law as on a balancing of the U.S. and West German national interests and on an analysis of the hardships Citibank would suffer, an approach suggested by Restatement Section 40.

113.   546 F.2d at 342. The court also implied that Andersen should not have purported to speak for the U.S. on the subject of international comity but should have sought to have appropriate officers and agencies of the U.S. make such representations to the court as they might deem suitable.

proxy provisions of the Exchange Act. Included among the defendants were four foreign banks, a foreign bank holding company, and four foreign mutual funds.

The prosecution of the *Vesco* case has been extremely difficult and complex and has been significantly impeded by the evasive efforts of certain of the defendants. Nevertheless, much has been accomplished since the institution of the case to prevent the further looting of the IOS Funds, thanks largely to an extraordinary, and probably unique, international cooperative effort. The Commission conferred with interested foreign governments, and a committee of regulatory authorities from the U. S., the federal government of Canada, the Provinces of Quebec and Ontario, Luxembourg, and the Netherlands Antilles was established for the purpose of coordinating the recovery, realization and administration of the assets of the various parts of the Vesco empire. Through the efforts of this committee, and with the cooperation of the courts, liquidators and trustees have been appointed abroad for many of these entities, including IOS, Ltd. itself.

　　　* * *

---

1. *International limitations of law and policy and judicial interpretations as to the reaches of statutes.* Normally courts—certainly those in the United States—will interpret ambiguous legislative intention as to reach so as to conform national law to customary international law. In the securities fraud cases discussed above it is clear that the federal courts have relied heavily on the Restatement's position as to prescriptive jurisdiction under general international law. During the formulation of the Restatement counsel for a multinational oil company tried to exclude economic effects from the objective territorial principle. The effort was motivated by a realization that a broad statement would have the influence on the interpretation of national law that it has in fact come to have. Yet, as the securities fraud cases also make clear, courts have not always held that the reach of national law is as wide as that permitted by international law. How do courts find this latter result? In Bersch v. Drexel Firestone, Inc., Judge Friendly wrote:

　　　* * * [There is no] subject matter jurisdiction if there was no intention that the securities should be offered to anyone in the United States, simply because in the long run there was an adverse effect on this country's general economic interests or on American security prices. *Moderation is all.* [Emphasis supplied.]

Is such moderation a canon or rule of interpretation or is it an overriding legal principle as suggested by Section 40 of the Restatement of Foreign Relations Law and Professor Currie's enlightened and restrained forum, note pp. 475–476? Is the ultimate question apt to be whether moderation is jurisdictional, in the sense that the particular court has competence only to the extent that it acts with moderation

as between forum and foreign rules? In the literature today there
are evidences of some revival of support for the notion that territorial jurisdiction based on the objective principle (acts outside, effects
within) ought to be—or is—more limited than the subjective principle is. Some Commonwealth countries recently have passed laws requiring authorization from national authorities before documents and
records kept within the territory may be removed in response to an
investigation by an extraterritorialist state, that is, one that is too as-
sertive in regard to the objective territorial principle as to economic
effects and the like. These laws are defended to some extent as having been enacted in defense of true international law as to jurisdiction. Moreover, the term comity, which in correct usage is not law
but reciprocal courtesy, is being used again in a somewhat peremptory way by some writers, academic and judicial.

2. *Judicial alignment of federal statutes as to reach.* After the
theorizing is over, the practical lawyer wants to know what the reach
of this or that federal statute is, where, as is normal, Congress has
not been specific. The problem has arisen very often in determining
whether a wide range of federal legislation applies to Puerto Rico,
the Virgin Islands and other associated territories. One simply has
to find what, if anything, the courts have held, for there are no assured legislative guidelines. In addition to antitrust statutes (mainly
the Sherman Act) and securities fraud statutes and regulations
thereunder, there are federal precedents on the "intended reach" of
federal legislation as to unionization of seamen, foreign seamen's
right to pay in American ports, and maritime torts (including
wrongful death statutes). In these cases, ordinarily, judicial interpretation is of a statute that does not need to be based upon the "effects" doctrine. The act involved takes place within the United
States. But here, also, the "moderation" or a reasonableness test is
often applied.

3. OTHER LINES OF SOLUTION?

What lines of solution? Several possibilities, some of rules, some
of method, have been suggested already. An interesting question
arises whether, as the industrialized nations of the world move toward the specific regulation of the same types of private economic activity, the differences in their approaches, remedies and tolerations
will exacerbate or relieve conflicts of jurisdiction. From one point of
view, that of achieving the general objective of social control of particular types of economic conduct, it does not seem to make much difference which set of rules actually gets applied. But administrators
and legislators in nation states as well as in the European Economic
Community proceed in economic matters from localized senses of mission. Thus the increased number of potentially applicable sets of
rules may threaten the effective conduct of transnational business enterprise and create a common need for some system of rationalization
or harmonization of regulatory principles. In the period 1948–52,

roughly, the first major effort to create a set of international rules for restrictive trade practices and monopoly, the Havana Charter of the aborted International Trade Organization (see p. 1084), failed through lack of sufficient agreement among states. Later efforts for the creation of new, positive, universal law in this sector has been slight so far. But perhaps circumstances are changing, due both to the increased array of particularistic regulatory systems and the growth of multinational enterprise.

STATEMENT OF KY P. EWING, JR., DEPUTY ASSISTANT ATTORNEY GENERAL, ANTITRUST DIVISION, DEPARTMENT OF JUSTICE, CONCERNING § 1010, A BILL TO ESTABLISH A COMMISSION ON THE INTERNATIONAL APPLICATION OF ANTITRUST LAWS

Department of Justice Press Release, October 31, 1979.

* * * § 1010 would direct the Commission to address seven topics: (1) sovereign immunity, (2) the act-of-state doctrine, (3) the defense of "foreign compulsion", (4) the effects doctrine, (5) the statutory exemptions from the antitrust laws provided by the Webb-Pomerene Act and the Edge Act, (6) the difficulties of enforcing U. S. court orders extraterritorially, and (7) the problems relating to reciprocal enforcement of antitrust laws between nations.

* * *

* * * [T]he Department of Justice can express agreement that the seven specific topics listed in section 2(b) of § 1010 represent key elements in the sensible application of our antitrust law jurisdiction to reflect both the international limits on our authority and the comity due other nations.

Having noted these areas of broad agreement, let me also in candor note our disagreement with three propositions that may have played some role in triggering the introduction of § 1010. We disagree with the idea that U. S. companies are unreasonably barred from setting up joint ventures, and that they forfeit business abroad as a result. We also disagree with the contention that uncertainty about the enforcement of U. S. antitrust laws extraterritorially is an inhibitor of foreign trade. Finally, we disagree with the idea that our courts have not kept pace with the real world ramifications of international commerce. Each of these propositions has recently been debated in other forums and has been found lacking in substance.
* * *

* * *

* * * [T]he courts have actively been considering these issues as they have arisen in an antitrust context. Admittedly, in the years immediately after Judge Hand's famous 1945 opinion in the Alcoa case, which enunciated the effects doctrine, there were few decided cases. More recently, however, the courts have been developing rational and sophisticated, yet practical, approaches to the questions of the so-called extraterritorial application of our antitrust laws. This developmental trend has been particularly evident recently in the 9th Circuit's 1976 Timberlane [2] decision and its recent offshoots, including this year's decisions in the Mannington Mills [3] and Mitsui [4] cases in the 3rd and 5th Circuits, respectively, and in the Southern District of New York's Bohio [5] decision.

Timberlane is illustrative of that aspect of our jurisprudence that resists an over-rigid codification of law in deference to the ability of the courts and the bar to reach practical resolutions of commercial problems by identifying relevant principles and applying them within the context of individual fact situations. The Timberlane court agreed with Judge Hand in Alcoa that our antitrust laws have no application where a restraint of trade has no effect in the United States. Timberlane went further to recognize that it is unreasonable to apply antitrust sanctions in every instance in which there is such an effect, even a substantial one, in the United States. Rather, an evaluation is required, said the court, that balances the interest of the United States against the foreign character of the activity in question. Specifically, the court stated that it should properly consider whether there is any conflict with foreign law or policy, the nationality and location of the firms involved, where the conduct occurred, whether enforcement will achieve compliance, the significance of effects in the United States as compared with those abroad, and whether the conduct was purposefully designed to affect United States commerce. The courts have been applying similar principles in conflict-of-laws cases for years. Considerations of comity, like those of equity, while sometimes complex, are peculiarly susceptible to judicial analysis.

* * *

A persistent contention we believe demonstrably wrong based on available evidence is the assertion that U. S. firms exporting services, such as engineering and construction firms, have been impeded from competing abroad by the reach of American antitrust laws to their actions outside this country. The hundreds of American construction and engineering consortia operating abroad in the past 25 years give the lie to this assertion. It is simply not so. We have said so in our past public statements. In 1970, for example, we gave a business review clearance to such a venture among eleven U. S. consulting engineering firms exporting their services to Southeast Asia. These firms wished to export their services and we advised them that they needed no antitrust exemption to do so legally.

* * *

2. Timberlane Lumber Co. v. Bank of America, 549 F.2d 597 (9th Cir. 1976).

3. Mannington Mills, Inc. v. Congoleum Corp., 595 F.2d 1287 (3rd Cir. 1979).

4. Industrial Inv. Development Corp. v. Mitsui & Co., 594 F.2d 48 (5th Cir. 1979).

5. Dominicus Americana Bohio v. Gulf & Western Industries, 1979—2 CCH Trade Cases ¶ 62,757 (S.D.N.Y.1979).

Comment and questions: Obviously, certain groups have sought to direct attention to the alleged harmful effects of the reach of American antitrust laws on American economic activities abroad. To what extent does the Department of Justice spokesman suggest that moderation may be jurisdictional? Suppose the United States should abandon the use of the effects doctrine in antitrust cases, either outright or by casting the balance against application. What assurance would American business have that the antitrust laws elsewhere, such as those of the German Federal Republic or the European Economic Community would not apply, either because of presence within the territory through controlled subsidiaries or the effects doctrine?

Part III

THE INDIVIDUAL IN THE INTERNATIONAL LEGAL SYSTEM

Chapter 8

PROTECTION AND ALLEGIANCE

A basic feature of today's system of nation states is the relative helplessness of the individual. At birth he finds himself a member of some political institution (typically a state in the international system) which, more or less, protects him from the violence of other individuals and groups of individuals. In the domestic legal system of that state, its police and courts may offer protection from harm inflicted within the state; its army may protect him from harm caused by aggression from outside the state.

If the individual steps outside his state and is injured by someone in another state, he is largely on his own. He must look for redress, if any, in the courts of that other state. Doctrines of sovereign immunity may bar him from redress for injuries caused by that state. As a last resort the individual must appeal to his own state's government to help him. If it chooses, it may come to his aid by espousing a claim against the wrongdoing state through diplomatic channels (or possibly through arbitration or through judicial means such as the International Court of Justice).

For the protection it offers him at home and the protection it may afford him against foreign injuries, the state demands obligations of the individual in return: to obey its laws, to pay its taxes, to help to defend it against aggression.

The physical fact of an individual's presence within a state has been the major basis from which the state exerts its power to protect the individual and to demand his allegiance. But the processes of history have developed legal relationships between the state and the individual that do not depend solely upon his physical presence in the territory of the state. The state has a special relationship to those it designates as its nationals. In broad and inexact terms, the state's nationals are entitled to greater rights than non-nationals (e. g., in states with voting systems, the national is permitted to vote, the non-national is not); the state is more ready to demand that the national perform obligations (e. g., the national may be subject to laws prescribed by his state even though he is not physically present in its territory).

The practices of states in creating the class of people upon whom they confer nationality vary widely. Some states accord nationality to individuals born within the territory; this right of nationality is referred to as jus soli. Some states accord nationality at birth only to individuals born of parents who are already nationals: this right of nationality is referred to as jus sanguinis. An increasing number of states recognize both bases. In addition to according nationality based upon facts associated with birth, states afford naturalization processes by which individuals may apply for and be granted nationality. With such a variety of bases for nationality existing in the international system it is possible for an individual to be designated a national and thus to have dual nationality or even multiple nationality. Indeed, there are circumstances under which he may have no nationality at all and thus be stateless.

From the perspective of the international legal system, several important questions arise:

    1.   Is a state free to set its own standards for conferring its nationality upon an individual? Or does international law set some minimum standard?

    2.   What is the significance of nationality as a base for the state's requiring the performance of obligations by an individual? For example, can the state draft into its army someone who is not its national?

This chapter explores these two questions. In succeeding chapters the question will be asked whether the developments in the law of human rights and individual responsibility significantly modify the legal situation of the individual as sketched above.

SECTION A. NATIONALITY: LOSS OF ITS BENEFITS

RE IMMIGRATION ACT AND HANNA

Canada, Supreme Court of British Columbia, 1957.
21 Western Weekly Rep. 400.*

SULLIVAN, J. This is a "hard case" of the kind of which it is said that bad law is made.

The applicant George Christian Hanna, whom I shall refer to as "Hanna" in these reasons for judgment, is a young man without a country—one of those unfortunate "stateless" persons of the world whose status is a matter of concern to humanitarians and has prompted men and women of good will of all countries to seek relief for such persons through the agency of the Economic and Social Council of the United Nations. A convention was adopted by that council in September, 1954, to which, however, Canada is not a signatory.

* Reprinted by permission of Burroughs
& Co., Ltd., Calgary, Alberta, Canada.

The matter comes before me by way of habeas corpus with certiorari in aid. Hanna seeks a judicial declaration that his detention under a deportation order made by F. Wragg, an immigration officer (acting as a special inquiry officer) dated January 18, 1957, and confirmed on appeal to an immigration appeal board duly constituted under the provisions of the Immigration Act, RSC, 1952, ch. 325, is illegal, (1) Because the deportation order is defective, incomplete, impossible of interpretation or enforcement and beyond the statutory authority of Mr. Wragg to make; and (2) Because the immigration appeal board improperly denied Hanna the right to be heard, either in person or by counsel, at the appeal proceedings before such board.

The issues thus presented for my determination are strictly legal in nature and narrow in their scope. I have no right to reflect upon and must guard against the danger that the strictly legal opinion which I am required to express should be influenced in any degree by considerations of human sympathy for this unfortunate (23-year-old) young applicant in the frustrating dilemma with which fate seems to have confronted him throughout his lifetime prior to his last arrival in Canada as ship-bound prisoner aboard a tramp motor-ship in her ceaseless meanderings from port to port throughout the world.

The deportation order in question is in the words and figures following:

CANADA

DEPARTMENT OF CITIZENSHIP AND IMMIGRATION
DEPORTATION ORDER AGAINST
CHRISTIAN GEORGE HANNA
of Djibouti, French Somaliland

under section 28 of the Immigration Act.

On the basis of the evidence adduced at an inquiry held at the Immigration Building, Vancouver, B. C., on January 18, 1957 I have reached the decision that you may not come into or remain in Canada as of right and that you are a member of the prohibited class described in paragraph (t) of Section 5 of the Immigration Act, in that you do not fulfil or comply with the conditions or requirements of Subsection (1), Subsection (3) and Subsection (8) of Section 18 of the Immigration Regulations.

I hereby order you to be detained and to be deported to the place whence you came to Canada, or to the country of which you are a national or citizen, or to the country of your birth, or to such country as may be approved by the minister.

Date 18 January 1957

[Sgd.] F. WRAGG
Special Inquiry Officer

Service Hereof Acknowledged by
[Sgd.] C. G. HANNA.

Subsecs. (1), (3) and (8) of sec. 18 of the regulations to which said deportation order refers require that an immigrant possess a passport and visa; and that his passport or other travel document bear a medical certificate in approved form.

It should be stated at the outset that no Canadian court has power to assist Hanna in his plea that he be given right of residence in Canada. That is a decision for immigration officials, and for them alone, to make. Similarly all right of exercise of discretionary power to exempt from strict compliance with the requirements of the Immigration Act or regulations made thereunder is vested in and is the prerogative of only the minister, deputy minister, director, or such other persons as may be authorized to act for the director. * * *

     * * *

It may be helpful to outline Hanna's history and background in brief detail as it is disclosed by the scanty material before me. Most of such material consists of Hanna's sworn testimony, given in the English language, when he was before Mr. Wragg on January 18, 1957, at which time his knowledge and proficiency in the use of our language was not as great as it may be now. He says that he was born at sea and that no known record of his birth is extant. The name of the vessel aboard which he was born, and particulars of her nationality or port of registry are unknown. His father was named George Hanna and supposedly travelled to French Somaliland from Liberia, a small republic situate on the west coast of Africa. His mother's maiden name was Marian Marika and she was a native of Ethiopia (or Abyssinia)—a country whose status either as empire or vassal of Italy at any given time can be determined only by reference to historical data bearing upon Emperor Haile Selassie's struggles in warfare with the late Benito Mussolini. Hanna understands that his parents met and were married at Djibouti, the capital city of French Somaliland. The accuracy of his information in this respect should be easy to check. French Somaliland is a very small country. It has been a French colony for about 80 years, and one imagines that statistical records of births, deaths and marriages are available at the capital city—a comparatively small place of about 22,000 population. Hanna was the only child born of his parents' marriage and both of his parents are dead. Continuing the narrative according to Hanna's understanding of events, his father left his mother to seek employment in Liberia. Subsequently his mother, being pregnant at the time, and seeking to rejoin her husband, took passage on a ship sailing out of Djibouti. She became ill and gave birth to Hanna when the ship was one day at sea, and because of her illness the ship was put about and returned to Djibouti where she and her newborn child were placed in a hospital or home for women. Thereafter Hanna was cared for by his mother who worked at various times at Addis Ababa and Dire Wawa (both in Ethiopia) and at Djibouti in French Somaliland, until Hanna was six years of age. She then died and thereafter Hanna more or less "raised himself" as he puts it, with some assistance from a kindly old Turkish gentleman at Djibouti and others, including a Japanese gentleman at Dire Wawa in Ethiopia.

During his years of infancy and adolescence Hanna seems to have crossed and recrossed the international boundaries of Ethiopia, French Somaliland, British Somaliland and Eritrea (formerly an Italian colony but now a province of Ethiopia by virtue of the recommendation of a United Nations' committee adopted by the General Assembly in 1952) without encountering difficulty with the immigration officials of those countries. I suppose that youth was in his favour at the outset, and I suppose, too, that the international boundaries referred to were not too well defined at that time. That still seems to be the case. I understand that the accurate fixation of the international borders convergent upon the small area of French Somaliland is a problem which presently engages the attention of the United Nations' General Assembly.

In this way Hanna lived and worked from time to time (inter alia) in the ports of Zeila and Berbera in British Somaliland where he picked up a smattering of English. He says that his mother spoke English and, although he never saw his father, it is his understanding that his parents conversed in English. This would be consistent with Hanna's theory that his father was a native of Liberia—a republic which most people look upon as a virtual protectorate of the United States of America, and where English is spoken.

As he grew older Hanna seems to have encountered and had difficulty with the immigration officers of these adjacent countries, in none of which he could claim right of residence. He thereby learned that possession of a birth certificate is an indispensable requirement of modern society. He learned "the hard way" that some of the fundamental human rights with which all men are endowed by their Creator at birth were not his to enjoy without the intervention and benevolent assistance of some temporal power—a power to be exercised in many cases according to the whim or opinion of immigration officers whose numbers are legion in most sovereign states. That is not to say, of course, that he or anyone else possesses an inherent right to enter or remain in Canada unless born here. The late Right Honourable W. L. Mackenzie King, Prime Minister of Canada, said in the House of Commons on May 1, 1947, that

> It is not a "fundamental human right" of an alien to enter Canada. It is a privilege. It is a matter of domestic policy.

The same thing might be said with respect to every sovereign state of the world, but one doubts that the Prime Minister intended his statement to be a repudiation of Canadian interest or sympathy in such a case of distress as this one, the like of which, I venture to say, has little chance of recurring. It is probable that the Prime Minister made use of the term "alien" in the popular sense of reference to a person who resides or seeks to reside in a country other than his own; and in that connotation it could be argued that a stateless person like Hanna is not an "alien" since he has no country of his own.

I think I should stop there by reminding myself again that the issue before me is a strictly legal one which I am required to divorce from any considerations of equity or humanitarianism. Those things must be deemed to have been embodied in the statute at the time of its enactment.

Almost three years ago, when he was in the port of Massaua, Eritrea, Hanna stowed away in an Italian tramp steamer in the hope of being carried in her to some country which would grant him asylum and right of residence. His plan met with frustration because upon arrival of such ship at any port he was immediately locked up and denied permission to land. After a year or more of such aimless wandering and imprisonment, Hanna escaped from the Italian vessel when she called at Beirut in the republic of Lebanon, and concealed himself in the hold of the Norwegian motor-ship "Gudveig." As a stowaway in such latter vessel he fared no better than before. He was held prisoner aboard The "Gudveig" for more than 16 months and made three or more trips to Canada in her until his release under writ of habeas corpus in these proceedings. He first came before Clyne, J. upon return of a show cause summons on January 18, 1957, wherein he challenged the legality of his detention by the master of The "Gudveig." My learned brother there held (correctly, in my respectful opinion) that the master's detention of Hanna was not illegal since the master was subject to and bound by the regulations applicable to "stowaways" as passed pursuant to the provisions of the Immigration Act. Thereafter Hanna made application to enter Canada and his status was thereby changed from that of "stowaway" to that of "immigrant." An immigrant is defined by sec. 2(i) of the Immigration Act as follows:

(i) "immigrant" means a person who seeks admission to Canada for permanent residence.

* * * And so, at a time when it had become a widely publicized matter of general public knowledge or repute that Hanna possessed no proof of birth nor documents of any kind, he was granted the privilege of appearing before three separate departmental tribunals for the purpose of proving—if he could—that he did in fact possess such documents. Of course, he was unable to discharge that onus, and the deportation order followed which is now under attack in these proceedings.

I now come to an examination of that deportation order. Was it an order which the special inquiry officer had legal authority to make in all of the circumstances existing at the time of its making? It contains four separate directives which are stated in the alternative and, presumably, in the order of their importance.

The most important directive is, No. 1, that Hanna be deported to the place whence he came to Canada.

The next directive is, No. 2, that he be deported to the country of which he is a national or citizen.

The next is, No. 3, that he be deported to the country of his birth.

The final alternative is, No. 4, that he be deported to such country as may be approved by the minister.

The No. 4 directive is meaningless in the absence of anything to show a possibility of the minister ever finding a country which would be willing to admit this young man in the face of Canada's refusal to admit him. It cannot be assumed that travel documents are of less significance in other countries than here. The thing goes further than that, however, because sec. 40(2) of our Act makes the minister's power of designation and approval of "such country" conditional upon the owners of the M. S. "Gudveig" first making request for such ministerial approval. Even then, as I interpret the statute, the approval of the minister could have no effect unless after finding "a country that is willing to receive him," Hanna were to indicate that such country is "acceptable" to him.

Directives No. 2 and No. 3 referring, respectively, to country of nationality or citizenship and country of birth, may be discussed together. Neither of these directives could possibly be complied with. In the absence of satisfactory evidence of nationality of a legitimate father and lack of any evidence as to the nationality or registry of the ship aboard which Hanna was born, these directives of the deportation order are meaningless.

The inescapable fact is that Hanna is a "stateless person," and the efforts of the department to prove otherwise have not been impressive. I was presented with evidence (consisting of affidavits by lawyers in Oslo, Norway, and a Canadian immigration officer) in support of the submission that Hanna is not "stateless" and that the words of the directive "country of your birth," therefore, are not meaningless. The trouble is that whilst the affidavit of the immigration officer fixes Hanna's birthplace as Djibouti in French Somaliland, the Norwegian lawyers suggest that he is an Egyptian who was born at Alexandria. None of this conflicting evidence is credible. It is all based on hearsay and, perhaps, the least said about it, the better.

That brings me to the consideration of directive No. 1—that Hanna be deported to the place whence he came to Canada. What does it mean?

The department's position, as I understand it, is that it could mean a number of things which it leaves to other people to determine for themselves. The place whence Hanna came to Canada might be the port of Beirut in the republic of Lebanon since that is the place where he first stowed away in the M. S. "Gudveig." Perhaps that interpretation is favoured by the department since it has presented certain material tending to show that if Lebanese authorities can be satisfied that Hanna stowed away at Beirut, they might permit him to land in their country—a country, incidentally, which is quite as foreign to Hanna as it is to me. Then again the department seems to suggest that the place whence Hanna came to Canada could be the United Kingdom and an affidavit is presented for the purpose of showing that The "Gudveig" sailed non-stop from the United Kingdom to Vancouver on her last voyage with Hanna aboard. Perhaps the place whence Hanna came to Canada could be the port of Massaua in Eritrea, since that was the starting point of his aimless wanderings as a stowaway in search of a country which would give him right of residence. Other interpretations are possible, but it seems to me that the matter of correct interpretation is of comparative unimportance here. The thing of importance, as I see it, is that the special inquiry officer here delegated to the master or owners of The "Gudveig" the responsibility for saying what his deportation order means; and, apart from the circumstances that he himself does not seem to know what it means, I am of opinion that he has not that power of delegation under the Act.

I have had reference to the authorities cited by counsel wherein it was held that deportation orders made (as this one was) in form approved by the minister were valid and enforceable notwithstanding their multiplicity of alternative directives, but in none of such cases were the facts comparable to the extraordinary facts of this amazing case. In each of such cases the meaning of the deportation order in the form used was clearly apparent to everyone concerned or affected by it. In no case did the deportation order require subsequent inquiry or investigation by anyone for determination of its meaning. In none of such cases was there a necessarily incidental delegation of his authority by the special inquiry officer who made the order for deportation. These are some of the things which, in my opinion, distinguish Hanna's case from all others.

From whatever angle one views it, so far as Hanna is concerned, this deportation order amounted to a sentence of imprisonment aboard The "Gudveig" for an indefinite term, and in my opinion and finding, no immigration officer has the legal right to exercise such drastic power.

*   *   *

For the reasons previously expressed, there will be judgment for Hanna in these proceedings, with costs. That does not mean that he has established any legal right to enter or remain in Canada. As previously stated, it is for immigration officials and for them alone to grant or withhold that privilege. This judgment does not mean that Hanna may not be deported legally from Canada by further proceedings properly instituted and conducted in accordance with the provisions and intent of the Immigration Act. It means only that the present deportation order is illegal and that Hanna is entitled to be released from detention thereunder; and I so order.

*   *   *

CONSEQUENCES OF STATELESSNESS

1. *What happens to Hanna now?* In Staniszewski v. Watkins, 80 F.Supp. 132 (S.D.N.Y.1948), a stateless seaman was released after being detained at Ellis Island for about seven months at the expense of his employer. The court observed that the government was "willing that he go back to the ship, but if he were sent back aboard ship and sailed to the port * * * from which he last sailed to the United States, he would probably be denied permission to land." The court said, "There is no other country that would take him without proper documents." (at 134) The court sustained the seamen's writ of habeas corpus and ordered his release: "He will be required to inform the immigration officials at Ellis Island by mail on the 15th of each month, stating where he is employed and where he can be reached by mail. If the government does succeed in arranging for petitioner's deportation to a country that will be ready to receive him as a resident, it may then advise the petitioner to that effect and arrange for his deportation in the manner provided by law." (at 135)

Similarly, in Public Prosecutor v. Zinger, France, Tribunal of the Seine, 1936, [1935–37] Ann.Dig. 307 (No. 138), the court ordered the release of a stateless person who had been imprisoned for failure to obey expulsion orders. The court weighed the alternatives of releasing the man or imprisoning him "at the cost of the French taxpayer" for an offence which he could not help committing, since he was unable to leave French territory. The court concluded that "release is the best solution from the legal point of view."

2. *Discrimination between aliens and stateless persons.* If a stateless person is allowed to remain in the United States, is he treated differently from an alien who has the nationality of some other state? Aliens have been held entitled to the benefits of the Fifth Amendment guarantee against expropriation of property without compensation. But suppose that the United States should discriminate between aliens with nationality and those without nationality, to the disadvantage of the latter? Would there be any international consequence? A state whose national has been the subject of discrimination could call the United States to account under international law. Who would, or could, espouse the claim of the stateless alien?

3. *Espousal of claims of stateless persons.* Suppose a stateless person is allowed to remain in the United States and does reside there for a number of years. Thereafter he enters a foreign state where he is subject to severe injury at the hands of state officials (e. g., he is imprisoned for a long period without charges or trial and is subjected to torture and other inhumane treatment). Will the United States espouse a claim on his behalf? Section 1732 of Title 22 of the United States Code provides as follows:

> Whenever it is made known to the President that any citizen of the United States has been unjustly deprived of his liberty by or under the authority of any foreign government, it shall be the

duty of the President forthwith to demand of that government the reasons of such imprisonment; and if it appears to be wrongful and in violation of the rights of American citizenship, the President shall forthwith demand the release of such citizen, and if the release so demanded is unreasonably delayed or refused, the President shall use such means, not amounting to acts of war, as he may think necessary and proper to obtain or effectuate the release; and all the facts and proceedings relative thereto shall as soon as practicable be communicated by the President to Congress.

The protection of the United States is not confined to native-born citizens. Title 22, Section 1731, of the United States Code provides:

> All naturalized citizens of the United States while in foreign countries are entitled to and shall receive from this Government the same protection of persons and property which is accorded to native-born citizens.

Suppose it is decided by the United States that it will espouse the stateless alien's claim. Is it permitted by international law to do so? See the Nottebohm case, below.

4. *Statelessness decreed against members of a class of persons.* Statelessness has resulted from a state's decree that members of a whole class of persons are no longer citizens of the state. During World War II, Germany withdrew German nationality from Jews permanently resident abroad. In France, this loss of nationality relieved an individual from the strictures applied by French law to enemy (German) subjects, even though the denationalization law was repealed by the Allies at the end of the war. Terhoch v. Daudin et Assistance Publique France, Court of Appeal of Paris, 1947, [1947] Ann.Dig. 121 (No. 54).

5. *Loss of nationality under the law of the United States.* Congress has provided that a person who is a national of the United States by birth or by naturalization shall lose his nationality for a variety of reasons. 8 U.S.C. § 1481. What is the meaning of the statutory phrase "lose his nationality"? In Kennedy v. Mendoza-Martinez, 372 U.S. 144, 160, 83 S.Ct. 554, 563 (1963), the Court said:

> We recognize at the outset that we are confronted here with an issue of the utmost import. Deprivation of citizenship—particularly American citizenship, which is "one of the most valuable rights in the world today," Report of the President's Commission on Immigration and Naturalization (1953), 235—has grave practical consequences. An expatriate who, like Cort, had no other nationality becomes a stateless person—a person who not only has no rights as an American citizen, but no membership in any national entity whatsoever. "Such individuals as do not possess any nationality enjoy, in general, no protection whatever, and if they are aggrieved by a State they have no means of redress, since there is no State which is competent to take up

their case. As far as the Law of Nations is concerned, there is, apart from restraints of morality or obligations expressly laid down by treaty * * * no restriction whatever to cause a State to abstain from maltreating to any extent such stateless individuals." I Oppenheim, International Law (8th ed., Lauterpacht, 1955), § 291, at 640. The calamity is "[n]ot the loss of specific rights, then, but the loss of a community willing and able to guarantee any rights whatsoever * * *." Arendt, The Origins of Totalitarianism (1951), 294.

In holding that denationalization as a punishment is barred by the Eighth Amendment, the court said in Trop v. Dulles, 356 U.S. 86, 101, 78 S.Ct. 590, 598 (1958):

> There may be involved no physical mistreatment, no primitive torture. There is instead the total destruction of the individual's status in organized society. It is a form of punishment more primitive than torture for it destroys for the individual the political existence that was centuries in the development. The punishment strips the citizen of his status in the national and international political community. His very existence is at the sufferance of the country in which he happens to find himself. While any one country may accord him some rights, and presumably as long as he remained in this country he would enjoy the limited rights of an alien, no country need do so because he is stateless. Furthermore, his enjoyment of even the limited rights of an alien might be subject to termination at any time by reason of deportation. In short, the expatriate has lost the right to have rights.

It is not only in Trop v. Dulles, supra, that the denationalization provisions have suffered badly at the hands of the United States Supreme Court. Although in Perez v. Brownell, 356 U.S. 44, 78 S.Ct. 568 (1958), the court had held that it was within Congress' foreign relations power to provide for loss of citizenship by one who votes in a foreign election, this case was overruled in Afroyim v. Rusk, 387 U.S. 253, 87 S.Ct. 1660 (1967). The court held in Vance v. Terrazas, 444 U.S. 252, 100 S.Ct. 540 (1980), that Congress cannot constitutionally deprive a citizen of citizenship without proving intent to renounce it.[a] In the Kennedy case, the court held that the provision for loss of nationality by remaining outside the United States to avoid military service was punitive and could not stand constitutionally because it lacked due process safeguards guaranteed by the Constitution of the United States. And in Schneider v. Rusk, 377 U.S. 163, 84 S. Ct. 1187 (1964), the court struck down the provision for loss of nationality by a naturalized citizen who had continuously resided for three years in the country of his origin.

a. The court was divided on other issues, including the issue of the standard of proof of intent to renounce citizenship. The court permitted a finding of intent based on a preponderance of the evidence rejecting the standard, required by the court of appeals, of clear and convincing evidence.

One of the grounds for loss of nationality is "making a formal renunciation of nationality before a diplomatic or consular officer of the United States in a foreign state." 8 U.S.C. § 1481(a)(6). If a citizen of the United States wishes such a renunciation and seeks return to the United States, can he be excluded? If he is later found in the United States, can be be deported? To what state? See Jolley v. Immigration and Naturalization Service, 441 F.2d 1245 (5th Cir. 1971), cert. denied 404 U.S. 946, 92 S.Ct. 302 (1971).

SECTION B.   INTERNATIONAL CRITERIA FOR STATE PROTECTION

NOTTEBOHM CASE (LIECHTENSTEIN v. GUATEMALA)

International Court of Justice, 1955.
[1955] I.C.J.Rep. 4.

By the Application filed on December 17th, 1951, the Government of Liechtenstein instituted proceedings before the Court in which it claimed restitution and compensation on the ground that the Government of Guatemala had "acted towards the person and property of Mr. Friedrich Nottebohm, a citizen of Liechtenstein, in a manner contrary to international law". In its Counter-Memorial, the Government of Guatemala contended that this claim was inadmissible on a number of grounds, and one of its objections to the admissibility of the claim related to the nationality of the person for whose protection Liechtenstein had seised the Court.

It appears to the Court that this plea in bar is of fundamental importance and that it is therefore desirable to consider it at the outset.

Guatemala has referred to a well-established principle of international law, which it expressed in Counter-Memorial, where it is stated that "it is the bond of nationality between the State and the individual which alone confers upon the State the right of diplomatic protection". * * *

Liechtenstein considers itself to be acting in conformity with this principle and contends that Nottebohm is its national by virtue of the naturalization conferred upon him.

Nottebohm was born at Hamburg on September 16th, 1881. He was German by birth, and still possessed German nationality when, in October 1939, he applied for naturalization in Liechtenstein.

In 1905 he went to Guatemala. He took up residence there and made that country the headquarters of his business activities, which increased and prospered; these activities developed in the field of commerce, banking and plantations. Having been an employee in the firm of Nottebohm Hermanos, which had been founded by his brothers Juan and Arturo, he became their partner in 1912 and later, in

1937, he was made head of the firm. After 1905 he sometimes went to Germany on business and to other countries for holidays. He continued to have business connections in Germany. He paid a few visits to a brother who had lived in Liechtenstein since 1931. Some of his other brothers, relatives and friends were in Germany, others in Guatemala. He himself continued to have his fixed abode in Guatemala until 1943, that is to say, until the occurrence of the events which constitute the basis of the present dispute.

In 1939, after having provided for the safeguarding of his interests in Guatemala by a power of attorney given to the firm of Nottebohm Hermanos on March 22nd, he left that country at a date fixed by Counsel for Liechtenstein as at approximately the end of March or the beginning of April, when he seems to have gone to Hamburg, and later to have paid a few brief visits to Vaduz where he was at the beginning of October 1939. It was then, on October 9th, a little more than a month after the opening of the second World War marked by Germany's attack on Poland, that his attorney, Dr. Marxer, submitted an application for naturalization on behalf of Nottebohm.

The Liechtenstein Law of January 4th, 1934, lays down the conditions for the naturalization of foreigners, specifies the supporting documents to be submitted and the undertakings to be given and defines the competent organs for giving a decision and the procedure to be followed. The Law specifies certain mandatory requirements, namely, that the applicant for naturalization should prove: (1) "that the acceptance into the Home Corporation (Heimatverband) of a Liechtenstein commune has been promised to him in case of acquisition of the nationality of the State"; (2) that he will lose his former nationality as a result of naturalization, although this requirement may be waived under stated conditions. It further makes naturalization conditional upon compliance with the requirement of residence for at least three years in the territory of the Principality, although it is provided that "this requirement can be dispensed with in circumstances deserving special consideration and by way of exception". In addition, the applicant for naturalization is required to submit a number of documents, such as evidence of his residence in the territory of the Principality, a certificate of good conduct issued by the competent authority of the place of residence, documents relating to his property and income and, if he is not a resident in the Principality, proof that he has concluded an agreement with the Revenue authorities, "subsequent to the revenue commission of the presumptive home commune having been heard". The Law further provides for the payment by the applicant of a naturalization fee, which is fixed by the Princely Government and amounts to at least one half of the sum payable by the applicant for reception into the Home Corporation of a Liechtenstein commune, the promise of such reception constituting a condition under the Law for the grant of naturalization.

* * *

As to the consideration of the application by the competent organs and the procedure to be followed by them, the Law provides that the Government, after having examined the application and the documents pertaining thereto, and after having obtained satisfactory information concerning the applicant, shall submit the application to the Diet. If the latter approves the application, the Government shall submit the requisite request to the Prince, who alone is entitled to confer nationality of the Principality.

* * *

This was the legal position with regard to applications for naturalization at the time when Nottebohm's application was submitted.

On October 9th, 1939, Nottebohm, "resident in Guatemala since 1905 (at present residing as a visitor with his brother, Hermann Nottebohm, in Vaduz)", applied for admission as a national of Liechtenstein and, at the same time, for the previous conferment of citizenship in the Commune of Mauren. He sought dispensation from the condition of three years' residence as prescribed by law, without indicating the special circumstances warranting such waiver. He submitted a statement of the Crédit Suisse in Zurich concerning his assets, and undertook to pay 25,000 Swiss francs to the Commune of Mauren, 12,500 Swiss francs to the State, to which was to be added the payment of dues in connection with the proceedings. He further stated that he had made "arrangements with the Revenue Authorities of the Government of Liechtenstein for the conclusion of a formal agreement to the effect that he will pay an annual tax of naturalization amounting to Swiss francs 1,000, of which Swiss francs 600 are payable to the Commune of Mauren and Swiss francs 400 are payable to the Principality of Liechtenstein, subject to the proviso that the payments of these taxes will be set off against ordinary taxes which will fall due if the applicant takes up residence in one of the Communes of the Principality". He further undertook to deposit as security a sum of 30,000 Swiss francs. He also gave certain general information as to his financial position and indicated that he would never become a burden to the Commune whose citizenship he was seeking.

* * *

A document dated October 15th, 1939, certifies that on that date the Commune of Mauren conferred the privilege of its citizenship upon Mr. Nottebohm and requested the Government to transmit it to the Diet for approval. A certificate of October 17th, 1939, evidences the payment of the taxes required to be paid by Mr. Nottebohm. On October 20th, 1939, Mr. Nottebohm took the oath of allegiance and a final arrangement concerning liability to taxation was concluded on October 23rd.

This was the procedure followed in the case of the naturalization of Nottebohm.

A certificate of nationality has also been produced, signed on behalf of the Government of the Principality and dated October 20th, 1939, to the effect that Nottebohm was naturalized by Supreme Resolution of the Reigning Prince dated October 13th, 1939.

Having obtained a Liechtenstein passport, Nottebohm had it visa-ed by the Consul General of Guatemala in Zurich on December 1st, 1939, and returned to Guatemala at the beginning of 1940, where he resumed his former business activities and in particular the management of the firm of Nottebohm Hermanos.

* * * Liechtenstein requests the Court to find and declare, first, "that the naturalization of Mr. Frederic Nottebohm in Liechtenstein on October 13th, 1939, was not contrary to international law", and, secondly, "that Liechtenstein's claim on behalf of Mr. Nottebohm as a national of Liechtenstein is admissible before the Court".

The Final Conclusions of Guatemala, on the other hand, request the Court "to declare that the claim of the Principality of Liechtenstein is inadmissible", and set forth a number of grounds relating to the nationality of Liechtenstein granted to Nottebohm by naturalization.

Thus, the real issue before the Court is the admissibility of the claim of Liechtenstein in respect of Nottebohm. Liechtenstein's first submission referred to above is a reason advanced for a decision by the Court in favour of Liechtenstein, while the several grounds given by Guatemala on the question of nationality are intended as reasons for the inadmissibility of Liechtenstein's claim. The present task of the Court is limited to adjudicating upon the admissibility of the claim of Liechtenstein in respect of Nottebohm on the basis of such reasons as it may itself consider relevant and proper.

In order to decide upon the admissibility of the Application, the Court must ascertain whether the nationality conferred on Nottebohm by Liechtenstein by means of a naturalization which took place in the circumstances which have been described, can be validly invoked as against Guatemala, whether it bestows upon Liechtenstein a sufficient title to the exercise of protection in respect of Nottebohm as against Guatemala and therefore entitles it to seise the Court of a claim relating to him. In this connection, Counsel for Liechtenstein said: "the essential question is whether Mr. Nottebohm, having acquired the nationality of Liechtenstein, that acquisition of nationality is one which must be recognized by other States". This formulation is accurate, subject to the twofold reservation that, in the first place, what is involved is not recognition for all purposes but merely for the purposes of the admissibility of the Application, and, secondly, that what is involved is not recognition by all States but only by Guatemala.

The Court does not propose to go beyond the limited scope of the question which it has to decide, namely whether the nationality conferred on Nottebohm can be relied upon as against Guatemala in justification of the proceedings instituted before the Court. It must decide this question on the basis of international law; to do so is consistent with the nature of the question and with the nature of the Court's own function.

          * * *

Since no proof has been adduced that Guatemala has recognized the title to the exercise of protection relied upon by Liechtenstein as being derived from the naturalization which it granted to Nottebohm, the Court must consider whether such an act of granting nationality by Liechtenstein directly entails an obligation on the part of Guatemala to recognize its effect, namely, Liechtenstein's right to exercise its protection. In other words, it must be determined whether that unilateral act by Liechtenstein is one which can be relied upon against Guatemala in regard to the exercise of protection. The Court will deal with this question without considering that of the validity of Nottebohm's naturalization according to the law of Liechtenstein.

It is for Liechtenstein, as it is for every sovereign State, to settle by its own legislation the rules relating to the acquisition of its nationality, and to confer that nationality by naturalization granted by its own organs in accordance with that legislation. It is not necessary to determine whether international law imposes any limitations on its freedom of decision in this domain. Furthermore, nationality has its most immediate, its most far-reaching and, for most people, its only effects within the legal system of the State conferring it. Nationality serves above all to determine that the person upon whom it is conferred enjoys the rights and is bound by the obligations which the law of the State in question grants to or imposes on its nationals. This is implied in the wider concept that nationality is within the domestic jurisdiction of the State.

But the issue which the Court must decide is not one which pertains to the legal system of Liechtenstein. It does not depend on the law or on the decision of Liechtenstein whether that State is entitled to exercise its protection, in the case under consideration. To exercise protection, to apply to the Court, is to place oneself on the plane of international law. It is international law which determines whether a State is entitled to exercise protection and to seise the Court.

The naturalization of Nottebohm was an act performed by Liechtenstein in the exercise of its domestic jurisdiction. The question to be decided is whether that act has the international effect here under consideration.

*　*　*

*　*　* International arbitrators, having before them allegations of nationality by the applicant State which were contested by the respondent State, have sought to ascertain whether nationality had been conferred by the applicant State in circumstances such as to give rise to an obligation on the part of the respondent State to recognize the effect of that nationality. In order to decide this question arbitrators have evolved certain principles for determining whether full international effect was to be attributed to the nationality invoked. The same issue is now before the Court: it must be resolved by applying the same principles.

The courts of third States, when confronted by a similar situation, have dealt with it in the same way. They have done so not in connection with the exercise of protection, which did not arise before them, but where two different nationalities have been invoked before them they have had, not indeed to decide such a dispute as between the two States concerned, but to determine whether a given foreign nationality which had been invoked before them was one which they ought to recognize.

International arbitrators have decided in the same way numerous cases of dual nationality, where the question arose with regard to the exercise of protection. They have given their preference to the real and effective nationality, that which accorded with the facts, that based on stronger factual ties between the person concerned and one of the States whose nationality is involved. Different factors are taken into consideration, and their importance will vary from one case to the next: the habitual residence of the individual concerned is an important factor, but there are other factors such as the centre of his interests, his family ties, his participation in public life, attachment shown by him for a given country and inculcated in his children, etc.

Similarly, the courts of third States, when they have before them an individual whom two other States hold to be their national, seek to resolve the conflict by having recourse to international criteria and their prevailing tendency is to prefer the real and effective nationality.

The same tendency prevails in the writings of publicists and in practice. This notion is inherent in the provisions of Article 3, paragraph 2, of the Statute of the Court. National laws reflect this tendency when, inter alia, they make naturalization dependent on conditions indicating the existence of a link, which may vary in their purpose or in their nature but which are essentially concerned with this idea. The Liechtenstein Law of January 4th, 1934, is a good example.

The practice of certain States which refrain from exercising protection in favour of a naturalized person when the latter has in fact, by his prolonged absence, severed his links with what is no longer for him anything but his nominal country, manifests the view of these States that, in order to be capable of being invoked against another State, nationality must correspond with the factual situation. * * *

The character thus recognized on the international level as pertaining to nationality is in no way inconsistent with the fact that international law leaves it to each State to lay down the rules governing the grant of its own nationality. The reason for this is that the diversity of demographic conditions has thus far made it impossible for any general agreement to be reached on the rules relating to nationality, although the latter by its very nature affects international relations. It has been considered that the best way of making such rules accord with the varying demographic conditions in different countries is to leave the fixing of such rules to the competence of each State. On the other hand, a State cannot claim that the rules it has thus laid down are entitled to recognition by another State unless it has acted in conformity with this general aim of making the legal bond of nationality accord with the individual's genuine connection with the State which assumes the defence of its citizens by means of protection as against other States.

The requirement that such a concordance must exist is to be found in the studies carried on in the course of the last thirty years upon the initiative and under the auspices of the League of Nations and the United Nations. * * *

According to the practice of States, to arbitral and judicial decisions and to the opinions of writers, nationality is a legal bond having as its basis a social fact of attachment, a genuine connection of existence, interests and sentiments, together with the existence of reciprocal rights and duties. It may be said to constitute the juridical expression of the fact that the individual upon whom it is conferred, either directly by the law or as the result of an act of the authorities, is in fact more closely connected with the population of the State conferring nationality than with that of any other State. Conferred by a State, it only entitles that State to exercise protection vis-à-vis another State, if it constitutes a translation into juridical terms of the individual's connection with the State which has made him its national.

Diplomatic protection and protection by means of international judicial proceedings constitute measures for the defence of the rights of the State. As the Permanent Court of International Justice has said and has repeated, "by taking up the case of one of its subjects and by resorting to diplomatic action or international judicial proceedings on his behalf, a State is in reality asserting its own rights —its right to ensure, in the person of its subjects, respect for the rules of international law" (P.C.I.J., Series A, No. 2, p. 12, and Series A/B, Nos. 20–21, p. 17).

Since this is the character which nationality must present when it is invoked to furnish the State which has granted it with a title to the exercise of protection and to the institution of international judicial proceedings, the Court must ascertain whether the nationality granted to Nottebohm by means of naturalization is of this character or, in other words, whether the factual connection between Nottebohm and Liechtenstein in the period preceding, contemporaneous with and following his naturalization appears to be sufficiently close, so preponderant in relation to any connection which may have existed between him and any other State, that it is possible to regard the nationality conferred upon him as real and effective, as the exact juridical expression of a social fact of a connection which existed previously or came into existence thereafter.

Naturalization is not a matter to be taken lightly. To seek and to obtain it is not something that happens frequently in the life of a human being. It involves his breaking of a bond of allegiance and his establishment of a new bond of allegiance. It may have far-reaching consequences and involve profound changes in the destiny of the individual who obtains it. It concerns him personally, and to consider it only from the point of view of its repercussions with regard to his property would be to misunderstand its profound significance. In order to appraise its international effect, it is impossible to disregard the circumstances in which it was conferred, the serious character which attaches to it, the real and effective, and not merely the verbal preference of the individual seeking it for the country which grants it to him.

At the time of his naturalization does Nottebohm appear to have been more closely attached by his tradition, his establishment, his interests, his activities, his family ties, his intentions for the near future to Liechtenstein than to any other State?

* * *

The essential facts are as follows: At the date when he applied for naturalization Nottebohm had been a German national from the time of his birth. He had always retained his connections with members of his family who had remained in Germany and he had always had business connections with that country. His country had been at war for more than a month, and there is nothing to indicate that the application for naturalization then made by Nottebohm was motivated by any desire to dissociate himself from the Government of his country.

He had been settled in Guatemala for 34 years. He had carried on his activities there. It was the main seat of his interests. He returned there shortly after his naturalization, and it remained the centre of his interests and of his business activities. He stayed there until his removal as a result of war measures in 1943. He subsequently attempted to return there, and he now complains of Guatemala's refusal to admit him. There, too, were several members of his family who sought to safeguard his interests.

In contrast, his actual connections with Liechtenstein were extremely tenuous. No settled abode, no prolonged residence in that country at the time of his application for naturalization: the application indicates that he was paying a visit there and confirms the transient character of this visit by its request that the naturalization proceedings should be initiated and concluded without delay. No intention of settling there was shown at that time or realized in the ensuing weeks, months or years—on the contrary, he returned to Guatemala very shortly after his naturalization and showed every intention of remaining there. If Nottebohm went to Liechtenstein in 1946, this was because of the refusal of Guatemala to admit him. No indication is given of the grounds warranting the waiver of the condition of residence, required by the 1934 Nationality Law, which waiver was implicitly granted to him. There is no allegation of any economic interests or of any activities exercised or to be exercised in Liechtenstein, and no manifestation of any intention whatsoever to transfer all or some of his interests and his business activities to Liechtenstein. It is unnecessary in this connection to attribute much importance to the promise to pay the taxes levied at the time of his naturalization. The only links to be discovered between the Principality and Nottebohm are the short sojourns already referred to and the presence in Vaduz of one of his brothers: but his brother's presence is referred to in his application for naturalization only as a reference to his good conduct. Furthermore, other members of his family have asserted Nottebohm's desire to spend his old age in Guatemala.

These facts clearly establish, on the one hand, the absence of any bond of attachment between Nottebohm and Liechtenstein and, on the other hand, the existence of a long-standing and close connection between him and Guatemala, a link which his naturalization in no way weakened. That naturalization was not based on any real prior connection with Liechtenstein, nor did it in any way alter the manner of life of the person upon whom it was conferred in exceptional circumstances of speed and accommodation. In both respects, it was lacking in the genuineness requisite to an act of such importance, if it is to be entitled to be respected by a State in the position of Guatemala. It was granted without regard to the concept of nationality adopted in international relations.

Naturalization was asked for not so much for the purpose of obtaining a legal recognition of Nottebohm's membership in fact in the population of Liechtenstein, as it was to enable him to substitute for his status as a national of a belligerent State that of a national of a neutral State, with the sole aim of thus coming within the protection of Liechtenstein but not of becoming wedded to its traditions, its interests, its way of life or of assuming the obligations—other than fiscal obligations—and exercising the rights pertaining to the status thus acquired.

Guatemala is under no obligation to recognize a nationality granted in such circumstances. Liechtenstein consequently is not entitled to extend its protection to Nottebohm vis-á-vis Guatemala and its claim must, for this reason, be held to be inadmissible.

The Court is not therefore called upon to deal with the other pleas in bar put forward by Guatemala or the Conclusions of the Parties other than those on which it is adjudicating in accordance with the reasons indicated above.

For these reasons, The COURT, by eleven votes to three,

Holds that the claim submitted by the Government of the Principality of Liechtenstein is inadmissible.

*   *   *

Judges KLAESTAD and READ, and M. GUGGENHEIM, Judge ad hoc, have availed themselves of the right conferred on them by Article 57 of the Statute and have appended to the Judgment statements of their dissenting opinion.

[Dissenting opinions omitted.]

1. *Earlier adjudication in the Permanent Court of International Justice.* In its Advisory Opinion on Nationality Decrees in Tunis and Morocco (France and Great Britain), 1923, P.C.I.J., Ser. B, No. 4, the court was asked whether a dispute between France and Great Britain as to nationality decrees in Tunis and Morocco was or was not, by international law, solely a matter of domestic jurisdiction under Article 15, paragraph 8, of the Covenant of the League of Nations. Apparently on the ground that the relations between France and Great Britain and their protectorates were determined by international agreements and that "it will be necessary to resort to international law in order to decide what the value of an agreement of this kind may be as regards third States," the court expressed the opinion that the dispute was not, by international law, solely a matter of domestic jurisdiction. But for the existence of the agreements, however, the court presumably would not have taken jurisdiction:

> The question whether a certain matter is or is not solely within the jurisdiction of a State is an essentially relative question; it depends upon the development of international relations. Thus, in the present state of international law, questions of nationality are, in the opinion of the Court, in principle within this reserved domain. (at 24)

2. *How far does Nottebohm reach?* Liechtenstein's claim was asserted against a state, Guatemala, with which Nottebohm had, in the language of the court, "a long-standing and close connection," "a link which his naturalization in no way weakened."

a. The opinion reveals that Nottebohm had been sent by Guatemala to the United States for internment during World War II. Suppose that the United States had injured Nottebohm by seizing and retaining, without compensation, property he had removed to a bank in the United States. Liechtenstein now brings an action against the United States in the International Court of Justice; the United States asks the court to declare the claim inadmissible on the grounds that Liechtenstein has no standing. How should the court rule? See Flegenheimer Case, XIV Rep. of Int'l Arb. Awards 327 (Italian-United States Conciliation Commission, 1958), p. 515 of this chapter.

b. Refer to the *Hanna* case, p. 489. Suppose that Hanna has resided in Canada for a period of twenty years, is married there, raises a family and conducts a business. As a result of the international operation of his business, he accumulates large sums of money in a bank in State X. State X expropriates his bank account without compensation. Although he has not been declared a national by Canada, Canada espouses his claim against State X and eventually brings an action against State X in the International Court of Justice. State X asks the court to declare the claim inadmissible on the ground that Hanna is not Canada's national. How should the court rule?

If Canada has in fact accorded Hanna its protection domestically over the years, and if in fact he has established a close link or tie with Canada, with its acquiescence, is the formal grant of nationality by Canada necessary? See Leigh, Nationality and Diplomatic Protection, 20 Int'l. & Comp.L. 453 (1971). What interest does State X have in Canada's according Hanna formal nationality?

c. If a stateless person is able to persuade *any* state to espouse his claim against a wrongdoing state with which he has previously had no link, why should that state not be permitted to claim on his behalf in the court?

d. Suppose a national of Czechoslovakia is kidnapped by Soviet agents and subjected to inhumane treatment in a USSR prison. His efforts from prison to enlist the aid of the Czechoslovakian government are in vain. At his request, communicated to the United States government, the United States brings an action against the USSR in the International Court of Justice. The USSR asks the court to declare the claim inadmissible on the ground that he is not a national of the United States. How should the court rule?

3. *Continuity of nationality of individual claimant.*

a. Oppenheim

A State which puts forward a claim before a claims commission or other international tribunal must be in a position to show that it has locus standi for that purpose. The principal, and almost the exclusive, factor creating that locus standi is the nationality of the claimant, and it may be stated as a general principle that from the time of the occurrence of the injury until the making of the award the claim must continuously and without interruption have belonged to a person or to a series of persons (a) having the nationality of the State by whom it is put forward, and (b) not having the nationality of the State against whom it is put forward. International Law 347 (8th ed. 1955) (Vol. I).*

b. Judge Van Eysinga

Those who maintain that this is a hard and fast rule rely mainly on the jurisprudence of the Claims Commissions (Mixed Commissions) * * *.

The Mixed Commissions are set up by treaty when, especially after stormy events such as a revolution or civil war, a great number of the nationals of both parties to the treaty have suffered injury. A desire to liquidate all these claims leads the two parties to refer them by treaty to a commission set up especially to deal with them. Accordingly the commission is a special tribunal for certain groups of the nationals of both sides, and it is obvious that such treaties have in view only the nationals of the two parties who have suffered injury but not non-nationals, who may be in the same situation and who, in order to take advantage of the existence of the commission, get themselves naturalized, or nationals who may have bought the claims of non-nationals. In the domain of treaties setting up Mixed Commis-

---

* Reprinted by permission of David   and Longmans, Green & Co., Ltd.,
McKay & Company, Inc., New York,   London.

sions, the rule relied on by the Lithuanian Agent is perfectly comprehensible and perhaps in this sphere it is possible to speak of a rule of international law in the sense that, in the absence of a definite treaty provision, it must be observed by the Mixed Commissions. Panevezys-Saldutiskis Railway Case (Estonia v. Lithuania), 1939, P.C.I.J., Ser. A/B, No. 76, at 33.

c. Schwarzenberger

International judicial practice interprets this test so strictly as to demand the continuity of nationality from the time of the injury (dies a quo) until the date of judgment (dies ad quem). If protection of the individual were the ratio legis behind the rule on the continuity of nationality, the hardships resulting from this rule would lay it open to serious objections. For instance, if, before the award is delivered, the claimant dies and his heirs have a different nationality, the claim lapses. Yet, in fact, the rule serves a completely different purpose. It is to limit intervention in the domestic affairs of other States even if, in marginal cases, this object can be attained only at the price of considerable hardship to the individual. A Manual of International Law 176 (5th ed. 1967).

MERGÉ CASE

Italian-United States Conciliation Commission, 1955.
XIV U.N.Rep. Int'l Arb. Awards 236.

I. The Facts

On October 26, 1948, the Embassy of the United States of America in Rome submitted to the Ministry of the Treasury of the Italian Republic on behalf of Mrs. Florence Strunsky Mergé, a national of the United States of America, a claim based upon Article 78 of the Treaty of Peace with Italy for compensation for the loss as a result of the war of a grand piano and other personal property located at Frascati, Italy, and owned by Mrs. Mergé.

As the Italian Ministry of the Treasury had rejected the claim on the grounds that Mrs. Mergé is to be deemed, under Italian law, an Italian national by marriage, the Agent of the United States of America, on August 28, 1950, submitted to this Commission the dispute which had arisen between the two Governments with respect to the claim of Mrs. Mergé.

* * *

The following facts relating to the two nationalities, Italian and United States, possessed by Mrs. Mergé are revealed by the record:

Florence Strunsky was born in New York City on April 7, 1909, thereby acquiring United States nationality according to the law of the United States.

On December 21, 1933, at the age of 24, Florence Strunsky married Salvatore Mergé in Rome, Italy. As Mr. Mergé is an Italian national, Florence Strunsky acquired Italian nationality by operation of Italian law.

The United States Department of State issued a passport to Mrs. Mergé, then Miss Strunsky, on March 17, 1931. This passport was renewed on July 11, 1933, to be valid until March 16, 1935.

Mrs. Mergé lived with her husband in Italy during the four years following her marriage until 1937. Her husband was an employee of the Italian Government, working as an interpreter and translator of the Japanese language in the Ministry of Communications. In 1937 he was sent to the Italian Embassy at Tokyo as a translator and interpreter.

Mrs. Mergé accompanied her husband to Tokyo, travelling on Italian passport No. 681688, issued on August 27, 1937 by the Ministry of Foreign Affairs in Rome. The passport was of the type issued by the Italian Government to employees and their families bound for foreign posts.

After her arrival in Japan, Mrs. Mergé on February 21, 1940 was registered, at her request, as a national of the United States at the American Consulate General at Tokyo.

Mrs. Mergé states that, when hostilities ceased between Japan and the United States of America, she refused to be returned to the United States by the United States military authorities, having preferred to remain with her husband.

On December 10, 1948, the American Consulate at Yokohama issued an American passport to Mrs. Mergé, valid only for travel to the United States, with which she travelled to the United States. She remained in the United States for nine months, from December, 1946, until September, 1947. The American passport issued to her at Yokohama and valid originally only for travel to the United States, was validated for travel to Italy, and the Italian Consulate General at New York, on July 31, 1947, granted Mrs. Mergé a visa for Italy as a visitor, valid for three months.

On September 19, 1947, Mrs. Mergé arrived in Italy where she has since resided with her husband.

Immediately after returning to Italy, on October 8, 1947, Mrs. Mergé registered as a United States national at the Consular Section of the American Embassy in Rome. On October 16, 1947, Mrs. Mergé executed an affidavit before an American consular officer at the American Embassy in Rome for the purpose of explaining her protracted residence outside of the United States. In that affidavit she lists her mother and father as her only ties with the United States, and states that she does not pay income taxes to the Government of the United States.

On September 11, 1950, Mrs. Mergé requested and was granted by the Consular Section of the American Embassy at Rome a new American passport to replace the one which had been issued to her on December 10, 1946, by the American Consulate at Yokohama and which had expired. In her application for the new American passport, Mrs. Mergé states that her "legal residence" is at New York, New York, and that she intends to return to the United States to reside permanently at some indefinite time in the future.

So far as the record indicates, Mrs. Mergé is still residing with her husband in Italy.

II. The Issue

It is not disputed between the Parties that the claimant possesses both nationalities. The issue is not one of choosing one of the two, but rather one of deciding whether in such case the Government of the United States may exercise before the Conciliation Commission the rights granted by the Treaty of Peace with reference to the property in Italy of United Nations nationals (Articles 78 and 83).

* * *

(1). Position of the Government of the United States of America:

(a) The Treaty of Peace between the United Nations and Italy provides the rules necessary to a solution of the case. The first subparagraph of paragraph 9(a) of Article 78 states:

> "United Nations nationals" means individuals who are nationals of any of the United Nations, or corporations or associations organized under the laws of any of the United Nations, at the coming into force of the present Treaty, provided that the said individuals, corporations or associations also had this status on September 3, 1943, the date of the Armistice with Italy.

All United Nations nationals are therefore entitled to claim, and it is irrelevant for such purpose that they possess or have possessed Italian nationality as well.

* * *

(c) The principle, according to which one State cannot afford diplomatic protection to one of its nationals against a State whose nationality such person also possesses, cannot be applied to the Treaty of Peace with Italy because such principle is based on the equal sovereignty of States, whereas this Treaty of Peace was not negotiated between equal Powers but between the United Nations and Italy, a State defeated and obliged to accept the clauses imposed by the victors who at that time did not consider Italy a sovereign State.

(2). Position of the Italian Government:

* * *

(b) A defeated State, even when it is obliged to undergo the imposition of the conqueror, continues to be a sovereign State. From the juridical point of view, the Treaty of Peace is an international convention, not a unilateral act. In cases of doubt, its interpretation must be that more favourable to the debtor.

(c) There exists a principle of international law, universally recognized and constantly applied, by virtue of which diplomatic protection cannot be exercised in cases of dual nationality when the claimant possesses also the nationality of the State against which the claim is being made.

* * *

V.   Considerations of law

(1).   The rules of the Hague Convention of 1930 and the customary law manifested in international precedents and in the legal writings of the authors attest the existence and the practice of two principles in the problem of diplomatic protection in dual nationality cases.

The first of these, specifically referring to the scope of diplomatic protection, as a question of public international law, is based on the sovereign equality of the States in the matter of nationality and bars protection in behalf of those who are simultaneously also nationals of the defendant State.

The second of the principles had its origin in *private* international law, in those cases, that is, in which the courts of a third State had to resolve a conflict of nationality Laws.   Thus, the principle of effective nationality was created with relation to the individual.   But decisions and legal writings, because of its evident justice, quickly transported it to the sphere of *public* international law.

(2).   It is not a question of adopting one nationality to the exclusion of the other.   Even less when it is recognized by both Parties that the claimant possesses the two nationalities.   The problem to be explained is, simply, that of determining whether diplomatic protection can be exercised in such cases.

(3).   A prior question requires a solution: are the two principles which have just been set forth incompatible with each other, so that the acceptance of one of them necessarily implies the exclusion of the other?   If the reply is in the affirmative, the problem presented is that of a choice; if it is in the negative, one must determine the sphere of application of each one of the two principles.

The Commission is of the opinion that no irreconcilable opposition between the two principles exists; in fact, to the contrary, it believes that they complement each other reciprocally.   The principle according to which a State cannot protect one of its nationals against a State which also considers him its national and the principle of effective, in the sense of dominant, nationality, have both been accepted by the Hague Convention (Articles 4 and 5) and by the International Court of Justice (Advisory Opinion of April 11, 1949 and the Nottebohm Decision of April 6, 1955).   If these two principles were irreconcilable, the acceptance of both by the Hague Convention and by the International Court of Justice would be incomprehensible.

(4).   The International Court of Justice, in its recent decision in the Nottebohm Case, after having said that " * * * international law leaves to each State to lay down the rules governing the grant of its own nationality", adds: "On the other hand, a State cannot claim that the rules it has thus laid down are entitled to recognition by another State unless it has acted in conformity with this general aim of making the legal bond of nationality accord with the individual's genuine connexion with the State which assumes the defence of its citizens by means of protection as against other States.   *   *   * Conferred by a State, it only entitles that State to exercise protection vis-à-vis another State, if it constitutes a translation into juridical terms of the individual's connexion with the State which has made him its national."   (Judgment of April 6, 1955, p. 23.)

For even greater reason, this theory must be understood to be applicable to the problem of dual nationality which concerns the two contesting States, in view of the fact that in such case effective nationality does not mean only the existence of a real bond, but means also the prevalence of that nationality over the other, by virtue of facts which exist in the case.

(5).   The principle, based on the sovereign equality of States, which excludes diplomatic protection in the case of dual nationality, must yield before the principle of effective nationality whenever such nationality is that of the claiming State.   But it must not yield when such predominance is not proved because the first of these two principles is generally recognized and may constitute a criterion of practical application for the elimination of any possible uncertainty.

(6).   *   *   *   In view of the principles accepted, it is considered that the Government of the United States of America shall be entitled to protect its nationals before this Commission in cases of dual nationality, United States and Italian, whenever the United States nationality is the effective nationality.

In order to establish the prevalence of the United States nationality in individual cases, habitual residence can be one of the criteria of evaluation, but not the only one.   The conduct of the individual in his economic, social, political, civic and family life, as well as the closer and more effective bond with one of the two States must also be considered.

(7).   It is considered that in this connexion the following principles may serve as guides:

(a) The United States nationality shall be prevalent in cases of children born in the United States of an Italian father and who have habitually lived there.

(b) The United States nationality shall also be prevalent in cases involving Italians who, after having acquired United States nationality by naturalization and having thus lost Italian nationality, have reacquired their nationality of origin as a matter of law as a result of having sojourned in Italy for more than two years, without the intention of retransferring their residence permanently to Italy.

(c) With respect to cases of dual nationality involving American women married to Italian nationals, the United States nationality shall be prevalent in cases in which the family has had habitual residence in the United States and the interests and the permanent professional life of the head of the family were established in the United States.

(d) In case of dissolution of marriage, if the family was established in Italy and the widow transfers her residence to the United States of America, whether or not the new residence is of an habitual nature must be evaluated, case by case, bearing in mind also the widow's conduct, especially with regard to the raising of her children, for the purpose of deciding which is the prevalent nationality.

(8). United States nationals who did not possess Italian nationality but the nationality of a third State can be considered "United Nations nationals" under the Treaty, even if their prevalent nationality was the nationality of the third State.

(9). In all other cases of dual nationality, Italian and United States, when, that is, the United States nationality is not prevalent in accordance with the above, the principle of international law, according to which a claim is not admissible against a State, Italy in our case, when this State also considers the claimant as its national and such bestowal of nationality is, as in the case of Italian law, in harmony (Article I of the Hague Convention of 1930) with international custom and generally recognized principles of law in the matter of nationality, will reacquire its force.

VI. Decision

Examining the facts of the case in bar, in the light of the aforementioned criteria, especially paragraph 6, in relation to paragraph 7(c), the Commission holds that Mrs. Mergé can in no way be considered to be dominantly a United States national within the meaning of Article 78 of the Treaty of Peace, because the family did not have its habitual residence in the United States and the interests and the permanent professional life of the head of the family were not established there. In fact, Mrs. Mergé has not lived in the United States since her marriage, she used an Italian passport in travelling to Japan from Italy in 1937, she stayed in Japan from 1937 until 1946 with her husband, an official of the Italian Embassy in Tokyo, and it does not appear that she was ever interned as a national of a country enemy to Japan.

Inasmuch as Mrs. Mergé, for the foregoing reasons, cannot be considered to be dominantly a United States national within the meaning of Article 78 of the Treaty of Peace, the Commission is of the opinion that the Government of the United States of America is not entitled to present a claim against the Italian Government in her behalf.

* * *

Effective nationality. Number (8) of the commission's Considerations of Law was further amplified in its 1958 decision in the Flegenheimer Case, Italian-United States Conciliation Commission, XIV

Rep. of Int'l Arb.Awards 327. Flegenheimer's claim (for cancellation of a sale of stock made under duress) depended upon his being a United States national. The commission found that he had lost his United States nationality upon acquiring German nationality in 1894 (and that this German nationality had been lost in 1940, so that he became stateless). Therefore, the claim was dismissed.

It had been argued by Italy, however, that because of close ties between Flegenheimer and Germany during the long period from 1894 until 1940 when he was a German national, "Italy therefore considers that no effective bond of nationality exists between the United States and Albert Flegenheimer, even if it were to be admitted that he was an American national on purely legal and nominal grounds." Thus, "the United States is not entitled to exercise, in his behalf, the right of diplomatic protection, nor can they resort to the commission to plead his case." (at 375) The commission's opinion further stated:

> The Commission is of the opinion that it is doubtful that the International Court of Justice intended to establish a rule of general international law in requiring, in the Nottebohm Case, that there must exist an effective link between the person and the State in order that the latter may exercise its right of diplomatic protection in behalf of the former. * * *
>
>   * * *
>
> The theory of effective or active nationality was established, in the Law of Nations, and above all in international private law, for the purpose of settling conflicts between two national States, or two national laws, regarding persons simultaneously vested with both nationalities, in order to decide which of them is to be dominant, whether that described as nominal, based on legal provisions of a given legal system, or that described as effective or active,[a] equally based on legal provisions of another legal system, but confirmed by elements of fact (domicile, participation in the political life, the center of family and business interests, etc.). It must allow one to make a distinction, between two bonds of nationality equally founded in law, which is the stronger and hence the effective one.
>
>   * * *
>
> But when a person is vested with only one nationality, which is attributed to him or her either jure sanguinis or jure soli, or by a valid naturalization entailing the positive loss of the former nationality, the theory of effective nationality cannot be applied without the risk of causing confusion. It lacks a sufficiently positive basis to be applied to a nationality which finds support in a state law. There does not in fact exist any criterion of proven effectiveness for disclosing the effectiveness of a bond

---

a.   See, e. g., Uzan v. Ministère Public, France, Court of Appeal of Paris, 1967, 48 Int'l L.Rep. 162 (1975).

with a political collectivity, and the persons by the thousands who, because of the facility of travel in the modern world, possess the positive legal nationality of a State, but live in foreign States where they are domiciled and where their family and business center is located, would be exposed to nonrecognition, at the international level, of the nationality with which they are undeniably vested by virtue of the laws of their national State, if this doctrine were to be generalized. (at 376–377)

SECTION C. OBLIGATIONS OF NATIONALITY OR ALLEGIANCE

It is not uncommon for a state to apply its law to acts performed by its own nationals beyond the territorial limits of the state.   As stated by Mr. Chief Justice Hughes in Blackmer v. United States, 284 U.S. 421, 436, 52 S.Ct. 252, 254 (1932),

> While it appears that the petitioner removed his residence to France in the year 1924, it is undisputed that he was, and continued to be, a citizen of the United States. He continued to owe allegiance to the United States. By virtue of the obligations of citizenship, the United States retained its authority over him, and he was bound by its laws made applicable to him in a foreign country. Thus although resident abroad, the petitioner remained subject to the taxing power of the United States. For disobedience to its laws through conduct abroad he was subject to punishment in the courts of the United States * * *. With respect to such an exercise of authority, there is no question of international law, but solely of the purport of the municipal law which establishes the duties of the citizen in relation to his own government. * * *

The basis for the rule permitting this reach of a state's law was the subject of speculation by the Mexican Supreme Court in a case involving jurisdiction over an offense committed by a Mexican national in Texas:

> It is well known that it is the federal judge who has jurisdiction notwithstanding that it is the principle of territoriality which fundamentally regulates the special application of the penal law in accordance with Article 4 of the Federal Criminal Code, even though this precept, in its first hypothesis—a crime committed abroad by a Mexican national—admits the principle of personal law. This is so because of the respect due * * * to the ties of allegiance which should bind the subject to his State, or because it is not possible to conceive that a State should be transformed into a safe refuge for its own nationals who have committed crimes outside its frontiers, or because the rule of prosecution is merely a just corollary to the nonextradition of nationals, which is the practice of the majority of countries. Re Gutierrez, 24 Int'l L.Rep. 265, 266 (1961).

Should this reach of a state's laws based upon the relationship of the individual with the state be confined to those who have the state's nationality? The question is posed below in connection with laws relating to (a) the crime of treason, (b) taxation and (c) compulsory military service.

1. THE CRIME OF TREASON

JOYCE v. DIRECTOR OF PUBLIC PROSECUTIONS

England, House of Lords, 1946.
[1946] A.C. 347.*

Appeal from the Court of Criminal Appeal.

The facts, stated by LORD JOWITT, L. C. and LORD PORTER, were as follows: The appellant, William Joyce, was charged at the Central Criminal Court on three counts, upon the third of which only he was convicted. That count was as follows

Statement of offence.

High Treason by adhering to the King's enemies elsewhere than in the King's Realm, to wit, in the German Realm, contrary to the Treason Act, 1351.

Particulars of offence.

William Joyce, on September 18, 1939, and on divers other days thereafter and between that day and July 2, 1940, being then—to wit on the several days—a person owing allegiance to our Lord the King, and whilst on the said several days an open and public war was being prosecuted and carried on by the German Realm and its subjects against our Lord the King and his subjects, then and on the said several days traitorously contriving and intending to aid and assist the said enemies of our Lord the King against our Lord the King and his subjects did traitorously adhere to and aid and comfort the said enemies in parts beyond the seas without the Realm of England to wit, in the Realm of Germany by broadcasting to the subjects of our Lord the King propaganda on behalf of the said enemies of our Lord the King.

*   *   *

The appellant was born in the United States of America, in 1906, the son of a naturalized American citizen who had previously been a British subject by birth. He thereby became himself a natural born American citizen. At about three years of age he was brought to Ireland, where he stayed until about 1921, when he came to England. He stayed in England until 1939. He was then thirty-three years of

---

* Reprinted by permission of the Incorporated Council of Law Reporting of
England and Wales, London.

age. He was brought up and educated within the King's Dominions, and he settled there. On July 4, 1933, he applied for a British passport, describing himself as a British subject by birth, born in Galway. He asked for the passport for the purpose of holiday touring in Belgium, France, Germany, Switzerland, Italy and Austria. He was granted the passport for a period of five years. The document was not produced, but its contents were duly proved. In it he was described as a British subject. On September 26, 1938, he applied for a renewal of the passport for a period of one year. He again declared that he was a British subject and had not lost that national status. His application was granted. On August 24, 1939, he again applied for a renewal of his passport for a further period of one year, repeating the same declaration. His application was granted, the passport, as appears from the endorsement on the declaration, being extended to July 1, 1940. On some day after August 24, 1939, the appellant left the realm, his parents, his brothers and his sister remaining in England. The exact date and manner of his departure were not proved. On his arrest in the year 1945 there was found on his person a "work book" issued by the German State on October 4, 1939, from which it appeared that he had been employed by the German radio company of Berlin as an announcer of English news from September 18, 1939. In this document his nationality was stated to be "Great Britain" and his special qualification "English." The passport was not found and nothing further was known of it. It was proved by uncontradicted evidence that he had, between September 3, 1939, and December 10, 1939, broadcast propaganda on behalf of the enemy. He did not give evidence but in a statement made after his arrest in Germany he said (inter alia): "In 1940 I acquired German nationality * * *. As, by reason of my opinions, I was not conscientiously disposed to fight for Britain against Germany, I decided to leave the country * * *. Realizing, however, that at this critical juncture I had declined to serve Britain I drew the logical conclusion that I should have no moral right to return to that country of my own free will and that it would be best to apply for German citizenship and make my home in Germany." After argument on the law, Tucker J. said to counsel for the Crown and for the appellant: "I shall direct the jury on count 3 that on August 24, 1939, when the passport was applied for, the prisoner beyond a shadow of doubt owed allegiance to the Crown of this country and that on the evidence given, if they accept it, nothing happened at the material time thereafter to put an end to the allegiance that he then owed. It will remain for the jury, and for the jury alone, as to whether or not at the relevant dates he adhered to the King's enemies with intent to assist the King's enemies. If both or either of you desire to address the jury on that issue, of course now is your opportunity." Both counsel proceeded to address the jury, the defence submitting that the appellant had not adhered to the King's enemies and the Crown that he had. No other topic was touched on and no argument was addressed to the question whether the appellant still had the passport in his possession and retained it for use or whether he still owed allegiance to the British Crown.   Tucker J. then summed up and the appellant was found guilty on the third count of the indictment, and sentenced to death on September 19, 1945.   An appeal was brought to the Court of Criminal Appeal on the following grounds: "(1.) The court wrongly assumed jurisdiction to try an alien for an offence against British law committed in a foreign country.   (2.) The learned judge was wrong in law in holding, and misdirected the jury in directing them, that the appellant owed allegiance to His Majesty the King during the period from September 18, 1939, to July 2, 1940.   (3.) That there was no evidence that the renewal of the appellant's passport afforded him or was capable of affording him any protection or that the appellant ever availed himself or had any intention of availing himself of any such protection.   *   *   *."   On November 7, 1945, the Court of Criminal Appeal dismissed the appeal.   The Attorney-General certified under s. 1, sub-s. 6, of the Criminal Appeal Act, 1907, that the decision of the Court of Criminal Appeal involved a point of law of exceptional public importance and that in his opinion it was desirable in the public interest that a further appeal should be brought.   The appellant accordingly appealed to the House of Lords.

> *   *   *

December 18, 1945.   LORD JOWITT, L.C.   I have come to the conclusion, in common with the majority of your Lordships, that the appeal should be dismissed.   I should propose to deliver my reasons at a later date.

> *   *   *

February 1, 1946.   Their Lordships delivered their reasons.

LORD JOWITT, L.C.

*   *   *   [I]t is clear that the question for your Lordships' determination is whether an alien who has been resident within the realm can be held guilty and convicted in this country of high treason in respect of acts committed by him outside the realm.   This is in truth a question of law of far-reaching importance.   *   *   *

The House is called upon in the year 1945 to consider the scope and effect of a statute of the year 1351, the twenty-fifth year of the reign of Edward III.   That statute, as has been commonly said and as appears from its terms, was itself declaratory of the common law: *   *   *   "Whereas divers opinions have been before this time in what case treason shall be said and in what not; the King, at the request of the Lords and of the Commons hath made a declaration in the manner as hereafter followeth, that is to say:"   [amongst other things] "if a man do levy war against our Lord the King in his realm, or be adherent to the King's enemies in his realm, giving them aid and comfort in the realm, or elsewhere" then (I depart from the text and use modern terms) he shall be guilty of treason.   It is not denied that the appellant has adhered to the King's enemies giving them aid and comfort elsewhere than in the realm.   Upon this part of the case the single question is whether, having done so, he can be and in the circumstances of the case is guilty of treason. Your Lordships will observe that the statute is wide enough in its terms to cover any man anywhere, "if a man do levy war," etc. Yet it is clear that some limitation must be placed upon the generality of the language, for the context in the preamble poses the question "in what case treason shall be said and in what not." It is necessary then to prove not only that an act was done but that, being done, it was a treasonable act. This must depend upon one thing only, namely the relation in which the actor stands to the King to whose enemies he adheres. An act that is in one man treasonable, may not be so in another. In the long discussion which your Lordships have heard upon this part of the case attention has necessarily been concentrated on the question of allegiance. The question whether a man can be guilty of treason to the King has been treated as identical with the question whether he owes allegiance to the King. An act, it is said, which is treasonable if the actor owes allegiance, is not treasonable if he does not. As a generalization, this is undoubtedly true and is supported by the language of the indictment but it leaves undecided the question by whom allegiance is owed * * *.

        * * * Allegiance is owed to their sovereign Lord the King by his natural born subjects; so it is by those who, being aliens, become his subjects by denization or naturalization (I will call them all "naturalized subjects"); so it is by those who, being aliens, reside within the King's realm. Whether you look to the feudal law for the origin of this conception or find it in the elementary necessities of any political society, it is clear that fundamentally it recognizes the need of the man for protection and of the sovereign lord for service. * * * The natural-born subject owes allegiance from his birth, the naturalized subject from his naturalization, the alien from the day when he comes within the realm. By what means and when can they cast off allegiance? The natural-born subject cannot at common law at any time cast it off. * * * Nor can the naturalized subjects at common law. It is in regard to the alien resident within the realm that the controversy in this case arises. Admittedly he owes allegiance while he is so resident, but it is argued that his allegiance extends no further. Numerous authorities were cited by the learned counsel for the appellant in which it is stated without any qualification or extension that an alien owes allegiance so long as he is within the realm and it has been argued with great force that the physical presence of the alien actor within the realm is necessary to make his act treasonable. It is implicit in this argument that during absence from the realm, however brief, an alien ordinarily resident within the realm cannot commit treason; he cannot in any circumstances by giving aid and comfort to the King's enemies outside the realm be guilty of a treasonable act. My Lords in my opinion this which is the necessary and logical statement of the appellant's case is not only at variance with the principle of the law, but is inconsistent with authority which your Lordships cannot disregard. I refer first to authority. It is said in Foster's Crown Cases (3rd ed.), p. 183—"Local

allegiance is founded in the protection a foreigner enjoyeth for his person, his family or effects, during his residence here; and it ceaseth, whenever he withdraweth with his family and effects." And then on p. 185 comes the statement of law upon which the passage I have cited is clearly founded "Section 4. And if such alien, seeking the protection of the Crown, and having a family and effects here, should during a war with his native country, go thither, and there adhere to the King's enemies for purposes of hostility, he might be dealt with as a traitor. For he came and settled here under the protection of the Crown; and, though his person was removed for a time, his effects and family continued still under the same protection. This rule was laid down by all the judges assembled at the Queen's command January 12, 1707." * * * In my view therefore it is the law that in the case supposed in the resolution of 1707 an alien may be guilty of treason for an act committed outside the realm. The reason which appears in the resolution is illuminating. The principle governing the rule is established by the exception: "though his person was removed for a time, his family and effects continued under the same protection," that is, the protection of the Crown. The vicarious protection still afforded to the family, which he had left behind in this country required of him a continuance of his fidelity. It is thus not true to say that an alien can never in law be guilty of treason to the sovereign of this realm in respect of an act committed outside the realm. My Lords, here no question arises of a vicarious protection. There is no evidence that the appellant left a family or effects behind him when he left this realm. I do not for this purpose regard parents or brothers or sister as a family. But though there was no continuing protection for his family or effects, of him too it must be asked, whether there was not such protection still afforded by the sovereign as to require of him the continuance of his allegiance. * * *

* * * The material facts are these, that being for long resident here and owing allegiance he applied for and obtained a passport and, leaving the realm, adhered to the King's enemies. It does not matter that he made false representations as to his status, asserting that he was a British subject by birth, a statement that he was afterwards at pains to disprove. It may be that when he first made the statement, he thought it was true. Of this there is no evidence. The essential fact is that he got the passport and I now examine its effect. The actual passport issued to the appellant has not been produced, but its contents have been duly proved. The terms of a passport are familiar. It is thus described by Lord Alverstone C. J., in R. v. Brailsford: "It is a document issued in the name of the sovereign on the responsibility of a minister of the Crown to a named individual, intended to be presented to the governments of foreign nations and to be used for that individual's protection as a British subject in foreign countries." By its terms it requests and requires in the name of His Majesty all those whom it may concern to allow the bearer to pass freely without let or hindrance and to afford him every assistance

and protection of which he may stand in need. It is, I think, true that the possession of a passport by a British subject does not increase the sovereign's duty of protection, though it will make his path easier. For him it serves as a voucher and means of identification. But the possession of a passport by one who is not a British subject gives him rights and imposes upon the sovereign obligations which would otherwise not be given or imposed. It is immaterial that he has obtained it by misrepresentation and that he is not in law a British subject. By the possession of that document he is enabled to obtain in a foreign country the protection extended to British subjects. By his own act he has maintained the bond which while he was within the realm bound him to his sovereign. The question is not whether he obtained British citizenship by obtaining the passport, but whether by its receipt he extended his duty of allegiance beyond the moment when he left the shores of this country. As one owing allegiance to the King he sought and obtained the protection of the King for himself while abroad.

* * * What is this protection upon which the claim to fidelity is founded? To me, my Lords, it appears that the Crown in issuing a passport is assuming an onerous burden, and the holder of the passport is acquiring substantial privileges. * * * Armed with that document the holder may demand from the State's representatives abroad and from the officials of foreign governments that he be treated as a British subject, and even in the territory of a hostile state may claim the intervention of the protecting power. * * * In these circumstances I am clearly of opinion that so long as he holds the passport he is within the meaning of the statute a man who, if he is adherent to the King's enemies in the realm or elsewhere commits an act of treason. There is one other aspect of this part of the case with which I must deal. It is said that there is nothing to prevent an alien from withdrawing from his allegiance when he leaves the realm. I do not dissent from this as a general proposition. It is possible that he may do so even though he has obtained a passport. But that is a hypothetical case. Here there was no suggestion that the appellant had surrendered his passport or taken any other overt step to withdraw from his allegiance, unless indeed reliance is placed on the act of treason itself as a withdrawal. That in my opinion he cannot do. For such an act is not inconsistent with his still availing himself of the passport in other countries than Germany and possibly even in Germany itself. * * *

The second point of appeal * * * was that in any case no English court has jurisdiction to try an alien for a crime committed abroad and your Lordships heard an exhaustive argument upon the construction of penal statutes. There is, I think, a short answer to this point. The statute in question deals with the crime of treason committed within or * * * without the realm: it is general in its terms and I see no reason for limiting its scope except in the way that I indicated earlier in this opinion, viz.: that, since it is declaratory of the crime of treason, it can apply only to those who are capable of committing that crime. No principle of comity demands that a state should ignore the crime of treason committed against it outside its territory. On the contrary a proper regard for its own security requires that all those who commit that crime, whether they commit it within or without the realm should be amenable to its laws.

* * *

Finally * * * it was urged on behalf of the appellant that there was no evidence that the renewal of his passport afforded him or was capable of affording him any protection or that he ever availed himself or had any intention of availing himself of any such protection * * *. The document speaks for itself. It was capable of affording the appellant protection. He applied for it and obtained it, and it was available for his use. * * *

* * *

[Other opinions omitted.]

REX v. NEUMANN

South Africa, Special Criminal Court of Transvaal, 1946.
[1949] 3 So.African L.Rep. 1238, 1263.*

[Neumann was indicted for high treason; he was charged with having enlisted and served in the military forces of Germany and with questioning members of the military forces of South Africa and its allies to obtain secret information for Germany. All the alleged acts took place outside the territory of South Africa while that state was at war with Germany. Although it was admitted by the Crown that the defendant was a German by birth and not naturalized in South Africa, the court declined to dismiss the indictment. After the Crown's evidence was heard, the court rejected the defendant's application for discharge (thus requiring the defendant to proceed with his defense). Portions of the court's opinion on the defendant's application appear below.]

* * * Some years before the outbreak of the present war the accused, a German national by birth, assumed permanent residence in the Cape Peninsula, and became domiciled in the Union. He married a Union national and established a home for her and their children in the vicinity of Cape Town. At one stage he had a business there, which for financial reasons he abandoned shortly before war broke out. He contemplated becoming naturalised and took certain steps in this direction, which were however not carried to completion. In 1940 he enlisted in the armed forces of the Union and in connection therewith took a certain oath to which reference in greater detail will be made later. He proceeded out of the Union as a member of such armed forces, firstly to Abyssinia and thereafter to Cyrenaica. He allotted portion of his military pay to his wife, to whom it was in due

* Reprinted with the permission of Juta
& Co. Ltd., Kenwin Cape, South Africa.

course paid. He was a member of such forces when captured by the German Forces. On various occasions even after capture he expressed his fixed intention to return to the Union. Shortly after his capture he was seen wearing an alleged German uniform. There is evidence that he was then interrogating Union and Allied prisoners of war. Later he served, with distinction, in a German military unit operating in Italy.

*   *   *

The present is, of course, a case of a conflict between two allegiances: on the one hand there is the accused's allegiance to the state of which he is a born subject. Of this allegiance he has never formally divested himself by the acquisition of citizenship by naturalisation. On the other hand there is the qualified, the less extensive, allegiance which was created by his having come to settle in the Union and having become a Union soldier.

It seems to be beyond question, from the authorities quoted to us, that not only in the law of England but also in the Roman-Dutch law an alien resident in a sovereign state foreign to him owes a qualified allegiance to that state, even when that state and his own are at war with one another.   *   *   *

Without doubt, then, allegiance is required of a resident alien while he himself is physically present in this country. Such allegiance does not, in my view, immediately terminate as soon as he departs from the country.   *   *   * The leaving of his family behind may per se involve a continuation, in respect of the family and for his benefit, of the protection until then enjoyed by him for himself and his family. It seems to me that where it is clear that his departure is of a purely temporary character, accompanied by a definite intention to return for permanent residence, the protection previously acquired does not cease on departure. Any uncertainty on this point, however, appears to disappear when his departure is permitted or facilitated by some positive act on his part, as in Joyce's case   *   *   * whereby he secures the extension, beyond the territorial limits of the country of residence, of the protection which he enjoyed in that country, and in return for which he incurred the *subjectio* referred to. If on principle (which I think is the case) it is the *protectio* which creates the obligation of allegiance, this Court should, in my opinion, follow the principle to be found in Joyce's case and hold that when the accused left the country temporarily in consequence of his enlistment as a soldier in the Union Forces, his existing allegiance continued precisely in the same way as if he had left the country after securing a Union passport.

When the accused enlisted in the Union Forces he stated clearly in his attestation form that he was a German subject and the military authorities accepted him as a soldier of this State with full knowledge of the allegiance he bore to Germany. There is the additional fact that   *   *   * it must have been realised (had the matter ever received specific consideration) that on the general principles of international law even naturalisation as a Union national during the existence of hostilities between the Union and the German Reich would in all probability not have been recognised by the German authorities.

On the other hand, the accused undertook certain obligations. On reference to the form of oath it will be seen that the first matter he swore to was to be faithful and bear true allegiance to His Majesty King George VI, his heirs and successors, according to law (meaning thereby in our view to be faithful and bear allegiance to the State of the Union of South Africa). In the next place he agreed to perform, to the best of his ability, the duties assigned to him as a volunteer member of the Union Defence Forces; he thirdly agreed that in accordance with the resolution of Parliament he would serve in the voluntary full-time Active Citizen Force in Africa, whether within or outside of the limits of South Africa, for the duration of the war; and finally, agreed to subject himself in so serving to the provisions of the South Africa Defence Act, as amended, and to the regulations in force from time to time and the Military Discipline Code.   *   *   *

The Attorney-General has submitted that the effect of the above oath, read in conjunction with the War Regulations permitting service outside the Union, and the raising of a foreign legion, was entirely to override the accused's natural allegiance to the Reich and to place him in exactly the same position as a Union national. I cannot agree that this is the correct position.   *   *   *   The oath taken by the accused was not contended by the Attorney-General to involve the creation of a new allegiance. At most it amounted to a reaffirmation, possibly an extension, of an existing allegiance. I am therefore, not prepared to go as far as the Crown here contends, and to treat the accused in all matters of allegiance on an equality with a Union citizen by birth or naturalisation. But at the same time I am of opinion that the allegiance in question did not terminate, ipso facto, on the accused's capture *   *   *. Leaving aside the problem presented by a case of voluntary desertion from the Union ranks, followed by enlistment in the German forces, it seems to be an impossible situation that the very moment after his capture the accused could with impunity have seized a rifle and opened fire on his previous comrades in arms, the members of the Union forces.   *   *   *

It seems to me that the only way to reconcile these two allegiances is to hold that even after capture by the German forces the accused was obliged to do nothing *voluntarily* to impair the safety of the Union or participate in any attack on the Union. If, while in German hands, he remained passive, he would not be committing a breach of his allegiance to the state of his birth, nor, obviously, to the Union of South Africa. But if without any compulsion from the German authorities, civil or military, he voluntarily (whether out of a sense of duty or not) embarked upon any course of action which, had he been a Union national, would have constituted an act or acts of high treason, then in my view he has deliberately failed to observe the *subjectio* which he incurred when on leaving South Africa he secured an extension of the *protectio* afforded to him. And if so he has, in my view, committed treason against the Union. If, on the other hand, all he has done is the result of enforcement by the German authorities of their claims against him as a natural-born citizen of the Reich, it seems that no complaint can fairly be made by the State of the Union of South Africa, which had full knowledge of his paramount allegiance when it accepted him as a Union soldier.

In the result, therefore, the question still to be ascertained is whether such otherwise treasonable acts as the accused performed after capture were performed voluntarily or under compulsion from the German authorities. I am not prepared to assume they were performed under compulsion. That question will have to be determined when the defence evidence has been heard. Until then there is a case for the accused to meet, and the application for discharge must be refused.   *   *   *

---

2.   TAXATION

UNITED STATES v. REXACH

United States Court of Appeals, First Circuit, 1977.
558 F.2d 37.

INGRAHAM, Circuit Judge.

This case and related lawsuits reflect the United States' efforts to tax income earned in the 1940's and 1950's by Felix Benitez Rexach, husband of Lucienne D'Hotelle de Benitez Rexach.[1] The deaths of Lucienne and Felix have not halted the litigation. We hold that the district court erred in ruling that Lucienne was not liable for taxes on one-half the income earned by Felix from November 10, 1949 to May 20, 1952. We do not disturb the refusal of the district court to dismiss Maria Benitez Rexach Viuda de Andreu as a party defendant.

Facts

Lucienne D'Hotelle was born in France in 1909. She became Lucienne D'Hotelle de Benitez Rexach upon her marriage to Felix in San Juan, Puerto Rico in 1928. She was naturalized as a United States citizen on December 7, 1942. The couple spent some time in the Dominican Republic, where Felix engaged in harbor construction projects. Lucienne established a residence in her native France on

---

1. The controversy can be followed, if not completely understood, in the reported cases: United States v. Rexach, 185 F.Supp. 465 (D.P.R.1960); United States v. Rexach, 200 F.Supp. 494 (D.P.R.1961); United States v. Rexach, 41 F.R.D. 180 (D.P.R.1966); Rexach v. United States, 390 F.2d 631 (1st Cir.), cert. denied 393 U.S. 833, 89 S.Ct. 103, 21 L.Ed.2d 103 (1968); United States v. Rexach, 331 F.Supp. 524 (D.P.R.1971), vacated and remanded, 482 F.2d 10 (1st Cir.), cert. denied 414 U.S. 1039 (1973); United States v. Rexach, 411 F.Supp. 1288 (D.P.R.1976).

November 10, 1946 and remained a resident until May 20, 1952. During that time § 404(b) of the Nationality Act of 1940 [2] provided

      * * *

that naturalized citizens who returned to their country of birth and resided there for three years lost their American citizenship. On November 10, 1947, after Lucienne had been in France for one year, the American Embassy in Paris issued her a United States passport valid through November 9, 1949. Soon after its expiration Lucienne applied in Puerto Rico for a renewal. By this time she had resided in France for three years. Nevertheless, the Governor of Puerto Rico renewed her passport on January 20, 1950 for a two year period beginning November 10, 1949. Three months after the expiration of this passport, Lucienne applied to the United States Consulate in Nice, France for another one. On May 20, 1952, the Vice-Consul there signed a Certificate of Loss of Nationality, citing Lucienne's continuous residence in France as having automatically divested her of citizenship under § 404(b). Her passport from the Governor of Puerto Rico was confiscated, cancelled and never returned to her. The State Department approved the certificate on December 23, 1952. Lucienne made no attempt to regain her American citizenship; neither did she affirmatively renounce it.

In October 1952 the Dominican Republic (then controlled by the dictator Rafael Trujillo) extended citizenship to Lucienne retroactive to January 2, 1952. Trujillo was assassinated in May 1961. The provisional government which followed revoked Lucienne's citizenship on January 20, 1962. On June 5, 1962 the French government issued her a passport.

For the years 1944 to 1958, Felix earned millions of dollars from harbor construction in the Dominican Republic. He was aided by Trujillo's favor and by his own undeniable skills as an engineer. Felix, an American citizen since 1917,[3] was sued by the United States for income taxes. The court held that Lucienne had a vested one-half interest in Felix's earnings under Dominican law, which established that such income was community property. Since the law of the situs where the income was earned determined its character, Felix

---

2. Section 404(b) of the Nationality Act of 1940, 54 Stat. 1170, 8 U.S.C. § 804(b) (1946), provided:
"A person who has become a national by naturalization shall lose his nationality by:
(b) Residing continuously for three years in the territory of a foreign state of which he was formerly a national or in which the place of his birth is situated, except as provided in section 406 hereof."

3. Felix was born in Puerto Rico on March 27, 1886. He became an American citizen under the Puerto Rico Organic Act of 1917, § 5, 39 Stat. 953. He was denaturalized on July 14, 1958 under § 349(a) of the Immigration and Naturalization Act of 1952, 8 U.S.C. § 1481(a). See United States v. Rexach, 185 F.Supp. 465, 467 (D.P.R.1960). However, the Board of Review on the Loss of Nationality later determined that the events which led to denaturalization were the result of coercion by Trujillo. It adjudged the denaturalization to be void ab initio. See United States v. Rexach, 331 F.Supp. 524, 527 (D.P. R.1971).

could be sued only for his half of the earnings. United States v. Rexach, 185 F.Supp. 465 (D.P.R.1960).

Predictably, the United States eventually sought to tax Lucienne for her half of that income. Whether by accident or design, the government's efforts began in earnest shortly after the Supreme Court invalidated the successor statute [4] to § 404(b). In Schneider v. Rusk, 377 U.S. 163, 84 S.Ct. 1187, 12 L.Ed.2d 218 (1964), the Court held that the distinction drawn by the statute between naturalized and native-born Americans was so discriminatory as to violate due process. In January 1965, about two months after this suit was filed, the State Department notified Lucienne by letter that her expatriation was void under *Schneider* and that the State Department considered her a citizen. Lucienne replied that she had accepted her denaturalization without protest and had thereafter considered herself not to be an American citizen.

Lucienne died on January 18, 1968. During her lifetime, Felix, as administrator of the marital community, retained and administered the community property, including Lucienne's share of the income earned in the Dominican Republic. Upon her death Felix did not return her share to the estate, but retained it. Lucienne's will named Maria Benitez Rexach Viuda de Andreu as executrix and Felix as sole beneficiary.

Lucienne's attorney officially notified the district court of Lucienne's death on October 25, 1973. The United States moved successfully to amend the complaint to add Maria and Felix as parties defendant. The amended complaint was filed on December 3, 1973. Maria failed to answer the complaint despite valid service of process. Default was entered against her on December 23, 1974. On April 14, 1975 Maria obtained an order from the Superior Court of Puerto Rico dismissing her as executrix. Her petition to that court included the admission that she had filed a tax return for the estate. The United States District Court denied her subsequent motion for dismissal as a party defendant.

The district court found that Lucienne was liable for taxes on her half of Felix's income from 1944 through November 9, 1949 in an amount to be computed in accordance with a stipulation of the parties. The court also found that Felix was obligated to pay this amount because (1) he was administrator of the marital community, (2) he had retained control and possession of the community property, thus making him a transferee at law of property subject to federal tax liens, and (3) he had tortiously converted property subject to federal tax liens. The district court absolved Lucienne of liability for

---

4. Section 352(a) of the Immigration and Naturalization Act of 1952, 8 U.S.C. § 1484(a), provided, in pertinent part:

"(a) A person who has become a national by naturalization shall lose his nationality by—

(1) having a continuous residence for three years in the territory of a foreign state of which he was formerly a national or in which the place of his birth is situated * * *."

taxes on income earned after November 9, 1949. Felix died on November 18, 1975. The United States filed a notice of death and moved to add Maria and Ramon Rodriguez as defendants in their capacities as co-executors of Felix's will. The motion was granted.

The United States appealed the denial of liability for the period November 10, 1949 to May 20, 1952. With this lengthy but skeletal summary we proceed to the merits.

Lucienne's Citizenship

The government contends that Lucienne was still an American citizen from her third anniversary as a French resident until the day the Certificate of Loss of Nationality was issued in Nice. This case presents a curious situation, since usually it is the individual who claims citizenship and the government which denies it. But pocketbook considerations occasionally reverse the roles. United States v. Matheson, 532 F.2d 809 (2nd Cir.), cert. denied 429 U.S. 823, 97 S.Ct. 75, 50 L.Ed.2d 85 (1976). The government's position is that under either Schneider v. Rusk, supra, or Afroyim v. Rusk, 387 U.S. 253, 87 S.Ct. 1660, 18 L.Ed.2d 757 (1967), the statute by which Lucienne was denaturalized is unconstitutional and its prior effects should be wiped out. *Afroyim* held that Congress lacks the power to strip persons of citizenship merely because they have voted in a foreign election. The cornerstone of the decision is the proposition that intent to relinquish citizenship is a prerequisite to expatriation.

Section 404(b) would have been declared unconstitutional under either *Schneider* or *Afroyim*. The statute is practically identical to its successor, which *Schneider* condemned as discriminatory. Section 404(b) would have been invalid under *Afroyim* as a congressional attempt to expatriate regardless of intent. Likewise it is clear that the determination of the Vice-Consul and the State Department in 1952 would have been upheld under then prevailing case law, even though Lucienne had manifested no intent to renounce her citizenship. Mackenzie v. Hare, 239 U.S. 299, 36 S.Ct. 106, 60 L.Ed. 297 (1915). Accord, Savorgnan v. United States, 338 U.S. 491, 70 S.Ct. 292, 94 L. Ed. 287 (1950). See also Perez v. Brownell, 356 U.S. 44, 78 S.Ct. 568, 2 L.Ed.2d 603 (1958), overruled, Afroyim v. Rusk, supra.

We think the principles governing retrospective application dictate that either *Schneider* or *Afroyim* apply to this case.[5] This circuit has applied *Afroyim* retroactively. Rocha v. Immigration and Naturalization Service, 450 F.2d 946 (1st Cir. 1971) (per curiam), withdrawing prior opinion, 351 F.2d 523 (1st Cir. 1965). Angela Rocha was born in Portugal in 1931. Her mother, a native American had married a Portuguese citizen in 1916 and moved to his homeland. Under the law then in effect Angela's mother was automatically divested of American citizenship by marrying a foreign national. Thus Angela was the daughter of two foreign nationals and, in the pre-*Af-*

---

5. We need not choose which decision should be given retrospective effect, since the principles discussed dictate the same result for either.

royim era, not an American citizen. In 1965 this court upheld the decision of the Board of Immigration Appeals that Angela was not a citizen. 351 F.2d 523. Upon granting a motion for reconsideration, the court held that *Afroyim* "clearly refutes" the notion that an American citizen can be involuntarily expatriated. 450 F.2d at 947. Thus Angela's mother was a citizen when Angela was born in 1931 and, since any procedural deficiencies were thereby cured, Angela was entitled to citizenship.

Although *Rocha* appears to be precisely on point, it involved a live person who wished to be an American citizen. The case mentions no benefits or duties dependent upon Angela's status for the first forty years of her life. In the case we now consider, however, the focus of the inquiry is whether Lucienne was a citizen. Thus in *Rocha* retrospective application of *Afroyim* was expected to have only prospective effect. A declaration that Lucienne was a citizen will have substantial retrospective effect. In light of her death, future benefits of citizenship cease to be a factor. This distinction justifies more complete treatment of the issue.

Retroactive application of constitutional decisions is not automatic. * * * The Supreme Court has opted for a flexible approach. * * * Equitable principles control in deciding whether cases should be applied retrospectively. * * *

The district court accurately summarized the law:

[T]he general principles that govern retroactivity should be applied on a case by case basis taking into consideration such factors as the reliance placed by the parties on the legislation in question, the balancing of the equities of the particular situation, and the foreseeability or lack thereof, that the legal doctrine or statute in question would be declared unconstitutional.

411 F.Supp. at 1293. However, the district court went too far in viewing the equities as between Lucienne and the government in strict isolation from broad policy considerations which argue for a generally retrospective application of *Afroyim* and *Schneider* to the entire class of persons invalidly expatriated. * * * The rights stemming from American citizenship are so important that, absent special circumstances, they must be recognized even for years past. Unless held to have been citizens without interruption, persons wrongfully expatriated as well as their offspring might be permanently and unreasonably barred from important benefits.[6] Application of *Afroyim* or *Schneider* is generally appropriate.

Of course, American citizenship implies not only rights but also duties, not the least of which is the payment of taxes. Cook v. Tait, 265 U.S. 47, 44 S.Ct. 444, 68 L.Ed. 895 (1924). And were *Schneider*

---

6. For example, if expatriation was void ab initio, the reinstated citizen will have the satisfaction of knowing that children born in the interim will have the right to become citizens. 8 U.S.C. §§ 1431, 1433, 1434. Cf. Rocha v. Immigration and Naturalization Service, 450 F.2d 946 (1st Cir. 1971) (per curiam).

or *Afroyim* used to compel payment of taxes by all persons who mistakenly thought themselves to have been validly expatriated, the calculus favoring retrospective application might shift markedly. We do think that the balance of the equities mandates that back income taxes be collectible for periods during which the involuntarily expatriated persons affirmatively exercised a specific right of citizenship. This is precisely the position taken by the Internal Revenue Service.[7] As to such periods, neither the government nor the expatriate can be said to have relied upon the constitutionality of § 404. Since the expatriate in fact received benefits of citizenship, the equities favor the imposition of federal income tax liability. Cf. Rexach v. United States, 390 F.2d 631 (1st Cir. 1968).

We now focus upon Lucienne's status. The years for which the government sought to collect taxes can be divided into three discrete periods: 1944 through November 9, 1949; November 10, 1949 through May 20, 1952; and May 21, 1952 through 1958. The district court's ruling that Lucienne was liable for taxes during the first period is not appealed. The district court refused to distinguish between the two remaining periods.

During the interval from late 1949 to mid-1952, Lucienne was unaware that she had been automatically denaturalized. In fact, she applied for, obtained and used an American passport for most of that period. On the passport application she stated that her travel outside the United States had consisted of "vacations," and her signature appeared below an oath that she had neither been naturalized by a foreign state nor declared her allegiance to a foreign state. Her subsequent application on February 11, 1952, which was eventually rejected, included an affidavit in which she stated that her mother's death and other business obligations caused her to remain in France. Ironically, on that same application, the following line appears:

"I (do/do not) pay the American Income Tax at ————."

Lucienne scratched out the words "do not" and filled in the blank with "San Juan, Puerto Rico."

As late as February 1952 Lucienne regarded herself as an American citizen and no one had disabused her of that notion. The Vice-Consul reported that Lucienne had told him "she was advised (by the State Department) that she could remain in France without endangering her American citizenship."

Fairness dictates that the United States recover income taxes for the period November 10, 1949 to May 20, 1952. Lucienne was privileged to travel on a United States passport; she received the protection of its government.

Although the government has not appealed the decision with respect to taxes from mid-1952 through 1958, the district court was

7. Rev.Rul. 75–357, 1975–34 Int.Rev. Bull. 8; Rev.Rul. 70–506, 1970–2 Cum. Bull. 1.

presented with the issue. We wish to explain why the government should be allowed to collect taxes for the two and one-half year interval but not for the subsequent period. The letter from Lucienne to the Department of State official in 1965, which appears in English translation in the record, states that after the Certificate of Loss of Nationality, "I have never considered myself to be a citizen of the United States." We think that in this case this letter can be construed as an acceptance and voluntary relinquishment of citizenship. We also find that in this particular case estoppel would have been proper against the United States. Although estoppel is rarely a proper defense against the government, there are instances where it would be unconscionable to allow the government to reverse an earlier position. Schuster v. Commissioner of Internal Revenue, 312 F. 2d 311, 317 (9th Cir. 1962). This is one of those instances. Lucienne cannot be dunned for taxes to support the United States government during the years in which she was denied its protection. In Peignand v. Immigration and Naturalization Service, 440 F.2d 757 (1st Cir. 1971), this court refused to decide whether estoppel could apply against the government. A decision on the question was unnecessary, since the petitioner had not been led to take a course of action he would not otherwise have taken. Id. at 761. Here, Lucienne severed her ties to this country at the direction of the State Department. The right hand will not be permitted to demand payment for something which the left hand has taken away. However, until her citizenship was snatched from her, Lucienne should have expected to honor her 1952 declaration that she was a taxpayer.

* * *

The case is reversed and remanded for a proper determination of taxes for the period November 10, 1949 to May 20, 1952, in accordance with the parties' stipulation.

Basis of taxation of aliens. As noted in Chapter 7, p. 421, international law has recognized a number of bases for the imposition of taxes. Here as elsewhere it is essential to distinguish between a state's jurisdiction to prescribe a rule imposing a tax and its jurisdiction to enforce such a rule. The practical difficulties of enforcing taxes upon persons not physically within its territory and not owning property within its territory realistically limit the voraciousness of the tax collecting state. International controversy as to jurisdiction to tax has been relatively infrequent. Consequently the only evidence of the international law on the subject is state practice.

The territorial base supports state taxation measured by property located and income produced within the state. States impose such taxes on the individuals owning such property, or producing or claiming such income, even though the individuals do not have a personal relationship with the taxing state such as that of nationality. At the other extreme, as in the *Rexach* case, states impose taxes upon their own nationals, even though the nationals are physically located outside the state and their property is located and income produced outside the state.

Will international law permit taxation measured by property located outside the state or income produced outside the state when the individual to be taxed is not its national? The United States, for example, imposes income tax upon aliens who are resident within the United States. "Resident aliens are, in general, taxable the same as citizens of the United States; that is, a resident alien is taxable on income derived from all sources, including sources without the United States." 26 C.F.R. Part 1, § 1.871–1. Residence is defined in the regulations as follows:

> An alien actually present in the United States who is not a mere transient or sojourner is a resident of the United States for purposes of the income tax. Whether he is a transient is determined by his intentions with regard to the length and nature of his stay. A mere floating intention, indefinite as to time, to return to another country is not sufficient to constitute him a transient. If he lives in the United States and has no definite intention as to his stay, he is a resident. One who comes to the United States for a definite purpose which in its nature may be promptly accomplished is a transient; but, if his purpose is of such a nature that an extended stay may be necessary for its accomplishment, and to that end the alien makes his home temporarily in the United States, he becomes a resident, though it may be his intention at all times to return to his domicile abroad when the purpose for which he came has been consummated or abandoned. An alien whose stay in the United States is limited to a definite period by the immigration laws is not a resident of the United States within the meaning of this section, in the absence of exceptional circumstances. 26 C.F.R. Part 1, § 1.871–2(b).

Consider the following more general definition of residence:

> It appears that most governments consider that an alien who remains in its territory for a certain period of time, six months or more, is resident in such territory for purposes of income taxation. Asst. Sec. of State Macomber to U. S. Senator Carl Hayden, letter quoted in 8 Whiteman, Digest of International Law 536 (1967).

If, then, nationality is not a necessary prerequisite to taxability, is there some minimum personal connection that must exist before a state can lawfully prescribe a tax based on events that occur outside the state? What should that connection be? Could a state lawfully tax a mere transient or sojourner? What would be a lawful measure of such a tax? "On the one hand it is agreed that a State cannot tax a transient on the whole of his year's income as if he were a resident, but on the other it is equally agreed that his presence may render him subject to poll tax, and sojourn tax, which, indeed, could be of an equivalent amount." 2 O'Connell, International Law 717 (2d ed. 1970).

———

3. COMPULSORY MILITARY SERVICE

UNITED STATES v. RUMSA

United States Court of Appeals, Seventh Circuit, 1954.
212 F.2d 927.[a]

SWAIM, Circuit Judge. This opinion disposes of two appeals by Antanas Juratis Rumsa, the first being an appeal in a criminal case and the second being an appeal from the order and judgment of the District Court dismissing Rumsa's amended complaint in an action to enjoin the defendants from inducting and causing him to be inducted and for a declaratory judgment.

* * *

We shall first consider the appeal of Rumsa from the judgment of the District Court entered on a verdict of guilty on an indictment which charged him with refusing to submit to induction into the armed forces of the United States in violation of Section 462, Title 50 Appendix, United States Code Annotated, and the prescribed rules and regulations thereunder.

The defendant was born in Lithuania on October 9, 1929, and resided there until sometime in 1944 when the Russians invaded that country and the defendant was forced to flee to Western Germany. In Germany he was placed in a labor camp and kept there until he was finally liberated by the American forces. On February 27, 1950, the defendant executed a printed form of Application for Immigration Visa and Alien Registration. This form stated that the defendant's purpose in going to the United States was "to reside" and that he intended "to remain permanently." This form also indicated that the defendant had had five years in elementary school and eight years in secondary school and that he was able to speak, read and write Lithuanian and a little English and German. The American Vice Counsul approved this application and granted the immigration visa to the defendant as a displaced person pursuant to Public Law 774, 50 U.S.C.A.Appendix, § 1951 et seq. Pursuant to the authority granted by the United States on this application, the defendant was admitted to, and did, enter the United States on April 6, 1950, coming to Chicago, Illinois, to live. On August 12, 1950, he registered under the Selective Service Act with Local Board No. 65, located at 63rd Street and Western Avenue in Chicago. A little more than a month later, September 15, 1950, the defendant filled out a Selective Service Questionnaire and on October 9, 1950, he was classified I–A (ready

a. Cert. denied 348 U.S. 838, 75 S.Ct. 36 (1954).

for service). On January 11, 1951, the defendant was ordered by the local board to report for physical examination on January 29, 1951.

* * *

The defendant seems to contend that, since he is an alien, he cannot be required to submit to induction into the armed forces of the United States; that requiring him to be inducted violates international law and also violates the Fifth Amendment to our Constitution; that, further, as a temporary resident alien, he had the right to be deferred from military service by waiving the right ever to become an American citizen; that by his executing and filing Form 130, he did waive his right to ever become an American citizen; and that he thereby acquired the right to be permanently classified as IV–C, a right to exemption which could not thereafter be taken away from him even by a change in the law by Congress.

It is true that the Selective Training and Service Act which was in effect when Rumsa came to this country and when he first registered did provide that any citizen or subject of a neutral country should be relieved from liability for training and service if, prior to his induction, he had made application (Form 130) to be relieved of such liability. But in 1951 the Congress, alarmed by the international situation, determined that the safety of this nation required that more men be inducted for training and service. See legislative history of Universal Military Training Act in U.S.Code Congressional and Administrative Service for 1951, Volume 2, pages 1472–1521. On page 1512 of this history, in the Conference Report, we find the recommendation that the law should be so changed that "All aliens admitted for permanent residence in the United States shall be immediately liable for induction into the Armed Forces or the National Security Training Corps under the same conditions applicable to citizens. * * *"

There can be no question but that the Universal Military Training and Service Act as amended authorized the selection and induction of aliens who had been admitted to the United States for permanent residence. Section 454(a) of 50 U.S.C.Appendix, § 4(a) of the Universal Military Training and Service Act, as amended June 19, 1951, expressly provided: "Except as otherwise provided in this title * * * every male alien *admitted for permanent residence* * * * shall be liable for training and service in the Armed Forces of the United States * * *." And Section 456 of 50 U.S.C.Appendix, which gave to the President broad powers to exempt various classes of aliens, expressly provided: "* * * except that *aliens admitted for permanent residence* in the United States shall not be so exempted." (Our emphasis.) This Act also provided, 50 U.S.C.Appendix, § 467(a): "Except as provided in this title all laws or any parts of laws in conflict with the provisions of this title are repealed." Such clear language leaves no ambiguity for interpretation. We may only apply such a law as it is written.

* * *

It necessarily remained within the province and was the duty of Congress to be constantly alert to impending danger, to appraise such danger, and to raise and support armies of a sufficient number of men to be able to meet the danger successfully. Signs of increasing danger in 1951 were apparent to all. This naturally called for increased numbers in the armed services. The increased numbers could be secured only by enlarging the field from which to draw. This was accomplished by certain amendments which, among other things, reduced the age at which men were eligible, reduced the physical and mental standards required for induction *and made all aliens admitted for permanent residence in the United States immediately available for induction.* No classification of any individual could be considered permanent as against changes in the law, changes in the circumstances of the individual on which the classification was made or changes in valid regulations promulgated under the changed law. To hold that a classification, once made, was binding on the Government regardless of changing conditions and amended laws to meet such changing conditions might, in effect, destroy the power of Congress to raise and support armies.

The defendant had come to the United States from Germany in 1950 with his father and mother. On August 12, 1950, he registered for Selective Service, giving the family address in Chicago as his residence. At that time he had already secured work with the National Video Corporation, and a short time later he enrolled in the Chicago Navy Pier Branch of the University of Illinois. He was a national of Lithuania and, since the Russians had taken over that country and had set up a puppet government, it was uncertain when, if ever, he might be able to return to his native land.

* * *

The conscription law which the defendant violated by refusing to submit to induction does not say that aliens who have come here intending to stay permanently shall be subject to military service; instead it says that those who are qualified for and who are *admitted* for permanent residence are to be inducted. The emphasis is therefore on the intention of the officials who approve the Application for Immigration Visa and those who consent to the alien's admission into the United States, not necessarily on the intention of the alien. With an application for a visa such as we have here before the officials whose duty it was to decide as to his admission, there cannot be much doubt but that Rumsa was *admitted* to the United States for permanent residence regardless of what his secret intention may actually have been.

When we consider this record as a whole, including the conflicting and patently untrue statements in the defendant's letters frantically urging that he be excused from military service, we have no hesitation in saying that there was a factual basis for the action of the local board in finding that he was admitted to the United States for permanent residence, and that he was, therefore, properly classified in January 1952 as I–A. Under the rule of the Cox and Estep decisions of the Supreme Court the District Court properly decided this and then left to the jury only the question of whether the defendant had "wilfully and knowingly failed, neglected or refused to submit to induction as ordered by his local board," a question which the jury decided against the defendant. The burden was on the defendant to establish facts before the local board which showed his right to exemption from military service. * * *

Counsel for the defendant have earnestly argued to us that the conscription of aliens is extremely bad policy on the part of the United States; that prior to the enactment of the Universal Military Training and Service Act the United States and most other nations had consistently refused to draft aliens; that the new policy which Congress adopted in 1951, if followed, will in effect invite other nations to force our nationals who may be residing in those countries to submit to service in their armies; and that, therefore, none of our nationals residing abroad will be safe from conscription by those countries or from the many dangers which service in foreign armies entail.

Even if all this be true there is nothing the courts can do about it. The question of whether or not aliens should be conscripted is a question of policy—a political question which is for the executive and legislative branches of the Government to solve. Such questions are entirely outside the realm of the judicial branch. * * *

The grant of power to Congress to raise and support armies is certainly sufficient to authorize the adoption of the present policy to conscript aliens. It is, of course, also within the power of Congress to change the conscription law to again excuse aliens from service in our armed forces at any time Congress determines that the services of aliens are either unnecessary or should not as a matter of policy be required. And as to this defendant and other aliens who have been convicted of violations of the present draft law, a pardon is always within the power of the President. Neither of these courses is open to the judiciary.

Finding no error, the judgment of the District Court is affirmed.

----

1. *United States legislation on the drafting of aliens.* During World War I, citizens and "male persons not alien enemies who have declared their intention to become citizens" were subject to the draft. Act of May 18, 1917, ch. 15, § 2, 40 Stat. 76.

The Selective Training and Service Act of 1940, ch. 720, § 3(a), 54 Stat. 885, contained similar provisions until amended in 1941, ch. 602, § 2, 55 Stat. 844. This World War II amendment made liable for training and service every male citizen and every other male person "residing in the United States," with the proviso that a citizen or subject of a neutral country could apply for and be granted relief, "but any person who makes such application shall thereafter be debarred from becoming a citizen of the United States." The phrase "residing in the United States" was held in McGrath v. Kristensen,

340 U.S. 162 (1950), not to include a Danish citizen who entered the United States on August 17, 1939 as a temporary visitor for sixty days (to attend the New York World's Fair and visit relatives) and was prevented from returning to Denmark by the outbreak of World War II in September of that year.

The Selective Service Act of 1948, ch. 625, § 4(a), 62 Stat. 604, broadened the category of resident aliens able to apply for relief to include "any citizen of a foreign country," retaining the provision for debarring such an applicant from citizenship.

The dramatic change in policy in the 1951 Universal Military Training and Service Act, ch. 144, § 1(d), 65 Stat. 75, as pointed out in the Rumsa case, was to apply the draft even-handedly to United States citizens and aliens admitted for permanent residence, with no provisions for relief. Non-resident aliens were also subject to the draft, but only if they had remained in the United States for a period exceeding one year; the provisions for application for relief (and debarring from citizenship) were retained as to those non-resident aliens. (In addition, the Act provided for "exemption of certain non-immigrant aliens holding diplomatic positions and of other non-immigrant aliens as determined by the President.) Thus, non-resident aliens might remain in the United States for up to one year without being subject to the draft; selected groups of non-resident aliens might remain for longer periods under exemptions provided by law and regulations. For the text of the relevant statutes referred to above in this note, see 8 Whiteman, Digest of International Law 549 (1967).

By amendments in 1971, which changed the title of the draft statute to Military Selective Service Act, a wider exclusion of aliens from the draft was provided for. The draft now applies to every male citizen and "every other male person residing in the United States" but not to any alien lawfully admitted as a "nonimmigrant" as defined in a long list of categories in the Immigration and Nationality Act. 8 U.S.C. § 1101(a)(15). In addition, induction of an alien who is draftable is not to take place until "such alien shall have resided in the United States for one year." Thus the statute applies to aliens admitted for permanent residence, who can be drafted only after a year's residence. There is no authorization for drafting any other class of aliens and no provision for application for relief or debarring from citizenship. 85 Stat. 348. Notwithstanding these changes in the draft statute, the Immigration and Nationality Act continues to provide in Title 18 of the United States Code, Section 1426(a): "* * * [A]ny alien who applies or has applied for exemption or discharge from training or service in the Armed Forces * * * on the ground that he is an alien, and is or was relieved or discharged from such training * * * on such ground, shall be permanently ineligible to become a citizen of the United States." Is this provision still viable? In McGrath v. Kristensen, 340 U.S. 162, 71 S.Ct. 224 (1950), in which the court was interpreting the provisions of the Selective Training and Service Act of 1940 debarring aliens from citizenship, the court state: "As there was no 'liability' for service, his act in applying for relief from a non-existent duty could not create the bar against naturalization. By the terms of the statute, that bar only comes into existence when an alien resident liable for service asks to be relieved." (at 172)

2. *International law on the drafting of aliens.* "* * * On the other hand, an alien does not fall under the personal supremacy of the local State; therefore he cannot, unless his own state consents, be made to serve in its army or navy, and cannot, like a citizen, be treated according to discretion." I Oppenheim, International Law 681 (Lauterpacht, 8th ed. 1955). Is this the law today? If a state should require military service of all persons *present* in its territory, whether resident or not and without regard to the length of time that person was present, would that state be in violation of international law? Does the state lack *jurisdiction* to prescribe a rule of law requiring military service of such a person in fact physically present in the state? If there is no lack of jurisdiction, for what reason is the state precluded from exercising that jurisdiction? Is the alien who is only temporarily within the state entitled to something akin to immunity? Can such an immunity be grounded on the customary behavior of states; on the expectations of aliens who are temporarily sojourning in host states?

3. *French point of view on the drafting of aliens.* In Chronique des Faits Internationaux, 71 Revue Générale de Droit International Public 143, 174 (1967), Rousseau comments on the Australian legislation of August 10, 1966. It subjected immigrant aliens to compulsory military service and hence some of them to duty in South Vietnam. Greece and Italy formally protested the legislation and Rousseau comments: "The most surprising aspect of the situation is that only two governments seem to have protested an act which constitutes a clear violation of the traditional status of aliens." (at 179)

He qualifies the French practice of declining even voluntary military service by aliens in time of peace as "perhaps [showing] an excessive respect for foreign sovereignty." He then discusses an exception to the practice, i. e. voluntary service in the French Foreign Legion and the difficulties to which this voluntary service had given rise between France and other states, notably Belgium, Germany and Switzerland. He reviews in particular a serious diplomatic dispute with Switzerland in 1959, concerning the service in the Foreign Legion of Swiss citizens who falsified documents to make it appear they were 21 years of age at the time they enlisted, but were in fact still below that age. Once they enlisted, the Foreign Legion refused to release them.

In time of war, Rousseau points out, the French practice is to permit voluntary military service by aliens and to subject them to compulsory service in the labor force. He then states that Anglo-Saxon states have a different point of view in the matter of drafting aliens and reviews critically the dispute between France and the

United States with respect to the drafting of French citizens in the American forces under the Service Act of 1951, the drafting of aliens by the United Kingdom during World War II, and an Australian decision of 1945 upholding the domestic validity of World War II legislation for the drafting of aliens while recognizing it was in violation of international law.

The Australian decision to which Rousseau refers is Polites v. The Commonwealth, and Kandiliotes v. The Commonwealth, High Court of Australia, 1945, [1943–1945] Ann.Dig. 208 (No. 61).

4. *Military service of Swiss nationals in the United States.* The report of the Federal Council of Switzerland for the year 1965 discusses the dispute between Switzerland and the United States concerning the drafting of Swiss nationals in the United States forces. It points out that a treaty of 1850 exempts the nationals of each from service in the forces of the other. Swiss nationals continue to be called for service in the United States, the report points out, but upon request by the Swiss ambassador, they are issued a deferment and hence do not actually serve. The report concludes that, even though the practical solution is satisfactory, the issue of principle needs to be resolved as soon as possible. XXIII Annuaire Suisse de Droit International 1966, at 88 (1967).

TELLECH (UNITED STATES) v. AUSTRIA AND HUNGARY

Tripartite Claims Commission, 1928.
VI U.N.Rep. Int'l Arb.Awards 248.

This claim is put forward by the United States on behalf of Alexander Tellech for compensation for time lost and for alleged suffering and privation to which he was subjected, first through internment in Austria, and then through enforced military service in the Austro-Hungarian army. The claimant was born in the United States of Austrian parents on May 14, 1895. Under the Constitution and laws of the United States he was by birth an American national. Under the laws of Austria he also possessed Austrian nationality by parentage. This created a conflict in citizenship, frequently described as "dual nationality". When the claimant was five years of age he accompanied his parents to Austria, where he continued to reside.

In August, 1914, the claimant, while residing in Austria a short distance from the Russian border, was subjected to preventive arrest as an agitator engaged in propaganda in favor of Russia. After investigation he was interned and confined in internment camps for 16 months. He then took the oath of allegiance to the Emperor of Austria and King of Hungary and was impressed into service in the Austro-Hungarian army. A decision of the sharply controverted claim that this oath was taken under duress and that he protested that he was an American citizen is not necessary to a disposition of this case. It appears that in 1915 and later representatives of the Government of the United States in Austria interested themselves in securing his release, but the application was denied.

In July, 1916, the claimant deserted from the Austro-Hungarian army and escaped into Russia, where he was arrested and held by the Russian army authorities as a prisoner of war until the outbreak of the Kerensky revolution, when he was released and thereupon returned to Prague, where he still lives and where he is practicing medicine.

The action taken by the Austrian civil authorities in the exercise of their police powers and by the Austro-Hungarian military authorities, of which complaint is made, was taken in Austria, where claimant was voluntarily residing, against claimant as an Austrian citizen. Citizenship is determined by rules prescribed by municipal law. Under the law of Austria, to which claimant had voluntarily subjected himself, he was an Austrian citizen. The Austrian and the Austro-Hungarian authorities were well within their rights in dealing with him as such. Possessing as he did dual nationality, he voluntarily took the risk incident to residing in Austrian territory and subjecting himself to the duties and obligations of an Austrian citizen arising under the municipal laws of Austria.

Assuming that the claimant suffered the loss and injury alleged and had not lost his American citizenship by taking the Austrian Army oath, the Commissioner finds no provision of the Treaty of Vienna or of Budapest obligating Austria and/or Hungary to make compensation therefor.

Wherefore the Commission decrees that under the Treaty of Vienna and the Treaty of Budapest the Government of Austria and the Government of Hungary are not obligated to pay to the Government of the United States any amount on behalf of the claimant herein.

---

1. *Authoritativeness of the Tellech decision.* The decision was rendered by a commissioner appointed under an agreement between the United States and Austria and Hungary to determine amounts to be paid by the latter two states under Treaties of Vienna and Budapest previously entered into with the United States in 1921. In Administrative Decision No. 1, VI U.N.Rep.Int'l Arb.Awards 203, 207, the commissioner stated:

> The liability of Austria and/or Hungary must be determined by the application of the terms of the Treaty or Treaties to the facts of each case. The Treaties embody in their terms contracts by which Austria and Hungary accorded to the United States, as one of the conditions of peace, rights in behalf of American nationals which had no prior existence. While these doubtless include some obligations of Austria and/or Hungary arising from violation of rules of international law or otherwise and existing prior to and independent of the Treaties, they also include obligations of Austria and/or Hungary which were created and fixed

by their terms. All of these obligations, whatever their nature, are merged in and fixed by the Treaties. The Commission's inquiry in this respect is confined solely to determining whether or not Austria and/or Hungary by the terms of the Treaty or Treaties assumed the pecuniary obligation asserted or accepted responsibility for the act causing the damage claimed, and it is not concerned with the quality of that act or whether it was legal or illegal as measured by rules of international law.

Does the opinion in the Tellech case embody any conclusions of significance to international law?

2. *Military service by the dual national.* If mere presence of the individual in the territory of a state is not sufficient to support the state's requiring him to perform military service, is the fact of nationality sufficient? The issue will not arise unless a state which claims that a person is its national complains to the drafting state and the latter defends its action on the ground that the individual was (also) its national.

IN RE M. M. AND X. M.

Greece, Conseil d'Etat, 1934 (No. 2).
[1933–1934] Ann.Dig. 295 (No. 117.)*

The Facts. The petitioners were born in England of a Greek father, in 1895 and 1898 respectively. By the Greek Law of Nationality (of October 9, 1856, amended by Law 120 of 1914) children of a Greek father, wheresoever they may be born, are Greek. Greek nationality is lost (i) by naturalisation with the consent of the Greek Government, (ii) in certain circumstances, by entering foreign public service, and (iii) by leaving Greek territory with no intention of returning. The petitioners contended (I) that they were British subjects, having opted for British nationality by declarations made at the British Consulate at Patras and by entering themselves as British subjects on the British census of 1915; that they had voted at an election in England; and that they had travelled with British passports.

They contended (II) that they had not registered as Greek nationals with the Greek Consulate in London, had no Greek domicile, and had not done their military service in Greece.

Held: that they were nevertheless Greek subjects. They had in fact two nationalities. The facts recited under (I) above were matters entirely for British law, which was irrelevant in this case. The facts recited under (II) were not sufficient to effect loss of Greek nationality. The provisions of Greek law for the loss of nationality were precise and were to be construed restrictively. Mere acquisition

* Reprinted by permission of E. Lauterpacht, ed., and Grotius Publications, Ltd., Cambridge, England.

of a foreign nationality without the consent of the Greek Government did not entail loss of Greek nationality (although this was so before the passing of the Law of 1914).

---

1. *Problem.* Although the foregoing case of M. M. and X. M. did not involve the question of Greece's right to draft those individuals, consider in the light of the Greek law of nationality expressed in the opinion the problem which follows.

Client's son was born in the United States. Client is a wealthy Greek alien resident of the U. S. The son went AWOL from the United States Army in Germany and began hitchhiking through Europe. In Greece he was picked up while visiting relatives in a remote village and inducted into the Greek army.

Client wants you to do all you can, vis-a-vis the Department of State, the Greek Embassy, and if necessary vis-a-vis the authorities in Greece, to get the son released from Greek military service. The son is presently serving a military prison sentence for insubordination, at hard labor along the Corinth Canal. The client says he would rather take chances on the AWOL charge (U. S.) than to leave his boy in the Greek military prison.

Does the state with whom an individual has a more effective link have a claim *on the merits* against the drafting state?

2. *The law in treaties.* The United States is a party to a Protocol Relating to Military Obligations in Certain Cases of Double Nationality which was concluded at the Hague April 12, 1930, and entered into force for the United States May 25, 1937. 50 Stat. 1317. Only 25 states were parties to this international agreement as of January 1, 1980. Article 1 provided: "A person possessing two or more nationalities who habitually resides in one of the countries whose nationality he possesses, and who is in fact most closely connected with that country, shall be exempt from all military obligations in the other country or countries. This exemption may involve the loss of the nationality of the other country or countries."

For bilateral agreements to which the United States is a party, dealing not only with the drafting of dual nationals but also with the drafting of aliens, see 8 Whiteman, Digest of International Law 561–573 (1967).

The Convention on the Reduction of Cases of Plurality of Nationalities and on Military Obligations in Cases of Plurality of Nationalities of May 6, 1963, was prepared by the Council of Europe. The provisions in Chapter 11 of the convention are designed to insure that a person having two or more nationalities shall discharge his military obligations only once and be dispensed from serving them again in other states parties to the convention. Documents, 95 Journal du Droit International 760, 781 (1968).

Chapter 9

THE GROWTH OF STATE RESPONSIBILITY TO INDIVIDUALS

The catalog of abuses to which human beings have subjected each other is one of unrelieved horror. Abuses range from murder through physical torture to the slaughter of religious and racial masses. They include human slavery, forced labor and deprivations of liberty of movement from one place or one state to another. Freedom to speak, to practice one's religion, to select one's own occupation, to marry whom one pleases have been repressed. Arbitrary arrest, imprisonment without trial, unfair trials and degrading punishments have been common ingredients of life. This has been true throughout history. And, what is worse, still is.

All of these abuses to the human personality, to what has been called in recent years human dignity, are committed by people upon people. Some, such as murder, are often matters of private endeavor. Others are perpetrated by people acting in some capacity as a part of the organizations of state. Protections against these abuses are frequently afforded by the internal laws of the state. Domestic laws are designed not only to deter private individuals from harming their fellows but also, as in the case of the United States Constitution, to protect the individual from abuses rendered by the state. But suppose the machinery of domestic law fails to operate to protect the individual, either in the United States or elsewhere? Does the international legal system offer any protection to the individual? In particular, does it afford protection against abuses by the individual's own state? A generation ago, it was suggested in a somewhat chilling phrase that a state could treat its own citizens "according to discretion." I Oppenheim, International Law 682 (Lauterpacht, 8th ed. 1955). Can this be the law today?

In this chapter, questions such as the following will be explored: what substantive legal norms have been developed in the international system for the protection of the individual; what classes of individuals are protected by such norms, aliens alone or citizens of the acting state as well; by what processes are those norms applied and the protections afforded?

SECTION A. RESPONSIBILITY OF STATES FOR INJURIES TO ALIENS

As the nation-state became the organizing unit of the European peoples there was an early, if halting, recognition that, in some circumstances, a state might be circumscribed in the way it treated some of its own nationals. Doctrines of natural law furnished a major impetus. Pressure for such recognition came from states to which those persons had formerly been attached. "The treaties by which States bound themselves to treat their own nationals in a certain way appear only as isolated phenomena inspired first by political interest and later by considerations of humanity. The series of particular agreements inaugurated in 1660 by the Treaty of Oliva after a century and a half of religious commotions bore this aspect. In these, states receiving cessions of territory guaranteed to the ceding states the continuance and protection of the religion existing in the ceded territories. This protection, granted first to individuals, was gradually extended to minority groups, to religious minorities first and afterwards ethnic or national minorities." DeVisscher, Theory and Reality in Public International Law 126 (Corbett trans., 1968).

This process of looking after one's own kind is reflected in the practice of diplomatic protection in the 18th and 19th centuries. By this practice the state sought protection for its own nationals when they had left its territory to travel, reside or trade in a foreign state. See Chapter 8, p. 488. If its nationals were injured by the foreign state, diplomatic protests were made, asserting that the foreign state had violated its treaty obligations or, in many cases, obligations imposed by international law generally. In theory, rights of the protecting state had been violated, not the rights of the injured individual. In the absence of an international judiciary in which the rights of the offended state could be litigated, states occasionally resorted to arbitration and authorized ad hoc tribunals to decide claims based upon alleged injuries to individuals. A substantial body of precedent, establishing a primitive law of human rights, was developed until the practice of arbitrating violations of personal rights began to slacken after World War II. The diplomatic protest remains a major vehicle for the assertion of human rights claims.

---

1. THE PRINCIPLE OF DIPLOMATIC PROTECTION

The theory that a claim for injury to an alien is the claim of the state of which he is a national has remained the underlying theory of international practice. But the reality of the claim as one on behalf of the individual has been recognized, as shown in the decision that follows.

ADMINISTRATIVE DECISION NO. V

Mixed Claims Commission (United States—Germany), 1924.
VII U.N.Rep. Int'l Arb. Awards 119, 152.

Ordinarily a nation will not espouse a claim on behalf of its national against another nation unless requested so to do by such national. When on such request a claim is espoused, the nation's absolute right to control it is necessarily exclusive. In exercising such control it is governed not only by the interest of the particular claimant but by the larger interests of the whole people of the nation and must exercise an untrammeled discretion in determining when and how the claim will be presented and pressed, or withdrawn or compromised, and the private owner will be bound by the action taken. Even if payment is made to the espousing nation in pursuance of an award, it has complete control over the fund so paid to and held by it and may, to prevent fraud, correct a mistake, or protect the national honor, at its election return the fund to the nation paying it or otherwise dispose of it. But where a demand is made on behalf of a designated national, and an award and payment is made on that specific demand, the fund so paid is not a national fund in the sense that the title vests in the nation receiving it entirely free from any obligation to account to the private claimant, on whose behalf the claim was asserted and paid and who is the real owner thereof. Broad and misleading statements susceptible of this construction are found in cases where lump-sum awards and payments have been made to the demanding nation covering numerous claims put forward by it and where the tribunal making the award did not undertake to adjudicate each claim or to allocate any specified amount to any designated claim. It is not believed that any case can be cited in which an award has been made by an international tribunal in favor of the demanding nation on behalf of its designated national in which the nation receiving payment of such award has, in the absence of fraud or mistake, hesitated to account to the national designated, or those claiming under him, for the full amount of the award received. So far as the United States is concerned it would seem that the Congress has treated funds paid the nation in satisfaction of specific claims as held "in trust for citizens of the United States or others".

The Umpire agrees with the American Commissioner that the control of the United States over claims espoused by it before this Commission is complete. But the generally accepted theory formulated by Vattel, which makes the injury to the national an injury to the nation and internationally therefore the claim a national claim which may and should be espoused by the nation injured, must not be permitted to obscure the realities or blind us to the fact that the ultimate object of asserting the claim is to provide reparation for the private claimant * * *.

     *   *   *

2. THE INTERNATIONAL MINIMUM STANDARD

ROBERTS (UNITED STATES) v. UNITED MEXICAN STATES

General Claims Commission, 1926.
IV U.N.Rep. Int'l Arb. Awards 77.

1. This claim is presented by the United States of America in behalf of Harry Roberts, an American citizen who, it is alleged in the

memorial, was arbitrarily and illegally arrested by Mexican authorities, who held him prisoner for a long time in contravention of Mexican law and subjected him to cruel and inhumane treatment throughout the entire period of confinement.

2.   From the memorial filed by the Government of the United States and accompanying documents, the allegations upon which the claim is based are briefly stated as follows: Harry Roberts, together with a number of other persons, was arrested by Mexican Federal troops on May 12, 1922, in the vicinity of Ocampo, Tamaulipas, Mexico, charged with having taken part in an assault on the house of E. F. Watts, near Ebano, San Luis Potosí, Mexico, on the night of May 5, 1922.   The claimant was taken prisoner and brought to Tampico, whence he was taken to Ciudad Valles, San Luis Potosí, where he was held under detention until he was placed at liberty on December 16, 1923, a period of nearly nineteen months.   It is alleged that there were undue delays in the prosecution of the trial of the accused which was not instituted within one year from the time of his arrest, as required by the Constitution of Mexico.   These delays were brought to the notice of the Government of Mexico, but no corrective measures were taken.   During the entire period of imprisonment, he was subject to rude and cruel treatment from which he suffered great physical pain and mental anguish.

3.   The United States asks that an indemnity be paid by the Government of Mexico in the sum of $10,000.00 for the wrongful treatment of the accused.   It is stated in the memorial that Roberts earned prior to the time of his arrest $350.00 a month; that he would have earned $6,650.00 during the nineteen months that he was under arrest; and that he spent $1,000.00 in fees paid to a lawyer resident in the United States to assist in obtaining his release.   A total indemnity is asked in the sum of $17,650.00 together with a proper allowance of interest.

4.   The evidence presented by the Agency of the United States consists of affidavits made by Roberts and by other persons; correspondence which Roberts and fellow prisoners exchanged with the American Consul at Tampico, and correspondence exchanged by the Consul with Mexican authorities and with the Department of State. The Mexican Government on its part presented records of judicial proceedings, including proceedings instituted against Roberts and others.

5.   It does not appear from this evidence that the Mexican authorities had not serious grounds for apprehending Roberts and his companions.   The record of the proceedings instituted by the Mexican authorities shows that at about twelve o'clock on the night of May 5, 1922, the Chief of the Detachment in the Ebano Station, San Luis Potosí, received a telephone message from Mr. Eduardo F. Watts to the effect that, at that moment, there had appeared in front of his house, which is situated on the limits of a small village, a band of outlaws consisting of several men, mounted and armed; that the

officer immediately left with the men under his orders to render assistance; that, upon arriving at the house he discovered several persons in hiding; that, having seen flashes of light and heard discharges from firearms, he ordered his men to return fire, whereupon the persons lying in ambush fled and succeeded in escaping due to their being mounted; that he picked up a dead man named Monte Michaels, who was suspected of being implicated in the blowing-up of a train belonging to a petroleum company; that the officer also picked up a rifle having a burnt cartridge and an unused one in the breech, a saddled mule, and other things; and that Watts furnished the information that the fugitives were three Americans. It further appears that an examination of Watts' house disclosed the impacts of several shots fired at the premises; that on May 12th, Harry Roberts and two of his companions were apprehended in the neighborhood of Chamal, where they had fled and where forces had been sent to capture them; that upon their being arrested, their preliminary statements were taken, in which they did not deny that they were the persons who were surprised by the detachment from Ebano on the night of May 5th in front of Watts' house, although they asserted that they had not gone there with criminal purposes. It is further shown by the official Mexican records that on May 15th, the prisoners were placed at the disposition of the agent of the Federal District Attorney, who immediately ordered a preliminary investigation; that from this time until the date when Roberts was placed at liberty judicial proceedings continued, first before the First District Court of Tampico, Tamaulipas, and afterwards before the Judge of First Instance of the District of Valles, San Luis Potosí; and that in the record of the proceedings instituted before those officials there are found statements of the accused and testimony of other persons indicating that there were grounds for suspecting that Harry Roberts and his companions had committed a crime—grounds sufficient to warrant the authorities to proceed with the arrest and trial of the accused.

6. The Commission is not called upon to reach a conclusion whether Roberts committed the crime with which he was charged. The determination of that question rested with the Mexican judiciary, and it is distinct from the question whether the Mexican authorities had just cause to arrest Roberts and to bring him to trial. Aliens of course are obliged to submit to proceedings properly instituted against them in conformity with local laws. In the light of the evidence presented in the case the Commission is of the opinion that the Mexican authorities had ample grounds to suspect that Harry Roberts had committed a crime and to proceed against him as they did. The Commission therefore holds that the claim is not substantiated with respect to the charge of illegal arrest.

7. In order to pass upon the complaint with reference to an excessive period of imprisonment, it is necessary to consider whether the proceedings instituted against Roberts while he was incarcerated exceeded reasonable limits within which an alien charged with crime may be held in custody pending the investigation of the charge

against him. Clearly there is no definite standard prescribed by international law by which such limits may be fixed. Doubtless an examination of local laws fixing a minimum length of time within which a person charged with crime may be held without being brought to trial may be useful in determining whether detention has been unreasonable in a given case. The Mexican Constitution of 1917, provides by its Article 20, section 8, that a person accused of crime "must be judged within four months if he is accused of a crime the maximum penalty for which may not exceed two years' imprisonment, and within one year if the maximum penalty is greater." From the judicial records presented by the Mexican Agent it clearly appears that there was a failure of compliance with this constitutional provision, since the proceedings were instituted on May 17, 1922, and that Roberts had not been brought to trial on December 16, 1923, the date when he was released. It was contended by the Mexican Agency that the delay was due to the fact that the accused repeatedly refused to name counsel to defend him, and that as a result of such refusal on his part proceedings were to his advantage suspended in order that he might obtain satisfactory counsel to defend him. We do not consider that this contention is sound. There is evidence in the record that Roberts constantly requested the American Consul at Tampico to take steps to expedite the trial. Several communications were addressed by American diplomatic and consular officers in Mexico to Mexican authorities with a view to hastening the trial. It was the duty of the Mexican judge under Article 20, section 9, of the Mexican Constitution to appoint counsel to act for Roberts from the time of the institution of the proceedings against him. The Commission is of the opinion that preliminary proceedings could have been completed before the lapse of a year after the arrest of Roberts. Even though it may have been necessary to make use of rogatory letters to obtain the testimony of witnesses in different localities, it would seem that that could have been accomplished at least within six or seven months from the time of the arrest. In any event, it is evident in the light of provisions of Mexican law that Roberts was unlawfully held a prisoner without trial for at least seven months. With respect to this point of unreasonably long detention without trial, the Mexican Agency contended that Roberts was undoubtedly guilty of the crime for which he was arrested; that therefore had he been tried he would have been sentenced to serve a term of imprisonment, of more than nineteen months; and that, since, under Mexican law, the period of nineteen months would have been taken into account in fixing his sentence of imprisonment, it cannot properly be considered that he was illegally detained for an unreasonable period of time. The Commission must reject this contention, since the Commission is not called upon to pass upon the guilt or innocence of Roberts but to determine whether the detention of the accused was of such an unreasonable duration as to warrant an award of indemnity under the principles of international law. Having in mind particularly that Roberts was held for several months without trial in contravention of Mexican

tamount to a denial of justice to the plaintiffs on the ground that they were contrary to Peruvian law; wherefore he called upon the Government of Peru to acknowledge that there had been a denial of justice and to make due reparation. The matter was referred by the Executive to the Supreme Court.

Held: That the claim, in so far as it is based on denial of justice, must fail. [A portion of the opinion of the court follows.]

Between Peru and Cuba there is no treaty regarding foreigners; but the tenor of our laws and the principles generally accepted, especially those proclaimed in American international law, are sufficient to make the question raised by the diplomatic representative of Cuba doctrinally simple.

The condition of foreigners in Peru, from the point of view of private rights, is not left entirely to the provisions of international convenience, nor subordinated to the simple fact of reciprocity, since Articles 32 and 33 of our Civil Code provide that "civil rights are independent of the status of the citizen," and that "foreigners enjoy in Peru all rights concerning the security of their persons and property and the free administration of the same."

Equality between natives and foreigners before the Civil Law implies their equality as to judicial competency and form of proceeding in the same subject-matter; hence, foreigners enjoy in Peru the same rights, means, recourses and guarantees as nationals to sue for and defend their rights; the cautio judicatum solvi (which, as a dilatory objection against the alien plaintiff, transient or without known assets, was allowed under the Code abrogated in 1912) is no longer in force, notwithstanding that it is still sanctioned by a legislation of some countries, including that of Cuba   *   *   *.

The diplomatic representative of Cuba agrees, as must be true, that the ordinary suit commenced by Cantero Herrera against Saco and Canevaro came to a close with the judgment of the Supreme Court, dated 11 August, 1921. As a result, that judgment has placed a final, absolute and definitive seal upon all questions of a legal and juridical character ventilated in the litigation between the said parties, in conformity with the precepts of the Constitution and the laws of Peru, from whose sovereignty the foreigner litigating in the national jurisdiction cannot abstract himself, and which merely give positive expression to the old classic adage res judicata pro veritate habetur.   *   *   *

There is no doubt that nations reciprocally owe one another justice, and are bound to extend it to foreigners having recourse to their tribunals and to give them the opportunity to obtain it in the like measure with nationals; but the good understanding among them, harmonising all interests, has raised to the category of an international law the authority of the thing adjudged, and no self-respecting country will countenance that any other country should impeach the force and legality of an executed judgment, rendered regularly by its authorities, as an emanation of sovereignty.

It is on this account that, in keeping with our political Constitution, it belongs to the President of the Republic, who represents abroad the national sovereignty, "to enforce, obligatorily, the judgments and resolutions of the tribunals and courts" (Article 121, par. 10); and Article 39 of the same Constitution contains this important provision, which it is timely to mention with respect to a claim growing out of litigation over territorial property: "foreigners are, as to their property, in the same condition as Peruvians, and cannot in any case invoke with regard thereto an exceptional situation, nor have recourse to diplomatic claims. * * *"

It is erroneous to suppose that the conclusion of a proceeding in which a foreigner has failed, marks the occasion for the transference of the issue to the diplomatic plane. If it were so, the passions accumulated around matters of an entirely private nature would constantly poison the best cemented international relations.

In the relations of nation to nation, the rule is respect for the sovereignty of friendly powers, typified in the authority of its judges and of its decisions. The exception is the claim based on the motive of denial of justice; but to make such claim conformably with the principles and usages of international law, it is necessary that the case be one of the utmost seriousness, that the denial of justice be manifest or notorious, that is, that the hearing which the foreigner claims, or the recourse which he interposes, has been denied him, and in general that the exercise of his rights and rights of action is interfered with contrary to law, or is subjected to unwarranted delays; because all this involves and constitutes an odious exception, a legal infringement which can be established objectively, without offending the jurisdiction of the country, and which compromises the responsibility of the State.

Cantero Herrera has not been denied a hearing by our tribunals, nor the interposition of any recourse or means of defence permitted by the law, nor has he been subjected to any objectionable treatment. Neither can he aver, as has been alleged in other cases, that he has been cited before a court lacking jurisdiction, or has been judged without being summoned; being the plaintiff, he has selected the court and the proceeding, and with the most absolute freedom has pleaded at every stage, by word of mouth and in writing, everything he has deemed necessary in support of his right. Of what, then, does he complain? Of not having won the action? It is not on that condition, nor on any other, that the portals of justice are thrown open to the public authorities, to foreigners, or to anyone else. * * *

---

1. *Standard for determining that there has been a denial of justice.* By what standard would the Peruvian Supreme Court decide that there has been a denial of justice? Must the complaining party show that there has been a failure to meet the standards of Peruvian law? Or may the standards of Peruvian law be so high that a failure

to meet those high standards is not, of itself, a denial of justice? Would the Peruvian court hold, on the other hand, that even though the standards of Peruvian law have been met there may be a denial of justice because those standards do not meet the higher standards of international law?

2. *The position of Latin American jurists.* These jurists have been in the forefront of those who deny that there is an international standard to which each state's jurisprudence must attain. A frequently stated position is that the alien is entitled only to equality of treatment with nationals. In analyzing this proposition it should be noted that the broad question of state responsibility for injury to aliens has been discussed somewhat indiscriminately in connection with two types of problems: injury to an alien individual in his personal rights (e. g., rights to physical security and personal freedom, rights to fair trial in cases involving personal liberty) on one hand and, on the other, the alien individual's (or corporation's) rights to property. In recent years, the latter rights have been the subject of considerable controversy, particularly with respect to the expropriation of property by states socializing and collectivizing the means of production. See Chapter 17.

Would you expect a system of international law to be more protective of personal rights than of property rights?

3. *Influence of the creation of new states on the question of the international standard.* The debate that was carried on in the Western World prior to World War II on the question of an international minimum standard versus a standard of national treatment may be viewed as one within an established legal system in which the members of that system sought to delineate the contours of a body of customary law acceptable to them. With the influx of new states into the community of nations, mostly former colonies, the debate has taken on a different tone:

> The international community in its inception was confined to only some Christian states of Europe. It expanded within very narrow limits to embrace, first, the other Christian states of Europe and next their own offshoots in other continents. It thus retained until recently its racial exclusiveness in full and its geographical and other limitations in part. The international law which the worldwide community of states today inherits is the law which owes its genesis and growth, first, to the attempts of these states to regulate their mutual intercourse in their own interests and, secondly, to the use made of it during the period of colonialism.
>
> The contacts of the members of the restricted international community of the past with other states and peoples of the much larger world outside its own charmed circle were not governed by any law or scruples beyond what expediency dictated. The history of the establishment and consolidation of empires overseas by some of the members of the old international community

and of the acquisition therein of vast economic interests by their nationals teems with instances of a total disregard of all ethical considerations. A strange irony of fate now compels those very members of the community of nations on the ebb tide of their imperial power to hold up principles of morality as shields against the liquidation of interests acquired and held by an abuse of international intercourse. Rights and interests acquired and consolidated during periods of such abuse cannot for obvious reasons carry with them in the mind of the victims of that abuse anything like the sanctity the holders of those rights and interests may and do attach to them. To the extent to which the law of responsibility of states for injuries to aliens favors such rights and interests, it protects an unjustified status quo or, to put it more bluntly, makes itself a handmaid of power in the preservation of its spoils.

* * *

The law of responsibility then, is not founded on any universal principles of law or morality. Its sole foundation is custom, which is binding only among states where it either grew up or came to be adopted. It is thus hardly possible to maintain that it is still part of universal international law. Whatever the basis of obligation in international law in the past, when the international community was restricted to only a few states, including those, fewer still, admitted into it from time to time, the birth of a new world community has brought about a radical change which makes the traditional basis of obligation outmoded.

Once it is found that the right of diplomatic protection of their nationals abroad, claimed by states as a customary right, is not universally binding, the structure of this law as part of universal international law crumbles, for this right is assumed to be the sole basis of a state's claim to stretch out its protecting hand to its nationals in the territory of another state independently of its consent. Its elimination from universal international law necessarily means that, even outside the limited zone of the applicability of this law, the responsibility of a state for injuries to aliens remains in every case in which it may be held to be responsible exactly in the same way as in the case of its own nationals, but it remains its responsibility not to the home state of the injured alien but to the injured alien himself. In other words, it ceases to be an international responsibility and becomes a responsibility only under the municipal law of the state concerned. Guha-Roy, Is the Law of Responsibility of States for Injuries to Aliens a Part of Universal International Law? 55 Am.J.Int'l L. 863, 866, 888 (1961).*

* Reprinted by permission of the American Society of International Law.

start here

CHATTIN (UNITED STATES) v. UNITED MEXICAN STATES

General Claims Commission, 1927.
IV U.N.Rep. Int'l Arb. Awards 282.

Broad scope of procedural objection

VAN VOLLENHOVEN, PRESIDING COMMISSIONER:

1. This claim is made by the United States of America against the United Mexican States on behalf of B. E. Chattin, an American national. Chattin, who since 1908 was an employee (at first freight conductor, thereafter passenger conductor) of the Ferrocarril Sud-Pacifico de Mexico (Southern Pacific Railroad Company of Mexico) and who in the Summer of 1910 performed his duties in the State of Sinaloa, was on July 9, 1910, arrested at Mazatlán, Sinaloa, on a charge of embezzlement; was tried there in January, 1911, convicted on February 6, 1911, and sentenced to two years' imprisonment; but was released from the jail at Mazatlán in May or June, 1911, as a consequence of disturbances caused by the Madero revolution. He then returned to the United States. It is alleged that the arrest, the trial and the sentence were illegal, that the treatment in jail was inhuman, and that Chattin was damaged to the extent of $50,000.00, which amount Mexico should pay.

* * *

3. The circumstances of Chattin's arrest, trial and sentence were as follows. In the year 1910 there had arisen a serious apprehension on the part of several railroad companies operating in Mexico as to whether the full proceeds of passenger fares were accounted for to these companies. The Southern Pacific Railroad Company of Mexico applied on June 15, 1910, to the Governor of the State of Sinaloa, in his capacity as chief of police of the State, co-operating with the federal police, in order to have investigations made of the existence and extent of said defrauding of their lines within the territory of his State. On or about July 8, 1910, one Cenobio Ramírez, a Mexican employee (brakeman) of the said railroad, was arrested at Mazatlán on a charge of fraudulent sale of railroad tickets of the said company, and in his appearance before the District Court in that town he accused the conductor Chattin—who since May 9, 1910, had charge of trains operating between Mazatlán and Acaponeta, Nayarit—as the principal in the crime with which he, Ramírez, was charged; whereupon Chattin also was arrested by the Mazatlán police, on July 9, (not 10), 1910. On August 3 (not 13), 1910, his case was consolidated not only with that of Ramírez, but also with that of three more American railway conductors (Haley, Englehart and Parrish) and of four more Mexicans. After many months of preparation and a trial at Mazatlán, during both of which Chattin, it is alleged, lacked proper information, legal assistance, assistance of an interpreter and confrontation with the witnesses, he was convicted on February 6, 1911, by the said District Court of Mazatlán as stated above. The case was carried on appeal to the Third Circuit Court at Mexico City, which court on July 3, 1911, affirmed the sentence. In the meantime (May

or June, 1911) Chattin had been released by the population of Mazatlán which threw open the doors of the jail in the time elapsing between the departure of the representatives of the Diaz regime and the arrival of the Modero forces.

* * *

Irregularity of court proceedings

12. The next allegation on the American side is that Chattin's trial was held in an illegal manner. The contentions are: (a) that the Governor of the State, for political reasons, used his influence to have this accused and three of his fellow conductors convicted; (b) that the proceedings against the four conductors were consolidated without reason; (c) that the proceedings were unduly delayed; (d) that an exorbitant amount of bail was required; (e) that the accused was not duly informed of the accusations; (f) that the accused lacked the aid of counsel; (g) that the accused lacked the aid of an interpreter; (h) that there were no oaths required of the witnesses; (i) that there was no such thing as a confrontation between the witnesses and the accused; and (j) that the hearings in open court which led to sentences of from two years' to two years and eight months' imprisonment lasted only some five minutes. It was also contended that the claimant had been forced to march under guard through the streets of Mazatlán; but the Commission in paragraph 3 of its opinion in the Faulkner case (Docket No. 47) rendered November 2, 1926, has already held that such treatment is incidental to the treatment of detention, and suspicion, and cannot in itself furnish a separate basis for a complaint.

13. As to illegal efforts made by the Governor of Sinaloa to influence the trial and the sentence (allegation a), the only evidence consists in hearsay or suppositions about such things as what the Governor had in mind, or what the Judge has said in private conversation; hearsay and suppositions which often come from persons connected with those colleagues of Chattin's who shared his fate. To uncorroborated talk of this kind the Commission should not pay any attention. * * *

* * *

15. For undue delay of the proceedings (allegation c), there is convincing evidence in more than one respect. The formal proceedings began on July 9, 1910. Chattin was not heard in court until more than one hundred days thereafter. The stubs and perhaps other pieces of evidence against Chattin were presented to the Court on August 3, 1910; Chattin, however, was not allowed to testify regarding them until October 28, 1910. Between the end of July and October 8, 1910, the Judge merely waited. * * * Another remarkable proof of the measure of speed which the Judge deemed due to a man deprived of his liberty, is in that, whereas Chattin appealed from the decree of his formal imprisonment on July 11, 1910—an appeal which would seem to be of rather an urgent character—"the corresponding

copy for the appeal" was not remitted to the appellate Court until September 12, 1910; this Court did not render judgment until October 27, 1910; and though its decision was forwarded to Mazatlán on October 31, 1910, its receipt was not established until November 12, 1910.

16. The allegation (d) that on July 25, 1910, an exorbitant amount of bail, to-wit a cash bond in the sum of 15,000.00 pesos, was required for the accused is true; but it is difficult to see how in the present case this can be held an illegal act on the part of the Judge.

17. The allegation (e) that the accused has not been duly informed regarding the charge brought against him is proven by the record, and to a painful extent. The real complainant in this case was the railroad company, acting through its general manager; this manager, an American, not only was allowed to make full statements to the Court on August 2, 3, and 26, 1910, without ever being confronted with the accused and his colleagues, but he was even allowed to submit to the Court a series of anonymous written accusations, the anonymity of which reports could not be removed (for reasons which he explained); these documents created the real atmosphere of the trial. Were they made known to the conductors? Were the accused given an opportunity to controvert them? There is no trace of it in the record, nor was it ever alleged by Mexico. It is true that, on August 3, 1910, they were ordered added to the court record; but that same day they were delivered to a translator, and they did not reappear on the court record until after January 16, 1911, when the investigations were over and Chattin's lawyer had filed his briefs. The court record only shows that on January 13, and 16, 1911, the conductors and one of their lawyers were aware of the existence, not that they knew the contents of these documents. * * *

18. The allegations (f) and (g) that the accused lacked counsel and interpreter are disproven by the record of the court proceedings. * * *

19. The allegation (h) that the witnesses were not sworn is irrelevant, as Mexican law does not require an "oath" (it is satisfied with a solemn promise, protesta, to tell the truth), nor do international standards of civilization.

20. The allegation (i) that the accused has not been confronted with the witnesses—Delgado and Sarabia—is disproven both by the record of the court proceedings and by the decision of the appellate tribunal. * * *

21. The allegation (j) that the hearings in open court lasted only some five minutes is proven by the record. This trial in open court was held on January 27, 1911. It was a pure formality in which only confirmations were made of written documents, and in which not even the lawyer of the accused conductors took the trouble to say more than a word or two.

22. The whole of the proceedings discloses a most astonishing lack of seriousness on the part of the Court. There is no trace of an effort to have the two foremost pieces of evidence explained. * * *

There is no trace of an effort to find one Manuel Virgen, who, according to the investigations of July 21, 1910, might have been mixed in Chattin's dealings, nor to examine one Carl or Carrol Collins, a dismissed clerk of the railroad company concerned, who was repeatedly mentioned as forging tickets and passes and as having been discharged for that very reason. One of the Mexican brakemen, Batriz, stated on August 8, 1910, in court that "it is true that the American conductors have among themselves schemes to defraud in that manner the company, the deponent not knowing it for sure"; but again no steps were taken to have this statement verified or this brakeman confronted with the accused Americans. No disclosures were made as to one pass, one "half-pass" and eight perforated tickets shown to Chattin on October 28, 1910, as pieces of evidence; * * *. No investigation was made as to why Delgado and Sarabia felt quite certain that June 29 was the date of their trip, a date upon the correctness of which the weight of their testimony wholly depended. No search of the houses of these conductors is mentioned. Nothing is revealed as to a search of their persons on the days of their arrest; when the lawyer of the other conductors, Haley and Englehart, insisted upon such an inquiry, a letter was sent to the Judge at Culiacán, but was allowed to remain unanswered. Neither during the investigations nor during the hearings in open court was any such thing as an oral examination or cross-examination of any importance attempted. It seems highly improbable that the accused have been given a real opportunity during the hearings in open court, freely to speak for themselves. It is not for the Commission to endeavor to reach from the record any conviction as to the innocence or guilt of Chattin and his colleagues; but even in case they were guilty, the Commission would render a bad service to the Government of Mexico if it failed to place the stamp of its disapproval and even indignation on a criminal procedure so far below international standards of civilization as the present one. If the wholesome rule of international law as to respect for the judiciary of another country * * * shall stand, it would seem of the utmost necessity that appellate tribunals when, in exceptional cases, discovering proceedings of this type should take against them the strongest measures possible under constitution and laws, in order to safeguard their country's reputation.
* * *

Conviction on insufficient evidence

24. In Mexican law, as in that of other countries, an accused can not be convicted unless the Judge is convinced of his guilt and has acquired this view from legal evidence. An international tribunal never can replace the important first element, that of the Judge's being convinced of the accused's guilt; it can only in extreme cases,

and then with great reserve, look into the second element, the legality and sufficiency of the evidence.

* * *

26.   From the record there is not convincing evidence that the proof against Chattin, scanty and weak though it may have been, was not such as to warrant a conviction.   Under the article deemed applicable the medium penalty fixed by law was imposed, and deduction made of the seven months Chattin had passed in detention from July, 1910, till February, 1911.   It is difficult to understand the sentence unless it be assumed that the Court, for some reason or other, wished to punish him severely.   The most acceptable explanation of this supposed desire would seem to be the urgent appeals made by the American chief manager of the railroad company concerned, the views expressed by him and contained in the record, and the dangerous collection of anonymous accusations which were not only inserted in the court record at the very last moment, but which were even quoted in the decision of February 6, 1911, as evidence to prove "illegal acts of the nature which forms the basis of this investigation".   The allegation that the Court in this matter was biased against American citizens would seem to be contradicted by the fact that, together with four Americans, five Mexicans were indicted as well, four of whom had been caught and have subsequently been convicted—that one of these Mexicans was punished as severely as the Americans were— and that the lower penalties imposed on the three others are explained by motives which, even if not shared, would seem reasonable. The fact that the Prosecuting Attorney who did not share the Judge's views applied merely for "insignificant penalties"—as the first decision establishes—shows, on the one hand, that he disagreed with the Court's wish to punish severely and with its interpretation of the Penal Code, but shows on the other hand that he also considered the evidence against Chattin a sufficient basis for his conviction.   If Chattin's guilt was sufficiently proven, the small amount of the embezzlement (four pesos) need not in itself have prevented the Court from imposing a severe penalty.

27.   It has been suggested as most probable that after Chattin's escape and return to the United States no demand for his extradition has been made by the Mexican Government, and that this might imply a recognition on the side of Mexico that the sentence had been unjust.   Both the disturbed conditions in Mexico since 1911, and the little chance of finding the United States disposed to extradite one of its citizens by way of exception, might easily explain the absence of such a demand, without raising so extravagant a supposition as Mexico's own recognition of the injustice of Chattin's conviction.

Mistreatment in prison

28.   The allegation of the claimant regarding mistreatment in the jail at Mazatlán refers to filthy and unsanitary conditions, bad food, and frequent compulsion to witness the shooting of prisoners. It is well known   * * *   how dangerous it would be to place too

great a confidence in uncorroborated statements of claimants regarding their previous treatment in jail. * * * The hot climate of Mazatlán would explain in a natural way many of the discomforts experienced by the prisoners; the fact that Chattin's three colleagues were taken to a hospital or allowed to go there when they were ill and that one of them had the services of an American physician in jail might prove that consideration was shown for the prisoner's conditions. Nevertheless, if a small town as Mazatlán could not afford— as Mexico seems to contend—a jail satisfactory to lodge prisoners for some considerable length of time, this could never apply to the food furnished, and it would only mean that it is Mexico's duty to see to it that prisoners who have to stay in such a jail for longer than a few weeks or months be transported to a neighboring jail of better conditions. The statement made in the Mexican reply brief that "a jail is a place of punishment, and not a place of pleasure" can have no bearing on the cases of Chattin and his colleagues, who were not convicts in prison, but persons in detention and presumed to be innocent until the Court held the contrary. On the record as it stands, however, inhuman treatment in jail is not proven.

Conclusion

29. Bringing the proceedings of Mexican authorities against Chattin to the test of international standards (paragraph 11), there can be no doubt of their being highly insufficient. Inquiring whether there is convincing evidence of these unjust proceedings (paragraph 11), the answer must be in the affirmative. Since this is a case of alleged responsibility of Mexico for injustice committed by its judiciary, it is necessary to inquire whether the treatment of Chattin amounts even to an outrage, to bad faith, to wilful neglect of duty, or to an insufficiency of governmental action recognizable by every unbiased man (paragraph 11); and the answer here again can only be in the affirmative.

30. An illegal arrest of Chattin is not proven. Irregularity of court proceedings is proven with reference to absence of proper investigations, insufficiency of confrontations, withholding from the accused the opportunity to know all of the charges brought against him, undue delay of the proceedings, making the hearings in open court a mere formality, and a continued absence of seriousness on the part of the Court. Insufficiency of the evidence against Chattin is not convincingly proven; intentional severity of the punishment is proven, without its being shown that the explanation is to be found in unfairmindedness of the Judge. Mistreatment in prison is not proven. Taking into consideration, on the one hand, that this is a case of direct governmental responsibility, and on the other hand, that Chattin, because of his escape, has stayed in jail for eleven months instead of for two years, it would seem proper to allow in behalf of this claimant damages in the sum of $5,000.00 without interest.

[Opinion of Nielsen, Commissioner, omitted.]

Decision

The Commission decides that the Government of the United Mexican States is obligated to pay to the Government of the United States of America, on behalf of B. E. Chattin, $5,000.00 (five thousand dollars), without interest.

Dissenting Opinion, FERNANDEZ MacGREGOR, Commissioner.

* * *

19. I consider that this is one of the most delicate cases that has come before the Commission and that its nature is such that it puts to a test the application of principles of international law. It is hardly of any use to proclaim in theory respect for the judiciary of a nation, if, in practice, it is attempted to call the judiciary to account for its minor acts. It is true that sometimes it is difficult to determine when a judicial act is internationally improper and when it is so from a domestic standpoint only. In my opinion the test which consists in ascertaining if the act implies damage, wilful neglect, or palpable deviation from the established customs becomes clearer by having in mind the damage which the claimant could have suffered. There are certain defects in procedure that can never cause damage which may be estimated separately, and that are blotted out or disappear, to put it thus, if the final decision is just. There are other defects which make it impossible for such decision to be just. The former, as a rule, do not engender international liability; the latter do so, since such liability arises from the decision which is iniquitous because of such defects. To prevent an accused from defending himself, either by refusing to inform him as to the facts imputed to him or by denying him a hearing and the use of remedies; to sentence him without evidence, or to impose on him disproportionate or unusual penalties, to treat him with cruelty and discrimination; are all acts which per se cause damage due to their rendering a just decision impossible. But to delay the proceedings somewhat, to lay aside some evidence, there existing other clear proofs, to fail to comply with the adjective law in its secondary provisions and other deficiencies of this kind, do not cause damage nor violate international law. Counsel for Mexico justly stated that to submit the decisions of a nation to revision in this respect was tantamount to submitting her to a régime of capitulations. All the criticism which has been made of these proceedings, I regret to say, appears to arise from lack of knowledge of the judicial system and practice of Mexico, and, what is more dangerous, from the application thereto of tests belonging to foreign systems of law. For example, in some of the latter the investigation of a crime is made only by the police magistrates and the trial proper is conducted by the Judge. Hence the reluctance in accepting that one same judge may have the two functions and that, therefore, he may have to receive in the preliminary investigation (instrucción) of the case all kinds of data, with the obligation, of course, of not taking them into account at the time of judgment, if they have no probative

weight. It is certain that the secret report, so much discussed in this case, would have been received by the police of the countries which place the investigation exclusively in the hands of such branch. This same police would have been free to follow all the clues or to abandon them at its discretion; but the Judge is criticized here because he did not follow up completely the clue given by Ramirez with respect to Chattin. The same domestic test—to call it such—is used to understand what is a trial or open trial imagining at the same time that it must have the sacred forms of common-law and without remembering that the same goal is reached by many roads. And the same can be said when speaking of the manner of taking testimony of witnesses, of cross-examination, of holding confrontations, etc.

20. In view of the above considerations, I am of the opinion that this claim should be disallowed.

————

1. *What variations in legal systems are comprehended by the international minimum standard?* National legal systems differ considerably as to how they deal with an accused in a criminal proceeding pending trial on the merits. In some countries, the accusation of a criminal offense results in the accused being put into detention pending investigation by a magistrate on the question of whether there is a probable case against him. In some of these countries, bail is not allowed, either for this period or pending trial. In many developing countries, and perhaps in some developed countries, the physical conditions of detention centers are rather grim. In many civil law countries, moreover, exclusionary rules of evidence are sparse and the defendant is not allowed in all cases to confront the witnesses against him. In view of these differences, it cannot be said that the international minimum standard of criminal procedural justice takes its contents from Anglo-American procedures. Does this mean that there is no international minimum standard? Or does this suggest that the task of determining the content of such a standard does not consist of asking whether the foreign state has conformed to the requirements of the United States Constitution as interpreted by the Supreme Court from time to time? Consider what elements in the Chattin case, in view of the differences in the criminal law systems of the United States and Mexico, violated any international minimum standard.

2. *Theory and practice.* Even states that in claims settlement proceedings assert the international minimum standard find it difficult to insure its application to their nationals as a basis for immediate relief. Consider for example the following announcement of the United States Department of State.

TRAVELERS WARNED OF PENALTIES FOR DRUG VIOLATIONS ABROAD

65 United States Department of State Bulletin 56 (1971).

At the end of May 1971, there were 747 Americans under detention in the jails of 50 foreign countries for violating local narcotic and marihuana laws. This represents an alarming fourfold increase in 2 years. Detentions in May 1969 totaled 190, and by May 1970 had risen to 556.

With more than 2 million Americans expected to go abroad this summer, the Department of State again warns travelers, particularly young Americans, of the serious consequences that may result from arrests abroad on charges of possessing, trafficking in, or smuggling illegal drugs.

The possibility of arrest is of particular concern because of the severe penalties involved, the primitive penal conditions in some countries, and the very limited ability of U. S. officials to assist those arrested.

Many of the young Americans arrested appear to have been under the impression that foreign governments are more tolerant of drug use and more permissive in their drug laws and law enforcement than is the case in the United States. In fact, however, prosecution of offenders is being intensified, partly as a result of the international effort to suppress the illicit drug trade, an effort in which the present administration has taken the lead. In many countries, the consequences of narcotics and marihuana violations are severe, ranging up to the death penalty.

* * *

Possession alone can result in a jail term of 6 years and a heavy fine in some countries. In others, possession or trafficking can result in sentences of 1 to 3 years in a detoxification asylum, usually a mental hospital. Penalties for trafficking can mean sentences of 10 years, 20 years, or life. Many countries have no provision for bail on drug charges and pretrial detention may be prolonged, in some cases up to a year.

Prison conditions in some countries are primitive: overcrowding, lack of sanitary facilities and bedding; limited, poor-quality food; little or no heat or light; damp, underground locations; rats and vermin; sometimes solitary confinement.

Case histories like the following illustrate the dangers facing Americans abroad who violate local drug laws:

—Two years ago a young American teacher, arrested in the Middle East for possessing a small quantity of hashish, spent several months in the one-room women's section of a provincial jail. The only light in the room filtered through the bars of the cell door, which, when covered to keep out winter drafts, left the cell in complete darkness.

—The diet of one young man has been nothing but beans and tortillas since his incarceration almost a year ago in a South American country on a drug charge. He has no money, and there are no local charitable sources to help supplement his diet. He has another year and a half to serve.

* * *

—A Latin American cabdriver urged a young American married couple to buy two marihuana cigarettes for 50 cents. Although they had not been looking for marihuana, they finally accepted the offer. The next night secret police arrested them as they sat by the waterfront smoking the cigarettes. They were placed in separate prisons. He was put with 14 other prisoners in a cell where wall bunks were designed to sleep four. Many slept on the cell floor. There were no sheets, blankets, or pillows. It was 6 months before the couple was brought to trial.

American travelers abroad are not protected by U. S. laws. They are subject solely to the laws of the country they are visiting. The authority of American consular officers to intercede on their behalf is very limited. The U. S. Government can only seek to insure that the American is not discriminated against; that is, that he receives the same treatment as do nationals of the country in which he is arrested who are charged with the same offense.

When a U. S. citizen is arrested abroad, U. S. consular officials move as quickly as possible to protect his rights, but the laws of the country where the arrest takes place determine what those rights are.

Whenever possible, an American consular officer visits the detainee on learning of his arrest, informs him of his rights, and provides him with a list of local attorneys from which to select defense counsel. If the detainee wishes, the consul helps him contact his family or friends to let them know what has happened and seek their assistance.

The consul reports the arrest and subsequent developments to the Department of State. He is in regular contact with the detainee, his attorney, and local officials to determine how the detainee is being treated and to make sure that processing of the legal charges is not unduly delayed. He also does whatever is possible to solve any difficulties which may result from the conditions of detention. (For example, in some foreign prisons a bare subsistence diet is provided, and families are expected to supply most of the prisoner's food.)

Under U. S. law, official U. S. funds cannot be used to pay legal fees or other expenses for an indigent American detainee.

------

1. *Transfer of American prisoners from Mexico by treaty arrangement.* See Rosado v. Civiletti, 621 F.2d 1179 (2d Cir. 1980), for an excruciatingly graphic account of brutal treatment of several Americans arrested by Mexican authorities and ultimately convicted in Mexico for illegal importation of cocaine. Sentenced to eight

years and nine months imprisonment, the Americans were subsequently transferred to the United States to complete their sentences there, under the terms of a United States-Mexican treaty permitting such transfers reciprocally. The Americans sought release from confinement in the United States on the ground that they had been coerced into giving their consents to transfer and that their continued detention in the United States was a deprivation of due process. The court denied their release, holding that they had voluntarily and intelligently given their consents. The court concluded its opinion as follows:

> We are satisfied * * * that the congressional decision to require offenders transferring to American custody to agree to abide by the jurisdictional provision was neither needless nor arbitrary. Moreover, we believe the conditional requirement that prisoners agree to challenge their convictions solely in the courts of the transferring nation legitimately serves two important interests that can be vindicated only by holding these prisoners to their agreements.

> In assessing the interacting interests of the United States and foreign nations, "we must move with the circumspection appropriate when [a court] is adjudicating issues inevitably entangled in the conduct of our international relations." Romero v. International Terminal Operating Co., 358 U.S. 354, 383, 79 S.Ct. 468, 486, 3 L.Ed.2d 368 (1959). Since Mexico was unwilling to enter a treaty that provided for review of its criminal judgments by United States courts, American negotiators did not have a completely free hand in structuring the Treaty's terms. Guided throughout by their humane concern to ameliorate the plight of hundreds of United States citizens imprisoned in Mexico, the negotiators obviously extracted a significant number of important concessions. At the same time, however, our negotiators were anxious to improve relations with Mexico and hopefully eliminate what had become an important source of tension between the two nations. See Letter from President Carter to the Senate of the United States (Feb. 15, 1977), reprinted in S.Exec.Doc.D., 95th Cong. 1st Sess. 1 (1977).

> Of paramount importance, however, is the interest of those Americans currently incarcerated in Mexico. Whatever hope the Treaty extends of escaping the harsh realities of confinement abroad will be dashed for hundreds of Americans [45] if we permit

---

45. As of March 28, 1980, 226 Americans were incarcerated in Mexico. Since ratification of the Treaty, 451 Americans have transferred to United States custody. Of this number, only 45 are still incarcerated in the United States. Letter of Richard Blumenthal, United States Attorney, to the Clerk of the United States Court of Appeals for the Second Circuit (Mar. 28, 1980).

In addition to the treaties with Mexico and Canada, the Senate has approved a similar treaty with Bolivia, and treaties with Panama, Peru, and Turkey have been approved for ratification by the Senate, but have not yet become effective. Each of

these three petitioners to rescind their agreement to limit their attacks upon their convictions to Mexico's courts. We refuse to scuttle the one certain opportunity open to Americans incarcerated abroad to return home, an opportunity, we note, the benefit of which Caban, Velez, and Rosado have already received. In holding these petitioners to their bargain, we by no means condone the shockingly brutal treatment to which they fell prey. Rather, we hold open the door for others similarly victimized to escape their torment.

2. *NATO Status of Forces Agreement.* The United States has concluded agreements with states on whose territory American military forces are stationed. Among other matters, these agreements deal with the division of jurisdiction, over criminal offenses committed by members of the forces, between the United States and the state on whose territory the forces are stationed. In general, military or duty-related offenses are triable by the United States, other offenses by the receiving state. In the Agreement between the Parties to the North Atlantic Treaty Regarding the Status of their Forces, June 19, 1951, [1953] 4 U.S.T. 1792, 199 U.N.T.S. 67, express provision is made regarding the principles which must govern a criminal trial conducted by the receiving state when it exercises its jurisdiction. Paragraph 9 of Article VII of the agreement provides:

Whenever a member of a force or civilian component or a dependent is prosecuted under the jurisdiction of a receiving State he shall be entitled

(a) to a prompt and speedy trial;

(b) to be informed, in advance of trial, of the specific charge or charges made against him;

(c) to be confronted with the witnesses against him;

(d) to have compulsory process for obtaining witnesses in his favor, if they are within the jurisdiction of the receiving State;

(e) to have legal representation of his own choice for his defence or to have free or assisted legal representation under the conditions prevailing for the time being in the receiving State;

(f) if he considers it necessary, to have the services of a competent interpreter; and

(g) to communicate with a representative of the Government of the sending State and, when the rules of the court permit, to have such a representative present at his trial.

Are these guarantees different from those which would be provided under the international minimum standard as defined in the

these treaties contains a provision similar to Article VI of the Mexican Treaty, conferring exclusive jurisdiction over challenges to convictions and sentences to the courts of the transferring nation. See, e. g. Treaty on the Execution of Penal Sentences, Feb. 10, 1978, United States-Bolivia, T.I.A.S. 9219, reprinted in S.Exec. Doc.G., 95th Cong., 2d Sess. (1978).

Roberts case, p. 547 (ordinary standards of civilization)? Would all the members of NATO provide these guarantees without reference to the agreement? Does paragraph 9 incorporate into status of forces jurisprudence the procedural guarantees of the United States Constitution?

      *   *   *   [T]he United States Senate, in advising ratification of the Status of Forces Agreement, resolved that the laws of all NATO countries be reviewed and analyzed to determine whether their legal systems afford the fundamental procedural safeguards of the Constitution of the United States, 99 Cong.Rec. 8780 (1953). If there is an absence or denial of these fundamental safeguards the military officials of the United States "shall request the authorities of the receiving state to waive jurisdiction." Ibid. In the operation of the jurisdictional aspects of the Agreement, the several territorial states have been co-operative with the United States authorities. Although the Agreement reserves primary jurisdiction to the territorial state in a substantial number of cases, practice indicates that the territorial state has often waived its right to exercise jurisdiction in response to a request by the military authorities of the United States. See generally, the annual Hearings before a Subcommittee of the Senate Committee on Armed Services to Review Operation of Art. VII of the Status of Forces Agreement. Reporters' Note (a) to Section 62 of the Restatement of the Foreign Relations Law of the United States (1965).*

    3. *Law applicable in international arbitrations.* In appraising the utility as precedent for international law, of such arbitral decisions as Roberts, p. 547, and Chattin, it is extremely important to determine the legal context in which the opinion was rendered. As noted in Chapter 1, p. 3, arbitrations are customarily conducted in accordance with an agreement between the contending states (the compromis) which not only sets the terms under which the arbitration will be conducted but also may indicate the governing rules to be applied by the arbitrators. In Roberts and Chattin those rules were set forth in the Convention of September 8, 1923, between the United States and Mexico. 43 Stat. 1730, IV U.N.Rep. Int'l Arb.Awards 11. The first article of the convention provided for the application of "principles of international law, justice and equity."

    In Perry (United States) v. Panama, General Claims Commission, 1933, VI U.N.Rep.Int'l Arb.Awards 315, the commission was similarly authorized to decide in accordance with these principles. In awarding the United States the sum of $10,000 because of Panama's arrest and imprisonment of an American citizen "without a proper order," who "remained imprisoned through the failure of the authorities to give to his case proper attention," the majority of the commissioners stated: "There is no reason to scrutinize whether these terms [i. e. international law, justice, and equity] embody an indivisible rule or mean that international law, justice and equity have to be considered in the order in which they are mentioned, because either of these constructions leads to the conclusion that the omission shall be guided rather by broad conceptions than by narrow interpretations." The dissenting Panamanian Commissioner stated that the majority opinion suggests "the Tribunal believes it proper to award Perry damages for simple reasons of equity."

NEER AND NEER (UNITED STATES) v. UNITED MEXICAN STATES

General Claims Commission, 1926.
IV U.N.Rep. Int'l Arb. Awards 60.

1.   This claim is presented by the United States against the United Mexican States in behalf of L. Fay H. Neer, widow, and Pauline E. Neer, daughter, of Paul Neer, who, at the time of his death, was employed as superintendent of a mine in the vicinity of Guanacevi, State of Durango, Mexico. On November 16, 1924, about eight o'clock in the evening, when he and his wife were proceeding on horseback from the village of Guanacevi to their home in the neighborhood, they were stopped by a number of armed men who engaged Neer in a conversation, which Mrs. Neer did not understand, in the midst of which bullets seem to have been exchanged and Neer was killed. It is alleged that, on account of this killing, his wife and daughter, American citizens, sustained damages in the sum of $100,000.00; that the Mexican authorities showed an unwarrantable lack of diligence or an unwarrantable lack of intelligent investigation in prosecuting the culprits; and that therefore the Mexican Government ought to pay to the claimants the said amount.

2.   As to the nationality of the claim, which is challenged, * * * [o]n the record as presented, the Commission decides that the claimants were by birth, and have since remained, American nationals.

3.   As to lack of diligence, or lack of intelligent investigation, on the part of the Mexican authorities, after the killing of Paul Neer had been brought to their notice, it would seem that in the early morning after the tragedy these authorities might have acted in a more vigorous and effective way than they did, and moreover, that both the special agent of the Attorney General of Durango (in his letter of November 24, 1924), and the Governor of that State, who proposed the removal of the Judge of Guanacevi, have shared this opinion. The Commission is mindful that the task of the local Mexican authorities was hampered by the fact that the only eyewitness of the murder was unable to furnish them any helpful information. There might have been reason for the higher authorities of the State to intervene in the matter, as they apparently did. But in the view of the

Commission there is a long way between holding that a more active and more efficient course of procedure might have been pursued, on the one hand, and holding that this record presents such lack of diligence and of intelligent investigation as constitutes an international delinquency, on the other hand.

4.   The Commission recognizes the difficulty of devising a general formula for determining the boundary between an international delinquency of this type and an unsatisfactory use of power included in national sovereignty.   *   *   *   Without attempting to announce a precise formula, it is in the opinion of the Commission possible to go a little further than the authors quoted, and to hold (first) that the propriety of governmental acts should be put to the test of international standards, and (second) that the treatment of an alien, in order to constitute an international delinquency, should amount to an outrage, to bad faith, to wilful neglect of duty, or to an insufficiency of governmental action so far short of international standards that every reasonable and impartial man would readily recognize its insufficiency.   Whether the insufficiency proceeds from deficient execution of an intelligent law or from the fact that the laws of the country do not empower the authorities to measure up to international standards is immaterial.

5.   It is not for an international tribunal such as this Commission to decide, whether another course of procedure taken by the local authorities at Guanaceví might have been more effective.   On the contrary, the grounds of liability limit its inquiry to whether there is convincing evidence either (1) that the authorities administering the Mexican law acted in an outrageous way, in bad faith, in wilful neglect of their duties, or in a pronounced degree of improper action, or (2) that Mexican law rendered it impossible for them properly to fulfil their task.   No attempt is made to establish the second point. The first point is negatived by the full record of police and judicial authorities produced by the Mexican Agent, though the Commission feels bound to state once more that in its opinion better methods might have been used.   From this record it appears that the local authorities, on the very night of the tragedy, November 16, went to the spot where the killing took place and examined the corpse; that on November 17 the Judge proceeded to the examination of some witnesses, among them Mrs. Neer; that investigations were continued for several days; that arrests were made of persons suspected; and that they were subsequently released for want of evidence.   The American Agency in rebuttal offers nothing but affidavits stating individual impressions or suppositions.   In the light of the entire record in this case the Commission is not prepared to hold that the Mexican authorities have shown such lack of diligence or such lack of intelligent investigation in apprehending and punishing the culprits as would render Mexico liable before this Commission.

Decision

6.   The Commission accordingly decides that the claim of the United States is disallowed.

[Separate opinion omitted.]

---

1.   *Exhaustion of local remedies.* "The rule that local remedies must be exhausted before international proceedings may be instituted is a well-established rule of customary international law; the rule has been generally observed in cases in which a state has adopted the cause of its national where rights are claimed to have been disregarded in another State in violation of international law. Before resort may be had to an international court in such a situation, it has been considered necessary that the State where the violation occurred should have an opportunity to redress it by its own means, within the framework of its own domestic legal system."   Interhandel Case (Switzerland v. United States), [1959] I.C.J.Rep. 6, 27. As stated, the rule is applicable to claims based upon violations of personal human rights as well as to claims arising from violations of rights of property.   Detailed examination of the rule is deferred to Chapter 17, dealing with economic interests.

It is said that the rule is subject to exceptions; for example, if it is clear that exhaustion of local remedies would not be effective, there is no need to pursue them.   Should the rule apply to diplomatic protests, or only to claims in litigation, before the International Court of Justice or an arbitral tribunal?

In view of the exhaustion of local remedies rule, how can a claimant state assert that the acting state has violated its own law? If, for example, an individual has been imprisoned for a long time before trial and complains of this through appropriate court proceedings until a court of final appeal has ruled that the local law does not prohibit such imprisonment, can an international tribunal properly hold that there has been a violation of local law?   See the Roberts case, at p. 547 where the commission asserted that Roberts' imprisonment was a violation of the Mexican Constitution.   Does the answer to this question lie in the fact that the compromis governing the Roberts arbitration provided in Article V as follows?

> The High Contracting Parties, being desirous of effecting an equitable settlement of the claims of their respective citizens thereby affording them just and adequate compensation for their losses or damages, agree that no claim shall be disallowed or rejected by the Commission by the application of the general principle of international law that the legal remedies must be exhausted as a condition precedent to the validity or allowance of any claim.

2.   *A new view of the older precedents.*   The flow of third party decisions on questions of violation of personal human rights practical-

ly ceased with World War II. It has been observed that the desire of states for freedom to act unilaterally has been strong during the whole life of the United Nations and that states have been reluctant to take disputes to the International Court of Justice. "It may be noted in this context that, whereas the number of arbitral decisions since 1945 was not spectacular, it was not insignificant, although it is probably true that, as the Secretary General of the United Nations pointed out, 'most of them concerned minor questions, many of them of a commercial nature, which were not in the least likely to disturb peace and security.' " Gross, The International Court of Justice: Consideration of Requirements for Enhancing its Role in the International Legal Order, 65 Am.J.Int'l L. 253, 268 (1971).

Although the body of arbitral precedents with respect to personal human rights is static, the United Nations has made the development of new legal norms in that field a major matter of concern. Query whether an arbitral tribunal deciding a case like Roberts or Chattin or Neer today could ignore the Universal Declaration of Human Rights or the relevant draft covenants and conventions that have flowed from the United Nations and regional organizations in recent decades.

SECTION B. THE HUMAN RIGHTS PROGRAM OF THE UNITED NATIONS

---

1. HUMAN RIGHTS PROVISIONS OF THE CHARTER OF THE UNITED NATIONS

CHARTER OF THE UNITED NATIONS

Article 1

The Purposes of the United Nations are:

*   *   *

3.   To achieve international cooperation in solving international problems of an economic, social, cultural, or humanitarian character, and in promoting and encouraging respect for human rights and for fundamental freedoms for all without distinction as to race, sex, language, or religion. *   *   *

*   *   *

Article 2

The Organization and its Members, in pursuit of the Purposes stated in Article 1, shall act in accordance with the following Principles.

*   *   *

2.   All Members, in order to ensure to all of them the rights and benefits resulting from membership, shall fulfil in good faith the obligations assumed by them in accordance with the present Charter.

* * *

Article 55

With a view to the creation of conditions of stability and well-being which are necessary for peaceful and friendly relations among nations based on respect for the principle of equal rights and self-determination of peoples, the United Nations shall promote:

a.   higher standards of living, full employment, and conditions of economic and social progress and development;

b.   solutions of international economic, social, health, and related problems; and international cultural and educational cooperation; and

c.   universal respect for, and observance of, human rights and fundamental freedoms for all without distinction as to race, sex, language or religion.

Article 56

All Members pledge themselves to take joint and separate action in cooperation with the Organization for the achievement of the purposes set forth in Article 55.

———

Highlights of the drafting history of Chapter IX, Article 56 of the Charter.   The question has been raised throughout the life of the United Nations whether Article 56 imposes on states an international legal obligation immediately to take national action to correct internal deficiencies in the area of human rights or serves merely as a statement of political principle, i. e. that states intend to do something about human rights.

The history of the drafting of Article 56 at the San Francisco Conference on International Organization discloses that two significant questions were discussed: one, the question of domestic jurisdiction and, two, the question of the nature of the commitment states should undertake.

The United States was particularly concerned that nothing in Chapter IX of the charter should "be construed as giving authority to the Organization to intervene in the domestic affairs of member states."   10 U.N.Conf.Int'l Org. 83 (1945).   The United States was, at one point, of the opinion that the reservation for domestic jurisdiction in Article 2(7) of the charter would not alone be sufficient to keep human rights from becoming matters of international concern if Article 56 were worded to include a pledge by members "to take such independent action as they deem appropriate to achieve these purposes within their own territories."   10 U.N.Conf.Int'l Org. 140

(1945). Nevertheless, the United States ultimately supported the language of Article 56 as it appears in the charter, without insisting upon a special reservation to retain domestic jurisdiction over human rights matters. 10 U.N.Conf.Int'l Org. 161 (1945).

As to the nature of the commitment, the following submission from a drafting sub-committee was rejected:

> All members undertake to cooperate jointly and severally with the Organization for the achievement of these purposes. 10 U.N.Conf.Int'l Org. 394 and 139 (1945).

The proposal noted above, for a pledge to take "independent action", was likewise not accepted. The ultimate language as found in the charter includes "*separate action* in cooperation with the Organization." [Emphasis supplied.]

What in fact was agreed to at San Francisco?

THE MEANING OF ARTICLE 56

THE QUESTION OF RACE CONFLICT IN SOUTH AFRICA RESULTING FROM THE POLICIES OF APARTHEID

United Nations, Resolution 721 (VIII) Adopted
by the General Assembly, Dec. 8, 1953

U.N.Gen.Ass., Off.Rec., 8th Sess.1953 Supp. No. 17(A/2630).

The General Assembly,

Having considered the report of the United Nations Commission on the Racial Situation in the Union of South Africa established by resolution 616A (VII) of 5 December 1952,

Noting with concern that the Commission, in its study of the racial policies of the Government of the Union of South Africa, has concluded that these policies and their consequences are contrary to the Charter and the Universal Declaration of Human Rights,

Noting that the Commission had also concluded that:

(a) "It is highly unlikely, and indeed improbable, that the policy of apartheid will ever be willingly accepted by the masses subjected to discrimination", and

(b) That the continuance of this policy would make peaceful solutions increasingly difficult and endanger friendly relations among nations,

Noting further that the Commission considers it desirable that the United Nations should request the Government of the Union of South Africa to reconsider the components of its policy towards various ethnic groups, * * *

Considering * * * the Commission's view that one of the difficulties encountered by it was the lack of cooperation from the

Sweeny, O. & L. Cs.Inter.Leg.Sys.2d Ed. UCB—15

Government of the Union of South Africa and, in particular, its refusal to permit the Commission to enter its territory,

1.   Reaffirms its resolutions 103(I) of 19 November 1946, 377 A(V), section E, of 3 November 1950 and 616B (VII) of 5 December 1952, particularly the passages in those resolutions which state respectively that "it is in the higher interests of humanity to put an immediate end to religious and so-called racial persecution and discrimination" ; that "enduring peace will not be secured solely by collective security arrangements against breaches of international peace and acts of aggression, but that a genuine and lasting peace depends also upon the observance of all the Principles and Purposes established in the Charter of the United Nations, * * * and especially upon respect for an observance of human rights and fundamental freedoms for all and on the establishment and maintenance of conditions of economic and social well-being in all countries"; and that "in a multi-racial society harmony and respect for human rights and freedoms and the peaceful development of a unified community are best assured when patterns of legislation and practice are directed towards ensuring the equality before the law of all persons regardless of race, creed or colour, and when economic, social, cultural and political participation of all racial groups is on a basis of equality";

2.   Expresses appreciation of the work of the United Nations Commission on the Racial Situation in the Union of South Africa;
        *   *   *
4.   Requests the Commission:

(a) To continue its study of the development of the racial situation in the Union of South Africa; *   *   *

(b) To suggest measures which would help to alleviate the situation and promote a peaceful settlement;

5.   Invites the Government of the Union of South Africa to extend its full co-operation to the Commission;

6.   Requests the Commission to report to the General Assembly at its ninth session.

UNITED NATIONS, EXTRACTS FROM DEBATE IN AD HOC POLITICAL COMMITTEE

U.N.Gen.Ass.Off.Rec., 8th Sess., Ad hoc Political Committee
20 Nov. 1953—5 Dec. 1953.

[In the course of the debate, the foregoing resolution was considered in draft form and adopted; a South African resolution denying the competence of the committee to deal with the matters covered by the resolution was defeated.]
        *   *   *

At the invitation of the Chairman, Mr. Santa Cruz, Chairman and Rapporteur of the Commission, took a seat at the Committee table.

5. Mr. SANTA CRUZ (Chairman and Rapporteur of the Commission appointed to study the racial situation in the Union of South Africa) * * *

* * *

7. The Commission had felt it necessary to include a chapter in the report in which it examined the question of its competence to deal with the racial problem in South Africa. * * * It had concluded * * * that the Assembly was empowered to undertake any investigations and make any recommendations to Member States that it deemed desirable concerning the application and enforcement of the purposes and principles of the Charter, and that, since the Commission was a subsidiary body of the Assembly, it was therefore not restricted in its activities by the provisions of the Charter. Finally, it had concluded that the exercise of the powers and functions devolving on the Assembly in such matters did not constitute an intervention within the meaning of Article 2, paragraph 7. Those conclusions were in keeping with the jurisprudence of the principal organs of the United Nations; they had been endorsed by the majority of Member States and were based on the views of the most eminent jurists who had dealt with the question. * * *

* * *

10. The Commission had assumed a formal obligation on the part of signatories to the Charter, who had undertaken, by adopting Article 56, to take the necessary measures to bring about the purposes of Article 55, including universal respect for human rights and fundamental freedoms, without distinction as to race, sex, language or religion. That obligation could not, however, mean that States were obliged either to eliminate overnight every internal situation which was contrary to the Charter or to be regarded as having violated it. It would be unreal to ignore the fact that in nearly all countries existing conditions were not always in accordance with the ideal principles proclaimed in the Charter. Imperfections in the social structure derived from historical circumstances and were associated with social, economic and religious factors which could not be eliminated by legislation. The obligation, therefore, amounted only to an undertaking by the signatories to do their best in good faith to amend their legislation and customs in accordance with those principles as quickly as practicable. No situation changing for the better should be regarded as contrary to the obligations laid down in the Charter. It was for that reason that the Commission had, when comparing the discriminatory legislation of the Union of South Africa with the provisions of the Charter and of the Universal Declaration of Human Rights, limited itself to analysing only those acts which had been promulgated since the Charter.

11. On the question of competence, the Commission had also come to the conclusion that United Nations agencies had the power to decide whether a matter concerning violation of fundamental human rights was "essentially within the domestic jurisdiction of any State". It was, however, the general conclusion, supported by the opinion of

eminent jurists, that United Nations agencies should not use their right in an arbitrary manner, and should avoid converting an institution meant to serve the interests of peace and human progress into an instrument of discord to make barren and unjustified attacks on one of its Members.

    *   *   *

1. Mr. JOOSTE (Union of South Africa) said that his delegation was very conscious of the serious implications of the debate upon which the Committee was about to embark. The South African delegation represented a sovereign and independent Member of the United Nations, with obligations under the Charter with which it was endeavouring to comply to the utmost of its ability and with rights which had been guaranteed to it and which it could expect to be honoured. Those rights were now at stake. The history of the matter before the Committee was well known to its members; as were the events that had culminated in the establishment on 5 December 1952 of a commission whose terms of reference amounted, despite his Government's most solemn protests, to intervention in the internal affairs of his country.

    *   *   *

5. It would probably be pointed out once again that the question had already been considered by the General Assembly and that that in itself rendered the Assembly competent in the matter. If that contention were accepted, the fact that the United Nations had asserted that it was itself competent to examine a question would ipso facto mean that the United Nations legally possessed such competence. In other words, a majority vote could render valid any action of the General Assembly which might be contrary to the provisions of the Charter. The argument that the United Nations had dealt with the matter in the past could therefore not justify the intervention of the General Assembly in the question of racial conflict in South Africa, unless the provisions of the Charter authorized the Assembly to intervene in matters of essentially domestic concern or the item in question did not relate to matters essentially within the domestic jurisdiction of South Africa. He wished to dwell upon those two points.

6. With regard to the first question, the Commission appointed to study the racial situation in the Union of South Africa had found it necessary to pronounce itself and had endeavoured to prove that the legal position of the Government of the Union of South Africa was not a valid one. But the Charter of the United Nations was a solemn contract between members of the family of nations, and must be interpreted as such. The Charter imposed obligations on all Members of the United Nations and guaranteed them certain rights; those obligations and rights were defined in the Charter. At San Francisco the great Powers had wished to safeguard their positions by reserving the right of veto. All Member States, and particularly the smaller States, had safeguarded themselves by introducing into Chapter I of the Charter a clause protecting them against any interference by the United Nations in their domestic affairs. That clause

was contained in Article 2, paragraph 7. It contained both an obligation and a right: an obligation on the United Nations not to intervene in the internal affairs of Member States; and the right of Member States to maintain absolute sovereignty in that field.

7. His delegation believed that the word "nothing" in Article 2, paragraph 7, precluded any intervention by the United Nations in domestic affairs, with the exception of the application of enforcement measures under Chapter VII of the Charter, which in any case lay outside the competence of the General Assembly. The word "intervene" in the same paragraph had the meaning assigned to it in dictionaries, and not the artificial, technical meaning given to it by certain jurists. The word necessarily included the act of interference. It could not be restricted to the meaning of "dictatorial interference", for if it were to be so restricted it would not apply to a measure taken by the General Assembly, which had only the power to recommend.

* * *

9. The South African delegation, therefore, reaffirmed its faith in the provisions of Article 2, paragraph 7, of the Charter as a protection against any interference in matters within the domestic jurisdiction of States; it did not recognize the United Nations as having any right to take action which would amount to such interference.

10. Turning to the question as to whether the racial conflict in South Africa could be regarded as essentially within the domestic jurisdiction of the Union of South Africa, he drew attention to the matters to which that conflict related: legislation on land tenure, conditions of employment in public services, regulation of transport, suppression of communism, combat service in the armed forces, nationality, the franchise, movement of population, residence, immigration, the work and practice of the professions, social security, education, public health, criminal law, taxation, housing, regulation of the liquor traffic, regulation of labour and wages, marriage, food subsidies, local government, pensions and workmen's compensation. Obviously, all those matters were without any doubt essentially within the domestic jurisdiction of the Union of South Africa; they covered the whole field of domestic administration in a modern State. To accept the thesis that the United Nations was entitled to intervene in such matters was tantamount to denying the principle and attributes of national sovereignty and to repudiating the provisions of Article 2, paragraph 1, of the Charter; it would signal the end of the United Nations as an organization of sovereign States.

11. It had been contended that the matters in question were outside the domestic jurisdiction of South Africa because they involved human rights; the Commission appointed to study the racial situation in the Union of South Africa had supported that contention. It should be pointed out, first, that human rights were not defined in the Charter of the United Nations and that the Charter imposed no obligation on States in respect of them; secondly, that the Universal Declaration of Human Rights was not a legally binding document;

and lastly, that there was as yet no international covenant of human rights in which such rights were defined. That was an especially important consideration, for the fact that the United Nations had deemed it necessary to embark on the drafting of an international covenant defining human rights clearly demonstrated that they had not yet been defined and that there was as yet no international instrument imposing specific obligations on Member States with respect to them.

12. Those who had attempted to justify intervention by the United Nations by alleging that human rights were involved had gone so far as to claim that the racial policy of the Union Government constituted a threat to international peace, and the Commission, in its report, had suggested that the policy was likely to impair friendly relations among nations and therefore called for action under Article 14 of the Charter.

13. Those preposterous and mischievous allegations reflected a desire to exploit the fundamental purpose of the United Nations, the maintenance of international peace and security, for tendentious purposes. It could not be seriously argued that the racial situation in South Africa constituted a threat to international peace. A threat to international peace could exist only when the territorial integrity or political independence of a State was threatened directly or indirectly. It could hardly be charged that the domestic laws of a State constituted such a threat.

* * *

12. Mr. DAYAL (India)

* * * [I]t was clear that the policy of apartheid was based on the idea that the interests of the white minority in South Africa could only be protected by a policy of racial domination. It was unnecessary to point out that such a solution was contrary to the Charter and was not supported by the experience of history or by the practice of the United Nations. It was true that racial differences existed, but it was perfectly possible to overcome them by recognizing the rights of each of the races concerned. A solution based on force and domination was no solution at all. It could only generate hatred and eventually make change by violence inevitable.

* * *

25. But social discrimination was the most humiliating type of discrimination. Apartheid did not manifest itself simply in the Group Areas Act or in measures designed to confine the native Bantu populations to reservations. It was practised in shops, hospitals, post offices, theatres, public parks and gardens, libraries, etc. It even existed in telephone booths and elevators. He quoted a series of examples, some of which had been given in the Commission's report.

26. The South African Government was not, of course, the only one to apply measures of racial and social discrimination. Such measures existed in other countries which had signed the United Nations Charter. But there was a vital difference between those countries,

which had undertaken to implement the provisions of the Charter without discrimination, and South Africa, which proclaimed that those measures were the only way to preserve white civilization. In all the other countries, discrimination was a diminishing social practice which enlightened opinion everywhere condemned. In South Africa, it was a norm of social behaviour, sanctified by the ideology of the State and enjoying the Government's full support. In the circumstances, a white citizen of South Africa who wished conscientiously to observe the provisions of the United Nations Charter would be guilty of a multitude of offences. Thus, the policy of apartheid not only contravened the Charter, but made the application of the Charter impossible and illegal in the territory of the Union.

27.   The memoranda submitted by the Governments of India and Pakistan, and reproduced in the annexes to the Commission's report, cited no less than twenty discriminatory laws promulgated in the Union after 1945, that was to say, after the signing of the Charter. Chapter VIII of the Commission's report alone cited ten of those laws which, according to the Commission, were not in harmony with the Universal Declaration of Human Rights. The non-European population of South Africa had, on 26 June 1952, embarked on a campaign of passive resistance to that policy of discrimination which was growing stronger. That campaign had been suspended soon after the Christmas holidays of 1952, after 8,065 persons had been sentenced to imprisonment. The Union Government had done its utmost to destroy the morale of the resisters by imposing excessively long prison terms, forced labour and corporal punishment. It had repeatedly utilized the Suppression of Communism Act to deal with resisters and had acquired very broad powers by promulgating the Public Safety Act and the Criminal Law Amendment Act which, according to the Rand Daily Mail, had been tantamount to setting up a dictatorship or reverting to barbaric despotism.

* * *

29.   The conclusions to be drawn from those facts were clear and the United Nations Commission had formulated them in unambiguous terms. It had stated that the doctrine of racial differentiation and superiority was scientifically false, extremely dangerous to internal peace and international relations, and contrary to the dignity and worth of the human person. The policy arising from it was contrary to the solemn declaration in the Preamble to the Charter, to Articles 55 and 56, to the Universal Declaration of Human Rights, to resolution 377(V) entitled "Uniting for peace", to resolutions 103(I) and 616B (VII) of the General Assembly—in short, to the whole doctrine upheld by the United Nations.

* * *

1.   Sir Walter HANKINSON (United Kingdom) said that in his delegation's opinion the item raised but one question, namely whether the United Nations was competent to discuss the question of apartheid. That did not mean, as he had pointed out at the 435th plenary

meeting of the General Assembly, that the United Kingdom's support for the progressive elimination of racial discrimination in the world was any less constant than it had always been.

2. Nevertheless, the United Kingdom Government considered that the item under discussion was outside the competence of the General Assembly for it related to matters essentially within the domestic jurisdiction of the Union of South Africa. That view was borne out by the provisions of Article 2, paragraph 7, of the Charter which should prevail over all other Articles of the Charter.

*   *   *

4. It was often said that by virtue of Articles 55 and 56 of the Charter, questions relating to human rights ceased to be purely domestic problems and acquired an international character. That interpretation was manifestly inaccurate, for if it were to be accepted the United Nations would acquire the right to intervene in all the internal affairs of its Member States, including economic, social and cultural problems. That argument would be valid only if specific international obligations were created with respect to particular rights. Article 56, however, created no such obligations. It merely pledged the Member States to cooperate with the Organization for the achievement of the purposes set forth in Article 55.

5. For all those reasons his delegation thought that the Commission appointed to study the racial situation in the Union of South Africa, whose report the Ad Hoc Political Committee was discussing, had been established illegally and that all its activities were therefore illegal.

*   *   *

8. The word "intervene", the key word in Article 2, had been interpreted by the Commission with an equal lack of objectivity. The authors of the report considered that the word related only to "dictatorial interference" and cited various authors in support of their view. On the other hand, they avoided mentioning authors holding the contrary view and in particular Professor Preuss himself who had said that the framers of the Charter had probably not even considered so direct and drastic a type of intervention and that nowhere in the Charter, save in Chapter VII, had they vested in any organ of the United Nations the power to interfere dictatorially in the domestic affairs of States. Elsewhere in his monograph Professor Preuss had expressed the view that United Nations practice hardly justified so restrictive an interpretation of the word "intervention" and had concluded that if recommendations and a general discussion were consistent with the pledge of States to undertake joint and separate action in co-operation with the United Nations for achieving the economic and social objectives set forth in the Charter, any specific recommendation relating to a matter within the domestic jurisdiction of a State would undoubtedly constitute interference, which the framers of the Charter had plainly wished to prohibit. *   *   *

12.   In short, the section of the report dealing with competence was by no means convincing. Consequently, he would support the South African draft resolution * * * relating to competence.

*   *   *

21.   Mrs. BOLTON (United States of America) said that the question of race conflict in South Africa brought before the General Assembly the entire programme of a Member State's policy and legislation concerning the status and treatment of its nationals on the basis of their racial origins.

22.   At the beginning of the session, the United States delegation had voted for the inclusion of the item in the agenda, stating that its attitude was governed by the fact that at its seventh session the Assembly had established a Commission and had asked it to report to the present session. It had noted on that occasion that an item of that character invited questions about the competence of the General Assembly under Article 2, paragraph 7, of the Charter; that the United States had observed with increasing concern the tendency of the General Assembly to place on its agenda subjects the international character of which was doubtful; and that that problem in the view of the United States, deserved most careful consideration by all Member Governments in preparing for the conference in reviewing the Charter.

23.   Some delegations, in particular that of the Union of South Africa, had contended that the General Assembly could not even discuss the item, in view of the reservation made in Article 2, paragraph 7. Most delegations, including that of the United States, did not share such an extreme view of the effect of the paragraph in question. At the same time, the United States was keenly aware of the serious problems in which the Organization might become involved in dealing with matters of that character if it did not constantly keep in mind the provision in the Charter on domestic jurisdiction.

24.   Many Member States considered that the programme of apartheid of the Government of the Union of South Africa imposed an inferior status on large sections of the population, by reason of their race, in disregard of provisions of the Charter, particularly of Articles 55 and 56. It was difficult to say how the United Nations could best play the part laid down for it in the Charter with respect to the advancement of human rights everywhere. The provisions on human rights in the Charter represented an important innovation in international political life. Action must be taken with the greatest circumspection and the highest degree of responsibility, in order not to blight the prospects of steady and wholesome growth for that new element in international relations. When the United Nations considered human rights problems within a particular country it should keep in mind developments throughout the world in the field of human rights and should state general conclusions relating to the objectives which all Member States should pursue in that field.

*   *   *

26.   The United States delegation had already had occasion to emphasize that progress in the field of race relations was necessarily slow.   The important thing was that there should be progress; no one could claim to have reached perfection.   The United States, from its own experience, recognized the difficulty of the problems confronting the Union of South Africa, and appreciated how acute the problems of racial relations could be rendered by shifts of population, consequent upon economic development and industrialization, and by the state of development of different groups within a population.   In South Africa those problems were further complicated by the numerical proportions of the various racial groups.   But for all that, the problem was not insoluble; in some parts of the United States and its territories the populations of different racial origins were approximately equal in number, but that did not prevent progress in the improvement of race relations.

*   *   *

MOVCHAN, THE HUMAN RIGHTS PROBLEM IN PRESENT-DAY INTERNATIONAL LAW

Contemporary International Law 233, 239 (Moscow 1969).

The Soviet science of international law is unequivocal in its claim that the "legal position of individuals is determined by national and not international law".   Professor S. B. Krylov, for instance, writes in his work on the U.N. history that the "individual is protected not directly by international law but only with the aid of national law".

International law proceeds from the recognition of the individual as a subject of national law and does not admit the direct protection of his rights by any international organ in circumvention of the state and disregard of the jurisdiction of the state organs in this sphere since this would be tantamount to interference in the domestic affairs of states and to impingement upon their sovereignty.

These principles are challenged by only a few international jurists (Scelle and Politis among them) who support the theory that the individual is a subject of international law, a theory advanced in the West before the Second World War and backed by some British and American scholars (Lauterpacht, Jessup and others).

This theory alleges that the individual is a subject of international law, enjoys international rights and, consequently, his rights must be defended not only by the state but directly by international organs with the aid of various measures involving interference in the domestic affairs of states.   The exponents of such a cosmopolitan interpretation of human rights in essence completely negate the sovereignty of states and in fact, negate international law by replacing it with "human right".

The theory that the individual is a subject of international law is incompatible with the nature of international law as interstate law and has very few supporters among international jurists.

––––––––––

1. *Domestic jurisdiction and Article 56.* If the position of the South African and United Kingdom representatives is correct, how is a state's performance under its pledge in Article 56 to be judged? Would it be irrational for a state to say that it has indeed accepted an obligation to promote human rights in its own territory but that it alone shall be the judge of both (a) the standard of human rights it is obligated to promote and (b) whether its own performance has reached that standard? Irrespective of the rationality of that position, is that what the Charter of the United Nations has provided?

2. *The contents of the obligations in Article 56.* If Article 56 has imposed an obligation upon members of the United Nations, what is the content of that obligation? Is a member state under an obligation to provide fair hearings in criminal cases, to guarantee freedom of expression, to ensure universal suffrage? Or is a member state merely under an obligation to move affirmatively toward some unstated ideal of rights and freedom? Or not to move negatively away from such an ideal? Or merely not to make distinctions, in the enjoyment of whatever rights may exist, in its domestic law, on the basis of race, sex, language or religion?

3. *Protracted debate in the United Nations.* The foregoing extract from the debates in the United Nations is but one example of a long line of similar discussions in which similar arguments have been made repeatedly. The United Nations' concern with South Africa's racial practices was first voiced in 1946 and continues to be expressed to this day. More recent resolutions of the Security Council and the General Assembly have been grounded in part upon the effect of those practices on international peace and security. This basis for United Nations action with respect to South Africa will be examined in Chapter 20.

––––––––––

ADVISORY OPINION ON THE CONTINUED PRESENCE OF SOUTH AFRICA IN NAMIBIA (SOUTH WEST AFRICA) [a]

International Court of Justice, 1971.
[1971] I.C.J.Rep. 16.

[At the conclusion of World War I, South Africa accepted a Mandate with respect to German South West Africa pursuant to the Covenant of the League of Nations. Upon the demise of the League, South Africa refused to accept the principle urged upon it by the

a. The full name of the case is: Legal Consequences for States of the Continued Presence of South Africa in

Namibia (South West Africa), notwithstanding Security Council Resolution 276 (1970), Advisory Opinion.

United Nations that the latter had the right to supervise its administration of South West Africa. After fruitless negotiations, and the
rendering of advisory opinions on various aspects of the matter by
the International Court of Justice, the General Assembly adopted a
resolution terminating the Mandate for South West Africa, now
called Namibia by the United Nations. South Africa having failed to
alter its policies with respect to South West Africa, the Security
Council adopted a resolution declaring the continued presence of
South Africa in Namibia to be illegal and called on states to act accordingly.

The council thereafter requested the court to render an advisory
opinion on the question: "What are the legal consequences for States
of the continued presence of South Africa in Namibia, notwithstanding Security Council resolution 276 (1970)?"

In the course of a comprehensive opinion answering this question, the following passages occurred.]

128.   In its oral statement and in written communications to the
Court, the Government of South Africa expressed the desire to supply
the Court with further factual information concerning the purposes
and objectives of South Africa's policy of separate development or
apartheid, contending that to establish a breach of South Africa's
substantive international obligations under the Mandate it would be
necessary to prove that a particular exercise of South Africa's legislative or administrative powers was not directed in good faith towards the purpose of promoting to the utmost the well-being and
progress of the inhabitants. It is claimed by the Government of
South Africa that no act or omission on its part would constitute a
violation of its international obligations unless it is shown that such
act or omission was actuated by a motive, or directed towards a purpose other than one to promote the interests of the inhabitants of the
Territory.

129.   The Government of South Africa having made this request, the Court finds that no factual evidence is needed for the purpose of determining whether the policy of apartheid as applied by
South Africa in Namibia is in conformity with the international obligations assumed by South Africa under the Charter of the United
Nations. In order to determine whether the laws and decrees applied
by South Africa in Namibia, which are a matter of public record,
constitute a violation of the purposes and principles of the Charter of
the United Nations, the question of intent or governmental discretion
is not relevant; nor is it necessary to investigate or determine the effects of those measures upon the welfare of the inhabitants.

130.   It is undisputed, and is amply supported by documents annexed to South Africa's written statement in these proceedings, that
the official governmental policy pursued by South Africa in Namibia
is to achieve a complete physical separation of races and ethnic
groups in separate areas within the Territory. The application of
this policy has required, as has been conceded by South Africa, re-

strictive measures of control officially adopted and enforced in the Territory by the coercive power of the former Mandatory. These measures establish limitations, exclusions or restrictions for the members of the indigenous population groups in respect of their participation in certain types of activities, fields of study or of training, labour or employment and also submit them to restrictions or exclusions of residence and movement in large parts of the Territory.

131.   Under the Charter of the United Nations, the former Mandatory had pledged itself to observe and respect, in a territory having an international status, human rights and fundamental freedoms for all without distinction as to race. To establish instead, and to enforce, distinctions, exclusions, restrictions and limitations exclusively based on grounds of race, colour, descent or national or ethnic origin which constitute a denial of fundamental human rights is a flagrant violation of the purposes and principles of the Charter.[a]

THE QUESTION OF THE SELF–EXECUTING CHARACTER OF ARTICLE 56

SEI FUJII v. STATE

United States, Supreme Court of California in Bank, 1952.
38 Cal.2d 718, 242 P.2d 617 (1952).

The text of the opinion appears at p. ——.

The court says that "The provisions in the charter pledging cooperation in promoting observance of fundamental freedoms lack the mandatory quality and definiteness which would indicate an intent to create justiciable rights in private persons immediately upon ratification." Is the court correct in its appraisal of the lack of "mandatory quality" of those provisions such as Article 56? Should the result of the case be different if "mandatory quality" were found? Can the "self-executing" analysis of the court lead to the conclusion, in a particular case, that the state is obligated internationally at some time after ratification not to discriminate on the basis of alienage but that the alien is at no time after ratification protected by internal law?

Compare Riesenfeld, Editorial Comment, The Doctrine of Self-Executing Treaties and GATT: A Notable German Judgment, 65 Am.J.Int'l L. 548, 550 (1971):

> Does it make sense to search for the intent of the parties, if some of the parties could not have had such an intent with respect to their own sphere? The United Kingdom is believed to be the standard example of such a party. Although the doctrine looking to the intent of the parties is widely supported by practice and theory, it seems much more reasonable to consider the self-executing or executory nature of international conventions a

---

a. For an analysis of this passage, see Schwelb, The International Court of Justice and the Human Rights Claus- es of the Charter, 66 Am.J.Int'l L. 337 (1972).

matter depending primarily upon the constitutional law of each nation rather than upon a dubious intent of the parties. Consequently in the United States a treaty ought to be deemed self-executing if it: (a) involves the rights and duties of individuals; (b) does not cover a subject for which legislative action is required by the Constitution; and (c) does not leave discretion to the parties in the application of the particular provision.

---

2. THE UNIVERSAL DECLARATION OF HUMAN RIGHTS[a]

The declaration was adopted by the United Nations General Assembly, Resolution 217A(III), on December 10, 1948, by a vote of 48 to 0, Gen.Ass.Off.Rec., 3rd Sess., Part 1, Resolutions, p. 71. Although there were no dissenting votes, the following states abstained: Byelorussia SSR, Czechoslovakia, Poland, Saudi Arabia, Ukranian SSR, USSR, Union of South Africa and Yugoslavia.

CONTENTS OF THE DECLARATION

The text of the Universal Declaration is set forth in full in the Documentary Supplement. The General Assembly of the United Nations proclaims the listed rights as a "common standard of achievement." These rights are applicable to "all human beings," to "everyone." The rights include such personal rights as equal protection of the law, right to a fair hearing, to be presumed innocent, to freedom of movement and asylum, to marry and found a family. Also included are economic and social rights such as to social security, to work, to form and join trade unions, to a standard of living adequate for health and well-being, to education. For example:

Article 5

No one shall be subjected to torture or to cruel, inhuman or degrading treatment or punishment.

a. **Other Human Rights Declarations.** In addition to the Universal Declaration, a number of other declarations dealing with particular aspects of human rights have been adopted by the General Assembly. Among them are:

Declaration of the Rights of the Child, November 20, 1959, G.A.Res. 1386 (XIV), U.N.Gen.Ass.Off.Rec., 14th Sess., Supp. 16(A/4354), p. 19.

Declaration on the Granting of Independence to Colonial Countries and Peoples, December 14, 1960, G.A.Res. 1514(XV), U.N.Gen.Ass.Off.Rec., 15th Sess., Supp. 16(A/4684), p. 66.

United Nations Declaration on the Elimination of All Forms of Racial Discrimination, November 20, 1963, G.A.Res. 1904(XVIII), U.N.Gen.Ass.

Off.Rec., 18th Sess., Supp. 15 (A/5515), p. 35.

Declaration on the Elimination of Discrimination Against Women, November 7, 1967, G.A.Res. 2263(XXII), U.N.Gen.Ass.Off.Rec., 22nd Sess., Supp. 16(A/6716), p. 35.

Declaration on Territorial Asylum, December 14, 1967, G.A.Res. 2312 (XXII), U.N.Gen.Ass.Off.Rec., 22nd Sess., Supp. 16(A/6716), p. 81.

Declaration on the Protection of all Persons from Being Subjected to Torture and Other Cruel, Inhuman or Degrading Treatment or Punishment, December 9, 1975, G.A.Res. 3452(XXX), U.N. Gen.Ass.Off.Rec., 30th Sess., Supp. 34(A/10034), p. 91.

Article 9

No one shall be subjected to arbitrary arrest, detention or exile.

Article 10

Everyone is entitled in full equality to a fair and public hearing by an independent and impartial tribunal, in the determination of his rights and obligations and of any criminal charge against him.

THE QUESTION OF THE DECLARATION AS LAW

A DRAFTSMAN'S VIEW

5 Whiteman, Digest of International Law 243 (1965).

As the General Assembly neared its final vote on the Declaration, Mrs. Franklin D. Roosevelt, as the Chairman of the Commission on Human Rights and a representative of the United States in the Assembly, stated:

In giving our approval to the declaration today, it is of primary importance that we keep clearly in mind the basic character of the document. It is not a treaty; it is not an international agreement. It is not and does not purport to be a statement of law or of legal obligation. It is a declaration of basic principles of human rights and freedoms, to be stamped with the approval of the General Assembly by formal vote of its members, and to serve as a common standard of achievement for all peoples of all nations.

A DIPLOMATIC VIEW

II Kiss, Répertoire de la Pratique Française en Matière de Droit International Public 651 (1966).ᵃ

Declaration of the French Government of August 1, 1951

The French Government has followed with the greatest attention the measures of deportation taken in Hungary against numerous components of the population [which have been] suddenly declared "undesirable." According to the information received [by the French Government] these measures appear to have been extraordinarily far reaching and harsh and to strike pitilessly a great diversity of persons within the population.

Such acts constitute a flagrant violation of the principle of respect for human beings and the rights of man [which is] recognized by the international community and embodied in the Declaration of the United Nations of December 10, 1948.

---

a. Translation by the editors. Reprinted by permission of Editions du   Centre National de la Recherche Scientifique, Paris.

The French Government notes with the greatest concern that the information has now been confirmed by official statements of the Hungarian authorities. Faithful to its traditions, the French Government regards it as its duty solemnly to denounce practices which openly violate the human rights that the Government of the People's Republic of Hungary has formally committed itself to observe in the Peace Treaty of February 10, 1947.[b]

A PUBLICIST'S VIEW

Humphrey, The UN Charter and the Universal Declaration of Human Rights,
The International Protection of Human Rights 51 (Luard, ed. 1967).

Even more remarkable than the performance of the United Nations in adopting the Declaration has been its impact and the role which it almost immediately began to play both within and outside the United Nations—an impact and a role which probably exceed the most sanguine hopes of its authors. No other act of the United Nations has had anything like the same impact on the thinking of our time, the best aspirations of which it incorporates and proclaims. It may well be that it will live in history chiefly as a statement of great moral principles. As such its influence is deeper and more lasting than any political document or legal instrument. Men of affairs, however, are more apt to be impressed by the political and legal authority which it has established for itself. Its political authority is now second only to that of the charter itself. Indeed its reception at all levels has been such that, contrary to the expressed intention of its authors, it may have now become part of international law.

A JURIST'S VIEW

Separate Opinion of Vice-President Ammoun in Advisory Opinion on the
Continued Presence of South Africa in Namibia (South West Africa)
[1971] I.C.J. Reports 16, 76.

The Advisory Opinion takes judicial notice of the Universal Declaration of Human Rights. In the case of certain of the Declaration's provisions, attracted by the conduct of South Africa, it would have been an improvement to have dealt in terms with their comminatory nature, which is implied in paragraphs 130 and 131 of the Opinion by the references to their violation.

b. The treaty of peace with Hungary, the signing of which antedated the Universal Declaration by twenty-two months, provides in Article 2:

1. Hungary shall take all measures necessary to secure to all persons under Hungarian jurisdiction, without distinction as to race, sex, language or religion, the enjoyment of human rights and of the fundamental freedoms, including freedom of expression, of press and publication, of religious worship, of political opinion and of public meeting.

2. Hungary further undertakes that the laws in force in Hungary shall not, either in their content or in their application, discriminate or entail any discrimination between persons of Hungarian nationality on the ground of their race, sex, language or religion, whether in reference to their persons, property, business, professional or financial interests, status, political or civil rights or any other matter.

In its written statement the French Government, alluding to the obligations which South Africa accepted under the Mandate and assumed on becoming a Member of the United Nations, and to the norms laid down in the Universal Declaration of Human Rights, stated that there was no doubt that the Government of South Africa had, in a very real sense, systematically infringed those rules and those obligations. Nevertheless, referring to the mention by resolution 2145(XXI) of the Universal Declaration of Human Rights, it objected that it was plainly impossible for non-compliance with the norms it enshrined to be sanctioned with the revocation of the Mandate, inasmuch as that Declaration was not in the nature of a treaty binding upon States.

Although the affirmations of the Declaration are not binding qua international convention within the meaning of Article 38, paragraph 1(a), of the Statute of the Court, they can bind States on the basis of custom within the meaning of paragraph 1(b) of the same Article, whether because they constituted a codification of customary law as was said in respect of Article 6 of the Vienna Convention on the Law of Treaties, or because they have acquired the force of custom through a general practice accepted as law, in the words of Article 38, paragraph 1(b), of the Statute. One right which must certainly be considered a preexisting binding customary norm which the Universal Declaration of Human Rights codified is the right to equality, which by common consent has ever since the remotest times been deemed inherent in human nature.

The equality demanded by the Namibians and by other peoples of every colour, the right to which is the outcome of prolonged struggles to make it a reality, is something of vital interest to us here, on the one hand because it is the foundation of other human rights which are no more than its corollaries and, on the other, because it naturally rules out racial discrimination and apartheid, which are the gravest of the facts with which South Africa, as also other States, stands charged. The attention I am devoting to it in these observations can therefore by no means be regarded as exaggerated or out of proportion.

It is not by mere chance that in Article 1 of the Universal Declaration of the Rights of Man there stands, so worded, this primordial principle or axiom: "All human beings are born free and equal in dignity and rights."

From this first principle flow most rights and freedoms. * * * The ground was thus prepared for the legislative and constitutional process which began with the first declarations or bills of rights in America and Europe, continued with the constitutions of the nineteenth century, and culminated in positive international law in the San Francisco, Bogota and Addis Ababa charters, and in the Universal Declaration of Human Rights which has been confirmed by numerous resolutions of the United Nations, in particular the above-mentioned declarations adopted by the General Assembly in resolutions 1514(XV), 2625(XXV) and 2627(XXV). The Court in its turn has now confirmed it.

*   *   *

---

3. THE HUMAN RIGHTS COVENANTS

Under the aegis of the League of Nations and the United Nations, a number of conventions on particular human rights matters have been prepared by a variety of conferences, committees and commissions. Drafts of these conventions have progressed through a variety of stages. They are typically given final approval by some plenary international body before being submitted to states for ratification or other indication of intention to be bound. In some cases that approval has been given by resolution of the General Assembly of the United Nations. In others, the final text is prepared and approved by an ad hoc United Nations conference. In still other cases, the final text has come from a specialized agency, such as the International Labor Organization.

The variety and range of the matters which have been dealt with concretely by international legislation are illustrated in the Documentary Supplement by lists of conventions dealing with human rights. Most of these conventions were in force as of January 1, 1980; some had not yet received a sufficient number of ratifications to bring them into force. The United States is a party to very few of these conventions. (See the Documentary Supplement.)

Included among the conventions in force are two that are the most general in scope of all of the human rights conventions. These are the International Covenant on Economic, Social and Cultural Rights and the International Covenant on Civil and Political Rights, set forth in full in the Documentary Supplement.[a] These two covenants comprehensively carry into detailed treaty form most of the provisions of the Universal Declaration of Human Rights, although it should be observed that they do not parallel the declaration. A close comparison should be made between the declaration on one hand and the covenants on the other. For example, the declaration provides for the right to asylum; the matter is not treated in the covenants. The right to compensation for unlawful arrest or detention is provided for by the Covenant on Civil and Political Rights, but not by the declaration. Other disparities include the right to own property and the right of self-determination. What other disparities exist? Is the fact of these disparities significant? Does the fact that certain rights were included in the declaration but not in the more detailed legislation weaken the general legal significance that has been accorded the declaration? Does the fact that certain rights appear

---

a. In 1978, the Office of Public Information of the United Nations published the texts of the Universal Declaration, these two covenants, and an official protocol relating to implementation of the latter covenant under the title: The International Bill of Human Rights.

in the covenants but not in the declaration (such as self-determination) suggest that they are less than universal, that they do not reflect general principles of international law? Or does the worldwide recognition of a particular right as international law depend upon factors more complex than whether the verbal recognition of that right was made in the declaration or one or the other of the covenants? If so, what are the factors?

The covenants were the product of many years' work, first in the Commission on Human Rights (from 1949 until 1954) and thereafter in the Third Committee of the General Assembly of the United Nations (from 1954 until 1966) and finally at the plenary session of the assembly in 1966. Although the original conception in the commission had been to prepare a single draft covenant, the insistence by some states that the covenant include provisions for economic, social and cultural rights resulted in a decision by the General Assembly while the draft covenant was still under consideration by the commission that two covenants be drafted, one dealing with those rights and the other with civil and political rights. Contrast the language of the two covenants as ultimately adopted with respect to the sense of assurance by which the various rights are asserted in each of the documents. Contrast also the wide difference between the two covenants with respect to methods of implementation. See p. 602 on questions of implementation.

The detail with which the Covenant on Civil and Political Rights has amplified and added to the rights that were listed in the Universal Declaration of Human Rights is illustrated by the following excerpt.

INTERNATIONAL COVENANT ON CIVIL AND POLITICAL RIGHTS

G.A. Res. 2200A(XXI) Dec. 16, 1966.
U.N. Gen. Ass. Off. Rec., 21st Sess, Supp. No. 16 (A/6316), p. 52.

Article 14

1. All persons shall be equal before the courts and tribunals. In the determination of any criminal charge against him, or of his rights and obligations in a suit at law, everyone shall be entitled to a fair and public hearing by a competent, independent and impartial tribunal established by law. The Press and the public may be excluded from all or part of a trial for reasons of morals, public order (ordre public) or national security in a democratic society, or when the interest of the private lives of the parties so requires, or to the extent strictly necessary in the opinion of the court in special circumstances where publicity would prejudice the interests of justice; but any judgment rendered in a criminal case or in a suit at law shall be made public except where the interest of juvenile persons otherwise

requires or the proceedings concern matrimonial disputes or the guardianship of children.

2. Everyone charged with a criminal offence shall have the right to be presumed innocent until proved guilty according to law.

3. In the determination of any criminal charge against him, everyone shall be entitled to the following minimum guarantees, in full equality:

(a) To be informed promptly and in detail in a language which he understands of the nature and cause of the charge against him;

(b) To have adequate time and facilities for the preparation of his defence and to communicate with counsel of his own choosing;

(c) To be tried without undue delay;

(d) To be tried in his presence, and to defend himself in person or through legal assistance of his own choosing; to be informed, if he does not have legal assistance, of this right; and to have legal assistance assigned to him, in any case where the interests of justice so require, and without payment by him in any such case if he does not have sufficient means to pay for it;

(e) To examine, or have examined, the witnesses against him and to obtain the attendance and examination of witnesses on his behalf under the same conditions as witnesses against him;

(f) To have the free assistance of an interpreter if he cannot understand or speak the language used in court;

(g) Not to be compelled to testify against himself or to confess guilt.

4. In the case of juvenile persons, the procedure shall be such as will take account of their age and the desirability of promoting their rehabilitation.

5. Everyone convicted of a crime shall have the right to his conviction and sentence being reviewed by a higher tribunal according to law.

6. When a person has by a final decision been convicted of a criminal offence and when subsequently his conviction has been reversed or he has been pardoned on the ground that a new or newly discovered fact shows conclusively that there has been a miscarriage of justice, the person who has suffered punishment as a result of such conviction shall be compensated according to law, unless it is proved that the non-disclosure of the unknown fact in time is wholly or partly attributable to him.

7. No one shall be liable to be tried or punished again for an offence for which he has already been finally convicted or acquitted in accordance with the law and penal procedure of each country.

1. *Comparison with the precedents on state responsibility.* How do the rights provided for in such conventions as the Covenant on Civil and Political Rights compare with those recognized in such cases as Chattin? Who is entitled to these rights? Aliens only? Others? Are the substantive standards different?

2. *Policy problems facing the United States in considering becoming a party.* In February, 1978, President Carter submitted four human rights conventions to the Senate for its advice and consent: The International Convention on the Elimination of All Forms of Racial Discrimination, the International Covenant on Economic, Social and Cultural Rights, the International Covenant on Civil and Political Rights and the American Convention on Human Rights. Certain reservations, understandings and declarations were recommended to the Senate. See the President's message, Executives C, D, E, and F, U.S.Sen., 95th Cong., 2d Sess. (Feb. 23, 1978). Examples of the numerous reservations are the following (refer to the relevant language of the conventions in the Documentary Supplement):

a. To the racial discrimination convention, Article 4: " * * * nothing in this convention shall be deemed to require or authorize legislation or other action by the United States which would restrict the right of free speech * * *."

b. To the economic, etc., rights covenant, Article 28: "The United States shall progressively implement all the provisions of the Covenant over whose subject matter the Federal Government exercises legislative and judicial jurisdiction; with respect to the provisions over whose subject matter constituent units exercise jurisdiction, the Federal Government shall take appropriate measures, to the end that the competent authorities of the constituent units may take appropriate measures for the fulfillment of this Covenant."

c. To the civil and political rights covenant, Article 6 (Paragraphs 2, 4 and 5): "The United States reserves the right to impose capital punishment on any person duly convicted under existing or future laws permitting the imposition of capital punishment." (The reason for this reservation, given by the Department of State in its letter of submittal to the President, is that "United States law is not entirely in accord with these standards.") A reservation, based upon the right of free speech, is recommended with respect to Article 20 of this covenant.

d. To the American convention, Article 9: "The United States does not adhere to the third sentence of Article 9." The Department of State's letter of submittal explains that this reservation is necessitated because the provision in question "goes beyond existing United States law."

In addition to these and other reservations, the Department of State also recommended declarations that the treaties are not self-executing. The explanation, given with respect to the racial discrimination convention and incorporated with respect to the substantive articles of the other three: "It is further recommended that a declaration indicate the non-self-executing nature of Articles 1 through 7 of the convention. Absent such a statement, the terms of the convention might be considered as directly enforceable law on a par with Congressional statutes. While the terms of the convention, with the suggested reservations and understanding, are consonant with United States law, it is nevertheless preferable to leave any further implementation that may be desired to the domestic legislative and judicial process."

If it is true that the United States already provides, by constitution or statute, most of the rights granted by these conventions, what is to be gained by binding the United States *by treaty* to provide for those rights? What is to be lost? To the extent that some of the rights granted by the conventions are not already provided for by constitution or statute in the United States, should they be? Presumably the main purpose of these conventions is to require states who become parties to raise their human rights standards to the level required by the conventions. Is that purpose served by the United States when it makes reservations to provisions in the convention because they go beyond United States law?

The United States is a party to only a very few of the human rights conventions already in force. It is still not a party to the Genocide Convention, although President Truman submitted that treaty to the Senate in 1949, and President Nixon called again for the Senate's advice and consent in 1970. The position of the Department of State with respect to the four human rights conventions recently submitted can fairly be described as cautious. Why has the United States been so hesitant?

-----

4. THE HELSINKI FINAL ACT

The Conference on Security and Cooperation in Europe, meeting from September 1973 to August 1975, concluded with a Final Act, signed at Helsinki by representatives of 35 states, including the countries of Western Europe, the Soviet-bloc countries of Europe, the United States and Canada. The legal status of this document was described by President Ford before he attended the closing days of the conference: "I would emphasize that the document I will sign is neither a treaty nor is it legally binding on any participating state. The Helsinki documents involve political and moral commitments aimed at lessening tensions and opening further the lines of communication between the peoples of East and West." 73 U.S. Dept. State Bull. 204, 205 (1975).

Thus, the text of the Final Act states that it "is not eligible for registration under Article 102 of the Charter of the United Nations" and the delegate of Finland (the depository government) informed the Coordinating Committee at the Conference of his government's intention to send the Final Act to the Secretary General of the United Nations with a letter containing the following statement: "I have also been asked   *   *   *   to draw your attention to the fact that this Final Act is not eligible, in whole or in part, for registration with the Secretariat under Article 102 of the Charter of the United Nations, as would be the case were it a matter of a treaty or international agreement, under the aforesaid Article."

The Final Act is a comprehensive document covering the following matters: Questions Relating to Security in Europe (so-called Basket I); Cooperation in the Field of Economics, of Science and Technology, and of the Environment (Basket II); Questions Relating to Security and Cooperation in the Mediterranean, and Cooperation in Humanitarian and Other Fields (Basket III).

A major outcome of the conference was an assurance that existing European territorial arrangements (e. g. borders) would not be disturbed by force. Human rights matters were also included in the Final Act, as Principle VII in a Declaration of Principles Guiding Relations between Participating States. The declaration contained in the Final Act is set forth in the Documentary Supplement. The complete text of the Final Act may be found at 73 U.S. Dept. State Bull. 323 (1975).

DEPARTMENT COMMENTS ON SUBJECT OF HUMAN RIGHTS IN CZECHOSLOVAKIA

76 United States Department of State Bulletin 154 (1977).

Following is a statement read to news correspondents on January 26 by Frederick Z. Brown, Director, Office of Press Relations.

I would like to make a brief statement on the subject of human rights in Czechoslovakia.

Some 300 individuals in that country have petitioned the government to guarantee the rights accorded them by the Czechoslovak Constitution, the international covenants on civil and political and on economic, social, and cultural rights, and by the Helsinki Final Act. We have noted that the signers of Charter 77 explicitly state that it is not a document of political opposition. Some of the signers have reportedly been detained or harassed.

As you know, the Helsinki Final Act provides that:

In the field of human rights and fundamental freedoms, the participating States will act in conformity with the purposes and principles of the Charter of the United Nations and with the Universal Declaration of Human Rights. They will also fulfill their obligations as set forth in the international declarations and agreements in this field, including inter alia the International Covenants on Human Rights, by which they may be bound.

All signatories of the Helsinki Final Act are pledged to promote, respect, and observe human rights and fundamental freedoms for all. We must strongly deplore the violation of such rights and freedoms wherever they occur.

EXTRACT FROM THE GENERAL DEBATE IN THE UNITED NATIONS GENERAL ASSEMBLY, 1977

XIV U.N. Monthly Chronicle, November 1977, p. 47.

CZECHOSLOVAKIA

Bohuslav CHNOUPEK, Minister for Foreign Affairs, said the policy of détente enhanced the democratization of international relations, strengthened the circulation of blood in the world organism of peace and opened up entirely new possibilities not only in the political sphere but in the sphere of the exchange of scientific and cultural values. Détente meant renouncing threats and coercion and embarking on the road of co-operation.

Since the signing of the Final Act of the Conference on Security and Cooperation in Europe two years ago, security in Europe had been strengthened and an atmosphere was being created which was conducive to complementing the political relaxation by a relaxation in the military sphere.

The new quality of international relations required not only general declarations but new constructive action. Czechoslovakia expected that the responsible leaders of the Western countries would display the necessary statesmanship and foresight in the interest of increasing the results in the basic sphere of human rights—the right to life and to peace and international security.

Czechoslovakia supported the USSR proposals relating to the expansion of all-European co-operation in important fields such as energy, transport and the protection of environment.

With regard to bilateral relations, during the past year Czechoslovakia had expanded contacts with many countries with different social systems, and had made some progress in the development of relations with the Federal Republic of Germany and Austria. There had also been favourable developments in relations with Canada, which unfortunately could not be said of relations with the United States because of issues which remained unsolved through no fault of Czechoslovakia.

Czechoslovakia welcomed the fact that the non-aligned countries considered it necessary for détente to become a dominant factor in international relations. However, imperialist circles were not interested in the stability of international relations. By causing conflicts among young independent States, they tried to destroy the unity of the anti-imperialist and anti-colonialist front.

    * * *

In the field of disarmament, an important step towards peace and co-operation would be the general prohibition of the further perfecting of nuclear weapons, including the so-called neutron bomb. There was an ironical and cynical contradiction between the decision on development of that bomb and the campaign launched at the same time for so-called protection of human rights.

* * *

IMPLEMENTATION OF THE HELSINKI ACCORD: SIXTH ANNUAL REPORT BY THE PRESIDENT OF THE UNITED STATES

Special Report No. 51, United States Department of State
(July 1979).

[The report was made to the Commission on Security and Cooperation in Europe on the Implementation of the Helsinki Final Act, December 1, 1978–May 31, 1979.]

Chapter Two

United States Implementation

Criticism of the American CSCE record has focused on charges that the United States violates provisions of Principle Seven concerning human rights, fails to promote the expansion of trade in accordance with Basket II, and fails to facilitate travel in accordance with Basket III.

Principle Seven calls for respect for human rights and fundamental freedoms. Specific criticisms have been directed at U.S. failure to ratify certain major international human rights agreements; continuing poverty and unemployment in the light of general affluence; discrimination against women and minorities such as blacks, migrant workers, Indians, and Hispanics; and imprisonment of individuals on criminal charges essentially because of their political beliefs or activities. It cannot be denied that some of these allegations reflect real problems. But neither can it be denied that the U.S. Government is working to solve them.

The United States is a party to nine of the 28 international agreements on human rights. President Carter in February 1978 submitted four additional agreements to the Senate, urging their ratification: the International Convention on the Elimination of All Forms of Racial Discrimination; the International Covenant on Economic, Social, and Cultural Rights; the International Covenant on Civil and Political Rights; and the American Convention on Human Rights. The President has, furthermore, urged the Senate to ratify the Convention on the Prevention and Punishment of the Crime of Genocide. Under the provisions of the Constitution, the Senate now has the responsibility of consenting to these agreements. While the United States has not formally ratified a number of international human rights agreements, U.S. human rights practices in fact meet many of the standards set in these agreements. Nonetheless, ratification of the agreements recommended by the President remains an important Administration goal, symbolic of our commitment to development of an international system protective of human rights and fundamental freedoms.

Poverty and unemployment are indeed social problems for the United States. They are, however, universal problems with which all societies are struggling. A few examples will illustrate the many programs of the U.S. Government aimed at reducing poverty and unemployment.

       *   *   *

Much has been achieved already. Affirmative Action programs have expanded the employment opportunities of minorities. Minority enrollment in higher education rose rapidly in the past decade. The number of black elected officials in the South has risen from 408 to 2,000 in the past 10 years, a direct result of changing public attitudes and of civil rights legislation which won an effective franchise for blacks. The educational level, health, and economic condition of Indians have been improved. Yet few could be satisfied with the progress which has been made in eliminating discrimination against minorities. Much remains to be done, and the U.S. Government is committed to that goal.

Amnesty International, the respected human rights organization which works on behalf of political prisoners, is among those who have charged that people are imprisoned for their political beliefs in the United States. Amnesty International identified four "prisoners of conscience" in the United States as of January 31, 1979: Ben Chavis, one of the so-called Wilmington 10; Earl Grant and T. J. Reddy, two members of the so-called Charlotte Three; and Inari Obadele, who was convicted of conspiracy to assault a federal officer. According to Amnesty, 15 prisoners of conscience had been held in the United States during the period July 1977 to June 1978.

American legal practice has been to expand to the maximum the area of free expression and permissible dissent, while according due process of law to accused persons—protecting their rights and the mechanism through which redress of wrongs can be sought. We believe that few political systems do as well in accomplishing these goals. None can succeed completely nor can any be satisfied with less than constant efforts to do better.

In the case of the Wilmington 10, the Civil Rights division of the Justice Department, after a lengthy investigation, filed a friend of the court brief urging the federal district court, before which the defendants' habeas corpus petitions are pending, to give serious consideration to the defendants' claims. Since the defendants were convicted on the basis of state criminal charges, the Federal Government's authority is somewhat limited.

* * *

On the whole, valid criticisms can be made of aspects of the U.S. performance in implementing the Helsinki Accords. Our record is not perfect, but we are open to criticism and change. While continuing to work on improvement of the U.S. record, the Administration will also continue to encourage other countries to fulfill the pledges they made at Helsinki.

CZECHOSLOVAK DISSIDENTS

United States Department of State Bulletin, December 1979, p. 44.

Department Statement, Oct. 24, 1979 [1]

We condemn both the trial and the unreasonably harsh sentences handed down in the trial of the Czechoslovak dissidents in Prague yesterday. It is a matter of serious concern to us that the Czechoslovak Government has again punished some of its own citizens for attempts to exercise their fundamental rights.

We cannot agree that the acts which the defendants were accused of committing were in any way criminal or that they warranted punishment. They were working to see that the government acted according to its own laws, legal procedures, and international commitments on human rights. We believe that the trial contradicts the spirit and letter of the CSCE [Conference on Security and Cooperation in Europe] Final Act.

We are and will continue to be concerned about violations of human rights wherever they occur. We have and will continue to speak out forcefully against these actions. In the case of Czechoslovakia, we are particularly disappointed, given its past tradition and experience of democracy and respect for law and the rights of individuals. The human rights of Czechs and Slovaks and their freedom to exercise these rights have obviously been a matter of interest to some of Czechoslovakia's neighbors who have had more than a little influence over the "internal affairs" of that country, in particular during the past 11 years.

1. Read to news correspondents by Department spokesman Hodding Carter III.

SECTION C.   IMPLEMENTATION OF THE INTERNATIONAL LAW OF HUMAN RIGHTS

1. THE CONTEXT OF IMPLEMENTATION AT THE UNITED NATIONS

STATEMENT ON HUMAN RIGHTS BY THE SECRETARY GENERAL OF THE INTERNATIONAL COMMISSION OF JURISTS, NOVEMBER 1978

Human Rights in United States and United Kingdom
Foreign Policy 23–26, 72 (Stewart ed. 1979).*

[Speaking at a colloquium on human rights in November 1978, Niall MacDermot, Secretary-General of the International Commission of Jurists, described the United Nations processes as follows.]

The UN bodies concerned with human rights are chiefly the Commission on Human Rights; its Sub-Commission on the Prevention of Discrimination and Protection of Minorities; and the Human Rights Committee set up under the International Covenant on Civil and Political Rights. Many other UN bodies also cope with human rights issues.

Because of the four-tier UN structure, there is an unending cycle of human rights meetings, all with almost identical agendas, producing the same discussions, speeches, arguments and resolutions throughout the year:

- In August/September the Sub-Commission meets in Geneva. Theoretically, it is a body of independent experts.
- In February/March the Human Rights Commission meets in Geneva for a six-week session. More than 30 nations are represented. The Commission reports to the Economic and Social Council (ECOSOC).
- In April/May ECOSOC meets in New York to deal with human rights.
- In September/December the General Assembly meets. Human rights are dealt with by the Third Committee in December.

There are clearly too many tiers. There is a movement to eliminate the ECOSOC, and to arrange twice-yearly meetings of the Human Rights Commission, with one session devoted to implementation, so that this aspect does not fail by default. The Commission could then report directly to the General Assembly.

Full-time government human rights officers tend to be in New York. UN mission staffs are larger there. The Western Group Poli-

* Reprinted with the permission of the American Association of the International Commission of Jurists.

cy Formulating Committee is also in New York. Final decisions are taken there.

The people in the Geneva missions deal with human rights as one aspect of their many duties. With the Human Rights Commission and the UN Division of Human Rights located in Geneva, it would probably be a better arrangement for governments to station their human rights experts there.

There is a frequent complaint about too much politics in the Human Rights Commission; but human rights are a very political subject. One must accept that. Paradoxically, it is very rare for politicians to attend the Human Rights Commission.

There is a need for people with continuing experience in human rights to head delegations. This is UK practice. The US changes its representatives on the Human Rights Commission frequently, to its disadvantage. It takes time to make influential contacts and understand the politicking that occurs.

A substantial delegation is needed by any government wanting to play a significant role. The UK's is often too small. In contrast, the Soviet Union sends a large body of experts. Its delegation plans strategy very carefully. Because of this it tends to be more successful. The Western Group does not seem to preplan to the same extent as the Soviet Group.

The Human Rights Commission and the Sub-Commission's work is threefold: standard setting, studies, and implementation.

STANDARD SETTING is the formulation of principles in Conventions or Declarations of Principles such as the two International Covenants prepared by the Commission, and the Draft Convention on Torture. The Draft Body of Principles for the Protection of Persons in All Forms of Detention or Imprisonment was delegated to the Sub-Commission.

STUDIES cover many subjects, some very political. Most start in the Sub-Commission. One recently completed is sponsored by the UK on the Rights of Non-Citizens, arising from the expulsion of the Ugandan Asians.

Two newer studies are worth mentioning: Human Rights under States of Exception or Emergency; and the Independence of the Judiciary, proposed by Sri Lanka.

Partly because the Sub-Commission is an independent body of experts, Western governments tend not to consider future studies. It should be part of government policy to think ahead and propose useful subjects.

When asked for information, governments normally respond only about their own countries. NGOs must provide information that governments do not give.

There is a feeling that the Human Rights Commission has done enough in the field of standard setting and should concentrate on implementation; but there is still a lot to do. Most of the Conventions state very general principles. Much detail needs to be worked out.

For example, the draft Convention on Torture implementing the general principles in the UN Declaration (which was based largely on the work of Amnesty International), will have specific provisions for the prevention and repression of torture at the national level. The ICJ is sponsoring a draft optional protocol to the proposed Convention on Torture, suggesting a much stronger implementation procedure than exists under any international declaration or covenant. The optional protocol as yet receives little support from Western governments, despite their complaints about the Commission's lack of implementation.

The Draft Body of Principles on Torture was passed unanimously by the Sub-Commission with a surprising degree of consensus. If adopted and applied, it will effectively end a great deal of torture. It will now go to the Human Rights Commission. Efforts will hopefully be made to ensure its place high on the agenda.

IMPLEMENTATION takes two forms:

Reports from States and Parties on legislative and administrative action to implement the various conventions and declarations. A number of them, such as on Freedom of Information and of the Press, go to the Commission. They do not form a large part of the Commission's activities and are not very effective. More impressive are the reporting procedures under the Convention on the Elimination of Racial Discrimination and under the Convention on Civil and Political Rights.

Alleged Violations Procedures can be public or private. They are public when a government raises an issue: the UK brought up Cambodia in the last session. Until recently, public investigations were confined to South Africa, Chile and Israel. An ad hoc committee is set up to study the subject and receive evidence, usually from NGOs and individuals. They tend to be one-sided in their views, often because the government under investigation has failed to cooperate. Governments do not regard them as fair tribunals.

The other system is the confidential so-called communications procedure directed to situations of a consistent pattern of gross violations of human rights, rather than to individual complaints.

The UN receives 30,000—40,000 complaints yearly, mostly from individuals and most of which do not begin to provide evidence of a consistent pattern. In practice, the Commission acts on complaints from NGOs.

The Human Rights Commission can set up a Commission of Enquiry with the consent of the concerned government; or it can order a thorough study. Neither has ever been done. Occasionally a complaint has been referred to a government for its comment. That is another delaying tactic. At that stage the government usually takes the matter very seriously, as it wants to avoid a condemnation by the Commission.

Very, very slowly progress is being made to strengthen and improve implementation. This year it was decided to send a former Nigerian judge to Uganda to discuss allegations against it with the Ugandan Government.

Certain conditions seem to be necessary for such an exercise to have any value:

- The persons sent must have a thorough knowledge of the situation. A general investigation is not sufficient.

- There must be a real possibility of seeing and hearing evidence on the spot.

- Linked with this, the UN must have a safe base in the country visited.

Those conditions were fulfilled in the recent mission to Chile, which worked well. They do not exist in Uganda, where it is unlikely that much will come of such a visit.

This year the President of the Human Rights Commission named nine countries on which action had been taken, although that seems to have been only to send a complaint to the government and invite its comments.

To be effective, the UN fact-finding capacity must be increased. At the moment the Human Rights Commission has neither the facilities nor staff to be an effective fact-finding body. This provides one of the strong arguments for a Human Rights Commissioner with his own staff to fulfill the function.

The Human Rights Committee under the International Covenant on Civil and Political Rights is in many ways the best UN body on human rights. Its independent experts are all lawyers. Their study of States-Parties' reports and cross-examination of States' representatives on those reports has been done very well. They have worked out their own rules of procedure and strengthened to the limit their own powers, under the rules.

Apart from the reports, they can investigate individual complaints under the Optional Protocol, but this has been publicized very little. To date only some 45 complaints have been received. If they build up to the number expected, the two meetings of three weeks yearly will not be adequate. The committee of experts will probably have to be paid an adequate salary if the standard is to be maintained.

Investigation of human rights violations. For the most part, the work of the United Nations bodies in implementation of its human rights policies consists of resolutions condemning massive violations of human rights standards, such as those claimed to have been committed by South Africa in the administration of its apartheid system over the years. Recently, resolutions have been addressed to Israel and Chile. Ad hoc groups of experts or working groups are occasionally created by the General Assembly or the Human Rights Commission, charged with the responsibility of investigating and publicizing human rights violations. From time to time, a special rapporteur may be asked to address a specific problem. The General Assembly may request the Secretary-General of the United Nations to investigate and publicize violations. A number of these United Nations activities are described in Carey, U.N. Protection of Civil and Political Rights (1970). For many years, the Human Rights Commission has discussed the creation of a High Commissioner for Human Rights, who could serve as an ombudsman, dealing with specific situations as the need might arise. The Soviets, among others, have vigorously opposed the creation of this office.

---

2. VINDICATION OF AN INDIVIDUAL'S RIGHTS

FILARTIGA v. PENA–IRALA

United States Court of Appeals, Second Circuit, 1980.
630 F.2d 876.

KAUFMAN, Circuit Judge:

Upon ratification of the Constitution, the thirteen former colonies were fused into a single nation, one which, in its relations with foreign states, is bound both to observe and construe the accepted norms of international law, formerly known as the law of nations. Under the Articles of Confederation, the several states had interpreted and applied this body of doctrine as a part of their common law, but with the founding of the "more perfect Union" of 1789, the law of nations became preeminently a federal concern.

Implementing the constitutional mandate for national control over foreign relations, the First Congress established original district court jurisdiction over "all causes where an alien sues for a tort only [committed] in violation of the law of nations." Judiciary Act of 1789, ch. 20, § 9(b), 1 Stat. 67, 77 (1789), codified at 28 U.S.C. § 1350. Construing this rarely-invoked provision, we hold that deliberate torture perpetrated under color of official authority violates universally accepted norms of the international law of human rights, regardless of the nationality of the parties. Thus, whenever an alleged torturer is found and served with process by an alien within our borders, § 1350 provides federal jurisdiction. Accordingly, we reverse the judgment of the district court dismissing the complaint for want of federal jurisdiction.

I

The appellants, plaintiffs below, are citizens of the Republic of Paraguay. Dr. Joel Filartiga, a physician, describes himself as a longstanding opponent of the government of President Alfredo Stroessner, which has held power in Paraguay since 1954. His daughter, Dolly Filartiga, arrived in the United States in 1978 under a visitor's visa, and has since applied for permanent political asylum. The Filartigas brought this action in the Eastern District of New York against Americo Norberto Pena-Irala (Pena), also a citizen of Paraguay, for wrongfully causing the death of Dr. Filartiga's seventeen-year old son, Joelito. Because the district court dismissed the action for want of subject matter jurisdiction, we must accept as true the allegations contained in the Filartigas' complaint and affidavits for purposes of this appeal.

The appellants contend that on March 29, 1976, Joelito Filartiga was kidnapped and tortured to death by Pena, who was then Inspector General of Police in Asuncion, Paraguay. Later that day, the police brought Dolly Filartiga to Pena's home where she was confronted with the body of her brother, which evidenced marks of severe torture. As she fled, horrified, from the house, Pena followed after her shouting, "Here you have what you have been looking for for so long and what you deserve. Now shut up." The Filartigas claim that Joelito was tortured and killed in retaliation for his father's political activities and beliefs.

Shortly thereafter, Dr. Filartiga commenced a criminal action in the Paraguayan courts against Pena and the police for the murder of his son. As a result, Dr. Filartiga's attorney was arrested and brought to police headquarters where, shackled to a wall, Pena threatened him with death. This attorney, it is alleged, has since been disbarred without just cause.

During the course of the Paraguayan criminal proceeding, which is apparently still pending after four years, another man, Hugo Duarte, confessed to the murder. Duarte, who was a member of the Pena household,[1] claimed that he had discovered his wife and Joelito in flagrante delicto, and that the crime was one of passion. The Filartigas have submitted a photograph of Joelito's corpse showing injuries they believe refute this claim. Dolly Filartiga, moreover, has stated that she will offer evidence of three independent autopsies demonstrating that her brother's death "was the result of professional methods of torture." Despite his confession, Duarte, we are told, has never been convicted or sentenced in connection with the crime.

In July of 1978, Pena sold his house in Paraguay and entered the United States under a visitor's visa. He was accompanied by Juana Bautista Fernandez Villalba, who had lived with him in Paraguay. The couple remained in the United States beyond the term of their visas, and were living in Brooklyn, New York, when Dolly Filartiga, who was then living in Washington, D.C., learned of their presence. Acting on information provided by Dolly, the Immigration and Naturalization Service arrested Pena and his companion, both of whom were subsequently ordered deported on April 5, 1979 following a hearing. They had then resided in the United States for more than nine months.

---

1. Duarte is the son of Pena's companion, Juana Bautista Fernandez Villal- ba, who later accompanied Pena to the United States.

Almost immediately, Dolly caused Pena to be served with a summons and civil complaint at the Brooklyn Navy Yard, where he was being held pending deportation. The complaint alleged that Pena had wrongfully caused Joelito's death by torture and sought compensatory and punitive damages of $10,000,000. The Filartigas also sought to enjoin Pena's deportation to ensure his availability for testimony at trial.[2] The cause of action is stated as arising under "wrongful death statutes; the U.N. Charter; the Universal Declaration on Human Rights; the U.N. Declaration Against Torture; the American Declaration of the Rights and Duties of Man; and other pertinent declarations, documents and practices constituting the customary international law of human rights and the law of nations," as well as 28 U.S.C. § 1350, Article II, sec. 2 and the Supremacy Clause of the U.S. Constitution. Jurisdiction is claimed under the general federal question provision, 28 U.S.C. § 1331 and, principally on this appeal, under the Alien Tort Statute, 28 U.S.C. § 1350.[3]

Judge Nickerson stayed the order of deportation, and Pena immediately moved to dismiss the complaint on the grounds that subject matter jurisdiction was absent and for forum non conveniens. On the jurisdictional issue, there has been no suggestion that Pena claims diplomatic immunity from suit. The Filartigas submitted the affidavits of a number of distinguished international legal scholars, who stated unanimously that the law of nations prohibits absolutely the use of torture as alleged in the complaint.[4] Pena, in support of his motion to dismiss on the ground of forum non conveniens, submitted the affidavit of his Paraguayan counsel, Jose Emilio Gorostiaga, who averred that Paraguayan law provides a full and adequate civil remedy for the wrong alleged.[5] Dr. Filartiga has not commenced

---

2. Several officials of the Immigration and Naturalization Service were named as defendants in connection with this portion of the action. Because Pena has now been deported, the federal defendants are no longer parties to this suit, and the claims against them are not before us on this appeal.

3. Jurisdiction was also invoked pursuant to 28 U.S.C. §§ 1651, 2201 & 2202, presumably in connection with appellants' attempt to delay Pena's return to Paraguay.

4. Richard Falk, the Albert G. Milbank Professor of International Law and Practice at Princeton University, and a former Vice President of the American Society of International Law, avers, that, in his judgment, "it is now beyond reasonable doubt that torture of a person held in detention that results in severe harm or death is a violation of the law of nations." Thomas Franck, professor of international law at New York University and Director of the New York University Center for International Studies offers his opinion that torture has now been rejected by virtually all nations, although it was once commonly used to extract confessions. Richard Lillich, the Howard W. Smith Professor of Law at the University of Virginia School of Law, concludes, after a lengthy review of the authorities, that officially perpetrated torture is "a violation of international law (formerly called the law of nations)." Finally, Myres MacDougal, a former Sterling Professor of Law at the Yale Law School, and a past President of the American Society of International Law, states that torture is an offense against the law of nations, and that "it has long been recognized that such offenses virtually affect relations between states."

5. The Gorostiaga affidavit states that a father whose son has been wrongfully killed may in addition to com-

such an action, however, believing that further resort to the courts of his own country would be futile.

Judge Nickerson heard argument on the motion to dismiss on May 14, 1979, and on May 15 dismissed the complaint on jurisdictional grounds.[6] The district judge recognized the strength of appellants' argument that official torture violates an emerging norm of customary international law. Nonetheless, he felt constrained by dicta contained in two recent opinions of this Court, Dreyfus v. von Finck, 534 F.2d 24 (2d Cir.), cert. denied 429 U.S. 835 (1976); IIT v. Vencap, Ltd., 519 F.2d 1001 (2d Cir. 1975), to construe narrowly "the law of nations," as employed in § 1350, as excluding that law which governs a state's treatment of its own citizens.

The district court continued the stay of deportation for forty-eight hours while appellants applied for further stays. These applications were denied by a panel of this Court on May 22, 1979, and by the Supreme Court two days later. Shortly thereafter, Pena and his companion returned to Paraguay.

II

Appellants rest their principal argument in support of federal jurisdiction upon the Alien Tort Statute, 28 U.S.C. § 1350, which provides: "The district courts shall have original jurisdiction of any civil action by an alien for a tort only, committed in violation of the law of nations or a treaty of the United States." Since appellants do not contend that their action arises directly under a treaty of the United States,[7] a threshold question on the jurisdictional issue is whether the conduct alleged violates the law of nations. In light of the universal condemnation of torture in numerous international agreements, and the renunciation of torture as an instrument of official policy by virtually all of the nations of the world (in principle if not in practice), we find that an act of torture committed by a state official against one held in detention violates established norms of the international law of human rights, and hence the law of nations.

mencing a criminal proceeding bring a civil action for damages against the person responsible. Accordingly, Mr. Filartiga has the right to commence a civil action against Mr. Duarte and Mr. Pena-Irala since he accuses them both of responsibility for his son's death. He may commence such a civil action either simultaneously with the commencement of the criminal proceeding, during the time that the criminal proceeding lasts, or within a year after the criminal proceeding has terminated. In either event, however, the civil action may not proceed to judgment until the criminal proceeding has been disposed of. If the defendant is found not guilty because he was not the author of the case under investigation in the criminal proceeding, no civil action for indemnity for damages based upon the same deed investigated in the criminal proceeding, can prosper or succeed.

6. The court below accordingly did not consider the motion to dismiss on forum non conveniens grounds, which is not before us on this appeal.

7. Appellants "associate themselves with" the argument of some of the amici curiae that their claim arises directly under a treaty of the United States, Brief for Appellants * * *, but nonetheless primarily rely upon treaties and other international instruments as evidence of an emerging norm of customary international law, rather than independent sources of law.

The Supreme Court has enumerated the appropriate sources of international law. The law of nations "may be ascertained by consulting the works of jurists, writing professedly on public law; or by the general usage and practice of nations; or by judicial decisions recognising and enforcing that law." United States v. Smith, 18 U.S. (5 Wheat.) 153, 160–61 (1820); Lopes v. Reederei Richard Schroder, 225 F.Supp. 292, 295 (E.D.Pa. 1963). In *Smith*, a statute proscribing "the crime of piracy [on the high seas] as defined by the law of nations," 3 Stat. 510(a) (1819), was held sufficiently determinate in meaning to afford the basis for a death sentence. The *Smith* Court discovered among the works of Lord Bacon, Grotius, Bochard and other commentators a genuine consensus that rendered the crime "sufficiently and constitutionally defined." *Smith*, supra, 18 U.S. (5 Wheat.) at 162.

The Paquete Habana, 175 U.S. 677 (1900), reaffirmed that

> where there is no treaty, and no controlling executive or legislative act or judicial decision, resort must be had to the customs and usages of civilized nations; and, as evidence of these, to the works of jurists and commentators, who by years of labor, research and experience, have made themselves peculiarly well acquainted with the subjects of which they treat. Such works are resorted to by judicial tribunals, not for the speculations of their authors concerning what the law ought to be, but for trustworthy evidence of what the law really is.

Id. at 700. Modern international sources confirm the propriety of this approach.[8]

Habana is particularly instructive for present purposes, for it held that the traditional prohibition against seizure of an enemy's coastal fishing vessels during wartime, a standard that began as one of comity only, had ripened over the preceding century into "a settled rule of international law" by "the general assent of civilized nations." Id. at 694; accord, id. at 686. Thus it is clear that courts must interpret international law not as it was in 1789, but as it has evolved and exists among the nations of the world today. See Ware v. Hylton, 3 U.S. (3 Dall.) 198 (1796) (distinguishing between "ancient" and "modern" law of nations).

The requirement that a rule command the "general assent of civilized nations" to become binding upon them all is a stringent one. Were this not so, the courts of one nation might feel free to impose idiosyncratic legal rules upon others, in the name of applying international law. Thus, in Banco Nacional de Cuba v. Sabbatino, 376 U.S. 398 (1964), the Court declined to pass on the validity of the Cuban government's expropriation of a foreign-owned corporation's assets, noting the sharply conflicting views on the issue propounded by the

8. [The court quotes Articles 38 and 59 of the Statute of the International Court of Justice.]

capital-exporting, capital-importing, socialist and capitalist nations. Id. at 428–30.

The case at bar presents us with a situation diametrically opposed to the conflicted state of law that confronted the *Sabbatino* Court. Indeed, to paraphrase that Court's statement, id. at 428, there are few, if any, issues in international law today on which opinion seems to be so united as the limitations on a state's power to torture persons held in its custody.

The United Nations Charter (a treaty of the United States, see 59 Stat. 1033 (1945)) makes it clear that in this modern age a state's treatment of its own citizens is a matter of international concern. It provides:

> With a view to the creation of conditions of stability and well-being which are necessary for peaceful and friendly relations among nations * * * the United Nations shall promote * * * universal respect for, and observance of, human rights and fundamental freedoms for all without distinctions as to race, sex, language or religion.

Id. Art. 55. And further:

> All members pledge themselves to take joint and separate action in cooperation with the Organization for the achievement of the purposes set forth in Article 55.

Id. Art. 56.

While this broad mandate has been held not to be wholly self-executing, Hitai v. Immigration and Naturalization Service, 343 F.2d 466, 468 (2d Cir. 1965), this observation alone does not end our inquiry.[9] For although there is no universal agreement as to the precise extent of the "human rights and fundamental freedoms" guaranteed to all by the Charter, there is at present no dissent from the view that the guaranties include, at a bare minimum, the right to be free from torture. This prohibition has become part of customary international law, as evidenced and defined by the Universal Declaration of Human Rights, General Assembly Resolution 217(III)(A) (Dec. 10, 1948) which states, in the plainest of terms, "no one shall be subjected to torture."[10] The General Assembly has declared that the Charter precepts embodied in this Universal Declaration "constitute basic principles of international law." G.A.Res. 2625 (XXV) (Oct. 24, 1970).

---

9. We observe that this Court has previously utilized the U.N. Charter and the Charter of the Organization of American States, another non-self-executing agreement, as evidence of binding principles of international law. United States v. Toscanino, 500 F.2d 267 (2d Cir. 1974). In that case, our government's duty under international law to refrain from kidnapping a criminal defendant from within the borders of another nation, where formal extradition procedures existed, infringed the personal rights of the defendant, whose international law claims were thereupon remanded for a hearing in the district court.

10. Eighteen nations have incorporated the Universal Declaration into their own constitutions. 48 Revue Internationale de Droit Penal Nos. 3 & 4, at 211 (1977).

Particularly relevant is the Declaration on the Protection of All Persons from Being Subjected to Torture, General Assembly Resolution 3452, 30 U.N. GAOR Supp., (n. 34) 91, U.S.Doc. A/1034 (1975), which is set out in full in the margin.[11] The Declaration expressly prohibits any state from permitting the dastardly and totally inhuman act of torture. Torture, in turn, is defined as "any act by which severe pain and suffering, whether physical or mental, is intentionally inflicted by or at the instigation of a public official on a person for such purposes as * * * intimidating him or other persons." The Declaration goes on to provide that "[w]here it is proved that an act of torture or other cruel, inhuman or degrading treatment or punishment has been committed by or at the instigation of a public official, the victim shall be afforded redress and compensation, in accordance with national law." This Declaration, like the Declaration of Human Rights before it, was adopted without dissent by the General Assembly. Nayar, "Human Rights: The United Nations and United States Foreign Policy," 19 Harv.Int'l L.J. 813, 816 n. 18 (1978).

These U.N. declarations are significant because they specify with great precision the obligations of member nations under the Charter. Since their adoption, "[m]embers can no longer contend that they do not know what human rights they promised in the Charter to promote." Sohn, "A Short History of United Nations Documents on Human Rights," in The United Nations and Human Rights, 18th Report of the Commission (Commission to Study the Organization of Peace ed. 1968). Moreover, a U.N. Declaration is, according to one authoritative definition, "a formal and solemn instrument, suitable for rare occasions when principles of great and lasting importance are being enunciated." 34 U.N. ESCOR, Supp. (No. 8) 15, U.N.Doc. E/cn. 4/1/610 (1962) (memorandum of Office of Legal Affairs, U.N. Secretariat). Accordingly, it has been observed that the Universal Declaration of Human Rights "no longer fits into the dichotomy of 'binding treaty' against 'non-binding pronouncement,' but is rather an authoritative statement of the international community." E. Schwelb, Human Rights and the International Community 70 (1964). Thus, a Declaration creates an expectation of adherence, and "insofar as the expectation is gradually justified by State practice, a declaration may by custom become recognized as laying down rules binding upon the States." 34 U.N. ESCOR, supra. Indeed, several commentators have concluded that the Universal Declaration has become, in toto, a part of binding, customary international law. Nayar, supra, at 816–17; Waldock, "Human Rights in Contemporary International Law and the Significance of the European Convention," Int'l & Comp.L.Q., Supp.Publ. No. 11 at 15 (1965).

Turning to the act of torture, we have little difficulty discerning its universal renunciation in the modern usage and practice of na-

11. [The text of the declaration is set forth in the Documentary Supplement.]

tions. *Smith,* supra, 18 U.S. (5 Wheat.) at 160–61. The international consensus surrounding torture has found expression in numerous international treaties and accords. E. g., American Convention on Human Rights, Art. 5, OAS Treaty Series No. 36 at 1, OAS Off.Rec. OEA/Ser 4 v/II 23, doc. 21, rev. 2 (English ed., 1975) ("No one shall be subjected to torture or to cruel, inhuman or degrading punishment or treatment"); International Covenant on Civil and Political Rights, U.N. General Assembly Res. 2200 (XXI)A, U.N.Doc. A/6316 (Dec. 16, 1966) (identical language); European Convention for the Protection of Human Rights and Fundamental Freedoms, Art. 3, Council of Europe, European Treaty Series No. 5 (1968), 213 U.N.T.S. 211 (semble). The substance of these international agreements is reflected in modern municipal—i. e. national—law as well. Although torture was once a routine concomitant of criminal interrogations in many nations, during the modern and hopefully more enlightened era it has been universally renounced. According to one survey, torture is prohibited, expressly or implicitly, by the constitutions of over fifty-five nations,[12] including both the United States [13] and Paraguay.[14] Our State Department reports a general recognition of this principle:

> There now exists an international consensus that recognizes basic human rights and obligations owed by all governments to their citizens * * *. There is no doubt that these rights are often violated; but virtually all governments acknowledge their validity.

Department of State, Country Reports on Human Rights for 1979, published as Joint Comm. Print, House Comm. on Foreign Affairs, and Senate Comm. on Foreign Relations, 96th Cong. 2d Sess. (Feb. 4, 1980), Introduction at 1. We have been directed to no assertion by any contemporary state of a right to torture its own or another nation's citizens. Indeed, United States diplomatic contacts confirm the universal abhorrence with which torture is viewed:

> In exchanges between United States embassies and all foreign states with which the United States maintains relations, it has been the Department of State's general experience that no government has asserted a right to torture its own nationals. Where reports of torture elicit some credence, a state usually responds by denial or, less frequently, by asserting that the conduct was unauthorized or constituted rough treatment short of torture.[15]

Memorandum of the United States as Amicus Curiae at 16 n. 34.

12. 48 Revue Internationale de Droit Penal Nos. 3 & 4 at 208 (1977).

13. U.S.Const. amend. VIII ("cruel and unusual punishments" prohibited); id. amend. XIV.

14. Constitution of Paraguay, Art. 45 (prohibiting torture and other cruel treatment).

15. The fact that the prohibition of torture is often honored in the breach

Having examined the sources from which customary international law is derived—the usage of nations, judicial opinions and the works of jurists—we conclude that official torture is now prohibited by the law of nations. The prohibition is clear and unambiguous, and admits of no distinction between treatment of aliens and citizens. Accordingly, we must conclude that the dictum in Dreyfus v. von Finck, supra, 534 F.2d at 31, to the effect that "violations of international law do not occur when the aggrieved parties are nationals of the acting state," is clearly out of tune with the current usage and practice of international law. The treaties and accords cited above, as well as the express foreign policy of our own government,[17] all make it clear that international law confers fundamental rights upon all people vis-a-vis their own governments. While the ultimate scope of those rights will be a subject for continuing refinement and elaboration, we hold that the right to be free from torture is now among them. We therefore turn to the question whether the other requirements for jurisdiction are met.

III

Appellee submits that even if the tort alleged is a violation of modern international law, federal jurisdiction may not be exercised consistent with the dictates of Article III of the Constitution. The claim is without merit. Common law courts of general jurisdiction regularly adjudicate transitory tort claims between individuals over whom they exercise personal jurisdiction, wherever the tort occurred. Moreover, as part of an articulated scheme of federal control over external affairs, Congress provided, in the First Judiciary Act, Sec. 9(b), 1 Stat. 73, 77 (1789), for federal jurisdiction over suits by aliens where principles of international law are in issue. The constitutional basis for the Alien Tort Statute is the Law of Nations, which has always been part of the federal common law.

It is not extraordinary for a court to adjudicate a tort claim arising outside of its territorial jurisdiction. A state or nation has a legitimate interest in the orderly resolution of disputes among those

does not diminish its binding effect as a norm of international law. As one commentator has put it, "The best evidence for the existence of international law is that every actual State recognizes that it does exist and that it is itself under an obligation to observe it. States often violate international law, just as individuals often violate municipal law; but no more than individuals do States defend their violations by claiming that they are above the law." J. Brierly, The Outlook for International Law 4–5 (Oxford 1944).

17. E. g., 22 U.S.C. § 2304(2) ("Except under circumstances specified in this section, no security assistance may be provided to any country the government of which engages in a consistent pattern of gross violations of internationally recognized human rights."); 22 U.S.C. § 2151(a) ("The Congress finds that fundamental political, economic, and technological changes have resulted in the interdependence of nations. The Congress declares that the individual liberties, economic prosperity, and security of the people of the United States are best sustained and enhanced in a community of nations which respect individual civil and economic rights and freedoms").

within its borders, and where the lex loci delicti commissi is applied, it is an expression of comity to give effect to the laws of the state where the wrong occurred. Thus, Lord Mansfield in Mostyn v. Fabrigas, 1 Cowp. 161 (1774), quoted in McKenna v. Fisk, 42 U.S. (1 How.) 241, 248 (1843) said:

> [I]f A becomes indebted to B, or commits a tort upon his person or upon his personal property in Paris, an action in either case may be maintained against A in England, if he is there found * * *. [A]s to transitory actions, there is not a colour of doubt but that any action which is transitory may be laid in any county in England, though the matter arises beyond the seas.

Mostyn came into our law as the original basis for state court jurisdiction over out-of-state torts, McKenna v. Fisk, supra, 42 U.S. (1 How.) 241 (personal injury suits held transitory); Dennick v. Railroad Co., 103 U.S. 11 (1880) (wrongful death action held transitory), and it has not lost its force in suits to recover for a wrongful death occurring upon foreign soil, Slater v. Mexican National Railroad Co., 194 U.S. 120 (1904), as long as the conduct complained of was unlawful where performed. Restatement (Second) of Foreign Relations Law of the United States § 19 (1965). Here, where in personam jurisdiction has been obtained over the defendant, the parties agree that the acts alleged would violate Paraguayan law, and the policies of the forum are consistent with the foreign law,[18] state court jurisdiction would be proper. Indeed, appellees conceded as much at oral argument.

Recalling that *Mostyn* was freshly decided at the time the Constitution was ratified, we proceed to consider whether the First Congress acted constitutionally in vesting jurisdiction over "foreign suits," Slater, supra, 194 U.S. at 124, alleging torts committed in violation of the law of nations. A case properly "aris[es] under the * * * laws of the United States" for Article III purposes if grounded upon statutes enacted by Congress or upon the common law of the United States. See Illinois v. City of Milwaukee, 406 U.S. 91, 99–100 (1972); Ivy Broadcasting Co., Inc. v. American Tel. & Tel. Co., 391 F.2d 486, 492 (2d Cir. 1968). The law of nations forms an integral part of the common law, and a review of the history surrounding the adoption of the Constitution demonstrates that it became a part of the common law of the United States upon the adoption of the Constitution. Therefore, the enactment of the Alien Tort Statute was authorized by Article III.

During the eighteenth century, it was taken for granted on both sides of the Atlantic that the law of nations forms a part of the common law. 1 Blackstone, Commentaries 263–64 (1st Ed. 1765–69); 4 id. at 67. Under the Articles of Confederation, the Pennsylvania Court of Oyer and Terminer at Philadelphia, per McKean, Chief Jus-

---

18. Conduct of the type alleged here would be actionable under 42 U.S.C. § 1983 or, undoubtedly, the Constitution, if performed by a government official.

tice, applied the law of nations to the criminal prosecution of the Chevalier de Longchamps for his assault upon the person of the French Consul-General to the United States, noting that "[t]his law, in its full extent, is a part of the law of this state * * *." Res-publica v. De Longchamps, 1 U.S. (1 Dall.) 113, 119 (1784). Thus, a leading commentator has written:

> It is an ancient and a salutary feature of the Anglo-American legal tradition that the Law of Nations is a part of the law of the land to be ascertained and administered, like any other, in the appropriate case. This doctrine was originally conceived and formulated in England in response to the demands of an expanding commerce and under the influence of theories widely accepted in the late sixteenth, the seventeenth and the eighteenth centuries. It was brought to America in the colonial years as part of the legal heritage from England. It was well understood by men of legal learning in America in the eighteenth century when the United Colonies broke away from England to unite effectively, a little later, in the United States of America.

Dickinson, "The Law of Nations as Part of the National Law of the United States," 101 U.Pa.L.Rev. 26, 27 (1952).

Indeed, Dickinson goes on to demonstrate, id. at 34–41, that one of the principal defects of the Confederation that our Constitution was intended to remedy was the central government's inability to "cause infractions of treaties or of the law of nations, to be punished." 1 Farrand, Records of the Federal Convention 19 (Rev. ed. 1937) (Notes of James Madison). And, in Jefferson's words, the very purpose of the proposed Union was "[t]o make us one nation as to foreign concerns, and keep us distinct in domestic ones." Dickinson, supra, at 36 n.28.

As ratified, the judiciary article contained no express reference to cases arising under the law of nations. Indeed, the only express reference to that body of law is contained in Article I, sec. 8, cl. 10, which grants to the Congress the power to "define and punish * * * offenses against the law of nations." Appellees seize upon this circumstance and advance the proposition that the law of nations forms a part of the laws of the United States only to the extent that Congress has acted to define it. This extravagant claim is amply refuted by the numerous decisions applying rules of international law uncodified in any act of Congress. E. g., Ware v. Hylton, 3 U.S. (3 Dall.) 198 (1796); The Paquete Habana, supra, 175 U.S. 677; Sabbatino, supra, 376 U.S. 398 (1964). A similar argument was offered to and rejected by the Supreme Court in United States v. Smith, supra, 18 U.S. (5 Wheat.) 153, 158–60, and we reject it today. As John Jay wrote in The Federalist No. 3, at 22 (1 Bourne ed. 1901), "Under the national government, treaties and articles of treaties, as well as the laws of nations, will always be expounded in one sense and executed in the same manner, whereas adjudications on the same points and questions in the thirteen states will not always accord or be consistent." Federal jurisdiction over cases involving international law is clear.

* * *

The Filartigas urge that 28 U.S.C. § 1350 be treated as an exercise of Congress's power to define offenses against the law of nations. While such a reading is possible, see Lincoln Mills v. Textile Workers, 353 U.S. 488 (1957) (jurisdictional statute authorizes judicial explication of federal common law), we believe it is sufficient here to construe the Alien Tort Statute, not as granting new rights to aliens, but simply as opening the federal courts for adjudication of the rights already recognized by international law. The statute nonetheless does inform our analysis of Article III, for we recognize that questions of jurisdiction "must be considered part of an organic growth—part of an evolutionary process," and that the history of the judiciary article gives meaning to its pithy phrases. Romero v. International Terminal Operating Co., 358 U.S. 354, 360 (1959). The Framers' overarching concern that control over international affairs be vested in the new national government to safeguard the standing of the United States among the nations of the world therefore reinforces the result we reach today.

Although the Alien Tort Statute has rarely been the basis for jurisdiction during its long history,[21] in light of the foregoing discussion, there can be little doubt that this action is properly brought in federal court.[22] This is undeniably an action by an alien, for a tort only, committed in violation of the law of nations. * * *

* * *

Since federal jurisdiction may properly be exercised over the Filartigas' claim, the action must be remanded for further proceedings. Appellee Pena, however, advances several additional points that lie beyond the scope of our holding on jurisdiction. Both to emphasize the boundaries of our holding, and to clarify some of the issues reserved for the district court on remand, we will address these contentions briefly.

IV

Pena argues that the customary law of nations, as reflected in treaties and declarations that are not self-executing, should not be applied as rules of decision in this case. In doing so, he confuses the

---

21. Section 1350 afforded the basis for jurisdiction over a child custody suit between aliens in Adra v. Clift, 195 F.Supp. 857. (D.Md.1961), with a falsified passport supplying the requisite international law violation. In Bolchos v. Darrell, 3 Fed.Cas. 810 (D.S.C.1795), the Alien Tort Statute provided an alternative basis of jurisdiction over a suit to determine title to slaves on board an enemy vessel taken on the high seas.

22. We recognize that our reasoning might also sustain jurisdiction under the general federal question provision, 28 U.S.C. § 1331. We prefer, however, to rest our decision upon the Alien Tort Statute, in light of that provision's close coincidence with the jurisdictional facts presented in this case. See Romero v. International Terminal Operating Co., 358 U.S. 354 (1959).

question of federal jurisdiction under the Alien Tort Statute, which requires consideration of the law of nations, with the issue of the choice of law to be applied, which will be addressed at a later stage in the proceedings. The two issues are distinct. Our holding on subject matter jurisdiction decides only whether Congress intended to confer judicial power, and whether it is authorized to do so by Article III. The choice of law inquiry is a much broader one, primarily concerned with fairness, see Home Insurance Co. v. Dick, 281 U.S. 397 (1930); consequently, it looks to wholly different considerations. See Lauritzen v. Larsen, 345 U.S. 571 (1954). Should the district court decide that the *Lauritzen* analysis requires it to apply Paraguayan law, our courts will not have occasion to consider what law would govern a suit under the Alien Tort Statute where the challenged conduct is actionable under the law of the forum and the law of nations, but not the law of the jurisdiction in which the tort occurred.[25]

Pena also argues that "[i]f the conduct complained of is alleged to be the act of the Paraguayan government, the suit is barred by the Act of State doctrine." This argument was not advanced below, and is therefore not before us on this appeal. We note in passing, however, that we doubt whether action by a state official in violation of the Constitution and laws of the Republic of Paraguay, and wholly unratified by that nation's government, could properly be characterized as an act of state. See Banco Nacional de Cuba v. Sabbatino, supra, 376 U.S. 398; Underhill v. Hernandez, 168 U.S. 250 (1897). Paraguay's renunciation of torture as a legitimate instrument of state policy, however, does not strip the tort of its character as an international law violation, if it in fact occurred under color of government authority. See Declaration on the Protection of All Persons from Being Subjected to Torture, supra note 11; cf. Ex parte Young, 209 U.S. 123 (1908) state official subject to suit for constitutional violations despite immunity of state).

Finally, we have already stated that we do not reach the critical question of forum non conveniens, since it was not considered below. In closing, however, we note that the foreign relations implications of this and other issues the district court will be required to adjudicate on remand underscores the wisdom of the First Congress in vesting

---

25. In taking that broad range of factors into account, the district court may well decide that fairness requires it to apply Paraguayan law to the instant case. See Slater v. Mexican National Railway Co., 194 U.S. 120 (1904). Such a decision would not retroactively oust the federal court of subject matter jurisdiction, even though plaintiff's cause of action would no longer properly be "created" by a law of the United States. See American Well Works Co. v. Lane & Bowler Co., 241 U.S. 257, 260 (1916) (Holmes, J.). Once federal jurisdiction is established by a colorable claim under federal law at a preliminary stage of the proceeding, subsequent dismissal of that claim (here, the claim under the general international proscription of torture) does not deprive the court of jurisdiction previously established. See Hagans v. Lavine, 415 U.S. 528 (1974); Romero v. International Terminal Operating Co., 358 U.S. 354 (1959); Bell v. Hood, 327 U.S. 678 (1946). Cf. Haynh Thi Ahn, supra, 586 F.2d at 633 (choice of municipal law ousts § 1350 jurisdiction when no international norms exist).

jurisdiction over such claims in the federal district courts through the Alien Tort Statute. Questions of this nature are fraught with implications for the nation as a whole, and therefore should not be left to the potentially varying adjudications of the courts of the fifty states.

In the twentieth century the international community has come to recognize the common danger posed by the flagrant disregard of basic human rights and particularly the right to be free of torture. Spurred first by the Great War, and then the Second, civilized nations have banded together to prescribe acceptable norms of international behavior. From the ashes of the Second World War arose the United Nations Organization, amid hopes that an era of peace and co-operation had at last begun. Though many of these aspirations have remained elusive goals, that circumstance cannot diminish the true progress that has been made. In the modern age, humanitarian and practical considerations have combined to lead the nations of the world to recognize that respect for fundamental human rights is in their individual and collective interest. Among the rights universally proclaimed by all nations, as we have noted, is the right to be free of physical torture. Indeed, for purposes of civil liability, the torturer has become—like the pirate and slave trader before him—hostis humani generis, an enemy of all mankind. Our holding today, giving effect to a jurisdictional provision enacted by our First Congress, is a small but important step in the fulfillment of the ageless dream to free all people from brutal violence.

Note. It has been suggested that the violation of the human rights of an alien can be vindicated at the international level through diplomatic protest by the injured individual's state, or through the processes of international arbitration or adjudication put in motion by the individual's state. The recent developments in human rights law under the aegis of the United Nations have emphasized that, either by the growth of international law or by convention, an individual's substantive rights may be claimed by him against even his own state. How can those rights be vindicated at the international level if the individual's state fails or refuses to accord them to him?

The hypothetical problem in the next sub-section illustrates the shortcomings of the adjudicatory process. In following sub-sections, certain procedures allowing individual access to United Nations are discussed. Test these procedures in the light of the immense variety of circumstances that may arise, e. g., a political opponent to a government is jailed, without charges, hearing or counsel; physical torture is applied to induce confession or the giving of information; a person is arbitrarily deprived of his citizenship, property or means of livelihood.

3. INTERNATIONAL ADJUDICATION

There is no universal court in which an individual can maintain an action to enforce the rights that international law has begun to recognize substantively. The only universal court is the International Court of Justice and only states may be parties in cases before the court. Are there nevertheless means by which an individual's rights can be vindicated in this court?

Problem. N is a national of State D, a party to the International Convention on the Elimination of All Forms of Racial Discrimination. (See the Documentary Supplement.) N claims that because of his race he has been denied equal opportunity by State D with respect to housing and employment, in violation of Article 5 of the convention. N persuades the foreign office of State P to become interested in his case by reason of the opportunity it affords State P to publicly embarrass State D over its racial policies. State P is unsuccessful in procuring any change in State D's policies or its treatment of N. All of the procedures provided for in the convention—see Articles 11, 12 and 13 in the Documentary Supplement—are exhausted without effect. Pursuant to Article 22 of the convention, State P refers its dispute with State D, over D's treatment of N, to the International Court of Justice. (Article 22 provides: "Any dispute between two or more States Parties with respect to the interpretation or application of this Convention, which is not settled by negotiation or by the procedures expressly provided for in this Convention, shall, at the request of any of the parties to the dispute, be referred to the International Court of Justice for decision, unless the disputants agree to another mode of settlement.")

Will the court take jurisdiction of such a claim? Will it recognize the standing or interest of the complainant state?

NOTTEBOHM CASE (LIECHTENSTEIN v. GUATEMALA)

International Court of Justice, 1955.
[1955] I.C.J.Rep. 4.

The opinion of the court is set forth at p. 499.

In the problem case the individual, N, whose rights were allegedly violated, is not a national of State P by any definition of nationality. Does the reasoning of Nottebohm suggest that P cannot maintain this proceeding?

SOUTH WEST AFRICA CASES (ETHIOPIA v. SOUTH AFRICA; LIBERIA v. SOUTH AFRICA)

International Court of Justice, 1966.
[1966] I.C.J.Rep. 6.

* * *

1.   In the present proceedings the two applicant States, the Empire of Ethiopia and the Republic of Liberia (whose cases are identical and will for present purposes be treated as one case), acting in the capacity of States which were members of the former League of Nations, put forward various allegations of contraventions of the League of Nations Mandate for South West Africa, said to have been committed by the respondent State, the Republic of South Africa, as the administering authority.

2.   In an earlier phase of the case, which took place before the Court in 1962, four preliminary objections were advanced, based on Article 37 of the Court's Statute and the jurisdictional clause (Article 7, paragraph 2) of the Mandate for South West Africa, which were all of them argued by the Respondent and treated by the Court as objections to its jurisdiction.   The Court, by its Judgment of 21 December 1962, rejected each of these objections, and thereupon found that it had "jurisdiction to adjudicate upon the merits of the dispute".

3.   In the course of the proceedings on the merits, * * * the Parties put forward various contentions on such matters as whether the Mandate for South West Africa was still in force,—and if so, whether the Mandatory's obligation under Article 6 of the Mandate to furnish annual reports to the Council of the former League of Nations concerning its administration of the mandated territory had become transformed by one means or another into an obligation to furnish such reports to the General Assembly of the United Nations, or had, on the other hand, lapsed entirely;—whether there had been any contravention by the Respondent of the second paragraph of Article 2 of the Mandate which required the Mandatory to "promote to the utmost the material and moral well-being and the social progress of the inhabitants of the territory",—whether there had been any contravention of Article 4 of the Mandate, prohibiting (except for police and local defence purposes) the "military training of the natives", and forbidding the establishment of military or naval bases, or the erection of fortifications in the territory.   The Applicants also alleged that the Respondent had contravened paragraph 1 of Article 7 of the Mandate (which provides that the Mandate can only be modified with the consent of the Council of the League of Nations) by attempting to modify the Mandate without the consent of the General Assembly of the United Nations which, so it was contended, had replaced the Council of the League for this and other purposes.   There were other allegations also, which it is not necessary to set out here.

4. * * * In this connection, there was one matter that appertained to the merits of the case but which had an antecedent character, namely the question of the Applicants' standing in the present phase of the proceedings,—not, that is to say, of their standing before the Court itself, which was the subject of the Court's decision in 1962, but the question, as a matter of the merits of the case, of their legal right or interest regarding the subject-matter of their claim, as set out in their final submissions.

* * *

10. The mandates system, as is well known, was formally instituted by Article 22 of the Covenant of the League of Nations. As there indicated, there were to be three categories of mandates, designated as "A", "B" and "C" mandates respectively, the Mandate for South West Africa being one of the "C" category. The differences between these categories lay in the nature and geographical situation of the territories concerned, the state of development of their peoples, and the powers accordingly to be vested in the administering authority, or mandatory, for each territory placed under mandate. But although it was by Article 22 of the League Covenant that the system as such was established, the precise terms of each mandate, covering the rights and obligations of the mandatory, of the League and its organs, and of the individual members of the League, in relation to each mandated territory, were set out in separate instruments of mandate which, with one exception to be noted later, took the form of resolutions of the Council of the League.

11. These instruments, whatever the differences between certain of their terms, had various features in common as regards their structure. For present purposes, their substantive provisions may be regarded as falling into two main categories. On the one hand, and of course as the principal element of each instrument, there were the articles defining the mandatory's powers, and its obligations in respect of the inhabitants of the territory and towards the League and its organs. These provisions, relating to the carrying out of the mandates as mandates, will hereinafter be referred to as "conduct of the mandate", or simply "conduct" provisions. On the other hand, there were articles conferring in different degrees, according to the particular mandate or category of mandate, certain rights relative to the mandated territory, directly upon the members of the League as individual States, or in favour of their nationals. Many of these rights were of the same kind as are to be found in certain provisions of ordinary treaties of commerce, establishment and navigation concluded between States. Rights of this kind will hereinafter be referred to as "special interests" rights, embodied in the "special interests" provisions of the mandates. * * * [The "special interest" provisions of "C" mandates] were confined to provisions for freedom for missionaries ("nationals of any State Member of the League of Nations") to "enter into, travel and reside in the territory for the purpose of prosecuting their calling"—(Mandate for South West Africa, Article 5). In the present case, the dispute between the Parties re-

lates exclusively to the former of these two categories of provisions, and not to the latter.

*   *   *

13.   In addition to the classes of provisions so far noticed, every instrument of mandate contained a jurisdictional clause which, with a single exception to be noticed in due course, was in identical terms for each mandate, whether belonging to the "A", "B" or "C" category. The language and effect of this clause will be considered later; but it provided for a reference of disputes to the Permanent Court of International Justice and, so the Court found in the first phase of the case, as already mentioned, this reference was now, by virtue of Article 37 of the Court's Statute, to be construed as a reference to the present Court.

*   *   *

33.   *   *   *   [E]ven in the time of the League, even as members of the League when that organization still existed, the Applicants did not, in their individual capacity as States, possess any separate self-contained right which they could assert, independently of, or additionally to, the right of the League, in the pursuit of its collective, institutional activity, to require the due performance of the Mandate in discharge of the "sacred trust". This right was vested exclusively in the League, and was exercised through its competent organs. *   *   *   But no right was reserved to them, individually as States, and independently of their participation in the institutional activities of the League, as component parts of it, to claim in their own name,—still less as agents authorized to represent the League, —the right to invigilate the sacred trust,—to set themselves up as separate custodians of the various mandates. This was the role of the League organs.

34.   To put this conclusion in another way, the position was that under the mandates system, and within the general framework of the League system, the various mandatories were responsible for their conduct of the mandates solely to the League—in particular to its Council—and were not additionally and separately responsible to each and every individual State member of the League. If the latter had been given a legal right or interest on an individual "State" basis, this would have meant that each member of the League, independently of the Council or other competent League organ, could have addressed itself directly to every mandatory, for the purpose of calling for explanations or justifications of its administration, and generally to exact from the mandatory the due performance of its mandate, according to the view which that State might individually take as to what was required for the purpose.

35.   Clearly no such right existed under the mandates system as contemplated by any of the relevant instruments. It would have involved a position of accountability by the mandatories to each and every member of the League separately, for otherwise there would have

been nothing additional to the normal faculty of participating in the collective work of the League respecting mandates.

* * *

49. * * * Throughout this case it has been suggested, directly or indirectly, that humanitarian considerations are sufficient in themselves to generate legal rights and obligations, and that the Court can and should proceed accordingly. The Court does not think so. It is a court of law, and can take account of moral principles only in so far as these are given a sufficient expression in legal form. Law exists, it is said, to serve a social need; but precisely for that reason it can do so only through and within the limits of its own discipline. Otherwise, it is not a legal service that would be rendered.

50. Humanitarian considerations may constitute the inspirational basis for rules of law, just as, for instance, the preambular parts of the United Nations Charter constitute the moral and political basis for the specific legal provisions thereafter set out. Such considerations do not, however, in themselves amount to rules of law. All States are interested—have an interest—in such matters. But the existence of an "interest" does not of itself entail that this interest is specifically juridical in character.

* * *

60. It is however contended that, even if the Judgment of 1962 was, for the above-mentioned reasons, not preclusive of the issue of the Applicants' legal right or interest, it did in essence determine that issue because it decided that the Applicants were entitled to invoke the jurisdictional clause of the Mandate, and that if they had a sufficient interest to do that, they must also have a sufficient interest in the subject-matter of their claim. This view is not well-founded. The faculty of invoking a jurisdictional clause depends upon what tests or conditions of the right to do so are laid down by the clause itself. To hold that the parties in any given case belong to the category of State specified in the clause,—that the dispute has the specified character,—and that the forum is the one specified,—is not the same thing as finding the existence of a legal right or interest relative to the merits of the claim. The jurisdictional clause of the Mandate for South West Africa (Article 7, paragraph 2), which appeared in all the mandates, reads as follows:

> The Mandatory agrees that, if any dispute whatever should arise between the Mandatory and another Member of the League of Nations relating to the interpretation or the application of the provisions of the Mandate, such dispute, if it cannot be settled by negotiation, shall be submitted to the Permanent Court of International Justice provided for by Article 14 of the Covenant of the League of Nations.

* * *

62. It is next contended that this particular jurisdictional clause has an effect which is more extensive than if it is considered as a simple jurisdictional clause: that it is a clause conferring a sub-

stantive right,—that the substantive right it confers is precisely the right to claim from the mandatory the carrying out of the "conduct of the Mandate" provisions of the instrument of mandate,—and that in consequence, even if the right is derivable from no other source, it is derivable from and implicit in this clause.

    *   *   *

64.   In truth however, there is nothing about this particular jurisdictional clause to differentiate it from many others, or to make it an exception to the rule that, in principle, jurisdictional clauses are adjectival not substantive in their nature and effect.   *   *   *   It is a universal and necessary, but yet almost elementary principle of procedural law that a distinction has to be made between, on the one hand, the right to activate a court and the right of the court to examine the merits of the claim,—and, on the other, the plaintiff party's legal right in respect of the subject-matter of that which it claims, which would have to be established to the satisfaction of the Court.

65.   In the present case, that subject-matter includes the question whether the Applicants possess any legal right to require the performance of the "conduct" provisions of the Mandate. This is something which cannot be predetermined by the language of a common-form jurisdictional clause such as Article 7, paragraph 2, of the Mandate for South West Africa. This provision, with slight differences of wording and emphasis, is in the same form as that of many other jurisdictional clauses. The Court can see nothing in it that would take the clause outside the normal rule that, in a dispute causing the activation of a jurisdictional clause, the substantive rights themselves which the dispute is about, must be sought for elsewhere than in this clause, or in some element apart from it,—and must therefore be established aliunde vel aliter. Jurisdictional clauses do not determine whether parties have substantive rights, but only whether, if they have them, they can vindicate them by recourse to a tribunal.

66.   Such rights may be derived from participation in an international instrument by a State which has signed and ratified, or has acceded, or has in some other manner become a party to it; and which in consequence, and subject to any exceptions expressly indicated, is entitled to enjoy rights under all the provisions of the instrument concerned. Since the Applicants cannot bring themselves under this head, they must show that the "conduct" provisions of the mandates conferred rights in terms on members of the League as individual States, in the same way that the "special interests" provisions did. It is however contended that there is a third possibility, and that on the basis of the jurisdictional clause alone, the Applicants, as members of the League, were part of the institutional machinery of control relative to the mandates, and that in this capacity they had a right of action of the same kind as, for instance, members of the League Council had under the jurisdictional clauses of the minorities treaties of that period, for the protection of minority rights.

On this footing the essence of the contention is that the Applicants do not need to show the existence of any substantive rights outside the jurisdictional clause, and that they had—that all members of the League had—what was in effect a policing function under the mandates and by virtue of the jurisdictional clause.

67. The Court has examined this contention, but does not think that the two cases are in any way comparable. When States intend to create a right of action of this kind they adopt a different method. Such a right has, in special circumstances, been conferred on States belonging to a body of compact size such as the Council of the League of Nations, invested with special supervisory functions and even a power of intervention in the matter, as provided by the jurisdictional clause of the minorities treaties—see for instance Article 12 of the minorities treaty with Poland, signed at Versailles on 28 June 1919, which was typical. Even so the right, as exercisable by members of the League Council, in effect as part of the Council's work, with which they would ex hypothesi have been fully familiar, was characterized at the time by an eminent Judge and former President of the Permanent Court as being "in every respect very particular in character" and as going "beyond the province of general international law". The intention to confer it must be quite clear; and the Court holds that for the reasons which have already been given, and for others to be considered later, there was never any intention to confer an invigilatory function of this kind on each and every member of the League.

*   *   *

69. The Court finds itself unable to reconcile the two types of case except upon the assumption, strongly supported by every other factor involved, that, as regards the mandates, the jurisdictional clause was intended to serve a different purpose, namely to give the individual members of the League the means, which might not otherwise be available to them through League channels, of protecting their "special interests" relative to the mandated territories. In the minorities case, the right of action of the members of the Council under the jurisdictional clause was only intended for the protection of minority populations. No other purpose in conferring a right of action on members of the League Council would have been possible in that case. *   *   *

70. In this last connection it is of capital importance that the right as conferred in the minorities case was subjected to certain characterizations which were wholly absent in the case of the jurisdictional clause of the mandates. Any "difference of opinion" was characterized in advance as being justiciable, because it was to be "held to be a dispute of an international character" within the meaning of Article 14 of the Covenant (this was the well-known "deeming" clause), so that no question of any lack of legal right or interest could arise. The decisions of the Court were moreover, to be final and, by means of a reference to Article 13 of the Covenant, were giv-

en an effect erga omnes as a general judicial settlement binding on all concerned. The jurisdictional clause of the mandates on the other hand, was essentially an ordinary jurisdictional clause, having none of the special characteristics or effects of those of the minorities treaties.

* * *

99.   In the light of these various considerations, the Court finds that the Applicants cannot be considered to have established any legal right or interest appertaining to them in the subject-matter of the present claims, and that, accordingly, the Court must decline to give effect to them.

100.   For these reasons,

The COURT, by the President's casting vote—the votes being equally divided, decides to reject the claims of the Empire of Ethiopia and the Republic of Liberia.

* * *

Dissenting Opinion of Judge JESSUP.

* * *

The Applicants have not asked for an award of damages or for any other material amend for their own individual benefit. They have in effect, and in part, asked for a declaratory judgment interpreting certain provisions of the Mandate for South West Africa. The Court having decided in 1962 that they had standing (locus standi) to bring the action, they are now entitled to a declaratory judgment without any further showing of interest. (at 328)

* * *

In the minority treaties, one sees a further illustration of the fact that the statesmen of 1919 recognized the right of States to invoke the jurisdiction of the Court in the interest of special groups even when their individual interests were not affected. This is brought out very clearly in the dissenting opinion of Judge Huber in the case of Minority Schools in Upper Silesia (P.C.I.J., Series A, No. 15 (1928), at p. 50):

> Article 72, paragraph 3 [of the Geneva Convention] is the literal reproduction of Article 12 of the Minorities Treaty of June 28th, 1919, and of analogous provisions of other treaties. The jurisdiction conferred by this clause is in every respect very particular in character and goes beyond the province of general international law; for Article 72, paragraph 3, confers on every Power being a Member of the Council, *even if it is not a contracting Party to the Minority Treaties* or to the Geneva Convention, the right of appealing to the Court, and *such judicial action is based upon stipulations which relate not to rights of the applicant State or to those of its nationals on whose behalf it might take action*, but to the relations between the respondent State and its own nationals. (Italics added.)

The principle that States were entitled to bring to the Court cases which did not involve their own direct interests is not affected by the fact that the right of recourse in the minority treaties was limited to Members of the Council of the League. Although in the Memel case, the Powers who could resort to the Court were all parties to the treaty, in several of the minority cases, the right of recourse belonged not only to the Permanent Members of the Council who may have been parties, but also to the non-permanent Members who were elected from time to time and who, as Judge Huber pointed out, did not need to be, and often were not, parties to the minority treaties which gave them the right to invoke the Court. The States in question derived their "standing" before the Court from the adjudication clause, not from some other conferment of a substantive right. (at 377)

* * *

My separate opinion in 1962 also called attention (at p. 426) to the fact that in more recent times, the same general appreciation of a right to turn to the International Court of Justice for interpretation, application or fulfilment of a treaty having a broad humanitarian interest, is recognized in—

the Genocide Convention, which came into force on 12 January 1951 on the deposit of the twentieth ratification. [It] provides in Article IX:

Disputes between the Contracting Parties relating to the interpretation, application or fulfilment of the present Convention, including those relating to the responsibility of a State for genocide or for any of the other acts enumerated in article III, shall be submitted to the International Court of Justice at the request of any of the parties to the dispute. (Vol. 78, United Nations Treaty Series, pp. 278 at 282).

As this Court said of the Genocide Convention: "In such a convention the contracting States do not have any interests of their own; they merely have, one and all, a common interest, namely the accomplishment of those high purposes which are the raison d'être of the convention. Consequently, in a convention of this type one cannot speak of individual advantages or disadvantages to States, or of the maintenance of a perfect contractual balance between rights and duties. The high ideals which inspired the Convention provide, by virtue of the common will of the parties the foundation and measure of all its provisions." (I.C.J. Reports 1951, at p. 23) (at 379)

* * *

---

1. *Comparison of the Mandate for South West Africa with the International Convention on the Elimination of All Forms of Racial Discrimination.* Is the convention comparable to the mandate so as to bring the Article 22 provisions (for reference of a dispute to the court) under the same strictures as to interest and standing that were articulated in the South West Africa cases? Are there compa-

rable institutional arrangements in the convention which would suggest that state parties cannot bring each other directly into the court? Does the convention contain both special interest provisions and conduct provisions? Is a state limited, in referring a dispute to the court under Article 22, to disputes relating to its own special interests in its own nationals? Do the references in the opinions to the minorities treaties suggest that the court would deal differently with the convention than it dealt with the mandate?

2. *The case concerning the Barcelona Traction, Light and Power Company, Limited (Belgium v. Spain).* The case was decided in 1970, [1970] I.C.J.Rep. 3. A portion of the text of the decision appears in Chapter 17. The case concerned claimed injury to a corporation's property. In the course of an opinion dealing with the question of the proper state to maintain an action to redress this injury, the court stated:

> 33. When a State admits into its territory foreign investments or foreign nationals, whether natural or juristic persons, it is bound to extend to them the protection of the law and assumes obligations concerning the treatment to be afforded them. These obligations, however, are neither absolute nor unqualified. In particular, an essential distinction should be drawn between the obligations of a State towards the international community as a whole, and those arising vis-à-vis another State in the field of diplomatic protection. By their very nature the former are the concern of all States. In view of the importance of the rights involved, all States can be held to have a legal interest in their protection; they are obligations erga omnes.

> 34. Such obligations derive, for example, in contemporary international law, from the outlawing of acts of aggression, and of genocide, as also from the principles and rules concerning the basic rights of the human person, including protection from slavery and racial discrimination. Some of the corresponding rights of protection have entered into the body of general international law (Reservations to the Convention on the Prevention and Punishment of the Crime of Genocide, Advisory Opinion, I.C.J. Reports 1951, p. 23); others are conferred by international instruments of a universal or quasi-universal character.

> 35. Obligations the performance of which is the subject of diplomatic protection are not of the same category. It cannot be held, when one such obligation in particular is in question, in a specific case, that all States have a legal interest in its observance. In order to bring a claim in respect of the breach of such an obligation, a State must first establish its right to do so, for the rules on the subject rest on two suppositions:

>> The first is that the defendant State has broken an obligation towards the national State in respect of its nationals. The second is that only the party to whom an international obligation is due can bring a claim in respect of its breach.

(Reparation for Injuries Suffered in the Service of the United Nations, Advisory Opinion, I.C.J. Reports 1949, pp. 181–182.)

* * *

3. *Remedies.* If a state refers to the court a dispute about a second state's treatment of the second state's own nationals, what relief should be requested or granted? Would monetary relief be administrable? Would a declaratory judgment be more workable? Would it be effective? See Judge Jessup's dissenting opinion in the South West Africa cases, [1966] I.C.J.Rep. at 329.

4. *Advisory Opinions.* How could an individual injured by his own state seek relief by way of an advisory opinion? The individual would need the support of some other state, to enlist the aid of the General Assembly or the Security Council (or some other body authorized under Article 65 of the Statute of the International Court of Justice) to ask for the opinion. The question put to the court would have to be constructed in terms that would permit the court to find it had been asked for an opinion on a legal question under Article 65 of the statute. In addition, the court might have to be persuaded it was not in effect deciding a dispute involving a state without that state's consent to its jurisdiction. Cf. Status of Eastern Carelia, P.C.I.J., Ser. B, No. 5 (1923), (Advisory Opinion).

ADVISORY OPINION ON THE WESTERN SAHARA

International Court of Justice, 1975.
[1975] I.C.J.Rep. 12, 22.

* * *

27. Spain considers that the subject of the dispute which Morocco invited it to submit jointly to the Court for decision in contentious proceedings, and the subject of the questions on which the advisory opinion is requested are substantially identical; thus the advisory procedure is said to have been used as an alternative after the failure of an attempt to make use of the contentious jurisdiction with regard to the same question. Consequently, to give a reply would, according to Spain, be to allow the advisory procedure to be used as a means of bypassing the consent of a State, which constitutes the basis of the Court's jurisdiction. If the Court were to countenance such a use of its advisory jurisdiction, the outcome would be to obliterate the distinction between the two spheres of the Court's jurisdiction, and the fundamental principle of the independence of States would be affected, for States would find their disputes with other States being submitted to the Court, by this indirect means, without their consent; this might result in compulsory jurisdiction being achieved by majority vote in a political organ. Such circumvention of the well-established principle of consent for the exercise of international jurisdiction would constitute, according to this view, a compelling reason for declining to answer the request.

28.   In support of these propositions Spain has invoked the fundamental rule, repeatedly reaffirmed in the Court's jurisprudence, that a State cannot, without its consent, be compelled to submit its disputes with other States to the Court's adjudication. It has relied, in particular, on the application of this rule to the advisory jurisdiction by the Permanent Court of International Justice in the Status of Eastern Carelia case (P.C.I.J., Series B, No. 5), maintaining that the essential principle enunciated in that case is not modified by the decisions of the present Court in the cases concerning the Interpretation of Peace Treaties with Bulgaria, Hungary and Romania, First Phase (I.C.J. Reports 1950, p. 65) and the Legal Consequences for States of the Continued Presence of South Africa in Namibia (South West Africa) notwithstanding Security Council Resolution 276 (1970) (I.C.J. Reports 1971, p. 16). Morocco and Mauritania, on the other hand, have maintained that the present case falls within the principles applied in those two decisions and that the ratio decidendi of the Status of Eastern Carelia case is not applicable to it.

29.   It is clear that Spain has not consented to the adjudication of the questions formulated in resolution 3292 (XXIX). It did not agree to Morocco's proposal for the joint submission to the Court of the issue raised in the communication of 23 September 1974. Spain made no reply to the letter setting out the proposal, and this was properly understood by Morocco as signifying its rejection by Spain. As to the request for an advisory opinion the records of the discussions in the Fourth Committee and in the plenary of the General Assembly confirm that Spain raised objections to the Court's being asked for an opinion on the basis of the two questions formulated in the present request. The Spanish delegation stated that it was prepared to join in the request only if the questions put were supplemented by another question establishing a satisfactory balance between the historical and legal exposition of the matter and the current situation viewed in the light of the Charter of the United Nations and the relevant General Assembly resolutions on the decolonization of the territory. In view of Spain's persistent objections to the questions formulated in resolution 3292 (XXIX), the fact that it abstained and did not vote against the resolution cannot be interpreted as implying its consent to the adjudication of those questions by the Court. Moreover, its participation in the Court's proceedings cannot be understood as implying that it has consented to the adjudication of the questions posed in resolution 3292 (XXIX), for it has persistently maintained its objections throughout.

30.   In other respects, however, Spain's position in relation to the present proceedings finds no parallel in the circumstances of the advisory proceedings concerning the Status of Eastern Carelia in 1923. In that case, one of the States concerned was neither a party to the Statute of the Permanent Court nor, at the time, a Member of the League of Nations, and lack of competence of the League to deal with a dispute involving non-member States which refused its intervention was a decisive reason for the Court's declining to give an an-

swer. In the present case, Spain is a Member of the United Nations and has accepted the provisions of the Charter and Statute; it has thereby in general given its consent to the exercise by the Court of its advisory jurisdiction. It has not objected, and could not validly object, to the General Assembly's exercise of its powers to deal with the decolonization of a non-self-governing territory and to seek an opinion on questions relevant to the exercise of those powers. In the proceedings in the General Assembly, Spain did not oppose the reference of the Western Sahara question as such to the Court's advisory jurisdiction; it objected rather to the restriction of that reference to the historical aspects of that question.

31. In the proceedings concerning the Interpretation of Peace Treaties with Bulgaria, Hungary and Romania, First Phase, this Court had to consider how far the views expressed by the Permanent Court in the Status of Eastern Carelia case were still pertinent in relation to the applicable provisions of the Charter of the United Nations and the Statute of the Court. It stated, *inter alia*:

> "This objection reveals a confusion between the principles governing contentious procedure and those which are applicable to Advisory Opinions.
>
> The consent of States, parties to a dispute, is the basis of the Court's jurisdiction in contentious cases. The situation is different in regard to advisory proceedings even where the Request for an Opinion relates to a legal question actually pending between States. The Court's reply is only of an advisory character: as such, it has no binding force. It follows that no State, whether a Member of the United Nations or not, can prevent the giving of an Advisory Opinion which the United Nations considers to be desirable in order to obtain enlightenment as to the course of action it should take. The Court's Opinion is given not to the States, but to the organ which is entitled to request it; the reply of the Court, itself an 'organ of the United Nations', represents its participation in the activities of the organization, and, in principle, should not be refused." I.C.J. Reports 1950, p. 71.)

32. The Court, it is true, affirmed in this pronouncement that its competence to give an opinion did not depend on the consent of the interested States, even when the case concerned a legal question actually pending between them. However, the Court proceeded not merely to stress its judicial character and the permissive nature of Article 65, paragraph 1, of the Statute but to examine, specifically in relation to the opposition of some of the interested States, the question of the judicial propriety of giving the opinion. Moreover, the Court emphasized the circumstances differentiating the case then under consideration from the Status of Eastern Carelia case and explained the particular grounds which led it to conclude that there was no reason requiring the Court to refuse to reply to the request. Thus the Court recognized that lack of consent might constitute a ground for declining to give the opinion requested if, in the circumstances of

a given case, considerations of judicial propriety should oblige the Court to refuse an opinion. In short, the consent of an interested State continues to be relevant not for the Court's competence, but for the appreciation of the propriety of giving an opinion.

33.   In certain circumstances, therefore, the lack of consent of an interested State may render the giving of an advisory opinion incompatible with the Court's judicial character. An instance of this would be when the circumstances disclose that to give a reply would have the effect of circumventing the principle that a State is not obliged to allow its disputes to be submitted to judicial settlement without its consent. If such a situation should arise, the powers of the Court under the discretion given to it by Article 65, paragraph 1, of the Statute, would afford sufficient legal means to ensure respect for the fundamental principle of consent to jurisdiction.

34.   The situation existing in the present case is not, however, the one envisaged above. There is in this case a legal controversy, but one which arose during the proceedings of the General Assembly and in relation to matters with which it was dealing. It did not arise independently in bilateral relations. In a communication addressed on 10 November 1958 to the Secretary-General of the United Nations, the Spanish Government stated: "Spain possesses no non-self-governing territories, since the territories subject to its sovereignty in Africa are, in accordance with the legislation now in force, considered to be and classified as provinces of Spain". This gave rise to the "most explicit reservations" of the Government of Morocco, which, in a communication to the Secretary-General of 20 November 1958, stated that it "claim[ed] certain African territories at present under Spanish control as an integral part of Moroccan national territory".

---

4. INDIVIDUAL PETITIONS

Gross and reliably attested violations. The Human Rights Commission and the Economic and Social Council decided in 1947 that the Commission "has no power to take any action in regard to any complaints concerning human rights." ECOSOC Off.Rec., 4th Sess., Supp. 3, Report of the Commission on Human Rights, First Sess., p. 6. Although attempts were made for two decades to reverse this position, the many communications from individuals that came to the United Nations informally each year were not acted upon, although a state named in a complaint was sent an anonymous copy.

This situation was changed by ECOSOC Resolution 1503 (XLVIII) of May 27, 1970, ECOSOC Off.Rec., Resumed 48th Sess., Resolutions, Supp. 1A, p. 8. It provides that the Sub-Commission on Prevention of Discrimination and Protection of Minorities may appoint a working group to consider communications from individuals and to bring to the sub-commission's attention those communications "which appear to reveal a consistent pattern of gross and reliably attested violations of human rights and fundamental freedoms within the terms of reference of the sub-commission." The resolution provides for consideration of the communications by the sub-commission, with reference thereafter to the Human Rights Commission and possibly a study and report by the commission or an investigation by an ad hoc committee appointed by the commission and recommendation to ECOSOC. Limitations of significance are that the ad hoc investigation can be made only with the consent of the state concerned and that the matter must remain confidential until the commission decides to make a recommendation to ECOSOC. The text of the resolution is set forth in the Documentary Supplement.

Procedures to carry out ECOSOC Resolution 1503 were adopted by the sub-commission in August 1971. The text of the procedures is set forth in the Documentary Supplement. Paragraph 2 of the procedures discloses that a broad range of persons and groups is empowered to originate communications. Paragraph 1 indicates that the procedures are useful for a single individual only if he is a victim of a "consistent pattern of gross and reliably attested violations of human rights and fundamental freedoms." It is significant, however, that the injured person can communicate directly with the United Nations without the necessity of enlisting the aid of a foreign state.

The requirement that matters being considered under the Resolution 1503 procedure remain confidential raises questions. First, how is the confidential 1503 procedure to be coordinated with the Human Rights Commission's normal, plenary agenda (which can include discussion of a particular country's violations of human rights)? Second, since the 1503 procedure is confidential, how is it possible to determine whether that procedure has produced any concrete results? These two questions are reflected in the following report.

THE RESOLUTION 1503 PROCEDURE

20 Review of the International Commission of Jurists 33 (1978).

Important steps forward were made this year under the Resolution 1503 procedure, by which allegations of gross violations of human rights are examined in closed session. Previously the Commission had not reached any decision in the terms of the resolution either to order a thorough study or to institute an investigation by an ad hoc committee with the consent of the State concerned. This year, before the public discussion on gross violations of human rights, the President of the Commission announced that some action had been decided upon in the private session with respect to the following nine countries: Bolivia, Equatorial Guinea, Ethiopia, Indonesia, Malawi, Paraguay, South Korea, Uganda and Uruguay.

It was reported by Reuters on 9 March that the action decided on included a special representative to investigate the situation in Uganda. There was no indication what actions were authorised with respect to the other countries, so that the real significance of the Commission's decisions remains to be seen. A resolution was adopted asking the Secretariat to report quarterly to members of the Commission on actions taken to implement its decisions under Resolution 1503.

The announcement of the names of these nine countries was unexpected, since in principle the procedure remains confidential until the Commission reports to ECOSOC upon completion of its action. The announcement was the result of a temporary compromise on a fundamental question—whether human rights violations can be raised in public when they concern a country being examined under the confidential procedure of Resolution 1503. The question arose last year when Canada and the UK introduced a draft resolution concerning events in Uganda. Although allegations concerning Uganda were then being considered under Resolution 1503, the events referred to in the draft resolution were so recent that they were not included in the communications referred to the Commission.

Since progress under Resolution 1503 tends to be very slow, the question whether a case "under consideration" precludes all public debate concerning the same country is of considerable importance. The immunity from public comment which the nine countries enjoyed, for example, was in marked contrast to the extensive presentations, questions and commentary addressed to Argentina and Democratic Kampuchea, neither of which was being considered under Resolution 1503.

With respect to Argentina, much of the discussion consisted of interventions by NGOs which had recently completed missions in that country. Although several member states expressed concern, no resolutions were introduced. With respect to Kampuchea, a resolution was introduced by the United Kingdom. After some compromise, a resolution was adopted by consensus which asks the Secretariat to send the record of the discussion of alleged violations to the government of Kampuchea, and to transmit back to the Commission the government's response "together with all the information that might be available about the situation". This development is also an innovation in the procedure of the Commission.

Despite a lengthy report prepared by the Secretariat concerning the compatibility of public and confidential procedures (E/CN. 4/1273 and addenda), no progress was made in resolving the question of principle. As a temporary solution an agreement was reached that no debate would be allowed regarding the countries with respect to which some action had been authorised under Resolution 1503. This necessitated announcing the names of the nine countries.

During the public debate several representatives of NGOs described recent missions to Latin America. Following the established practice, they refrained from naming the country about which they were speaking. Fearing that the speakers were making veiled references to countries upon which public discussion has been barred, members of the Commission asked the speakers to name the states to which they were referring. This demand, a clear departure from the rule that countries not be named by NGOs, caused a discussion of the wisdom of the rule itself. Several members commented that it makes little sense to permit NGOs to make grave charges of human rights violations without naming the country concerned. As the delegate from Panama noted, the Commission must know what country the information submitted refers to in order to fulfil its duty to evaluate the allegations and determine what response, if any, is called for.

---

1. *Racial discrimination.* A procedure for hearing individual communications is contained in the International Convention on the Elimination of All Forms of Racial Discrimination and a Committee on the Elimination of Racial Discrimination exists under Article 8 of that convention. Under Article 14 of the convention, no communication from individuals is to be received by the committee if it concerns a state party that has not made a declaration recognizing the competence of the committee.

2. *Civil and political rights.* The right to make individual communications is also provided by the Optional Protocol to the International Covenant on Civil and Political Rights. The Human Rights Committee, established by Part IV of the covenant, is the mechanism for dealing with such communications. Under Article 1 of the protocol, a state party to the protocol "recognizes the competence of the Committee to receive and consider communications from individuals subject to its jurisdiction who claim to be victims of a violation by that State Party of any of the rights set forth in the Covenant." It should be noted that this provision allows an individual to claim a single violation (i. e. it is not necessary to identify a pattern of violations as under the 1503 procedure). In addition, although Article 5(3) of the protocol calls for closed meetings, the committee is not held to the level of confidentiality that surrounds the 1503 procedure, as evidenced by the following material.

REPORT OF THE HUMAN RIGHTS COMMITTEE

XVI U.N. Monthly Chronicle, June 1979, p. 66.

The Committee also concluded, for the first time, consideration of a communication submitted to it by a Uruguayan national in accordance with the Optional Protocol to the International Covenant on Civil and Political Rights. Under the terms of the Protocol, individuals who claimed that any of their rights enumerated in the Covenant had been violated and who had exhausted all available remedies, might submit written communications to the Committee for consideration. The Committee, after examining the communication in question, took the view that it revealed a number of violations by Uruguay, the State Party concerned, of the Covenant provisions.

It held that the State Party was under an obligation to take immediate steps to ensure strict observance of the Covenant provisions and to provide effective remedies to the victims.

The communication was written by a Uruguayan national residing in Mexico, who submitted it on her own behalf, as well as on behalf of her husband, Luis María Bazzano Ambrosini, her stepfather, José Luis Massera, and her mother, Martha Valentini de Massera.

The author alleged, with regard to herself, that she was detained in Uruguay from 25 April to 3 May 1975 and subjected to psychological torture. She stated that she was released on 3 May 1975 without having been brought before a judge.

The author claimed that her husband, Luis María Bazzano Ambrosini, was detained on 3 April 1975 and immediately thereafter subjected to various forms of torture.

She also claimed that her stepfather, José Luis Massera, professor of mathematics and former Deputy to the National Assembly, had been arrested on 22 October 1975 and held incommunicado until his detention was made known in January 1976, and that her mother, Martha Valentini de Massera, had been arrested on 28 January 1976 without any formal charges and that in September 1976 she was accused of "assistance to subversive association", an offence which carried a penalty of two to eight years imprisonment.

* * * The Committee decided to base its views on the following facts which had not been contradicted by the State Party. Luis María Bazzano Ambrosini was arrested on 3 April 1975 on the charge of complicity in "assistance to subversive association". Although his arrest had taken place before the coming into force of the International Covenant on Civil and Political Rights and of the Optional Protocol thereto, on 23 March 1976, his detention without trial continued after that date. After being detained for one year, he was granted conditional release, but that judicial decision was not respected and the prisoner was taken to an unidentified place, where he was confined and held incommunicado until 7 February 1977. On that date he was tried on the charge of "subversive association" and remained imprisoned in conditions seriously detrimental to his health.

José Luis Massera, a professor of mathematics and former Deputy to the National Assembly, was arrested in October 1975 and has remained imprisoned since that date. He was denied the remedy of habeas corpus and another application for remedy made to the Commission on Respect for Human Rights of the Council of State went unanswered. On 15 August 1976 he was tried on charges of "subversive association" and remained in prison.

Martha Valentini de Massera was arrested on 28 January 1976. In September 1976 she was charged with "assistance to subversive association." She was kept in detention and was initially held incommunicado. In November 1976 for the first time a visit was permitted, but thereafter she was again taken to an unknown place of detention. She was tried by a military court and sentenced to three-and-a-half years imprisonment.

The Committee, acting under article 5(4) of the Optional Protocol to the International Covenant on Civil and Political Rights, took the view that those facts, in so far as they had occurred after 23 March 1976, disclosed violations of the International Covenant on Civil and Political Rights.

---

5.   SELF–HELP: ASYLUM AND REFUGE

So long as the level of human rights protections varies among the states of the world, the individual will continue the age-old human practice of leaving a state where he is oppressed to live in another state where, he believes, his rights will be protected.   But it is said: "The reception of aliens is a matter of discretion, and every state is by reason of its territorial supremacy competent to exclude aliens from the whole, or any part, of its territory."   I Oppenheim, International Law 675 (Lauterpacht, 8th ed. 1955).   The writer further asserts that the Universal Declaration of Human Rights does not give an alien a right to demand asylum.   The declaration provides:

Article 13

1.   Everyone has the right to freedom of movement and residence within the borders of each State.

*   *   *

Article 14

1.   Everyone has the right to seek and to enjoy in other countries asylum from persecution.

2.   This right may not be invoked in the case of prosecutions genuinely arising from non-political crimes or from acts contrary to the purposes and principles of the United Nations.

If an alien cannot lawfully demand that a state grant him asylum, what is the content of the right to seek asylum?

The United Nations adopted a Declaration on Territorial Asylum, Resolution 2312 (XXII) of December 14, 1967, U.N.Gen.Ass. Off.Rec., 22nd Sess., Supp. 16 (A/6716), p. 81.   It stated:

Article 1

1.   Asylum granted by a State, in the exercise of its sovereignty, to persons entitled to invoke article 14 of the Universal Declaration of Human Rights, including persons struggling against colonialism, shall be respected by all other States.

*   *   *

Article 3

1.   No person referred to in article 1, paragraph 1, shall be subjected to measures such as rejection at the frontier or, if he has already entered the territory in which he seeks asylum, expulsion or compulsory return ᵃ to any State where he may be subjected to persecution.

It is doubtful that the international community is presently prepared to accept an absolute obligation on the part of each state to grant asylum. In the preparation of a draft convention designed to give real effect to the apparent rights proclaimed in Article 14, what interests should be taken into account? Would a convention binding a state to "use its best endeavors to grant asylum in its territory" promote the humanitarian objectives of the Universal Declaration of Human Rights?

INDOCHINESE REFUGEES

United States Department of State Bulletin, October 1979, p. 1.

In the 4½ years since the collapse of the governments of South Vietnam, Cambodia (now called Kampuchea), and Laos, more than a million Indochinese have fled their homelands to seek temporary or permanent asylum elsewhere. Some 350,000 refugees have resettled in non-Communist countries, and about 350,000 remain in countries of first-asylum in Southeast Asia. In addition, an estimated 250,000 Indochinese have fled to the People's Republic of China, and about 150,000 Kampucheans are in camps in the Socialist Republic of Vietnam.

The exodus from the countries of Indochina initially consisted primarily of those who had fought the Communists, who had been associated with the previous regimes or with the U.S. Government, or who had opposed the new authorities.

In 1978, however, conditions within Indochina began to change radically. The Hanoi government instituted policies designed to restructure society, shift city dwellers to the countryside, and eliminate the business and professional class. These policies were principally aimed at Vietnam's 1.5 million ethnic Chinese, who were seen as a security threat at a time of worsening relations with China. The ethnic Chinese, including those who had lived peacefully in the north since 1954, were increasingly faced with the threat of dismissal from jobs, conscription, or transfer to remote areas of the country without services, called "new economic zones."

As a result, by the summer of 1978 there was a marked increase in both the number of people fleeing Indochina and the percentage of

---

ᵃ. A provision similar to this prohibition against explusion or return (refoulement) appears in a treaty in force, the Convention Relating to the Status of Refugees, 1951, 189 U.N.T. S. 137, as amended by the Protocol of 1967, 606 U.N.T.S. 267.

ethnic Chinese among the refugees. Other factors contributing to the outflow of refugees were the war between China and Vietnam, the occupation of areas of Laos and Kampuchea by Vietnamese forces, military operations against the Hmong tribesmen in Laos, deteriorating economic conditions (particularly food shortages), and violations of political and other rights. In addition, Vietnamese authorities began to assist the departures of ethnic Chinese and others they considered undesirable.

The number of Indochinese seeking asylum in non-Communist countries in Southeast Asia jumped from about 6,000 a month in August 1978 to a peak of 65,000 in May 1979. Partially as a result of the Vietnamese decision announced at the Geneva refugee conference in July to stem "illegal departures" from Vietnam, the arrival rate dropped to about 12,000 in August 1979. These figures reflect only the numbers of people who succeed in seeking asylum. It is not known how many people actually attempt to leave Indochina, but there are estimates that from 30% to 60% perish before arriving at a safe haven.

Since the beginning of 1979, about 240,000 Indochinese have joined the more than 200,000 refugees who were already in camps in first-asylum countries awaiting resettlement elsewhere. In this period, however, some 75,000 have been moved from the camps to permanent homes in other countries.

Despite increased international efforts to resettle the Indochinese, the presence of large refugee populations in the countries of first-asylum continues to be a source of domestic concern and regional instability. The first-asylum countries have resisted efforts to resettle any Indochinese within their borders because they already feel overburdened by their own population pressures, economic problems, and religious and ethnic tensions, and they are concerned about the possibility of subversion and insurgency. The lack of resettlement opportunities in Southeast Asia has increased the need for greater international participation in the refugee assistance program. The U. N. High Commissioner for Refugees (UNHCR) is responsible for the protection and care of refugees in camps in Southeast Asia until permanent resettlement can be arranged.

In May and June 1979 the refugee situation reached crisis proportions, as the countries of first asylum reacted in desperation to the mounting refugee populations, the increasing arrival rates, and the apparently inadequate response to the problem by the rest of the world community. Southeast Asian governments began refusing to grant asylum to new arrivals—causing death to tens of thousands of refugees pushed back out to sea or back across land borders—and in some cases they threatened to expel refugees already admitted to U. N.-sponsored camps. * * *

Additional problems. Several additional problems concerning asylum and the reception of refugees require notice. (1) Is a state that grants asylum to the national of another state violating the rights of that state? See the language of Article 1 of the Declaration on Territorial Asylum, above. (2) If a state admits individuals seeking asylum or refuge, how must they be treated? On a basis of equality with other aliens; with nationals of the asylum state? See the Convention Relating to the Status of Refugees, 1951, noted in the Documentary Supplement.

At what locations may a state receive persons seeking asylum so as not to violate the rights of the state of which he is a national or from which he is fleeing? Compare the following two cases.

DEFECTION FROM THE "UKRAINA"

8 Whiteman, Digest of International Law 669 (1967).

In connection with the circumstances in which a refugee escaping from a Soviet fishing fleet off Shetland was pursued by Soviets across British soil in June 1958, the Secretary of State for the Home Department and Lord Privy Seal, R. A. Butler, furnished the House of Commons with the following information:

A man named Erich Teayn, stated to be an Estonian, came ashore in the Shetland Islands early this morning from the Russian fishing vessel "Ukraina", one of three Russian trawlers anchored in a bay at Walls. He made his way to a crofter's house and indicated that he did not want to go back to the Russian vessel. He was followed by a party of Russians, said to number about 30, who landed from two small boats in pursuit of him. He was taken into custody for interrogation under the Aliens Order. Three Russians subsequently called at Lerwick police station and sought access to him. This was refused. * * *

In response to a question whether immediate protest would be made to the Russians if the facts as stated were confirmed, and the person involved were a genuine political refugee, Mr. Butler replied: "First, we have to examine the case. If this man asks for political asylum, it will certainly be considered." * * *

ASYLUM ON A VESSEL

II Hackworth, Digest of International Law 641 (1941).

The American Minister in Guatemala reported to the Department of State, in October 1922, that in reply to an inquiry of the Mexican Minister as to whether a certain Guatemalan to whom the Mexican Legation had given asylum would be safe from arrest if placed aboard an American vessel in a Guatemalan harbor, he had informed the Minister that the Guatemalan authorities would have the right to effect the arrest of a person in such circumstances so long as the vessel was within Guatemalan waters. In an instruction of November 3, 1922 the Department approved the attitude assumed by the Minister.

Would the result be different if the Guatemalan were placed aboard a United States *naval* vessel in Guatemalan waters? That is, could Guatemala lawfully arrest the man; would Guatemala have a basis for diplomatic protest in such a case? Asylum on diplomatic premises is dealt with at p. 849.

For the United States Department of State statement of general policy for dealing with requests for asylum by foreign nationals, see 66 U.S.Dept. of State Bull. 124 (1972).

SECTION D. THE HUMAN RIGHTS PROGRAMS OF REGIONAL ORGANIZATIONS

---

1. THE COUNCIL OF EUROPE

The Council of Europe was created in 1949 by European states with the aim, in the language of the statute, 87 U.N.T.S. 103, "to achieve a greater unity between its Members for the purpose of safeguarding and realising the ideals and principles which are their common heritage," this aim to be pursued "by discussion of questions of common concern * * * and in the maintenance and further realization of human rights and fundamental freedoms." Pursuant to that aim, and in the light of the Universal Declaration of Human Rights, the European Convention for the Protection of Human Rights and Fundamental Freedoms was brought into force in 1953, 213 U. N.T.S. 221.[a] Compare with counterpart provisions of the International Covenant on Civil and Political Rights the following provisions in the convention.

a. States that had ratified the Convention as of December 31, 1978, were Austria, Belgium, Cyprus, Denmark, Federal Republic of Germany, France, Greece, Iceland, Ireland, Italy, Luxembourg, Malta, Netherlands, Norway, Portugal, Sweden, Switzerland, Turkey and the United Kingdom. Liechtenstein and Spain had signed but had not ratified the convention. See 1978 Yearbook of the European Convention on Human Rights 27 (1979). (The Council of Europe is a different institution from the European Community and is not to be confused therewith.)

EUROPEAN CONVENTION FOR THE PROTECTION OF HUMAN RIGHTS AND FUNDAMENTAL FREEDOMS OF NOVEMBER 4, 1950

213 U.N.T.S. 221.

Article 5

(1) Everyone has the right to liberty and security of person.

No one shall be deprived of his liberty save in the following cases and in accordance with a procedure prescribed by law:

(a) the lawful detention of a person after conviction by a competent court;

(b) the lawful arrest or detention of a person for noncompliance with the lawful order of a court or in order to secure fulfilment of any obligation prescribed by law;

(c) the lawful arrest or detention of a person effected for the purpose of bringing him before the competent legal authority on reasonable suspicion of having committed an offense or when it is reasonably considered necessary to prevent his committing an offence or fleeing after having done so;

(d) the detention of a minor by lawful order for the purpose of educational supervision or his lawful detention for the purpose of bringing him before the competent legal authority;

(e) the lawful detention of persons for the prevention of the spreading of infectious diseases, of persons of unsound mind, alcoholics or drug addicts or vagrants;

(f) the lawful arrest or detention of a person to prevent his effecting an unauthorised entry into the country or of a person against whom action is being taken with a view to deportation or extradition.

(2) Everyone who is arrested shall be informed promptly, in a language which he understands, of the reasons for his arrest and of any charge against him.

(3) Everyone arrested or detained in accordance with the provisions of paragraph 1(c) of this Article shall be brought promptly before a judge or other officer authorised by law to exercise judicial power and shall be entitled to trial within a reasonable time or to release pending trial. Release may be conditioned by guarantees to appear for trial.

(4) Everyone who is deprived of his liberty by arrest or detention shall be entitled to take proceedings by which the lawfulness of his detention shall be decided speedily by a court and his release ordered if the detention is not lawful.

(5) Everyone who has been the victim of arrest or detention in contravention of the provisions of this Article shall have an enforceable right to compensation.

Article 6

(1) In the determination of his civil rights and obligations or of any criminal charge against him, everyone is entitled to a fair and public hearing within a reasonable time by an independent and impartial tribunal established by law. Judgment shall be pronounced publicly but the press and public may be excluded from all or part of the trial in the interests of morals, public order or national security in a democratic society, where the interests of juveniles or the protection of the private life of the parties so require, or to the extent strictly necessary in the opinion of the court in special circumstances where publicity would prejudice the interests of justice.

(2) Everyone charged with a criminal offence shall be presumed innocent until proved guilty according to law.

(3) Everyone charged with a criminal offence has the following minimum rights:

 (a) to be informed promptly, in a language which he understands and in detail, of the nature and cause of the accusation against him;

 (b) to have adequate time and facilities for the preparation of his defence;

 (c) to defend himself in person or through legal assistance of his own choosing or, if he has not sufficient means to pay for legal assistance, to be given it free when the interests of justice so require;

 (d) to examine or have examined witnesses against him and to obtain the attendance and examination of witnesses on his behalf under the same conditions as witnesses against him;

 (e) to have the free assistance of an interpreter if he cannot understand or speak the language used in court.

Article 7

(1) No one shall be held guilty of any criminal offence on account of any act or omission which did not constitute a criminal offence under national or international law at the time when it was committed. Nor shall a heavier penalty be imposed than the one that was applicable at the time the criminal offence was committed.

(2) This Article shall not prejudice the trial and punishment of any person for any act or omission which, at the time when it was committed, was criminal according to the general principles of law recognised by civilised nations.

European Commission and European Court of Human Rights. The convention is notable because it is a working system for the international protection of human rights. The international organs of enforcement are the European Commission on Human Rights and the European Court of Human Rights; these organs have established a substantial body of precedent under the convention. The function of the commission is to ascertain the facts as to alleged breaches of the Convention and to secure a friendly settlement. There are two ways in which the commission can be activated. One, any state party to the convention may refer an alleged breach by another party. Second, individual victims [a] of a violation by a state party can petition the commission; but this right of petition can be exercised against a state only if it has declared that it recognizes the competence of the commission to receive petitions. The commission has received hundreds of petitions but, under provisions of the convention relating to admissibility (such as the requirement of the exhaustion of domestic remedies), has declared only a small number of them to be admissible. In the event a friendly settlement is not reached through its conciliation processes, the commission renders a report in which it states "its opinion as to whether the facts found disclose a breach by the State concerned of its obligations under the Convention." The convention provides for further decision and the requirement of measures by the Committee of Ministers, an organ of the Council of Europe.

The court on the other hand, has a jurisdiction which is more remote from the individual. Its jurisdiction comprises cases referred to it by the commission or by a state party to the convention; a state may refer the case to the court if its national is alleged to be a victim, or if it referred the case to the commission or was the state against which the complaint had been lodged. As in the case of the International Court of Justice, jurisdiction depends upon the consent of the state concerned. A case cannot be brought to the court until after the commission's efforts for a friendly settlement have failed. From the individual victim's point of view, he is protected only derivatively in a case before the court. Why are states, even in a regional organization of states with a common heritage, reluctant to permit individuals to have direct access to a court of human rights?

A number of cases that have been considered by the commission and the court are to be found in Sohn and Buergenthal, International Protection of Human Rights 999 (1973). A textual exposition of the work of these two institutions is Robertson, Human Rights in Europe (2d ed. 1977).

---

2. THE ORGANIZATION OF AMERICAN STATES

In the Charter of the Organization of American States, which entered into force on December 13, 1951, the American states "proclaim the fundamental rights of the individual without distinction as to race, nationality, creed or sex." 2 U.S.T. 2394, 119 U.N.T.S. 3.

---

a. Article 25 of the convention: "Any person, non-governmental organization or group of individuals claiming to be the victim of a violation * * *."

Amendments to the Charter entered into force February 27, 1970, 21 U.S.T. 607 (1970).ᵃ

At the 1948 Conference of the American States which gave birth to the Charter, there was also adopted the American Declaration of the Rights and Duties of Man. In 1959, by resolution of the Ministers of Foreign Affairs meeting as an organ of the Organization, the Inter-American Commission on Human Rights was created. In addition to its powers of study and advice, the commission was given the power to receive and examine individual communications charging the violation of fundamental human rights set forth in the American Declaration and to make recommendations to governments with respect thereto.

A conference in 1969 approved the American Convention on Human Rights, which contains provisions widening the American Declaration, re-establishing the Inter-American Commission and establishing the Inter-American Court of Human Rights. Individuals do not have access to the court, since only states parties and the commission have the right to submit a case to the court; as usual, the court's jurisdiction depends upon the state's consenting thereto. For the statute of the court, see XIX International Legal Materials 634 (1980).

President Carter submitted this convention to the Senate for its advice and consent in 1978. However, ratification of the convention does not, of itself, constitute a state's consent to the court's jurisdiction. As in the case of the International Court of Justice, a further declaration of submission to the court's jurisdiction (or a special agreement) is necessary. See Article 62 of the convention, in the Documentary Supplement. The President did not call upon the Senate to make such a declaration.

SECTION E. GENOCIDE: BORDERLINE OF STATE AND INDIVIDUAL RESPONSIBILITY UNDER INTERNATIONAL LAW

THE UNITED STATES AND THE GENOCIDE CONVENTION REPORT OF SECRETARY OF STATE ROGERS TO PRESIDENT NIXON

62 United States Department of State Bulletin 351 (1970).ᵃ

* * *

The Convention was adopted unanimously by the General Assembly of the United Nations on December 9, 1948, and signed by the United States two days later. It was submitted to the Senate by

---

a. Members of the organization are the states of the Western Hemisphere except Canada. The present government of Cuba has been declared by two-thirds of the member states to have "voluntarily placed itself outside the inter-American system."

a. For the text of the convention, see the Documentary Supplement.

President Truman on June 16, 1949 (Executive O, 81st Congress, 1st Session). Hearings were held in 1950 by a Subcommittee of the Foreign Relations Committee which reported it favorably to the full Committee. Neither the Committee nor the Senate as a whole has yet taken action on the Convention.

The Convention entered into force on January 12, 1951. So far seventy-four countries have become parties. It is anomalous that the United States, which firmly opposes the crime of genocide and which played a leading role in bringing about the recognition of genocide as a crime against international law, is not among the parties to the Convention.

Genocide has been perpetrated many times throughout history. Although man has always expressed his horror at this crime, little was done to prevent or punish it before the 1930's. World War II witnessed the most drastic series of genocidal acts ever committed. The revulsion of civilized society manifested itself in a United Nations General Assembly resolution of December 11, 1946, declaring genocide to be a crime under international law and recommending international cooperation in its prevention and punishment. This resolution was the impetus for the drafting of the Convention on the Prevention and Punishment of the Crime of Genocide.

* * *

The contracting parties undertake to enact legislation necessary to give effect to the provisions of the Convention "in accordance with their respective constitutions." It is clear, therefore, that the Convention was not expected to be self-executing. I do not recommend, however, that the Executive Branch propose any specific implementing legislation at this time. The Departments of State and Justice will be prepared to discuss this question should the Congress request our views.

* * *

[President Nixon urged the senate to give its advice and consent to ratification of the convention. 62 U. S. Dept. of State Bull. 350 (1970). The convention remains in committee a decade later.]

Questions. Does the convention impose any obligations upon the state aside from the obligation to enact legislation under Article V? If legislation is enacted making genocide a domestic crime, is the state under an obligation to use that legislation? Even if legislation is not enacted, does the state (as distinct from the individuals under its jurisdiction) have any treaty obligation not to commit genocide?

If a state has not become a party to the convention, does it violate international law if it commits genocide as a matter of state policy? If it condones genocide by individuals under its jurisdiction? Or if it fails to take action to prevent or punish genocide by individuals?

MASSACRE IN THE HEART OF AFRICA

The New York Times, June 4, 1972.
Sec. 4, p. 2, col. 1.*

Bujumbura, Burundi—Just before Christmas of 1968, Ntare V, the 19-year-old Mwame, or King, of Burundi, paid a visit to the neighboring country of the Congo, or Zaire, as it now calls itself. * * * He left behind a ceremonial drum, a symbol of his power. During the King's absence, the commander of the Burundi army, Capt. Michel Micombero, drove up to the royal palace, seized the drum, went to the state radio station and proclaimed himself President.

So began an internecine struggle that in the past two months has grown into bloody civil war. Reports in this Burundi capital indicate that the toll in lives has been as high as 120,000.

King Ntare and President Micombero are both members of the Tutsi tribe, a tall race of warriors that for centuries has dominated the less bellicose Hutus, who account for 85 percent of the country's 3.5 million people. Within the Tutsi tribe, however, the King and the army commander belonged to rival factions. It is out of this rivalry that the 1968 coup emerged.

As self-proclaimed President, Captain—now Colonel—Micombero ruled Burundi with an iron hand. Earlier this year, he decided that he had consolidated his power sufficiently to let the King return from exile in West Germany. (Burundi had once been a German—and later a Belgian—colony.) The President gave assurances for the monarch's safety.

But shortly after the King's return at the end of March, the authorities announced discovery of a royalist plot. Ntare was placed under arrest. Then, on April 29, an abortive attempt to overthrow the Micombero regime was staged by Tutsi royalists backed by Hutus, who have been supporters of the monarchy. In the melée, Ntare was assassinated.

Thereupon the Hutus, taking advantage of the general confusion, launched an insurrection of their own. The Burundi authorities claim that 50,000 persons, mostly members of the Tutsi tribe, were killed. Independent sources put the number at 20,000. Members of President Micombero's family and the families of many of his army officers were among the slain, though he himself is safe.[a]

The Tutsi minority had lived in dread of just such a Hutu rebellion ever since the bloody events of a decade ago in the sister republic

---

a. Tribal rivalries have endured for centuries, are to a degree associated with sorcery, and often exceedingly bloody. Pamphlets have been found on Hutu rebels against the Burundian Tutsi aristocracy, saying: "Kill every man, woman and child. Do not take prisoners. Do not judge. Kill every Tutsi." Sulzberger, "To Be Obscurely Massacred," New York Times, July 2, 1972, Sec. 4, p. 9, col. 1.

of Rwanda. There too the Tutsi tribe was in control and the Hutus were the overwhelming majority. There too the Hutus rebelled. They overthrew the Tutsi regime of Rwanda, massacred 20,000 Tutsis and forced the rest into exile.

But in Burundi the Hutu rebellion was met head-on. The country's Tutsi-dominated army, police and militant youth organization retaliated savagely. Some 100,000 Hutus are reported to have been killed in the past few weeks.

Word of the massacres has been carried by missionaries and other foreign residents and by refugees who have fled to Zaire. According to these reports, the Tutsis have waged a deliberate campaign to wipe out the Hutu elite. Those slain are said to have included three Hutu ministers in the Micombero Cabinet, Parliamentary deputies, teachers, church leaders and even school children.

"They have eliminated the Hutu intellectuals for the next generation," said one missionary who fled the country last week. Another churchman who had just crossed the border into Zaire said, "It's worse than Biafra ever was."

Last week, however, the picture apparently began to change. According to foreign sources in this Burundi capital, the Government sought to curb the violence. Army and police chiefs have been counseled to show moderation and punish those of their men who take the law into their own hands.

The Government's efforts came in response to growing international concern over the bloodshed in Burundi. Pope Paul, in a public address last Sunday, denounced the "organized massacre of innocent people." Belgium, which exercised a trusteeship over Burundi for 40 years and still provides aid that constitutes 25 per cent of Burundi's national budget, has threatened to cut off all further assistance. At the same time, the Burundi state radio has begun to talk about "an imperialist plot," alleging that the Belgians were behind the Hutu rising.

An uneasy calm reigns over this bucolic city of 75,000 where life seems to have resumed its quiet routine despite the gruesome tales from the interior. The only evidence of the troubles here is an 8 P. M. curfew and an occasional paratroop patrol.

Yet, the outlook in Burundi remains grim. There is fear that the Hutus in the northern section of the country, who have played a passive role thus far, may mount a violent response to the Tutsi repression. "That," as one foreign observer put it last week, "would be the blood bath to end all blood baths."

Questions. Do the actions of the rival tribes in Burundi fall within the definition of genocide in Article II of the convention? Is the answer affected by the fact that the tribes are engaged, in part at least, in a struggle for control of the government of the state, i. e. a

least, in a struggle for control of the government of the state, i. e. a civil war? (Note, however, that neither Burundi nor Rwanda is a party to the Genocide Convention.)

What is the legal position of the individuals responsible for the Burundian massacres? The Burundian domestic law of murder is relevant. There is probably no domestic law of genocide such as that described in Article V of the convention. Is there, beyond the domestic law, an international responsibility imposed upon the individual? See the preamble to the convention and consider the significance of the Nuremberg precedent, discussed in the next chapter.

Chapter 10

THE GROWTH OF INDIVIDUAL RESPONSIBILITY

SECTION A. TRADITIONAL WAR CRIMES

JUDGMENT IN CASE OF LIEUTENANTS DITHMAR AND BOLDT
HOSPITAL SHIP "LLANDOVERY CASTLE"

Germany, Supreme Court of Leipzig, 1921.
16 American Journal of International Law 708 (1922).*

* * *

Up to the year 1916 the steamer Llandovery Castle, had, according to the statements of the witnesses Chapman and Heather, been used for the transport of troops. In that year she was commissioned by the British Government to carry wounded and sick Canadian soldiers home to Canada from the European theatre of war. The vessel was suitably fitted out for the purpose and was provided with the distinguishing marks, which the Tenth Hague Convention of the 18th October, 1907 (relating to the application to naval warfare of the principles of the Geneva Convention) requires in the case of naval hospital ships. The name of the vessel was communicated to the enemy powers. From that time onwards she was exclusively employed in the transport of sick and wounded. She never again carried troops, and never had taken munitions on board. * * *

* * *

At the end of the month of June, 1918, the Llandovery Castle was on her way back to England from Halifax, after having carried sick and wounded there. She had on board the crew consisting of 164 men, 80 officers and men of the Canadian Medical Corps, and 14 nurses, a total of 258 persons. There were no combatants on board, and, in particular, no American airmen. The vessel had not taken on board any munitions or other war material. * * *

In the evening of 27th June, 1918, at about 9:30 (local time) the Llandovery Castle was sunk in the Atlantic Ocean, about 116 miles south-west of Fastnet (Ireland), by a torpedo from the German U-boat 86. Of those on board only 24 persons were saved, 234 having been drowned. The commander of U-boat 86 was First-Lieutenant Patzig, who was subsequently promoted captain. His present whereabouts are unknown. The accused Dithmar was the first officer of the watch, and the accused Boldt the second. Patzig recognized the character of the ship, which he had been pursuing for a long time, at

* Reprinted with the permission of the
American Society of International
Law.

the latest when she exhibited at dusk the lights prescribed for hospital ships by the Tenth Hague Convention. In accordance with international law, the German U-boats were forbidden to torpedo hospital ships. According both to the German and the British Governments' interpretation of the said Hague Convention, ships, which were used for the transport of military persons wounded and fallen ill in war on land, belonged to this category. The German Naval Command had given orders that hospital ships were only to be sunk within the limits of a certain barred area. However, this area was a long way from the point we have now under consideration. Patzig knew this and was aware that by torpedoing the Llandovery Castle he was acting against orders. But he was of the opinion, founded on various information (including some from official sources, the accuracy of which cannot be verified, and does not require to be verified in these proceedings), that on the enemy side, hospital ships were being used for transporting troops and combatants, as well as munitions. He, therefore, presumed that, contrary to international law, a similar use was being made of the Llandovery Castle. In particular, he seems to have expected (what grounds he had for this has not been made clear) that she had American airmen on board. Acting on this suspicion, he decided to torpedo the ship, in spite of his having been advised not to do so by the accused Dithmar and the witness Popitz. Both were with him in the conning tower, the accused Boldt being at the depth rudder.

The torpedo struck the Llandovery Castle amidship on the port side and damaged the ship to such an extent that she sank in about 10 minutes. There were 19 lifeboats on board. Each could take a maximum of 52 persons. Only two of them (described as cutters) were smaller, and these could not take more than 23 persons. Some of the boats on the port side were destroyed by the explosion of the torpedo. A good number of undamaged boats were, however, successfully lowered. The favorable weather assisted life-saving operations. There was a light breeze and a slight swell.

The men who were saved from the Llandovery Castle do not agree as regards the number of boats which got away safely. This is sufficiently explained by the circumstances, and particularly by the state of excitement, into which the majority of them were plunged, by the torpedoing and sinking of the ship. *   *   *

It is quite possible that out of these five boats which left the steamer safely, one or two may have been drawn into the vortex made by the sinking ship. But the evidence has shown that at least three of these five boats survived the sinking of the ship. *   *   *
        *   *   *

Thus, after the sinking of the Llandovery Castle, there were still left three of her boats with people on board.

Some time after the torpedoing, the U-boat came to the surface and approached the lifeboats, in order to ascertain by examination whether the Llandovery Castle had airmen and munitions on board.

The witness Popitz, who was steersman on board the U-boat, took part in the stopping of several lifeboats for that purpose. *   *   *
*   *   *

After passing by the second time, the U-boat once more went away. The lifeboat, which had hoisted a sail in the meantime, endeavored to get away. But after a brief period, the occupants of the boat noticed firing from the U-boat. The first two shells passed over the lifeboat. Then firing took place in another direction; about 12 to 14 shots fell all told. The flash at the mouth of the gun and the flash of the exploding shells were noticed almost at the same time, so that, as the expert also assumes, the firing was at a very near target. After firing had ceased, the occupants of the lifeboat saw nothing more of the U-boat.

The captain's boat cruised about for some 36 hours altogether. On the 29th June, in the morning, it was found by the English destroyer Lysander. The crew were taken on board and the boat left to its fate. During the 29th June, the commander of the English Fleet caused a search to be made for the other lifeboats of the Llandovery Castle. The English sloop Snowdrop and four American destroyers systematically searched the area, where the boats from the sunken ship might be drifting about. The Snowdrop found an undamaged boat of the Llandovery Castle 9 miles from the spot on which the Lysander had found the captain's boat. The boat was empty, but had been occupied, as was shown by the position of the sail. *   *   * Otherwise the search which was continued until the evening of the 1st July, in uniformly good weather, remained fruitless. No other boat from the Llandovery Castle and no more survivors were found.

The firing from the U-boat was not only noticed by the occupants of the captain's boat. It was also heard by the witnesses Popitz, Knoche, Ney, Tegtmeier and Käss, who were members of the crew of the U-boat. According to their statements a portion of the crew of the U-boat were on deck during the evolutions of the U-boat, during the holding up of the lifeboat and during the interrogation of the Englishmen. *   *   *

After the examination was completed the command "Ready for submerging" was given. *   *   * [T]he whole of the crew went below deck, as is the case when the order to be ready for diving is given. There only remained on deck Commander Patzig, the accused, as his officers of the watch and, by special order, the first boatswain's mate, Meissner, who had since died. *   *   * Firing commenced some time after the crew had gone below. The witnesses heard distinctly that only the stern gun, a 8.8 c/m gun was in action. While firing, the U-boat moved about. It did not submerge even after the firing had ceased, but continued on the surface.

The prosecution assumes that the firing of the U-boat was directed against the lifeboats of the Llandovery Castle. The court has arrived at the same conclusion as the result of the evidence given at this time. * * *

* * *

In this connection we must refer to the opinion of the actual witnesses, both English and German. [The court analyzes the testimony of the witnesses.]

* * *

If finally the question is asked—what can have induced Patzig to sink the lifeboats, the answer is to be found in the previous torpedoing of the Llandovery Castle. Patzig wished to keep this quiet and to prevent any news of it reaching England. * * * He may have argued to himself that, if the sinking of the ship became known (the legality of which he, in view of the fruitlessness of his endeavors to prove the misuse of the ship, was not able to establish) great difficulties would be caused to the German Government in their relations with other powers. Irregular torpedoings had already brought the German Government several times into complications with other states and there was the possibility that this fresh case might still further prejudice the international position of Germany. This might bring powers, that were still neutral, into the field against her. Patzig may have wished to prevent this, by wiping out all traces of his action. The false entries in the log-book and the chart, which have already been mentioned, were intended, having regard to his position in the service, to achieve this object. This illusion could be, however, of but short duration, if the passengers in the lifeboats, some of whom had been on board the U-boat, and who, therefore could fully describe it, were allowed to get home. It was, therefore, necessary to get rid of them, if Patzig did not wish the sinking of the Llandovery Castle to be known. Herein is to be found the explanation of the unholy decision, which he came to and promptly carried out after his fruitless examination of the boats.

On these various grounds the court has decided that the lifeboats of the Llandovery Castle were fired on in order to sink them. This is the only conclusion possible, in view of what has been stated by the witnesses. It is only on this basis that the behavior of Patzig and of the accused men can be explained.

The court finds that it is beyond all doubt that, even though no witness had direct observation of the effect of the fire, Patzig attained his object so far as two of the boats were concerned. * * *

For the firing on the lifeboats only those persons can be held responsible, who at the time were on the deck of the U-boat; namely Patzig, the two accused and the chief boatswain's mate Meissner. Patzig gave the decisive order, which was carried out without demur in virtue of his position as commander. It is possible that he asked the opinion of the two accused beforehand, though of this there is no evidence. As Meissner was the gunlayer and remained on deck by special orders, it may be assumed with certainty that he manned the after gun which was fired. In the opinion of the naval expert, he was able to act without assistance. According to this view, owing to the nearness of the objects under fire, there was no need for the fire to be directed by an artillery officer, such as the accused Dithmar. The only technical explanation, which both the accused have given and which fits in with the facts, is that they themselves did not fire. Under the circumstances this is quite credible. They confined themselves to making observations while the firing was going on. The naval expert also assumes that they kept a look-out. Such a look-out must have brought the lifeboats, which were being fired on, within their view. By reporting their position and the varying distances of the lifeboats and such like, the accused assisted in the firing on the lifeboats, and this, quite apart from the fact that their observations saved the U-boat from danger from any other quarter, and that they thereby enabled Patzig to do what he intended as regards the lifeboats. The statement of the accused Boldt that "so far as he took part in what happened, he acted in accordance with his orders" has reference to the question whether the accused took part in the firing on the lifeboats. He does not appear to admit any participation. But the two accused must be held guilty for the destruction of the lifeboats.

With regard to the question of the guilt of the accused, no importance is to be attached to the statements put forward by the defence, that the enemies of Germany were making improper use of hospital ships for military purposes, and that they had repeatedly fired on German lifeboats and shipwrecked people. * * * [T]hroughout the German fleet it was a matter of general belief that improper use of hospital ships was made by the enemy. It must, therefore, be assumed for the benefit of the accused, that they also held this belief. Whether this belief was founded on fact or not, is of less importance as affecting the case before the court, than the established fact that the Llandovery Castle at the time was not carrying any cargo or troops prohibited under clause 10 of the Hague Convention.

The act of Patzig is homicide, according to para. 212 of the Penal Code. By sinking the lifeboats he purposely killed the people who were in them. * * *

            * * *

The firing on the boats was an offence against the law of nations. In war on land the killing of unarmed enemies is not allowed (compare the Hague regulations as to war on land, para. 23(c)), similarly in war at sea, the killing of shipwrecked people, who have taken refuge in lifeboats, is forbidden. It is certainly possible to imagine exceptions to this rule, as, for example, if the inmates of the lifeboats take part in the fight. But there was no such state of affairs in the present case, as Patzig and the accused persons were well aware, when they cruised around and examined the boats.

Any violation of the law of nations in warfare is, as the Senate has already pointed out, a punishable offence, so far as in general, a penalty is attached to the deed. The killing of enemies in war is in accordance with the will of the State that makes war, (whose laws as to the legality or illegality on the question of killing are decisive), only in so far as such killing is in accordance with the conditions and limitations imposed by the law of nations. The fact that his deed is a violation of international law must be well-known to the doer, apart from acts of carelessness, in which careless ignorance is a sufficient excuse. In examining the question of the existence of this knowledge, the ambiguity of many of the rules of international law, as well as the actual circumstances of the case, must be borne in mind, because in war time decisions of great importance have frequently to be made on very insufficient material. This consideration, however, cannot be applied to the case at present before the court. The rule of international law, which is here involved, is simple and is universally known. No possible doubt can exist with regard to the question of its applicability. The court must in this instance affirm Patzig's guilt of killing contrary to international law.

The two accused knowingly assisted Patzig in this killing, by the very fact of their having accorded him their support in the manner, which has already been set out. It is not proved that they were in agreement with his intentions. The decision rested with Patzig as the commander. The others who took part in this deed carried out his orders. It must be accepted that the deed was carried out on his responsibility, the accused only wishing to support him therein. A direct act of killing, following a deliberate intention to kill, is not proved against the accused. They are, therefore, only liable to punishment as accessories. (Para. 49 of the Penal Code.)

Patzig's order does not free the accused from guilt. It is true that according to para. 47 of the Military Penal Code, if the execution of an order in the ordinary course of duty involves such a violation of the law as is punishable, the superior officer issuing such an order is alone responsible. According to No. 2, however, the subordinate obeying such an order is liable to punishment, if it was known to him that the order of the superior involved the infringement of civil or military law. This applies in the case of the accused. It is certainly to be urged in favor of the military subordinates, that they are under no obligation to question the order of their superior officer, and they can count upon its legality. But no such confidence can be held to exist, if such an order is universally known to everybody, including also the accused, to be without any doubt whatever against the law. This happens only in rare and exceptional cases. But this case was precisely one of them, for in the present instance, it was perfectly clear to the accused that killing defenceless people in the lifeboats could be nothing else but a breach of the law. As naval officers by profession they were well aware, as the naval expert Saalwächter has strikingly stated, that one is not legally authorized to kill defenceless people. They well knew that this was the case here. They quickly found out the facts by questioning the occupants in the boats when these were stopped. They could only have gathered, from the order given by Patzig, that he wished to make use of his subordinates to carry out a breach of the law. They should, therefore, have refused to obey. As they did not do so, they must be punished.

* * *

The defence finally points out that the accused must have considered that Patzig would have enforced his orders, weapon in hand, if they had not obeyed them. This possibility is rejected. If Patzig had been faced by refusal on the part of his subordinates, he would have been obliged to desist from his purpose, as then it would have been impossible for him to attain his object, namely, the concealment of the torpedoing of the Llandovery Castle. This was also quite well-known to the accused, who had witnessed the affair. From the point of view of necessity (para. 52 of the Penal Code), they can thus not claim to be acquitted.

In estimating the punishment, it has, in the first place, to be borne in mind that the principal guilt rests with Commander Patzig, under whose orders the accused acted. They should certainly have refused to obey the order. This would have required a specially high degree of resolution. A refusal to obey the commander on a submarine would have been something so unusual, that it is humanly possible to understand that the accused could not bring themselves to disobey. That certainly does not make them innocent, as has been stated above. They had acquired the habit of obedience to military authority and could not rid themselves of it. This justifies the recognition of mitigating circumstances. In determining the punishment under para. 213, 49, para. 2, 44 of the State Penal Code, a severe sentence must, however, be passed. The killing of defenceless shipwrecked people is an act in the highest degree contrary to ethical principles. It must also not be left out of consideration that the deed throws a dark shadow on the German fleet, and specially on the submarine weapon which did so much in the fight for the Fatherland. For this reason a sentence of four years' imprisonment on both the accused persons has been considered appropriate.

In accordance with Section 34, para. 1, No. 2, Section 40, para. 1, No. 1, and Section 36 of the Military Penal Code, the accused, Dithmar, is dismissed from the service, and the accused, Boldt, is condemned to lose the right to wear officer's uniform.

TAYLOR, NUREMBERG AND VIETNAM 20 (1970) *

What, then, are the "laws of war"? They are of ancient origin, and followed two main streams of development. The first flowed from medieval notions of knightly chivalry. Over the course of the centuries the stream has thinned to a trickle; it had a brief spurt during the days of single-handed aerial combat, and survives today in rules (often violated) prohibiting various deceptions such as the use

* Reprinted with permission of Quadrangle Books, Inc., New York.

of the enemy's uniforms or battle insignia, or the launching of a war without fair warning by formal declaration.

The second and far more important concept is that the ravages of war should be mitigated as far as possible by prohibiting needless cruelties, and other acts that spread death and destruction and are not reasonably related to the conduct of hostilities. The seeds of such a principle must be nearly as old as human society, and ancient literature abounds with condemnation of pillage and massacre. In more recent times, both religious humanitarianism and the opposition of merchants to unnecessary disruptions of commerce have furnished the motivation for restricting customs and understandings. In the 17th century these ideas began to find expression in learned writings, especially those of the Dutch jurist-philosopher Hugo Grotius.

The formalization of military organization in the 18th-century brought the establishment of military courts, empowered to try violations of the laws of war as well as other offenses by soldiers. During the American Revolution, both Captain Nathan Hale and the British Major John André were convicted as spies and ordered to be hanged, the former by a British military court and the latter by a "Board of General Officers" appointed by George Washington. During the Mexican War, General Winfield Scott created "military commissions," with jurisdiction over violations of the laws of war committed either by American troops against Mexican civilians, or vice versa.

Up to that time the laws of war had remained largely a matter of unwritten tradition, and it was the United States, during the Civil War, that took the lead in reducing them to systematic, written form. In 1863 President Lincoln approved the promulgation by the War Department of "Instructions for the Government of Armies of the United States in the Field," prepared by Francis Lieber, a German veteran of the Napoleonic wars, who emigrated to the United States and became professor of law and political science at Columbia University. These comprised 159 articles, covering such subjects as "military necessity," "punishment of crimes against the inhabitants of hostile countries," "prisoners of war," and "spies." It was by a military commission appointed in accordance with these instructions that Mary Surratt and the others accused of conspiring to assassinate Lincoln were tried.

In the wake of the Crimean War, the Civil War and the Franco-Prussian War of 1870 there arose, in Europe and America, a tide of sentiment for codification of the laws of war and their embodiment in international agreements. The principal fruits of that movement were the series of treaties known today as the Hague and Geneva Conventions. For present purposes, the most important of these are the Fourth Hague Convention of 1907, and the Geneva Prisoner of War, Red Cross, and Protection of Civilians Conventions of 1929 and 1949.[a]

a. Protocols supplementing the 1949 conventions were adopted in 1977. See note 1, page 670.

"The right of belligerents to adopt means of injuring the enemy is not unlimited," declared Article 22 of the Fourth Hague Convention, and ensuing articles specify a number of limitations: Enemy soldiers who surrender must not be killed, and are to be taken prisoner; captured cities and towns must not be pillaged, nor "undefended" places bombarded; poisoned weapons and other arms "calculated to cause unnecessary suffering" are forbidden. Other provisions make it clear that war is not a free-for-all between the populations of the countries at war; only members of the armed forces can claim protection of the laws of war, and if a noncombatant civilian takes hostile action against the enemy he is guilty of a war crime. When an army occupies enemy territory, it must endeavor to restore public order, and respect "family honor and rights, the lives of persons, and private property, as well as religious convictions and practices."

Rules requiring humane treatment of prisoners, and for protection of the sick and wounded, are prescribed in the Geneva Conventions. While there is no general treaty on naval warfare, the Ninth Hague Convention prohibited the bombardment of undefended "ports," and the London Naval Treaty of 1930 condemned submarine sinkings of merchant vessels, unless passengers and crews were first placed in "safety."

In all of these treaties, the laws of war are stated as general principles of conduct, and neither the means of enforcement nor the penalties for violations are specified. The substance of their provisions, however, has been taken into the military law of many countries, and is often set forth in general orders, manuals of instruction, or other official documents. In the United States, for example, the Lieber rules of 1863 were replaced in 1914 by an army field manual which, up-dated, is still in force under the title "The Law of Land Warfare." It is set forth therein that the laws of war are part of the law of the United States, and that they may be enforced against both soldiers and civilians, including enemy personnel, by general courts-martial, military commissions, or other military or international tribunals.

Comparable though not identical publications have been issued by the military authorities of Britain, France, Germany and many other countries. These documents, and the treaties on which they are largely based, are regarded as a comprehensive but not necessarily complete exposition of what is really a body of international common law—the laws of war.

Since the mid-19th century, with increasing frequency, the major powers have utilized military courts for the trial of persons accused of war crimes. An early and now famous trial, depicted in a successful Broadway play, was the post-Civil War proceeding against the Confederate Major Henry Wirz on charges of responsibility for the death of thousands of Union prisoners in the Andersonville prison camp, of which he had been commandant. War crimes tribunals were convened by the United States after the Spanish-American War, and by the British after the Boer War.

Following the defeat of Germany in the First World War, the Allies demanded that nearly 900 Germans accused of war crimes, including military and political leaders, be handed over for trial on war crimes charges. The Germans resisted the demand, and in the upshot they were allowed to try their own "war criminals." The trials in 1921 and 1922 were not conducted by military courts, but by the Supreme Court of Germany, sitting in Leipzig. From the Allied standpoint they were a fiasco, as only a handful of accused were tried, and of these nearly all were acquitted or allowed to escape their very short prison sentences. The German court did, however, affirm that violations of the laws of war are punishable offenses, and in the Llandovery Castle case sentenced two German U-boat officers to four-year prison terms (from which both soon escaped) for complicity in the torpedoing of a British hospital ship and the shelling and sinking of her lifeboats.

IN RE YAMASHITA

United States Supreme Court, 1946.
327 U.S. 1, 66 S.Ct. 340.

Mr. Chief Justice STONE delivered the opinion of the Court.

No. 61 Miscellaneous is an application for leave to file a petition for writs of habeas corpus and prohibition in this Court. No. 672 is a petition for certiorari to review an order of the Supreme Court of the Commonwealth of the Philippines (28 U.S.C. § 349), denying petitioner's application to that court for writs of habeas corpus and prohibition. * * *

From the petitions and supporting papers it appears that prior to September 3, 1945, petitioner was the Commanding General of the Fourteenth Army Group of the Imperial Japanese Army in the Philippine Islands. On that date he surrendered to and became a prisoner of war of the United States Army Forces in Baguio, Philippine Islands. On September 25th, by order of respondent, Lieutenant General Wilhelm D. Styer, Commanding General of the United States Army Forces, Western Pacific, which command embraces the Philippine Islands, petitioner was served with a charge prepared by the Judge Advocate General's Department of the Army, purporting to charge petitioner with a violation of the law of war. On October 8, 1945, petitioner, after pleading not guilty to the charge, was held for trial before a military commission of five Army officers appointed by order of General Styer. The order appointed six Army officers, all lawyers, as defense counsel.

* * *

On the same date a bill of particulars was filed by the prosecution, and the commission heard a motion made in petitioner's behalf to dismiss the charge on the ground that it failed to state a violation of the law of war. On October 29th the commission was reconvened, a supplemental bill of particulars was filed, and the motion to dismiss was denied. The trial then proceeded until its conclusion on December 7, 1945, the commission hearing two hundred and eighty-six witnesses, who gave over three thousand pages of testimony. On that date petitioner was found guilty of the offense as charged and sentenced to death by hanging.

The petitions for habeas corpus set up that the detention of petitioner for the purpose of the trial was unlawful for reasons which are now urged as showing that the military commission was without lawful authority or jurisdiction to place petitioner on trial, as follows:

(a) That the military commission which tried and convicted petitioner was not lawfully created, and that no military commission to try petitioner for violations of the law of war could lawfully be convened after the cessation of hostilities between the armed forces of the United States and Japan;

(b) That the charge preferred against petitioner fails to charge him with a violation of the law of war;

     *   *   *

On the same grounds the petitions for writs of prohibition set up that the commission is without authority to proceed with the trial.

The Supreme Court of the Philippine Islands, after hearing argument, denied the petition for habeas corpus presented to it, on the ground, among others, that its jurisdiction was limited to an inquiry as to the jurisdiction of the commission to place petitioner on trial for the offense charged, and that the commission, being validly constituted by the order of General Styer, had jurisdiction over the person of petitioner and over the trial for the offense charged.

In Ex parte Quirin, 317 U.S. 1, 63 S.Ct. 2, we had occasion to consider at length the sources and nature of the authority to create military commissions for the trial of enemy combatants for offenses against the law of war. We there pointed out that Congress, in the exercise of the power conferred upon it by Article I, § 8, Cl. 10 of the Constitution to "define and punish * * * Offences against the Law of Nations * * *" of which the law of war is a part, had by the Articles of War (10 U.S.C.A. §§ 1471–1593) recognized the "military commission" appointed by military command, as it had previously existed in United States Army practice, as an appropriate tribunal for the trial and punishment of offenses against the law of war. Article 15 declares that the "provisions of these articles conferring jurisdiction upon courts martial shall not be construed as depriving military commissions * * * or other military tribunals of concurrent jurisdiction in respect of offenders or offenses that by statute or by the law of war may be triable by such military commissions * * * or other military tribunals." a * * * *

We further pointed out that Congress, by sanctioning trial of enemy combatants for violations of the law of war by military commission, had not attempted to codify the law of war or to mark its precise boundaries. Instead, by Article 15 it had incorporated, by reference, as within the preexisting jurisdiction of military commissions created by appropriate military command, all offenses which are defined as such by the law of war, and which may constitutionally be included within that jurisdiction. It thus adopted the system of military common law applied by military tribunals so far as it should be recognized and deemed applicable by the courts, and as further defined and supplemented by the Hague Convention, to which the United States and the Axis powers were parties.

We also emphasized in Ex parte Quirin, as we do here, that on application for habeas corpus we are not concerned with the guilt or innocence of the petitioners. We consider here only the lawful power of the commission to try the petitioner for the offense charged. * * * If the military tribunals have lawful authority to hear, decide and condemn, their action is not subject to judicial review merely because they have made a wrong decision on disputed facts. Correction of their errors of decision is not for the courts but for the military authorities which are alone authorized to review their decisions. * * *

Finally, we held in Ex parte Quirin, supra, 24, 25, as we hold now, that Congress by sanctioning trials of enemy aliens by military commission for offenses against the law of war had recognized the right of the accused to make a defense. * * * It has not foreclosed their right to contend that the Constitution or laws of the United States withhold authority to proceed with the trial. It has not withdrawn, and the Executive branch of the Government could not, unless there was suspension of the writ, withdraw from the courts the duty and power to make such inquiry into the authority of the commission as may be made by habeas corpus.

* * *

* * * [W]e turn to the question whether the authority to create the commission and direct the trial by military order continued after the cessation of hostilities.

An important incident to the conduct of war is the adoption of measures by the military commander, not only to repel and defeat the enemy, but to seize and subject to disciplinary measures those enemies who, in their attempt to thwart or impede our military effort, have violated the law of war. * * * The trial and punishment of enemy combatants who have committed violations of the law of war is thus not only a part of the conduct of war operating as a preven-

a. The current provision is Art. 21 of
the Uniform Code of Military Justice,
10 U.S.C. § 821.

tive measure against such violations, but is an exercise of the authority sanctioned by Congress to administer the system of military justice recognized by the law of war. That sanction is without qualification as to the exercise of this authority so long as a state of war exists—from its declaration until peace is proclaimed. * * * The war power, from which the commission derives its existence, is not limited to victories in the field, but carries with it the inherent power to guard against the immediate renewal of the conflict, and to remedy, at least in ways Congress has recognized, the evils which the military operations have produced. * * *

We cannot say that there is no authority to convene a commission after hostilities have ended to try violations of the law of war committed before their cessation, at least until peace has been officially recognized by treaty or proclamation of the political branch of the Government. In fact, in most instances the practical administration of the system of military justice under the law of war would fail if such authority were thought to end with the cessation of hostilities. For only after their cessation could the greater number of offenders and the principal ones be apprehended and subjected to trial.

No writer on international law appears to have regarded the power of military tribunals, otherwise competent to try violations of the law of war, as terminating before the formal state of war has ended. In our own military history there have been numerous instances in which offenders were tried by military commission after the cessation of hostilities and before the proclamation of peace, for offenses against the law of war committed before the cessation of hostilities.

The extent to which the power to prosecute violations of the law of war shall be exercised before peace is declared rests, not with the courts, but with the political branch of the Government, and may itself be governed by the terms of an armistice or the treaty of peace. Here, peace has not been agreed upon or proclaimed. Japan, by her acceptance of the Potsdam Declaration and her surrender, has acquiesced in the trials of those guilty of violations of the law of war. The conduct of the trial by the military commission has been authorized by the political branch of the Government, by military command, by international law and usage, and by the terms of the surrender of the Japanese government.

The charge. Neither congressional action nor the military orders constituting the commission authorized it to place petitioner on trial unless the charge preferred against him is of a violation of the law of war. The charge, so far as now relevant, is that petitioner, between October 9, 1944 and September 2, 1945, in the Philippine Islands, "while commander of armed forces of Japan at war with the United States of America and its allies, unlawfully disregarded and failed to discharge his duty as commander to control the operations of the members of his command, permitting them to commit brutal atrocities and other high crimes against people of the United States and of its allies and dependencies, particularly the Philippines; and he * * * thereby violated the laws of war."

Bills of particulars, filed by the prosecution by order of the commission, allege a series of acts, one hundred and twenty-three in number, committed by members of the forces under petitioner's command during the period mentioned. The first item specifies the execution of "a deliberate plan and purpose to massacre and exterminate a large part of the civilian population of Batangas Province, and to devastate and destroy public, private and religious property therein, as a result of which more than 25,000 men, women and children, all unarmed noncombatant civilians, were brutally mistreated and killed, without cause or trial, and entire settlements were devastated and destroyed wantonly and without military necessity." Other items specify acts of violence, cruelty and homicide inflicted upon the civilian population and prisoners of war, acts of wholesale pillage and the wanton destruction of religious monuments.

It is not denied that such acts directed against the civilian population of an occupied country and against prisoners of war are recognized in international law as violations of the law of war. Articles 4, 28, 46, and 47, Annex to the Fourth Hague Convention, 1907, 36 Stat. 2277, 2296, 2303, 2306–7. But it is urged that the charge does not allege that petitioner has either committed or directed the commission of such acts, and consequently that no violation is charged as against him. But this overlooks the fact that the gist of the charge is an unlawful breach of duty by petitioner as an army commander to control the operations of the members of his command by "permitting them to commit" the extensive and widespread atrocities specified. The question then is whether the law of war imposes on an army commander a duty to take such appropriate measures as are within his power to control the troops under his command for the prevention of the specified acts which are violations of the law of war and which are likely to attend the occupation of hostile territory by an uncontrolled soldiery, and whether he may be charged with personal responsibility for his failure to take such measures when violations result. That this was the precise issue to be tried was made clear by the statement of the prosecution at the opening of the trial.

It is evident that the conduct of military operations by troops whose excesses are unrestrained by the orders or efforts of their commander would almost certainly result in violations which it is the purpose of the law of war to prevent. Its purpose to protect civilian populations and prisoners of war from brutality would largely be defeated if the commander of an invading army could with impunity neglect to take reasonable measures for their protection. Hence the law of war presupposes that its violation is to be avoided through the control of the operations of war by commanders who are to some extent responsible for their subordinates.

This is recognized by the Annex to the Fourth Hague Convention of 1907, respecting the laws and customs of war on land. Article 1 lays down as a condition which an armed force must fulfill in order to be accorded the rights of lawful belligerents, that it must be "commanded by a person responsible for his subordinates." 36 Stat. 2295. Similarly Article 19 of the Tenth Hague Convention, relating to bombardment by naval vessels, provides that commanders in chief of the belligerent vessels "must see that the above Articles are properly carried out." 36 Stat. 2389. And Article 26 of the Geneva Red Cross Convention of 1929, 47 Stat. 2074, 2092, for the amelioration of the condition of the wounded and sick in armies in the field, makes it "the duty of the commanders-in-chief of the belligerent armies to provide for the details of execution of the foregoing articles, [of the convention] as well as for unforeseen cases * * *." And, finally, Article 43 of the Annex of the Fourth Hague Convention, 36 Stat. 2306, requires that the commander of a force occupying enemy territory, as was petitioner, "shall take all the measures in his power to restore, and ensure, as far as possible, public order and safety, while respecting, unless absolutely prevented, the laws in force in the country."

These provisions plainly imposed on petitioner, who at the time specified was military governor of the Philippines, as well as commander of the Japanese forces, an affirmative duty to take such measures as were within his power and appropriate in the circumstances to protect prisoners of war and the civilian population. This duty of a commanding officer has heretofore been recognized, and its breach penalized by our own military tribunals. A like principle has been applied so as to impose liability on the United States in international arbitrations. Case of Jeannaud, 3 Moore, International Arbitrations, 3000; Case of The Zafiro, 5 Hackworth, Digest of International Law, 707.

We do not make the laws of war but we respect them so far as they do not conflict with the commands of Congress or the Constitution. There is no contention that the present charge, thus read, is without the support of evidence, or that the commission held petitioner responsible for failing to take measures which were beyond his control or inappropriate for a commanding officer to take in the circumstances. We do not here appraise the evidence on which petitioner was convicted. We do not consider what measures, if any, petitioner took to prevent the commission, by the troops under his command, of the plain violations of the law of war detailed in the bill of particulars, or whether such measures as he may have taken were appropriate and sufficient to discharge the duty imposed upon him. These are questions within the peculiar competence of the military officers composing the commission and were for it to decide. See Smith v. Whitney, 116 U.S. 167, 178, 6 S.Ct. 570, 576. It is plain that the charge on which petitioner was tried charged him with a breach of his duty to control the operations of the members of his command, by permitting them to commit the specified atrocities. This was enough to require the commission to hear evidence tending to establish the culpable failure of petitioner to perform the duty imposed on him by the law of war and to pass upon its sufficiency to establish guilt.

    *   *   *

Petitioner further urges that by virtue of Article 63 of the Geneva Convention of 1929, 47 Stat. 2052, he is entitled to the benefits afforded by the 25th and 38th Articles of War to members of our own forces.[a] Article 63 provides: "Sentence may be pronounced against a prisoner of war only by the same courts and according to the same procedure as in the case of persons belonging to the armed forces of the detaining Power." Since petitioner is a prisoner of war, and as the 25th and 38th Articles of War apply to the trial of any person in our own armed forces, it is said that Article 63 requires them to be applied in the trial of petitioner. But we think examination of Article 63 in its setting in the Convention plainly shows that it refers to sentence "pronounced against a prisoner of war" for an offense committed while a prisoner of war, and not for a violation of the law of war committed while a combatant.

    *   *   *

It thus appears that the order convening the commission was a lawful order, that the commission was lawfully constituted, that petitioner was charged with violation of the law of war, and that the commission had authority to proceed with the trial, and in doing so did not violate any military, statutory or constitutional command. We have considered, but find it unnecessary to discuss, other contentions which we find to be without merit. We therefore conclude that the detention of petitioner for trial and his detention upon his conviction, subject to the prescribed review by the military authorities, were lawful, and that the petition for certiorari, and leave to file in this Court petitions for writs of habeas corpus and prohibition should be, and they are denied.

Mr. Justice JACKSON took no part in the consideration or decision of these cases.

[Dissenting opinions omitted.]

NOTE, THE GENEVA CONVENTION AND THE TREATMENT OF PRISONERS OF WAR IN VIETNAM

80 Harvard Law Review 851 (1967).*

As early as the spring of 1965 the International Committee of the Red Cross took the position that: "The hostilities raging at the present time in Vietnam both North and South of the 17th parallel

---

a. The petitioner had argued that these provisions of the Articles of War would have prevented the prosecution's use of deposition, hearsay and opinion evidence against members of the United States armed forces and thus, by operation of Article 63 of the Geneva Convention, should have prevented their use against himself.

* Copyright 1967 by the Harvard Law Review Association.

have assumed such proportions recently that there can be no doubt they constitute an armed conflict to which the regulations of humanitarian law as a whole should be applied." The Committee was referring to the four Geneva Conventions of 1949,[3] which not only set out provisions for the benefit of war victims, both civilian and military, in case of armed conflict between two or more of the signatory States but also establish in Article 3, common to all four Conventions, minimum standards to be respected even in the case of civil war.

The actual participants in the Vietnam conflict have disputed among themselves the applicability of the Conventions, even though all are signatories except the Viet Cong's political arm—the National Liberation Front of South Vietnam (NLF).[4] The United States, the Republic of Vietnam (South Vietnam), and New Zealand support the Red Cross opinion, but the Democratic Republic of Vietnam (North Vietnam) and the NLF consider the Conventions inapplicable, though both avow that the prisoners they hold are accorded humane treatment. This Note will evaluate the claims of the NLF and North Vietnam in relation to the Geneva Convention Relative to the Treatment of Prisoners of War.

The 143 articles of this Convention regulate, among other things, the internment, the labor, the medical care, the discipline, and the trial of captives. They provide for the safeguarding of prisoners' rights by the supervision of protecting powers and by the punishment of "grave breaches" of the Convention according to national legislation which each party agrees to enact. * * *

* * *

North Vietnam maintains that it need not treat American captives as prisoners of war under the Convention. One reason given is that neither country has formally declared war. Article 2 states that "the present Convention shall apply to all cases of declared war or of any other armed conflict which may arise between two or more of the

3. Geneva Convention for the Amelioration of the Condition of the Wounded and Sick in Armed Forces in the Field, Aug. 12, 1949, [1955] 3 U.S.T. 3114, T.I.A.S. No. 3362, 75 U.N.T.S. 31; Geneva Convention for the Amelioration of the Condition of Wounded, Sick and Shipwrecked Members of Armed Forces at Sea, Aug. 12, 1949, [1955] 3 U.S.T. 3217, T.I.A.S. No. 3363, 75 U.N.T.S. 85; Geneva Convention Relative to the Treatment of Prisoners of War, Aug. 12, 1949, [1955] 3 U.S.T. 3316, T.I.A.S. No. 3364, 75 U.N.T.S. 135 [hereinafter cited as Convention]; Geneva Convention Relative to the Protection of Civilian Persons in Time of War, Aug. 12, 1949, [1955] 3 U.S.T. 3516, T.I.A.S. No. 3365, 75 U.N.T.S. 287.

4. Prior to partition, Vietnam acceded to the Prisoners of War Convention, 181 U.N.T.S. 351 (1953), and North Vietnam acceded separately in 1957, 274 U.N.T.S. 339. The Soviet Union —which has military advisers serving in North Vietnam, N.Y. Times, Oct. 3, 1966, at 1, col. 1—ratified in 1954, 191 U.N.T.S. 365, and Communist China acceded in 1956, 260 U.N.T.S. 442. The United States ratified in 1955, 213 U.N.T.S. 383; the Philippines in 1952, 141 U.N.T.S. 384; Australia in 1958, 314 U.N.T.S. 332; and New Zealand in 1959, 330 U.N.T.S. 356. Thailand acceded in 1954, 202 U.N.T.S. 332, and South Korea has recently acceded as well, 6 Int'l Rev. of the Red Cross 547 (1966). The last five countries are allies of the United States with forces fighting in Vietnam. See N.Y. Times, Sept. 28, 1966, at 1, col. 1.

High Contracting Parties, even if the state of war is not recognized by one of them"; the argument seems to be that a formal recognition by at least one country is necessary, based on the negative implication of the last phrase and aided by the fact that preliminary drafts of the Article provided for application even when no participant recognizes a state of war. But the language of the article as a whole can also be read plausibly to suggest that the Convention was intended to apply to all armed conflicts between signatories. Moreover in light of the purposes of the Convention, no legitimate interest could be served by the narrower reading. A declaration of war is not an empty formality, and it should have important legal consequences as to some issues, but lack of a declaration in no way makes less necessary the humanitarian safeguards established by the Convention.

North Vietnam also seeks to justify its position by alleging that American pilots who have bombed its territory are war criminals under the Nuremberg Charter.ᵃ * * *

* * * But North Vietnam has also alleged perpetration of traditional war crimes and crimes against humanity—the second and third categories [of the Nuremberg Charter]. * * *

Even if North Vietnam can assert colorable charges of war crimes within one of the Nuremberg categories, American pilots would still be entitled to substantial protection under the Geneva Convention. Article 85 declares: "Prisoners of war prosecuted under the laws of the Detaining Power for acts committed prior to capture shall retain, even if convicted, the benefits of the present Convention." This provision was adopted in response to a line of decisions following the Second World War which held that prisoners of war charged with the commission of war crimes before capture were not guaranteed certain safeguards of the 1929 Geneva Convention (the immediate predecessor to the current treaty). The leading case was In re Yamashita, in which a Japanese general, sentenced to death for failure to restrain his troops from committing atrocities against Americans and their allies, sought a writ of habeas corpus in the United States Supreme Court on the ground that the procedure at his trial violated Article 63 of the 1929 Convention. That article required the detaining power to try prisoners of war by the same procedure used in trials of its own soldiers, and hearsay and opinion evidence had been admitted at Yamashita's trial, even though the American Articles of War proscribed the use of such evidence in trials of American soldiers. The Court held that "examination of Article 63 in its setting in the Convention plainly shows that it refers to sentence 'pronounced against a prisoner of war' for an offense committed while a prisoner of war, and not for a violation of the law of war committed while a combatant."

One case after Yamashita arrived at the same conclusion by relying not only on the "setting" of Article 63 in the 1929 Convention but

a. The Nuremberg Charter and its application are dealt with at p. 704.

also on a rule of customary law that those who have abused the laws of war are not entitled to the protection they offer. But the tendency of these decisions was to prejudge the guilt of the accused by denying him the guarantees of a prisoner of war before he was proved to be a war criminal. Article 85 not only cures this defect but accomplishes a major change in the rule of customary law by continuing the guarantees even after conviction. This does not mean, however, that prisoners of war may no longer be tried, convicted, and executed for war crimes. It does mean that the determination of guilt must be made according to the same procedures used by the detaining power for trial of its own military personnel and in conformity with certain minimal standards established in the Convention. For example:

> The prisoner of war shall be entitled to assistance by one of his prisoner comrades, to defence by a qualified advocate or counsel of his own choice, to the calling of witnesses and, if he deems necessary, to the services of a competent interpreter.

The Soviet-bloc countries, however, have made reservations to Article 85; the Soviet Union's statement is generally representative:

> The Union of Soviet Socialist Republics does not consider itself bound by the obligation, which follows from Article 85, to extend the application of the Convention to prisoners of war who have been convicted under the law of the Detaining Power, in accordance with the principles of the Nuremberg trial, for war crimes and crimes against humanity, it being understood that persons convicted of such crimes must be subject to the conditions obtaining in the country in question for those who undergo their punishment.

The Soviet Union has given its assurance that this reservation does not alter the effect of Article 85 until "the sentence has become legally enforceable." If so, the result of the reservation is to maintain the rule that war criminals do not enjoy the privileges of a prisoner of war, but to reject Yamashita's deprivation of such privileges before conviction.

The North Vietnamese reservation varies only slightly from the Soviet Union's, and the difference may well have been accidental. Potentially, however, this difference may be of considerable significance:

> The Democratic Republic of Viet-Nam declares that prisoners of war *prosecuted for and convicted of* war crimes or crimes against humanity, in accordance with the principles established by the Nuremberg Tribunal, will not enjoy the benefits of the provisions of the present Convention as provided in article 85.

[The note continues with a detailed analysis of the reservations problem. Reservations to multipartite international agreements are considered at p. 967.]

1. *Protocols I and II to the Geneva Conventions of 1949.* On June 8, 1977, the Geneva Diplomatic Conference on the Reaffirmation and Development of International Humanitarian Law Applicable in Armed Conflicts adopted two protocols supplementing these conventions: the Protocol Additional to the Geneva Conventions of 12 August 1949, and relating to the Protection of Victims of International Armed Conflicts (Protocol I), with annexes, and the Protocol Additional to the Geneva Conventions of August 12, 1949, and relating to the Protection of Victims of Non-International Armed Conflicts (Protocol II). The protocols entered into force December 7, 1978; they were not in force for the United States as of January 1, 1980. The text of the protocols appears at 72 Am.J.Int'l L. 457 (1978).

2. *Effect of Protocol I (1977).* The report, submitted to the Secretary of State, of the United States Delegation to the 1977 Geneva Diplomatic Conference just discussed, stated:

> * * * Similarly, we welcome the clear statement in the Preamble that no person protected by the Geneva Conventions or the Protocol could be denied [their] protections on the basis of charges of aggression and the statement in article 44 that a combatant may not be deprived of his status as a prisoner of war by allegations of war crimes. Although this latter provision does not, by itself, undo the Communist reservation to article 85 of the Third Convention, it does make it clear that the interpretation given it by the Vietnamese (i. e., that it was a basis for denying PW [prisoner of war] status merely upon charges of war crimes and prior to conviction and exhaustion of rights of appeal) is untenable. Boyd, Digest of United States Practice in International Law 1977, at 918 (1979).

The statement in the Preamble referred to reads as follows:

> Reaffirming further that the provisions of the Geneva Conventions of 12 August 1949 and of the Protocol must be fully applied in all circumstances to all persons who are protected by these instruments, without any adverse distinction based on the nature or origin of the armed conflict or on the causes espoused by or attributed to the Parties to the conflict.

The relevant provision of Article 44 referred to in the delegation's report states:

> 2. While all combatants are obliged to comply with the rules of international law applicable to armed conflicts, violations of these rules shall not deprive a combatant * * *, if he falls into the power of an adverse Party, of his right to be a prisoner of war * * *.

UNITED STATES v. CALLEY

United States Court of Military Appeals, 1973.
22 C.M.A. 534, 48 C.–M. Rep. 19.

QUINN, Judge:

First Lieutenant Calley stands convicted of the premeditated murder of 22 infants, children, women, and old men, and of assault with intent to murder a child of about 2 years of age. All the killings and the assault took place on March 16, 1968 in the area of the village of My Lai in the Republic of South Vietnam. The Army Court of Military Review affirmed the findings of guilty and the sentence, which, as reduced by the convening authority, includes dismissal and confinement at hard labor for 20 years. The accused petitioned this Court for further review, alleging 30 assignments of error. We granted three of these assignments.

We consider first whether the public attention given the charges was so pernicious as to prevent a fair trial for the accused. At the trial, defense counsel moved to dismiss all the charges on the ground that the pretrial publicity made it impossible for the Government to accord the accused a fair trial. The motion was denied. It is contended that the ruling was wrong.

The defense asserts, and the Government concedes, that the pretrial publicity was massive. The defense perceives the publicity as virulent and vicious. At trial, it submitted a vast array of newspaper stories, copies of national news magazines, transcripts of television interviews, and editorial comment. Counsel also referred to comments by the President in which he alluded to the deaths as a "massacre" and to similar remarks by the Secretary of State, the Secretary of Defense, the Secretary of the Army, and various members of Congress. Before us, defense counsel contend that the decisions of the United States Supreme Court in Marshall v. United States, 360 U.S. 310 (1959), Irvin v. Dowd, 366 U.S. 717 (1961), and Sheppard v. Maxwell, 384 U.S. 333 (1966) require reversal of this conviction. In our opinion, neither the cited cases, nor others dealing with pretrial publicity and its effect upon an accused's constitutional right to a fair trial, mandate that result.

[The court's discussion of this issue is omitted.]

In his second assignment of error the accused contends that the evidence is insufficient to establish his guilt beyond a reasonable doubt. Summarized, the pertinent evidence is as follows:

Lieutenant Calley was a platoon leader in C Company, a unit that was part of an organization known as Task Force Barker, whose mission was to subdue and drive out the enemy in an area in the Republic of Vietnam known popularly as Pinkville. Before March 16, 1968, this area, which included the village of My Lai 4, was a Viet Cong stronghold. C Company had operated in the area several times. Each time the unit had entered the area it suffered casualties by sniper fire, machine gun fire, mines, and other forms of attack. Lieutenant Calley had accompanied his platoon on some of the incursions.

On March 15, 1968, a memorial service for members of the company killed in the area during the preceding weeks was held. After the service Captain Ernest L. Medina, the commanding officer of C Company, briefed the company on a mission in the Pinkville area set for the next day. C Company was to serve as the main attack formation for Task Force Barker. In that role it would assault and neutralize My Lai 4, 5, and 6 and then mass for an assault on My Lai 1. Intelligence reports indicated that the unit would be opposed by a veteran enemy battalion, and that all civilians would be absent from the area. The objective was to destroy the enemy. Disagreement exists as to the instructions on the specifics of destruction.

Captain Medina testified that he instructed his troops that they were to destroy My Lai 4 by "burning the hootches, to kill the livestock, to close the wells and to destroy the food crops." Asked if women and children were to be killed, Medina said he replied in the negative, adding that, "You must use common sense. If they have a weapon and are trying to engage you, then you can shoot back, but you must use common sense." However, Lieutenant Calley testified that Captain Medina informed the troops they were to kill every living thing—men, women, children, and animals—and under no circumstances were they to leave any Vietnamese behind them as they passed through the villages enroute to their final objective. Other witnesses gave more or less support to both versions of the briefing.

On March 16, 1968, the operation began with interdicting fire. C Company was then brought to the area by helicopters. Lieutenant Calley's platoon was on the first lift. This platoon formed a defense perimeter until the remainder of the force was landed. The unit received no hostile fire from the village.

Calley's platoon passed the approaches to the village with his men firing heavily. Entering the village, the platoon encountered only unarmed, unresisting men, women, and children. The villagers, including infants held in their mothers' arms, were assembled and moved in separate groups to collection points. Calley testified that during this time he was radioed twice by Captain Medina, who demanded to know what was delaying the platoon. On being told that a large number of villagers had been detained, Calley said Medina ordered him to "waste them." Calley further testified that he obeyed the orders because he had been taught the doctrine of obedience throughout his military career. Medina denied that he gave any such order.

One of the collection points for the villagers was in the southern part of the village. There, Private First Class Paul D. Meadlo guarded a group of between 30 to 40 old men, women, and children. Lieutenant Calley approached Meadlo and told him, "You know what to do," and left. He returned shortly and asked Meadlo why the people were not yet dead. Meadlo replied he did not know that Calley had meant that they should be killed. Calley declared that he wanted them dead. He and Meadlo then opened fire on the group, until all but a few children fell. Calley then personally shot these children. He expended 4 or 5 magazines from his M-16 rifle in the incident.

Lieutenant Calley and Meadlo moved from this point to an irrigation ditch on the east side of My Lai 4. There, they encountered another group of civilians being held by several soldiers. Meadlo estimated that this group contained from 75 to 100 persons. Calley stated, "We got another job to do, Meadlo," and he ordered the group into the ditch. When all were in the ditch, Calley and Meadlo opened fire on them. Although ordered by Calley to shoot, Private First Class James J. Dursi refused to join in the killings, and Specialist Four Robert E. Maples refused to give his machine gun to Calley for use in the killings. Lieutenant Calley admitted that he fired into the ditch, with the muzzle of his weapon within 5 feet of people in it. He expended between 10 to 15 magazines of ammunition on this occasion.

With his radio operator, Private Charles Sledge, Calley moved to the north end of the ditch. There, he found an elderly Vietnamese monk, whom he interrogated. Calley struck the man with his rifle butt and then shot him in the head. Other testimony indicates that immediately afterwards a young child was observed running toward the village. Calley seized him by the arm, threw him into the ditch, and fired at him. Calley admitted interrogating and striking the monk, but denied shooting him. He also denied the incident involving the child.

Appellate defense counsel contend that the evidence is insufficient to establish the accused's guilt. They do not dispute Calley's participation in the homicides, but they argue that he did not act with the malice or mens rea essential to a conviction of murder; that the orders he received to kill everyone in the village were not palpably illegal; that he was acting in ignorance of the laws of war; that since he was told that only "the enemy" would be in the village, his honest belief that there were no innocent civilians in the village exonerates him of criminal responsibility for their deaths; and, finally, that his actions were in the heat of passion caused by reasonable provocation.

* * *

The testimony of Meadlo and others provided the court members with ample evidence from which to find that Lieutenant Calley directed and personally participated in the intentional killing of men, women, and children, who were unarmed and in the custody of armed soldiers of C Company. If the prosecution's witnesses are believed, there is also ample evidence to support a finding that the accused deliberately shot the Vietnamese monk whom he interrogated, and that he seized, threw into a ditch, and fired on a child with the intent to kill.

Enemy prisoners are not subject to summary execution by their captors. Military law has long held that the killing of an unresisting prisoner is murder. Winthrop's Military Law and Precedents, 2d ed., 1920 Reprint, at 788–91.

> While it is lawful to kill an enemy "in the heat and exercise of war," yet "to kill such an enemy after he has laid down his arms * * * is murder."

Digest of Opinions of the Judge Advocates General of the Army, 1912, at 1074–75 n. 3.

Conceding for the purposes of this assignment of error that Calley believed the villagers were part of "the enemy," the uncontradicted evidence is that they were under the control of armed soldiers and were offering no resistance. In his testimony, Calley admitted he was aware of the requirement that prisoners be treated with respect. He also admitted he knew that the normal practice was to interrogate villagers, release those who could satisfactorily account for themselves, and evacuate the suspect among them for further examination. Instead of proceeding in the usual way, Calley executed all, without regard to age, condition, or possibility of suspicion. On the evidence, the court-martial could reasonably find Calley guilty of the offenses before us.

At trial, Calley's principal defense was that he acted in execution of Captain Medina's order to kill everyone in My Lai 4. Appellate defense counsel urge this defense as the most important factor in assessment of the legal sufficiency of the evidence. The argument, however, is inapplicable to whether the evidence is *legally* sufficient. Captain Medina denied that he issued any such order, either during the previous day's briefing or on the date the killings were carried out. Resolution of the conflict between his testimony and that of the accused was for the triers of the facts. United States v. Guerra, 13 USCMA 463, 32 CMR 463 (1963). The general finding of guilty, with exceptions as to the number of persons killed, does not indicate whether the court members found that Captain Medina did not issue the alleged order to kill, or whether, if he did, the court members believed that the accused knew the order was illegal. For the purpose of the legal sufficiency of the evidence, the record supports the findings of guilty.

In the third assignment of error, appellate defense counsel assert gross deficiencies in the military judge's instructions to the court members. Only two assertions merit discussion. One contention is that the judge should have, but did not, advise the court members of the necessity to find the existence of "malice aforethought" in connection with the murder charges; the second allegation is that the defense of compliance with superior orders was not properly submitted to the court members.

The existence vel non of malice, say appellate defense counsel, is the factor that distinguishes murder from manslaughter. *   *   *

* * * In enactment of the Uniform Code of Military Justice, Congress eliminated malice as an element of murder by codifying the common circumstances under which that state of mind was deemed to be present. * * * One of the stated purposes of the Code was the "listing and definition of offenses, redrafted and rephrased in modern legislative language." S.Rep.No. 486, 81st Cong., 1st Sess. 2 (1949). That purpose was accomplished by defining murder as the unlawful killing of a human being, without justification or excuse. * * *

The trial judge delineated the elements of premeditated murder for the court members in accordance with the statutory language. He instructed them that to convict Lieutenant Calley, they must be convinced beyond a reasonable doubt that the victims were dead; that their respective deaths resulted from specified acts of the accused; that the killings were unlawful; and that Calley acted with a premeditated design to kill. The judge defined accurately the meaning of an unlawful killing and the meaning of a "premeditated design to kill." These instructions comported fully with requirements of existing law for the offense of premeditated murder, and neither statute nor judicial precedent requires that reference also be made to the pre-Code concept of malice.

We turn to the contention that the judge erred in his submission of the defense of superior orders to the court. After fairly summarizing the evidence, the judge gave the following instructions pertinent to the issue:

The killing of resisting or fleeing enemy forces is generally recognized as a justifiable act of war, and you may consider any such killings justifiable in this case. The law attempts to protect those persons not actually engaged in warfare, however; and limits the circumstances under which their lives may be taken.

Both combatants captured by and noncombatants detained by the opposing force, regardless of their loyalties, political views, or prior acts, have the right to be treated as prisoners until released, confined, or executed, in accordance with law and established procedures, by competent authority sitting in judgment of such detained or captured individuals. Summary execution of detainees or prisoners is forbidden by law. Further, it's clear under the evidence presented in this case, that hostile acts or support of the enemy North Vietnamese or Viet Cong forces by inhabitants of My Lai (4) at some time prior to 16 March 1968, would not justify the summary execution of all or a part of the occupants of My Lai (4) on 16 March, nor would hostile acts committed that day, if, following the hostility, the belligerents surrendered or were captured by our forces. I therefore instruct you, as a matter of law, that if unresisting human beings were killed at My Lai (4) while within the effective custody and control of our military forces, their deaths cannot be considered justified, and any order to kill such people would be, as a matter of law, an illegal order. Thus, if you find that Lieutenant Calley received an order directing him to kill unresisting Vietnamese within his control or within the control of his troops, *that order would be an illegal order.*

A determination that an order is illegal does not, of itself, assign criminal responsibility to the person following the order for acts done in compliance with it. Soldiers are taught to follow orders, and special attention is given to obedience of orders on the battlefield. Military effectiveness depends upon obedience to orders. On the other hand, the obedience of a soldier is not the obedience of an automaton. A soldier is a reasoning agent, obliged to respond, not as a machine, but as a person. The law takes these factors into account in assessing criminal responsibility for acts done in compliance with illegal orders.

The acts of a subordinate done in compliance with an unlawful order given him by his superior are excused and impose no criminal liability upon him unless the superior's order is one which a man of *ordinary sense and understanding* would, under the circumstances, know to be unlawful, or if the order in question is actually known to the accused to be unlawful.

* * *

* * * In determining what orders, if any, Lieutenant Calley acted under, if you find him to have acted, you should consider all of the matters which he has testified reached him and which you can infer from other evidence that he saw and heard. Then, unless you find beyond a reasonable doubt that he was not acting under orders directing him in substance and effect to kill unresisting occupants of My Lai (4), you must determine whether Lieutenant Calley actually knew those orders to be unlawful.

* * * In determining whether or not Lieutenant Calley had knowledge of the unlawfulness of any order found by you to have been given, you may consider all relevant facts and circumstances, including Lieutenant Calley's rank; educational background; OCS schooling; other training while in the Army, including basic training, and his training in Hawaii and Vietnam; his experience on prior operations involving contact with hostile and friendly Vietnamese; his age; and any other evidence tending to prove or disprove that on 16 March 1968, Lieutenant Calley knew the order was unlawful. If you find beyond a reasonable doubt, on the basis of all the evidence, that *Lieutenant Calley actually knew* the order under which he asserts he operated was unlawful, the fact that the order was given operates as no defense.

Unless you find beyond reasonable doubt that the accused acted with actual knowledge that the order was unlawful, you must proceed to determine whether, under the circumstances, *a man of ordinary sense and understanding would have known the order was unlawful. Your deliberations on this question do not focus on Lieutenant Calley and the manner in which he perceived the legality of the order found to have been given him. The standard is that of a man of ordinary sense and understanding under the circumstances.*

Think back to the events of 15 and 16 March 1968. * * * *Then determine, in light of all the surrounding circumstances, whether the order, which to reach this point you will have found him to be operating in accordance with, is one which a man of ordinary sense and understanding would know to be unlawful. Apply this to each charged act which you have found Lieutenant Calley to have committed. Unless you are satisfied from the evidence, beyond a reasonable doubt, that a man of ordinary sense and understanding would have known the order to be unlawful, you must acquit Lieutenant Calley for committing acts done in accordance with the order.* (Emphasis added.)

Appellate defense counsel contend that these instructions are prejudicially erroneous in that they require the court members to determine that Lieutenant Calley knew that an order to kill human beings in the circumstances under which he killed was illegal by the standard of whether "a man of ordinary sense and understanding" would know the order was illegal. They urge us to adopt as the governing test whether the order is so palpably or manifestly illegal that a person of "the commonest understanding" would be aware of its illegality. They maintain the standard stated by the judge is too strict and unjust; that it confronts members of the armed forces who are not persons of ordinary sense and understanding with the dilemma of choosing between the penalty of death for disobedience of an order in time of war on the one hand and the equally serious punishment for obedience on the other. Some thoughtful commentators on military law have presented much the same argument.[1]

The "ordinary sense and understanding" standard is set forth in the present Manual for Courts-Martial, United States, 1969 (Rev.) and was the standard accepted by this Court in United States v. Schultz, 18 USCMA 133, 39 CMR 133 (1969) and United States v. Keenan, 18 USCMA 108, 39 CMR 108 (1969). It appeared as early as 1917. Manual for Courts-Martial, U.S. Army, 1917, paragraph 442. Apparently, it originated in a quotation from F. Wharton, Homicide § 485 (3d ed. 1907). Wharton's authority is Riggs v. State,

1. In the words of one author: "If the standard of reasonableness continues to be applied, we run the unacceptable risk of applying serious punishment to one whose only crime is the slowness of his wit or his stupidity. The soldier, who honestly believes that he must obey an order to kill and is punished for it, is convicted not of murder but of simple negligence." Finkelstein, Duty to Obey as a Defense, March 9, 1970 (unpublished essay, Army War College). See also L. Norene, Obedience to Orders as a Defense to a Criminal Act, March 1971 (unpublished thesis presented to The Judge Advocate General's School, U.S. Army).

3 Coldwell 85, 91 American Decisions 272, 273 (Tenn.1866), in which the court approved a charge to the jury as follows:

> [I]n its substance being clearly illegal, so that a man of ordinary sense and understanding would know as soon as he heard the order read or given that such order was illegal, would afford a private no protection for a crime committed under such order.

Other courts have used other language to define the substance of the defense. Typical is McCall v. McDowell, 15 F.Cas. 1235, 1240 (C.C.D.Cal.1867), in which the court said:

> But I am not satisfied that Douglas ought to be held liable to the plaintiff at all. He acted not as a volunteer, but as a subordinate in obedience to the order of his superior. Except in a plain case of excess of authority, where at first blush it is apparent and palpable to the commonest understanding that the order is illegal. I cannot but think that the law should excuse the military subordinate when acting in obedience to the orders of his commander. Otherwise he is placed in the dangerous dilemma of being liable in damages to third persons for obedience to an order, or to the loss of his commission and disgrace for disobedience thereto. * * * The first duty of a soldier is obedience, and without this there can be neither discipline nor efficiency in an army. If every subordinate officer and soldier were at liberty to question the legality of the orders of the commander, and obey them or not as they may consider them valid or invalid, the camp would be turned into a debating school, where the precious moment for action would be wasted in wordy conflicts between the advocates of conflicting opinions.

Colonel William Winthrop, the leading American commentator on military law, notes:

> But for the inferior to assume to determine the question of the lawfulness of an order given him by a superior would of itself, as a general rule, amount to insubordination, and such an assumption carried into practice would subvert military discipline. Where the order is apparently regular and *lawful on its face*, he is not to go behind it to satisfy himself that his superior has proceeded with authority, but is to obey it according to its terms, *the only exceptions recognized to the rule of obedience being cases of orders so manifestly beyond the legal power or discretion of the commander as to admit of no rational doubt of their unlawfulness.* * * *
>
> Except in such instances of palpable illegality, which must be of rare occurrence, the inferior should presume that the order was lawful and authorized and obey it accordingly, and in obeying it can scarcely fail to be held justified by a military court.

Winthrop's Military Law and Precedents, 2d ed., 1920 Reprint, at 296–297 (footnotes omitted) (emphasis added).

In the stress of combat, a member of the armed forces cannot reasonably be expected to make a refined legal judgment and be held criminally responsible if he guesses wrong on a question as to which there may be considerable disagreement. But there is no disagreement as to the illegality of the order to kill in this case. For 100 years, it has been a settled rule of American law that even in war the summary killing of an enemy, who has submitted to, and is under, effective physical control, is murder. Appellate defense counsel acknowledge that rule of law and its continued viability, but they say that Lieutenant Calley should not be held accountable for the men, women and children he killed because the court-martial could have found that he was a person of "commonest understanding" and such a person might not know what our law provides; that his captain had ordered him to kill these unarmed and submissive people and he only carried out that order as a good disciplined soldier should.

Whether Lieutenant Calley was the most ignorant person in the United States Army in Vietnam, or the most intelligent, he must be presumed to know that he could not kill the people involved here. The United States Supreme Court has pointed out that "[t]he rule that 'ignorance of the law will not excuse' [a positive act that constitutes a crime] * * * is deep in our law." Lambert v. California, 355 U.S. 225, 228 (1957). An order to kill infants and unarmed civilians who were so demonstrably incapable of resistance to the armed might of a military force as were those killed by Lieutenant Calley is, in my opinion, so palpably illegal that whatever conceptional difference there may be between a person of "commonest understanding" and a person of "common understanding," that difference could not have had any "impact on a court of lay members receiving the respective wordings in instructions," as appellate defense counsel contend. In my judgment, there is no possibility of prejudice to Lieutenant Calley in the trial judge's reliance upon the established standard of excuse of criminal conduct, rather than the standard of "commonest understanding" presented by the defense, or by the new variable test postulated in the dissent, which, with the inclusion of such factors for consideration as grade and experience, would appear to exact a higher standard of understanding from Lieutenant Calley than that of the person of ordinary understanding.

In summary, as reflected in the record, the judge was capable and fair, and dedicated to assuring the accused a trial on the merits as provided by law; his instructions on all issues were comprehensive and correct. Lieutenant Calley was given every consideration to which he was entitled, and perhaps more. We are impressed with the absence of bias or prejudice on the part of the court members. They were instructed to determine the *truth* according to the law and this they did with due deliberation and full consideration of the evidence. Their findings of guilty represent the truth of the facts as they determined them to be and there is substantial evidence to support those findings. No mistakes of procedure cast doubt upon them.

Consequently, the decision of the Court of Military Review is affirmed.

DUNCAN, Judge (concurring in the result):

My difference of opinion from Judge Quinn's view of the defense of obedience to orders is narrow. The issue of obedience to orders was raised in defense by the evidence. Contrary to Judge Quinn, I do not consider that a presumption arose that the appellant knew he could not kill the people involved. The Government, as I see it, is not entitled to a presumption of what the appellant knew of the illegality of an order. It is a matter for the factfinders under proper instructions.

Paragraph 216, Manual for Courts-Martial, United States, 1969 (Rev.), provides for special defenses: excuse because of accident or misadventure; self-defense; entrapment; coercion or duress; physical or financial inability; and obedience to apparently lawful orders. Subparagraph *d* of paragraph 216 is as follows:

> An order requiring the performance of a military duty may be inferred to be legal. An act performed manifestly beyond the scope of authority, or pursuant to an order that a man of ordinary sense and understanding would know to be illegal, or in a wanton manner in the discharge of a lawful duty, is not excusable.

The military judge clearly instructed the members pursuant to this provision of the Manual. The heart of the issue is whether, under the circumstances of this case, he should have abandoned the Manual standard and fashioned another. The defense urges a purely subjective standard; the dissent herein yet another. I suggest that there are important general as well as certain specific considerations which convince me that the standard should not be abandoned. The process of promulgating Manual provisions is geared to produce requirements for the system only after most serious reflection by knowledgeable and concerned personnel.[2] These persons have full regard for the needs of the armed forces and genuine concern for the plight of one accused. Those who prepared the Manual provision and the President of the United States, the Commander-in-Chief, who approved and made the provision a part of our law,[3] were aware that disobedience to orders is the anathema to an efficient military force. Judge Quinn points out that this Court has established as precedent the applicability of the special defense upon proof adduced pursuant

---

2. The draft of the Manual for Courts-Martial, United States, 1951, its predecessor, was prepared through the cooperation of the Judge Advocates General of the Army, Navy, Air Force, and the General Counsel, Office of the Secretary of Defense. The draft was then approved by the Secretary of Defense. The draft was further reviewed by the Office of the Attorney General and the Director of the Archives. After study by the Executive Office of the President, it was promulgated as Executive Order 10214 on February 8, 1951. See Legal and Legislative Basis, MCM, 1951.

3. See Article 36, UCMJ, 10 U.S.C. § 836; United States v. Smith, 13 USCMA 105, 32 CMR 105 (1962).

to the Manual standard. These are important general reasons for not aborting a standard that has been long in existence and often used.

It is urged that in using the Manual test of "a man of ordinary sense and understanding" those persons at the lowest end of the scale of intelligence and experience in the services may suffer conviction while those more intelligent and experienced would possess faculties which would cause them to abjure the order with impunity. Such an argument has some attraction but in my view falls short of that which should impel a court to replace that which is provided to us as law.

It appears to me that all tests which measure an accused's conduct by an objective standard—whether it is the test of "palpable illegality to the commonest understanding" or whether the test establishes a set of profile considerations by which to measure the accused's ability to assess the legality of the order—are less than perfect, and they have a certain potential for injustice to the member having the slowest wit and quickest obedience. Obviously the higher the standard, the likelihood is that fewer persons will be able to measure up to it. Knowledge of the fact that there are other standards that are arguably more fair does not convince me that the standard used herein is unfair, on its face, or as applied to Lieutenant Calley.

Perhaps a new standard, such as the dissent suggests, has merit; however, I would leave that for the legislative authority or for the cause where the record demonstrates harm from the instructions given. I perceive none in this case. The general verdict in this case implies that the jury believed a man of ordinary sense and understanding would have known the order in question to be illegal.[4] Even conceding arguendo that this issue should have been resolved under instructions requiring a finding that almost every member of the armed forces would have immediately recognized that the order was unlawful, as well as a finding that as a consequence of his age, grade, intelligence, experience, and training, Lieutenant Calley should have recognized the order's illegality, I do not believe the result in this case would have been different.

DARDEN, Chief Judge (dissenting):

Although the charge the military judge gave on the defense of superior orders was not inconsistent with the Manual treatment of this subject, I believe the Manual provision is too strict in a combat environment.[5] Among other things, this standard permits serious punishment of persons whose training and attitude incline them either to be enthusiastic about compliance with orders or not to challenge the authority of their superiors. The standard also permits conviction of members who are not persons of ordinary sense and understanding.

---

4. This assumes that the jury found that the order the appellant contends he obeyed was given.

5. I agree with the majority opinion that the military judge was eminently fair and I do not blame him for this error.

The principal opinion has accurately traced the history of the current standard. Since this Manual provision is one of substantive law rather than one relating to procedure or modes of proof, the Manual rule is not binding on this Court, which has the responsibility for determining the principles that govern justification in the law of homicide. United States v. Smith, 13 USCMA 105, 32 CMR 105 (1962). My impression is that the weight of authority, including the commentators whose articles are mentioned in the principal opinion, supports a more liberal approach to the defense of superior orders. Under this approach, superior orders should constitute a defense except "in a plain case of excess of authority, where at first blush it is apparent and palpable to the commonest understanding that the order is illegal." McCall v. McDowell, 15 F.Cas. 1235, 1240 (No. 8,673) (C.C.D.Cal.1867); In re Fair, 100 F. 149, 155 (C.C.D.Neb.1900); Winthrop's Military Law and Precedents, 2d ed., 1920 Reprint, at 296–97.

While this test is phrased in language that now seems "somewhat archaic and ungrammatical," [6] the test recognizes that the essential ingredient of discipline in any armed force is obedience to orders and that this obedience is so important it should not be penalized unless the order would be recognized as illegal, not by what some hypothetical reasonable soldier would have known, but also by "those persons at the lowest end of the scale of intelligence and experience in the services." [7] This is the real purpose in permitting superior orders to be a defense, and it ought not to be restricted by the concept of a fictional reasonable man so that, regardless of his personal characteristics, an accused judged after the fact may find himself punished for either obedience or disobedience, depending on whether the evidence will support the finding of simple negligence on his part.

It is true that the standard of a "reasonable man" is used in other areas of military criminal law, e. g., in connection with the provocation necessary to reduce murder to voluntary manslaughter; what constitutes an honest and reasonable mistake; and, indirectly, in connection with involuntary manslaughter. But in none of these instances do we have the countervailing consideration of avoiding the subversion of obedience to discipline in combat by encouraging a member to weigh the legality of an order or whether the superior had the authority to issue it. See Martin v. Mott, 25 U.S. 19, 30 (1827).

The preservation of human life is, of course, of surpassing importance. To accomplish such preservation, members of the armed forces must be held to standards of conduct that will permit punishment of atrocities and enable this nation to follow civilized concepts of warfare. In defending the current standard, the Army Court of Military Review expressed the view that:

6. L. Norene, Obedience to Orders as a Defense to a Criminal Act, March 1971 (unpublished thesis presented to The Judge Advocate General's School, U.S. Army).

7. Id.

Heed must be given not only to the subjective innocence-through-ignorance in the soldier, but to the consequences for his victims. Also, barbarism tends to invite reprisal to the detriment of our own force or disrepute which interferes with the achievement of war aims, even though the barbaric acts were preceded by orders for their commission. Casting the defense of obedience to orders solely in subjective terms of *mens rea* would operate practically to abrogate those objective restraints which are essential to functioning rules of war.

United States v. Calley, 46 CMR 1131, 1184 (ACMR 1973).

I do not disagree with these comments. But while humanitarian considerations compel us to consider the impact of actions by members of our armed forces on citizens of other nations, I am also convinced that the phrasing of the defense of superior orders should have as its principal objective fairness to the unsophisticated soldier and those of somewhat limited intellect who nonetheless are doing their best to perform their duty.

The test of palpable illegality to the commonest understanding properly balances punishment for the obedience of an obviously illegal order against protection to an accused for following his elementary duty of obeying his superiors. Such a test reinforces the need for obedience as an essential element of military discipline by broadly protecting the soldier who has been effectively trained to look to his superiors for direction. It also promotes fairness by permitting the military jury to consider the particular accused's intelligence, grade, training, and other elements directly related to the issue of whether he should have known an order was illegal. Finally, that test imputes such knowledge to an accused not as a result of simple negligence but on the much stronger circumstantial concept that almost anyone in the armed forces would have immediately recognized that the order was palpably illegal.

I would adopt this standard as the correct instruction for the jury when the defense of superior orders is in issue. Because the original case language is archaic and somewhat ungrammatical, I would rephrase it to require that the military jury be instructed that, despite his asserted defense of superior orders, an accused may be held criminally accountable for his acts, allegedly committed pursuant to such orders, if the court members are convinced beyond a reasonable doubt (1) that almost every member of the armed forces would have immediately recognized that the order was unlawful, and (2) that the accused should have recognized the order's illegality as a consequence of his age, grade, intelligence, experience, and training.

The temptation is to say that even under this new formulation Lieutenant Calley would have been found guilty. No matter how such a position is phrased, essentially it means that the appellate judge rather than the military jury is functioning as a fact finder.

My reaction to this has been expressed by the former chief justice of the California Supreme Court in these words:

> If an erroneous instruction or an erroneous failure to give an instruction relates to a substantial element of the appellant's case, an appellate court would not find it highly probable that the error did not influence the verdict.

R. Traynor, The Riddle of Harmless Error 74 (1970).

The same authority also expressed this thought:

> The concept of fairness extends to reconsideration of the merits when a judgment has been or might have been influenced by error. In that event there should be a retrial in the trial court, time consuming or costly though it may be. The short-cut alternative of reconsidering the merits in the appellate court, because it is familiar with the evidence and aware of the error, has the appeal of saving time and money. Unfortunately it does not measure up to accepted standards of fairness.

Id. at 20.

In the instant case, Lieutenant Calley's testimony placed the defense of superior orders in issue even though he conceded that he knew prisoners were normally to be treated with respect and that the unit's normal practice was to interrogate Vietnamese villagers, release those who could account for themselves, and evacuate those suspected of being a part of the enemy forces. Although crucial parts of his testimony were sharply contested, according to Lieutenant Calley, (1) he had received a briefing before the assault in which he was instructed that every living thing in the village was to be killed, including women and children; (2) he was informed that speed was important in securing the village and moving forward; (3) he was ordered that under no circumstances were any Vietnamese to be allowed to stay behind the lines of his forces; (4) the residents of the village who were taken into custody were hindering the progress of his platoon in taking up the position it was to occupy; and (5) when he informed Captain Medina of this hindrance, he was ordered to kill the villagers and to move his platoon to a proper position.

In addition to the briefing, Lieutenant Calley's experience in the Pinkville area caused him to know that, in the past, when villagers had been left behind his unit, the unit had immediately received sniper fire from the rear as it pressed forward. Faulty intelligence apparently led him also to believe that those persons in the village were not innocent civilians but were either enemies or enemy sympathizers. For a participant in the My Lai operation, the circumstances that could have obtained there may have caused the illegality of alleged orders to kill civilians to be much less clear than they are in a hindsight review.[8]

---

8. A New York Times Book Reviewer has noted, "One cannot locate the exact moment in his [Calley's] narrative when one can be absolutely certain that one would have acted differently given the same circumstances." See Paris ed., New York Herald Tribune, September 13, 1971.

Since the defense of superior orders was not submitted to the military jury under what I consider to be the proper standard, I would grant Lieutenant Calley a rehearing.

I concur in Judge Quinn's opinion on the other granted issues.

---

1. *Standard applied in the Calley case.* Should a soldier be convicted of murder (as opposed to, say, manslaughter) only if he *subjectively knew* that an order to kill was illegal? Or can he be convicted of murder even if he did not in his own mind know of its illegality but other soldiers knew it was illegal? Was Calley convicted because of what he knew or because of what other people knew? The debate in the opinions in the Calley case centers around what some other person would know: i. e. a man of ordinary sense and understanding, or a man of commonest understanding. Are all the judges saying that Calley can be found guilty, even though he didn't know subjectively, if the man meeting that standard would have known? Or is the standard some rule of evidence, e. g., since a man of ordinary sense and understanding would know the order was illegal and since Calley is a man of ordinary sense and understanding, therefore Calley must have known the order was illegal?

In Public Prosecutor v. Leopold L, Austria, Supreme Court 1967, 47 Int'l L.Rep. 464 (1974), defendant was convicted of the murder of Poles and Jews, inmates of a labor camp in Poland during the Second World War. Defendant was a German S.S. deputy troop leader, a member of the guard at the labor camp, who claimed to be acting pursuant to orders. The defendant's appeal asserted, inter alia, that he was "unable, owing to his limited intelligence, to realize the criminal nature of the execution of an illegal order." In denying the appeal, the court stated:

> *   *   *   [I]t must be said that orders to kill, given without previous proceedings, in respect of individual or groups of inmates of this labour camp could not even as a matter of form have any legal justification. They were therefore *straightaway recognizable as illegal.* Furthermore, the fact must be considered that orders to kill inmates of the labour camp, irrespective of their form and extent, which were *clearly recognizable by anybody as illegal,* could never have justified the person executing such orders but could only, in certain circumstances, have excused him from the point of view of absolute coercion (§ 2(g) Penal Code), that is, only if non-execution of such orders would have meant immediate danger to life for the person disregarding them. The reference in the appeal to the power of a commander under martial law to reinforce his orders, in face of the enemy, if necessary immediately by the use of his weapon (which incidentally—as is generally known—was only applied in the last phase of the Second World War), is out of place in this context, since the defendant was not involved in belligerent action by a

fighting unit but performed only a guarding function. [Emphasis supplied.]

2. *Further proceedings in the Calley case.* In Calley v. Callaway, 382 F.Supp. 650 (M.D.Georgia 1974), Calley was ordered released on habeas corpus because of pretrial publicity. This was reversed, 519 F.2d 184 (5th Cir. 1975), cert. denied sub. nom. Calley v. Hoffman, 425 U.S. 911, 96 S.Ct. 1505 (1976). While these cases were in process, Calley was first paroled by the United States Army and then released on bail by the District Court in November 1974, pending appeal. After the Supreme Court denied certiorari, the United States Army announced in April 1976 that it would not seek to return Calley to custody for the remaining ten days of his sentence (previously reduced). See The New York Times, Nov. 9, 1974, p. 1, col. 4; Nov. 10, 1974, p. 1, col. 2; Sept. 11, 1975, p. 26, col. 3; Apr. 6, 1976, p. 1, col. 5.

COMMENT, PUNISHMENT FOR WAR CRIMES: DUTY OR DISCRETION?

69 Michigan Law Review 1312 (1971).*

* * * Immediately prior to the adoption of the 1949 Conventions, it was remarked in reference to one of these earlier conventions that "[i]t is one of the greatest weaknesses of the existing rules on prisoners of war that they do not contain definite and written provisions on sanctions." In view of such criticisms and the ad hoc measures taken to deal with the war crimes of World War II, negotiators in 1949 agreed that specific provisions for punishment of breaches of the new Conventions were essential. Accordingly, each of the Four Conventions adopted in 1949 contained an article requiring each Party to "enact any legislation necessary to provide effective penal sanctions for persons committing * * * grave breaches" of the Conventions.

On March 16, 1968, the most notorious American atrocity yet documented in the Vietnam war took place in the Vietnamese province of Quang Ngai. Soldiers of the United States Army's Americal Division participated in an operation in which scores of unarmed South Vietnamese civilians were slain. If the 1949 Conventions are applicable in the Vietnam War and to the civilian victims at My Lai, the massacre undoubtedly was a grave breach of the standards of wartime conduct imposed on the Parties by the Conventions. Thus, the United States, as a Party to the Conventions, would be obligated to act in compliance with the penal-sanctions provision of the applicable Convention or Conventions. Acting consistently with the possible existence of such an obligation, the United States brought to trial, and convicted of murder, Army First Lieutenant William L. Calley, Jr., Paul Meadlo's platoon leader. Because of his disclosures on na-

* Reprinted by permission of the Michigan Law Review.

tional television, Meadlo, by then discharged from the Army, was subpoenaed as a witness for the prosecution. Meadlo, however, invoked his fifth amendment privilege against self-incrimination and refused to testify. Although granted a writ of immunity from military prosecution by the Commanding General of Fort Benning, Georgia, where the trial by court-martial of Lieutenant Calley was conducted, Meadlo consistently refused to testify until the Government issued a federal immunity order protecting him from civilian prosecution. Finally, under threat of arrest for further refusal to testify after having been granted federal immunity, Meadlo took the witness stand on January 11, 1971. Ten days later, Assistant United States Attorney General William H. Rehnquist struck a disquieting note that has been overlooked in the wake of the Calley conviction: Has the United States violated its treaty obligation under the 1949 Geneva Conventions to prosecute those persons accused of "grave breaches" of the Conventions by granting immunity to a confessed participant in the My Lai slayings?

BISHOP, JUSTICE UNDER FIRE 290 (1974) *

* * * All of the Geneva Conventions obligate each signatory power to search for persons alleged to have committed "grave breaches" of those Conventions and to "bring such persons, regardless of their nationality, before its own courts." There is still too little precedent for such enforcement of the law of war. I know of no instance in which North Vietnam or any other totalitarian government has ever accused a member of its own forces of a violation of the Geneva Conventions or any other war crime. But the most recent available figures show that, as of April, 1971, American courts-martial had tried 117 servicemen and convicted 60 on charges of murdering civilians in Vietnam; an unknown, but probably larger, number had been tried for lesser offenses, such as rape and robbery, against civilians. Murder and other violence against the persons of noncombatants or captured enemies violate the Geneva Conventions, but they are also, of course, violations of the Uniform Code of Military Justice and have been charged as such. The main practical difference is that trial by court-martial for a violation of the Code guarantees the accused procedural protections and appellate review to which he might not be entitled if he were tried by a military commission for a war crime.

Some of the acquittals were probably unjustified, and in at least one case, that of Captain Ernest Medina, the acquittal may have been based on the military judge's erroneous instruction that Medina had no responsibility for the My Lai massacre unless he had "actual knowledge" of it: as laid down by the Supreme Court in General Yamashita's case, the law is that a commander is responsible for war

* Reprinted by permission of Joseph W.
Bishop, Jr.

crimes committed by his subordinates if he knew, *or should have known,* that they were going on and failed to do what he could to prevent or punish them. It is also safe to assume that many war crimes committed by Americans have never been investigated, tried, or punished. The Pentagon has not shown much enthusiasm for investigating the possible failures of commanders at divisional and higher levels to take adequate measures to prevent and punish war crimes. Moreover, the Department of Justice seems to take the position that an honorably discharged serviceman cannot be tried for a war crime committed prior to his discharge. The Supreme Court did hold some years ago that such a discharged soldier could not be tried for an ordinary offense—i. e., one that was not a war crime—committed prior to his discharge. But it had earlier held, in World War II, that a Nazi saboteur who was an American civilian could constitutionally be tried by a military commission for a war crime, and it did not overrule that decision. I am myself of the opinion (though I seem to be in the minority) that a discharged serviceman *can* be tried by a military court on a charge of violating the law of war. In any case, Congress could and should give the federal courts jurisdiction to try such cases: under the Geneva Conventions, in fact, the United States is obligated to "enact any legislation necessary to provide effective penal sanctions" for persons committing "grave breaches."

The record is thus very far from perfect. All that can be said is that it is a better record than that of any other nation in the world and that it lends a degree of credibility to the Pentagon's numerous orders and regulations that aim to prevent and punish war crimes by requiring a report and an investigation of such incidents, and the training and indoctrination of the troops on the subject.[a]

THE LAW OF LAND WARFARE

United States, Department of the Army Field Manual
[FM 27–10] at 4 (1956) (as amended by Change No. 1, 1976).

4.   Sources

The law of war is derived from two principal sources:

a.   Lawmaking Treaties (or Conventions), such as the Hague and Geneva Conventions.

---

a.   Air Force Pamphlet 110–31, 19 Nov. 1976. "This document represents a well-researched and balanced analysis of the legal controls applicable to air operations. It completes the trilogy of instruction for the armed forces on the law of war. The instructions on the law of land warfare are contained in Army Field Manual 27–10, and those concerning naval warfare in Navy instructions NWIP 10–2.
"The Air Force pamphlet is different in tone and style from the manuals of its sister services. For example, FM 27–10 is pronounced to be 'authoritative guidance' and an 'official publication of the U.S. Army.' AFP 110–31 however is not 'directive in nature' and does not represent 'official Government policy.' Despite this disclaimer, however, it marks the most authoritative American source of the law of air warfare to date." DeSaussure, Book Review, 72 Am.J. Int'l L. 174 (1978).

b. Custom. Although some of the law of war has not been incorporated in any treaty or convention to which the United States is a party, this body of unwritten or customary law is firmly established by the custom of nations and well defined by recognized authorities on international law.

Lawmaking treaties may be compared with legislative enactments in the national law of the United States and the customary law of war with the unwritten Anglo-American common law.

5.   Lawmaking Treaties

a.   Treaties to Which the United States Is a Party. The United States is a party to the following conventions pertinent to warfare on land:

(1) Hague Convention No. III of 18 October 1907, Relative to the Opening of Hostilities (36 Stat. 2259, Treaty Series 538), cited herein as H. III.

(2) Hague Convention No. IV of 18 October 1907, Respecting the Laws and Customs of War on Land (36 Stat. 2277; Treaty Series 539), cited herein as H. IV, and the Annex thereto, embodying the Regulations Respecting the Laws and Customs of War on Land (36 Stat. 2295; Treaty Series 539), cited herein as HR.

(3) Hague Convention No. V of 18 October 1907, Respecting the Rights and Duties of Neutral Powers and Persons in Case of War on Land (36 Stat. 2310; Treaty Series 540), cited herein as H. V.

(4) Hague Convention No. IX of 18 October 1907, Concerning Bombardment by Naval Forces in Time of War (36 Stat. 2351; Treaty Series 542), cited herein as H. IX.

(5) Hague Convention No. X of 18 October 1907, for the Adaptation to Maritime Warfare of the Principles of the Geneva Convention (36 Stat. 2371; Treaty Series No. 543), cited herein as H. X.

(6) Geneva Convention Relative to the Treatment of Prisoners of War of 27 July 1929 (47 Stat. 2021; Treaty Series 846), cited herein as GPW 1929.

(7) Geneva Convention for the Amelioration of the Condition of the Wounded and Sick of Armies in the Field of 27 July 1929 (47 Stat. 2074; Treaty Series 847), cited herein as GWS 1929.

(8) Treaty on the Protection of Artistic and Scientific Institutions and Historic Monuments of 15 April 1935 (49 Stat. 3267; Treaty Series 899), cited herein as the Roerich Pact. Only the United States and a number of the American Republics are parties to this treaty.

(9) Geneva Convention for the Amelioration of the Condition of the Wounded and Sick in Armed Forces in the Field of 12 August 1949 (T.I.A.S. 3362), cited herein as GWS.

(10) Geneva Convention for the Amelioration of the Condition of Wounded, Sick and Shipwrecked Members of Armed Forces at Sea of 12 August 1949 (T.I.A.S. 3363), cited herein as GWS Sea.

(11) Geneva Convention Relative to the Treatment of Prisoners of War of 12 August 1949 (T.I.A.S. 3364), cited herein as GPW.

(12) Geneva Convention Relative to the Protection of Civilian Persons in Time of War of 12 August 1949 (T.I.A.S. 3365), cited herein as GC.

* * *

6. Custom

Evidence of the customary law of war, arising from the general consent of States, may be found in judicial decisions, the writings of jurists, diplomatic correspondence, and other documentary material concerning the practice of States. Even though individual States may not be parties to or otherwise strictly bound by H. IV and GPW 1929, the former convention and the general principles of the latter have been held to be declaratory of the customary law of war, to which all States are subject.

The Preamble to the HR specifically provides:

Until a more complete code of the laws of war has been issued, the High Contracting Parties deem it expedient to declare that, in cases not included in the Regulations adopted by them, the inhabitants and the belligerents remain under the protection and the rule of the principles of the law of nations, as they result from the usages established among civilized peoples, from the laws of humanity, and the dictates of the public conscience.

Similarly, a common article of the Geneva Conventions of 1949 (GWS, art. 63; GWS Sea, art. 62; GPW, art. 142; GC, art. 158) provides that the denunciation of (withdrawal from) any of the Geneva Conventions of 1949

* * * shall in no way impair the obligations which the Parties to the conflict shall remain bound to fulfil by virtue of the principles of the law of nations, as they result from the usages established among civilized peoples, from the laws of humanity and the dictates of the public conscience.

* * *

SECTION II.   FORBIDDEN CONDUCT WITH RESPECT TO PERSONS

28. Refusal of Quarter

It is especially forbidden * * * to declare that no quarter will be given.   (HR, art. 23, par. (d).)

29. Injury Forbidden After Surrender

It is especially forbidden * * * to kill or wound an enemy who having laid down his arms, or having no longer means of defense, has surrendered at discretion.   (HR, art. 23, par. (c).)

30.   Persons Descending by Parachute

The law of war does not prohibit firing upon paratroops or other persons who are or appear to be bound upon hostile missions while such persons are descending by parachute.   Persons other than those mentioned in the preceding sentence who are descending by parachute from disabled aircraft may not be fired upon.

31.   Assassination and Outlawry

HR provides:

It is especially forbidden * * * to kill or wound treacherously individuals belonging to the hostile nation or army. (HR, art. 23, par. (b).)

This article is construed as prohibiting assassination, proscription, or outlawry of an enemy, or putting a price upon an enemy's head, as well as offering a reward for an enemy "dead or alive".   It does not, however, preclude attacks on individual soldiers or officers of the enemy whether in the zone of hostilities, occupied territory, or elsewhere.

32.   Nationals Not To Be Compelled to Take Part in Operations Against Their Own Country

A belligerent is likewise forbidden to compel the nationals of the hostile party to take part in the operations of war directed against their own country, even if they were in the belligerent's service before the commencement of the war.   (HR, art. 23, 2d par.)

SECTION III.   FORBIDDEN MEANS OF WAGING WARFARE

33.   Means of Injuring the Enemy Limited

a.   Treaty Provision.

The right of belligerents to adopt means of injuring the enemy is not unlimited.   (HR, art. 22.)

b.   The means employed are definitely restricted by international declarations and conventions and by the laws and usages of war.

34.   Employment of Arms Causing Unnecessary Injury

a.   Treaty Provision.

It is especially forbidden * * * to employ arms, projectiles, or material calculated to cause unnecessary suffering. (HR, art. 23, par. (e).)

b.   Interpretation.   What weapons cause "unnecessary injury" can only be determined in light of the practice of States in refraining from the use of a given weapon because it is believed to have that effect.   The prohibition certainly does not extend to the use of explosives contained in artillery projectiles, mines, rockets, or hand grenades.   Usage has, however, established the illegality of the use of lances with barbed heads, irregular-shaped bullets, and projectiles filled with glass, the use of any substance on bullets that would tend unnecessarily to inflame a wound inflicted by them, and the scoring of the surface or the filing off of the ends of the hard cases of bullets.

35.   Atomic Weapons

The use of explosive "atomic weapons," whether by air, sea, or land forces, cannot as such be regarded as violative of international law in the absence of any customary rule of international law or international convention restricting their employment.

36.   Weapons Employing Fire

The use of weapons which employ fire, such as tracer ammunition, flamethrowers, napalm and other incendiary agents, against targets requiring their use is not violative of international law. They should not, however, be employed in such a way as to cause unnecessary suffering to individuals.

37.   Poison

a.   Treaty Provision.

It is especially forbidden * * * to employ poison or poisoned weapons. (HR, art. 23, par. (a).)

b.   Discussion of Rule. The foregoing rule prohibits the use in war of poison or poisoned weapons against human beings. Restrictions on the use of herbicides as well as treaty provisions concerning chemical and bacteriological warfare are discussed in paragraph 38.

38.   Chemical and Bacteriological Warfare

a.   Treaty Provision. Whereas the use in war of asphyxiating, poisonous or other gases, and of all analogous liquids, materials or devices, has been justly condemned by the general opinion of the civilized world; and

Whereas the prohibition of such use has been declared in Treaties to which the majority of Powers of the world are Parties; and

To the end that this prohibition shall be universally accepted as a part of International Law, binding alike the conscience and the practice of nations:

* * * the High Contracting Parties, so far as they are not already Parties to Treaties prohibiting such use, accept this prohibition, agree to extend this prohibition to the use of bacteriological methods of warfare and agree to be bound as between themselves according to the terms of this declaration. (Geneva Protocol of 1925.)

b.   United States Reservation to the Geneva Protocol of 1925. [T]he said Protocol shall cease to be binding on the government of the United States with respect to the use in war of asphyxiating, poisonous or other gases, and of all analogous liquids, materials, or devices, in regard to an enemy State if such State or any of its allies fails to respect the prohibitions laid down in the Protocol.

c.   Renunciation of Certain Uses in War of Chemical Herbicides and Riot Control Agents. The United States renounces, as a matter of national policy, first use of herbicides in war except use, under regulations applicable to their domestic use, for control of vegetation within US bases and installations or around their immediate defensive perimeters, and first use of riot control agents in war except in defensive military modes to save lives such as:

(1) Use of riot control agents in riot control situations in areas under direct and distinct US military control, to include controlling rioting prisoners of war.

(2) Use of riot control agents in situations in which civilians are used to mask or screen attacks and civilian casualties can be reduced or avoided.

(3) Use of riot control agents in rescue missions in remotely isolated areas, of downed aircrews and passengers, and escaping prisoners.

(4) Use of riot control agents in rear echelon areas outside the zone of immediate combat to protect convoys from civil disturbances, terrorists and paramilitary organizations.

* * *

NOW, THEREFORE, by virtue of the authority vested in me as President of the United States of America by the Constitution and laws of the United States and as Commander-in-Chief of the Armed Forces of the United States, it is hereby ordered as follows:

SECTION 1. The Secretary of Defense shall take all necessary measures to ensure that the use by the Armed Forces of the United States of any riot control agents and chemical herbicides in war is prohibited unless such use has Presidential approval, in advance.

SECTION 2. The Secretary of Defense shall prescribe the rules and regulations he deems necessary to ensure that the national policy herein announced shall be observed by the Armed Forces of the United States. (Exec. Order No. 11850, 40 Fed.Reg. 16187 (1975).)

d. Discussion. Although the language of the 1925 Geneva Protocol appears to ban unqualifiedly the use in war of the chemical weapons within the scope of its prohibition, reservations submitted by most of the Parties to the Protocol, including the United States, have, in effect, rendered the Protocol a prohibition only of the first use in war of materials within its scope. Therefore, the United States, like many other Parties, has reserved the right to use chemical weapons against a state if that state or any of its allies fails to respect the prohibitions of the Protocol.

The reservation of the United States does not, however, reserve the right to retaliate with bacteriological methods of warfare against a state if that state or any of its allies fails to respect the prohibitions of the Protocol. The prohibition concerning bacteriological methods of warfare which the United States has accepted under the Protocol, therefore, proscribes not only the initial but also any retaliatory use of bacteriological methods of warfare. In this connection, the United States considers bacteriological methods of warfare to include not only biological weapons but also toxins, which, although not living organisms and therefore susceptible of being characterized as chemical agents, are generally produced from biological agents. All toxins, however, regardless of the manner of production, are regarded by the United States as bacteriological methods of warfare within the meaning of the proscription of the Geneva Protocol of 1925.

Concerning chemical weapons, the United States considers the Geneva Protocol of 1925 as applying to both lethal and incapacitating chemical agents. Incapacitating agents are those producing symptoms that persist for hours or even days after exposure to the agent has terminated. It is the position of the United States that the Geneva Protocol of 1925 does not prohibit the use in war of either chemical herbicides or riot control agents, which are those agents of a type widely used by governments for law enforcement purposes because they produce, in all but the most unusual circumstances, merely transient effects that disappear within minutes after exposure to the agent has terminated. In this connection, however, the United States has unilaterally renounced, as a matter of national policy, certain uses in war of chemical herbicides and riot control agents (see Exec. Order No. 11850 above). The policy and provisions of Executive Order No. 11850 do not, however, prohibit or restrict the use of chemical herbicides or riot control agents by US armed forces either (1) as retaliation in kind during armed conflict or (2) in situations when the United States is not engaged in armed conflict. Any use in armed conflict of herbicides or riot control agents, however, requires Presidential approval in advance.

The use in war of smoke and incendiary materials is not prohibited or restricted by the Geneva Protocol of 1925.

39. Bombardment of Undefended Places Forbidden

a. Treaty Provision. The attack or bombardment, by whatever means, of towns, villages, dwellings, or buildings which are undefended is prohibited. (HR, art. 25.)

b. Interpretation. An undefended place, within the meaning of Article 25, HR, is any inhabited place near or in a zone where opposing armed forces are in contact which is open for occupation by an adverse party without resistance. In order to be considered as undefended, the following conditions should be fulfilled:

(1) Armed forces and all other combatants, as well as mobile weapons and mobile military equipment, must have been evacuated, or otherwise neutralized;

(2) no hostile use shall be made of fixed military installations or establishments;

(3) no acts of warfare shall be committed by the authorities or by the population; and,

(4) no activities in support of military operations shall be undertaken.

The presence, in the place, of medical units, wounded and sick, and police forces retained for the sole purpose of maintaining law and order does not change the character of such an undefended place.

40. Permissible Objects of Attack or Bombardment

a. *Attacks Against the Civilian Population as Such Prohibited.* Customary international law prohibits the launching of attacks (including bombardment) against either the civilian population as such or individual civilians as such.

b. *Defended Places.* Defended places, which are outside the scope of the proscription of Article 25, HR, are permissible objects of attack (including bombardment). In this context, defended places include—

(1) A fort or fortified place.

(2) A place that is occupied by a combatant military force or through which such a force is passing. The occupation of a place by medical units alone, however, is not sufficient to render it a permissible object of attack.

(3) A city or town surrounded by detached defense positions, if under the circumstances the city or town can be considered jointly with such defense positions as an indivisible whole.

c. *Military Objectives.* Military objectives—i. e., combatants, and those objects which by their nature, location, purpose, or use make an effective contribution to military action and whose total or partial destruction, capture or neutralization, in the circumstances ruling at the time, offers a definite military advantage—are permissible objects of attack (including bombardment). Military objectives include, for example, factories producing munitions and military supplies, military camps, warehouses storing munitions and military supplies, ports and railroads being used for the transportation of military supplies, and other places that are for the accommodation of troops or the support of military operations. Pursuant to the provisions of Article 25, HR, however, cities, towns, villages, dwellings, or buildings which may be classified as military objectives, but which are undefended (para 39b), are not permissible objects of attack.

41. Unnecessary Killing and Devastation

Particularly in the circumstances referred to in the preceding paragraph, loss of life and damage to property incidental to attacks must not be excessive in relation to the concrete and direct military advantage expected to be gained. Those who plan or decide upon an attack, therefore, must take all reasonable steps to ensure not only that the objectives are identified as military objectives or defended places within the meaning of the preceding paragraph but also that these objectives may be attacked without probable losses in lives and damage to property disproportionate to the military advantage anticipated. Moreover, once a fort or defended locality has surrendered, only such further damage is permitted as is demanded by the exigencies of war, such as the removal of fortifications, demolition of military buildings, and destruction of military stores (HR, art. 23, par. (g); GC, art. 53).

42. Aerial Bombardment

There is no prohibition of general application against bombardment from the air of combatant troops, defended places, or other legitimate military objectives.

43. Notice of Bombardment

a. Treaty Provision.

The officer in command of an attacking force must, before commencing a bombardment, except in cases of assault, do all in his power to warn the authorities. (HR, art. 26.)

b. Application of Rule. This rule is understood to refer only to bombardments of places where parts of the civil population remain.

c. When Warning is To Be Given. Even when belligerents are not subject to the above treaty, the commanders of the United States ground forces will, when the situation permits, inform the enemy of their intention to bombard a place, so that the noncombatants, especially the women and children, may be removed before the bombardment commences.

* * *

Section III.   General Protection of Prisoners of War

84. Duration of Protection

a. Treaty Provision.

The present Convention shall apply to the persons referred to in Article 4 from the time they fall into the power of the enemy and until their final release and repatriation * * *. (GPW, art. 5; see par. 71 herein.)

b. Power of the Enemy Defined. A person is considered to have fallen into the power of the enemy when he has been captured by, or surrendered to members of the military forces, the civilian police, or local civilian defense organizations or enemy civilians who have taken him into custody.

85. Killing of Prisoners

A commander may not put his prisoners to death because their presence retards his movements or diminishes his power of resistance by necessitating a large guard, or by reason of their consuming supplies, or because it appears certain that they will regain their liberty through the impending success of their forces. It is likewise unlawful for a commander to kill his prisoners on grounds of self-preservation, even in the case of airborne or commando operations, although the circumstances of the operation may make necessary rigorous supervision of and restraint upon the movement of prisoners of war.

88. Responsibility for the Treatment of Prisoners

Prisoners of war are in the hands of the enemy Power, but not of the individuals or military units who have captured them.

Irrespective of the individual responsibilities that may exist, the Detaining Power is responsible for the treatment given them.

Prisoners of war may only be transferred by the Detaining Power to a Power which is a party to the Convention and after the Detaining Power has satisfied itself of the willingness and ability of such transferee Power to apply the Convention. When prisoners of war are transferred under such circumstances, responsibility for the application of the Convention rests on the Power accepting them while they are in its custody.

Nevertheless, if that Power fails to carry out the provisions of the Convention in any important respect, the Power by whom the prisoners of war were transferred shall, upon being notified by the Protecting Power, take effective measures to correct the situation or shall request the return of the prisoners of war. Such requests must be complied with. (GPW, art. 12.)

89. Humane Treatment of Prisoners

Prisoners of war must at all times be humanely treated. Any unlawful act or omission of the Detaining Power causing death or seriously endangering the health of a prisoner of war in its custody is prohibited, and will be regarded as a serious breach of the present Convention. In particular, no prisoner of war may be subjected to physical mutilation or to medical or scientific experiments of any kind which are not justified by the medical, dental or hospital treatment of the prisoner concerned and carried out in his interest.

Likewise, prisoners of war must at all times be protected, particularly against acts of violence or intimidation and against insults and public curiosity.

Measures of reprisal against prisoners of war are prohibited. (GPW, art. 13.)

90. Respect for the Person of Prisoners

Prisoners of war are entitled in all circumstances to respect for their persons and their honour.

Women shall be treated with all the regard due to their sex and shall in all cases benefit by treatment as favourable as that granted to men.

Prisoners of war shall retain the full civil capacity which they enjoyed at the time of their capture. The Detaining Power may not restrict the exercise, either within or without its own territory, of the rights such capacity confers except in so far as the captivity requires. (GPW, art. 14.)

* * *

497. Reprisals

a. Definition. Reprisals are acts of retaliation in the form of conduct which would otherwise be unlawful, resorted to by one belligerent against enemy personnel or property for acts of warfare committed by the other belligerent in violation of the law of war, for the purpose of enforcing future compliance with the recognized rules of civilized warfare. For example, the employment by a belligerent of a weapon the use of which is normally precluded by the law of war would constitute a lawful reprisal for intentional mistreatment of prisoners of war held by the enemy.

b. *Priority of Other Remedies.* Other means of securing compliance with the law of war should normally be exhausted before resort is had to reprisals. This course should be pursued unless the safety of the troops requires immediate drastic action and the persons who actually committed the offenses cannot be secured. Even when appeal to the enemy for redress has failed, it may be a matter of policy to consider, before resorting to reprisals, whether the opposing forces are not more likely to be influenced by a steady adherence to the law of war on the part of their adversary.

c. *Against Whom Permitted.* Reprisals against the persons or property of prisoners of war, including the wounded and sick, and protected civilians are forbidden (GPW, art. 13; GC, art. 33). Collective penalties and punishment of prisoners of war and protected civilians are likewise prohibited (GPW, art. 87; GC, art. 33). However, reprisals may still be visited on enemy troops who have not yet fallen into the hands of the forces making the reprisals.

d. *When and How Employed.* Reprisals are never adopted merely for revenge, but only as an unavoidable last resort to induce the enemy to desist from unlawful practices. They should never be employed by individual soldiers except by direct orders of a commander, and the latter should give such orders only after careful inquiry into the alleged offense. The highest accessible military authority should be consulted unless immediate action is demanded, in which event a subordinate commander may order appropriate reprisals upon his own initiative. Ill-considered action may subsequently be found to have been wholly unjustified and will subject the responsible officer himself to punishment for a violation of the law of war. On the other hand, commanding officers must assume responsibility for retaliative measures when an unscrupulous enemy leaves no other recourse against the repetition of unlawful acts.

e. *Form of Reprisal.* The acts resorted to by way of reprisal need not conform to those complained of by the injured party, but should not be excessive or exceed the degree of violence committed by the enemy.

f. *Procedure.* The rule requiring careful inquiry into the real occurrence will always be followed unless the safety of the troops requires immediate drastic action and the persons who actually committed the offense cannot be ascertained.

g. *Hostages.* The taking of hostages is forbidden (GC, art. 34). The taking of prisoners by way of reprisal for acts previously committed (so-called "reprisal prisoners") is likewise forbidden. (See GC, art. 33.)

* * *

502.   Grave Breaches of the Geneva Conventions of 1949 as War Crimes

The Geneva Conventions of 1949 define the following acts as "grave breaches," if committed against persons or property protected by the Conventions:

a.   GWS and GWS Sea.

Grave breaches to which the preceding Article relates shall be those involving any of the following acts, if committed against persons or property protected by the Convention: wilful killing, torture or inhuman treatment, including biological experiments, wilfully causing great suffering or serious injury to body or health, and extensive destruction and appropriation of property, not justified by military necessity and carried out unlawfully and wantonly.   (GWS, art. 50; GWS Sea, art. 51.)

b.   GPW.

Grave breaches to which the preceding Article relates shall be those involving any of the following acts, if committed against persons or property protected by the Convention: wilful killing, torture or inhuman treatment, including biological experiments, wilfully causing great suffering or serious injury to body or health, compelling a prisoner of war to serve in the forces of the hostile Power, or wilfully depriving a prisoner of war of the rights of fair and regular trial prescribed in this Convention. (GPW, art. 130.)

c.   GC.

Grave breaches to which the preceding Article relates shall be those involving any of the following acts, if committed against persons or property protected by the present Convention: wilful killing, torture or inhuman treatment, including biological experiments, wilfully causing great suffering or serious injury to body or health, unlawful deportation or transfer or unlawful confinement of a protected person, compelling a protected person to serve in the forces of a hostile Power, or wilfully depriving a protected person of the rights of fair and regular trial prescribed in the present Convention, taking of hostages and extensive destruction and appropriation of property, not justified by military necessity and carried out unlawfully and wantonly. (GC, art. 147.)

503.   Responsibilities of the Contracting Parties

No High Contracting Party shall be allowed to absolve itself or any other High Contracting Party of any liability incurred by itself or by another High Contracting Party in respect of breaches referred to in the preceding Article.   (GWS, art. 51; GWS Sea, art. 52; GPW, art. 131; GC, art. 148.)

504.   Other Types of War Crimes

In addition to the "grave breaches" of the Geneva Conventions of 1949, the following acts are representative of violations of the law of war ("war crimes"):

a.   Making use of poisoned or otherwise forbidden arms or ammunition.

b.   Treacherous request for quarter.

c.   Maltreatment of dead bodies.

d.   Firing on localities which are undefended and without military significance.

e.   Abuse of or firing on the flag of truce.

f.   Misuse of the Red Cross emblem.

g.   Use of civilian clothing by troops to conceal their military character during battle.

h.   Improper use of privileged buildings for military purposes.

i.   Poisoning of wells or streams.

j.   Pillage or purposeless destruction.

k.   Compelling prisoners of war to perform prohibited labor.

l.   Killing without trial spies or other persons who have committed hostile acts.

m.   Compelling civilians to perform prohibited labor.

n.   Violation of surrender terms.

"THE CHRISTMAS BOMBING" [a]

The New York Times, Dec. 31, 1972, Sec. 4, p. 1, col. 1.

Saigon—Air raid sirens scream day and night. The earth trembles with the violence of an earthquake, and whole sections of the city crumble in a roar of flames and flying jagged steel. For the first time in the war the people seem afraid.

This is Hanoi under attack by American B–52's, as described by Westerners who have been there. The big bombers, flying in wedges of three, lay down more than 65 tons of bombs at a time in a carpet pattern a mile and a half long and a half mile wide.

For nearly two weeks now the city has been the focal point of a siege by American bombers that has extended across the densely populated heart of North Vietnam. Hundreds, if not thousands, of civilians are believed to have been killed. Even during a 36-hour bombing halt at Christmas, reconnaissance planes swooped over Hanoi keeping the people's nerves on edge.

The destruction, said one Westerner who left Hanoi last week, is "unbelievable."

The B–52's reportedly have destroyed about 80 per cent of the Gia Lam International Airport buildings in the capital. The main railroad station and yards in downtown Hanoi have been smashed, and much of the Bach Mai Hospital also is said to have been reduced to rubble.

Although North Vietnamese officials have been advising city dwellers for some time to move into the countryside as a precaution against just this kind of intensive raids, intelligence sources here say that many persons disregarded the advice and only now are evacuating the prime target areas.

For the first 10 days of the raids that started Dec. 18 the United States military command here maintained official silence on the scope of the operations and the damage, saying that "military security" was at stake.

Last Wednesday it released a report of some 50 targets that had been bombed at least once in the first seven days of the raids. The command further disclosed that there had been more than 1,000 strikes by fighter-bombers during the week and 147 B–52 missions, each presumed to consist of at least three planes.

Nineteen of the targets were within 10 miles of the center of Hanoi. Among them were the city's thermal power plant and its port facilities. Another seven of them were within six miles of the center of Haiphong, including a shipyard, a naval base and an airfield. There were several other targets in and around the cities of Thai Nguyen to the north and Thanh Hoa on the southern coast.

The American command maintained that all of these were "military targets," and spokesmen would not respond to questions about the international airport or the hospital in Hanoi, or even acknowledge that some of the small brick homes with red tiled roofs packed closely together in the cities were being flattened. It also would not acknowledge that there were any civilian casualties.

"We have targeted and continue to target only military targets," Maj. Gilbert L. Whiteman, a spokesman for the command, said.

The command likewise would not comment on reports from Radio Hanoi that B–52's had cut swaths through several of the compact, circular farming villages that dot the fertile delta. Several of the "military targets" were being bombed for the first time, the command admitted, without adding that they had previously been proscribed because to attack them increased the chances of killing civilans.

One of the major reasons that B–52's had not previously been used in North Vietnam in great numbers, a senior Air Force officer said in a recent interview, was the increased threat they posed to the civilian population. "Even with the accuracy we get," the officer said, "we're still not sure we would not get a little more than military targets."

The North Vietnamese Foreign Ministry charged at midweek that the bombing had "caused thousands of deaths [and] destroyed thousands of homes."

Losses on the American side have been grave, too. By Friday evening the American command had acknowledged the loss of 25 aircraft—including 15 B-52's which are valued at about $8-million each —and indicated that at least 82 American airmen were missing or captured. One American official said the losses were a measure of Mr. Nixon's intention to "go all out."

"In May the policy was 'If you lose a B-52 you're in trouble,'" the official said. "When we start losing as many B-52's as we've lost in the last few days, you know that a lot of scruples and constraints have been done away with. We've always tried to avoid civilian casualties, but now it looks like someone has said, 'Well, it may not be nice, but we've just got to do it.'"

It is widely believed here that the massive new bombing is being closely supervised by President Nixon. He has shrouded the operation in extremely tight military security, withholding the sketchiest of information from some of the highest ranking civilian and military officials in Saigon. Informed officers say that the daily staff briefings at the command headquarters here have been restricted to intelligence and operations officers only and their commanders.

Some officials have suggested that part of the reason for this is that the South Vietnamese Government is believed to have been "penetrated" by enemy agents. Other officials and some newsmen, however, said they failed to understand the secrecy and believed strongly that it was a conscious attempt to allow only the barest details of the bombing to reach the American public.

Military spokesmen here and in Washington initially said that the bombing had been ordered to head off preparations for a new offensive by the North. That line of reasoning could have been called into play at almost any time in the history of the conflict because the North Vietnamese have always either been engaged in an offensive or planning one. But officials here said they saw no activity by the North Vietnamese prior to the latest air raids that in itself would have warranted such a massive response.

The only genuine reason universally accepted here for the new bombing was that Mr. Nixon was determined to bring the North Vietnamese to their knees, bludgeoning them with bombs into accepting terms for peace that the President believed were favorable to the United States and South Vietnam.

South Vietnamese Government officials thoroughly endorse the bombing. It might bring about a settlement, some of them say. If not, at least it will weaken the North for future battles.

KISSINGER, WHITE HOUSE YEARS, 1454, 1460 (1979)

"Indiscriminate carpet bombing of heavily populated areas" was the principal accusation. Once the phrase caught on among commentators, it took on a life of its own. The facts were otherwise. A scholar who has examined the evidence writes:

These charges are disproven by evidence available then and by later reports from the scene. The North Vietnamese themselves at the time claimed between 1,300 and 1,600 fatalities, and even though both Hanoi and Haiphong were partially evacuated, such a number of victims—regrettable as any civilian casualties always are—is surely not indicative of terror-bombing. Attacks explicitly aimed at the morale of the population took place against Germany and Japan during World War II and killed tens of thousands. According to an East German estimate, 35,000 died in the triple raid on Dresden in February 1945; the official casualty toll of the bombing of Tokyo with incendiaries on 9–10 March 1945, stands at 83,793 dead and 40,918 wounded. The Hanoi death toll, wrote the London Economist, "is smaller than the number of civilians killed by the North Vietnamese in their artillery bombardment of An Loc in April or the toll of refugees ambushed when trying to escape from Quang Tri at the beginning of May. This is what makes the denunciation of Mr. Nixon as another Hitler sound so unreal." Part of the death toll was undoubtedly caused by the North Vietnamese themselves, for they launched about 1,000 SAMs, many of which impacted in the cities of Hanoi and Haiphong and took their toll on their own people.

* * *

Malcolm W. Browne of the New York Times was greatly surprised by the condition in which he found Hanoi and wrote that "the damage caused by American bombing was grossly overstated by North Vietnamese propaganda. * * *." "Hanoi has certainly been damaged," noted Peter Ward of the Baltimore Sun on 25 March 1973 after a visit, "but evidence on the ground disproves charges of indiscriminate bombing. Several bomb loads obviously went astray into civilian residential areas, but damage there is minor, compared to the total destruction of selected targets." a

* * *

No foreign policy event of the Nixon Presidency evoked such outrage as the Christmas bombing. On no issue was he more unjustly treated. It was not a barbarous act of revenge. It did not cause exorbitant casualties by Hanoi's own figures; certainly it cost much less than the continuation of the war, which was the alternative. It is hard to avoid the impression that a decade of frustration with Vietnam, a generation of hostility to Nixon, and—let me be frank—

a. From America in Vietnam by Guenter Lewy, pp. 413–414. Copyright © 1978 by Guenter Lewy. Reprinted by permission of Oxford University Press.

frustration over his electoral triumph coalesced to produce a unanimity of editorial outrage that suppressed all judgment in an emotional orgy. Any other course would almost certainly have witnessed an endless repetition of the tactics of December. Faced with the prospect of an open-ended war and continued bitter divisions, considering that the weather made the usual bombing ineffective, Nixon chose the only weapon he had available. His decision speeded the end of the war; even in retrospect I can think of no other measure that would have.

SECTION B. THE INNOVATIONS OF NUREMBERG:
CRIMES AGAINST PEACE AND CRIMES
AGAINST HUMANITY

CHARTER OF THE INTERNATIONAL MILITARY TRIBUNAL

59 Stat. 1544, 1546.

Article 1. In pursuance of the Agreement signed on the 8th day of August 1945 by the Government of the United States of America, the Provisional Government of the French Republic, the Government of the United Kingdom of Great Britain and Northern Ireland and the Goverment of the Union of Soviet Socialist Republics, there shall be established an International Military Tribunal (hereinafter called "the Tribunal") for the just and prompt trial and punishment of the major war criminals of the European Axis.

Article 2. The Tribunal shall consist of four members, each with an alternate. One member and one alternate shall be appointed by each of the Signatories. *   *   *

   *   *   *

Article 6. The Tribunal established by the Agreement referred to in Article 1 hereof for the trial and punishment of the major war criminals of the European Axis countries shall have the power to try and punish persons who, acting in the interests of the European Axis countries, whether as individuals or as members of organizations, committed any of the following crimes.

The following acts, or any of them, are crimes coming within the jurisdiction of the Tribunal for which there shall be individual responsibility:

  (a) CRIMES AGAINST PEACE: namely, planning, preparation, initiation or waging of a war of aggression, or a war in violation of international treaties, agreements or assurances, or participation in a common plan or conspiracy for the accomplishment of any of the foregoing;

  (b) WAR CRIMES: namely, violations of the laws or customs of war. Such violations shall include, but not be limited to, murder, ill-treatment or deportation to slave labor or for any

other purpose of civilian population of or in occupied territory, murder or ill-treatment of prisoners of war or persons
on the seas, killing of hostages, plunder of public or private
property, wanton destruction of cities, towns or villages, or
devastation not justified by military necessity;

(c) CRIMES AGAINST HUMANITY: namely, murder, extermination, enslavement, deportation, and other inhumane
acts committed against any civilian population, before or
during the war;[1] or persecutions on political, racial or religious grounds in execution of or in connection with any
crime within the jurisdiction of the Tribunal, whether or not
in violation of the domestic law of the country where perpetrated.

Leaders, organizers, instigators and accomplices participating in
the formulation or execution of a common plan or conspiracy to commit any of the foregoing crimes are responsible for all acts performed
by any persons in execution of such plan.

Article 7.   The official position of defendants, whether as Heads
of State or responsible officials in Government Departments, shall not
be considered as freeing them from responsibility or mitigating punishment.

Article 8.   The fact that the Defendant acted pursuant to order
of his Government or of a superior shall not free him from responsibility, but may be considered in mitigation of punishment if the Tribunal determines that justice so requires.

Article 9.   At the trial of any individual member of any group
or organization the Tribunal may declare (in connection with any act
of which the individual may be convicted) that the group or organization of which the individual was a member was a criminal organization.

After receipt of the Indictment the Tribunal shall give such notice as it thinks fit that the prosecution intends to ask the Tribunal to
make such declaration and any member of the organization will be
entitled to apply to the Tribunal for leave to be heard by the Tribunal
upon the question of the criminal character of the organization.   The
Tribunal shall have power to allow or reject the application.   If the
application is allowed, the Tribunal may direct in what manner the
applicants shall be represented and heard.

Article 10.   In cases where a group or organization is declared
criminal by the Tribunal, the competent national authority of any
Signatory shall have the right to bring individuals to trial for membership therein before national, military or occupation courts.   In
any such case the criminal nature of the group or organization is considered proved and shall not be questioned.

[1] [The contracting governments signed a protocol at Berlin on Oct. 6, 1945 * * * which provides that this semi-colon in the English text should be changed to a comma.]

Article 11. Any person convicted by the Tribunal may be charged before a national, military or occupation court, referred to in Article 10 of this Charter, with a crime other than of membership in a criminal group or organization and such court may, after convicting him, impose upon him punishment independent of and additional to the punishment imposed by the Tribunal for participation in the criminal activities of such group or organization.

Article 12. The Tribunal shall have the right to take proceedings against a person charged with crimes set out in Article 6 of this Charter in his absence, if he has not been found or if the Tribunal, for any reason, finds it necessary, in the interests of justice, to conduct the hearing in his absence.

* * *

Article 26. The judgment of the Tribunal as to the guilt or the innocence of any Defendant shall give the reasons on which it is based, and shall be final and not subject to review.

Article 27. The Tribunal shall have the right to impose upon a Defendant, on conviction, death or such other punishment as shall be determined by it to be just.

JUDGMENT OF THE INTERNATIONAL MILITARY TRIBUNAL, NUREMBERG, GERMANY, 1946

Nazi Conspiracy and Aggression
(U.S. Gov't Printing Office, 1947).

III. THE COMMON PLAN OF CONSPIRACY AND AGGRESSIVE WAR

The Tribunal now turns to the consideration of the crimes against peace charged in the indictment. Count one of the indictment charges the defendants with conspiring or having a common plan to commit crimes against peace. Count two of the indictment charges the defendants with committing specific crimes against peace by planning, preparing, initiating, and waging wars of aggression against a number of other States. It will be convenient to consider the question of the existence of a common plan and the question of aggressive war together, and to deal later in this judgment with the question of the individual responsibility of the defendants.

The charges in the indictment that the defendants planned and waged aggressive wars are charges of the utmost gravity. War is essentially an evil thing. Its consequences are not confined to the belligerent states alone, but affect the whole world.

To initiate a war of aggression, therefore, is not only an international crime; it is the supreme international crime differing only from other war crimes in that it contains within itself the accumulated evil of the whole.

The first acts of aggression referred to in the indictment are the seizure of Austria and Czechoslovakia; and the first war of aggression charged in the indictment is the war against Poland begun on the 1st September 1939.

Before examining that charge it is necessary to look more closely at some of the events which preceded these acts of aggression. The war against Poland did not come suddenly out of an otherwise clear sky; the evidence has made it plain that this war of aggression, as well as the seizure of Austria and Czechoslovakia, was premeditated and carefully prepared, and was not undertaken until the moment was thought opportune for it to be carried through as a definite part of the preordained scheme and plan.

For the aggressive designs of the Nazi Government were not accidents arising out of the immediate political situation in Europe and the world; they were a deliberate and essential part of Nazi foreign policy.

From the beginning, the National Socialist movement claimed that its object was to unite the German people in the consciousness of their mission and destiny, based on inherent qualities of race, and under the guidance of the Fuehrer.

For its achievement, two things were deemed to be essential: The disruption of the European order as it had existed since the Treaty of Versailles, and the creation of a Greater Germany beyond the frontiers of 1914. This necessarily involved the seizure of foreign territories.

War was seen to be inevitable, or at the very least, highly probable, if these purposes were to be accomplished. The German people, therefore, with all their resources, were to be organized as a great political-military army, schooled to obey without question any policy decreed by the State.

*   *   *

IV. VIOLATIONS OF INTERNATIONAL TREATIES

The Charter defines as a crime the planning or waging of war that is a war of aggression or a war in violation of international treaties. The Tribunal has decided that certain of the defendants planned and waged aggressive wars against 10 nations, and were therefore guilty of this series of crimes. This makes it unnecessary to discuss the subject in further detail, or even to consider at any length the extent to which these aggressive wars were also "wars in violation of international treaties, agreements. or assurances." These treaties are set out in appendix C of the indictment. Those of principal importance are the following:

(A) Hague Conventions

In the 1899 Convention the signatory powers agreed: "before an appeal to arms * * * to have recourse, as far as circumstances allow, to the good offices or mediation of one or more friendly powers." A similar clause was inserted in the Convention for Pacific Settlement of International Disputes of 1907. In the accompanying Convention Relative to Opening of Hostilities, article I contains this far more specific language:

> The Contracting Powers recognize that hostilities between them must not commence without a previous and explicit warning, in the form of either a declaration of war, giving reasons, or an ultimatum with a conditional declaration of war.

Germany was a party to these conventions.

(B) Versailles Treaty

Breaches of certain provisions of the Versailles Treaty are also relied on by the prosecution—not to fortify the left bank of the Rhine (art. 42–44); to "respect strictly the independence of Austria" (art. 80); renunciation of any rights in Memel (art. 99) and the Free City of Danzig (art. 100); the recognition of the independence of the Czecho-Slovak State; and the Military, Naval, and Air Clauses against German rearmament found in part V. There is no doubt that action was taken by the German Government contrary to all these provisions, the details of which are set out in appendix C. With regard to the Treaty of Versailles, the matters relied on are:

1. The violation of articles 42 to 44 in respect of the demilitarized zone of the Rhineland.

2. The annexation of Austria on the 13th March 1938, in violation of article 80.

3. The incorporation of the district of Memel on the 22d March 1939, in violation of article 99.

4. The incorporation of the Free City of Danzig on the 1st September 1939, in violation of article 100.

5. The incorporation of the provinces of Bohemia and Moravia on the 16th March 1939, in violation of article 81.

6. The repudiation of the military, naval and air clauses of the treaty in or about March of 1935.

On the 21st May 1935, Germany announced that, whilst renouncing the disarmament clauses of the treaty, she would still respect the territorial limitations, and would comply with the Locarno Pact. (With regard to the first five breaches alleged, therefore, the Tribunal finds the allegation proved.)

* * *

(E) The Law of the Charter

The jurisdiction of the Tribunal is defined in the Agreement and Charter, and the crimes coming within the jurisdiction of the Tribunal, for which there shall be individual responsibility, are set out in Article 6. The law of the Charter is decisive, and binding upon the Tribunal.

The making of the Charter was the exercise of the sovereign legislative power by the countries to which the German Reich unconditionally surrendered; and the undoubted right of these countries to legislate for the occupied territories has been recognized by the civilized world. The Charter is not an arbitrary exercise of power on the part of the victorious nations, but in the view of the Tribunal, as will be shown, it is the expression of international law existing at the time of its creation; and to that extent is itself a contribution to international law.

*   *   *

*   *   * [T]he very essence of the Charter is that individuals have international duties which transcend the national obligations of obedience imposed by the individual State. He who violates the laws of war cannot obtain immunity while acting in pursuance of the authority of the State if the State in authorizing action moves outside its competence under international law.

It was also submitted on behalf of most of these defendants that in doing what they did they were acting under the orders of Hitler, and therefore cannot be held responsible for the acts committed by them in carrying out these orders. The Charter specifically provides in Article 8:

> The fact that the defendant acted pursuant to order of his Government or of a superior shall not free him from responsibility, but may be considered in mitigation of punishment.

The provisions of this Article are in conformity with the law of all nations. That a soldier was ordered to kill or torture in violation of the international law of war has never been recognized as a defense to such acts of brutality, though, as the Charter here provides, the order may be urged in mitigation of the punishment. The true test, which is found in varying degrees in the criminal law of most nations, is not the existence of the order, but whether moral choice was in fact possible.

V. The Law as to the Common Plan or Conspiracy

In the previous recital of the facts relating to aggressive war, it is clear that planning and preparation had been carried out in the most systematic way at every stage of the history.

*   *   *

In the opinion of the Tribunal, the evidence establishes the common planning to prepare and wage war by certain of the defendants. It is immaterial to consider whether a single conspiracy to the extent and over the time set out in the indictment has been conclusively proved. Continued planning, with aggressive war as the objective, has been established beyond doubt. The truth of the situation was well stated by Paul Schmidt, official interpreter of the German Foreign Office, as follows:

> "The general objectives of the Nazi leadership were apparent from the start, namely the domination of the European Continent, to be achieved first by the incorporation of all German-speaking groups in the Reich, and, secondly, by territorial expansion under the slogan "Lebensraum." The execution of these ba-

sic objectives, however, seemed to be characterized by improvisation. Each succeeding step was apparently carried out as each new situation arose, but all consistent with the ultimate objectives mentioned above."

The argument that such common planning cannot exist where there is complete dictatorship is unsound. A plan in the execution of which a number of persons participate is still a plan, even though conceived by only one of them; and those who execute the plan do not avoid responsibility by showing that they acted under the direction of the man who conceived it. Hitler could not make aggressive war by himself. He had to have the cooperation of statesmen, military leaders, diplomats, and businessmen. When they, with knowledge of his aims, gave him their cooperation, they made themselves parties to the plan he had initiated. They are not to be deemed innocent because Hitler made use of them, if they knew what they were doing. That they were assigned to their tasks by a dictator does not absolve them from responsibility for their acts. The relation of leader and follower does not preclude responsibility here any more than it does in the comparable tyranny of organized domestic crime.

* * *

VI.   WAR CRIMES AND CRIMES AGAINST HUMANITY

The evidence relating to war crimes has been overwhelming, in its volume and its detail. It is impossible for this judgment adequately to review it, or to record the mass of documentary and oral evidence that has been presented. The truth remains that war crimes were committed on a vast scale, never before seen in the history of war. They were perpetrated in all the countries occupied by Germany, and on the high seas, and were attended by every conceivable circumstance of cruelty and horror. There can be no doubt that the majority of them arose from the Nazi conception of "total war," with which the aggressive wars were waged. For in this conception of "total war" the moral ideas underlying the conventions which seek to make war more humane are no longer regarded as having force or validity. Everything is made subordinate to the overmastering dictates of war. Rules, regulations, assurances, and treaties, all alike, are of no moment; and so, freed from the restraining influence of international law, the aggressive war is conducted by the Nazi leaders in the most barbaric way. Accordingly, war crimes were committed when and wherever the Fuehrer and his close associates thought them to be advantageous. They were for the most part the result of cold and criminal calculation.

On some occasions war crimes were deliberately planned long in advance. In the case of the Soviet Union, the plunder of the territories to be occupied, and the ill-treatment of the civilian population, were settled in minute detail before the attack was begun. As early as the autumn of 1940, the invasion of the territories of the Soviet Union was being considered. From that date onwards, the methods to be employed in destroying all possible opposition were continuously under discussion.

Similarly, when planning to exploit the inhabitants of the occupied countries for slave labor on the very greatest scale, the German Government conceived it as an integral part of the war economy, and planned and organized this particular war crime down to the last elaborate detail.

Other war crimes, such as the murder of prisoners of war who had escaped and been recaptured, or the murder of commandos or captured airmen, or the destruction of the Soviet commissars, were the result of direct orders circulated through the highest official channels.

The Tribunal proposes, therefore, to deal quite generally with the question of war crimes, and to refer to them later when examining the responsibility of the individual defendants in relation to them. Prisoners of war were ill-treated and tortured and murdered, not only in defiance of the well-established rules of international law, but in complete disregard of the elementary dictates of humanity. Civilian populations in occupied territories suffered the same fate. Whole populations were deported to Germany for the purposes of slave labor upon defense works, armament production and similar tasks connected with the war effort. Hostages were taken in very large numbers from the civilian populations in all the occupied countries, and were shot as suited the German purposes. Public and private property was systematically plundered and pillaged in order to enlarge the resources of Germany at the expense of the rest of Europe. Cities and towns and villages were wantonly destroyed without military justification or necessity.

(A) Murder and Ill-Treatment of Prisoners of War

Article 6(b) of the Charter defines war crimes in these words:

War Crimes: namely, violations of the laws or customs of war. Such violations shall include, but not be limited to, murder, ill-treatment or deportation to slave labor or for any other purpose of civilian population of or in occupied territory, murder or ill-treatment of prisoners of war or persons on the seas, killing of hostages, plunder of public or private property, wanton destruction of cities, towns, or villages, or devastation not justified by military necessity.

In the course of the war, many Allied soldiers who had surrendered to the Germans were shot immediately, often as a matter of deliberate, calculated policy.   *   *   *

*   *   *

When Allied airmen were forced to land in Germany they were sometimes killed at once by the civilian population. The police were instructed not to interfere with these killings, and the Ministry of Justice was informed that no one should be prosecuted for taking part in them.

The treatment of Soviet prisoners of war was characterized by particular inhumanity. The death of so many of them was not due merely to the action of individual guards, or to the exigencies of life in the camps. It was the result of systematic plans to murder. * * *

* * *

(B) Murder and Ill-Treatment of Civilian Population

Article 6(b) of the Charter provides that "ill-treatment * * * of civilian population of or in occupied territory * * * killing of hostages * * * wanton destruction of cities, towns, or villages" shall be a war crime. In the main, these provisions are merely declaratory of the existing laws of war as expressed by the Hague Convention, Article 46, which stated:

Family honor and rights, the lives of persons and private property, as well as religious convictions and practice, must be respected.

The territories occupied by Germany were administered in violation of the laws of war. The evidence is quite overwhelming of a systematic rule of violence, brutality, and terror. On the 7th December 1941, Hitler issued the directive since known as the "Nacht und Nebel Erlass" (night and fog decree), under which persons who committed offenses against the Reich or the German forces in occupied territories, except where the death sentence was certain, were to be taken secretly to Germany and handed over to the SIPO and SD for trial or punishment in Germany. * * *

Even persons who were only suspected of opposing any of the policies of the German occupation authorities were arrested, and on arrest were interrogated by the Gestapo and the SD in the most shameful manner. * * *

* * *

The practice of keeping hostages to prevent and to punish any form of civil disorder was resorted to by the Germans; an order issued by the defendant Keitel on the 16th September 1941, spoke in terms of fifty or a hundred lives from the occupied areas of the Soviet Union for one German life taken. The order stated that "it should be remembered that a human life in unsettled countries frequently counts for nothing, and a deterrent effect can be obtained only by unusual severity." The exact number of persons killed as a result of this policy is not known, but large numbers were killed in France and the other occupied territories in the west, while in the east the slaughter was on an even more extensive scale. * * *

* * *

(D) Slave Labor Policy

Article 6(b) of the Charter provides that the "ill-treatment or deportation to slave labor or for any other purpose, of civilian population of or in occupied territory" shall be a war crime. The laws relating to forced labor by the inhabitants of occupied territories are found in Article 52 of the Hague Convention, which provides:

> Requisition in kind and services shall not be demanded from municipalities or inhabitants except for the needs of the army of occupation. They shall be in proportion to the resources of the country, and of such a nature as not to involve the inhabitants in the obligation of taking part in military operations against their own country.

The policy of the German occupation authorities was in flagrant violation of the terms of this convention. Some idea of this policy may be gathered from the statement made by Hitler in a speech on November 9, 1941:

> The territory which now works for us contains more than 250,000,000 men, but the territory which works indirectly for us includes now more than 350,000,000. In the measure in which it concerns German territory, the domain which we have taken under our administration, it is not doubtful that we shall succeed in harnessing the very last man to this work.

The actual results achieved were not so complete as this, but the German occupation authorities did succeed in forcing many of the inhabitants of the occupied territories to work for the German war effort, and in deporting at least 5,000,000 persons to Germany to serve German industry and agriculture.

*   *   *

(E) Persecution of the Jews

The persecution of the Jews at the hands of the Nazi Government has been proved in the greatest detail before the Tribunal. It is a record of consistent and systematic inhumanity on the greatest scale. *   *   *

*   *   *

*   *   * Adolf Eichmann, who had been put in charge of this program by Hitler, has estimated that the policy pursued resulted in the killing of 6,000,000 Jews, of which 4,000,000 were killed in the extermination institutions.

(F) The Law Relating to War Crimes and Crimes Against Humanity

*   *   *

The Tribunal is of course bound by the Charter, in the definition which it gives both of war crimes and crimes against humanity. With respect to war crimes, however, as has already been pointed out, the crimes defined by Article 6, section (b), of the Charter were already recognized as war crimes under international law. They were covered by Articles 46, 50, 52, and 56 of the Hague Convention of 1907, and Articles 2, 3, 4, 46, and 51 of the Geneva Convention of 1929. That violation of these provisions constituted crimes for which the guilty individuals were punishable is too well settled to admit of argument.

But it is argued that the Hague Convention does not apply in this case, because of the "general participation" clause in Article 2 of the Hague Convention of 1907. That clause provided:

> The provisions contained in the regulations (rules of land warfare) referred to in Article I as well as in the present convention do not apply except between contracting powers, and then only if all the belligerents are parties to the convention.

Several of the belligerents in the recent war were not parties to this convention.

In the opinion of the Tribunal it is not necessary to decide this question. The rules of land warfare expressed in the convention undoubtedly represented an advance over existing international law at the time of their adoption. But the convention expressly stated that it was an attempt "to revise the general laws and customs of war," which it thus recognized to be then existing, but by 1939 these rules laid down in the convention were recognized by all civilized nations, and were regarded as being declaratory of the laws and customs of war which are referred to in Article 6 (b) of the Charter.

A further submission was made that Germany was no longer bound by the rules of land warfare in many of the territories occupied during the war, because Germany had completely subjugated those countries and incorporated them into the German Reich, a fact which gave Germany authority to deal with the occupied countries as though they were part of Germany. In the view of the Tribunal it is unnecessary in this case to decide whether this doctrine of subjugation, dependent as it is upon military conquest, has any application where the subjugation is the result of the crime of aggressive war.

*   *   *

With regard to crimes against humanity, there is no doubt whatever that political opponents were murdered in Germany before the war, and that many of them were kept in concentration camps in circumstances of great horror and cruelty. The policy of terror was certainly carried out on a vast scale, and in many cases was organized and systematic. The policy of persecution, repression, and murder of civilians in Germany before the war of 1939, who were likely to be hostile to the Government, was most ruthlessly carried out. The persecution of Jews during the same period is established beyond all doubt. To constitute crimes against humanity, the acts relied on before the outbreak of war must have been in execution of, or in connection with, any crime within the jurisdiction of the Tribunal. The Tribunal is of the opinion that revolting and horrible as many of these crimes were, it has not been satisfactorily proved that they were done in execution of, or in connection with, any such crime. The Tribunal therefore cannot make a general declaration that the acts before 1939 were crimes against humanity within the meaning of the Charter, but from the beginning of the war in 1939 war crimes were committed on a vast scale, which were also crimes against humanity; and insofar as the inhumane acts charged in the indictment, and committed after the beginning of the war, did not constitute war crimes, they were all committed in execution of, or in connection with, the aggressive war, and therefore constituted crimes against humanity.

*   *   *

VERDICTS AND SENTENCES OF THE INTERNATIONAL MILITARY TRIBUNAL

Calvocaressi, Nuremberg 141 (1947).

	Charges Counts				Verdicts Counts				Sentences
	1	2	3	4	1	2	3	4	
Goering [a]	X	X	X	X	X	X	X	X	Death.
Ribbentrop	X	X	X	X	X	X	X	X	
Keitel	X	X	X	X	X	X	X	X	
Jodl	X	X	X	X	X	X	X	X	
Rosenberg	X	X	X	X	X	X	X	X	
Frick	X	X	X	X		X	X	X	
Seyss-Inquart	X	X	X	X		X	X	X	
Sauckel	X	X	X	X			X	X	
Bormann [b]	X		X	X			X	X	
Kaltenbrunner	X		X	X			X	X	
Frank	X		X	X			X	X	
Streicher	X			X				X	
Raeder	X	X	X	X	X	X	X		Life.
Funk	X	X	X	X		X	X	X	
Hess [c]	X	X	X	X	X	X			
Speer	X	X	X	X			X	X	20 years.
Schirach	X			X				X	
Neurath	X	X	X	X	X	X	X	X	15 years.
Doenitz	X	X	X			X	X		10 years.
Fritzsche	X		X	X					Acquitted.
von Papen	X	X							
Schacht	X			X					

Other trials in Germany. In an article entitled The Eichmann Case and the Nuremberg Trials, 48 A.B.A.J. 738 (1962), Lippert states:

As a follow-up to the International Military Tribunal (IMT) case, the United States had planned to prosecute high-ranking

---

a. Committed suicide.

b. Tried in absentia; never found.

c. The only defendant still imprisoned.

officials of the security and police services, but after investigation it was realized that few were available for trial. Justice Jackson's successor as United States Prosecutor, Brigadier General Telford Taylor, reported that "Many of them were known to be dead and others missing could not be located." It cannot be doubted that the missing Eichmann, the very man named by the IMT, was one of those whose trial had been contemplated, such to be held before one of the United States courts that were established in Nuremberg in 1946 after the IMT finished its work.

These courts which were known as United States Military Tribunals, were staffed by judges who were drawn from the Bench and Bar of the United States. Before one or the other of them, there appeared 177 members of the SS and police, doctors, judges, lawyers, industrialists, government ministers and military leaders. Of this total 142 were found guilty, in greater or less degree, of the war crimes, crimes against peace, and crimes against humanity, of which they were charged, and twelve were executed pursuant to the death penalty imposed. The trial of the jurists has become well known by reason of the fictional version of it portrayed in the film "Judgment at Nuremberg."

Moreover, there were still other United States courts in Germany which could have taken jurisdiction of Eichmann's case at the time. Concurrently with the trials in Nuremberg an equally monumental judicial undertaking was in progress in Dachau, a suburb of Munich, and previously the site of one of the infamous extermination camps, complete with gas chamber and ovens. Here the United States Army in a staggering total of 489 trials prosecuted those charged with crimes committed against United States soldiers and those having complicity in the operation of the concentration camps liberated by United States troops. Of the 1,672 persons accused, 1,347 were found guilty and 258 suffered the death penalty. * * *

UNITED STATES v. VON LEEB (THE HIGH COMMAND CASE)

American Military Tribunal (Tribunal V), 1948.
XI Trials of War Criminals 462 (1950).

Presiding Judge YOUNG: The Tribunal will now proceed to read the judgment.

This Tribunal is composed of Presiding Judge John C. Young (formerly Chief Justice of the Supreme Court of Colorado), and Associate Judges Justin W. Harding (formerly U. S. District Judge, First Division, District of Alaska) and Winfield B. Hale (Justice, Tennessee Court of Appeals, on leave of absence).

It was created under and by virtue of Military Government Ordinance No. 7, effective 18 October 1946 adopted pursuant to Control Council Law No. 10, enacted 20 December 1945, in order to give effect to the London Agreement of 8 August 1945, and the Charter issued pursuant thereto for the prosecution of war criminals.

In Nuernberg, on 28 November 1947, in accordance with Ordinance No. 7 (Article III(a)) supra, an indictment was lodged against the defendants by Telford Taylor, Brigadier General, U.S.A., Chief of Counsel for War Crimes, acting in behalf of the United States of America. A copy of the indictment in the German language was served upon each defendant at least thirty days prior to arraignment on 30 December 1947, at which time each, in the presence of counsel of his own selection, entered a plea of "not guilty."

The indictment named as defendants:

Generalfeldmarschall (General of the Army) Wilhelm von Leeb, Generalfeldmarschall (General of the Army) Hugo Sperrle, Generalfeldmarschall (General of the Army) Georg Karl Friedrich-Wilhelm von Kuechler, Generaloberst (General) Johannes Blaskowitz, Generaloberst (General) Hermann Hoth, Generaloberst (General) Hans Reinhardt, Generaloberst (General) Hans von Salmuth, Generaloberst (General) Karl Hollidt, Generaladmiral (Admiral) Otto Schniewind, General der Infanterie (Lieutenant General, Infantry) Karl von Roques, General der Infanterie (Lieutenant General, Infantry) Hermann Reinecke, General der Artillerie (Lieutenant General, Artillery) Walter Warlimont, General der Infanterie (Lieutenant General, Infantry) Otto Woehler, and Generaloberstabsrichter (Lieutenant General, Judge Advocate) Rudolf Lehmann.

* * *

The indictment is in four counts charging (1) crimes against peace; (2) war crimes; (3) crimes against humanity; and (4) a common plan or conspiracy to commit the crimes charged in counts one, two, and three.

* * *

Count one of the indictment, heretofore set out, charges the defendants with crimes against peace.

Before seeking to determine the law applicable it is necessary to determine with certainty the action which the defendants are alleged to have taken that constitutes the crime. As a preliminary to that we deem it necessary to give a brief consideration to the nature and characteristics of war. We need not attempt a definition that is all-inclusive and all-exclusive. It is sufficient to say that war is the exerting of violence by one state or politically organized body against another. In other words, it is the implementation of a political policy by means of violence. Wars are contests by force between political units but the policy that brings about their initiation is made and the actual waging of them is done by individuals. What we have said thus far is equally as applicable to a just as to an unjust war, to the initiation of an aggressive and, therefore, criminal war as to the waging of a defensive and, therefore, legitimate war against criminal aggression. The point we stress is that war activity is the implementation of a predetermined national policy.

Likewise, an invasion of one state by another is the implementation of the national policy of the invading state by force even though the invaded state, due to fear or a sense of the futility of resistance in the face of superior force, adopts a policy of nonresistance and thus prevents the occurrence of any actual combat.

In the light of this general characterization and definition of war and invasions we now consider the charge contained in the indictment. The essence of the charge is *participation in the initiation of aggressive invasions and in the planning, preparation, and waging of aggressive wars.* * * *

The prosecution does not seek, or contend that the law authorizes, a conviction of the defendants simply by reason of their positions as shown by the evidence, but it contends only that such positions may be considered by the Tribunal with all other evidence in the case for such light as they may shed on the personal guilt or innocence of the individual defendants. The prosecution does contend, and we think the contention sound, that the defendants are not relieved of responsibility for action which would be criminal in one who held no military position, simply by reason of their military positions. This is the clear holding of the judgment of the IMT, and is so provided in Control Council Law No. 10, Article II, paragraph 4(a).

The initiation of war or an invasion is a unilateral operation. When war is formally declared or the first shot is fired the initiation of the war has ended and from then on there is a waging of war between the two adversaries. Whether a war be lawful, or aggressive and therefore unlawful under international law, is and can be determined only from a consideration of the factors that entered into its initiation. In the intent and purpose for which it is planned, prepared, initiated and waged is to be found its lawfulness or unlawfulness.

As we have pointed out, war whether it be lawful or unlawful is the implementation of a national policy. If the policy under which it is initiated is criminal in its intent and purpose it is so because the individuals at the policy-making level had a criminal intent and purpose in determining the policy. If war is the means by which the criminal objective is to be attained then the waging of the war is but an implementation of the policy, and the criminality which attaches to the waging of an aggressive war should be confined to those who participate in it at the policy level.

This does not mean that the Tribunal subscribes to the contention made in this trial that since Hitler was the Dictator of the Third Reich and that he was supreme in both the civil and military fields, he alone must bear criminal responsibility for political and military policies. No matter how absolute his authority, Hitler alone could not formulate a policy of aggressive war and alone implement that policy by preparing, planning, and waging such a war. Somewhere between the Dictator and Supreme Commander of the Military Forces of the nation and the common soldier is the boundary between the criminal and the excusable participation in the waging of an aggressive war by an individual engaged in it. Control Council Law No. 10 does not definitely draw such a line.

It points out in paragraph 2 of Article II certain fact situations and established relations that are or may be sufficient to constitute guilt and sets forth certain categories of activity that do not establish immunity from criminality. Since there has been no other prosecution under Control Council Law No. 10 with defendants in the same category as those in this case, no such definite line has been judicially drawn. This Tribunal is not required to fix a general rule but only to determine the guilt or innocence of the present defendants.

The judgment of the IMT held that:

The Charter is not an arbitrary exercise of power on the part of the victorious nations, but in view of the Tribunal, as will be shown, it is the expression of international law existing at the time of its creation; and to that extent is itself a contribution to international law.

We hold that Control Council Law No. 10 likewise is but an expression of international law existing at the time of its creation. We cannot therefore construe it as extending the international common law as it existed at the time of the Charter to add thereto any new element of criminality, for so to do would give it an ex post facto effect which we do not construe it to have intended. Moreover, that this was not intended is indicated by the fact that the London Charter of 8 August 1945, is made an integral part of the Control Council Law.

Since international common law grows out of the common reactions and the composite thinking with respect to recurring situations by the various states composing the family of nations, it is pertinent to consider the general attitude of the citizens of states with respect to their military commanders and their obligations when their nations plan, prepare for and initiate or engage in war.

While it is undoubtedly true that international common law in case of conflict with state law takes precedence over it and while it is equally true that absolute unanimity among all the states in the family of nations is not required to bring an international common law into being, it is scarcely a tenable proposition that international common law will run counter to the consensus within any considerable number of nations.

Furthermore, we must not confuse idealistic objectives with realities. The world has not arrived at a state of civilization such that it can dispense with fleets, armies, and air forces, nor has it arrived at a point where it can safely outlaw war under any and all circumstances and situations. In as much as all war cannot be considered outlawed then armed forces are lawful instrumentalities of state, which have internationally legitimate functions. An unlawful war of aggression connotes of necessity a lawful war of defense against aggression. There is no general criterion under international common law for determining the extent to which a nation may arm and prepare for war. As long as there is no aggressive intent, there is no evil inherent in a nation making itself militarily strong. An example is Switzerland which for her geographical extent, her population and resources is proportionally stronger militarily than many nations of the world. She uses her military strength to implement a national policy that seeks peace and to maintain her borders against aggression.

There have been nations that have initiated and waged aggressive wars through long periods of history, doubtless there are nations still disposed to do so; and if not, judging in the light of history, there may be nations which tomorrow will be disposed so to do. Furthermore, situations may arise in which the question whether the war is or is not aggressive is doubtful and uncertain. We may safely assume that the general and considered opinions of the people within states—the source from which international common law springs are not such as to hamper or render them impotent to do the things they deem necessary for their national protection.

We are of the opinion that as in ordinary criminal cases, so in the crime denominated aggressive war, the same elements must all be present to constitute criminality. There first must be actual knowledge that an aggressive war is intended and that if launched it will be an aggressive war. But mere knowledge is not sufficient to make participation even by high ranking military officers in the war criminal. It requires in addition that the possessor of such knowledge, after he acquires it shall be in a position to shape or influence the policy that brings about its initiation or its continuance after initiation, either by furthering, or by hindering or preventing it. If he then does the former, he becomes criminally responsible; if he does the latter to the extent of his ability, then his action shows the lack of criminal intent with respect to such policy.

If a defendant did not know that the planning and preparation for invasions and wars in which he was involved were concrete plans and preparations for aggressive wars and for wars otherwise in violation of international laws and treaties, then he cannot be guilty of an offense. If, however, after the policy to initiate and wage aggressive wars was formulated, a defendant came into possession of knowledge that the invasions and wars to be waged, were aggressive and unlawful, then he will be criminally responsible if he, being on the policy level, could have influenced such policy and failed to do so.

If and as long as a member of the armed forces does not participate in the preparation, planning, initiating, or waging of aggressive war on a policy level, his war activities do not fall under the definition of crimes against peace. It is not a person's rank or status, but his power to shape or influence the policy of his state, which is the relevant issue for determining his criminality under the charge of crimes against peace.

International law condemns those who, due to their actual power to shape and influence the policy of their nation, prepare for, or lead their country into or in an aggressive war. But we do not find that, at the present stage of development, international law declares as criminals those below that level who, in the execution of this war policy, act as the instruments of the policy makers. Anybody who is on the policy level and participates in the war policy is liable to punishment. But those under them cannot be punished for the crimes of others. The misdeed of the policy makers is all the greater in as much as they use the great mass of the soldiers and officers to carry out an international crime; however, the individual soldier or officer below the policy level is but the policy makers' instrument, finding himself, as he does, under the rigid discipline which is necessary for and peculiar to military organization.

We do not hesitate to state that it would have been eminently desirable had the commanders of the German armed forces refused to implement the policy of the Third Reich by means of aggressive war. It would have been creditable to them not to contribute to the cataclysmic catastrophe. This would have been the honorable and righteous thing to do; it would have been in the interest of their State. Had they done so they would have served their fatherland and humanity also.

But however much their failure is morally reprimandable, we are of the opinion and hold that international common law, at the time they so acted, had not developed to the point of making the participation of military officers below the policy making or policy influencing level into a criminal offense in and of itself.

International law operates as a restriction and limitation on the sovereignty of nations. It may also limit the obligations which individuals owe to their states, and create for them international obligations which are binding upon them to an extent that they must be carried out even if to do so violates a positive law or directive of state. But the limitation which international common law imposes on national sovereignty, or on individual obligations, is a limitation self-imposed or imposed by the composite thinking in the international community, for it is by such democratic processes that common law comes into being. If there is no generality of opinion among the nations of the world as to a particular restriction on national sovereignty or on the obligations of individuals toward their own state, then there is no international common law on such matter.

By the Kellogg-Briand Pact 63 nations, including Germany, renounced war as an instrument of national policy. If this, as we believe it is, is evidence of a sufficient crystallization of world opinion to authorize a judicial finding that there exist crimes against peace under international common law, we cannot find that law to extend further than such evidence indicates. The nations that entered into the Kellogg-Briand Pact considered it imperative that existing international relationships should not be changed by force. In the preamble they state they they are:

> Persuaded that the time has come when * * * all changes in their relationships with one another should be sought only by pacific means * * * .

This is a declaration that from that time forward each of the signatory nations should be deemed to possess and to have the right to exercise all the privileges and powers of a sovereign nation within the limitations of international law, free from all interference by force on the part of any other nation. As a corollary to this, the changing or attempting to change the international relationships by force of arms is an act of aggression and if the aggression results in war, the war is an aggressive war. It is, therefore, aggressive war that is renounced by the pact. It is aggressive war that is criminal under international law.

The crime denounced by the law is the use of war as an instrument of national policy. Those who commit the crime are those who participate at the policy making level in planning, preparing, or in initiating war. After war is initiated, and is being waged, the policy question then involved becomes one of extending, continuing or discontinuing the war. The crime at this stage likewise must be committed at the policy making level.

The making of a national policy is essentially political, though it may require, and of necessity does require, if war is to be one element of that policy, a consideration of matters military as well as matters political.

It is self-evident that national policies are made by man. When men make a policy that is criminal under international law, they are criminally responsible for so doing. This is the logical and inescapable conclusion.

The acts of commanders and staff officers below the policy level, in planning campaigns, preparing means for carrying them out, moving against a country on orders and fighting a war after it has been instituted, do not constitute the planning, preparation, initiation, and waging of war or the initiation of invasion that international law denounces as criminal.

Under the record we find the defendants were not on the policy level, and are not guilty under count one of the indictment. With crimes charged to have been committed by them in the *manner* in which they behaved in the waging of war, we deal in other parts of this judgment.

　　　* * *

---

1. *Trial of Japanese leaders.* An International Military Tribunal for the Far East conducted a trial of Japanese leaders in Tokyo and rendered a judgment in November, 1948. Examples from the

judgment and other opinions are reported in Sohn, Cases on United Nations Law 898 (1956).

2. *The Nuremberg principles in the United Nations.* In December, 1946, the General Assembly of the United Nations adopted a resolution affirming "the principles of international law recognized by the Charter of the Nuremberg Tribunal and the judgment of the Tribunal." Resolution 95(1). The International Law Commission, an organ of the United Nations established by the General Assembly to carry out Article 13 of the Charter, was requested by the General Assembly to formulate the Nuremberg principles. In 1950, the Commission submitted a draft of seven principles which were discussed by the General Assembly but never formally affirmed by the assembly. Extensive efforts in the United Nations to prepare and agree upon a Draft Code of Offenses against the Peace and Security of Mankind and to establish an international criminal court have come to naught. A detailed report of this work of the United Nations is set forth in Sohn, Cases on United Nations Law 969–1019 (1956).

3. *Nuremberg's aftermath: an appraisal.* In Justice Under Fire (1974), Bishop asks, at 284:

What, then, has the Magna Carta of international law done for the welfare of humanity since its promulgation? The answer is clear and simple: nothing. Since Nuremberg, there have been at least eighty or ninety wars (some calculators exclude armed invasions of neighbors too weak to attempt resistance), some of them on a very large scale. The list includes the Korean war, the Suez invasion of 1956, the Algerian rebellion, the four Arab-Israeli wars, the Vietnam wars (including the accompanying fighting in Laos and Cambodia), and the invasion of Czechoslovakia by the Soviet Union and its myrmidons. In none of these cases, nor in any other, was an aggressor arrested and brought to the bar of international justice, and none is likely to be. For all the good it has done, the doctrine that aggressive war is a crime might as well be relegated to the divinity schools.

As to some of the wars referred to by Bishop, the relevance of the provisions of the United Nations Charter is examined in Chapters 19 and 20.

SECTION C. UNIVERSAL JURISDICTION AND THE NUREMBERG PRINCIPLES

ATTORNEY GENERAL OF ISRAEL v. EICHMANN

Israel, Supreme Court 1962.
36 Int'l L.Rep. 277 (1968).*

1. The appellant, Adolf Eichmann, was found guilty by the District Court of Jerusalem of offenses of the most extreme gravity against the Nazi and Nazi Collaborators (Punishment) Law, 1950 (hereinafter referred to as "the Law") and was sentenced to death. These offences may be divided into four groups:

(a) Crimes against the Jewish people, contrary to Section I (a)(1) of the Law;

(b) Crimes against humanity, contrary to Section I(a)(2);

(c) War crimes, contrary to Section I(a)(3);

(d) Membership of hostile organizations, contrary to Section 3.

2. The acts constituting these offences, which the Court attributed to the appellant, have been specified in paragraph 244 of the judgment of the District Court * * *.

The acts comprised in Group (a) are:

(1) that during the period from August 1941 to May 1945, in Germany, in the Axis States and in the areas which were subject to the authority of Germany and the Axis States, he, together with others, caused the killing of millions of Jews for the purpose of carrying out the plan known as "the Final Solution of the Jewish Problem" with the intent to exterminate the Jewish people;

(2) that during that period and in the same places he, together with others, placed millions of Jews in living conditions which were calculated to bring about their physical destruction, for the purpose of carrying out the plan above mentioned with the intent to exterminate the Jewish people;

(3) that during that period and in the same places he, together with others, caused serious physical and mental harm to millions of Jews with the intent to exterminate the Jewish people;

(4) that during the years 1943 and 1944 he, together with others, "devised measures the purpose of which was to prevent births among Jews by his instructions forbidding child bearing and ordering the interruption of pregnancies of Jewish women

* Reprinted by permission of E. Lauterpacht, ed., and Grotius Publications, Ltd., Cambridge, England.

in the Theresin Ghetto with the intent to exterminate the Jewish people".

The acts constituting the crimes in Group (b) are as follows:

(5) that during the period from August 1941 to May 1945 he, together with others, caused in the territories and areas mentioned in clause (1) the murder, extermination, enslavement, starvation and deportation of the civilian Jewish population;

(6) that during the period from December 1939 to March 1941 he, together with others, caused the deportation of Jews to Nisco, and the deportation of Jews from the areas in the East annexed to the Reich, and from the Reich area proper, to the German Occupied Territories in the East, and to France;

(7) that in carrying out the above-mentioned activities he persecuted Jews on national, racial, religious and political grounds;

(8) that during the period from March 1938 to May 1945 in the places mentioned above he, together with others, caused the spoliation of the property of millions of Jews by means of mass terror linked with the murder, extermination, starvation and deportation of these Jews;

(9) that during the years 1940–1942 he, together with others, caused the expulsion of hundreds of thousands of Poles from their places of residence;

(10) that during 1941 he, together with others, caused the expulsion of more than 14,000 Slovenes from their places of residence;

(11) that during the Second World War he, together with others, caused the expulsion of scores of thousands of gipsies from Germany and German-occupied areas and their transportation to the German-occupied areas in the East;

(12) that in 1942 he, together with others, caused the expulsion of 93 children of the Czech village of Lidice.

The acts comprised in Group (c) are:

that he committed the acts of persecution, expulsion and murder mentioned in Counts 1 to 7, in so far as these were done during the Second World War against Jews from among the populations of the States occupied by the Germans and by the other Axis States.

The acts comprised in Group (d) are:

that as from May 1940 he was a member of three Nazi Police organizations which were declared criminal organizations by the International Military Tribunal which tried the Major War Criminals, and as a member of such organizations he took part in acts which were declared criminal in Article 6 of the London Charter of August 8, 1945.

3.   The appellant has appealed to this Court against both conviction and sentence.

4.   The oral and written submissions of learned counsel who supported the appeal, Dr. Servatius, may, in so far as they are directed against conviction, be classified under two heads:

(1) Purely legal contentions, the principal object of which was to undermine the jurisdiction of a court in Israel to try the appellant for the crimes in question;

(2) Factual contentions the object of which was in essence to upset the finding of the District Court that there was no foundation for the defence of the appellant that he played the part of a "small cog" in the machine of Nazi destruction, that in all the above-mentioned chapters of events he functioned as a minor official without any independent initiative, and that nothing but the compulsion of orders and blind obedience to commands from above guided him in carrying out his work at all stages.

*   *   *

5.   The District Court has in its judgment dealt with both categories of contentions in an exhaustive, profound and most convincing manner.   We should say at once that we fully concur, without hesitation or reserve, in all its conclusions and reasons.   *   *   *

[The Jurisdiction of the Court]

6.   Most of the legal contentions of counsel for the appellant revolve around the argument that in assuming jurisdiction to try the appellant the District Court acted contrary to the principles of international law.   These contentions are as follows:

(1) The Law of 1950, which is the only source of the jurisdiction of the Court in this case, constitutes ex post facto penal legislation which prescribes as offences acts that were committed before the State of Israel came into existence;   therefore the validity of this Law is confined to its citizens alone.

(2) The offences for which the appellant was tried are "extra-territorial offences", that is to say, offences that were committed outside the territory of Israel by a citizen of a foreign State, and even though the Law confers jurisdiction in respect of such offences, it conflicts in so doing with the principle of territorial sovereignty, which postulates that only the country within whose territory the offence was committed or to which the offender belongs—in this case, Germany—has the right to punish therefor.

(3) The acts constituting the offence of which the appellant was convicted were at the time of their commission Acts of State.

(4) The appellant was brought to Israel territory, to be tried for the offences in question, unwillingly and without the consent of the country in which he resided, and this was done through agents of the State of Israel, who acted on the orders of their Government.

(5) The judges of the District Court, being Jews and feeling affinity with the victims of the plan of extermination and Nazi persecution, were psychologically incapable of giving the appellant an objective trial.

* * *

7. We reject all these contentions.

* * *

[Portions of the court's opinion dealing with the second contention—the "extraterritoriality" of the offences—are set forth as follows.]

[*Universal Jurisdiction*]

12. * * * [I]t is the universal character of the crimes in question which vests in every State the authority to try and punish those who participated in their commission. This proposition is closely linked with the one advanced in the preceding paragraph, from which indeed it follows as a logical outcome. The grounds upon which it rests are as follows:

(a) One of the principles whereby States assume in one degree or another the power to try and punish a person for an offence is the principle of universality. Its meaning is substantially that such power is vested in every State regardless of the fact that the offence was committed outside its territory by a person who did not belong to it, provided he is in its custody when brought to trial. This principle has wide currency and is universally acknowledged with respect to the offence of piracy jure gentium. But while general agreement exists as to this offence, the question of the scope of its application is in dispute * * *.

* * *

(b) The brief survey of views set out above shows that, notwithstanding the differences between them, there is full justification for applying here the principle of universal jurisdiction since the international character of "crimes against humanity" (in the wide meaning of the term) dealt with in this case is no longer in doubt, while the unprecedented extent of their injurious and murderous effects is not to be disputed at the present time. In other words, the basic reason for which international law recognizes the right of each State to exercise such jurisdiction in piracy offences—notwithstanding the fact that its own sovereignty does not extend to the scene of the commission of the offence (the high seas) and the offender is a national of another State or is stateless—applies with even greater force to the above-mentioned crimes. That reason is, it will be recalled, that the interest to prevent bodily and material harm to those who sail the seas and to persons engaged in trade between nations, is a vital interest common to all civilized States and of universal scope * * *.

It follows that the State which prosecutes and punishes a person for piracy acts merely as the organ and agent of the international community and metes out punishment to the offender for his breach of the prohibition imposed by the law of nations * * *.

The above explanation of the substantive basis upon which the exercise of the principle of universal jurisdiction in respect of the crime of piracy rests, justifies its exercise in regard also to the crimes which are the subject of the present case.

(c) The truth is—and this further supports our conclusion— that the application of this principle has for some time been moving beyond the international crime of piracy. We have in mind its application to conventional war crimes as well. As we observed in paragraph 11(c) of this judgment, whenever a "belligerent" country tries and punishes a member of the armed forces of the enemy for an act contrary to "the laws and customs of war", it does so because the matter involves an international crime in the prevention of which the countries of the whole world have an interest. * * *

* * *

(f) We sum up our views on this subject as follows. Not only do all the crimes attributed to the appellant bear an international character, but their harmful and murderous effects were so embracing and widespread as to shake the international community to its very foundations. The State of Israel therefore was entitled, pursuant to the principle of universal jurisdiction and in the capacity of a guardian of international law and an agent for its enforcement, to try the appellant. That being the case, no importance attaches to the fact that the State of Israel did not exist when the offences were committed. Here therefore is an additional reason—and one based on a positive approach—for rejecting the second, "jurisdictional", submission of counsel for the appellant.

* * *

SECTION D. DEFENSIVE USE OF NUREMBERG PRINCIPLES UNDER UNITED STATES LAW

UNITED STATES v. MITCHELL

United States Court of Appeals, Second Circuit, 1966.
369 F.2d 323.

MEDINA, Circuit Judge. David Henry Mitchell, III appeals from a conviction, after a trial to Judge Clarie and a jury, of wilful failure to report for induction into the Armed Forces in violation of 50 U.S.C., Appx., Section 462.

After initially registering with Selective Service Local Board 17, appellant "disaffiliated" himself from the Selective Service and thereafter refused to cooperate with his Board in any respect. In August, 1964, appellant was classified 1A and did not appeal. Subsequently, he was ordered to report for induction on January 11, 1965. Appellant acknowledged receipt of this notice by letter but did not report as ordered.

Appellant was indicted for violation of 50 U.S.C., Appx., Section 462, tried and found guilty. This Court reversed the first conviction because the trial judge had failed to allow sufficient time for appellant to obtain counsel. United States v. Mitchell, 354 F.2d 767 (2 Cir. 1966). He was retried before Judge Clarie and a jury. The wilfulness of his failure to report for induction was all too apparent, and he was again convicted and sentenced to five years imprisonment. At trial appellant made no claim to be a conscientious objector but sought to produce evidence to show that the war in Vietnam was being conducted in violation of various treaties to which the United States is a signatory and that the Selective Service system was being operated as an adjunct of this military effort. Judge Clarie ruled out all such evidence as immaterial and this ruling is assigned as error.

The government, citing a line of cases beginning with Falbo v. United States, 320 U.S. 549, 64 S.Ct. 346, 88 L.Ed. 305 (1944), would preclude consideration of appellant's claims because of his failure to exhaust his administrative remedies. But, as appellant does not seek any relief which the Selective Service is empowered to grant, we will assume these cases are not in point. Rather, he seeks a declaration, in effect, that the Service must cease to function. It would be pointless in this case to require appellant to press his claims before a Board which he claims is illegal.

Similarly, as appellant asserts that the Selective Service, and not merely the conduct of the war in Vietnam, is illegal, his defenses would seem not to be premature.

Nevertheless, appellant's allegations are not a defense to a prosecution for failure to report for induction into the Armed Forces and his evidence was properly excluded. Regardless of the proof that appellant might present to demonstrate the correlation between the Selective Service and our nation's efforts in Vietnam, as a matter of law the congressional power "to raise and support armies" and "to provide and maintain a navy" is a matter quite distinct from the use which the Executive makes of those who have been found qualified and who have been inducted into the Armed Forces. Whatever action the President may order, or the Congress sanction, cannot impair this constitutional power of the Congress.

Thus we need not consider whether the substantive issues raised by appellant can ever be appropriate for judicial determination. See United States v. Hogans, 2 Cir., 369 F.2d 359, decided by this Court on November 28, 1966.

Affirmed.

MITCHELL v. UNITED STATES

United States Supreme Court, 1967.
386 U.S. 972, 87 S.Ct. 1162.

Certiorari denied.

Mr. Justice DOUGLAS, dissenting.

Petitioner did not report for induction as ordered, was indicted, convicted, and sentenced to five years' imprisonment and his conviction was affirmed. 369 F.2d 323. His defense was that the "war" in Vietnam was being conducted in violation of various treaties to which we were a signatory, especially the Treaty of London of August 8, 1945, 59 Stat. 1544, which in Article 6(a) declares that "waging of a war of aggression" is a "crime against peace" imposing "individual responsibility." Article 8 provides:

"The fact that the Defendant acted pursuant to order of his Government or of a superior shall not free him from responsibility, but may be considered in mitigation of punishment if the Tribunal determines that justice so requires."

Petitioner claimed that the "war" in Vietnam was a "war of aggression" within the meaning of the Treaty of London and that Article 8 makes him responsible for participating in it even though he is ordered to do so.[1]

Mr. Justice Jackson, the United States prosecutor at Nuremberg, stated: "If certain acts in violation of treaties are crimes, they are crimes whether the United States does them or whether Germany does them, and we are not prepared to lay down a rule of criminal conduct against others which we would not be willing to have invoked against us." (International Conference on Military Trials, Dept. of State Pub. No. 3080, p. 330.)

Article VI, cl. 2, of the Constitution states that "Treaties" are a part of the "supreme Law of the Land; and the Judges in every State shall be bound thereby."

There is a considerable body of opinion that our actions in Vietnam constitute the waging of an aggressive "war."

This case presents the questions:

(1) whether the Treaty of London is a treaty within the meaning of Art. VI, cl. 2;

(2) whether the question as to the waging of an aggressive "war" is in the context of this criminal prosecution a justiciable question;

(3) whether the Vietnam episode is a "war" in the sense of the Treaty;

(4) whether petitioner has standing to raise the question;

---

1. The trial court charged the jury that the Treaty of London did not interfere "in any manner in respect to this defendant fulfilling his duty under this order."

(5) whether, if he has, the Treaty may be tendered as a defense in this criminal case or in amelioration of the punishment.

These are extremely sensitive and delicate questions. But they should, I think, be answered. Even those who think that the Nuremberg judgments were unconstitutional by our guarantee relating to ex post facto laws would have to take a different view of the Treaty of London that purports to lay down a standard of future conduct for all the signatories.

I intimate no opinion on the merits. But I think the petition for certiorari should be granted. We have here a recurring question in present-day Selective Service cases.[a]

UNITED STATES v. SAMAS

United States, Board of Review (Army), 1967.
37 C.–M. Rep. 708.

The Board of Review finds the findings of guilty and the sentence as approved by proper authority correct in law and fact and determines, on the basis of the entire record, that the findings of guilty and only so much of the sentence as provides for dishonorable discharge, confinement at hard labor for three (3) years, forfeiture of all pay and allowances and reduction to the grade of Private (E–1) should be approved. The sentence is modified accordingly. The findings and sentence as thus modified are affirmed.

CRIMMINS and CHALK, Judge Advocates. 27 June 1967.

FENIG, Judge Advocate:

I concur. The discussion which follows may be helpful.

The accused is one of three from Fort Dix appealing military convictions for disobedience. They refused to go to Viet Nam. In appealing they would substitute for themselves as accused a more transcendent matter: American policy in Viet Nam.

The basic facts concerning the disobedience are not in dispute. The accused, at Ford Hood, Texas, received orders transferring them to Viet Nam and pursuant to such orders took preembarkation leave. All three, plus one other soldier who subsequently fell away, met in New York City. There they and their supporters conceived and implemented a plan—to test the legality of the war in Viet Nam by filing suit in a federal court seeking an injunction to prevent their deployment to Viet Nam. After suit was filed they held a press conference and announced their intention not to obey their then existent orders.

After some few days' delay the Army had their orders amended to show Fort Dix, New Jersey, rather than the west coast, as their de-

---

a. Problems posed by this case are more fully analyzed in Forman, The Nuremberg Trials and Conscientious Objection to War: Justiciability Under United States Municipal Law, 1969 Proceedings of the American Society of International Law 157 and comments by Telford Taylor and others, 165 ff.

parture point. Then their leave was curtailed and the men were apprehended and taken to Fort Dix. After about a week of administrative segregation the men, on 14 July 1966, their originally scheduled departure date, were individually ordered to board a plane in the case of Samas and Johnson, and a sedan in the case of Mora, which would commence their westward journey to the Viet Nam combat area. Each accused clearly understood the order and at each trial has acknowledged he intentionally refused to obey.

I find the order was legal and not given with a view to increasing potential punishment; in addition, in accord with the law officer's ruling, that the American effort in Viet Nam is legal.

Defense counsel apparently decries the fact that no charges were brought against the accused for his conduct prior to apprehension in New York and from this they reason the later order to board the plane was a sham to punish the soldier's exercise of a right to free speech or to increase the possible maximum sentence imposable for his possibly planned unauthorized absence. But, at trial this issue of possible increased punishment was litigated. Inherent in the finding of the military jury is the conclusion that the Army's action actually appears to have been given to afford the accused a last chance—with the hope that compliance would result. One of the original four evidently did comply. The failure of the military to charge the accused with a pre-apprehension crime may have been a bonanza to him. It is quite conceivable that if four soldiers get together and agree they will defy military authority and take overt action designed to publicize their insubordinate intent * * * they may be guilty of a military crime. Such conduct might almost be described as mutinous. (Par. 173, MCM, 1951).

It is important to remember that the accused, prior to curtailment of his leave and New York liberty, was already in possession of valid orders assigning him to Viet Nam. This order was not reiterated on 14 July 1966 for punishment purposes; it was repeated for reenforcement purposes. The federal courts did not have jurisdiction of the accused nor of his complaint. Luftig v. McNamara, 373 F.2d 664 (D.C.Cir. 1967). The military have a duty to see that their orders are complied with. A captain who failed to put the power and prestige of his office behind an effort to prevent a crime being committed in his presence would be guilty of dereliction of duty.

Free speech, like other rights of the military, are modified to meet overriding demands of discipline and duty in the military services. See Burns v. Wilson, 346 U.S. 137 (1953). CM 413739, Howe, 3 November 1966. It cannot be a cover for disobedience of deployment orders.

The accused before the disobedience consulted with a lawyer and then sought two forums—the federal courts and public opinion. Being intelligent and well read young soldiers they should have relied, prior to the disobedience, on American law, both military and civilian, and the lessons of history.

It is, of course, axiomatic that no military organization can continue to exist if each man in it is free to decide which war he will participate in and which he will merely sit out. See United States v. Macintosh, 283 U.S. 605, 625 (1931). Appellate defense counsel know of no nation which accords a military accused the luxury of choice. American military precedent is clearly to the contrary. Winthrop, Military Law and Precedent, 2d Ed. (1920), makes this clear:

> " * * * The obligation to obey is one to be fulfilled without hesitation, with alacrity, and to the full; nothing short of a physical impossibility ordinarily excusing a complete performance * * * the inferior cannot, as a general rule, be permitted to raise a question as to the propriety, expedience, or feasibility of a command given him * * *" (p. 572).

Military law recognizes exceptions—instances of palpable illegality. Cf. ACM 7321 Kinder, 14 CMR 742. The accused, in effect, contends that the war in Viet Nam is an instance of palpable illegality. The accused claims that merely to go to Viet Nam in an American uniform would be to commit a war crime subjecting him to international censure and possible punishment at some time by some international tribunal.

The legality of the American war effort in Viet Nam was one for the law officer to decide. In United States v. Carson (No. 18,277), 51 USCMA 407, 35 CMR 379, it was held:

> "Whether an act comports with law, that is, whether it is legal or illegal, is a question of law, not an issue of fact for determination by the triers of fact. For example, in a prosecution for disobedience of an order * * * the court-martial must determine whether the order was given to the accused, but it may not consider whether the order was legal or illegal in relation to a constitutional or statutory right of the accused." (citations omitted).

In the present case the defense efforts were concentrated on proving the violation of accused's constitutional, statutory, and international rights. Those attacks went exclusively to questions of law and thus were "within the sole cognizance of the law officer." (Id., at 35 CMR 381).

The President is the Commander in Chief. The immortal literature on the subject of the American Constitution needs no reenforcement by an expatiation by me on its virtues. But both the President and Congress evidently regard Communism as a monolithic doctrine intent on world domination; they feel it is in our national interests to make a stand in Viet Nam in opposition to Communism. Historical experience would appear to support this view; the apparently innocuous "agrarian reformers" of China in 1948 became the "volunteer" invaders of Korea in 1950.

A declaration of war is not necessary. Winthrop, supra, p. 668. Many Presidents, as Commander in Chief, have sent men into combat, or situations where combat was likely, without such a declaration. Berlin, Korea, Lebanon, and the Dominican Republic are some examples. Besides, Congress has repeatedly approved the military action in Viet Nam. In August 1964 Congress overwhelmingly adopted a resolution approving the taking of all necessary measures to prevent further aggression by the forces of North Viet Nam. Since then Congress has voted large sums of money for the prosecution of the war, voted extension of the draft law, and authorized the equivalent of combat pay for troops serving in Viet Nam.

No conflict between domestic law and our own treaty obligations is perceived. Thus, we need not resolve whether the United States Constitution or our treaty obligations are supreme. See Reid v. Covert, 354 U.S. 1, 18 (1956). I do not know of any international agreements that the accused would be called upon to violate by merely going to Viet Nam in an American uniform. I know of no recognized international tribunal which has denounced American armed participation in Viet Nam.

Appellant argues that American troops commit atrocities in Viet Nam and that he might be regarded as an accomplice because of his mere presence. With strained hyperbole, the accused thus might be regarded as being the driver of a "get away car" for the actual perpetrators. The Army has not ordered this accused to commit any atrocity. If he had, but disobeyed, military law would have protected him. Cf. ACM 7321, Kinder, supra. But this accused disobeyed a different kind of order, a deployment order.

Counsel for the accused quote the Kellogg-Briand Pact and many other impeccable pronouncements. The Nuremberg rationale for our own prosecution of war criminals is also invoked. But the defense right of first quotation does not confer an exclusive proprietary interest. The American government is also against war crimes. If an American accused commits an atrocity we punish him. United States v. Schreiber (No. 5468,), 5 USCMA 602, 18 CMR 226.

In matters of conscience the law does not give carte blanche for individual stirrings and sincerity of purpose is often of dubious legal merit. So are political opinions. In a recent Supreme Court decision involving a deliberate violation of a state court injunction it was held: " * * * that in the fair administration of justice no man can be judge in his own case, however exalted his station, however righteous his motives and irrespective of his race, color, politics or religion. * * * " Walker v. City of Birmingham, 35 LW 4584 (13 Jun 67). See Winthrop, supra, p. 576.

FENIG, Judge Advocate. 27 June 1967.

Samas case on review.　Samas' petition for review was denied, sub nom.　United States v. Johnson, Mora and Samas, 38 C.M.R. 44 (1967–68):

Under domestic law, the presence of American troops in Vietnam is unassailable.　United States v. Smith, 13 USCMA 105, 32 CMR 105.　The legality under international law of the American presence in Vietnam is not a justiciable issue.　As long ago as Martin v. Mott, 12 Wheat 19, 29 (U.S.1827), the Supreme Court rejected the idea that the orders of the President as Commander-in-Chief may be so questioned, either by the individual concerned or the judiciary.　*Inter alia,* it said:

*　*　* If it be a limited power, the question arises, by whom is the exigency to be judged of and decided? Is the President the sole and exclusive judge whether the exigency has arisen, or is it to be considered as an open question, upon which every officer to whom the orders of the President are addressed, may decide for himself, and equally open to be contested by every militia-man who shall refuse to obey the orders of the President? We are all of opinion that the authority to decide whether the exigency has arisen, belongs exclusively to the President, and that his decision is conclusive upon all other persons.

Part IV

THE STRUCTURE OF THE INTERNATIONAL SYSTEM

Chapter 11

THE CONCEPT OF STATEHOOD

In spite of increasing concern for the individual in the international legal system, the fact remains that the fulcrum of that system is still the nation state. It is the major institution governing the affairs of men today. No other institution offers serious competition as the center for law-making and for the protection (well or poorly executed) of the interests of individuals. International organizations such as the United Nations have not pushed the state off the power center; religious organizations, the corporation, the tribe and the family are largely subordinate to the state. Political entities such as cities, "states" members of a federal system, commonwealths, trusteeships, mandates and colonies are likewise subordinated to the state.

In a functional sense, the states are the major actors in the international system, the political entities that operate the system. Most of them are members of the United Nations; they may be parties in cases before the International Court of Justice, can expect to be accorded immunity in the courts of sister states, can and do prescribe and enforce laws applicable to individuals and institutional aggregates of individuals, send diplomatic representatives to each other, demand from each other protection of their citizens, make protests to sister states over invasions of their territory, territorial seas and airspace, wage war in their self-defense and so forth. These entities in the international community exist for years, even centuries, despite wars, revolutions and changes of government by peaceful or other means.

Up to this point in this book, several major problems of the powers of states have been examined without an exploration of the concept of statehood. For the most part, there has been no need to question whether the institution or entity involved in those cases was a state as that term is understood in international law. Thus, in the Cutting case, p. 95, the United States did not ground its objection to Mexico's extension of its jurisdiction to Mr. Cutting on any notion that Mexico was not a state with general power to legislate. And in the Letelier case, p. 319, Chile's failure to be accorded immunity did not rest upon Chile not being a state. But legal controversies do arise in which the concept of statehood becomes significant: a treaty or domestic statute may apply in terms only to states; a rule of positive law may have been articulated in terms of statehood; one or more of the parties may verbalize the controversy in terms of states or statehood. In this chapter, the concept of statehood is examined from the point of view of the international lawyer who must decide specific cases or advise on their resolution.

Analytically, the concept of statehood embraces two very different components: first, the minimum set of facts which must exist before one can say that a state exists; second, the normal legal consequences that follow from the existence of that set of facts.

1. *The question of minimum facts.* The definition of state in Section 4 of the Restatement of the Foreign Relations Law of the United States (1965) may be useful: " *   *   * an entity that has a defined territory and population under the control of a government and that engages in foreign relations." It is instructive to note that this definition does not make reference to any central legal process by which those facts are to be determined. The lack of a central legal process for this purpose stands in contrast to domestic legal systems in which new entities such as corporations are created by legal processes: frequently by the issuance of a charter or certificate of incorporation by an official after the applicants have satisfied minimum factual criteria set forth in the relevant statute. In such a domestic system a corporation can be defined as an entity that has been created by compliance with that statutorily prescribed process. No such legal process exists in the case of the formation of entities called states.

The nearest analogues are (a) the process by which new members are admitted to the United Nations and (b) the phenomenon known as recognition in the international system. These analogues are imperfect. Admission to the United Nations is not automatically accorded to every entity that meets the factual criteria for statehood, since Article 4 of the Charter lays down additional criteria. As for the process of recognition, it should be noted that (i) there is no central recognizing authority, for each state in the international community makes its own unilateral determination to recognize a new state (or a new government of an existing state) and (ii) there is disagreement among legal theorists on the question whether the fact of recognition by other states is one of the minimum facts necessary for a new state to come into existence or is merely a neutral acknowledgment of an historical fact, i. e., that a new state has come into existence. (The question of recognition will be explored in Chapter 12.)

2. *The question of the normal legal consequences of statehood.* Once a state exists in the factual sense referred to above (i. e., there exist the elements of territory, population, government and engagement in foreign relations), what normal legal consequences follow

from this? Some of these consequences can be gleaned from an examination of the charters of international organizations. Extracts from the United Nations Charter, the Statute of the International Court of Justice and the Charter of the Organization of American States are set out below.

There are two additional documents of interest in this connection. They appear in the Documentary Supplement: a Draft Declaration on Rights and Duties of States, proposed by the International Law Commission to the General Assembly in 1949, and The Declaration on Principles of International Law Concerning Friendly Relations and Cooperation among States, adopted by the General Assembly.

CHARTER OF THE UNITED NATIONS

Article 2

The Organization and its Members, in pursuit of the Purposes stated in Article 1, shall act in accordance with the following Principles.

1. The Organization is based on the principle of the sovereign equality of all its Members.

    * * *

4. All Members shall refrain in their international relations from the threat or use of force against the territorial integrity or political independence of any state, or in any other manner inconsistent with the Purposes of the United Nations.

    * * *

6. The Organization shall ensure that states which are not Members of the United Nations act in accordance with these Principles so far as may be necessary for the maintenance of international peace and security.

7. Nothing contained in the present Charter shall authorize the United Nations to intervene in matters which are essentially within the domestic jurisdiction of any state or shall require the Members to submit such matters to settlement under the present Charter; but this principle shall not prejudice the application of enforcement measures under Chapter VII.

Article 3

The original Members of the United Nations shall be the states which, having participated in the United Nations Conference on International Organization at San Francisco, or having previously signed the Declaration by United Nations of 1 January 1942, sign the present Charter and ratify it in accordance with Article 110.

Article 4

1. Membership in the United Nations is open to all other peace-loving states which accept the obligations contained in the present Charter and, in the judgment of the Organization, are able and willing to carry out these obligations.

Article 31

Any Member of the United Nations which is not a member of the Security Council may participate, without vote, in the discussion of any question brought before the Security Council whenever the latter considers that the interests of that Member are specially affected.

Article 32

Any Member of the United Nations which is not a member of the Security Council or any state which is not a Member of the United Nations, if it is a party to a dispute under consideration by the Security Council, shall be invited to participate, without vote, in the discussion relating to the dispute. The Security Council shall lay down such conditions as it deems just for the participation of a state which is not a Member of the United Nations.

Article 35

1. Any Member of the United Nations may bring any dispute, or any situation of the nature referred to in Article 34, to the attention of the Security Council or of the General Assembly.

2. A state which is not a Member of the United Nations may bring to the attention of the Security Council or of the General Assembly any dispute to which it is a party if it accepts in advance, for the purposes of the dispute, the obligations of pacific settlement provided in the present Charter.

    *   *   *

STATUTE OF THE INTERNATIONAL COURT OF JUSTICE

Article 34—1. Only states may be parties in cases before the Court.

CHARTER OF THE ORGANIZATION OF AMERICAN STATES

2 U.S.T. 2394, 119 U.N.T.S. 3, as amended February 27, 1967, 21 U.S.T. 607.

Article 1

The American States establish by this Charter the international organization that they have developed to achieve an order of peace and justice, to promote their solidarity, to strengthen their collaboration, and to defend their sovereignty, their territorial integrity and their independence. Within the United Nations, the Organization of American States is a regional agency.

Article 4

All American States that ratify the present Charter are Members of the Organization.

Article 9

States are juridically equal, enjoy equal rights and equal capacity to exercise these rights, and have equal duties. The rights of each State depend not upon its power to ensure the exercise thereof, but upon the mere fact of its existence as a person under international law.

Article 10

Every American State has the duty to respect the rights enjoyed by every other State in accordance with international law.

Article 11

The fundamental rights of States may not be impaired in any manner whatsoever.

Article 12

The political existence of the State is independent of recognition by other States. Even before being recognized, the State has the right to defend its integrity and independence, to provide for its preservation and prosperity, and consequently to organize itself as it sees fit, to legislate concerning its interests, to administer its services, and to determine the jurisdiction and competence of its courts. The exercise of these rights is limited only by the exercise of the rights of other States in accordance with international law.

Article 13

Recognition implies that the State granting it accepts the personality of the new State, with all the rights and duties that international law prescribes for the two States.

Article 14

The right of each State to protect itself and to live its own life does not authorize it to commit unjust acts against another State.

Article 15

The jurisdiction of States within the limits of their national territory is exercised equally over all the inhabitants, whether nationals or aliens.

Article 16

Each State has the right to develop its cultural, political and economic life freely and naturally. In this free development, the State shall respect the rights of the individual and the principles of universal morality.

Article 17

Respect for and the faithful observance of treaties constitute standards for the development of peaceful relations among States. International treaties and agreements should be public.

Article 18

No State or group of States has the right to intervene, directly or indirectly, for any reason whatever, in the internal or external affairs of any other State. The foregoing principle prohibits not only armed force but also any other form of interference or attempted threat against the personality of the State or against its political, economic and cultural elements.

Article 19

No State may use or encourage the use of coercive measures of an economic or political character in order to force the sovereign will of another State and obtain from it advantages of any kind.

Article 20

The territory of a State is inviolable; it may not be the object, even temporarily, of military occupation or of other measures of force taken by another State, directly or indirectly, on any grounds whatever. No territorial acquisitions or special advantages obtained either by force or by other means of coercion shall be recognized.

Article 21

The American States bind themselves in their international relations not to have recourse to the use of force, except in the case of self-defense in accordance with existing treaties or in fulfillment thereof.

Article 22

Measures adopted for the maintenance of peace and security in accordance with existing treaties do not constitute a violation of the principles set forth in Articles 18 and 20.

Minimum facts for statehood not clearly present. It is easy enough to identify entities of long standing as states and to concede that whatever one normally believes to be the rights and duties of states inheres in those entities. France is a state, without doubt, and has the normal rights and duties of a state. And the same can be said for most of the more than 150 members of the United Nations.

But cases may arise when the factual criteria to support a finding of statehood are either not clearly discernible, or when parties to a controversy take differing views on the existence or non-existence of the facts, or when essential facts clearly do not exist. What, then, are the rights and duties of such an entity? For example, as a result of political compromise it was agreed at the founding of the United Nations that two of the federal states of the Union of Soviet Socialist Republics would be admitted to the United Nations as members: Byelorussian Soviet Socialist Republic and Ukranian Soviet Socialist Republic. This compromise was agreed to by the founders of the United Nations even though these units of the USSR did not freely engage in international relations with the rest of the world.

Thus political entities which did not satisfy the minimum factual criteria for statehood were treated, at least for purposes of membership in the United Nations, as though they were states. Did they thereby become states? The international lawyer is not presented with such a question in the abstract. Rather, the question is whether such entities, not fully meeting the factual criteria for statehood, will or will not have one of the legal attributes normally accorded to states, this attribute to be identified as problems arise. Under international law, are the Byelorussian Soviet Socialist Republic and the Ukranian Socialist Soviet Republic proper parties to treaties? See the following list of parties to the Nuclear Test Ban Treaty. Other issues may illustrate the problem. Are these two entitles entitled to sovereign immunity in the courts of foreign states, such as the United States? Are such questions to be answered by first determining whether these entities are states? Or by an analysis of the purposes which would be served by according these entities in the particular case the particular attribute of statehood in question? If the latter question is the one to be answered, the subsidiary processes of inquiry may be enormously complex.

PARTIES TO THE NUCLEAR TEST BAN TREATY
OF AUGUST 5, 1963

Treaties in Force on Jan. 1, 1980 (United States Department of State).

Ratification, accession or notification of succession deposited by:

Afghanistan	Hungary	Philippines
Australia	Iceland	Poland
Austria	India	Romania
Bahamas, The	Indonesia	Rwanda
Belgium	Iran	San Marino
Benin	Iraq	Senegal
Bhutan	Ireland	Sierra Leone
Bolivia	Israel	Singapore
Botswana	Italy	South Africa
Brazil	Ivory Coast	Spain
Bulgaria	Japan	Sri Lanka
Burma	Jordan	Sudan
Byelorussian Soviet	Kenya	Swaziland
Socialist Rep.[1]	Korea	Sweden
Canada	Kuwait	Switzerland
Cape Verde	Laos	Syrian Arab Rep.
Central African Rep.	Lebanon	Tanzania
Chad	Liberia	Thailand
Chile	Libya	Togo
China (Taiwan)	Luxembourg	Tonga
Costa Rica	Madagascar	Trinidad & Tobago
Cyprus	Malawi	Tunisia
Czechoslovakia	Malaysia	Turkey
Denmark	Malta	Uganda
Dominican Rep.	Mauritania	Ukrainian Soviet
Ecuador	Mauritius	Socialist Rep.[1]
Egypt	Mexico	Union of Soviet
El Salvador	Mongolia	Socialist Reps.
Fiji	Morocco	United Kingdom
Finland	Nepal	United States
Gabon	Netherlands	Uruguay
Gambia, The	New Zealand	Venezuela
German Dem. Rep.	Nicaragua	Western Samoa
Germany, Fed. Rep.	Niger	Yemen (Aden)
Ghana	Nigeria	Yugoslavia
Greece	Norway	Zaire
Guatemala	Panama	Zambia
Honduras	Peru	

1. With reference to the reported signature and deposit of ratification at Moscow by the Byelorussian Soviet Socialist Republic and the Ukrainian Soviet Socialist Republic, the Government of the United States considers those two constituent republics as already covered by the signature and deposit of ratification of the treaty by the Union of Soviet Socialist Republics.

Treaty relations with entities not otherwise treated as states. A number of footnotes to this table have been omitted; these notes identify the place or places when the parties deposited their accessions or ratifications. Ratifications and accessions were deposited in Washington, London and Moscow: sometimes in all those cities, sometimes in two of them, sometimes in but one. This means of recording adherence to the treaty was deliberately chosen instead of depositing ratifications and accessions at a single place, such as the Secretariat of the United Nations. See Chapter 12, p. 824.

The Holy See is a party to the Geneva Conventions of 1949 (dealing with prisoners of war, 6 U.S.T. 3316, 75 U.N.T.S. 135; wounded and sick in armed forces in the field, 6 U.S.T. 3114, 75 U.N. T.S. 31; wounded, sick and shipwrecked members of armed forces at sea, 6 U.S.T. 3217, 75 U.N.T.S. 85). "The problem of personality divorced from territorial base is difficult to isolate because of the interaction of the Vatican City, the Holy See, and the Roman Catholic Church." Brownlie, Principles of Public International Law 68, n. 1 (3rd ed. 1979).

Also parties to the Geneva Conventions of 1949 are the Republic of Korea, the Democratic People's Republic of Korea, the Federal Republic of Germany and the Democratic Republic of Germany.

ADMISSION OF RUANDA AND BURUNDI TO UNITED NATIONS MEMBERSHIP

Higgins, The Development of International Law through the
Political Organs of the United Nations 22 (1963).*

The United Nations role in the coming to nationhood of Ruanda and Burundi, and their admission to membership at the seventeenth session of the Assembly, is also of interest in this context. Ruanda-Urundi—originally two separate kingdoms, each headed by a Mwami (King)—came under Belgian administration in 1923, and was a mandate under the League and a trust territory under the United Nations. In 1959 tribal fighting broke out, and in September 1961 a United Nations Commission supervised legislative elections and a referendum on the institution of the Mwami. The result of the vote was a declared preference for two separate states—a republic in Ruanda and a kingdom in Burundi. On 23 February 1962 the General Assembly sent a new commission, which was given certain specific tasks, to Ruanda-Urundi. The Assembly declared at this time its view that the best course for the territory would be to become independent as a single sovereign state. At the end of June 1962 the Assembly discussed the report of the most recent commission. The Commission noted the refusal of the Governments of the two parts to

* From THE DEVELOPMENT OF INTERNATIONAL LAW THROUGH THE POLITICAL ORGANS OF THE UNITED NATIONS by Rosalyn Higgins. Published by Oxford University Press under the auspices of the Royal Institute of International Affairs.

become independent as a single state, and expressed its disappointment with this attitude. The Commission supported the Belgian view that the national forces were in an embryonic state, and that there might well be difficulties in keeping law and order. In Burundi the Government in power had "indisputable popular support", the Commission reported. It was therefore felt that in spite of the inadequate training of officials and army, the government should prove capable of ensuring law and order in its territory. In Ruanda, where different ethnic groups (primarily the Tutsi aristocracy of warriors and the formerly subservient Hutu majority) had yet to be reconciled, and the question of the future of the Mwami still remained unsettled, the Commission was less hopeful about the ability of the government to maintain order.

Nevertheless, to prevent further tension and violence, it was felt that the scheduled date of 1 July 1962 for independence should be adhered to. But so inadequate were the governmental resources at Burundi's disposal, and so uncertain was the nature and degree of governmental control, that the Commission stated that:

 * * * [T]he granting of independence on July 1 and the simultaneous adoption of a body of measures designed to make up for the country's lack of preparation in the Economic, Social, Educational and other spheres, will be an essential contribution to Burundi's free and independent development. * * *

 The situation in [Ruanda] is not calculated to dispel the many misgivings which the General Assembly has always felt with regard to the conditions in which the people of Ruanda are approaching statehood.

It is quite clear, then, that these two territories, when emerging from trusteeship, lacked at least one of the traditional requirements of statehood. This view is confirmed by an examination of Assembly resolution 1746 (XVI), passed after considering the report of the Commission. This resolution, implicitly acknowledging the difficulties the new Governments will face in keeping law and order, calls for Belgium to withdraw its forces by 1 August 1962—that is to say, a full month after independence. A Soviet amendment to this resolution, which would have called on Belgium to withdraw its troops before independence, was rejected by 24 votes to 46, with 33 abstentions. The Ruanda and Burundi applications for United Nations membership were received soon after their independence, and upon Security Council recommendation they were admitted to the Organization.

The problem is this: that the traditional requirement of a stable and effective government in a territory claiming statehood runs counter to the developments in international law regarding a legal right of self-determination. It is also often at variance with political reality: the anti-colonial pressures upon Western European states, and uneconomic costs for them to remain by force in their colonial possessions, have caused these states in several cases to withdraw from territories which they previously governed before any adequate indigenous system of government has been formed. Are these territories, no longer under colonial rule, to be denied the dignity of statehood, and the rights and duties that follow therefrom? Bearing in mind that such marginal legal problems are invariably graded by policy preference rather than by juridical preference, it can hardly be in the interests of the international community to refuse to acknowledge such territories as states. To do so would be to set up a class of "territories-in-Limbo", and with it a host of unnecessary problems. It would also seem to involve a visitation on the children of the sins of the fathers. In purely political terms, to adhere rigidly to the requirement of a stable and effective government is in neither the Communist nor the Afro-Asian interest, as these groups perceive it. It becomes more and more doubtful whether it is in the interests of the West either.

Statehood in United Nations practice. Denial of United Nations membership to a political entity is at best ambiguous on the question of statehood, since Article 4 of the charter opens membership to states that meet other criteria besides statehood. In addition, since admission is not automatic but requires affirmative action by two political bodies, the Security Council and the General Assembly, reasons for non-admission can be both numerous and unspecified. Major political entities that are not members of the United Nations are Switzerland and the two Koreas.

When an entity is admitted to membership in the United Nations before meeting the standard minimum criteria for statehood as defined by international law, is one to assume that the members have acted illegally or, at least, outside the law? Or are the members saying that the purposes of the charter may be fulfilled when an entity is well on the way to meeting those criteria and that it is thus a state as that term is used in Article 4 of the Charter?

What is meant by the legal right of self-determination referred to in the extract from Higgins?

THE ARANTZAZU MENDI

England, House of Lords, 1939.
[1939] A.C. 256.*

* * *

[The Arantzazu Mendi] was a Spanish ship registered at Bilbao. After that port was captured by General Franco's forces she was requisitioned by the Republican Government. She was then on the high seas, and on August 11, 1937, on her arrival in London, her owners issued a writ in rem for possession, and in pursuance thereof the ship

---

* Reprinted by permission of the Incorporated Council of Law Reporting for England and Wales, London.

was arrested by the Admiralty Marshal in the Surrey Commercial Docks. To that writ the Republican Government entered a conditional appearance. On March 28, 1938, General Franco issued a decree requisitioning the ship in question and other vessels for public services. On April 11, 1938, the owners' possession action was discontinued, but the vessel still remained under arrest. On April 13 the managing director of the owners made a notarial declaration that he consented to the order of requisition and held the vessel at the disposal of the Nationalist Government. The master made a similar declaration. On the same day the Republican Government issued the present writ, which the Nationalist Government sought to set aside on the ground that it impleaded a foreign sovereign State which was unwilling to submit to the jurisdiction of the Court.

* * *

Lord ATKIN. My Lords, * * * [t]he question is whether the Nationalist Government of Spain represents a foreign sovereign State in the sense that entitles them to immunity from being impleaded in these Courts, and, if so, whether they are impleaded in the action by reason of being in possession of the ship in question. I state the question in that form as being sufficient to dispose of the present case. * * * On the question whether the Nationalist Government of Spain was a foreign sovereign State, Bucknill, J., took the correct course of directing a letter, dated May 25, 1938, to be written by the Admiralty Registrar to the Secretary of State for Foreign Affairs, asking whether the Nationalist Government of Spain is recognized by His Majesty's Government as a foreign sovereign State. I pause here to say that not only is this the correct procedure, but that it is the only procedure by which the Court can inform itself of the material fact whether the party sought to be impleaded, or whose property is sought to be affected, is a foreign sovereign State.

* * * The reason is, I think, obvious. Our State cannot speak with two voices on such a matter, the judiciary saying one thing, the executive another. Our Sovereign has to decide whom he will recognize as a fellow sovereign in the family of States; and the relations of the foreign State with ours in the matter of State immunities must flow from that decision alone.

The answer of the Foreign Secretary was given in a letter dated May 28, 1938. After stating that His Majesty's Government recognizes Spain as a foreign sovereign State, and recognizes the Government of the Spanish Republic as the only de jure Government of Spain or any part of it, the letter proceeds:

5. His Majesty's Government recognizes the Nationalist Government as a Government which at present exercises de facto administrative control over the larger portion of Spain.

6. His Majesty's Government recognizes that the Nationalist Government now exercises effective administrative control over all the Basque Provinces of Spain.

8.   The Nationalist Government is not a Government subordinate to any other Government in Spain.

My Lords, this letter appears to me to dispose of the controversy. By "exercising de facto administrative control" or "exercising effective administrative control," I understand exercising all the functions of a sovereign government, in maintaining law and order, instituting and maintaining courts of justice, adopting or imposing laws regulating the relations of the inhabitants of the territory to one another and to the Government. It necessarily implies the ownership and control of property whether for military or civil purposes, including vessels whether warships or merchant ships. In those circumstances it seems to me that the recognition of a Government as possessing all those attributes in a territory while not subordinate to any other Government in that territory is to recognize it as sovereign, and for the purposes of international law as a foreign sovereign State. It does not appear to be material whether the territory over which it exercises sovereign powers is from time to time increased or diminished. In the present case we appear to be dealing with a claim based upon a legislative decree affecting merchant shipping registered at Bilbao in the Basque Provinces, the territory specially designated in the sixth paragraph of the Foreign Office letter. That the decree therefore emanated from the sovereign in that territory there can be no doubt. There is ample authority for the proposition that there is no difference for the present purposes between a recognition of a State de facto as opposed to de jure. All the reasons for immunity which are the basis of the doctrine in international law as incorporated into our law exist. There is the same necessity for reciprocal rights of immunity, the same feeling of injured pride if jurisdiction is sought to be exercised, the same risk of belligerent action if Government property is seized or injured. The non-belligerent State which recognizes two Governments, one de jure and one de facto, will not allow them to transfer their quarrels to the area of the jurisdiction of its municipal Courts.

For these reasons I think that it was established by the Foreign Office letter that the Nationalist Government of Spain at the date of the writ was a foreign sovereign State and could not be impleaded.

* * *

* * * For these reasons, my Lords, the appeal was, in my opinion, rightly dismissed.

* * *

[Other opinions omitted.]

---

1.   *Questions.* Lord Atkin says that "the Nationalist Government of Spain at the date of the writ was a foreign sovereign State." Were there, then, two governments of the single territory formerly known as Spain? Or was that territory now divided into two territories, each with its own government? Was it necessary for the court

to find that the Nationalist Government was a state in order to reach the result in the case?

2. *Belligerent and insurgent entities.* During the 19th century, processes were developed by which revolutionary groups were treated as something different from merely bands of private persons defying legal governments. As will be discussed in Chapter 19, older ideas about the lawfulness of war have been altered by the Pact of Paris of 1928 and the United Nations Charter; the law of war, civil war, neutrality and intervention has undergone substantial change. Thus the processes of recognition of belligerency and recognition of insurgency are today more interesting than useful in international practice. They are described in the Reporters' note to Section 94 of the Restatement of the Foreign Relations Law of the United States (1965),* as follows:

Recognition of belligerency. Recognition of belligerency by a state is an act by which the state, in issuing a declaration of neutrality, asserts that it (a) is neutral in an armed conflict, (b) assumes certain neutral duties toward the parties to the conflict, and (c) has certain rights with respect to trade between its nationals and persons within the territory of the belligerency subject to the rules of international law regarding visitation, search, contraband, blockade, and prize. Recognition of belligerency for an otherwise unrecognized entity or regime may arise from a declaration of neutrality by another state as between a constitutional government and rebels in a civil war. This occurred in the American Civil War when Great Britain recognized the belligerency of the Confederacy, declared its neutrality, and claimed neutral trading rights. It is well-established, as in that instance, that recognition of a rebel's belligerency does not have the effect, standing alone, of committing the second state to treat the rebel regime as the government, or the rebel entity (if one is claimed to have come into existence) as a state.

Recognition of insurgency. In customary practice, recognition of insurgency has considerably less legal significance than recognition of belligerency. Historically, the object of recognition of insurgency by non-contending states was to obtain for rebels carrying on organized military operations the protections given by international law. Recognition of insurgency has often been the first official notice that other states have taken of the eventual possible success of a revolutionary regime.

The more recent tendency has been to rely on ad hoc assurances in revolutionary situations that the basic principles underlying the rules of warfare will be respected. * * *

THE CASE OF KOREA IN THE UNITED NATIONS

United Nations Security Council, Off.Rec., V, No. 24, Aug. 3, 1950; No. 27,
Aug. 10, 1950; No. 28, Aug. 11, 1950; No. 31, Aug. 22, 1950;
No. 36, Sept. 1, 1950.

[Korea had existed independently for centuries prior to falling under Japanese rule in 1905; it was still under Japanese rule during the Second World War. Allied leaders had first planned to place Korea under a trusteeship after the war, but these plans fell through. As a military matter, Korea was divided at the 38th parallel in 1945, when Japanese troops surrendered to the USSR north of that parallel and to the United States in the south.

The United Nations addressed itself to Korean independence but no way could be found to provide a single government for all Korea. In 1948, elections were held in the south under United Nations supervision and the United Nations General Assembly adopted a resolution declaring that "there has been established a lawful government (the Government of the Republic of Korea) having effective control and jurisdiction over the part of Korea where the Temporary Commission was able to observe and consult and in which the great majority of the people of all Korea reside; that this Government is based on elections which were a valid expression of the free will of the electorate of that part of Korea and which were observed by the Temporary Commission; and that this is the only such Government in Korea." Also in that year, a Democratic People's Republic of Korea was proclaimed by a Supreme People's Assembly. The Republic claimed jurisdiction over all Korea. Elections to the assembly were not observed by the United Nations.

The USSR and the United States announced withdrawal of forces from Korea in 1948 and 1949. The United Nations was informed that the North Koreans had invaded South Korea on June 25, 1950. The Security Council met; the Russians were not present, since they had left the council some months earlier over the refusal of the council to oust the Nationalist Chinese in favor of the Communist Chinese. In a series of resolutions the council recommended "that the members of the United Nations furnish such assistance to the Republic of Korea as may be necessary to repel the armed attack and to restore international peace and security in the area," recommended that the members provide forces to a unified command under the United States, requested the United States to designate the commander of such forces and authorized the "use of the United Nations flag in the course of operations against North Korean forces concurrently with the flags of the various nations participating." [a]

The USSR entered into the debate on the Korean question for the first time when it returned to the council on August 1, 1950, with Mr. Malik then taking his turn in the chair.]

a. These events are more fully described in Higgins, United Nations Peacekeeping, 1946–67, II Asia 153 (1970); Sohn, Cases and Materials on United Nations Law (2d ed. 1967).

1. Debate on the Adoption of the Agenda (No. 24, Aug. 3, 1950).

[The representatives of the following countries were present: China, Cuba, Ecuador, Egypt, France, India, Norway, Union of Soviet Socialist Republics, United Kingdom of Great Britain and Northern Ireland, United States of American and Yugoslavia.

The president of the Security Council, Mr. MALIK, had proposed a provisional agenda which included an item entitled "Peaceful Settlement of the Korean Question." The council rejected this item in favor of one proposed by the United States, entitled: "Complaint of Aggression upon the Republic of Korea." In the course of the debate on the adoption of the agenda, the president made a speech, a portion of which appears below.]

The President (translated from Russian):

*   *   *

It is clear to anyone with a grain of impartiality that a civil war is in progress in Korea between the North and South Koreans. The military operations between the North and South Koreans are of an internal character; they bear the character of a civil war. There is therefore no justification for regarding these military operations as aggression.

Aggression takes place where one State attacks another. The U.S.S.R. Government has taken this line in defining aggression since 1933, when the delegation of the Soviet Union put forward a definition of aggression in the Committee on Security Questions of the Conference for the reduction and limitation of armaments in Geneva. This definition contains instructions for the guidance of international organs which may be called upon to determine the side guilty of attack, the attacking side, in other words, the aggressor.

As is known, this definition of aggression includes such acts as a declaration of war by a State against another State; invasion of a territory by the armed forces of another State even without a declaration of war; the invasion of the territory of one State by the armed forces of another State and so forth.

According to this definition no political, strategic or economic considerations can justify aggression. Nor can the denial that a territory which is attacked has the specific attributes of statehood serve as a justification for an attack. Nor can a revolutionary or counter-revolutionary movement, or a civil war, serve as a justification, or the establishment or the maintenance of a particular political, economic or social order.

*   *   *

United States armed forces have invaded Korean territory, although without a formal declaration of war. The above-mentioned definition qualifies such action as aggression. United States land, sea and air forces are bombing Korean territory and attacking Korean vessels and aircraft. According to the above-mentioned definition, such acts are acts of aggression, and the United States is the attacking State—the aggressor. United States land, sea and air forces have landed on Korean territory and are carrying on military action there against the Korean people which is at present in a state of domestic civil war. Such acts constitute aggression on the part of the United States. The United States has established a naval blockade of the Korean coast and ports. Such acts constitute aggression in accordance with the definition referred to.

* * *

Thus if the action taken by the United States in Korea is considered in the light of the above definition of aggression, it is clear beyond question that the United States Government has interfered in an internal conflict in Korea between two groups in a single State and has thereby undertaken an act of aggression upon the Korean people.

As regards the war between the North and South Koreans, it is a civil war and therefore does not come under the definition of aggression, since it is a war, not between two States, but between two parts of the Korean people temporarily split into two camps under two separate authorities.

The conflict in Korea is thus an internal conflict. Consequently rules relating to aggression are just as inapplicable to the North and South Koreans as the concept of aggression was inapplicable to the northern and southern states of America, when they were fighting a civil war for the unification of their country. We know that the role of aggressor at that time was played by Great Britain, which attempted to intervene in that civil war and to prevent the unification of the North and South in the United States. Similarly, the United Kingdom is now, together with the United States, intervening in the civil war in Korea in the attempt to impede the unification of that country.

A similar situation arises in China also where, as we know, the struggle between the Chiang Kai-shek group and the national liberation movement of the north has not been regarded as aggression, and foreign Powers have accordingly abstained from intervention in this domestic conflict, in this civil war.

All this goes to show that the only aggressors in Korea are those Powers which are maintaining their forces on Korean territory and are intervening in the struggle between the North and South Koreans, thereby extending the sphere of military operations.

Hence we have in Korea on the one hand an internal conflict between the North and South Koreans—a civil war—and on the other hand the armed intervention of the Government of the United States in this internal Korean civil war in the form of armed aggression, which falls completely within the definition of aggression contained in the declaration on aggression, which was adopted in May 1933 by the League of Nations Committee on Security Questions, on which seventeen States were represented, including the United States of America.

As is known, the United Nations Charter also directly prohibits intervention by the United Nations in the domestic affairs of any State when the conflict is an internal one between two groups within a single State and a single nation. Accordingly, the United Nations Charter provides for intervention by the Security Council only in events of an international rather than of an internal nature.

That is the essence of the Korean question and of the United States armed aggression against the Korean people.

Thus the peoples of the whole world and the United Nations are at present confronted with open armed aggression in Korea on the part of the United States Government and with attempts by the United States to involve the United Nations in that aggression.

*   *   *

2. Complaint of Aggression upon the Republic of Korea. (No. 27, Aug. 10, 1950).

[The agenda having been adopted, Mr. MALIK, proposed that the council invite representatives of both North and South Korea to the council. The Chinese representative raised a point of order, namely that the council had previously invited a representative of South Korea and should not vote on that matter again. In the course of the debate on the question of invitation of representatives, the following statements were made.]

Mr. AUSTIN (United States of America):

*   *   * During the recent world war, the leading allies, including the U.S.S.R., pledged the freedom and independence of Korea. By agreement between the United States and the Soviet Union at the time of Japan's surrender, the 38th parallel was selected as an administrative boundary line for convenience in accepting the surrender of Japanese troops. That was a temporary, military, division; it was not a permanent, political, division. It was interpreted differently, however, by the U.S.S.R. Government, which proceeded to turn the 38th parallel into a hard and fast frontier. In an effort to correct that obvious violation of war-time pledges made to the Korean people, my Government has consistently urged the abolition of the military frontier and the creation of a democratic and independent government of unified Korea.

In 1947, in 1948 and in 1949, the General Assembly by an overwhelming majority urged the same things. It has maintained in Korea for nearly three years a Commission charged with the completion of those tasks. The Commission has been denied access to North Korea—that is, that part of Korea north of the 38th parallel—by the Soviet Union as the occupying Power. South of that parallel, the United Nations Commission on Korea has supervised two elections, certified the establishment of a democratic government and verified the withdrawal of United States occupation forces. The General

Assembly itself, by its resolution 195 (III), accepted the Government of the Republic of Korea as the only valid and lawful government in Korea. Many Members of the United Nations have recognized the Republic of Korea, whose admission to the United Nations was blocked by the U.S.S.R. veto.

This summary of political history should make it clear what Government has blocked the unity and independence of Korea, what Government has established a puppet government in its zone of military control, and what Government has defied the recommendations of the United Nations.

*   *   *

If the efforts of the United Nations had not been blocked by the Soviet Union and the authorities in North Korea, then Korea today would be free and independent. Below the line of the 38th parallel, the light of day has shone. The United Nations observers could watch and report. They could tell us what was happening—the faults of a new nation, as well as its virtues. They could certify to us that democracy was having its struggles, but that it was succeeding.

Above that line, all was darkness. The arbitrary action of one great Power—and one great Power alone—kept the United Nations observers from fulfilling, above that line, the task assigned to them by the General Assembly. That great Power was free to pick and choose its instruments as it wished, to carry out its imperialist purposes in North Korea.

*   *   *

On 25 June, the mists that for five years had covered North Korea parted. Out of the fog came a mighty military machine to launch an unexpected and unprovoked attack on the Republic of Korea.

Although the representative of the Soviet Union did not feel able to attend the meetings of the Security Council called when Korea was invaded, he must have read the reports submitted to us by the United Nations Commission on Korea.

On 24 June, the day before the attack, the observers for the Commission reported that their "principal impression" was that the Republican army "is organized entirely for defence and is in no condition to carry out attack on large scale against forces of north" [S/1518]. The Commission itself, composed of representatives of Australia, China, El Salvador, France, India, the Philippines and Turkey, found on 26 June [S/1507] that "judging from actual progress of operations, Northern régime is carrying out well-planned, concerted, and full-scale invasion of South Korea".

*   *   *

Subsequent military developments have proved to anyone with a knowledge of warfare that the invasion by the North Koreans was carefully planned and had been prepared over a long period of time. I am sure the representative of the U.S.S.R. will agree that it must have taken many months to train the drivers and gunners who are now massacring their fellow countrymen and defying the United Nations.

In the face of the unprovoked aggression launched by the North Koreans, the Security Council met within twenty-four hours of the attack and adopted [473rd meeting] a resolution calling for the immediate cessation of hostilities, for the withdrawal of the North Korean forces to the 38th parallel, and for the rendering of "every assistance" by all Members to the United Nations "in the execution of this resolution". That was addressed to all Members.

As the attack continued, the President of the United States, at noon on 27 June, announced support for this resolution by ordering the United States air and sea forces to assist the troops of the Korean Government. On the same day, 27 June, the Security Council recommended [474th meeting] that all Members of the United Nations should furnish such aid to the Republic of Korea as might be necessary to repel the attack and restore international peace and security in the area. Since that time, fifty-three Members have supported the Security Council's action to restore peace in Korea. Many of them have offered, and some have already sent, military support or other types of assistance. All are working and fighting together under the United Nations flag and under a Unified Command in a great common effort to put down lawless aggression. To call such a United Nations function "aggression" is like calling aid to a peaceful citizen, attacked by a thief in the night, aggression.

Yet the representative of the Soviet Union obstructs all efforts of the Security Council to perform its peacemaking functions by speeches charging the United States as the aggressor.

Those are the facts of recent Korean history.

* * *

3. Complaint of Aggression upon the Republic of Korea, Continued (No. 28, Aug. 11, 1950).

* * *

Sir Gladwyn JEBB (United Kingdom): It is, I fear, only too true that the refusal of our President to admit the representative of the Republic of Korea and his insistence on inviting a representative of the North Korean authorities raise most important and, indeed, basic matters of principle, some of which, but not all, have already been alluded to in the long debate which we have now had on this subject.

* * *

The Soviet Union representative's basic intention, as I understand it, is based on the premise that what we are dealing with in Korea is a civil war. He proceeds to argue that, as is indeed natural, there are two sides to most civil wars and, therefore, two sides to this one. Consequently, if we invite the representative of one side to be present, we are bound in logic and in equity—and, indeed, I think he said in accordance with the dictates of common sense—to invite the representative of the other side also.

This would all be very obvious were it not for the fact that the Soviet Union representative, in his desire to impress public opinion with the rightness of his cause, has omitted to draw attention to the fact that the Government of the Republic of Korea has already been declared the lawful government by the United Nations; that United Nations observers were stationed on its de facto northern frontier; and that, therefore, the whole State was, as it were, existing under the mantle of this great international Organization.

The Government of the Korean Republic was, however, attacked —and I shall not here proceed to demonstrate that it was attacked or to counter Soviet propaganda to the effect that it was Mr. Dulles and Mr. Muccio who attacked the Northern Koreans first—incidently I must apologize for omitting to refer to Mr. Muccio previously, since clearly Mr. Muccio's presence doubled the total number of the interventionist force—since that is so obviously absurd that it is hard to think that it can be swallowed even by the automata who listen to the Moscow radio. It was attacked, I say, by soldiers coming under the authority of a rival Korean government, not acceptable to the United Nations, and established at Pyongyang. It is quite true that the soldiers I refer to were Koreans, and therefore were, so to speak, blood brothers of the people whom they attacked; but to argue that this fact in itself constitutes a civil war, or that it necessarily in itself puts both sides on an equal footing, is patent nonsense. The President made what he thought were some very telling observations regarding the American Civil War, but they would only have been relevant if he had gone on to show that in 1861 either the northern states or the southern had been recognized by an international organization, which he could not do for the simple reason that no international organization existed at that time.

* * *

Quite apart from this, there is absolutely no reason to suppose that wars between people of the same race, even if they do not involve a government which has been set up under the aegis of the United Nations, are necessarily exempt from the decisions of the Security Council. A civil war in certain circumstances might well, under Article 39 of the Charter, constitute a "threat to the peace", or even a "breach of the peace", and if the Security Council so decided, there would be nothing whatever to prevent its taking any action it liked in order to put an end to the incident, even if it should involve two or more portions of the same international entity. Indeed, paragraph 7 of Article 2 of the Charter so provides. This reads:

> Nothing contained in the present Charter shall authorize the United Nations to intervene in matters which are essentially within the domestic jurisdiction of any State or shall require the Members to submit such matters to settlement under the present Charter; but this principle shall not prejudice the application of enforcement measures under Chapter VII.

It will be seen that the last few words make it quite clear that the United Nations has full authority to intervene actively in the internal affairs of any country if this is necessary for the purpose of enforcing its decisions as regards the maintenance of international peace and security. I do honestly hope that, for the reasons given, we shall hear no more of this "civil war" argument from the mouth of the Soviet Union spokesman.

It is equally true that, under the Charter, the Security Council might be unlikely to make a recommendation or a decision under Article 39 in regard to another such incident as the present, since such action could and no doubt would be vetoed by the Soviet Union. But when the Security Council very properly decided that the Government of the Republic of Korea should be defended against a brutal attack, and decided on the appropriate measures to that effect, it did so unanimously, and no permanent member present at this table objected in the slightest degree, or even made any reservations. On the contrary, they were all horrified at the outrage which had occurred, and the Council machinery therefore worked smoothly and easily and in entire accord with the purposes and principles of the Charter.
* * *

* * *

4. Complaint of Aggression upon the Republic of Korea, Continued (No. 31, Aug. 22, 1950).

Sir Gladwyn JEBB (United Kingdom):
* * *

Quite apart from this, however, the "civil war" argument simply does not make sense on general grounds. First of all, you divide a State into two, then you organize a special Government in one part of it, not allowing anybody else to see how this Government is formed or what it is doing. You give it full governmental powers and you recognize it, even though most States have recognized the other Government. Then the Government organized in this way, possessing de facto authority over half the territory, attacks the lawful Government of the other half which has been set up under the international protection of the United Nations. Nobody, however, is allowed to interfere with this process on the grounds that it is a "civil war". The result, of course, is that, in defiance of international authority, you get control of the whole country and you get what you want. It is quite easy to think of other cases in which this interesting, if rather sinister, theory might be applied.
* * *

5. Complaint of Aggression upon the Republic of Korea, Continued (No. 36, Sept. 1, 1950).

[The president of the council, Mr. MALIK, neither invited a representative of South Korea to the council nor put to a vote his proposal to invite a representative of North Korea. At the beginning of the next month, the presidency of the council rotated to Sir Gladwyn, Jebb, who immediately invited the South Korean representative to sit at the council table. This action was upheld by the council (the USSR opposed). A draft resolution by the USSR to invite representatives of North and South Korea was interpreted by the president (the council agreeing) to relate only to the question of the representation of North Korea. The USSR draft resolution was rejected. Prior to the vote, the following statements were made.]

Sir Benegal N. RAU (India): * * *
* * *

It has been urged that Article 32 of the Charter requires us to invite the North Korean representative. If this contention were correct, not only must the North Korean representative be invited to our future discussions, but any past proceedings to which he was not invited would stand vitiated as a violation of the Charter. This, to my mind, is a serious matter. Some of these past proceedings have been endorsed by India, and it is therefore necessary for me to examine the contention carefully. I shall proceed to do so even at the risk of being tedious.

The relevant portion of Article 32 provides that any State which is not a Member of the United Nations, "if it is a party to a dispute under consideration by the Security Council", must be invited to participate without vote in the discussion relating to the dispute. So three conditions must be satisfied if the Article is to apply to the present case: North Korea must be a State; so must South Korea; and the Security Council must be considering a dispute between the two. But if North Korea and South Korea are separate States, the contention that the conflict between them is a civil war is untenable. That is by the way. There is, however, a more fundamental flaw in the argument: what we are discussing at present with respect to Korea is not a dispute. If I may use a hackneyed analogy of which some of the members of the Council may be rather tired, when the police are quelling a riot or the fire brigade is putting out a fire, they are not considering a dispute; they are taking action to remove a serious danger.

So, here, at this moment, we are not investigating or considering a dispute; we are in the midst of enforcement action to suppress a dangerous breach of the peace. The two things are quite distinct. The Security Council has, in fact, a dual function under the Charter: it investigates disputes under Chapter VI of the Charter, and it takes action with respect to breaches of the peace under Chapter VII. It is only when it is considering disputes that Article 32 of the Charter applies. The wording, if I may repeat it, makes this clear: "if it is a party to a dispute under consideration by the Security Council".

Of course, when the enforcement action that is now in progress has been concluded, there may supervene a dispute, and at that stage Article 32 may come into operation, if we regard North Korea and South as separate States.

In his recent book on The Law of the United Nations, Professor Kelsen states: "A 'dispute' exists in the relation between two States only if the one has addressed a claim to the other State and if the latter has refused to comply with this claim. When a State attacks another State without previously having demanded anything from the attacked State and without this State's having refused to comply with a demand of the other, there exists a conflict between the two States, but no 'dispute'."

Therefore it seems to me that Article 32 of the Charter has no application to the present situation at this stage. The Council will remember that when we invited the representative of the Republic of Korea on 25 June and subsequent dates, we did so not under Article 32 of the Charter, but under rule 39 of our provisional rules of procedure.[a] This, I hope, is not a small legal point. I think there is more in it than that.

From time to time, we receive reports from the Unified Command describing the progress of the campaign in Korea. I am not a military expert myself but it is conceivable that the contents of these reports, and any disclosures in the course of our discussions upon those reports, might be of value to the enemy. So far as I am aware, no representative of the United Nations is allowed to participate in the discussions conducted by the North Korean authorities on the Korean campaign.

Briefly, what we are engaged in at the present moment is not the discussion of the Korean dispute, but, rather of the Korean campaign. In the view of my Government, the question of hearing the representative of the North Korean authorities cannot arise until the campaign is over; that is to say, until at least hostilities have ceased and withdrawal of the North Korean forces has been agreed upon. I shall therefore have to vote against the proposal that their representative should be invited to the Council table at this stage—and I emphasize the words "at this stage".

Mr. MALIK (Union of Soviet Socialist Republics) (translated from Russian): * * *

It is impossible to agree that Article 32 of the Charter is applicable only in the consideration of questions relating to Chapter VI. Article 40, in Chapter VII, provides that in case of international conflict, the Security Council should not rush headlong into that conflict, that it should not make the situation more complicated or allow aggression or military action to spread. It specifically states: "In order to prevent an aggravation of the situation, the Security Council may, before making the recommendations or deciding upon the measures provided for in Article 39, call upon the parties concerned to comply with such provisional measures as it deems necessary or desirable."

Article 41 states: "The Security Council may decide what measures not involving the use of armed force are to be employed to give effect to its decisions".

---

a. Rule 39 provides: "The Security Council may invite members of the secretariat or other persons, whom it considers competent for the purpose, to supply it with information or to give other assistance in examining matters within its competence."

If the Council considers and decides on such measures, then where in Chapter VII or elsewhere is it said that the representative of the party which, rightly or wrongly, legitimately or illegitimately, is accused of aggression, has no right to be present at the meetings of the Council? Would the jurists show me a sentence, a word, a provision or an Article in the Charter to that effect? There are no such provisions in the Charter and when questions falling within Chapters VI and VII are discussed, the representative of the party against which charges of aggression have been brought must attend in order that the Council may better clarify the facts of the dispute and take all the necessary measures to halt aggression and to prevent the war from spreading.

Was anything done here to that end? No. On 25 June, when the conflict which had arisen in Korea was discussed, no decision was taken as to what Article of the Charter should be applied and on what legal basis action should be taken. The representative of North Korea was not admitted to the meeting. No jurist could have explained, or can explain, on what grounds he was voting against inviting the representative of North Korea; yet when the question of not admitting the representative of North Korea was discussed on 25 June, no decision was taken regarding the application of sanctions, even of illegal ones. I am not even speaking about the illegal character of that resolution. Any truly objective jurist will be obliged to state that the decisions on the Korean question were taken in violation of the Charter, without the participation of two permanent members of the Security Council who were unable to attend the meeting for reasons which are well known, and at a time when one of the permanent members of the Security Council, relying on the support of a group of members of the Council, was blocking the admission to the Council of the legitimate representative of China. This is common knowledge.

What happened on 25 June? On that day the Security Council adopted by a majority the illegal decision to refuse to admit a representative of North Korea to the Security Council meeting. On what grounds was this done, on what legal basis? No objective jurist would find a justification for such a decision. * * *

Lastly, let us take a document such as the definition of aggression proposed by the USSR delegation as early as May 1933 in the Committee on Security Questions of the League of Nations and taken by that Committee as a basis. It contains a specific provision that the fact that a territory has not been recognized as a State cannot be used as a justification for aggression against that State. I can cite the exact words of that document. It states that a people's political, economic or cultural backwardness, or the alleged shortcomings of its administration, may not be used to justify any act of aggression. Nor may the fact that a territory has no distinct attributes of statehood or that its possession of such attributes is denied.

In the present case, the jurist invokes the argument that since there is no State of North Korea, North Korea does not exist at all.

This, however, is absurd. There is a North Korea which has nine million or more inhabitants, its own authorities, an army—and a very good one at that, as events have shown; for that army has been able to deal not only with the mercenary troops of the Syngman Rhee regime of South Korea, but also with the troops of the United States aggressor who has invaded foreign territory. How then can it be denied that we are dealing with a people and their authorities? What jurist will take it upon himself to prove the contrary—that there is nothing and no one there?

In any case, the document on the definition of aggression, on the basis of which the organs called upon to consider international conflicts must determine who is the aggressor, and who the victim of aggression, states plainly that the fact that a specific territory is not a State, or lacks the distinguishing signs of a State, cannot be used to justify aggression.

Thus no legal tricks will help in this case. There is a North Korea with a population of from nine to ten million, if not more, a government, an army, local and central authorities and legislative organs. What right has the Security Council to examine the Korean question without inviting and hearing the representatives of those authorities? Only because the United States Government wishes it? That is no reason, and cannot be used as a legal justification, as a ground for not inviting the representative of North Korea. *   *   *

Commentary and questions. The foregoing extracts, lengthy as they are, are but a small trickle in the torrent of words emanating from the Security Council during the debate on the agenda and the question of representation. The formal issues before the council were the matters of agenda and invitation of representatives. The more pervasive issue was the question of the military operation of the United Nations, although this issue was not precisely focussed by draft resolutions before the council.

What was the relevance of the arguments on Korean statehood on the formal issues of agenda and representation? On the issues of the legality of the United Nations military operations? Analytically Korea could be characterized as one state or two states. Or as no state. Is characterization the beginning or the end of the inquiry?

If the legal problem before the council is not to be phrased as "Is Korea a single state?", then what is the problem? By what legal criteria should it be solved?

IN RE HARSHAW CHEMICAL CO.'S PATENT

England, Comptroller of Patents, 1964.
41 Int'l L.Rep. 15 (1970).*

The Facts. This was an application for an extension of their patent by the Harshaw Chemical Company, the registered proprietors of letters patent relating to a method of bright nickel plating. The application was made under section 24(1) of the Patents Act, 1949, which provides:

> If upon application made by a patentee in accordance with this section the court or the comptroller is satisfied that the patentee as such has suffered loss or damage * * * by reason of hostilities between His Majesty and any foreign state, the court or comptroller may by order extend the term of the patent subject to such restrictions, conditions * * * as may be specified in the order * * *.

Section 24(8) of the Act provides:

> No order shall be made under this section on the application of—
>
> (a) a person who is a subject of such a foreign state as is mentioned in subsection (1) of this section * * *.

The application was opposed by three other companies.

The applicants asked for an extension of six years based entirely on the shortage of nickel between 1950 and 1957 which they alleged was caused by the Korean war. The opponents contended that the shortage of nickel was not occasioned "by reason of hostilities between His Majesty and any foreign state", and asked that the Comptroller of Patents or one of the opponents should inquire from the Foreign Office as to whether there were any hostilities with a foreign State. The Foreign Office's reply to an inquiry by the Comptroller was in these terms:—

> The United Kingdom was one of the States which as Members of the United Nations participated in the hostilities against the so-called Democratic People's Republic of Korea. These hostilities lasted from June 25, 1950, to July 27, 1953. The decision to send United Kingdom troops to Korea was taken on July 26, 1950; these troops arrived in Korea on August 29, 1950.
>
> The Democratic People's Republic of Korea was not recognized by either His late Majesty's Government or Her Majesty's Government as an independent sovereign State at any time during the above-mentioned period of hostilities, and it has not subsequently been so recognized by Her Majesty's Government.

The remaining facts and the arguments presented by counsel appear from the decision of the Comptroller.

* Reprinted by permission of E. Lauterpacht, ed., and Grotius Publications, Ltd., Cambridge, England.

Held: that the application must fail. The patentee had not shown a loss within section 24 because the Democratic People's Republic of Korea was not a "State" recognized by Her Majesty's Government at any relevant time.

The Comptroller stated the facts substantially as set out above * * *. [A portion of the decision by the Comptroller appears below.]

Mr. Price argued [for the applicants] that the absence of recognition did not alter the fact that the Democratic People's Republic is a "state". A "state" is merely a country with certain sovereignty, as, for example, a member state of the U.S.A. The Foreign Office statement admits the existence of the Democratic People's Republic as an entity, and it is clear from the reference thereto in Whittaker's Almanac that it is just as much a "state" as the Republic of Korea.

Mr. Ford, on the other hand, submitted [for two of the opponents] that the reference in section 24(8) of the Act to "a person who is a subject of such a foreign state as is mentioned in subsection (1) of this section" necessarily infers that a "state" within the meaning of section 24 must have subjects. This in turn introduces the concept of sovereignty, which the Democratic People's Republic does not possess because it has not been recognised as an "independent sovereign state". Mr. Ford referred to International Law by L. Oppenheim, Volume I, seventh edition, page 145, in support of his contention that recognition is a declaration, on the part of the recognising States, that a foreign community or authority is in possession of the necessary qualifications of statehood, these qualifications being the existence of a people, a country, a government and a sovereign government. It followed that in the absence of recognition there was no evidence that the facts are such that the Democratic People's Republic of Korea comprised a state. Its name implied a claim for authority over the whole state of Korea whereas there existed also a government in South Korea representing the "Republic of Korea". The necessary qualification of sovereignty was therefore not satisfied.

Later, Mr. Ford referred to Halsbury's Laws of England, third edition, volume 15, paragraph 612, on page 336, as the authority that the courts take notice of the existence and titles of foreign states which are recognised by the British Government as independent, and, as appears from the footnote (r), that the existence and status of foreign states not so recognised are not noticed by the judges.

Dr. White [for the third opponent company] supported Mr. Ford's arguments and stressed that the applicants had failed to supply any evidence to prove that the hostilities in Korea were between the Crown and a foreign state. He submitted that section 24 must be construed strictly and that it would be wrong for the Comptroller to hold that the Democratic People's Republic was a state under section 24 in the face of the Foreign Office statement. The history of events shows that Korea was a single unitary state divided in itself, and the

United Nations intervened in Korea to restore order and unify the country. Crown intervention in a civil war does not qualify for loss under section 24.

In reply, Mr. Price argued that the Democratic People's Republic clearly possessed all the qualifications of statehood, and it was not necessary for sovereignty to be complete for a "state" to exist. On recognition, the concern in the present case is with facts and not the niceties of international diplomacy. The acceptance of North Korea is evidenced by the references in the Post Office Guide on the sending of letters to North or South Korea, and the Comptroller can act accordingly under section 24 without prejudicing the position of the Crown.

In deciding on this question I am impressed with the force of Dr. White's argument that section 24(1) must be construed strictly. * * * Whilst none of the cases mentioned have any direct bearing on the present issue, nevertheless I agree that they point to a strict interpretation of the wording of the relevant sections of the Act. As I see it, therefore, I should regard the word "state" in section 24(1) as meaning a state which exists manifestly with all the qualifications required for statehood in international law, and not just any entity, whatever its status. Indeed, if it was the intention of section 24 to provide relief for loss sustained by reason of any hostilities involving the Crown, then presumably the section would have been worded accordingly. It does not appear to me that such was the intention and I take the view that the reference to "state" in the wording of section 24 is intended to limit the scope of the section. To be effective, therefore, the word "state" must be construed rigidly, and to be consistent it must be defined in accordance with established law as implying independence and sovereignty. This appears to me to follow also from the reference in section 24(8) to a person who is "a subject of such a foreign state", because unless such significance is attached to the word "state" then considerable difficulty may arise in deciding on questions under section 24(8) * * *.

Having reached the conclusion that the word "state" must be construed rigidly, then as I see it, on the authority to which Mr. Ford referred, I cannot ignore the dictum that the courts cannot take judicial notice of the existence and status of "states" which are not recognised by the British Government as independent. The footnote (r) to paragraph 612 of Halsbury's Laws of England, which I have already mentioned, refers to a number of cases in which this dictum has been followed and in which it is established that the proper course on any question of the status of a foreign country is to ascertain the facts from H.M. Government, and that the court is bound to act on the information given to it through the proper department. As Lord Atkin stated in the case of The Arantzazu Mendi [1939] A.C. 256, H.L.; at page 264,

> Our state cannot speak with two voices on such a matter, the judiciary saying one thing, the executive another.

This being so, then, in the light of the Foreign Office statement, I am bound to decide that the Democratic People's Republic of Korea, or, as it is more commonly referred to, North Korea, cannot be regarded at any relevant time as comprising a "state" within the meaning of section 24 of the Act.   *   *   *

However, in view of the submissions made at the hearing on the necessary qualifications of statehood and particularly the submission of Mr. Price that the absence of recognition by the Crown does not alter the fact that the Democratic People's Republic of Korea is a "state", it is perhaps desirable that I should also state my views on the matter in the light of these submissions.

The applicants have not adduced any evidence to show that the Democratic People's Republic of Korea constitutes a "state" despite the fact that they have been aware of the Foreign Office statement since the end of May, 1963. Of course, the facts on Korea as set out in Whittaker's Almanac are within recent memory, and it may be that the applicants feel that these known facts are sufficient to prove the existence of the Democratic People's Republic as a "state", but in my view the contrary is the case. As I see it, since the end of Japanese rule in 1945, the country of Korea has been a focal point of East-West conflict, with the country divided into North and South areas. Prior to the outbreak of hostilities in June, 1950, each area had set up its own government and constitution, with South Korea calling itself the "Republic of Korea", and North Korea "The Democratic People's Republic of Korea". It may fairly be said that the Republic of Korea, which was formally inaugurated in August, 1948 and has been recognised by Her Majesty's Government and by most other countries except the U.S.S.R. and her satellites, came into existence in accordance with a resolution passed by the General Assembly of the United Nations in November, 1947. On the other hand, the Democratic People's Republic was set up in September, 1948 under the auspices of the U.S.S.R. and has been recognised by the U.S.S.R. and her satellites.

The names adopted by the two areas each suggest a claim to represent the whole territory of Korea, and certainly the aim of the United Nations at all times has been to bring about the unification of the country. There is but one Korean people and, for reasons which are of no concern in these proceedings, this people is divided among itself. It is significant in this respect that the government of the Republic of Korea did not accept the armistice agreement, signed by the U. N. Commander-in-Chief and the commanders of the North Korean forces in July, 1953, wherein the line of division between North and South Korea remained in the neighbourhood of the 38th parallel.

It seems to me, therefore, that the hostilities in Korea were more in the nature of a civil war rather than a war between two "states". The United Nations intervened on the side of the government of the Republic of Korea, which had come into being under United Nations sponsorship and which was recognised by the majority of the member states of the United Nations including the United Kingdom. The armistice of 1953 brought about the cessation of hostilities, and in 1954 the Geneva Conference discussed Korea with a view to agreeing measures for reunifying the country. No agreement was reached, but the fact that such discussion took place suggests to me that, up to then at least, the Democratic People's Republic was considered to be no more than a "belligerent power". On the facts available to me nothing has happened since to so consolidate the division of Korea as would confer the status of statehood on the so-called Democratic People's Republic. In my view, therefore, the Democratic People's Republic has not at any time been a "state" for the purposes of section 24.

Having reached this conclusion, it is unnecessary for me to decide the second question, namely, whether the hostilities in North Korea were "between His Majesty and any foreign state". I think I should say, however, that if, contrary to this conclusion, I had formed the opinion that the Democratic People's Republic could be regarded as a state for the purposes of section 24, I would have had no hesitation in concluding that the Korean hostilities were hostilities within the meaning of section 24. * * *

———

Questions. The comptroller feels bound by the fact that North Korea had not been recognized by the Foreign Office. Is the constitutional question of the relationship between the comptroller and the Foreign Office relevant to the question presented in the application? He also apparently decided on his own analysis of Korean history that the hostilities in Korea were more like a civil war than a war between two states. By what criteria did he make that determination?

In the opinion that follows, the same issue was before a court five years later, on application of a different patentee. Although the court doubted its own jurisdiction in the peculiar procedural posture of the case, it nevertheless offered its opinion on the merits. By what criteria did the court arrive at a different conclusion from the comptroller? Is statehood to be determined by international legal principles? Why did the English Parliament exclude all but hostilities between states from the operation of the provisions of Section 24(1) of the Patents Act? Does either opinion consider that question? Should it have?

———

IN RE AL–FIN CORPORATION'S PATENT

Chancery Division, 1969.
[1969] 2 W.L.R. 1405.*

ORIGINATING SUMMONS.

Patentees, Al-Fin Corporation, took out this originating summons in connection with an application for extension of their patent

* Reprinted by permission of the Incorporated Council of Law Reporting for England and Wales, London.

No. 689,129 for the determination of whether on a true construction of section 24 of the Patents Act, 1949, the Democratic Peoples Republic of Korea in the events which happened was a foreign state within the meaning of subsection 1 of section 24 at the time of the Korean war. *   *   *

*   *   * An affidavit of Mr. Victor Frank dated April 24, 1968, set out a factual account of the history of Korea over the relevant period. By paragraphs 22 to 25:

22.   Elections for local People's Committees were held in November, 1946; only one list of candidates, all members of the National Democratic Front, was presented, and, it was announced, gained 97 per cent. of the votes cast. These local People's Committees appointed a Convention of People's Committees which met in 1947 in Pyongyang. This convention set up a further body, a "Supreme People's Assembly," which drafted and, in April 1948, approved a constitution based on that of the U.S.S.R. Elections for the new Assembly were held in August 1948—360 of the 572 seats being nominally for South Korea, where clandestine "elections" were held by Communist canvassers. In September 1948, the formation of a "People's Democratic Republic of Korea" was announced, and, in October, the Soviet Union accorded it diplomatic recognition, the other Communist countries following suit. No other members of the United Nations accorded the Government diplomatic recognition. The Soviet Government announced that it had withdrawn all its forces from North Korea by January 1, 1949. Thus, two Governments had been established, one in the South, the other in the North. Both Governments claimed to be Governments of the whole of Korea, and each of them denied its rival any legal or constitutional validity.

23.   When the Russian forces withdrew in 1949 they left behind them in North Korea a government which, though not wholly subject to the direction of the Kremlin, was nonetheless bound both economically and politically to the will of the Soviet Government. The North Korean military forces were built up with Russian arms (and arms captured from the Japanese), by Russian instructors, the members of the forces being conscripted from 1949 onwards by the effective Government of the country. It should be emphasised that between 1949 and 1950 the Government of North Korea exercised effective rule over the area of Korea defined already, that its rule was accepted by the population as being the sole source of civil and military authority in the said area, and that the government entered into diplomatic relations with other sovereign states which recognised its existence.

24.   On June 25, 1950, North Korean forces launched a large scale offensive against the territory of the Republic of Korea. On the same day, the Security Council held a meeting which, in the absence of the Soviet representative, passed a resolution describing the North Korean invasion as a breach of the peace and calling upon all U.N. member-states "to render every assistance to the United Nations and to refrain from giving assistance to the North Korean au-

thorities." Two days later, in view of an imminent collapse of South Korean resistance, the Security Council adopted a resolution which recommended "that the members of the United Nations furnish such assistance to the Republic of Korea as may be necessary to repel the armed attack and to restore international peace and security in the area." On June 29, 1950, the North Korean authorities rejected the decisions of the U.N. Security Council as "unlawful." In this attitude North Korea was supported by the U.S.S.R. and all other Soviet-orbit states. An overwhelming majority of U.N. member-states, however, endorsed the council's actions. Immediate and substantial naval and air support was furnished by the British Commonwealth. On June 28, the United Kingdom Prime Minister, Mr. Attlee, announced that ships of the Royal Navy then in Japanese waters would be sent to aid the Republic of Korea. In the succeeding months the majority of U.N. member-states including members of the British Commonwealth, gave further substantial military or economic support to the United Nations action.

25. The attack on the Republic of Korea was an act of war by the effective government of North Korea and was not in any sense comparable to a civil disturbance arising out of an insurrection against a lawful government, or an act of civil war within a single country. The Government of North Korea launched its offensive with the approval and consent of the Soviet Union. Indeed, so close were the political, military and economic ties then existing between North Korea and the Soviet Union, that it could not have made the attack other than with Soviet approval and consent.

Further facts appear from the judgment.

GRAHAM, J. By notice of motion dated July 31, 1967, the applicants the Al-Fin Corporation of 1 Paul Street, Bethel, Connecticut, in the United States of America, ask for the determination of the court of the question whether, on the true construction of section 24 of the Patents Act, 1949, the Democratic People's Republic of Korea in the events which happened was a foreign state within the meaning of section 24(1) at the time of the Korean war. The Comptroller General of Patents Designs and Trade Marks is the respondent to the motion.

The applicants are the owners of British letters patent No. 689,129, which was applied for on November 9, 1950, and claims priority from an American application dated November 10, 1949. The British letters patent were granted in 1953 and on May 6, 1966, the applicants applied to the comptroller under section 24 for an extension of five years on the ground of war loss due to hostilities between His late Majesty and the government of the Democratic People's Republic of Korea during the period June 25, 1950, until July 27, 1953.

It is sufficient for present purposes to note that the letters patent relate to the use of ferrous metal incorporated in pistons of either a high nickel cast iron or gray cast iron and which require the use of quantities of nickel in their manufacture. It is alleged that by reason of the war in question nickel was in short supply in this country and that the applicants suffered loss because they were not able to manufacture and sell as many pistons as they would have been able to do had there been no such shortage.

*   *   *

The position of North Korea. I will now deal with the question whether North Korea is a "state" within the meaning of section 24 as a preliminary point in the hearing of the application for extension by the court, which I will treat as before the court in accordance with the undertaking to refer previously mentioned.

The question depends primarily on the proper construction of section 24 and the difference between the parties may be succinctly stated as follows: Must the section be read as if the words "recognised as such by Her Majesty" were included after the words "any foreign state" in subsection (1), or is it correct to read the section in a broader sense without the necessity for the qualification of recognition?

Mr. MacCrindle argued that the court is not here construing a contract between parties but ascertaining the intention of the legislature which is an arm of state. The words hostilities "between His Majesty and any foreign state" demonstrate that it is not sufficient to point to any hostilities—they must be hostilities against a "state," and he took the example of the Eoka disturbances in Cyprus which he submitted would clearly not qualify under these words. Section 8, he says, makes it clear that the foreign state is one which has "subjects." Subjects have their counterpart in their sovereign and the former owe allegiance to the latter and it is not enough that those called subjects merely carry out the orders of some government exercising practical authority over them. In English law a person cannot be a national or subject of a foreign state unless by the laws of that state such person is recognised as a subject of that state. So, if a person is alleged to be a subject of North Korea, the approach of the English court would involve the inquiry whether under the system of law which the English courts would regard as valid in North Korea that individual is a subject of North Korea. In establishing the law prevailing in North Korea, the English courts must look and see if the government which has made the law in question is entitled so to do. The court must therefore first inquire which government is recognised as being in authority in the territory of that foreign state and it can consider only laws passed by that government, and on the question of recognition the Foreign Office certificate is conclusive. The corollary follows that, if there is no formal recognition, there is no government and no state whose laws can be inquired into for the purpose of establishing whether a person is the subject of such a state. To apply section 8 you must be able to examine the relevant law as to status and you are not entitled to regard as a competent law giver a foreign body not recognised by Her Majesty as Sovereign. There are insoluble problems, says Mr. MacCrindle, unless you can establish that the person in question is a subject or national of the state in question, since, once the strict legal meaning of "subject" in that sense is abandoned, how far can one go in considering the question of status.

* * *

Mr. Dillon, on the other hand, for the applicants argued that the obvious intention of the section was to give a right to an extension for loss where the applicant could show that hostilities between this country and another country had occasioned such loss, and that the definition of "state" should certainly not be limited in such a way that it depended on the technical fact of recognition. He said the matter must be looked at from a practical point of view and that, if the facts were sufficient to show that there was a government in effective control over a defined area of territory, then this should qualify as a state within the section whether in fact recognition by the Foreign Office had been made or not. In recent times it has frequently been the case that governments for political or other reasons are not prepared to give de facto or de jure recognition of other governments sometimes for short and sometimes for long periods of time after the stability of such other governments has in fact been clearly established. To this the Foreign Office is no exception and the present certificate is interesting in this respect, since, though recognition has not been made, it is clear on the face of the certificate, paragraph 4, that there was a government exercising control over North Korea during the relevant period, and, secondly, from the point of view of the Foreign Office the question in issue here is regarded as one for the court.

As regards the meaning of "subject" in subsection (8), Mr. Dillon argued that the word should be construed in a general sense as meaning a person who was in fact under the control of an established foreign government whether recognised or not, and should be tested by such matters as the fact of such control, the place of his birth, the place of his father's birth, his residence and generally having regard to all the facts relating to his status and freedom of action.

* * *

* * * In my judgment, the correct principle is that the word must be construed in its context and given the meaning which it is considered was intended by the legislature.

Applying these principles to section 24, I have no hesitation in holding that the phrase "any foreign state," although of course it includes a foreign state which has been given Foreign Office recognition, is not limited thereto. It must at any rate include a sufficiently defined area of territory over which a foreign government has effective control. Whether or not the state in question satisfies these conditions is a matter primarily of fact in each case and no doubt there will be difficult cases for decision from time to time, but difficult cases of fact do not prevent the court from coming to a conclusion when the relevant facts are proved before it.

In the present case, * * * there is the evidence of Mr. Frank in his affidavit of April 24, 1968, which satisfies me, see paragraphs 22 to 25 in particular, that at the relevant time North Korea had a defined territory over which a government had effective control and that His late Majesty was engaged in hostilities with this state albeit his troops were under the command and formed part of the United Nations' forces fighting in the area.

I hold therefore that North Korea was a foreign state within the meaning of section 24 and that the applicants are entitled to proceed with the application for extension on that basis.

In so saying it is clear that I consider that the Harshaw case [1965] R.P.C. 97 was on this point wrongly decided for the reasons which I have given above. It is not necessary to analyse the decision in detail, since in my judgment the question is one of construction and the conclusion of the superintending examiner was wrong. * * *

Order accordingly.

THE TERRITORIAL ELEMENT IN STATEHOOD

1. *Acquisition of land territory.* The existence of a state is conditioned upon its occupation of a defined area of the earth, its land territory. Only if it does have such a territory can it also meet the other organic requirements for membership in the international community, i. e. the requirement of a defined population and the requirement of a government in control of it.

Historically, competition for the acquisition of land territory has been a main feature of the rise of the nation state and the source of bitter and violent conflicts as well. Conquest was a common and legally recognized form of acquisition of title to territory, and this mode of establishing a right to permanent occupation of a defined area of the earth is not extinct, though it occurs much less frequently than it used to. Peaceful means of acquisition of title also developed, such as cession, prescription and occupation. But the last two at least presuppose the availability of earth areas not already occupied or firmly occupied, else conquest would be the only recourse. Yet there are not many land areas left on earth which are not already occupied by a state.

The outstanding exception is the Antarctic and it is symptomatic of modern attitudes, and the result as well no doubt of the harsh climate, that states with potential claims of sovereignty in the area, such as Great Britain, Norway, Chile and Argentina, and others which disclaimed any intention of territorial acquisition there, such as the United States, agreed to establish an international regime for Antarctica. Antarctic Treaty of December 1, 1959, 12 U.S.T. 794, 402 U.N.T.S. 71. It entered into force on June 23, 1961, upon the deposit of ratifications by all the signatory states: Argentina, Australia, Belgium, Chile, France, Japan, New Zealand, Norway, Union of South Africa, Union of Soviet Socialist Republics, United Kingdom and the United States.

The intent of the treaty is to ensure that Antarctica shall be used exclusively for peaceful purposes and not become the object of international discord, and to promote freedom of scientific investigation in the area and international cooperation to that end. Article 4 provides that nothing in the treaty shall be interpreted as a renunciation of asserted rights of sovereignty or bases for claims of sovereignty by the parties, or prejudice their recognition or non-recognition of claims by other states. It further states that the acts or activities of the parties taking place in Antarctica shall not constitute a basis for asserting, supporting or denying claims of sovereignty in the area or creating rights of sovereignty therein.

As to the maritime territory of states, see Chapter 3, and as to their airspace above their land and maritime territory, see Chapter 4.

2. *Territorial boundaries.* Over the centuries, many contests between states concerning territorial questions have been over the location of land boundaries delimiting their respective areas of sovereignty. For even when allocations of territory have been agreed upon by two or more states, there still remain the problem of agreeing on the description of the boundaries and the problem of actually laying down the boundaries by demarcation.

In parts of the earth where allocations of territory have been stable for a long time, and descriptions and demarcations of boundaries made long ago, there are still portions of boundaries, often involving small areas, in controversy. The issue may be resolved by litigation before the International Court of Justice, as in the Case Concerning Sovereignty over Certain Frontier Land, (Belgium v. Netherlands), [1959] I.C.J. 209. Or it may be resolved on the occasion of some other settlement, as in the Italian Peace Treaty of February 10, 1948, where provisions were made for changes in the Franco-Italian boundary. 61 Stat. 1245, 49 and 50 U.N.T.S. A border issue was also involved in the case before the International Court of Justice concerning the Temple of Preah Vihear (Cambodia v. Thailand), [1962] I.C.J.Rep. 6. Hostilities over a border question broke out between India and Pakistan in 1965 and the issue was submitted to arbitration. Rann of Kutch Arbitration, 1968, VII International Legal Materials 633 (1968). Communist China and India have been embroiled over the years in border disputes which flare up occasionally into limited hostilities. And an old boundary dispute was the cause of the armed conflict between Iraq and Iran which began in March-April 1980.

It would be quite pointless to try elucidating from boundary cases specific principles of international law, since the issues nearly always come down to a matter of interpretation of agreements between the parties. There is an exception to this proposition, however, when the boundary between two states is a navigable river. In such a case, the location of the boundary is the *thalweg,* i. e. the middle of the channel of navigation. Restatement of the Foreign Relations Law of the United States, § 12 (1965). The same section also states that when the boundary between two states is a non-navigable river or lake, its location is in the middle of the river or lake. For the settlement of the Chamizal Boundary Dispute between the United States and Mexico, which involved the Rio Grande, see Chapter 1.

3. *Newly independent states.* Since World War II, the breaking-up of colonial empires has proceeded at an accelerated pace. As a result, a substantial number of independent states have come into being which previously were dependent territories of a colonial power or were subjected in various degrees to administrative control by another state, as in the case of mandates or trusteeships. The emergence of new states has created difficult problems of succession, including those concerning succession to treaties dealing with the boundaries of their territory or certain uses of their territory.

At its 1972 Session, the International Law Commission adopted Draft Articles on the Succession of States in Respect of Treaties. II Yearbook of the International Law Commission 1972, at 223. Part V of the draft is entitled: Boundary Regimes or Other Territorial Regimes Established by a Treaty. It consists of two articles. Article 29 provides:

Boundary regimes

A succession of States shall not as such affect:

(a) a boundary established by a treaty; or

(b) obligations and rights established by a treaty and relating to the regime of a boundary.

The commentary on this article states in part:

There was general agreement in the Commission upon the basic principle that a succession of States does not, as such, affect a boundary or a boundary regime established by treaty. Having regard to the various considerations mentioned * * * and to the trend of modern opinion on the matter, the Commission concluded that it should formulate the rule not in terms of the treaty itself but of a boundary established by a treaty and of a boundary regime so established. Accordingly, article 29 provides that a succession of States shall not as such affect: (a) a boundary established by a treaty; or (b) obligations and rights established by a treaty and relating to the regime of a boundary. In accepting this formulation the Commission underlined the purely negative character of the rule, which goes no further than to deny that any succession of States simply by reason of its occurrence affects a boundary established by a treaty or a boundary regime so established. As already pointed out in paragraph (16), it leaves untouched any legal ground that may exist for challenging the boundary, such as self-determination or the invalidity of the treaty, just as it also leaves untouched any legal ground of defence to such a challenge. The Commission was also agreed that this negative rule must apply equally to any boundary regime established by a treaty, whether the same treaty as established the boundary or a separate treaty.

Article 30 provides:

Other territorial regimes

1. A succession of States shall not as such affect:

    (a) obligations relating to the use of a particular territory, or to restrictions upon its use, established by a treaty specifically for the benefit of a particular territory of a foreign State and considered as attaching to the territories in question;

    (b) rights established by a treaty specifically for the benefit of a particular territory and relating to the use, or to restrictions upon the use of a particular territory of a foreign State and considered as attaching to the territories in question.

2. A succession of States shall not as such affect:

    (a) obligations relating to the use of a particular territory, or to restrictions upon its use, established by a treaty specifically for the benefit of a group of States or of all States and considered as attaching to that territory;

    (b) rights established by a treaty specifically for the benefit of a group of States or of all States and relating to the use of a particular territory, or to restrictions upon its use, and considered as attaching to that territory.

This article is intended to deal with situations in which the predecessor state granted to another state by treaty certain rights in the territory such as lease of a port in perpetuity, operation of commercial aircraft for certain bases, rights of navigation on rivers or canals, and rights to use water resources.

The commentary states in part:

Some further precedents of one kind or another might be examined, but it is doubtful whether they would throw any clearer light on the difficult question of territorial treaties. Running through the precedents and the opinions of writers are strong indications of a belief that certain treaties attach a regime to territory which continues to bind it in the hands of any successor State. Not infrequently other elements enter into the picture, such as an allegation of fundamental change of circumstances or the allegedly limited competence of the predecessor State, and the successor State in fact claims to be free of the obligation to respect the regime. Nevertheless, the indications of the general acceptance of such a principle remain. At the same time, neither the precedents nor the opinions of writers give clear guidance as to the criteria for determining when this principle operates. The evidence does not, however, suggest that this category of treaties should embrace a very wide range of so-called territorial treaties. On the contrary, this category seems to be limited to cases where a State by a treaty grants a right to use territory, or to restrict its own use of territory, which is intended to attach to territory of a foreign State or, alternatively, to be for the benefit of a group of States or of all States generally. There must in short be something in the nature of a territorial regime.

It should be noted that draft article 30 restricts the devolution by succession of the types of rights involved to those situations where the right either benefits the particular territory of another state and attaches to it, or benefits a group of states or all states. Can you see why? What would happen to the lease of a port in perpetuity, or to a right to operate commercial aircraft from bases in the territory, under draft article 30?

At its 1974 session, The International Law Commission modified Articles 29 and 30 of the draft by replacing in both the word "shall" by the word "does," deleting in Article 30 the adverb "specifically," and replacing in Article 30 the words "a particular territory" by "any territory." I Yearbook of the International Law Commission 1974, at 261. They were in that form when the United Nations Conference on Succession of States in Respect of Treaties adopted the draft as a convention on the subject on August 22, 1978. XVII International Legal Materials 1488 (1978).

4. *Rights over territory short of title.* A state may cede to another a portion of its territory, just as a person may pass title to his property in private law. But just as rights in property may be created in private law which fall short of title, so it is in international law with respect to the territory of a state.

Thus a state may lease to another a portion of its territory for a term of years. The United Kingdom holds Hong Kong in lease from China for 99 years. The convention between the United States and Panama of November 18, 1903, 33 Stat. 2234, granted to the United States in perpetuity the use, occupation and control of a ten-mile strip of Panamanian territory for the purpose of constructing and operating a ship canal, and in this zone the United States exercised all the rights it "would possess and exercise if it were the sovereign of the territory" to the entire exclusion of the exercise by Panama of any such sovereign rights. For the termination of the convention, see Chapter 15 p. 1007.

The trusteeship system set up under Articles 75–91 of the Charter of the United Nations presents obvious analogies to the institution of the trust in the common law system. See the Documentary Supplement for these articles. It does not follow, however, that a state holding a territory in trusteeship is vested with title to it because a trustee is usually vested with title to the trust at common law. The common core of the concept which underlies the system of trusteeship under the Charter of the United Nations and the preceding systems of mandates under the League of Nations is the vesting of power of control in the mandatory and the trustee for the benefit of the people in the territory under mandate or trusteeship. The most absolute power of control available, i. e. title to or sovereignty over the territory, is not given however to the mandatory or the trustee state, though of course the scope of the power is very broad.

The arrangements just described and involving rights over territory falling short of title must be distinguished from arrangements where a state gives to another the right to exercise a certain amount of jurisdiction in its territory with respect to certain persons. Under the system of extraterritorial jurisdiction once in effect in many states of Africa and Asia, the United States like many European states had jurisdiction over its nationals when they were defendants in certain civil and criminal cases. This jurisdiction, based on nationality, was personal and did not rest on any right over the territory.

Chapter 12

RECOGNITION OF STATES AND GOVERNMENTS

Recognition is a political act, taken by a government of a state in reference to foreign affairs operations. In this chapter we consider the extent to which the international legal system has rules about the performance of this political act and attempt to project some of the legal-political consequences of the act of recognition, once it has occurred.

THE THEORY OF RECOGNITION

1 O'Connell, International Law 127–128 (2d ed. 1970).*

There is no topic of international law more theoretically confusing than that of recognition. The term "recognition" itself is used with distressing imprecision by both lawyers and political scientists, while only an arbitrary selection and rejection of evidence has made the mass of contradictory State practice on the subject intelligible. Even the most dedicated positivist has been forced into a priori reasoning, and in the result there are several intellectual constructions claiming exclusive authority as to the legal value of an act of recognition and as to its legal consequence. It would seem, however, that too much has been made of the theoretical issue between the rival schools of thoughts. Many of the puzzles of recognition as a legal concept are only linguistic, and careful definition will cause them to vanish. This is not to suggest that the topic is thereby simplified. Far from it. But at least confusion is not worse confounded by mistaking what we are talking about and what we are trying to do.

Recognition as a term covers a variety of factual situations calling for acknowledgment by foreign States. They are: the appearance of new States, changes of government outside the constitutional forms, territorial changes, especially those achieved by force and involving the extinction of States, and the parties to civil war. The common factor in all these cases is that certain governmental authorities claim competence over territory and people, and foreign States are faced with the choice of recognising or not recognising that the claim is valid. Recognition is a political action whereby the recognising State indicates a willingness to acknowledge the factual situation and to bring about certain legal consequences of that acknowledgment. Acknowledgment is not recognition if it is limited to noting the factual situation. * * *

In order to distinguish an acknowledgment of facts which has consequences in international law from one which has not it is useful to

* Reprinted with the permission of Sweet & Maxwell, Ltd., London.

distinguish three processes, cognition, cognisance and recognition. The taking notice of the facts may be described as cognition. Until the facts are noted, and until indeed they are facts, there is no proper cognition, without which there can be no proper recognition. Cognisance is the act of some body other than the executive taking note of the facts and allowing consequences to follow therefrom. This is what a judge does when he draws legal conclusions from the existence of an unrecognised as well as from a recognised State or government. Recognition is the act of the executive taking note of the facts and indicating a willingness to allow all the legal consequences of that noting to operate. These are consequences in international law. Whether consequences also follow in municipal law is a matter for municipal law itself to determine. In fact most of the material on recognition is not international law at all, but municipal law dealing with the respective roles of the executive and non-executive branches of government inter se in this matter of fact-finding and of drawing legal conclusions. The first point to be settled, therefore, is that there is no necessary logic in the process of recognition, whereby uniform conclusions must be drawn in every legal system, so that the case law of any one system would form part of the corpus of internaional law.

* * *

Recognition involves only extraordinary political changes. The need for recognition arises only when the appearance on the world scene of a new state or the rise to power of a new government of an existing state is an extraordinary political event. In the case of the recognition of entities as new states, the element of the extraordinary usually occurs only when there has been a revolutionary separation from another state. It is true that every new state holds itself out for recognition, but recognition is routine if the new entity is a peaceful—or at least not militarily contested—separation from an old state.

By far the majority of recognition problems that arise involve recognition of regimes as the governments of already recognized states. If the succession from one government to another is in keeping with the ordinary processes (usually as specified in constitutions) for changes of government, there is no occasion for an act of recognition. It is only when the change of government is discontinuous such as by a coup d'état or some other departure from legitimacy in the succession, that a question arises as to whether the new regime should be considered for recognition.

Thus there is a close relationship between the need for recognition and the unorthodoxy of how the new political authority in the state came to power. One school of thought and action—so far not the prevailing view—holds that even revolutionary changes of government should not require a new act of recognition. This viewpoint originated in Mexico and is known as the Estrada doctrine, being so named for the foreign minister of Mexico who first asserted it. Mexican motivation for the assertion of such a doctrine—that change by bullets is as valid as change by ballots so far as the external world is concerned—is grounded in that country's feeling that its big neighbor to the north manipulates the withholding of recognition of successful revolutionary regimes to interventionist ends.

The Mexican reaction was brought about by the no doubt well-intentioned efforts of President Woodrow Wilson during the Mexican Revolution (1911–1921) to create a pressure for democratic and orderly changes of government, p. 822. Why should the Mexicans reject so well-intentioned a viewpoint?

SECTION A.   THE EFFECT OF NONRECOGNITION IN JUDICIAL PROCEEDINGS

By far the majority of legal problems concerning recognition and nonrecognition have arisen in domestic courts. The classic problem has been this: in the absence of diplomatic recognition of an entity as a state or of a regime as the government of a state by the department or branch of the forum state government having control of foreign affairs, may such entity or regime be treated by domestic courts as having juridical existence? It might be possible in such cases for the courts of a country to find themselves incapable of acting at all. Or, the courts might feel that the characterizations of parties as state entities or as governments of states should be made for all national purposes by the diplomatic arm. Or, the courts might make such decisions for themselves upon the basis of law. If so, what law? International? Principles of law common to the world's major legal systems? Judicial notice? Analogies to the private law of entities, such as that of corporations? Judicial responses of various types are discernible in the materials that follow in this section.

---

1.   ON ACTIONS IN DOMESTIC COURTS: STANDING TO SUE AND RIGHT TO CONTROL STATE ASSETS

RUSSIAN SOCIALIST FEDERATED SOVIET REPUBLIC v. CIBRARIO

United States, New York Court of Appeals, 1923.
235 N.Y. 255, 139 N.E. 259.

ANDREWS, J.   In Wulfsohn v. Russian Federated Soviet Republic, 234 N.Y. 372, 138 N.E. 24, we held that our courts would not entertain jurisdiction of an action brought without its consent against an existing foreign government, in control of the political and military power within its own territory, whether or not such government had been recognized by the United States. We have now to determine whether such a government may itself become a plaintiff here.

If recognized, undoubtedly it may. * * * Conceivably this right may depend on treaty. But if no treaty to that effect exists the privilege rests upon the theory of international comity. This is so with regard to all foreign corporations. * * * Their power to sue may be regulated as is done by section 15 of our General Corporation Law (Cons.Laws, ch. 23). (Paul v. Virginia, 75 U.S. [8 Wall.] 168.) And except as limited by constitutional provisions the same thing is true of those not citizens of our state. Much more true is it that the right of a foreign government to sue is likewise based upon the same consideration. Neither a natural person nor a corporation, ordinarily we would not recognize it as a proper party plaintiff. * * * It represents, however, the general interests of the nation over which it has authority. We permit it to appear and protect those interests as a body analogous to one possessing corporate rights, but solely because of comity. * * *

Comity may be defined as that reciprocal courtesy which one member of the family of nations owes to the others. It presupposes friendship. It assumes the prevalence of equity and justice. Experience points to the expediency of recognizing the legislative, executive and judicial acts of other powers. We do justice that justice may be done in return. * * *

* * *

Does any rule of comity then require us to permit a suit by an unrecognized power? In view of the attitude of our government should we permit an action to be brought by the Soviet government? To both queries we must give a negative answer.

* * *

We reach the conclusion, therefore, that a foreign power brings an action in our courts not as a matter of right. Its power to do so is the creature of comity. Until such government is recognized by the United States, no such comity exists. The plaintiff concededly has not been so recognized. There is, therefore, no proper party before us. We may add that recognition and consequently the existence of comity is purely a matter for the determination of the legislative or executive departments of the government. Who is the sovereign of a territory is a political question. In any case where that question is in dispute the courts are bound by the decision reached by those departments. * * *

* * *

With regard to the present Russian government the case is still stronger, even did comity not depend on recognition. We not only refuse to recognize it. Our state department gives the reasons. Secretary Colby has stated them in an official note, dated August 10, 1920. He begins by saying that our government will not participate in any plan for the expansion of the armistice negotiations between Russia and Poland into a general European conference, "which would in all probability involve two results, from both of which this country strongly recoils, viz.: The recognition of the Bolshevist regime and a settlement of the Russian problem almost inevitably upon the basis of a dismemberment of Russia." He continues, "We are unwilling that while it is helpless in the grip of a non-representative government whose only sanction is brutal force, Russia shall be weakened still further by a policy of dismemberment, conceived in other than Russian interests. * * * The Bolsheviki, although in number an inconsiderable minority of the people, by force and cunning seized the powers and machinery of government, and have continued to use them with savage oppression to maintain themselves in power. * * * It is not possible for the government of the United States to recognize the present rulers of Russia as a government with which the relations common to friendly governments can be maintained. * * * The existing regime in Russia is based upon the negation of every principle of honor and good faith, and every usage and convention, underlying the whole structure of international law, the negation, in short, of every principle upon which it is possible to base harmonious and trustful relations, whether of nations or of individuals. The responsible leaders of the regime have frequently and openly boasted that they are willing to sign agreements and undertakings with foreign powers while not having the slightest intention of observing such undertakings or carrying out such agreements. * * * They have made it quite plain that they intend to use every means * * * to promote revolutionary movements in other countries. * * * In the view of this government, there cannot be any common ground upon which it can stand with a power whose conceptions of international relations are so entirely alien to its own, so utterly repugnant to its moral sense. There can be no mutual confidence or trust, no respect even, if pledges are to be given and agreements made with a cynical repudiation of their obligations already in the mind of one of the parties. We cannot recognize, hold official relations with, or give friendly reception to the agents of a government which is determined and bound to conspire against our institutions, whose diplomats will be the agitators of dangerous revolt, whose spokesmen say that they sign agreements with no intention of keeping them."

Our government has not receded from this position. Secretary Hughes in rejecting trade proposals of the Soviet, said on March 25, 1921, "It is only in the productivity of Russia that there is any hope for the Russian people, and it is idle to expect resumption of trade until the economic bases of production are securely established. Production is conditioned upon the safety of life, the recognition by firm guarantees of private property, the sanctity of contract and the rights of free labor," and he postpones any consideration of trade relations until such time as our government has convincing evidence of fundamental changes that will fulfill these conditions.

In the face of these declarations it is impossible to hold that today any such relations exist between the United States and Russia as call upon our courts to enforce rules in favor of the latter depending on the comity of nations.

The judgment appealed from should be affirmed, with costs.

WULFSOHN v. RUSSIAN SOCIALIST FEDERATED SOVIET REPUBLIC

United States, New York Court of Appeals, 1923.
234 N.Y. 372, 138 N.E. 24.

ANDREWS, J. The Russian Federated Soviet Republic is the existing de facto government of Russia. This is admitted by the plaintiff. Otherwise there is no proper party defendant before the court. It is claimed by the defendant. The Appellate Division states that it is a matter of common knowledge. It has not been recognized by the government of the United States. The plaintiffs owned a quantity of furs. They were stored in Russia and they were confiscated by the Russian government. Treating this act as a conversion the present action is brought. The litigation is not, therefore, with regard to title to property situated within the jurisdiction of our courts where the result depends upon the effect to be given to the action of some foreign government. Under such circumstances it might be that the theory of the comity of nations would have a place. * * * A different case is presented to us. The government itself is sued for an exercise of sovereignty within its own territories on the theory that such an act if committed by an individual here would be a tort under our system of municipal law. It is said that because of non-recognition by the United States such an action may be maintained. There is no relation between the premise and the conclusion.

The result we reach depends upon more basic considerations than recognition or non-recognition by the United States. Whether or not a government exists clothed with the power to enforce its authority within its own territory, obeyed by the people over whom it rules, capable of performing the duties and fulfilling the obligations of an independent power, able to enforce its claims by military force, is a fact not a theory. For it recognition does not create the state although it may be desirable. So only are diplomatic relations permitted. Treaties made with the government which it succeeds may again come into effect. It is a testimony of friendly intentions. * * * We have an existing government sovereign within its own territories. There necessarily its jurisdiction is exclusive and absolute. It is susceptible of no limitation not imposed by itself. This is the result of its independence. It may be conceded that its actions should accord with natural justice and equity. If they do not, however, our courts are not competent to review them. They may not bring a foreign sovereign before our bar, not because of comity, but because he has not submitted himself to our laws. Without his consent he is not subject to them. Concededly that is so as to a foreign government that has received recognition. * * * But whether recognized or not the evil of such an attempt would be the same. "To cite a foreign potentate into a municipal court for any complaint against him in his public capacity is contrary to the law of nations and an insult which he is entitled to resent." (De Haber v. Queen of Portugal, 17 Q.B. 171.) In either case to do so would "vex the peace of nations." In either case the hands of the state department would be tied. Unwillingly it would find itself involved in disputes it might think unwise. Such is not the proper method of redress if a citizen of the United States is wronged. The question is a political one, not confided to the courts but to another department of government. Whenever an act done by a sovereign in his sovereign character is questioned it becomes a matter of negotiation, or of reprisals or of war.

If the complaint and the affidavits upon which the warrant of attachment was based in the case before us clearly indicate that the plaintiffs must ultimately fail the warrant should be vacated. It does so appear in this case.

The orders, therefore, appealed from should be reversed, with costs in all courts, and motions to vacate attachment granted, with costs, and the question certified to us should be answered in the negative.

HISCOCK, Ch. J., HOGAN, CARDOZO, POUND and McLAUGHLIN, JJ., concur; CRANE, J., dissents.

Ordered accordingly.

UPRIGHT v. MERCURY BUSINESS MACHINES CO.

United States, New York Supreme Court, Appellate Division, 1961.
13 A.D.2d 36, 213 N.Y.S.2d 417.

BREITEL, Justice Presiding.

Plaintiff, an individual, sues as the assignee of a trade acceptance drawn on and accepted by defendant in payment for business typewriters sold and delivered to it by a foreign corporation. The trade acceptance is in the amount of $27,307.45 and was assigned to plaintiff after dishonor by defendant.

Involved on this appeal is only the legal sufficiency of the first affirmative defense. It alleges that the foreign corporation is the creature of the East German Government, a government not recognized by the United States. It alleges, moreover, that such corporation is an enterprise controlled by and that it is an arm and instrument of such government.

On motion addressed to its sufficiency Special Term sustained the defense. For the reasons that follow the defense should have been stricken as legally insufficient * * *.

A foreign government, although not recognized by the political arm of the United States Government, may nevertheless have de facto existence which is juridically cognizable. The acts of such a de facto government may affect private rights and obligations arising either as a result of activity in, or with persons or corporations within, the territory controlled by such de facto government. This is traditional law. * * *

In the Russian Reinsurance Co. case, Lehman, J., later Chief Judge, summarized the principles:

> The fall of one governmental establishment and the substitution of another governmental establishment which actually governs, which is able to enforce its claims by military force and is obeyed by the people over whom it rules, must profoundly affect all the acts and duties, all the relations of those who live within the territory over which the new establishment exercises rule. Its rule may be without lawful foundation; but lawful or unlawful, its existence is a fact, and that fact cannot be destroyed by juridical concepts. The State Department determines whether it will recognize its existence as lawful, and, until the State Department has recognized the new establishment, the court may not pass upon its legitimacy or ascribe to its decrees all the effect which inheres in the laws or orders of a sovereign. The State Department determines only that question. It cannot determine how far the private rights and obligations of individuals are affected by acts of a body not sovereign, or with which our government will have no dealings. That question does not concern our foreign relations. It is not a political question, but a judicial question. The courts in considering that question assume as a premise that until recognition these acts are not in full sense law. Their conclusion must depend upon whether these have nevertheless had such an actual effect that they may not be disregarded. In such case we deal with result rather than cause. We do not pass upon what such an unrecognized governmental authority may do, or upon the right or wrong of what it has done; we consider the effect upon others of that which has been done, primarily from the point of view of fact rather than of theory. * * *

So, too, only limited effect is given to the fact that the political arm has not recognized a foreign government. Realistically, the courts apprehend that political nonrecognition may serve only narrow purposes. While the judicial arm obligates itself to follow the suggestions of the political arm in effecting such narrow purposes, nevertheless, it will not exaggerate or compound the consequences required by such narrow purposes in construing rights and obligations affected by the acts of unrecognized governments. * * *

  * * *

Applying these principles, it is insufficient for defendant merely to allege the nonrecognition of the East German Government and that plaintiff's assignor was organized by and is an arm and instrumentality of such unrecognized East German Government. The lack of jural status for such government or its creature corporation is not determinative of whether transactions with it will be denied enforcement in American courts, so long as the government is not the suitor. (Actually, on the present pleadings no issue is raised that plaintiff assignee is that government, or is an arm of that government, or that the assignment to him of the trade acceptance is invalid or does not represent a genuine transfer.)

     *   *   *

This case does not involve the issues, tendered by defendant in its argument, of jural status of the East German corporation, or of its incapacity to transfer title, or even of its capacity to sue in our courts.   These have been long recognized as issues to be resolved by reference to the actual facts—the realities of life—occurring in the territory controlled by a de facto government, unless, of course, the contemplated juridical consequences of such "facts" can be properly related as inimical to the aims and purposes of our public or national policy.   *   *   *   Even the power of a rebel government in one of the Confederate States to create a corporation with capacity to sue the United States Government was admitted where such creation was not directly in furtherance of the rebellion (United States v. Insurance Companies, 22 Wall. 99, 89 U.S. 99, 22 L.Ed. 816).

It is a false notion, if it prevail anywhere, that an unrecognized government is always an evil thing and all that occurs within its governmental purview are always evil works.   There are many things which may occur within the purview of an unrecognized government which are not evil and which will be given customary legal significance in the courts of nations which do not recognize the prevailing de facto government.   In a time in which governments with established control over territories may be denied recognition for many reasons, it does not mean that the denizens of such territories or the corporate creatures of such powers do not have the juridical capacity to trade, transfer title, or collect the price for the merchandise they sell to outsiders, even in the courts of nonrecognizing nations (cf. Sokoloff v. National City Bank, 239 N.Y. 158, 165–166, 145 N.E. 917, 918–919, supra).

Of course, nonrecognition is a material fact but only a preliminary one.   The proper conclusion will depend upon factors in addition to that of nonrecognition.   Such is still the case even though an entity involved in the transaction be an arm or instrumentality of the unrecognized government.   Thus, in order to exculpate defendant from payment for the merchandise it has received, it would have to allege and prove that the sale upon which the trade acceptance was based, or that the negotiation of the trade acceptance itself, was in violation of public or national policy.   Such a defense would constitute one in the nature of illegality and if established would, or at least might, render all that ensued from the infected transaction void and unenforceable.   Defendant buyer cannot escape liability merely by alleging and proving that it dealt with a corporation created by and functioning as the arm of and instrumentality of an unrecognized government.

Put more concretely: The public policy which denies juridical recognition to the East German Government is determined by the refusal of the political arm to recognize it. That means the East German Government cannot sue in our courts. The question whether its corporate instrumentality can sue is not so clear. Perhaps it could sue. But another, not otherwise lacking in capacity to sue, may, by way of transfer or other mesne assignment, sue on the underlying transaction, unless such transaction itself or the assignment is shown to violate the national or public policy. In order for such transaction or the assignment to violate national or public policy, it must be shown either to violate our laws or some definite policy. If the national government does not administratively forbid, or if it facilitates, the purchase and delivery into this country of East German typewriters, and no law forbids it, then defendant buyer will be hard put to show the "illegality" of the underlying transaction, or the assignment, and thereby avoid payment of the price for such merchandise.

Moreover, the status of the East German territory is that of territory, once belligerent, but now occupied by a wartime ally, the Soviet Union, with the consent of the other allies. Nonrecognition, in the past, of the East German Government simply meant that, pending a reunification plan and free secret elections, the State Department refused to recognize the displacement of the Soviet Union as the power responsible for the territory and for the conduct of affairs there.

* * *

Accordingly, the order of Special Term should be reversed, on the law, and the motion to strike the first affirmative defense granted * * *

[Concurring opinion omitted.]

IN RE ALEXANDRAVICUS

United States, New Jersey Superior Court, Appellate Division, 1964.
83 N.J.Super. 303, 199 A.2d 662.

The opinion of the court was delivered by LEWIS, J. A. D.

This is one of several appellate reviews incident to the estate of Joseph Alexandravicus, deceased. Death occurred February 15, 1953, and the litigated issue as to the right to administer decedent's estate is still a matter of controversy.

* * * Jonas Budrys, Consul General of the Republic of Lithuania, instituted proceedings in the Hudson County Court, Probate Division, demanding that he be granted letters of administration. The crucial allegations set forth in his verified complaint may be summarized:

Joseph Alexandravicus of the County of Hudson died intestate leaving him surviving two brothers, Vincas and Antanas, residents of the Republic of Lithuania.

Said Republic was unlawfully subjugated on June 15, 1940, and, shortly thereafter, it was illegally annexed into the Union of Soviet Socialist Republics. The occupied government is not recognized by the United States of America.

Plaintiff's consular status with the Republic of Lithuania is evidenced by an exequatur issued to him by the Government of the United States. Pursuant to the "laws and treaties" of our country and the Republic of Lithuania, he, as consul general has the power and authority to act as attorney-in-fact for his nationals who inherit American property in the State of New Jersey.

The application of Jesse Moskowitz, Esq., for such an appointment was predicated upon a power of attorney (dated February 19, 1959), executed by decedent's two brothers empowering the New York law firm of Messrs. Wolf, Popper, Ross, Wolf & Jones, or its nominee, to apply for letters of administration. Said power was not executed before officials of the Republic of Lithuania * * *.

* * * After a full hearing before the County Court, the trial judge entered an order on August 3, 1962 vacating the order to show cause and dismissing the complaint.

On appeal to this court plaintiff advances two major arguments to support a reversal: (1) the power of attorney and designation under which the authority of Moskowitz emanates is invalid; and (2) the consul general has the exclusive right to be appointed administrator.

* * *

The documentary facts are not in dispute. The identity of the surviving brothers, the authenticity of their signatures and their legal capacity, were certified February 19, 1959 by a notary of the Ministry of Justice of the Lithuanian Soviet Socialist Republic. The notary's qualification and signature were certified by the Chief of the Revisionary Department of the Ministry of Justice of the Lithuanian Soviet Socialist Republic whose signature was visaed by the Consular Administration of the Ministry of Foreign Affairs of U. S. S. R. There was an accompanying certificate by an American consul certifying the authenticity of the Russian minister's signature and the official Russian seal; a caveat thereto stated, "This authentication is not to be interpreted as implying recognition of Soviet sovereignty over Lithuania."

The trial judge received a letter dated January 31, 1962, addressed to him from the United States Department of State which included the following information: the Government of the United States does not recognize the forced incorporation of Lithuania into the Union of Soviet Socialist Republics; it continues to recognize the diplomatic and consular officers of the Republic of Lithuania, and the position of the Department is the same as declared in a communique of October 1, 1959 declaring that the effect to be given a power of attorney executed in the Soviet Union by nationals of Lithuania is for the courts to decide.

It is well settled that the laws, acts, judgments and decrees of foreign governments have extraterritorial effect only as a matter of comity, sometimes called "comity of nations," which in a legal sense is "neither a matter of absolute obligation, on the one hand, nor of mere courtesy and good will, upon the other." Hilton v. Guyot, 159 U.S. 113, 163–164, 16 S.Ct. 139, 143, 40 L.Ed. 95, 108 (1895), approvingly cited in Banco Nacional de Cuba v. Sabbatino, 84 S.Ct. 923 (decided March 23, 1964). Political recognition, however, is exclusively a function of the Executive. Ibid. When our Federal Government has determined upon a policy of recognition of a foreign country, it is binding upon the courts. United States v. Pink, 315 U.S. 203, 229–230, 62 S.Ct. 552, 565, 86 L.Ed. 796, 817 (1942). Similarly, a policy of non-recognition when demonstrated by the Executive must be deemed to be "as affirmative and positive in effect as the policy of recognition." The Maret, 145 F.2d 431, 442 (3 Cir. 1944). Accord, Latvian State Cargo & Passenger S. S. Line v. McGrath, 88 U.S.App. D.C. 226, 188 F.2d 1000, 1003 (D.C.Cir.), cert. denied 342 U.S. 816, 72 S.Ct. 30, 96 L.Ed. 617 (1951).

Appellant contends that because the power of attorney here at issue was executed in subjugated Lithuania and the notarial acts appended to the power were sealed and consummated by officers of an unrecognized sovereignty, the document should be declared a total nullity. He relies upon the authority of cases typified by In re Adler's Estate, 197 Misc. 104, 93 N.Y.S.2d 416 (Surr.Ct.1949), appeal dismissed 279 App.Div. 745, 109 N.Y.S.2d 175 (App.Div.1951), wherein it was said that a court may not give effect to an act of an unrecognized government, since to do so would invade the domain of the political authority. It was then declared, "If, therefore, the court may not give effect to an act of an unrecognized government, it may not give effect to an act of an official acting in behalf of that regime." * * *

The argument continues that it would be an anomalous situation if we were to give recognition to the notarial acts of those appointed under the laws of the "puppet regime" now in control of Lithuania, because it would be tantamount to an acknowledgment that the Russian laws were applicable to the Baltic country of Lithuania. But that does not necessarily follow. In the first place, the American consul's certification was specifically qualified to negate such a conclusion, and, secondly, it is not every act of an official of an unrecognized government that is regarded as a nullity. While judicially a government that is unrecognized may be viewed as no government at all, it was pointed out many years ago by Justice (then Judge) Cardozo that in practice "juridical conceptions are seldom, if ever, carried to the limit of their logic, the equivalence is not absolute, but is subject to self-imposed limitations of common sense and fairness * * *." Sokoloff v. National City Bank, 239 N.Y. 158, 165, 145 N.E. 917, 918, 37 A.L.R. 712 (Ct.App.1924).

It is only where the acts are political in nature that the courts are precluded from considering their validity and effectiveness. Russian Reinsurance Co. v. Stoddard, 240 N.Y. 149, 147 N.E. 703 (Ct. App.1925). Thus, where the controversy is concerned exclusively with private rights and obligations of the subjects of an unrecognized state, the law of that state may prevail. * * *

A significant approach was taken to this issue in the recent case of In re Luberg's Estate, 19 A.D.2d 370, 243 N.Y.S.2d 747 (App.Div. 1963), wherein two powers of attorney were involved—one executed and notarized in Estonia and the other at Leningrad, Russia. In considering the former, it was declared, by way of obiter dictum, that the judiciary is not required to disregard a power of attorney merely because it was authenticated by an official of a de facto rather than a de jure government. If this were not so, rationalized the court,

> many situations would become intolerable. It would be impossible to establish the elementary facts of birth, marriage, death or the like where the certification of the same was made by, or the official before whom proof was to be taken was an appointee of, the unrecognized regime. Moreover, we would perforce have to refuse nationals of the regime that we do recognize access to our shores because the only persons who could in fact authenticate their passports would be officials of the regime that is not recognized. In that way we would be acting in a manner that was in practical effect more oppressive to those nationals whose independence we are seeking to further than is the government which usurped authority over them. * * * (243 N.Y.S.2d, at p. 750.)

* * *

Against the force of the evidence before us, we find appellant's countervailing arguments, attacking the validity of the power of attorney in question, to be unpersuasive.

* * *

We conclude that plaintiff did not have an exclusive right to be appointed administrator and that any standing he might have had prior to February 19, 1959, terminated at that time when decedent's brothers designated attorneys in this country to represent them.

The judgment of the trial court is affirmed.

———

IN RE ESTATE OF LUKS

United States, New York Surrogate Court, N.Y. County, 1965.
45 Misc.2d 72, 256 N.Y.S.2d 194.

JOSEPH A. COX, Surrogate. The Consuls General of the governments in exile of Latvia and Estonia have moved for orders dismissing the objections to the Public Administrator's accounts and striking the notices of appearance filed by purported attorneys-in-fact for alleged distributees in the accounting proceedings. The motions are founded upon the alleged invalidity of the powers of attorney. The attorneys-in-fact on their part have moved to strike the appearances of the Consuls General, alleging that they are not proper parties to these proceedings by reason of the designation of specified persons as attorneys-in-fact authorized to appear on behalf of the claimants in these proceedings * * *. The Attorney General of the State of New York has joined in the motions to have the powers of attorney declared invalid. Except for the fact that in the Luks case the powers of attorney were executed in Latvia and in the Kask and Tiit cases the powers were executed in Estonia, the fact situations surrounding the execution of the powers and their authentication present like issues.

In each case the powers were executed in the country where the claimants reside and were purportedly acknowledged before a notary in that country whose signature was authenticated by an official of the Notarial Department of the Soviet Latvian or Soviet Estonian Supreme Court as the case might be. The authority of the authenticating official was in turn certified by an official of the Consular Administration of the Ministry of Foreign Affairs of the Union of Soviet Socialist Republics whose signature was attested to by the Consul of the United States in Moscow. Each certification of the United States Consul contained a provision that the certification was not to be interpreted as implying a recognition of Soviet sovereignty in the occupied country. In addition to the foregoing documents, Certificates of Conformity have been filed which certify that the powers of attorney conformed to and were executed, acknowledged and authenticated in accordance with the laws of the Union of Soviet Socialist Republics and which attest to the correctness of the translations of the texts of the powers from the Russian into the English language. These Certificates of Conformity are signed by the Third Secretary of the Embassy of the Union of Soviet Socialist Republics at Washington, D. C. who is also the Deputy Chief of the Consular Division of the Embassy of the Union of Soviet Socialist Republics.

The Government of the United States has never recognized the forceful occupation of Estonia and Latvia by the Union of Soviet Socialist Republics nor does it recognize the absorption and incorporation of Latvia and Estonia into the Union of Soviet Socialist Republics. The legality of the acts, laws and decrees of the puppet regimes set up in these countries by the Union of Soviet Socialist Republics is not recognized by the United States, diplomatic or consular officers are not maintained in either Estonia or Latvia and full recognition is given to the Legations of Estonia and Latvia established and maintained here by the governments in exile of those countries.

*   *   *

The problems here presented arise from the facts that a powerful aggressor nation overwhelmed its small neighboring nations, ousted their chosen governments and installed instead puppet governments not responsive to the needs or wants of the citizens of those nations. The policy of our government has been to refuse recognition to such acts of aggression. Questions of recognition of governments lie exclusively within the realm of the executive branch of our government and our courts can give no effect to an act of an unrecognized government which either by implication or otherwise would indicate recognition of that government * * *.

* * *

* * * In the cases at bar the Certificates of Conformity were issued by a consular official of the Union of Soviet Socialist Republics who certified that the said powers were executed in accordance with the laws of the Union of Soviet Socialist Republics. This country does not recognize the law of the Union of Soviet Socialist Republics in Latvia and Estonia and, for such reason, the Certificates of Conformity are defective. As the powers were executed in Latvia and Estonia the Certificates of Conformity must show that they were executed in accordance with the laws of Latvia and Estonia as independent governments.

The acknowledgement of the alleged claimants' signatures by the notaries and the authentications of the notaries' signatures by the Notarial Department of the Soviet Estonian and Soviet Latvian Supreme Courts were acts performed by officials whose presence in and dominion over those countries is not recognized by the United States Government. As such they are invalid from their inception and such invalid acts cannot be validated by the acts of the Soviet officials in Moscow who certified as to the authority of their officials in Estonia and Latvia.

* * * The powers of attorney filed in these matters are not entitled to recognition and the motions to dismiss the objections and the notices of appearance filed by the attorneys-in-fact designated in such powers are granted. The cross-motions to strike the appearances of the Consuls General are denied. The claimants in the above entitled matters are citizens of Latvia and Estonia and the Consuls General of those countries are by treaty vested with power to represent their nationals.

BANK OF CHINA v. WELLS FARGO BANK & UNION TRUST CO.

United States District Court, N.D. California, 1952.
104 F.Supp. 59.ᵃ

GOODMAN, District Judge. Plaintiff, a Chinese corporation, filed these actions to recover the total sum of $798,584.64 on deposit in the defendant Bank. Defendant Bank filed answers asserting its willingness to pay the sum, but alleging that it was unable to do so because of conflicting claims of corporate authority to receive payment. Thereafter the attorneys for the plaintiff moved for summary judgment in plaintiff's favor. Later a second group of attorneys,

a. Reversed as to other issues 209 F.
2d 467 (9th Cir. 1953).

claiming that they were the only attorneys empowered to represent the plaintiff Bank of China, filed a motion to dismiss these actions or in the alternative to substitute themselves as the attorneys for the plaintiff. * * *

* * *

The question now presented is essentially one of law. The attorneys who initiated this action contend that the controlling corporate authority of the Bank of China is vested by its Articles of Association in the Nationalist Government of China. They note that the Bank of China was directed by representatives of that Government when the deposit in suit was made. The Nationalist Government, they point out, not only still exists, but is the only government of China recognized by the United States. The Bank of China, they assert, still functions under the control of the Nationalist Government at its present seat on the Island of Formosa and at branch offices in various parts of the world. The Bank of China, so functioning, is the plaintiff in this action, they say, and the rightful claimant to the deposit in suit.

The intervening attorneys contend that the Peoples Government of China, as the successor in fact to the Nationalist Government in continental China, has succeeded to the corporate rights of the Chinese State in the Bank of China. They allege that the operations of the Bank of China throughout the Chinese Mainland and in certain branch offices abroad are now conducted by new Government directors appointed by the Peoples Government in conjunction with the directors representing private stockholders. It is only through these banking operations, they argue, that the corporate purposes of the Bank of China are now being realized. Only through operations so conducted, they say, can the rights of the Chinese State as majority stockholder and those of the private investors be given any substance. Such corporate operations, the intervening attorneys urge, are the true indicia of rightful ownership of the deposit.

The issue before the Court has therefore been reduced to a comparatively narrow one. It appears from the record, that there are two Banks of China now functioning. The question is: Which Bank of China is legally entitled to the deposit in suit? For convenience, the plaintiff will hereafter be referred to as the "Nationalist" Bank of China, and the Bank of China represented by the intervening attorneys as the "Peoples" Bank of China.

At the outset, the Court must determine whether these causes may finally be disposed of by summary judgment. Rule 56(c), F.R. C.P., 28 U.S.C. If there is "a genuine issue as to a material fact," summary disposition of the causes cannot be made. This does not mean that any factual dispute bars summary judgment. The dispute must be as to material facts; and the issue thus resulting must be "genuine."

* * *

The affidavits, certificates, and other documents proffered by the plaintiff and the intervening attorneys are in conflict only in the sense that they allege facts in support of adverse claims to the funds deposited with the defendant Bank. The events and transactions set forth by both sides are not reciprocally denied. Only the legal effect of the factual occurrences and the conclusions to be drawn from them are in dispute. Thus the Court may assume the truth of the facts set forth by both sides and be required to decide only the legal effect. Consequently there is no genuine issue of material fact requiring a further hearing or trial.

* * *

Consequently, we now reach the question: Which Bank of China is legally entitled to the funds deposited with the defendant Bank?

The controlling corporate authority of the Bank of China is effectively vested in the Government of China by virtue of its majority stock ownership, its dominant voice in the managing directorate, and the supervisory powers accorded by the Articles of Association to the Minister of Finance. A determination of what government, if any, should be recognized by this court as now entitled to exercise this corporate authority over the deposit in suit, will govern the disposition of these causes.

The issue thus posed focuses attention at the outset on the fact that of the two governments asserting corporate authority, one is recognized by the United States while the other is not. If this fact, per se, is determinative, the issue is resolved. If whenever this court is called upon to determine whether there is a government justly entitled to act on behalf of a foreign state in respect to a particular matter, the court is bound to say, without regard to the facts before it, that the government recognized by our executive is that government, then nothing more need be said here. To permit this expression of executive policy to usurp entirely the judicial judgment would relieve the court of a burdensome duty, but it is doubtful that the ends of justice would thus be met. It has been argued that such is the accepted practice. But the authorities do not support this view.

* * *

Some more recent decisions of the federal courts, involving Soviet nationalization of corporations of the Baltic states, give great weight to the executive policy of non-recognition. But it cannot be said that these decisions establish an all-embracing rule that no extra-territorial effect may ever be given the acts of an unrecognized government.

* * *

The decisions just set forth, as well as others in this field, reveal no rule of law obliging the courts to give conclusive effect to the acts of a recognized government to the exclusion of all consideration of the acts of an opposing unrecognized government. Nor does it appear that such a sweeping rule would be a sound one.

Even were the court solely concerned with the implementation of our executive foreign policy, it would be presumptuous to blindly effectuate every act of a recognized government or to treat every act of an unrecognized government as entirely fictional. Early in our national history, our recognition policy was generally based on the executive's view of the stability and effectiveness of the government in question. More recently recognition has been granted and withheld at the diplomatic bargaining table. Our policy has thus become equivocal. Conflicting considerations are balanced in the executive decision. Moreover, an act of recognition does not necessarily mark a sudden reversal in executive policy. It may come as a culmination of a gradual change in attitude. Thus the import of recognition or non-recognition may vary with time and circumstance.

Recognition is not intended to sanctify every act, past and future, of a foreign government. The withholding of recognition may cast a mantle of disfavor over a government. But, it does not necessarily stamp all of its acts with disapproval or brand them unworthy of judicial notice. Our executive, on occasion, has even entered into a treaty with an unrecognized government.

This is not to suggest that the courts should regard executive policy in respect to recognition and non-recognition of foreign governments as meaningless or of little consequence. In any particular situation, executive policy may be crucial, as indeed it appears to be in the present case. But, it is a fact which properly should be considered and weighed along with the other facts before the court.

Turning to the record in this case, it appears that two governments are governments in fact of portions of the territory of the State of China. The "Peoples" Government has supplanted the "Nationalist" Government in dominion over the entire Chinese Mainland with an area of more than 3,700,000 square miles, and a population of more than 460,000,000. The "Nationalist" Government controls one of the 35 provinces of China, the Island of Formosa, which has an area of 13,885 square miles and a population in excess of 6,000,000. It is obvious that the "Peoples" Government is now the government in fact of by far the greater part of the territory of the Chinese State. Nevertheless the "Nationalist" Government controls substantial territory, exceeding in area that of either Belgium or the Netherlands, and in population that of Denmark or Switzerland.

Each government, in its respective sphere, functions effectively. Each is recognized by a significant number of the nations of the world. Each maintains normal diplomatic intercourse with those nations which extend recognition. This has been the status quo for more than two years.

Each government is in a position to exercise corporate authority in behalf of the Bank of China. That is, each government is capable of utilizing the corporate structure and certain corporate assets to promote the corporate purposes. The Bank of China was chartered primarily to facilitate Chinese international commercial activities. It was organized as an international exchange bank to deal in domestic and foreign exchange and gold and silver bullion, to discount, purchase, and collect commercial bills and drafts, to issue, service, and redeem government bonds in foreign markets, and to handle public funds deposited abroad.   It was also authorized to engage in a general domestic banking business including the acceptance of deposits and valuables for safe keeping, the granting of loans, and the issuance and service of domestic government loans.   Each government is in a position to act through the corporate structure of the Bank of China to carry on these international functions in the areas abroad where such Government is recognized and these domestic functions within the territory such Government controls.   Each government is in fact doing so.   The Bank of China, as controlled by the Nationalist Government, continues to function on the Island of Formosa and through its foreign branches in the United States, Cuba, Australia, Japan, Indo China, and elsewhere where the Nationalist Government is recognized.

The Peoples Government as successor in fact to the Nationalist Government on the Chinese Mainland is exercising the prerogatives of the Government in respect to the Bank of China there.   The Peoples Government has not nationalized the Bank of China, nor confiscated its assets, nor denied the rights of private stockholders.   It exercises the authority vested in the Government of China as majority stockholder.   The Bank of China continues to function in accordance with its Articles of Association under the guidance of the appointees of the Peoples Government and the majority of the directors previously elected by private stockholders on the Chinese Mainland and through branches in London, Hong Kong, Singapore, Penang, Kuala Lumpur, Batavia, Calcutta, Bombay, Karachi, Chittagong, and Rangoon.

* * *

* * * Both the Nationalist and Peoples Governments have maintained and strengthened their positions.   Our national policy toward these governments is now definite.   We have taken a stand adverse to the aims and ambitions of the Peoples Government.   The armed forces of that Government are now engaged in conflict with our forces in Korea.   We recognize only the Nationalist Government as the representative of the State of China, and are actively assisting in developing its military forces in Formosa.   The Bank of China now operates as two corporate entities, each performing within the area of its operations the functions bestowed upon the Bank of China by its Articles of Association.   Each Bank of China is in a position to employ the deposit in suit for corporate purposes.

From a practical standpoint, neither of the rival Banks of China is a true embodiment of the corporate entity which made the deposit in the Wells Fargo Bank.   The present Nationalist Bank of China is more nearly equivalent in the sense of continuity of management. The Peoples Bank is more representative in ability to deal with the greater number of private stockholders and established depositors and creditors. Were the Court to adopt a strictly pragmatic approach, it might attempt a division of the deposit between these two banks in the degree that each now exercises the functions of the Bank of China. Or the Court might award the entire deposit to the bank it deems to be the closest counterpart of the corporation contemplated by the Articles of Association.

But this, the Court could not do merely by balancing interests of a private nature. Such a course would ultimately entail determining which bank best serves the corporate interests of the State of China. That determination could not be made, while the State, itself, remains divided, except by an excursion into the realm of political philosophy. Were there only one government, in fact, of the Chinese State, or only one government in a position to act effectively for the State in respect to the matter before the Court, the Court might be justified in accepting such a government as the proper representative of the State, even though our executive declined to deal with it. Here, there co-exist two governments, in fact, each attempting to further, in its own way, the interests of the State of China, in the Bank of China. It is not a proper function of a domestic court of the United States to attempt to judge which government best represents the interests of the Chinese State in the Bank of China. In this situation, the Court should justly accept, as the representative of the Chinese State, that government which our executive deems best able to further the mutual interests of China and the United States.

Since the Court is of the opinion that it should recognize the Nationalist Government of China as legally entitled to exercise the controlling corporate authority of the Bank of China in respect to the deposit in suit, the motion for summary judgment in favor of the Bank of China, as controlled by the Nationalist Government, is granted. The motion of the intervening attorneys to dismiss, or, in the alternative, for their substitution as attorneys for the plaintiff, is denied.

* * *

No legal change until 1979. Richard M. Nixon re-established political relations with the People's Republic of China (see infra, p. 825), having begun to indicate a shift in the United States position early in his first administration. But it was not until 1979 that diplomatic relations between the United States and Beijing were formally established by the Joint Communiqué on the Establishment of Diplomatic Relations between the United States of America and the People's Republic of China, January 1, 1979, U.S. Dept. of State Bull., January 1979, pp. 25–26, in which each of the parties agreed to recognize the other, a formula that the People's Republic had insisted upon with other well-recognized states, such as the United Kingdom and France, when these, some years earlier, shifted relations from Taiwan to Beijing. Agreement on Consular Relations, Cultural Relations, Cooperation in the Field of High Energy Physics, Exchange of

Students and Scholars, Agricultural Exchange, and Space Technology became effective at signature, January 31, 1969. 18 International Legal Materials 337 (1979). On May 11, 1979 an Agreement on the Settlement of Claims was signed (effective at signature). 18 International Legal Materials 551 (1979). The United States waives the nationalization claims of itself and its nationals for takings on or after October 1, 1949, for a lump sum payment of $80.5 million, the United States to be solely responsible for its distribution among claimants. The People's Republic waives claims arising from the blocking of Chinese assets after December 17, 1950; and the United States agrees to unblock these assets and further agrees [Art. II(b)] " * * * that prior to unblocking * * * it will notify the holders of blocked assets which the records of the Government of the United States indicate are held in the name of residents of the PRC that the Government of the PRC requests * * * not be transferred or withdrawn without its consent."

An Agreement on Trade Relations was signed at Beijing on July 7, 1979. See 18 International Legal Materials 1041 (1979) for the text.

The President also "derecognized" the regime on Taiwan as the government of China and invoked the termination clause in the Mutual Defense Treaty with Taiwan as the government of China. As to the former, see Unger (the last American ambassador to Taiwan), Derecognition Worked, Foreign Policy No. 36,105 (Fall 1979). The termination of the mutual defense treaty resulted in the litigation dealt with in Chapter 16.

HAILE SELASSIE v. CABLE AND WIRELESS, LTD. (NO. 2)

England, Court of Appeal, 1938.
[1939] Ch. 182.*

* * *

SIR WILFRID GREENE M. R. This is an appeal from a judgment of Bennett J. in an action by the late Emperor of Abyssinia against Cable and Wireless Limited. The claim in the action was for an account of all dealings between the plaintiff and the defendant company under a certain agreement, and payment of the amount found due. The agreement in question was an agreement between the competent Minister of the then Government of Ethiopia and the defendant company in relation to the establishment of a wireless station at Addis Ababa, the capital city of Abyssinia. Under that agreement certain sums admittedly became due from the defendant company. The dispute between the parties turned on the fact that the defendants asserted that the plaintiff had no title to sue for those moneys. Bennett J. decided in favour of the plaintiff. At the date of the trial the

* Reprinted by permission of the Incorporated Council of Law Reporting for England and Wales, London.

evidence available which was before the learned Judge, so far as it relates to the essential question raised in this appeal, showed that the annexation of Ethiopia by His Majesty the King of Italy had not yet been recognized by His Majesty's Government, but that His Majesty's Government recognized the plaintiff as the de jure Emperor of Ethiopia, and that His Majesty's Government recognized the Italian Government as the Government de facto of virtually the whole of Ethiopia, and such recognition had existed since the second half of December, 1936, that is to say, since a date earlier than the date of the issue of the writ, which was issued on January 4, 1937. Bennett J. held that the events which had taken place in Ethiopia and the other matters which were established before him were not sufficient to divest the plaintiff as still de jure Emperor of Ethiopia, of the right to recover the debt in suit in this country. From that judgment this appeal is brought. The appeal stood in the list for hearing on November 3 last, and it was called to our attention by Mr. Wynn Parry that, on the day before, an announcement had been made by the Prime Minister in the House of Commons from which it appeared that in the course of a few days, or at any rate a very short time, it was the intention of His Majesty's Government to recognize His Majesty the King of Italy as Emperor of Abyssinia, that is to say, that his position would be recognized de jure and no longer merely de facto. It was obvious from that announcement that, if it were carried into effect, the situation of this action would be profoundly affected, because circumstances would then be brought to the knowledge of the Court which would have a very important bearing upon the position of the plaintiff and his rights in respect of the debt in question in the action. Accordingly we thought right to adjourn the hearing of the appeal until a date after the probable date of recognition. * * * Events have proved that that decision was a right and just one.

What has happened is this. As appears from a certificate signed by the direction of His Majesty's Principal Secretary of State for Foreign Affairs, dated November 30, 1938, His Majesty's Government no longer recognizes His Majesty Haile Selassie as de jure Emperor of Ethiopia; His Majesty's Government now recognizes His Majesty the King of Italy as de jure Emperor of Ethiopia. From that certificate two things emerge as the result of the recognition thereby evidenced. It is not disputed that in the Courts of this country His Majesty the King of Italy as Emperor of Abyssinia is entitled by succession to the public property of the State of Abyssinia, and the late Emperor of Abyssinia's title thereto is no longer recognized as existent. Further, it is not disputed that that right of succession is to be dated back at any rate to the date when the de facto recognition, recognition of the King of Italy as the de facto Sovereign of Abyssinia, took place. That was in December, 1936. Accordingly the appeal comes before us upon a footing quite different to that upon which the action stood when it was before Bennett J. We now have the position that in the eye of the law of this country the right to sue in respect of what was held by Bennett J. to be (and no dispute is raised with regard to it) part of the public State property, must be treated in the Courts of this country as having become vested in His Majesty the King of Italy as from a date, at the latest, in December, 1936, that is to say, before the date of the issue of the writ in this action.   Now that being so, the title of the plaintiff to sue is necessarily displaced.   When the matter was before Bennett J., the de jure recognition not having taken place, the question that he had to deal with was whether the effect of the de facto conquest of Abyssinia and the recognition de facto of the Italian Government's position in Abyssinia, operated to divest the plaintiff of his title to sue. Whether that decision was right or whether it was wrong is a question we are not called upon to answer, but what is admittedly the case is that if Bennett J. had had before him the state of affairs which we have before us, his decision would have been the other way.

*   *   *

That being so, the order of the Court will be that the appeal be allowed, that the action be dismissed, but that the order as to costs made by Bennett J. shall not be disturbed, and there will be no costs of the appeal.

*   *   *

-----

1.   *Retroactive effect of recognition.*   Suppose that in the Haile Selassie case, the decision below in favor of the King of Ethiopia had become final and the next day the King of Italy had been recognized by the British Government as the de jure sovereign of Ethiopia.   If the Court of Appeal meant literally what it said in stating that, for the purpose of succession to property, recognition was retroactive to the time of recognition of the King of Italy as de facto sovereign of Ethiopia, what would the situation be?   Does the statement really mean that the King of Italy would be entitled to funds that a person had previously paid to the King of Ethiopia?

One can argue that in any event the King of Italy would not sue the King of Ethiopia in the British courts because they would uphold a defense of sovereign immunity and hence the issue is really moot. But the same issue can be posed in terms which get around this point. Consider the case of Gdynia Ameryka Linie v. Boguslawski, [1953] A.C. 11.   The case involved the Polish Government in exile in London and the Lublin regime in Poland.   A department of the Polish Government in exile agreed on behalf of the Polish shipping companies it controlled in England to give severance pay to the seamen of Polish vessels it controlled.   The British Government then recognized the Lublin government.   Next some of the crewmen sued one of the Polish shipping companies for the severance pay.   It defended that the recognition of the Lublin government retroactively invalidated all the acts of the former government in exile.

The contention was rejected and the result can be explained by pointing out that the British Government had specified it recognized the London government until midnight July 5–6, 1945, and from that moment it recognized the Lublin government. Hence, the explanation runs, the British Government had specified that its recognition had no retroactive effect. Suppose the British Government had not been so careful, and assume further the Polish Government in London had paid the severance pay before recognition. Does it follow that the Lublin government could claim the payment was invalid?

A great deal of confusion has arisen over the meaning of so-called retroactivity in both the British courts and the courts of the United States. Whatever the rationale advanced, the result of the decisions in the United States and the United Kingdom is that rights acquired or obligations incurred by the previously recognized government are not denied effect as a result of the recognition of the successor government. The question then is whether it is proper to speak at all of retroactivity, as the courts do, or whether it would be better to accept the fact that, in the kind of situations presented in the cases appearing in this subsection, there is neither need nor justification for doing so.

In the kind of situations involved in these cases, the government of a state continues to recognize a government of another state which has lost control of all or a major part of its territory. Even so, the dispossessed government still has some matters under its effective control so long as other governments continue to recognize it. Thus in the Wells Fargo case, the Nationalist Government of China, because it was recognized still as the government of China even though it had lost control of the Chinese territory or most of it, remained in effective control of funds of the state of China. What this really means is that the United States had the choice of continuing the Nationalist Government in effective control of the funds or else shifting the effective control of the funds to the communist regime by the simple process of recognizing it.

To speak of retroactivity in this kind of situation is to suggest that the United States, by recognizing the Nationalist Government all along and then recognizing the successor regime, is the real party in error and thus at fault in failing to acknowledge that the successor regime was entitled from the start to control of the assets of China in the United States. Yet the rule of international law in point is precisely the reverse and the issue created by talk of retroactivity is false. The United States and the United Kingdom are not under a legal duty to recognize a successor regime even though it occupies the territory at stake and have a right to maintain the government they recognize in effective control of matters still within its grasp.

In this kind of situation, the effect of recognition is clean cut. One day the King of Ethiopia is entitled to the funds due the state of Ethiopia, and the next day the government of Italy is. One day he can sue in the name of his state and the next day cannot. There is no question of invalidating his act and much less of invalidating the continuing recognition given him by the state in which he has taken refuge. In short there is no issue of retroactivity.

The issue is somewhat different, however, when the time comes for the newly recognized government to present itself in the courts of the state which has recognized it and discarded, so to speak, the previous government. Though yesterday the King of Italy was told he could not claim the funds of Ethiopia because he was not recognized as its government, today, because of the act of recognition, he cannot be turned down. But what if he should rely for his claim on some act he previously took in the territory of Ethiopia, when he was in effective control of it and its population, and long before he was recognized? May he be told he was not then the recognized government and cannot therefore be treated now for what he was in fact at the time?

The answer, of course, is no, and the newly recognized government cannot be told there is a vacuum—sometimes of many years duration—between the time it acquired effective control of territory and population and the time the fact was formally acknowledged by way of the act of recognition. What that government did then cannot now be denied and to this extent and in this sense, the act of recognition may be labeled as having a retroactive effect. It operates to suppress the defense of non-recognition with respect to past as well as future occurrences.

This is not to say, nevertheless, that all acts previously done, or which may be done in the future, by the newly recognized government will be given effect by the recognizing state. It simply means that whatever legal rules would be operative aside from non-recognition now come into effect. See the next subsection.

2. *Decisions in other legal systems.* Access to courts has been denied to a non-recognized regime in a number of states outside the common law system. Thus the Soviet Government was refused the right to sue in Soviet Government v. Ericsson, Sweden, Supreme Court, 1921, [1919–1922] Ann.Dig. 54 (No. 30). The outcome was the same in Société Despa v. USSR, Belgium, Court of Appeal of Liège, 1931 Pasicrisie II, 108, 1931. In USSR v. Luxembourg and Saar Company, Luxembourg, Tribunal of Commerce of Luxembourg, 1935, Sirey, IV, 26, 1936, the USSR was allowed to sue but on the ground it had been impliedly recognized by Luxembourg and hence the bar against bringing the suit had been removed. In some cases, however, the unrecognized regime has been allowed to sue even though it may not claim under international law a right to do so. Commercial Representation of the USSR v. Levant Red Sea Coal Co., Egypt, Tribunal of Alexandria, 1933, 62 Journal du Droit International 199 (1935); Republic of the South Moluccas v. Netherlands New Guinea, Netherlands, District Court of the Hague, 1954, 21 Int'l L.Rep. 48 (1957).

It has been held in France that an unrecognized regime is entitled to sovereign immunity to the extent demanded by international law. Clerget v. Commercial Representation of the Democratic Republic of Vietnam, Court of Appeal of Paris, 1969, 96 Journal du Droit International 895 (1969). The court said that a state becomes part of the international legal order as soon as it exists and this is so the moment it effectively exercises powers of government over a defined territory and its government is obeyed by a majority of the population. Immunity results from the independence and sovereignty of a state and not from its recognition by other states. In this case, the defendant state was not entitled to immunity from jurisdiction, but was entitled to immunity from attachment or execution for its bank assets.

In the case of The Spanish Government v. Felipe Campuzano, Norway, Supreme Court, 1938, 33 Am.J.Int'l 609 (1939), the Spanish minister in Oslo resigned at the start of the Civil War and informed the Norwegian authorities he was joining the party of General Franco. His second in command removed the furniture of the legation, including the archives, and refused to turn them over to the new appointee of the Republican Government, claiming he was holding the articles for the government of General Franco. The court upheld the right to the articles of the representative of the Republican Government so long as it was recognized by the Norwegian Government.

In Case No. ke–162, Japan, Tokyo High Court, 1973, a company organized in the German Democratic Republic, not recognized by Japan, was held entitled to sue in Japan under multipartite industrial property conventions to which the GDR had acceded on a showing that Japanese nationals would be allowed to sue under similar laws in the GDR, it being permissible to treat the unrecognized GDR as a country under Article 32 of the former Japanese Patent Law. 19 Japanese Annual of International Law 187 (1975). For a possible doctrinal shift in Italy from a retroactivity theory to acceptance of the capacity of an unrecognized regime to create rights under private international law see the analysis in II Italian Yearbook of International Law 314 (1976) especially at 319:

> The Court's view does not necessarily rest on the assumption that States become subjects of international law irrespective of recognition. The Court adopted the current argument that the applicability of the law of a non-recognized State depends only on the rules of conflict of laws and that the Italian rules do not set recognition * * * as a pre-requisite.

> The Court gave as a secondary reason the fact that the German Democratic Republic had in the meantime been recognized by the Italian Government and that this recognition must be given a retroactive effect * * *.

2. ON THE AUTHORITY OF UNRECOGNIZED GOVERNMENTS TO MAKE LAW

SALIMOFF & CO. v. STANDARD OIL CO. OF NEW YORK

United States, New York Court of Appeals, 1933.
262 N.Y. 220, 186 N.E. 679.

POUND, Ch. J. The Soviet government, by a nationalization decree, confiscated all oil lands in Russia and sold oil extracted therefrom to defendants. The former owners of the property, Russian nationals, join in an equitable action for an accounting on the ground that the confiscatory decrees of the unrecognized Soviet government and the seizure of oil lands thereunder have no other effect in law on the rights of the parties than seizure by bandits. (Luther v. Sagor & Co., [1921] 1 K.B. 456; s. c., 3 K.B. 532; cited in Sokoloff v. National City Bank, 239 N.Y. 158, 164, 145 N.E. 917.) The complaints have been dismissed.

The question is as to the effect on the title of a purchaser from the unrecognized confiscating Soviet Russian government. Does title pass or is the Soviet government no better than a thief, stealing the property of its nationals and giving only a robber's title to stolen property? Plaintiffs contend that the Soviet decrees of confiscation did not divest them of title.

When a government which originates in revolution is recognized by the political department of our government as the de jure government of the country in which it is established, such recognition is retroactive in effect and validates all the actions of the government so recognized from the commencement of its existence. (Oetjen v. Central Leather Co., 246 U.S. 297, 38 S.Ct. 309; Terrazas v. Holmes, 115 Tex. 32, 275 S.W. 392.) The courts of one independent government will not sit in judgment upon the validity of the acts of another done within its own territory, even when such government seizes and sells the property of an American citizen within its boundaries. If the Soviet government were a de jure government, it would follow that title to the property in this case must be determined by the result of the confiscatory Soviet decrees.

The status of the Soviet government is defined by the Secretary of State's office as follows:

1. The Government of the United States accorded recognition to the Provisional Government of Russia as the successor of the Russian Imperial Government, and has not accorded recognition to any government in Russia since the overthrow of the Provisional Government of Russia.

2. The Department of State is cognizant of the fact that the Soviet regime is exercising control and power in territory of the former Russian Empire and the Department of State has no disposition to ignore that fact.

3. The refusal of the Government of the United States to accord recognition to the Soviet regime is not based on the ground that that regime does not exercise control and authority in territory of the former Russian Empire, but on other facts.

It follows that the question as to the validity of acts and decrees of a regime, not the subject of diplomatic recognition, becomes a matter to be decided by the courts in an appropriate case. Thus it was held that out of respect for the political departments of the United States government only a recognized government may be a plaintiff in the courts of this State. (Russian Socialist Federated Soviet Republic v. Cibrario, 235 N.Y. 255, 139 N.E. 259.)

It has been held by the Appellate Division: "Whatever may be said of the propriety or justice of the nationalizing decrees promulgated by the Soviet government of Russia, those decrees were made by the de facto government of that country and are there in full force and effect and binding upon all Russian nationals. * * * "

"Under well-established principles of international law and in accordance with the decisions of our courts, the Soviet law and decrees must be given internal effect in that country." (237 App.Div. 686, 689, 690, 262 N.Y.S. 693, 697.)

* * *

* * * The oil property confiscated was taken in Russia from Russian nationals. A recovery in conversion is dependent upon the laws of Russia. (Riley v. Pierce Oil Corp., 245 N.Y. 152, 154, 156 N. E. 647.) When no right of action is created at the place of wrong, no recovery in tort can be had in any other State on account of the wrong. The United States government recognizes that the Soviet government has functioned as a de facto or quasi government since 1917, ruling within its borders. It has recognized its existence as a fact although it has refused diplomatic recognition as one might refuse to recognize an objectionable relative although his actual existence could not be denied. It tells us that it has no disposition to ignore the fact that such government is exercising control and power in territory of the former Russian empire. As was said by this court in Sokoloff v. National City Bank (supra, p. 165): "Juridically, a government that is unrecognized may be viewed as no government at all, if the power withholding recognition chooses thus to view it. In practice, however, since juridical conceptions are seldom, if ever, carried to the limit of their logic, the equivalence is not absolute, but is subject to self-imposed limitations of common sense and fairness, as we learned in litigations following our Civil War."

As a juristic conception, what is Soviet Russia? A band of robbers or a government? We all know that it is a government. The State Department knows it, the courts, the nations and the man on the street. If it is a government in fact, its decrees have force within its borders and over its nationals. "Recognition does not create the state." (Wulfsohn v. Russian S. F. S. Republic, 234 N.Y. 372, 375, 138 N.E. 24, 25.) It simply gives to a de facto state international status. Must the courts say that Soviet Russia is an outlaw and that the Provisional government of Russia as the successor of the Russian Imperial government is still the lawful government of Russia although it is long since dead? * * * The courts may not recognize the Soviet government as the de jure government until the State Department gives the word. They may, however, say that it is a government, maintaining internal peace and order, providing for national defense and the general welfare, carrying on relations with our own government and others. To refuse to recognize that Soviet Russia is a government regulating the internal affairs of the country, is to give to fictions an air of reality which they do not deserve.

The courts cannot create a foreign wrong contrary to the law of the place of the act. * * * The cause of action herein arose where the act of confiscation occurred and it must be governed by the law of Soviet Russia. According to the law of nations it did no legal wrong when it confiscated the oil of its own nationals and sold it in Russia to the defendants. Such conduct may lead to governmental refusal to recognize Russia as a country with which the United States may have diplomatic dealings. The confiscation is none the less effective. The government may be objectionable in a political sense. It is not unrecognizable as a real governmental power which can give title to property within its limits.

* * *

Orders affirmed * * *.

PETROGRADSKY M. K. BANK v. NATIONAL CITY BANK OF NEW YORK

United States, New York Court of Appeals, 1930.
253 N.Y. 23, 170 N.E. 479.[a]

CARDOZO, Ch. J. The plaintiff, a Russian bank, chartered in 1869 by the Imperial Russian Government, has deposit accounts with the defendant, opened in 1911 and 1915, with a balance of $66,749.45 to its credit at the trial.

Following the Soviet revolution of November, 1917, the assets of the bank in Russia were seized by the revolutionary government, and the directors driven into exile. By decrees of the Russian Soviet Republic in 1917, the bank was declared to be merged in the People's or State Bank, its assets were confiscated, its liabilities canceled, and its shares extinguished, and by a later decree, in January, 1920, the People's or State Bank was itself abolished, a banking system having been found to be unnecessary to the new economic life.

The terms of the plaintiff's charter or "statutes" are printed in the record. The governing body was to be a directorate consisting of seven members, of whom three were to form a quorum. One of the

a. Cert. denied 282 U.S. 878, 51 S.Ct.

directors lost his life in the revolution. The other six made their way to Paris, where they held meetings from time to time, and did such business as they could. All six were alive in October, 1925, when this action was begun. Three have since died, but a quorum, three, survive.

At the time of the revolution the bank had assets of large value outside the territorial limits of the Soviet Republic. The refugee directors have sought and are still seeking to bring these assets together at their present domicile in Paris. Branch banks were in existence in London, Paris, Brussels and Geneva. The assets in these branches, with the exception of those in Geneva, have been paid to the directors, and are held in the name of the bank to be distributed hereafter as justice may require. At times the payments have been voluntary, and at times in obedience to judgments of the courts. In fulfilment of the same policy, the directors have attempted to collect the balance on deposit with the defendant in New York. They requested payment, but the defendant declined to recognize their authority. They presented a check, signed by directors who had been accredited in former years as competent to draw, but the check was dishonored. In this action, which followed, the defendant insists: (1) That the plaintiff corporation has been dissolved and is no longer a juristic person; (2) that if it be a juristic person, its former directors are without authority to speak for it; and (3) that the court, in any event, should decline jurisdiction since a judgment for the plaintiff will leave the defendant unprotected against the danger of conflicting claims. The Trial Term gave judgment in favor of the defendant, and the Appellate Division unanimously affirmed.

(1) We think the plaintiff is not dissolved, but is still a juristic person with capacity to sue.

The decrees of the Soviet Republic nationalizing the Russian banks are not law in the United States, nor recognized as law * * *. They are exhibitions of power. They are not pronouncements of authority. "Acts or decrees, to be ranked as governmental, must proceed from some authority recognized as a government de facto" * * *. Exhibitions of power may be followed or attended by physical changes, legal or illegal. These we do not ignore, however lawless their origin, in any survey of the legal scene. They are a source at times of new rights and liabilities. Ex facto jus oritur. Exhibitions of power may couple the physical change with declarations of the jural consequences. These last we ignore, if the consequences, apart from the declaration, do not follow from the change itself * * *. There may be exceptions to this as there are to most principles of equal generality. If so, it is only when "violence to fundamental principles of justice or to our own public policy might otherwise be done" * * *. The every-day transactions of business or domestic life are not subject to impeachment, though the form may have been regulated by the command of the usurping government * * *. To undo them would bring hardship or confusion to the helpless and the innocent without compensating benefit. On the other hand, there is no shelter in such exceptions for rapine or oppression. We do not recognize the decrees of Soviet Russia as competent to divest the plaintiff of the title to any assets that would otherwise have the protection of our law. At least this must be so where the title thus divested is transferred to the very government not recognized as existent. * * *

 * * *

 Putting aside, then, as irrelevant the fiat of the Soviet Government that the jural consequence shall be death, we are brought to the question whether the law of the Imperial Government of Russia or of the later Provisional Government would have ascribed the consequence of death to the supervening changes irrespective of the fiat. These changes in briefest summary are the loss of the Russian assets, the dispersion of the stockholders, and the exclusion of the directors as well as all subordinate agents from the soil of the old empire.

 * * *

 The corporation once existing, the burden was on the defendant to overthrow the presumption of continuance and to show that life had ceased * * *. We cannot say upon this record that the burden has been borne. * * *

 * * *

 We find no statute or precedent that points with reasonable clarity to the conclusion that by the law of pre-Soviet Russia there has been an extinguishment of life as well as a suspension of activity. We find nothing in the Russian concept of juristic personality that leads to that conclusion, for there is nothing to show that the concept differs from our own. This being so, the presumption of continuance must tilt the balanced scales. The corporation survives in such a sense and to such a degree that it may still be dealt with as a persona in lands where the decrees of the Soviet Republic are not recognized as law. We think there is no substantial basis in the evidence for an opinion to the contrary * * *.

 (2)   The corporation surviving, the question must still be answered whether the former directors have authority to speak for it.

 * * *

 * * * We think their authority is sufficient in default of other representatives to permit them to sue in our courts in the name and for the benefit of the corporation they represent * * *.

 * * *

 (3)   The possibility of adverse claims does not relieve the defendant from liability when sued in an action at law by a depositor who is successful in proving a title to the fund.

 * * *

 The case comes down to this: A fund is in this State with title vested in the plaintiff at the time of the deposit. Nothing to divest that title has ever happened here or elsewhere. The directors who made the deposit in the name of the corporation or continued it in that name now ask to get it back. Either it must be paid to the depositor, acting by them, or it must be kept here indefinitely. Either they must control the custody, or for the present and the indefinite future it is not controllable by any one. The defendant expresses the fear that the money may be misapplied if the custody is changed. The fear has its basis in nothing more than mere suspicion. The directors, men of honor presumably, will be charged with the duties of trustees, and will be subject to prosecution, civil or criminal, if those duties are ignored. The defendant is not required to follow the money into their hands and see how they apply it. Its duty is to pay.

The judgment of the Appellate Division and that of the Trial Term should be reversed and judgment directed in favor of the plaintiff for $66,749.45 with interest from December 21, 1920, and costs in all the courts.

CRANE, LEHMAN, KELLOGG and HUBBS, JJ., concur; POUND and O'BRIEN, JJ., dissent.

Judgment accordingly.

A. M. LUTHER v. JAMES SAGOR & CO.

England, Court of Appeal, 1921.
[1921] 3 K.B. 532.*

BANKES, L. J. The action was brought to establish the plaintiff company's right to a quantity of veneer or plywood which had been imported by the defendants from Russia. The plaintiffs' case was that they are a Russian company having a factory or mill at Staraja Russia in Russia for the manufacture of veneer or plywood, and that in the year 1919 the so-called Republican Government of Russia without any right or title to do so seized all the stock at their mill and subsequently purported to sell the quantity in dispute in this action to the defendants. The plaintiffs contended that the so-called Republican Government had no existence as a government, that it had never been recognized by His Majesty's Government, and that the seizure of their goods was pure robbery. As an alternative they contended that the decree of the so-called government nationalizing all factories, as a result of which their goods were seized, is not a decree which the Courts of this country would recognize.

The answer of the defendants was two-fold. In the first place they contended that the Republican Government which had passed the decree nationalizing all factories was the de facto Government of Russia at the time, and had been recognized by His Majesty's Government as such, and that the decree was one to which the Courts of this country could not refuse recognition. Secondly they contended that

* Reprinted by permission of the Incorporated Council of Law Reporting for England and Wales, London.

the plaintiff company was an Esthonian and not a Russian company * * *. Roche, J. decided the two main points in the plaintiffs' favour. Upon the evidence which was before the learned judge I think that his decision was quite right. As the case was presented in the Court below the appellants relied on certain letters from the Foreign Office as establishing that His Majesty's Government had recognized the Soviet Government as the de facto Government of Russia. The principal letters are referred to by the learned judge in his judgment. He took the view that the letters relied on did not establish the appellants' contention. In this view I entirely agree.

In this Court the appellants asked leave to adduce further evidence, and as the respondents raised no objection, the evidence was given. It consisted of two letters from the Foreign Office dated respectively April 20 and 22, 1921. The first is in reply to a letter dated April 12, which the appellants' solicitors wrote to the Under Secretary of State for Foreign Affairs, asking for a "Certificate for production to the Court of Appeal that the Government of the Russian Socialist Federal Soviet Republic is recognized by His Majesty's Government as the de facto Government of Russia." To this request a reply was received dated April 20, 1921, in these terms: "I am directed by Earl Curzon of Kedleston to refer to your letter of April 12, asking for information as to the relations between His Majesty's Government and the Soviet Government of Russia. (2.) I am to inform you that His Majesty's Government recognize the Soviet Government as the de facto Government of Russia." The letter of April 22 is in reply to a request for information whether His Majesty's Government recognized the Provisional Government of Russia, and as to the period of its duration, and the extent of its jurisdiction. The answer contains (inter alia) the statement that the Provisional Government came into power on March 14, 1917, that it was recognized by His Majesty's Government as the then existing Government of Russia, and that the Constituent Assembly remained in session until December 13, 1917, when it was dispersed by the Soviet authorities. The statement contained in the letter of April 20 is accepted by the respondents' counsel as the proper and sufficient proof of the recognition of the Soviet Government as the de facto Government of Russia.

     * * *

     * * * [U]pon the construction which I place upon the communication of the Foreign Office to which I have referred, this Court must treat the Soviet Government, which the Government of this country has now recognized as the de facto Government of Russia, as having commenced its existence at a date anterior to any date material to the dispute between the parties to this appeal.

An attempt was made by the respondents' counsel to draw a distinction between the effect of a recognition of a government as a de facto government and the effect of a recognition of a government as a government de jure, and to say that the latter form of recognition might relate back to acts of state of a date earlier than the date of recognition, whereas the former could not. Wheaton quoting from

Mountague Bernard states the distinction between a de jure and a de facto government thus (1): "A de jure government is one which, in the opinion of the person using the phrase, ought to possess the powers of sovereignty, though at the time it may be deprived of them. A de facto government is one which is really in possession of them, although the possession may be wrongful or precarious." For some purposes no doubt a distinction can be drawn between the effect of the recognition by a sovereign state of the one form of government or of the other, but for the present purpose in my opinion no distinction can be drawn. The Government of this country having, to use the language just quoted, recognized the Soviet Government as the Government really in possession of the powers of sovereignty in Russia, the acts of that Government must be treated by the Courts of this country with all the respect due to the acts of a duly recognized foreign sovereign state.

* * *

* * * Although I consider that upon the materials before him the learned judge's judgment was quite correct, I think that upon the fresh materials before this Court the appeal succeeds and the judgment must be set aside and entered for the appellants. As the respondents succeeded, as I consider, rightly upon the evidence upon which the appellants relied in the Court below, I think that the respondents should have the costs of the action, and the appellants should have the costs of this appeal.

Since writing this judgment a further communication from the Foreign Office dated May 4, 1921, has been supplied by the respondents' solicitors to the members of the Court, and to the appellants' solicitors. The communication was made to a firm of solicitors interested in some other litigation. In the communication the writer states that he is instructed to state that His Majesty's Government recognize the Soviet Government of Russia as the de facto Government of that country as from March 16, 1921. I have ascertained that the words "as from" should be read "as on." So read the communication adds nothing to the information already before the Court and I need not refer to it further.

[Other opinions omitted.]

Decisions in other legal systems. Effect has been denied to acts of an unrecognized regime done in its own territory by a number of courts outside the common law system in cases where they would otherwise have determined the issue by applying their rules of private international law, i. e. conflict of laws. The exclusive reliance on non-recognition as a ground for refusing effect to the act involved has led on occasion to peculiar results.

Lhoest-Siniawskaia v. Officier de l'Etat Civil, Belgium, Tribunal Civil of Liège, 1929, 56 Journal du Droit International 1158 (1929), involved an action to compel the registrar to record an act of marriage established in Russia in 1919. In view of the non-recognition of the USSR by Belgium, there was no Russian official whose act could be recognized as valid in Belgium and in any case the signatures on the document were not certified. In Krimtchansky v. Officier de l'Etat Civil of Belgium, Tribunal Civil of Liège, 1929, 56 Journal du Droit International 1159 (1929), the action was to compel the registrar to accept a document as evidence of a divorce in Russia in 1928 so that the plaintiff could get a marriage license. The document had been recorded in Odessa. But since Belgium did not recognize the government of the USSR, the document, quite apart from other defects, could not be recognized as a valid act by a Russian official.

An heir claimed the money deposited in a bank account by the deceased in Hamarvy v. Credit Lyonnais, Egypt, Tribunal of Alexandria, 1925, 52 Journal du Droit International 475 (1925). Proof of his identity as heir depended on a certification by the appropriate Russian authorities. Since Egypt did not recognize the USSR, however, the proof would have to be furnished by consuls from the former Russian Government who were still in Egypt. In Decision No. 5641, Greece, Tribunal of Athens, 1924, 52 Journal du Droit International 1111 (1925), a will was given effect though contrary to Soviet law which would normally govern, on the ground that since Greece did not recognize the government of the Soviet Union, it would be contrary to the public order to give effect to Soviet law.

There were cases of Russian companies whose directors in France could not, as a practical matter, comply with the Russian law in force prior to the taking of power by the Soviet government. Still that law controlled, rather than that of the unrecognized regime, and the directors were to follow it as much as feasible and otherwise do the best they could under the circumstances. Vlasto v. Banque Russo Asiatique, France, Tribunal of Commerce of the Seine, 1922, 50 Journal du Droit International 933 (1923); Shramchenko v. Tcheloff, France, Tribunal of Commerce of Marseille, 1920, 51 Journal du Droit International 141 (1924). A similar type of issue and ruling was also involved in Katsikis v. Societá Fati Svoroni di Pallone, Italy, Tribunal of Genoa, 1923, 50 Journal du Droit International 1021 (1923).

In Attorney General v. Salomon Toledano, Morocco, Court of Appeal of Rabat, 1963, 40 Int'l L.Rep. 40 (1970), Toledano was granted by the court below an exequatur (i. e. an order giving full force and effect) for a notarial act executed in Tel Aviv. On appeal by the Attorney General, the order was reversed. Morocco did not recognize Israel as a state; hence it is deemed not to exist, all the rules regulating its functioning are deemed to be non-existent, and the notarial act is non-existent.

Stroganoff-Scherbatoff v. Bensimon, Tribunal of General Jurisdiction of the Seine, 1966, 56 Revue Critique du Droit International Privé 120 (1967), involved the following facts. By laws of succession of 1817 and 1847, Lieutenant Stroganoff became owner of certain properties. In 1918, the Soviet government abolished the legislation under which he had title to them, took in particular some of the art objects and sold them in Berlin to the defendant company. A nephew of Stroganoff claimed as heir the objects involved. Part of the issue turned on whether the art objects continued to be immovables under the Russian laws of 1817 and 1847 or became movables by the Soviet law of 1918. The court said that the non-recognition of the Soviet government did not entitle French courts to disregard Soviet legislation on succession enacted before recognition of the Soviet government by France. It went on to apply the appropriate choice of law rules and found that Lieutenant Stroganoff lost possession of the objects in 1918 and hence the thirty year prescription (i. e. statute of limitations) had run long before the plaintiff brought his action.

---

3. NONRECOGNITION DISTINGUISHED FROM BREAKING DIPLOMATIC RELATIONS

BANCO NACIONAL DE CUBA v. SABBATINO

United States, Supreme Court, 1964.
376 U.S. 398, 84 S.Ct. 923.

[This case is reported at p. 372, above. Banco Nacional, an instrumentality of the Cuban government, brought an action in the Federal District Court for the Southern District of New York alleging conversion of bills of lading representing sugar previously expropriated by the Cuban government; the action seeks recovery of proceeds from the sale of the sugar. At the outset several procedural questions were presented to the court, one of which was dealt with when Mr. Justice HARLAN delivered the opinion of the court, as follows.]

It is first contended that this petitioner, an instrumentality of the Cuban Government, should be denied access to American courts because Cuba is an unfriendly power and does not permit nationals of this country to obtain relief in its courts. * * * If the courts of this country should be closed to the government of a foreign state, the underlying reason is one of national policy transcending the interests of the parties to the action, and this Court should give effect to that policy sua sponte even at this stage of the litigation.

Under principles of comity governing this country's relations with other nations, sovereign states are allowed to sue in the courts of the United States * * *. [P]rior to some recent lower court cases which have questioned the right of instrumentalities of the Cuban Government to sue in our courts, the privilege of suit has been denied only to governments at war with the United States * * *.

Respondents, pointing to the severance of diplomatic relations, commercial embargo, and freezing of Cuban assets in this country, contend that relations between the United States and Cuba manifest such animosity that unfriendliness is clear, and that the courts should be closed to the Cuban Government. We do not agree. This Court would hardly be competent to undertake assessments of varying degrees of friendliness or its absence, and, lacking some definite touchstone for determination, we are constrained to consider any relationship, short of war, with a recognized sovereign power as embracing the privilege of resorting to United States courts. Although the severance of diplomatic relations is an overt act with objective significance in the dealings of sovereign states, we are unwilling to say that it should inevitably result in the withdrawal of the privilege of bringing suit. Severance may take place for any number of political reasons, its duration is unpredictable, and whatever expression of animosity it may imply does not approach that implicit in a declaration of war.

It is perhaps true that nonrecognition of a government in certain circumstances may reflect no greater unfriendliness than the severance of diplomatic relations with a recognized government, but the refusal to recognize has a unique legal aspect. It signifies this country's unwillingness to acknowledge that the government in question speaks as the sovereign authority for the territory it purports to control * * *. Political recognition is exclusively a function of the Executive. The possible incongruity of judicial "recognition," by permitting suit, of a government not recognized by the Executive is completely absent when merely diplomatic relations are broken.

The view that the existing situation between the United States and Cuba should not lead to a denial of status to sue is buttressed by the circumstance that none of the acts of our Government have been aimed at closing the courts of this country to Cuba, and more particularly by the fact that the Government has come to the support of Cuba's "act of state" claim in this very litigation.

There are good reasons for declining to extend the principle to the question of standing of sovereign states to sue. Whether a foreign sovereign will be permitted to sue involves a problem more sensitive politically than whether the judgments of its courts may be re-examined, and the possibility of embarrassment to the Executive Branch in handling foreign relations is substantially more acute. Re-examination of judgments, in principle, reduces rather than enhances the possibility of injustice being done in a particular case; refusal to allow suit makes it impossible for a court to see that a particular dispute is fairly resolved. The freezing of Cuban assets exemplifies the capacity of the political branches to assure, through a variety of techniques * * * that the national interest is protected against a country which is thought to be improperly denying the rights of United States citizens.

Furthermore, the question whether a country gives res judicata effect to United States judgments presents a relatively simple inquiry. The precise status of the United States Government and its nationals before foreign courts is much more difficult to determine.

To make such an investigation significant, a court would have to discover not only what is provided by the formal structure of the foreign judicial system, but also what the practical possibilities of fair treatment are. The courts, whose powers to further the national interest in foreign affairs are necessarily circumscribed as compared with those of the political branches, can best serve the rule of law by not excluding otherwise proper suitors because of deficiencies in their legal systems.

We hold that this petitioner is not barred from access to the federal courts.

---

4. IN INTERNATIONAL TRIBUNALS

ARBITRATION BETWEEN GREAT BRITAIN AND COSTA RICA (THE TINOCO CLAIMS)

William H. Taft, Sole Arbitrator, 1923.
1 U.N.Rep.Int'l Arb.Awards 375 (1948).

[There has been very little consideration by international tribunals of the subject of recognition, either as to its legal effects in the sense of this section, or as to international rights and duties in regard to recognition. One of the few legal decisions at the international level is this arbitration by a former President of the United States and (at the time) Chief Justice of the United States. Chief Justice Taft as sole arbitrator had to decide, basically, whether rights against the Costa Rican state could vest in favor of persons entitled to British diplomatic protection as a result of governmental monetary activities and contractual undertakings by Tinoco, a coupist president of Costa Rica whose regime had not been recognized by the United Kingdom, the United States, and a number of other leading countries. After Tinoco fell, a new government enacted a Law of Nullities, purporting to invalidate currency issued by Tinoco's regime and held by British subjects and an oil concession granted by Tinoco to a British company. Although the arbitrator found no injury to the plaintiff as to either claim for reasons not relevant at this point, he determined that the Tinoco regime could bind the state internationally. A portion of his award follows.]

Dr. John Bassett Moore, now a member of the Permanent Court of International Justice, in his Digest of International Law, Volume 1, p. 249, announces the general principle which has had such universal acquiescence as to become well settled international law:

Changes in the government or the internal policy of a state do not as a rule affect its position in international law. A monarchy may be transformed into a republic or a republic into a monarchy; absolute principles may be substituted for constitutional, or the reverse; but, though the government changes, the nation remains, with rights and obligations unimpaired.

* * *

First, what are the facts to be gathered from the documents and evidence submitted by the two parties as to the de facto character of the Tinoco government?

In January, 1917, Frederico A. Tinoco was Secretary of War under Alfredo Gonzalez, the then President of Costa Rica. On the ground that Gonzalez was seeking reelection as President in violation of a constitutional limitation, Tinoco used the army and navy to seize the government, assume the provisional headship of the Republic and become Commander-in-Chief of the army. Gonzalez took refuge in the American Legation, thence escaping to the United States. Tinoco constituted a provisional government at once and summoned the people to an election for deputies to a constituent assembly on the first of May, 1917. At the same time he directed an election to take place for the Presidency and himself became a candidate. An election was held. Some 61,000 votes were cast for Tinoco and 259 for another candidate. Tinoco then was inaugurated as the President to administer his powers under the former constitution until the creation of a new one. A new constitution was adopted June 8, 1917, supplanting the constitution of 1871. For a full two years Tinoco and the legislative assembly under him peaceably administered the affairs of the Government of Costa Rica, and there was no disorder of a revolutionary character during that interval. No other government of any kind asserted power in the country. The courts sat, Congress legislated, and the government was duly administered. Its power was fully established and peaceably exercised. The people seemed to have accepted Tinoco's government with great good will when it came in, and to have welcomed the change. * * *

But it is urged that many leading Powers refused to recognize the Tinoco government, and that recognition by other nations is the chief and best evidence of the birth, existence and continuity of succession of a government. Undoubtedly recognition by other Powers is an important evidential factor in establishing proof of the existence of a government in the society of nations. What are the facts as to this? The Tinoco government was recognized by Bolivia on May 17, 1917; by Argentina on May 22, 1917; by Chile on May 22, 1917; by Haiti on May 22, 1917; by Guatemala on May 28, 1917; by Switzerland on June 1, 1917; by Germany on June 10, 1917; by Denmark on June 18, 1917; by Spain on June 18, 1917; by Mexico on July 1, 1917; by Holland on July 11, 1917; by the Vatican on June 9, 1917; by Colombia on August 9, 1917; by Austria on August 10, 1917; by Portugal on August 14, 1917; by El Salvador on September 12, 1917; by Roumania on November 15, 1917; by Brazil on November 28, 1917; by Peru on December 15, 1917; and by Ecuador on April 23, 1917.

What were the circumstances as to the other nations?

The United States, on February 9, 1917, two weeks after Tinoco had assumed power, took this action:

> The Government of the United States has viewed the recent overthrow of the established government in Costa Rica with the gravest concern and considers that illegal acts of this character tend to disturb the peace of Central America and to disrupt the unity of the American continent. In view of its policy in regard to the assumption of power through illegal methods, clearly enunciated by it on several occasions during the past four years, the Government of the United States desires to set forth in an emphatic and distinct manner its present position in regard to the actual situation in Costa Rica which is that it will not give recognition or support to any government which may be established unless it is clearly proven that it is elected by legal and constitutional means.

And again on February 24, 1917:

> In order that citizens of the United States may have definite information as to the position of this Government in regard to any financial aid which they may give to, or any business transaction which they may have with those persons who overthrew the constitutional Government of Costa Rica by an act of armed rebellion, the Government of the United States desires to advise them that it will not consider any claims which may in the future arise from such dealings, worthy of its diplomatic support.

The Department of State issued the following in April, 1918:

> The Department of State has received reports to the effect that those citizens of Costa Rica now exercising the functions of government in the Republic of Costa Rica have been led to believe by those persons who are acting as their agents, that the Government of the United States was considering granting recognition to them as constituting the Government of Costa Rica.
>
> In order to correct any such impression which is absolutely erroneous, the Government of the United States desires to state clearly and emphatically that it has not altered the attitude which it has assumed in regard to the granting of recognition to the above mentioned citizens of Costa Rica and which was conveyed to them in February, 1917, and further that this attitude will not be altered in the future.

Probably because of the leadership of the United States in respect to a matter of this kind, her then Allies in the war, Great Britain, and France and Italy, declined to recognize the Tinoco government. Costa Rica was, therefore, not permitted to sign the Treaty of Peace at Versailles, although the Tinoco government had declared war against Germany.

The merits of the policy of the United States in this non-recognition it is not for the arbitrator to discuss, for the reasons that in his consideration of this case, he is necessarily controlled by principles of international law, and however justified as a national policy non-recognition on such a ground may be, it certainly has not been acquiesced in by all the nations of the world, which is a condition precedent to considering it as a postulate of international law.

The non-recognition by other nations of a government claiming to be a national personality, is usually appropriate evidence that it has not attained the independence and control entitling it by international law to be classed as such. But when recognition vel non of a government is by such nations determined by inquiry, not into its de facto sovereignty and complete governmental control, but into its illegitimacy or irregularity of origin, their non-recognition loses something of evidential weight on the issue with which those applying the rules of international law are alone concerned. What is true of the non-recognition of the United States in its bearing upon the existence of a de facto government under Tinoco for thirty months is probably in a measure true of the non-recognition by her Allies in the European War. Such non-recognition for any reason, however, cannot outweigh the evidence disclosed by this record before me as to the de facto character of Tinoco's government, according to the standard set by international law.

Second.   It is ably and earnestly argued on behalf of Costa Rica that the Tinoco government cannot be considered a de facto government, because it was not established and maintained in accord with the constitution of Costa Rica of 1871. To hold that a government which establishes itself and maintains a peaceful administration, with the acquiescence of the people for a substantial period of time, does not become a de facto government unless it conforms to a previous constitution would be to hold that within the rules of international law a revolution contrary to the fundamental law of the existing government cannot establish a new government. This cannot be, and is not, true. The change by revolution upsets the rule of the authorities in power under the then existing fundamental law, and sets aside the fundamental law in so far as the change of rule makes it necessary. To speak of a revolution creating a de facto government, which conforms to the limitations of the old constitution is to use a contradiction in terms. The same government continues internationally, but not the internal law of its being. The issue is not whether the new government assumes power or conducts its administration under constitutional limitations established by the people during the incumbency of the government it has overthrown. The question is, has it really established itself in such a way that all within its influence recognize its control, and that there is no opposing force assuming to be a government in its place? Is it discharging its functions as a government usually does, respected within its own jurisdiction?

* * *

Liability of the state for acts of ordinary governmental administration by an unrecognized regime. There is international arbitral, as well as national decisional, support for the proposition that even a revolutionary regime that is not successful in establishing itself, albeit temporarily, as the only effective government in a state is capable in territory under its control of creating legal obligations against the state and in favor of aliens as a result of the conduct of ordinary governmental administration, such as collecting and giving quittances for taxes, issuing postal money orders, etc. See generally, Restatement of the Foreign Relations Law of the United States, Reporters' Notes to Section 110 (1965).

It is frequently assumed a fortiori, cf. the Tinoco arbitration, that a revolutionary regime that does establish itself as the effective government in control of a state can create concession and other investment rights in favor of aliens that will bind a future de jure government. While this may be so in law, the political problems for a foreign investor who has dealt with a dictator, especially if the transaction is unusually favorable to the investor, can and have been many. Thus, in foreign investment practice there is a very difficult problem for international transactions lawyers whose clients want to know: "Do you advise me to take up or reject this really good opportunity that old General Dictadura is offering me?" Try your hand at responding to hypotheticals that you can easily think of about direct foreign investments involving special acts of grant by, inter alia, the regimes presently in control of Argentina, Bolivia, Brazil, Ecuador, Haiti, Libya, Paraguay, and Peru.

SECTION B. INTERNATIONAL LEGAL EFFECTS OF NATIONAL RECOGNITION POLICIES

---

1. SKETCHES OF NATIONAL POLICIES

1. *Recognition of entities as states.* It is not often that the recognition of a state is in doubt. Most such recognitions are as routine as the acts that bring new states into existence, such as by the voluntary granting of independence to a former colony. Under these circumstances a classic doctrinal dispute has fallen into desuetude: is recognition of a state *constitutive*, in the sense that the state cannot exist legally as a state without recognition? Much ink has been spilled on this question, with inconclusive results, because almost all entities (including micro-mini states) that mount drives for statehood get recognized as such. About the only failure is the Island of Anguilla, but it is by no means clear that the Anguillans wanted independence so much as freedom from association in semi-statehood with the neighboring islands of Nevis and St. Kitts. The Anguillans seemed happy to settle for renewed British colonial status. The British seemed less happy to have to keep the colony.

2. *De facto recognition of regimes as governments.* As an act of cognition, see p. 778, recognition obviously must be based on what

is perceived about an entity as a state or about a regime as a government. While there is no rule or doctrine of international law that a regime perceived as a government must be recognized as such by the diplomatic arm of another state, the general practice of states is to recognize or extend recognition to a new regime that has come to power in abnormal ways and is perceived in fact as having established itself as a government. Therefore, in this sense recognition practice, at least, as to regimes as governments is de facto, i. e. based on the facts perceived. Notwithstanding the simplicity of the basic situation just described, the terms de facto and de jure have unfortunately been used with imprecision in international relations and law. The Restatement of the Foreign Relations Law of the United States (1965) * attempts clarification as follows in Reporters' Note 2 to Section 96:

> *Uses of term de facto in connection with recognition.* The term de facto is used by writers and in judicial decisions dealing with recognition in a variety of ways.
>
> a.   The term de facto is used to indicate that the recognition extended to a regime is tentative and hence, under the rule stated in Subsection (2) of this section, may be withdrawn. In this sense, a regime may be recognized as a de facto government or, to make it even more tentative, as a de facto authority. For an example of British practice regarding tentative recognition see § 102, Reporters' Note.
>
> b.   The term de facto is used to describe the policy followed by some states in determining whether to extend recognition. Even in this context two separate uses of the term de facto must be distinguished:
>
> (i)   The term de facto has been used, in contrast to the term de jure, to describe a recognition policy that does not interpose as an objection to recognition of a government the fact that the government came into power in violation of the constitution of the state. This sense of the term is now obsolete since no state now requires constitutional legitimacy as a necessary condition for recognition of a new government.
>
> (ii)   The term de facto has been used to describe a policy under which a state will recognize any new regime satisfying the requirements stated in § 101 with respect to actual control of the state. This is in contrast to a policy under which legal considerations, such as the ability and intention of the regime to carry out the obligations of the state under international law and agreements, are applied as additional requirements for recognition.

c. The term de facto has been used by national courts and international tribunals in dealing with the effect to be given the acts of non-recognized regimes that are in actual control of the state. Arbitrator Taft referred to the Tinoco regime as the de facto government of Costa Rica in the Tinoco Arbitration (Great Britain v. Costa Rica), [1923–1924] Ann.Dig. 34, 176, 177, 379, 380 (Nos. 15, 95, 96, 211, 212), 18 Am.J. Int'l L. 147 (Oct. 18, 1923). The New York Court of Appeals described the Soviet Union in the same terms in Salimoff & Co. v. Standard Oil Co., 262 N.Y. 220, 186 N.E. 679 (1933). In neither case did the court's characterization of the non-recognized regime as a de facto government involve recognition of the regime, although the facts that led to this characterization resulted in a decision, in each case, giving legal effect to the acts of the regime under the rules stated in §§ 109 and 113.

British recognition policy is commonly described as being de facto in the sense of both a and b(ii) above. In the United States, which has oscillated as between a de facto and a de jure policy as to recognition of governments, de facto recognition was classically stated by Thomas Jefferson, as Secretary of State, and elaborated by his successors in that office, as requiring satisfaction *in fact* that three pre-conditions had been met by the regime being considered for recognition: (i) it is in substantial control of the territory of the state, (ii) with the acquiescence (not necessarily the electoral approval) of the people and (iii) is willing to carry out the international obligations of the state. Prior to the recognition of the People's Republic of China a scholarly British ambassador explained British and American recognition policies as follows:

Sir Roger Makins, British Ambassador to the United States, speaking in 1954, discussed American and British viewpoints with reference to diplomatic recognition and explained particularly with reference to the viewpoint of Great Britain:

* * * As you all know, the British Government recognized the Communist Government of China in 1950, in company with a number of other Governments. We continue to recognize it and have no present intention of changing our position. The United States has not recognized the Peking regime, and the administration has recently reaffirmed its refusal to do so.

Now, there are no differences between us in our objectives in the Far East, even if we sometimes differ on the timing, and the method of our approach to them. We are both equally concerned to oppose and to prevent the spread of Communist imperialism. How is it, therefore, that we should be found at variance on this question of recognition? And what is the significance of this divergent position?

The practice of governments in giving diplomatic recognition to each other has fluctuated through the years, and the attitudes of the British and United States governments have sometimes approximated and sometimes diverged. Broadly speaking, there are two main lines of approach to be found in the writings of the authorities, and in the policies of governments. The one treats recognition as an act based solely on the facts, an act which follows upon the fulfillment of certain objective criteria; the other regards it as an act of policy which signifies something more than the recognition of a situation of fact and law. I shall call the former the de facto principle, the latter the principle of legitimacy. * * *

The practice of Great Britain has always conformed fairly closely to the de facto principle. If a government is in effective control of the country in question; if it seems to have a reasonable expectancy of permanence; if it can act for a majority of the country's inhabitants; if it is able (though possibly not willing) to carry out its international obligations; if, in short, it can give a convincing answer to the question, "Who's in charge here?," then we recognize that government. We are not conferring a favor, we are recognizing a situation of fact. The conduct of foreign affairs (as distinct from the formation of foreign policy) is, after all, not essentially different from the conduct of any other business. You do not have to like a man's face, or manners, or even morals, in doing business with him. And even if you do not want to do business with an ugly customer, shutting your eyes won't make him go away.

* * *

There have been other periods in American history when this realistic, Jeffersonian, de facto-type view of recognition has yielded to the belief that what Chief Justice Taft called "legitimacy" was a further requirement. The Union took that view, naturally enough, under Secretary Seward at the time of the Civil War, and later, during President Wilson's first term, there were emphatic reversions to the principle of legitimacy. Britain also applied this principle to some extent during the 19th century. For example, in 1870 Britain refused to recognize the government of the Third Republic in France until it had been elected by a constituent assembly, and again in Portugal in 1910 Britain refused to recognize the revolutionary government until a constitution had been voted and a President elected.

But since 1924 Britain has followed the de facto principle closely in a series of cases, the Soviet Union, Chile, Peru, Ecuador, Argentina, and the Nationalist government of Gen. Franco in Spain. So we arrive at the situation today in which Britain and the United States find themselves at opposite points in applying the doctrine of diplomatic recognition in the case of China: we have applied the de facto principle, you are applying a contemporary version of the legitimacy principle.

Before commenting on this there is a question of timing and circumstances to be mentioned. Britain recognized Communist China before the Korean war began, before Chinese intervention in the struggle, before the natural indignation to which these events gave rise. * * *

2 Whiteman, Digest of International Law 110 (1963).

3. *Recognition and revolution.* When a mother country in an orderly manner spins off a former colony as a new state—"mini" or normal—or when a sharp change in political preference within a country comes at the ballot box, recognition is either routine, as in the case of new states, or does not recur at all, as when the Chileans elected Dr. Allende as the world's first freely elected communist chief of state. Hence both the policy and the consequent legal problems related to recognition are closely linked to abnormal political change within particular geographic areas. Established governments of existing states respond in various ways, over time, to revolutionary changes elsewhere. Not even the United Kingdom has always been rigorously faithful to a de facto view of diplomatic recognition. As to the recognition of revolutionary regimes, the United States, although over the longer span being more or less faithful to the Jeffersonian Prescription where old-line countries and fairly remote new ones have had coups d'état, has followed a zig-zag course as to Latin America and as to revolutionary socialism (the USSR and the People's Republic of China).

The most dramatic and possibly still the most far-reaching departure of the United States from a detached and clinical viewpoint as to coups was that of President Woodrow Wilson, who under the influence of his Secretary of State, William Jennings Bryan, withheld recognition of Francisco Madero, and later others, who in Mexico rose up against the dictatorship of Porfirio Diaz.

What had begun with an excess of virtue, p. 779, ended with an excess of national espousal of questionable property rights given to American concerns by Diaz. That is, the Harding administration withheld recognition of the Obregon government of Mexico, after conditions had stabilized in the country, until the government of Mexico agreed, as a condition to recognition by the United States, to validate the Diaz grants of property rights.

These pages of history have had great influences. Out of Latin America's observation of the Wilson-Harding episode came the Estrada doctrine and an attitudinal conditioning in Latin America that the withholding of recognition is an act of inadmissible intervention in the internal affairs of the state that has had the coup. With ethnocentric insensitivity, however, United States diplomatic practice and strong mass media opinion continued to support a United States recognition policy for Latin America different from the one applied to coups elsewhere, excluding the major socialist ones.

In 1962, President Kennedy for nearly a month withheld recognition of a coup in Peru, on the grounds that the change of government had not occurred democratically. But in the 1960's, coup after coup in sub-Sahara Africa and southeast Asia were met with routine applications of the Jeffersonian criteria.

Latin America has become extremely sensitive as to the discrimination. But even before the announcement by President Nixon, pursuant to his low profile doctrine, that we would deal with governments as we find them—even in Latin America, United States recognition policy had begun to shift toward what might be called a modified Estrada doctrine. In the Panamanian and Peruvian coups of 1968, the Department of State took the position that the occurrence of a coup did not necessarily mean that a new act of recognition would have to take place. Instead, the practice of the government came to be to adjust relations in accordance with the stage of the coup and the stability of the regime within the country and to continue relations in such cases and situations as the national interests of the United States might indicate as provident for contact between the United States and the coupists. The ambassadors were not withdrawn, and the resumptions of full relations were not marked by formal acts, such as presentations of credentials. The United States did continue a practice of consulting with other members of the Organization of American States and of issuing press statements at the time of return to full relationships. These recent practices and utterances have tended to reduce sharply the former difference in treatment of coups in the other American republics from those elsewhere.

UNITED STATES POLICY ON NONRECOGNITION OF COMMUNIST CHINA

39 United States Department of State Bulletin 385 (1958).

[Excerpts from a memorandum sent by the Department of State to its missions abroad when the United States policy was not to recognize Communist China.]

Policy toward Communist China has been an important issue since the Communists came to power there, and it is of critical significance to the United States and the free world today. In the United States the issue is a very real one to the vast majority of the people. As a result of Korean and Chinese Communist aggression in Korea, the United States suffered 142,000 casualties, bringing tragedy to communities all over the country. * * *

The basic considerations on which United States policy toward China rests are twofold. First, the Soviet bloc, of which Communist China is an important part, is engaged in a long-range struggle to destroy the way of life of the free countries of the world and bring about the global dominion of communism. The Chinese Communist regime has made no secret of its fundamental hostility to the United States and the free world as a whole nor of its avowed intention to effect their downfall. Today its defiance of and attacks on the non-Communist world have reached a level of intensity that has not been witnessed since the Korean war. The second basic factor is that East Asia is peculiarly vulnerable to the Communist offensive because of the proximity of the free countries of that area to Communist China, the inexperience in self-government of those which have recently won their independence, their suspicions of the West inherited from their colonial past, and the social, political, and economic changes which inevitably accompany their drive toward modernization.

* * *

An argument often heard is that the Chinese Communists are here "to stay"; that they will have to be recognized sooner or later; and that it would be the course of wisdom to bow to the inevitable now rather than be forced to do so ungracefully at a later date. It is true that there is no reason to believe that the Chinese Communist regime is on the verge of collapse; but there is equally no reason to accept its present rule in mainland China as permanent. In fact, unmistakable signs of dissatisfaction and unrest in Communist China have appeared in the "ideological remodeling" and the mass campaign against "rightists" which have been in progress during the past year. Dictatorships often create an illusion of permanence from the very fact that they suppress and still all opposition, and that of the Chinese Communists is no exception to this rule. The United States holds the view that communism's rule in China is not permanent and that it one day will pass. By withholding diplomatic recognition from Peiping it seeks to hasten that passing.

In public discussions of China policy one of the proposals that has attracted widest attention is that known as the "two Chinas solution." Briefly, advocates of this arrangement propose that the Chinese Communist regime be recognized as the government of mainland China while the Government at Taipei remains as the legal government of Taiwan. They argue that this approach to the Chinese problem has the merit of granting the Communists only what they already control while retaining for the free world the military strategic bastion of Taiwan. However, it overlooks or ignores certain facts of basic importance. * * *

The "two Chinas" concept is bitterly opposed by both Peiping and Taipei. Hence, even if such a solution could be imposed by outside authority, it would not be a stable one. Constant policing would be required to avert its violent overthrow by one side or the other. * * *

---

1. *Can there be implied or inadvertent recognition?* Once at Geneva in the 1950s, Secretary of State John Foster Dulles found himself in the same room with Chou En-lai of the People's Republic

of China. Fearing a handshake or some other greeting from Chou, Dulles rushed from the room, exclaiming, "I cannot, I cannot!" Aside from personal and ideological factors, the Secretary seems to have been motivated by the fear that an act of social intercourse would amount to recognition of the Mao regime as the government of mainland China. In his instructions to American diplomatic missions, Mr. Dulles also expressed great concern lest American foreign service officers, by appearing at the same social functions with representatives of unrecognized regimes representing international communism, effectuate inadvertent recognition of them.

Need the Secretary have worried? Section 104 of the Restatement of the Foreign Relations Law of the United States (1965) makes the sensible and widely accepted point that, although recognition by implication can occur, a disclaimer is sufficient to negate it. Hence an implication of intention to recognize from propinquity or other associative conduct is largely an illusory fear.

The best subsequent support of the effect of a disclaimer—mutual in this case—is that in 1971 the President of the United States made an official visit to the government of the People's Republic of China, without previously having extended it recognition.

2. *What, if anything, should be done to regulate internationally long term or intensive relations without recognition?* The disclaimer principle makes it possible for governments to carry on over many years fairly intensive sets of relationships without recognition. For instance, the United States did not recognize the Bolshevists as the government of the state of Russia until 16 years after the 1917 Russian Revolution. However, in that period trade delegates were exchanged and the largest volume of private sector United States trade and technology transfers to date took place.

Franco took Madrid and the Spanish Civil War ended in April 1939. Mexico for years had quite intensive commercial, cultural (including exchanges of bullfighters) and other relations with the Franco regime. There was a Mexican official in Madrid to give visas for travel to Mexico. But Mexico had no diplomatic mission to the Franco regime. Are these peculiarities significant or not in the conduct of international relations? Should diplomatic recognition be regulated by positive international law in this respect? Why or why not?

SCHWEBEL, "COGNITION" AND THE PEKING VISIT, IS THE RECOGNITION OF GOVERNMENTS OBSOLETE?

The Washington Post, Feb. 23, 1972.
Sec. A, p. 16, col. 3, 4, 5.*

One of the many extraordinary aspects of President Nixon's visit to Peking is that it is an official visit by the chief of state of a government that does not recognize the government by whose chief of state he has been officially received.

Not only, in fact, does the United States not recognize what it calls the Government of the People's Republic of China as the Government of China; it recognizes another government, the Government of the Republic of China, as the Government of China.

Great importance is attached by the three governments concerned—in Washington, Peking and Taipei—to which government is acknowledged as the recognized government. Yet at the same time, as President Nixon's journey so dramatically demonstrates, the content of recognition is, internationally speaking, unimpressive.

For two governments may in fact know, appreciate and act on the conclusion of their respective existence, even though they do not "recognize" one another. They may conclude treaties (such as that for a Korean armistice), conduct negotiations between ambassadors (as with the Warsaw talks), trade (as U.S. citizens may now lawfully do with mainland China), promote cultural exchanges (as of ping-pong teams), collaborate or contest in international organs (such as the United Nations Security Council), attend each other's diplomatic receptions (as in New York), and coordinate their foreign policies (as China and the United States appear to have done, in effect if not by design, on Bengal). Viewed against that background of not inconsiderable relations, President Nixon's official visit to the unrecognized government in Peking seems less anomalous.

Not only does the absence of recognition admit extensive relations; recognition itself does not require substantial, still less cordial relations. For example, the United States recognized the State of Cuba with the Spanish-American War. It recognized the Castro government soon after it seized power. But diplomatic relations between the two governments have been severed for years. Trade is interdicted, travel is limited, the most minimal diplomatic intercourse seems to be carried on through the good offices of third states, indeed sanctions are in force.

If then the reality of recognition is so arid, why the fuss about it? Whether or not one government accords recognition to a foreign state or government remains a matter of much political significance. Sheikh Mujibur Rahman is triumphant when more than a score of states recognize the statehood of Bangladesh. The senators of the opposition scent a political point in the administration's delaying the recognition of Bangladesh, a matter which, ironically enough, President Nixon suggests he will deal with on his return from talks with the unrecognized government in Peking.

Presumably there is something to all this controversy about recognition or there would be less controversy. Something, but not much.

Under international law, an entity is generally acknowledged to be a state if it has a reasonably defined territory, a population, a government substantially independent of other governments, and a measure of stability.

Under international law, a political authority qualifies as a government if it is in effective control of the state.

When these conditions are fulfilled, other governments act as if they know that the entities that fulfill these conditions are there. This they can do short of recognition—as American relations with the government in Peking demonstrate.

And short of recognition, other governments must nevertheless accord unrecognized states and governments certain rights—most notably respect for their territorial integrity. The Arab States are not legally permitted to attack the State of Israel because they do not recognize it; nor is the United States entitled to attack forces of the Government of the People's Republic of China because it does not recognize it.

In other words, short of recognition, there is what the legal adviser of the Swedish Ministry for Foreign Affairs, Hans Blix, terms "cognition." States know when in fact foreign states and governments exist, even though they have not extended recognition to them; and they must act on that knowledge up to a limited point.

What then is left to the function of recognition?

Recognition is a declaration (or occasionally, an action) by which the recognizing government in effect affirms that the new state or regime fulfils the criteria of statehood or government and that it is ready to accept it as such. It implies (but does not require) that the recognizing government is prepared to regularize relations by the establishment of diplomatic relations. It suggests that the recognizing government is ready to extend to the newly recognized at least a measure of cooperation and courtesy.

But recognition does not necessarily manifest readiness for close and cordial relations. Thus, on Sept. 25, 1969, the United States Senate resolved: " * * * that it is the sense of the Senate that when the United States recognizes a foreign government and exchanges diplomatic relations with it, this does not of itself imply that the United States approves of the form, ideology or policy of that foreign government."

In other words, recognition, on the international plane, does little more than manifest the willingness of the recognizing government to maintain relations on a more regularized and possibly more intimate basis than heretofore. It may not even imply that. India recognized Israel years ago; it has yet to exchange ambassadors with it.

On the domestic plane, the effects of recognition are larger. In most national courts, questions like the capacity of a foreign state or government to sue, and to claim sovereign immunity from suit, turn on whether it is recognized by the national government in question.

The substantive aridity of recognition on the international level —coupled with the considerable emotional confusion which issues of recognition nevertheless continue to generate—have led to suggestions that the term and concept of recognition be dropped. States would act on the basis of cognition alone. They would establish diplomatic relations, and pragmatically develop other relations, as they please.

Possibly national courts might be left to themselves to make decisions about the existence of foreign states and governments as cases arise, without the benefit of executive guidance.

Abandonment of recognition as an international practice would seem to present few problems. *   *   *

Certainly a good deal of international misunderstanding and domestic hyperbole would disappear with the disappearance of the doctrine of recognition. *   *   *

ACADEMY OF SCIENCES OF THE U.S.S.R. INSTITUTE OF STATE AND LAW, INTERNATIONAL LAW 117 (MOSCOW, 1961)

*   *   *

Political factors play a certain part in deciding upon recognition of a State.

Recognition is an act undertaken by a State which expresses the desire of the ruling class of that State. The emergence of a socialist State as a rule gives rise to strong opposition on the part of the imperialist States. This is expressed by their attitude to the problem of recognition (the United States did not recognize the Soviet Union until 1933, and it has still not recognized the Chinese People's Republic).

Something similar may also be observed in the case of the recognition of States emerging as a result of the national-liberation struggle. The governments of some imperialist States not only do not recognise these States, but attempt to keep them in a state of dependence by force of arms, and in this way to maintain unchanged the shameful system of colonialism.

All these measures are illegal, in that they contradict a most important principle of International Law—the principle of the self-determination of nations.

*   *   *

DIPLOMATIC RECOGNITION
A FOREIGN AFFAIRS OUTLINE

77 United States Department of State Bulletin 462 (1977).[1]

Recently President Carter expressed his desire that the United States work toward establishment and maintenance of normal diplo-

---

1. Based on a Department of State publication in the Gist series, released August 1977. This outline is designed to be a quick reference aid on U. S. foreign relations. It is not intended as a comprehensive U.S. policy statement.

matic relations with the governments of all states. The United States now has diplomatic relations with over 130 governments of states. It has no diplomatic relations, or is in the process of normalizing relations, with 11 other governments of entities widely recognized as states. * * * In a few cases, the United States has withheld recognition from, or has suspended relations with, another government; in other cases, governments have suspended relations with us.

Under our constitutional system, recognition and the establishment of diplomatic relations are Presidential prerogatives. Establishing and maintaining diplomatic relations with governments, however, is not a unilateral process; both states must agree that it serves their national interests.

The United States maintains relations with other governments because it helps us achieve our basic foreign policy objectives: By communicating directly with governments on a full range of issues—by stating our views and listening to theirs—we can help avoid misunderstandings and affect the decisions and actions of other governments. This is particularly true in crises, when good communication is essential.

Criteria for Recognition

Diplomatic recognition of governments is a comparatively recent practice in the history of international relations. Traditionally some European governments used nonrecognition of revolutionary change to protect monarchies and to emphasize the unique legitimacy of dynastic heirs and their governments. France ignored this tradition by recognizing the United States during our Revolutionary War. Later, when the revolutionary French Government took power in 1792, Thomas Jefferson, our first Secretary of State, instructed the U.S. envoy in Paris to deal with it because it had been "formed by the will of the nation substantially declared."

Throughout most of the 19th century, the United States recognized stable governments without thereby attempting to confer approval. U. S. recognition policy grew more complex as various Administrations applied differing criteria for recognition and expressed differently the reasons for their decisions. For example, Secretary of State William Seward (1861–69) added as a criterion the government's ability to honor its international obligations; President Rutherford Hayes (1877–81) required a demonstration of popular support for the new government; and President Woodrow Wilson (1913–21) favored using recognition to spread democracy around the world by demanding free elections.

Other criteria have been applied since then. These include the degree of foreign involvement in the government as well as the government's political orientation, attitude toward foreign investment, and treatment of U. S. citizens, corporations, and government representatives.

One result of such complex recognition criteria was to create the impression among other nations that the United States approved of those governments it recognized and disapproved of those from which it withheld recognition. This appearance of approval, in turn, affected our decisions in ways that have not always advanced U. S. interests. In recent years, U. S. practice has been to deemphasize and avoid the use of recognition in cases of changes of governments and to concern ourselves with the question of whether we wish to have diplomatic relations with the new governments.

The Administration's policy is that establishment of relations does not involve approval or disapproval but merely demonstrates a willingness on our part to conduct our affairs with other governments directly. In today's interdependent world, effective contacts with other governments are of ever-increasing importance.

Status of Relations

Albania. There has been no Albanian expression of interest in establishing diplomatic relations.

Angola. The United States looks forward eventually to establishing relations with Angola.

Cambodia. The new government of what is now Democratic Kampuchea has expressed no interest in establishing relations with the United States.

People's Republic of China. The P.R.C. and the United States maintain liaison offices in each other's capitals. The goal of U. S. policy is normalization of U.S.–P.R.C. relations on the basis of the Shanghai communique (1972).

Cuba. The United States is seeking to normalize relations with Cuba through negotiations based on strict reciprocity.

Equatorial Guinea. The United States suspended relations following a dispute over treatment of the U.S. Ambassador.

Iraq. The United States will reestablish diplomatic relations, which Iraq suspended, whenever Iraq desires.

North Korea. The United States is prepared to move toward improved relations, provided North Korea's allies take steps to improve relations with South Korea.

Mongolia. The United States has made clear to the Mongolian People's Republic that we are prepared to continue negotiations begun in 1973 aimed at establishing diplomatic relations.

Vietnam. The United States and Vietnam have begun discussions to explore the possibility of normalizing relations.

South Yemen. The United States looks forward to normalizing relations with South Yemen.

STATUS OF PALESTINIANS IN PEACE NEGOTIATIONS

77 United States Department of State Bulletin 463 (1977).

Department Statement [1]

Along with the issues of the nature of peace, recognition, security, and borders, the status of the Palestinians must be settled in a comprehensive Arab-Israeli peace agreement. This issue cannot be ignored if the others are to be solved.

Moreover, to be lasting, a peace agreement must be positively supported by all of the parties to the conflict, including the Palestinians. This means that the Palestinians must be involved in the peace-making process. Their representatives will have to be at Geneva for the Palestinian question to be solved.

As cochairman of the Geneva conference, the United States has a special responsibility for insuring the success of the conference. We have therefore been exploring with the confrontation states and Saudi Arabia a number of alternatives with regard to the participation of the Palestinians in the peace negotiations.

       *   *   *

---

1. *Questions*: What is the situation as to the status of the Palestinian people as you read this? Has the Palestine Liberation Organization (PLO) become a state? Have the Palestinians become a part of the population of Jordan? Or of any other state? What factors brought about whatever has taken place as to their legal status?

2. *Governments and diplomatic missions in exile.* Charles II bided his time with a very modest retinue on the continent during the Cromwellian era. Many another deposed ruler or pretender has also waited abroad. During World War II a number of governments in exile came into being. Because of occupation of their territories by German forces, the de jure governments of Belgium, the Netherlands, Norway, Yugoslavia, and Poland had to flee to the territory of allied states, mainly to the United Kingdom, where they arranged to carry on acts of governance. A contemporary legal analysis presented the ensuing legal problems as follows:

> The appointment of the American Ambassador to Poland, Mr. Biddle, as diplomatic representative to Belgium, The Netherlands, Norway, and Yugoslavia, raises a nice point of international law and procedure. Is this unique embassy to governments-in-exile in England a fiction or a fact?

> When Poland was occupied by Germany, Ambassador Biddle accompanied the Polish Government in its flight and re-established the Embassy near the remnant of Polish sovereignty rep-

1. Read to news correspondents on Sept. 12, 1977, by Department spokesman Hodding Carter III.

resented in London. This government exercises no authority whatever within the boundaries of Poland. Can it therefore be truly said that Poland still exists as a member of the family of nations?

The status of Norway and Yugoslavia is similar to that of Poland, but the situation of Belgium and The Netherlands is much different. The King of Belgium, it is true, is a German prisoner, while the Queen of The Netherlands is free to serve as the standardbearer of Dutch sovereignty. The significant fact in the case of both these countries, however, is that they possess vast colonial territories still under the direct administration of their respective governments in London. They continue to exist as international entities and are able to maintain diplomatic relations with other nations.

Poland, Norway, and Yugoslavia, on the other hand, have no territory left on which to find pied à terre. Their governments are in large measure simulacra, symbols rather than active administrative entities. And yet both Poland and Norway possess and control navies and merchant marines. Their airplanes and submarines are inflicting serious damage on Germany.

While the status of these governments-in-exile is unique and not identical in every case, it would seem clear that they are facts and not fictions. Until their countries shall have been definitely integrated with the German Reich they must be considered as international entities. Their sovereignty has not been extinguished. Its freedom of exercise has merely been restricted or suspended.

Military occupation by itself does not confer title or extinguish a nation. Nor does a proclamation of annexation so long as the claims of the occupying Power are effectively challenged and remain unrecognized. The Emperor of Abyssinia in exile never accepted the occupation of his country by Italy and now once again is its sovereign head. Such may be the good fortune of all those nations which have been over-run by the German armies. Brown, Sovereignty in Exile, 35 Am.J.Int'l Law 666 (1941).

The analyst was right. The overrun European states had the same good fortune as the Emperor of Abyssinia (despite his earlier setback in the British courts, p. 797). But the problem continues on another front, that of the Soviet occupations of the formerly independent states of Estonia, Latvia and Lithuania. A number of states, following a practice pioneered by the United States in 1932 at the time of the Japanese occupation of Manchuria and the creation there of a puppet state of Manchukuo, have refused to "recognize" (in what sense?) that these Baltic states and their governments disappeared when the USSR by force reconstituted the old Czarist territorial hegemony in the Baltic area. However, in the cases of the three invaded and incorporated Baltic states, the governments did not escape to set up elsewhere. Only their diplomatic representatives are still free of Soviet sway. What, from the standpoint of the international legal system, especially as to diplomatic immunity, do you think about the situation described in the extract that follows?

PHANTOM DIPLOMATS CARRY ON IN BRITAIN— MEN WITH NO COUNTRY

The Wall Street Journal, Dec. 9, 1970, p. 1, col. 4.*

London—By all rights, His Excellency August Torma should easily qualify as dean of the diplomatic corps here.

Mr. Torma is Estonia's Envoy Extraordinary and Minister Plenipotentiary—a post he has occupied since 1934, when he presented his credentials to King George V. "It was on December 12th or 13th," he recalls.

Of 112 foreign envoys here, Mr. Torma alone has had official business with either King George V or his successor, King Edward VIII, who became the Duke of Windsor after his abdication.

And yet the 76-year-old Mr. Torma wasn't even invited last month to the Queen's annual reception for the diplomatic corps at Buckingham Palace. In fact, Mr. Torma and Queen Elizabeth II haven't met since her coronation in 1952, although he knew her as a young princess during the reign of her father, King George VI.

A Buckingham Palace official, after confirming that last month's guest list had excluded Mr. Torma, confesses "I didn't know Estonia had a legation here."

The Royal Family, however, hasn't committed an unpardonable gaffe by snubbing Mr. Torma. For the past 30 years, Mr. Torma hasn't existed. At least officially. Mr. Torma is, in effect, an envoy without a country. He and four other such "phantom diplomats" have been granted diplomatic privileges by the British government— but they aren't quite recognized by it.

This unusual state of diplomatic affairs dates to 1940, when Russia invaded Estonia and its Baltic Sea neighbors, Latvia and Lithuania. The three Baltic states were unwillingly "absorbed" by the Soviet Union, which now numbers them among its 15 republics. Britain acknowledges the political realities of the situation. It concedes that Russia occupies and governs the Baltic states—but it doesn't recognize the legality of the Soviet absorption.

*   *   *

The Baltic legations continue to function—issuing passports, displaying their flags on national holidays, keeping alive memories of their brief period of independence between the two world wars. But they function in diminished elegance, existing mostly on private con-

* Reprinted with the permission of The
Wall Street Journal.

tributions and carefully watching expenses: Furniture hasn't been replaced in 30 years, rugs are threadbare, old maps curl against faded wallpaper. Only the outside brass plates that identify the stately buildings as legations are kept as shiny as those of the busiest embassy.

* * *

The United States goes beyond Britain and recognizes neither the Soviet Union's legal nor de facto occupation of the Baltic states, a position that gratifies the three legations. "The world owes us some justice," says Mr. Torma, "but we have only right on our side, not might." Nevertheless, he's confident that there will be a change. "Not tomorrow nor the next day and I probably won't see it," he says, "but things won't be like this forever."

Meantime, the phantom diplomats try to remind the world that their nations once existed and governed about six million people without Russian assistance. And, occasionally, European border authorities are reminded of the Baltic states when someone like Mr. Zilinskis [Secretary of the Latvian legation] presents them with a Latvian passport.

"Of course, only on holiday," he says. "There are no business trips for me anymore."

Directory listing. The embassies of Estonia, Latvia and Lithuania were still listed among the embassy chanceries as recently as the spring of 1979 in the directory of the Department of State of the United States.

---

2. EMERGING INTERNATIONAL LAW ISSUES RELATED TO RECOGNITION

1. *Withdrawal of recognition and tacit re-recognition.* As the basic notion of recognition is cognition or perception, p. 778, there is an inherent illogic in later attempts to say, when no change has intervened, "What we said we saw we now say we no longer see." Withdrawal of the recognition of states, moreover, would involve doctrinal problems about the declaratory versus the constitutive theory of the recognition of states, p. 818. Some states, including the United States, have viewpoints on record that do not exclude the possibility that the recognition of a regime as a government can be withdrawn; see Restatement of the Foreign Relations Law of the United States (1965), Section 96, and especially Reporters' Note 1. When it recognized the People's Republic of China as the government of all the territory of the state of China the United States derecognized the regime on Taiwan as the government of even a part of the territory (Taiwan) of the state of China. What is United States cognition of the regime on Taiwan following the resumption of relations with a government on the mainland? The Joint Communiqué, supra, p. 796,

states that "the people of the United States will maintain cultural, commercial, and other unofficial relations with the people of Taiwan." A Presidential memorandum, Relations with the People on Taiwan, December 30, 1978, 15 Weekly Comp. of Pres. Doc. 1, provides that all programs with the people of Taiwan will be carried out through "an unofficial instrumentality in corporate form, to be identified shortly." The Taiwan Relations Act, PL 96–8, 96th Cong., April 19, 1979, 22 USC § 3301 et seq., identifies this instrumentality as The American Institute of Taiwan, 22 USC § 3305. Section 4 of the Public Law, 22 USC § 3303, provides very interestingly for the continuation in legal effect so far as the United States is concerned "of laws of the United States with respect to Taiwan." Congressional oversight of the act is provided, 22 USC § 3313. For detail as to the institute, consult 22 USC §§ 3306 through 3312, and 3315.

In October, 1980, an arrangement as to immunities for the United States personnel of the American Institute was concluded with the regime on Taiwan. The Chinese People's Republic has strongly criticized this arrangement as violative of the Joint Communiqué above.

The notion of withdrawal of recognition seems to have no international legal content. And it is a concept not known to have been used in modern times, except by the unlearned, such as the mass media, which never seem able to distinguish, in the case of the United States and the government of Cuba, between recognition, derecognition and the breaking of diplomatic relations; see p. 812.

2.   *Recognition conditioned upon performance.*   Again, here, the situation seems to be one in which state practice in past times has in some instances involved the granting of recognition of a regime as a government upon the basis of its acceptance of some stipulations or pre-conditions by the recognizing state. In such instances the promise of certain performance by the regime seeking recognition may be sought and obtained in a negotiation relating to recognition; but there is no practice of using a divesting condition subsequent that would authorize the withdrawal of recognition if the promise should not be carried out.

The most famous negotiation leading to recognition was the Litvinov-Roosevelt Agreement of 1933 under which the Soviet Union made several promises (some that it has not yet entirely performed) and was recognized. The Mexicans and other Latin Americans base a good deal of their objection to the withholding of recognition (seen as an instrument of intervention) upon the fact that well after the Mexican Revolution had settled down into a new government, the United States continued to withhold recognition until Mexico made certain promises about American private property claims in Mexico.

In a 1966 study of the differences between intervention and collective action, the Latin America members of the Inter-American

Juridical Committee of the Organization of American States listed as an illegal act of intervention:

> 1.   The abusive use of recognition of governments in contravention of the norms established by international law as a means of obtaining unjustified advantages.

The recommendation of which this entry is one item has not yet been acted upon by the member states through the competent organs of the OAS.   There is little doubt, however, that Latin America (Mexico in particular) considers that historically the United States has misused its power not to recognize revolutionary regimes, or to impose conditions for recognition of them.

3.   *The American shift away from recognition of governments.* Until recently the shift in United States practice from any requirement of formal new recognition of a coupist regime to a modified Estrada doctrine (i. e. vary the intensity of relationships but do not consider a coup a discontinuity requiring re-recognition) was unevenly applied, say as between new countries in sub-Sahara Africa and in Latin America.   By now, it is believed, the United States no longer differentiates in this manner.   Galloway, Recognizing Foreign Governments: The Practice of the United States (1978) is a digest-like presentation of United States recognition (and alternatives thereto) over the life of the nation, with more detail from the Kennedy presidency forward.   The reference to Latin America in the Johnson era does not make clear the significance of the adoption of a modified Estrada doctrine in connection with the 1968 coups in Peru and Panama.   In those instances the Department of State instructed the embassies not to deal with the situations in terms of recognition, but in terms of the intensity of the diplomatic relations.

---

3.   RECOGNITION OF BELLIGERENCY AND OF INSURGENCY

REPORTERS' NOTES TO SECTION 94 OF THE RESTATEMENT OF THE FOREIGN RELATIONS LAW OF THE UNITED STATES (1965) *

1.   *Recognition of belligerency.* Recognition of belligerency by a state is an act by which the state, in issuing a declaration of neutrality, asserts that it (a) is neutral in an armed conflict, (b) assumes certain neutral duties toward the parties to the conflict and (c) has certain rights with respect to trade between its nationals and persons within the territory of the belligerency subject to the rules of international law regarding visitation, search, contraband, blockade and prize.   Recognition of belligerency for an otherwise unrecognized entity or regime may arise from a declaration of neutrality by anoth-

er state as between a constitutional government and rebels in a civil war. This occurred in the American Civil War when Great Britain recognized the belligerency of the Confederacy, declared its neutrality and claimed neutral trading rights. It is well-established, as in that instance, that recognition of a rebel's belligerency does not have the effect, standing alone, of committing the second state to treat the rebel regime as the government or the rebel entity (if one is claimed to have come into existence) as a state.

2. *Recognition of insurgency.* In customary practice, recognition of insurgency has considerably less legal significance than recognition of belligerency. Historically, the object of recognition of insurgency by non-contending states was to obtain for rebels carrying on organized military operations the protections given by international law. Recognition of insurgency has often been the first official notice that other states have taken of the eventual possible success of a revolutionary regime.

The more recent tendency has been to rely on ad hoc assurances in revolutionary situations that the basic principles underlying the rules of warfare will be respected. *   *   *

---

1. *Legal responsibility for premature recognition.* Recognition problems are almost always closely linked to revolutionary situations, p. 822. Revolutions usually begin as insurgencies, that is, are conducted by organized military or para-military units. In the past century and earlier, the insurgents might later be recognized as belligerents if successful enough to become of economic significance to traders in neutral states. Recognition of belligerency in this sense, one that invoked an elaborate set of rights and duties as between neutrals and belligerents as to trade, is passé. The rules of the Declaration of Paris, 1856, as to free ships make free goods; a blockade to be legal must be effective, etc., were not followed in either of the twentieth century world wars; and today a formal recognition of belligerency, statement of neutrality and assertion of the right to trade in non-contraband with the rebels—or with the established government in some cases—would surely be treated as a quaint anachronism—and in the United Nations, possibly, as a violation of basic obligations of United Nations membership.

But the fact remains that there have been modern problems about long, drawn out revolutions—or civil wars. If the rebels quickly win or are quickly put down, problems of premature recognition do not often arise. But if the rebels have their successes, acquire control of important state territory and installations, such as ports and airfields, are recognized and then eventually lose, are the states that have recognized them liable to the established state? A number of only slightly analyzed questions are: (a) Under what circumstances is recognition actionably premature? (b) Are actual damages caused by premature recognition essential to the cause of action, or does something like punitive damages in domestic law obtain? (c) Does the cause of action die if later the plaintiff loses the revolution and is ousted (to other territory if a state, to government in exile status if a defeated de jure regime)?

Consider, briefly, these examples (some hypothetically varied from history) of lengthy rebellions:

a. The American Revolution, if the United States had been recognized by Prussia, Russia and Turkey as a state and the Continental Congress as its government, and then the British had won.

b. The American Civil War, if the Confederacy had been recognized by Spain as a new, separate state, and thereafter it was defeated.

c. The Spanish Civil War, if after the United Kingdom and other states had recognized the Franco regime as the government of that portion of Spain that it then controlled, the Spanish Republic had won.

d. The Nigerian Civil War, if Biafra had been recognized by the United States as an independent state and government, and thereafter it was defeated.

e. The Chinese Civil War, if after the Nationalists had been forced off the mainland to Taiwan, the Chinese People's Republic had been recognized by France as the government of mainland China and then Chiang had unleashed himself and regained the mainland.

These instances reveal a basic political reality, that foreign recognition of rebels is in every sense a disservice or threat to the established state and its de jure government; and if that state or government is able to overcome the threat to its existence that the rebellion is, it will remember to resent recognition extended to the rebels during the crisis.

At what point does premature recognition become a resentment that the injured state may pursue as a legal claim under international law? There is very little authority in international decisional law. In treatises it is usually assumed that a cause of action exists, although its point of maturation—on the scale of events during the rebellion—is not clearly specified by the writers. See Restatement of the Foreign Relations Law of the United States (1955), Sections 100 and 101.

In the celebrated arbitral award in the Alabama Claims (1872), Great Britain was found liable for actual damages inflicted upon Union shipping by Confederate raiders allowed to be fitted out in British ports. This is about as close as one can come so far to an international decision on state responsibility for premature recognition. In this case the status of the Confederacy as a belligerent had been recognized by the United Kingdom. However, it is to be noted that: (a) the award was made under an agreement to arbitrate that excluded decision on principles of international law; (b) the award was for the damage caused to plaintiff's shipping by the failure of the respondent to use due diligence to prevent the fitting out and arming of Confederate sea raiders within its jurisdiction; and (c) recognition of belligerency per se was not the burden of the United States claim. Although as a general proposition premature recognition of a rebel group as a state and government would be an a fortiori case for liability if there is liability for a premature recognition of belligerency, the Alabama Claims award does not go to recognition so much as to the improper discharge of neutral duties by Great Britain after the belligerent status of the Confederate States of America had been recognized.

2. *Problems.*

a.   An insurgency begins in the remote mountain areas of State A, a developing country. The insurgent chieftain is colorful and immensely popular with the foreign mass media. The insurgency is presented by the press to the world as very apt to succeed. As a result 75 states recognize the insurgents as the de jure government of State A, and this causes a severe flight of capital from State A that slows its rate of development from six percent to one percent per year, resulting in an estimated national accounts loss of one billion dollars. State A easily puts down the insurgency and then sues the 75 states that recognized the insurgents as the de jure government of State A for the above amount in damages. On the merits, what would be your opinion as a judge of the International Court of Justice?

b.   What if the insurgents had been recognized as the government de facto of State A, all other facts being the same?

3. *Reprise on recognition.* On the whole, the international relations (political) problems of recognition seem to outweigh the legal effects of recognition. Is it possible that, if the political problems of recognition should decline in importance, as a result of doctrinal change about recognition, detente between the socialist and the non-socialist states, or a drastic drop in the number of revolutions, the legal problems of recognition would also drop to a very low level of significance, or disappear entirely? There are some straws in the wind that indicate that recognition is not as much of a problem on any front as it used to be.

From one viewpoint, it is seen as unlikely that many more new states will come into existence by revolutionary secession. But, on the other hand, what may happen in the new Africa as tribal boundaries press against the frontiers that new states defend as a result of how white colonialists drew lines?

One of the major difficulties with older recognition notions after World War II was the inability of these to deal with—or to be permitted to deal with—the notorious divided somethings (states? governments?), viz: two Germanies, two Koreas, two Vietnams, two

Chinas. By the time of the preparation of this edition, however, a number of these stalemates of the cold war have been moved toward political (and therefore legal?) resolution:

    a.   The existence of two de jure German states is now established; and no destabilization factors are presently discernible.

    b.   The recent mutual recognition arrangements between the United States and the People's Republic of China clearly mark the end of a two-Chinas era, most of the rest of the world having abandoned this concept some years ago.

    c.   The two Vietnams have become one (possibly to include Cambodia as well?) due to the military defeat by former North Vietnam of the French, the Americans, and the former South Vietnamese.

    d.   The two Koreas remain, arms poised against each other, but with some question now as to whether their respective patron states feel as involved as they once did.

Meanwhile, recognition problems are now being created by political movements within developing countries themselves, sometimes with developed-state patrons, see infra, p. 838, and in territories seeking the end of foreign rule and the achievement of statehood. Consider North and South Yemen, Namibia, Palestine, and the shadow-nation of Kurdistan within the territories of Iran and Iraq.

Chapter 13

DIPLOMATIC AND CONSULAR PROTECTION
AND IMMUNITY

SECTION A. PROTECTION OF FOREIGN
REPRESENTATIVES

---

1. *Risks of diplomatic life: in former times.* Diplomatic representation is essential to the operation of the international legal system. As a concomitant of this proposition it has been recognized for
a long time that, in order for diplomatic representation to function
effectively, diplomatic representatives must be protected from interference with the discharge of their duties by the authorities in the receiving state. Some sense of the early and ready acceptance of this
verity is reflected in the entertaining account by Lord Mansfield in
Triquet v. Bath of the incident which led to the enactment in England
of the Diplomatic Privileges Act of 1708:

> This privilege of foreign ministers and their domestic serv-
> ants depends upon the law of nations. The Act of Parliament of
> 7 Ann. c. 12, is declaratory of it. All that is new in this Act, is
> the clause which gives a summary jurisdiction for the punish-
> ment of the infractors of this law.

> The Act of Parliament was made upon occasion of the
> Czar's Ambassador being arrested. If proper application had
> been immediately made for his discharge from the arrest, the
> matter might and doubtless would have been set right. Instead
> of that, bail was put in, before any complaint was made. An in-
> formation was filed by the then Attorney General against the
> persons who were thus concerned, as infractors of the law of na-
> tions: and they were found guilty; but never brought up to
> judgment.

> The Czar took the matter up, highly. No punishment would
> have been thought, by him, an adequate reparation. Such a sen-
> tence as the Court could have given, he might have thought a
> fresh insult.

> Another expedient was fallen upon and agreed to: this Act
> of Parliament passed, as an apology and humiliation from the
> whole nation. It was sent to the Czar, finely illuminated by an
> ambassador extraordinary, who made excuses in a solemn ora-
> tion. 3 Burr. 1478, 1480 (K.B.1764).

Protection from the authorities in the receiving state has not always been sufficient, however, to insure the inviolability of diplomatic representatives. Over the many years that diplomatic representa-

tion and immunity have existed, private individuals have at times felt compelled physically to vent frustrations of one kind or another upon the persons of foreign ambassadors. A celebrated instance in the history of the United States involved an assault upon a French diplomat, for which the culprit was convicted of a crime against the law of nations. Respublica v. De Longchamps, 1 Dall. 111 (1784).

On the whole, though, interference with the function of diplomatic representation, either by the authorities of the receiving states or by individuals resorting to violence, seems to have been minimal in the past. In recent years, unfortunately, the situation has changed.

2. *Risks of diplomatic life: in modern times.* The Revue Générale de Droit International Public publishes in each of its quarterly issues a Chronique des Faits Internationaux. This chronicle of diplomatic happenings is kept by Rousseau and is based on official and unofficial sources, including newspaper reports. The first year the chronicle appeared, 1958, it made no report of violence involving diplomatic personnel. The next, it reported the sentencing in France of a person charged with an attack upon the Hungarian legation and a demonstration before the embassy of the United States in Bolivia. (Vol. 63, at 115, 299). Again in 1960, there was nothing to report along those lines. Soon thereafter, however, the Chronique became a lengthy catalogue of violence and other illegal acts against diplomatic (and consular) representatives.

For example it shows that during the period running from about the fall of 1964 to the fall of 1965, diplomatic premises of the United States were attacked in 16 different states. The attacks, by groups large and small, included the breaking down of doors and windows, the ransacking of the interior, the throwing of Molotov cocktails or more effective bombs, and attempted or successful destruction by fire. (Vol. 69 at 120, 154, 155, 461, 479, 482, 483, 485, 803, 804, 806 and 1110.) During the same period, the embassies of other states were also attacked in 16 instances. (Vol. 69 at 108, 111, 118, 123, 131, 176, 177, 443, 474, 762, 770, 794, 1096 and 1106.)

The Chronique for the period running from about the spring of 1970 to about the fall of 1971 shows no improvement. A rough count of attacks on diplomatic premises which involved violence would come to at least 39, not to mention attacks on consular premises. In addition some diplomatic and consular representatives were personally assaulted or shot at. What is worse, diplomatic or consular representatives were either kidnapped, or made the object of an attempted kidnapping, in at least 11 instances which occurred in Guatemala, Paraguay, Brazil, Uruguay, Venezuela, Spain and Canada. The ambassador of the Federal Republic of Germany to Guatemala was killed by his abductors when their political demands were not met. (Vol. 75, at 143, 152, 157, 474, 483, 805, 856, 1087, 1098 and 1107.)

The total number of incidents, including attacks upon embassies, the taking of hostages, kidnappings and attempted and successful killings, reached a peak in the period running roughly from the fall of 1973 to the spring of 1976. (About 118 reported in Volumes 79 and 80.) Since then this total seems to have declined somewhat though violence against the persons of diplomats still remains high. (Seven reported killings in Volumes 81 and 82, not to mention attempted killings.) The taking of the hostages at the American embassy in Teheran on November 4, 1979, was the ultimate in the particular genre.

3. *United States legislation to protect foreign representatives.* Threats of violence and violent acts against foreign representatives have also been on the rise in the United States. The situation in New York, with repeated hostile demonstrations and attacks on diplomatic representatives to the United Nations, led the General Assembly to pass a resolution urging the United States to take measures for ensuring the protection and security of the United Nations Headquarters and the missions accredited to it and their personnel. See the statements of the Deputy Under Secretary of State for Management and of the United States Representative to the United Nations, 67 U. S. Dept. of State Bull. 609 (1972). At the request of the United States Department of State, legislation was enacted on October 24, 1972, 86 Stat. 1070. It makes it a federal offense to commit certain crimes, e. g. murder, kidnapping, assault, harassment, property damage, against foreign embassy personnel and their families and representatives to international organizations and their families.

4. *International agreement for the protection of diplomats.* The Convention on the Prevention and Punishment of Crimes Against Internationally Protected Persons Including Diplomatic Agents, signed December 14, 1973, is designed to deny safe haven to those who attack, kidnap or inflict grievous bodily harm upon diplomats or officials of foreign governments or international organizations. The convention requires the state where the offender is found to prosecute him if it does not extradite him. 28 (Part 2) U.S.T. 1975 (1976–1977). The United States enacted legislation implementing the convention on October 8, 1976, 90 Stat. 1997. The convention entered into force for the United States February 20, 1977. As of January 1, 1980, 43 states were parties.

SECTION B. DIPLOMATIC IMMUNITY

1. INVIOLABILITY OF DIPLOMATIC PREMISES

RADWAN v. RADWAN

England, Family Division, 1972.
[1972] 3 W.L.R. 735.*

CUMMING–BRUCE J.   Mrs. Mary Isobel Radwan filed a petition for dissolution of marriage on November 27, 1970, seeking dissolution on the ground of her husband's cruelty.   *   *   *

*   *   *

The facts are as follows.   The husband was born in Cairo.   He is and at all material times was a Mohammedan.   He was and remains a subject of the United Arab Republic.   By the date of the institution of these proceedings, and by the date of the pronouncement of divorce by talaq in April 1970, he had acquired a domicile of choice in England.   On April 1, 1970, he entered the Egyptian Consulate in London; the procedure stated in the affidavit of the deputy consul of the Consulate General was followed.   The husband three times declared the prescribed form of divorce in the presence of two witnesses.   All the steps were carried out in accordance with Egyptian law.   After the prescribed 90 days the divorce was finalised in accordance with Egyptian law, and in accordance with that law it was no impediment to the efficacy of the proceedings that the wife knew nothing about it at all.

The deputy consul states   *   *   *   that the Egyptian Consulate in London is regarded as being Egyptian territory on Egyptian soil. I take it that he means so regarded by the sending sovereign state *   *   *.

The question for my decision is whether by English law the Egyptian Consulate General is part of a country outside the British Isles within the meaning of section 2(a) of the Recognition of Divorces and Legal Separations Act 1971.   By that Act the relevant sections providing for recognition will have effect in respect of overseas divorces if they have been obtained by means of judicial or other proceedings in any country outside the British Isles, and it is necessary for the efficacy of the talaq divorce that it should have been obtained outside the British Isles by reason of the fact that at the material time the husband had acquired English domicile.

Curiously, the question has not arisen for decision in England before, that is, the question whether the premises of an embassy or

* Reprinted by permission of the Incorporated Council of Law Reporting for England and Wales, London.

consulate are part of the territory of the sending state as compared to the territory of the receiving state. *   *   *

*   *   *

The term "extraterritorial" has been used to describe in a compendious phrase that bundle of immunities and privileges which are accorded by receiving civilised states to the envoys sent by foreign states. One such immunity included in the term is the inviolable character of the premises of a mission, which the agents of the receiving state may not enter without the consent of the head of the mission. The phrase was used by Grotius *   *   *. The word "extra-territorialitas" was used by Wolff in 1749 and has been in use in English, French and German for some 250 years.

Three theories have been invoked to explain the admitted principles that diplomatic premises and property are inviolable by the agents of the receiving state:

(a) The strict extraterritorial fiction. The premises are regarded by a legal fiction as outside the territory of the receiving state and as part of the territory of the sending state. (b) The representative theory. The premises are immune from entry without consent of the head of the mission, as the mission represents or personifies the sovereignty of the sending state. (c) The theory of functional necessity. The immunity is granted by the receiving state because it is necessary to enable the mission to carry out its functions.

Mr. Ewbank submits, and I agree, that (a) should be discarded as obsolete in the sense that international lawyers have long regarded it as unsound, and it is inconsistent with modern foreign decisions and international convention. He asks me to prefer (c) to (b), though both avoid the practical dangers which (a) is liable to produce.

This view is rested on the foundation of the consensus of authors learned in international law, the approach of courts of law abroad in such cases in modern times as have involved consideration of the immunity of diplomatic land and buildings, and inferences from the international conventions by which civilised states in modern times have sought to define the immunities which they will accord to diplomatic missions. I develop these three heads separately.

1. *The opinion of authors.*

[There follows a list of the 11 works examined by the judge.]

In all of them I find a consensus of opinion that there is no valid foundation for the proposition, or alleged rule, that diplomatic premises are to be regarded as outside the territory of the receiving state. The history of the confusion is given concisely by Professor Lauterpacht in Oppenheim's International Law, vol. 1, 8th ed. (1955), pp. 792, 793, which I quote:

The exterritoriality which must be granted to diplomatic envoys by the municipal laws of all the members of the international community is not, as in case of sovereign Heads of States, based on the principle par in parem non habet imperium, but on the necessity that envoys must, for the purpose of fulfilling their duties, be independent of the jurisdiction, control, and the like, of the receiving states. Exterritoriality, in this as in every other case, is a fiction only, for diplomatic envoys are in reality not without, but within, the territories of the receiving states. The term 'exterritoriality' is nevertheless valuable because it demonstrates clearly the fact that envoys must, in most respects, be treated as though they were not within the territory of the receiving states. * * *

* * * Nowadays the official residences of envoys are, *in a sense and in some respects only*, considered as though they were outside the territory of the receiving states.

And he continues, at pp. 795–796:

But such immunity of domicile is granted only so far as it is necessary for the independence and inviolability of envoys, and the inviolability of their official documents and archives.

A little further down:

If a crime is committed inside the house of an envoy by an individual who does not enjoy personally the privilege of exterritoriality, the criminal must be surrendered to the local government.

I quote and adopt the observations of Mr. J. E. S. Fawcett in *The Law of Nations*, at p. 64:

But there are two popular myths about diplomats and their immunities which we must clear away; one is that an embassy is foreign territory * * *

The premises of a mission are inviolable, and the local authorities may enter them only with the consent of the head of the mission. But this does not make the premises foreign territory or take them out of the reach of the local law for many purposes: for example, a commercial transaction in an embassy may be governed by the local law, particularly tax law; marriages may be celebrated there only if conditions laid down by the local law are met; and a child born in it will, unless his father has diplomatic status, acquire the local nationality.

This so exactly represents the conclusion to which I have come, after looking at the textbooks to which I have referred, that I think it unnecessary in this judgment to quote other passages of eminent authorities. * * *

2. *Approach of courts of law abroad.*

I now turn to the decisions of Commonwealth or foreign courts for such indication as they may give as to the view taken in foreign or Commonwealth civilised states. Australia: in Ex Parte Petroff (unreported), 1971, Fox J. of the Supreme Court of the Australian Capital Territory was dealing with a case where two persons had been throwing explosive substances at the Chancery of the Soviet Union's Embassy in Canberra:

> * * * it was sought to argue in prerogative writ proceedings that the magistrate concerned had no jurisdiction to deal with the alleged offences as these were committed on foreign territory. Fox J. * * * rejected this contention and expressly held, after a full review of the authorities, that an embassy is not a part of the territory of the sending state, and that the accused could be prosecuted for such alleged offences against the local law.

France: Cour de Cassation (Crim.), 1865. See Briggs, The Law of Nations, Cases, Documents, Notes, 2nd ed. (1952). The court was dealing with murderous assaults on the First Secretary of the Russian Embassy in the Russian Embassy in Paris, and an argument was submitted that the place of the crime being the premises of the Russian Embassy was a place situated outside the territory of France and not governed by French law. * * *

The court stated:

> * * * this legal fiction cannot be extended but constitutes an exception to the rule of territorial jurisdiction * * * and is strictly limited to the ambassador or minister whose independence it is designed to protect and to those of his subordinates who are clothed with the same public character;

The report continues:

> Whereas the accused is not attached in any sense to the Russian Embassy but, as a foreigner residing for the time in France, was subject to French law; and whereas the place where the crime which he is charged with committing cannot, in so far as he is concerned, be regarded as outside the limits of (French) territory; * * * the jurisdiction of the French judiciary is clearly established.

The contention advanced was held to be without validity. I refer also to Trochanoff, Tribunal Correctionnel de la Seine [1910] J.D.I.P. 551; Basiliadis, Cour d'Appel de Paris (1922) 49 J.D.I.P. 407; Munir Pasha v. Aristarchi Bey, the Civil Tribunal of the Seine [1910] J.D. I.P. 549.

Germany: the Afghan Embassy Case, Annual Digest, 1933–1934, Case No. 166.

Italy: Trenta v. Ragonesi, Court of Appeal of Rome, May 31, 1938, Annual Digest, 1938–1940, Case No. 173; In re Moriggi, Annual Digest, 1938–1940, Case No. 172; In re Couhi in the Court of Cassation, Annual Digest, 1922, Case No. 218.

In all these cases the court rejected the argument that diplomatic premises were not part of the territory of the receiving state * * *.

* * *

3. *International conventions.*

Though international conventions do not have the force of law unless embodied in municipal legislation, they may in the field of international law be valuable as a guide to the rules of international law which this country as a signatory respects. There are two conventions relevant to this problem, the Vienna Convention on Consular Relations in 1963, (Command Paper 2113), by article 31 sets out the agreed immunities adherent to consular premises under the heading: "Inviolability of the consular premises": "1. Consular premises shall be inviolable to the extent provided in this article," and the article then sets out that extent in its several different ways. There is no suggestion that it was in the mind of any of the signatories that the premises themselves were part of the territory of the sending state. So, too, the Vienna Convention on Diplomatic Relations 1961, by article 22: [a]

1. The premises of the mission shall be inviolable. The agents of the receiving state may not enter them, except with the consent of the head of the mission.

The next paragraph deals with protection, and the third:

3. The premises of the mission, their furnishings and other property thereon and the means of transport of the mission shall be immune from search, requisition, attachment or execution.

What is significant about those articles is not so much what they say as what they do not say. If it was the view of the high contracting parties that the premises of missions were part of the territory of the sending state, that would undoubtedly be formulated and it would have been quite unnecessary to set out the immunities in the way in which it has been done.

* * *

For those reasons the husband, being at the material time a gentleman of English domicile, did not go through a proceeding for divorce in a country outside the British Isles when he pronounced the talaq three times in the Consulate General of the United Arab Republic of London in 1970.

* * *

---

1. *Fiction of extraterritoriality rejected in Belgium.* The Belgian National Office for Employment denied unemployment compensation to a British national formerly employed in the British embassy on the ground he did not qualify under Belgian law because he had not been employed in Belgium. The Labor Court of Brussels dismissed the argument of extraterritoriality of foreign embassies, stating the fiction was clearly rejected by the Vienna Convention. Smith

a. The United Kingdom had enacted on July 31, 1964 the Diplomatic Privileges Act 1964, giving force of law in the Kingdom to the Vienna Convention on Diplomatic Relations. Public General Acts and Measures of 1964, Elizabeth II, Part II, Chapter 81, p. 1261.

v. National Office for Employment, 1972, X Revue Belge de Droit International 715 (1974).

2. *Inviolability of premises bars service of process by mail.* This is the position of the U.S. Department of State. It cited Article 22(1) of the Vienna Convention in support of its view and undertook to obtain a modification of proposed legislation on sovereign immunity which contemplated service of process by registered or certified mail to the ambassador or chief of mission of the foreign government concerned. Rovine, Digest of United States Practice in International Law 1974, at 171 (1975). The Foreign Sovereign Immunities Act of 1976 does not contain a provision for such service of process. The act is in the Documentary Supplement.

3. *Freedom of communication of the mission.* Whether a mission could install and use a wireless transmitter was much debated during the drafting of the Vienna Convention. Eventually it was permitted by Article 27, but only with the consent of the receiving state. See Report of the United States Delegation to the United Nations Conference on Diplomatic Intercourse and Immunities, reprinted in U. S. Senate Committee on Foreign Relations, 96th Cong., 1st Sess., Legislative History of the Diplomatic Relations Act 754–755 (1979).

During a dispute between France and Australia over French nuclear tests in the Pacific, Australian unions refused to handle postal and telegraphic communications of the French embassy. France protested that the Australian government had violated Article 27 of the Vienna Convention by not sufficiently protecting the freedom of communications of the French embassy. XIX Annuaire Français de Droit International 1051 (1973).

4. *Jurisdiction of sending state over crimes committed within diplomatic premises.* In United States v. Erdos, 474 F.2d 157 (4th Cir. 1973), the chargé d'affairs at the American embassy in the Republic of Equitorial Guinea was convicted of killing another embassy employee within the embassy compound. The court construed 18 U. S.C. § 7(3), which deals with the special maritime and territorial jurisdiction of the United States, as embracing an embassy in a foreign country.

In 1978, the former ambassador of Austria to Yugoslavia was sentenced by an Austrian court to a heavy fine for accidentally killing the French ambassador to Yugoslavia upon their return from a hunting trip. The court relied on Article 31(4) of the Vienna Convention which specifies that immunity from the jurisdiction of the receiving state does not exempt the diplomat from the jurisdiction of the sending state. 82 Revue Générale de Droit International Public 1086 (1978).

5. *Diplomatic Asylum.* The states of Latin America assert that a right to grant asylum in the diplomatic premises exists by virtue of a regional custom peculiar to them. The existence of such a right was tested and denied in the Asylum Case (Colombia v. Peru),

[1950] I.C.J. Rep. 266. Sharply critical comments on the decision by Nascimento e Silva appear supra, Chapter 1, at p. 69.

The holding of the court that the Colombian government had failed to prove the existence of a regional custom of asylum may have induced the adoption of a new convention on asylum by the Tenth Inter-American Conference at Caracas in 1954. 6 Whiteman Digest of International Law 436 (1968).

The Department of State of the United States has consistently maintained that a state does not have a right to grant asylum under international law. The granting of asylum to Cardinal Mindszenty by the American embassy in Budapest in 1956 was explained as "exceptional." 6 Whiteman Digest of International Law 463–464 (1968). It lasted for 15 years.

---

2. IMMUNITY OF DIPLOMATIC AGENTS

The Vienna Convention on Diplomatic Relations was signed on April 18, 1961, at a conference of 81 states. It entered into force on April 24, 1964; as of January 1, 1980, 134 states were parties to the convention. For its text, see the Documentary Supplement. The convention entered into force for the United States on December 13, 1972. The long delay between the signature of the convention and its ratification by the United States was caused by efforts of the Department of State to obtain before ratification the enactment of new legislation to resolve inconsistencies between existing legislation and the convention.

The legislation then in existence dated from the eighteenth century, Act of 30 April 1790, ch. 9, § 25, 1 Stat. 117, 22 U.S.C. § 252, and conferred broad immunity from both criminal and civil jurisdiction upon ambassadors and their domestic servants, and upon other diplomatic personnel. The convention on the other hand granted a narrower measure of immunity to all diplomatic personnel. The Department of Justice took the position that the convention did not repeal or supersede the greater measure of immunity provided by existing legislation. Rovine, Digest of United States Practice in International Law 1973, at 143 (1974).

The Diplomatic Relations Act, repealing the previous legislation and giving effect to the convention as controlling domestic law, was enacted on September 30, 1978. 22 U.S.C. §§ 254a–254e, 28 U.S.C. § 1364.

IMMEUBLE DE LA RUE DE CIVRY v. ISSAKIDES AND KONSTANTIS

France, Tribunal de Grande Instance of the Seine, 1966.
48 Int'l L.Rep. 205 (1975).*

[An action was brought against Konstantis and Issakides with respect to apartments occupied by them. Konstantis pleaded diplomatic immunity.

A portion of the opinion appears below.]

Fotios Konstantis * * * states that in January 1966 * * * he was designated as "Secretary to the Delegation of Greece to the North Atlantic Treaty Organization, (N.A.T.O.)". In support of his statements he has produced a photocopy of his identity card issued on 31 January 1966 by the Ministry for Foreign Affairs, in which he is in fact described as a member of the Greek Delegation to N.A.T.O. and which contains the statement that he is "assimilated to a member of a diplomatic mission".

The plaintiff company submits that the objection to the jurisdiction raised by Konstantis should be dismissed. It contends in fact that the status of members of the delegations forming N.A.T.O., the only status which might be pleaded by the defendant, does not confer the immunity which he claims. It states that the international Ottawa Agreement [on the Status of the North Atlantic Treaty Organization, National Representatives and International Staff], dated 20 September 1951 and published in France on 3 February 1955, which determines that status, "does not accord jurisdictional immunity to N.A.T.O. personnel except in respect of acts performed by them in their official capacity", and adds that the transaction which is the subject of this dispute can only be regarded as a private one.

The plaintiff company declares, moreover, that on account of the private character of the transaction Konstantis is incorrect in relying on diplomatic immunity, even if he could claim the general status of diplomatic agents who are not subject to a special régime as are the members of a N.A.T.O. Delegation.

* * *

Fotios Konstantis must be counted amongst the agents on whom Article 12 [of the 1951 convention] confers the benefit of the "immunities and privileges accorded to diplomatic representatives and their official staff of comparable rank", since this provision may be pleaded, as it states, both by "Every person designated by a Member State as its principal permanent representative to the Organization in the territory of another Member State", and by "members of his official staff". It appears from the documents produced by Konstantis that he is a member of the official staff of the principal permanent representative of Greece to N.A.T.O.

* Reprinted by permission of E. Lauterpacht, ed., and Grotius Publications, Ltd., Cambridge, England.

The resolution of the dispute must therefore be based on the general status of diplomatic agents. The Vienna Convention of 18 April 1961, which defines this status, provides that a diplomatic agent shall enjoy "immunity from civil jurisdiction" except in certain cases, in which disputes, such as that with which we are seised, concerning accommodation are not included. Konstantis is therefore well-founded in pleading the principle of diplomatic immunity.

The Vienna Convention on which the decision of this matter must be based does not permit the application of the distinction which the plaintiff company wishes to make between acts performed by the diplomatic agent in the exercise of his mission and those which he performs in his own private interest.

* * *

For these reasons, adjudicating on the order with regard to Miltiades Issakides the Court declares null, * * * the transaction which Issakides and Konstantis concluded regarding the apartments which they occupied, situated respectively at 16 and 18 Rue de Civry, Paris, and at 10 Avenue Lenotre, Sceaux. The Court declares that this decision is only binding on Issakides * * * and further declares that the objection to the jurisdiction raised by Konstantis is well-founded. Costs are awarded against Issakides.

———

Rationale of immunity of diplomatic agents. Diplomatic immunity rests on two grounds: one, it ensures the effective performance by the diplomatic agent of his duties; and two, it protects the person and dignity of the diplomatic agent. Before the Vienna Convention, however, a number of states rejected the *representational* considerations, i. e. those pertaining to the personal dignity of diplomatic agents and took the position that *functional* necessity was the sole basis of diplomatic immunity.

In the states adopting the rationale of functional necessity, the courts distinguished between the official acts and the private acts of a diplomatic representative, immunity being granted for the former, but not for the latter. The distinction had an obvious parallel in the distinction made by many courts in civil law states between the public acts of a foreign state (for which immunity is granted) and its private acts (for which no immunity is given). See Chapter 5.

———

SOVIET OPPOSITION TO FUNCTIONAL BASIS FOR DIPLOMATIC IMMUNITY

Romanov, The Vienna Convention on Diplomatic Intercourse and Fundamental Questions of the Codification of International Law Regarding Diplomatic Privileges and Immunities, Soviet Year Book of International Law 1961, at 89 (1962).

The delegations of several countries, especially small countries, sought to ensure that the principle of functional necessity should be set down in the Convention as the sole basis of diplomatic immunities and privileges. The Soviet delegation like those of many other countries, pointed out that it was impossible to restrict the question to this principle alone, because it is insufficient to constitute a basis for diplomatic privileges and immunities. * * *

The adherents of the principle of functional requirements did not succeed in getting its recognition as the sole basis for diplomatic privileges and immunities in the Vienna Convention. At the suggestion of the Soviet delegation, a reference to the representational character of Embassies and Missions as one of the foundations for diplomatic privileges and immunities was included in the Preamble to the Convention.

* * *

The draft convention granted the possibility of civil actions against diplomats unrelated to their official functions. At the conference the representatives of many countries called for the extension of the range of exceptions to immunity from civil jurisdiction envisaged in the draft. It was, for example, proposed that in the event of an action seeking compensation for damages caused by a diplomat as a result of a motor accident, he should enjoy immunity from civil jurisdiction only if an insurance company in the host-state had previously assumed liability for such damage.

The majority of representatives, including that of the U.S.S.R., pointed out that such proposals undermine the very principle of the immunity of the diplomat. If it is possible to take an action for damages caused by a diplomat against an insurance company of the host-country, there is no necessity to include this in the Convention. In so far as such insurance does not exist in all countries, a clause in the Convention to this effect would create inequality in the legal position of diplomats.

A special resolution regarding compensation for damages caused by a diplomat was adopted at the conference. The resolution recommends that in appropriate cases the accrediting state should waive the immunity of officials of its diplomatic mission as regards civil suits by persons in the host-state when this is possible without violation of the function of representation, and that when there is no waiver of immunity, the accrediting state should do everything possible for the legitimate satisfaction of such demands.

Exceptions to immunity. Even though the representational approach prevailed and as a result the immunity of diplomatic agents is very broad, Article 31(1) of the convention makes exceptions to the immunity of diplomatic agents from the civil jurisdiction of the receiving state in three types of situations involving his private acts. See infra, p. 867. See also the denial of immunity to members of the administrative and technical staff of a diplomatic mission for all acts performed outside the course of their duties as discussion infra, p. 875 -.

BEYOND THE LAW

Newsweek, August 8, 1977, p. 42.*

[Before passage of the Diplomatic Relations Act, a number of articles appeared in the American press expressing resentment of diplomatic privileges.]

A foreign diplomat living in the U.S. can ignore his bills, let his dog bite the neighbors and injure or even kill people with his automobile, and nothing can be done. Not only are diplomats above the law, but so are their wives and children and every foreign national in their employ, including maids at the embassy. The U.S. Government treats international emissaries more leniently than almost any other nation in the world. * * *

* * * In the suburban New York town of Pelham, for instance, a Barbados diplomat threatened "possible international consequences" if police shot his German shepherd dog, which had bitten eight neighbors. Many foreign envoys think nothing of clogging traffic by double-parking outside a restaurant while they take a leisurely lunch. "Every time I see a DPL license I feel like kicking it," says Virginia Schlundt, a House staff lawyer who helped draft the new bill. In New York, where the hard-pressed city government spends more than $2 million a year to protect the United Nations, diplomats pile up 200,000 traffic tickets annually, about $4 million worth, and pay few. A survey last year showed that three cars registered to Idi Amin's Uganda Mission had collected 1,761 tickets in eleven months.

Parking violators may be simple nuisances, but reckless foreign drivers are something worse. In 1974, a cultural attaché at the Panamanian Embassy ran a red light and smashed broadside into the auto of Dr. Halla Brown, a 62-year-old clinical professor of medicine at George Washington University. The impact damaged Brown's spinal cord and turned her into a quadriplegic. The Panamanian was not insured. After spending $250,000 on medical bills and exhausting her own insurance, Brown still requires round-the-clock nursing care and exercises her active mind principally by reading, turning the pages with a marker held in her mouth. The Panamanian ambassador offered his condolences—and nothing else.

* * *

---

1. *Resentment of diplomatic privileges.* Articles in the same vein as the one quoted from Newsweek appeared in Time Magazine (Oct. 16, 1978, p. 38), U. S. News and World Report (Sept. 4, 1978, p. 33), the New York Times (July 18, 1978, Sec. B, p. 8, col. 4), and the Wall Street Journal (Oct. 3, 1978, p. 18, col. 1). From these and

other articles it appears no single issue provoked more resentment than the violation with impunity by diplomats of parking and traffic regulations.

The more serious issue was, however, the invocation of immunity in cases of accidents, as illustrated by the dramatic case of Dr. Halla Brown in the Newsweek article. Her case was cited in all the press articles listed supra and was referred to repeatedly during the congressional hearings on the proposed legislation to implement the Vienna Convention. See U. S. Senate Committee on Foreign Relations, 96th Cong., 1st Sess., Legislative History of the Diplomatic Relations Act 124, 226, 372, 595 (1979).

The suspicion that immunity encourages reckless driving was confirmed in Japan, at least, by an extensive survey of accidents in Tokyo involving diplomatic personnel and accidents involving other persons. Ribot Hatano, Traffic Accidents and Diplomatic Immunity, 11 Japanese Annual of International Law 18 (1967). The author stated:

> * * * The accident ratio of DPL-numbered vehicles averages 175% that of all other types of motor vehicles including buses, trucks, and so-called Kamikaze (suicide) taxis, and more than 200% that of owner-driven passenger cars (some 80% of the DPL numbered vehicles are presumed to be driven by their owners) * * *. Furthermore, the ratio seems to be increasing: The accident ratio of non-DPL numbered vehicles was halved during the five years covered by [the survey], while the ratio of DPL-numbered vehicles varied only slightly during the same period. (at 20)

The problem was solved, in part, in many states by making liability insurance compulsory for diplomatic personnel. The United States adopted this solution in the Diplomatic Relations Act.

2. *Liability insurance required for diplomatic personnel in the United States.* Section 254e of Title 22 of the United States Code states the requirement and directs the President to promulgate regulations for the purpose, while Section 1364 of Title 28 provides for direct actions against insurers of diplomatic personnel. The Department of State published the regulations mandated by the legislation. They became effective June 1, 1979. 22 C.F.R. Part 151.

3. *Taking of insurance not a waiver of diplomatic immunity.* In the case of Armour v. Katz, Ghana, Court of Appeal of Accra, 1976, [1976] 2 Ghana Law Reports 115, the plaintiff sued the first secretary of the Israeli embassy for the injuries caused by his son, a minor, while driving his father's car. He had taken liability insurance in compliance with legislation in effect in Ghana since 1958. The court of appeal reversed on the grounds that the requirements for waiver, as stated in Article 32 of the Vienna Convention, in force in Ghana, were not met and that waiver could not reasonably be implied by insuring a car.

SANCTIONS AGAINST DIPLOMATS

Statement of the Minister for Foreign Affairs of the Netherlands
2 Netherlands Yearbook of International Law 170 (1971).

During a * * * debate in the Parliamentary Standing Committee for Foreign Affairs, the Minister for Foreign Affairs made, *inter alia*, the following remarks:

> * * * a foreign diplomat cannot be prosecuted, unless his Government or he himself waives his right to immunity * * *

> Yet, there are some sanctions. First, expulsion from the host country, which goes further than recall. * * * Secondly, the person in question can be called to account through his ambassador * * * and one can ensure that civil liability, at least, be assumed. Thirdly, the foreign government does sometimes take this liability on itself. There have been cases of ordinary offences such as nonpayment of large amounts for the purchase of cars, food, etc. being committed; in these cases the nomination of a new ambassador was made conditional on previous settlement of those questions. * * * [I]t is a principle of public international law that the host country should put nothing in the way of a diplomat which would hinder him from complete freedom to exercise his functions and should remove any existing hindrances. [But there] are of course limits; for instance, when a diplomat obviously abuses his position. I am thinking of cases in which espionage activities lead to expulsion. Then there are local customs: one should behave according to local standards. One also oversteps the limit, therefore, by violating unwritten morals of a host country, by behaving in a provocative manner, by being drunk in a public place or, in countries where ladies go veiled, by insisting on seeing what is going on behind the veil. I just give a few examples that do not require the exercise of much imagination on the part of this illustrious assembly. In these cases of what I would call overstepping the limit, the diplomat concerned may be declared *persona non grata;* this will imply recall.

CASE CONCERNING UNITED STATES DIPLOMATIC AND CONSULAR STAFF IN TEHERAN (UNITED STATES v. IRAN)

International Court of Justice, 1980.
XIX International Legal Materials 553 (1980).*

[On November 27, 1979, the United States instituted proceedings in the International Court of Justice against Iran with respect to the seizure and holding as hostages in Teheran on November 4, 1979, of American diplomatic and consular personnel.

* Reprinted by permission of the American Society of International Law.

Iran did not file any pleading and did not appoint an agent to appear on its behalf. It sent to the court, however, two letters in which it defined its position and contended that the taking of the hostages might be justified by the existence of special circumstances.

The court examined that contention as follows.]

*   *   *

81. In his letters of 9 December 1979 and 16 March 1980, as previously recalled, Iran's Minister for Foreign Affairs referred to the present case as only "a marginal and secondary aspect of an overall problem". This problem, he maintained, "involves, inter alia, more than 25 years of continual interference by the United States in the internal affairs of Iran, the shameless exploitation of our country, and numerous crimes perpetrated against the Iranian people, contrary to and in conflict with all international and humanitarian norms". In the first of the two letters he indeed singled out amongst the "crimes" which he attributed to the United States an alleged complicity on the part of the Central Intelligence Agency in the coup d'état of 1953 and in the restoration of the Shah to the throne of Iran. Invoking these alleged crimes of the United States, the Iranian Foreign Minister took the position that the United States' Application could not be examined by the Court divorced from its proper context, which he insisted was "the whole political dossier of the relations between Iran and the United States over the last 25 years".

82. [From other information before the court it appeared that the criminal activities asserted in the letter consisted of espionage and interference in Iran by the United States centered upon its embassy in Teheran.]

*   *   *

85. *   *   * it is for the very purpose of providing a remedy for such possible abuses of diplomatic functions that Article 9 of the 1961 Convention on Diplomatic Relations stipulates:

1. The receiving State may at any time and without having to explain its decision, notify the sending State that the head of the mission or any member of the diplomatic staff of the mission is persona non grata or that any other member of the staff of the mission is not acceptable. In any such case, the sending State shall, as appropriate, either recall the person concerned or terminate his functions with the mission. A person may be declared non grata or not acceptable before arriving in the territory of the receiving State.

2. If the sending State refuses or fails within a reasonable period to carry out its obligations under paragraph 1 of this Article, the receiving State may refuse to recognize the person concerned as a member of the mission.

The 1963 Convention contains, in Article 23, paragraphs 1 and 4, analogous provisions in respect of consular officers and consular staff. Paragraph 1 of Article 9 of the 1961 Convention, and para-

graph 4 of Article 23 of the 1963 Convention, take account of the difficulty that may be experienced in practice of proving such abuses in
every case or, indeed, of determining exactly when exercise of the
diplomatic function, expressly recognized in Article 3(1)(d) of the
1961 Convention, of "ascertaining by all lawful means conditions and
developments in the receiving State" may be considered as involving
such acts as "espionage" or "interference in internal affairs". The
way in which Article 9, paragraph 1, takes account of any such difficulty is by providing expressly in its opening sentence that the receiving State may "at any time and without having to explain its decision" notify the sending State that any particular member of its diplomatic mission is "persona non grata" or "not acceptable" (and similarly Article 23, paragraph 4, of the 1963 Convention provides that
"the receiving State is not obliged to give to the sending State reasons for its decision"). Beyond that remedy for dealing with abuses
of the diplomatic function by individual members of a mission, a receiving State has in its hands a more radical remedy if abuses of
their functions by members of a mission reach serious proportions.
This is the power which every receiving State has, at its own discretion, to break off diplomatic relations with a sending State and to call
for the immediate closure of the offending mission.

86.   The rules of diplomatic law, in short, constitute a self-contained regime which, on the one hand, lays down the receiving State's
obligations regarding the facilities, privileges and immunities to be
accorded to diplomatic missions and, on the other, foresees their possible abuse by members of the mission and specifies the means at the
disposal of the receiving State to counter any such abuse. These
means are, by their nature, entirely efficacious, for unless the sending State recalls the member of the mission objected to forthwith, the
prospect of the almost immediate loss of his privileges and immunities, because of the withdrawal by the receiving State of his recognition as a member of the mission, will in practice compel that person,
in his own interest, to depart at once. But the principle of the inviolability of the persons of diplomatic agents and the premises of diplomatic missions is one of the very foundations of this long-established
regime, to the evolution of which the traditions of Islam made a substantial contribution. The fundamental character of the principle of
inviolability is, moreover, strongly underlined by the provisions of
Articles 44 and 45 of the Convention of 1961 (cf. also Articles 26 and
27 of the Convention of 1963). Even in the case of armed conflict or
in the case of a breach in diplomatic relations those provisions require that both the inviolability of the members of a diplomatic mission and of the premises, property and archives of the mission must
be respected by the receiving State. Naturally, the observance of this
principle does not mean—and this the Applicant Government expressly acknowledges—that a diplomatic agent caught in the act of committing an assault or other offence may not, on occasion, be briefly
arrested by the police of the receiving State in order to prevent the

commission of the particular crime. But such eventualities bear no relation at all to what occurred in the present case.

* * *

[By 13 votes to 2, the court decided, inter alia, that the conduct of Iran was in violation of the rules of international law on diplomatic immunity and by 12 votes to 3 decided that Iran was under an obligation to make reparation to the United States for the injury. Subsequently, however, the United States waived its claims under the judgment in the agreement for the release of the hostages, as indicated in Chapter 1, p. 75.]

SEIZURE OF ARMS IN BAGGAGE OF DIPLOMAT IN TRANSIT

Rousseau, Chronique des Faits Internationaux
78 Revue Générale de Droit International Public 247 (1974).[a]

* * * Five hand grenades, five revolvers, eight kilos of explosive devices and 21 letter bombs not yet addressed, rifles and ammunition were discovered on the evening of October 23, 1972, by Dutch customs officers at the airport of Schiphol in the baggage of an Algerian diplomatic agent accredited to a South American nation which the Dutch Minister of Justice refused to identify. Aged 32, born in Jordan, but carrying an Algerian diplomatic passport, the diplomat, who was identified only by the initials H.R., came from Damascus via Frankfurt and was en route to Rio de Janeiro. He declared himself to be entirely ignorant of the contents of his baggage, explaining only he thought he was carrying documents delivered to him in Damascus and destined for an Algerian embassy in a South American republic, which he declined to identify further. He added nevertheless he had bought the rifles, which were found separately, for diplomatic colleagues. The Queen's prosecutor did not institute judicial proceedings against the diplomat because in his judgment it had not at all been established that the diplomat was actually aware of the contents of his baggage. As a result the diplomat was authorized to continue his trip to South America, but his bags were retained for an investigation.

Following the discovery, the Israeli government—which was convinced the arms seized were to be used in organizing an attack upon its embassy in Brazil—requested an explanation from the Dutch government, because in its opinion the Algerian diplomat should have been held by the authorities at the airport "because diplomatic immunity applies only in the countries where diplomatic agents are accredited and not in the countries through which they are only in transit." One should have some reservations about this assertion which is contrary to established practice and is contradicted by Article 40 of the Vienna Convention of April 18, 1961, on Diplomatic Re-

a. Translation by the editors. Reprinted by permission of Charles   Rousseau and Editions A. Pedone, Paris.

lations by whose terms a diplomatic agent in transit through the territory of a third state is given "inviolability and every other immunity necessary for his passage or return."   But, inasmuch as the acts here were outside official functions, the immunity of agents in transit, already subject to strict limitations, obviously ceases in a case of flagrant offense.

---

1. *Abuse of privilege of transit.*   Article 40 of the convention does not contain any language dealing with possible abuse of transit. In this connection, the Report of the United States Delegation to the United Nations Conference on Diplomatic Intercourse and Immunities at Vienna states:

> The Conference did not adopt two perfecting amendments proposed by the United States.   The United States proposed amendments to provide that the passage must be immediate and continuous, and that a third State might deny to any person the privilege of transit through its territory, require that the transit be subject to such conditions as it may specify, and apply its laws to effect the departure of any person who abused the privilege of transit or violated its conditions.   These were considered desirable amendments, but the inclusion of language limiting the obligation of a third State under the article to persons to whom a passport visa has been granted, if such visa is necessary, may serve the same purpose.   It was brought out during the discussion that delegations did not interpret the article as granting an absolute right of transit.   Reprinted in U. S. Senate Committee on Foreign Relations, 96th Cong., 1st Sess., Legislative History of the Diplomatic Relations Act 737, 765 (1979).

2. *Pre-flight checks of diplomatic agents.*   The Bureau of Legal and Consular Affairs of the Department of External Affairs of Canada was requested to give an opinion on the right of an airline to check Canadian diplomats before allowing them to board aircraft. The Bureau replied it would be better for the diplomats not to create difficulties by objecting to routine inspection of baggage or search of the person before boarding for the purpose of detecting arms, subject to protesting under Article 36(2) of the Vienna Convention, should it turn out the checks were conducted for other purposes. Such would be the case if things other than arms were confiscated or documents in the baggage were read.

Strictly speaking, however, said the Bureau, the systematic inspection, and the more so the systematic body search, are in derogation of the Vienna Convention because it contemplates inspection only when there are serious grounds for presuming the baggage contains prohibited articles.   IX Canadian Yearbook of International Law 279 (1971).

3. *Airport check of diplomatic bag.* A question was raised in the House of Commons concerning the reported use of the diplomatic bag to introduce arms into the United Kingdom illegally. On behalf of the Foreign Office it was stated that the diplomatic bags could not be opened or detained under the Vienna Convention. 83 Revue Générale de Droit International Public 527 (1979).

---

3. WHEN DOMESTIC LAW DOES APPLY

REGINA v. GOVERNOR OF PENTONVILLE PRISON, EX PARTE TEJA

United Kingdom, Divisional Court, 1971.
[1971] 2 Q.B. 274.*

[The defendant, a national of India, had been chairman of the board of an Indian company before coming to the United States. After his arrival, the government of India requested his extradition for various criminal breaches of trust. He jumped bail and absconded to Costa Rica, which did not have a treaty of extradition with India.

In June 1970, the government of Costa Rica gave him a diplomatic passport and a letter of reference in which he was identified as "economic adviser to Costa Rica in special mission." The letter also stated he was to establish himself in Switzerland and would "soon be accredited as an economic counselor for the Costa Rican embassy" in that country. The letter requested he be given the privileges and immunities inherent to his diplomatic condition.

In pursuance of his mission—a study of the possible development of an integral steel industry in Central Latin America—he travelled to various European countries, including the United Kingdom where he was arrested and held for extradition to India. He applied for a writ of habeas corpus on the ground, inter alia, that he was a diplomatic agent not liable to any form of arrest or detention.

The court had received from the Foreign and Commonwealth Office a certificate stating that he had not been accredited to the Court of St. James as a diplomatic agent of the Costa Rican Government.

A portion of the opinion appears below.]

Lord PARKER, C. J. In these proceedings Sir Dingle Foot moves on behalf of the applicant, one Jayanti Dharma Teja, who is now detained in Her Majesty's Prison at Pentonville, for a writ of habeas corpus. * * *
* * *

* Reprinted by permission of the Incorporated Council of Law Reporting for England and Wales, London.

Article 29 [of the Vienna Convention on Diplomatic Relations] provides categorically that: "The person of a diplomatic agent shall be inviolable. He shall not be liable to any form of arrest or detention." Article 31 goes on to provide that he shall enjoy immunity from the criminal jurisdiction of a receiving state, and finally by article 39, paragraph 1 it is provided that:

> Every person entitled to privileges and immunities shall enjoy them from the moment he enters the territory of the receiving state on proceeding to take up his post or, if already in its territory, from the moment when his appointment is notified to the Ministry for Foreign Affairs or such other ministry as may be agreed.

Accordingly, Sir Dingle puts the matter in a very simple form. He says: here is a man who was head of a mission, the mission being that referred to in the letter of credence; as such he was entitled to the privileges and immunities under articles 29 and 31 of the Schedule to the Act of 1964 from the moment he enters the territory of the receiving state. Accordingly, from the very moment he lands in this country he is immune from any form of arrest or detention or criminal proceedings.

I confess that at the very outset this argument, simple as it was, seemed to me to produce a frightening result in that any foreign country could claim immunity for representatives sent to this country unilaterally whether this country agreed or not. As I see it, it is fundamental to the claiming of immunity by reason of being a diplomatic agent that that diplomatic agent should have been in some from accepted or received by this country. In the case to which the court has been referred of Fenton Textile Association Ltd. v. Krassin (1921) 38 T.L.R. 259, the court were considering the immunities and privileges attaching to a representative of a foreign country who had come pursuant to a trade agreement, and the facts do not matter in the least. At the end of his judgment Bankes L. J. said, at p. 261: "That status is clearly insufficient to carry with it the immunity accorded to accredited and recognised representatives of foreign states." * * * Accordingly, it was recognised in that case that no immunity can be conferred by reason of diplomatic status unless the representative of the foreign country in question has been accepted or received by this country. In other words, immunity depends on mutual agreement on the person entitled to the immunity.

I think Sir Dingle would accept that certainly in the case of an ambassador it is implicit that he cannot come to this country claiming immunity until his presence has been indicated as persona grata in this country, and the same it seems to me is true of any diplomatic agent of whatever status.

It is not without interest in this connection to see that in the Vienna Convention of 1961 itself, in articles 2 and 4, which are not set out in the Schedule to the Act of 1964,[a] it is provided by article 2:

The establishment of diplomatic relations between states, and of permanent diplomatic missions, takes place by mutual consent,

and article 4:

1. The sending state must make certain that the agreement of the receiving state has been given for the person it proposes to accredit as head of the mission through that state. 2. The receiving state is not obliged to give reasons to the sending state for a refusal of agreement.

I only refer to that incidentally because I am by no means clear that it would be proper to construe the Act of 1964 by reference to articles in the Vienna Convention, which were not incorporated in that Act, but it does bear out what I have always understood to be the general principle that there must be prior agreement between the two countries before any particular person can be the subject of immunity.

* * *

[The court also ruled the defendant was not a diplomat in transit to or from Geneva because Costa Rica had no embassy there and there was no evidence he had been accepted as a diplomat by the Swiss government.

The application was denied.]

———

Beginning of diplomatic immunity. In the report of the United States delegation to the United Nations Conference on Diplomatic Intercourse and Immunities at Vienna, the following language appears:

A U.S. proposal to include language requiring acceptance by the receiving State of the appointment to a mission of a person already in its territory as a condition to his becoming entitled to privileges and immunities was not adopted. Consequently, the U.S. delegate placed in the record of the plenary session a statement that he considered the text must be read as if the word "provisionally" appeared between the words "if already in its territory," and the words "from the moment when his appointment is notified." Reprinted in U.S. Senate Committee on Foreign Relations, 96th Cong., 1st. Sess., Legislative History of the Diplomatic Relations Act 737, 764 (1979).

a. The act came into force July 31, 1964. See note a on p. 848.

DAME NZIE v. VESSAH

France, Court of Appeal of Paris, 1978.
105 Journal du Droit International 605 (1978).[a]

[The wife of Vessah, Julienne Nzie, from the Republic of Cameroon, filed for divorce under both French law and the law of Cameroon. The court held that it had no jurisdiction because Vessah, as First Secretary of the Embassy of Cameroon in Paris, and as such registered on the diplomatic list, was entitled to immunity and had not waived it.

The plaintiff appealed on two grounds. First, the court should not have declared itself without jurisdiction on its own initiative. Second, her husband had written to her family, in accordance with the customary law in force in Cameroon, that he agreed to divorce her according to her wishes. Hence, she contended, he had waived his diplomatic immunity.

She finally argued only French courts could assure her physical safety by giving her permission to live separately from her husband.

A portion of the opinion of the court appears below.]

* * * The Vienna Convention of April 18, 1961, on diplomatic relations, made effective in France by the decree of March 29, 1971, * * * and ratified by the [Republic of] Cameroon in March, 1977, provides in Article 31 that a diplomatic agent enjoys immunity from jurisdiction save in exceptional cases, which are limited to those enumerated, and do not include a divorce proceeding. According to the terms of Article 32 of the Convention, the accrediting state may waive the immunity of jurisdiction of its diplomatic agents, but the waiver must always be express, [and] if a diplomatic agent brings suit, he may not invoke his immunity with regard to any counterclaim directly connected with the principal claim.

It follows that the waiver by a diplomatic agent who is summoned to appear before a court must always be expressly authorized by his government.

* * * In the case at bar, the Republic of Cameroon has not indicated any waiver of immunity.

* * * In the absence of a waiver of immunity, the judge for matrimonial matters did not have the power to proceed with attempts at reconciliation, nor could he continue in force his preliminary ruling of December 17, 1976, by which * * * he authorized Julienne Nzie to live apart from her husband.

The appeal is thus without foundation.

a. Translation by the editors. Reprinted by permission of Editions Techniques, S.A., Paris.

J. A. HELINSKI v. B. B. 't HART

Netherlands, Local Court of The Hague, 1976.
VIII Netherlands Yearbook of International Law 279 (1977).

[Helinski, a diplomatic agent, deducted from his rent the cost of repairs he had done on his residence. His landlord sued him and obtained a judgment for a much larger sum than Helinski was awarded on his counterclaim. The landlord sought execution of his judgment. Helinski invoked his diplomatic status for the first time and the execution was stopped on the advice of the Ministry of Justice, but he eventually paid the judgment.

As a result of the legal wrangling, Helinski discovered he had been paying all along a much larger amount of rent than permitted by the rent control legislation. He obtained advice on the point from the Rent Tribunal and then applied for a court order to determine his financial obligations to his landlord; in turn, the landlord's defense was that Helinski could not personally waive his diplomatic immunity and institute civil proceedings in the Netherlands without the consent of his own government. Helinski asserted that he could.

A portion of the opinion of the court appears below.]

This is the first point to be decided. The Court considers Helinski's view to be correct. There is no rule of international law recognised by the Netherlands to prohibit him from acting as a plaintiff or petitioner in the Netherlands without first getting the express consent of his own Government. Such a rule cannot be found in either Dutch or foreign literature. Reliance on the 1961 Vienna Convention on Diplomatic Relations would also be of no avail; * * * neither the text of the Convention nor its history give sufficient pointers. Although the Convention has been signed by the Netherlands it has still not been ratified. * * * In the meantime, it must be assumed that the Convention, although not yet formally in force in the Netherlands, has to be regarded as a consolidation of international customary law. Should it clearly answer the question referred to this answer would be of particular importance. This is, however, not the case. It would seem that the authors of the text have not always drawn a sharp distinction between those cases in which the diplomat must be protected against the acts of other persons * * * and those in which the diplomat himself wishes to go to Court in the receiving State to protect his interests. Thus, Article 32 of the Convention is a mixture of provisions, and it cannot be said clearly if they apply to both categories of cases. What is clear, is that in the event of waiver of diplomatic immunity, both in criminal proceedings and in civil actions against the diplomat, an express declaration is required to grant jurisdiction to the Court of the receiving State. Para. 3 of this Article would, however, rather suggest the contrary in cases where a diplomat has instituted civil proceedings against a private individual. He is then precluded from invoking immunity from jurisdiction in respect of any counter-claim made by the opposing

party. This provision thus proceeds on the assumption that the diplomat has the power to initiate proceedings. The intention is that, in
such a case, he is not allowed both to use this power of initiating proceedings against another, and to prevent this person from making a
counter-claim. In other words, the diplomat cannot have it both
ways. But even this provision gives no explicit answer to the question with which we are here concerned.

In the absence of an express and unambiguous provision, it will
be the purport of the rules of international customary law concerned
with the protection of diplomats which has to be considered. This
purport has traditionally found expression in the principle of *ne im-
pediatur legatio* but this principle should be strictly applied. It must
result in protection of the diplomat (in the interests of his country),
but is not intended to protect others against acts of the diplomat.
Therefore, it cannot, in the Court's view, be advanced by other persons *against* the diplomat. This was most clearly expressed by Roberto Ago during the discussion in the International Law Commission
which made a draft for the Vienna Convention; see Yearbook ILC,
1957, Vol. I, p. 114: "Enjoying immunity from jurisdiction meant
simply enjoying the right not to be the object of judicial proceedings,
in other words, not being bound to appear as defendant in the courts
in consequence of proceedings instituted against him. The immunity
in question had never meant the inability to appear as plaintiff before the same courts." But, again, this statement was not in so many
words included in the Convention itself.

No doubt, any State has the power to deny its diplomats the
rights to initiate civil proceedings in the receiving State. In that
case it is an internal instruction that cannot be invoked by the opposing party.

Generally speaking, a Court should not decline jurisdiction in the
absence of an unambiguous rule to that effect. Since, in this case,
there is no such rule, the plea that this Court should decline jurisdiction, must fail * * *.

---

1. *Waiver of immunity of diplomatic agent by initiation of proceedings.*

In Diplomatic Immunities, Austria, Supreme Court, 1977, 105
Journal du Droit International 165 (1979), a high official of the International Agency for Atomic Energy (I.A.A.E.) was divorced from
his wife. Some three years later, he brought an action in which he
claimed custody of their child, who until then had remained with the
mother. She counterclaimed to obtain custody of the child for herself. He thereupon discontinued his action and pleaded diplomatic
immunity to hers. The court ruled that under Articles 33(1) and
(2) of the Vienna Convention his plea was valid because no express
waiver of his immunity had been supplied by either the state of his
nationality or the I.A.A.E.

Is it consistent to require the express authorization of waiver by the sending state when the diplomatic agent is sued and not require any authorization of waiver when he brings the proceeding himself? Can the apparent inconsistency be resolved by saying that, when the diplomatic agent brings a proceeding, it is likely to be a private matter in which the sending state would have little interest?

2. *Waiver of inviolability of private residence of diplomatic agent.* The Office for Public International Law of the Swiss Federal Political Department has given an opinion in answer to the question whether a diplomatic agent—or a member of the administrative and technical staff of a mission—could waive the inviolability of his private residence.

It first stated that the Vienna Convention did not provide a clear answer as to who could give the authorities of the receiving state consent to enter the private residence of a diplomatic agent. It declined to assimilate the inviolability of the personal residence of the agent to the inviolability of the premises of the mission and thus to conclude that, since the consent of the head of the mission was required for entry into the premises of the mission, it was required as well for entry into the personal residence of the agent.

From an examination of the "travaux préparatoires" of the convention, the Office concluded the inviolability of the premises of the mission availed the sending state while the inviolability of the private residence of the agent attached to his person, thus providing him with it even in a temporary residence. Accordingly, the agent could validly waive the inviolability of his residence. XXXII Annuaire Suisse de Droit International 147 (1976).

3. *Private acts of diplomatic agent not covered by immunity.* The Division of the Juridical Affairs of the Swiss Federal Political Department has given an opinion as to whether a lien could be secured on a building owned by a high official of an international organization.

First the opinion discussed the facts. Under the Swiss code, workmen who provide services and materials for the construction of a building are protected for their payment by a lien against the property, even if the owner is not the one owing the debt. In order to be effective, the lien must be recorded and this can be done only if the debtor acknowledges the debt or a court orders the recordation following a summary proceeding. In the case at hand, a cantonal court has ordered provisional recordation of a lien upon the property of a high official of the United Nations.

The opinion then noted that under Article 31(1) of the Vienna Convention a diplomatic agent shall enjoy immunity from civil and administrative jurisdiction of the receiving state, but not with respect to private immovable property in the territory of the receiving state. Since the property was private in this case, the opinion concluded there was no need to seek a waiver of diplomatic immunity. XXXII Annuaire Suisse de Droit International 143 (1976).

For the other two types of private acts not covered by diplomatic immunity, see Article 31(1) in the Documentary Supplement.

4. *Ending of diplomatic function: effect upon diplomatic immunity.* Under Article 39(2) of the Vienna Convention, the effect differs as between the diplomat's official and private acts.

Thus with respect to a car accident, the following statement appears in 11 Japanese Annual of International Law 94 (1967):

On February 17, 1964, a secretary of the Malaysian Embassy in Tokyo, while driving home from a reception, ran over a Japanese student causing his death. The police made the necessary inquest and found that the accident was caused by his reckless driving, but, in view of the diplomatic status of the driver, no further action was taken by way of criminal proceedings against him. In August 1964, the secretary was recalled back home after completion of his term in Tokyo, and he left Japan without coming to a settlement with the family of the victim on the question of the damages. When this case was taken up for debate in the House of Councillors, the Director of the Treaties Bureau of the Ministry of Foreign Affairs stated that although the Civil Code of Japan was applicable to such a case of car accident, which might constitute a tort in civil law, the man had been immune from the jurisdiction of the court to entertain an action against him at the time of the accident because of his status as a [member of the] diplomatic staff of the Embassy. Further to a question whether he continued to enjoy the immunity from jurisdiction after returning to his own country, the Director of the Treaties Bureau stated that in accordance with the provisions of the Vienna Convention on Diplomatic Relations, the jurisdictional immunity of a diplomat will cease to exist when the sending State gives notice of the termination of his mission to the receiving State, and that in law the secretary was now not immune from the civil jurisdiction of the court in Japan.

Suppose, however, a diplomatic agent performs an official act such as the preparation of a report on a highly sensitive political matter in the receiving state, at the request of his chief of mission. The report is made public in the sending state and is eventually reprinted in a newspaper in the receiving state. The diplomatic agent retires from the diplomatic service of the sending state and remains in the state where he formerly exercised his function. Thereupon he is sued for libel in the report he prepared as an official act. He is entitled to immunity. See Section 39(2) of the Vienna Convention.

4. OTHER PERSONS ENTITLED TO DIPLOMATIC IMMUNITY

1. *Organization of a diplomatic mission.* The Vienna Convention divides the personnel of a diplomatic mission into four categories and assigns different privileges and immunities to each. In assessing

the difference in treatment of each of these categories, it is useful to know who are the persons in each and what they do.   The information below is a simplified table of organization of a diplomatic mission.

The first category is the diplomatic staff.   Its members have diplomatic rank.   They are the ones who are engaged in the performance of the diplomatic function in the strict sense of the term.   These diplomatic agents, as they are called in the Vienna Convention, include the chief of mission (ambassador, or minister or chargé d'affaires), counsellor or deputy chief of mission, the first, second and third secretaries (of embassy), the military attachés (air, army, navy) and such other attachés (for commerce, labor, treasury and other matters) as the receiving state may agree to recognize as diplomatic agents.

The next two categories—which may be looked upon as part of the official family of the diplomatic agent—are the administrative and technical staff on the one hand and the service staff on the other. The administrative staff includes administrative officers, persons in charge of communications (code and mail), secretary-typists and file clerks.   The service staff includes drivers of the mission cars, butlers, cooks, maids and gardeners.   The last category—which may be looked upon as part of the personal family of the diplomatic agent— consists of private servants.

2.   *Variant state interests as to the reach of immunity.*   Many diplomatic missions, including those of the United States, make heavy use of local employees, i.e., nationals of the host state.   These states have had reason to be concerned about the position of the local employees before national authorities of the host state.   It is in the general interest of states in this group to have a fairly wide reach of immunity for all members of the embassy community, including the local employees.   On the other hand, states such as the United States have to take into account the objections of those of their citizens (and their elected representatives) who would develop a sense of outrage if diplomatic immunity were widely accorded to fellow nationals and resident aliens because of their employment by a foreign mission.

3.   *Effect of nationality upon diplomatic immunity.*   Under Article 38 of the Vienna Convention, a diplomatic agent who is a national of, or a permanent resident in, the receiving state is entitled to immunity only in respect of acts performed in the exercise of his functions.

Thus in Querouil v. Breton, France, Court of Appeal of Paris, 1976, 57 Revue Critique de Droit International Privé 478 (1968), the plaintiffs were owners of an apartment rented to a Frenchman who was counsellor of the embassy of Chad in Paris.   They brought a proceeding for the eviction of the defendant who pleaded diplomatic immunity.   The court held that, even though the Vienna Convention was not yet ratified by France, it was a codification of current practice.   Thus, being French, the defendant could not claim diplomatic immunity for a suit arising from his private act.

As to all other personnel, they are not entitled to any immunity if they are nationals of the receiving state, unless and except to the extent such state cares to accord it to them.

PERSONAL FAMILY

STATUS OF HUSBAND–IN–FACT OF WOMAN DIPLOMAT

Opinion of the Office for Public International Law of
the Swiss Federal Political Department.
XXXIII Annuaire Suisse De Droit International 224 (1977).[a]

[In a note dated July 13, 1976, the Office for Public International Law of the Federal Political Department handed down a ruling on the question whether the de facto husband of a woman diplomat accredited to Switzerland could avail himself of the privileges and immunities accorded by Article 37, paragraph 1, of the Vienna Convention on Diplomatic Relations of April 18, 1961, " * * * to members of the family of a diplomatic agent who are part of his household and not nationals of the accrediting state."]

Doctrine [scholarly writing] is silent on this question. Jurisprudence [case law] appears to be nonexistent. Albeit, we can cite a decision of the Tribunal Civil of the Seine in 1907 holding that the wife of a diplomat, who had been authorized to establish a separate domicile as a result of a suit for separation, continued to enjoy diplomatic privileges and immunities.

The working papers of the International Law Commission (ILC) do not address themselves to the precise question of a spouse in fact. But they do furnish useful guidelines as to the circle of members of the family entitled to diplomatic privileges. The ILC has noted in particular that the chief, or member, of a mission may be elderly or a bachelor and be assisted by a sister, an adult daughter or even a sister-in-law, who acts as lady of the house * * *.

In its comments on Article 36 (practically identical to the future Article 37 of the Convention) of the draft articles (concerning diplomatic relations and immunities), the ILC comments as follows * * *:

So far as concerns diplomatic agents * * * who enjoy the full range of privileges and immunities, the Commission, in conformity with existing practice, proposed that these prerogatives, be equally accorded to members of their families, on the condition they be members of their households and they not be nationals of the accrediting state. The Commission did not want to go so far as precisely to define the meaning of the term "members of the family" or to set a maximum age for children. The spouse and the minor children, at least, are universally ac-

---

a. Translation by the editors. Reprinted by permission of Schulthess Polygraphischer Verlag AG, Zurich.

knowledged to be members of the family, but there can be cases where other relatives also qualify if they are part of the household. In stipulating that in order to claim privileges and immunities, a member of the family must be part of the household, the Commission means to indicate that close relationships or special circumstances must be involved. These special circumstances may exist when a relative keeps house for the ambassador though they may not be closely related or when a distant relative has lived in the bosom of the family for so long he ends up being a part of it.

Strictly speaking the term *family* means a group of persons linked to each other by marriage (relationship by affinity), by descent (relationship by consanguinity) or by adoption. But the commentary clearly leads one to think that the ILC preferred to put the emphasis on the common household rather than on the links of marriage. Therefore it seems to be in conformity with the spirit of the Convention to include a spouse in fact among the members of the family. The Convention never made it its goal to regulate the private lives of diplomatic agents, but [rather made it its goal] to regulate the granting of diplomatic privileges.

In conformity with the preamble to the Vienna Convention, the purpose of the convention's privileges is not to create advantages for individuals but to insure the effective performance of the functions of diplomatic missions insofar as they represent states. They are extended to the family that is part of the household of the diplomatic agent because the family is supposed to represent that which is dearest to him and because, by threats to it, one would be able to compromise the free exercise of the mission of the agent. Besides, the family in the sense of the Convention includes a limited number of persons. Giving a privileged status to its members would not in itself involve major risks of abuse. The family does not vary every day in its composition. It is relatively stable. It exists within the orbit of the diplomatic agent who can exert upon it a certain control.

All of these elements are present in the case at bar. The theoretical foundation of the law of diplomatic privileges and immunities rests on the idea that certain persons—first of all the members of his family—may be considered as an extension of the personality of the diplomatic agent * * *. As it were, there are sometimes circumstances under which one must hold them to be special and assimilate a person, even though a stranger to the agent (diplomat) by blood or by marriage, to a member of the family within the meaning of Article 37, paragraph 1, of the Convention. Such is the case with a long-time liaison, officially recognized as such by the accrediting state, between two spouses in fact who travel together, each with an official passport. The closeness of the bond seems to us further strengthened when the husband in fact, far from wanting to create his own center of interests and exercise a gainful activity in the accrediting state, manifests an intention to live under the same roof and in the financial orbit of the diplomatic agent. * * *

STATUS OF PRIVATE SERVANT OF COUNSELOR
OF EMBASSY

Austria, Supreme Court, 1971.
101 Journal du Droit International 630 (1974).[a]

In a proceeding to establish natural paternity, the defendant, a Greek national, objected that he was not subject to Austrian jurisdiction in his occupation as a private servant of a counselor of the Embassy of Greece in Vienna. The Federal Minister of Justice had expressed an opinion on the subject to the effect that the defendant in the case did not enjoy any immunity. But, as a result of a decision of the Austrian Constitutional Court of October 14, 1970, such opinions do not bind the courts. Following an examination of the state of the law, the supreme court reached the same conclusion.

According to Article 37, paragraph 4, of the Convention on Diplomatic Relations, the private servants of members of a mission, who are not nationals of the state to which they are accredited or who do not have their permanent residence there, are exempt from taxes on the salaries they receive for their services; in all other respects, they enjoy privileges and immunities only to the extent allowed by the state to which they are accredited. The lower courts recognized the immunity of the defendant by virtue of a provision in an Austrian decree of February 7, 1834, which granted diplomatic immunity to private servants of accredited diplomats * * *.

This provision was abolished by the law of April 3, 1919, however. This law recognized the privilege of extraterritoriality only for those persons who had a right to it according to the principles of public international law. Such a right, though, does not exist in this case. Even before the law of April 3, 1919, went into effect, it was doubtful that personnel employed in the private service of diplomats enjoyed immunity. Today, it results from the very terms of Article 37, Paragraph 4, of the Convention on Diplomatic Relations that such privileges no longer exist in favor of private servants. The significance of this prudent drafting will be properly appreciated if one remembers that the outcome * * * was influenced only to a small degree by juridical considerations. Indeed almost all the heads of delegations were diplomats who, in doubtful cases, tended to opt for the strengthening of privileges. If, nevertheless, they accord generally to private domestics no exemption from the civil jurisdiction of the accrediting state, they are manifestly inspired by the idea that the immunity of the group of persons in question is devoid of functional necessity, one of the controlling ideas of the Diplomatic Conference of Vienna.

Anglo-American precedents. See Triquet v. Bath, supra, p. 841 and the Act of 1790, supra, p. 850.

a. Translation by the editors. Reprinted by permission of Editions Techniques, S.A., Paris.

OFFICIAL FAMILY

ROMANOV, THE VIENNA CONVENTION ON DIPLOMATIC INTERCOURSE AND FUNDAMENTAL QUESTIONS OF THE CODIFICATION OF INTERNATIONAL LAW REGARDING DIPLOMATIC PRIVILEGES AND IMMUNITIES

Soviet Year Book of International Law 1961, at 92 (1962).

The most prolonged and acute discussion at the Vienna Conference developed around the question of the privileges and immunities of the administrative and technical personnel of Embassies and Missions.

The draft convention drawn up by the International Law Commission envisaged the establishment of general rules which would oblige all signatories to extend all diplomatic privileges and immunities to administrative and technical personnel of Embassies without exception. Such a rule has not hitherto existed in international law, and the practice of states has been extremely varied.

Some delegations proposed that the administrative and technical personnel of Embassies and Missions should enjoy immunity only in regard to actions committed by them in the execution of their duties, which would equate this category of official to the auxiliary personnel of diplomatic missions. A proposal that no general rule envisaging concrete privileges and immunities for administrative and technical personnel should be incorporated in the Convention, as a result of which the question would be left to the discretion of the parties concerned, was also submitted.

The majority of delegations, while not objecting to the granting of diplomatic privileges and immunities to this category of official, considered, however, that the draft convention went too far in fully equating administrative and technical personnel with diplomatic personnel.

*   *   *

During plenary session the proposal adopted by the Committee was amended somewhat. A reservation was incorporated to the effect that the immunity from civil and administrative jurisdiction is granted to administrative and technical personnel only in relation to actions committed in the course of the fulfilment of their official duties. In all other respects the Vienna Convention accords the administrative and technical personnel of Embassies and Missions the same privileges and immunities as diplomats.

Hence, whereas in other respects regarding diplomatic privileges and immunities the Vienna Convention in the main reinforced already-existing rules of international law, it established a new rule as regards the privileges and immunities of the administrative and technical personnel of Embassies and Missions. The Convention substantially alters the legal status of this category of official or diplomatic missions   *   *   *.

VULCAN IRON WORKS, INC. v. POLISH AMERICAN MACHINERY CORP.

United States District Court, S.D. New York, 1979.
472 F.Supp. 77.

LASKER, District Judge.

In connection with litigation pending in the United States District Court for the District of New Jersey, the plaintiffs in that action served deposition subpoenas on the Commercial Attache and Vice Commercial Attache of the Polish Commercial Counselor's Office in New York City, Anatoliusz Inowolski and Woadyslaw Golab, who are not parties to the New Jersey action. Inowolski and Golab did not appear for the depositions noticed in the subpoenas, and the plaintiffs move for an order finding them in contempt of court for failing to obey the subpoenas "without adequate excuse." Fed.R.Civ.P. 45(f). Inowolski and Golab assert that their failure to appear is excused because they enjoy diplomatic immunity from the jurisdiction and compulsory process of this court.

The immunity of representatives of foreign nations (and their staffs and households) from criminal and civil jurisdiction has long been a precept of international law. In the United States this precept is embodied in the Vienna Convention on Diplomatic Relations and the Diplomatic Relations Act, which extends to diplomatic representatives of non-signatories to the Vienna Convention the immunities specified in the Convention, and in various bilateral agreements, including the Consular Convention between the United States and the Polish People's Republic (Polish Consular Convention).

The provisions of the Vienna Convention and the Polish Consular Convention respecting immunity differ. Thus the initial question here is which of the two applies in the circumstances of this case. The Vienna Convention delimits the immunity of heads of "diplomatic missions," their families, staff, and servants, whereas the Consular Convention does so for officers and employees of "consular establishments." The issue, then, is what is the status of the Polish Commercial Counselor's Office.

* * *

First, both the head of the Polish Commercial Counselor's Office and the Minister-Counselor of the Polish Embassy state, in letters to the court, that the Commercial Counselor's Office is a part of the Embassy. Second, their assertions are indirectly supported by a State Department note dated January 30, 1979, which, though it states only that the Commercial Counselor's Office "is a recognized official office of the Polish People's Republic in the United States," notes that "[t]he Department has formally extended to the head of that office the status of a diplomatic agent and the privileges and immunities attendant to that status." Article 1(e) of the Vienna Convention defines a "diplomatic agent" as the head of a "diplomatic mission." The term does not appear in the Consular Convention. Finally, the plaintiffs, who bear the ultimate burden of proof on this motion, have not submitted a copy of the exequatur or other official document recognizing the head of the Commercial Counselor's Office as the head of a consular establishment. In the circumstances, we conclude that the Commercial Counselor's Office is an arm of the Polish Embassy, and that the treaty applicable in this case is the Vienna Convention, not the Polish Consular Convention.

Article 31 of the Vienna Convention deals with the immunity of "diplomatic agents." Article 37(2) provides that "[m]embers of the administrative and technical staff of the mission * * * shall * * * enjoy the privileges and immunities specified in Articles 29 to 35, except that the immunity from civil and administrative jurisdiction of the receiving state specified in paragraph 1 of Article 31 shall not extend to acts performed outside the course of their duties." Accordingly, Inowolski and Golab, as members of the "administrative and technical staff" of the Commercial Counselor's Office, are entitled to the protection accorded diplomatic agents by Article 31(2), which provides that "[a] diplomatic agent is not obligated to give evidence as a witness." Thus, their failure to appear for depositions in response to the plaintiffs' subpoenas was excusable, and the plaintiffs' motion for an order of contempt must be denied.

* * *

----

1. *Inviolability of person and private residence of members of administrative and technical staff.* The case of Immunity of Trade Representative, France, Court of State Security, 1975, 80 Revue Générale de Droit International Public 1277 (1976), involved espionage.

Pursuant to warrants issued by the magistrate in charge of the proceedings, police officers searched the person and domicile, and seized documents, of the Trade Representative of the embassy of a foreign country. (The report discloses the name of neither the subject nor his country.) The court held that because he was a member of the administrative and technical staff, the searches had breached the inviolability of his person, residence and property in violation of Article 37(2) of the Vienna Convention. It ordered the restitution of the documents seized and declared null the searches and records made of them.

2. *Limited immunity of members of service staff.* Under Article 37(3) of the Vienna Convention, they have no immunity from criminal jurisdiction and immunity from civil jurisdiction only for acts performed in the course of their duties.

U.S.—U.S.S.R. AGREEMENT EXTENDING DIPLOMATIC IMMUNITY TO ALL EMBASSY PERSONNEL

73 American Journal of International Law 284 (1979).*

Prior to enactment of the Diplomatic Relations Act, Public Law 95–393, approved Sept. 30, 1978 * * * the Soviet Union had expressed concern that it would curtail the full diplomatic immunity enjoyed by the administrative, technical, and service staffs of its embassy in Washington, pursuant to the Agreement Concerning the Extension of Diplomatic Privileges and Immunities to Non-Diplomatic Personnel, by exchange of notes October 17, 1967, and March 1, 1968 * * *. A Soviet aide mémoire, handed to the American Embassy in Moscow on October 12, 1978, proposed that the status of personnel of Soviet diplomatic and consular establishments in the United States under the existing agreement be reconfirmed with respect to the new legislation, on the basis of reciprocity, as before.

The Department of State considered that the existing reciprocal arrangement had been mutually beneficial, and that its continuation would be in the U.S. interest. Section 4 of the act, specifically authorizing the grant of more (or less) favorable treatment, on the basis of reciprocity, than that under the 1961 Vienna Convention on Diplomatic Relations, had, in fact, been drafted with such a circumstance in mind. Accordingly, after exchanging views, the United States and the Soviet Union entered into a new agreement, by notes dated December 14, 1978, to take effect December 29, 1978, the effective date of the Diplomatic Relations Act. Under the new agreement, the United States and the Soviet Union have agreed to accord the privileges and immunities of diplomatic agents, as specified in the 1961 Vienna Convention, to all members of the other's embassy in its territory and to the members of their families, who are nationals of the sending state. An Agreed Minute to the exchange of notes provided, among other things, for continuation of existing Department of State practice, under which the Department certified to a court or other appropriate authority the status of an individual and the scope of immunity resulting from that status. * * *

        * * *

_____

1. *Proving diplomatic status.* Where the Secretary of State, or the person designated by him, certifies that an individual is a person accepted as a diplomatic agent, or as a member of another category of diplomatic personnel, the certification is conclusive on the courts in the United States. See Comment *i* to Section 73 and Comment *b* to Section 74 of the Restatement of the Foreign Relations of the United States (1965).

* Reprinted with the permission of American Society of International Law.

Decisions in matters of diplomatic immunity by the national courts of other states often mention that the ministry of foreign affairs has certified the diplomatic status of the person involved in the case and thus suggest that decision-making by the executive with respect to diplomatic status is widespread.

A diplomatic passport is not proof of diplomatic status and indeed may be issued on occasion to important officials who are not diplomatic agents. On the other hand, the special identity cards issued by the Department of State to foreign diplomatic agents in the United States are of great practical value in readily establishing their diplomatic identity.

2. *Immunities associated with international organizations.* These immunities are considered in Chapter 14.

---

5. SPECIAL MISSIONS AND HEADS OF STATE OR PERSONS OF HIGH RANK

a. *Special missions.* On December 8, 1969, the General Assembly of the United Nations adopted and opened for signature on December 16, 1969, a Convention on Special Missions. For its text, see U.N. Document A/Res/2530 (XXIV) of December 16, 1969 and A/Res/2530 (XXIV)/Corr. 1 of January 2, 1970. As of December 31, 1979, 19 states were parties to the convention, but it was not yet in force.

In Article I of the convention, a special mission is defined as a "temporary mission, representing the State, which is sent by one State to another State with the consent of the latter for the purpose of dealing with it on specific questions or of performing in relation to it a specific task."

Like the Vienna Convention on Diplomatic Relations, the Convention on Special Missions breaks down their personnel into four categories—diplomatic staff, administrative and technical staff, service staff and private staff—and grants to the members in each the same immunities, subject to one qualification, as are granted to personnel in the corresponding categories by the Vienna Convention on Diplomatic Relations. The qualification is that in addition to the three types of private acts for which a diplomatic agent is not entitled to immunity from civil and administrative jurisdiction under the Vienna Convention on Diplomatic Relations, a member of the diplomatic staff of a special mission has no immunity from civil and administrative jurisdiction in the case of "an action for damages arising out of an accident caused by a vehicle used outside the official functions of the person concerned." Article 31, 2, (d). By Article 25, the premises of a special mission are made inviolable, and the members of its diplomatic staff enjoy personal inviolability under Article 29.

b. *Heads of state and persons of high rank.* Article 21 of the Convention on Special Missions provides:

> 1. The Head of the sending State, when he leads a special mission, shall enjoy in the receiving State or in a third State the facilities, privileges and immunities accorded by international law to Heads of State on an official visit.

> 2. The Head of the Government, the Minister for Foreign Affairs and other persons of high rank, when they take part in a special mission of the sending State, shall enjoy in the receiving State or in a third State, in addition to what is granted by the present Convention, the facilities, privileges and immunities accorded by international law.

In the message sent by the Federal Council of Switzerland to the legislature when proposing ratification of the convention, the following comment on paragraph 2 of Article 21 appears: "This provision is defective to the extent that *   *   *   the general rules of international law—in contrast to those concerning heads of state—are controverted." XXXIII Annuaire Suisse de Droit International 231, 232 (1977).

SECTION C. CONSULAR IMMUNITY

THE CONSULAR FUNCTION

2 O'Connell, International Law 914 (2d ed. 1970).*

Consular Functions as Compared with Diplomatic Functions

The institution of the consul derives from the practice in medieval Italy of electing a representative from among the foreign merchants resident in a city, and until very recently consular functions were principally commercial and not diplomatic, though judicial jurisdiction over nationals of the consul's State was sometimes vested in consuls, especially in undeveloped countries. Today, however, the distinction between commercial and diplomatic activity is difficult to maintain. Much formal diplomatic negotiation is in fact trade promotion, and much trade promotion leads to diplomatic overtures. This fusion of functions has led inevitably to a fusion of the diplomatic and consular services, so that a career officer may be posted on one tour to an embassy secretariat, on the next to a trade mission, and on the next to a consulate proper. Some embassies make no pretence even of keeping the consular service distinct, and house it in the same building, and to some extent with the same personnel.

Traditionally, consuls were concerned only with commercial and like matters, but in recent times they have come to represent all man-

* Reprinted with the permission of
Sweet & Maxwell, Ltd., London.

ner of governmental activity, such as supervising treaty implementation and performing duties with respect to government-owned merchant ships. These functions are not very distinguishable from those of diplomats.

In 1963 a Convention on Consular Relations was signed at Vienna, and Article 5 lists consular functions at length.

(a) Promotion of commerce. Consuls prepare trade reports, make trade inquiries, supply commercial information, arrange trade fairs, investigate infractions of commercial treaties, and visa invoices and certificates of origin.

(b) Supervision of shipping. They also supervise the papers of their national ships, and assist in matters of customs clearance, quarantine, immigration and seamen's regulations. They inspect their national ships to enable them to procure whatever information is necessary to prepare necessary documents. They take protective measures with respect to wrecked national ships. They also settle disputes according to national law among seamen or between seamen and the ship, supervise the signing on of seamen, and their discharge, and arrange their repatriation, or disposal of their property on decease.

(c) Protection of nationals. The United Kingdom Consular Instructions refer to the duty of a consul to watch over and take all proper steps to safeguard the interests of British subjects. These steps include advice and assistance to nationals in their dealings with the local authorities, and intervention where necessary to secure for them the benefit of treaty rights or rights under international law. Consuls report to the diplomatic authorities any failure to secure redress, and intervene in judicial proceedings if a denial of justice occurs. They see that their nationals have proper legal advice, are detained under satisfactory conditions and have necessary access to the outside world. Certain consular conventions require that consuls be informed immediately of the arrest of their nationals.

Sometimes consuls are instructed to assist their nationals who became ill or indigent.

(d) Representational functions. Many countries authorise their consuls to represent their nationals in civil litigation and in the administration of deceased estates. Obviously their competence so to do will depend greatly upon the law of the receiving country. Accordingly, United States consuls are instructed to discharge these functions only if treaty, usage or the local law permits, but in any event are prohibited from acting as agents or trustees of deceased estates. Some legal systems acknowledge the right of foreign consuls to represent their nationals, even in the absence of treaties. The laws of several of the United States tend in this direction, especially those of New York, although in the absence of treaties consuls will not be allowed to exercise rights "personal" to the national. Also, the right of consuls to take bona vacantia as against the right of the host State is dependent upon treaty. The United States has, however, been reluctant to accord foreign consuls broad representative and administrative functions, and the 1949 consular convention with the United Kingdom which contained provisions to this effect, was not ratified, and was replaced in 1951 with a convention conferring on British consuls only the right to receive for transmission abroad the proceeds of a court administration of deceased estates. United States consuls abroad are authorised to take possession of personal estates of deceased nationals, list the assets, dispose of them, collect and pay debts, and account to the successors. United Kingdom consuls may fully or partially administer estates of British subjects if the local law permits and this is reasonably necessary for the protection of British interests. Foreign consuls of countries specified by Order in Council may exercise certain powers relating to the administration of deceased estates in England.

Vienna Convention on Consular Relations. The Vienna Convention on Consular Relations was signed on April 24, 1963. The convention entered into force on March 19, 1967; as of January 1, 1980, 95 states were parties to the convention. It entered into force for the United States on December 24, 1969. 21 U.S.T. 77, 596 U.N.T.S. 261.

RE RISSMANN

Italy, Court of Genoa, 1970.
1 Italian Yearbook of International Law 254 (1975).*

Facts.—By complaint lodged with the Public Prosecutor of Genoa dated 13 July 1966, Mrs. Mancuso Santa in Cucco declared:

that by decision dated 21 July 1964 the Genoa Minors Court had given her custody of her minor daughter Muller Maria Luisa, born in Genoa on 7 June 1947 from her first marriage with the German citizen Muller Werner; which marriage was dissolved by the Hannover Court with a sentence of divorce on 2 October 1956, recognized and made effective in Italy by the Court of Appeal of Genoa by judgment dated 31 March 1961;

that following such judgment the minor had acquired Italian citizenship, in accordance with a note dated 5 July 1965 from the Prefettura of Genoa;

that by letter dated 8 March 1966 addressed to the Consul General for Germany in Genoa and, with a copy to the Head of the Police, she, as legitimate guardian of the said minor child, had given notice of her disapproval to the issuing of a passport or of any other equivalent document to the said minor, even if requested by a third party;

* * *

that in March 1966, she, the complainant, following a serious act of indiscipline by the minor * * * had agreed for her to stay in the boarding house Istituto Madri Pie, Via Galata 40, Genoa * * *;

* * *

that, however, on the morning of 11 July 1966 a nun of the Institute had informed her that her daughter had gone out * * * and had not come back * * *.

* * *

Therefore the complainant formally called for punishment of whoever was responsible for the disappearance of her daughter, a minor of less than 21 years of age, of the removal of her from her mother's guardianship and of any other criminal action arising from the facts reported by her or subsequently arising therefrom * * *.

Following the summons the Public Prosecutor proceeded to verify the facts reported therein and the further circumstances arising therefrom * * *.

On the basis of such results and after acquiring copies of the statements made during the guardianship proceedings by the minor to the President of the Genoa Court for Minors, * * * the Public Prosecutor made the charge referred to in the heading against Dr. Rissmann, sending a copy thereof to the Consulate of the German Federal Republic in Genoa under cover of a note dated 8 August 1966.

However, the German Embassy in Rome, by memorandum dated 25 August 1966 addressed to the Ministry of Foreign Affairs and through it transmitted to the Ministry of Justice who also sent a copy to the Public Prosecutor in Genoa, stated that Dr. Rissmann had "in the exercise of his functions and following written request by the father of the German national Maria Luisa Muller, born 7 June 1947, whom he had the right to legally represent, issued her with a German passport", and invoked for the Consul Rissmann the consular immunity provided for in the first paragraph of art. 43 of the Vienna Convention on Consular Relations dated 24 October 1963, ratified by both Italy and Germany, stating that in view of this the Consul Rissmann had been ordered not to appear in Court.

* * *

Law.—The question as to whether or not consular immunity exists is clearly a preliminary question to be decided since it is relevant to whether or not Dr. Rissmann is exempt from the jurisdiction of this criminal Court. First and foremost, it calls for consideration as to the nationality of the minor Maria Luisa Muller.

There is no doubt that she, German iure sanguinis having been born of parents who were both German at that time, never lost German nationality according to the German law on citizenship dated 22 July 1913.

* * *

It is * * * established that in the same way as Italy, maintaining that Muller had acquired Italian nationality iure communicationis, could legitimately consider her purely as an Italian citizen ignoring her dual nationality, so also could the German Federal Republic, and consequently also the Consul, Rissmann, who was one of the representatives operating abroad, legitimately consider her a German citizen.

Clearly, in view of the fact that, inter alia, the minor had been legally entrusted by the Italian judge to her mother, the Consul in issuing her with a passport as a German citizen and facilitating her return to Germany was certainly acting in conflict with the Italian legal system and behaving in a manner liable to give rise to the criminal charge contained in the indictment in this case.

But at this point it is necessary to clarify the question as to whether or not there exist in the present case the necessary conditions and circumstances for the application of consular immunity.

According to agreed doctrine (developed from jurisprudence of the principal States) and to general international law, even prior to the last Convention on Consular Relations concluded in Vienna on 24 April 1963 in conformity with the principles of the Charter of the United Nations, there existed functional immunity for Consuls: namely, exemption from local jurisdiction in civil and criminal matters in respect of acts performed in the exercise of their office. Following the same doctrine, a demonstration of the common feeling of states on this matter was afforded by Article II of the Convention of Montreux dated 8 May 1937. This provided that "foreign consuls are subject to the jurisdiction of mixed Courts subject always to the exceptions recognised by international law. In particular, they are not subject to indictment in respect of actions carried out in the exercise of their office".

It should be added that functional immunity, already then generally recognised even in the absence of specific provisions in consular conventions, finds its justification in the general principle according to which the consul's acts, even though they may be valid within the legal system of territorial State and thus produce legal consequences therein, constitute an activity of the State to which the Consul belongs, and not of the consul personally, since, in the exercise of his office, he must answer to his government. Such an immunity is not, therefore, confined to judicial proceedings. It is based on a principle of substantive law, and continues even after his tour of office as consul has terminated.

* * *

We now come to the Convention on Consular Relations signed in Vienna 24 April 1963 by 92 States members of the United Nations, including Italy and the German Federal Republic, and implemented by law No. 804 of 9 August 1967. The Court observes that the functional immunity of consuls is explicitly covered by Art. 43 of the Convention, under the title "Immunity from Jurisdiction", the first paragraph of which provides as follows: "Consular officers and consular employees shall not be amenable to the jurisdiction of the judicial or administrative authorities of the receiving State in respect of acts performed in the exercise of consular functions".   *   *   *

We must now examine whether or not the action of the Consul Rissmann which gives rise to this case fell within the scope of his consular functions. As far as concerns the present judgment, suffice to observe that Art. 5 of the Convention includes among consular functions at letters *d*) and *e*) respectively, the issuing of passports and travel documents to citizens of the State concerned and the giving of assistance to the same: textually "Consular functions consist in: *   *   *   *d*) issuing passports and travel documents to nationals of the sending State, *   *   *   *e*) helping and assisting nationals, both individuals and bodies corporate, of the sending State".

Now, since it is certain that Muller was a German citizen, there can be no doubt that Rissmann, in issuing her with a German passport, was carrying out a true and proper official act as Consul, and this is because, in view of the fact that a minor was in question, he had not only the consent but even the express request on the part of the father, a German citizen, entitled to guardianship of her which entitlement had never lapsed *   *   *.

It should not be forgotten that Consuls, being State agents operating abroad, do not exceed the scope of their functions when they act in accordance with the laws of their country which they must comply with in so far as these laws are to be applied abroad.

As far as concerns the cooperation of Rissmann in furthering the return of the minor to Germany by means of booking and acquiring the air ticket and the assistance given to her for this purpose, it must be stressed that this undoubtedly pertains to the consular office. First and foremost, such an assistance was given to a minor German citizen, upon the request of the father, a German national, exercising guardianship rights over her. Secondly, from the knowledge that the Consul had of the history of Muller, as it had been referred to him by her and her father, he had valid reason—even independently from actual truth of the case that, as proved by evidence before the Court, had been explained to him only by the afore-mentioned as a situation of dramatic tension and intolerability—to respond to the appeal for assistance directed to him by a fellow country woman who, among other things, was by then 19 years of age.

    *   *   *

    *   *   *   [W]e must, therefore, hold that proceedings cannot be brought against Rissmann in respect of the charges made against him, since, as a person who enjoys consular immunity, he is exempted from criminal action *   *   *.

1. *Immunity from jurisdiction.* Article 43 of the convention specifies:

> 1. Consular officers and consular employees shall not be amenable to the jurisdiction of the judicial or administrative authorities of the receiving State in respect of acts performed in the exercise of consular functions.
>
> 2. The provisions of paragraph 1 of this Article shall not, however, apply in respect of a civil action either:
>
> > (a) arising out of a contract concluded by a consular officer or a consular employee in which he did not contract expressly or impliedly as an agent of the sending State; or
> >
> > (b) by a third party for damage arising from an accident in the receiving State caused by a vehicle, vessel or aircraft.

2. *Personal inviolability of consular officers.* Article 41 of the convention provides:

> 1. Consular officers shall not be liable to arrest or detention pending trial, except in the case of a grave crime and pursuant to a decision by the competent judicial authority.
>
> 2. Except in the case specified in paragraph 1 of this Article, consular officers shall not be committed to prison or liable to any other form of restriction on their personal freedom save in execution of a judicial decision of final effect.
>
> 3. If criminal proceedings are instituted against a consular officer, he must appear before the competent authorities. Nevertheless, the proceedings shall be conducted with the respect due to him by reason of his official position and, except in the case specified in paragraph 1 of this Article, in a manner which will hamper the exercise of consular functions as little as possible. When, in the circumstances mentioned in paragraph 1 of this Article, it has become necessary to detain a consular officer, the proceedings against him shall be instituted with the minimum of delay.

3. *Inviolability of the consular premises.* Article 31 of the convention provides:

> 1. Consular premises shall be inviolable to the extent provided in this Article.
>
> 2. The authorities of the receiving State shall not enter that part of the consular premises which is used exclusively for the purpose of the work of the consular post except with the consent of the head of the consular post or of his designee or of the head of the diplomatic mission of the sending State. The consent of the head of the consular post may, however, be assumed in case of fire or other disaster requiring prompt protective action.

3.   Subject to the provisions of paragraph 2 of this Article, the receiving State is under a special duty to take all appropriate steps to protect the consular premises against any intrusion or damage and to prevent any disturbance of the peace of the consular post or impairment of its dignity.

4.   The consular premises, their furnishings, the property of the consular post and its means of transport shall be immune from any form of requisition for purposes of national defence or public utility. If expropriation is necessary for such purposes, all possible steps shall be taken to avoid impeding the performance of consular functions, and prompt, adequate and effective compensation shall be paid to the sending State.

Chapter 14

SOME STRUCTURAL PROBLEMS OF INTERNATIONAL ORGANIZATIONS

When individuals decide to associate with each other in a long-term business venture or to carry out a long-term charitable purpose, they organize their efforts with reference to the laws of some nation, state or, indeed, as in the case of the United States, the laws of one of its constituent states (e.g., Delaware). Thus they create associations such as partnerships and corporations and their analogues in various countries. Under the relevant domestic laws, these associations have defined legal attributes, such as, in Anglo-American law applicable to corporations, the right of the association to be treated as a separate legal entity (to sue or be sued in its own name, to insulate its members from personal liability for its debts). Indeed under domestic legal systems, there are frequently central legal processes by which such associations are created, as discussed at paze 734. Whether the legal attributes accorded such an association under the domestic law of the state of its creation will be recognized in other states will be determined in turn by the domestic law of such other states.

If two or more states desire to enter into a long-term relationship for the accomplishment of general goals they too might create an association (say, a non-profit corporation) under the domestic laws of some particular nation state. On the other hand, to escape the control of a single domestic legal system, they may organize themselves purely by entering into an international agreement with each other, purporting to create a new entity without reference to the creative powers of a domestic legal system. Such an agreement may carry any of the variety of labels referred to on page 952, not infrequently the label of charter. But just as there is no central legal process by which states are created in the international legal system, so also there is no central legal process by which intergovernmental organizations or international organizations are created in the international legal system. This lack of a central legal process or of a developed body of international law creates questions relating to the structure of such organizations. A few of these structural questions are explored in this chapter, following a short sketch of some major organizations.

SECTION A. PROFILE OF SOME INTERNATIONAL ORGANIZATIONS

JACOB AND ATHERTON, THE DYNAMICS OF INTERNATIONAL ORGANIZATION 18 (1965).*

Evolution of International Organizations

Three main types of international organization have developed over the last hundred years. First, administrative agencies have been set up for specialized technical tasks, such as regulation of international means of communication. Second, machinery for adjudication or conciliation of international disputes was established. Third, general international organizations were created on either a regional or global basis to provide collective security and promote cooperative action on a broad range of other international problems.

International Administration

International administration started with private associations that attempted to advance their particular interests across national frontiers. The problems of international rail traffic led to organization of the International Railway Union, a body representing the individual railroad managements in Europe. The International Red Cross was created as a private effort to assist the wounded and ease the suffering of other war victims. Gradually, governments agreed to support or even participate in some private bodies; and, ultimately, a number of "public international unions," usually representing only governments, were formed to carry out administrative tasks that required public authority. In 1856, for instance, the Treaty of Paris created two international commissions to regulate and improve navigation on the Danube River. The Universal Postal Union, as mentioned above, was established in 1874, the first International Telegraphic Union in 1865, the International Commission for Air Navigation and the International Labor Organization at the Paris Peace Conference in 1919. The structure and powers of such bodies have changed from time to time. Some have merged into new and different organizations. But the machinery for international administration has expanded and become permanent.

*   *   *

League of Nations

The League of Nations was the first attempt to develop a comprehensive global international organization to preserve peace. It was born a compromise between the vision of a world parliament championed by Woodrow Wilson and a pact among the victorious Allies to maintain the peace treaties as demanded by French leaders. It was designed, in part, to provide the machinery for mutual aid among its members if they were victims of attack. At the same time,

* Reprinted with permission from Jacob and Atherton, The Dynamics of International Organization (Homeward, Ill., The Dorsey Press, 1965 c).

it had a much broader group of functions aimed at preventing war. It had specific responsibilities for encouraging peaceful settlement of disputes, developing plans for limitation of armaments, and supervising administration of the former German and Turkish colonies. The League was furthermore entrusted with supervision over international agreements relating to traffic in drugs and women and children, collection of information in all matters of international interest, and direction of international bureaus. The organization, though far from a government, nevertheless had broad competence to care for the world's welfare, and it quickly came to occupy a position in international affairs far beyond the status of the more specialized agencies that had previously existed. It served at once as a world forum, an instrument for continuous diplomatic negotiation, an international civil service, and an organ of economic and social collaboration. The League could not fulfill its political role as custodian of international security in the face of the resurgent nationalism of the 1930's and, in particular, the aggressive policies of Nazi Germany, Fascist Italy, and Japan. The organization was also seriously weakened because the United States had failed to become a member; the U.S. Senate insisted on reservations to the Covenant that were unacceptable to President Wilson. But the League's economic, financial, statistical, and social services grew so significant that they were continued even during the second world war.

The United Nations System

The framework of international society was so badly shattered by the war that Britain, Russia, the United States, and China decided not to revive the League but, instead, to build a new general international organization through which they could continue their wartime collaboration and attempt to assure a durable peace. Concrete proposals for the organization were worked out while the war was still in full progress, in joint discussions of the four powers at Dumbarton Oaks (an estate in Washington, D. C.) from August 21 to October 7, 1944. They placed primary emphasis on the security functions of the agency and provided for the big powers to assume major responsibility for the maintenance of peace. On the other hand, formation of the organization was divorced from the process of making the peace with the Axis so that it might be less hampered than the League by identification with the specific settlements imposed by the victors. The Dumbarton Oaks proposals were made public and were discussed intensively for over six months, particularly in the United States and Great Britain. Criticisms and suggestions were invited from other governments, from private organizations, and individuals. In April, 1945, 50 nations assembled at San Francisco for the United Nations Conference on International Organization, which reconsidered the proposals, modified and amended them in important respects, and finally, on June 26, signed the Charter of the United Nations.

The new organization, as tailored by the smaller states, has broader functions and a more democratic division of responsibility than originally envisaged by the four sponsoring powers. It has fused the predominant power interests of the postwar world with the heritage of functional cooperation left by the League of Nations. As a matter of fact, its powers extend well beyond those of the League. In addition to providing for peaceful settlement of international disputes and for collective action to prevent or stop aggression, the Charter endowed the United Nations with very wide responsibility for promoting economic and social welfare, exercising trusteeship over the former mandates, and encouraging respect for human rights and fundamental freedoms. While five powers—Britain, the United States, U.S.S.R., France, and China—received special prerogatives, particularly in regard to peace and security, all members of the organization, large and small, were given equal voice in most of the other United Nations' activities. The United Nations has been from the beginning, therefore, more than a mere league of victors; it is, in fact, a comprehensive system for the conduct and oversight of the entire range of international affairs.

The basic organization established by the Charter includes six major organs: the General Assembly, the Security Council, the Economic and Social Council, the Trusteeship Council, the Secretariat, and the International Court of Justice. In addition, there is a vast network of subsidiary commissions, committees, and other bodies, some established by the Charter and others by the U.N. organs themselves in the course of their operations. Completing the United Nations "system" are a group of affiliated but autonomous "specialized agencies."

* * *

Specialized Agencies

In addition to the United Nations organization, * * * intergovernmental specialized agencies, functioning under their own constitutions, carry out separate programs of international action in their respective fields. They are, however, related to the United Nations by formal agreements providing that they submit reports and, in some cases, budgets to the Economic and Social Council for its consideration and approval. They agree to consider recommendations made to them by the United Nations and, in particular, to assist the regular organs of the U.N. in carrying out decisions related to the maintenance of peace and security. Most of the specialized agencies are also organizationally involved with the U.N. as participants in the United Nations Expanded Program of Technical Assistance.

Three of these agencies are public international unions that existed prior to creation of the United Nations, but their constitutions are slightly changed in order to bring about their integration with the United Nations system. These are: Universal Postal Union (UPU), established 1875; International Telecommunications Union (ITU), originally established 1865; International Labor Organization (ILO), established 1919.

[O]ther specialized agencies, newly organized during or after the second World War, are:

Food and Agricultural Organization (FAO), 1944.

International Monetary Fund, 1944.

International Bank for Reconstruction and Development, 1944.

United Nations Educational, Scientific, and Cultural Organization (UNESCO), 1945.

World Health Organization (WHO), 1946.

International Civil Aviation Organization (ICAO), 1947.

World Meteorological Organization (WMO), 1950.

International Finance Corporation (IFC), 1956.

Intergovernmental Maritime Consultative Organization (IMCO), 1958.

Another specialized agency, the International Refugee Organization ceased operations at the end of 1951.

The International Atomic Energy Agency (IAEA), established in 1957, has a working relationship with the United Nations, although it is not formally designated a specialized agency.[a]

----

1. *Regional organizations and the Charter of the United Nations.* Article 51 (Chapter VII) and Chapter VIII (Articles 52–54) of the charter make it clear that states members of the universal organization and of the universal specialized international agencies may also belong to regional groupings of states. Chapter VIII does not use the term regional organizations but the looser regional arrangements, a usage criticized by Professor Hans Kelsen in his Law of the United Nations but understandable to negotiators, especially in the light of the problems about regional arrangements that arose at the San Francisco Conference, at which the charter was prepared in final form.

Behind the San Francisco debates lay a basic question: Should the United Nations be a worldwide association of states or an association of regional associations of states? Within the United States government the issue was an open one for some time, in part because one of the proposed reservations of the Senate minority that blocked United States ratification of the Covenant of the League of Nations in 1919 had sought to ensure that regional arrangements in the Western Hemisphere would not be affected by the covenant. Cordell Hull

a. Other inter-governmental organizations related to the United Nations are the International Development Association (IDA), 1960, the World Intellectual Property Organization (WIPO), 1977, the International Fund for Agricultural Development (IFAD), 1977, and the General Agreement on Tariffs and Trade (GATT), 1948 (for which the International Commission for the International Trade Organization, ICITO, serves as the secretariat). For descriptions of the functions of the specialized and other related agencies, see the Yearbooks of the United Nations.

recalls in his memoirs that President Franklin D. Roosevelt himself made the decision that the United States would support a universalistic concept of a United Nations. The Dumbarton Oaks Draft (U.S.) reflected this viewpoint, but at San Francisco the Latin American countries and smaller states elsewhere (such as Australia) were dissatisfied with the role provided for regional aggregations of states. The charter reflects what is known as the Vandenberg Compromise (proposed by the late Senator Arthur Vandenberg), authorizing collective defense "if an armed attack occurs." The result is that pre-attack treaty arrangements have been made for purposes of collective security within regions (but not limited to states actually within such regions). These regional arrangements are always based on Article 51 and sometimes on Chapter VIII as well. Such arrangements and the activities of the institutions created by them must under the charter be consistent with the Purposes and Principles (Chapter I) of the United Nations. Moreover, Article 53 makes it clear that regional arrangements cannot take enforcement action (as distinguished from collective self-defense) except as authorized or required by the Security Council.

It will be noted that the charter says nothing for or against regional organizations that are not related to self-defense, collective security, and peace-keeping. States members of the United Nations are not limited by the charter as to a preference for regional over universal mechanisms for such things as economic and social development, scientific and cultural improvement, and even common, peaceful political objectives. There are few regional organizations that seem to fit entirely into the category of those not covered at all by the charter. Perhaps the Organization of African Unity does. The Organization of American States (OAS), which did not come into existence until after the charter of the United Nations was in effect, has many goals and functions that lie outside the force-security-defense field, but the OAS also has subtle and somewhat complicated relationships with its companion arrangement, the Inter-American (Rio) Pack of Reciprocal Assistance. The latter, like the North Atlantic Treaty Organization (NATO) and the eastern socialist bloc's Warsaw Pact, is basically an Article 51 organization for collective self-defense. For its part, though, NATO is seen by some as having evolved a few functions that are not directly related to the primary defense purpose of the organization.

Regional arrangements in some instances have sub-institutions or organs that in name and function overlap similar sub-institutions of the United Nations. Thus, there are an Inter-American Economic and Social Council (IA–ECOSOC) under the OAS and the Economic and Social Council of the United Nations. There are Inter-American and European human rights commissions and also one in the United Nations.

The jurisdictional lines between the U.N., the universal international organization, its organs and its linked specialized agencies, and regional organizations and their organs and linked specialized agencies are by no means clear on paper or in practice. The only rule that seems clearly laid down is that a regional organization cannot engage in enforcement action. See Chapter 19. One of the important activities of national decision makers with a legal bent and a political sense is to decide which channel to use to achieve particular objectives, the universal or a regional one. Of course, even with both universal and regional international organizations available, the state-to-state channel may not be foreclosed either. This is particularly so as to agreements related to coordinated or unified positions within such organizations, such as how to vote on particular proposals.

2. *What is the European Community (EC)?* [a] An arrangement between states in a particular area to create free trade between themselves could be a regional international organization. But if free trade were no more than a treaty undertaking, with no transnational structure for administration, the treaty might not create an international organization (entity) at all. Military alliances without structure of earlier centuries are not regarded today—and certainly were not then—as entities.

Probably, however, most of the free trade associations and common markets that exist today are regional international organizations, e. g., entities. (As yet there is no worldwide or even transregional free trade area or common arrangement.) The European Free Trade Association (EFTA), the Latin American Free Trade Association (LAFTA), the Central American Common Market (CACM) and the Andean Community (ANCOM) all have some organs of a transnational nature. The Caribbean, African and Southeast Asian trade arrangements are somewhat harder to analyze at this time.

But the European Economic Community, the world's most outstanding economic association of states, has reached such a high level of development as to have moved beyond the field of international organizations as they are presently understood. The EEC is more than a common market (with zero tariffs between its members and a common external tariff as to the rest of the world)—thus differing from a free trade association (in which each member state keeps its own tariff structures as against non-members). It is a limited federated structure for some economic and some social purposes.

a. On the basis of the authorities granted to them in the international agreements that create them, there are three European communities with identical state membership. They are the European Coal and Steel Community (ECSC), the European Economic Community (EEC, created by the Treaty of Rome), and the European Atomic Community (EURATOM). The first became operational in 1953, the other two in 1958. In 1965 the member countries entered into a Merger Treaty that provided a single council and a single commission for the three communities. This treaty also provided for a single staff. The assembly and the court were dealt with in the same way in all three of the earlier treaties, so the Merger Treaty did not have to make new provisions as to them. In a technically correct way there are today still three communities, but in ordinary usage the term European Community is correct enough.

But, granted its advanced stage of institutional development (council of ministers, commission, court, assembly, large technical staff), *why* is the European Community more akin to a federated state than to an international organization? Its members are still states in every sense. It is because the community has the power, once its relevant organs have reached decisions in accordance with the voting and other allocations of decision-making authority, to act directly within the territory of the member states. The Court of the Communities has even declared national legislation and the national constitutional authority therefor unavailing as against the commands of the Treaty of Rome. The commission, subject to judicial review by the court, can assess nationals of member states for violations of the community antitrust and other regulatory laws.

The Grand Design of the first conceptualizers of European unification was that Western Europe would evolve into a new, federated state by movement from a customs union, to economic unification, to a common defense force, to political fusion. Resurgences of nationalism in France have twice slowed or stopped this movement. At the present time the community has expanded from six to ten members; and the United Kingdom has called for the strengthening of the assembly, to make it into a law-making, rather than a law-advising body, through direct election of its members by the people of the member states. Such expectations and the growing realization of the member states that they must develop a common monetary policy (which cannot be done without a common budgetary and tax policy) are seen in some quarters as justifying a revival of expectations for the complete federation of Western Europe.

The EC has already developed so much law-stuff of its own that its treatment in a general course on international law is impossible. Some with long sight and high idealism see in what has and may come to pass in Western Europe the possibility that evolution beyond the present state system will proceed through the development of regional governments to coalescence into world government.

3. *Voting formulas.* A fundamental principle of conventional international relations practice is that all states are juridically and politically equal and sovereign (not subject to external command). Equality requires that each state in a decision-making relationship with another state or states have the same vote as any other state. Sovereignty means that no state may be compelled without its consent to accept a decision or action. Thus there have developed the twin principles of one-state, one-vote and of unanimity.

As to undertakings looking to future developments, in old-fashioned politico-military alliances, these twin principles did not cause much difficulty. Indeed, sometimes they were seen as having a desirable stabilizing influence or as a protection for one or the other of the parties. Obviously they do not cause problems as to bilateral agreements.

But most types of modern international organizations, universal and regional, are set up primarily to deal with a continuum of events. The international agreements that create the organizations are only frameworks of principles and procedures for decisions that can be made only as events unfold, situations develop and foreseen general needs become specific. Here the twin principles cannot but get in the way of, complicate or abort decision-making. The architects of international organizations have tried in various ways to reduce the dimensions of the problems thus created.

One approach is to reduce the principle of one-state, one-vote. The weighted voting formulas of the World Bank Group and of the International Monetary Fund are examples of this approach. In these organizations decisions are made by a majority of the votes cast, but the votes themselves are mathematical functions of the invested capital of the member states. Needless to say, weighted voting is not popular with states with slight voting rights; but sometimes such states organize themselves into blocs that by aggregation can increase their combined voting strength. Or states with low voting strength may align themselves with one or more of the states with high voting strength.

Weighted voting of a different sort is seen in the rule requiring the concurrence of the permanent members of the Security Council (Article 27 of the charter).

The other approach to the problem of freeing-up decision-making in international organizations is to reduce the required vote for a decision from "all" to various fractions of "all." The approach leaves all members with equal votes, but the outcome is determined by some type of majority (three-fourths, two-thirds, plurality) of the votes cast. The nearer the required voting strength approaches unanimity, of course, the easier it is for groups of states to band together in blocs to block action.

In your study of the United Nations, you will note various approaches to the definition of effective majorities. See, especially, Article 18, dealing with voting in the General Assembly. In the Organization of American States many types of questions, such as the exclusion or re-inclusion of the Castro government of Cuba, must be taken by a two-thirds vote, and the votes of Brazil and El Salvador, of the United States and Bolivia, are equal.

The use of voting formulas during the transition period (1958–70) of the EEC, from partial to full economic union as to trade, eased the shift from a strictly national control of events. Even today the allocation among the community members of portions of the total voting strength established for decisions that still require national assent is carefully, almost cunningly, arranged. What is sought is to ensure that possible blocs of two big states cannot dominate all the other states of the community (big and small) and that the small ones not be able to form blocs capable of stopping action.

In 1965, France under President de Gaulle almost stopped the evolution—and even threatened the continued existence—of the community. One motivation was fear that majority voting in the final phases of the transition period would permit unacceptable decisions to be forced on France as to the common agricultural policy of the community. France simply quit participating in the Council of Ministers, and the other five decided to do nothing of importance without France's participation. The impasse was finally resolved by a tacit political understanding that the voting strength of the community would never—or almost never—be used against a strongly dissident, important member. Whether this understanding or the careful efforts to anticipate and avoid possible voting blocs will survive in the expanded community is a very interesting and important matter. Perhaps one day a member state whose nationalism has not yet been transferred to the community will have to face the question of what to do if soundly outvoted on an issue of importance to it. The three merged treaties that establish the community do not carry provisions for terms of years, termination, or secession.

SECTION B. THE INTERNATIONAL CIVIL SERVANT

Law governing the relationships between the United Nations and its employees. The basic law is, of course, the charter. Articles of special significance to the question of the status of the employees of the organization (international civil servants) are Articles 97 through 101, defining the powers and duties of the Secretary-General of the United Nations and his staff, and Articles 104 and 105, dealing with questions of capacity, privileges and immunities.

In addition to the charter, there are basic international agreements detailing in more specific form the broad provisions of the charter. A major document is the Convention on the Privileges and Immunities of the United Nations, 21 U.S.T. 1418, 1 U.N.T.S. 15, which came into force early in the life of the organization, but was not ratified by the United States until April 1970. The organization has also entered into conventions with states in which it has located its principal offices; the agreement governing the United Nations premises in New York City is the Headquarters Agreement with the United Nations, 61 Stat. 756, 11 U.N.T.S. 11.

Beyond agreements of general applicability are those the organization has entered into with states on whose territory it is carrying on a specific, temporary project. For example, the Secretary-General of the United Nations concluded an agreement with the government of Egypt in 1957 on the status of the United Nations Emergency Forces in that country, dealing with such matters as civil and criminal jurisdiction over members of the force, privileges and immunities and the like. U.N. Doc. A/3526, Gen.Ass.Off.Rec. XI, Annexes,

Agenda Item 66, pp. 52–57; Sohn, Recent Cases on United Nations Law 225 (1963).

In determining what law governs a particular situation arising in the United States, it is of course necessary to analyze the several possibly applicable treaties and legislation not only in terms of their substantive provisions but also, in case of conflict, in terms of the chronology of their enactment or coming into force. See p. 25 for a discussion of the relationship between treaties and legislation under the law of the United States.

The Convention on the Privileges and Immunities of the United Nations and excerpts from the Headquarters Agreement and the International Organizations Immunities Act are set forth in the Documentary Supplement.

CONVENTION ON THE PRIVILEGES AND IMMUNITIES OF THE UNITED NATIONS OF FEBRUARY 13, 1946

21 U.S.T. 1418, 1 U.N.T.S. 15.

Article VII
United Nations Laissez-Passer

Section 24. The United Nations may issue United Nations laissez-passer to its officials. These laissez-passer shall be recognized and accepted as valid travel documents by the authorities of Members, taking into account the provisions of Section 25.

Section 25. Applications for visas (where required) from the holders of United Nations laissez-passer, when accompanied by a certificate that they are travelling on the business of the United Nations, shall be dealt with as speedily as possible. In addition, such persons shall be granted facilities for speedy travel.

Section 26. Similar facilities to those specified in Section 25 shall be accorded to experts and other persons who, though not the holders of United Nations laissez-passer, have a certificate that they are travelling on the business of the United Nations.

Section 27. The Secretary-General, Assistant Secretaries-General and Directors travelling on United Nations laissez-passer on the business of the United Nations shall be granted the same facilities as are accorded to diplomatic envoys.

Section 28. The provisions of this article may be applied to the comparable officials of specialized agencies if the agreements for relationship made under Article 63 of the Charter so provide.

8 WHITEMAN, DIGEST OF INTERNATIONAL LAW
334 (1967)

On July 9, 1959, the United Nations Secretariat addressed the following note to the United States Mission to the United Nations at New York:

* * * the United States Mission has invited the views of the Secretariat as to the implications of a possible accession [to the Convention on the Privileges and Immunities of the United Nations, February 13, 1946, 1 UNTS 15] by the United States subject to a reservation as to the United Nations laissez-passer established by Article VII of the Convention.

In reply the Secretariat wishes to take this opportunity to emphasize the great importance to the United Nations of the fullest recognition of the laissez-passer. Of the States Members of the Organization sixty-one have to date acceded to the Convention and none has yet proposed a reservation with respect to the laissez-passer. Moreover, it has from the beginning been a constant preoccupation of the Organization to obtain from other States, pending their accession, a recognition in practice of the laissez-passer as a valid travel document.

* * * Both its issuance and its use are subject to strict control, with the result that it may be carried only by officials and then only during actual travel in the interests of the Organization; on official duty, on home leave at the expense of the Organization, or in similar circumstances specially authorized by the Secretary-General. In this manner it serves to establish the identity of United Nations officials; to bring to the attention of various government authorities throughout the world the specific texts, in each of the official languages, of the articles of the Convention determining the legal status of officials; to enable governments to enter visas in a travel document which they can know will be used by the bearer only in his capacity as a member of the staff of the international organization; to serve as a travel document for officials who are stateless or otherwise unable to avail themselves of a national passport for travel on behalf of the Organization; and, finally, to permit members of an international Secretariat to travel strictly as such, without impediments in any particular country which might otherwise be imposed upon bearers of given national passports.

Because of this very real practical importance of the laissez-passer to a world-wide organization, it will be understood that the United Nations must necessarily view with genuine concern any measure which might undermine the effectiveness of this essential travel document. It seems inevitable that a reservation to Article VII of the Convention on the part of the very Government which is host to the Headquarters of the United Nations— the Government to and from whose territory more international personnel must travel than in any other country—must gravely impair the status of the laissez-passer as an effective travel document. In this connection it will also be recalled that a major purpose in the decision to adopt a Convention pursuant to Article 105 of the Charter was to secure "the greatest uniformity in application" of the privileges necessary for the fulfillment of the purposes of the Organization. (First Report of the Sub-Committee on Privileges and Immunities, Official Records of the General Assembly, First Part of the First Session, Sixth Committee, Annex 3 to Summary Records, para. 3.)

In view of the value of the laissez-passer as a practical device to facilitate the travel of United Nations personnel, it is permissible to inquire whether practical advantage would be retained by the United States if it were to enter a reservation to Article VII. To do so could not effect the entry and exit, the transit to the Headquarters, of officials of the United Nations, since Section 18(d) of the Convention would still assure them right of entry and freedom from immigration restrictions for themselves and their immediate families * * *. [The United States] has already conferred unimpeded right of transit on such persons by the terms of Sections 11(1) of the Headquarters Agreement between the United Nations and the United States.

Inasmuch as it is only officials who are entitled to the United Nations laissez-passer, and inasmuch as this class of persons is already assured transit to and from the Headquarters by Section 11 of the Headquarters Agreement, it would appear that a reservation to Article VII could constitute no more than a reservation to the existence of an official travel document as such, without affecting the substantive right of staff to travel * * *.[a]

UNITED STATES CHANGES PROCEDURES GOVERNING TRAVEL OF HUNGARIAN OFFICIALS

45 United States Department of State Bulletin 67 (1961).

The U.S. Government was informed by the Government of the Hungarian People's Republic on June 21, 1961, that, effective July 1, 1961, the existing authorization requirement for travel of U.S. Government personnel in Hungary would be replaced by a procedure under which U.S. personnel may travel within Hungary upon advance notification to the Hungarian Government of the planned travel. The U.S. Government has, therefore, informed the Government of the Hungarian People's Republic that, effective July 1, 1961, personnel of

----

a. When the United States acceded to the convention it did not enter a reservation to the provisions on laissez-passer. It did, however, enter a reservation to the provisions on privileges and immunities: "Nothing * * * shall be construed to grant any person who has abused his privileges of residence by activities in the United States outside his official capacity exemption from the laws and regulations of the United States regarding the continued residence of aliens * * *." 21 U.S.T. 1418, 1442.

the Hungarian Legation in Washington and the Hungarian Mission to the United Nations in New York may travel within the United States upon advance notification to the U.S. Government of the planned travel.

These procedures apply, as heretofore, only to travel which exceeds a radius of 25 miles from Washington or New York City or 40 kilometers from Budapest, as appropriate.

RESTRICTIONS ON MOVEMENT—THE PALESTINE LIBERATION ORGANIZATION

Rovine, Digest of United States Practice in International Law
1974, at 27 (1975).

In Anti-Defamation League v. Kissinger, et al., Civil Action No. 74C1545 before the U.S. District Court for the Eastern District of New York, the League obtained on October 31, 1974, an Order directing the Departments of State, Justice and the Treasury to show cause why the Palestine Liberation Organization (PLO) representatives, invited to participate in the 29th Session of the U.N. General Assembly, should not be denied entry into the United States, or in the alternative, granted only a restricted C–2 visa limiting their freedom of movement to the purposes of their visit to the United Nations. Before the case was heard, the Department of State decided to issue only the limited C–2 visas.

After oral argument on November 1, 1974, U.S. District Judge Mark A. Costantino denied the petitioner's motion without prejudice, subject to the condition that the members of the PLO invited to the General Assembly be issued the limited C–2 visas. The Court said, in pertinent part:

*   *   *

*   *   * This court has jurisdiction to review an alleged abuse of administrative discretion in the issuance of visas to certain members of the Palestine Liberation Organization.

This problem must be viewed in the context of the special responsibility which the United States has to provide access to the U.N. under the Headquarters Agreement. It is important to note for the purposes of this case that a primary goal of the U.N. is to provide a forum where peaceful discussion may displace violence as a means of resolving disputed issues. At times our responsibility to the U.N. may require us to issue visas to persons who are objectionable to certain segments of our society.

Although the fears expressed by counsel for the Anti-Defamation League may have some basis, this court trusts that the law enforcement authorities will provide adequate security for the individual petitioners as they have apparently done in the past. It is worth noting that the denial of visas to these PLO representatives would not necessarily enhance petitioners' security.

The government's concern for security is evidenced by its recent decision to issue restrictive C–2 visas to the PLO representatives. For the reasons this court has outlined, the relief requested is denied without prejudice, subject to the condition that the C–2 visas be issued.

The court would like, however, to express its view that serious consideration should be given to the imposition of more restrictive territorial limitations on the movement of the PLO representatives.

*   *   *

In a letter dated November 7, 1974, to the Departments of State and Justice, counsel for the Anti-Defamation League requested, in light of Judge Costantino's suggestion for "more restrictive territorial limitations," that the two Departments explicitly delineate the right of movement of the PLO representatives who received the C–2 visas. (The C–2 visas issued limited the PLO delegation to a 25-mile radius from Columbus Circle in Manhattan.) The League requested an explicit limitation to bar the PLO representatives "from activity of any kind outside the physical limits of the United Nations headquarters; that it forbid any participation in demonstrations, forums, public meetings, radio and television appearances or the like off the United Nations premises. We do not ask that these restrictions apply to the activities of the PLO leaders undertaken within the territorial confines of the United Nations headquarters." The League asked that the PLO leaders "be permitted to move about in the U.S. only as necessary to fulfill the requirements of the U.N. invitation. *   *   * "

On November 18, 1974, Robert O. Blake, Deputy Assistant Secretary of State for International Organization Affairs, replied to the League as follows:

I have been asked by the Secretary of State to reply to your letter of November 7, 1974. Having considered Judge Costantino's decision and the arguments contained in your letter, as well as all aspects of the presence here of the PLO delegation for the Palestine debate and giving due regard to our responsibilities under the Headquarters Agreement, the Department has concluded that further restrictions on the activities of the PLO delegation above the strict ones already applied would not be appropriate.

You may be sure that we are fully conscious of and sympathetic with your preoccupations. Furthermore, you will recognize that the U.S. delegation strongly opposed the hearing of the PLO representatives in the manner in which they were invited. We appreciate receiving your letter, and you may be sure that we continue to give the closest attention to the concerns that motivated it.

REPARATION FOR INJURIES SUFFERED IN THE SERVICE OF THE UNITED NATIONS (ADVISORY OPINION)

International Court of Justice, 1949.
[1949] I.C.J. Rep. 174.

The COURT   *   *   * gives the following advisory opinion:

On December 3rd, 1948, the General Assembly of the United Nations adopted the following Resolution:

Whereas the series of tragic events which have lately befallen agents of the United Nations engaged in the performance of their duties raises, with greater urgency than ever, the question of the arrangements to be made by the United Nations with a view to ensuring to its agents the fullest measure of protection in the future and ensuring that reparation be made for the injuries suffered; and

Whereas it is highly desirable that the Secretary-General should be able to act without question as efficaciously as possible with a view to obtaining any reparation due; therefore

The General Assembly

Decides to submit the following legal questions to the International Court of Justice for an advisory opinion:

I. In the event of an agent of the United Nations in the performance of his duties suffering injury in circumstances involving the responsibility of a State, has the United Nations, as an Organization, the capacity to bring an international claim against the responsible de jure or de facto government with a view to obtaining the reparation due in respect of the damage caused (a) to the United Nations, (b) to the victim or to persons entitled through him?

II. In the event of an affirmative reply on point I(b), how is action by the United Nations to be reconciled with such rights as may be possessed by the State of which the victim is a national?

Instructs the Secretary-General, after the Court has given its opinion, to prepare proposals in the light of that opinion, and to submit them to the General Assembly at its next regular session.

*   *   *

The questions asked of the Court relate to the "capacity to bring an international claim"; accordingly, we must begin by defining what is meant by that capacity, and consider the characteristics of the Organization, so as to determine whether, in general, these characteristics do, or do not, include for the Organization a right to present an international claim.

Competence to bring an international claim is, for those possessing it, the capacity to resort to the customary methods recognized by international law for the establishment, the presentation and the settlement of claims. Among these methods may be mentioned protest, request for an enquiry, negotiation, and request for submission to an arbitral tribunal or to the Court in so far as this may be authorized by the Statute.

This capacity certainly belongs to the State; a State can bring an international claim against another State. Such a claim takes the form of a claim between two political entities, equal in law, similar in form, and both the direct subjects of international law. It is dealt with by means of negotiation, and cannot, in the present state of the law as to international jurisdiction, be submitted to a tribunal, except with the consent of the States concerned.

When the Organization brings a claim against one of its Members, this claim will be presented in the same manner, and regulated by the same procedure. It may, when necessary, be supported by the political means at the disposal of the Organization. In these ways the Organization would find a method for securing the observance of its rights by the Member against which it has a claim.

But, in the international sphere, has the Organization such a nature as involves the capacity to bring an international claim? In order to answer this question, the Court must first enquire whether the Charter has given the Organization such a position that it possesses, in regard to its Members, rights which it is entitled to ask them to respect. In other words, does the Organization possess international personality? This is no doubt a doctrinal expression, which has sometimes given rise to controversy. But it will be used here to mean that if the Organization is recognized as having that personality, it is an entity capable of availing itself of obligations incumbent upon its Members.

* * *

The subjects of law in any legal system are not necessarily identical in their nature or in the extent of their rights, and their nature depends upon the needs of the community. Throughout its history, the development of international law has been influenced by the requirements of international life, and the progressive increase in the collective activities of States has already given rise to instances of action upon the international plane by certain entities which are not States. This development culminated in the establishment in June 1945 of an international organization whose purposes and principles are specified in the Charter of the United Nations. But to achieve these ends the attribution of international personality is indispensable.

The Charter has not been content to make the Organization created by it merely a centre "for harmonizing the actions of nations in the attainment of these common ends" (Article I, para. 4). It has equipped that centre with organs, and has given it special tasks. It has defined the position of the Members in relation to the Organization by requiring them to give it every assistance in any action undertaken by it (Article 2, para. 5), and to accept and carry out the decisions of the Security Council; by authorizing the General Assembly to make recommendations to the Members; by giving the Organization legal capacity and privileges and immunities in the territory of each of its Members; and by providing for the conclusion of agreements between the Organization and its Members. Practice—in particular the conclusion of conventions to which the Organization is a party—has confirmed this character of the Organization, which occupies a position in certain respects in detachment from its Members, and which is under a duty to remind them, if need be, of certain obligations. It must be added that the Organization is a political body, charged with political tasks of an important character, and covering a wide field namely, the maintenance of international peace and security, the development of friendly relations among nations, and the achievement of international co-operation in the solution of problems of an economic, social, cultural or humanitarian character (Article I); and in dealing with its Members it employs political means. The "Convention on the Privileges and Immunities of the United Nations" of 1946 creates rights and duties between each of the signatories and the Organization (see, in particular, Section 35). It is difficult to see how such a convention could operate except upon the international plane and as between parties possessing international personality.

In the opinion of the Court, the Organization was intended to exercise and enjoy, and is in fact exercising and enjoying, functions and rights which can only be explained on the basis of the possession of a large measure of international personality and the capacity to operate upon an international plane. It is at present the supreme type of international organization, and it could not carry out the intentions of its founders if it was devoid of international personality. It must be acknowledged that its Members, by entrusting certain functions to it, with the attendant duties and responsibilities, have clothed it with the competence required to enable those functions to be effectively discharged.

Accordingly, the Court has come to the conclusion that the Organization is an international person. That is not the same thing as saying that it is a State, which it certainly is not, or that its legal personality and rights and duties are the same as those of a State. Still less is it the same thing as saying that it is "a super-State," whatever that expression may mean. It does not even imply that all its rights and duties must be upon the international plane, any more than all the rights and duties of a State must be upon that plane. What it does mean is that it is a subject of international law and capable of possessing international rights and duties, and that it has capacity to maintain its rights by bringing international claims.

The next question is whether the sum of the international rights of the Organization comprises the right to bring the kind of international claim described in the Request for this Opinion. That is a claim against a State to obtain reparation in respect of the damage caused by the injury of an agent of the Organization in the course of the performance of his duties. Whereas a State possesses the totality of international rights and duties recognized by international law, the rights and duties of an entity such as the Organization must depend upon its purposes and functions as specified or implied in its constituent documents and developed in practice. The functions of the Organization are of such a character that they could not be effectively discharged if they involved the concurrent action, on the international plane, of fifty-eight or more Foreign Offices, and the Court concludes that the Members have endowed the Organization with capacity to bring international claims when necessitated by the discharge of its functions.

What is the position as regards the claims mentioned in the request for an opinion? Question I is divided into two points, which must be considered in turn.

Question I(a) is as follows:

> In the event of an agent of the United Nations in the performance of his duties suffering injury in circumstances involving the responsibility of a State has the United Nations, as an Organization, the capacity to bring an international claim against the responsible de jure or de facto government with a view to obtaining the reparation due in respect of the damage caused (a) to the United Nations * * * ?

The question is concerned solely with the reparation of damage caused to the Organization when one of its agents suffers injury at the same time. It cannot be doubted that the Organization has the capacity to bring an international claim against one of its Members which has caused injury to it by a breach of its international obligations towards it. The damage specified in Question I(a) means exclusively damage caused to the interests of the Organization itself, to its administrative machine, to its property and assets, and to the interests of which it is the guardian. It is clear that the Organization has the capacity to bring a claim for this damage. As the claim is based on the breach of an international obligation on the part of the Member held responsible by the Organization, the Member cannot contend that this obligation is governed by municipal law, and the Organization is justified in giving its claim the character of an international claim.

When the Organization has sustained damage resulting from a breach by a Member of its international obligations, it is impossible to see how it can obtain reparation unless it possesses capacity to bring an international claim. It cannot be supposed that in such an event all the Members of the Organization, save the defendant State, must combine to bring a claim against the defendant for the damage suffered by the Organization.

The Court is not called upon to determine the precise extent of the reparation which the Organization would be entitled to recover. It may, however, be said that the measure of the reparation should depend upon the amount of the damage which the Organization has suffered as the result of the wrongful act or omission of the defendant State and should be calculated in accordance with the rules of international law. Amongst other things, this damage would include the reimbursement of any reasonable compensation which the Organization had to pay to its agent or to persons entitled through him. Again, the death or disablement of one of its agents engaged upon a distant mission might involve very considerable expenditure in replacing him. These are mere illustrations, and the Court cannot pretend to forecast all the kinds of damage which the Organization itself might sustain.

Question I(b) is as follows:

* * * has the United Nations, as an Organization, the capacity to bring an international claim * * * in respect of the damage caused

* * * (b) to the victim or to persons entitled through him?

In dealing with the question of law which arises out of Question I(b), it is unnecessary to repeat the considerations which led to an affirmative answer being given to Question I(a). It can now be assumed that the Organization has the capacity to bring a claim on the international plane, to negotiate, to conclude a special agreement and to prosecute a claim before an international tribunal. The only legal question which remains to be considered is whether, in the course of bringing an international claim of this kind, the Organization can recover "the reparation due in respect of the damage caused * * * to the victim. * * *"

The traditional rule that diplomatic protection is exercised by the national State does not involve the giving of a negative answer to Question I(b).

In the first place, this rule applies to claims brought by a State. But here we have the different and new case of a claim that would be brought by the Organization.

In the second place, even in inter-State relations, there are important exceptions to the rule, for there are cases in which protection may be exercised by a State on behalf of persons not having its nationality.

In the third place, the rule rests on two bases. The first is that the defendant State has broken an obligation towards the national State in respect of its nationals. The second is that only the party to whom an international obligation is due can bring a claim in respect of its breach. This is precisely what happens when the Organization, in bringing a claim for damage suffered by its agent, does so by invoking the breach of an obligation towards itself. Thus, the rule of the nationality of claims affords no reason against recognizing that the Organization has the right to bring a claim for the damage referred to in Question I(b). On the contrary, the principle underlying this rule leads to the recognition of this capacity as belonging to the Organization, when the Organization invokes, as the ground of its claim, a breach of an obligation towards itself.

Nor does the analogy of the traditional rule of diplomatic protection of nationals abroad justify in itself an affirmative reply. It is not possible, by a strained use of the concept of allegience, to assimilate the legal bond which exists, under Article 100 of the Charter, between the Organization on the one hand, and the Secretary-General and the staff on the other, to the bond of nationality existing between a State and its nationals.

The Court is here faced with a new situation. The questions to which it gives rise can only be solved by realizing that the situation is dominated by the provisions of the Charter considered in the light of the principles of international law.

The question lies within the limits already established; that is to say it presupposes that the injury for which the reparation is demanded arises from a breach of an obligation designed to help an agent of the Organization in the performance of his duties. It is not a case in which the wrongful act or omission would merely constitute a breach of the general obligations of a State concerning the position of aliens; claims made under this head would be within the competence of the national State and not, as a general rule, within that of the Organization.

The Charter does not expressly confer upon the Organization the capacity to include, in its claim for reparation, damage caused to the victim or to persons entitled through him. The Court must therefore begin by enquiring whether the provisions of the Charter concerning the functions of the Organization, and the part played by its agents in the performance of those functions, imply for the Organization power to afford its agents the limited protection that would consist in the bringing of a claim on their behalf for reparation for damage suffered in such circumstances. Under international law, the Organization must be deemed to have those powers which, though not expressly provided in the Charter, are conferred upon it by necessary implication as being essential to the performance of its duties. This principle of law was applied by the Permanent Court of International Justice to the International Labour Organization in its Advisory Opinion No. 13 of July 23rd, 1926 (Series B., No. 13, p. 18), and must be applied to the United Nations.

Having regard to its purposes and functions already referred to, the Organization may find it necessary, and has in fact found it necessary, to entrust its agents with important missions to be performed in disturbed parts of the world. Many missions, from their very nature, involve the agents in unusual dangers to which ordinary persons are not exposed. For the same reason, the injuries suffered by its agents in these circumstances will sometimes have occurred in such a manner that their national State would not be justified in bringing a claim for reparation on the ground of diplomatic protection, or, at any rate, would not feel disposed to do so. Both to ensure the efficient and independent performance of these missions and to afford effective support to its agents, the Organization must provide them with adequate protection.

This need of protection for the agents of the Organization, as a condition of the performance of its functions, has already been realized, and the Preamble to the Resolution of December 3rd, 1948 * * * shows that this was the unanimous view of the General Assembly.

For this purpose, the Members of the Organization have entered into certain undertakings, some of which are in the Charter and others in complementary agreements. The content of these undertakings need not be described here; but the Court must stress the importance of the duty to render to the Organization "every assistance" which is accepted by the Members in Article 2, paragraph 5, of the Charter. It must be noted that the effective working of the Organization—the accomplishment of its task, and the independence and effectiveness of the work of its agents—require that these undertakings should be strictly observed. For that purpose, it is necessary that, when an infringement occurs, the Organization should be able to call upon the responsible State to remedy its default, and, in particular, to obtain from the State reparation for the damage that the default may have caused to its agent.

In order that the agent may perform his duties satisfactorily, he must feel that this protection is assured to him by the Organization, and that he may count on it. To ensure the independence of the agent, and, consequently, the independent action of the Organization itself, it is essential that in performing his duties he need not have to rely on any other protection than that of the Organization (save of course for the more direct and immediate protection due from the State in whose territory he may be). In particular, he should not have to rely on the protection of his own State. If he had to rely on that State, his independence might well be compromised, contrary to the principle applied by Article 100 of the Charter. And lastly, it is essential that—whether the agent belongs to a powerful or to a weak State; to one more affected or less affected by the complications of international life; to one in sympathy or not in sympathy with the mission of the agent—he should know that in the performance of his duties he is under the protection of the Organization. This assurance is even more necessary when the agent is stateless.

Upon examination of the character of the functions entrusted to the Organization and of the nature of the missions of its agents, it becomes clear that the capacity of the Organization to exercise a measure of functional protection of its agents arises by necessary intendment out of the Charter.

The obligations entered into by States to enable the agents of the Organization to perform their duties are undertaken not in the interest of the agents, but in that of the Organization. When it claims redress for a breach of these obligations, the Organization is invoking its own right, the right that the obligations due to it should be respected. On this ground, it asks for reparation of the injury suffered, for "it is a principle of international law that the breach of an engagement involves an obligation to make reparation in an adequate form"; as was stated by the Permanent Court in its Judgment No. 8 of July 26th, 1927 (Series A., No. 9, p. 21). In claiming reparation based on the injury suffered by its agent, the Organization does not represent the agent, but is asserting its own right, the right to secure respect for undertakings entered into towards the Organization.

Having regard to the foregoing considerations, and to the undeniable right of the Organization to demand that its Members shall fulfil the obligations entered into by them in the interest of the good working of the Organization, the Court is of the opinion that, in the case of a breach of these obligations, the Organization has the capacity to claim adequate reparation, and that in assessing this reparation it is authorized to include the damage suffered by the victim or by persons entitled through him.

The question remains whether the Organization has "the capacity to bring an international claim against the responsible de jure or de facto government with a view to obtaining the reparation due in respect of the damage caused (a) to the United Nations, (b) to the victim or to persons entitled through him" when the defendant State is not a member of the Organization.

In considering this aspect of Question I(a) and (b) it is necessary to keep in mind the reasons which have led the Court to give an affirmative answer to it when the defendant State is a Member of the Organization. It has now been established that the Organization has capacity to bring claims on the international plane, and that it possesses a right of functional protection in respect of its agents. Here again the Court is authorized to assume that the damage suffered involves the responsibility of a State, and it is not called upon to express an opinion upon the various ways in which that responsibility might be engaged. Accordingly the question is whether the Organization has capacity to bring a claim against the defendant State to recover reparation in respect of that damage or whether, on the contrary, the defendant State, not being a member, is justified in raising the objection that the Organization lacks the capacity to bring an international claim. On this point, the Court's opinion is that fifty States, representing the vast majority of the members of the international community, had the power, in conformity with international law, to bring into being an entity possessing objective international personality, and not merely personality recognized by them alone, together with capacity to bring international claims.

Accordingly, the Court arrives at the conclusion that an affirmative answer should be given to Question I(a) and (b) whether or not the defendant State is a Member of the United Nations.

    *   *   *

Question II is as follows:

In the event of an affirmative reply on point I(b), how is action by the United Nations to be reconciled with such rights as may be possessed by the State of which the victim is a national?

The affirmative reply given by the Court on point I(b) obliges it now to examine Question II. When the victim has a nationality, cases can clearly occur in which the injury suffered by him may engage the interest both of his national State and of the Organization. In such an event, competition between the State's right of diplomatic protection and the Organization's right of functional protection might arise, and this is the only case with which the Court is invited to deal.

In such a case, there is no rule of law which assigns priority to the one or to the other, or which compels either the State or the Organization to refrain from bringing an international claim. The Court sees no reason why the parties concerned should not find solutions inspired by goodwill and common sense, and as between the Organization and its Members it draws attention to their duty to render "every assistance" provided by Article 2, paragraph 5, of the Charter.

Although the bases of the two claims are different, that does not mean that the defendant State can be compelled to pay the reparation due in respect of the damage twice over. International tribunals are already familiar with the problem of a claim in which two or more national States are interested, and they know how to protect the defendant State in such a case.

The risk of competition between the Organization and the national State can be reduced or eliminated either by a general convention or by agreements entered into in each particular case. There is no doubt that in due course a practice will be developed, and it is worthy of note that already certain States whose nationals have been injured in the performance of missions undertaken for the Organization have shown a reasonable and co-operative disposition to find a practical solution.

* * *

The question of reconciling action by the Organization with the rights of a national State may arise in another way; that is to say, when the agent bears the nationality of the defendant State.

The ordinary practice whereby a State does not exercise protection on behalf of one of its nationals against a State which regards him as its own national, does not constitute a precedent which is relevent here. The action of the Organization is in fact based not upon the nationality of the victim but upon his status as agent of the Organization. Therefore it does not matter whether or not the State to which the claim is addressed regards him as its own national, because the question of nationality is not pertinent to the admissibility of the claim.

In law, therefore, it does not seem that the fact of the possession of the nationality of the defendant State by the agent constitutes any obstacle to a claim brought by the Organization for a breach of obligations towards it occurring in relation to the performance of his mission by that agent.

For These Reasons, the Court is of opinion

On Question I(a):

(i) unanimously,

That, in the event of an agent of the United Nations in the performance of his duties suffering injury in circumstances involving the responsibility of a Member State, the United Nations as an Organization has the capacity to bring an international claim against the responsible de jure or de facto government with a view to obtaining the reparation due in respect of the damage caused to the United Nations.

(ii) unanimously,

That, in the event of an agent of the United Nations in the performance of his duties suffering injury in circumstances involving the responsibility of a State which is not a member, the United Nations as an Organization has the capacity to bring an international claim against the responsible de jure or de facto government with a view to obtaining the reparation due in respect of the damage caused to the United Nations.

On Question I(b):

(i) by eleven votes against four,

That, in the event of an agent of the United Nations in the performance of his duties suffering injury in circumstances involving the responsibility of a Member State, the United Nations as an Organization has the capacity to bring an international claim against the responsible de jure or de facto government with a view to obtaining the reparation due in respect of the damage caused to the victim or to persons entitled through him.

(ii) by eleven votes against four,

That, in the event of an agent of the United Nations in the performance of his duties suffering injury in circumstances involving the responsibility of a State which is not a member, the United Nations as an Organization has the capacity to bring an international claim against the responsible de jure or de facto government with a view to obtaining the reparation due in respect of the damage caused to the victim or to persons entitled through him.

On Question II:

By ten votes against five,

When the United Nations as an Organization is bringing a claim for reparation of damage caused to its agent, it can only do so by basing its claim upon a breach of obligations due to itself; respect for this rule will usually prevent a conflict between the action of the United Nations and such rights as the agent's national State may possess, and thus bring about a reconciliation between their claims; moreover, this reconciliation must depend upon considerations applicable to each particular case, and upon agreements to be made between the Organization and individual States, either generally or in each case.

* * *

[Concurring and dissenting opinions omitted.]

Freedom of the staff of the United Nations Secretariat from national control. Article 100 of the charter provides that the Secretary-General of the United Nations and his staff "shall not seek or receive instructions from any government or from any other authority external to the organization;" members of the United Nations are committed not to seek to influence the Secretary-General and his staff in the discharge of their responsibilities. In realistic terms the staff can retain freedom from national control only if the staff members are not dependent on their home state. But complete lack of dependency is not attainable, since the United Nations cannot confer a permanent citizenship upon its employees. (Indeed, the judges of the International Court of Justice do not have life-time tenure, as do federal judges in the United States.)

The opinion of the court in the Reparation case, however, suggests that at least in one area the dependency of the staff member on his state is reduced. The Legal Department of the United Nations Secretariat has interpreted this opinion as conferring on the United Nations a right of diplomatic protection which goes beyond the bare right to present a claim to an alleged wrong-doing state: "* * * [W]hen a United Nations staff member is arrested or detained by the authorities of a State, the Organization always has a right to send representatives to visit and converse with him with a view to ascertaining whether or not an injury has occurred to the United Nations or to him through non-observance by the State concerned of its international obligations, and whether or not such injury is connected with the performance of his duties. Furthermore, at least when the staff member is not a national of the detaining State, there are reasons for recognizing a broader interest of the United Nations in the matter, so that the staff member will not have to rely exclusively on the protection of his own State." United Nations Juridical Yearbook 1963, at 191–192; 13 Whiteman, Digest of International Law 187–188 (1968).

KEENEY v. UNITED STATES

United States Court of Appeals, D.C. Circuit, 1954.
218 F.2d 843.

EDGERTON, Circuit Judge. Appellant, a former employee of the United Nations, was a witness before a Subcommittee of the Committee on the Judiciary of the United States Senate. She was asked whether anyone in the State Department had aided her in obtaining employment with the United Nations. She did not answer, and asserted a privilege not to answer by reason of the Charter and the Staff Rules of the United Nations. On the theory that she had "refused" to answer, she was prosecuted for contempt of Congress. Rev.Stat. § 102, as amended, 52 Stat. 942, 2 U.S.C.A. § 192. The District Court overruled her claim of privilege and she was convicted. United States v. Keeney, D.C., 111 F.Supp. 233.

Appellant was not asked whether anyone in the State Department *told her he would try* to aid her. Perhaps it was a mistake not to ask her that question, but if so, the mistake was not hers. We need not speculate whether she would have answered that question if it had been asked, or whether she would have been punishable if she had not answered it. She was asked whether anyone in the State Department *did* aid her: "Did anyone in the State Department aid you in obtaining employment with the United Nations?" Whether she realized it or not, this was equivalent to asking her whether the United Nations officials who decided to appoint her had received and been influenced by communications from anyone in the State Department recommending that she be appointed.

Staff Rule 7 of the United Nations provides that "Staff members shall exercise the utmost discretion in regard to all matters of official business. They shall not communicate to any other person any unpublished information known by them by reason of their official position except in the course of their duties or by authorization of the Secretary-General." In my opinion both the first sentence and the second sentence of this Rule support appellant's failure to answer. (1) Since the appointment of official personnel is official business, appellant could not answer without violating her obligation to "exercise the utmost discretion in regard to all matters of official business." She could not, consistently with "the utmost discretion", even answer that she did not know, for that would have meant that her superiors had not told her. Whether officials do or do not tell an employee who aided her in obtaining employment is a matter of official policy and official business. (2) The question related to "unpublished information." The United Nations does not tell the world what recommendations underlie appointments of staff members. The United Nations Administrative Manual even defines "unpublished information" to include "the appointment * * * [of] or any other confidential information concerning" a staff member. I think it plain that staff members would not have such unpublished and confidential information unless it had been made "known to them by reason of their official position."

The Charter of the United Nations supports Staff Rule 7. The Charter provides:

Article 100

1. In the performance of their duties the Secretary-General and the staff shall not seek or receive instructions from any government or from any other authority external to the Organiza-

tion. They shall refrain from any action which might reflect on their position as international officials responsible only to the Organization.

2. Each Member of the United Nations undertakes to respect the exclusively international character of the responsibilities of the Secretary-General and the staff and not to seek to influence them in the discharge of their responsibilities. * * *

Article 105

1. The Organization shall enjoy in the territory of each of its Members such privileges and immunities as are necessary for the fulfillment of its purposes.

2. Representatives of the Members of the United Nations and officials of the Organization shall similarly enjoy such privileges and immunities as are necessary for the independent exercise of their functions in connection with the Organization. 59 Stat. 1052, 1053.

Compulsory disclosure of the persons who influence appointments to the staff of the United Nations would not be consistent with the independence of the Organization or "the exclusively international character of the responsibilities of the Secretary-General and the staff * * *." (Art. 100, Par. 2.) And the prospect of such disclosure might influence staff members, in one degree or another, to regulate their official conduct with a view to avoiding embarrassment of sponsors. The privilege of nondisclosure is therefore "necessary for the independent exercise of their functions in connection with the Organization." (Art. 105, Par. 2.)

Thus the Charter and the Staff Rules of the United Nations establish, in my opinion, the privilege on which appellant relied. And her failure to answer is within the spirit if not the letter of the International Organizations Immunities Act, which provides in § 7(b), 59 Stat. 672, 22 U.S.C.A. § 288d(b): "Representatives of foreign governments in or to international organizations and officers and employees of such organizations shall be immune from suit and legal process relating to acts performed by them in their official capacity and falling within their functions as such representatives, officers, or employees except insofar as such immunity may be waived by the foreign government or international organization concerned."

So far in this opinion I speak only for myself. But we all agree that appellant's conviction must be reversed because of errors in the admission of evidence.

* * *

The result of our several opinions is this. The conviction is reversed with instructions to grant a new trial. In so far as the answer depends upon data in the files of the United Nations or upon information derived from those files, it was privileged by the Charter and the Staff Rules and could not legally be revealed. Evidence as to pertinency will be taken in the absence of the jury. The question whether the appellant's action was under all the circumstances a deliberate and intentional refusal to answer will be put to the jury with the other jury issues.

Reversed.

DANAHER, Circuit Judge (concurring).

I agree that the conviction should be reversed and a new trial be ordered. The error requiring this result stems from the failure to exclude the jury while highly prejudicial evidence was received to establish the element of pertinency.

From the very outset the jury heard the appellant linked to a nefarious, world-wide Communist movement, with her associates numbered among those performing acts of espionage and sabotage even as they purloined secrets of the United States in favor of the Russian government.

* * *

The witness testified that the Committee was attempting to learn a number of facts about the Institute of Pacific Relations, how it operated, what it sought to accomplish, and the degree to which it had accomplished it. "The Institute of Pacific Relations was an institution which had been taken over by Communists and was being operated for their purposes." The Institute had sought to place and had in fact placed "its persons" in high places in government and elsewhere in positions of influence. The Committee came across the name of Mary Jane Keeney in a document which had been seized from the files of the Institute; the document indicated that appellant was active in the Washington Advisory Committee of the Institute; and "the Committee found that Mrs. Keeney had a long record of what appeared to be Communist affiliation—"

Mr. Donner. I object to this, Your Honor.

The Court. Objection overruled. This testimony is not given as proof of any fact, but merely as proof of the pertinency of the inquiry * * *.

Defense counsel again insisted that the question of pertinency was a matter of law for the court, and upon a ruling that the trial judge saw no reason for excluding the jury, defense counsel moved for a mistrial.

The witness continued that appellant in San Francisco prior to 1940 had attended a number of Communist meetings and after coming to Washington had entered a circle of acquaintanceship which included Communists and suspected Communists, numbering among her friends Nathan Gregory Silvermaster and Leonard Ullman. The Committee had "unevaluated" information that Mrs. Keeney had been placed in the United Nations with the help of persons in the IPR and the assistance of persons in the State Department.

Defense counsel renewed his motion for a mistrial and moved to strike the testimony and both motions were denied. That the admission of such evidence over appellant's objections was highly prejudicial can not be doubted, and the rulings with reference thereto and denial of appellant's motion for mistrial constitute reversible error. A new trial must be granted.

On the record presented we do not, in my view, reach the question of privilege. Appellant in her brief and in oral argument has urged us to adopt the sophistry which both before the Senate committee and the District Court she applied to the question: "Did anyone in the State Department aid you in obtaining employment with the United Nations?"

Cited to us are the United Nations charter, its rules and interpretations, and section 7(b) of the International Organizations Immunities Act, 59 Stat. 669, 22 U.S.C.A. § 288 et seq. The question asked does not lead us within the fold of privilege so predicated. There is not the slightest suggestion at any stage that by virtue of her official position the appellant gleaned knowledge from the official files as to how her employment came about. On the contrary, after her conviction, the appellant took the witness stand and was sworn and testified " * * * I do not know to whom the United Nations wrote for references, *because that information is never disclosed to the applicant*, to the Secretariat * * *." (Emphasis supplied.)

When a witness before the Senate committee, if appellant did not know the answer to the question, all she had to say was "I don't know"—if she did not know. If, either before obtaining employment with the United Nations or after such employment had been terminated, she learned—other than from official sources—that someone in the State Department had aided her in obtaining employment she was bound to answer "Yes." If she had personal knowledge—other than from official sources—that no one in the State Department had been of "aid" in her procuring employment, she was bound to answer "No."

In short, even if we were to reach the question of the claimed privilege, unless she acquired information by virtue of her official position during the period of her employment by the United Nations that someone in the State Department did aid her in obtaining such employment, she was bound to answer according to the fact. Whatever privilege may be said to stem from the charter and the staff rules and regulations of the United Nations would apply only with respect to information known to the witness by reason of official position, past or present.

The International Organizations Immunities Act, § 7(b), 59 Stat. 671, 22 U.S.C.A. § 288d(b), provides: "Representatives of foreign governments in or to international organizations and officers and employees of such organizations shall be immune from suit and legal process *relating to acts performed by them in their official capacity and falling within their functions as such representatives, officers, or employees * * *.*" (Emphasis supplied.) This witness was not subjected to suit or legal process relating to acts performed by her in her official capacity.   There is no need to give strained and extended interpretation to the very useful Immunities Act which by its terms has no application here.

After trial when the very question was put to her, with her own particular qualification she answered "I don't know."   She specified "that information is never disclosed to the applicant   *   *   *."   When she applied for employment in the United Nations she "did not know anyone in the State Department."   "Q.   Did anyone intercede for you?   A.   Not to my knowledge."

The answer to the question was clearly within the power of the witness to provide, and a reading of her testimony in the Joint Appendix discloses that the jury might properly be asked to pass upon the issue as to her contumacy as alleged.

* * *

PRETTYMAN, Circuit Judge (concurring).

I concur in the result, and I agree with both of my brethren in the parts of their opinions dealing with the reception before the jury of the evidence relating to pertinency.

* * *

On the other point, concerning the accused's privilege not to answer the question put to her, I find myself midway between my two brethren.   I think that, in so far as the answer to the question, "Did anyone in the State Department aid you in obtaining employment with the United Nations?", depended upon data in the files of the United Nations or upon information derived from those files, it was privileged by the Charter and the Staff Rules and could not legally be revealed.   To that extent the witness could and should have refused to answer.   But it is conceivable that wholly apart from any files or information gleaned from them the witness had knowledge that someone at the State Department did aid her in getting employment. Some such matters are frequently known personally and altogether outside official channels.   Information thus obtained was not privileged, and if this witness knew of any of that sort in her case she should have said so.   If she did not know of any, she should have answered to that effect.   As the event turned out, that was the view of the United Nations Secretariat and also the view later adopted by the witness.   It seems to me that her initial position in response to the question was not fully protected.

At the same time it seems to me that this witness's course might not be deemed by a jury to be a refusal to answer.

* * *

DUBERG v. UNITED NATIONS EDUCATIONAL, SCIENTIFIC AND CULTURAL ORGANIZATION

International Labor Organization Administrative Tribunal, 1955.
38 I.L.O. Off. Bull. 251.

[Duberg, an American citizen who was employed by the defendant organization, was denied a renewal of his employment contract by the Director-General because he had not complied with an invitation to appear before the International Organizations Employees Loyalty Board of the United States Civil Service Commission in 1953. The Director-General had informed Duberg that his conduct could not be accepted as consistent with "the high standards of integrity which are required of those employed by the Organization."]

(10) By a letter of 10 September 1954 the Director-General received communication of the report of the Loyalty Board (advisory determination) in which it was stated: "It has been determined on all the evidence that there is a reasonable doubt as to the loyalty of Norwood Peter Duberg to the Government of the United States" and that "this determination, together with the reasons therefor, in as much detail as security considerations permit, are submitted for your use in exercising your rights and duties with respect to the integrity of the personnel employed by the United Nations Educational, Scientific and Cultural Organisation";

(11) The complainant was himself informed of the conclusions of the Loyalty Board by letter of the Chairman of the Loyalty Board dated 10 September 1954, and was also informed of the fact that the report of the Loyalty Board had been transmitted to the Director-General of the defendant Organisation;

(12) On 23 September 1954 the complainant submitted an appeal to the U.N.E.S.C.O. Appeals Board asking that the above-mentioned decision should be rescinded;

(13) On 2 November 1954 the Appeals Board, by a majority opinion, expressed the opinion that the decision should be rescinded;

(14) By a letter dated 25 November 1954 the Director-General informed the Chairman of the Appeals Board that he could not act in accordance with this opinion;

(15) Before the Appeals Board had taken its decision the Director-General, on 28 September 1954, set up a Special Advisory Board consisting of members of the staff, whose task was to "examine the cases of certain staff members on the basis of certain information which has been brought to the knowledge of the Director-General, and in the light of the standards of employment and conduct prescribed by the Constitution and Staff Regulations";

(16) The complainant appeared and explained his position before this Special Advisory Board. However, in a letter to the Director-General dated 4 October 1954, he expressed certain reservations to

the procedure followed and asked for any measures affecting him which might result from this procedure to be cancelled;

(17) By a letter dated 11 October 1954 the Chief of the Bureau of Personnel and Management informed the complainant of the rejection of this request;

* * *

On the Substance:

A. Considering that the defendant Organisation holds that the renewal or the non-renewal of a fixed-term appointment depends entirely on the personal and sovereign discretion of the Director-General, who is not even required to give his reason therefor;

Considering that, if this were to be so, any unmotivated decision would not be subject to the general legal review which is vested in the Tribunal, and would be liable to become arbitrary;

Considering that, in fact, it may be conceived that this might exceptionally be the case when, for example, it is a matter of assessing the technical suitability of the person concerned for carrying out his duties;

Considering, however, that in this matter the question does not affect the issue inasmuch as the Director-General has not only given the reason for the decision taken by him but has also made it public in a communiqué issued to the press;

That this reason is based solely on the refusal of the complainant to co-operate in the measures of investigation provided in respect of certain of its nationals by the Government of the State of which he is a citizen, and in particular on his refusal to appear before a commission invested by that Government with the power to investigate his loyalty to that State;

That the Director-General declares that he concludes from this that he can no longer retain his confidence in the complainant and offer him a new appointment, his attitude being incompatible with the high standards of integrity required of those who are employed by the Organisation and being, furthermore, capable of harming the interests of the Organisation;

Considering in relation hereto that it is necessary expressly to reject all uncertainty and confusion as to the meaning of the expression "loyalty towards a State" which is entirely different from the idea of "integrity" as embodied in the Staff Regulations and Rules; and that this is evident and requires no further proof;

B. Considering that if the Director-General is granted authority not to renew a fixed-term appointment and so to do without notice or indemnity, this is clearly subject to the implied condition that this authority must be exercised only for the good of the service and in the interest of the Organisation;

Considering that it is in the light of this principle that the facts in this case should be examined;

Considering that Article 1.4 of the Staff Regulations of the defendant Organisation, as it stood at the moment when the decision complained of was taken, was as follows:

Members of the Secretariat shall conduct themselves at all times in a manner consonant with the good repute and high purposes of the Organisation and their status as international civil servants. They shall not engage in any activity that is incompatible with the proper discharge of their duties. They shall avoid any action, and in particular any kind of public pronouncement, which would adversely reflect upon their status. While they are not expected to give up religious or political convictions or national sentiments, they shall at all times exercise the reserve and tact incumbent upon them by reason of their international responsibilities;

Considering that, in thus clearly establishing the entire freedom of conscience recognised to international officials in respect of both their philosophical convictions and their political opinions, the Regulations impose on them the duty to abstain from all acts capable of being interpreted as associating them with propaganda or militant proselytism in any sense whatever:

That this abstention is rigorously imposed on them by the overriding interest of the international organisation to which they owe their loyalty and devotion;

C.   Considering that, when consulted by the Staff Association of the defendant organisation on the obligation incumbent on members of the staff to reply to questionnaires issued by authorities of their respective countries, the Director-General declared that the answer must depend only on the conscience of the individual, except that he should not lie and should have regard to the consequences which the refusal to reply might have for him;

* * *

Considering that it is desirable to determine whether the attitude adopted by the complainant in this respect may be considered as justifying the loss of confidence pledged by the Director-General;

* * *

E.   Considering that it is quite different when the ground for complaint of the Director-General is based solely on the refusal of the official to participate in measures of verbal or written inquiry to which his national Government considers it necessary to subject him;

That the Director-General of an international organisation cannot associate himself with the execution of the policy of the government authorities of any State Member without disregarding the obligations imposed on all international officials without distinction and, in consequence, without misusing the authority which has been conferred on him solely for the purpose of directing that organisation towards the achievement of its own, exclusively international, objectives;

That this duty of the Director-General is governed by Article VI, paragraph 5 of the Constitution of the defendant Organisation, in the following terms:

> The responsibilities of the Director-General and of the staff shall be exclusively international in character. In the discharge of their duties they shall not seek or receive instructions from any government or from any authority external to the Organisation. They shall refrain from any action which might prejudice their position as international officials. Each State Member of the Organisation undertakes to respect the international character of the responsibilities of the Director-General and the staff, and not to seek to influence them in the discharge of their duties;

Considering that the fact that in this case the matter involved is an accusation of disloyalty brought by a Government which enjoys in all respects the highest prestige must be without any influence upon the consideration of the facts in the case and the determination of the principles whose respect the Tribunal must ensure;

That it will suffice to realise that if any one of the 72 States and Governments involved in the defendant Organisation brought against an official, one of its citizens, an accusation of disloyalty and claimed to subject him to an inquiry in similar or analogous conditions, the attitude adopted by the Director-General would constitute a precedent obliging him to lend his assistance to such inquiry and, moreover, to invoke the same disciplinary or statutory consequences, the same withdrawal of confidence, on the basis of any opposal by the person concerned to the action of his national Government;

That if this were to be the case there would result for all international officials, in matters touching on conscience, a state of uncertainty and insecurity prejudicial to the performance of their duties and liable to provoke disturbances in the international administration such as cannot be imagined to have been in the intention of those who drew up the Constitution of the defendant Organisation;

Considering, therefore, that the only ground for complaint adduced by the Director-General to justify the application to the complainant of an exception to the general rule of renewal of appointments, that is to say his opposal to the investigations of his own Government, is entirely unjustified;

Considering that it results therefrom that the decision taken must be rescinded; but that nevertheless the Tribunal does not have the power to order the renewal of a fixed-term appointment, which requires a positive act of the Director-General over whom the Tribunal has no hierarchical authority;

That in the absence of such a power, and unless the Director-General should consider himself in a position to reconsider his decision in this manner, the Tribunal is none the less competent to order equitable reparation of the damage suffered by the complainant by reason of the discriminatory treatment of which he was the object;

That redress will be ensured ex aequo et bono by the granting to the complainant of the sum set forth below;

Considering that, on the one hand, there should be granted to the complainant the amount of the salary which he would have received had he not been subject to the measure of exception of which he complains, that is to say one year's basic salary;

That, on the other hand, there should be granted to him a second year's basic salary in order to compensate for the moral prejudice and in particular the difficulties which he will encounter in seeking new means of subsistence;

That, in this calculation, there should be added to the salary the statutory amount of children's allowance;

On the grounds as aforesaid:

The Tribunal,

*   *   *

Orders the decision taken to be rescinded and declares in law that it constitutes an abuse of rights causing prejudice to the complainant;

In consequence, should the defendant not reconsider the decision taken and renew the complainant's appointment, orders the said defendant to pay to the complainant the sum of 15,500 dollars, plus children's allowance for two years, the whole together with interest at 4 per centum from 1 January 1955;

Orders the defendant Organisation to pay to the complainant the sum of 300 dollars by way of participation in the costs of his defence
*   *   *.

---

1. *Affirmance by the International Court of Justice.* The court subsequently rendered an advisory opinion that the administrative tribunal had acted within its jurisdiction in the Duberg and companion cases. Judgments of the Administrative Tribunal of the International Labour Organization upon Complaints Made against the United Nations Educational, Scientific and Cultural Organization, [1956] I.C.J.Rep. 77.

2. *Questions.*

a. Has the independence of the international civil service been vindicated in this case?

b. Why did the tribunal not order Mr. Duberg's reinstatement to his job? (Note that the Duberg case arose during the McCarthy era in the United States.)

c. How can international organizations deal with the problem of national influence on selection of international civil servants?

SECTION C. CAPACITIES AND IMMUNITIES

BALFOUR, GUTHRIE & CO., LTD. v. UNITED STATES

United States District Court, N.D. California, 1950.
90 F.Supp. 831.

GOODMAN, District Judge. The competency of the United Nations to sue the United States in Federal Court under the Suits in Admiralty Act, 46 U.S.C.A. § 741 et seq., is the principal and unique question tendered by the exceptions to the libel of the United Nations and other joint libelants. As well do the exceptions question the right of the United Nations to maintain the libel against American Pacific Steamship Co., a co-respondent.

The libel alleges that in the autumn of 1947, the United Nations' International Children's Emergency Fund shipped from the ports of Tacoma and Oakland aboard the SS Abraham Rosenberg a large quantity of powdered milk destined for Italy and Greece. A portion of the shipment, it is alleged, was never delivered to the consignee and another portion arrived in a damaged condition. The Abraham Rosenberg was owned by the United States and was operated under a bareboat charter by respondent American Pacific Steamship Company. The United Nations and six other shippers, whose merchandise allegedly suffered a similar fate, have joined in the libel against the United States and the American Pacific Steamship Company.

Whether the United Nations may maintain these proceedings against respondent American Pacific Steamship Company can be first and more easily answered.

The International Court of Justice has held that the United Nations is a legal entity separate and distinct from the member States. While it is not a state nor a super-State, it is an international person, clothed by its Members with the competence necessary to discharge its functions.

Article 104 of the Charter of the United Nations, 59 Stat. 1053, provides that "the Organization shall enjoy in the territory of each of its Members such legal capacity as may be necessary for the exercise of its functions and the fulfillment of its purposes." As a treaty ratified by the United States, the Charter is part of the supreme law of the land. No implemental legislation would appear to be necessary to endow the United Nations with legal capacity in the United States. But the President has removed any possible doubt by designating the United Nations as one of the organizations entitled to enjoy the privileges conferred by the International Organizations Immunities Act, 59 Stat. 669, 22 U.S.C.A. §§ 288–288f. Section 2(a) of that Act, 22 U.S.C.A. § 288a(a), states that "international organizations shall, to the extent consistent with the instrument creating them, possess the capacity—(i) to contract; (ii) to acquire and dispose of real and personal property; (iii) to institute legal proceedings."

The capacity of the United Nations to maintain the libel against the American Pacific Steamship Company is completely consistent with its charter. The libel asserts rights flowing from a contract made by a specialized agency of the United Nations in the performance of its duties. The agency, the International Children's Emergency Fund, was created by resolution of the General Assembly of the United Nations on December 11, 1946. (Resolution 57(1), United Nations Yearbook 1946–47, 162). Its function is to promote child health generally and in particular to assist the governments of countries, that were the victims of aggression, to rehabilitate their children. The solution of international health problems is one of the responsibilities assumed by the United Nations in Article 55 of its Charter, 59 Stat. 1045.

Whether the United Nations may sue the United States is a more difficult question. It is apparent that Article 104 of the Charter of the United Nations was never intended to provide a method for settling differences between the United Nations and its members. It is equally clear that the International Organizations Immunities Act does not amount to a waiver of the United States' sovereign immunity from suit. The precise question posed is whether the capacity to institute legal proceedings conferred on the United Nations by that Act includes the competence to sue the United States in cases in which the United States has consented to suits by other litigants.

The broad purpose of the International Organizations Immunities Act was to vitalize the status of international organizations of which the United States is a member and to facilitate their activities. A liberal interpretation of the Act is in harmony with this purpose.

The considerations which might prompt a restrictive interpretation are not persuasive. It is true that history has recorded few, if any, instances in which international entities have submitted their disputes to the courts of one of the disputing parties. But international organizations on a grand scale are a modern phenomena. The wide variety of activities in which they engage is likely to give rise to claims against their members that can most readily be disposed of in national courts. The present claim is such a claim. No political overtones surround it. No possible embarrassment to the United States in the conduct of its international affairs could result from such a decree as this court might enter. A claim for cargo loss and damage is clearly susceptible of judicial settlement. Particularly is this so in this litigation inasmuch as the United Nations' claim is one of several of the same nature arising out of the same transaction or occurrence.

International organizations, such as the United Nations and its agencies, of which the United States is a member, are not alien bodies. The interests of the United States are served when the United Nations' interests are protected. A prompt and equitable settlement of any claim it may have against the United States will be the settlement most advantageous to both parties. The courts of the United

States afford a most appropriate forum for accomplishing such a settlement.

It may be contended that since international organizations are granted immunity from suit by the International Organizations Immunities Act, an equitable and complete judicial settlement of claims asserted against the United States may not be had. But this possible objection is more fancied than real. For the United Nations submits to our courts when it urges its claim and cannot consequently shut off any proper defenses of the United States.

Finally, it cannot be denied that when the Congress conferred the privileges specified in the International Organizations Immunities Act, it neither explicitly nor implicitly limited the kind or type of legal proceedings that might be instituted by the United Nations. There appears to be no good reason for the judicial imposition of such limitations.

The exceptions of the respondents are severally overruled.

Convention on the Privileges and Immunities of the United Nations. The United States became a party to the convention after the date of the foregoing opinion. Compare the language of the immunities provision of the convention (Section 2) with the language of the International Organization Immunities Act (22 U.S.C. § 288a; Documentary Supplement) referred to in the opinion. Both provide for express waiver. The act provides for the same immunity "as is enjoyed by foreign governments"; the convention provides for immunity from every form of legal process without mentioning foreign governments. Under the convention, if the United Nations is a plaintiff in a law suit, does it submit to counterclaims by the defendant?

BROADBENT v. ORGANIZATION OF AMERICAN STATES

United States Court of Appeals, District of Columbia Circuit, 1980.
628 F.2d 27.

LEVENTHAL, Circuit Judge: This is an appeal from a District Court judgment dismissing an action by the appellants [1] claiming they had been improperly discharged by the Organization of American States (OAS). The district court held the OAS was absolutely immune from suit. We affirm on the ground that, even assuming for discussion the applicability of the lesser, "restrictive" immunity doctrine, which permits a lawsuit based on "commercial" activity to be maintained against a sovereign without its consent, this case does not present such "commercial" activity.

---

1. Amici Curiae briefs were submitted by the International Bank for Reconstruction and Development and the Inter-American Development Bank, the International Telecommunications Satellite Organization, the United Nations, and the United States.

I. Background

The plaintiffs-appellants are seven former staff members of the General Secretariat of OAS. Before their termination, they had been employed at the permanent headquarters of the organization in Washington, D.C., for periods ranging from six to twenty-four years. They are all United States citizens or foreign nationals admitted to permanent residency in the United States.

The appellants were dismissed from the Secretariat on August 31, 1976, due to a reduction in force mandated by the OAS General Assembly. At various times between October 31 and November 8, 1976, they filed complaints with the Administrative Tribunal of the OAS, the internal court created to resolve personnel disputes. On June 1, 1977, the Tribunal held that the discharges had been improper and that the appellants should be reinstated at the grades they held when they were separated from service. In accordance with its governing statute, the Tribunal also fixed an indemnity to be paid to each appellant should the Secretary General choose to exercise the option of refusing to reinstate them. Subsequently, the Secretary General denied reinstatement, and each appellant received the indicated indemnity.[3]

On November 16, 1977, the appellants brought this action in the district court, alleging breach of contract and seeking damages totalling three million dollars. The OAS moved to quash service and dismiss the complaint, asserting that the district court lacked subject matter jurisdiction and that the OAS is immune from service of process; but the district court denied the motion in an order dated January 25, 1978. On February 28, the OAS filed a request for certification under 28 U.S.C. § 1292(b) so as to take an interlocutory appeal of the January order to this court. In a final order dated March 28, 1978, the district court vacated its order of January 25 and dismissed the lawsuit. The March 28 order stated in pertinent part:

> On January 25, 1978, this Court held that the express language of 22 U.S.C. § 288a(b) and the statutory purposes underlying the International Organizations Immunities Act of 1945 bring international organizations within the terms of the Foreign Sovereign Immunities Act of 1976, and that pursuant to 28 U.S.C. § 1330 this Court had jurisdiction over the parties and controversy involved in the case. Upon careful review of that decision, the Court finds that it did not properly weigh the facts that international organizations, and particularly the Organization of American States, are creatures of treaty and by virtue of treaty stand in a different position with respect to the issue of immunity than sovereign nations. The Court is persuaded that international organizations are immune from every form of legal

---

3. The amounts of the indemnities ranged from $9,000 to $12,000 plus attorney's fees.

process except insofar as that immunity is expressly waived by treaty or expressly limited by statute. The Court is further persuaded that this Court has jurisdiction over lawsuits involving international organizations only insofar as such jurisdiction is expressly provided for by statute.

The Foreign Sovereign Immunities Act of 1976 makes no mention of international organizations. The jurisdictional grant of 28 U.S.C. § 1330 refers only to foreign states. Nothing in the International Organizations Immunities Act of 1945 provides for jurisdiction in the district courts over civil actions against international organizations.

On April 19, 1978, appellants filed their notice of appeal from this ruling.

II. ANALYSIS

A. Jurisdiction

In its final order, the district court concluded that it lacked subject matter jurisdiction, and the OAS advances that position on appeal. Appellants—and the district court in its January 25 order—rely upon a conjunctive reading of the International Organizations Immunity Act (IOIA) of 1945, 22 U.S.C. § 288a(b) (1979), and the Foreign Sovereign Immunities Act (FSIA) of 1976, 28 U.S.C. § 1330 (1979), to establish jurisdiction.[a] The OAS counters that § 288a(b) confers immunity, not jurisdiction, and that § 1330 establishes jurisdiction over suits against foreign *states*, not international organizations.

The United Nations (U.N.), appearing amicus curiae, offers a different approach to the question of jurisdiction. It contends that jurisdiction over suits involving international organizations exists under 28 U.S.C. § 1331(a). In support of this contention, amicus cited International Refugee Organization v. Republic Steamship Co., 189 F.2d 858, 861 (4th Cir. 1951), which held that "an international organization created by treaties to which the United States is a party may invoke [federal question] jurisdiction because it is created by a treaty of the United States." That case also found an alternate basis for federal court jurisdiction over suits brought by international organizations in the provisions of 28 U.S.C. § 288a(a) that confer capacity to sue upon international organizations. Id. at 860. Counsel for the U.N. reasons from this alternative holding that, if international organizations may institute suits in a federal court, they should be permitted to defend them there; thus, he argues that § 1331 should be construed to confer federal jurisdiction over such suits.

Because clear and adequate non-judicial grounds for the disposal of this case exist, we need not and do not decide the difficult jurisdictional issues it presents.

a. The Foreign Sovereign Immunities Act and portions of the International Organizations Immunities Act are set forth in the Documentary Supplement.

B.   The Immunity of International Organizations

The International Organizations Immunities Act of 1945, 22 U. S.C. § 288a(b) (1979), grants to international organizations which are designated by the President [10] "the same immunity from suit and every form of judicial process as is enjoyed by foreign governments, except to the extent that such organizations may expressly waive their immunity for the purpose of any proceedings or by the terms of any contract."   As of 1945, the statute granted absolute immunity to international organizations, for that was the immunity then enjoyed by foreign governments.

The Foreign Sovereign Immunities Act of 1976, 28 U.S.C. § 1602 et seq. (1979), codified what, in the period between 1946 and 1976,[12] had come to be the immunity enjoyed by sovereign states—*restrictive immunity*.   The central feature of restrictive immunity is the distinction between the governmental or sovereign activities of a state (acts jure imperii) and its commercial activities (acts jure gestionis). Foreign states may not be found liable for their governmental activities by American courts; but they enjoy no immunity from liability for their commercial activities.

Contention for restrictive immunity

Appellants—and the United States as amicus curiae—submit the following syllogism: the IOIA conferred on international organizations the same immunity enjoyed by foreign governments; the FSIA indicates that foreign governments now enjoy only restrictive immunity; therefore, international organizations enjoy only restrictive immunity.   They are supported by the general doctrine that ordinarily, "[a] statute which refers to the law of a subject generally adopts the law on the subject as of the time the law was invoked * * * includ[ing] all the amendments and modifications of the law subsequent to the time the reference statute was enacted." [13]

Contention for absolute immunity

The OAS and several other international organizations as amici curiae counter that Congress granted international organizations absolute immunity in the IOIA, and it has never modified that grant. They rely on three implications of a legislative intent *not* to apply to international organizations the post World War II evolutions in the doctrine of sovereign immunity.

First, the FSIA is generally silent about international organizations.   No reference to such organizations is made in the elaborate definition of "state" in § 1603, and only § 1611 even alludes to their existence.   True, § 1611, dealing as it does with the attachment of property belonging to international organizations, presupposes a suc-

---

10. By Executive Order 10533 (June 3, 1954), 19 Fed.Reg. 3289 (1954). President Eisenhower designated the OAS an international organization entitled to the privileges and immunities conferred by the IOIA.

12. See, e. g., the "Tate Letter," 26 Dept. State Bull. 984–85 (1952), quoted in Alfred Dunhill of London, Inc. v. Cuba, 425 U.S. 682, 711 (1975).

13. Sands (ed.), Sutherland Statutory Construction § 51.08 (4th ed. 1975).

cessful action against an international organization. However, that could follow a waiver of immunity. Alternatively, § 1611 would have application in case of an attempt to execute a judgment against a foreign state by attaching funds of that foreign state held by an international organization.[16]

Second, by its own terms the IOIA provides for the modification, where appropriate, of the immunity enjoyed by one or more international organizations.

Under the statute, the President can withdraw or restrict the immunity and privileges thereby conferred. Specifically, it provides:

> The president (is) authorized, in the light of the functions performed by any such international organization, by appropriate executive order to withhold or withdraw from any such organization or its officers or employees any of the privileges, exemptions, and immunities provided for in this title * * * or to condition or limit the enjoyment by any such organization or its officers or employees of any such privilege, exemption, or immunity.[17]

The Senate Report on the IOIA stated: "This provision will permit the adjustment or limitation of the privileges in the event that any international organization should engage for example, in activities of a commercial nature."[18] And, in floor debate on the legislation, its supporters pointed again to this provision as a limitation on commercial abuses by an international organization.[19] Hence this provision may reveal that Congress intended to grant absolute immunity to international organizations giving to the President the authority to relax that immunity, including removal or restriction of immunity in cases involving the commercial activities of international organizations.

Finally, Congress may have concluded that the policies and considerations that led to the development of the restrictive immunity concept for foreign nations do not apply to international organizations like the OAS.[20]

16. According to the House Report: The purpose of this section is to permit international organizations designated by the President pursuant to the International Organization Immunities Act, 22 U.S.C. 288 et seq., to carry out their functions from their offices located in the United States without hindrance by private claimants seeking to attach the payment of funds to a foreign state; such attachments would also violate the immunities accorded to such international institutions.

H.R.Rep. No. 94–1487, 94th Cong., 2d Sess. 30 (1976). The Report continues, even more pointedly

This reference to "international organizations" in this subsection is not intended to restrict any immunity accorded to such international organizations under any law or international agreement.
Id. at 31.

17. 22 U.S.C. § 288a(a) (1979).

18. S.R.Rep. No. 861, 79th Cong., 1st Sess. 2 (1945).

19. See 91 Cong.Rec. 12,432 (daily ed. Dec. 20, 1945) and 12,530 (daily ed. Dec. 21, 1945).

20. Prior to its modification, the absolute immunity of states was justified by "the desirability of avoiding adjudication which might affront a foreign nation and thus embarrass the

We need not decide this difficult question of statutory construction. On *either* theory of immunity—absolute or restrictive—an immunity exists sufficient to shield the organization from lawsuit on the basis of acts involved here.

C. The "Commercial" Activity Concept in the Restrictive Immunity Doctrine

Even under the restrictive immunity doctrine, there is immunity from lawsuits based on governmental or sovereign activities—the jure imperii—as distinct from commercial activities. We discuss the narrower standard of restrictive immunity not because it is necessarily the governing principle, but because we discern that an organization conducting the activities at issue in this case is shielded even under the restrictive immunity formula, and a fortiori on the absolute immunity theory.

Section 1605 of the FSIA provides that foreign states shall not be immune from the jurisdiction of American courts in any case based upon their commercial activity in the United States, with the commercial character of an activity determined by reference to its "nature" rather than to its "purpose." The conceptual difficulties involved in differentiating jure questionis from jure imperii have led some commentators to declare the distinction unworkable.[22] The restrictive immunity doctrine is designed to accommodate the legal interests of citizens doing business with foreign governments on the one hand, with the interests of foreign states in avoiding the embarrassment of defending the propriety of political acts before a foreign court.

In our view, the employment by a foreign state or international organization of internal administrative personnel—civil servants—is not properly characterized as "doing business." That view is sup-

executive branch in its conduct of foreign relations." See Hearings on H.R. 11315 before the Subcommittee on Administrative Law and Governmental Relations, House Committee on the Judiciary, 94th Cong., 2d Sess. 29 (1976). As sovereign nations become more and more involved in the market place, as merchants rather than sovereigns, claims arising out of commercial transactions do not affront the sovereignty of the nations involved. Id. Recognition of this growing involvement in commercial activity was the basis of the movement to a restrictive concept. Moreover, most other commercial nations embrace restrictive immunity with regard to sovereigns. Thus, when our government and its instrumentalities are sued abroad in commercial litigation, the sovereign immunity defense is rarely available. H.R.Rep. No. 94–2487, 94th Cong., 2d Sess. 9

(1976). Congressional proponents of the restrictive immunity could thus indicate that use of the restrictive immunity concept would bring the United States into step with foreign nations. Id. at 54. But neither rationale for adopting the restrictive notion of immunity would seem to apply to international organizations. Such organizations do not regularly engage in commercial activities, nor do other nations apply the concept of restrictive immunity to them. Cf. Alfred Dunhill of London, Inc. v. Cuba, 425 U.S. 682, 699–702 (1975).

22. See, e. g., Comment, The Jurisdictional Immunity of Foreign Sovereigns, 63 Yale L.J. 1148, 1161–62 (1954); Lauterpacht, The Problem of Jurisdictional Immunities of Foreign States, 28 Brit.Y.B.Int'l.L. 220, 225–26 (1951).

ported by the legislative history of the FSIA, and the definition of "commercial activity" in § 1603. The House Report commented:

> (d) Commercial activity.—Paragraph (c) of section 1603 defines the term "commercial activity" as including a broad spectrum of endeavor, from an individual commercial transaction or act to a regular course of commercial conduct. A "regular course of commercial conduct" includes the carrying on of a commercial enterprise such as a mineral extraction company, an airline or a state trading corporation. Certainly, if an activity is customarily carried on for profit, its commercial nature could readily be assumed. At the other end of the spectrum, a single contract, if of the same character as a contract which might be made by a private person, could constitute a "particular transaction or act."

> As the definition indicates, the fact that goods or services to be procured through a contract are to be used for a public purpose is irrelevant; it is the essentially commercial nature of an activity or transaction that is critical. Thus, a contract by a foreign government to buy provisions or equipment for its armed forces or to construct a government building constitutes a commercial activity. The same would be true of a contract to make repairs on an embassy building. Such contracts should be considered to be commercial contracts, even if their ultimate object is to further a public function.

> By contrast, a foreign state's mere participation in a foreign assistance program administered by the Agency for International Development (AID) is an activity whose essential nature is public or governmental, and it would not itself constitute a commercial activity. By the same token, a foreign state's activities in and "contacts" with the United States resulting from or necessitated by participation in such a program would not in themselves constitute a sufficient commercial nexus with the United States so as to give rise to jurisdiction (see sec. 1330) or to assets which could be subjected to attachment or execution with respect to unrelated commercial transactions (see sec. 1610(b)). However, a transaction to obtain goods or services from private parties would not lose its otherwise commercial character because it was entered into in connection with an AID program. *Also public or governmental and not commercial in nature, would be the employment of diplomatic, civil service,* or military personnel, but not the employment of American citizens or third country nationals by the foreign state in the United States.[23]

This report clearly marks employment of civil servants as noncommercial for purposes of restrictive immunity. The Committee Reports establish an exception from the general rule in the case of employment of American citizens or third country nationals by for-

23. H.Rep. No. 94–1487, 94th Cong., 2d Sess. 16 (1976) (emphasis added), U.S.   Code Cong. & Admin.News 1976, p. 6614.

eign states.   The exception leaves foreign states free to conduct "governmental" matters through their own citizens.   A comparable exception is not applicable to international organizations, because their civil servants are inevitably drawn from either American citizens or "third" country nations.   In the case of international organizations, such an exception would swallow up the rule of immunity for civil service employment disputes.

The United States has accepted without qualification the principles that international organizations must be free to perform their functions and that no member state may take action to hinder the organization.[24]   The unique nature of the *international* civil service is relevant.   International officials should be as free as possible, within the mandate granted by the member states, to perform their duties free from the peculiarities of national politics.   The OAS charter, for example, imposes constraints on the organization's employment practices.[25]   Such constraints may not coincide with the employment policies pursued by its various member states.[26]   It would seem singularly inappropriate for the international organization to bind itself to the employment law of any particular member, and we have no reason to think that either the President or Congress intended this result.   An attempt by the courts of one nation to adjudicate the personnel claims of international civil servants would entangle those courts in the internal administration of those organizations.   Denial of immunity opens the door to divided decisions of the courts of different member states passing judgment on the rules, regulations, and decisions of the international bodies.   Undercutting uniformity in the application of staff rules or regulations would undermine the ability of the organization to function effectively.[27]

24. See e. g. XIII Documents of the United Nations Conference on International Organizations 704–05 (1945), reprinted in 13 Whitman, Digest of International Law 36 (1968).

25. See e. g., OAS Charter, Article 143 (forbidding discrimination on the basis of "race, creed or sex"), Article 126 (requiring staff recruitment on as wide a geographic basis as possible).

26. For example, the Age Discrimination in Employment Act of 1978, (ADEA) 29 U.S.C. § 621 et seq., forbids in most circumstances a requirement that a person retire at a particular age.   Yet other countries consider early retirement an important social goal, the achievement of which facilitates advancement by younger people.   Since there is no inconsistent provision in the OAS Charter (and since, even if there were, the ADEA was enacted after the latest amendment to the OAS Charter), the ADEA presumably would govern, and unless its provisions were construed not to cover international employment, see 29 U.S.C. §§ 630 and 633a, the OAS and other international organizations who are thought not immune from suit would be required to abide by the terms of the Act in their employment here.

Or for another example, the rigid quotas employed as an integral part of recruiting a "balanced" international civil service, see, e. g., General Assembly resolution 33/143, December 18, 1978, might run afoul of the emerging law of "affirmative action" in the United States.

27. Treatise writers on the law of international organizations have recognized the force of the argument made in text. See, e. g., M. B. Akehurst, The Law Governing Employment in International Organizations 12 (1967), which discusses suits such as the instant case in the following terms:

We hold that the relationship of an international organization with its internal administrative staff is noncommercial, and, absent waiver, activities defining or arising out of that relationship may not be the basis of an action against the organization—regardless of whether international organizations enjoy absolute or restrictive immunity.

D.   The Activities at Issue Here

The appellants were staff members of the General Secretariat of the OAS. Their appointments, terms of employment, salaries and allowances, and the termination of employment were governed by detailed "Staff Rules of the General Secretariat" promulgated by the OAS. The Staff Rules further establish an elaborate grievance procedure within the OAS, with ultimate appeal to the Administrative Tribunal of the OAS.

The Tribunal is competent to determine the lawfulness of an employee's termination of employment. If an employee has been wrongfully discharged, the Tribunal may order reinstatement. If reinstatement is ordered, the Tribunal may also establish an indemnity to be paid to the employee in the event the Secretary General exercises his authority to indemnify the employee rather than effect the reinstatement.

The employment disputes between the appellants and OAS were disputes concerning the internal administrative staff of the Organization. The internal administration of the OAS is a non-commercial activity shielded by the doctrine of immunity. There was no waiver, and accordingly the appellant's action had to be dismissed.

Affirmed.

----

1. *Convention on the Privileges and Immunities of the Specialized Agencies.* When acceding to this convention, the text of which is at 33 U.N.T.S. 261, states indicate to which of the special-

At first sight, disputes of this sort could be referred to municipal tribunals. The organization normally possesses immunity, but immunity can be waived. However, the special nature of the law governing employment in international organizations, closely linked as it is with delicate questions of administrative policy, makes municipal tribunals totally unsuited to deal with it. It would be like an English court trying to judge a dispute between the French Government and one of its officials. Courts in all countries usually refuse to handle questions of foreign *public* law, and, in the same way, a number of municipal courts have held themselves incompetent to judge claims brought by international civil servants against the organizations which employ them, not on the grounds of immunity, but on the grounds of the special law applicable.

There is therefore a vacuum which needs to be filled by the organizations themselves. The creation of an independent body, empowered to make binding decisions in legal disputes between an organization and its staff, is by no means an altruistic gesture from the organization's point of view; without it, officials might suffer from a sense of injustice which would impair the smooth running of the Secretariat.

The court notes that the OAS, like most international organizations, has established elaborate internal grievance machinery.

ized agencies they choose to apply it. The United States is not a party to the convention, although, pursuant to the International Organization Immunities Act, 22 U.S.C. § 288, the President of the United States has designated virtually all these agencies as entitled to the benefits of the act.

2. *Effect of inviolability of headquarters of the United Nations.* In People v. Coumatos, 224 N.Y.S.2d 507, 32 Misc.2d 1085 (1962), the defendant, an American citizen, was indicted on multiple counts of grand larceny, for crimes alleged to have been committed by him within the United Nations Headquarters where he was employed as a payroll clerk by the United Nations. He was arrested in Bronx County, outside the Headquarters. Defendant claimed that the court lacked jurisdiction over acts committed within the premises of the United Nations. This defense was rejected:

> What does the defendant offer as evidence regarding his claimed immunity? His claim is rested upon the Headquarters Agreement, Secs. 8 and 9. * * *

> * * * [T]he question remains as to whether we have jurisdiction over the acts as allegedly committed within the premises of the United Nations. This is the vital question that has not heretofore been clearly presented in the reported cases.

> While it is true that the United States in ceding certain powers and lands to international control did agree that "the Headquarters District shall be under the control and authority of the United Nations" (Laws of 80th Congress, First Session, Ch. 482, Public Law 357); and, under Section 9(a), supra, did agree further that the "Headquarters District shall be inviolate" such agreement meant only that Federal, State and local officers shall not enter the Headquarters District to perform any official duties except upon the consent of the Secretary-General.

> Without prejudice to any of its charter provisions, the United Nations as part of its agreement with the United States, consented to prevent the Headquarters District from being used as a refuge by those seeking to avoid arrest or service of local processes under the Federal, State or local law of the United States. (See Sec. 9(b))

> The United Nations has full power to formulate its own rules and regulations for execution of its functions. (See Sec. 8) Moreover, it has the power only to expel or exclude persons from the Headquarters District for violation of its regulations. (See Sec. 10)

> However, any other penalty or arrest can be made "only in accordance with the provisions of such laws or regulations as may be adopted by the appropriate American authorities." Therefore, it would appear that the United Nations is without jurisdiction or authority to hear and determine either criminal or civil cases. (See Opinion by Culkin, J., 224 N.Y.S.2d 504). Such power is reserved to the appropriate American authori-

ties who may remove any person from the Headquarters District "as requested under the authority of the United Nations". See Article VI, Sec. 16.

Once having removed a person from the Headquarters District under these circumstances, what can further be done?—or, what if a person is arrested within the United Nations upon consent of the Secretary-General for allegedly committing acts done in violation of local statutes within the premises of the United Nations or is arrested outside the premises as was the defendant in this case, and upon the complaint of someone within in New York State or elsewhere; here again, what can be done? Have we jurisdiction if the person is not one to whom diplomatic immunity has been given? The answers seem to be contained in Article III, Section 7(b): "except as otherwise provided in this agreement or in the General Convention, the federal, state and local law of the United States shall apply within the headquarters district." Further, Section 7(c) provides: "except as otherwise provided in this agreement or in the General Convention, the federal, state and local courts of the United States shall have jurisdiction over acts done and transactions taking place in the headquarters district as provided in applicable federal, state and local laws."

Accordingly, it would appear from this agreement that the local law shall have jurisdiction over any acts done or transactions taking place within the Headquarters District which are in violation of such laws and the courts of the appropriate American authorities shall have jurisdiction to try and determine issues between the parties. However, such Federal, State or local laws shall, of course, not be inconsistent with any regulation that has been authorized by the United Nations. (See Article III, Sec. 8)

INTERNATIONAL REFUGEE ORGANIZATION v. REPUBLIC S. S. CORP.

United States Court of Appeals, Fourth Circuit, 1951.
189 F.2d 858.

PARKER, Chief Judge. These cases arise out of a controversy between the International Refugee Organization, an agency of the United Nations, and the Republic of Panama, and one Jose Jacintho de Medeiros, a citizen of Portugal. * * * No. 6202 involves a charge of fraud and deceit made by the I.R.O. against the corporation and Medeiros in a suit instituted against them to recover damages and establish a constructive trust.

* * *

The allegations of fraud in both cases are that the corporation and Medeiros obtained $840,000 from I.R.O. by means of false and fraudulent representations with respect to the ownership, title and speed of the S. S. San Francisco, a vessel chartered to the I.R.O. by the Republic Steamship Company represented by Medeiros as president.

In No. 6202, the action against Medeiros and the Republic Steamship Company was dismissed by the lower court for lack of jurisdiction.

* * *

The dismissal for lack of jurisdiction in No. 6202 is based upon the holding that a suit by the I.R.O. is not one of which the federal courts have been given jurisdiction. We think that this is error. The United Nations is an international organization of which the United States is a member, and article 104 of its charter provides that it shall enjoy in the territory of each of its members "such legal capacity as may be necessary for the exercise of its functions and the fulfillment of its purposes." 59 Stat. 1053. Article 13 of the Constitution of the I.R.O., which is an agency of the United Nations, contains a provision to like effect. In the International Organization Immunities Act, 59 Stat. 669, 22 U.S.C.A. § 288a, Congress has undertaken to discharge the obligations assumed under these provisions by providing that international organizations such as I.R.O. shall "to the extent consistent with the instrument creating them, possess the capacity—

"(i) to contract;

"(ii) to acquire and dispose of real and personal property;

"(iii) *to institute legal proceedings.*" (Italics supplied.) This means, by necessary implication, that Congress has opened the doors of the federal courts to suits by such international organizations; for the right to institute legal proceedings means the right to go into court, and the federal courts are the only courts whose doors Congress can open.

As pointed out by the Secretary of State (hearings on U. N. Charter, 77th Congress, 1st Session, pp. 33, 134–135) and the Senate Committee on Foreign Affairs (S.Report, exec. No. 8, 77th Congress, 1st Session, p. 6), "It is apparent that an organization like the United Nations which will have offices and employees, will purchase supplies, and presumably rent or purchase office space, must have the legal capacity to enter into contracts, to take title to real and personal property and to appear in court (although its position as a defendant is protected by Article 105). The purpose of Article 104 is to make clear that the Organization has that legal capacity." Certainly an organization like the I.R.O., which is purchasing and chartering vessels and entering into all sorts of contracts in connection with the transportation of refugees, must have the right to go into court for the protection of its rights and interests; and in this country the logical courts for it to go into are the courts of the nation which has adhered to the international organization, not the local courts of the several states which have had no part therein. In determining its rights in this regard, we should give a liberal interpretation to the International Organization Immunities Act.

* * *

We think also that there is jurisdiction to entertain the suit by reason of 28 U.S.C.A. § 1331, which provides that the District Courts shall have jurisdiction of civil actions arising under the "Constitution, laws or treaties of the United States." Under the principles laid down in Osborn v. United States Bank, 9 Wheat. 738, 6 L.Ed. 204, this was certainly a civil action arising not only under the treaties creating the United Nations and the International Refugee Organization into both of which the United States had entered, but also under the act of Congress which gives the right to sue to public international organizations in which the United States participates. The right of federal corporations to invoke the jurisdiction of the federal courts has been curtailed by act of Congress but this involves no limitation of the doctrine of Osborne v. United States Bank, supra. On the contrary, it is an express recognition of that doctrine. It will be noted that the statute, 28 U.S.C.A. § 1349, denying jurisdiction to a corporation created by act of Congress unless the United States is the owner of more than one-half its capital stock can have no application because the I.R.O. is not a corporation created by act of Congress but an international organization to which the United States itself is a party. If, as said by the Supreme Court in the case of Gully v. First National Bank, 299 U.S. 109, 114, 57 S.Ct. 96, 81 L.Ed. 70, there is no thought of disturbing the doctrine of the charter cases, that doctrine must be held to support the jurisdiction here. If a corporation may invoke the federal jurisdiction because created by a law of the United States, an international organization created by treaties to which the United States is a party may invoke the jurisdiction because created by a treaty of the United States. Especially is this true where the international organization is clothed by a law of the United States with the essential corporate functions of contracting, acquiring and disposing of property and suing in court.

It has been suggested that the jurisdiction of the court can be sustained under 28 U.S.C.A. § 1345 on the theory that a suit by an international organization is a suit by the United States as well as by the other nations which are parties to the organization and that jurisdiction of a suit by the United States is not defeated because other parties are joined as plaintiffs in the suit. See Erickson v. United States, 264 U.S. 246, 249, 44 S.Ct. 310, 68 L.Ed. 661. We need not pass upon this, however, as we think there can be no question as to the jurisdiction for the reasons already given.

* * *

PEOPLE v. LEO

United States, Criminal Court of the City of New York, 1978.
407 N.Y.S.2d 941, 95 Misc.2d 408.

BETTY WEINBERG ELLERIN, Judge:

Defendant moves for dismissal of the complaint charging him with assault in the third degree (Penal Law § 120.00) and resisting arrest (Penal Law § 205.30) on the ground that he "is a person who has international diplomatic immunity and as such the court lacks jurisdiction".

The relevant facts underlying the charges arose on July 29, 1977, when defendant, who was then working at his office in the United Nations Building at about 10 P.M., received a telephone call from his wife advising him of the uninvited presence of complainant in their apartment and her refusal to leave despite requests that she do so. Defendant then left his office and returned home, where a scuffle with complainant ensued resulting in the arrival of the police to place defendant under arrest for assault and his resistance to such arrest.

Defendant contends that a dismissal is mandated in this case because he is insulated from prosecution by the cloak of diplomatic immunity and, further, because this court lacks jurisdiction over the subject matter which, according to defendant, constitutes the commission of a federal crime by the complainant. In regard to the latter argument, it may be noted that defendant has pressed a cross-complaint against complainant in this court and has also made a formal complaint to the U.S. Attorney's office against her apparently under Title 18, Sect. 112 of the United States Code.

At the outset, it is essential to establish the precise status occupied by defendant in this country. It is uncontradicted that he is a Tanzanian national who is employed by the United Nations at its headquarters in New York in the capacity of Economic Affairs Officer, Economic Affairs Section, Centre for Natural Resources, Energy, and Transportation. While defendant is concededly sponsored for this position by the government of Tanzania, he holds no other diplomatic position on behalf of the government of Tanzania, has never been issued a diplomatic passport and he resides in the United States under a G4 visa which is issued to international civil servants. Thus, it is clear that defendant's status is solely that of an employee of the United Nations with whatever rights and immunities may inure to him by virtue of that position.

The controlling authorities are set forth in Article 105 of the United Nations Charter (59 U.S.Stat. 1053), of which the United States is a signatory, and in the International Organizations Immunities Act (22 U.S.C. § 288d[b]) which was enacted in 1945 to implement the immunities provisions embodied in the United Nations Charter and was made applicable to that organization by Executive

Order No. 9698 of February 19, 1946. (U.S.Code Cong.Serv., 1946, p. 1771.)

Article 105 of the United Nations Charter, provides that:

1. The Organization shall enjoy in the territory of each of its Members such privileges and immunities as are necessary for the fulfillment of its purposes.

2. Representatives of the Members of the United Nations and officials of the Organization shall similarly enjoy such privileges and immunities as are necessary for the independent exercise of their functions in connection with the Organization. (Underscoring added.)

Section 288d, sub-paragraph (b) of Title 22 of the United States Code states that:

Representatives of foreign governments in or to international organizations and officers and employees of such organization shall be immune from suit and legal process relating to acts performed by them in their official capacity and falling within their function as such representatives, officers, or employees except insofar as such immunity may be waived by the foreign government or international organization concerned. (Underscoring added.)

The underscored language clearly delineates the perimeters of the immunity applicable to defendant, as an employee of the United Nations. It is limited in scope and purpose to protection for acts committed by United Nations officials in the course of accomplishing their functions as United Nations' employees in distinction to the unlimited form of immunity traditionally accorded to diplomats. (See U. S. v. Melekh, 190 F.Supp. 67 [S.D.N.Y. 1960]; People v. Weiner, 85 Misc.2d 161, 378 N.Y.S.2d 966.)

While defendant asserts that the statutory immunity under Section 288d(b) applies in this instance because complainant did in fact obstruct him "in the performance of his duties", an analysis of the facts in this case, in the most liberal perspective possible, fails to demonstrate any basis whatsoever upon which to conclude that defendant was acting in his official capacity or that there was some reasonable relationship between the alleged altercation and defendant's United Nations employment. On the contrary, the acts underlying the charges took place away from defendant's office when he returned home in response to his wife's call concerning an unwanted visitor whose presence at defendant's residence has not been shown to have been in any way connected with defendant's employment. The defendant's acts took place wholly within the context of a personal, domestic matter and as such are outside the scope of the limited immunity to which he is entitled as a United Nations' employee. The tenuous circumstance that he was at his office when he received his wife's call affords no rational basis for holding that his subsequent acts of violence in ejecting complainant and in resisting arrest were in some way related to the purposes of the United Nations or to the performance or fulfillment of defendant's duties and functions as an Economic Affairs Officer of that organization. (See U. S. v. Egorov, 222 F.Supp. 106 [E.D.N.Y. 1963]; Cty. of Westchester v. Ranollo, 187 Misc. 777, 67 N.Y.S.2d 31.)

Nor is there merit to defendant's argument that this court lacks jurisdiction over the subject matter herein because such jurisdiction is vested solely in the Federal Courts. In support of this contention defendant points to the fact that, under his version of the incident, complainant is chargeable with a violation of the federal law (i. e. 18 U.S.C. § 112[a] and [b]) which provides for the imposition of criminal penalties for injury to the person or property of a foreign official, including trespass upon the residence of such official. It is apparently defendant's position that if he initiates charges against complainant under such statute, he is thereby rendered immune from criminal prosecution for any acts committed against complainant, however egregious. Aside from the fact that defendant does not fall within the category of "foreign official" covered by the statute, he seriously misapprehends its scope and purpose. The statute is designed to provide foreign officials with a protective shield against harm by imposing severe criminal penalties upon those who would interfere with such foreign officials in the performance of their functions and duties. There is no language whatsoever in Section 112(a) and (b) of Title 18 which deals with the granting of immunity or which can give rise to a construction of the statute permitting it to be converted into a sword authorizing the perpetration of criminal acts with impunity by those whom the statute seeks to protect. (See Legislative History of the "Act For The Prevention and Punishment of Crimes Against Internationally Protected Persons", 90 U.S.Stat. 1997, P.L. 94–467, 4 U.S. Code Congressional and Administrative News, p. 4480 [1976].) The purpose of this legislation is simply to deal with the protection of diplomatic officials by preventing and discouraging crimes against such persons. Any immunities from prosecution which they or other persons may enjoy derive from other statutory provisions. Insofar as defendant is concerned the controlling statute is Section 288d(b) of Title 22 which, as has already been discussed, affords him only the limited diplomatic immunity applicable to a United Nations employee, an immunity which in no way proscribes the instant prosecution. It is undoubtedly in recognition of the limited scope of Section 288 of title 22 that defendant seeks to create a more expansive immunity by a strained and distorted interpretation of Section 112 of title 18. Significantly, defendant has submitted no authority whatsoever in support of such untenable construction of that statute.

*   *   *

Accordingly, defendant's motion to dismiss on the ground of diplomatic immunity is in all respects denied.

1. *Is immunity derivative?* In Westchester County v. Ranollo, 187 Misc. 777, 67 N.Y.S.2d 31 (1946), defendant was prosecuted for speeding. Defendant automobile operator claimed immunity as an employee of the United Nations; he asserted that, in fact, he was accompanied at the time by the Secretary General of the United Nations, Trygve Lie. The court noted that the International Organizations Immunities Act accorded immunity to "officers and employees of such organizations * * * from suit and legal process relating to acts performed by them in their official capacity and falling within their functions * * *." It held that "the defendant is not entitled to immunity as a matter of law without a trial of the issue of fact * * *." What issue of fact remains to be tried? Suppose that defendant proves that he was chauffering the Secretary General to an official United Nations meeting (cocktail party?) and was speeding because the Secretary was late for the appointment.

2. *The Vienna Convention on the Representation of States in Their Relations with International Organizations of a Universal Character.* This convention was adopted by a United Nations conference in March 1975 and was not in force as of December 31, 1979. The United States abstained on the vote adopting the text of the convention and did not become a signatory. The head of the United States delegation to the conference explained that the United States viewed the convention as needlessly expanding the obligations of host states. "Article 66, for example, is an expansion of current privileges and immunities for which no justification whatsoever has been given. Administrative and technical staff, who have no representational functions, are accorded virtually the same privileges and immunities for all intents and purposes as would be accorded, for example, the ambassador to the host state." McDowell, Digest of United States Practice in International Law 1975, at 40 (1976).

3. *When the state of nationality of a United Nations employee confers diplomatic rank upon him.* United States v. Melekh, 190 F. Supp. 67 (S.D.N.Y.1960), involved an indictment of a Russian citizen for a conspiracy to obtain United States defense information. Melekh was employed in the Secretariat of the United Nations as chief of the Russian language section in the office of Conference Services. Melekh's defense of immunity was based upon the assertion that the Soviet Union had conferred on him the diplomatic rank of Second Secretary of the Ministry of Foreign Affairs of the USSR. The court rejected Melekh's claim of immunity. The defendant had not been designated as a representative of the USSR to the United Nations, was not a member of the staff of the Soviet delegation, was not assigned by the USSR to diplomatic duties with the United States or any other government and had not been received by the United States as a diplomat. Diplomatic immunity was therefore unavailable under 22 U.S.C. § 252 and the Headquarters Agreement. Functional immunity was unavailable under the International Organizations Immunities Act: " * * * the defendant does not argue that the alleged criminal acts * * * grew out of or were incidental to his official

activities as a United Nations officer or employee." (at 79). The court also found no basis for immunity in Article 105 of the charter or international law. In response to the argument that diplomatic status arose out of the relationship between the defendant's government and the United Nations, the court stated: "It is neither the defendant's position with his own government, as such, nor the relationship of the defendant's government, as such, with the United Nations that is decisive. What counts is the actual position occupied by the defendant in the United Nations and his actual duties and functions in the United Nations." (at 85)

In support of an identical holding in United States v. Enger, 472 F.Supp. 490 (D.N.J.1978), the court remarked, drily: "Espionage, the crime with which the defendants are charged, is, of course, not one of the functions performed in the defendants' official capacities with the United Nations." (at 502). (The defendants' titles within the United Nations secretariat were, in one case, "Political Affairs Officer attached to the Unit for Coordination and Political Information, Office of the Undersecretary General for Political Information" and, in the other, "Administrative Officer, * * * a member of the Training and Examination Service, Office of Personnel Service." In explaining why diplomatic status is not accorded to all employees of the United Nations the court stated:

> There is, as well, a practical justification based on the legitimate self-interest of the United States. The fact that the United Nations has its headquarters in the United States requires a large number of foreign government representatives and foreign national employees to reside in the New York City area for substantial periods of time. From the standpoint of providing diplomatic immunity, it would be impractical for all concerned if each of those individuals had to be "approved" by the United States in advance. The accommodation reached is not to afford all such foreign nationals full immunity status. Rather, it is to permit the foreign government or international organization to undertake the selection of representatives and employees but, as a means of protecting this country's interests, to limit the availability and scope of immunity. Accordingly, under the Headquarters Agreement and 22 U.S.C. § 288d(b), only a limited number of persons may receive full immunity and then only after prior government approval; all others are cloaked with immunity only when acting within the scope of their employment. (at 503)

UNITED STATES EX REL. CASANOVA v. FITZPATRICK

United States District Court, S.D. New York, 1963.
214 F.Supp. 425.

WEINFELD, District Judge. The petitioner, Roberto Santiesteban Casanova, seeks his release from custody on a writ of habeas corpus on the ground of lack of the Court's jurisdiction over his person. He is under arrest and detention by virtue of a two-count indictment wherein he, two codefendants and two others not named as defendants are charged with conspiracy to commit sabotage and to violate the Foreign Agents Registration Act. He was originally arrested on a warrant issued by the United States Commissioner, based upon a complaint, and held in $250,000 bail fixed by the Commissioner. Thereafter, following his indictment by a grand jury, this Court set bail in the sum of $75,000, which it later reduced to $50,000. Petitioner has been confined since his arrest in default of bail.

Petitioner contends he is entitled to diplomatic immunity and is not subject to Federal arrest, detention or prosecution. The basic facts upon which his claim to immunity rests are not in dispute. He is a Cuban national, appointed by his government as an attache and Resident Member of the Staff of the Permanent Mission of Cuba to the United Nations, hereafter referred to as the "Cuban Mission." He entered the United States on October 3, 1962 with a diplomatic passport issued by his own government, a nonimmigrant visa issued by our Department of State, and a landing card issued by the Immigration and Naturalization Service. From the time of his admission to the United States to the date of his arrest on November 16th he was employed as a Resident Member of the staff of the Cuban Mission.

Petitioner contends that he enjoys diplomatic immunity from arrest and prosecution under (1) Article 105 of the United Nations Charter, (2) Section 15(2) of the Headquarters Agreement of the United Nations, and (3) the Law of Nations. He further contends that even if his claim to immunity is overruled, nonetheless the writ must be sustained, since the Supreme Court of the United States has exclusive and original jurisdiction to try him under Article III of the Constitution of the United States and section 1251 of Title 28, United States Code.

Before considering his contentions, it is desirable to localize the issue with which we deal. The petitioner is not a member of a diplomatic staff accredited to, and recognized by, the United States Government. He is not a representative to, or an employee of, the United Nations. His claim to diplomatic immunity derives solely from his status as a Resident Member of the Cuban Permanent Mission to the United Nations. Whatever right to immunity exists must be considered within the context of that status.

A. THE CLAIM OF DIPLOMATIC IMMUNITY UNDER THE UNITED NATIONS CHARTER.

     * * *

The thrust of the relator's contention is that the declaration in section 2 is self-executing and requires absolute diplomatic immunity be accorded to representatives of members and their staffs. The argument rests upon the postulate, universally recognized in international law, that diplomatic agents are accorded immunity from judicial process so that their governments may not be hampered in their foreign relations by the arrest or harassment of, or interference with, their diplomatic representatives. Petitioner urges that this rationale applies with equal force to the members of a mission to the United Nations and its staff; that unless they enjoy diplomatic immunity they can be prevented from fulfilling their diplomatic functions vis-a-vis the United Nations, if the host country, in this instance the United States, were able to arrest and detain them—in short, that diplomatic immunity is required to assure the independence of the Organization and its members in the discharge of their duties and functions. Accordingly, he contends that Article 105 intended, and in fact confers, full diplomatic immunity. The language of Article 105, its history, as well as subsequent acts by the United States and the United Nations, require rejection of petitioner's claim that by its own force full diplomatic immunity was either intended or granted by the Article.

* * *

The Court concludes that Article 105 of the Charter does not purport to nor does it confer diplomatic immunity. The broadest claim that can be made is that it is self-operative with respect to functional activities. And even if it were so construed, it avails not the petitioner, since by its very language the immunity is confined to acts necessary for the independent exercise of functions in connection with the United Nations. Conspiracy to commit sabotage against the Government of the United States is not a function of any mission or member of a mission to the United Nations. Accordingly, the Court holds that the petitioner does not enjoy diplomatic immunity against prosecution on the indictment by virtue of Article 105 of the United Nations Charter.

B. THE CLAIM OF DIPLOMATIC IMMUNITY UNDER THE HEADQUARTERS AGREEMENT.

(1) Is the Court concluded by the certificate of the State Department?

The development and growth of international organizations over the past two decades, particularly the United Nations as a world force, have brought into being new problems and concepts relating to the immunities and privileges to be accorded the organization, its officials and representatives of member states and their staffs. From the start it was evident that unless adequate immunity was provided to protect them in the exercise of their respective functions, the independence of the organization would be undermined and its effectiveness greatly hampered, if not destroyed. The location of the headquarters presents special problems to the host country and the organization. Access to the headquarters to all persons having legitimate business with the organization is required and, on the other hand, the host country is entitled to protection against the admission of persons likely to engage in activities subversive of its national interests and internal security. These matters are usually provided for by the basic charter or constitution, special agreements or national legislation. With the United States as the site of the United Nations headquarters, our Government was particularly sensitive to the problem of assuring the independence and proper functioning of the United Nations, and also to the protection of its own security. The Headquarters Agreement was one of the means adopted to protect the respective interests.

* * *

Under the above provisions, those who come within its embrace are entitled to the broad diplomatic privileges and immunities enjoyed by diplomatic envoys accredited to the United States. And there would appear to be no question that if the petitioner is entitled to the benefits of Article 15, he is immune from prosecution upon the charges contained in the indictment. Petitioner relies upon section 15(2) as conferring diplomatic immunity upon him by reason of his position as an attache and a Resident Member of the Cuban Mission. The Government challenges his claim, pointing out that the subsection expressly provides that immunity thereunder is accorded only to "such resident members * * * as may be agreed upon between the Secretary-General, the Government of the United States and the Government of the Member concerned." It denies that any such agreement was ever manifested, although it admits that an application therefor was made by the Secretary-General of the United Nations pursuant to the request of the Cuban Mission.

The prosecution has filed an authenticated affidavit of the Chief Protocol Officer of the Department of State certifying that the Government of the United States has not agreed to grant diplomatic immunity to petitioner under section 15(2) of the Headquarters Agreement, "and that he does not enjoy any diplomatic privileges and immunities under the aforesaid Article 15 of the Agreement." Accordingly, it presses that the Court is concluded by this certification.

Thus, a threshold question is presented. The precise issue before the Court is whether, in the light of section 15(2) of the Headquarters Agreement, certification by the Department of State that an individual acknowledged to be a resident attache of the Permanent Cuban Mission to the United Nations has not been "agreed upon" by the Government as entitled to diplomatic privileges and immunities thereunder, concludes the question.

A number of leading authorities do hold that the State Department certification is conclusive where the issue pertains to a diplomatic envoy accredited to the United States. This Court is of the view that such authorities do not control the question here presented. There is a sharp distinction between a diplomatic envoy accredited to the Government of the United States and a representative of a member state to the United Nations, an international organization. The status of each is different and immunity rests upon and is derived from entirely different desiderata.

Acceptance of a diplomatic envoy from a foreign government to the United States rests upon the exercise by our Executive of its power to conduct foreign affairs. It either accepts or rejects the diplomat in its sole and absolute discretion and, if he is received, he thereby is entitled, without more, under the Law of Nations, to full diplomatic immunity. These are political judgments by the Executive Branch of the Government and the Court is concluded thereby. In contrast, a representative of a member state to an international organization, such as the United Nations, is designated by his Government entirely independent of the views of other member states and indeed of the Organization. The United States has no say or veto power with respect to such representative of any member state. These representatives acquire immunity only to the extent that it is granted by legislation, or by agreement, whether under the basic charter, a general convention, or a separate agreement, as in the instant case by the Headquarters Agreement. Accordingly, whether or not a particular individual is entitled to immunity is to be decided within the framework of the applicable document. The Headquarters Agreement simply provides that the three designated parties are to agree upon those entitled to immunity.

* * *

Whether, upon the facts presented by both the Government and the individual involved or his government, immunity exists by reason of the agreement, is not a political question, but a justiciable controversy involving the interpretation of the agreement and its application to the particular facts. In this instance the decision is for the Court and it is not concluded by the unilateral statement of the Government, a party to that agreement and to this controversy, that the individual is not entitled to immunity thereunder.

* * *

The scope of the inquiry is narrowly confined. Did the United States of America, as one of the parties to the Headquarters Agreement, make its decision under section 15(2) either that it agreed or did not agree that petitioner was entitled to diplomatic immunity? The Government's statement that it did not so agree is evidential but not conclusive. Petitioner asserts that by various acts the necessary agreement was manifested; the Government denies it.

* * *

Thus we proceed to consider the petitioner's contention upon the merits.

(2) The claim that section 15(2) of the Headquarters Agreement contemplates agreement only as to categories and not as to individuals.

The petitioner's contention is that the clause "such resident members as may be agreed upon" contemplates an agreement with respect to categories of persons and does not require agreement upon persons within the category. The petitioner's main props in support of his contention are comments and reports of committees of the

United Nations with respect to immunity proposals. While the unilateral views of any United Nations committee or member cannot serve to defeat the express language of the final agreement (the Headquarters Agreement), nonetheless, analysis of such comments and reports negates rather than supports the plaintiff's position.

* * *

The argument that unless petitioner's construction of class agreement is adopted the United States would obtain "a discriminatory, unilateral and effective control of and sanctions against nations of equal sovereignty in the United Nations" is unpersuasive. As already demonstrated, full diplomatic immunity is accorded under subdivision 1 of section 15 to top echelon representatives of member nations identical to that accorded to accredited diplomats to the United States. As to their staff members, pending agreement by the United States under section 15(2), which would entitle them to diplomatic immunity, there is available under the International Organizations Immunities Act the immunity necessary for the independent exercise of their functions, apart from Article 105 of the Charter, if in fact it is self-executing. No member state is prevented from appointing whomever it will to serve on the resident staff of its mission to the United Nations, but the United States, under section 15(2), is not required, simply by reason of one's employment in a particular category, to grant diplomatic immunity. It retains the rights thereunder to agree or not to agree that diplomatic immunity shall extend to individuals who qualify under the broad category "Resident Members of their Staffs." While it has exercised this right sparingly, it has refused, in the instance of at least five individuals, to agree to the request for immunity, without objection by either the Secretary-General or the member state who submitted the request.

The construction advanced would mean that a member state of the United Nations which may be hostile to our interests is free to send to the United States individuals designated as resident members of their staffs, to engage in conduct destructive of our national interest and security and yet have them protected from criminal prosecution on the theory that their designated status cloaked them with diplomatic immunity. It would open the flood gates for the entry of saboteurs, agents provocateur and others under a built-in guarantee that no matter what the criminal conduct, the Government could not prosecute them.

The language of the section controls. There is nothing in its history or in the practice under it to support petitioner's claim. To accept his contention would in effect amend section 15(2) by inserting therein the words "classes of" to read "such classes of resident members * * *."

The Court holds that the status of petitioner as an attache and resident member of the Cuban Mission does not by itself entitle him to diplomatic immunity under section 15(2) and that unless there was the agreement of the United States, as provided therein, the prosecution is not barred. The petitioner claims there was such agreement.

(3) The claim that the United States did agree that petitioner was entitled to diplomatic immunity.

The essence of petitioner's claim is that the issuance of the visa and the landing permit constituted, under the facts and law, the agreement of the Government of the United States that he was entitled to diplomatic privileges and immunities under section 15(2) of the Headquarters Agreement. * * *

   *   *   *

I am of the view that petitioner's contention cannot be upheld. To do so is to transmute the G–1 visa issued by the State Department into the agreement of the United States required under section 15(2) before diplomatic immunity extends to staff members of missions to the United Nations. The fact that the G–1 visa recognized that petitioner had the status encompassed within section 15(2) does not mean that by reason thereof the United States gave the required agreement thereunder. The visa was issued at the request of the Cuban Mission upon presentation of a diplomatic passport issued by the Cuban government and its representation of petitioner's appointment as "diplomatic attache." Since the designation rested with the Cuban government, the United States was obligated under sections 11 and 13 of the Headquarters Agreement not to impose any impediment in his transit to and from the Headquarters District and to provide him with the necessary visa. The visa was the basic document of entry into the United States enroute to his post with his mission.

Petitioner argues that the State Department did not have to issue a G–1 visa in order to fulfill its obligations under the Headquarters Agreement; that so long as petitioner was accorded free access to the Headquarters District, the obligations of the United States Government were met. But as the prosecution contends, once the State Department determined that petitioner, upon the documents and representations contained therein, qualified for a G–1 visa, its issuance to the petitioner was pursuant to rules promulgated under the Immigration and Naturalization Act. The question of the agreement of the United States Government to diplomatic immunity was entirely separate from facilitating petitioner's entry to assume his duties with his mission.

I conclude that the Government of the United States did not, by the issuance of the visa and the landing permit, give its agreement that petitioner, on his entry into the United States to assume his duties as a member of the Cuban Mission, was thereby entitled to diplomatic immunity under section 15(2) of the Headquarters Agreement.

C. THE CLAIM OF DIPLOMATIC IMMUNITY UNDER THE LAW OF NATIONS.

Here the petitioner's position is that under the Law of Nations he had diplomatic immunity from the time of his entry until the Government of the United States took definitive action upon the request of the Cuban Mission that he be "agreed upon" for diplomatic immunity under the Headquarters Agreement. Again, the claim centers in part about the G–1 visa and landing permit. He urges in substance that by this issuance the United States acknowledged his status for the purpose of entry into the United States to assume his duties with his mission, aware that he was eligible for diplomatic immunity. Accordingly, he contends that he was entitled to diplomatic immunity from the time of his entry on the same principle as that applicable under the Law of Nations to diplomats awaiting acknowledgment by governments to which they are accredited and which attaches even before they have been received by it—in fine, that until he was either agreed upon or rejected in response to his government's request, he was protected. *   *   *

   *   *   *

  Petitioner's path is blocked by the same reasoning upon which the Court rejected the Government's position that its unilateral determination that he was not entitled to diplomatic immunity under the Headquarters Agreement was conclusive. As the Government's suggestion of an analogy to diplomats accredited to the United States was refused above, so is petitioner's in this instance. It is the Headquarters Agreement, the Charter and the applicable statutes of the United States that govern the determination of his rights, not the Law of Nations. The Law of Nations comes into play and has applicability in defining the nature and scope of diplomatic immunity only once it is found a person is entitled thereto under an applicable agreement or statute.

  The Court concludes that petitioner is not entitled to diplomatic immunity by virtue of the Law of Nations.

   *   *   *

  The petition for a writ of habeas corpus is dismissed upon the merits.

ANONYMOUS v. ANONYMOUS

United States, Family Court of the City of New York, 1964.
252 N.Y.S.2d 913, 44 Misc.2d 14.

LOUIS A. PAGNUCCO, Judge.

  This case arises from a verified petition filed in Filiation Term of the Family Court of the State of New York in the City of New York. Petitioner alleges that she is pregnant with child which is likely to be born out of wedlock, offers a certificate of pregnancy, and asks this Court to issue a warrant of arrest to require the Respondent to show cause why the Court should not enter against him a declaration of paternity, an order of support and such other and further relief as may be appropriate under the circumstances. *   *   *

In support of her application for the warrant of arrest, the petitioner alleges that the respondent is the _____ Ambassador attached to the _____ Mission to the United Nations, that he is likely to leave the jurisdiction and that a summons would be unavailing. A special appearance has been entered on behalf of the "Embassy of the Republic of _____ amici curiae," urging that this court lacks jurisdiction because of diplomatic immunity and status.

The Embassy predicates its claim on the "Headquarters Agreement" between the United Nations and the United States, as conferring on resident representatives of Member Nations to the United Nations the privileges and immunities of ambassadors accredited to the United States, Public Law 357, 80th Cong., 1st Sess., Ch. 482, 61 Stat. 756, (1947); * * * and on 22 U.S.Code Section 252, declaring that any Federal or State writ of process "whereby the person of any ambassador or public minister of any foreign prince or State, authorized and received as such by the President" is arrested or imprisoned, or his goods or chattels seized or attached shall be void.

   *   *   *

   *   *   *   [I]n the case at hand both the attorney for the petitioner and the lawyers for the Embassy of the Republic of _____ agree that the Respondent is the _____ Ambassador attached to the _____ mission to the United Nations. The brief on behalf of the Embassy shows that the Respondent is designated by the Republic of _____, a member of the United Nations, as its Permanent Representative and Ambassador Extraordinary and Plenipotentiary to the United Nations, and that he holds a card issued by Secretary of State Herter, certifying that he is entitled as the Permanent Representative of the _____, "to the privileges and immunities set forth in Public Law 357, 80th Congress" (1947). [Although not determinative of the application, we note a letter from the United States Mission to the United Nations, appended by counsel for the petitioner, informing him that, pursuant to his request, the matter of certain allegations made by the petitioner were discussed with the respondent Ambassador, and that he categorically denied them.]

Public Law 357 of the 80th Congress, supra, Tit. 22 of the U.S. Code, § 287, is known as the "Headquarters Agreement". It was entered into between the United States and the United Nations. Article V, section 15, subdivision 1 provides that every person designated by a Member of the United Nations as its principal resident representative to the United Nations or as its resident representative with the rank of Ambassador or Minister Plenipotentiary, shall "be entitled in the territory of the United States to the same privileges and immunities, subject to corresponding conditions and obligations, as it accords to diplomatic envoys accredited to it. * * *" It is clear from the context and purpose of the statute that "it" refers to the United States, and that the respondent Ambassador to the United Nations having been so designated is entitled, by virtue of the Headquarters Agreement, to whatever privileges and immunities are "accorded to diplomatic envoys accredited to the United States" (Senate

Report 559, 80th Cong., 1st Sess., at p. 4, submitted by Senator Vandenberg, Committee on Foreign Relations, to accompany S.J.Res. 144 and S.J.Res. 136; and see, to same effect, Tsiang v. Tsiang, 194 Misc. 259, 260, 86 N.Y.S.2d 556 (Sup.Ct., Sp.T.N.Y.Co., 1949), upholding diplomatic immunity in a separation suit against the permanent resident representative of the Chinese Government to the United Nations; Arcaya v. Paez, 145 F.Supp. 464 (S.D.N.Y., 1956), aff'd on op. below, 244 F.2d 958 (2nd Cir.), applying diplomatic immunity in a suit for libel against envoy to United Nations *   *   * .

The scope of diplomatic immunity from local jurisdiction, predicated as it is upon the national and international need to avoid impediments to effective diplomatic intercourse has been set forth in the "Instructions to Diplomatic Officers of the United States, March 8, 1927," prescribed by Executive Order (Collection of the Diplomatic and Consular Laws and Regulations of Various Countries, by Feller and Hudson, Carnegie Endowment for International Peace, at pp. 1263–4) * * *.

Having ascertained that the respondent _____ is the accredited ambassador and principal representative of the _____ to the United Nations, this court reaches the conclusion that the motion for a warrant of arrest must be denied. From reading the pertinent cases and statutes, in relation to the law of nations, the court concludes that it has no jurisdiction to entertain paternity proceedings against the respondent while he is serving in his present official capacity, and accordingly the petition is dismissed. This, of course, is without prejudice to any right of the petitioner to renew if and when the respondent is not clothed with diplomatic immunity, and this judgment of the court shall not be construed as limiting or abridging any rights to assert any claim by or on behalf of the yet unborn child in any future proceedings in this or in any other forum.

Part V

METHODS OF OPERATION IN THE
INTERNATIONAL SYSTEM

Chapter 15

INTERNATIONAL AGREEMENTS: THE
INTERNATIONAL LAW

1. *The "treaty on treaties": present status and significance as evidence of customary law.* In our own uses of this casebook we ask our students to read the Vienna Convention on the Law of Treaties at the outset. The Convention entered into force January 27, 1980. It is in the Documentary Supplement. Although not yet acted upon in the Senate of the United States, to which the President referred it on November 21, 1971, the Vienna Convention is the best evidence of what present customary international law about treaties and other international agreements is, at least with respect to most of its provisions. The Department of State has stated since 1973 that it considers the convention as a codification of customary international law and thus as authoritative with respect to the executive's treatment of international agreements issues arising after May 22, 1969. See Rovine, Digest of United States Practice in International Law 1973, at 307, 482–83 (1974). Several judicial decisions in the United States have also followed the convention. While these executive and judicial acceptances may raise problems of separation of powers and of "supreme law" under Article VI of the Constitution (cf. the material on this in the next chapter), especially if the Senate buries the convention or rejects it as a result of the opposition of one-third of the Senate plus one, study of the law about treaties during the usable life of this edition ought to be undertaken with knowledge of the convention's treatment of the various international legal issues that follow. Ask yourselves when you finish this chapter: Is the Vienna Convention either silent or a poor guide on any of the issues raised in this chapter? What issues does it clarify well or seem to settle? Where, if anywhere, does the convention expand doctrine?

The convention was developed from draft articles prepared by the International Law Commission. Four rapporteurs over many years presented four different approaches to the commission. The work of the last rapporteur (Sir Humphrey Waldock, now a judge of the International Court of Justice) was overwhelmingly the most influential on the commission as it prepared the draft that went to the

Convention at Vienna. The International Law Commission's Draft Articles, with commentary, can be found in 61 Am.J.Int'l L. 263 (1967). The convention itself is authoritatively commented upon by two of the American negotiators, Kearney and Dalton, in The Treaty on Treaties, 64 Am.J.Int'l Law 495 (1970). These authors give this useful perspective:

> The Convention on the Law of Treaties sets forth the code of rules that will govern the indispensable element in the conduct of foreign affairs, the mechanism without which international intercourse could not exist, much less function. It is possible to imagine a future in which the treaty will no longer be the standard device for dealing with any and all international problems —a future in which for example, the use of regulations promulgated by international organizations in special fields of activity, such as the World Health Organization's sanitary regulations, will become the accepted substitute for the lawmaking activity now effected through international agreement. But, in the present state of international development, this is crystal-gazing. For the foreseeable future, the treaty will remain the cement that holds the world community together.

2. *The wide range of utilization of international agreements.* Undertakings between states are major tools of operations in the international legal system. Rules of customary law, derived from the usual modes of conduct of international relations, custom, right reason, judicial decisions, general principles of law common to the world's major legal systems and the like, usually lags behind developing needs within the international community; and for technologically complicated and politically sophisticated situations they lack specificity. International agreements, on the other hand, are often made because the parties thereto have realized a need to reach specific accord upon some issue, matter or common concern. Like contracts or trusts in private law, international agreements are cut to the cloth of the interests of the parties.

Functionally, international agreements cover a wide range of interests, extending from certain types of agreements that are in effect conveyances of real estate (treaties of lease, cession and admeasurement of boundaries) through mutual promises to pursue common lines of action (military alliances, mutual defense, safety at sea) to organic arrangements that function much as constitutions (the Charter of the United Nations). Some international agreements are regarded as executed internationally as between the parties when made (boundary treaties). Others are executory, such as the mutual promises of the members of the North Atlantic Treaty Organization to consider an attack on one an attack on all and to respond effectively in such context.

International agreements carry many labels: treaty, convention, modus vivendi, concordat, charter, articles of agreement, etc. Basically, the labels are not legally significant, except that some are used mainly to denominate agreements of two or at most, several states, while others refer to multipartite agreements, which, as such, may have special rules governing their applicability (e. g., reservations).

In Chapter 17 we shall see that international agreements have given the international legal system almost all the rules that exist as to trade and investment. In the more traditional political areas, international agreements alter or expand customary international law. Also, they may restate or codify it. Finally, given the lack so far of an effective international parallel to national legislatures, international agreements of the multipartite sort are used to make new law such as with respect to pollution of the high seas, uses of the moon, aerial hi-jacking, human rights. Sometimes these latter are referred to as law-making treaties, and it is with respect to them that the analytical issue whether the rules therein stated are themselves international law arises. Here it suffices to note that the modern international practitioner must of necessity have a lot to do with international agreements and that the International Court of Justice has subject-matter jurisdiction as to issues concerning international agreements.

One of the most significant new types of international agreements is the Treaty of Rome, which created the European Economic Community (EEC). It establishes new structures, binds the member states to stated courses of action in the field of the integration of their economies and has an in-built capacity to generate new rules of law through the operations of the authorized agencies of the community. Is the legal system of the EEC international law among the member states, or is it a new species of semi-federal domestic law? There is probably no clear answer to this question at this stage of the EEC's life; but, again the law in and deriving from the Treaty of Rome is of great professional interest or concern to lawyers everywhere.

SECTION A. INTERNATIONAL AGREEMENTS AS BASES OF LEGAL RIGHTS AND DUTIES

Pacta sunt servanda. Before the Vienna Convention, the authorities were not always clearly in agreement as between the notions that the Latin phrase pacta sunt servanda meant that international agreements should be performed in good faith or with utmost fidelity (uberrima fides). Article 26 of the convention states the former as the standard; and the negotiating history shows that it would have been difficult to go beyond it, because other differences arose as to the formulation of the article. The ILC draft was adopted in principle to avoid putting the other differences to a vote, and it had used good faith. Notice that Article 26 states that every treaty in force is binding on the parties and must be performed in good faith, whereas some delegates at Vienna wanted it stated that only valid treaties in force should be so entitled, and some others wished to confine the performance standard to treaties in force in conformity with the convention, which, of course, would have raised a serious retroactivity problem. See the Kearney and Dalton article at p. 516. What is the difference between the two standards?

YALTA CONFERENCE, AGREEMENT REGARDING ENTRY OF THE SOVIET UNION INTO THE WAR AGAINST JAPAN, FEB. 11, 1945

59 Stat. 1823.

The leaders of the three Great Powers—the Soviet Union, the United States of America and Great Britain—have agreed that in two or three months after Germany has surrendered and the war in Europe has terminated the Soviet Union shall enter into the war against Japan on the side of the Allies on condition that:

1.   The status quo in Outer-Mongolia (The Mongolian People's Republic) shall be preserved;

2.   The former rights of Russia violated by the treacherous attack of Japan in 1904 shall be restored, viz:

(a)   the southern part of Sakhalin as well as all the islands adjacent to it shall be returned to the Soviet Union,

(b)   the commercial port of Dairen shall be internationalized, the preeminent interests of the Soviet Union in this port being safeguarded and the lease of Port Arthur as a naval base of the USSR restored,

(c)   the Chinese-Eastern Railroad and the South-Manchurian Railroad which provides an outlet to Dairen shall be jointly operated by the establishment of a joint Soviet-Chinese Company it being understood that the preeminent interests of the Soviet Union shall be safeguarded and that China shall retain full sovereignty in Manchuria;

3.   The Kuril islands shall be handed over to the Soviet Union.

It is understood, that the agreement concerning Outer-Mongolia and the ports and railroads referred to above will require concurrence of Generalissimo Chiang Kai-Shek. The President will take measures in order to obtain this concurrence on advice from Marshal Stalin.

The Heads of the three Great Powers have agreed that these claims of the Soviet Union shall be unquestionably fulfilled after Japan has been defeated.

For its part the Soviet Union expresses its readiness to conclude with the National Government of China a pact of friendship and alliance between the USSR and China in order to render assistance to

China with its armed forces for the purpose of liberating China from the Japanese yoke.

И. Сталин [a]
Franklin D. Roosevelt
Winston S. Churchill

UNITED STATES POSITION ON SOVIET–JAPANESE PEACE TREATY NEGOTIATIONS

35 United States Department of State Bulletin 484 (1956).

Following is the text of an aide memoire which was given to the Japanese Ambassador at Washington on September 7 and to the Japanese Foreign Minister at Tokyo on September 8.

Pursuant to the request made by the Japanese Foreign Minister, Mr. Shigemitsu, in the course of recent conversations in London with the Secretary of State, Mr. Dulles, the Department of State has reviewed the problems presented in the course of the current negotiations for a treaty of peace between the Union of Soviet Socialist Republics and Japan, with particular reference to the interest of the United States as a signatory of the San Francisco Peace Treaty, and on the basis of such review makes the following observations.

The Government of the United States believes that the state of war between Japan and the Soviet Union should be formally terminated. Such action has been overdue since 1951, when the Soviet Union declined to sign the San Francisco Peace Treaty. Japan should also long since have been admitted to the United Nations, for which it is fully qualified; and Japanese prisoners of war in Soviet hands should long since have been returned in accordance with the surrender terms.

With respect to the territorial question, as the Japanese Government has been previously informed, the United States regards the so-called Yalta agreement as simply a statement of common purposes by the then heads of the participating powers, and not as a final determination by those powers or of any legal effect in transferring territories. The San Francisco Peace Treaty (which conferred no rights upon the Soviet Union because it refused to sign) did not determine the sovereignty of the territories renounced by Japan, leaving that question, as was stated by the Delegate of the United States at San Francisco, to "international solvents other than this treaty".

* * *

Department of State,
        Washington, September 7, 1956.

a.   J. Stalin

LEGAL STATUS OF EASTERN GREENLAND
(DENMARK v. NORWAY)

Permanent Court of International Justice, 1933.
P.C.I.J., ser. A/B, No. 53.

* * *

By an Application instituting proceedings, filed with the Registry of the Court on July 12th, 1931, in accordance with Article 40 of the Statute and Article 35 of the Rules of Court, the Royal Danish Government, relying on the optional clause of Article 36, paragraph 2, of the Statute, brought before the Permanent Court of International Justice a suit against the Royal Norwegian Government on the ground that the latter Government had, on July 10th, 1931, published a proclamation declaring that it had proceeded to occupy certain territories in Eastern Greenland, which, in the contention of the Danish Government, were subject to the sovereignty of the Crown of Denmark. The Application, after thus indicating the subject of the dispute, proceeds, subject to the subsequent presentation of any cases, counter-cases and any other documents or evidence, to formulate the claim by asking the Court for judgment to the effect that "the promulgation of the above-mentioned declaration of occupation and any steps taken in this respect by the Norwegian Government constitute a violation of the existing legal situation and are accordingly unlawful and invalid."

* * *

The Danish submission in the written pleading, that the Norwegian occupation of July 10th, 1931, is invalid, is founded upon the contention that the area occupied was at the time of the occupation subject to Danish sovereignty; that the area is part of Greenland, and at the time of the occupation Danish sovereignty existed over all Greenland; consequently it could not be occupied by another Power.

In support of this contention, the Danish Government advances two propositions. The first is that the sovereignty which Denmark now enjoys over Greenland has existed for a long time, has been continuously and peacefully exercised and, until the present dispute, has not been contested by any Power. This proposition Denmark sets out to establish as a fact. The second proposition is that Norway has by treaty or otherwise herself recognized Danish sovereignty over Greenland as a whole and therefore cannot now dispute it.

* * *

The Court will now consider the second Danish proposition that Norway had given certain undertakings which recognized Danish sovereignty over all Greenland. These undertakings have been fully discussed by the two Parties, and in three cases the Court considers that undertakings were given.

* * *

In addition to the engagements dealt with above, the Ihlen declaration, viz. the reply given by M. Ihlen, the Norwegian Minister for

Foreign Affairs, to the Danish Minister on July 22nd, 1919, must also be considered.   *   *   *

  *   *   *   [T]he point which must now be considered is whether the Ihlen declaration—even if not constituting a definitive recognition of Danish sovereignty—did not constitute an engagement obliging Norway to refrain from occupying any part of Greenland.

The Danish request and M. Ihlen's reply were recorded by him in a minute, worded as follows:

I.   The Danish Minister informed me to-day that his Government has heard from Paris that the question of Spitzbergen will be examined by a Commission of four members (American, British, French, Italian). If the Danish Government is questioned by this Commission, it is prepared to reply that Denmark has no interests in Spitzbergen, and that it has no reason to oppose the wishes of Norway in regard to the settlement of this question.

Furthermore, the Danish Minister made the following statement:

The Danish Government has for some years past been anxious to obtain the recognition of all the interested Powers of Denmark's sovereignty over the whole of Greenland, and it proposes to place this question before the above-mentioned Committee at the same time. During the negotiations with the U.S.A. over the cession of the Danish West Indies, the Danish Government raised this question in so far as concerns recognition by the Government of the U.S.A., and it succeeded in inducing the latter to agree that, concurrently with the conclusion of a convention regarding the cession of the said islands, it would make a declaration to the effect that the Government of the U.S.A. would not object to the Danish Government extending their political and economic interests to the whole of Greenland.

The Danish Government is confident (he added) that the Norwegian Government will not make any difficulties in the settlement of this question.

I replied that the question would be examined.

14/7—19 Ih.

II.   To-day I informed the Danish Minister that the Norwegian Government would not make any difficulties in the settlement of this question.

22/7—19 Ih.

The incident has, therefore, reference, first to the attitude to be observed by Denmark before the Committee of the Peace Conference at Paris in regard to Spitzbergen, this attitude being that Denmark would not "oppose the wishes of Norway in regard to the settlement of this question"; as is known, these wishes related to the sovereignty over Spitzbergen. Secondly, the request showed that "the Danish Government was confident that the Norwegian Government would not make any difficulty" in the settlement of the Greenland question;

the aims that Denmark had in view in regard to the last-named island were to secure the "recognition by all the Powers concerned of Danish sovereignty over the whole of Greenland," and that there should be no opposition "to the Danish Government extending their political and economic interests to the whole of Greenland." It is clear from the relevant Danish documents which preceded the Danish Minister's démarche at Christiania on July 14th, 1919, that the Danish attitude in the Spitzbergen question and the Norwegian attitude in the Greenland question were regarded in Denmark as interdependent, and this interdependence appears to be reflected also in M. Ihlen's minute of the interview. Even if this interdependence—which, in view of the affirmative reply of the Norwegian Government, in whose name the Minister for Foreign Affairs was speaking, would have created a bilateral engagement—is not held to have been established, it can hardly be denied that what Denmark was asking of Norway ("not to make any difficulties in the settlement of the [Greenland] question") was equivalent to what she was indicating her readiness to concede in the Spitzbergen question (to refrain from opposing "the wishes of Norway in regard to the settlement of this question"). What Denmark desired to obtain from Norway was that the latter should do nothing to obstruct the Danish plans in regard to Greenland. The declaration which the Minister for Foreign Affairs gave on July 22nd, 1919, on behalf of the Norwegian Government, was definitely affirmative: "I told the Danish Minister to-day that the Norwegian Government would not make any difficulty in the settlement of this question."

The Court considers it beyond all dispute that a reply of this nature given by the Minister for Foreign Affairs on behalf of his Government in response to a request by the diplomatic representative of a foreign Power, in regard to a question falling within his province, is binding upon the country to which the Minister belongs.

* * *

It follows that, as a result of the undertaking involved in the Ihlen declaration of July 22nd, 1919, Norway is under an obligation to refrain from contesting Danish sovereignty over Greenland as a whole, and a fortiori to refrain from occupying a part of Greenland.

* * *

For these reasons, the court, by twelve votes to two,

(1) decides that the declaration of occupation promulgated by the Norwegian Government on July 10th, 1931, and any steps taken in this respect by that Government, constitute a violation of the existing legal situation and are accordingly unlawful and invalid;

* * *

Dissenting Opinion of Mr. ANZILOTTI:

* * *

The question whether the so-called Ihlen declaration was merely a provisional indication (Norwegian contention) or a definitive undertaking (Danish contention) has been debated at length. * * *

The outcome of all this is therefore an agreement, concluded between the Danish Minister at Christiania, on behalf of the Danish Government, and the Norwegian Minister for Foreign Affairs, on behalf of the Norwegian Government, by means of purely verbal declarations.

The validity of this agreement has been questioned, having regard, in the first place, to its verbal form, and to the competence of the Minister for Foreign Affairs.

As regards the form, it should be noted, to begin with, that as both Parties are agreed as to the existence and tenor of these declarations, the question of proof does not arise. Moreover, there does not seem to be any rule of international law requiring that agreements of this kind must necessarily be in writing, in order to be valid.

The question of the competence of the Minister for Foreign Affairs is closely connected with the contents of the agreement in question; and these have already been determined.

No arbitral or judicial decision relating to the international competence of a Minister for Foreign Affairs has been brought to the knowledge of the Court; nor has this question been exhaustively treated by legal authorities. In my opinion, it must be recognized that the constant and general practice of States has been to invest the Minister for Foreign Affairs—the direct agent of the chief of the State—with authority to make statements on current affairs to foreign diplomatic representatives, and in particular to inform them as to the attitude which the government, in whose name he speaks, will adopt in a given question. Declarations of this kind are binding upon the State.

As regards the question whether Norwegian constitutional law authorized the Minister for Foreign Affairs to make the declaration, that is a point which, in my opinion, does not concern the Danish Government: it was M. Ihlen's duty to refrain from giving his reply until he had obtained any assent that might be requisite under the Norwegian laws.

[Observations and a dissenting opinion omitted.]

RIGHTS AND OBLIGATIONS OF STATES NOT PARTIES TO AN INTERNATIONAL AGREEMENT

Read Articles 34 through 37 of the Vienna Convention, Documentary Supplement.

FREE ZONES OF UPPER SAVOY AND THE DISTRICT OF GEX (FRANCE v. SWITZERLAND)

Permanent Court of International Justice, 1932.
P.C.I.J., ser. A/B, No. 46.

[France contended that the Treaty of Versailles (1919) abrogated certain tariff-free areas within France, on the border with Switzerland in the region of Geneva. Switzerland claimed that her rights in these areas had been provided in the post-Napoleonic settlement of Europe, by various treaties stemming from the Congress of Vienna, in the years 1814–15. The court found that Switzerland had sufficiently participated in the earlier arrangements as to have acquired rights as to the free zones. It also decided that the Treaty of Versailles was not intended to abrogate these rights. Nevertheless, the court expressed a viewpoint on the question whether rights that Switzerland might have acquired as a non-party to the 1814–15 treaties could have been taken away by France and other parties to the Versailles treaty, to which Switzerland was not a party. On third party rights the court made a statement which a common law lawyer would call obiter dictum. It appears below.]

It cannot be lightly presumed that stipulations favourable to a third State have been adopted with the object of creating an actual right in its favour. There is however nothing to prevent the will of sovereign States from having this object and this effect. The question of the existence of a right acquired under an instrument drawn between other States is therefore one to be decided in each particular case: it must be ascertained whether the States which have stipulated in favour of a third State meant to create for that State an actual right *which the latter has accepted as such.* [Emphasis supplied.]

Question. Before the Vienna Convention the statement above was the main authority on the point. Does the convention follow the dictum squarely? See Article 36 of the convention.

JUS COGENS

Question. Are there overriding restrictions on what states may do by international agreements? The Latin term jus cogens (compelling law) may supply an answer.

INTERNATIONAL LAW COMMISSION, DRAFT ARTICLES ON THE LAW OF TREATIES

61 American Journal of International Law 263, 409 (1967).

Article 50 [a]

Treaties conflicting with a peremptory norm of general international law (jus cogens)

A treaty is void if it conflicts with a peremptory norm of general international law from which no derogation is permitted and which

---

a.   Draft Article 50, with changes, corresponds to Article 53 in the convention.

can be modified only by a subsequent norm of general international law having the same character.

Commentary

(1) The view that in the last analysis there is no rule of international law from which states cannot at their own free will contract out has become increasingly difficult to sustain, although some jurists deny the existence of any rules of jus cogens in international law, since in their view even the most general rules still fall short of being universal. The Commission pointed out that the law of the Charter concerning the prohibition of the use of force in itself constitutes a conspicuous example of a rule in international law having the character of jus cogens. Moreover, if some governments in their comments have expressed doubts as to the advisability of this article unless it is accompanied by provision for independent adjudication, only one questioned the existence of rules of jus cogens in the international law of today. Accordingly, the Commission concluded that in codifying the law of treaties it must start from the basis that today there are certain rules from which states are not competent to derogate at all by a treaty arrangement, and which may be changed only by another rule of the same character.

(2) The formulation of the article is not free from difficulty, since there is no simple criterion by which to identify a general rule of international law as having the character of jus cogens. Moreover, the majority of the general rules of international law do not have that character, and states may contract out of them by treaty. It would therefore be going much too far to state that a treaty is void if its provisions conflict with a rule of general international law. Nor would it be correct to say that a provision in a treaty possesses the character of jus cogens merely because the parties have stipulated that no derogation from that provision is to be permitted, so that another treaty which conflicted with that provision would be void. Such a stipulation may be inserted in any treaty with respect to any subject matter for any reasons which may seem good to the parties. The conclusion by a party of a later treaty derogating from such a stipulation may, of course, engage its responsibility for a breach of the earlier treaty. But the breach of the stipulation does not, simply as such, render the treaty void (see Article 26). It is not the form of a general rule of international law but the particular nature of the subject matter with which it deals that may, in the opinion of the Commission, give it the character of jus cogens.

(3) The emergence of rules having the character of jus cogens is comparatively recent, while international law is in process of rapid development. The Commission considered the right course to be to provide in general terms that a treaty is void if it conflicts with a rule of jus cogens and to leave the full content of this rule to be worked out in state practice and in the jurisprudence of international tribunals. Some members of the Commission felt that there might be advantage in specifying, by way of illustration, some of the most ob-

vious and best settled rules of jus cogens in order to indicate by these examples the general nature and scope of the rule contained in the article. Examples suggested included (a) a treaty contemplating an unlawful use of force contrary to the principles of the Charter, (b) a treaty contemplating the performance of any other act criminal under international law, and (c) a treaty contemplating or conniving at the commission of acts, such as trade in slaves, piracy or genocide, in the suppression of which every state is called upon to co-operate. Other members expressed the view that, if examples were given, it would be undesirable to appear to limit the scope of the article to cases involving acts which constitute crimes under international law; treaties violating human rights, the equality of states or the principle of self-determination were mentioned as other possible examples. The Commission decided against including any examples of rules of jus cogens in the article for two reasons. First, the mention of some cases of treaties void for conflict with a rule of jus cogens might, even with the most careful drafting, lead to misunderstanding as to the position concerning other cases not mentioned in the article. Secondly, if the Commission were to attempt to draw up, even on a selective basis, a list of the rules of international law which are to be regarded as having the character of jus cogens, it might find itself engaged in a prolonged study of matters which fall outside the scope of the present articles.

(4) Accordingly, the article simply provides that a treaty is void "if it conflicts with a peremptory norm of general international law from which no derogation is permitted and which can be modified only by a subsequent norm of general international law having the same character." This provision makes it plain that nullity attaches to a treaty under the article only if the rule with which it conflicts is a peremptory norm of general international law from which no derogation is permitted, even by agreement between particular states. On the other hand, it would clearly be wrong to regard even rules of jus cogens as immutable and incapable of modification in the light of future developments. As a modification of a rule of jus cogens would today most probably be effected through a general multilateral treaty, the Commission thought it desirable to indicate that such a treaty would fall outside the scope of the article. The article, therefore defines rules of jus cogens as peremptory norms of general international law from which no derogation is permitted "and which can be modified only by a subsequent norm of general international law having the same character."

     *   *   *

SCHWELB, SOME ASPECTS OF INTERNATIONAL JUS COGENS AS FORMULATED BY THE INTERNATIONAL LAW COMMISSION

61 American Journal of International Law 946, 949 (1967).*

Jurisprudence on International Jus Cogens

The only instances involving the authoritative invocation of something akin to international jus cogens which can be traced are the four judicial pronouncements mentioned below, two of which were dissenting opinions, while the other two were those of national courts. Certain United Nations proceedings on the Cyprus question have also a bearing on the problem. There appears to be no case on record in which an international court or arbitral tribunal decided that an international treaty was void because of repugnancy to a peremptory rule, in which an international political organ made a decision or recommendation to this effect, or where, in settling a dispute, governments have agreed on such a proposition.

In the case of the S. S. Wimbledon the question at issue was whether Germany, as a neutral in the Polish-Russian war, was in 1921 under the obligation to permit contraband destined for Poland to pass through the Kiel Canal. The Court decided that Article 380 of the Peace Treaty of Versailles applied, under which the Canal was to be maintained open to the vessels of all nations at peace with Germany. Mr. Schücking, the German national judge, dissented. One of his arguments was the consideration that, by permitting the passage of the ship carrying contraband, Germany would have violated the duties of a neutral. It cannot have been the intention of the victorious states, he said, to bind Germany to commit offenses against third states. It would have been impossible to give effect to such an intention because it is impossible to undertake by treaty a valid obligation to perform acts which would violate the rights of third parties. Judges Anzilotti and Huber, who also dissented from the decision of the Court, did not adduce an argument based on the partial invalidity of the Peace Treaty article.

State Practice on Jus Cogens

In the Treaty of Guarantee between Cyprus on the one hand and Greece, Turkey and the United Kingdom on the other, signed at Nicosia on August 16, 1960, it is provided that, in the event of a breach of certain provisions of the treaty, the three guarantor Powers undertake to consult together with respect to the representations or measures necessary to insure observance of those provisions. Insofar as common or concerted action may not prove possible, each of the three guaranteeing Powers reserves the right to take action with the sole aim of re-establishing the state of affairs created by the treaty.

* Reprinted by permission of the American Society of International Law.

When, after the outbreak of inter-communal violence on Cyprus in December, 1963, the Security Council was seised of the situation, the treaty provisions just summarized became one of the contested points, particularly the right of unilateral and possibly armed intervention of any of the guaranteeing Powers. One of the reasons adduced in support of the claim that the provision was invalid was the contention that it conflicted with a peremptory rule of international law (jus cogens) within the meaning of what is now Article 50 of the draft articles on the law of treaties, particularly with the rule prohibiting the threat or use of force as formulated in Article 2(4) of the Charter. The claim was also made that the contested provision was an unequal or "leonine" treaty, a concept to which further reference will be made later in the present article. The immediate outcome was the Security Council resolution of March 4, 1964, which recommended the creation of a United Nations peacekeeping force in Cyprus and the designation of a mediator for the purpose of promoting a peaceful solution and an agreed settlement. The Security Council abstained from expressing an opinion on the validity or otherwise of the treaty. It said in the Preamble to the resolution, however, that it considered "the positions taken by the parties in relation to the Treaties signed at Nicosia" and that it "had in mind" the relevant provisions of the Charter and its Article 2, paragraph 4, thus leaving the question open whether or not the treaties were repugnant to the peremptory rule codified in that paragraph.

In 1965 the General Assembly was seised of the Cyprus question and adopted a resolution in which it took "cognizance of the fact that the Republic of Cyprus, as *an equal Member* of the United Nations is, in accordance with the Charter of the United Nations, entitled to enjoy, *and should enjoy*, full sovereignty and complete independence *without any foreign intervention or interference.*" The General Assembly further called upon all states, "in conformity with their obligations under the Charter, and in particular Article 2, paragraphs 1 and 4, to respect the sovereignty, unity, independence and territorial integrity of the Republic of Cyprus *and to refrain from any intervention directed against it.*" The vote on this resolution indicates, however, that the authority which can be attributed to it is not very great, as only 47 Members voted for it, five against, and 54 Members abstained. For the purposes of the present article it should also be noted that the jus cogens rules which were invoked (sovereign equality and the prohibition of the threat of force) are expressly set forth in the Charter.

THE NEGOTIATING HISTORY OF JUS COGENS
AT VIENNA

Kearney and Dalton, Treaty on Treaties, 64 American Journal
of International Law 495, 535 (1970).*

From this heated discussion the committee of the whole moved immediately to one of the most controversial articles produced by the Commission—Article 53 on treaties conflicting with a peremptory norm of international law or, as it is customarily described, the Jus Cogens Doctrine. The Commission's proposal was:

> A treaty is void if it conflicts with a peremptory norm of general international law from which no derogation is permitted and which can be modified only by a subsequent norm of general international law having the same character.

Although the principle that there are fundamental requirements of international behavior that cannot be set aside by treaty is considered a fairly recent development, it has been incorporated into Section 116 of the Restatement of the Foreign Relations Law of the United States in the following terms:

> An international agreement may be made with respect to any matter except to the extent that the agreement conflicts with
>
> a) the rules of international law incorporating basic standards of international conduct.   *   *   *

Both the Commission's article and the Restatement, however, present the same difficulty: they leave open the question what is a peremptory norm of international law or what is a basic standard of international conduct.

     *   *   *

In his second report Waldock had proposed three categories of jus cogens: (a) the use or threat of force in contravention of the principles of the United Nations Charter; (b) international crimes so characterized by international law; (c) acts or omissions whose suppression is required by international law. The discussion in the Commission indicated such varying viewpoints on what constituted jus cogens that the categories were dropped. A comment regarding the resulting draft is pertinent: "Mr. Bartoš explained that the drafting committee had been compelled to refrain from giving any definition of jus cogens whatever, because two-thirds of the Commission had been opposed to each formula proposed."

The position in the conference reflected the position in the Commission. There was no substantial attack made upon the concept of jus cogens. Indeed, it would be very difficult to make a sustainable case that two states are free to make a treaty in which they agree to attack and carve up a third state or to sell some of their residents to each other as slaves. But as Minagawa points out, "examples such as

* Reprinted by permission of the American Society of International Law.

the treaty permitting piracy or re-establishing slavery appear to concern merely 'une pure hypothèse d'école'." The real problem was how to define the test for recognizing a rule of jus cogens.

* * *

The Austrian jurist, Hanspeter Neuhold, gives in his analysis of the 1968 session a lively account of the conclusion of debate:

> After five meetings had been devoted to discussing the various problems of jus cogens, the scene was set for the final showdown at a night meeting on 7 May which lasted almost till midnight. It was fought with all the weapons which the arsenal of the rules of procedure offered the delegates. Thus, the representative of the USA introduced a motion to defer the vote on article [53] and to refer all amendments to the Drafting Committee with a view to working out a more acceptable text. This proposal was endorsed by the United Kingdom and France. Conversely, the Ghanaian delegate, who was supported by the representatives of India and the USSR, moved to take a vote immediately, since the various delegations had made their positions sufficiently clear. Motions to adjourn the debate and to close the discussion were defeated. Other motions requesting a division of the original United States proposal caused considerable confusion. At last, a roll call was taken on the motion submitted by the USA to defer voting on article [53] and the amendments thereto, which failed to obtain the necessary majority by the narrowest margin possible: 42 votes were cast in favour, the same number against, with 7 abstentions! Ironically enough, if a request by Ghana for priority of her motion to vote at once had been adopted and the votes cast in the same way, the United States motion would have prevailed indirectly * * *. The first part of the substantive amendment introduced by the USA which specified the non-retroactive character of article [53]—which had been stressed by the ILC in its commentary—was adopted, whereas reference to recognition of jus cogens by the national and regional legal systems of the world was rejected. The somewhat similar amendment co-sponsored by Finland, Greece and Spain requesting [sic] recognition by the international community of a peremptory norm was, on the contrary, referred to the Drafting Committee * * *.

A dispute then arose as to the meaning of that vote and whether the principle of jus cogens had been adopted. The chairman settled the matter by ruling that the jus cogens principle had been adopted and that the drafting committee was to see if the text could be made clearer. In the drafting committee, Dean [Joseph M.] Sweeney performed superbly in helping frame, against substantial opposition, an addition to Article 53 that achieved the objective of the United States. A peremptory norm was defined as "a norm accepted and recognized by the international community of States as a whole * * *." At the eightieth meeting, the chairman of the drafting committee, in introducing the revised text, stated that the phrase "as a whole" had been included to avoid any implication that an individual state had a right of veto. The Ghanaian delegate, on the basis that the phrase might be interpreted otherwise, asked for a separate vote on those three words. The phrase was approved 57 votes to 3 with 27 abstentions. No change was made in 1969.

* * *

SECTION B.   RESERVATIONS TO INTERNATIONAL AGREEMENTS

1.   *Why are reservations ever made?*   A state that is interested in entering into a treaty relationship will attempt during the negotiations to shape the agreement to its wishes. If it succeeds, there is no further problem. But if it cannot convince its negotiating partner or partners and if its wish then is to protect itself against becoming obligated in a manner or to a degree that in the negotiations it unsuccessfully sought to provide against, it may want to attempt to enter into the treaty relationship under the safeguard of a reservation.

Where the negotiations are between two, or at most several, states, reservations have little utility. Either the parties agree or they do not agree during the negotiations; if they do not, there is not going to be any agreement at all. In the context of bilateral negotiations it is sometimes said that a reservation is a counter-offer, which if not accepted by the offeree, means no contract. If it is accepted, there is a contract on the terms of the counter-offer.

In the case of some multipartite international agreements, such as the Vienna Convention on the Law of Treaties, we have already seen the intensity with which particular issues are disputed and voted on in the negotiating conference. If a state tries hard to make its point and is voted down but still is interested in the general idea of being a party to such a convention, it may consider trying to enter the treaty community thus created with a reservation.

A reservation will be put forward by a state that has made the decision just alluded to simultaneously with its manifestation of intent to become bound. In times past, when most chiefs of state were autocrats, this was at the time their representatives purported to sign for them. But today it is rare indeed that a multipartite convention should come into effect at signing. Today, the signature of the final act of the negotiating conference is almost always ad referendum to an internal authorization process, leading to ratification. Even so, reservations are sometimes made at signature, so as to give a clear showing of viewpoint to the other states involved or to protect the negotiators from criticism at home. An international agreement may provide that it is open for acceptance or accession by states that did not participate in the negotiation. In such cases, obviously, an acceding state wishing to make a reservation would do so at the time of attempted accession.

In many states the internal authorization to become bound involves the consent of the legislative branch. In the case of the United States, as the following chapter discloses, the Senate, by a two-thirds majority of the senators present, gives the legislative authorization. The legislative authorization may itself be conditioned upon the making of a reservation. Under most constitutional systems when this happens the executive has no alternative, if it wishes to go forward with the treaty association, but to put the reservation forward internationally. Such a second stage reservation often reflects imperfect foresight on the part of the executive at the time of the negotiations as to the views of the legislature on the particular point. The classic and tragic case is that of President Woodrow Wilson and a minority (more than one-third) of the Senate as to the Covenant of the League of Nations. In negotiating the covenant at Paris in 1919, the President did not take into account that a group of dissident senators would block the approval of the covenant unless their reservations were accepted. When he discovered that they did have such power, it was too late. The covenant was an annex to the Versailles peace treaty with Germany, and a re-convention of the peace conference was politically impossible because Germany was in internal turmoil, with the Weimar Republic weak, hyperinflation raging, and the revanchist elements that Hitler later mobilized already active against the treaty. Eventually the Nazis terminated the treaty.

The relationships between the President and the Senate of the United States with respect to the conclusion of treaties makes for both domestic and international complications. The Restatement of the Foreign Relations Law of the United States (1965) sketches them at pp. 413–425.

2. *Effect of reservation on other states.* When a reservation is put forward, it presents the other states with this problem: shall State X come in on its altered version of the treaty or shall we try to exclude State X from the agreement? This issue has a substantive and a procedural aspect. The old rule was clear: State X could not come in, unless its reservation was unanimously accepted. In modern times as reflected in the Vienna Convention, there has been a shift in this viewpoint with the result that the rules provide greater flexibility. The materials that follow deal with this shift.

RESERVATIONS TO THE CONVENTION ON GENOCIDE (ADVISORY OPINION)

International Court of Justice, 1951.
[1951] I.C.J. Rep. 15.

[On November 16th, 1950, the General Assembly of the United Nations requested the Court to respond to the following questions concerning the Genocide Convention:]

I. Can the reserving State be regarded as being a party to the Convention while still maintaining its reservation if the reservation is objected to by one or more of the parties to the Convention but not by others?

II. If the answer to Question I is in the affirmative, what is the effect of the reservation as between the reserving State and:

   (a) The parties which object to the reservation?

   (b) Those which accept it?

III. What would be the legal effect as regards the answer to Question I if an objection to a reservation is made:

   (a) By a signatory which has not yet ratified?

   (b) By a State entitled to sign or accede but which has not yet done so?

* * *

The Court observes that the three questions which have been referred to it for an Opinion have certain common characteristics.

All three questions are expressly limited by the terms of the Resolution of the General Assembly to the Convention on the Prevention and Punishment of the Crime of Genocide, and the same Resolution invites the International Law Commission to study the general question of reservations to multilateral conventions both from the point of view of codification and from that of the progressive development of international law. The questions thus having a clearly defined object, the replies which the Court is called upon to give to them are necessarily and strictly limited to that Convention. The Court will seek these replies in the rules of law relating to the effect to be given to the intention of the parties to multilateral conventions.

The three questions are purely abstract in character. They refer neither to the reservations which have, in fact, been made to the Convention by certain States, nor to the objections which have been made to such reservations by other States. They do not even refer to the reservations which may in future be made in respect of any particular article; nor do they refer to the objections to which these reservations might give rise.

Question I is framed in the following terms:

Can the reserving State be regarded as being a party to the Convention while still maintaining its reservation if the reservation is objected to by one or more of the parties to the Convention but not by others?

The Court observes that this question refers, not to the possibility of making reservations to the Genocide Convention, but solely to the question whether a contracting State which has made a reservation can, while still maintaining it, be regarded as being a party to the Convention, when there is a divergence of views between the contracting parties concerning this reservation, some accepting the reservation, others refusing to accept it.

It is well established that in its treaty relations a State cannot be bound without its consent, and that consequently no reservation can be effective against any State without its agreement thereto. It is also a generally recognized principle that a multilateral convention is the result of an agreement freely concluded upon its clauses and that consequently none of the contracting parties is entitled to frustrate or impair, by means of unilateral decisions or particular agreements, the purpose and raison d'être of the convention. To this principle was linked the notion of the integrity of the convention as adopted, a notion which in its traditional concept involved the proposition that no reservation was valid unless it was accepted by all the contracting parties without exception, as would have been the case if it had been stated during the negotiations.

This concept, which is directly inspired by the notion of contract, is of undisputed value as a principle. However, as regards the Genocide Convention, it is proper to refer to a variety of circumstances which would lead to a more flexible application of this principle. Among these circumstances may be noted the clearly universal character of the United Nations under whose auspices the Convention was concluded, and the very wide degree of participation envisaged by Article XI of the Convention. Extensive participation in conventions of this type has already given rise to greater flexibility in the international practice concerning multilateral conventions. More general resort to reservations, very great allowance made for tacit assent to reservations, the existence of practices which go so far as to admit that the author of reservations which have been rejected by certain contracting parties is nevertheless to be regarded as a party to the convention in relation to those contracting parties that have accepted the reservations—all these factors are manifestations of a new need for flexibility in the operation of multilateral conventions.

It must also be pointed out that although the Genocide Convention was finally approved unanimously, it is nevertheless the result of a series of majority votes. The majority principle, while facilitating the conclusion of multilateral conventions, may also make it necessary for certain States to make reservations. This observation is confirmed by the great number of reservations which have been made of recent years to multilateral conventions.

In this state of international practice, it could certainly not be inferred from the absence of an article providing for reservations in a multilateral convention that the contracting States are prohibited from making certain reservations. Account should also be taken of the fact that the absence of such an article or even the decision not to insert such an article can be explained by the desire not to invite a multiplicity of reservations. The character of a multilateral convention, its purpose, provisions, mode of preparation and adoption, are factors which must be considered in determining, in the absence of any express provision on the subject, the possibility of making reservations, as well as their validity and effect.

Although it was decided during the preparatory work not to insert a special article on reservations, it is none the less true that the faculty for States to make reservations was contemplated at successive stages of the drafting of the Convention. In this connection, the following passage may be quoted from the comments on the draft Convention prepared by the Secretary-General: " * * * (1) It would seem that reservations of a general scope have no place in a convention of this kind which does not deal with the private interests of a State, but with the preservation of an element of international order * * *; (2) perhaps in the course of discussion in the General Assembly it will be possible to allow certain limited reservations."

Even more decisive in this connection is the debate on reservations in the Sixth Committee at the meetings (December 1st and 2nd, 1948) which immediately preceded the adoption of the Genocide Convention by the General Assembly. Certain delegates clearly announced that their governments could only sign or ratify the Convention subject to certain reservations.

Furthermore, the faculty to make reservations to the Convention appears to be implicitly admitted by the very terms of Question I.

The Court recognizes that an understanding was reached within the General Assembly on the faculty to make reservations to the Genocide Convention and that it is permitted to conclude therefrom that States becoming parties to the Convention gave their assent thereto. It must now determine what kind of reservations may be made and what kind of objections may be taken to them.

The solution of these problems must be found in the special characteristics of the Genocide Convention. The origins and character of that Convention, the objects pursued by the General Assembly and the contracting parties, the relations which exist between the provisions of the Convention, inter se, and between those provisions and these objects, furnish elements of interpretation of the will of the General Assembly and the parties. The origins of the Convention show that it was the intention of the United Nations to condemn and punish genocide as "a crime under international law" involving a denial of the right of existence of entire human groups, a denial which shocks the conscience of mankind and results in great losses to humanity, and which is contrary to moral law and to the spirit and aims of the United Nations (Resolution 96(I) of the General Assembly, December 11th 1946). The first consequence arising from this conception is that the principles underlying the Convention are principles which are recognized by civilized nations as binding on States, even without any conventional obligation. A second consequence is the universal character both of the condemnation of genocide and of the co-operation required "in order to liberate mankind from such an odious scourge" (Preamble to the Convention). The Genocide Convention was therefore intended by the General Assembly and by the contracting parties to be definitely universal in scope. It was in fact approved on December 9th, 1948, by a resolution which was unanimously adopted by fifty-six States.

The objects of such a convention must also be considered. The Convention was manifestly adopted for a purely humanitarian and civilizing purpose. It is indeed difficult to imagine a convention that might have this dual character to a greater degree, since its object on the one hand is to safeguard the very existence of certain human groups and on the other to confirm and endorse the most elementary principles of morality. In such a convention the contracting States do not have any interests of their own; they merely have, one and all, a common interest, namely, the accomplishment of those high purposes which are the raison d'être of the convention. Consequently, in a convention of this type one cannot speak of individual advantages or disadvantages to States, or of the maintenance of a perfect contractual balance between rights and duties. The high ideals which inspired the Convention provide, by virtue of the common will of the parties, the foundation and measure of all its provisions.

The foregoing considerations, when applied to the question of reservations, and more particularly to the effects of objections to reservations, lead to the following conclusions.

The object and purpose of the Genocide Convention imply that it was the intention of the General Assembly and of the States which adopted it that as many States as possible should participate. The complete exclusion from the Convention of one or more States would not only restrict the scope of its application, but would detract from the authority of the moral and humanitarian principles which are its basis. It is inconceivable that the contracting parties readily contemplated that an objection to a minor reservation should produce such a result. But even less could the contracting parties have intended to sacrifice the very object of the Convention in favour of a vain desire to secure as many participants as possible. The object and purpose of the Convention thus limit both the freedom of making reservations and that of objecting to them. It follows that it is the compatability of a reservation with the object and purpose of the Convention that must furnish the criterion for the attitude of a State in making the reservation on accession as well as for the appraisal by a State in objecting to the reservation. Such is the rule of conduct which must guide every State in the appraisal which it must make, individually and from its own standpoint, of the admissibility of any reservation.

Any other view would lead either to the acceptance of reservations which frustrate the purposes which the General Assembly and the contracting parties had in mind, or to recognition that the parties to the Convention have the power of excluding from it the author of a reservation, even a minor one, which may be quite compatible with those purposes.

It has nevertheless been argued that any State entitled to become a party to the Genocide Convention may do so while making any reservation it chooses by virtue of its sovereignty. The Court cannot share this view. It is obvious that so extreme an application of the idea of State sovereignty could lead to a complete disregard of the object and purpose of the Convention.

On the other hand, it has been argued that there exists a rule of international law subjecting the effect of a reservation to the express or tacit assent of all the contracting parties. This theory rests essentially on a contractual conception of the absolute integrity of the convention as adopted. This view, however, cannot prevail if, having regard to the character of the convention, its purpose and its mode of adoption, it can be established that the parties intended to derogate from that rule by admitting the faculty to make reservations thereto.

It does not appear, moreover, that the conception of the absolute integrity of a convention has been transformed into a rule of international law. The considerable part which tacit assent has always played in estimating the effect which is to be given to reservations scarcely permits one to state that such a rule exists, determining with sufficient precision the effect of objections made to reservations. In fact, the examples of objections made to reservations appear to be too rare in international practice to have given rise to such a rule. It cannot be recognized that the report which was adopted on the subject by the Council of the League of Nations on June 17th, 1927, has had this effect. At best, the recommendation made on that date by the council constitutes the point of departure of an administrative practice which, after being observed by the Secretariat of the League of Nations, imposed itself, so to speak, in the ordinary course of things on the Secretary-General of the United Nations in his capacity of depositary of conventions concluded under the auspices of the League. But it cannot be concluded that the legal problem of the effect of objections to reservations has in this way been solved. The opinion of the Secretary-General of the United Nations himself is embodied in the following passage of his report of September 21st, 1950: "While it is universally recognized that the consent of the other governments concerned must be sought before they can be bound by the terms of a reservation, there has not been unanimity either as to the procedure to be followed by a depositary in obtaining the necessary consent or as to the legal effect of a State's objecting to a reservation."

It may, however, be asked whether the General Assembly of the United Nations, in approving the Genocide Convention, had in mind the practice according to which the Secretary-General, in exercising his functions as a depositary, did not regard a reservation as definitively accepted until it had been established that none of the other contracting States objected to it. If this were the case, it might be argued that the implied intention of the contracting parties was to make the effectiveness of any reservation to the Genocide Convention conditional on the assent of all the parties.

The Court does not consider that this view corresponds to reality. It must be pointed out, first of all, that the existence of an administrative practice does not in itself constitute a decisive factor in ascertaining what views the contracting States to the Genocide Convention may have had concerning the rights and duties resulting therefrom. It must also be pointed out that there existed among the American States members both of the United Nations and of the Organization of American States, a different practice which goes so far as to permit a reserving State to become a party irrespective of the nature of the reservations or of the objections raised by other contracting States. The preparatory work of the Convention contains nothing to justify the statement that the contracting States implicitly had any definite practice in mind. Nor is there any such indication in the subsequent attitude of the contracting States: neither the reservations made by certain States nor the position adopted by other States towards those reservations permit the conclusion that assent to one or the other of these practices had been given. Finally, it is not without interest to note, in view of the preference generally said to attach to an established practice, that the debate on reservations to multilateral treaties which took place in the Sixth Committee at the fifth session of the General Assembly reveals a profound divergence of views, some delegations being attached to the idea of the absolute integrity of the Convention, others favouring a more flexible practice which would bring about the participation of as many States as possible.

It results from the foregoing considerations that Question I, on account of its abstract character, cannot be given an absolute answer. The appraisal of a reservation and the effect of objections that might be made to it depend upon the particular circumstances of each individual case.

Having replied to Question I, the Court will now examine Question II, which is framed as follows:

If the answer to Question I is in the affirmative, what is the effect of the reservation as between the reserving State and:

(a) the parties which object to the reservation?

(b) those which accept it?

The considerations which form the basis of the Court's reply to Question I are to a large extent equally applicable here. As has been pointed out above, each State which is a party to the Convention is entitled to appraise the validity of the reservation, and it exercises this right individually and from its own standpoint. As no State can be bound by a reservation to which it has not consented, it necessarily follows that each State objecting to it will or will not, on the basis of its individual appraisal within the limits of the criterion of the object and purpose stated above, consider the reserving State to be a party to the Convention. In the ordinary course of events, such a decision will only affect the relationship between the State making the reservation and the objecting State; on the other hand, as will be pointed out later, such a decision might aim at the complete exclusion from the Convention in a case where it was expressed by the adoption of a position on the jurisdictional plane.

The disadvantages which result from this possible divergence of views—which an article concerning the making of reservations could have obviated—are real; they are mitigated by the common duty of the contracting States to be guided in their judgment by the compatibility or incompatibility of the reservation with the object and purpose of the Convention. It must clearly be assumed that the contracting States are desirous of preserving intact at least what is essential to the object of the Convention; should this desire be absent, it is quite clear that the Convention itself would be impaired both in its principle and in its application.

It may be that the divergence of views between parties as to the admissibility of a reservation will not in fact have any consequences. On the other hand, it may be that certain parties who consider that the assent given by other parties to a reservation is incompatible with the purpose of the Convention, will decide to adopt a position on the jurisdictional plane in respect of this divergence and to settle the dispute which thus arises either by special agreement or by the procedure laid down in Article IX of the Convention.

Finally, it may be that a State, whilst not claiming that a reservation is incompatible with the object and purpose of the Convention, will nevertheless object to it, but that an understanding between that State and the reserving State will have the effect that the Convention will enter into force between them, except for the clauses affected by the reservation.

Such being the situation, the task of the Secretary-General would be simplified and would be confined to receiving reservations and objections and notifying them.

Question III is framed in the following terms:

What would be the legal effect as regards the answer to Question I if an objection to a reservation is made:

(a) By a signatory which has not yet ratified?

(b) By a State entitled to sign or accede but which has not yet done so?

The Court notes that the terms of this question link it to Question I. This link is regarded by certain States as presupposing a negative reply to Question I.

The Court considers, however, that Question III could arise in any case. Even should the reply to Question I not tend to exclude, from being a party to the Convention, a State which has made a reservation to which another State has objected, the fact remains that the Convention does not enter into force as between the reserving State and the objecting State. Even if the objection has this reduced legal effect, the question would still arise whether the States mentioned under (a) and (b) of Question III are entitled to bring about such a result by their objection.

An extreme view of the right of such States would appear to be that these two categories of States have a *right to become* parties to the Convention, and that by virtue of this right they may object to reservations in the same way as any State which is a party to the Convention with full legal effect, i. e. the exclusion from the Convention of the reserving State. By denying them this right, it is said, they would be obliged either to renounce entirely their right of participating in the Convention, or to become a party to what is, in fact, a different convention. The dilemma does not correspond to reality, as the States concerned have always a right to be parties to the Convention in their relations with other contracting States.

From the date when the Genocide Convention was opened for signature, any Member of the United Nations and any non-member State to which an invitation to sign had been addressed by the General Assembly, had the *right to be a party* to the Convention. Two courses of action were possible to this end: either signature, from December 9th, 1948, until December 31st, 1949, followed by ratification, or accession as from January 1st, 1950 (Article XI of the Convention). The Court would point out that the right to become a party to the Convention does not express any very clear notion. It is inconceivable that a State, even if it has participated in the preparation of the Convention, could, before taking one or the other of the two courses of action provided for becoming a party to the Convention, exclude another State. Possessing no rights which derive from the Convention, that State cannot claim such a right from its status as a Member of the United Nations or from the invitation to sign which has been addressed to it by the General Assembly.

The case of a signatory State is different. Without going into the question of the legal effect of signing an international convention, which necessarily varies in individual cases, the Court considers that signature constitutes a first step to participation in the Convention.

It is evident that without ratification, signature does not make the signatory State a party to the Convention; nevertheless, it establishes a provisional status in favour of that State. This status may decrease in value and importance after the Convention enters into force. But, both before and after the entry into force, this status would justify more favourable treatment being meted out to signatory States in respect of objections than to States which have neither signed nor acceded.

As distinct from the latter States, signatory States have taken certain of the steps necessary for the exercise of the right of being a party. Pending ratification, the provisional status created by signature confers upon the signatory a right to formulate as a precautionary measure objections which have themselves a provisional character. These would disappear if the signature were not followed by ratification, or they would become effective on ratification.

Until this ratification is made, the objection of a signatory State can therefore not have an immediate legal effect in regard to the reserving State. It would merely express and proclaim the eventual attitude of the signatory State when it becomes a party to the Convention.

The legal interest of a signatory State in objecting to a reservation would thus be amply safeguarded. The reserving State would be given notice that as soon as the constitutional or other processes, which cause the lapse of time before ratification, have been completed, it would be confronted with a valid objection which carries full legal effect and consequently, it would have to decide, when the objection is stated, whether it wishes to maintain or withdraw its reservation. In the circumstances, it is of little importance whether the ratification occurs within a more or less long time-limit. The resulting situation will always be that of a ratification accompanied by an objection to the reservation. In the event of no ratification occurring, the notice would merely have been in vain.

For these reasons,

The COURT is of opinion,

In so far as concerns the Convention on the Prevention and Punishment of the Crime of Genocide, in the event of a State ratifying or acceding to the Convention subject to a reservation made either on ratification or on accession, or on signature followed by ratification,
On Question I:

by seven votes to five,

that a State which has made and maintained a reservation which has been objected to by one or more of the parties to the Convention but not by others, can be regarded as being a party to the Convention if the reservation is compatible with the object and purpose of the Convention; otherwise, that State cannot be regarded as being a party to the Convention.

On Question II:

by seven votes to five,

(a) that if a party to the Convention objects to a reservation which it considers to be incompatible with the object and purpose of the Convention, it can in fact consider that the reserving State is not a party to the Convention;

(b) that if, on the other hand, a party accepts the reservation as being compatible with the object and purpose of the Convention, it can in fact consider that the reserving State is a party to the Convention;

On Question III:

by seven votes to five,

(a) that an objection to a reservation made by a signatory State which has not yet ratified the Convention can have the legal effect indicated in the reply to Question I only upon ratification. Until that moment it merely serves as a notice to the other State of the eventual attitude of the signatory State;

(b) that an objection to a reservation made by a State which is entitled to sign or accede but which has not yet done so, is without legal effect.

    *   *   *

[Dissenting opinions omitted.]

------

1. *Vienna Convention provisions on reservations.* See Articles 19–23. These articles are the end product of the General Assembly's invitation to the International Law Commission, referred to in the Genocide case, to deal with the matter of reservations. How do the convention's provisions compare with the decision of the International Court of Justice? Do other states have to consent to reservations and if so how is consent to be determined? Are the needs of the United Nations Secretariat as a treaty depositary well met in the convention?

2. *Problems.*

a. State X, with nuclear capability, has not yet acceded to the Nuclear Test Ban Treaty, Documentary Supplement. What would be the legal consequences (a) under the Genocide case and (b) under the Vienna Convention if State X were to deposit the following instrument with the three depositary governments? "State X accedes to the Treaty Banning Nuclear Weapons in the Atmosphere, in Outer Space and under Water done at Moscow, August 5, 1963, subject to the reservation that the treaty shall not be deemed to inhibit the use of nuclear weapons in armed conflict."

b. State Y, a new state that has just come into existence, proposes to accede to a number of multipartite international agreements open for accession including the Geneva Convention Relative to the Treatment of Prisoners of War, 6 U.S.T. 3316, 75–76 U.N.T.S. 135. It offers for deposit this reservation: "Provided, however, that persons guilty of war crimes shall not be entitled in State Y to treatment as prisoners of war under this Convention." At the time this proposal is made, military personnel of State A, which is engaged in armed conflict with State Y, have been captured in large numbers by State Y. State A is a party to the Geneva Convention. Assume the Vienna Convention is in force. What position would you as the relevant official of State A take as to this reservation under the Vienna Convention?

c. The United States and Canada negotiated a Treaty Concerning the Uses of the Waters of the Niagara River, 1 U.S.T. 694 (1950). The major purpose of the treaty was to allocate as between the two countries the amount of hydro-static potential each could use for the generation of electrical power. The Senate resolution of advice and consent included a reservation that the United States for its part reserves the right to provide by legislation for the use of the United States' share of the waters of the Niagara and that no project for the use of the United States' share should be undertaken until specifically authorized by Congress. This reservation was officially called to the attention of the government of Canada. What, if any, response do you think Canada should make? See Reporters' Note 7 to Section 133 of the Restatement of the Foreign Relations Law of the United States. Internal legal aspects of this situation, in relationship to the Federal Power Act of 1920 and the jurisdiction of the Federal Power Commission in the absence of any new legislation, were involved in Power Authority of New York v. Federal Power Commission, 101 U.S.App.D.C. 132, 247 F.2d 538 (1957), cert. vacated as moot 355 U.S. 64, 78 S.Ct. 141 (1957).

SECTION C. INTERPRETATION OF INTERNATIONAL AGREEMENTS

A hypothetical problem involving the interpretation provisions of the Vienna Convention (Articles 31–33, Documentary Supplement). Article 5 of the Convention on the High Seas (Documentary Supplement) provides:

> Each state shall fix the conditions for the grant of its nationality to ships, for the registration of ships in its territory, and for the right to fly its flag. Ships have the nationality of the state whose flag they are entitled to fly. There must exist a genuine link between the state and the ship; in particular, the state must effectively exercise its jurisdiction and control in administrative, technical and social matters over ships flying its flag.

A national of State X wholly owns a vessel registered in and flying the flag of State Y. The law of State Y purports only to impose a small property tax on such vessels. While in a port of State Z, the vessel is nationalized without compensation by State Z, because the military dictator of State Z believes that State X has given military assistance to State A in hostilities between Z and A. State Y asserts a claim against State Z for the taking of the vessel. State Z defends that the vessel does not have (for diplomatic protection purposes) the nationality of State Y (under a rule of general international law, accepted here arguendo, that such claims can only be espoused by the state of nationality). State Z cites Article 5 of the Convention on the High Seas and the Vienna Convention on the Law of Treaties, both of which, it is assumed, are in force as to all parties concerned. How do you interpret Article 5 of the High Seas Convention in the light of the materials below?

INTERNATIONAL LAW COMMISSION, DRAFT ARTICLES ON THE LAW OF TREATIES

61 American Journal of International Law 255, 349 (1967).*

Commentary on Rules of Interpretation

(1) The utility and even the existence of rules of international law governing the interpretation of treaties are sometimes questioned. The first two of the Commission's Special Rapporteurs on the law of treaties in their private writings also expressed doubts as to the existence in international law of any general rules for the interpretation of treaties. Other jurists, although they express reservations as to the obligatory character of certain of the so-called canons of interpretation, show less hesitation in recognizing the existence of some general rules for the interpretation of treaties. * * *

(2) Jurists also differ to some extent in their basic approach to the interpretation of treaties according to the relative weight which they give to:

　　(a) The text of the treaty as the authentic expression of the intentions of the parties;

　　(b) The intentions of the parties as a subjective element distinct from the text; and

　　(c) The declared or apparent objects and purposes of the treaty. * * *

* * *

(3) Most cases submitted to international adjudication involve the interpretation of treaties, and the jurisprudence of international tribunals is rich in reference to principles and maxims of interpretation. In fact, statements can be found in the decisions of international tribunals to support the use of almost every principle or maxim of which use is made in national systems of law in the interpretation of statutes and contracts. Treaty interpretation is, of course, equally part of the everyday work of Foreign Ministries. * * *

* * *

(11) The article as already indicated is based on the view that the text must be presumed to be the authentic expression of the intentions of the parties; and, that, in consequence, the starting point of interpretation is the elucidation of the meaning of the text, not an investigation ab initio into the intentions of the parties. The Institute of International Law adopted this—the textual—approach to treaty interpretation. The objections to giving too large a place to the intentions of the parties as an independent basis of interpretation find expression in the proceedings of the Institute. The textual approach on the other hand, commends itself by the fact that, as one authority

* Reprinted with the permission of the American Society of International Law.

has put it, "le texte signé est, sauf de rares exceptions, la seule et la plus récente expression de la volonté commune des parties." Moreover, the jurisprudence of the International Court contains many pronouncements from which it is permissible to conclude that the textual approach to treaty interpretation is regarded by it as established law. In particular, the Court has more than once stressed that it is not the function of interpretation to revise treaties or to read into them what they do not, expressly or by implication, contain.

THE INTERNATIONAL LAW COMMISSION'S DRAFT ARTICLES UPON INTERPRETATION: TEXTUALITY REDIVIVUS

McDougal, 61 American Journal of International Law 992 (1967).*

The great defect, and tragedy, in the International Law Commission's final recommendations about the interpretation of treaties is in their insistent emphasis upon an impossible, conformity-imposing textuality. * * *

In explicit rejection of a quest for the "intentions of the parties as a subjective element distinct from the text," the Commission adopts a "basic approach" which demands merely the ascription of a meaning to a text. The only justification offered, and several times repeated as if in an effort to carry conviction, is that "the text [of a treaty] must be presumed to be the authentic expression of the intentions of the parties" and hence that "the starting point of interpretation is the elucidation of the meaning of the text, not an investigation ab initio into the intentions of the parties." This arbitrary presumption is described as "established law" because of approval by the Institute of International Law and pronouncements by the International Court of Justice * * *.

* * *

It can scarcely be doubted, further, that the "basic approach" of the Commission in generally arrogating to one particular set of signs —the text of a document—the rôle of serving as the exclusive index of the shared expectations of the parties to an agreement is an exercise in primitive and potentially destructive formalism. The parties to any particular agreement may have sought to communicate their shared expectations of commitment by many other signs and acts of collaboration; and it is hubris of the highest order to assume that the presence or absence of shared subjectivities at the outcome phase of any sequence of communications, much less that of an international agreement, can be read off in simple fashion from a manifest content or "ordinary meaning" of words imprinted or embossed in a document. * * * To foreclose or impede inquiry about features of the process of making and performing agreements which in fact affect

* Reprinted with the permission of the American Society of International Law.

the parties' expectations about commitment, and to establish in advance of inquiry fixed hierarchies in significance among features of the process whose significance in fact is a function of the configuration of all other features in any particular context, may be to impose upon one or both of the parties an agreement they never made and completely to disrupt that stability in expectation which is indispensable to effective cooperation. The truth is that in the absence of a comprehensive, contextual examination of all the potentially significant features of the process of agreement, undertaken without the blinders of advance restrictive hierarchies or weightings, no interpreter can be sure that his determinations bear any relation to the genuine shared expectations of the parties. If it be suggested that the Commission's formulations are so vague and imprecise and so impossible of effective application that a sophisticated decision-maker can easily escape their putative limits, surely it must be answered that not all decision-makers are so sophisticated and that it is not the expected function of the International Law Commission to create myth for cloaking arbitrary decision.

The insight had appeared widespread, prior to the appearance of the Commission's formulations, that the most appropriate function of all principles of interpretation, including both "general rules" and "so-called canons," is that of guiding interpreters to potentially relevant features of the process of agreement and its context and, hence, of assisting in the making of that comprehensive and systematic examination regarded as indispensable to rational decision. The great bulk of the principles historically employed by international and national tribunals, as well as by other interpreters, has in fact, with the exception of some formulations of the travaux préparatoires and the "ordinary meaning" principles, been primarily permissive, opening up features for inquiry, rather than restrictive in character; and expositions of relevant principles, whether by authoritative decision-makers or private scholars, have largely differed only in the comprehensiveness and systematization of their presentation. In such a context, it has made little difference whether principles of interpretation were regarded as "obligatory" prescriptions or mere optional aids; only occasional impediments to inquiry have been imposed by even the "obligatory" view. The International Law Commission, in contrast, not only projects the highly restrictive principles which we have noted above, but also recommends that these principles be made obligatory prescription—which of course they will become if the states of the world accept in present form the proposed convention on the law of treaties. * * *

Fortunately, an excellent model both in statement of appropriate goal and in perception of relevant features of the process of agreement and its context is readily available for any critic who may choose to seek alternatives to the Commission's formulations. The Harvard Research in International Law, more than thirty years ago, put the essential understanding for such a model into black-letter nutshell:

A treaty is to be interpreted in the light of the general purpose which it is intended to serve. The historical background of the treaty, travaux préparatoires, the circumstances of the parties at the time the treaty was entered into, the change in these circumstances sought to be effected, the subsequent conduct of the parties in applying the provisions of the treaty, and the conditions prevailing at the time interpretation is being made, are to be considered in connection with the general purpose which the treaty is intended to serve.[35]

What the Harvard Research does not offer, in implementation of its insight about appropriate goal and necessary context, is a comprehensive and systematic set of principles of content and procedure designed effectively to assist interpreters in the economic examination of particular contexts in pursuit of their appropriate goal. Even the task of fashioning such a set of principles should not, however, be beyond the reach of contemporary scholars who enjoy the advantages both of a rich inheritance in tested principles and of access to modern studies in semantics, syntactics, and other aspects of communication.

KEARNEY AND DALTON, THE TREATY ON TREATIES

64 American Journal of International Law 495, 518 (1970).*

* * *

The articles on interpretation demonstrate that a quite conservative (even old-fashioned) series of rules would be accepted by the conference if endorsed by the Commission. Articles 31 and 32 deal, respectively, with the general rule and supplementary means of interpretation. The Commission's formulation established a hierarchy of sources in which primacy was accorded to the text.

Paragraph 1 of Article 31 requires that a treaty be "interpreted in good faith in accordance with the ordinary meaning to be given to the terms of the treaty in their context and the light of its object and purpose." Context is narrowly defined as comprising, "in addition to the text, including its preamble and annexes," related agreements made by all the parties and instruments made by less than all the parties but accepted by all as related to the treaty. Paragraph 3 of Article 31, listing elements "extrinsic to the text" which shall be "taken into account" in interpretation, is limited to subsequent agreements between the parties, subsequent practice establishing agreement and relevant rules of international law.

Article 32 allows "supplementary means of interpretation" to be resorted to, "including preparatory work on the treaty and the circumstances of its conclusion, in order to confirm the meaning resulting from the application of article 31, or to determine the meaning when the interpretation according to article 31: (a) leaves the mean-

35. Harvard Research in International Law, Law of Treaties, 29 A.J.I.L. Supp. 653 at 937 (1935), Art. 19.

* Reprinted with the permission of the American Society of International Law.

ing ambiguous or obscure; or (b) leads to a result which is manifestly absurd or unreasonable."

A member of the Commission has observed that the method of presentation in both Articles 31 and 32 "is designed to stress the dominant position of the text itself in the interpretative process."

In the Commission Messrs. Briggs, El Erian, Rosenne and Tsuruoka supported a proposal to combine the substance of Articles 31 and 32 into a single article. In addition, Mr. Bartoš stated that he was inclined to favor the proposal, and Mr. Amado that he had no strong feelings either way. Among the governments which in their comments on the Commission's articles criticized treating the travaux préparatoires as a secondary means of interpretation were Hungary and the United States.

In light of the division in the Commission on the subject, the expressions of concern in governmental comments, and the traditional United States position in favor of according equal weight to travaux, the United States formally proposed an amendment, the principal objective of which was to eliminate the hierarchy between the sources of evidence for interpretation of treaties by combining the articles containing the general rule and the supplementary means of interpretation:

> A treaty shall be interpreted in good faith in order to determine the meaning to be given to its terms in the light of all relevant factors, including in particular:
>
> (a) the context of the treaty;
>
> (b) its objects and purposes;
>
> (c) any agreement between the parties regarding the interpretation of the treaty;
>
> (d) any instrument made by one or more parties in connexion with the conclusion of the treaty and accepted by the other parties as an instrument related to the treaty;
>
> (e) any subsequent practice in the application of the treaty which establishes the common understanding of the meaning of the terms as between the parties generally;
>
> (f) the preparatory work of the treaty;
>
> (g) the circumstances of its conclusion;
>
> (h) any relevant rules of international law applicable in the relations between the parties;
>
> (i) the special meaning to be given to a term if the parties intended such term to have a special meaning.

In introducing the amendment Professor McDougal adverted to the practice of Ministries of Foreign Affairs in looking at the travaux when considering a problem of treaty interpretation and to the practice of international tribunals, as illustrated by the Lotus case, of looking at the preparatory work before reaching a decision on the interpretation of a treaty described as "sufficiently clear in itself."

In the ensuing debate in the committee of the whole, the U.S. amendment received scant support. A principal source of arguments against it was the 1950 debates in the Institute of International Law which had adopted the textual approach. Fear was expressed that "too ready admission of the preparatory work" would afford an opportunity to a state which had "found a clear provision of a treaty inconvenient" to allege a different interpretation "because there was generally something in the preparatory work that could be found to support almost any intention." Other arguments advanced included the assertion that recourse to travaux would favor wealthy states with large and well-indexed archives, fear that non-negotiating states would hesitate to accede to multilateral conventions, since they could hardly be aware of or wish to have their rights based on recourse to the travaux, and the characterization of the International Law Commission text as a "neutral and fair formulation of the generally recognized canons of treaty interpretation." Given the tenor of the debate, the rejection of the amendment was a foregone conclusion.

The adoption by the conference of two articles which the United States viewed as somewhat archaic and unduly rigid does not seriously weaken the value of the convention. It seems unlikely that Foreign Offices will cease to take into consideration the preparatory work and the circumstances of the conclusion of treaties when faced with problems of treaty interpretation, or that international tribunals will be less disposed to consult Article 32 sources in determining questions of treaty interpretation.

The reaction of the conference to a United States amendment to Article 33, which deals with interpretation of plurilingual treaties, was more favorable. The amendment was referred to the drafting committee, which incorporated it in paragraph 4. The new rule provides that when a treaty has been authenticated in two or more languages, neither of which has been accorded priority, and a difference in meaning persists after recourse to the other articles on interpretation, "the meaning which best reconciles the texts, having regard to the object and purpose of the treaty, shall be adopted."

FITZMAURICE, VAE VICTIS OR WOE TO THE NEGOTIATORS! YOUR TREATY OR OUR "INTERPRETATION" OF IT?

65 American Journal of International Law 358, 370 (1971).*

[Taken from an article-length book review of McDougal, Lasswell and Miller, The Interpretation of Agreements and World Public Order: Principles of Content and Procedure (1967).]

* * * But this is and remains a very difficult work to assimilate and, partly for that reason, to be fair to. We doubt whether we shall in fact succeed in being fair to it, and think it best to declare

* Reprinted with the permission of the American Society of International Law.

ourselves in that sense at the outset. Not only do the authors make the task exceptionally difficult, for reasons that will appear and which indeed constitute a major part of our complaint, but, in addition, the book is peculiarly well calculated to run foul of some of our most dearly cherished predilections! Having said this, however, we hope we can claim to have complied, or tried to comply, with at least one of the recommendations the authors make to "decision-makers," namely * * *, to carry out the operation of *"examining the self * * * for bias"* (italics in the original), as a first step towards modifying one's outlook. * * *

　　　　* * *

The most striking feature of the authors' system is, however, that it subordinates the interpretation of a treaty—or rather (for the matter has little to do with interpretation stricto sensu) its application—to the attainment of certain objectives,—a process which is summed up * * * under the head of the "policing * * * goal." This is defined in general terms * * * as "requiring the rejection of the parties' explicit expectations which [sc. if and insofar as they] contradict community policies." In other words the intentions of the parties, even if clear and ascertained and—what is even more important—common to them both, or all (in short the intentions of the *treaty*—* * *), are not to be given effect to if, in the opinion of the "decision-maker," such intentions are inconsistent with * * * "the goals of public order." Since it is thus left to the adjudicator to decide not only whether there is such inconsistency but also what *are* the goals of public order (and of which public order) to be taken into account, it is evident that on this wideranging, indeed almost illimitable basis, the parties could never be sure how their treaty would be applied or whether it would be applied at all. The process would, in fact, confer on the "decision-maker" a discretion of a kind altogether exceeding the normal limits of the judicial function, amounting rather to the exercise of an administrative rôle.

This is well illustrated by the character of the only "community goal" which, so far as this reviewer can see, the authors themselves actually specify, namely, that of the preservation of "human dignity" which is coupled with what is called * * * "the operation of *examining the self* (italics in the original) for predispositions incompatible with the goal of human dignity"—an admirable desideratum, one aspect of which (the duty of impartiality) has already received some comment earlier herein. No one of course can quarrel with the ideal of the preservation of human dignity, and the avoidance of action incompatible with it, as an essential objective. But without further and much more precise definition, this criterion and others like it which the authors specify, such as "overriding community goals" or "basic constitutive policies," etc. are too subjective to be of practical value to the adjudicator, or in the alternative would invest him with an almost arbitrary power. As Professor Leo Gross has well said, such concepts "are pregnant with ambiguity far greater than ever confronted an international tribunal in interpreting * * * a treaty." He adds, pointing to a further difficulty: "Reference is apparently made to communities of various orders ranging from a relatively compact community comprising the parties and the tribunal * * * to a world-wide community." Everyone knows, for instance, that in private life some people will regard as an affront to their dignity things which others will not even notice; and in the international field also there is a wide range of possible variables.

> * * *

The *second* goal contemplates the case where the search for * * * the "genuine shared expectations" of the parties "must falter or fail because of gaps, contradictions or ambiguities" in their "communication"—(an unclear term which might mean in the course of the negotiations leading up to the agreement, or in the agreement itself). In such event (ibid.) "a decision-maker should supplement or *augment* (our italics) the relatively more explicit expressions of the parties [sc. what they actually wrote into the agreement] by making reference to the basic constitutive policies of the larger community * * *." Here again, therefore, community policies come in as a criterion, and also, once more, human dignity,—for (ibid.) "no conceivable alternative goal" could be "in accord with the aspiration to defend and expand a social system compatible with the overriding objectives of human dignity."

This, of course, however excellent, is not law but sociology; and although the aim is said to be "in support of search for the genuine shared expectations of the parties," it would in many cases have— and is perhaps subconsciously designed to have—quite a different effect, namely, in the guise of interpretation, to substitute the will of the adjudicator for that of the parties, since the intentions of the latter are, by definition (in the given circumstances) unascertainable because not sufficiently clearly or fully expressed,—and therefore presumed intentions, based on what the adjudicator thinks would be good for the community, or in accordance with "overriding objectives of human dignity" etc., must be attributed to them.

Now the process of, so to speak, curing the deficiencies of a text is, within certain limits, a perfectly legitimate one, constantly employed by courts and tribunals. For instance, where the intention or object of the agreement is plain, no court would allow a party to get out of what was a clear undertaking, merely on account of some drafting lapse, wrong reference, incorrect description or manifest omission, and such like deficiencies of a technical not substantive character—(this indeed, when the "explicit rationality" is cut away, can be seen to be the real basis of the decision of the International Court in the first (preliminary objection) phase of the Temple case). Another example is afforded by the principle ut res magis valeat quam pereat, the effect of which is that where a text is ambiguous or defective, but a possible, though uncertain, interpretation of it would give the agreement some effect, whereas otherwise it would have none, a court is entitled to adopt that interpretation, on the legitimate assumption that the parties must have intended their agreement to have some effect, not none.

Significantly, however, the maxim ut magis is all too frequently misunderstood as denoting that agreements should always be given their maximum possible effect, whereas its real object is merely ("quam pereat") to prevent them failing altogether. This affords a very good pointer to the limits of a doctrine which, if allowed free play, would result in parties finding themselves saddled with obligations they never intended to enter into, in relation to situations they never contemplated, and which often they could not even have anticipated. Is it unfair to ascribe to the authors of this work the championship of such a doctrine? Let them * * * be heard for themselves:

> Modern logical tools may disclose implications that were undreamed of when the parties were hammering out their understanding.

Of what use then is it to "hammer out" an understanding (not surely any casual process) if implications then "undreamed of" are later to be imported, and given obligatory force?

ANGLO–IRANIAN OIL CO. CASE (UNITED KINGDOM v. IRAN)

International Court of Justice, 1952.
[1952] I.C.J. Rep. 4.

* * *

On April 29th, 1933, an agreement was concluded between the Imperial Government of Persia (now the Imperial Government of Iran, which name the Court will use hereinafter) and the Anglo-Persian Oil Company, Limited (later the Anglo-Iranian Oil Company, Limited), a company incorporated in the United Kingdom. This agreement was ratified by the Iranian Majlis on May 28th, 1933, and came into force on the following day after having received the Imperial assent.

On March 15th and 20th, 1951, the Iranian Majlis and Senate, respectively, passed a law enunciating the principle of nationalization of the oil industry in Iran. On April 28th and 30th, 1951, they passed another law "concerning the procedure for enforcement of the law concerning the nationalization of the oil industry throughout the country". These two laws received the Imperial assent on May 1st, 1951.

As a consequence of these laws, a dispute arose between the Government of Iran and the Anglo-Iranian Oil Company, Limited. The Government of the United Kingdom adopted the cause of this British Company and submitted, in virtue of the right of diplomatic protection, an Application to the Court on May 26th, 1951, instituting proceedings in the name of the Government of the United Kingdom of Great Britain and Northern Ireland against the Imperial Government of Iran.

On June 22nd, 1951, the Government of the United Kingdom submitted, in accordance with Article 41 of the Statute and Article 61 of the Rules of Court, a request that the Court should indicate provisional measures in order to preserve the rights of that Government. In view of the urgent nature of such a request, the Court, by Order of July 5th, 1951, indicated certain provisional measures by virtue of the power conferred on it by Article 41 of the Statute. The Court stated expressly that "the indication of such measures in no way prejudges the question of the jurisdiction of the Court to deal with the merits of the case and leaves unaffected the right of the Respondent to submit arguments against such jurisdiction".

While the Court derived its power to indicate these provisional measures from the special provisions contained in Article 41 of the Statute, it must now derive its jurisdiction to deal with the merits of the case from the general rules laid down in Article 36 of the Statute. These general rules, which are entirely different from the special provisions of Article 41, are based on the principle that the jurisdiction of the Court to deal with and decide a case on the merits depends on the will of the Parties. Unless the Parties have conferred jurisdiction on the Court in accordance with Article 36, the Court lacks such jurisdiction.

In the present case the jurisdiction of the Court depends on the Declarations made by the Parties under Article 36, paragraph 2, on condition of reciprocity, which were, in the case of the United Kingdom, signed on February 28th, 1940, and, in the case of Iran, signed on October 2nd, 1930, and ratified on September 19th, 1932. By these Declarations, jurisdiction is conferred on the Court only to the extent to which the two Declarations coincide in conferring it. As the Iranian Declaration is more limited in scope than the United Kingdom Declaration, it is the Iranian Declaration on which the Court must base itself. This is common ground between the Parties.

The Iranian Declaration, which was drafted in French, is as follows:

[Translation]

The Imperial Government of Persia recognizes as compulsory ipso facto and without special agreement in relation to any other State accepting the same obligation, that is to say, on condition of reciprocity, the jurisdiction of the Permanent Court of International Justice, in accordance with Article 36, paragraph 2, of the Statute of the Court, in any disputes arising after the ratification of the present declaration with regard to situations or facts relating directly or indirectly to the application of treaties or conventions accepted by Persia and subsequent to the ratification of this declaration, with the exception of:

    (a) disputes relating to the territorial status of Persia, including those concerning the rights of sovereignty of Persia over its islands and ports;

    (b) disputes in regard to which the Parties have agreed or shall agree to have recourse to some other method of peaceful settlement;

    (c) disputes with regard to questions which, by international law, fall exclusively within the jurisdiction of Persia;

However, the Imperial Government of Persia reserves the right to require that proceedings in the Court shall be suspended in respect of any dispute which has been submitted to the Council of the League of Nations.

The present declaration is made for a period of six years. At the expiration of that period, it shall continue to bear its full effects until notification is given of its abrogation.

According to the first clause of this Declaration, the Court has jurisdiction only when a dispute relates to the application of a treaty or convention accepted by Iran. The Parties are in agreement on this point. But they disagree on the question whether this jurisdiction is limited to the application of treaties or conventions accepted by Iran after the ratification of the Declaration, or whether it comprises the application of treaties or conventions accepted by Iran at any time.

The Government of Iran contends that the jurisdiction of the Court is limited to the application of treaties or conventions accepted by Iran after the ratification of the Declaration. It refers to the fact that the words "et postérieurs à la ratification de cette déclaration" follow immediately after the expression "traités ou conventions acceptés par la Perse".

The Government of the United Kingdom contends that the words "et postérieurs à la ratification de cette déclaration" refer to the expression "au sujet de situations ou de faits". Consequently, the Government of the United Kingdom maintains that the Declaration relates to the application of treaties or conventions accepted by Iran at any time.

If the Declaration is considered from a purely grammatical point of view, both contentions might be regarded as compatible with the text. The words "et postérieurs à la ratification de cette déclaration" may, strictly speaking, be considered as referring either to the expression "traités ou conventions acceptés par la Perse", or to the expression "au sujet de situations ou de faits".

But the Court cannot base itself on a purely grammatical interpretation of the text. It must seek the interpretation which is in harmony with a natural and reasonable way of reading the text, having due regard to the intention of the Government of Iran at the time when it accepted the compulsory jurisdiction of the Court.

The text itself conveys the impression that the words "postérieurs à la ratification de cette déclaration" relate to the expression which immediately precedes them, namely, to "traités ou conventions acceptés par la Perse", to which they are linked by the word "et". This is, in the opinion of the Court, the natural and reasonable way of reading the text. It would require special and clearly established reasons to link the words "et postérieurs à la ratification de cette déclaration", to the expression "au sujet de situations ou de faits", which is separated from them by a considerable number of words, namely, "ayant directement ou indirectement trait à l'application des traités ou conventions acceptés par la Perse".

The Government of the United Kingdom has endeavoured to invoke such special reasons. It has relied on the fact that the Iranian Declaration is copied from the corresponding clause adopted by Belgium in 1925, which refers to "tous les différends qui s'élèveraient après la ratification de la présente déclaration au sujet de situations ou de faits postérieurs à cette ratification". It is argued that thereafter this formula or a similar one was adopted by numerous States and that the Iranian Declaration must be understood in the same sense, namely, that the expression "et postérieurs à la ratification de cette déclaration" relates only to the expression "au sujet de situations ou de faits".

But these expressions, which in the Belgian Declaration are closely linked to each other, are in the Iranian Declaration separated by the words "ayant directement ou indirectement trait à l'application des traités ou conventions acceptés par la Perse". By the interpolation of these words, the substance of the usual formula was so much altered that it is impossible to seek the real meaning of the Iranian Declaration in that formula. This Declaration must be interpreted as it stands, having regard to the words actually used.

The Government of the United Kingdom has further argued that the Declaration would contain some superfluous words if it is interpreted as contended by Iran. It asserts that a legal text should be interpreted in such a way that a reason and a meaning can be attributed to every word in the text.

It may be said that this principle should in general be applied when interpreting the text of a treaty. But the text of the Iranian Declaration is not a treaty text resulting from negotiations between two or more States. It is the result of unilateral drafting by the Government of Iran, which appears to have shown a particular degree of caution when drafting the text of the Declaration. It appears to have inserted, ex abundanti cautela, words which, strictly speaking, may seem to have been superfluous. This caution is explained by the special reasons which led the Government of Iran to draft the Declaration in a very restrictive manner.

On May 10th, 1927, the Government of Iran denounced all treaties with other States relating to the régime of capitulations, the denunciation to take effect one year thereafter, and it had commenced negotiations with these States with a view to replacing the denounced treaties by new treaties based on the principle of equality. At the time when the Declaration was signed in October 1930, these negotiations had been brought to an end with some States, but not with all. The Government of Iran considered all capitulatory treaties as no longer binding, but was uncertain as to the legal effect of its unilateral denunciations. It is unlikely that the Government of Iran, in such circumstances, should have been willing, on its own initiative, to agree that disputes relating to such treaties might be submitted for adjudication to an international court of justice by virtue of a general clause in the Declaration.

It is reasonable to assume, therefore, that when the Government of Iran was about to accept the compulsory jurisdiction of the Court, it desired to exclude from that jurisdiction all disputes which might relate to the application of the capitulatory treaties, and the Declaration was drafted on the basis of this desire. In the light of these considerations it does not seem possible to hold that the term "traités ou conventions", used in the Declaration, could mean treaties or conventions concluded at any time, as contended by the Government of the United Kingdom.

It is objected that the Government of Iran, at or about the time when it signed the Declaration, concluded with a number of other States bilateral treaties which provided for arbitration of disputes relating to treaties already concluded or to be concluded. This attitude is said to be contrary to the view that the Government of Iran desired to exclude from the jurisdiction of the Court treaties accepted by it before the ratification of the Declaration.

This objection loses all weight when it is viewed in the light of the special reasons which prompted the formulation by the Iranian Government of its Declaration on the one hand, and of the arbitration clauses inserted in certain treaties on the other. That Government was dealing with two different situations, one being particular, the other general. It is quite understandable that it was disposed to accept the arbitration clause as it is expressed in the treaties concluded with certain States which were willing to give up capitulatory rights. But the Government of Iran was confronted with an entirely different problem when it was preparing a Declaration under Article 36, paragraph 2, of the Court's Statute, binding itself to submit to the jurisdiction of the Court in relation to all States which had signed similar Declarations or which might do so in the future, whether such States had concluded with Iran treaties replacing the régime of capitulations or not.

Having regard to these considerations, the Court is satisfied that it was the manifest intention of the Government of Iran to exclude from the jurisdiction of the Court disputes relating to the application of all treaties or conventions accepted by it before the ratification of the Declaration. This intention has found an adequate expression in the text of the Declaration as interpreted above by the Court.

That such was the intention of the Government of Iran is confirmed by an Iranian law of June 14th, 1931, by which the Majlis approved the Declaration. This law was passed some months after the Declaration was signed and some months before it was ratified. It was stated in that law that the Majlis approved the Declaration relating to the compulsory jurisdiction of the Court "as it was signed by the representative of Iran" on October 2nd, 1930; it was further stated that the law comprised a single article and the text of Article 36 of the Court's Statute, "together with the conditions of the Iranian Government's accession to the aforesaid Article". One of these conditions was mentioned as follows:

> In respect of all disputes arising out of situations or facts relating, directly or indirectly, to the execution of treaties and conventions which the Government will have accepted after the ratification of the Declaration.

This clause, referring as it does to "treaties and conventions which the Government will have accepted after the ratification of the Declaration", is, in the opinion of the Court, a decisive confirmation of the intention of the Government of Iran at the time when it accepted the compulsory jurisdiction of the Court.

It is argued that the terms used in the law are not identical with the text of the Declaration. That is true. But it is irrelevant, since the law only paraphrases the Declaration without repeating it textually. Had the Iranian Government been of the opinion that the terms of the law differed from the true meaning of the Declaration, as it was signed in October 1930, it could easily have altered the Declaration. But it did not do so. It ratified it in September 1932 without any modification. It must therefore have considered that the Declaration corresponded to the explanation given in the law of 1931.

It is contended that this evidence as to the intention of the Government of Iran should be rejected as inadmissible and that this Iranian law is a purely domestic instrument, unknown to other governments. The law is described as "a private document written only in the Persian language which was not communicated to the League or to any of the other States which had made declarations".

The Court is unable to see why it should be prevented from taking this piece of evidence into consideration. The law was published in the Corpus of Iranian laws voted and ratified during the period from January 15th, 1931, to January 15th, 1933. It has thus been available for the examination of other governments during a period of about twenty years. The law is not, and could not be, relied on as affording a basis for the jurisdiction of the Court. It was filed for the sole purpose of throwing light on a disputed question of fact, namely, the intention of the Government of Iran at the time when it signed the Declaration.

Having regard to the foregoing considerations, the Court concludes that the Declaration is limited to disputes relating to the application of treaties or conventions accepted by Iran after the ratification of the Declaration.

* * *

Dissenting Opinion of Judge ALVAREZ

I

* * *

The case now before the Court has given rise to long discussions, both in the written proceedings and in the oral arguments. All the legal questions relating to jurisdiction involved in the dispute have not, however, in my opinion, been fully brought out.

There are four important questions which have to be considered by the Court:

(1) What is the scope of the Declaration by which Iran accepted the provisions of Article 36, paragraph 2, of the Statute of the Court, or rather, how is this Declaration to be construed?

(2) Is the nationalization by Iran of the oil industry, which directly affected the Anglo-Iranian Oil Company, a measure solely within the reserved domain of Iran, and thus outside the jurisdiction of the Court?

(3) What is the nature of the United Kingdom Government's intervention in this case?

(4) What is the scope of Article 36, paragraph 2, of the Statute of the Court? Is the Court competent to deal with questions other than those expressly specified in the said article?

I shall follow the scheme of my previous individual and dissenting opinions, and consider the questions indicated above from the point of view of the law, after which I shall apply the law to the facts of the present dispute.

One preliminary observation of cardinal importance must be made in this connection. As a result of the profound and sudden transformations which have recently occurred in the life of peoples, it is necessary to consider in respect of the above questions, first the way they have been settled until recent times, that is to say, in accordance with classical international law, and secondly, how they are settled to-day, that is to say, in accordance with the new international law.

There is a fundamental difference between the two. Classical international law was static, it scarcely altered at all, because the life of peoples was subject to few changes; moreover, it was based on the individualistic regime. The new international law is dynamic; it is subject to constant and rapid transformations in accordance with the new conditions of international life which it must ever reflect. This law, therefore, has not the character of quasi-immutability; it is constantly being created. Moreover, it is based upon the regime of interdependence which has arisen and which has brought into being the law of social interdependence, the outcome of the revitalized juridical conscience, which accords an important place to the general interest. This is social justice. This law is not, therefore, mere speculation; nor is it the ideal law of the future, but it is a reality; it is in conformity with the spirit of the Charter as it appears from the Preamble and from Chapter I thereof.

The Court must not apply classical international law, but rather the law which it considers exists at the time the judgment is delivered, having due regard to the modifications it may have undergone following the changes in the life of peoples; in other words, the Court must apply the new international law.

II

Scope of the Declaration by which Iran accepted the provisions of Article 36, paragraph 2, of the Statute of the Court

It was this question which gave rise to the most lengthy argument. The Parties resorted to arguments of all kinds, especially to arguments based on the rules of grammar. The question whether Iran's Declaration of adherence was unilateral or bilateral in character was also argued. I shall not dwell long upon this latter point; the Declaration is a multilateral act of a special character; it is the basis of a treaty made by Iran with the States which had already adhered and with those which would subsequently adhere to the provisions of Article 36, paragraph 2, of the Statute of the Court.

The Iranian Declaration of adherence should not be construed by the methods hitherto employed for the interpretation of unilateral instruments, conventions and legal texts, but by methods more in accordance with the new conditions of international life.

The traditional methods of interpretation may be summarized by the following points:

(1) It is considered that the texts have an everlasting and fixed character as long as they have not been expressly abrogated.

(2) Strict respect for the letter of the legal or conventional texts.

(3) Examination of these texts, considered by themselves without regard to their relations with the institution or convention as a whole.

(4) Recourse to travaux préparatoires in case of doubt as to the scope of these texts.

(5) Use, in reasoning, of out-and-out logic, almost as in the case of problems of mathematics or philosophy.

(6) Application of legal concepts or doctrines of the law of nations as traditionally conceived.

(7) Application of the decisions of the present International Court, or of the earlier Court, in similar cases which arise, without

regard to the question whether the law so laid down must be modified by reason of the new conditions of international life.

(8) Disregard for the social or international consequences which may result from the construction applied.

Some form of reaction is necessary against these postulates because they have had their day.

In the first place the legal or conventional texts must be modified and even regarded as abrogated if the new conditions of international life or of States which participated in the establishment of those texts, have undergone profound change.

Then it is necessary to avoid slavish adherence to the literal meaning of legal or conventional texts; those who drafted them did not do so with a grammar and a dictionary in front of them; very often, they used vague or inadequate expressions. The important point is, therefore, to have regard above all to the spirit of such documents, to the intention of the parties in the case of a treaty, as they emerge from the institution or convention as a whole, and indeed from the new requirements of international life.

Recourse should only be had to travaux préparatoires when it is necessary to discover the will of the parties with regard to matters which affect their interests alone. A legal institution, a convention, once established, acquires a life of its own and evolves not in accordance with the ideas or the will of those who drafted its provisions, but in accordance with the changing conditions of the life of peoples.

A single example will suffice to show the correctness of this assertion. Let us assume that in a commercial convention there is a stipulation that all questions relating to maritime trade are to be governed by the principles of international law in force. These principles may have been followed by the parties for a century, perhaps, without any disputes arising between them; but one of the parties may, at the present time, by reason of the changes which have recently taken place in such matters, come to Court to claim that the century-old practice hitherto followed should be changed on the ground that it must be held that the will of the parties is no longer the same as it was at the time when the convention was signed. This is in many ways similar to the rebus sic stantibus clause which is so well known in the law of nations.

It is, moreover, to be observed that out-and-out reliance upon the rules of logic is not the best method of interpretation of legal or conventional texts, for international life is not based on logic; States follow, above all, their own interests and feelings in their relations with one another. Reason, pushed to extremes, may easily result in absurdity.

It is also necessary to bear in mind the fact that certain fundamental legal conceptions have changed and that certain institutions and certain problems are not everywhere understood in the same way: democracy is differently understood in Europe and in America, and in the countries of the Eastern group and those of the Western group in Europe; the institution of asylum is not understood in the same way and is not governed by the same rules in Europe and in Latin America; the Polar question, particularly in the Antarctic, is not looked at in the same way in America as on other continents, and so forth.

Finally, it is necessary to take into consideration the consequences of the interpretation decided upon in order to avoid anomalies.

Applying the foregoing considerations to the determination of the scope of Iran's adherence to the provisions of Article 36, paragraph 2, of the Statute of the Court, this adherence must be interpreted as giving the Court jurisdiction to deal with the present case. The scope of this adherence is not to be restricted by giving too great an importance to certain grammatical or secondary considerations. Justice must not be based upon subtleties but upon realities.

I shall not dwell on this point, because I think it is necessary to consider other elements, perhaps more important than the will of the Parties, in order to decide as to the Court's jurisdiction, as will subsequently be seen.

* * *

CASE ON INTERPRETATION OF THE AUSTRIAN STATE TREATY

Seidl-Hohenveldern, Notes on Austrian Judicial Decisions
86 Journal du Droit International 835, 837 (1959).[a]

The German text of Article 16, Austrian State Treaty (BGBl., Nr. 152/1955; J. O. 2nd Sept. 1955; 49 AJIL, 1955, Off.Doc., p. 162), is worded as follows: "Prohibition relating to Civil Aircraft of German and Japanese Design". "Austria shall not acquire or manufacture civil aircraft which are of German or Japanese design or which embody major assemblies of German or Japanese manufacture or design". Pursuant to this regulation, the Federal Ministry of communications and electric power—Air Navigation Division—denied the request filed by an Austrian glider club for licensing a glider of German construction type; and the glider club, in protest, brought an action before the Verwaltungsgerichtshof. It pointed out, to start with, that in the German language version of the Treaty there was an inherent contradiction, since the Title of Article 16 read "Zivilflugzeuge" (airplanes), whereas in the Article proper one referred to "Luftfahrtzeugen" (aircraft). In Austrian terminology, the plaintiff asserted, "Zivilflugzeuge" indicates in principle that the plane is engine-driven, while "Luftfahrtzeuge" covers gliders as well. Pursuant to Article 38, State Treaty, the Russian, English, French and Ger-

a. English text in the Journal. Reprinted by permission of Editions Techniques, S.A., Paris.

man texts are authentic. The French version makes use, for both title and text of Article 16, of the word "Avion", which corresponds to the "Zivilflugzeug" concept, instead of using "aéronef", which would render "Luftfahrtzeug"; and so does the Russian text. The English version, on the contrary, reads—for both title and text of Article 16—"aircraft", which corresponds to "Luftfahrtzeug", whereas "Zivilflugzeug", in English, would be "airplane".

The glider club considered that, account being taken of the aforementioned discrepancies between texts, one was faced here, essentially, with an error in the translation into German. Article 16 certainly brings about a limitation of Austrian sovereignty, but even according to the basic principles of international law the existence of diverging authentic texts of a State Treaty results in considering that version which infringes least on sovereignty, as the only one which may be regarded as consonant with the will of the contracting parties and the principles of International Law. Moreover, it claimed, the French text of the State Treaty is most authoritative, because in the Convention on International Civil Aviation French terminology is clearly defined—French being the official language of ICAO. If taken into account, the French wording does not provide any reason for further limiting Austria's sovereignty.

The Verwaltungsgerichtshof decided that, for the purpose of implementing the State Treaty—which in the domestic sphere is to be regarded as directly applicable law—one must infer from its Article 39, paragraph 1, that the State Treaty in its German version became domestic law. Pursuant to Austrian practice, headings are to be called upon for construing a legal text only in the event that the text proper is not clear or does not make sense—which is not the case here. In the light of the purpose which, among others, underlies Part II of the State Treaty—namely, to prevent coordination of the Austrian Air Force and civilian aviation with those of Germany and Japan—, the importance of civil aviation as a whole in war time, together with the widespread use of all types of aircraft, including gliders and balloons, for war aims, make a prohibition against any aircraft (even one which is not engine-propelled) appear perfectly logical, however harsh such a rule may seem to glider pilots.

Nor is anything to be gained in favour of thus construing this legal text by underlining the existing contradictions between the German version and those in other languages, since the latter turn out to be just as diverging. Therefore, as long as the differences are not settled by an authentic interpretation of Article 16, made in accordance with the procedure provided for in Article 35 of the Treaty—a procedure which can only be initiated at the international public law level—, the Austrian authorities must continue to abide by the German text, application of which as positive law is mandatory for them and in which the wording does not admit—as already pointed out—of the kind of interpretation proposed by the plaintiff. A legal text may be interpreted in the manner most favourable to the sovereignty of the country concerned only when there exists a doubt as to how that regulation ought to be interpreted; since the provisions of Article 16, in its German version, are unambiguous, this does not apply here.

*   *   *

JAMES BUCHANAN & CO. LTD. v. BABCO FORWARDING & SHIPPING (U.K.) LTD.

England, Court of Appeal, 1976.
[1977] Q.B. 208.*

Lord DENNING M.R.: *   *   * One thousand cases of whisky were stolen. It was on Friday evening, 24 January 1975. A lorry driver drove into a lorry park at North Woolwich. He was driving a prime mover pulling a trailer on which was a big container. Inside it there were 1,000 cases of Buchanan's Scotch whisky. He left the trailer and container unattended over the week-end. He did not return until Tuesday morning. By that time it had gone. Someone had come with another prime mover and taken the whole lot away, stolen it and disposed of it.

Now here is the point of the case. The value of that whisky in England was £ 37,000. If it had been sold to a trader in England, that is the sum it would fetch. But four-fifths of that sum was made up of excise duty payable to the revenue. The actual value in bond of the 1,000 cases was only £ 7,000, but the excise duty was £ 30,000. That duty had to be paid before the whisky could be got out of bond and marketed in England. Buchanan, the owners of the whisky, had not actually paid the excise duty to the revenue. The reason was because the whisky was intended for export. It was on its way from Glasgow to Teheran. It had come out of the bonded warehouse in Glasgow. It had been loaded immediately into the container and secured. Seals were affixed. The container, so secured, was to have been driven to Felixstowe, lifted on board a container ship, carried across to the Europort at Rotterdam, driven thence across Europe and the Bosphorus, through Turkey to Iran. If everything had gone according to that plan, Buchanan would not have had to pay any excise duty. The buyers in Iran might have had to pay Iranian customs duty, but Buchanan would have paid no duty at all. But when it was stolen in England, Buchanan came under our own Customs and Excise Act 1952. Under section 85 of the Act the revenue authorities were entitled to—and did—call upon Buchanan to pay the whole of the duty themselves. The reason is plain. It is to prevent any abuse of the facilities granted to exporters. It is done so as to deter Buchanan or their men from disposing of the whisky in England "on the sly." Buchanan paid the £ 30,000 excise duty to the revenue. But if the whisky had been stolen in Holland or any other country on the way to its destination—other than England—Buchanan would not have had to pay that £ 30,000 or any of it. The consignees might have had to pay something in the country of loss—depending on the law of that country—but Buchanan would not have had to pay anything.

Now Buchanan sue the carriers for the loss of the goods. The carriers admit that they are liable, but the question is: what is the amount which Buchanan can recover? Is it only the £ 7,000, the value of the whisky in bond at Glasgow? Or is it the £ 7,000 plus the £ 30,000 excise duty? The carriers say it is only £ 7,000. Buchanan says it is £ 37,000. It is clear beyond doubt that Buchanan have suffered damage in the full £ 37,000, but can they recover it?

If this case rested on the common law of England, Buchanan would recover the whole £ 37,000: for it was plainly damage directly caused by the negligence of the carriers. But the case does not rest on the common law. The carriage was undertaken by the carriers subject to "CMR conditions". Those are the terms and conditions which were agreed at an international convention signed in Geneva in 1956. They were designed so as to cover the important transcontinental traffic by road. They are given the force of law in England by the Carriage of Goods by Road Act 1965. Section 1 says that the provisions of the Convention "as set out in the Schedule to this Act, shall have the force of law in the United Kingdom".

Article 23, paragraph 1

The compensation provisions are contained in Article 23. Compensation is to be assessed very differently from the rules of the common law. The common law takes the value of the goods at the place and time at which they ought to have been delivered by the carrier. Article 23, paragraph 1, says that compensation is to be "calculated by reference to the value of the goods at the place and time at which they were accepted for carriage". What was the place and time of acceptance here? It was at Glasgow. The whisky was accepted at the door of the bonded warehouse. It was accepted for delivery to Felixstowe for export.

Article 23, paragraph 2, says:

The value of the goods should be fixed according to the commodity exchange price or, if there is no such price, according to the current market price, or, if there is no commodity exchange price or current market price, by reference to the normal value of goods of the same kind and quality.

It is agreed that there was here no commodity exchange price. But was there a market price? Buchanan submit that it was the market price at which the whisky could be sold at the door of the warehouse in Glasgow to a purchaser for the home market. That is, £ 37,000. Alternatively they say that £ 37,000 was the normal value in Glasgow of goods of the same kind and quality. That argument sounds fair enough. But I do not think it should be accepted. Test it by supposing that the loss was not occasioned by theft but by an Act of God or inevitable accident—on the way from Glasgow to Felixstowe—so that all the bottles were broken and the whisky ran out and went literally "down the drain". Buchanan would not have been liable to pay the excise duty of £30,000. The loss would have been due to a 'legitimate cause' which would excuse Buchanan from payment under section 85. Take another instance. Suppose that the whisky was not stolen in England but somewhere on the continent of Europe or in Asia before it was delivered to the consignee in Teheran. Buchanan would not have been liable to pay the excise duty of £30,000. The consignee might have had to pay something somewhere depending on the law of the country where it was stolen: but Buchanan would not have had to pay anything. I cannot think that Buchanan could claim compensation for the £30,000 if they were never liable to pay it. This throws much light on the words "the value of the goods at the place and time where they were accepted for carriage". That value must be ascertained at that place and time. It cannot vary according to subsequent events, that is, whether they are lost or stolen in England or anywhere else.

It follows to my mind that for the purpose of paragraph 1 of Article 23 the value of this whisky was its value when it was in bond at the door of the bonded warehouse in Glasgow before excise duty was paid. That value was £7,000 and no more. That deals with Article 23, paragraph 1.

Article 23, paragraph 4, says:

In addition, the carriage charges, customs duties and other charges incurred in respect of the carriage of the goods shall be refunded in full in case of total loss and in proportion to the loss sustained in case of partial loss, but no further damages shall be payable.

Buchanan submit that the £30,000 excise duty was a charge "incurred in respect of the carriage of the goods". I must say that, if this Article is to be construed according to our traditional rules of interpretation, the £30,000 was not such a charge. Strictly interpreted, those words comprehend only charges for the actual carriage of the goods and other charges incurred *in respect of the carriage*, such as packing, insurance, certificate of quality, and so forth. Buchanan did not pay this £30,000 "in respect of the carriage of the goods". They paid it in consequence of the theft of the goods, that is, the non-carriage of them.

But, here comes the point. This Article 23, paragraph 4, is an agreed clause in an international convention. As such it should be given the same interpretation in all the countries who were parties to the convention. It would be absurd that the courts of England should interpret it differently from the courts of France, or Holland, or Germany. Compensation for loss should be assessed on the same basis, no matter in which country the claim is brought. We must, therefore, put on one side our traditional rules of interpretation. We have for years tended to stick too closely to the letter—to the literal interpretation of the words. We ought, in interpreting this convention, to adopt the European method. I tried to describe it in H. P. Bulmer Ltd. v. J. Bollinger S.A.[1] Some of us recently spent a couple of days in Luxembourg discussing it with the members of the European Court, and our colleagues in the other countries of the nine.

We had a valuable paper on it by the President of the court (Judge H. Kutscher) which is well worth studying: "Methods of interpretation as seen by a judge at the Court of Justice, Luxembourg 1976". They adopt a method which they call in English by strange words—at any rate they were strange to me—the "schematic and teleological" method of interpretation. It is not really so alarming as it sounds. All it means is that the judges do not go by the literal meaning of the words or by the grammatical structure of the sentence. They go by the design or purpose which lies behind it. When they come upon a situation which is to their minds within the spirit—but not the letter—of the legislation, they solve the problem by looking at the design and purpose of the legislature—at the effect which it was sought to achieve. They then interpret the legislation so as to produce the desired effect. This means that they fill in gaps, quite unashamedly, without hesitation. They ask simply: what is the sensible way of dealing with this situation so as to give effect to the presumed purpose of the legislation? They lay down the law accordingly. If you study the decisions of the European Court, you will see that they do it every day. To our eyes—shortsighted by tradition—it is legislation, pure and simple. But, to their eyes, it is fulfilling the true role of the courts. They are giving effect to what the legislature intended, or may be presumed to have intended. I see nothing wrong in this. Quite the contrary. It is a method of interpretation which I advocated long ago in Seaford Court Estates Ltd. v. Asher.[2] It did not gain acceptance at that time. It was condemned by Lord Simonds in the House of Lords in Magor and St. Mellons Rural District Council v. Newport Corporation,[3] as a "naked usurpation of the legislative power". But the time has now come when we should think again. In interpreting the Treaty of Rome (which is part of our law) we must certainly adopt the new approach. Just as in Rome, you should do as Rome does. So in the European Community, you should do as the European Court does. So also in interpreting an international convention (such as we have here) we should do likewise. We should interpret it in the same spirit and by the same methods as the judges of the other countries do. So as to obtain a uniform result. Even in interpreting our own legislation, we should do well to throw aside our traditional approach and adopt a more liberal attitude. We should adopt such a construction as will "promote the general legislative purpose" underlying the provision. This has been recommended by Sir David Renton and his colleagues in their most valu-

---

1.   [1974] Ch. 401, 425–426, [1974] 2 C.   2.   [1949] 2 K.B. 481, 498–499.
    M.L.R. 108, 118–120.

                                  3.   [1952] A.C. 189, 191.

able report on The Preparation of Legislation (1975).[4] There is no reason why we should not follow it at once without waiting for a statute to tell us.

Looking at paragraph 4 of Article 23 in this light, it seems to me that there is a gap in it—or, at any rate—in the English version of it. It speaks only of the charges incurred "in respect of the carriage of the goods", but says nothing of the charges consequent on the loss of the goods. I think we should fill that gap. I ask myself: what was the intention—the design or purpose—behind it all? It seems to me that it was intended that the sender should not be limited to the value of the goods as defined in paragraph 1 of Article 23, that is, to the value at the place and time of acceptance for carriage. But that he should also be compensated for any additional expense that he incurred directly by reason of the loss. So he should be compensated for any expense which had been rendered useless by reason of the loss of the goods", but says nothing of the charges consequent on the loss put as a direct consequence of the loss. We should fill the gap left by the English text so as to achieve this result. Take this very case. The carrier negligently left the whisky unattended, and it was stolen. As a direct consequence, Buchanan have had to pay £ 30,000 to the revenue. It would be most unjust that they should have to bear this expense themselves when it has been brought about solely by the negligence of the carrier. The only sensible solution is that the carrier should compensate the sender for the expense. The men who framed the Convention and agreed to it must be presumed to have intended this. So we should give effect to it. By way of contrast, I do not think the sender could recover his loss of profit. He could not recover any additional value which the goods might have had at their destination over and above their value at the place of sending. That would not be an expense at all. Loss of profit comes within the prohibition at the end of paragraph 4 of Article 23—"no further damages shall be payable".

I would say a word about William Tatton & Co. Ltd. v. Ferrymasters Ltd.[5] On one item Browne, J., there applied the traditional method of interpretation of paragraph 4 of Article 23. He rejected the expense of the return carriage from Le Havre to England and the subsequent warehousing. But, applying the new method, it seems to me that he should have allowed this expense. It was an expense reasonably incurred in consequence of the negligent carriage.

Article 23, paragraph 6, and article 26

If the owner of the goods has "a special interest in delivery" he can declare it in the consignment note and pay a surcharge. On so doing, he can claim higher compensation on that account. This seems to me to cover cases where the sender is expecting a good profit on the goods when they reach their destination; or where he may suffer consequential damage which is not in the nature of an expense in-

---

4. Cmnd. 6053 at pp. 135–148.   5. [1974] 1 Lloyd's Rep. 203.

curred by him. In that case he must declare his special interest and pay a surcharge. Otherwise he cannot recover it.

Conclusion

We are told that there have been no decisions so far in other countries on this Article of the Convention. So we feel an especial responsibility in expressing our views on it. Where we lead, others may follow. But I would like to assure them that if it had come first before them, we should only be too glad to follow them.

In my opinion Buchanan are entitled to recover the full £ 37,000 from the carriers. I would, therefore, dismiss the appeal.

SECTION D. PROBLEMS OF PERFORMANCE, SUCCESSION, BREACH, SUSPENSION AND TERMINATION

1. *Similarities and contrasts between problems of treaty performance and the performance of ordinary contracts.* The satisfaction of the promisee's expectation by the promisor's compliance with the undertaking is at the heart of most treaties and almost all private bargains. Pacta sunt servanda has its counterpart in private law, but in private law to a greater degree than in public transnational law the notion obtains that a bad man may weigh paying damages as a legal alternative to living up to his promise. In Anglo-American private law some undertakings are so highly regarded as to make the promisor subject to the powerful weapons of equity, acting (as always) in personam. The notion that a person may be jailed indefinitely to compel compliance with the chancellor's decree is, to put it bluntly, shocking to other legal systems. Hence, for this reason as well as those of international relations realism, states almost always have the bad man's option; and even then it is not always easy to get payment of damages. Although theoretically it is possible for states to sue each other for damages for nonperformance of treaty obligations, it is almost never done. Have you seen such a case so far in your study of international law? Most international litigation about treaty obligations that gets to the merits involves what the promise was (interpretation), not what the plaintiff is entitled to for its breach. Thus, it is fair to say that parties to treaties, generally speaking, have to trust each other more than parties to most (at least, commercial) contracts need to, for the best assurance to the expectant party is the reliability of the other party. Pacta sunt servanda, then, is not merely a statement of the standard for performance; it is also the best assurance of performance. In entering into a relationship of trust, parties to treaties know that states, like most people, see their duties relatively, not absolutely. Thus factors of change of circumstances, original and continued essential fairness of the bargain, degree of equality in making the bargain and the passage of time itself are important variables that bear upon the performance-content of pacta sunt servanda. Does it follow from this that treaties as obligations are no more enduring than the continued willing-

ness of the obligated party to perform? Bear in mind, whilst pondering this, that most treaties, like most contracts, are routinely performed, without issues arising. In this section we deal with the pathology of treaty performance, not with the preponderant reality that normally treaties are carried out adequately, if not always with the absolute and utmost fidelity.

2. *Other remedies for non-performance.* If suits for damages are rarely resorted to and specific performance is normally not available, what can the claiming state do, in the legal realm, as distinguished from publicity, blacklisting, and withholding of new benefits to the obligated state? Practice in the international community tolerates (i) slow-downs in counter-performance and even suspension of treaty application, in the sense that such slow-downs or suspensions, if themselves sued upon, can be used defensively; (ii) the application, where suitable to the type of agreement involved, of principles analogous to those in private law relating to conditions precedent to performance, concurrent conditions, mutuality, and, possibly frustration. What about a principle analogous to failure of consideration? (Do international agreements need consideration?) The rather big unresolved question is whether a disappointed state may as a matter of general law, as distinguished from termination provisions in the treaty, abrogate it by denunciation for the failure of the other party to perform. What does the Vienna Convention say as to this? Suppose State A denounces the treaty for State B's failure to perform but B defends its conduct as compelled by force majeure (vis major), hardship, change of condition, or jus cogens? You probably will not be able to find authoritative answers to all of these variations but imagine that you had to argue them for State A. For State B.

3. *Durability of international agreements: general.* Where an international agreement is not made for a term of years, it continues to be in force as a basis of an international obligation until it is terminated. Normal types of termination are renegotiation (comparable to novation in private law), substitution, and cancellation (sometimes called denunciation) by a party having that capacity under the terms of the treaty or by the practice of states as to treaties of the particular type. Extraordinary types of termination include desuetude for very old and now-inapt international agreements, although ordinarily the problem of over-age treaties is dealt with through a process that begins with national analysis to identify them and continues with a proposal for novation or cancellation by mutual consent. Additionally, extraordinary termination may result, dependent upon the function of the agreement, from external developments, such as the complete disappearance of one or more of the states that entered into a bilateral or several-party treaty, through its absorption into another state and the break-up into a number of states of a former state, no one of which is juridically the same state (now reduced) as the treaty state. The effect of jus cogens, under Article 64 of the Vienna Convention on the Law of Treaties is to give a new extraordinary ground for termination, even of multipartite conventions, inas-

much as the article says that the emergence in future of a new peremptory norm of international law makes void and terminates a pre-existing treaty in conflict therewith.

In the view of some critics, the agreement of January 19, 1981 for the release of the American hostages in Teheran (which is in the Documentary Supplement) ought to be invalidated for duress. Is this possible under the terms of Article 52 of the Vienna Convention on The Law of Treaties? Would invalidation be possible under Article 53?

In some situations, extrinsic happenings are held to suspend rather than end international agreements. Such suspension may be as to mutual promissory and continuing undertakings, or it may arise from the fact that the extrinsic situation gives one of the parties, by stipulation in the agreement or by interpretation, the privilege of not performing a promise until a condition precedent or concurrent has been met.

4. *Relative durability of various types of international agreements.* While international agreements are in strict legal analysis all equally durable, in the actual practices of states some agreements are more durable than others. Bilateral treaties that are or become out of balance as to mutuality of interests between the parties are susceptible to unilateral denunciation that politically the advantaged party may be unable effectively to complain of. In international relations practice treaties, bipartite and multipartite, that create territorial rights (said to be executed treaties) are usually stable. So are treaties that deal equitably with a common problem or need shared by the parties. Where, in the past, war has either terminated or suspended international agreements, peace treaties may clarify the situation by stipulating the pre-war bilateral treaties that the parties deem still to be in force and by stating for the negotiating history of the peace treaty that multipartite treaties, unless specifically stipulated against, continue in force. The peace treaties negotiated with Italy, Finland, Rumania and Bulgaria at Paris in 1946 followed the method just described.

When the issue is whether an international agreement has an internal legal effect, as in cases in national courts where a party claims under a treaty, the court looks to the element of the national government that is in charge of international relations for guidance as to whether the agreement is still in effect. In some states subsequent inconsistent national law may affect the internal legal standing of the international agreement, although internationally it has not been legally ended. Various cases in the next chapter illustrate aspects of this problem in United States law.

5. *Two significant instances of treaty instability.*

The Treaty of Versailles, 1919. This treaty was negotiated to end World War I with Germany. The Covenant of the League of Nations was an annex to it. President Woodrow Wilson went to Paris to negotiate it. The stroke that led to his death happened while he was trying to go to the American people in support of the treaty after far less than half the Senate balked at approving it without reservations that politically could not have been re-negotiated with Germany and the other Allies. A very young John Maynard Keynes became famous for his attack on its reparations provisions and his study of the disintegration of Wilson's principles under the pounding of vengeful European leaders, especially Georges Clémenceau, premier of France. Keynes, The Economic Consequences of the Peace (1919). In addition to reparations that Germany claimed it could not pay without an expansion of its export trade unacceptable to the Allies, Germany from the beginning evaded the arms limitations provisions of the treaty. Hitler, after he was elected chancellor in 1933, denounced the treaty, armed openly and stated as an objective of his 1,000 year Reich the elimination of the injustices done to Germany under Versailles, including the Allies' imposition on Germany of onerous terms that would not have been acceptable in the first instance but for disintegration of the German economy following the Armistice of November 11, 1918. Many asked themselves, as World War II approached and during that war, whether a more benign Versailles Treaty would have avoided a second terrible war in Europe, or whether a more severe and effectively policed 1919 treaty would have prevented World War II. Unconditional surrender and Allied military occupation were imposed upon Germany following World War II. No peace treaty has yet been made with either the Federal German Republic or the German Democratic Republic. The western Allies successfully resisted Soviet demands for heavy reparations charges (20 billion dollars in current production), so far as the occupation zones administered by France, the United Kingdom and the United States were concerned; and this resistance is historically directly linked to the division of Germany into two states today.

The Panama Canal Treaty of 1903. A zone eleven miles wide through the fledgling state of Panama was granted to the United States in perpetuity, along with authority to act there " * * * as if sovereign." In 1964 internal objection in Panama erupted into riot at a high school within the zone when the Panamanian flag was hauled down by U.S. students. To avoid further unrest negotiations to replace the treaty of 1903 began in 1965 but did not result in mutually agreed terms until after a military coup in Panama in 1968 and the subsequent mobilization by Panama of world opinion in its favor, including a special session of the Security Council held in Panama. Under two treaties now in force Panama and the United States are jointly responsible for the security of the Panama Canal, United States law has been replaced in the zone by Panamanian law and courts, various public installations in the zone are in the process of being transferred to Panama, and by the year 2000 the canal itself is to pass to Panamanian ownership and control.

See, generally and as to other instances, Malawer, Imposed Treaties and International Law, 7 Calif. Western Law Journal 1 (1977); Stone, De Victoribus: The International Law Commission and Imposed Treaties of Peace, 8 Va.J. of Int'l Law 356 (1968); Bilder, Breach of Treaty and Response Thereto, 1967 Proceedings of the American Society of International Law 193; David, The Strategy of Treaty Termination—Lawful Breaches and Retaliations (1975). Cf., the meta-legal literature of conflict resolution and negotiating science, such as M. Deutsch, Cooperation and Trust, Some Theoretical Notes, Nebraska Symposium on Motivation (1962); Bilder, Helping Nations Cooperate: Risk Management Techniques in International Agreements (1980).

6. *State continuation and succession* [a] *and the durability and ambit of applicability of international agreements.* In international practice a state can survive a great deal and continue to exist. The Western Allies of World War II debated, at the time (1950) when they began the process which led to the coming into existence of what is now the Federal German Republic, whether the German state (Reich) had survived defeat, unconditional surrender and the complete exercise of governmental authority in the territory of the Reich for some years by Allied military governments. The United Kingdom and the United States said that the German state had survived all this. The French thought that the German state had died. The practical issue—there were political ones as well—was about treaty relationships. If the German state had died and the entity in the western zones of occupation of the former Germany was to be a new something, then all treaty relationships would have to be negotiated again by it. Finally, the French gave in, and "Germany's" treaty relationships continued, except for such effects as war might have had on suspension or termination.

Complete split-up of states (the Austro-Hungarian Empire after World War I) and the growth of states by aggregation (the expansion of the Kingdom of Savoy into the Kingdom of Italy) have become historic phenomena. Theoretically, in a complete split-up the pre-existing state would disappear and its treaty relationships with it. The expansion of the territory of a state merely makes its treaty law more widely applicable, unless, of course, the treaty itself contains some indication that the other party should not be held to have impliedly agreed to such a possibility.

The separation of a territory and its people from a metropole through the creation of a new state (a spin-off, to continue the corporate analogy) creates many important problems about state succession. If the spin-off is orderly and itself based upon an international agreement or agreements, there is no problem, usually, as to state succession to the rights and duties of the former mother state, insofar as the territory, installations and inhabitants of the new state are

a. A (Vienna) Convention on Succession of States in Respect of Treaties was concluded on August 23, 1978. It was not in force on December 31, 1979. The Vienna Convention on the Law of Treaties does not " * * * prejudge any question that may arise in regard to a treaty from a succession of states * * *." Art. 73. The text of the convention is in XVII International Legal Materials 1488 (1978).

concerned. New states, of which we have seen there are so many to-day, are free to decide for themselves what relationships they shall accept as to those multipartite conventions that are always open for accession, such as the United Nations Charter, the Articles of Association of the International Bank for Reconstruction and Development, the Charter of the Food and Agriculture Organization and the Convention on Safety of Life at Sea, to list just a sample of the large number of agreements that the foreign affairs decision-makers of such a country have to consider in the light of the interests of the new state as seen by them. It is a politically popular attitude sometimes in very new states to exhibit great sensitivity about being bound to pre-existing law. The targets of doubt include customary international law and rules in treaties. In point of fact, except for fully-executed international agreements about such things as boundaries, the new states have had very little law in treaties imposed upon them. Nonetheless, from a politico-anthropological viewpoint, the new states in sub-Sahara Africa do have serious problems, where boundaries fixed between colonies by European imperial powers have determined the boundaries of the new states with each other, even though they cut across the territorial dispersion of various tribal groups in Africa. It well may be that the principle that a deed of grant treaty is almost invulnerable to subsequent changes of circumstances will meet a challenge of survival in Africa. There is nothing in the Vienna Convention on state succession and existing treaties.

The creation of new states (as distinguished from new governments) by violent revolution is not, so far, a common experience in the modern world. It is inferable that states beginning life in this manner will be less subject to pre-existing metropole treaties than states that spun-off peacefully would be, but even in such cases the freezing effect of a boundary or territorial arrangement would probably be felt, because of the interests of a third state or states.

The treaties creating the European Economic Community contain no provisions limiting the life of the association or for withdrawal. Although only an economic union, the parallel between these treaties and the Constitution of the United States of America in this particular is striking. Undoubtedly, in both cases omissions of time limits were deliberate.

In connection with treaty draftsmanship attention should be paid to whether the matters of duration, effect of hostilities, change of condition and circumstances, hardship and the like should be dealt with in the negotiations with a view to the inclusion of provisions in the agreement.

7. *Treaty provisions on termination and related matters.* Treaties contained in the Documentary Supplement display a variety of approaches to the question of termination.

    a. No express provision appears in the following:

        (i) International Covenant on Economic, Social and Cultural Rights.

(ii) International Covenant on Civil and Political Rights.

(iii) Vienna Convention on the Law of Treaties.

(iv) Vienna Convention on Diplomatic Relations.

(v) Conventions on the Law of the Sea.

b. Denunciation at anytime by notice to Secretary-General of United Nations (to take effect one year after receipt of notice): International Convention on the Elimination of all forms of Racial Discrimination, Article 21.

c. After ten years, convention in force for successive periods of five years, for parties that have not denounced (by notice to Secretary-General) six months before end of current period: Convention on the Prevention and Punishment of the Crime of Genocide, Article XIV.

d. Notice of withdrawal may be given to Depository Governments after one year after treaty in force (to take effect one year after receipt of notice): Space Treaty, Article XVI.

Some conventions provide an amendment process (e. g., Nuclear Test Ban, Space Treaty, United Nations Charter).

Some conventions provide that parties may request revision by notifying the Secretary General of the United Nations, in which event the General Assembly shall decide what steps to take (e. g., conventions on Racial Discrimination, the Territorial Sea, the High Seas, the Continental Shelf). The 1958 Law of the Sea conventions provide that such requests can be made only after five years from the date the relevant convention has come into force.

Article 56 of the Vienna Convention on the Law of Treaties provides that if there is no provision for termination, denunciation or withdrawal, a treaty is not subject to denunciation unless "it is established that the parties intended to admit the possibility of denunciation or withdrawal" or "a right of denunciation or withdrawal may be implied by the *nature* of the treaty." [Emphasis supplied.]

ACADEMY OF SCIENCES OF THE U.S.S.R., INSTITUTE OF STATE AND LAW, INTERNATIONAL LAW 280 (MOSCOW, 1961)

Annulment of Treaties. The annulment of an international treaty can be defined as a unilateral declaration by a State that it repudiates the treaty concerned.

Annulment may take the form of a recognition of the treaty as having been ineffective from the outset, or regarding its termination in the future.

Not every annulment is impermissible under International Law. The annulment of a treaty by one signatory in the event of the nonfulfilment by the other of key terms is held to be legal.

It will be recalled that the British and French governments, by their remilitarisation of Western Germany, the creation of a West European army and the inclusion of a remilitarised Western Germany in the military groupings of the Western European Union and the North Atlantic bloc—actions directed against the Soviet Union— in effect annulled the Anglo-Soviet Treaty of May 26, 1942 and the Franco-Soviet Treaty of December 10, 1944.

Therefore on May 7, 1955 the Presidium of the Supreme Soviet of the U.S.S.R. annulled these treaties as ineffective.

It has already been noted that unequal treaties and treaties of a similar character are not binding. Their annulment does not contradict generally recognised democratic principles of present-day International Law. From this point of view, the Egyptian Parliament's decision of October 15, 1951 to repudiate the Anglo-Egyptian Treaty of 1936 and the 1899 Convention regarding the condominium over the Sudan was legal in that it corresponded to the principles of democracy supported by all progressive mankind, since these treaties violated the elementary sovereign rights of the Egyptian people.

A treaty may be annulled by the fact that a signatory ceases to exist.

The annulment of an international treaty is justified, in the opinion of some international jurists, by a vital change of circumstances when the signatories based themselves upon the fact that such circumstances could not change (that is, when a treaty is subject to the reservation rebus sic stantibus).

We may cite as examples the Franco-Moroccan Declaration of March 2, 1956, regarding the Treaty of March 30, 1912 and the Franco-Tunisian Protocol of March 22, 1956 regarding the Treaty of May 12, 1881.

It must, however, be borne in mind that this clause is frequently interpreted extremely broadly by capitalist States, in the sense that any change in the international situation gives the right to annul a treaty. Such an interpretation has been used by aggressor countries to justify expansionist foreign policies.[1]

Only a fundamental, radical change in the international situation can constitute grounds for the application of the clause rebus sic stantibus.

The unilateral, arbitrary dissolution of international treaties contradicts International Law. Nevertheless, it is a frequent phenomenon in the practice of capitalist States, particularly in the period of imperialism. Imperialist States not only grossly violate the United Nations Charter and the international undertakings which they have assumed during and since the Second World War, but in effect unilaterally annul them.

---

1. It should at the same time be noted that in bourgeois literature a negative attitude to this reservation is also to be found (See Hans Kelsen, "Théorie du droit international public". Recueil des Cours, t. 84, 1955, pp. 162–64).

The U.S.S.R. unswervingly champions the stability of international treaties concluded on the basis of the sovereign equality of the parties.

Question. Should the Academicians' statements be taken with some grains of salt?

NEDERLANDSCHE RIJNVAARTVEREENIGING v. DAMCO SCHEEPVAART MAATSCHAPPIJ

Netherlands, District Court of Rotterdam, 1954.
21 Int'l L.Rep. 276 (1957).*

The Facts. In Swiss Corporation Tanutra v. N.V. Nederlandsche Rijnvaartvereeniging (see International Law Reports, 1953, p. 164), the same Court, on April 17, 1953, had ex officio declared itself not competent to adjudicate on a claim for damages arising out of a collision which had taken place on the Rhine near Cologne after the British High Commissioner for the Western Zone of Germany had reinstated the Rhine Navigation Courts. In the present case the collision had taken place at a point between the bridges across the Rhine at Mainz near the thalweg of the river which was the boundary line between the United States and the French Zones of Occupation. The date of the collision was April 1, 1946. The claim for damages was presented on November 6, 1948. During 1946 and 1947 the United States and the French authorities had reinstated the Rhine Navigation Courts in their respective Zones. It does not appear that either party raised the issue of jurisdiction. However, the Court raised the matter ex officio.

Held: that the Court's decision in the Tanutra case be adhered to and that, therefore, the Court was not competent to adjudicate in this action. [A portion of the opinion of the court appears below.]

* * * In November 1936 the German Government denounced the Revised Convention of Mannheim of 1868 concerning Navigation on the Rhine [hereinafter called the Rhine Convention] and dissolved the German Rhine Navigation Courts. Since the Rhine Convention is a treaty which cannot be denounced unilaterally no legal consequences could, therefore, according to international law, follow from such denunciation. In the Netherlands the Convention remained in full force. With regard to Germany it could, as a consequence of the dissolution of the German Rhine Navigation Courts, no longer be observed by the other States. Germany was henceforth not in a position to demand that the other States should apply the provisions on jurisdiction laid down in Articles 33, 34 and 35 of the Rhine Convention in connection with collisions occurring on the Rhine in Germany.

---

* Reprinted by permission of E. Lauterpacht, ed., and Grotius Publications, Ltd., Cambridge, England.

These provisions with regard to Germany remained in force de jure, but they could no longer be observed de facto. After 1936, the Netherlands courts applied to such collisions the provision concerning competence ratione materiae laid down in Article 543 of the Netherlands Commercial Code. This was a provisional solution fully justified by Germany's illegal acts. The multilateral Rhine Convention, which had always remained in full operation between the Netherlands and Belgium, France and Switzerland had, as far as the legal relations between the Netherlands and Germany were concerned, been suspended, according to generally recognized principles of international law, by the outbreak of war between the Netherlands and Germany on May 10, 1940. That suspension must be deemed to have ended in the autumn of 1945. At that time all the Governments concerned promoted by their words and acts the restoration of the use of the Rhine for commerce within the scope of the Rhine Convention. Since the autumn of 1945 the Rhine Convention again completely regulated navigation on the Rhine between the Netherlands and the Occupying Powers which then exercised the sovereignty of the German State. In the course of the years 1946 and 1947, these Occupying Powers established courts which could fulfil the task which the Rhine Convention imposed on the navigation courts envisaged by it. The present collision took place at a time when navigation on the Rhine was once more controlled by the Rhine Convention save for the fact that the functions allotted to the courts constituted by the Convention could not yet be exercised. This was, however, possible by the time the writ of summons was served in the present proceedings. In these circumstances there is no reason why the interim solution based on Article 543 of the Commercial Code should take priority over the time-honoured regulation of the jurisdiction of the Rhine Navigation Courts.

       *   *   *

Outbreak of hostilities. In Clark v. Allen, 331 U.S. 503, 508, 67 S.Ct. 1431 (1947), the court said:

We start from the premise that the outbreak of war does not necessarily suspend or abrogate treaty provisions. Society for the Propagation of the Gospel v. New Haven, 8 Wheat. 464, 494–495. There may of course be such an incompatibility between a particular treaty provision and the maintenance of a state of war as to make clear that it should not be enforced. Karnuth v. United States, 279 U.S. 231, 49 S.Ct. 274. Or the Chief Executive or the Congress may have formulated a national policy quite inconsistent with the enforcement of a treaty in whole or in part. This was the view stated in Techt v. Hughes * * * [229 N.Y. 222, 128 N.E. 185 (1920), cert. denied 254 U.S. 643, 41 S.Ct. 14 (1920)] and we believe it to be the correct one. That case concerned the right of a resident alien enemy to inherit real property in New York. Under New York law, as it then stood, an alien enemy had no such right. The question was whether the right was granted by a reciprocal inheritance provision in a treaty with Austria which was couched in terms practically identical with those we have here. The court found nothing incompatible with national policy in permitting the resident alien enemy to have the right of inheritance granted by the treaty.

Article 73, Vienna Convention on the Law of Treaties provides: "The provisions of the present Convention shall not prejudge any question that may arise in regard to a treaty * * * from the outbreak of hostilities between States."

BREMEN (FREE HANSA CITY OF) v. PRUSSIA

Germany, Staatsgerichtshof, 1925.
[1925–1926] Ann.Dig. 352 (No. 266).*

The Facts. A treaty entered into on 21 May, 1904, between Bremen and Prussia provided for an exchange of portions of territory belonging to each of the two States mainly with the view of enabling Bremen to extend the facilities for transport by sea. Article 13 of the Treaty laid down that a specified portion of the territory received by Bremen in exchange should be used by Bremen only for the purpose of constructing ports and other works connected with navigation, and Article 22 provided that no works connected with the fishing industry should be constructed or allowed by Bremen. The area of the territories exchanged was 595 and 597 hectares, but it appears from the judgment that the territory received by Prussia was only useful for agricultural purposes and, therefore, less valuable. Prussia, therefore, asked for a further consideration, and received it in the form of the above restrictive clauses calculated to safeguard the interests of her adjoining provinces menaced by the competition of the neighbouring Bremen fishing industry. Before the Staatsgerichtshof Bremen asked for a rescission of the restrictive clauses, subject, if necessary, to adequate compensation to be paid by her. She claimed that, as a result of the outcome of the War of 1914–1918, there had taken place a total change in the circumstances which underlay the conclusion of the Treaty. It was expected in 1904 that not only would the commercial fleet of Bremen, especially the North German Lloyd, continue to exist, but also that a rapid development of that fleet would take place. It was in view of this expectation that Bremen agreed to the restrictions contemplated in Articles 13 and 22. Bremen pointed out before the court that the Treaty of Versailles effected a complete change in the situation in that the German commercial fleet was handed over to the Allied Powers; that the position of Bremen as a centre of shipping and navigation was irretrievably lost;

* Reprinted with the permission of E. Lauterpacht and Grotius Publications, Ltd., Cambridge, England.

and that the operation of the restrictive clauses had become most oppressive as the prohibited activities had now become the only sphere open to Bremen as a maritime State.

Held: That the application of Bremen must be refused.

1.   International Law recognises to a large extent the possibility of termination of treaties on account of changed circumstances in accordance with the principle rebus sic stantibus.

2.   This principle applies also to treaties concluded between State members of the German Reich.   Although rules of International Law do not eo ipso form part of German constitutional law, they may be resorted to in order to supplement the latter.   The regard for the interests of the other contracting party which International Law expects from a State, cannot be regarded as inequitable and devoid of a legal foundation within the German Federation.

3.   However, as the two restrictive clauses formed an integral part of the treaties in question and as Prussia would not, in the opinion of the Court, have agreed to the treaties but for the restrictive clauses they could not be abrogated without her consent.

4.   Neither could the clauses in question be abrogated subject to compensation to be paid to Prussia by Bremen.   No such alteration of individual provisions of the treaty is admissible as would compel one contracting party to remain subject to the obligation while surrendering what it intended to achieve as the principal object of the treaty, at the time of the conclusion of the treaty.

5.   The above decision does not amount in fact to a rejection of the doctrine rebus sic stantibus.   The doctrine could still be applied in regard to certain payments or time limits contemplated in several provisions of the treaty.

––––––––

1.   *The clause rebus sic stantibus.*   The Vienna Convention on the Law of Treaties provides in Article 62 (in somewhat negative language) for terminating, withdrawing from or suspending a treaty because of a fundamental change of circumstances.   This provision should be read in conjunction with the procedures established in Articles 65–68, with respect to invalidity, termination, withdrawal from or suspension of a treaty.

Suppose a state simply ceases to comply with a treaty and is subsequently called to account by the other party.   Is rebus sic stantibus a defense?   Under the Vienna Convention, is a fundamental change of circumstances a defense, i. e. can either doctrine be invoked unilaterally by a state?

In order to avoid the doctrinal implication of the term rebus sic stantibus, the International Law Commission decided not to use it either in the text or the title of the article on fundamental change.   See the Commentary of the International Law Commission in its draft

Article 59 (now Treaty Article 62), 61 Am.J.Int'l L. 428 (1967). It is clear, however, that the commission was carefully and narrowly stating its preferred version of the rule of rebus sic stantibus. In its commentary, the commission noted that the International Court of Justice had avoided taking a position on the existence of the rule by finding, in the one case which posed the question, that the facts of that case did not warrant application of the rule. Free Zones of Savoy and Gex, P.C.I.J., 1932, Series A/B, No. 46. The commission further noted that, although municipal courts "have not infrequently recognized the relevance of the principle in international law," they have "always ended by rejecting the application of it in the particular circumstances of the case before them." (One such case was Bremen v. Prussia.) However, the commission found in state practice "a wide acceptance of the view that a fundamental change of circumstances may justify a demand for termination or revision of a treaty."

The doctrine of rebus sic stantibus, either in those terms or in other words, is to be found in the domestic law of states in cases not involving treaties but, rather, commercial contracts between private persons. Article 610 of the German Civil Code provides that one who promises to make a loan can revoke the promise in case of misgivings if a material deterioration develops in the pecuniary circumstances of the other party, through which the claim for repayment is jeopardized. See also Article 321 of the German Civil Code, on bilateral contracts. Article 2–615 of the United States Uniform Commercial Code provides: " * * * (a) Delay in delivery in whole or in part by a seller * * * is not a breach of his duty under a contract for sale if performance as agreed has been made impracticable by the occurrence of a contingency the nonoccurrence of which was a basic assumption on which the contract was made * * *."

2. *Questions.* If notions of rebus sic stantibus are common to municipal systems of law, why should there be such hesitancy to recognize that the rule is a rule of international law? Are there any peculiar risks to its application in international law that do not exist, or exist to a lesser extent, in municipal law? Is the weakness of international adjudication one such risk?

CHARLTON v. KELLY, SHERIFF

United States Supreme Court, 1913.
229 U.S. 447, 33 S.Ct. 945.

Mr. Justice LURTON delivered the opinion of the court.

[This is an appeal from a judgment dismissing a petition for a writ of habeas corpus and remanding the petitioner to custody under a warrant for his extradition as a fugitive from the justice of the Kingdom of Italy.]

     * * *

The objections which are relied upon for the purpose of defeating extradition may be conveniently summarized and considered under four heads:

* * *

3. That appellant is a citizen of the United States, and that the treaty in providing for the extradition of "persons" accused of crime does not include persons who are citizens or subjects of the nation upon whom the demand is made.

4. That if the word "person" as used in the treaty includes citizens of the asylum country, the treaty, in so far as it covers that subject, has been abrogated by the conduct of Italy in refusing to deliver up its own citizens upon the demand of the United States, and by the enactment of a municipal law, since the treaty, forbidding the extradition of citizens.

We will consider these objections in their order:

* * *

3. By Article I of the extradition treaty with Italy the two governments mutually agree to deliver up all persons, who, having been convicted of or charged with any of the crimes specified in the following article, committed within the jurisdiction of one of the contracting parties, shall seek an asylum in the other, etc. It is claimed by counsel for the appellant that the word "persons" as used in this article does not include persons who are citizens of the asylum country.

That the word "persons" etymologically includes citizens as well as those who are not, can hardly be debatable. The treaty contains no reservation of citizens of the country of asylum. The contention is that an express exclusion of citizens or subjects is not necessary, as by implication, from accepted principles of public law, persons who are citizens of the asylum country are excluded from extradition conventions unless expressly included. * * *

* * * This interpretation has been consistently upheld by the United States, and enforced under the several treaties which do not exempt citizens. That Italy has not conformed to this view, and the effect of this attitude will be considered later. But that the United States has always construed its obligation as embracing its citizens is illustrated by the action of the executive branch of the Government in this very instance. A construction of a treaty by the political department of the Government, while not conclusive upon a court called upon to construe such a treaty in a matter involving personal rights, is nevertheless of much weight. * * *

4. We come now to the contention that by the refusal of Italy to deliver up fugitives of Italian nationality, the treaty has thereby ceased to be of obligation on the United States. The attitude of Italy is indicated by its Penal Code of 1900 which forbids the extradition of citizens, and by the denial in two or more instances to recognize this obligation of the treaty as extending to its citizens.

* * *

This adherence to a view of the obligation of the treaty as not requiring one country to surrender its nationals while it did the other, presented a situation in which the United States might do either of two things, namely: abandon its own interpretation of the word "persons" as including citizens, or adhere to its own interpretation and surrender the appellant, although the obligation had, as to nationals, ceased to be reciprocal. The United States could not yield its own interpretation of the treaty, since that would have had the most serious consequence on five other treaties in which the word "persons" had been used in its ordinary meaning, as including, all persons, and, therefore, not exempting citizens. If the attitude of Italy was, as contended, a violation of the obligation of the treaty, which, in international law, would have justified the United States in denouncing the treaty as no longer obligatory, it did not automatically have that effect. If the United States elected not to declare its abrogation, or come to a rupture, the treaty would remain in force. It was only voidable, not void; and if the United States should prefer, it might waive any breach which in its judgment had occurred and conform to its own obligation as if there had been no such breach.

* * *

That the political branch of the Government recognizes the treaty obligation as still existing is evidenced by its action in this case. In the memorandum giving the reasons of the Department of State for determining to surrender the appellant, after stating the difference between the two governments as to the interpretation of this clause of the treaty, Mr. Secretary Knox said:

The question is now for the first time presented as to whether or not the United States is under obligation under treaty to surrender to Italy for trial and punishment citizens of the United States fugitive from the justice of Italy, notwithstanding the interpretation placed upon the treaty by Italy with reference to Italian subjects. In this connection it should be observed that the United States, although, as stated above, consistently contending that the Italian interpretation was not the proper one, has not treated the Italian practice as a breach of the treaty obligation necessarily requiring abrogation, has not abrogated the treaty or taken any step looking thereto, and has, on the contrary, constantly regarded the treaty as in full force and effect and has answered the obligations imposed thereby and has invoked the rights therein granted. It should, moreover, be observed that even though the action of the Italian Government be regarded as a breach of the treaty, the treaty is binding until abrogated, and therefore the treaty not having been abrogated, its provisions are operative against us.

The question would, therefore, appear to reduce itself to one of interpretation of the meaning of the treaty, the Government of the United States being now for the first time called upon to declare whether it regards the treaty as obliging it to surrender its citizens to Italy, notwithstanding Italy has not and insists it can not surrender its citizens to us. It should be observed, in the first place, that we have always insisted not only with reference to the Italian extradition treaty, but with reference to the other extradition treaties similarly phrased that the word "persons" includes citizens. We are, therefore, committed to that interpretation. The fact that we have for reasons already given ceased generally to make requisition upon the Government of Italy for the surrender of Italian subjects under the treaty, would not require of necessity that we should, as a matter of logic or law, regard ourselves as free from the obligation of surrendering our citizens, we laboring under no such legal inhibition regarding surrender as operates against the government of Italy. Therefore, since extradition treaties need not be reciprocal, even in the matter of the surrendering of citizens, it would seem entirely sound to consider ourselves as bound to surrender our citizens to Italy even though Italy should not, by reason of the provisions of her municipal law be able to surrender its citizens to us.

The executive department having thus elected to waive any right to free itself from the obligation to deliver up its own citizens, it is the plain duty of this court to recognize the obligation to surrender the appellant as one imposed by the treaty as the supreme law of the land and as affording authority for the warrant of extradition.

Judgment affirmed.

INTERNATIONAL LAW COMMISSION DRAFT ARTICLES ON THE LAW OF TREATIES

61 American Journal of International Law 263, 422 (1967).*

Commentary ᵃ

(1) The great majority of jurists recognize that a violation of a treaty by one party may give rise to a right in the other party to abrogate the treaty or to suspend the performance of its own obligations under a treaty. A violation of a treaty obligation, as of any other obligation, may give rise to a right in the other party to take non-forcible reprisals, and these reprisals may properly relate to the defaulting party's rights under the treaty. Opinion differs, however, as to the extent of the right to abrogate the treaty and the conditions under which it may be exercised. Some jurists, in the absence of effective international machinery for securing the observance of treaties, are more impressed with the innocent party's need to have this right as a sanction for the violation of the treaty. They tend to formulate the right in unqualified terms, giving the innocent party a general right to abrogate the treaty in the event of a breach. Other jurists are more impressed with the risk that a State may allege a trivial or even fictitious breach simply to furnish a pretext for denouncing a treaty which it now finds embarrassing. These jurists

---

* Reprinted by permission of the American Society of International Law.

a. On Draft Article 57 (now Treaty Article 60).

tend to restrict the right of denunciation to "material" or "fundamental" breaches and also to subject the exercise of the right to procedural conditions.

(2) State practice does not give great assistance in determining the true extent of this right or the proper conditions for its exercise. In many cases, the denouncing state has decided for quite other reasons to put an end to the treaty and, having alleged the violation primarily to provide a pretext for its action, has not been prepared to enter into a serious discussion of the legal principles involved. The other party has usually contested the denunciation primarily on the basis of the facts; and, if it has sometimes used language appearing to deny that unilateral denunciation is ever justified, this has usually appeared rather to be a protest against the one-sided and arbitrary pronouncements of the denouncing state than a rejection of the right to denounce when serious violations are established.

(3) Municipal courts have not infrequently made pronouncements recognizing the principle that the violation of a treaty may entitle the innocent party to denounce it. But they have nearly always done so in cases where their government had not in point of fact elected to denounce the treaty, and they have not found it necessary to examine the conditions for the application of the principle at all closely.

(4) In the case of the Diversion of Water from the Meuse, Belgium contended that, by constructing certain works contrary to the terms of the Treaty of 1863, Holland had forfeited the right to invoke the treaty against it. Belgium did not claim to denounce the treaty, but it did assert a right, as a defence to Holland's claim, to suspend the operation of one of the provisions of the treaty on the basis of Holland's alleged breach of that provision, although it pleaded its claim rather as an application of the principle inadimplenti non est adimplendum. The Court, having found that Holland had not violated the treaty, did not pronounce upon the Belgian contention. In a dissenting opinion, however, Judge Anzilotti expressed the view that the principle underlying the Belgian contention is "so just, so equitable, so universally recognized that it must be applied in international relations also." The only other case that seems to be of much significance is the Tacna-Arica Arbitration. There Peru contended that by preventing the performance of Article 3 of the Treaty of Ancon, which provided for the holding of a plebiscite under certain conditions in the disputed area, Chile had discharged Peru from her obligations under that article. The Arbitrator, after examining the evidence, rejected the Peruvian contention, saying:

> It is manifest that if abuses of administration could have the effect of terminating such an agreement, it would be necessary to establish such serious conditions as the consequence of administrative wrongs as would operate to frustrate the purpose of the agreement, and, in the opinion of the Arbitrator, a situation of such gravity has not been shown.

This pronouncement seems to assume that only a "fundamental" breach of Article 3 by Chile could have justified Peru in claiming to be released from its provisions.

(5) The Commission was agreed that a breach of a treaty, however serious, does not ipso facto put an end to the treaty, and also that it is not open to a state simply to allege a violation of the treaty and pronounce the treaty at an end. On the other hand, it considered that within certain limits and subject to certain safeguards the right of a party to invoke the breach of a treaty as a ground for terminating it or suspending its operation must be recognized. Some members considered that it would be dangerous for the Commission to endorse such a right, unless its exercise were to be made subject to control by compulsory reference to the International Court of Justice. The Commission, while recognizing the importance of providing proper safeguards against arbitrary denunciation of a treaty on the ground of an alleged breach, concluded that the question of providing safeguards against arbitrary action was a general one which affected several articles. It, therefore, decided to formulate in the present article the substantive conditions under which a treaty may be terminated or its operation suspended in consequence of a breach, and to deal with the question of the procedural safeguards in Article 62.

Chapter 16

INTERNATIONAL AGREEMENTS: THE LAW OF THE UNITED STATES

SECTION A. THE TREATY POWER, THE FEDERAL LEGISLATIVE POWER, AND THE BILL OF RIGHTS

CONSTITUTION OF THE UNITED STATES

Article I, Section 10

Clause 3. No State shall, without the Consent of Congress, * * *, enter into any Agreement or Compact with another State or with a foreign Power * * *.

Article II, Section 2

Clause 2. He [the President] shall have Power, by and with the Advice and Consent of the Senate, to make Treaties, provided two-thirds of the Senators present concur; and he shall nominate, and by and with the Advice and Consent of the Senate, shall appoint Ambassadors, other public Ministers and Consuls, * * *.

Article II, Section 3

Clause 1. * * * [H]e shall receive Ambassadors and other public Ministers * * *.

Article VI

Clause 2. This Constitution, and the laws of the United States which shall be made in Pursuance thereof; and all Treaties made, or which shall be made, under the Authority of the United States, shall be the supreme Law of the Land; and the Judges in every State shall be bound thereby, any Thing in the Constitution or Laws of any State to the Contrary notwithstanding.

Amendment 10

The powers not delegated to the United States by the Constitution, nor prohibited by it to the States, are reserved to the States respectively, or to the people.

MISSOURI v. HOLLAND

United States, Supreme Court, 1920.
252 U.S. 416, 40 S.Ct. 382.

Mr. Justice HOLMES delivered the opinion of the court.

This is a bill in equity brought by the State of Missouri to prevent a game warden of the United States from attempting to enforce the Migratory Bird Treaty Act of July 3, 1918, c. 128, 40 Stat. 755, and the regulations made by the Secretary of Agriculture in pursuance of the same. The ground of the bill is that the statute is an unconstitutional interference with the rights reserved to the States by the Tenth Amendment, and that the acts of the defendant done and threatened under that authority invade the sovereign right of the State and contravene its will manifested in statutes. The State also alleges a pecuniary interest, as owner of the wild birds within its borders and otherwise, admitted by the Government to be sufficient, but it is enough that the bill is a reasonable and proper means to assert the alleged quasi sovereign rights of a State. Kansas v. Colorado, 185 U.S. 125, 142, 22 S.Ct. 552; Georgia v. Tennessee Copper Co., 206 U.S. 230, 237, 27 S.Ct. 618; Marshall Dental Manufacturing Co. v. Iowa, 26 U.S. 460, 462, 33 S.Ct. 168. A motion to dismiss was sustained by the District Court on the ground that the act of Congress is constitutional. 258 Fed. 479. Acc. United States v. Thompson, 258 Fed. 257; United States v. Rockefeller, 260 Fed. 346. The State appeals.

On December 8, 1916, a treaty between the United States and Great Britain was proclaimed by the President. It recited that many species of birds in their annual migrations traversed certain parts of the United States and of Canada, that they were of great value as a source of food and in destroying insects injurious to vegetation, but were in danger of extermination through lack of adequate protection. It therefore provided for specified close[d] seasons and protection in other forms, and agreed that the two powers would take or propose to their law-making bodies the necessary measures for carrying the treaty out. 39 Stat. 1702. The above mentioned Act of July 3, 1918, entitled an act to give effect to the convention, prohibited the killing, capturing or selling any of the migratory birds included in the terms of the treaty except as permitted by regulations compatible with those terms, to be made by the Secretary of Agriculture. Regulations were proclaimed on July 31, and October 25, 1918. 40 Stat. 1812; 1863. It is unnecessary to go into any details, because, as we have said, the question raised is the general one whether the treaty and statute are void as an interference with the rights reserved to the States.

To answer this question it is not enough to refer to the Tenth Amendment, reserving the powers not delegated to the United States, because by Article II, § 2, the power to make treaties is delegated expressly, and by Article VI treaties made under the authority of the

United States, along with the Constitution and laws of the United States made in pursuance thereof, are declared the supreme law of the land. If the treaty is valid there can be no dispute about the validity of the statute under Article I, § 8, as a necessary and proper means to execute the powers of the Government. The language of the Constitution as to the supremacy of treaties being general, the question before us is narrowed to an inquiry into the ground upon which the present supposed exception is placed.

It is said that a treaty cannot be valid if it infringes the Constitution, that there are limits, therefore, to the treatymaking power, and that one such limit is that what an act of Congress could not do unaided, in derogation of the powers reserved to the States, a treaty cannot do. An earlier act of Congress that attempted by itself and not in pursuance of a treaty to regulate the killing of migratory birds within the States had been held bad in the District Court. United States v. Shauver, 214 Fed. 154; United States v. McCullagh, 221 Fed. 288. Those decisions were supported by arguments that migratory birds were owned by the States in their sovereign capacity for the benefit of their people, and that under cases like Geer v. Connecticut, 161 U.S. 519, 16 S.Ct. 600, this control was one that Congress had no power to displace. The same argument is supposed to apply now with equal force.

Whether the two cases cited were decided rightly or not they cannot be accepted as a test of the treaty power. Acts of Congress are the supreme law of the land only when made in pursuance of the Constitution, while treaties are declared to be so when made under the authority of the United States. It is open to question whether the authority of the United States means more than the formal acts prescribed to make the convention. We do not mean to imply that there are no qualifications to the treaty-making power; but they must be ascertained in a different way. It is obvious that there may be matters of the sharpest exigency for the national well being that an act of Congress could not deal with but that a treaty followed by such an act could, and it is not lightly to be assumed that, in matters requiring national action, "a power which must belong to and somewhere reside in every civilized government" is not to be found. Andrews v. Andrews, 188 U.S. 14, 33, 23 S.Ct. 237. What was said in that case with regard to the powers of the States applies with equal force to the powers of the nation in cases where the States individually are incompetent to act. We are not yet discussing the particular case before us but only are considering the validity of the test proposed. With regard to that we may add that when we are dealing with words that also are a constituent act, like the Constitution of the United States, we must realize that they have called into life a being the development of which could not have been foreseen completely by the most gifted of its begetters. It was enough for them to realize or to hope that they had created an organism; it has taken a century and has cost their successors much sweat and blood to prove that they created a nation. The case before us must be considered in the light of our whole experience and not merely in that of what was said a hundred years ago. The treaty in question does not contravene any prohibitory words to be found in the Constitution. The only question is whether it is forbidden by some invisible radiation from the general terms of the Tenth Amendment. We must consider what this country has become in deciding what that Amendment has reserved.

The State as we have intimated founds its claim of exclusive authority upon an assertion of title to migratory birds, an assertion that is embodied in statute. No doubt it is true that as between a State and its inhabitants the State may regulate the killing and sale of such birds, but it does not follow that its authority is exclusive of paramount powers. To put the claim of the State upon title is to lean upon a slender reed. Wild birds are not in the possession of anyone; and possession is the beginning of ownership. The whole foundation of the State's rights is the presence within their jurisdiction of birds that yesterday had not arrived, tomorrow may be in another State and in a week a thousand miles away. If we are to be accurate we cannot put the case of the State upon higher ground than that the treaty deals with creatures that for the moment are within the state borders, that it must be carried out by officers of the United States within the same territory, and that but for the treaty the State would be free to regulate this subject itself.

As most of the laws of the United States are carried out within the States and as many of them deal with matters which in the silence of such laws the State might regulate, such general grounds are not enough to support Missouri's claim. Valid treaties of course "are as binding within the territorial limits of the States as they are elsewhere throughout the dominion of the United States." Baldwin v. Franks, 120 U.S. 678, 683, 7 S.Ct. 656, 657. No doubt the great body of private relations usually fall within the control of the State, but a treaty may override its power. We do not have to invoke the later developments of constitutional law for this proposition; it was recognized as early as Hopkirk v. Bell, 3 Cranch, 454, with regard to statutes of limitation, and even earlier, as to confiscation, in Ware v. Hylton, 3 Dall. 199. It was assumed by Chief Justice Marshall with regard to the escheat of land to the State in Chirac v. Chirac, 2 Wheat. 259, 275; Hauenstein v. Wynham, 100 U.S. 483; Geofroy v. Riggs, 133 U.S. 258, 10 S.Ct. 295; Blythe v. Hinckley, 180 U.S. 333, 340, 21 S.Ct. 390. So as to a limited jurisdiction of foreign consuls within a State. Wildenhus's Case, 120 U.S. 1, 7 S.Ct. 385. See Ross v. McIntyre, 140 U.S. 453, 11 S.Ct. 897. Further illustration seems unnecessary, and it only remains to consider the application of established rules to the present case.

Here a national interest of very nearly the first magnitude is involved. It can be protected only by national action in concert with that of another power. The subject-matter is only transitorily within the State and has no permanent habitat therein. But for the treaty and the statute there soon might be no birds for any powers to deal with. We see nothing in the Constitution that compels the Government to sit by while a food supply is cut off and the protectors of our forests and our crops are destroyed. It is not sufficient to rely upon the States. The reliance is vain, and were it otherwise, the question is whether the United States is forbidden to act. We are of opinion that the treaty and statute must be upheld. Carey v. South Dakota, 250 U.S. 118, 39 S.Ct. 403.

Decree affirmed.

Mr. Justice VAN DEVANTER and Mr. Justice PITNEY dissent.

REID v. COVERT

United States Supreme Court, 1957.
354 U.S. 1, 77 S.Ct. 1222.

Mr. Justice BLACK announced the judgment of the Court and delivered an opinion, in which The Chief Justice, Mr. Justice DOUGLAS, and Mr. Justice BRENNAN join.

These cases raise basic constitutional issues of the utmost concern. They call into question the role of the military under our system of government. They involve the power of Congress to expose civilians to trial by military tribunals, under military regulations and procedures, for offenses against the United States thereby depriving them of trial in civilian courts, under civilian laws and procedures and with all the safeguards of the Bill of Rights. These cases are particularly significant because for the first time since the adoption of the Constitution wives of soldiers have been denied trial by jury in a court of law and forced to trial before courts-martial.

In No. 701 Mrs. Clarice Covert killed her husband, a sergeant in the United States Air Force, at an airbase in England. Mrs. Covert, who was not a member of the armed services, was residing on the base with her husband at the time. She was tried by a court-martial for murder under Article 118 of the Uniform Code of Military Justice (UCMJ). The trial was on charges preferred by Air Force personnel and the court-martial was composed of Air Force officers. The court-martial asserted jurisdiction over Mrs. Covert under Article 2(11) of the UCMJ, which provides:

The following persons are subject to this code:

    *   *   *

(11) Subject to the provisions of any treaty or agreement to which the United States is or may be a party or to any accepted rule of international law, all persons serving with, employed by, or accompanying the armed forces without the continental limits of the United States * * *.

Counsel for Mrs. Covert contended that she was insane at the time she killed her husband, but the military tribunal found her guilty of murder and sentenced her to life imprisonment. The judgment was affirmed by the Air Force Board of Review, 16 CMR 465, but was reversed by the Court of Military Appeals, 6 USCMA 48, because of prejudicial errors concerning the defense of insanity. While Mrs. Covert was being held in this country pending a proposed retrial by court-martial in the District of Columbia, her counsel petitioned the District Court for a writ of habeas corpus to set her free on the ground that the Constitution forbade her trial by military authorities. Construing this Court's decision in United States ex rel. Toth v. Quarles, 350 U.S. 11, 76 S.Ct. 1, as holding that "a civilian is entitled to a civilian trial" the District Court held that Mrs. Covert could not be tried by court-martial and ordered her released from custody. The Government appealed directly to this Court under 28 U.S.C.A. § 1252. See 350 U.S. 985, 76 S.Ct. 476.

In No. 713 Mrs. Dorothy Smith killed her husband, an Army officer, at a post in Japan where she was living with him. She was tried for murder by a court-martial and despite considerable evidence that she was insane was found guilty and sentenced to life imprisonment. The judgment was approved by the Army Board of Review, 10 CMR 350, 13 CMR 307, and the Court of Military Appeals, 5 USCMA 314. Mrs. Smith was then confined in a federal penitentiary in West Virginia. Her father, respondent here, filed a petition for habeas corpus in a District Court for West Virginia. The petition charged that the court-martial was without jurisdiction because Article 2(11) of the UCMJ was unconstitutional insofar as it authorized the trial of civilian dependents accompanying servicemen overseas. The District Court refused to issue the writ, 137 F.Supp. 806, and while an appeal was pending in the Court of Appeals for the Fourth Circuit we granted certiorari at the request of the Government, 350 U.S. 986, 76 S.Ct. 476.

The two cases were consolidated and argued last Term and a majority of the Court, with three Justices dissenting and one reserving opinion, held that military trial of Mrs. Smith and Mrs. Covert for their alleged offenses was constitutional. 351 U.S. 470, 76 S.Ct. 886; 351 U.S. 487, 76 S.Ct. 880. The majority held that the provisions of Article III and the Fifth and Sixth Amendments which require that crimes be tried by a jury after indictment by a grand jury did not protect an American citizen when he was tried by the American Government in foreign lands for offenses committed there and that Congress could provide for the trial of such offenses in any manner it saw fit so long as the procedures established were reasonable and consonant with due process. The opinion then went on to express the view that military trials, as now practiced, were not unreasonable or arbitrary when applied to dependents accompanying members of the armed forces overseas. In reaching their conclusion the majority found it unnecessary to consider the power of Congress "To make Rules for the Government and Regulation of the land and naval Forces" under Article I of the Constitution.

Subsequently, the Court granted a petition for rehearing, 352 U. S. 901, 77 S.Ct. 124. Now, after further argument and consideration, we conclude that the previous decisions cannot be permitted to stand. We hold that Mrs. Smith and Mrs. Covert could not constitutionally be tried by military authorities.

* * *

At the time of Mrs. Covert's alleged offense, an executive agreement was in effect between the United States and Great Britain which permitted United States' military courts to exercise exclusive jurisdiction over offenses committed in Great Britain by American servicemen or their dependents.[29] For its part, the United States agreed that these military courts would be willing and able to try and to punish all offenses against the laws of Great Britain by such persons. In all material respects, the same situation existed in Japan when Mrs. Smith killed her husband.[30] Even though a court-martial does not give an accused trial by jury and other Bill of Rights protections, the Government contends that Art. 2(11) of the UCMJ, insofar as it provides for the military trial of dependents accompanying the armed forces in Great Britain and Japan, can be sustained as legislation which is necessary and proper to carry out the United States' obligations under the international agreements made with those countries. The obvious and decisive answer to this, of course, is that no agreement with a foreign nation can confer power on the Congress, or on any other branch of Government, which is free from the restraints of the Constitution.

Article VI, the Supremacy Clause of the Constitution, declares:

> This Constitution, and the Laws of the United States which shall be made in Pursuance thereof; and all Treaties made, or which shall be made, under the Authority of the United States, shall be the supreme Law of the Land * * *.

There is nothing in this language which intimates the treaties and laws enacted pursuant to them do not have to comply with the provisions of the Constitution. Nor is there anything in the debates which accompanied the drafting and ratification of the Constitution which

---

29. Executive Agreement of July 27, 1942, 57 Stat. 1193. The arrangement now in effect in Great Britain and the other North Atlantic Treaty Organization nations, as well as in Japan, is the NATO Status of Forces Agreement, 4 U.S. Treaties and Other International Agreements 1792, T.I. A.S. 2846, which by its terms gives the foreign nation primary jurisdiction to try dependents accompanying American servicemen for offenses which are violations of the law of both the foreign nation and the United States. Art. VII, §§ 1(b), 3(a). The foreign nation has exclusive criminal jurisdiction over dependents for offenses which only violate its laws. Art. VII, § 2(b). However, the Agreement contains provisions which require that the foreign nations provide procedural safeguards for our nationals tried under the terms of the Agreement in their courts. Art. VII, § 9. Generally, see Note, 70 Harv.L. Rev. 1043.

Apart from those persons subject to the Status of Forces and comparable agreements and certain other restricted classes of Americans, a foreign nation has plenary criminal jurisdiction, of course, over all Americans—tourists, residents, businessmen, government employees and so forth—who commit offenses against its law within its territory.

30. See Administrative Agreement, 3 U. S. Treaties and Other International Agreements, 3341, T.I.A.S. 2492.

even suggests such a result. These debates as well as the history that surrounds the adoption of the treaty provision in Article VI make it clear that the reason treaties were not limited to those made in "pursuance" of the Constitution was so that agreements made by the United States under the Articles of Confederation, including the important peace treaties which concluded the Revolutionary War, would remain in effect. It would be manifestly contrary to the objectives of those who created the Constitution, as well as those who were responsible for the Bill of Rights—let alone alien to our entire constitutional history and tradition—to construe Article VI as permitting the United States to exercise power under an international agreement without observing constitutional prohibitions. In effect, such construction would permit amendment of that document in a manner not sanctioned by Article V. The prohibitions of the Constitution were designed to apply to all branches of the National Government and they cannot be nullified by the Executive or by the Executive and the Senate combined.

There is nothing new or unique about what we say here. This Court has regularly and uniformly recognized the supremacy of the Constitution over a treaty.[33] For example, in Geofroy v. Riggs, 133 U.S. 258, 267, 10 S.Ct. 295, 297, it declared:

> The treaty power, as expressed in the Constitution, is in terms unlimited except by those restraints which are found in that instrument against the action of the government or of its departments, and those arising from the nature of the government itself and of that of the States. It would not be contended that it extends so far as to authorize what the Constitution forbids, or a change in the character of the government or in that of one of the States, or a cession of any portion of the territory of the latter, without its consent.

This Court has also repeatedly taken the position that an Act of Congress, which must comply with the Constitution, is on a full parity with a treaty, and that when a statute which is subsequent in time is inconsistent with a treaty, the statute to the extent of conflict renders the treaty null.[34] It would be completely anomalous to say that

---

33. E. g., United States v. Minnesota, 270 U.S. 181, 207–208, 46 S.Ct. 298, 305–306; Holden v. Joy, 17 Wall. 211, 242–243; The Cherokee Tobacco, 11 Wall. 616, 620–621; Doe v. Braden, 16 How. 635, 657. Cf. Marbury v. Madison, 1 Cranch 137, 176–180. We recognize that executive agreements are involved here but it cannot be contended that such an agreement rises to greater stature than a treaty.

34. In Whitney v. Robertson, 124 U.S. 190, 8 S.Ct. 456, at page 458, the Court stated, at p. 194: "By the Constitution a treaty is placed on the same footing, and made of like obligation, with an act of legislation. Both are declared by that instrument to be the supreme law of the land, and no superior efficacy is given to either over the other * * *. [I]f the two are inconsistent, the one last in date will control the other * * *." Head Money Cases, 112 U.S. 580, 5 S.Ct. 247; Botiller v. Dominguez, 130 U.S. 238, 9 S.Ct. 525; Chae Chan Ping v. United States, 130 U.S. 581, 9 S.Ct. 623. See Clark v. Allen, 331 U.S. 503, 509–510, 67 S.Ct. 1431, 1435–1436; Moser v. United States, 341 U.S. 41, 45, 71 S.Ct. 553, 555.

a treaty need not comply with the Constitution when such an agreement can be overridden by a statute that must conform to that instrument.

There is nothing in Missouri v. Holland, 252 U.S. 416, 40 S.Ct. 382, which is contrary to the position taken here. There the Court carefully noted that the treaty involved was not inconsistent with any specific provision of the Constitution. The Court was concerned with the Tenth Amendment which reserves to the States or the people all power not delegated to the National Government. To the extent that the United States can validly make treaties, the people and the States have delegated their power to the National Government and the Tenth Amendment is no barrier.

In summary, we conclude that the Constitution in its entirety applied to the trials of Mrs. Smith and Mrs. Covert. Since their court-martial did not meet the requirements of Art. III, § 2 or the Fifth and Sixth Amendments we are compelled to determine if there is anything *within* the Constitution which authorizes the military trial of dependents accompanying the armed forces overseas.

* * *

In No. 701, Reid v. Covert, the judgment of the District Court directing that Mrs. Covert be released from custody is affirmed.

In No. 713, Kinsella v. Krueger, the judgment of the District Court is reversed and the case is remanded with instructions to order Mrs. Smith released from custody.

Reversed and remanded.

Mr. Justice WHITTAKER took no part in the consideration or decision of these cases.

Mr. Justice FRANKFURTER, concurring in the result.

* * *

A further argument is made that a decision adverse to the Government would mean that only a foreign trial could be had. Even assuming that the NATO Status of Forces Agreement, 4 U.S. Treaties and Other International Agreements 1792, T.I.A.S. 2846, covering countries where a large part of our armed forces are stationed, gives jurisdiction to the United States only through its military authorities, this Court cannot speculate that any given nation would be unwilling to grant or continue such extraterritorial jurisdiction over civilian dependents in capital cases if they were to be tried by some other manner than court-martial. And, even if such were the case, these civilian dependents would then merely be in the same position as are so many federal employees and their dependents and other United States citizens who are subject to the laws of foreign nations when residing there. * * *

[Opinion of Mr. Justice HARLAN, concurring in the result, omitted.]

Mr. Justice CLARK, with whom Mr. Justice BURTON joins, dissenting.

*   *   *

Before discussing the power of the Congress under Art. I, § 8, cl. 14, of the Constitution it is well to take our bearings. These cases do not involve the jurisdiction of a military court-martial sitting within the territorial limits of the United States. Nor are they concerned with the power of the Government to make treaties or the legal relationship between treaties and the Constitution. Nor are they concerned with the power of Congress to provide for the trial of Americans sojourning, touring, or temporarily residing in foreign nations. Essentially, we are to determine only whether the civilian dependents of American servicemen may constitutionally be tried by an American military court-martial in a foreign country for an offense committed in that country.

*   *   *

The only alternative remaining—probably the alternative that the Congress will now be forced to choose—is that Americans committing offenses on foreign soil be tried by the courts of the country in which the offense is committed. Foreign courts have exclusive jurisdiction under the principles of international law and many nations enjoy concurrent jurisdiction with the American military authorities pursuant to Article VII of the Agreement Regarding Status of Forces of Parties to the North Atlantic Treaty. Where the American military authorities do have jurisdiction, it is only by mutual agreement with the foreign sovereign concerned and pursuant to carefully drawn agreements conditioned on trial by the American military authorities. Typical of these agreements was the one concluded between the United States and Japan on February 28, 1952, and in force at the time one of these cases arose. Under this and like agreements, the jurisdiction so ceded to the United States military courts will surely be withdrawn if the services are impotent to exercise it. It is clear that trial before an American court-martial in which the fundamentals of due process are observed is preferable to leaving American servicemen and their dependents to the widely varying standards of justice in foreign courts throughout the world. Under these circumstances it is untenable to say that Congress could have exercised a lesser power adequate to the end proposed.

*   *   *

Questions on the constitutionality of the human rights conventions.

a. Are there constitutional impediments to the United States becoming a party to the human rights conventions sponsored by the United Nations? Refer in particular to the conventions in the Documentary Supplement: Economic, Social and Cultural Rights; Civil and Political Rights; Elimination of All Forms of Racial Discrimination; Genocide. Consider Article 4 of the Convention on Racial Discrimination and Article 19 of the Convention on Civil and Political Rights. Is Article 5 of the Convention on Civil and Political Rights relevant to the question of the constitutionality of that convention as a whole?

b. Do the human rights treaties embody a bargain with foreign states? Must they, to be within the treaty power? If a treaty does not involve a bargaining of concessions between the negotiating states, some have argued that it does not involve a matter of international concern. If a putative treaty does not involve a matter of international concern, the argument continues, the arrangement is not really a treaty within the meaning of the Constitution, and hence the overriding power given to the federal government in Article VI, Clause 2 is not activated. This argument assumes that a decision-maker, presumably a court, would pass on the question whether the supposedly necessary international concern exists in the particular case. Is this evaluation a proper function for courts in the United States? How would the Supreme Court go about making a determination as to whether a treaty was or was not a matter of international concern? Could it ever find a treaty not of international concern without impugning the good faith of the executive branch, including the President? Of course, even if the courts were not to review a treaty at the constitutional level on the basis of international concern, senators in giving their advice and consent to the treaty are also obligated, by their oath of office, to consider the question. And even if the senators should find that the treaty is constitutional in this respect, it lies within their responsibilities and prerogatives to determine that the treaty is, nonetheless, undesirable from a policy point of view. The term international concern is also used in this latter sense. Nonetheless, as to the human rights treaties, the fundamental question still remains: is it a legitimate use of a treaty power for the President and the Senate to make a human rights treaty supreme law of the land simply if it is desirable to have as many nations as possible promise to adhere to the human rights standards stated in them?

c. Between roughly 1948 and 1953 a determined effort was made by a group of senators, elements of the American Bar Association, and others to amend the Constitution to limit the internal legal effect of treaties to the limitations on the federal legislative power. The political history of the period shows that the proponents of the Bricker Amendment (the Ohio senator who led the fight) were neo-isolationists in general alignment, but it also shows among them a serious concern lest the conventions on human rights then being negotiated in the United Nations might be given internal effect within the United States in such matters as segregated education and travel facilities. The amendment effort failed not too long before the Supreme Court, in 1954, interpreted the due process and equal protection clauses of the XIVth Amendment to prohibit different treatment based on race in public education, thus setting the stage for the general dismantling of all forms of racial discrimination involving state action. In other areas of differentiation that may amount to discrimination, the relationship between the potential of the treaty power to bring about change through internal legal effect and the alternative of change in the Constitution, either by judicial interpretation or formal amendment, still exists. The proposed Equal Rights Amendment is still in controversy domestically. Groups opposing this effort to reduce discrimination based on gender have already testified against four conventions on human rights that the Senate has under consideration. The objection is that ERA would be achieved by the treaty route.

EDWARDS v. CARTER

United States Court of Appeals, District of Columbia Circuit, 1978.
580 F.2d 1055.[a]

PER CURIAM:

This is an appeal from the District Court's dismissal of a challenge to appellee's use of the treaty power to convey to the Republic of Panama United States properties, including the Panama Canal, located in the Panama Canal Zone.[1] Appellants, sixty members of the

a. Cert. denied, 436 U.S. 907, 98 S.Ct. 2240 (1978).

1. PROPERTY TRANSFER AND ECONOMIC PARTICIPATION BY THE REPUBLIC OF PANAMA

1. Upon termination of this Treaty, the Republic of Panama shall assume total responsibility for the management, operation, and maintenance of the Panama Canal, which shall be turned over in operating condition and free of liens and debts, except as the two Parties may otherwise agree.

2. The United States of America transfers, without charge, to the Republic of Panama all right, title and interest the United States of America may have with respect to all real property, including non-removable improvements thereon, as set forth below:

(a) Upon the entry into force of this Treaty, the Panama Railroad and such property that was located in the former Canal Zone but that is not within the land and water areas the use of which is made available to the United States of America pursuant to this Treaty. However, it is agreed that the transfer on such date shall not include buildings and other facilities, except hous-

ing, the use of which is retained by the United States of America pursuant to this Treaty and related agreements, outside such areas;

(b) Such property located in an area or a portion thereof at such time as the use by the United States of America of such area or portion thereof ceases pursuant to agreement between the two Parties.

(c) Housing units made available for occupancy by members of the Armed Forces of the Republic of Panama in accordance with paragraph 5(b) of Annex B to the Agreement in Implementation of Article IV of this Treaty at such time as such units are made available to the Republic of Panama.

(d) Upon termination of this Treaty, all real property and non-removable improvements that were used by the United States of America for the purposes of this Treaty and related agreements and equipment related to the management, operation and maintenance of the Canal remaining in the Republic of Panama.

3. The Republic of Panama agrees to hold the United States of

House of Representatives, sought a declaratory judgment that the exclusive means provided in the Constitution for disposal of United States property requires approval of both Houses of Congress, *see* Art. IV, § 3, cl. 2, and that therefore the Panama Canal Zone may not be returned to Panama through the Treaty process, which invests the treaty-making power in the President by and with the advice and consent of two-thirds of the Senators present, see Art. II, § 2, cl. 2. Appellee contends that the Constitution permits United States territory to be disposed of either through congressional legislation or through the treaty process, and that therefore the President's decision to proceed under the treaty power is constitutionally permissible.

The District Court did not reach the merits of this controversy; rather, it dismissed the complaint for lack of jurisdiction after concluding that appellants lacked standing because they had failed to demonstrate injury in fact from the President's invocation of the treaty process. A notice of appeal and a request for a preliminary injunction pending appeal were immediately filed with this court. Appellee has moved for summary affirmance of the District Court's judgment either on the jurisdictional ground stated by the District Court or on the merits of appellants' contention; appellants have moved for summary reversal. We have heard oral argument and have considered the case on an expedited basis. For the reasons appearing below, we affirm the dismissal of the complaint, not on the jurisdictional ground relied on by the District Court but for failure to state a claim on which relief may be granted.

I

* * *

* * * [T]he precise question we address is whether the constitutional delegation found in Art. IV, § 3, cl. 2 is exclusive so as to prohibit the disposition of United States property by self-executing treaty—i. e., a treaty enacted in accordance with Art. II, § 2, cl. 2, which becomes effective without implementing legislation.

II

Article IV, § 3, cl. 2 of the Constitution states in its entirety:

The Congress shall have Power to dispose of and make all needful Rules and Regulations respecting the Territory or other Property belonging to the United States; and nothing in this Constitution shall be so construed as to Prejudice any Claims of the United States, or of any particular State.

America harmless with respect to any claims which may be made by third parties relating to rights, title and interest in such property.

4. The Republic of Panama shall receive, in addition, from the Panama Canal Commission a just and equitable return on the national resources which it has dedicated to the efficient management, operation, maintenance, protection and defense of the Panama Canal * * *.

Appellants contend that this clause gives Congress exclusive power to convey to foreign nations any property, such as the Panama Canal, owned by the United States. We find such a construction to be at odds with the wording of this and similar grants of power to the Congress, and, most significantly, with the history of the constitutional debates.[4]

The grant of authority to Congress under the property clause states that "The Congress shall have Power * * *," not that only the Congress shall have power, or that the Congress shall have exclusive power. In this respect the property clause is parallel to Article I, § 8, which also states that "The Congress shall have Power * * *." Many of the powers thereafter enumerated in § 8 involve matters that were at the time the Constitution was adopted, and that are at the present time, also commonly the subject of treaties. The most prominent example of this is the regulation of commerce with foreign nations, Art. 1, § 8, cl. 3, and appellants do not go so far as to contend that the treaty process is not a constitutionally allowable means for regulating foreign commerce. It thus seems to us that, on its face, the property clause is intended not to restrict the scope of the treaty clause, but, rather, is intended to permit Congress to accomplish through legislation what may concurrently be accomplished through other means provided in the Constitution.

4. The Senate Foreign Relations Committee has thoroughly considered and rejected appellants' argument. That Committee reported the treaties with Panama to the full Senate by a 14 to 1 vote, and the one dissenting Senator did not dispute the power of the President, by and with the advice and consent of two-thirds of the Senate present, to transfer United States property. See Exec. Rept. No. 95–12 (95th Cong., 2d Sess., Feb. 3, 1978).

In addition to the American Law Institute's Restatement of Foreign Relations Law, see infra, other authorities in agreement with this conclusion include Professor Louis Henkin, see L. Henkin, Foreign Affairs and the Constitution 159–60 (1965); Dean Louis Pollak, see 124 Cong.Rec., No. 8, at 5729 (95th Cong., Jan 30, 1978); Professor Covey Oliver, see Hearings Before the Committee on Foreign Relations, Part IV, at 95, 103, 112–13 (Jan. 19, 1978); and Professor John Norton Moore, see id. at 89, 93–94. The Attorney General and the State Department Legal Adviser have also issued opinions that the Panama Canal may be disposed of through self-executing treaty. See Opinion of the Attorney General to the Secretary of State, Aug. 11, 1977; Hearings Before the Subcommittee on the Separation of Powers of the Senate Judiciary Committee, Part I, at 3–25 (July 29, 1977). Raoul Berger, in testimony before the Subcommittee on Separation of Powers of the Senate Judiciary Committee in the fall of 1977, expressed a contrary position. His thesis seems to be that the President and Senate cannot exercise under the treaty power any power granted to Congress, see Hearings Before the Subcommittee on Separation of Powers, (95th Cong. 1st Sess., Nov. 3, 1977). We agree with Professor Henkin that such a narrow view of the treaty power would, by "outlaw[ing] treaties on matters as to which Congress could legislate domestically," "virtually wipe out the treaty power." L. Henkin, supra at 149.

We note that Professor Henkin's treatise leaves no doubt but that he is in agreement with our position. The passage quoted by the dissent, as is realized upon a careful reading of the passage itself (with its references to "unilateral" Presidential action and "executive order[s]"), concerns the limitations upon the President's power to dispose of property through unilateral executive action. See note 24 infra.

The American Law Institute's Restatement of Foreign Relations, Law, directly addressing this issue, comes to the same conclusion we reach:

> The mere fact, however, that a congressional power exists does not mean that the power is exclusive so as to preclude the making of a self-executing treaty within the area of that power.

ALI Restatement of Foreign Relations Law (2d), § 141, at 435 (1965). The section of the Restatement relied on by the dissent merely states that the treaty power, like all powers granted to the United States, is limited by other restraints found in the Constitution on the exercise of governmental power. (Rest.For.Rel. § 117). Of course the correctness of this proposition as a matter of constitutional law is clear. See Reid v. Covert, 354 U.S. 1, 77 S.Ct. 1222, 1 L. Ed.2d 1148 (1957); Geoffroy v. Riggs, 133 U.S. 258, 10 S.Ct. 295, 33 L.Ed. 642 (1890); Asakura v. Seattle, 265 U.S. 332, 44 S.Ct. 515, 68 L.Ed. 1041 (1924), also relied on by the dissent. To urge, as does the dissent, that the transfer of the Canal Zone property by treaty offends this well-settled principle—that the treaty power can only be exercised in a manner which conforms to the Constitution—begs the very question to be decided, namely, whether Art. IV, § 3, cl. 2 places in the Congress the *exclusive* authority to dispose of United States property.

There are certain grants of authority to Congress which are, by their very terms, exclusive. In these areas, the treaty-making power and the power of Congress are not concurrent; rather, the only department of the federal government authorized to take action is the Congress. For instance, the Constitution expressly provides only one method—congressional enactment—for the appropriation of money:

> No Money shall be drawn from the Treasury, but in Consequence of Appropriations made by Law.

Art. I, § 9, cl. 7. Thus, the expenditure of funds by the United States cannot be accomplished by self-executing treaty; implementing legislation appropriating such funds is indispensable. Similarly, the constitutional mandate that "all Bills for raising Revenue shall originate in the House of Representatives," Art. 1, § 7, cl. 1, appears, by reason of the restrictive language used, to prohibit the use of the treaty power to impose taxes.

These particular grants of power to Congress operate to limit the treaty power because the language of these provisions clearly precludes any method of appropriating money or raising taxes other than through the enactment of laws by the full Congress. This is to be contrasted with the power-granting language in Art. 1, § 8, and in Art. IV, § 3, cl. 2. Rather than stating the particular matter of concern and providing that the enactment of a law is the only way for the federal government to take action regarding that matter, these provisions state simply that Congress shall have power to take action on the matters enumerated.

Thus it appears from the very language used in the property clause that this provision was not intended to preclude the availability of self-executing treaties as a means for disposing of United States property. The history of the drafting and ratification of that clause confirms this conclusion. The other clause in Art. IV, § 3 concerns the procedures for admission of new states into the Union, and the debates at the Constitutional Convention clearly demonstrate that the property clause was intended to delineate the role to be played by the central government in the disposition of Western lands which were potential new states. Several individual states had made territorial claims to portions of these lands; and as finally enacted the property clause, introduced in the midst of the Convention's consideration of the admission of new states, sought to preserve both federal claims and conflicting state claims to certain portions of the Western lands.

The proceedings of the Virginia state ratifying convention provide further evidence of the limited scope of the property clause. During a debate in which the meaning of the clause was questioned, Mr. Grayson noted that the sole purpose for including this provision was to preserve the property rights of the states and the federal government to the Western territory as these rights existed during the Confederation.

This history demonstrates the limited concerns giving rise to the inclusion of Article IV, § 3, cl. 2 in the Constitution. Whether or not this historical perspective might serve as a basis for restricting the scope of congressional power under the property clause, we view it as persuasive evidence for rejecting the claim that Article IV is an express limitation on the treaty power, foreclosing the availability of that process as a constitutionally permissible means of disposing of American interests in the Panama Canal Zone.

* * *

IV

In view of the lack of ambiguity as to the intended effects of the treaty and property clauses, it may be surprising that judicial pronouncements over the past two centuries relating to these constitutional provisions are somewhat vague and conflicting. However, none of the actual holdings in these cases addressed the precise issue before us—whether the property clause prohibits the transfer of United States property to foreign nations through self-executing treaties. While, therefore, neither the holdings nor the dicta of these previous cases are dispositive of the case before us, we believe that in the main they support the conclusions we have stated heretofore.

* * *

As is true of most of the cases in which the Supreme Court has addressed the scope of the treaty power, Holden, Jones, and Francis involved the federal government's interaction with Indian tribes. Because of the sui generis nature of the relationship between the Indian tribes and the federal government, it might be argued that these decisions are not dispositive. We think, however, that they are persuasively supportive of the authority of the President and the Senate under the treaty clause.

V

While certain earlier judicial interpretations of the interplay between the property clause and the treaty clause may be somewhat confused and less than dispositive of the precise issue before us, past treaty practice is thoroughly consistent with the revealed intention of the Framers of these clauses. In addition to the treaties with Indian tribes upheld in the cases discussed above, there are many other instances of self-executing treaties with foreign nations, including Panama, which cede land or other property assertedly owned by the United States. That some transfers have been effected through a congressional enactment instead of, or in addition to, a treaty signed by the President and ratified by two-thirds of the Senate present lends no support to appellants' position in this case, because, as stated previously, self-executing treaties and congressional enactments are alternative, concurrent means provided in the Constitution for disposal of United States property.

For instance, the Treaty with Panama of 1955, 6 U.S.T. 2273, transferred certain property (a strip of water and other sites within the Canal Zone) to Panama without concurring legislation by the Congress, while transfer of other property (owned by the United States but within the jurisdiction of Panama) was, under the terms of the treaty itself, dependent upon concurring legislation by the Congress. The decision to cast some but not all of the articles of conveyance in non-self-executing form was a policy choice; it was not required by the Constitution.

The transfer of property contemplated in the current instance is part of a broader effort in the conduct of our foreign affairs to strengthen relations with another country, and indeed with the whole of Latin America. The Framers in their wisdom have made the treaty power available to the President, the chief executant of foreign relations under our constitutional scheme, by and with the advice and consent of two-thirds of the members of the Senate present, as a means of accomplishing these public purposes.

We do not think it is relevant that many previous treaties couched in self-executing terms have been different in scope, dealing with boundary issues or otherwise ceding land which was claimed both both by the United States and by a foreign nation. * * *

For the foregoing reasons, the judgment of the District Court dismissing the complaint is

Affirmed.

[Dissenting opinion of MacKINNON, Circuit Judge, omitted.]

SECTION B.   EXECUTIVE AGREEMENTS AND THE CONSTITUTION

---

1. PRESIDENTIAL POWER

The President, the Senate and the House of Representatives. What institutions of the federal government should participate in the formulation of foreign policy and in the making of internal law by international agreement? Despite the experience of President Washington, detailed below, Senate leaders in recent years have contended that the power as to advice and consent to treaties gives the Senate a special role of collaboration with the executive in the formulation of United States foreign policy, even where no specific international agreement is involved. Leaders of the House of Representatives have not shown much enthusiasm for this concept of senatorial special responsibility.

Sometimes, as in the case of tax treaties, the special responsibility of the House as to revenue measures is respected by the practice of making such treaties subject to the enactment of tax legislation by Congress. Further, in a revenue measure, Congress delegates to the executive, before the fact, the power to make certain types of international agreements, such as those for the reduction of tariffs or the elimination of non-tariff trade barriers. These delegations fix time limits, state maximum cuts and require periodic reports to Congress. More recently, they specify procedural steps. See Chapter 17, Section A.

Concern as to the possibility that executive agreements not authorized by Congress might force it to go along with the executive, either as to foreign policy lines of action or as to internal legal effect, has from time to time been expressed in both chambers, although the Senate has usually taken the lead in expressing it, as in the celebrated Bricker Amendment crisis in the early 1950s. In recent years reviews of executive-congressional responsibilities have been conducted by the Senate Committee on Foreign Relations and resulted in the legislation which appears at p. 1047. The hearings were significant because they covered many current aspects of the basic problem. Selected portions of the hearings are in the Documentary Supplement.

If the people of the United States should ever consider a full-scale review of the Constitution what would you think of making those international agreements that now require the approval of two-thirds of the senators subject only to approval by simple majorities in both houses? If you are generally favorable, would you wish to see all international agreements subject to such approval? If generally favorable to both suggestions, would you be willing to include in the revision a provision that an international agreement of the United States, as so approved, could not be contradicted by subsequent inconsistent legislation? See Chapter 1, p. 34.

II SCHWARTZ, A COMMENTARY ON THE CONSTITUTION OF THE UNITED STATES: THE POWERS OF GOVERNMENT 101, 150 (1963)*

The conception of the Senate as a Presidential council in the diplomatic field broke down as soon as it was tried in practice. In August, 1789, Washington came personally to the Senate to seek its advice on a proposed treaty. As might have been expected, an independent legislative chamber (even one composed of only twenty-six members) was scarcely suited to perform the role of Council of State. Instead of giving the President the speedy advice he sought, the Senators made lengthy speeches on the procedure to be followed. "This defeats every purpose of my coming here!" Washington exclaimed. As he left the Senate Chamber, he is reported to have declared "That he would be damned if he ever went there again." The account is probably apocryphal, but the fact remains that, after Washington's experience in this respect, neither he nor any other President ever again sought the formal advice of the Senate on a proposed negotiation. The concept of the Senate as an executive council in the field of foreign affairs was thus all but still-born at the outset of the Republic.

* * *

That an executive agreement can, in fact, be employed to accomplish the identical purpose as a treaty covering the same subject-matter is dramatically demonstrated by Theodore Roosevelt's action in connection with a proposed treaty with the Dominican Republic. Plenipotentiaries of the two countries had signed an agreement in 1905 in treaty form providing for the collection and disbursement of Dominican customs revenues. The treaty was submitted to the Senate, but that body failed to give its constitutional consent. President Roosevelt then proceeded to put the proposed treaty provisions into effect as an executive agreement. As T. R. put it in his Autobiography: "Somebody had to do that duty, and accordingly I did it. I went ahead and administered the proposed treaty anyhow, considering it as a simple agreement on the part of the Executive."

Having regard only to the legal questions involved, there is no doubt that any President can do what Theodore Roosevelt did in the case of the Dominican treaty. The executive agreement may thus be used as a means of circumventing the treaty-making procedure prescribed in Article II and avoiding the Senatorial control provided for therein. This can be done by the negotiation, in any particular case, of an executive agreement, which the President alone can make, rather than a treaty, which must be confirmed by the Senate.

This is true because, as this section has shown, there is no hard and fast legal line between executive agreements and treaties and they have come to be employed interchangeably in most areas of our foreign relations. That even experts in the field cannot really draw other than a purely formal line between treaties and executive agreements is shown by a request addressed to the State Department by a Senator asking them how to distinguish a treaty, which must be approved by the Senate, from an executive agreement, which need not. The State Department unhelpfully defined a treaty as "something they had to send to the Senate in order to get approval by a two-thirds vote. An executive agreement was something they did not have to send to the Senate." This reply, said the Senator who had sent the request, "reminded me of the time when I was a boy on the farm, and asked the hired man how to tell the difference between a male and a female pigeon. He said, 'You put corn in front of the pigeon. If he picks it up, it is a he; if she picks it up, it is a she.'" (at 150)

---

1 O'CONNELL, INTERNATIONAL LAW 206 (2d ed. 1970)*

The Constitution of the United States requires the approval of treaties by a two-third majority of the Senate. If, in constitutional law, a mere agreement is not a treaty, and thereby does not require Senate endorsement, the President may, by resort to informal methods of contracting, oblige the nation without the democratic control that the legislative process aims at. Actually the President is rarely so isolated in the matter of executive agreements from Congressional action of some sort as to be independent of legislative control or approval. The term "executive agreement" is a wide one, designed to mark off the boundary between treaties which require the advice and consent of the Senate and those documents, widely but loosely described in international practices as "treaties," which do not. Three main categories of instruments are comprehended: (a) agreements or understandings entered into pursuant to or in accordance with specific directives or authorisation of Congress given antecedently; (b) those not given effect to without such direction or authorisation given subsequently; and (c) those made by the Executive solely in virtue of its constitutional power. Actually, those in the third category are relatively few. The critics of the executive agreements, therefore, must be taken to be attacking, not principally the dangers of Presidential commitment without legislative check, so much as the constitutional rule concerning the effect internally on the States of informal international agreements; implied in the argument is that State sovereignty is insufficiently protected by Joint Resolution of both Houses, and that the more obstructive process of a two-third Senate majority is necessary.

The principal example of an executive agreement in the third category was the Litvinov Agreement between President Roosevelt

* Reprinted with the permission of
Sweet & Maxwell, Ltd., London.

and the Soviet Ambassador which affected suits between private claimants and the Soviet. * * *

      * * *

The question is whether an international commitment of the United States is required by the Constitution to be in treaty as distinct from agreement form. The question is usually resolved on an ad hoc basis by consultation between the Executive and Congress, taking into account the extent to which the agreement can be carried out by the former without encroaching on the domain of the latter. Whenever there is a serious doubt as to whether an international agreement should be in the form of a treaty or in the form of an executive agreement the matter must be brought to the attention of the Secretary of State by memorandum with comments of the Legal Adviser. It is then referred to Congress through the office of the Assistant Secretary for Congressional Relations. If it is decided that the matter may be dealt with by executive agreement the next question that arises is whether such agreement should be supported, antecedently or subsequently by a Joint Resolution or an Act so as to acquire legislative character, or whether it may be left within the President's constitutional authority. It is accepted that this authority is to be deduced from those provisions of the Constitution which confer exclusive power on the President, such as command of the armed forces, and it is quite certain that it is limited by the stated guarantees of the Constitution. Since the field of executive action proper is necessarily limited the bulk of executive agreements are made with Congressional co-operation, and this, in fact, is the case with some 90 per cent. of those actually contracted.

Annex

Select List of Executive Agreements

Category 1 (prior Congressional approval)

Agriculture:	Migration of Mexican agricultural workers. 57 Stat. 70, 73; 58 Stat. 15; 59 Stat. 645; 61 Stat. 55; 50 U.S.C.App. 1355(g). Co-operative agricultural pro-grammes. 61 Stat. 780.
Aid, Foreign:	Assistance agreements with Greece and Turkey. 61 Stat. 103, 610; 62 Stat. 157.
Anthropology:	Co-operation in research. 53 Stat. 1290; 22 U.S.C. 501–502.
Civil Air Routes:	International Civil Aviation Convention. T.I.A.S. 1591; 61 Stat., pt. 2, 1180.

Civil Defence:	Defence Agreement with Canada. Public Law 920, 81st Cong.; 64 Stat. 1245.
Claims:	War Damage Act. 55 Stat. 880; 57 Stat. 66; 59 Stat. 511; 31 U.S.C. 224 d—224 i–1; 63 Stat. 279, 878.
Copyright:	Extension of time agreements. 55 Stat. 732. Rights affected by war. 60 Stat. 568, 940; 61 Stat. 413. Lend-Lease Act. 55 Stat. 732; 22 U.S.C. 411–419.
Economic Co-operation:	Foreign Assistance Act 1948. 62 Stat. 137, 150, 153. Foreign Aid Appropriation Act 1949. 62 Stat. 1054.
Educational Programmes:	Fulbright Act. 61 Stat. 780; 60 Stat. 754; Public Law 584. 79th Cong.
Lend-Lease:	Lend-Lease Act 1941. 55 Stat. 31; 57 Stat. 222; 58 Stat. 223; 59 Stat. 52; 22 U.S.C. 411–419.
Military Service:	Reciprocal agreements for service of aliens. 50 U.S.C.App. 301–318.
Passport Visas:	Abolition of. 43 Stat. 976; 8 U.S.C. 202(i).
Postal Conventions:	Rev.Stat., sec. 398; 48 Stat. 943. This confers on the Postmaster-General power to conclude postal agreements.
Shipping:	International Convention for the Safety of Life at Sea. 50 Stat. 1121.
Taxation, Double:	Internal Revenue Code. 26 U.S.C. 212(b), 231(d).
Trade:	Trade Agreement with Iceland. 57 Stat. 1075, 1094; E.A.S. No. 342; U.N.T.S., Vol. 29, p. 317. GATT (Tariff Act 1950). 19 U.S.C. 1351(a).

Category 2 (subsequent Congressional approval)

ILO	Joint Resolution,	1934, 48 Stat. 1182.
	" "	1938, 62 Stat. 1151.
UNNRA	" "	1944, 58 Stat. 122; 59 Stat. U.S.C. 1571–1578.
PAO	" "	1945, 59 Stat. 539.
IMF	Act	1945, 59 Stat. 512; 22 U.S. C. 286–286K; 59 Stat. 669.
IBRD	ibid.	ibid.
UNESCO	Joint Resolution,	1946, 60 Stat. 712; Act, 59 Stat. 669.
WHO	" "	1948, 62 Stat. 441; Act, 59 Stat. 669.
IRO	" "	1947, 61 Stat. 214; Act, 59 Stat. 669.
U.N.H.Q. Agmt.	" "	1946, 61 Stat. 756; Act, 59 Stat. 669.
Trusteeship Agmt.	" "	1947, 61 Stat. 397.
Fur Seal Agmt. with Canada Act	" "	1944, 58 Stat. 100; 61 Stat. 450; 16 U.S.C. 631a– 631r.

Category 3 (inherent executive powers)

Armistice Agreements (five).

Understandings with certain countries after the Second World War that U. S. armed forces were present on their territory with permission.

Understandings with Syria and Lebanon regarding most-favour-ed-nation treatment to American nationals.

Agreements regarding aid by certain countries to U. S. armed forces stationed in their territory.

Arrangements recognising jurisdiction of the U. S. over criminal offences by U. S. armed forces in foreign countries.

Arrangements dealing with various phases of the movement and treatment of U. S. armed forces.

Arrangements for Red Cross facilities to U. S. armed forces.

Claims settlement not involving rights of U. S. citizens.

Arrangement with the LON for registration of treaties.

Modi vivendi, e. g. Preparatory Commissions for UN, UNESCO, IRO.

Arrangements with Panama for emergency use of highways.

Arrangements for military occupation of territory.

UNITED STATES DEPARTMENT OF STATE
CIRCULAR NUMBER 175

50 American Journal of International Law 784 (1956).*

1. Purpose of Circular

1.1 The purpose of this circular is to insure (a) that the function of making treaties and other international agreements is carried out within traditional and constitutional limits; (b) that the objectives to be sought in the negotiation of particular treaties and other international agreements are approved by the Secretary or Under Secretary; (c) that firm positions resulting from negotiations are not undertaken without the approval of the interested Assistant Secretaries or their Deputies; (d) that the final texts developed are approved by the interested Assistant Secretaries or their Deputies and brought to the attention of the Secretary or Under Secretary a reasonable time before signature; and (e) that authorization to sign the final text is secured and appropriate arrangements for signature are made.

1.2 It is a further purpose of this circular to insure that full implementation shall be given to the policy stated in the Secretary's testimony before the Senate Committee on the Judiciary on April 6, 1953, in which he said:

"The Constitution provides that the President shall have power to make treaties by and with the advice and consent of the Senate. This administration recognizes the significance of the word "advice". It will be our effort to see that the Senate gets its opportunity to "advise and consent" in time so that it does not have to choose between adopting treaties it does not like, or embarrassing our international position by rejecting what has already been negotiated out with foreign governments.

" * * * I am authorized by the President to advise this Committee, the Senate Foreign Relations Committee, and the House Foreign Affairs Committee as follows:

"It has long been recognized that difficulties exist in the determination as to which international agreements should be submitted to the Senate as treaties, which ones should be submitted to both Houses of the Congress, and which ones do not require any Congressional approval.

" * * * [T]he Congress is entitled to know the considerations that enter into the determinations as to which procedures are sought to be followed. To that end, when there is any serious question of this nature and the circumstances permit, the Executive Branch will consult with appropriate Congressional leaders and Committees in determining the most suitable way of handling international agreements as they arise."

* Reprinted by permission of the American Society of International Law.

2.   Scope of the Treaty-Making Power

Treaties should be designed to promote United States interests by securing action by foreign governments in a way deemed advantageous to the United States. Treaties are not to be used as a device for the purpose of effecting internal social changes or to try to circumvent the constitutional procedures established in relation to what are essentially matters of domestic concern.

3.   Scope of the Executive Agreement-Making Power

Executive agreements shall not be used when the subject matter should be covered by a treaty. The executive agreement form shall be used only for agreements which fall into one or more of the following categories:

  a.   Agreements which are made pursuant to or in accordance with existing legislation or a treaty;

  b.   Agreements which are made subject to Congressional approval or implementation; or *[handwritten]*

  c.   Agreements which are made under and in accordance with the President's Constitutional power. *vague & broad [handwritten]*

* * *

5.   Action Required

* * *

5.2   Questions as to Treaty or Executive Agreement Form

Where there is any serious question as to whether an international agreement should be made in the form of a treaty or in the form of an executive agreement made by the President alone or with the consent of both Houses of Congress, the matter shall be brought to the attention of the Secretary by a memorandum prepared by the officer responsible for the contemplated negotiations. This memorandum shall first be routed to the Legal Adviser and the Assistant Secretary for Congressional Relations for their clearance and comment. Thereafter, whenever circumstances permit, consultation shall be had with appropriate Congressional leaders and committees in determining the most suitable way of handling such international agreements, such consultation to be had by the office responsible for the negotiations with the assistance of the Assistant Secretary for Congressional Relations.

* * *

The monitoring and management of undertakings to other countries. Circular 175 is still in the Foreign Affairs Manual (FAM). If the Department of State is to discharge effectively the reporting duty imposed on it in the statute that follows, it must have some way of keeping track of all commitments made by departments and agencies of the United States that carry on executive functions. Circular 175 may help in this regard. The statute assumes [subsections (c) and (d)] that the Secretary of State will effectively manage the making of international commitments throughout the departments and agencies of the government, in the sense of insuring coordination of such agreements with each other and with foreign policy generally. Whether the Secretary through the Department of State is actually able to discharge this function is not known by us. In past, presidential efforts to direct the supremacy of state as to matters bearing on foreign policy have not been successful, especially as to the National Security Council and other units in the Executive Office of the President and the Department of Defense. Cf. Kissinger, The White House Years (1979).

TRANSMITTAL OF UNITED STATES INTERNATIONAL AGREEMENTS TO CONGRESS

1 U.S.C. 112b, as amended.

§ 112b. United States international agreements; transmission to Congress

(a) The Secretary of State shall transmit to the Congress the text of any international agreement (including the text of any oral international agreement, which agreement shall be reduced to writing), other than a treaty, to which the United States is a party as soon as practicable after such agreement has entered into force with respect to the United States but in no event later than sixty days thereafter. However, any such agreement the immediate public disclosure of which would, in the opinion of the President, be prejudicial to the national security of the United States shall not be so transmitted to the Congress but shall be transmitted to the Committee on Foreign Relations of the Senate and the Committee on International Relations of the House of Representatives under an appropriate injunction of secrecy to be removed only upon due notice from the President. Any department or agency of the United States Government which enters into any international agreement on behalf of the United States shall transmit to the Department of State the text of such agreement not later than twenty days after such agreement has been signed.

(b) Not later than March 1, 1979, and at yearly intervals thereafter, the President shall, under his own signature, transmit to the Speaker of the House of Representatives and the chairman of the Committee on Foreign Relations of the Senate a report with respect to each international agreement which, during the preceding year, was transmitted to the Congress after the expiration of the 60-day period referred to in the first sentence of subsection (a), describing fully and completely the reasons for the late transmittal.

(c) Notwithstanding any other provision of law, an international agreement may not be signed or otherwise concluded on behalf of the United States without prior consultation with the Secretary of

State. Such consultation may encompass a class of agreements rather than a particular agreement.

(d) The Secretary of State shall determine for and within the executive branch whether an arrangement constitutes an international agreement within the meaning of this section.

(e) The President shall, through the Secretary of State, promulgate such rules and regulations as may be necessary to carry out this section.

As amended Pub.L. 95–45, § 5, June 15, 1977, 91 Stat. 224; Pub.L. 95–426, Title VII, § 708, Oct. 7, 1978, 92 Stat. 993. [For excerpts from the hearings on the bill, see the Documentary Supplement.]

---

2. AGREEMENTS UNDER PRESIDENTIAL POWER: INTERNAL LAW?

UNITED STATES v. PINK

United States Supreme Court, 1942.
315 U.S. 203, 62 S.Ct. 552.

[The Litvinov Agreement referred to in the quotation from O'Connell on p. 1041, was the subject of litigation in United States v. Belmont, 301 U.S. 324, 57 S.Ct. 758 (1937), and United States v. Pink. In the Pink case, the relevant document is referred to as the Litvinov Assignment. As an incident to the United States recognition of the USSR on November 16, 1933, the Soviet foreign minister, Litvinov, delivered a letter to the President of the United States by which the Soviet Union assigned to the United States amounts due to the Soviet Union from United States nationals. This assignment was stated to be preparatory to a final settlement mainly of United States claims for nationalization of property of citizens of the United States situated in the USSR. In Pink the United States, assignee of the Soviet Union, sued the New York Superintendent of Insurance, who had succeeded by a court order to the assets of the New York branch of a Russian insurance company (previously nationalized by Soviet law). One defense was that the Russian nationalization decrees were extraterritorial, confiscatory and contrary to the public policy of New York. The New York courts had dismissed the United States complaint, but the Supreme Court reversed. In the court's opinion, Mr. Justice DOUGLAS stated, in part:]

* * * The powers of the President in the conduct of foreign relations included the power, without consent of the Senate, to determine the public policy of the United States with respect to the Russian nationalization decrees. "What government is to be regarded here as representative of a foreign sovereign state is a political rather than a judicial question, and is to be determined by the political department of the government." Guaranty Trust Co. v. United States, supra, 304 U.S. page 137, 58 S.Ct. page 791. That authority is not limited to a determination of the government to be recognized.

It includes the power to determine the policy which is to govern the question of recognition. Objections to the underlying policy as well as objections to recognition are to be addressed to the political department and not to the courts. See Guaranty Trust Co. v. United States, supra, 304 U.S. page 138, 58 S.Ct. page 791; Kennett v. Chambers, 14 How. 38, 50–51. As we have noted, this Court in the Belmont case recognized that the Litvinov Assignment was an international compact which did not require the participation of the Senate. It stated (301 U.S. pages 330–331, 57 S.Ct. pages 760, 761): "There are many such compacts, of which a protocol, a modus vivendi, a postal convention, and agreements like that now under consideration are illustrations." And see Monaco v. Mississippi, 292 U.S. 313, 331, 54 S.Ct. 745, 751; United States v. Curtiss-Wright Corp., 299 U.S. 304, 318, 57 S.Ct. 216, 220. Recognition is not always absolute; it is sometimes conditional. 1 Moore, International Law Digest (1906), pp. 73–74; 1 Hackworth, Digest of International Law (1940), pp. 192–195. Power to remove such obstacles to full recognition as settlement of claims of our nationals (Levitan, Executive Agreements, 35 Ill.L.Rev. 365, 382–385) certainly is a modest implied power of the President who is the "sole organ of the federal government in the field of international relations." United States v. Curtiss-Wright Corp., supra, 299 U.S. page 320, 57 S.Ct. page 221. Effectiveness in handling the delicate problems of foreign relations requires no less. Unless such a power exists, the power of recognition might be thwarted or seriously diluted. No such obstacle can be placed in the way of rehabilitation of relations between this country and another nation, unless the historic conception of the powers and responsibilities of the President in the conduct of foreign affairs (see Moore, Treaties and Executive Agreements, 20 Pol.Sc.Q. 385, 403–417) is to be drastically revised. It was the judgment of the political department that full recognition of the Soviet Government required the settlement of all outstanding problems including the claims of our nationals. Recognition and the Litvinov Assignment were interdependent. We would usurp the executive function if we held that that decision was not final and conclusive in the courts.

"All constitutional acts of power, whether in the executive or in the judicial department, have as much legal validity and obligation as if they proceeded from the legislature, * * *." The Federalist, No. 64. A treaty is a "Law of the Land" under the supremacy clause (Art. VI, Cl. 2) of the Constitution. Such international compacts and agreements as the Litvinov Assignment have a similar dignity. United States v. Belmont, supra, 301 U.S. page 331, 57 S.Ct. page 761. See Corwin, The President, Office & Powers (1940), pp. 228–240.

It is, of course, true that even treaties with foreign nations will be carefully construed so as not to derogate from the authority and jurisdiction of the States of this nation unless clearly necessary to effectuate the national policy. Guaranty Trust Co. v. United States, supra, 304 U.S. page 143, 58 S.Ct. page 793, and cases cited. For ex-

ample, in Todok v. Union State Bank, 281 U.S. 449, 50 S.Ct. 363, this
Court took pains in its construction of a treaty, relating to the power
of an alien to dispose of property in this country, not to invalidate
the provisions of state law governing such dispositions. Frequently
the obligation of a treaty will be dependent on state law. Prevost v.
Greneaux, 19 How. 1. But state law must yield when it is inconsistent with, or impairs the policy or provisions of, a treaty or of an international compact or agreement. See Nielsen v. Johnson, 279 U.S.
47, 49 S.Ct. 223. Then, the power of a State to refuse enforcement of
rights based on foreign law which runs counter to the public policy of
the forum (Griffin v. McCoach, 313 U.S. 498, 506, 61 S.Ct. 1023,
1027) must give way before the superior Federal policy evidenced by
a treaty or international compact or agreement. Santovincenzo v.
Egan, supra, 284 U.S. 30, 52 S.Ct. 81; United States v. Belmont, supra [301 U.S. 324, 57 S.Ct. 758].

Enforcement of New York's policy as formulated by the Moscow
case would collide with and subtract from the Federal policy, whether
it was premised on the absence of extraterritorial effect of the Russian decrees, the conception of the New York branch as a distinct
juristic personality, or disapproval by New York of the Russian program of nationalization. * * *

UNITED STATES v. GUY W. CAPPS, INC.

United States Court of Appeals, Fourth Circuit, 1953.
204 F.2d 655.[a]

PARKER, Chief Judge. This is an appeal by the United States
from a judgment entered on a verdict directed for the defendant, Guy
W. Capps, in an action instituted to recover damages alleged to have
been sustained by the United States as the result of alleged breach by
defendant of a contract with respect to the importation of seed potatoes from Canada. The District Court denied a motion to dismiss the
action. United States v. Guy W. Capps, Inc., 100 F.Supp. 30. Upon
the subsequent trial, however, the court directed a verdict and entered judgment for defendant on the ground that there was no sufficient showing of breach of contract or damage to the United States.

The contract sued on has relation to the potato price support
program of 1948 and the executive agreement entered into between
Canada and the United States through the Canadian Ambassador and
the Acting Secretary of State of the United States. Pursuant to the
Agricultural Act of 1948, Public Law 897, 80th Cong.2d Sess., 62
Stat. 1247, the United States committed itself to purchase from eligible potato growers, directly or through dealers, all table stock and
seed potatoes that could not be sold commercially at a parity price.
The purchase and disposal of potatoes under this program was
carried out by the Commodity Credit Corporation. In a manifest at-

a. Aff'd 348 U.S. 296, 75 S.Ct. 326
(1955), on other grounds.

tempt to protect the American Potato Market in which this price support program was operating from an influx of Canadian grown potatoes, the Acting Secretary of State of the United States, on November 23, 1948, entered into an executive agreement with the Canadian Ambassador, who was acting for the Canadian Government, to the effect that the Canadian Government would place potatoes in the list of commodities for which export permits were required and that export permits would be granted therefor only to Canadian exporters who could give evidence that they had firm orders from legitimate United States users of Canadian seed potatoes and that "Canadian exporters would also be required to have included in any contract into which they might enter with a United States seed potato importer a clause in which the importer would give an assurance that the potatoes would not be diverted or reconsigned for table stock purposes." In consideration of this agreement on the part of the Canadian Government, the United States Government undertook that it would not impose "any quantitative limitations or fees on Canadian potatoes of the 1948 crop exported to the United States" under the system of regulating the movement of potatoes to the United States outlined in the Canadian proposal and would not consider the Canadian Government's guarantee of a floor price with respect to certain potatoes to be the payment of a bounty or grant and would not levy any countervailing duty on such potatoes under the provisions of section 303 of the Tariff Act of 1930. On November 26, 1948, the Canadian Privy Council added potatoes to the list of products under export permit control and exporters of seed potatoes to the United States could not secure an export permit without complying with the conditions required by the executive agreement.

Defendant, a corporation engaged in business in Norfolk, Virginia, entered into a contract in December 1948 with H. B. Willis, Inc., a Canadian exporter, to purchase 48,544 sacks of Canadian seed potatoes, containing 100 lbs. each, to be shipped on the S. S. Empire Gangway docking in Jacksonville, Florida, in January 1949. Defendant's officers admittedly knew of the agreement with Canada and stated in a telegram to an official of the United States Department of Agriculture that the potatoes were being brought in for seed purposes. Defendant sent a telegram to the exporter in Canada on the same day that the potatoes were billed stating that they were for planting in Florida and Georgia. Defendant sold the potatoes while in shipment to the Atlantic Commission Company, a wholly owned agency of Great Atlantic & Pacific Tea Company, a retail grocery organization. No attempt was made to restrict their sale so that they would be used for seed and not for food, and there is evidence from which the jury could properly have drawn the conclusion that they were sold on the market as food displacing potatoes grown in this country and causing damage to the United States by requiring greater purchases of American grown potatoes in aid of the price support program than would have been necessary in the absence of their importation.

On these facts we think that judgment was properly entered for the defendant, but for reasons other than those given by the District Court. We have little difficulty in seeing in the evidence breach of contract on the part of defendant and damage resulting to the United States from the breach. We think, however, that the executive agreement was void because it was not authorized by Congress and contravened provisions of a statute dealing with the very matter to which it related and that the contract relied on, which was based on the executive agreement, was unenforceable in the courts of the United States for like reason. We think, also, that no action can be maintained by the government to recover damages on account of what is essentially a breach of a trade regulation, in the absence of express authorization by Congress. The power to regulate foreign commerce is vested in Congress, not in the executive or the courts; and the executive may not exercise the power by entering into executive agreements and suing in the courts for damages resulting from breaches of contracts made on the basis of such agreements.

In the Agricultural Act of 1948, Congress had legislated specifically with respect to the limitations which might be imposed on imports if it was thought that they would render ineffective or materially interfere with any program or operation undertaken pursuant to that act. Section 3 of the act, which amended prior statutes, provided in the portion here pertinent, 62 Stat. 1248–1250, 7 U.S.C.A. § 624:

> (a) Whenever the President has reason to believe that any article or articles are being or are practically certain to be imported into the United States under such conditions and in such quantities as to render or tend to render ineffective, or materially interfere with, any program or operation undertaken under this title * * * he shall cause an immediate investigation to be made by the United States Tariff Commission, which shall give precedence to investigations under this section to determine such facts. Such investigation shall be made after due notice and opportunity for hearing to interested parties, and shall be conducted subject to such regulations as the President shall specify.

> (b) If, on the basis of such investigation and report to him of findings and recommendations made in connection therewith, the President finds the existence of such facts, he shall by proclamation impose such * * * quantitative limitations on any article or articles which may be entered * * * for consumption as he finds and declares shown by such investigation to be necessary in order that the entry of such article or articles will not render or tend to render ineffective, or materially interfere with, any program or operation referred to in subsection (a), of this section * * * Provided, That no proclamation under this section shall impose any limitation on the total quantity of any article or articles which may be entered * * * for consumption which reduces such permissible total quantity to pro-

portionately less than 50 per centum of the total quantity of such article or articles which was entered   *   *   *   for consumption during a representative period as determined by the President: *   *   *.

There was no pretense of complying with the requirements of this statute. The President did not cause an investigation to be made by the Tariff Commission, the Commission did not conduct an investigation or make findings or recommendations, and the President made no findings of fact and issued no proclamation imposing quantitative limitations and determined no representative period for the application of the 50% limitation contained in the proviso. All that occurred in the making of this executive agreement, the effect of which was to exclude entirely a food product of a foreign country from importation into the United States, was an exchange of correspondence between the Acting Secretary of State and the Canadian Ambassador. Since the purpose of the agreement as well as its effect was to bar imports which would interfere with the Agricultural Adjustment program, it was necessary that the provisions of this statute be complied with and an executive agreement excluding such imports which failed to comply with it was void. Morgan v. United States, 304 U.S. 1, 58 S.Ct. 773, 999, 82 L.Ed. 1129; Panama Refining Co. v. Ryan, 293 U. S. 388, 55 S.Ct. 241, 253, 79 L.Ed. 446. As was said by Chief Justice Hughes in the case last cited: "We are not dealing with action which, appropriately belonging to the executive province, is not the subject of judicial review or with the presumptions attaching to executive action.   *   *   *   [W]e are concerned with the question of the delegation of legislative power.   *   *   * "

It is argued, however, that the validity of the executive agreement was not dependent upon the Act of Congress but was made pursuant to the inherent powers of the President under the Constitution. The answer is that while the President has certain inherent powers under the Constitution such as the power pertaining to his position as Commander in Chief of Army and Navy and the power necessary to see that the laws are faithfully executed, the power to regulate interstate and foreign commerce is not among the powers incident to the Presidential office, but is expressly vested by the Constitution in the Congress. It cannot be upheld as an exercise of the power to see that the laws are faithfully executed for, as said by Mr. Justice Holmes in his dissenting opinion in Myers v. United States, 272 U.S. 52, 177, 47 S.Ct. 21, 85, 71 L.Ed. 160, "The duty of the President to see that the laws be executed is a duty that does not go beyond the laws or require him to achieve more than Congress sees fit to leave within his power."   *   *   *

We think that whatever the power of the executive with respect to making executive trade agreements regulating foreign commerce in the absence of action by Congress, it is clear that the executive may not through entering into such an agreement avoid complying with a regulation prescribed by Congress. Imports from a foreign country are foreign commerce subject to regulation, so far as this country is concerned, by Congress alone. The executive may not by-pass congressional limitations regulating such commerce by entering into an agreement with the foreign country that the regulation be exercised by that country through its control over exports. Even though the regulation prescribed by the executive agreement be more desirable than that prescribed by Congressional action, it is the latter which must be accepted as the expression of national policy.

* * *

For the reasons stated, we do not think that the United States can maintain the action for damages. The judgment for defendant will accordingly be affirmed.

Affirmed.

---

1. *Problem.* The Nuclear Test Ban Treaty entered into force on October 10, 1963, following its ratification by the United States, the United Kingdom and the Soviet Union. 110 states were parties to the treaty by January 1, 1980. For the text, see the Documentary Supplement. In its operative Article I "[e]ach of the Parties to this Treaty undertakes to prohibit, to prevent, and not to carry out any nuclear weapon test explosion, or any other nuclear explosion, at any place under its jurisdiction or control: (a) in the atmosphere; beyond its limits, including outer space; or underwater, including territorial waters or high seas; or (b) in any other environment if such explosion causes radioactive debris to be present outside the territorial limits of the State under whose jurisdiction or control such explosion is conducted. * * *" Article II of the treaty provides for amendment as follows:

1. Any Party may propose amendments to this Treaty. The text of any proposed amendment shall be submitted to the Depositary Governments which shall circulate it to all Parties to this Treaty. Thereafter, if requested to do so by one-third or more of the Parties, the Depositary Governments shall convene a conference, to which they shall invite all the Parties, to consider such amendment.

2. Any amendment to this Treaty must be approved by a majority of the votes of all the Parties to this Treaty, including the votes of all of the Original Parties. The amendment shall enter into force for all Parties upon the deposit of instruments of ratification by a majority of all the Parties, including the instruments of ratification of all of the Original Parties.

The resolution of the United States Senate giving its advice and consent to the ratification of the treaty provides as follows:

Whereas the President has submitted a limited nuclear test ban treaty, providing a method of amendment, to the Senate for its advice and consent in accordance with article II, section 2 of the Constitution; and

Whereas the Constitution in article II, section 2, provides "He shall have Power, by and with the Advice and Consent of the Senate, to make Treaties, provided two-thirds of the Senators present concur"; and

Whereas amendments to treaties are subject to this constitutional provision: Now, therefore, be it

Resolved (two-thirds of the Senators present concurring therein), That the Senate advise and consent to the ratification of the treaty banning nuclear weapon tests in the atmosphere, in outer space, and underwater, signed at Moscow on August 5, 1963, on behalf of the United States of America, the United Kingdom of Great Britain and Northern Ireland, and the Union of Soviet Socialist Republics.

Suppose that in conjunction with the negotiation of an arms limitation treaty the United States and the USSR agree to ban underground testing and that the President, because of expected delays in the Senate as to the approval of the entire treaty, undertakes to enforce the underground testing prohibition as an executive agreement pending Senate consent to the entire treaty:

(i) Is the United States bound internationally not to test nuclear weapons underground?

(ii) Does this executive agreement legally justify no further underground testing in the United States as against prior legislation directing a certain number of such tests and appropriating money for them?

2. *What of the Pink case today?* After Pink was decided, the Supreme Court held in Youngstown Sheet and Tube Co. v. Sawyer, 343 U.S. 579, 72 S.Ct. 863 (1952), that the President has neither explicit nor inherent power to set aside an act of Congress for the benefit of United States foreign affairs interests as seen by the President. The decision was based upon the separation of powers, a principle underlying the structure of the Constitution, though not stated as such therein. Whether Pink survived *Youngstown* is conjectural. The court has not addressed the issue whether executive action at the federal level may still supersede state legislation, even if such action may not supersede federal legislation.

Another question concerning presidential powers arises from Article 11 of the first Declaration by the government of Algeria in the agreement of January 19, 1981, for the release of American hostages in Teheran. The article provides, inter alia, that the United States will "bar and preclude" the prosecution against Iran of any pending or future claims of United States nationals. See the Documentary Supplement.

In Electronic Data Systems Corp. v. Iran, 508 F.Supp. 1350 (D.Tex., 1981) the plaintiff had won a judgment against Iran that was on appeal at the effective date of the agreement and Iranian assets had been attached to secure the judgment. Judge Robert W. Porter issued a preliminary injunction against transfer of the attached assets to Iran under the terms of Article 11 and was quoted by the press as having ruled that the executive agreement was an "unwarranted intrusion into the realm of the judicial branch of the government." Compare United States v. Pink and the above situation in the light of Youngstown Sheet and Tube Co. v. Sawyer. What if the President were to refer the agreement to the Senate and over two-thirds of the Senate should approve it? What if the House and the Senate by a joint resolution or an "act of ratification" were to approve the agreement by ordinary majorities in both houses: would the issue be resolved by either of these actions?

Senator Charles H. Percy, speaking for the White House, announced on February 16, 1981, that the Reagan Administration would abide by the agreement and was convinced executive power sufficed to make it entirely effective, so far as United States undertakings were concerned. In the same period, lawyers for claimants were telling congressional committees that the President could not effectively transfer their clients' claims to the Iran-United States Claims Tribunal created by the agreement. Is the basic problem a structural one under the terms of the Constitution?

2. SEPARATION OF POWERS AND THE TERMINATION OF TREATIES BY THE PRESIDENT

The issue of judicial authority to resolve disputes between groups of legislators and the federal executive has arisen in connection with a presidential order ending a mutual security treaty between the United States and the regime on Taiwan formerly known here as the Republic of China. Note where the lines seem to be drawn in the opinions that follow.

GOLDWATER v. CARTER

United States Court of Appeals, District of Columbia Circuit, 1979.[a]
617 F.2d 697.[b]

PER CURIAM: The court *en banc* has before it for review the judgment of the District Court that the notice of termination given by the President pursuant to the terms of the Mutual Defense Treaty with the Republic of China is ineffective absent either (1) a manifestation of the consent of the Senate to such termination by a two-thirds vote or (2) an approving majority vote therefor by both houses of Congress. The preliminary questions we confront are, first, whether the District Court was without jurisdiction because appellees

---

a. Heard en banc on accelerated appeal at the request of the executive branch.

b. Cert. granted and dismissal of the complaint was directed, without argument, 444 U.S. 996, 100 S.Ct. 533 (1979), 7–2.

lacked standing, and, second, whether it should in any event have declined to exercise jurisdiction by reason of the political nature of the question it was called upon to decide. Since a majority of the court does not exist to dispose of the appeal on either of these bases, we reach the merits and reverse.

In doing so, however, we think it important at the outset to stress that the Treaty, as it was presented to the Senate in 1954 and consented to by it, contained an explicit provision for termination by either party on one year's notice. The Senate, in the course of giving its consent, exhibited no purpose and took no action to reserve a role for itself—by amendment, reservation, or condition—in the effectuation of this provision. Neither has the Senate, since the giving of the notice of termination, purported to take any final or decisive action with respect to it, either by way of approval or disapproval. The constitutional issue we face, therefore, is solely and simply the one of whether the President in these precise circumstances is, on behalf of the United States, empowered to terminate the Treaty in accordance with its terms. It is our view that he is, and that the limitations which the District Court purported to place on his action in this regard have no foundation in the Constitution.

BACKGROUND

On December 22, 1978 plaintiffs-appellees filed this suit in District Court, seeking declaratory and injunctive relief to prevent termination of the Treaty without senatorial or congressional consent. The complaint alleged that the President violated his sworn duty to uphold the laws, including the treaties, of the United States. It asserted that the President has no unilateral power under the Constitution to abrogate treaties, and that the United States, not the President, is the party invested by Article X of the Treaty with the power of termination.

On June 6, 1979 the District Court dismissed the suit, without prejudice, for lack of standing. The court observed that three resolutions then pending in the Senate might resolve the controversy without need for judicial intervention. The court concluded:

> If the Congress approves the President's action, the issue presently before the Court would be moot. If the Senate or the Congress takes action, the result of which falls short of approving the President's termination effort, then the controversy will be ripe for a judicial declaration. * * *

JA 631–632.

Within hours of the District Court order the Senate called up Senate Resolution 15 which, as amended by the Foreign Relations Committee, would have recognized some fourteen grounds that would justify unilateral action by the President to terminate treaty obligations of the United States. By a vote of 59 to 35 the Senate substi-

tuted for its consideration an amendment drafted by Senator Harry
Byrd, Jr.:

> That it is the sense of the Senate that approval of the United
> States Senate is required to terminate any mutual defense treaty
> between the United States and another nation.

125 Cong.Rec. S7015, S7038–S7039 (daily ed. June 6, 1979). Later
that day, during the course of debate on the amended resolution, a
dispute arose among the Senators over whether the resolution would
have retrospective, or merely prospective, effect. No final vote was
ever taken on the resolution, and the Majority Leader returned the
resolution to the calendar.

On June 12, 1979, after the Byrd amendment was voted on, the
plaintiffs-appellees filed a motion in District Court for alteration or
amendment of the June 6 order of dismissal. They contended that
the Senate's action on the Byrd amendment satisfied the court's stated criteria for creating a justiciable controversy. On October 17,
1979 the District Court granted this motion, ruling that the plaintiffs
had suffered the requisite injury in fact because of the denial of their
right to be consulted and to vote on treaty termination. The court
also ruled that the case did not present a nonjusticiable political question. Reaching the constitutional question, the court granted plaintiffs' cross-motion for summary judgment. This appeal followed.

I

For purposes of the standing issue, we accept, as we must, appellees' pleaded theories as valid. A majority of the court is of the
view that, at least as their principal theory has evolved—that the
Senate has a constitutional right to vote on the President's proposed
treaty termination and to block such termination with a one-third
plus one vote—the appellee Senators have standing.

* * *

In the present case, appellees plead an objective standard in the
Constitution as giving them a right to vote on treaty termination.
They further allege disenfranchisement in the context of a specific
measure, i. e., the proposed termination of the Mutual Defense
Treaty. Whether the President's action amounts to a complete disenfranchisement depends on whether appellees have left to them any
legislative means to vote in the way they claim is their right. In other words, do they have effective power to block the termination of
this treaty despite the President's action? This is the crucial issue,
and the focus of our disagreement with the concurring opinion.

* * *

* * * The only way the Senate can effectively vote on treaty
termination, with the burden on termination proponents to secure a
two-thirds majority, is for the President to submit the proposed
treaty termination to the Senate as he would a proposed treaty. This
is the concrete remedy appellees seek. For the court to require of

them some other legislative action before allowing them standing to pursue this claim would be to require a useless act.

Since the President has not afforded an opportunity for an up-or-down vote as appellees request, we do not know whether the Senate would actually block the President's action if given the opportunity. Yet courts consistently vindicate the right to vote without first demanding that the votes when cast will achieve their intended end. A live controversy exists in appellees' claim of an opportunity to cast a binding vote. The President's action has deprived them of this opportunity completely, in the sense that they have no legislative power to exercise an equivalent voting opportunity. Therefore, appellee Senators have standing.

II

Various considerations enter into our determination that the President's notice of termination will be effective on January 1, 1980. The result we reach draws upon their totality, but in listing them hereinafter we neither assign them hierarchical values nor imply that any one factor or combination of factors is determinative.

1.　We turn first to the argument, embraced by the District Court, drawn from the language of Article II, § 2, of the Constitution. It is that, since the President clearly cannot enter into a treaty without the consent of the Senate, the inference is inescapable that he must in all circumstances seek the same senatorial consent to terminate that treaty. As a matter of language alone, however, the same inference would appear automatically to obtain with respect to the termination by the President of officers appointed by him under the same clause of the Constitution and subject to Senate confirmation. But the Supreme Court has read that clause as not having such an inevitable effect in any and all circumstances. Compare Myers v. United States, 272 U.S. 52, 47 S.Ct. 21 (1926) with In Re Humphrey's Executor v. United States, 295 U.S. 602, 55 S.Ct. 869 (1935). In the area of foreign relations in particular, where the constitutional commitment of powers to the President is notably comprehensive, it has never been suggested that the services of Ambassadors—appointed by the President, confirmed by the Senate, and of critical importance as they are to the successful conduct of our foreign relations—may not be terminated by the President without the prior authorization of that body.

Expansion of the language of the Constitution by sequential linguistic projection is a tricky business at best. Virtually all constitutional principles have unique elements and can be distinguished from one another. As the Supreme Court has recognized with respect to the clause in question, it is not abstract logic or sterile symmetry that controls, but a sensible and realistic ascertainment of the meaning of the Constitution in the context of the specific action taken.

2.　The District Court's declaration, in the alternative, that the necessary authority in this instance may be granted by a majority of each house of Congress presumably has its source in the Supremacy Clause of Article VI. The argument is that a treaty, being a part of the "supreme Law of the Land," can only be terminated at the least by a subsequent federal statute.

The central purpose of the Supremacy Clause has been accepted to be that of causing each of the designated supreme laws—Constitution, statute, and treaty—to prevail, for purposes of domestic law, over state law in any form. Article VI speaks explicitly to the judges to assure that this is so. But these three types of supreme law are not necessarily the same in their other characteristics, any more than are the circumstances and terms of their creation the same. Certainly the Constitution is silent on the matter of treaty termination. And the fact that it speaks to the common characteristic of supremacy over state law does not provide any basis for concluding that a treaty must be unmade either by (1) the same process by which it was made, or (2) the alternative means by which a statute is made or terminated.

3. The constitutional institution of advice and consent of the Senate, provided two-thirds of the Senators concur, is a special and extraordinary condition of the exercise by the President of certain specified powers under Article II. It is not lightly to be extended in instances not set forth in the Constitution. Such an extension by implication is not proper unless that implication is unmistakably clear.

The District Court's absolutist extension of this limitation to termination of treaties, irrespective of the particular circumstances involved, is not sound. The making of a treaty has the consequences of an entangling alliance for the nation. Similarly, the amending of a treaty merely continues such entangling alliances, changing only their character and therefore also requires the advice and consent of the Senate. It does not follow, however, that a constitutional provision for a special concurrence (two-thirds of the Senators) prior to entry into an entangling alliance necessarily applies to its termination in accordance with its terms.

4. The Constitution specifically confers no power of treaty termination on either the Congress or the Executive. We note, however, that the powers conferred upon Congress in Article I of the Constitution are specific, detailed, and limited, while the powers conferred upon the President by Article II are generalized in a manner that bespeaks no such limitation upon foreign affairs powers. "Section 1. The executive Power shall be vested in a President. * * *" Although specific powers are listed in Section 2 and Section 3, these are in many instances not powers necessary to an Executive, while "The executive Power" referred to in Section 1 is nowhere defined. There is no required two-thirds vote of the Senate conditioning the exercise of any power in Section 1.

In some instances this difference is reflective of the origin of the particular power in question. In general, the powers of the federal government arise out of specific grants of authority delegated by the states—hence the enumerated powers of Congress in Article I, Section 8. The foreign affairs powers, however, proceed directly from the sovereignty of the Union. "[I]f they had never been mentioned in the Constitution, [they] would have vested in the federal government as necessary concomitants of nationality." United States v. Curtiss-Wright Export Corp., 299 U.S. 304, 318, 57 S.Ct. 216, 220 (1936).

The President is the constitutional representative of the United States with respect to external affairs. It is significant that the treaty power appears in Article II of the Constitution, relating to the executive branch, and not in Article I, setting forth the powers of the legislative branch. It is the President as Chief Executive who is given the constitutional authority to enter into a treaty; and even after he has obtained the consent of the Senate it is for him to decide whether to ratify a treaty and put it into effect. Senatorial confirmation of a treaty concededly does not obligate the President to go forward with a treaty if he concludes that it is not in the public interest to do so.

Thus, in contrast to the lawmaking power, the constitutional initiative in the treaty-making field is in the President, not Congress. It would take an unprecedented feat of judicial construction to read into the Constitution an absolute condition precedent of congressional or Senate approval for termination of all treaties, similar to the specific one relating to initial approval. And it would unalterably affect the balance of power between the two Branches laid down in Articles I and II.

5. Ultimately, what must be recognized is that a treaty is sui generis. It is not just another law. It is an international compact, a solemn obligation of the United States and a "supreme Law" that supersedes state policies and prior federal laws. For clarity of analysis, it is thus well to distinguish between treaty-making as an international act and the consequences which flow domestically from such act. In one realm the Constitution has conferred the primary role upon the President; in the other, Congress retains its primary role as lawmaker. The fact that the Constitution, statutes, and treaties are all listed in the Supremacy Clause as being superior to any form of state law does not mean that the making and unmaking of treaties can be analogized to the making and unmaking of domestic statutes any more than it can be analogized to the making or unmaking of a constitutional amendment.

The recognized powers of Congress to implement (or fail to implement) a treaty by an appropriation or other law essential to its effectuation, or to supersede for all practical purposes the effect of a treaty on domestic law, are legislative powers, not treaty-making or treaty termination powers. The issue here, however, is not Congress' legislative powers to supersede or affect the domestic impact of a treaty; the issue is whether the Senate (or Congress) must in this case give its prior consent to discontinue a treaty which the President thinks it desirable to terminate in the national interest and pursuant to a provision in the treaty itself. The existence, in practical terms, of one power does not imply the existence, in constitutional terms, of the other.

6. If we were to hold that under the Constitution a treaty could only be terminated by exactly the same process by which it was made, we would be locking the United States into all of its international obligations, even if the President and two-thirds of the Senate minus one firmly believed that the proper course for the United States was to terminate a treaty. Many of our treaties in force, such as mutual defense treaties, carry potentially dangerous obligations. These obligations are terminable under international law upon breach by the other party or change in circumstances that frustrates the purpose of the treaty. In many of these situations the President must take immediate action. The creation of a constitutionally obligatory role in all cases for a two-thirds consent by the Senate would give to one-third plus one of the Senate the power to deny the President the authority necessary to conduct our foreign policy in a rational and effective manner.

7. Even as to the formal termination of treaties, as the District Court pointed out, "a variety of means have been used to terminate treaties." There is much debate among the historians and scholars as to whether in some instances the legislature has been involved at all; they are agreed that, when involved, that involvement with the President has taken many different forms. It appears moreover that the Senate may wish to continue to determine the nature of its involvement on a case by case basis. 125 Cong.Rec. S16683–S16692 (daily ed. Nov. 15, 1979).

The District Court concluded that the diversity of historical precedents left an inconclusive basis on which to decide the issue of whether the President's power to terminate a treaty must always be "shared" in some way by the Senate or Congress. We agree. Yet we think it is not without significance that out of all the historical precedents brought to our attention, in no situation has a treaty been continued in force over the opposition of the President.

There is on the other hand widespread agreement that the President has the power as Chief Executive under many circumstances to exercise functions regarding treaties which have the effect of either terminating or continuing their vitality. Prominent among these is the authority of the President as Chief Executive (1) to determine whether a treaty has terminated because of a breach, Charlton v. Kelly, 229 U.S. 447, 473–76, 33 S.Ct. 945(1913); and (2) to determine whether a treaty is at an end due to changed circumstances.

In short, the determination of the conduct of the United States in regard to treaties is an instance of what has broadly been called the "foreign affairs power" of the President. We have no occasion to define that term, but we do take account of its vitality. The Curtiss-Wright opinion, written by a Justice who had served in the United States Senate, declares in oft-repeated language that the President is "the sole organ of the federal government in the field of international relations." That status is not confined to the service of the President as a channel of communication, as the District Court suggested, but embraces an active policy determination as to the conduct of the United States in regard to a treaty in response to numerous problems and circumstances as they arise.

8. How the vital functions of the President in implementing treaties and in deciding on their viability in response to changing events can or should interact with Congress' legitimate concerns and powers in relating to foreign affairs is an area into which we should not and do not prematurely intrude. History shows us that there are too many variables to lay down any hard and fast constitutional rules.

We cannot find an implied role in the Constitution for the Senate in treaty termination for some but not all treaties in terms of their relative importance. There is no judicially ascertainable and manageable method of making any distinction among treaties on the basis of their substance, the magnitude of the risk involved, the degree of controversy which their termination would engender, or by any other standards. We know of no standards to apply in making such distinctions. The facts on which such distinctions might be drawn may be difficult of ascertainment; and the resolution of such inevitable disputes between the two Branches would be an improper and unnecessary role for the courts. To decide whether there was a breach or changed circumstances, for example, would involve a court in making fundamental decisions of foreign policy and would create insuperable problems of evidentiary proof. This is beyond the acceptable judicial role. All we decide today is that two-thirds Senate consent or majority consent in both houses is not necessary to terminate this treaty in the circumstances before us now.

* * *

10. Finally, and of central significance, the treaty here at issue contains a termination clause. The existence of Article X of the ROC treaty, permitting termination by either party on one year's notice, is an over-arching factor in this case, which in effect enables all of the other considerations to be knit together.

Without derogating from the executive power of the President to decide to act contrary to the wording of a treaty—for example, because of a breach by the other party (Charlton v. Kelly, supra), or because of a doctrine of fundamental change of circumstances (rebus sic stantibus)—the President's authority as Chief Executive is at its zenith when the Senate has consented to a treaty that expressly provides for termination on one year's notice, and the President's action is the giving of notice of termination.

In our holding in this case we do not ignore the question of justiciability. We regard the only issue here to be whether the constitutional allocation of governmental power between two branches requires prior legislative consent to the termination of this treaty under the circumstances presented by this record. Viewing the issue before us so narrowly and in the circumstances of this treaty and its history to date, we see no reason which we could in good conscience invoke to refrain from judgment, and conclude that it is the duty of the court to confront and decide that issue.

Reversed.

WRIGHT, Chief Judge, with whom TAMM, Circuit Judge, joins, concurring in the result: We agree that the judgment and opinion of the District Court must be vacated and that appellees' complaint must be dismissed. Because we believe the appellees lack standing, we reach no other issue.

* * *

MACKINNON, Circuit Judge, dissenting in part and concurring in part. I concur in the decision of a majority of my colleagues that the Senators and Representatives who are the plaintiffs in this action possess standing to have their grievance decided by this court, and that the question raised is not a "political" one that we should decline to adjudicate. We are not deciding a political question, but merely determining the procedure to be followed under the Constitution for the termination of a treaty. I disagree, however, with the majority's conclusion on the merits that the Constitution confers the absolute power on the President, acting alone, to terminate this Mutual Defense Treaty. No prior President has ever claimed the absolute power to terminate such a treaty.

* * *

[The per curiam opinion contains this note:

We note that Judge MacKinnon's position also requires a reversal of the District Court. Judge Gasch's judgment forbids further action to terminate the treaty without *either* consent of the Senate by a two-thirds vote *or* a vote by a majority of both Houses of Congress. Judge MacKinnon clearly would require action by both Houses; hence Judge Gasch's approval of Senate advice and consent as sufficient is reversed without dissent.]

GOLDWATER v. CARTER

Memorandum Decision.
United States Supreme Court, 1979.
444 U.S. 996, 100 S.Ct. 533.

ORDER

Dec. 13, 1979. The petition for a writ of certiorari is granted. The judgment of the Court of Appeals is vacated and the case is remanded to the District Court with directions to dismiss the complaint.

Mr. Justice MARSHALL concurs in the result.

Mr. Justice POWELL concurs in the judgment and has filed a statement.

Mr. Justice REHNQUIST concurs in the judgment and has filed a statement in which Mr. Chief Justice BURGER, Mr. Justice STEWART, and Mr. Justice STEVENS join.

Mr. Justice WHITE and Mr. Justice BLACKMUN join in the grant of the petition for a writ of certiorari but would set the case for argument and give it plenary consideration. Mr. Justice BLACKMUN has filed a statement in which Mr. Justice WHITE joins.

Mr. Justice BRENNAN would grant the petition for certiorari and affirm the judgment of the Court of Appeals and has filed a statement.

Mr. Justice POWELL, concurring.

Although I agree with the result reached by the Court, I would dismiss the complaint as not ripe for judicial review.

I

This Court has recognized that an issue should not be decided if it is not ripe for judicial review. Buckley v. Valeo, 424 U.S. 1, 113–114, 96 S.Ct. 612, 46 L.Ed.2d 659 (1976) (per curiam). Prudential considerations persuade me that a dispute between Congress and the President is not ready for judicial review unless and until each branch has taken action asserting its constitutional authority. Differences between the President and the Congress are commonplace under our system. The differences should, and almost invariably do, turn on political rather than legal considerations. The Judicial Branch should not decide issues affecting the allocation of power between the President and Congress until the political branches reach a constitutional impasse. Otherwise, we would encourage small groups or even individual Members of Congress to seek judicial resolution of issues before the normal political process has the opportunity to resolve the conflict.

In this case, a few Members of Congress claim that the President's action in terminating the treaty with Taiwan has deprived them of their constitutional role with respect to a change in the supreme law of the land. Congress has taken no official action. In the present posture of this case, we do not know whether there ever will be an actual confrontation between the Legislative and Executive Branches. Although the Senate has considered a resolution declaring that Senate approval is necessary for the termination of any mutual defense treaty, see 125 Cong.Rec. S7015, S7038–S7039 (daily ed. June 6, 1979), no final vote has been taken on the resolution. See id., at S16683–S16692 (daily ed. Nov. 15, 1979). Moreover, it is unclear whether the resolution would have retroactive effect. See id., at S7054–S7064 (daily ed. June 6, 1979); id., at S7862 (daily ed. June 18, 1979). It cannot be said that either the Senate or the House has rejected the President's claim. If the Congress chooses not to confront the President, it is not our task to do so. I therefore concur in the dismissal of this case.

II

Mr. Justice Rehnquist suggests, however, that the issue presented by this case is a nonjusticiable political question which can never be considered by this Court. I cannot agree. In my view, reliance upon the political-question doctrine is inconsistent with our precedents. As set forth in the seminal case of Baker v. Carr, 369 U.S. 186, 217, 82 S.Ct. 691, 7 L.Ed.2d 663 (1962), the doctrine incorporates three inquiries: (i) Does the issue involve resolution of questions committed by the text of the Constitution to a coordinate branch of government? (ii) Would resolution of the question demand that a court move beyond areas of judicial expertise? (iii) Do prudential considerations counsel against judicial intervention? In my opinion the answer to each of these inquiries would require us to decide this case if it were ready for review.

First, the existence of "a textually demonstrable constitutional commitment of the issue to a coordinate political branch," ibid., turns on an examination of the constitutional provisions governing the exercise of the power in question. Powell v. McCormack, 395 U.S. 486, 519, 89 S.Ct. 1944, 23 L.Ed.2d 491 (1969). No constitutional provision explicitly confers upon the President the power to terminate treaties. Further, Art. II, § 2 of the Constitution authorizes the President to make treaties with the advice and consent of the Senate. Article VI provides that treaties shall be a part of the supreme law of the land. These provisions add support to the view that the text of the Constitution does not unquestionably commit the power to terminate treaties to the President alone. Cf. Gilligan v. Morgan, 413 U.S. 1, 6, 93 S.Ct. 2440, 37 L.Ed.2d 407 (1973); Luther v. Borden, 7 How. 1, 42, 12 L.Ed. 581 (1849).

Second, there is no "lack of judicially discoverable and manageable standards for resolving" this case; nor is a decision impossible "without an initial policy determination of a kind clearly for nonjudicial discretion." Baker v. Carr, 369 U.S., at 217, 82 S.Ct. 691. We are asked to decide whether the President may terminate a treaty under the Constitution without congressional approval. Resolution of the question may not be easy, but it only requires us to apply normal principles of interpretation to the constitutional provisions at issue. See Powell v. McCormack, 395 U.S., at 548–549, 89 S.Ct. 1944. The present case involves neither review of the President's activities as Commander-in-Chief nor impermissible interference in the field of foreign affairs. Such a case would arise if we were asked to decide, for example, whether a treaty required the President to order troops into a foreign country. But "it is error to suppose that every case or controversy which touches foreign relations lies beyond judicial cognizance." Baker v. Carr, supra, 369 U.S., at 211, 82 S.Ct. 691. This case "touches" foreign relations, but the question presented to us concerns only the constitutional division of power between Congress and the President.

A simple hypothetical demonstrates the confusion that I find inherent in Mr. Justice Rehnquist's concurring opinion. Assume that the President signed a mutual defense treaty with a foreign country and announced that it would go into effect despite its rejection by the Senate. Under Mr. Justice Rehnquist's analysis that situation would present a political question even though Art. II, § 2, clearly would resolve the dispute. Although the answer to the hypothetical case seems self-evident because it demands textual rather than interstitial analysis, the nature of the legal issue presented is no different from the issue presented in the case before us. In both cases, the Court would interpret the Constitution to decide whether congressional approval is necessary to give a Presidential decision on the validity of a treaty the force of law. Such an inquiry demands no special competence or information beyond the reach of the judiciary. Cf. Chicago & Southern Air Lines v. Waterman Steamship Corp., 333 U.S. 103, 111, 68 S.Ct. 431, 92 L.Ed. 568 (1948).[1]

Finally, the political-question doctrine rests in part on prudential concerns calling for mutual respect among the three branches of government. Thus, the Judicial Branch should avoid "the potentiality of embarrassment [that would result] from multifarious pronouncements by various departments on one question." Similarly, the doctrine restrains judicial action where there is an "unusual need for unquestioning adherence to a political decision already made." Baker v. Carr, supra, 369 U.S., at 217, 82 S.Ct. 691.

If this case were ripe for judicial review, see Part I supra, none of these prudential considerations would be present. Interpretation of the Constitution does not imply lack of respect for a coordinate branch. Powell v. McCormack, 395 U.S., at 548, 89 S.Ct. 1944. If the President and the Congress had reached irreconcilable positions, final disposition of the question presented by this case would eliminate, rather than create, multiple constitutional interpretations. The spectre of the Federal Government brought to a halt because of the mutual intransigence of the President and the Congress would require this Court to provide a resolution pursuant to our duty "to say what the law is." United States v. Nixon, 418 U.S. 683, 703, 94 S.Ct. 3090, 41 L.Ed.2d 1039 (1974), quoting Marbury v. Madison, 1 Cranch 137, 177, 2 L.Ed. 60 (1803).

---

1. The Court has recognized that, in the area of foreign policy, Congress may leave the President with wide discretion that otherwise might run afoul of the nondelegation doctrine. United States v. Curtiss-Wright Export Corp., 299 U.S. 304, 57 S.Ct. 216, 81 L.Ed. 255 (1936). As stated in that case, "the President alone has the power to speak or listen as a representative of the Nation. He *makes* treaties with the advice and consent of the Senate; but he alone negotiates." Id., at 319, 57 S.Ct. 216 (emphasis in the original). Resolution of this case would interfere with neither the President's ability to negotiate treaties nor his duty to execute their provisions. We are merely being asked to decide whether a treaty, which cannot be ratified without Senate approval, continues in effect until the Senate or perhaps the Congress take further action.

III

In my view, the suggestion that this case presents a political question is incompatible with this Court's willingness on previous occasions to decide whether one branch of our government has impinged upon the power of another. See Buckley v. Valeo, 424 U.S. 1, 138, 96 S.Ct. 612, 46 L.Ed.2d 659 (1976); United States v. Nixon, 418 U.S. 683, 707, 94 S.Ct. 3090, 41 L.Ed.2d 1039 (1974); The Pocket Veto Case, 279 U.S. 655, 676–678, 49 S.Ct. 463, 73 L.Ed. 894 (1929); Myers v. United States, 272 U.S. 52, 47 S.Ct. 21, 71 L.Ed. 160 (1926). Under the criteria enunciated in Baker v. Carr, we have the responsibility to decide whether both the Executive and Legislative Branches have constitutional roles to play in termination of a treaty. If the Congress, by appropriate formal action, had challenged the President's authority to terminate the treaty with Taiwan, the resulting uncertainty could have serious consequences for our country. In that situation, it would be the duty of this Court to resolve the issue.

Mr. Justice REHNQUIST, with whom The Chief Justice, Mr. Justice STEWART, and Mr. Justice STEVENS join, concurring.

I am of the view that the basic question presented by the petitioners in this case is "political" and therefore nonjusticiable because it involves the authority of the President in the conduct of our country's foreign relations and the extent to which the Senate or the Congress is authorized to negate the action of the President. * * *

SECTION C. PROBLEMS OF THE SELF-EXECUTING TREATY, AN AMERICAN PHENOMENON

The self-executing versus non self-executing dichotomy as to international agreements within a single state. Most states either have one or the other of these systems. Absolute monarchies and dictatorships have the power to bring treaties into effect without legislative participation. Most democratic states in the world have cabinet forms of government, and in many of these both international validation and internal implementation of an international agreement are within the power of the legislature, with the result that all international agreements are non self-executing. In some democracies with constitutional monarchs, such as the countries of the Commonwealth, the Crown can theoretically commit the state internationally, but in fact the cabinet controls the foreign affairs process even as to this. In the Commonwealth countries, also, the omnipotence of Parliament as to law-making means that no international agreement may have internal effect as a self-executing treaty. Thus, in these countries the possibility of having both self-executing treaties and non self-executing possibilities exists but is only theoretical.

In the United States the Constitution empowers the President and two-thirds of the senators both to bring treaties into effect internationally and to give them internal effect as law (under the supremacy clause, Article VI). Jefferson thought otherwise, but he was not a draftsman of the Constitution and his view has not prevailed. Thus the self-executing treaty exists in American foreign affairs law; but it is also established by practice and judicial decisions that the President and two-thirds of the Senate may choose only to bind the United States internationally by their action, leaving implementation by legislation to the action of both houses of the Congress by simple majority vote. The existence in a single country of both systems, side by side, is quite rare.

Sometimes the President and the Senate are not clear as to the choice. Then the courts must decide whether the treaty is self-executing or not. What factors might influence explicit choice of one or the other of these modalities? Suppose the treaty requires an appropriation of funds, fixes a tariff, levies a tax or defines a crime: would the President and the Senate choose the self-executing treaty route? If they did, would the treaty have valid internal legal effect? See Constitution, Article I, § 7.

Even where the House of Representatives does not have special interests as to legislation, there is a problem as to how far the President and two-thirds of the Senate should go in excluding the House from participation. Would it have been feasible to effect the environmental protections laws of the United States by self-executing treaty? The energy laws? The Civil Rights Act of 1964?

Under the American arrangement, however, non self-executing treaties also present difficulties. One is that the Congress might refuse to implement an international commitment made by the President and two-thirds of the Senate, as it seemed for a critical time would happen as to the Canal Zone treaties with Panama. Another is that in the implementing legislation Congress might depart from the terms of the treaty. This has happened for several law-making treaties, such as the 1924 Convention on Carriage of Goods by Sea.

On the other hand, sometimes countries where international agreements must come into effect as internal law in order to have effect internationally, as under the Constitution of the Federal German Republic, find themselves unduly limited as to their capacity to make assured commitments internationally because of uncertainty as to legislative approval. In the United States the President and the Senate can, if it is deemed necessary, legally make an international commitment and take the risk that the House will not acquiesce with implementing legislation. In fact, often in such situations the House has, with delays and grumblings, done just this. Again, the legislative history of the implementing legislation for the Canal Zone treaties is instructive.

The British system, too, gives a degree of flexibility useful in diplomacy. For a description of the Ponsonby Rule, under which treaties requiring legislation for implementation are laid on the table of the House of Commons, see Oliver, Enforcement of Treaties by a Federal State, [1974] Académie de Droit International, Recueil des Cours 362 et seq., and Reporters' Note to Section 154, Restatement of the Foreign Relations Law of the United States (1965).

ASAKURA v. CITY OF SEATTLE

United States Supreme Court, 1924.
265 U.S. 332, 44 S.Ct. 515.

Mr. Justice BUTLER delivered the opinion of the Court.

Plaintiff in error is a subject of the Emperor of Japan, and, since 1904, has resided in Seattle, Washington. Since July, 1915, he has been engaged in business there as a pawnbroker. The city passed an ordinance, which took effect July 2, 1921, regulating the business of pawnbroker and repealing former ordinances on the same subject. It makes it unlawful for any person to engage in the business unless he shall have a license, and the ordinance provides "that no such license shall be granted unless the applicant be a citizen of the United States." Violations of the ordinance are punishable by fine or imprisonment or both. Plaintiff in error brought this suit in the Superior Court of King County, Washington, against the city, its Comptroller and its Chief of Police to restrain them from enforcing the ordinance against him. He attacked the ordinance on the ground that it violates the treaty between the United States and the Empire of Japan, proclaimed April 5, 1911, 37 Stat. 1504 * * *. It was shown that he had about $5,000 invested in his business, which would be broken up and destroyed by the enforcement of the ordinance. The Superior Court granted the relief prayed. On appeal, the Supreme Court of the State held the ordinance valid and reversed the decree. * * *

Does the ordinance violate the treaty? Plaintiff in error invokes and relies upon the following provisions: "The citizens or subjects of each of the High Contracting Parties shall have liberty to enter, travel and reside in the territories of the other to carry on trade, wholesale and retail, to own or lease and occupy houses, manufactories, warehouses and shops, to employ agents of their choice, to lease land for residential and commercial purposes, and generally to do anything incident to or necessary for trade upon the same terms as native citizens or subjects, submitting themselves to the laws and regulations there established. * * * The citizens or subjects of each * * * shall receive, in the territories of the other, the most constant protection, and security for their persons and property * * *."

A treaty made under the authority of the United States "shall be the supreme law of the land; and the judges in every State shall be bound thereby, any thing in the constitution or laws of any State to the contrary notwithstanding." Constitution, Art. VI, § 2.

The treaty-making power of the United States is not limited by any express provision of the Constitution, and, though it does not extend "so far as to authorize what the Constitution forbids," it does extend to all proper subjects of negotiation between our government and other nations.

* * * The treaty was made to strengthen friendly relations between the two nations. As to the things covered by it, the provision quoted establishes the rule of equality between Japanese subjects while in this country and native citizens. Treaties for the protection of citizens of one country residing in the territory of another are numerous, and make for good understanding between nations. The treaty is binding within the State of Washington. * * * The rule of equality established by it cannot be rendered nugatory in any part of the United States by municipal ordinances or state laws. It stands on the same footing of supremacy as do the provisions of the Constitution and laws of the United States. It operates of itself without the aid of any legislation, state or national; and it will be applied and given authoritative effect by the courts. * * *

The purpose of the ordinance complained of is to regulate, not to prohibit, the business of pawnbroker. But it makes it impossible for aliens to carry on the business. It need not be considered whether the State, if it sees fit, may forbid and destroy the business generally. Such a law would apply equally to aliens and citizens, and no question of conflict with the treaty would arise. The grievance here alleged is that plaintiff in error, in violation of the treaty, is denied equal opportunity.

It remains to be considered whether the business of pawnbroker is "trade" within the meaning of the treaty.

* * * The language of the treaty is comprehensive. The phrase "to carry on trade" is broad. That it is not to be given a restricted meaning is plain. * * *

* * * There is nothing in the character of the business of pawnbroker which requires it to be excluded from the field covered by the above quoted provision, and it must be held that such business is "trade" within the meaning of the treaty. The ordinance violates the treaty. * * *

Decree reversed.

SEI FUJII v. STATE

United States, Supreme Court of California, in Bank, 1952.
38 Cal.2d 718, 242 P.2d 617.

GIBSON, Chief Justice. Plaintiff, an alien Japanese who is ineligible to citizenship under our naturalization laws, appeals from a judgment declaring that certain land purchased by him in 1948 had escheated to the state. There is no treaty between this country and Japan which confers upon plaintiff the right to own land, and the sole question presented on this appeal is the validity of the California alien land law.[1]

United Nations Charter

It is first contended that the land law has been invalidated and superseded by the provisions of the United Nations Charter pledging the member nations to promote the observance of human rights and fundamental freedoms without distinction as to race. Plaintiff relies on statements in the preamble and in Articles 1, 55 and 56 of the Charter, 59 Stat. 1035.[2]

It is not disputed that the charter is a treaty, and our federal Constitution provides that treaties made under the authority of the United States are part of the supreme law of the land and that the judges in every state are bound thereby. U.S.Const., art. VI. A

---

[1]. The pertinent portions of the alien land law, 1 Deering's Gen.Laws, Act 261, as amended in 1945, are as follows:

§ 1. All aliens eligible to citizenship under the laws of the United States may acquire, possess, enjoy, use, cultivate, occupy, transfer, transmit and inherit real property, or any interest therein, in this state, and have in whole or in part the beneficial use thereof, in the same manner and to the same extent as citizens of the United States, except as otherwise provided by the laws of this state.

§ 2. All aliens other than those mentioned in section one of this act may acquire, possess, enjoy, use, cultivate, occupy and transfer real property, or any interest therein, in this state, and have in whole or in part the beneficial use thereof, in the manner and to the extent, and for the purposes prescribed by any treaty now existing between the government of the United States and the nation or country of which such alien is a citizen or subject, and not otherwise.

§ 7. Any real property hereafter acquired in fee in violation of the provisions of this act by any alien mentioned in section 2 of this act, * * * shall escheat as of the date of such acquiring, to, and become and remain the property of the state of California. * * *

[2]. The preamble recites that "We the peoples of the United Nations determined * * * to reaffirm faith in fundamental human rights * * * and for these ends * * * to employ international machinery for the promotion of the economic and social advancement of all peoples, have resolved to combine our efforts to accomplish these aims."

Article 1 states that The Purposes of the United Nations are: * * * 3. To achieve international co-operation in solving international problems of an economic, social, cultural, or humanitarian character, and in promoting and encouraging respect for human rights and for fundamental freedoms for all without distinction as to race, sex, language, or religion; * * *.

Articles 55 and 56 appear in Chapter IX, entitled "International Economic and Social Cooperation." Article 55 provides: "With a view to the creation of conditions of stability and well-being which are necessary for peaceful and friendly relations among nations based on respect for the principle of equal rights and self-determination of peoples, the United Nations shall promote:

a. higher standards of living, full employment, and conditions of economic and social progress and development;

b. solutions of international economic, social, health, and related problems; and international cultural and educational cooperation; and

c. universal respect for, and observance of, human rights and fundamental freedoms for all without distinction as to race, sex, language, or religion.

Article 56 provides: All Members pledge themselves to take joint and separate action in cooperation with the Organization for the achievement of the purposes set forth in Article 55.

treaty, however, does not automatically supersede local laws which are inconsistent with it unless the treaty provisions are self-executing. In the words of Chief Justice Marshall: A treaty is "to be regarded in courts of justice as equivalent to an act of the Legislature, whenever it operates of itself, without the aid of any legislative provision. But when the terms of the stipulation import a contract— when either of the parties engages to perform a particular act, the treaty addresses itself to the political, not the judicial department; and the Legislature must execute the contract, before it can become a rule for the court." Foster v. Neilson, 1829, 2 Pet. 253, 314, 7 L.Ed. 415.[3]

In determining whether a treaty is self-executing courts look to the intent of the signatory parties as manifested by the language of the instrument, and, if the instrument is uncertain, recourse may be had to the circumstances surrounding its execution. * * *

In order for a treaty provision to be operative without the aid of implementing legislation and to have the force and effect of a statute, it must appear that the framers of the treaty intended to prescribe a rule that, standing alone, would be enforceable in the courts. * * *

It is clear that the provisions of the preamble and of Article 1 of the charter which are claimed to be in conflict with the alien land law are not self-executing. They state general purposes and objectives of the United Nations Organization and do not purport to impose legal obligations on the individual member nations or to create rights in private persons. It is equally clear that none of the other provisions relied on by plaintiff is self-executing. Article 55 declares that the United Nations "shall promote: * * * universal respect for, and observance of, human rights and fundamental freedoms for all without distinction as to race, sex, language, or religion," and in Article 56, the member nations "pledge themselves to take joint and separate action in cooperation with the Organization for the achievement of the purposes set forth in Article 55." Although the member nations have obligated themselves to cooperate with the international organization in promoting respect for, and observance of, human rights, it is plain that it was contemplated that future legislative action by the several nations would be required to accomplish the declared objectives, and there is nothing to indicate that these provisions were intended to become rules of law for the courts of this country upon the ratification of the charter.

3. In Foster v. Neilson, certain treaty provisions were held not to be self-executing on the basis of construction of the English version of the document. Subsequently, upon consideration of the Spanish version, the provisions in question were held to be self-executing. United States v. Percheman, 7 Pet. 51, 8 L.Ed. 604.

Chief Justice Marshall's language in the Foster case, however, has been quoted with approval in later cases. United States v. Rauscher, 119 U.S. 407, 417–418, 7 S.Ct. 234, 239–240, 30 L.Ed. 425; Valentine v. United States, 299 U.S. 5, 10, 57 S.Ct. 100, 103, 81 L.Ed. 5.

The language used in Articles 55 and 56 is not the type customarily employed in treaties which have been held to be self-executing and to create rights and duties in individuals. For example, the treaty involved in Clark v. Allen, 331 U.S. 503, 507–508, 67 S.Ct. 1431, 1434, 91 L.Ed. 1633, relating to the rights of a national of one country to inherit real property located in another country, specifically provided that "such national shall be allowed a term of three years in which to sell the [property] * * * and withdraw the proceeds * * *" free from any discriminatory taxation. See, also, Hauenstein v. Lynham, 100 U.S. 483, 488–490, 25 L.Ed. 628. In Nielsen v. Johnson, 279 U.S. 47, 50, 49 S.Ct. 223, 73 L.Ed. 607, the provision treated as being self-executing was equally definite. There each of the signatory parties agreed that "no higher or other duties, charges, or taxes of any kind, shall be levied" by one country on removal of property therefrom by citizens of the other country "than are or shall be payable in each state, upon the same, when removed by a citizen or subject of such state respectively." In other instances treaty provisions were enforced without implementing legislation where they prescribed in detail the rules governing rights and obligations of individuals or specifically provided that citizens of one nation shall have the same rights while in the other country as are enjoyed by that country's own citizens. * * *

It is significant to note that when the framers of the charter intended to make certain provisions effective without the aid of implementing legislation they employed language which is clear and definite and manifests that intention. For example, Article 104 provides: "The Organization shall enjoy in the territory of each of its Members such legal capacity as may be necessary for the exercise of its functions and the fulfillment of its purposes." Article 105 provides: "1. The Organization shall enjoy in the territory of each of its Members such privileges and immunities as are necessary for the fulfillment of its purposes. 2. Representatives of the Members of the United Nations and officials of the Organization shall similarly enjoy such privileges and immunities as are necessary for the independent exercise of their functions in connection with the Organization." In Curran v. City of New York, 191 Misc. 229, 77 N.Y.S.2d 206, 212, these articles were treated as being self-executory. See, also, Balfour, Guthrie & Co. v. United States, D.C., 90 F.Supp. 831, 832.

The provisions in the charter pledging cooperation in promoting observance of fundamental freedoms lack the mandatory quality and definiteness which would indicate an intent to create justiciable rights in private persons immediately upon ratification. Instead, they are framed as a promise of future action by the member nations. Secretary of State Stettinius, Chairman of the United States delegation at the San Francisco Conference where the charter was drafted, stated in his report to President Truman that Article 56 "pledges the various countries to cooperate with the organization by joint and separate action in the achievement of the economic and social objectives of the organization without infringing upon their right to order their national affairs according to their own best ability, in their own way, and in accordance with their own political and economic institutions and processes." Report to the President on the Results of the San Francisco Conference by the Chairman of the United States Delegation, the Secretary of State, Department of State Publication 2349, Conference Series 71, p. 115; Hearings before the Committee on Foreign Relations, United States Senate [Revised] July 9–13, 1945, p. 106. The same view was repeatedly expressed by delegates of other nations in the debates attending the drafting of article 56. * * *

The humane and enlightened objectives of the United Nations Charter are, of course, entitled to respectful consideration by the courts and Legislatures of every member nation, since that document expresses the universal desire of thinking men for peace and for equality of rights and opportunities. The charter represents a moral commitment of foremost importance, and we must not permit the spirit of our pledge to be compromised or disparaged in either our domestic or foreign affairs. We are satisfied, however, that the charter provisions relied on by plaintiff were not intended to supersede existing domestic legislation, and we cannot hold that they operate to invalidate the alien land law.

Fourteenth Amendment of the Federal Constitution

The next question is whether the alien land law violates the due process and equal protection clauses of the Fourteenth Amendment. * * *

    * * *

* * * The California alien land law is obviously designed and administered as an instrument for effectuating racial discrimination, and the most searching examination discloses no circumstances justifying classification on that basis. There is nothing to indicate that those alien residents who are racially ineligible for citizenship possess characteristics which are dangerous to the legitimate interests of the state, or that they, as a class, might use the land for purposes injurious to public morals, safety or welfare. Accordingly, we hold that the alien land law is invalid as in violation of the Fourteenth Amendment.

The judgment is reversed.
    * * *

SCHAUER, Justice (dissenting and concurring). * * *
    * * *

I agree that the United Nations Charter, as presently constituted and accepted was not intended to, and does not, supersede existing domestic legislation of the United States or of the several states and territories.

I would hold that provisions of the Alien Land Law here invoked by the State of California do not contravene either the federal or state constitutions; and would affirm the judgment of the trial court.

* * *

[Concurring and dissenting opinions omitted.]

Self-execution when the intention of states parties on that issue not specified. Aside from the instances in which the treaty makes it reasonably clear that the only immediate obligation the parties wanted from each was the enactment of legislation (so that the treaty can easily be described as non self-executing), there are instances in which the treaty is fairly opaque on the question of how the parties will put into effect, domestically, what they have promised internationally. Riesenfeld has suggested, as we have seen, p. 587, that it may not be useful to search for the intention of the states parties on this domestic question. At least in multilateral treaties a state may have multiple expectations about what the other parties will do as a matter of domestic law, since states vary in their practices with respect to implementing legislation.

The significant first question in the analysis is: did each state expect the other states immediately to be bound to perform the substance that was promised (e. g., to recognize a new boundary, to refrain from going to war, to cease racial discrimination, to pay certain sums of money, to impose criminal sanctions on certain behavior)? If so, according to the Riesenfeld suggestion, the only functional question for the United States is whether by its Constitution it is required to enact legislation as a matter purely of internal law (as presumably it would in cases involving the appropriation of money or the designation of certain behavior as criminal); in such a case the treaty could be described as non self-executing. On the other hand, if a court could constitutionally apply a rule of law without the aid of Congress, as it did in the Asakura case in its invalidation of the local ordinance, then it need not await legislation action; the treaty can then be described as self-executing. The resolution of this problem is especially significant in the field of human rights, since such rights are so frequently of the kind that courts have in the past been able to recognize under our own constitutional Bill of Rights without the aid of legislation.

It bears reiteration, however, that the first question is whether the states expected of each other immediate international responsibility with respect to the substance of the treaty.

---

1. *A review question of possible moment.* A proposal that the Senate advise and consent to treaties by simple majority vote lost narrowly in the Constitutional Convention. Considering what you know of important treaties that have died in the Senate or have been

there for years without a vote, would you support an amendment providing for the reduction of the required majority for approval? Would the fact that senators are now popularly elected under the XVIIth Amendment influence your decision? Do you consider it desirable or undesirable that the United States requirement as to Senate approval imposes a far stronger bias against international commitment than do the legal systems of the vast majority of states?

2. *Another such question.* Suppose the presidency should develop as a generally-used alternative to the present two-step procedure for non self-executing treaties, that of entering into a presidential executive agreement internationally, understood by the other party to be made subject to congressional implementation, and seeking effective approval of the arrangement by simple majority votes in both houses on the implementing legislation. Are there any constitutional problems? Political problems? See McDougal and Lans, Treaties and Congressional-Executive or Presidential Agreements: Interchangeable Instruments of National Policy, 54 Yale L.J. 181, 534 (1945); cf. Oliver, editorial, Getting the Senators to Accept Reference of Treaties to Both Houses for Approval by Simple Majorities; Does the Sense Resolution in the 1979 Foreign Relations Authorization Point a Way?, 74 Am.J.Int'l Law 142 (1980).

3. *Attempting to control uncertainty as to whether a treaty is or is not self-executing.* The rules of interpretation have not always been clear guides to classification of treaties as self-executing or not. Cf. Riesenfeld, editorial, The Doctrine of Self-Executing Treaties and United States v. Postal: Win at Any Price? 74 Am.J.Int'l Law 892 (1980). The decision by the Fifth Circuit Court of Appeals is at 589 F.2d 862, 876–885 (1979). In submitting four human rights conventions to the Senate in 1978, the executive reported that it had examined these treaties for any conflicts with existing United States law and as to conflicting provisions recommended Senate reservations. Such reservations would reduce the necessity for implementation by change of existing legislation. Do you see any disadvantages in the practice?

Chapter 17

THE LAW OF INTERNATIONAL TRADE AND INVESTMENT

1. *Problems.* The four problems set forth below are intended to be an introduction to the subject matter in this chapter.

Problem A. Denial of entry of foreign goods. For a long time private enterprise in State X has exported large quantities of electric home appliances to consumers in State Y, paying normal import duties. Suddenly, the authorities in State Y decree a very low quota on foreign-made electric home appliances, stating that this is done to save the domestic home appliance industry from extinction. Business failures and serious unemployment result in the home appliance industry of State X.

Problem B. Denial of entry of foreign business capital. Home appliance manufacturers in State X decide to set up production in State Y for the State Y market, using Y labor. State Y refuses to permit the transfer of the requisite business capital from State X to it.

Problem C. Denial of rights flowing from ownership. A corporation organized in State Z owns 100% a corporation chartered in State Y that under State Y law owns subsurface rights to mine certain minerals. These rights are now worth $50,000,000. State Y expropriated these rights and pays no compensation, charging that the alien group from State Z only paid $500,000 for the rights to begin with and has since profited $100,000,000 from their exploitation.

Problem D. Denial of developmental opportunity. State M has a population growth rate of three percent a year and a Gross National Product per capita of $62 a year—a very poor state indeed. It has been receiving from State N and from International Organization O foreign assistance grants to help with its population problem and development loans on concessional terms (below the market cost of the money to the lenders) to support a National Development Plan designed to boost GNP per capita to $200 over ten years. In the fifth year of the assistance program State N objects to the denial of basic human rights in State M. N cuts off its bilateral development assistance to M and successfully prevents O from providing multilateral assistance.

2. *Lack of customary international law.* Persons in states and states themselves have long engaged in the movement of goods and capital across national frontiers. The velocity, frequency and quantity of such movements have increased tremendously in modern industrial times.

1078

Whether for moral, political or trade investment reasons, a foreign aid dimension has been added to transnational economic activity in response to the troublesome gap, still widening, between rich and poor nations.

Economic power is a prime factor in the assessment of the capacity of a state, a group of states or an international organization to be effective in the achievement of its objectives and values. Where military force is illegal or inadvisable, economic strength is now the principal source of a state's authority in the international system.

Notwithstanding these major activities and needs, there is no customary international law imposing duties and creating correlative rights in the above cases, except possibly Case C, where capital-exporting states (or some of them) would argue that there is a rule of customary law requiring fair compensation and some capital-receiving (usually also poor and developing) nations would assert the contrary.

Except for the increasingly disputed nationalization area of Case C and some rules about the trading rights of neutrals in pre-UN wars—rules that in World War I and II were not followed because the enemy continued to breach closely related rules—the rules of the international legal systems as to economic activity are in international agreements. These rules are incomplete. The lawyer's role in the transnational economic field is presently active and highly important, although his international lawyering takes him more often than not into national centers of law and policy and to the law in treaties, rather than to decisions of international tribunals or the doctrines of international law publicists.

This chapter affords only a sketch of a subject matter that largely falls in the curricula of law schools in the United States to courses in International Transactions or The Regulation of International Trade and Investment.

SECTION A.   TRADE LAW

1. UNCONDITIONAL MOST FAVORED NATION TREATMENT OF TRADE

Problem. At a time when its own tariffs were highly protectionist, State A analyzed world trade conditions and came to the conclusion that tariff barriers were undesirably high worldwide including the tariffs of States B, C and D. Up to that time, State A had given another state only such tariff cuts for its exports to State A as were paid for by some corresponding cut in that state's duty on State A's exports to it. This requirement of compensation applied even where the other state had been promised most favored nation treatment in a treaty with State A, and State A had given a cut to a third state, which, in turn, had conceded a trade benefit to State A.

When State A decided to launch a worldwide effort to lower tariff barriers, it announced that it was changing its concept of most favored nation provisions to an unconditional form. Thereafter, States A, B, C and D each entered into unconditional most favored nation agreements (MFNs) with all three other states. States A, B and C are highly-developed, producing wide ranges of manufactured goods. State D is a less well-developed country, largely an agricultural producer and non-competitive as to costs with A, B and C insofar as manufactured goods are concerned. If D did not have its very high tariffs on goods (say automobiles) manufactured in A, B and C, its high cost domestic market would yield to the foreign imports and D would lose scarce foreign exchange to pay for the imports.

States A and B enter into wide-ranging and hard-bargained negotiations that result in average tariff cuts of 50% from schedules on both sides. C and D, under their MFN treaties with A and B, claim the benefits of these cuts but offer none in return, with the result that their tariff walls loom higher than ever as clogs on international trade.

Considering the materials on pp. 1080–1085, answer these questions:

1. Why did A ever move to unconditional MFN?

2. Why did A and B make their arrangement, assuming they knew that C and D would not offer cuts?

3. Could A and B legally withdraw their promises to C and D?

METZGER, INTERNATIONAL LAW, TRADE AND FINANCE: REALITIES AND PROSPECTS 18 (1962)

Under the nation-state system a country can buy what it wants from anyone, or discriminate among foreigners in what it buys and in how it treats the goods at the border; it can exclude foreigners from entering the country for any purpose, including investment purposes; it can sell its goods abroad at any time in any manner, and at any price; it can manipulate its currency any way it pleases; it can maintain exchange controls, quotas, and any other device it chooses under any circumstances; it can broadcast over the entire spectrum at any strength regardless of interference with other countries' radio stations and listeners. These and many other things which in the modern world can result in serious injury to others can be done without trenching upon the customary rules which international law has evolved from days when the problems were different from those which now beset us. The fast pace which the industrial revolution has set in creating more complicated economic arrangements, to speak of only one segment, has created more problems of a complex character than could possibly be coped with by the old tort technique of international law.

What to do? The statutory technique, which was the principal domestic addition to the common law in order to respond to the industrial revolution, was not available because there was no legislature to enact statutes. And there was not ever a court of general compulsory jurisdiction to perform the ancillary functions of interpretation and application. The nations did the best they could with the only available techniques. For centuries they had made many contracts with each other on extremely general and sometimes specific matters. These contracts or treaties established rules of behavior of a limited or general type as between signatories. They were flexible instruments, able to be filled with high-sounding protestations of friendship, or detailed rules regarding customs formalities, or both. They came into increasing use for both purposes. During the past one hundred years, and especially during the past fifty years, it is fair to say that contract rules—or treaty law as it is sometimes called—have far overshadowed customary international law rules, from the viewpoint of coping with the main problems of modern international relations.

PATTERSON, DISCRIMINATION IN INTERNATIONAL TRADE, THE POLICY ISSUES 1945–1965, at 6 (1966)*

Discriminatory policies were sometimes defended on the much wider grounds that they fostered freer trade. In a world in which there are problems of unemployment and in which tariff barriers exist and are reduced by a process of negotiation and exchange of "concessions," in such a world a policy of nondiscrimination (unconditional-most-favored-nation treatment) by A and B reduces their future bargaining power in the quest for larger markets in C and D. The consequence, many held, could easily be a slowing down in tariff reductions all around the world. This case for discrimination was more difficult to deal with by those who favored more liberal trade policies and it was commonly accepted as a potent case for discrimination. Ways were found to partially meet the problem—notably, the development of the "principal supplier" rule and specialized tariff classification [6] —but at the cost of impairing the most-favored-nation principle.[7]

---

6. The principal supplier—or chief source—rule requires that a nation negotiate reductions in import barriers on a given product only with the country which had been supplying the greatest portion of the former's import of that product. It is thus intended that each concession will be negotiated with the country having the greatest interest in it. This practice preserves bargaining power when the unconditional-most-favored-nation practice is followed, because there is a tendency under it for some products of prime interest to other countries (those goods for which each is a major supplier) not to be the subject of negotiation between other pairs of countries. Specialized tariff classification facilitates the application of the principal supplier rule by so defining products for trade barrier cutting purposes that fewer, rather than more, of the exports important to those not participating in a given bilateral negotiation qualify for the bilaterally agreed cuts.

7. The argument lost some more of its potency when, immediately after

Trade liberalization and the rise of most favored national treatment in the unconditional form. Broadly, both the conditional and unconditional forms of most favored nation treatment reduce the discrimination that exists in international trade when two states restrict exclusively to themselves the trade advantages they give to each other. Bilateral and strictly exclusive trade bargains were the norm over much of the historical period of the modern state, often being linked to treaties of military and political alliance. To a considerable extent for some countries such arrangements existed until sometime after World War II in the Western world, usually those with foreign exchange difficulties. Bilateral trade arrangements of the exclusive sort still characterize the trading practices of the Eastern European socialist bloc.

However, there is evidence that, in past centuries, states sometimes found it in their respective national interests to make trade liberalization arrangements in the knowledge that there were outstanding most favored nation promises to third states, and in some instances these promises were of the unconditional type.

Between the two World Wars and after the second down to date, subject to questions that arise in relationship to material to follow in this section, the United States has been the prime mover toward trade liberalization (lower tariffs and the reduction of quotas on imports, i. e. quantitative restrictions). Exclusive trade agreements were not favored by the United States even when political parties favoring highly protective tariffs were in power. Until shortly before the exchange of notes with Brazil that follows, the United States adhered to the practice of entering into conditional most favored nation treaty relationships. See Whitney v. Robertson, 124 U.S. 190, 8 S.Ct. 456 (1888), where an importer of goods from San Domingo (today the Dominican Republic) failed to get the lower than tariff schedule rate the United States had given the King of Hawaii on the same product, because the United States treaty with the country of the import's origin was of the conditional most favored nation variety and that country did not give American imports concessions comparable to those that the King of Hawaii had given. It was so held even though the treaty had not specifically stated that the United States treaty promise to that country was conditioned upon the giving of such compensation.

Nonetheless, the general level of United States and other tariffs remained high. What is said to be the highest general level of tariffs in United States history was reached in the Tariff Act of 1930, coinciding with the Great Depression and European defaults on war debts to the United States, because of the debtor's inability to sell enough for dollars and gold to pay without seriously impairing the credibility of their own monies and their capacity to pay for neces-

World War II, arrangements were made for simultaneous bilateral negotiations, a procedure which Germany had followed before World War I, and which became the hallmark of the General Agreement on Tariffs and Trade.

sary imports. Franklin D. Roosevelt came to power in 1933 committed to trade liberalization through the negotiation of bilateral tariff reductions that by unconditional most favored nation treatment would spread throughout the world trading system. It was assumed that the maximum use of the principal supplier technique (see the excerpt from Patterson above) would ensure the requisite network of tariff-cutting agreements.

Congress responded with the Reciprocal Trade Agreements Act of 1933, which as codified and from time to time extended and amplified as to the scope of the President's delegated power to cut tariffs, is still the basis of United States trade liberalization treaties and for United States participation in the General Agreement on Tariffs and Trade (GATT).[a]

TREATY OF FRIENDSHIP, COMMERCE AND NAVIGATION BETWEEN THE UNITED STATES AND JAPAN OF APRIL 2, 1953

4 U.S.T. 2063, 206 U.N.T.S. 143.

Article XIV

1.   Each Party shall accord most-favored-nation treatment to products of the other Party, from whatever place and by whatever type of carrier arriving, and to products destined for exportation to the territories of such other Party, by whatever route and by whatever type of carrier, with respect to customs duties and charges of any kind imposed on or in connection with importation or exportation or imposed on the international transfer of payments for imports or exports, and with respect to the method of levying such duties and charges, and with respect to all rules and formalities in connection with importation and exportation.

*   *   *

Article XXII

*   *   *

2.   The term "most-favored-nation treatment" means treatment accorded within the territories of a Party upon terms no less favorable than the treatment accorded therein, in like situations, to nationals, companies, products, vessels or other objects, as the case may be, of any third country.

GENERAL AGREEMENT ON TARIFFS AND TRADE OF OCTOBER 30, 1947

61 Stat. Part 5, A12, 55 U.N.T.S. 187.

Article I

1.   With respect to customs duties and charges of any kind imposed on or in connection with importation or exportation or imposed

a.   84 states were parties as of January 1, 1980.

on the international transfer of payments for imports or exports, and with respect to the method of levying such duties and charges, and with respect to all rules and formalities in connection with importation and exportation, and with respect to all matters referred to in paragraphs 1 and 2 of Article III, any advantage, favour, privilege or immunity granted by any contracting party to any product originating in or destined for any other country shall be accorded immediately and unconditionally to the like product originating in or destined for the territories of all other contracting parties.

2.   The provisions of paragraph 1 of this Article shall not require the elimination of any preferences in respect of import duties or charges which do not exceed the levels provided for in paragraph 3 of this Article and which fall within the following descriptions:

[There follow specified excepted trade preferences, i. e. tariff advantages that are to remain exclusive. Generally, these were those between the United Kingdom and other Commonwealth entities; France and Territories of the French Union; the Customs Union of Belgium, Luxembourg and the Netherlands and the overseas territories of Belgium and the Netherlands; the United States and the Republics of Cuba and the Philippines and dependent territories of the United States; preferences between a few neighboring countries, the United States and Canada-Mexico not being included.]

The institutional history of GATT. The GATT, as a set of multipartite treaty rules about international trade and as a slightly developed international organization, is all that survives of an ambitious post-World War II, early UN effort to establish an International Trade Organization (ITO). The Charter of the International Trade Organization died aborning, chiefly because it attempted to regulate internationally restrictive trade practices and cartels and monopolies, as well as tariffs and quotas. GATT was put into effect pending sufficient state approvals to permit the ITO to come into being, which it never did. As the prospects for the ITO dimmed, GATT institutionalized itself, although it still is not, strictly speaking, a full-fledged international organization.

As to the expectations for the ITO, see Rubin, The Judicial Review Problem in the International Trade Organization, 63 Harv.L. Rev. 78 (1949). As to the early period of GATT, consult Gorter, GATT after Six Years, VIII Int'l Orgs. 1 (1954). The failure of the ITO also cost the less-developed countries (LDCs) their effort to write into most favored nation treatment an explicit exception for their development-related exports; the developed countries having agreed to such a principle (Art. XV of the ITO) for the ITO, successfully resisting its inclusion in the GATT part of that arrangement. As things turned out GATT was the only part of the total effort to regulate all major aspects of international trade that went into effect. As to the work of GATT, consult Hudec, The GATT Legal System and World Trade Diplomacy (1975) and Jackson, World Trade and the Law of GATT (1970).

---

2.   DEPARTURES FROM UNCONDITIONAL MOST FAVORED NATION TREATMENT

Types of departures. The most favored nation principle, along with provisions for national treatment in some instances, has a wider use in modern commercial treaties than terms of trade (tariffs and quotas) alone. Custom has dictated certain exclusions from most favored nation provisions as to the right of an alien to do business within a state, civil aviation for example. Certain other activities are also excluded, sometimes explicitly or by the general understanding of the mutually promising states: defense industries, administration of aliens' estates, for example. As to trade in the strict sense, there is a customary exclusion of preferences given to "frontier traffic"; see GATT, Article XXIV(3), which codifies this exception.

The more important departures are those that arise where customs unions and free trade areas provide trade advantages for the participating states in their trade with each other that if extended to non-participating states having most favored nation treaties with the member states individually would destroy a major incentive toward the elimination of tariffs and quotas between the member states. Article XXIV of GATT lays down the contours of the exception under reference, but in practice few of the arrangements that have been made have fitted GATT like a glove, with the result that waivers have been sought and usually granted, as was the case (with strong United States approval) in the formative period of the European Economic Community (EEC).

The EEC has now completed its transitional phases (except for new entrants), and the general rule is zero tariff between the members. Non-members are subject to a common external tariff, except where the EEC has made special arrangements; and the EEC is bound to unconditional most favored nation treatment with third states only as to its external tariff. The EEC is subject to GATT, because its members are all GATT states. The same general principle applies to the European Free Trade Association (EFTA) as to the tariff and quota preferences the member states give each other. But as there is no common external tariff in EFTA, each EFTA state, through GATT, is responsible for dealing properly with third states in the administration of its national tariff. The Central American Common Market (CACM) is in the situation of the EEC; and the Latin American Free Trade Association (LAFTA), allowing for a few uncertainties, is like EFTA, as to unconditional most favored nation treatment. Other groupings in developing Africa, Southeast Asia and Latin America (the Andean Group within LAFTA) are similarly classifiable as either common markets or customs unions.

The greatest problems raised as to departures from unconditional most favored nation treatment are those created by emergency foreign exchange stringencies suffered by a state (whether developed or developing) and by the insistent demands of the developing countries that the rich countries grant them non-reciprocal, non-discriminatory, generalized trade preferences for the products of their industrialization. As to trade preference, the battle lost at ITO/GATT has brought into being the Group of 77 (actually many more) of the poorer, developing countries, which through the United Nations Conference on Trade and Development (UNCTAD) fight on for preferences and other special trade advantages.

Why do they? What have preferences to do with development? In a nutshell the LDC's argument is: "Development requires a net inflow of resources in excess of our subsistence needs; we are too poor and too far behind to grow, as urgently we must, from what our societies can save from our internal trade and our disadvantaged exports of agricultural commodities and other raw materials." No matter what comes to us from external assistance and from foreign investment, greater export earnings are absolutely essential as a source of the development capital we need. But our exports are at a comparative disadvantage in world markets, because (a) we are just getting started and our market base is too narrow for economies of scale, (b) we have to use large components of manpower in our production due to underemployment, (c) we lack technology. If we have to pay the same tariffs as our developed competitors do in any significant foreign market, we will lose the export opportunity because our costs are higher." To this they usually add: "While developing, we need many kinds of manufactured imports ourselves. They always cost too much and the costs of what we have to buy are always rising faster than the prices of our traditional (raw materials) exports."

This viewpoint is sometimes theorized by poor country groups claiming that unconditional most favored nation treatment is a modern version of Mercantilism. This is hard for grizzled trade liberationists in developed countries to accept if they look back to the battles they have won or tried to win, instead of facing the new reality of Rich Nations-Poor Nations.

TREATY ESTABLISHING THE EUROPEAN ECONOMIC COMMUNITY OF MARCH 25, 1957

298 U.N.T.S. 3, 11.

Article 9

1. The Community shall be based upon a customs union covering the exchange of all goods and comprising both the prohibition, as between Member States, of customs duties on importation and exportation and all charges with equivalent effect and the adoption of a common customs tariff in their relations with third countries.

2.   The provisions of Chapter 1, Section 1 and of Chapter 2 of this Title shall apply   *   *   *   also to products coming from third countries and having been entered for consumption in Member States.

Article 10

1.   Products having been entered for consumption in a Member State shall be deemed to be products coming from a third country in cases where, in respect of such products, the necessary import formalities have been complied with and the appropriate customs duties or charges with equivalent effect have been levied in such Member State and where such products have not benefited by any total or partial drawback on such duties or charges.   *   *   *

*   *   *

Article 18

Member States hereby declare their willingness to contribute to the development of international commerce and the reduction of barriers to trade by entering into reciprocal and mutually advantageous arrangements directed to the reduction of customs duties below the general level which they could claim as a result of the establishment of a customs union between themselves.

Article 19

1.   Under the conditions and within the limits laid down below, the duties under the common customs tariff shall be at the level of the arithmetical average of the duties applied in the four customs territories covered by the Community.

*   *   *

Article 30

Quantitative restrictions on importation and all measures with equivalent effect shall, without prejudice to the following provisions, hereby be prohibited between Member States.

AGREEMENT CONCERNING AUTOMOTIVE PRODUCTS BETWEEN THE UNITED STATES AND CANADA OF JANUARY 16, 1965

17 U.S.T. 1372.

Article II

(a) The Government of Canada, not later than the entry into force of the legislation contemplated in paragraph (b) of this Article, shall accord duty free treatment to imports of the products of the United States described in Annex A [automotive vehicles and parts].

(b) The Government of the United States   *   *   *   shall seek enactment of legislation authorizing duty-free treatments of imports of the products of Canada described in [the same products, with the exception of stated percentages of components manufactured outside Canada].

_____

Problems.

a. Mexico complains of the preference given a Canadian-made truck over one made entirely in Mexico, say at the huge, integrated Volkswagen factory at Puebla. Does the United States have a defense as against its unconditional most favored nation promises to Mexico?

b. Under the third country component provision in (b), what is legally permissible to Canada as to the claim that a United States-made small car with a German-made engine and a British transmission is entitled to duty-free entry into Canada?

c. In the early stages of the 1980 presidential campaign at least one candidate from each party called for a common market between the United States, Canada and Mexico. If consulted what do you think the President of Mexico would say?

_____

The developing countries' demand for generalized, non-reciprocal trade preferences. Latin American developmental theoreticians quite early, after United States and other developed countries' attention finally turned to the development needs of the poorer world, about 1959–60, saw it as essential to the capital flows necessary for development that the developing countries expand their export markets for manufactured and semi-manufactured goods. (These states also wished to stabilize their agricultural exports at prices insuring substantial and inflation-proof levels.) The unconditional most favored nation principle conflicts with the trade intensification export efforts of developing countries. Why? Does the extract that follows give the answer? Gingerly, the United States, the European Economic Community and, to an extent, Japan have given carefully limited trade preferences to developing countries that an importing country does not extend to similar goods from non-developing countries. How do you suppose this is managed legally?

A question the developing countries dislike to address is whether, if trade preferences are given as development assistance, the assisted country should link such advantages to development goals and agree to substantive post-audit on performance in regard to such goals. Such reviews are commonplace as to development assistance loans even though the reaction to them ranges from bemusement to fury.

JOINT DECLARATION OF THE DEVELOPING COUNTRIES OF NOVEMBER 11, 1963

UNCTAD, Basic Documents 8, 10 (1963).

2.   International trade could become a more powerful instrument and vehicle of economic development not only through the expansion of the traditional exports of the developing countries, but also through the development of markets for their new products and a general increase in their share of world exports under improved terms of trade. For this purpose, a new international division of labour, with new patterns of production and trade, is necessary. Only in this way will the economic independence of the developing countries be strengthened and a truly interdependent and integrated world economy emerge. The development of production and the increase in productivity and purchasing power of the developing countries will contribute to the economic growth of the industrialized countries as well, and thus become a means to world-wide prosperity.

3.   The existing principles and patterns of world trade still mainly favour the advanced parts of the world. Instead of helping the developing countries to promote the development and diversification of their economies, the present tendencies in world trade frustrate their efforts to attain more rapid growth. These trends must be reversed. The volume of trade of the developing countries should be increased and its composition diversified; the prices of their exports should be stabilized at fair and remunerative levels, and international transfers of capital should be made more favourable to those countries so as to enable them to obtain through trade more of the means needed for their economic development.

4.   To achieve these objectives, a dynamic international trade policy is required. This policy should be based on the need for providing special assistance and protection for the less developed parts of the world economy. The removal of obstacles to the trade of the developing countries is important, but the accelerated development of the parts of the world which are lagging behind requires more than the unconditional application of the most-favoured-nation principle and the mere reduction of tariffs. More positive measures aimed at achieving a new international division of labour are essential to bring about the necessary increase in productivity and diversification of economic activity in the developing countries. The measures taken by developed countries to promote the development of the relatively backward areas within their national boundaries provide a guide for the purposeful and dynamic action which needs to be taken in the field of international economic co-operation.

5.   The fundamental trade problems of developing countries are well identified. What the world lacks today is, therefore, not the awareness of the problem, but the readiness to act. Many constructive proposals were advanced during the second session of the Pre-

paratory Committee of the United Nations Conference on Trade and Development. The representatives of developing countries making the present Declaration recommend to all Members of the United Nations that they give earnest consideration to these proposals and that they explore, before the beginning of the Conference, all practical means for their implementation, so as to make it possible to reach at the Conference basic agreement on a new international trade and development policy.   *   *   *

Foreign exchange stringencies. What happens legally when a GATT member finds that its trade liberalization policy has brought it a flood of imports priced in a scarce foreign currency at a time when its own exports are lagging, with the result that its adverse balance of trade (trade deficit) affects or threatens to affect its balance of payments or even its reserves to back its own currency? See the materials that follow.

GENERAL AGREEMENT ON TARIFFS AND TRADE OF OCTOBER 30, 1947

61 Stat. Part 5, A12, 55 U.N.T.S. 187.

Article XII

1. Notwithstanding the provisions of paragraph 1 of Article XI [eliminating quotas], any contracting party, in order to safeguard its external financial position and its balance of payments, may restrict the quantity or value of merchandise permitted to be imported, subject to the provisions of the following paragraphs of this Article.

2. (a) Import restrictions instituted, maintained or intensified by a contracting party under this Article shall not exceed those necessary:

   (i)   to forestall the imminent threat of, or to stop, a serious decline in its monetary reserves, or

   (ii)   in the case of a contracting party with very low monetary reserves, to achieve a reasonable rate of increase in its reserves   *   *   *

(b) Contracting parties applying restrictions under subparagraph (a) of this paragraph shall progressively relax them as such conditions improve   *   *   *.

    *   *   *

Article XXXVII

1. The developed contracting parties shall to the fullest extent possible—that is, except when compelling reasons, which may include

legal reasons, make it impossible—give effect to the following provisions:

* * *

(b) refrain from introducing, or increasing the incidence of, customs duties * * * on products currently and potentially of particular export interest to less-developed contracting parties * * *.

IMPOSITION OF SUPPLEMENTAL DUTY FOR BALANCE OF PAYMENTS PURPOSES BY THE PRESIDENT OF THE UNITED STATES OF AMERICA

36 Fed. Reg. 15724 (1971).

A Proclamation

Whereas, there has been a prolonged decline in the international monetary reserves of the United States, and our trade and international competitive position is seriously threatened and, as a result, our continued ability to assure our security could be impaired;

Whereas, the balance of payments position of the United States requires the imposition of a surcharge on dutiable imports;

Whereas, pursuant to the authority vested in him by the Constitution and the statutes, including, but not limited to, the Tariff Act of 1930, as amended (hereinafter referred to as "the Tariff Act"), and the Trade Expansion Act of 1962 (hereinafter referred to as "the TEA"), the President entered into, and proclaimed tariff rates under, trade agreements with foreign countries;

Whereas, under the Tariff Act, the TEA, and other provisions of law, the President may, at any time, modify or terminate, in whole or in part, any proclamation made under his authority;

Now, Therefore, I, Richard Nixon, President of the United States of America, acting under the authority vested in me by the Constitution and the statutes, including, but not limited to, the Tariff Act, and the TEA, respectively, do proclaim as follows:

A.   I hereby declare a national emergency during which I call upon the public and private sector to make the efforts necessary to strengthen the international economic position of the United States.

B.   (1) I hereby terminate in part for such period as may be necessary and modify prior Presidential Proclamations which carry out trade agreements insofar as such proclamations are inconsistent with, or proclaim duties different from, those made effective pursuant to the terms of this Proclamation.

(2) Such proclamations are suspended only insofar as is required to assess a surcharge in the form of a supplemental duty amounting to 10 percent ad valorem. Such supplemental duty shall be imposed on all dutiable articles imported into the customs territory of the United States from outside thereof, which are entered, or with-

drawn from warehouse, for consumption after 12:01 a. m., August 16, 1971, provided, however, that if the imposition of an additional duty of 10 percent ad valorem would cause the total duty or charge payable to exceed the total duty or charge payable at the rate prescribed in column 2 of the Tariff Schedules of the United States, then the column 2 rate shall apply.

C. To implement section B of this Proclamation, the following new subpart shall be inserted after subpart B of part 2 of the Appendix to the Tariff Schedules of the United States:

Subpart C—Temporary Modifications for Balance of Payments Purposes

Subpart C headnotes:

1. This subpart contains modifications of the provisions of the tariff schedules proclaimed by the President in Proclamation 4074.

2. Additional duties imposed—The duties provided for in this subpart are cumulative duties which apply in addition to the duties otherwise imposed on the articles involved. The provisions for these duties are effective with respect to articles entered on and after 12:01 a. m., August 16, 1971, and shall continue in effect until modified or terminated by the President or by the Secretary of the Treasury (hereinafter referred to as the Secretary) in accordance with headnote 4 of this subpart.

3. Limitation on additional duties—The additional 10 percent rate of duty specified in rate of duty column numbered 1 of item 948.00 shall in no event exceed that rate which, when added to the column numbered 1 rate imposed on the imported article under the appropriate item in schedules 1 through 7 of these schedules, would result in an aggregated rate in excess of the rate provided for such article in rate of duty column numbered 2.

    *   *   *

Item	Article	Rates of duty	
		1	2
948.00	Articles, except as exempted under headnote 5 of this subpart, which are not free of duty under these schedules and which are the subject of tariff concessions granted by the United States in trade agreements.	10% ad val. . . . (See headnote 3 of this subpart.)	No change.

D. This Proclamation shall be effective 12:01 a. m., August 16, 1971.

In Witness Whereof, I have hereunto set my hand this fifteenth day of August in the year of our Lord nineteen hundred and seventy-one, and of the Independence of the United States of America the one hundred and ninety-sixth.

Richard Nixon

Question: Does this action square with the President's power under national law? Under international law? See Yoshida Int'l, Inc. v. United States, 526 F.2d 560 (C.C.P.A.1975).

Has there been a shift of the focus of concern from rates of duty to non-tariff barriers? The conventional wisdom of the 1970's was that amongst developing countries rates of duty have not been a serious problem to trade expansion since the Kennedy Round of GATT-extended cuts was negotiated between the United States and the European Economic Community in 1967; whereas quantitative restrictions, specifications damaging to foreign products and legal requirements that government agencies buy domestic products, to list a core group of non-tariff barriers, are still serious impediments to free movement. Thus in the Trade Reform Act of 1974 (signed by the President in January, 1975) Congress spent little time on authorizing the President to cut tariffs but many pages on authorizing him to negotiate international agreements as to non-tariff barriers and providing for itself a legislative veto on agreements so negotiated, even when these are within the black letter of the delegation. The legislation was needed to clear the way for the Tokyo Round (so-called even though negotiated in Geneva, at GATT headquarters). For some time the other GATT members had to wait on the United States, as the President's earlier authority to negotiate any trade liberalization agreement expired at midnight of the day the Kennedy Round agreement was signed in 1967. The President signed the Trade Reform Act with its legislative veto provisions, it seems clear by inference, because otherwise the no-authority situation would have continued. The Tokyo Round resulted in another trade agreement, and the Congress has approved and brought it into internal effect as United States trade law by the Trade Agreements Act of 1979, 19 U.S.C. § 2501 et seq.

The new trade law of the world community (even non-GATT members such as the Soviet Union may get its benefit under bilateral treaties with a GATT member) does indeed focus mainly on non-tariff barriers. But in the United States and elsewhere in recent years low rates of duty themselves have created some tensions and difficulties. In the United States the sole surviving American color television manufacturer mounted a determined legal offensive to get Japanese television sets charged a higher-than-schedule duty through a claimed countervailing duty in the amount of asserted Japanese subsidies to exporters through the refund (in trade jargon, drawback) of purchase taxes imposed on consumers in Japan. American producers have also been active—with the support of organized labor—in claiming that certain importers should be assessed additional duties (called anti-dumping duties) for allegedly selling goods here, after normal tariffs and shipping charges have been absorbed, cheaper than they are sold in the home market of the producing country or below a constructed cost of production there. If these efforts do not produce results, domestic manufacturers and their labor confrères may seek, under the Trade Reform Act of 1974, to move the government to raise schedule duties (tariff relief under Title II of the Act, 19 U.S.C. § 2251 et seq.). Since the Trade Reform Act of 1962, which expired just after the Kennedy Round you may recall, an alternative to tariff relief is Adjustment Assistance for business, labor and now communities badly hurt by foreign goods coming in at the lower duties that the GATT rounds have produced.

Do you have a guess as to which alternative, adjustment assistance or protection by higher duties, American businesses and the labor force prefer? Why?

The foregoing also suggests why customs law is a bustling transnational law specialty in the United States. It is still a fairly small specialty, but the volume of litigation is surprisingly high. Customs classifications for rates of duty are rather frequently litigated before two special Article III courts, the Customs Court—renamed as of November 1, 1980, the United States Court of International Trade—and the Court of Customs and Patent Appeals. Issues of executive branch authority may to some extent come up in the regular federal courts.

Tariff Schedules of the United States. They are made up of very narrow categories of products, with the result that the customs classification problem is often litigated. Is a pregnant Holstein heifer weighing over 700 pounds a "cow imported specially for dairy purposes" and thus entitled a lower rate of duty per pound than "cattle generally"? See Dillingham, Inc. v. United States, 490 F.2d 967 (C.C. PA.1974).

UNITED STATES v. TEXAS INSTRUMENTS, INC.

United States Court of Customs and Patent Appeals, 1980.
620 F.2d 269.

MARKEY, Chief Judge. The Government appeals from the judgment of the Customs Court * * * sustaining Texas Instruments, classification protest relating to imported integrated circuit devices used as components in solid state digital watches. We affirm.

     *   *   *

The Customs Service classified the imported articles under TSUS item 720.75 [2] as assemblies and subassemblies for watch movements. Texas Instruments claimed classification under TSUS item 687.60.[3] The Government asserted an alternate classification under TSUS item 720.86 [4] as assemblies and subassemblies for clock movements.

Judge Nils A. Boe held: (1) the legislative history of TSUS item 720.75 does not evidence a congressional intent to include every device capable of measuring time within the meaning of "watch movement"; (2) "watch movement" refers to a mechanism possessing moving parts to which or from which motion is transferred; (3) the molecular vibration within the quartz crystal of an electronic watch module does not satisfy that motion requirement; (4) the imported articles do not bear an essential resemblance to watch movements, and are specifically provided for under TSUS item 687.60; (5) the imported articles are not more than integrated circuits; and (6) the imported articles are not classifiable as "clock movements" under TSUS item 720.86, the sole distinction between clock and watch movements being size.

Issue

The dispositive issue is whether the Customs Court erred in holding the articles properly classified under TSUS item 687.60 as transistor and other related electronic crystal components rather than as subassemblies for watch or clock movements.

2. Assemblies and subassemblies for watch movements consisting of two or more parts or pieces fastened or joined together:

* * *

720.75 Other assemblies and subassemblies ..... 4.5¢ for each jewel (if any) + the column 1 rate specified in item 720.65 for bottom or pillar plates or their equivalent therein . . . but the total duty on the assembly or subassembly shall not . . . be less than 22.5% ad val.

. . .

3. Electronic tubes (except X-ray tubes): photo-cells; transistors and other related electronic crystal components; mounted piezoelectric crystals; all the foregoing and parts thereof:

* * *

687.60 Other ....6% ad val.

4. Assemblies and subassemblies for clock movements, consisting of two or more parts or pieces fastened or joined together:

* * *

Other assemblies and subassemblies:

* * *

720.86 For other movements.. 16% ad val. + 6.25¢ for each jewel (if any) + 0.75¢ for each other piece or part.

OPINION

The Government argues the Customs Court erred because: (1) legislative history shows a congressional intent to include electronic movements within the term "watch movements"; (2) the quartz crystal incorporated into the imported articles after importation provides movement; (3) the imported articles bear an essential resemblance to watch movement subassemblies in existence when the TSUS was enacted; (4) the articles are more than integrated circuits; and (5) if the articles are not watch movements, they are clock movements.

(1) Legislative History

The Government cites portions of the Tariff Classification Study and the Congressional Record that indicate a congressional intent that electronically regulated movements be classified with conventional movements. Those citations do not, however, persuasively show that a solid state module having no moving parts was intended by Congress to be included within the provision for "watch movements." [5] Accordingly, the Customs Court properly determined the meaning of the term "watch movements" by reference to texts and dictionaries in use at the time the TSUS was enacted, the common understanding of the term in the horological industry at that time, and the testimony of experts as to what the term meant when the TSUS was enacted. The conclusion of the Customs Court that the term refers to a mechanism incorporating "moving parts to which or from which motion is transferred," 82 Cust.Ct. at 278, 475 F.Supp. at 1187, has not been shown to be erroneous by the Government. We agree with the Customs Court that the term requires a mechanism for the transfer of motion. Indeed, until 1972, every watch sold contained a movement meeting that definition. Electronically regulated watch movements, the subject of much discussion when the TSUS were enacted (and of the legislative history cited by the Government), also have moving parts and thus meet that definition. The Customs Court correctly decided that the articles at issue here, having no mechanism for the transfer of motion, were not "movements" or subassemblies of "movements" within the meaning of that term as it was understood in 1962.

(2) Quartz Crystal Motion

The Government argues that even if motion is required by the definition of watch movement, that requirement is satisfied by the vibration of the quartz crystal later incorporated into the imported articles. We do not accept that contention. The magnitude of the motion within the crystal is roughly one angstrom (one ten-billionth of a

5. Congress rejected an attempt to amend the relevant TSUS items in 1975 and 1976 to include components of solid state watches under the TSUS provisions for watches. H.R. 10176, 94th Cong., 1st Sess. (1975); H.R. 14600, 94th Cong., 2d Sess. (1976).

meter); the motion is essentially molecular vibration; and the motion does not transmit mechanical energy or transfer motion to or from any other part.

(3) Essential Resemblance

The Government argues that the imported articles bear an essential resemblance to subassemblies for watch movements in existence when the TSUS were enacted and thus should be classified with them. That argument is supported by a functional analysis: because the imported articles and prior subassemblies are used to keep time and meet certain dimensional requirements, they should be classified together.

The required essential resemblance is to those characteristics established by the TSUS as the criteria of classification. Davies Turner & Co. v. United States, 45 CCPA 39, 41–42, C.A.D. 669 (1957). The criteria established by the TSUS for classification as a watch movement are: (1) a timepiece movement, (2) less than 1.77 inches wide and 0.5 inch thick. Though the dimensional requirements are met by the imported article, it does not bear an essential resemblance to a timepiece movement because the imported article is not and does not contain a movement. We agree with the Customs Court that the articles are more specifically provided for as transistors and other related electronic crystal components.

(4) "More Than" Integrated Circuits

Arguing that the imported articles are more than integrated circuits, the Government says classification in a TSUS item for integrated circuits is improper because: (1) the encapsulation material serves as a housing for other components; (2) the lead frame serves as the device's substrate; and (3) not all the usable terminals are connected to external leads.

"Only the most general of rules can be ascertained from the previous decisions dealing with the 'more than' doctrine, and it appears that each case must in the first analysis be determined on its own facts." E. Green & Son (New York), Inc. v. United States, 59 CCPA 31, 34, C.A.D. 1032, 450 F.2d 1396, 1398 (1971). This court will not reverse on questions of fact unless the findings are unsupported by substantial evidence or are clearly contrary to the weight of the evidence. Pollard Bearings Corp. v. United States, 62 CCPA 61, 64, C.A.D. 1146, 511 F.2d 568, 571 (1975); United States v. F. W. Myers & Co., 45 CCPA 48, 52, C.A.D. 671 (1958).

The Customs Court's finding that the articles are not more than integrated circuits is fully supported by the evidence. We agree with the Customs Court that the features the Government points to are subordinate to the articles' use as integrated circuits.

(5) Clock Movement

The Government argues that if the articles are not classifiable as watch movements they are classifiable as "clock movements or mechanisms" under TSUS item 720.86, because Schedule 7, Part 2, Subpart E, Headnote 2(c), says for the purpose of Subpart E: "the term 'clock movements' means any movement or mechanism, other than 'watch movements' as defined in headnote 2(b), above, intended or suitable for measuring time." That language, says the Government, requires that any timekeeping device not meeting the dimensional and physical requirements of "watch movement" be classified as a "clock movement or mechanism."

That argument turns on the meaning of "mechanism" at the time the TSUS were enacted. That meaning is of a breadth insufficient to encompass a solid state module having no moving parts. Webster's Third New International Dictionary (1961) defines mechanism as "a piece of machinery: a structure of working parts functioning together to produce an effect," with machine defined as "[a]ny device consisting of two or more * * * parts, which * * * may serve to transmit and modify force and motion ⊩ * *." That that meaning has long been accepted is evidenced by Lockwood's Dictionary of Mechanical Engineering Terms (1913), defining mechanism as "an assemblage of parts * * * which embraces the essential principles on which the machine is constructed," and "machine" "an assemblage of parts * * * by which motion and force are transmitted."

The integrated circuit before us is not a subassembly of a mechanism for the same reason it is not a subassembly of a movement: there is simply no physical movement or motion generated in or by the circuit.

SUMMARY

The judgment of the Customs Court, that encapsulated integrated circuits, used in solid state watches, are properly classified as transistors and other related electronic crystal components rather than subassemblies for watch movements, is affirmed.

Companion case. The Court of Customs and Patent Appeals ruled similarly for Texas Instruments as to imported visible light emitting diode display devices used as components in solid state digital watches. Briefs amici were filed in both cases by the trade association for the domestic watchmaking industry and several companies.

EXCERPT FROM THE TRADE AGREEMENTS ACT OF 1979

19 U.S.C. § 2501 et seq.

SEC. 2.   APPROVAL OF TRADE AGREEMENTS.

(a) Approval of Agreements and Statements of Administrative Action.—In accordance with the provisions of sections 102 and 151 of the Trade Act of 1974 (19 U.S.C. 2112 and 2191), the Congress approves the trade agreements described in subsection (c) submitted to the Congress on June 19, 1979, and the statements of administrative action proposed to implement such trade agreements submitted to the Congress on that date.

(b) Acceptance of Agreements by the President.—

(1) In general.—The President may accept for the United States the final legal instruments or texts embodying each of the trade agreements approved by the Congress under subsection (a). The President shall submit a copy of each final instrument or text to the Congress on the date such text or instrument is available, together with a notification of any changes in the instruments or texts, including their annexes, if any, as accepted and the texts of such agreements as submitted to the Congress under subsection (a). Such final legal instruments or texts shall be deemed to be the agreements submitted to and approved by the Congress under subsection (a) if such changes are—

(A) only rectifications of a formal character or minor technical or clerical changes which do not affect the substance or meaning of the texts as submitted to the Congress on June 19, 1979, or

(B) changes in annexes to such agreements, and the President determines that the balance of United States rights and obligations under such agreements is maintained.

(2) Application of agreement between the United States and other countries.—No agreement accepted by the President under paragraph (1) shall apply between the United States and any other country unless the President determines that such country—

(A) has accepted the obligations of the agreement with respect to the United States, and

(B) should not otherwise be denied the benefits of the agreement with respect to the United States because such country has not accorded adequate benefits, including substantially equal competitive opportunities for the commerce of the United States to the extent required under section 126(c) of the Trade Act of 1974 (19 U.S.C. 2136(c)), to the United States.

(3) Limitation on acceptance concerning major industrial countries.—The President may not accept an agreement de-

scribed in paragraph (1), (2), (3), (4), (5), (6), (7), (9), (10), or (11) of subsection (c), unless he determines that each major industrial country (as defined in section 126(d) of the Trade Act of 1974 (19 U.S.C. 2136(d)) is also accepting the agreement. Notwithstanding the preceding sentence, the President may accept such an agreement, if he determines that only one major industrial country is not accepting that agreement and the acceptance of that agreement by that country is not essential to the effective operation of the agreement, and if—

     (A) that country is not a major factor in trade in the products covered by that agreement,

     (B) the President has authority to deny the benefits of the agreement to that country and has taken steps to deny the benefits of the agreement to that country, or

     (C) a significant portion of United States trade would benefit from the agreement, notwithstanding such nonacceptance, and the President determines and reports to the Congress that it is in the national interest of the United States to accept the agreement.

For purposes of this paragraph, the acceptance of an agreement by the European Communities on behalf of its member countries shall also be treated as acceptance of that agreement by each member country, and acceptance of an agreement by all the member countries of the European Communities shall also be treated as acceptance of that agreement by the European Communities.

(c) Trade Agreements to Which this Act Applies.—The trade agreements to which subsection (a) applies are the following:

     (1) The Agreement on Implementation of Article VII of the General Agreement on Tariffs and Trade (relating to customs valuation).

     (2) The Agreement on Government Procurement.

     (3) The Agreement on Import Licensing Procedures.

     (4) The Agreement on Technical Barriers to Trade (relating to product standards).

     (5) The Agreement on Interpretation and Application of Articles VI, XVI, and XXIII of the General Agreement on Tariffs and Trade (relating to subsidies and countervailing measures).

     (6) The Agreement on Implementation of Article VI of the General Agreement on Tariffs and Trade (relating to antidumping measures).

     (7) The International Dairy Arrangement.

     (8) Certain bilateral agreements on cheese, other dairy products, and meat.

     (9) The Arrangement Regarding Bovine Meat.

(10) The Agreement on Trade in Civil Aircraft.

(11) Texts Concerning a Framework for the Conduct of World Trade.

(12) Certain Bilateral Agreements to Eliminate the Wine-Gallon Method of Tax and Duty Assessment.

(13) Certain other agreements to be reflected in Schedule XX of the United States to the General Agreement on Tariffs and Trade, including Agreements—

(A) to Modify United States Watch Marking Requirements, and to Modify United States Tariff Nomenclature and Rates of Duty for Watches,

(B) to Provide Duty-Free Treatment for Agricultural and Horticultural Machinery, Equipment, Implements, and Parts Thereof, and

(C) to Modify United States Tariff Nomenclature and Rates of Duty for Ceramic Tableware.

(14) The Agreement with the Hungarian People's Republic.

SEC. 3. RELÁTIONSHIP OF TRADE AGREEMENTS TO UNITED STATES LAW.

(a) United States Statutes to Prevail in Conflict.—No provision of any trade agreement approved by the Congress under section 2(a), nor the application of any such provision to any person or circumstance, which is in conflict with any statute of the United States shall be given effect under the laws of the United States.

*   *   *

---

1. *Some headlines from Le Figaro.*

"Cri d'alarme de l'industrie française face à la concurrence étrangère"

"Alerte aux importations sauvages"

July 5, 1977

"Textiles: la Communauté adopte les mesures restrictives à l'importation prises par la France"

July 7, 1977

2. *British lambs in France.* France refused to obey a final judgment by the European Court of Justice that under the European Economic Community Treaty it must admit "sheep meat" from the United Kingdom. Great Britain, claiming to be contributing more than any other member to the existing agricultural price support systems of the Community—ones that the British say have produced "wheat mountains, wine lakes, and butter hills"—objects to price supports that take away the comparative advantage of British agricultural producers.

The perspective of a developing country on trade negotiations is presented in the material which follows.

EDITORIAL, THE RECENT INTERNATIONAL ECONOMIC NEGOTIATIONS

29 Comercio Exterior No. 6 (June, 1979) 203.
Banco Nacional de Comercio Exterior, S.A., Mexico City, D.F., Mexico.

* * * International economic negotiations have been carried on of late primarily in two forums: the General Agreement on Tariffs and Trade (GATT) and the United Nations Conference on Trade and Development (UNCTAD).

GATT was set up by the developed nations originally and gradually a good proportion of underdeveloped and developing countries have joined. Given the fact that it is they that carry on the majority of international trade, the developed nations have continued to dominate negotiations in this forum. The major advantage achieved by the developing countries has been the tacit application of the principle of non-reciprocity, for they have been allowed to retain all their measures to protect domestic industry virtually intact without reciprocal restrictions being imposed. In GATT, at least, they have not succeeded in achieving preferential access to the industrialized countries' markets. UNCTAD, by contrast, has recognized the right of the developing countries to non-reciprocal preferential treatment with regard to process to such markets. The Generalized System of Preferences (GSP) establishes that the developed countries should allow manufactured products from the developing nations access to their markets under favorable tariff conditions without demanding any kind of reciprocity.

Unfortunately, the precise scope of this preference has never been determined, thus leaving it up to each developed country to decide on the amount and the conditions of any advantages it might grant. As a consequence, these advantages have turned out to be less significant in practice than was envisaged when the GSP was instituted. Concessions have been limited and precarious. Benefits of a concrete nature did accrue to the countries of the Third World, but they were not sufficiently secure or stable to permit the setting up, or even the expansion, of industrial concerns that might take advantage of them.

However that may be, UNCTAD, which is a forum for North-South negotiations, has attributed greater importance to the voice of the developing countries. At the same time, however, its meetings have hardly ever culminated in basic agreements and they have rarely translated into tangible benefits. Thus, it can hardly come as a surprise that the Conference's fifth meeting has come to an end without any significant agreement having been reached.

As far as GATT is concerned, the Tokyo Round negotiations have almost come to a close; the reciprocal concessions made known so far do not represent a step forward that specifically favors the developing countries. Let us hope that these nations' hopes will not be completely frustrated and that in the few remaining days of negotiations some positive advances are made in this direction.

The truth of the matter is that the present international situation is not favorable. Most of the industrialized nations have still to fully recover from the recession of 1974–1975. The United States, the country which achieved the greatest degree of recovery, did so by concentrating on the fight against unemployment. But its expansionist measures fostered inflation and gave rise to an increase trade deficit. As a result, the United States Government has now decided to concentrate its efforts on the fight against inflation, which demands contractionist measures that will certainly reduce the demand for imports in the greatest market in the world.

This situation is leading to increased unemployment in the industrialized countries and giving a boost to protectionist tendencies.

The developing countries will only be able to raise their exports to the developed world when these latter overcome the conditions described and their demand grows.

    *   *   *

SECTION B. THE LAW OF FOREIGN INVESTMENT

Dimensions of the problem. This section deals mainly with the nationalization problem where aliens' property or economic interests are affected. The existing international legal system is under stress in this area. The problem is an old one; but it has become more acute than ever before, as states, particularly new and developing ones, embark upon various types of social experimentation.

First of all, there is a sharp cleavage between the rich states and some of the developing countries on the question whether there is an international minimum standard, that is, a legal restraint upon the taking state as to the (i) purpose of nationalization and the (ii) payment of compensation.

Second, there is a question as to whether only certain types of traditional property rights are included, or whether impairment of aliens' economic interests more broadly viewed are within the ambit of the rules and principles governing nationalization and its counterpart in diplomacy, the extension of diplomatic protection (espousal) by the state of nationality.

A third modern issue, dealt with in Chapter 6 on aspects of the act of state doctrine, concerns the scope of the remedies for nationalizations, especially as to whether invalidation of the title given by the taking state to a purchaser from it is a remedy that customary international law recognizes.

The modern nationalization problem in international law must be viewed against the backdrop of strong psycho-political pressures in certain taking states. These tend to induce irrationality, not only in the decision to nationalize, but also in the stance of the nationalizing state in relationship to its international interests and obligations. Also, the dispossessed alien owners, even when from rich and highly developed states, tend to become emotional about the issues involved. Thus where, as is usually the case, such owners are influential persons in the essentially democratically responsive rich nation, both the sending and the host states become involved in escalations of tension that make it necessary for things to cool before either diplomacy or law can act effectively.

However, despite the foregoing, it is reasonably accurate to generalize that in time most nationalization issues get settled, by negotiation, by arbitration or by adjudication. International claims law is a specialty in international practice; and sometimes, as where there is a lump sum settlement calling for a division among claimants by one of its indigenous institutions, a parallel specialty in domestic law also develops. Also the lawyer who is called upon to counsel foreign investors needs to know about the nationalization problem and its law, both substantive and procedural.

Almost no one is satisfied with the international law of nationalization as it is. It is not only disputed. It is slow. An old quip of its practitioners is that the claims of the grandparents are settled by the parents for the benefit of the children. In the field of foreign capital movements, the accelerated pace of planet-wide activity chafes against the slow, Dickensian tempo of nationalization settlements.

The final and most important question is: what *should* the law be—reliance, rationality, equity, economic development, reasonable universality and effectiveness all considered? Some day, before too long, lawyers and statesmen are going to have to answer the question multinationally, not by legislative fiat in a single state. To answer it effectively they have to know what exists now as to legal regulation of nationalization of aliens' economic interests and go on from there.

---

1. STATE RESPONSIBILITY FOR TAKINGS

LAUTERPACHT, THE DEVELOPMENT OF INTERNATIONAL LAW BY THE INTERNATIONAL COURT 314 (1958)*

The Plea of Non-Discrimination

In the sphere of State responsibility the jurisprudence of the Court has assisted—indirectly, but emphatically—in discouraging a view closely connected with an extreme assertion of sovereignty, namely, that a State incurs no international responsibility if, with regard to measures adopted by it, it treats aliens and nationals alike. The Court has repeatedly laid down that the so-called plea of nondis-

* Reprinted by permission of Frederick A. Praeger, Inc., New York, and Sweet & Maxwell, Ltd., London.

crimination is not a valid defence against a charge of violation of international law. This the Court has done in the numerous cases, referred to elsewhere in this book, in which it affirmed the principle that equality of treatment must be an equality of both fact and law, and that a State cannot avoid its obligations by the device of framing its law in general terms equally applicable to all. However, the jurisprudence of the Court goes further than that. A measure, even if genuinely applicable both to nationals and to aliens, does not, for that reason, become lawful if it is otherwise prohibited by treaty. After finding, in the case of Certain German Interests in Polish Upper Silesia, that expropriation without indemnity was contrary to the Convention between Poland and Germany, the Court held expressly that "a measure prohibited by the Convention cannot become lawful under this instrument by reason of the fact that the State applies it to its own nationals." It invoked that principle once more in its Judgment in the Peter Pázmány University case. Previously, in the Advisory Opinion on German Settlers in Poland, the Court considered as irrelevant the fact that in a few instances the Polish law in question applied also to non-German Polish nationals who took as purchasers from original holders of German race.

It is legitimate to assume that these principles apply not only to international obligations established by treaty but also to customary international law. The plea of non-discrimination as a defence against a charge of violation of international law amounts, upon analysis, to a claim of the sovereign State to disregard international law and to erect its own law as the sole standard of the legitimacy of its action so long as such action is of general application. That claim the Court has declined to countenance. The attitude of the Court on the subject is fully in accordance with its repeated affirmation, as a matter of course, of the priority of the obligations of international law over municipal law. It did so in particular by refusing to permit the parties to plead their municipal law as a justification for non-compliance with an international obligation; that, in the words of the Court, "would amount to relying upon the non-fulfilment of an obligation imposed * * * by an international agreement."

Measure of Damages

In connection with State responsibility it is of interest to note the attitude of the Court to the question of the measure of damages due as compensation for a breach of an international obligation. In the international sphere the principle established in general jurisprudence to the effect that damages must, as a rule, include full restitution in integrum [a] did not at first secure ready acceptance by writers. It was asserted that the responsibility of States must be limited to damages arising directly out of the injurious event, to the exclusion of all indirect and consequential damages. This was, to some extent,

---

[a]. As used here the term merely means full damages, not invalidation of title to the nationalized property.

in accordance with certain tendencies in national law—now in process of disappearing in countries under the rule of law—to limit both the amenability of the State to suit and the consequences of its liability. While discouraging the award of purely speculative and remotely consequential damages, international jurisprudence has not, in general, accepted these assertions.

The suggestion of a general limitation of the responsibility of States in this matter was rejected by the Court in the Judgment in the case concerning the Chorzów Factory. The Court declined to agree that the compensation due to the German Government was limited to the value of the undertaking at the moment of dispossession, plus interest to the day of payment. The Court distinguished between expropriation which was lawful but for the fact of the State having failed to pay the just price of the property taken—in which case the compensation might properly be limited to the value of the undertaking at the time of the dispossession—and expropriation which had been resorted to in violation of an international undertaking. In the latter case, the Court said, the reparation "must, so far as possible, wipe out all the consequences of the illegal act and re-establish the situation which would, in all probability, have existed if that act had not been committed." The Court laid down in detail the principles governing compensation in these cases: "Restitution in kind, or, if this is not possible, payment of a sum corresponding to the value which a restitution in kind would bear; the award, if need be, of damages for loss sustained which cannot be covered by restitution in kind or payment in place of it." The Court then proceeded to assess compensation for losses in a manner which might have caused a less authoritative tribunal some apprehension lest it be charged with awarding damages for speculative profits.

GERMAN INTERESTS IN POLISH UPPER SILESIA—THE SO–CALLED CASE OF THE FACTORY AT CHORZOW (GERMANY v. POLAND)

Permanent Court of International Justice, 1926.
P.C.I.J., Ser. E, No. 2, 99, 114–115.

[Acting under a national law and claiming authorization under the Treaty of Versailles and a Germano-Polish Convention Concerning Upper Silesia, a Polish tribunal nullified in the land records a conveyance from the German state to a German national made after the Armistice but before the effective date of the Treaty of Versailles. To Germany's claim under general international law, as incorporated into the convention as a general standard by Heading III thereof, the Polish defense was that it did not lie because of what the court in the excerpt below refers to as treaty exceptions.]

* * * This right constitutes an exception to the principle of respect for vested rights recognized by international law and confirmed as regards Upper Silesia generally under Heading II of the

Convention; the derogation is therefore strictly in the nature of an exception and, for this reason, exclusive. Any measure affecting the property, rights and interests of German subjects covered by Head III of the Convention, which would overstep the limits set by the generally accepted principles of international law and were not justified on special grounds taking precedence over the Convention, would be incompatible with the régime established under the Convention.

Again, one of the formal conditions for the exercise of the right of expropriation is that previous notice of an intention to expropriate should be given; this notice must only cover property liable to expropriation and therefore presupposes a preliminary enquiry as to the existence of the necessary conditions. The Court infers from this that there may be no dispossession of property except in the form intended by the Convention, unless it be first established that the Convention is not applicable.

Considering next the law of July 14th, 1920, in the light of these principles, the Court observes that Article 2 of the law treats as null and non-existing rights which private persons may have acquired by deeds of alienation executed by the Crown, the German Reich, etc., if such deeds were drawn after November 11th, 1918. And, by authorizing the Polish Treasury to demand the eviction of any persons who, after the coming into force of the law, remain, in virtue of a contract of the kind contemplated in Article 5, in occupation of one of the landed properties in question, this article, in the Court's view, recognizes a right to disregard even private rights derived from contracts previous to November 11th, 1918. These articles, therefore, may affect private property and withdraw it from the protective régime instituted by Heading III, subjecting it to measures prohibited by the Convention; and they are applied automatically, without any investigation as to the title of ownership or validity of each transfer or contract. No means of redress is given to interested Parties and no indemnification is provided for. The Court arrives at the conclusion that both in form and in substance the application of Articles 2 and 5 of the Polish law is not compatible with the system established by Heading III of the * * * Convention.

THE PANEVEZYS–SALDUTISKIS RAILWAY CASE
(ESTONIA v. LITHUANIA)

Permanent Court of International Justice, 1939.
P.C.I.J., Ser. A/B, No. 76, 4, 16.

[This nationalization case turned on issues related to the nationality of the private party and exhaustion of remedies considered at pp. 1152–1159. The excerpt that follows tends to show that the parties and the court assumed, in going on to these issues, the existence of an underlying general principle of customary international law as to the taking state's responsibility. To what extent is it valid to argue from such assumptions that the weight of opinion among states supports the underlying principle when it is not specifically challenged in the particular case?]

* * *

In the opinion of the Court, the rule of international law on which the first Lithuanian objection is based is that in taking up the case of one of its nationals, by resorting to diplomatic action or international judicial proceedings on his behalf, a State is in reality asserting its own right, the right to ensure in the person of its nationals respect for the rules of international law. This right is necessarily limited to intervention on behalf of its own nationals because, in the absence of a special agreement, it is the bond of nationality between the State and the individual which alone confers upon the State the right of diplomatic protection, and it is as a part of the function of diplomatic protection that the right to take up a claim and to ensure respect for the rules of international law must be envisaged. Where the injury was done to the national of some other State, no claim to which such injury may give rise falls within the scope of the diplomatic protection which a State is entitled to afford nor can it give rise to a claim which that State is entitled to espouse.

* * *

STATEMENT OF POLICY BY THE PRESIDENT OF THE UNITED STATES CONCERNING THE INTERNATIONAL MINIMUM STANDARD

8 Weekly Compilation of Presidential Documents 64 (1972).

[The statement was made by President Nixon.]

We live in an age that rightly attaches very high importance to economic development. The people of the developing societies in particular see in their own economic development the path to fulfillment of a whole range of national and human aspirations. The United States continues to support wholeheartedly, as we have done for decades, the efforts of those societies to grow economically—out of our deep conviction that, as I said in my Inaugural Address, "To go forward at all is to go forward together"; that the well-being of mankind is in the final analysis indivisible; and that a better-fed, better-clothed, healthier, and more literate world will be a more peaceful world as well.

* * *

I also wish to make clear the approach of this administration to the role of private investment in developing countries, and in particular to one of the major problems affecting such private investment: upholding accepted principles of international law in the face of expropriations without adequate compensation.

A principal objective of foreign economic assistance programs is to assist developing countries in attracting private investment. A nation's ability to compete for this scarce and vital development in-

gredient is improved by programs which develop economic infra-
structure, increase literacy, and raise health standards. Private investment, as a carrier of technology, of trade opportunities, and of
capital itself, in turn becomes a major factor in promoting industrial
and agricultural development. Further, a significant flow of private
foreign capital stimulates the mobilization and formation of domestic
capital within the recipient country.

A sort of symbiosis exists—with government aid efforts not only
speeding the flow of, but actually depending for their success upon,
private capital both domestic and foreign. And, of course, from the
investor's point of view, foreign private investment must either yield
financial benefits to him over time, or cease to be available. Mutual
benefit is thus the sine qua non of successful foreign private investment.

Unfortunately, for all concerned, these virtually axiomatic views
on the beneficial role of and necessary conditions for private capital
have been challenged in recent and important instances. U. S. enterprises, and those of many other nations, operating abroad under valid
contracts negotiated in good faith, and within the established legal
codes of certain foreign countries, have found their contracts revoked
and their assets seized with inadequate compensation, or with no
compensation.

Such actions by other governments are wasteful from a resource
standpoint, shortsighted considering their adverse effects on the flow
of private investment funds from all sources, and unfair to the legitimate interests of foreign private investors.

The wisdom of any expropriation is questionable, even when adequate compensation is paid. The resources diverted to compensate
investments that are already producing employment and taxes often
could be used more productively to finance new investment in the domestic economy, particularly in areas of high social priority to which
foreign capital does not always flow. Consequently, countries that
expropriate often postpone the attainment of their own development
goals. Still more unfairly, expropriations in one developing country
can and do impair the investment climate in other developing countries.

In light of all this, it seems to me imperative to state—to our citizens and to other nations—the policy of this Government in future
situations involving expropriatory acts.

1. Under international law, the United States has a right to expect:

> —That any taking of American private property will be nondis-
> criminatory;
>
> —that it will be for a public purpose; and
>
> —that its citizens will receive prompt, adequate, and effective
> compensation from the expropriating country.

Thus, when a country expropriates a significant U. S. interest without making reasonable provision for such compensation to U. S. citizens, we will presume that the U. S. will not extend new bilateral economic benefits to the expropriating country unless and until it is determined that the country is taking reasonable steps to provide adequate compensation or that there are major factors affecting U. S. interests which require continuance of all or part of these benefits.

2. In the face of the expropriatory circumstances just described, we will presume that the United States Government will withhold its support from loans under consideration in multilateral development banks.

3. Humanitarian assistance will, of course, continue to receive special consideration under such circumstances.

4. In order to carry out this policy effectively, I have directed that each potential expropriation case be followed closely. A special inter-agency group will be established under the Council on International Economic Policy to review such cases and to recommend courses of action for the U. S. Government.

     *   *   *

1. *Significance of presidential statement.* According to the New York Times of January 20, 1972, p. 1, col. 1, the foregoing is the first known explicit presidential statement of the international minimum standard. In the practice of the Department of State, its assertion in diplomatic notes and in claims presentations is well established. Congress, in the two Hickenlopper amendments, pp. 389–393. 22 U.S.C. § 2370(e)(1) and (2), assumes (and thus asserts) its existence. However, the Supreme Court of the United States has been more reserved. In Banco Nacional de Cuba v. Sabbatino, 376 U.S. 398, 84 S.Ct. 923 (1964), the celebrated act of state decision considered in Chapter 6 above, Mr. Justice Harlan, speaking for the majority, observed:

     *   *   *

There are few if any issues in international law today on which opinion seems to be so divided as the limitations on a state's power to expropriate the property of aliens. There is, of course, authority, in international judicial and arbitral decisions, in the expressions of national governments, and among commentators for the view that a taking is improper under international law if it is not for a public purpose, is discriminatory, or is without provision for prompt, adequate, and effective compensation. However, Communist countries, although they have in fact provided a degree of compensation after diplomatic efforts, commonly recognize no obligation on the part of the taking country. Certain representatives of the newly independent and underdeveloped countries have questioned whether rules of state responsibility toward aliens can bind nations that have not consented to them and it is argued that the traditionally articulated standards governing expropriation of property reflect "imperialist" interests and are inappropriate to the circumstances of emergent states.

The disagreement as to relevant international law standards reflects an even more basic divergence between the national interests of capital importing and capital exporting nations and between the social ideologies of those countries that favor state control of a considerable portion of the means of production and those that adhere to a free enterprise system. It is difficult to imagine the courts of this country embarking on adjudication in an area which touches more sensitively the practical and ideological goals of the various members of the community of nations. (at 428–430)

* * *

However, Mr. Justice White, dissenting, stated:

* * *

The Court accepts the application of rules of international law to other aspects of this litigation, accepts the relevance of international law in other cases and announces that when there is an appropriate degree of "consensus concerning a particular area of international law, the more appropriate it is for the judiciary to render decisions regarding it, since the courts can then focus on the application of an agreed principle to circumstances of fact rather than on the sensitive task of establishing a principle not inconsistent with the national interest or with international justice." Ante, p. 428. The Court then, rather lightly in my view, dispenses with its obligation to resolve controversies in accordance with "international justice" and the "national interest" by assuming and declaring that there are no areas of agreement between nations in respect to expropriations. There may not be. But without critical examination, which the Court fails to provide, I would not conclude that a confiscatory taking which discriminates against nationals of another country to retaliate against the government of that country falls within that area of issues in international law "on which opinion seems to be so divided." Nor would I assume, as the ironclad rule of the Court necessarily implies, that there is not likely to be a consensus among nations in this area, as for example upon the illegality of discriminatory takings of alien property based upon race, religion or nationality. But most of all I would not declare that even if there were a clear consensus in the international community, the courts must close their eyes to a lawless act and validate the transgression by rendering judgment for the foreign state at its own request. This is an unfortunate declaration for this Court to make. It is, of course, wholly inconsistent with the premise from which the Court starts, and, under it, banishment of international law from the courts is complete and final in cases like this. I cannot so cavalierly ignore the obligations of a court to dispense justice to the litigants before it. (at 455–56)

*   *   *

2. *Carter administration continued to follow presidential statement.* In connection with the preparation of this edition of the casebook, a very high level official of the Department of State was asked whether the Carter administration accepts and follows the Nixon Doctrine, considering the strong position to the contrary taken by the developing countries (see pp. 1122–1127). By letter that official stated that the presidential policy statement continued to be followed.

3. *The Calvo doctrine.* The doctrinal source of opposition to the concept of an international minimum standard is to be found in the 1868 treatise on international law of Carlos Calvo, Argentine diplomat and publicist. As explained in 5 Hackworth, Digest of International Law 635 (1943), the Calvo doctrine is based upon two fundamental propositions: (i) the sovereign equality of states requires that a state be free from foreign state interference of any sort; (ii) diplomatic protection of an alien's interests is proscribed interference and hence an alien " *   *   *   may seek redress for grievances only before the local [national] authorities." The result of this doctrine is that the alien is entitled to national treatment and no more, thus negating the concept that, whatever a state does to its nationals, it must treat aliens permitted to enter in accordance with the rules of international law setting a minimum standard for such treatment.

Reporter's Note to § 202, Restatement of the Foreign Relations Law of the United States (1965) gives useful information as to the development of Calvo clauses in constitutions, legislation and state contracts with aliens. These clauses require the alien, as a condition of entry, to accept the principles of equality of treatment with nationals and to undertake not to seek diplomatic protection from the state of his nationality. See p. 1161.

4. *The Drago doctrine.* Also of Argentinian origin (1902), it rejects specifically the threat of external force to collect past due public debts; see p. 1123. However, it is postulated on the same derivation from concepts of sovereignty, independence and absolute equality of states as is the Calvo doctrine. The twin doctrines have been widely accepted by scholars and applied by governments in the other American republics.

NOTE FROM THE MEXICAN MINISTER FOR FOREIGN AFFAIRS (HAY) TO THE AMERICAN AMBASSADOR IN MEXICO (DANIELS)

[1940] 5 Foreign Relations of the United States 1019 (1961).

Mexico, May 1, 1940.

Mr. Ambassador: I have the honor to refer to the note sent on the third of last April by the Government of Your Excellency to the Ambassador of Mexico in Washington. * * *

* * * Once more the Government of the United States admits the right of expropriation which for reasons of public utility pertains to every sovereign State, adding that such right is united to and conditioned by the obligation to make an effective, prompt and adequate compensation. For this purpose, it is recalled that in a previous note the government of Your Excellency stated that the structure of international relations in its different phases rests in the respect of governments and peoples for reciprocal rights, according to International Law, and that a prompt and just compensation was part of that structure; a principle professed by all the governments of the world and to which the Government of Mexico has lent its support.

Based on the indisputable facts, it cannot be denied that my Government has shown its utmost respect, by its legal dispositions, to the principle of compensation, as well as its resolution to put it into effect. In a conciliatory spirit, it has avoided introducing into this matter the point of view supported and confirmed by numerous cases that there is not, in International Law, any accepted universal policy in theory or in practice that makes obligatory the payment of immediate compensation, and therefore that immediate indemnization does not constitute an inherent element or a condition to the right of expropriation. Nevertheless, though on different bases, it is pleasing to my Government to recognize that there does not exist any disagreement with the Government of your country regarding the obligation of making payment of due indemnization as imposed on the Mexican Nation by its own laws.

* * *

The Government of Your Excellency concludes proposing that both Governments agree to submit to arbitration the petroleum question, investing a court of justice with the necessary authority, not only to determine the amount to be paid to American nationals deprived of their properties, "but also the means so that its decision may be executed and to assure that an effective and adequate compensation be soon paid".

With this in mind, the Government of Your Excellency makes an appeal to continental solidarity for the principle of arbitration, its use being more commendable because it comes at a time when an increasing contempt for order appears to be in the ascendent and there is a tendency to substitute force for peaceful measures in the friendly solution of these matters.

It pleases me to recognize that Mexico concurs with the ideas of the Government of Your Excellency in a manifestation of its persevering and firmly renewed faith that the moment will come when force will be eliminated as a means of resolving conflicts between States, using only the pacific means adopted by our Continent. If a country of America has constantly maintained its faith in arbitration, it has been Mexico, which has always scrupulously fulfilled the arbitral decisions, even in those cases where the award had been adverse, as in the recent case of Clipperton Island; neither has it failed to recognize the utility of using this means of settling international differences, even though as in the case of Chamizal, an award which was favorable to it has been pending fulfillment on the part of the Government of Your Excellency since 1911.

Nevertheless, my Government does not believe that arbitration should be accepted unless the Nation has fully exercised its rights of sovereignty through the action of its tribunals and it can be proved that denial of justice exists.

* * *

Eduardo Hay

PERMANENT SOVEREIGNTY OVER NATURAL RESOURCES GENERAL ASSEMBLY RESOLUTION 1803 (XVII), DEC. 14, 1962

U.N.Gen.Ass.Off.Rec. 17th Sess., Supp. No. 17 (A/5217), p. 15.

The General Assembly,

Recalling its resolutions 523(VI) of 12 January 1952 and 626(VII) of 21 December 1952,

Bearing in mind its resolution 1314(XIII) of 12 December 1958, by which it established the Commission on Permanent Sovereignty over Natural Resources and instructed it to conduct a full survey of the status of permanent sovereignty over natural wealth and resources as a basic constituent of the right to self-determination, with recommendations, where necessary, for its strengthening and decided further that, in the conduct of the full survey of the status of the permanent sovereignty of peoples and nations over their natural wealth and resources, due regard should be paid to the rights and duties of States under international law and to the importance of encouraging international co-operation in the economic development of developing countries,

Bearing in mind its resolution 1515(XV) of 15 December 1960, in which it recommended that the sovereign right of every State to dispose of its wealth and its natural resources should be respected,

Considering that any measure in this respect must be based on the recognition of the inalienable right of all States freely to dispose of their natural wealth and resources in accordance with their national interests, and on respect for the economic independence of States,

Considering that nothing in paragraph 4 below in any way prejudices the position of any Member State on any aspect of the question of the rights and obligations of successor States and Governments in respect of property acquired before the accession to complete sovereignty of countries formerly under colonial rule,

*   *   *

Desiring that there should be further consideration by the United Nations of the subject of permanent sovereignty over natural resources in the spirit of international co-operation in the field of economic development, particularly that of the developing countries,

I

Declares that:

1.   The right of peoples and nations to permanent sovereignty over their natural wealth and resources must be exercised in the interest of their national development and of the well-being of the people of the State concerned.

2.   The exploration, development and disposition of such resources, as well as the import of the foreign capital required for these purposes, should be in conformity with the rules and conditions which the peoples and nations freely consider to be necessary or desirable with regard to the authorization, restriction or prohibition of such activities.

3.   In cases where authorization is granted, the capital imported and the earnings on that capital shall be governed by the terms thereof, by the national legislation in force, and by international law. The profits derived must be shared in the proportions freely agreed upon, in each case, between the investors and the recipient State, due care being taken to ensure that there is no impairment, for any reason, of that State's sovereignty over its natural wealth and resources.

4.   Nationalization, expropriation or requisitioning shall be based on grounds or reasons of public utility, security or the national interest which are recognized as overriding purely individual or private interests, both domestic and foreign. In such cases the owner shall be paid appropriate compensation, in accordance with the rules in force in the State taking such measures in the exercise of its sovereignty and in accordance with international law. In any case where the question of compensation gives rise to a controversy, the national jurisdiction of the State taking such measures shall be exhausted. However, upon agreement by sovereign States and other parties concerned, settlement of the dispute should be made through arbitration or international adjudication.

5.   The free and beneficial exercise of the sovereignty of peoples and nations over the their natural resources must be furthered by the mutual respect of States based on their sovereign equality.

*   *   *

8.   Foreign investment agreements freely entered into by or between sovereign States shall be observed in good faith; States and international organizations shall strictly and conscientiously respect the sovereignty of peoples and nations over their natural wealth and resources in accordance with the Charter and the principles set forth in the present resolution.

*   *   *

Comment on the 1962 Resolution. The capital exporting countries were seriously taxed, even in 1962, to get modifications favorable to an international minimum standard for direct foreign investment into an initiative taken by a group of developing countries to assert permanent sovereignty over natural resources. The 1962 Resolution also called for "further consideration" of the permanent sovereignty issue " *   *   * in the field of economic development." Somewhat over a decade later there were the developments at the United Nations which are presented in the material following the next case.

BARCELONA TRACTION, LIGHT AND POWER CO., LTD. (BELGIUM v. SPAIN)

International Court of Justice, 1970.
[1970] I.C.J.Rep. 3.

[The decision was on a narrow issue, the question whether Belgium had standing to espouse claims of its nationals who owned the majority of the shares of a corporation organized in Canada. In the course of 303 pages of separate opinions by members of a court, who except for one judge ad hoc, agreed on the disposition of the case almost every aspect of the nationalization problem as it concerns investments in the corporate form is discussed by one or more of the judges. The selections that follow deal with the international minimum standard. It is perhaps revealing that the dispositive opinion and some of the separate opinions assume it exists. Other views, pro and con, are more explicitly stated.]

Separate Opinion of Judge TANAKA, at pp. 115, 116.

*   *   *

Here, it is not necessary to emphasize the spirit of a universally recognized rule of customary international law concerning every State's right of diplomatic protection over its nationals abroad, that is, a right to require that another State observe a certain standard of decent treatment to aliens in its territory. *   *   *

*   *   *

Briefly, the idea of diplomatic protection does not seem to be a blind extension of the sovereign power of a State to the territory of other countries; the spirit of this institution signifies the collaboration of the protecting State for the cause of the rule of law and justice.

* * *

Separate Opinion of Judge JESSUP at p. 162, 164–167

* * *

10.   In adjudicating upon the Barcelona Traction case the Court must apply rules from one of the most controversial branches of international law.   The subject of the responsibility of States for injuries to aliens (otherwise referred to as the diplomatic protection of nationals), evokes in many current writings recollections of political abuses in past eras.   The Court is not involved here in any conflict between great capital-exporting States and States in course of development.   Belgium and Spain are States which, in those terms, belong in the same grouping.   I do not agree with the Spanish contention on 20 May 1969 that Belgium was merely trying to get the Court to internationalize a private litigation, but it is true that basically the conflict was between a powerful Spanish financial group and a comparable non-Spanish group.   This case cannot be said to evoke problems of "neo-colonialism".

Moreover, the Court is not here in the least concerned with such provocative problems as State sovereignty over natural resources or the rules applicable to compensation in case of nationalizations or expropriations.   Professor F. V. García Amador, in his sixth report as Special Rapporteur of the International Law Commission on State responsibility (Yearbook of the International Law Commission, 1961, Vol. II, p. 2 at p. 46), set forth an admirable attitude:

> * * * his purpose was to take into account the profound changes which are occurring in international law, in so far as they are capable of affecting the traditional ideas and principles relating to responsibility.   The only reason why, in this endeavour, he rejected notions or opinions for which acceptance is being sought in our time, is that he firmly believes that any notion or opinion which postulates extreme positions—whatever may be the underlying purpose or motive—is incompatible and irreconcilable with the idea of securing the recognition and adequate legal protection of all the legitimate interests involved. That has been the policy followed by the Commission hitherto and no doubt will continue to be its policy in the future.

11.   The institution "of the right to give diplomatic protection to nationals abroad was recognized in * * * the Vienna Convention on Diplomatic Relations, 1961", as Mr. Gros (as he then was) reminded the sub-committee of the International Law Commission (Yearbook of the International Law Commission, 1963, Vol. II, p. 230).   The institution of the right to give diplomatic protection is surely not obsolete although new procedures are emerging.

With reference to diplomatic protection of corporate interests, the customary international law began to change in the latter half of

the nineteenth century. As Jennings writes, in somewhat pictur-
esque and Kiplingesque language:

> It is small wonder that difficulties arise when 19th century
> precedents about outrageous behaviour towards aliens residing in
> outlandish parts are sought to be pressed into service to yield
> principles apposite to sophisticated programmes of international
> investment. (121 Hague Recueil 1967, II, p. 473.)

Since the critical date in this case is 1948, developments in the law
and procedures during the ensuing last two decades are not controlling.

12. Any court's application of a rule of law to a particular case,
involves an interpretation of the rule. Historical and logical and teleological tools may be used by the judge, consciously or unconsciously. If the Court in the instant case had decided to include more factors in its Judgment, it could have clarified the traditional system in
the light of clearer understandings of business practices and forms of
corporate organization, as these were already well developed two decades ago when the events called into question in this case transpired.
Legal norms applicable to those events should not be swept aside on
the assumption that they have already become mere cobwebs in the
attics of legal history. Corporations today and tommorow may well
utilize other methods of financing and controlling foreign enterprises,
and governments will have adapted or will adapt their own laws and
practices to meet the realities of the economic factors which affect
the general interests of the State. The "law of international economic development" will mature. Thus joint business ventures, State
guarantees of foreign investment, the use of international organizations such as the IBRD and UNDP, may in the course of time rele-
gate the case of Barcelona Traction to the status now occupied by De-
lagoa Bay—a precedent to be cited by advocates if helpful to the
pleading of a cause, but not a guiding element in the life of the international business community.

Nevertheless, the Court has the duty to settle a specific dispute
between Belgium and Spain which arose out of Spain's exercising
jurisdiction over a complex of foreign corporate enterprises.

13. There is a trend in the direction of extending the jurisdictional power of the State to deal with foreign enterprises which have
contact with the State's territorial domain; " * * * all that can
be required of a State is that it should not overstep the limits which
international law places upon its jurisdiction; within these limits, its
title to exercise jurisdiction rests in its sovereignty." But what are
the limits placed by international law? Do the courts of the United
States, for example, go too far in applying its anti-trust laws to foreign enterprises, following the statement of principle by Judge Hand
in Alcoa? But that principle is accepted in at least six other countries. Are the jurisdictional limits on national jurisdiction exceeded
in the cases dealing with product liability of a "giant octopus corporation" with multiple subsidiaries abroad? Rules valid enough for

interstate conflicts within the constitutional system of the United States, may be improper when placing a burden on international commerce. The Committee on International Law of the Association of the Bar of the City of New York concluded that " * * * the extension of the regulatory and penal provisions of the Securities Exchange Act of 1934 * * * to foreign corporations which have neither listed securities in the United States nor publicly offered securities within the United States is a violation of international law".

14. In States having different types of economic and financial problems, international law has become increasingly permissive of actions involving nationalizations. In place of what used to be denounced as illegal expropriation, the issues now turn largely on the measure of compensation, since even the famous General Assembly Resolution on Permanent Sovereignty Over Natural Resources, provides that compensation is due.

Separate Opinion of Judge PADILLA NERVO at p. 244, 246–250

* * *

The history of the responsibility of States in respect to the treatment of foreign nationals is the history of abuses, illegal interference in the domestic jurisdiction of weaker States, unjust claims, threats and even military aggression under the flag of exercising rights of protection, and the imposing of sanctions in order to oblige a government to make the reparations demanded.

Special agreements to establish arbitral tribunals were on many occasions concluded under pressure, by political, economic or military threats.

The protecting States, in many instances, are more concerned with obtaining financial settlements than with preserving principles. Against the pressure of diplomatic protection, weaker States could do no more than to preserve and defend a principle of international law, while giving way under the guise of accepting friendly settlements, either giving the compensation demanded or by establishing claims commissions which had as a point of departure the acceptance of responsibility for acts or omissions, where the government was, neither in fact nor in law, really responsible.

In the written and in the oral pleadings the Applicant has made reference, in support of his thesis, to arbitral decisions of claims commissions—among others those between Mexico and the United States, 1923.

These decisions do not necessarily give expression to rules of customary international law, as * * * the Commissions were authorized to decide these claims "in accordance with principles of international law, justice and equity" and, therefore, may have been influenced by other than strictly legal considerations. (Schwarzenberger, International Law, Vol. I, p. 201.)

In the Special Claims Commission: Mexico-United States, established by the convention of 10 September 1923, Article II states:

> * * * each member of the Commission * * * shall make and subscribe a solemn declaration stating that he will * * * examine and decide, according to the best of his judgment and in accordance with the principles of *justice and equity* all claims presented for decision * * *. (Italics are mine.)

The second paragraph of the same Article II reads as follows:

> The Mexican Government desires that the claims shall be so decided because Mexico wishes that her responsibility shall not be fixed according to the generally accepted rules and principles of international law, but ex gratia feels morally bound to make full indemnification and agrees, therefore * * * (U.N.R.I. A.A., Vol. IV, p. 780.)

Article VI of the same convention makes another exception to the accepted general rules, when it states:

> * * * the Mexican Government agrees that the Commission shall not disallow or reject any claim by the application of the general principle of international law that the legal remedies must be exhausted as a condition precedent to the validity or allowance of any claim. (Ibid., p. 781.)

Some of the decisions of claims commissions invoked during the pleadings are not, in my view, relevant precedents in respect to this case.

Now the evolution of international law has other horizons and its progressive development is more promising, as Rosenne wrote:

> There is prevalent in the world today a widespread questioning of the contemporary international law. This feeling is based on the view that for the greater part international law is the product of European imperialism and colonialism and does not take sufficient account of the completely changed pattern of international relations which now exists. * * *

> Careful scrutiny of the record of the Court may lead to the conclusion that it has been remarkably perceptive of the changing currents of internationalist thought. In this respect it has performed a major service to the international community as a whole, because the need to bring international law into line with present-day requirements and conditions is real and urgent. (Rosenne, The Law and Practice of the International Court, 1965, Vol. I, pp. 17–18.)

The law, in all its aspects, the jurisprudence and the practice of States change, as the world and the everyday requirements of international life change, but those responsible for its progressive evolution should take care that their decisions do, in the long run, contribute to the maintenance of peace and security and to the betterment of the majority of mankind.

In considering the needs and the good of the international community in our changing world, one must realize that there are more important aspects than those concerned with economic interests and profit making; other legitimate interests of a political and moral nature are at stake and should be considered in judging the behaviour and operation of the complex international scope of modern commercial enterprises.

It is not the shareholders in those huge corporations who are in need of diplomatic protection; it is rather the poorer or weaker States, where the investments take place, who need to be protected against encroachment by powerful financial groups, or against unwarranted diplomatic pressure from governments who appear to be always ready to back at any rate their national shareholders, even when they are legally obliged to share the risk of their corporation and follow its fate, or even in case of shareholders who are not or have never been under the limited jurisdiction of the State of residence accused of having violated in respect of them certain fundamental rights concerning the treatment of foreigners. It can be said that, by the mere fact of the existence of certain rules concerning the treatment of foreigners, these have certain fundamental rights that the State of residence cannot violate without incurring international responsibility; but this is not the case of foreign shareholders as such, who may be scattered all over the world and have never been or need not be residents of the respondent State or under its jurisdiction.

In the case of the Rosa Gelbtrunk claim between Salvador and the United States, the President of the arbitration commission expressed a view which may summarize the position of foreigners in a country where they are resident. This view was expressed as follows:

> A citizen or subject of one nation who, in the pursuit of commercial enterprise, carries on trade within the territory and under the protection of the sovereignty of a nation other than his own, is to be considered *as having cast in his lot* with the subjects or citizens of the State in which he *resides* and carries on business. (Italics added.)

"In this case", Schwarzenberger remarks, "the rule was applied to the loss of foreign property in the course of a civil war. The decision touches, however, one aspect of a much wider problem: the existence of international minimum standards, by which, regarding foreigners, territorial jurisdiction is limited."

As the Permanent Court of International Justice said in the Lotus case in 1927 (P.C.I.J., Series A, No. 10, p. 19)—

> all that can be required of a State is that it should not overstep the limits which international law places upon its jurisdiction; within these limits, its title to exercise jurisdiction rests in its sovereignty.

The rules concerning the treatment of foreigners are a limitation of a State's jurisdiction ratione personae. Schwarzenberger says in this respect:

> States generally exercise exclusive jurisdiction over their nationals within their territory, concurrent jurisdiction over their nationals abroad, and limited jurisdiction over, for example, individuals and groups within their territory who are protected by international customary or treaty law.
>
> While, in principle, territorial sovereignty applies to nationals and foreigners alike, the home State retains a concurrent jurisdiction over its nationals abroad. * * * Furthermore, the unrestricted exercise of territorial jurisdiction over foreigners on the part of the State of residence may be limited by rules of international customary law or treaties. If such exercise of territorial jurisdiction happens to come into conflict with international law, the question turns into an issue between the subjects of international law concerned. The home State is entitled to demand respect for international limitations of territorial jurisdiction, and the State of residence may have to answer for its interference "with the rights which each State may claim for its national in foreign territory." As the World Court laid down in the case of the Mavrommatis Palestine Concessions (1924), "it is an elementary principle of international law that a State is entitled to protect its subjects, when injured by acts contrary to international law committed by another State, from whom they have been unable to obtain satisfaction through the ordinary channels." (Schwarzenberger, International Law, Vol. I, pp. 189–190.)

Much has been said about the justification for not leaving the shareholders in those enterprises without protection.

Perhaps modern international business practice has a tendency to be soft and partial towards the powerful and the rich, but no rule of law could be built on such flimsy bases.

Investors who go abroad in search of profits take a risk and go there for better or for worse, not only for better. They should respect the institutions and abide by the national laws of the country where they chose to go.

　　* * *

Separate Opinion of Judge AMMOUN at p. 287, 290–295

　　* * *

5. In this connection, it is essential to stress the trends of Latin-American law and that of Asia and Africa, and their undeniable influence on the development of traditional international law.

It seems indeed that among the principles and norms which have sprung from the regional law peculiar to Latin America are the norms and principles whose aim is to protect countries in that part of the world against the more powerful industrialized States of North America and Europe.

An Afro-Asian law also seems to be developing as a result of the same preoccupations, springing from the same causes. In the field of the responsibility of States and of diplomatic protection, the same points of view have been adopted in the countries of the three continents, thus initiating a form of co-operation which will not be of slight effect on the renewal of law.

The first reaction to the rules of traditional law came however from the countries of Latin America; witness the vehement speech made by Mr. Seijas, a former Venezuelan minister, at the 1891 Session of the Institut de droit international at Hamburg, which was no mere display of bad temper. Evidence of this too is the appearance of the Calvo Clause, excluding recourse to international adjudication in favour of internal remedies, on which the jurists of Latin America have never compromised, because of their lack of confidence in diplomatic protection as conceived by traditional law and the practices of western nations. This reaction on the part of the Latin American States would, moreover, explain their opposition from 1948 onwards to the draft insurance guarantee agreement proposed by the United States, providing for the exercise of diplomatic protection by that power without local remedies having been exhausted.

This attitude on the part of the Hispanic States, which is shared by the Afro-Asian States, is the more readily understandable if the extra-legal forms and means to which diplomatic protection formerly had recourse are borne in mind. It will be recalled that the claims of great States and their nationals abroad often led, during the period preceding the renewal of the law consequent upon two world wars and the creation of a means of international adjudication, to acute conflicts and to acts of deliberate violence going so far as armed intervention and permanent occupation, or to demonstrations of force, against which the Drago doctrine, which was endorsed by the Pan-American Conference of 1906 and has since become one of the basic principles of Latin American international law, has, since 1926, reacted not without success. Recourse to force, subject to an offer of arbitration, was nevertheless tolerated by The Hague Peace Conference of 1907, which admitted intervention sub modo by virtue of the Porter Convention, against which Convention Drago and his Latin American colleagues vainly protested at the Conference. This was not the least of the contradictions which attended it, contradictions which bespeak the still predominant influence of the colonialist era. Accordingly, one is entitled to suspect certain arbitral decisions of having been agreed to or accepted under duress, those decisions having been preceded by ultimata or menaces or by a deployment of force more or less in the spirit of the said Conference, which was struggling to free itself from a tyrannical tradition.

If the Drago doctrine has finally triumphed, and if the Porter Convention, on the insistence of Mexico, expressing Latin American opinion at the Chapultepec Conference in 1945, is now recognized as incompatible with the terms of Article 103 of the United Nations Charter, it is nevertheless the case that many decisions have not avoided all confusion between reparation sticto sensu, as in private municipal law, and the "satisfaction" demanded by powerful States, which gives reparation lato sensu the character of a measure aimed at deterrence or punishment. This right to punish, which is arrogated to themselves by certain States, and to which such eminent writers as Bluntschli, Liszt and Fauchille, as well as a 1927 resolution of the Institut de droit international have lent their authority, seems to have been rejected by Anzilotti, who noted that in all forms of reaction against the unlawful act there were present " * * * an element of satisfaction and an element of reparation, the notion of punishment of the unlawful act and that of reparation for the wrong suffered". Thus, the opposition of Latin American or Afro-Asian jurists to the western conception of responsibility and diplomatic protection is founded not only on memories of a painful past, but also on serious apprehensions.

The development of Latin American thought concerning diplomatic protection and its limits must be particularly stressed in the present discussion, on account of the influence which it can have on the development of that institution. This thought is at present centered on the following aspects of the problem:

A. The 20 States of South and Central America all reject the rule laid down by Vatel and endorsed by the Permanent Court of International Justice, according to which the right of diplomatic protection is "to ensure, in the person of its subjects, respect for the rules of international law". They hold it to be a fiction, which one of their most eminent jurists, Garcia Robles, has described as "a product of Hegelian influence, resulting from the expansionism of the nineteenth century". And all these States, at inter-American conferences, in the writings of publicists, in the positions adopted by governments, are united in their efforts for its elimination, on the understanding that the individual's status as a subject of the law is to be recognized thus enabling him to seek legal redress himself, and not under the cloak of his national State. But before what tribunal? Before an American regional tribunal. The resolution submitted to the Inter-American Conference at Buenos Aires and adopted almost unanimously reads: "American legal controversies should be decided by American judges * * * and a correct understanding of acts pertaining to the Americas is more readily to be obtained by Americans themselves".

Since the same causes produce the same effects, the States of the Organization of African Unity wrote into the Addis Ababa Charter the same objective of the creation of a regional tribunal.

The countries of Latin America have gone further still. In 1948 they unanimously adopted a resolution at Bogotá whereby they undertook not to bring a claim before a court of international jurisdiction, not excluding the International Court of Justice.

B.   The States of Latin America remain firmly attached to the Calvo Clause, which they habitually insert in contracts entered into with foreign undertakings.   Their constitutions and laws generally make it compulsory.   Their doctrine with regard thereto, founded upon the two principles of equality between States and non-intervention, was forcefully expressed by Judge Guerrero, a former President of the Court, in the report which he submitted on behalf of the Subcommittee set up by the Committee of Experts of the League of Nations to study the responsibility of States.   Several non-American countries were not hostile to this point of view.   China, Holland and Finland were frankly favourable to it.   Finally, the United States, which had found in Borchard a vigorous defender of the thesis that the individual cannot dispose of a right which, according to Vatelian doctrine, is that of the State and not his own, allowed itself to be won over, with the inauguration of the "good neighbour" policy of F. D. Roosevelt, to the doctrine of its southern neighbours.

C.   The Calvo Clause, which on the other side of the Atlantic is regarded merely as a compromise, was destined to prepare the way for the adoption of the Calvo doctrine, which is aimed at nothing less than the abolition of unilateral diplomatic protection in order to substitute for it a protection exercised by the collectivity on the basis of human rights.

The path towards this unconcealed objective is certainly a long and arduous one; its success seems bound up with the progress of mankind towards an inter-American or international organization less removed than the United Nations from the concept of the Super-State.

*   *   *

It was the more necessary to recall these features of American law in that other States are treading the same path towards the limitation of diplomatic protection.   The States of Africa and of Asia, since they too have come to participate in international life, share the same concerns,—as witness the proceedings of the International Law Commission.   At its Ninth Session in 1957, Mr. Padilla Nervo stated that:

*   *   *   the history of the institution of State responsibility was the history of the obstacles placed in the way of the new Latin American countries—obstacles to the defence of their *   *   *   independence, to the ownership and development of their resources, and to their social integration.

And he added:

With State responsibility   *   *   *   international rules were established, not merely without reference to small States but against them.

And Mr. El-Erian, of the United Arab Republic, stressed the twofold consequence of the privileged condition accorded to nationals of Western countries in their relations with the countries of Africa or Asia, which on the one hand had led to the system of capitulations and on the other afforded a pretext for intervention in the domestic affairs of States.

The similarity of the essential views and objectives of the States of the three continents of America, Africa and Asia, and the action they are able to take to develop a positive international law of world-wide ambit, will tend to direct them toward a universalist concept of law and bring them back to a system of international adjudication which will no longer be of an exclusive nature but will, through its effective composition, meet the wishes expressed in the United Nations Charter, which would have it represent the main legal systems and principal forms of civilization of the world.

It is in the light of these preliminary considerations that the connected problem of diplomatic protection and the jus standi of the applicant State should have been approached.

*   *   *

A WORLD DIVIDED ON AN ISSUE: THE LAW GOVERNING NATIONALIZATIONS OF DIRECT FOREIGN INVESTMENT

1. *Further consideration at the General Assembly.* Judge Jessup, at the end of the excerpt from his separate opinion, cites the 1962 Resolution to support a proposition that "the issues now turn largely on the measure of compensation." However, later developments in the General Assembly at the initiative of the Group of Seventy-Seven Countries (the developing countries in the United Nations Commission on Trade and Development (UNCTAD) that actually number perhaps 130) challenge the notion of an international minimum standard, even as to substantive rights of investors, to say nothing of the existence of rules as to international remedies. In brief summary: (a) in May, 1972, UNCTAD called for the formulation of a charter to establish a just and stable world order based on the protection of the rights of all countries but in particular the developing states; (b) a working group was designated to deal with this task by the General Assembly; (c) the General Assembly by various intermediate resolutions continued to favor this project and on May 1, 1974, approved Resolutions 3201 (S-VI) and 3202 (S-VI), the first a declaration and the second an action plan on the Establishment of a New International Economic Order, 28 Yearbook of the United Nations 305–339 (1974); and (d) on December 12, 1974, the General Assembly voted 120 to 6, with 10 abstentions, for a Charter of Economic Rights and Duties of States. The six negative votes came from Belgium, Denmark, the Federal Republic of Germany, Luxembourg, the United Kingdom and the United States. Canada, France, Japan and the Netherlands were among the abstaining countries. 28

Yearbook of the United Nations 381, 391, 402, 402–407 (1974).   Article 2 specifies the rights of states to include the right:

> (c) To nationalize, expropriate or transfer ownership of foreign property, in which case appropriate compensation should be paid by the State adopting such measures, taking into account its relevant laws and regulations and all circumstances that the State considers pertinent.   In any case where the question of compensation gives rise to a controversy, it shall be settled under the domestic law of the nationalizing State and by its tribunals, unless it is freely and mutually agreed by all States concerned that other peaceful means be sought on the basis of the sovereign equality of States and in accordance with the principle of free choice of means.

2.   *What is the law today?*   Is the charter law?   If not, is the heavy supporting majority in the General Assembly the best evidence today of customary international law?   Developing countries have claimed validity for the charter, either as an overriding political principle or as law from one source or the other.   The following nationalization dispute has directly involved these questions, but you must judge the strength of the arbitrator's disposition as a resolution of the issue because of the peculiar circumstances of the arbitral proceedings.

TEXACO OVERSEAS PETROLEUM CO. AND CALIFORNIA ASIATIC OIL CO v. THE GOVERNMENT OF THE LIBYAN ARAB REPUBLIC

Dupuy, Sole Arbitrator
Award on the Merits, 1977.
53 Int'l L.Rep. 389, 486 (1979).*

[Had the Sole Arbitrator's award been a judgment of the International Court of Justice, it would have had to be excerpted herein as many times as the Barcelona Traction case is, for it reaches many points and decides them in the foreign investor's favor.   It deals with the effect of the General Assembly resolutions discussed supra.

The arbitrator decided that the arbitration clause in the concession agreements referred to international law as the rule of decision, rather than the national law of the host state.   Then the Sole Arbitrator directed himself to the content of the "international law" that was to govern.   One aspect of that problem is the one dealt with here.

A portion of the arbitral award appears below.]

83.   The general question of the legal validity of the Resolutions of the United Nations has been widely discussed by the *writers.* [Emphasis supplied.]   *   *   *

* Reprinted by permission of E. Lauterpacht, ed., and Grotius Publications,
Ltd., Cambridge, England.

84. * * * Resolution 1803 (XVII) of 14 December 1962 was passed by the General Assembly by 87 votes to 2, with 12 abstentions. It is particularly important to note that the majority voted for this text, including many States of the Third World, but also several Western developed countries with market economies, including the most important one, the United States. The principles stated in this Resolution were therefore assented to by a great many States representing not only all geographical areas but also all economic systems.

From this point of view, this Tribunal notes that the affirmative vote of several developed countries with a market economy was made possible in particular by the inclusion in the Resolution of two references to international law; and one passage relating to the importance of international cooperation for economic development. According to the representative of Tunisia:

> * * * the result of the debate on this question was that the balance of the original draft resolution was improved—a balance between, on the one hand, the unequivocal affirmation of the inalienable right of States to exercise sovereignty over their natural resources and, on the other hand, the reconciliation or adaptation of this sovereignty to international law, equity and the principles of international cooperation. (17 U.N. GAOR 1122, U.N. Doc. A/PV. 1193 (1962).)

The reference to international law, in particular in the field of nationalization, was therefore an essential factor in the support given by several Western countries to Resolution 1803 (XVII).

85. * * *

The conditions under which Resolution 3281 (XXIX) proclaiming the Charter of Economic Rights and Duties of States, was adopted also show unambiguously that there was no general consensus of the States with respect to the most important provisions and in particular those concerning nationalization. Having been the subject matter of a roll-call vote, the Charter was adopted by 118 votes to 6, with 10 abstentions. The analysis of votes on specific sections of the Charter is most significant insofar as the present case is concerned. From this point of view, paragraph 2(c) of Article 2 of the Charter, which limits consideration of the characteristics of compensation to the State and does not refer to international law, was voted by 104 to 16, with 6 abstentions, all of the industrialized countries with market economies having abstained or having voted against it.

86. * * *

As this Tribunal has already indicated, the legal value of the resolutions which are relevant to the present case can be determined on the basis of circumstances under which they were adopted and by analysis of the principles which they state:

With respect to the first point, the absence of any binding force of the resolutions of the General Assembly of the United Nations implies that such resolutions must be accepted by the members of the

United Nations in order to be legally binding. In this respect, the Tribunal notes that only Resolution 1803 (XVII) of 14 December 1962 was supported by a majority of Member States representing all of the various groups. By contrast, the other Resolutions mentioned above, and in particular those referred to in the Libyan Memorandum, were supported by a majority of States but not by any of the developed countries with market economies which carry on the largest part of international trade.

87. With repect to * * * the appraisal of the legal value on the basis of the principles stated, it appears essential to this Tribunal to distinguish between those provisions stating the existence of a right on which the generality of the States has expressed agreement and those provisions introducing new principles which were rejected by certain representative groups of States and having nothing more than a *de lege ferenda* value only in the eyes of the States which have adopted them; as far as the others are concerned, the rejection of these same principles implies that they consider them as being *contra legem*. With respect to the former, which proclaim rules recognized by the community of nations, they do not create a custom but confirm one by formulating it and specifying its scope, thereby making it possible to determine whether or not one is confronted with a legal rule. As has been noted by Ambassador Castañeda, "[such resolutions] do not create the law; they have a declaratory nature of noting what does exist" (129 R.C.A.D.I. 204 (1970), at 315).

On the basis of the circumstances of adoption mentioned above and by expressing an *opinio juris communis*, Resolution 1803 (XVII) seems to this Tribunal to reflect the state of customary law existing in this field. Indeed, on the occasion of the vote on a resolution finding the existence of a customary rule, the States concerned clearly express their views. The consensus by a majority of States belonging to the various representative groups indicates without the slightest doubt universal recognition of the rules therein incorporated, *i. e.*, with respect to nationalization and compensation the use of the rules in force in the nationalizing State, but all this in conformity with international law.

* * *

89. Such an attitude is further reinforced by an examination of the general practice of relations between States with respect to investments. This practice is in conformity, not with the provisions of Article 2(c) of the above-mentioned Charter conferring exclusive jurisdiction on domestic legislation and courts, but with the exception stated at the end of this paragraph. Thus a great many investment agreements entered into between industrial States or their nationals, on the one hand, and developing countries, on the other, state, in an objective way, the standards of compensation and further provide, in case of dispute regarding the level of such compensation, the possibility of resorting to an international tribunal. In this respect, it is

particularly significant in the eyes of this Tribunal that no fewer than 65 States, as of 31 October 1974, had ratified the Convention on the Settlement of Investment Disputes between States and Nationals of other States, dated March 18, 1965.

* * *

Question. How do you think each of the four judges whose separate opinions are excerpted in Barcelona Traction (p. 1116) would have ruled, seriatim, on the issue of the resolutions as international law?

BP EXPLORATION CO. (LIBYA) LTD. v. GOVERNMENT OF THE LIBYAN ARAB REPUBLIC

Lagergren, Sole Arbitrator (1973 and 1974).
53 Int'l.L.Rep. 297, 327, 329, 354 (1979).

[The plaintiffs in the arbitration proceeding reported immediately above distributed widely copies of the award by Dupuy, Sole Arbitrator, in 1979. Not until 1979 did a contradictory award in an earlier, parallel case come to light. The Dupuy and the Lagergren awards are published one after the other in the above volume of the International Law Reports. Why do you suppose the Lagergren award was, if not kept secret, not given any publicity?]

3. *Applicable Law*

* * *

The Tribunal cannot accept the submission that international law applies. * * * Nor does the BP Concession itself constitute a source of law controlling the relationship between the Parties * * *.

[The arbitrator discusses the legal fundamentals:]

A rule of reason therefore dictates a result which conforms both to international law, as evidenced by State practice and the law of treaties, and to the governing principle of English and American contract law. This is that, when by the exercise of sovereign power a State has committed a fundamental breach of a concession agreement by repudiating it through a nationalisation of the enterprise and its assets in a manner which implies finality, the concessionaire is not entitled to call for specific performance by the Government of the agreement and reinstatement of his contractual rights, but his sole remedy is an action for damages.

For these reasons, the Tribunal cannot accept the Claimant's principal proposition with respect to the issue now under consideration, and the Claimant cannot be granted the relief asked for in the requested Declarations Nos. 2, 3 and 4 (see Part V above); the requested Declaration No. 6, being predicated on Nos. 2 and 3, also cannot be made. The BP Concession can be said to remain in force and effect as a contractual instrument only in the sense that it forms the basis of the jurisdiction of the Tribunal and of the right of the Claimant to claim damages from the Respondent before the Tribunal.

---

2. TYPES OF ECONOMIC INTERESTS TREATED AS ENTITLED TO DIPLOMATIC PROTECTION

Perspective. Here the focus is on what types of economic interests the state of nationality or other state entitled to make the claim will recognize and the host state will accept as constituting a taking of property. In many situations there is no problem in this regard. There is common agreement that land, physical things (artifacts), patents, copyrights, bank balances and other book assets are property for nationalization claims purposes. At the other extreme, the mere prospect of having made a gain is not property. When a business enterprise is taken from an alien the manner in which he holds his ownership interests therein may become important in the context of the present inquiry. In the field of direct foreign investment in minerals extraction and disposal for profit, the civil and the common law tend to have different viewpoints as to whether authorizations to explore, mine or drill, and remove create interests in property. In the common law world they do. The recipient of the authorization either has an estate in determinable fee simple in the subsurface, an incorporeal hereditament (profit à prendre), or a lessee's rights under a mining lease. But in most of Latin America, all subsurface minerals property pertains to the state, and the state is not authorized to alienate such property. A concession contract in such a country is not a grant of a real property interest; it is a contract with the state under which the private party is licensed to explore, extract and market.

In several notable instances in Latin America, some governments sought to convey to foreign investors property in sub-surface minerals in disregard of this fundamental notion. Nonetheless, it is usually not argued in extractive industries nationalization cases that a minerals concession is not property. There is less general agreement about losses by aliens due to the cancellation or non-performance by the state of other types of contracts with aliens.

In nationalization cases valuation is often a serious problem. However, in several nationalizations in Latin America the regime in control of the state has not contested its general responsibility to pay compensation, or even the amount, but has sought to offset the claim with charges for alleged back taxes, improper exploitation or illegality ab initio of removals, despite the good faith nature of the alien's operation. Whether such situations will fall into the category of denial of justice or be dealt with as defenses to taking cannot now be foretold.

CREDITORS' CLAIMS: EARLY POLICY OF UNITED STATES DEPARTMENT OF STATE

VI Moore, Digest of International Law 707 (1906).

* * *

How far it may be justifiable or expedient formally to press all the claims upon the French Government for immediate payment is a consideration to be distinguished from the clear opinion which is entertained of their intrinsic justice. Wherever they originated in compulsory measures practiced upon the claimants, they are entitled to a full and immediate interposition of their Government; but where the bills have been received by virtue of voluntary contracts, whether with the agents of the French Government or individuals, the receivers, having regard, as they must have had, to the degree of credit and punctuality ascribed to that Government, at the period of their speculation, any calculation and consequent disappointment ought not to be permitted to embarrass their own Government by binding it to pursue very pointed measures for their relief. (at 707)

You appear not fully to have understood your powers and duties under the law of nations in regard to claims of American citizens on foreign governments. I can not explain these more clearly than by extracting a few sentences from a letter dated on the 11th November, 1847, and addressed by this Department to Vice-President Dallas, in answer to an application made by him in behalf of an American citizen. The extract follows: "It has been the practice of this Department to confine its official action in the recovery of indemnity from foreign governments to tortious acts committed under their authority against the persons and property of our citizens. In the case of violation of contract, the rule has been not to interfere, unless under very peculiar circumstances, and then only to instruct our diplomatic agents abroad to use their good offices in behalf of American citizens with the Governments to which they are accredited. The distinction between claims arising from torts and from contracts is, I believe, recognized by all nations, and the reasons for this distinction will readily occur to your own mind." This letter was carefully considered and adopted by the President and the entire Cabinet. I might add, that if this were not the rule, governments, and especially our Government, would be involved in endless difficulties. Our citizens go abroad over the whole world and enter into contracts with all foreign governments. In doing this they must estimate the character of those with whom they contract and assume the risk of their ability and will to execute their contracts. Upon a different principle, it would become the duty of the Government of our country to enforce the payment of loans made by its citizens and subjects to the government of another country. This might prove exceedingly inconvenient to some of the States of this Union as well as to other sovereign States. (at 708, 709)

* * *

CREDITORS' CLAIMS: LATER POLICY OF UNITED STATES DEPARTMENT OF STATE

8 Whiteman, Digest of International Law 933 (1967).

In response to a letter requesting information on steps which the United States Government could take to protect the interests of United States bondholders affected by the default of the Government of Cuba on payments of principal and interest on bonds, the policy of the Department of State with regard thereto was explained as follows:

A default in the payment of principal or interest on bonds of foreign governments is considered by the Department primarily a matter for direct negotiation and settlement by the American bondholders or their representatives and the foreign government concerned. The Department is, however, always ready to facilitate such negotiations and settlements when possible, but it has been its consistent policy, repeatedly stated by various Secretaries of State, generally to decline to intervene in the enforcement of such obligations, except under very unusual circumstances, as, for example, where American nationals are discriminated against in connection with payments made by a foreign government on its obligations.

It was because of this policy that the Government in the fall of 1933 encouraged the creation of the Foreign Bondholders Protective Council, a private nonprofit organization, with the view that it would assist the numerous and scattered American holders of defaulted foreign government securities in the protection of their interests. The Council has offices at 90 Broad Street, New York, New York. As it functions entirely independently of the Government, this reference to it is, of course, made without responsibility on the part of the Department.

The Department will consider the bonds to which you have referred in the event that a general settlement of claims against Cuba becomes feasible or in the event that unusual circumstances arise with respect to the bonds, such as those mentioned above.

* * *

* * * [The Foreign Bondholders Protective Council, Inc.] was formed in 1933 by its original directors upon request of Mr. Cordell Hull, Secretary of State, Mr. W. H. Woodin, Secretary of the Treasury, and Mr. Charles H. March, Chairman of the Federal Trade Commission, who expressed the need for "an adequate and disinterested organization for the protection of American holders of foreign securities," this problem being of such "great and urgent importance to American investors, and of such public significance as to make its proper handling a public service."

The White House announcement to the press on October 20, 1933 stated that the making of satisfactory arrangements and protecting

American interests was "a task primarily for private initiative and interests. The traditional policy of the American Government has been that such loan and investment transactions were primarily private actions, to be handled by the parties directly concerned. The Government realizes a duty, within the proper limits of international law and international amity, to defend American interests abroad. However, it would not be wise for the Government to undertake directly the settlement of private debt situations."

As a consequence, the Council was incorporated December 13, 1933 under the laws of the State of Maryland as a non-stock, non-profit organization. Among the purposes for which the corporation was formed is that of protecting the rights and interests of American holders of publicly offered dollar bonds issued or guaranteed by foreign governments and their political subdivisions.

BOND CLAIMS AGAINST BLOCKED ASSETS

8 Whiteman, Digest of International Law 952 (1967).

Public Law 285, 84th Congress, approved August 9, 1955, further amending the International Claims Settlement Act of 1949, contained provision (section 202) that in accordance with article 29 of the Treaty of Peace with Hungary, which entered into force September 15, 1947, any property blocked by the United States in accordance with Executive Order No. 8389 of April 10, 1940, as amended, and remaining blocked on the date of the Act, and which, as of September 15, 1947, was owned by Hungary or a national thereof, should vest in such officer or agency as the President of the United States might designate, such property to be sold or otherwise liquidated as expeditiously as possible after vesting and the net proceeds thereof to be covered into the U. S. Treasury. (Provision was also contained in the same section for the divesting and restoration to blocked status (subject to release) of property "directly owned at the date of vesting by a natural person".) The 1949 Act as amended, provided (section 302 of title III) that there was thereby created in the U. S. Treasury, the Hungarian Claims Fund comprised of net proceeds of vested Hungarian assets covered into the Treasury (as provided in the Act). By section 303 the Foreign Claims Settlement Commission was authorized to receive and determine "in accordance with applicable substantive law, including international law, the validity and amounts of claims of nationals of the United States" against the Government of Hungary, Bulgaria, and Rumania, for failure to comply with obligations in three categories of cases, the first of which had to do with restoration of or payment for property under the Peace Treaties, the second, with payment of "effective compensation for the nationalization, compulsory liquidation, or other taking, prior to the effective date of this title" of property of U. S. nationals, and the third, with failure to meet obligations expressed in currency of the United States arising out of contractual or other rights acquired by U. S. nationals prior to September 1, 1939 (in the case of Hungary), and which became payable prior to September 15, 1947. The Foreign Claims Settlement Commission made awards in favor of U. S. nationals in certain bond claims against Hungary.   [The opinion of the commission stated:]

> The essential part of this section [303(3)] as it relates to the question provides, for the determination of claims against the Governments of Bulgaria, Hungary, and Rumania, arising out of the failure to meet obligations expressed in dollars arising out of contractual or other rights acquired prior to certain dates and which became payable prior to September 15, 1947.
>
> It has been concluded * * * that under section 303(3) of the Act only those dollar bond claims and interest coupon claims which became payable prior to September 15, 1947, are deemed compensable.
>
> The legislative history of the Act suggests that the term "against the Governments of Bulgaria, Hungary, and Rumania or any of them, arising out of the failure to * * * meet obligations * * *" are claims against the three governments. The Senate Committee on Foreign Relations in reporting on the amendments to the Act in its discussion of H.R. 6382, stated, with respect to section 303(3), the following:
>
>> The purpose of the present bill is to establish a claims program for the benefit of American nationals * * * for * * * prewar governmental debt (bond) claims, against the Governments of Bulgaria, Hungary, and Rumania, * * *. (S. Report No. 1050, 84th Congress, 1st Sess., p. 1.)
>
> Prewar government debt claims contemplate those claims based upon the failure of any of these governments to meet their bond obligations or other debts. * * * Claims dealt with in section 303(3) of the bill relate to contractual obligations, principally rights in bonds, issued by the Governments of Bulgaria, Hungary, and Rumania.
>
> Other congressional reports and debates pertaining to section 303(3) further substantiates [sic] the interpretation of this section as claims dealing in bonds issued by the three governments or other contractual obligations of such governments. The legislative history is void of any reference to the contractual obligations of the political subdivisions of the three governments.
>
> * * * [T]his bond issue has never been considered a government bond. These bonds were issued on the credit of the Municipality of the City of Budapest and the purchasers of such bonds did so with the knowledge of this fact. It is a well-established fact that a political subdivision cannot pledge the credit of its national government since they are distinct and separate entities.

Claims based upon bonds of private banking institutions in Hungary were likewise found to be not compensable under Section 303(3) of the Act inasmuch as they involved no obligations for which the Government of Hungary was responsible.

* * *

SAUDI ARABIA v. ARABIAN AMERICAN OIL CO. (ARAMCO)

Arbitration Tribunal, 1958.
27 Int'l L.Rep. 117, 168, 170, 171 (1963).*

[This was an arbitration by an ad hoc panel pursuant to an agreement between the Arabian American Oil Co. (Aramco), a Delaware corporation, and the State of Saudi Arabia. A 1933 concession arrangement grants the company's predecessor in title (a company with a slightly different name and organized in California) " * * * the exclusive right * * * to explore, prospect, drill for, extract, treat, manufacture, transport, deal with, carry away and export petroleum * * *" within an "Exclusive Area" which included islands, territorial waters and all offshore areas as to which the Saudi State has or may claim dominion. In 1954 Aristotle Socrates Onassis made an agreement with Saudi Arabia under which Onassis' Saudi Arabian Tankers Company (Satco) was granted " * * * the right of priority to ship and transport oil and its products exported from Saudi Arabia to foreign countries by way of the sea * * *." This priority was conditioned upon a first priority for shipment by concessionaires up to the extent they actually engaged in the regular transportation of Saudi Arabian oil before December 31, 1953. Aramco asked the tribunal to declare the contracts in conflict and the second a nullity as to Aramco, i. e. that Aramco have an unlimited right to ship oil from Saudi Arabia. A majority of the panel did so declare. The appointee of Saudi Arabia dissented.

A portion of the opinion by the arbitral tribunal appears below.]

* * *

Inasmuch as the law in force in Saudi Arabia did not contain any definite rule relating to the exploitation of oil deposits, because no such exploitation existed in that State before 1933, this lacuna was filled by the 1933 Concession Agreement, whose validity and legality under Saudi Arabian law are not disputed by either side. The present dispute only concerns the effects of the provisions contained in the Agreement.

The Concession Agreement is thus the fundamental law of the Parties, and the Arbitration Tribunal is bound to recognize its particular importance owing to the fact that it fills a gap in the legal system of Saudi Arabia with regard to the oil industry. The Tribunal

---

* Reprinted by permission of E. Lauterpacht, ed., and Grotius Publications,
Ltd., Cambridge, England.

holds that the Concession has the nature of a constitution which has the effect of conferring acquired rights on the contracting Parties.

* * *

In so far as doubts may remain on the content or on the meaning of the agreements of the Parties, it is necessary to resort to the general principles of law and to apply them in order to interpret, and even to supplement, the respective rights and obligations of the Parties.

The Arbitration Tribunal relies, by analogy, on the precedent of the Lena Goldfields Arbitration between the U.S.S.R. and a British corporation, with respect to mining concessions, and on the award given in that case on 3 September 1930. According to Article 75 of the concession contract, the concessionary company was subject to the whole present and future legislation of the U.S.S.R., but with the following important reservation: "in so far as special provisions are not contained in the present agreement". Further, under Article 76, the Government had undertaken not to modify the contract in any way, by order, by decree or by any other unilateral act, without the approval of the Lena Goldfields Ltd. The arbitrators (in the absence of the Government's arbitrator who refused to take part in the proceedings) adopted the following standpoint, in conformity with the submissions of the plaintiff:

> * * * On all domestic matters in the U.S.S.R., the laws of Soviet Russia applied except in so far as they were excluded by the contract, and accordingly that in regard to performance of the contract by both parties inside the U.S.S.R. Russian law was the "proper law of the contract."

> But * * * for other purposes the general principles of law such as those recognised by Article 38 of the Statute of the Permanent Court of International Justice at The Hague should be regarded as the "proper law of the contract."

The latter solution seemed justified to the arbitrators because several provisions in the Concession called for the application of international law rather than that of municipal law (Cornell Law Quarterly, vol. 36, 1930, p. 50).

* * *

Aramco's right of ownership in the oil it extracts and the oil derivatives it produces is not expressly mentioned in the 1933 Concession Agreement and it has been questioned by the Government, although the latter admits that the Company does possess private rights of a sacred character. (Answering Memorial No. 46, p. 56.)

In the course of the oral hearings, the Government claimed that this omission was intentional and that neither one nor the other Party had any absolute right of ownership in the oil. Aramco has no such right, it was argued, because it is not entitled to enjoy and dispose freely of the object of the Concession. Under Moslem law, it cannot base its alleged right of ownership on the fact of prior discovery and extraction of the oil because the right of the first discoverer in Hanbali law is not an exclusive right and is only attributed to Moslems and to non-Moslems who are among the residents of the Moslem State (Ahl al Dar); Aramco, it was further argued, cannot claim to be the first discoverer of the oil by virtue of its exclusive right to explore the vast area reserved to it in the Concession for the following reason: as no one else had the right to explore and prospect, Aramco's privilege would destroy the rules of Hanbali law according to which the first discoverer cannot prevent others from taking their needs of the mineral resources he has discovered.

But these rules, evolved some centuries ago in respect of mineral deposits other than oil, have precisely been supplemented by the 1933 Concession Agreement, ratified by Royal Decree No. 1135 in the proper exercise of the powers vested, under Hanbali law, in the Ruler of the State. The right to sell the products of the conceded oil deposits is not disputed by the Government, for it is explicitly mentioned in Article I of the 1933 Concession, as follows:

> It is understood, however that such right does not include the exclusive right to sell crude or refined products within the area described below or within Saudi Arabia.

It follows, by an inescapable argument a contrario, that the concessionaire has the exclusive right to sell outside Saudi Arabia. This right of sale, which entails a transfer of title, implies a recognition of Aramco's right of ownership in the oil and oil products.

     * * *

In conclusion, this analysis shows that, in Saudi Arabian law as in the laws of Western Countries, the oil concession is an institution which implies an authorization by the State, on the basis of a statute or of a contract, and necessarily entails the grant to the concessionaire of property rights in the oil. As a result of this, the Concession, even in the absence of an express clause to that effect, confers upon Aramco the right to dispose of the oil. Because of this fundamental similarity, the Tribunal will be led, in the case of gaps in the law of Saudi Arabia, of which the Concession Agreement is a part, to ascertain the applicable principles by resorting to the world-wide custom and practice in the oil business and industry; failing such custom and practice, the Tribunal will be influenced by the solutions recognized by world case-law and doctrine and by pure jurisprudence.

As regards the international effects of the Concession, such as the effects of the sale and transport of the oil and oil products to foreign countries, and in particular the f. o. b. sales, the Tribunal holds that these effects are governed by the custom and practice prevailing in maritime law and in the international oil business. Because of the American nationality of the concessionaire, a particular importance must be ascribed, in this connection, to the custom and practice followed by producers in the United States and their buyers all over the world. This does not mean that American law, as the law of the nationality and of the domicile of one of the Parties, should be given any priority in relation to the law of Saudi Arabia, as the national law of the grantor and the law of the place of exploration. What the Tribunal intends to take into account is only the world-wide practice adopted in the oil industry and business.

Lastly, the Tribunal holds that public international law should be applied to the effects of the Concession, when objective reasons lead it to conclude that certain matters cannot be governed by any rule of the municipal law of any State, as is the case in all matters relating to transport by sea, to the sovereignty of the State on its territorial waters and to the responsibility of States for the violation of its international obligations.

* * *

[Dissenting opinion omitted.]

TEXAS OVERSEAS PETROLEUM CO. AND CALIFORNIA ASIATIC OIL CO. v. THE GOVERNMENT OF THE LIBYAN ARAB REPUBLIC

Dupuy, Sole Arbitrator, 1977.
53 Int'l L.Rep. 389, 431 (1979).*

[An excerpt from the arbitral award on a different point is at p. 1127. The question here is whether, under the choice of law provision in the concession contracts, these contracts are to be governed by Libyan law or international law. The applicable provision read:

This concession shall be governed by and interpreted in accordance with the principles of the law of Libya common to the principles of international law and, in the absence of such common principles, then by and in accordance with the general principles of law, including such of those principles as may have been applied by international tribunals.]

* * *

B. The Law Governing the Arbitration

11. The Arbitral Tribunal must now state precisely what law or what system of law is applicable to this arbitration, it being understood that the parties themselves are entitled freely to choose the law of procedure applicable to the arbitration and it is only, as is the case here, in the absence of any express agreement between them that the Arbitral Tribunal must determine the law or system of law applicable to the arbitration. Two solutions are theoretically possible:

12. (a) The first solution, which was adopted with respect to the arbitration between Sapphire International Petroleum Limited and the National Iranian Oil Company (NIOC), consists in submitting the arbitration to a given municipal law which will generally, but not necessarily, be that of the place of arbitration * * *. [The Sole Arbitrator rejected this alternative.]

* Reprinted by permission of E. Lauterpacht, ed., and Grotius Publications, Ltd., Cambridge, England.

13.   (b) All the elements of this case support, on the contrary, the adoption of a second solution which is to consider this arbitration as being directly governed by international law.

    *   *   *

[Reasoning and arbitral precedents omitted. The Sole Arbitrator then developed the following thesis.]

32.   For the time being, it will suffice to note that the evolution which has occurred in the old case law of the Permanent Court of International Justice is due to the fact that, while the old case law viewed the contract as something which could not come under international law because it could not be regarded as a treaty between States, under the new concept treaties are not the only type of agreements governed by such law. And it should be added that, although they are not to be confused with treaties, contracts between States and private persons can, under certain conditions, come within the ambit of a particular and new branch of international law: the international law of contracts.

33.   As Dr. F. A. Mann wrote (Studies in International Law (1973), at 223):

>   *   *   * [I]n regard to treaties between international persons, the nature and subject matter of which frequently are not substantially different from contracts between international and private persons, those legal rules have been, or are capable of being, and, in any event, must be developed. The law which is available for application to the one type of contractual arrangement can, without difficulty, be applied to the other group of contracts.

    *   *   *

---

1. *Question.* From this excerpt, what is the holding? Concessions contracts are economic interests of aliens that, as such, are protected by international law? Or the parties may choose international law to govern?

2. *Management-service contracts with the state.* As an alternative to foreign direct investment in enterprises within the territory, some developing countries are paying for foreign skills, technology and, to some extent, capital, by making contracts with foreign enterprise for the conduct of a particular type of economic operation on a fee basis. For example, Mexico, despite its state-owned oil industry and the full rigor of a constitutional prohibition on any kind of foreign-owned capital interest in oil and gas in place, has made many contracts with foreign oil companies for exploration and production of oil and gas. Another example: when in the 1940's the Franco regime in Spain bought out ITT's interest in the Spanish telephone company, an ITT subsidiary was given a contract to operate, maintain and supply the nationalized public utility. The foreign compa-

nies are usually paid an agreed percentage of the net returns from the operation, but they have only contract rights with the host state.

As to espousal of claims based on management-service contracts, so far there has been too little experience with unilateral cancellation, outside of contract stipulations, for any clear trend to have developed as to whether such cancellations would fall into the category of interests of aliens for which espousal is accepted or into that for which espousal is not generally recognized. It is likely that the foreign investment history of such arrangements (that of having developed as alternatives to foreign private sector entrepreneurial activity based on ownership of the means of production) will incline both capital-exporting and capital-importing states to regard management-service contracts as eligible for espousal—if, of course, the receiving country does not under Calvo Clause doctrines or otherwise deny the validity of diplomatic protection in any case.

3.   *Question.* Your client has been offered a management-service contract in a state where the constitution requires a Calvo Clause undertaking from a foreign investor. Would you advise your client to reject the offer out of hand? Why or why not?

4.   *Cancellation of the right to engage in business where no contract, franchise or concession right is involved.* Suppose you represent a Brazilian manufacturer of Saturday night specials and that Congress enacts legislation prohibiting the sale of such handguns in the United States. The Brazilian manufacturer has a sales agency in the United States and has imported, under proper munitions control procedures, 350,000 Saturday night specials before the effective date of the act of Congress. The Brazilian national stands to lose his normal profit of $22 each on these arms and claims that existing arms control laws in most other countries prevent him from mitigating his damages by removing the arms from the United States for sale elsewhere. Suppose (i) that in an FCN treaty between Brazil and the United States the nationals of either are entitled to engage in general manufactures and commerce in the other; (ii) that there is no such treaty undertaking. Under each assumption: if Brazil espouses the claim, what should the Legal Adviser of the Department of State recommend to the Secretary?

Do the following provisions of the Restatement give you adequate guidance?

PROHIBITION OF GAINFUL ACTIVITY

Restatement of the Foreign Relations Law
of the United States §§ 196, 197 (1965).*

§ 196. **General Rule**

(1) Conduct attributable to a state that forbids an alien to engage in previously lawful gainful activity is wrongful under international law unless either

(a) the alien receives reasonable notice and opportunity to engage in other gainful activities or to depart from the territory of the state,

(b) the prohibition is promulgated for bona fide reasons of public policy of the state and is equally applicable to nationals and to aliens similarly situated, or

(c) under the law and practice of the state in effect when the prohibition becomes effective there is reasonable provision for the determination and payment of just compensation.

(2) Failure of a state to pay just compensation under the circumstances, indicated in Subsection (1)(c) is wrongful under international law.

§ 197. **Police Power and Law Enforcement**

(1) Conduct attributable to a state and causing damage to an alien does not depart from the international standard of justice indicated in § 165 if it is reasonably necessary for

(a) the maintenance of public order, safety, or health, or

(b) the enforcement of any law of the state (including any revenue law) that does not itself depart from the international standard.

*   *   *

Comment:

a. General. The essential criterion in determining whether exercise of police power, or enforcement of a law of a state, that causes damage to an alien is consistent with the international standard, is whether the conduct, in each case, is reasonably necessary to achieve the indicated objective, and whether that objective is consistent with the international standard.

Illustrations:

1. State A enacts a law requiring periodical inspection of livestock and destruction of animals that are found to have certain communicable diseases. The law provides for compensation only in cases where more than five percent of a herd is destroyed. Pursuant to such inspection, the state destroys two percent of a herd belonging to X, an alien. The destruction does not violate the rule stated in § 185

---

* Copyright 1965. Reprinted with the
permission of the American Law Institute.

regarding the taking of an alien's property without just compensation.

* * *

Questions. Suppose the legislation prohibiting the sale of Saturday night specials also provided for their confiscation and destruction? Would Brazil clearly have a claim?

Suppose the change of national policy involves, as in land reform, the taking of property from one group (large landowners) and its transfer to another (small holders). What then as to the rights of foreign large landowners?

THE REQUIREMENT OF PUBLIC PURPOSE

EL AGUILA NATIONALIZATION

8 Whiteman, Digest of International Law 1272 (1967).

Pursuant to a Decree of the Mexican Government of March 18, 1938, that Government expropriated property, including oilfields in Mexico, of a Mexican joint stock company, Compañía Mexicana de Petróleo El Aguila, S.A. (Mexican Eagle Oil Company), the shareholders of which were mainly British. Article 1 of the decree stated that the company's assets were being expropriated "on grounds of public interest (utilidad publica)". The British Government by a note to the Mexican Government of April 8, 1938, protested and requested restoration of the property to the company. In the note it was stated that "His Majesty's Government in the United Kingdom do not question the general right of a Government to expropriate in the public interest and on payment of adequate compensation; but this principle does not serve to justify expropriations essentially arbitrary in character." In its reply of April 12, 1938, the Government of Mexico took the position that the company was "a Mexican enterprise, and therefore the defence of its interests does not appertain to a foreign State, either in the realm of the internal affairs of the Mexican State or in the sphere of international life." The Mexican Government stated further in this note that it desired to place on record that—

* * * there is a universally accepted principle of international law which attributes to all sovereign and independent countries the right to expropriate in the public interest with the payment of adequate compensation; moreover, this principle has been considered and held to mean that the grounds of public interest may be determined by every State at its own discretion, with such latitude as conditions, social and of every other kind, may require in each case.

In a further note of April 20, 1938, the British Government insisted on its right to protect the interest of British shareholders in the company, stating:

His Majesty's Government are not intervening on behalf of the Mexican Eagle Company but on behalf of the very large majority of shareholders who are of British nationality.

They are perfectly well aware of the Mexican nationality of the Mexican Eagle Company itself in the sense that it is incorporated under Mexican law, and in no way seek to deny this.

But the fact remains that the majority of shareholders who are the ultimate sufferers from the action of the Mexican Government are British, and the undertaking in question is essentially a British interest.

For this reason alone His Majesty's Government have the right, which cannot be affected by anything in the Mexican Constitution, to protest against an action which they regard as unjustified * * *.

The British note pointed out in this connection that—

If the doctrine were admitted that a Government can first make the operation of foreign interests in its territories depend upon their incorporation under local law, and then plead such incorporation as the justification for rejecting foreign diplomatic intervention, it is clear that the means would never be wanting whereby foreign Governments could be prevented from exercising their undoubted right under international law to protect the commerical interests of their nationals abroad.[a]

By notes exchanged between the two Governments, February 7, 1946, procedure was agreed upon for determining the amount to be paid to British subjects affected by the acts of expropriation or otherwise (subsequent to March 17, 1938) in respect of certain petroleum industrial properties in Mexico. Experts, appointed by the two Governments, were to determine an adequate valuation of the properties, rights, and interests, at the time they were affected by the acts of the Government of Mexico, on the basis of justice and equity. The experts, however, failed to reach agreement within the time allotted (3 months).

        * * *

Thereafter, in August 1947, the Government of Mexico and the the several companies whose properties were affected as a consequence of the Mexican Decree of March 18, 1938, reached a settlement whereby the Government of Mexico undertook to pay $81,250,000, with interest, in U. S. currency, to the companies. The Agreement was incorporated in notes exchanged on August 29, 1947, between the British Embassy at Mexico City and the Mexican Foreign Office. * * *

a. For a discussion of this type of situation, see paragraph 92 of the opinion of the International court of Justice in the Barcelona Traction case, which appears at p. 1173.

CLAIMS FOR TAKING OF CORPORATE ASSETS

Agreement for the release of American hostages in Teheran of January 19, 1981. It is in the Documentary Supplement. See Article VII, paragraphs 1 and 2 of the second Declaration by the Algerian government for definitions of nationality in relationship to ownership of interests in corporations. Suppose that under paragraph 1, American natural persons owed 51% of the shares of a corporation organized under the laws of Iran. Would the corporation be eligible to claim against Iran under this agreement? If the corporation could not, what about the American shareholders under paragraph 2?

PEACE TREATY BETWEEN THE ALLIED POWERS AND ITALY OF FEBRUARY 10, 1947

61 Stat. 1245, 49 U.N.T.S. 3.

Section 1—United Nations Property in Italy

Article 78

(1) In so far as Italy has not already done so, Italy shall restore all legal rights and interests in Italy of the United Nations and their nationals as they existed on June 10, 1940, and shall return all property in Italy of the United Nations and their nationals as it now exists.

* * *

(4)(a) The Italian Government shall be responsible for the restoration to complete good order of the property returned to United Nations nationals under paragraph 1 of this Article. In cases where property cannot be returned or where, as a result of the war, a United Nations national has suffered a loss by reason of injury or damage to property in Italy, he shall receive from the Italian Government compensation in lire to the extent of two-thirds of the sum necessary, at the date of payment, to purchase similar property or to make good the loss suffered. In no event shall United Nations nationals receive less favourable treatment with respect to compensation than that accorded to Italian nationals.

(b) United Nations nationals who hold, directly or indirectly, ownership interests in corporations or associations which are not United Nations nationals within the meaning of paragraph 9(a) of this Article, but which have suffered a loss by reason of injury or damage to property in Italy, shall receive compensation in accordance with sub-paragraph (a) above. This compensation shall be calculated on the basis of the total loss or damage suffered by the corporation or association and shall bear the same proportion to such loss or damage as the beneficial interests of such nationals in the corporation or association bear to the total capital thereof.

(c) Compensation shall be paid free of any levies, taxes or other charges. It shall be freely usable in Italy but shall be subject to the foreign exchange control regulations which may be in force in Italy from time to time.

* * *

(9) As used in this Article:

(a) "United Nations nationals" means individuals who are nationals of any of the United Nations, or corporations or associations organised under the laws of any of the United Nations, at the coming into force of the present Treaty, provided that the said individuals, corporations or associations also had this status on September 3, 1943, the date of the Armistice with Italy.

The term "United Nations nationals" also includes all individuals, corporations or associations which, under the laws in force in Italy during the war, have been treated as enemy;

(b) "Owner" means the United Nations national, as defined in sub-paragraph (a) above, who is entitled to the property in question, and includes a successor of the owner, provided that the successor is also a United Nations national as defined in sub-paragraph (a). If the successor has purchased the property in its damaged state, the transferor shall retain his rights to compensation under this Article, without prejudice to obligations between the transferor and the purchaser under domestic law;

(c) "Property" means all movable or immovable property, whether tangible or intangible, including industrial, literary and artistic property, as well as all rights or interests of any kind in property. Without prejudice to the generality of the foregoing provisions, the property of the United Nations and their nationals includes all seagoing and river vessels, together with their gear and equipment, which were either owned by United Nations or their nationals, or registered in the territory of one of the United Nations, or sailed under the flag of one of the United Nations and which, after June 10, 1940, while in Italian waters, or after they had been forcibly brought into Italian waters, either were placed under the control of the Italian authorities as enemy property or ceased to be at the free disposal in Italy of the United Nations or their nationals, as a result of measures of control taken by the Italian authorities in relation to the existence of a state of war between members of the United Nations and Germany.

* * *

BARCELONA TRACTION, LIGHT AND POWER CO., LTD. (BELGIUM v. SPAIN)

International Court of Justice, 1970.
[1970] I.C.J. Rep. 3, 168.

Separate Opinion of Judge JESSUP.

* * *

16. In connection with the instant case, the question arises from the argument that there can be no international right to dam-

ages for shareholders indirectly injured by damage to the company in which they hold shares, since no such right is generally established in municipal law.   Much reliance is placed upon the proposition that under most systems of municipal law, shareholders have no rights in or to the assets of the corporation until after it is dissolved or wound up.   Shareholders' suits are indeed provided by law in the United States and somewhat less extensively in Great Britain.   In the United States "The derivative stockholder-plaintiff is not only a nominal plaintiff, but at the same time a real party in interest.   He sues not solely upon a corporate cause of action but also upon his own cause of action".   See Koessler, "The Stockholder's Suit: A Comparative View", 46 Columbia Law Review 1946, pages 238 and 242.   The provisions for shareholder suits in the European countries seem to be somewhat less favourable to the shareholder.   But the trend in France is toward more protection of shareholders, as Judge Gros points out in paragraph 11 of his separate opinion.

17.   Although the concept of corporate personality is a creature of municipal law, none of the theories evolved in that frame of reference can be relied on universally to explain the legal relations surrounding that "technical legal device".

> Gierke's theory was based upon Germanic village communities, medieval guilds and similar truly corporate entities.   But such a theory hardly fits the modern holding company * * *.
> The result is that those who administer the law, whether as judges, revenue authorities, or as administrators, in civilian and common law systems alike [and I would add in the international law system] have had to discard all known theories of corporate personality, and to relativise the conception of juristic personality, respecting it for some purposes, disregarding it for others, in accordance with the nature of the problem before them.   (Friedmann, Legal Theory, 5th ed. 1967, pp. 522–523.   See also p. 571.)

I would paraphrase and adapt a dictum from a recent decision of the Supreme Court of the United States in an anti-trust case: the International Court of Justice in the instant case is "not bound by formal conceptions of" corporation law.   "We must look at the economic reality of the relevant transactions" and identify "the overwhelmingly dominant feature".   The overwhelmingly dominant feature in the affairs of Barcelona Traction was not the fact of incorporation in Canada, but the controlling influence of far-flung international financial interests manifested in the Sofina grouping.

It may well be that the new structures of international enterprise will be increasingly important, but any glance at the world-wide picture today shows that non-governmental corporations still have a major role to play.   That is why so many new States, and the United Nations itself, encourage the investment of private capital.

The Right to Extend Diplomatic Protection
to Corporate Enterprises

18.   The decision of the Court, in this case, is based on the legal conclusion that only Canada had a right to present a diplomatic claim on behalf of Barcelona Traction which was a company of Canadian nationality. My own conclusion is that, for reasons which I shall explain, Canada did not have, in this case, a right to claim on behalf of Barcelona Traction. As a matter of general international law, it is also my conclusion that a State, under certain circumstances, has a right to present a diplomatic claim on behalf of shareholders who are its nationals. As a matter of proof of fact, I find that Belgium did not succeed in proving the Belgian nationality, between the critical dates, of those natural and juristic persons on whose behalf it sought to claim. The Belgian claim must therefore be rejected.

                    *   *   *

———————

1.   *Creeping nationalization.* It is sometimes difficult to find a positive act of nationalization such as a statute or decree. Major political changes in the host country may alter the whole investment climate in reliance on which the investment was made. Or the tax laws of the host country may become much more severe. The zeal with which the police power is used may increase. At some point, in some situations, a design of harassment and discrimination against all, or a particular, foreign investment may become sufficiently clear as to be the basis of formal or informal diplomatic remonstrance by a state entitled to espouse the interests of the investor affected. But it is extremely difficult for such diplomatic actions to go to the point of claiming a constructive taking of the alien's economic interests thus making the objection one under international law.

In a few instances, such as in that of a deliberate course of police intimidation of foreign enterprise, some states of nationality have declared that the conduct of the host state was a constructive taking. Other states have been disinclined to make claims based on constructive nationalization. Whyever not?

2.   *Question.* From the standpoint of a host state, if a foreign investment has become internally unpopular or undesirable, why should the state nationalize instead of squeezing the foreign interest out? Would the host state not have an easier time internationally if it followed the latter course? Would the Hickenlooper amendments [see 22 U.S.C. § 2370(e)(1) and (2)] be activated by a program of tightening the noose to the point of practical strangulation of the foreign enterprise, but without taking title? Mexico has developed some refined ways of inducing foreign enterprises, such as the American sulphur industry in Mexico, to scale down the foreign stock ownership through sale at fair prices. The inducement in the sulphur case was to cut down almost to zero on export licenses for sulphur, most of which was sold in the world market, not in Mexico. After the

American interests sold down to a minority position, export licensing on a large scale was resumed. Eventually the American interest sold out entirely.

IN THE MATTER OF THE CLAIM OF JENO HARTMANN

8 Whiteman, Digest of International Law 1011 (1967).

[Foreign Claims Settlement Commission of the United States, 1958.[a]]

This is a claim under Section 303(2) of the International Claims Settlement Act of 1949, as amended, for $27,901.26 by Jeno Hartmann, a national of the United States since his naturalization in the United States on July 23, 1946, for the nationalization, compulsory liquidation, or other taking of property in Hungary.

The Commission finds that the claimant was the owner of a plot of land at 6 Epreskert Street, Ryiregyhazs, improved with a building containing living quarters and a bakery consisting of installed equipment, and furnishings, all of which belonged to claimant, although the business was conducted by another, to whom any profits belonged. The Government of Hungary nationalized the bakery on January 6, 1950, under the provisions of Law-Decree 1949: 20 tvr. (Magyar Kozlony, December 28, 1949).

The operation of the bakery by the Government of Hungary is made possible only through the use of the claimant's real property, for which he has received no compensation. Although the Government of Hungary has stated that title to the real estate in question has not been taken into state ownership, it is hard to conceive of a more effective method of taking of property than appears in the instant case with respect to claimant's realty. Claimant has been prohibited from entering upon his property, from using and enjoying it, and from alienating it. Accordingly, while the method of taking of claimant's realty utilized in the present situation, leaves the claimant endowed with the indicia of ownership, the Commission nevertheless finds that such realty has been effectively taken from claimant within the meaning of Section 303(2) of the International Claims Settlement Act of 1949, as amended.

3. THE FUNDAMENTALS OF INTERNATIONAL CLAIMS

1. *Tour d'horizon.* The existing international legal system does not provide very effective rules for assuring direct foreign private sector investors against nationalization. The possibilities for im-

---

a. The decisional law of the commission is important, although it sometimes results from the application of particular statutory principles in the United States authorizing legislation, 64 Stat. 12 (1949), as amended, rather than from general international law. Unfortunately these decisions are not officially published but are included only in semi-annual reports to the Congress. The use by Whiteman of some of them makes the digest the semi-official reporter for Claims Commission decisions—to the extent that the digest reproduces them.

provement are sketched later on in this chapter. But when a nationalization occurs and the host state does not behave in a normal way, that is, provide that such takings be only for public purposes (including social policy purposes, as in land reform), be executed with procedural fairness and on the payment of compensation, the injured foreign investor has a natural grievance. When a series of abnormal takings occurs (either in a single country or in a group of countries) or in sensational cases, a degree of neurosis is added to the sense of grievance. The investor under these latter circumstances—or its lawyers (it is usually a corporation that has been nationalized)—wants lessons taught as well as compensation. Probably the subconscious wish in many cases is to be freed of the nationalization threat and to resume business as usual. But usually this wish is not within the range of achievement and this adds to the frustrations.

Thus it is that abnormal nationalizations tend to involve the emotions, as well as the law. Naturally, in such cases, emotions, political or genuinely deeply held, also rise in the nationalizing country if it begins to sense foreign opprobrium or pressure. One result of this syndrome is that time must pass before passions cool and a settlement of the claim can be worked out, whether by private arrangements, diplomatic protection activities, arbitration, adjudication or other means of conflicts resolution. The truth of this observation can be verified by studying the time-lag in the claims settlements between the United States and Mexico following the highly charged atmosphere engendered by the Mexican Revolution and its aftermath. Also, when will it be that the United States and Cuba will find themselves calmly and clinically able to work out mutual solutions to the wholesale nationalizations carried out by Fidel Castro?

In the main the materials that follow relate to the process of claims settlement in a calm environment. Some of the applications of the principles sketched, it is true, were made during periods of tension. Such uses are often tactical gambits, designed to put off as long as possible—or until tempers have cooled—the real work of settlement. The analyst should always be aware of the psycho-political atmosphere in which a claims settlement rule is being invoked or rejected.

Another consequence of the emotions aroused in certain instances of nationalization is that the aggrieved former owners of expropriated property turn to varieties of self-help, either on their own or through the enlistment of national legislation such as the Hickenlooper amendments (see p. 1179) and, in the case of the United States also, to the registration of claims with the Department of State and, more recently, to pre-international settlement declarations of right to compensation by the Foreign Claims Settlement Commission of the United States. Self-help is also induced, no doubt, by the reality that except through it, save in the rare case of an arbitration contract with the host state, the private party has no standing on his own to pursue his rights by a suit against the nationalizing state.

2. *The fundamentals in a nutshell.* The basic rules for international claims settlements are set out in a number of useful sources, including the Restatement of the Foreign Relations Law of the United States § 184–214 (1965), 8 Whiteman, Digest of International Law 1216–1291 (1967) and 2 O'Connell, International Law, Ch. 33 (1970). Whatever the instrumentality or means of settlement, the major rules usually followed are:

a.   Local (nationalizing state) remedies must have been exhausted, if any exist in law and are not clearly unavailable in fact.

b.   The private claimant must have had the nationality, through a genuine link, of the espousing state at the time of the taking. This rule creates obvious problems where dual or corporate nationality is involved; distinguish as to the latter the question considered at pp. 1143–1146 as to the rights of foreign shareholders in relationship to their equities in corporations of the nationality of the taking state. In the settlements of the nationalizations that occurred in socialist states in Eastern Europe after World War II, sensitive issues arose as to persecuted persons who had had the nationality of the taking state at the time of the taking but had been naturalized in other states before the claims settlement.

c.   The claimant must have continued to be a national of the espousing state down to the time of espousal, and possibly to the time of settlement. This rule has also created certain stresses of a politico-moral nature.

d.   The most widely recognized remedy is compensation. Restitution or invalidation of title to the nationalized property has not been granted by international adjudication as a clear alternative to compensation possibly because international cases are not presented in the form of suits against private parties purchasing from the nationalizing states. However, some national courts have given these remedies in cases involving such parties, but others have not. See Chapter 6.

e.   The doctrine of sovereign immunity bars suits against the taking state in the courts of another state.

f.   Internationally the state authorized to espouse the claim has the power to bar it in whole or in part by arrangement with the taking state, even though no—or no adequate—compensation has been obtained.

g.   Use of force by the espousing state to redress the injury suffered by the owner whose economic interests are taken in violation of international law is illicit under the United Nations Charter and the Charter of the Organization of American States. Also, for political reasons, it is extremely unlikely today that intervention in pursuit of such redress would be undertaken. The aborted British-French action at Suez, 1956, in redress of the nationalization of the Suez Canal by the United Arab Republic, is likely not to be often imitated. The Bay of Pigs and Dominican Republic actions involved no property protection elements whatsoever. As to the denial by the espousing state of economic advantages or development assistance to the taking state, see p. 1110.

EXHAUSTION OF REMEDIES AND OTHER PRECONDITIONS

LETTER OF ACTING SECRETARY OF STATE WELLES TO SENATOR BUNKER (1942)

8 Whiteman, Digest of International Law 769 (1967).

I have received your letter of April 1 in which you urge that this Government request the British Government to effect a dismissal of the Prize Court proceedings instituted against the oil cargoes of the vessels Chas. Racine and Petter and to transmit the proceeds of the sale of the cargoes to the United States for delivery to Davis and Company, Incorporated, the alleged owner.

It appears from the Department's records that in relation to a similar request which you addressed to Mr. Berle [Assistant Secretary of State] and Mr. Hackworth [The Legal Adviser], respectively, the Secretary [Mr. Hull], on January 28, 1942, informed you of the long standing practice of this Government to decline to intervene in cases of this character pending in the courts of a foreign country.

* * * I should like to invite your attention to a few of the many authorities in support of the general rule of international law and practice in this respect.

In an opinion of February 22, 1792, Attorney General Randolph stated that states do not interfere with the regular course of the administration of justice in cases in which an alien is a party until he shall have taken his case to the court of last resort. (1 Op.Atty.Gen. 25, 26). In an opinion of Attorney General Lee it was held that American citizens were bound to apply to the tribunals of the Province of Florida "for the recovery of their property in that Province, as well as for redress of injury done them there." (Ibid. 68, 69.)

In a communication of June 1, 1885, to the British Minister, Secretary Bayard cited with approval the following statement of Sir R. Phillimore (International Law, II, 4):

> The State must be satisfied that its citizen has exhausted the means of legal redress offered by the tribunals of the country in which he has been injured.

He also cited the following statement of Chief Justice Waite in the case of New Hampshire v. Louisiana (108 U.S., 90):

> There is no principle of international law which makes it the duty of one nation to assume the collection of the claims of its citizens against another nation, if the citizens themselves have ample means of redress without the intervention of their Government. (Foreign Relations 1885, Page 458.)

In a report of February 5, 1896 to the President, Secretary Olney stated:

> This position of the French Government—that claims of aliens cognizable by the courts of a foreign country can not be made the subject of diplomatic intervention unless there has been a palpable failure of justice after all local judicial remedies have been exhausted—is one upon which this Government has often insisted and of which it has often availed itself. (Foreign Relations 1895, Part I, Page 259.)

On more than one occasion the Court of Claims has dismissed claims because of the failure of the claimants to exhaust the legal remedies available to them in the courts of a foreign state. (See 29 Ct.Cls. 68, and 45 Ct.Cls. 555.) Similar action has been taken by international arbitral tribunals in a large number of cases.

In the [sic] declining to intervene in the case of the steamship Dacia pending in the French Prize Court, the Department in a communication of August 31, 1915 stated:

> * * * the Department desires to call your attention to the generally accepted rule of international law, that, in cases of the character of the present one, the interested party must exhaust his local legal remedies before diplomatic intervention is appropriate. (Foreign Relations, 1915, Supplement, Page 530.)

The position of the British Government in this regard was set forth in the excerpt from a memorandum, accompanying the British Embassy's note of April 24, 1916, which was quoted in the Secretary's letter to you of January 28, 1942. In that relation I may say that the Department has recently received a despatch from the American Embassy at London reporting the receipt by it of a communication from the Procurator General enclosing a copy of a letter addressed to you by the latter on February 5, 1942 in which it was stated that since the present case is pending in the Prize Court any intervention, whether through the diplomatic channel or otherwise, is in principle inappropriate and inadmissible.

In the light of the foregoing consideration I feel sure that you will appreciate that the Department is not in a position to intervene in the present case. I should also point out the possibility that any rights which Davis and Company, Incorporated, may have in the matter may be seriously prejudiced should the Company fail to present to the Prize Court the evidence and arguments upon which it rests its claim for compensation.

THE AMBATIELOS CLAIM

Commission of Arbitration, 1956.
XII U.N.Rep.Int'l Arb.Awards 82, 91 (1963).

[This claim arose out of a 1919 contract between Ambatielos, a Greek national, and the United Kingdom government for the purchase by the former of several vessels being built for the government at Hong Kong. Ambatielos was unable to complete payment for the vessels, allegedly because an undue delay in their delivery deprived him of favorable freight rates; and he gave mortgages to the British government for the balance owed on them. On foreclosure proceedings in an English court, the defense of undue delay was rejected and the vessels ordered sold. Ambatielos lost the vessels and what he had paid on them. In the trial court and on appeal Ambatielos tried to get support for his defense from British official files and from the British officials who had negotiated with him. He was unsuccessful, and thereupon Ambatielos abandoned his appeal in the British case and got the Greek government to espouse the claim. The International Court of Justice held that the United Kingdom was under an international agreement obligation to submit the claim to arbitration, and in the arbitration that followed one of the British defenses was that Ambatielos had not exhausted his remedies in the English courts. Great Britain won the arbitration on Claim A on the ground that in fact Ambatielos had not exhausted his domestic judicial remedies, as to calling witnesses. Other claims were rejected because it was found that they had not been presented in the British courts at all.]

In countering the claim of the Greek Government the Government of the United Kingdom relies on the non-exhaustion by Mr. Ambatielos of the legal remedies which English law put at his disposal.

One of the questions which the Commission is requested to determine is "The question raised by the United Kingdom Government of the non-exhaustion of legal remedies in the English Courts in respect of the acts alleged to constitute breaches of the Treaty." The Commission notes that the question raised by the United Kingdom Government covers all the acts alleged to constitute breaches of the Treaty.

The Commission will therefore examine the validity of the United Kingdom objection independently of the conclusions it has reached concerning the validity of the Ambatielos claim under the Treaty of 1886.

The rule thus invoked by the United Kingdom Government is well-established in international law. Nor is its existence contested by the Greek Government. It means that the State against which an international action is brought for injuries suffered by private individuals has the right to resist such an action if the persons alleged to have been injured have not first exhausted all the remedies available to them under the municipal law of that State. The defendant State has the right to demand that full advantage shall have been taken of all local remedies before the matters in dispute are taken up on the international level by the State of which the persons alleged to have been injured are nationals.

In order to contend successfully that international proceedings are inadmissible, the defendant State must prove the existence, in its system of internal law, of remedies which have not been used. The views expressed by writers and in judicial precedents, however, coincide in that the existence of remedies which are obviously ineffective is held not to be sufficient to justify the application of the rule. Remedies which could not rectify the situation cannot be relied upon by the defendant State as precluding an international action.

The Greek Government contends that in the present case the remedies which English law offered to Mr. Ambatielos were ineffective and that, accordingly, the rule is not applicable.

The ineffectiveness of local remedies may result clearly from the municipal law itself. That is the case, for example, when a Court of Appeal is not competent to reconsider the judgment given by a Court of first instance on matters of fact, and when, failing such reconsideration, no redress can be obtained. In such a case there is no doubt that local remedies are ineffective.

Furthermore, however, it is generally considered that the ineffectiveness of available remedies, without being legally certain, may also result from circumstances which do not permit any hope of redress to be placed in the use of those remedies. But in a case of that kind it is essential that such remedies, if they had been resorted to, would have proved to be obviously futile.

Here a question of considerable practical importance arises.

If the rule of exhaustion of local remedies is relied upon against the action of the claimant State, what is the test to be applied by an international tribunal for the purpose of determining the applicability of the rule?

As the arbitrator ruled in the Finnish Vessels Case of 9th May, 1934, the only possible test is to assume the truth of the facts on which the claimant State bases its claim. As will be shown below, any departure from this assumption would lead to inadmissible results.

In the Finnish Vessels Case the issue was whether a means of appeal which had not been used by the claimants ought to be regarded as ineffective.

In the Ambatielos Case, failure to use certain means of appeal is likewise relied upon by the United Kingdom Government, but reliance is also placed on the failure of Mr. Ambatielos to adduce before Mr. Justice Hill evidence which it is now said would have been essential to establish his claims. There is no doubt that the exhaustion of local remedies requires the use of the means of procedure which are essential to redress the situation complained of by the person who is alleged to have been injured.

In paragraph 109 of its Counter-Case, the United Kingdom Government says the following concerning this point:

> The "local remedies" rule * * * finds its principal field of application in the two requirements (a) that the complainant should have availed himself of any right given him by the local law to take legal proceedings in the local courts; and (b) that

having done so, he should have exhausted the possibilities of appealing to a higher court against any adverse decision of a lower one. The application of the rule is not, however, confined to these two cases. It also requires that during the progress, and for the purposes of any particular proceedings in one of the local courts, the complainant should have availed himself of all such procedural facilities in the way of calling witnesses, procuring documentation, etc., as the local system provides.

The Commission shares this view in principle. At the same time it feels that it must add some clarifications and reservations to it. Although this question has hardly been studied by writers and although it does not seem, hitherto, to have been the subject of judicial decisions, it is hardly possible to limit the scope of the rule of prior exhaustion of local remedies to recourse to local courts.

The rule requires that "local remedies" shall have been exhausted before an international action can be brought. These "local remedies" include not only reference to the courts and tribunals, but also the use of the procedural facilities which municipal law makes available to litigants before such courts and tribunals. It is the whole system of legal protection, as provided by municipal law, which must have been put to the test before a State, as the protector of its nationals, can prosecute the claim on the international plane. In this sense the statement in paragraph 109 of the Counter-Case seems to be sound.

It is clear, however, that it cannot be strained too far. Taken literally, it would imply that the fact of having neglected to make use of some means of procedure—even one which is not important to the defence of the action—would suffice to allow a defendant State to claim that local remedies have not been exhausted, and that, therefore, an international action cannot be brought. This would confer on the rule of the prior exhaustion of local remedies a scope which is unacceptable.

In the view of the Commission the non-utilisation of certain means of procedure can be accepted as constituting a gap in the exhaustion of local remedies only if the use of these means of procedure were essential to establish the claimant's case before the municipal courts.

It is on the assumption that the statements of the claimant Government are correct that the international tribunal will be able to say whether the non-utilisation of this or that method of procedure makes it possible to raise against a claim a plea of inadmissibility on the ground of non-exhaustion of local remedies.

Have the local remedies been exhausted with regard to Claim A?

Claim A is a claim for compensation for breach of the contract of sale by the United Kingdom Government. The breach alleged is that the vessels which Mr. Ambatielos bought at an agreed price and on condition that they were to be delivered to him on certain fixed dates, which had been agreed upon between the Parties, were not in fact delivered on those dates.   Compensation is claimed for the damage caused to Mr. Ambatielos as a result of this breach of contract.

The United Kingdom Government has raised the question of the non-exhaustion of local remedies in the English Courts in so far as concerns the acts which are alleged to constitute breaches of the Treaty of 1886.

The principal act which is alleged by the Greek Government to constitute a breach of that Treaty is the alleged breach of contract aforesaid.

As regards Claim A, the questions of the non-exhaustion of local remedies thus raised are:

(1) In the 1922 proceedings Mr. Ambatielos failed to call (as he could have done) the witnesses who, as he now says, were essential to establish his case.

With regard to Major Laing, the Greek Government has primarily contended that Mr. Ambatielos was prevented from calling Major Laing as a witness before Mr. Justice Hill because Major Laing—though not heard—had been subpoenaed to appear as a witness for the Crown.   In the course of the proceedings before the Commission, however, the Parties agreed that the fact that Major Laing had been subpoenaed by the Crown would not, under English law, have precluded Mr. Ambatielos from calling Major Laing as a witness before Mr. Justice Hill.

The Greek Government further contends that if Mr. Ambatielos had called Major Laing as a witness, the decision of Mr. Justice Hill would have been favourable to him; this is a contention which is disputed by the United Kingdom Government.

It is not possible for the Commission to decide on the evidence before it the question whether the case would have been decided in favour of Mr. Ambatielos if Major Laing had been heard as a witness.   The Commission has not heard the witnesses called before Mr. Justice Hill and cannot solely on the documentary evidence put before the Commission form an opinion whether the testimony of Major Laing would have been successful in establishing the claim of Mr. Ambatielos before Mr. Justice Hill.   The Commission cannot put itself in the position of Mr. Justice Hill in this respect.

The test as regards the question whether the testimony of Major Laing was essential must therefore be what the claimant Government in this respect has contended, viz. that the testimony of Major Laing would have had the effect of establishing the claim put forward by Mr. Ambatielos before Mr. Justice Hill.

Under English law Mr. Ambatielos was not precluded from calling Major Laing as a witness.

In so far as concerns Claim A, the failure of Mr. Ambatielos to call Major Laing as a witness at the hearing before Mr. Justice Hill must therefore be held to amount to non-exhaustion of the local remedy available to him in the proceedings before Mr. Justice Hill.

It may be that the decision of Mr. Ambatielos not to call Major Laing as a witness, with the result that he did not exhaust local remedies, was dictated by reasons of expediency—quite understandable in themselves—in putting his case before Mr. Justice Hill. This, however, is not the question to be determined. The Commission is not concerned with the question as to whether he was right or wrong in acting as he did. He took his decision at his own risk.

* * *

1. *Recognition of the exhaustion requirement by international adjudication.* The Interhandel case, abstracted at p. 66 was a 1959 holding by the International Court of Justice that Switzerland could not sue the United States there for a claimed illicit taking of the property of alleged Swiss nationals until it had exhausted its remedies in United States courts. This Swiss resort to the International Court came after a United States federal district court had dismissed with prejudice a Swiss suit in the United States, because the plaintiff refused to permit discovery of records kept in Switzerland and claimed by the Department of Justice to have a possible bearing on the basic issue being litigated. The issue: was General Aniline and Film Corporation, organized in the United States, beneficially owned by enemy-national Germans or by Swiss? Noting that the Supreme Court of the United States had, shortly after the international suit was instituted, granted certiorari to review a court of appeals affirmance of the above holding of the district court and, further, had, before the instant hearing of preliminary objections in the ICJ, reversed the lower courts as to dismissal with prejudice, the International Court of Justice upheld the United States' objection that domestic remedies had not been exhausted. In doing so the court recognized the rule requiring exhaustion of local remedies before resort to international proceedings as " * * * a well-established rule of customary international law * * * " that clearly " * * * must be observed when domestic proceedings are pending * * * [that] are designed to obtain the same result: the restitution of the assets of Interhandel vested in the United States * * * ".

2. *Questions about exhaustion of remedies.* The Swiss have stringent laws against the unauthorized revelation of business records and usually react negatively to foreign official efforts to command the use as evidence of records kept in Switzerland. Suppose the Swiss, after having suffered dismissal with prejudice on discovery rules grounds in the federal district court, had not appealed to the court of appeals but had dropped the American suit and had sued in the International Court of Justice. Might Switzerland have fared better on the exhaustion of remedies issue? Suppose the district court had dismissed the plaintiff's suit on motion for summary judg-

ment as having failed to make a prima facie case within the divestiture provisions of the United States Trading with the Enemy Act. Would the Swiss, nonetheless, have had to fight their way to a final decision by the United States Supreme Court before having satisfied a condition precedent to suit in the International Court of Justice? Suppose, in either of the above situations, that the Swiss had lost in the United States Supreme Court. Would they have to file a motion for rehearing in the United States Supreme Court as a condition precedent to suing effectively in the International Court of Justice? Or to appeal, after the denial of rehearing, to the Congress and the President to redress an alleged breach of international law compounded by the final action of the Supreme Court?

These questions raise the outer limits of exhaustion. There is little authority. The general view has been expressed that the claimant must have made reasonable efforts to obtain satisfaction within the domestic legal system. Cf. Restatement of the Foreign Relations Law of the United States, (1965), Section 207, which seems to assume that legal or quasi-legal trial and appellate systems in the respondent state must normally be exhausted.

3. *Where exhaustion is not required.* Exhaustion as a condition precedent to an international claims action is usually pleaded in bar by a state against a state. It is very rare indeed that a private party plaintiff would be in a litigation situation in which he would attempt to assert that the internal legal system of the respondent state is so under-developed, so corrupt, so unfair, or so predetermined as to make it clear that it would be useless to try to use it.

In state-to-state proceedings the plaintiff state's response to the defense of non-exhaustion must be made with due regard to the sensibilities of the respondent state. The safest contention, of course, is that all relevant local remedies have been tried and have proved to be unavailing.

4. *Waiver of the requirement of exhaustion by agreement.* Naturally, as between states wishing to settle issues between themselves through a general claims or a lump sum arrangement, exhaustion of remedies as to each of a large number of individual claims is waived, either expressly or tacitly. An agreement to waive the requirement of exhaustion also avoids, in sensitive situations (as both parties realize), any possibility of diplomatic indelicacy as to the honor of the respondent state's internal system of justice. As to the disputed effect of the existence of an agreement to arbitrate that does not expressly provide for waiver of exhaustion of domestic remedies, see the Reporters' Note to § 208, Restatement, Foreign Relations Law of the United States (1965).

WAIVER BY PRIVATE PARTY

OWNERS OF THE TATTLER (UNITED STATES)
v. GREAT BRITAIN

Arbitral Tribunal, Great Britain-United States, 1920.
VI U.N.Rep.Int'l Arb.Awards 48 (1955).

[The Canadian authorities in Nova Scotia arrested and detained a fishing vessel of United States nationality on charges of having engaged in fishing in violation of an 1818 treaty between the United States and Great Britain, which in 1886 became internal law in Canada, then and at the time of this suit still a British dominion. The Tattler was released upon the payment of a fine and the signing by the private party of a waiver of further claim.]

The record shows that by an agreement made at Liverpool, Nova Scotia, April 15, 1905 (United States memorial, exhibit 19, enclosure 1), the owners entered into the following undertaking:

"In consideration of the release of the American schooner Tattler of Gloucester, Mass., now under detention at the port of Liverpool, Nova Scotia (on payment of the fine of five hundred dollars, demanded by the Honourable, Minister of Marine and Fisheries of Canada, or by the Collector of Customs at said port), we hereby guarantee His Majesty King Edward the Seventh, his successors and assigns, represented in this behalf by the said Minister, and all whom it doth or may concern, against any and all claims made or to be made on account of or in respect to such detention or for deterioration or otherwise in respect to said vessel or her tackle or apparel, outfits, supplies or voyage, hereby waiving all such claims and right of libel or otherwise before any courts or Tribunal in respect to said detention or to such or any of such claims or for loss or damage in the premises."

It has been observed by the United States Government that on the same day the owners notified the Canadian authorities that the payment of the said sum of $500 was made under protest.

But neither this protest nor the receipt given by the Canadian authorities for the $500 contains any reservation to, or protest against, the guarantee given against "any and all claims made or to be made on account of or in respect to such detention". It does not appear, therefore, that the waiver in the undertaking of any claim or right "before any court or tribunal" was subject to any condition available before this tribunal.

It is proved by the documents that the consent of the British Government to the release of the vessel was given on two conditions, first, on payment of $500, and, second, on the owners undertaking to waive any right or claim before any court, and the protest against the payment does not extend and can not in any way be held by implication to extend to this waiver.

This protest appears to have been a precautionary measure in case the Canadian authorities should have been disposed to reduce the sum. Any protest or reserve as to the waiver of the right to damages would have been plainly inconsistent with the undertaking itself and would have rendered it nugatory if it had been accepted by the other party.

On the other hand, it has been objected that the renunciation of and guarantee against any claims are not binding upon the Government of the United States, which presents the claim.

But in this case the only right the United States Government is supporting is that of its national, and consequently in presenting this claim before this Tribunal, it can rely on no legal ground other than those which would have been open to its national.

For these reasons

This Tribunal decides that the claim relating to the seizure and detention of the American schooner Tattler on the between April 10 and April 16, 1905, must be dismissed.

---

1. *Settlement acceptable to the private claimant.* States usually espouse the claims of their nationals only because the claims have not otherwise been settled. If after causing or threatening to cause diplomatic problems, a claim is settled by the respondent state and the private claimant, the settlement is instinctively accepted as final. The potential plaintiff state's officials breathe a sigh of relief and go on to other business. This is clearly so if there is no related but independent plaintiff-state claim and if the settlement is reached before formal espousal has been made. Technically this would not be so for a settlement made after espousal, but the resistance to a second settlement that the respondent state would surely interpose makes the technicality rather illusory. The state of nationality, however, will tend to be sensitive to the interests of its national as against undue pressure or duress in the settlement itself.

But compare the provisions of Articles 9 and 11, in the first Declaration by the Algerian government in the agreement of January 19, 1981, for the release of American hostages in Teheran and the provisions in Article III-4 in the second Declaration by the Algerian government. The agreement is in the Documentary Supplement. See also Section 213 of the Restatement of the Foreign Relation Law of the United States (1965).

2. *Waiver as a condition precedent to entry as a foreign contractor or investor; the Calvo clause problem.* Some Latin American states in their constitutions, by statute, or by executive action make it a condition precedent to the entry of a foreign contractor or direct investor that the alien undertake at the time of entry and in consideration therefor not to invoke the diplomatic protection of the state of his nationality and to accept non-discriminatory national treatment

as his sole basis of right.   Contractually, this is an anticipatory waiver of claims.   The foreign minister of Argentina who gave his name in the latter part of the last century to the Calvo doctrine, which the clauses seek to implement, grounded the doctrine firmly on a negation of any right of diplomatic protection inhering in states of nationality and on a denial of the existence of an international minimum standard.   See p. 1112.

Calvo clauses raise these questions: (i) may the private party bind or bar the state of his nationality?   (ii) if the promisor, again the private party, breaches his promise and goes tattling to the state of his nationality, what happens as to: (a) the investor vis-á-vis the state to which he gave his promise, (b) any independent right of action that the state of nationality otherwise might have had?

The questions posed do not have clear and satisfactory answers in either doctrinal writings or in international arbitrations or adjudications.   Analytically, these questions raise the issue whether the notion that a nationalization claim is an injury to the state of espousal is an expression of a fundamental rule of customary international law, or whether it is really merely a doctrine of logical convenience, to get around under-development of individuals' rights in customary international law.

Capital exporting states other than the United States seem to have been only rarely troubled by Calvo clauses.   So far this device for subjecting the foreign investor to greater host state control has not spread throughout the developing half of the world.   But recall the separate opinion of Judge Ammoun in Barcelona Traction, p. 1122.

In diplomatic correspondence and in the position of at least one of its appointees to arbitral tribunals, the United States has rejected the notion that the international cause of action of the United States could be compromised by an agreement between a foreign state and a United States citizen.   United States Commissioner F. K. Neilsen dissented vigorously in the International Fisheries Case, U. S.-Mexican General Claims Commission 1926, Op. of Comms. 207 (1927).   There a majority of the arbitral body followed the general line of a previous case in the same arbitral series (U. S.-Mexico General Claims) to the effect that a Calvo clause undertaking must be given a reasonable and circumspect interpretation.   Such an interpretation includes these elements: (i) the undertaking covers only the economic and technical aspects of the contract or investment venture, not the general rights of alien private persons;   (ii) a Calvo clause does not mean that the private party must abstain from pursuing international legal remedies for denial of procedural justice or outrageous conduct by the host state;   (iii) a state's rights under international law cannot be taken away by a contract to which it is not a party;   (iv) where, in an arbitration involving a Calvo clause-affected claim, the plaintiff state acts strictly on behalf of its national and the national does not resort to (or exhaust) his local remedies but instead complains to his government and seeks espousal, provisions in the arbitration agreement that exhaustion of remedies will be waived do not apply. That is, a waiver of exhaustion between the states parties to the agreement to arbitrate does not cover non-exhaustion in Calvo clause cases.

Consult Restatement of the Foreign Relations Law of the United States (1965), Section 202, and particularly the authorities cited in the Reporters' Note. Both the arbitral decisions referred to above and state practice seem to negate the view that Calvo clauses are nullities in international claims law and practice. And there is some evidence that in United States diplomatic practice the presence of a Calvo clause is a factor in determining either willingness to espouse or the degree and intensity with which the diplomatic protection function of the Department of State is discharged. This is where the legal trail ends.

3. *Problem.* An American investor makes a Calvo clause investment in State X. Later the investment is nationalized without compensation satisfactory to the investor. The investor complains to the Department of State but does not pursue his remedies in X, which is under a military dictatorship that has made a big national issue out of this particular nationalization. Strictly on the bases of the two Hickenlooper amendments, see p. 389, one requiring the President to cut off foreign assistance to a country that does not give reasonable assurance of settling a nationalization claim in accordance with international law within six months of the taking and the other ordering the elimination of the act of state doctrine in Sabbatino-type nationalization cases, insofar as alleged violations of international law are concerned, what should be the effects, if any, of the disregard by the investor of his Calvo clause promises?

4. *Question.* Would it be reasonably accurate to say that the Hickenlooper amendments—see Chapter 6—are hard-nosed developed state responses to a too-clever developing state doctrinal device for making international law irrelevant in nationalization cases?

ESPOUSAL OF CLAIMS

General requirement of effective nationality. Judge Jessup discusses this requirement in the Barcelona Traction Case, [1970] I.C.J. Rep. 3, at 182. [A portion of his opinion follows.]

38. There is no question that, under international law, a State has in general a right to extend its diplomatic protection to a corporation which has its nationality, or national character as it is more properly called. The proposition raises two questions:

(1) What are the tests to determine the national character of a corporation?

(2) Assuming the appropriate tests are met, must that national character be "real and effective" as shown by the "link" between the corporation and the State, just as, in the Nottebohm

case, this Court decided that a certain claim to nationality is not enough in all situations to justify a State in extending its diplomatic protection to a natural person?

39. There are two standard tests of the "nationality" of a corporation. The place of incorporation is the test generally favoured in the legal systems of the common law, while the siège social is more generally accepted in the civil law systems. (See Kronstein, "The Nationality of International Enterprises", 52 Columbia Law Review (1952), p. 983.) There is respectable authority for requiring that both tests be met.

It is not possible to speak of a single rule for all purposes. The tests used in private international law have their own character, as well brought out by Caflisch, "La nationalité des sociétés commerciales en droit international privé", Annuaire suisse de droit international. Vol. XXIV, 1967, page 119.

Commercial treaties and claims conventions often contain their own definitions of which companies shall be considered to have the nationality of a State for purposes of the treaty. (Cf. Walker, "Provisions on Companies in United States Commercial Treaties", 50 American Journal of International Law, 1956, p. 373; Wilson, United States Commercial Treaties and International Law, 1960; and, for a more comprehensive survey, Ginther, "Nationality of Corporations", Österreichische Zeitschrift für Öffentliches Recht, Vol. XVI, 1966, p. 28 at pp. 31–59.) The tests used for such purposes may be quite different—even in the practice of the same State—from the tests used for other purposes. For example, the "control" test was widely used to determine the enemy character of property during war, but it is not established in international law as a general test of the nationality of a corporation. On the other hand, control may constitute the essential link which, when joined to nationality, gives the State the right to extend diplomatic protection to the corporation. It is a familiar fact that the laws of certain States provide favourable conditions for companies incorporating therein, especially in relation to taxation. Canada is one such State, Leichtenstein is another. In the United States, many companies find it advantageous, for various reasons, to incorporate in Delaware or New Jersey. Charters secured for such reasons may be called "charters of convenience".

40. The Judgment of the Court of Nottebohm, Second Phase, in 1955 (I.C.J. Reports 1955, p. 4), has been widely discussed in the subsequent literature of international law particularly with reference to the so-called "link theory" by which the effectiveness of nationality may be tested.

It has been argued that the doctrine is equally applicable in the case of ships flying "flags of convenience" and in relation to the diplomatic protection of corporations. I have maintained the view that it should apply in both those situations.

41.   In the instant case the Parties did not debate the applicability of the link principle to the Barcelona Traction Company, but they were certainly aware of the question. The Spanish side stated:

> * * * the Spanish Government never disputed the effective character of Barcelona Traction's Canadian nationality, because a number of factors were present which were sufficient proof of the existence of a real link between the company and the economic life of Canada. (P.O., 1963, p. 190.)

Counsel for Belgium argued on 4 July 1969 that "if the Canadian Government had been able to espouse in international judicial proceedings the cause of Barcelona Traction, its action could have been challenged on the ground of the lack of sufficient true Canadian interest". Counsel for Spain responded directly to this remark on 21 July.

42.   I am in full agreement with the proposition that the decisions of the International Court of Justice should not be based upon a legal rule or principle which has not been considered by the parties—indeed, I believe that the failure to heed that proposition is the only criticism which can properly be directed at the Court's decision in Nottebohm. When, however, both Parties have revealed a full awareness of the fact that the "link" principle might be applied to test the national quality of Barcelona Traction, the fact that they did not choose to develop their arguments on the ground of legal principle, rather than of fact, cannot operate to prevent the Court from dealing with the principle. Of course the question whether the link principle does apply to juristic persons is a question of international law and jura novit curia. The implication in the pleading of Belgian counsel just cited, intimated a conclusion that the link principle does apply to juristic persons.

It is indeed true that since Spain admitted that Canada had a right to extend diplomatic protection to Barcelona Traction, it may be argued that Spain is estopped to deny such a right although the elements of true estoppel may be lacking and such estoppel could be claimed (if at all) by Canada and not by Belgium. Aside from the fact that I believe the jurisprudence of the Court has tended to rely too heavily on estoppel or preclusion, the question posed here is in the first place a question of the Court's finding a rule of law. The Court in its Judgment does not accept the application of the link theory to juristic persons. Since I have reached the conclusion that the existence of a link between a corporation holding a "charter of convenience" and the State granting the charter, is the key to the diplomatic protection of multinational corporate interests, I cannot avoid the problems of law and fact on any such basis as the application of the doctrine of estoppel in this particular case.

43. It has also been argued that the Court should not pass judgment on the question whether there existed the necessary link between Canada and Barcelona Traction without hearing argument on behalf of Canada. Canada might have sought to intervene in the instant case under Article 62 of the Statute, but it did not do so. It is said that after judgment is pronounced in this case of Belgium v. Spain, Canada might find some jurisdictional ground to found an application to institute a case of Canada v. Spain. It is known that no such jurisdictional ground now exists. It seems quite unreal to suppose that Spain would now agree with Canada upon a compromise submitting to the Court a Canadian claim on behalf of Barcelona Traction, thus exposing Spain to the new hazard of being required to pay some two hundred millions of dollars of damages. But if the Court were properly seised of an application by Canada, it would have to take cognizance of the fact that following Article 59 of the Statute, "The decision of the Court has no binding force except between the parties and in respect of that particular case". Had the Court endorsed the application of the link principle to juristic persons, in its present decision in Belgium v. Spain, Canada could have argued against that conclusion in the hypothetical case of Canada v. Spain, or might have relied on Spanish admissions that Canada was entitled to protect the company.

44. It seems to be widely thought that the "link" concept in connection with the nationality of claims, originated in the International Court of Justice's Judgment in Nottebohm. I do not agree that in that instance the Court created a new rule of law. Indeed the underlying principle was already well established in connection with diplomatic claims on behalf of corporations. To look for the link between a corporation and a State is merely another example of what is now the familiar practice of "lifting the veil". See, for example Cohn and Simitis " 'Lifting the Veil' in the Company Laws of the European Continent", 12 International and Comparative Law Quarterly (1963), page 189; Drachsler in Report of the Section of International and Comparative Law of the American Bar Association, July 1964, page 29. The practice of such States as the United States and Switzerland had already given weight to the proposition that a corporation would not be protected solely because it was incorporated in the State, i. e., had the State's nationality; some other link was required and that link usually was related to the ownership of shares. Such abstention, being as it were "against interest", has special probative value.

Three years after the decision in Nottebohm, the Italian-United States Conciliation Commission, under the presidence of the late Professor Sauser Hall, in the Flegenheimer case stated:

> The right of challenge of the international court, authorizing it to determine whether, behind the nationality

certificate or the acts of naturalisation produced, the right to citizenship was regularly acquired, is in *conformity with the very broad rule* of *effectivity* which dominates the law of nationals entirely and allows the court to fulfill its legal function and remove the inconveniences specified. (Emphasis supplied.) (53 American Journal of International Law, 1959, p. 944.)

* * *

BARCELONA TRACTION, LIGHT AND POWER CO., LTD. (BELGIUM v. SPAIN)

International Court of Justice, 1970.
[1970] I.C.J.Rep. 3.

[In this case, the parent company in the corporate complex involved was incorporated in 1911 in Canada; but after the First World War approximately 85% of its shares came to be held by Belgian nationals, largely through complicated arrangements involving some very large Belgian holding companies. Belgium wished to be allowed to show that its nationals as shareholders had been seriously harmed by actions of the Spanish state after the Spanish Civil War. These included, according to the Belgian memorials in an earlier ICJ case dropped in 1961 in expectation of a diplomatic settlement: denial from 1940 on of foreign exchange licenses to the Traction Company and some of its Spanish subsidiaries to permit service on bonds payable in pounds sterling; a 1948 bankruptcy proceeding in Spain brought by Spanish purchasers of "defaulted" sterling bonds of which the Traction Company itself had not received fair notice; an unfair time limit on appeal in the bankruptcy case; and the eventual passage of very substantial influence over the corporate structures in Spain to one Juan March.[a]

Although the memorials do not mention the matter in just this way, March, known widely as the "Match King" of Spain, was often reported to have been a significant financial supporter of Franco's insurgency against the Spanish Republic and known as a highly skilled and secretive financial operator. The essence of the Belgian claim on the merits in the case that follows would have been that Belgians had been the victims of foreign exchange, bankruptcy and

---

a. J. Brooks, "Annals of Finance (Juan March—Part II)," *The New Yorker*, May 28, 1979, 42–87, details the skill with which a Catalan multimillionaire onetime smuggler (and great and good friend to Francisco Franco's Glorious Movement) acquired the assets of the Barcelona Traction Company in Spain through the orchestration of Spanish foreign exchange and other regulatory laws. Although the company was not itself in Spain, it was vulnerable through its subsidiaries there. The author points out that the Barcelona Traction Company was, in a sense, a multinational enterprise before that phrase was coined. In its day it was a not un-typical public utility holding company, organized in Canada, with its principal shareholders in Belgium (and elsewhere), owning subsidiaries in Spain that technically were Spanish national companies.

related official actions that squeezed out the Belgian equity investment in the Barcelona Traction corporate complex.

A portion of the opinion of the court appears below.]

28. For the sake of clarity, the Court will briefly recapitulate the claim and identify the entities concerned in it. The claim is presented on behalf of natural and juristic persons, alleged to be Belgian nationals and shareholders in the Barcelona Traction, Light and Power Company, Limited. The submissions of the Belgian Government make it clear that the object of its Application is reparation for damage allegedly caused to these persons by the conduct, said to be contrary to international law, of various organs of the Spanish State towards that company and various other companies in the same group.

29. In the first of its submissions, more specifically in the Counter-Memorial, the Spanish Government contends that the Belgian Application of 1962 seeks, though disguisedly, the same object as the Application of 1958, i. e., the protection of the Barcelona Traction Company as such, as a separate corporate entity, and that the claim should in consequence be dismissed. However, in making its new Application, as it has chosen to frame it, the Belgian Government was only exercising the freedom of action of any State to formulate its claim in its own way. The Court is therefore bound to examine the claim in accordance with the explicit content imparted to it by the Belgian Government.

30. The States which the present case principally concerns are Belgium, the national State of the alleged shareholders, Spain, the State whose organs are alleged to have committed the unlawful acts complained of, and Canada, the State under whose laws Barcelona Traction was incorporated and in whose territory it has its registered office ("head office" in the terms of the by-laws of Barcelona Traction).

31. Thus the Court has to deal with a series of problems arising out of a triangular relationship involving the State whose nationals are shareholders in a company incorporated under the laws of another State, in whose territory it has its registered office; the State whose organs are alleged to have committed against the company unlawful acts prejudicial to both it and its shareholders; and the State under whose laws the company is incorporated, and in whose territory it has its registered office.

32. In these circumstances it is logical that the Court should first address itself to what was originally presented as the subject-matter of the third preliminary objection: namely the question of the right of Belgium to exercise diplomatic protection of Belgian shareholders in a company which is a juristic entity incorporated in Canada, the measures complained of having been taken in relation not to any Belgian national but to the company itself.

* * *

35. * * * In order to bring a claim in respect of the breach of such an obligation, a State must first establish its right to do so, for the rules on the subject rest on two suppositions:

> The first is that the defendant State has broken an obligation towards the national State in respect of its nationals. The second is that only the party to whom an international obligation is due can bring a claim in respect of its breach. (Reparation for Injuries Suffered in the Service of the United Nations, Advisory Opinion, I.C.J. Reports 1949, pp. 181–182.)

In the present case it is therefore essential to establish whether the losses allegedly suffered by Belgian shareholders in Barcelona Traction were the consequence of the violation of obligations of which they were the beneficiaries. In other words: has a right of Belgium been violated on account of its nationals' having suffered infringement of their rights as shareholders in a company not of Belgian nationality?

36. Thus it is the existence or absence of a right, belonging to Belgium and recognized as such by international law, which is decisive for the problem of Belgium's capacity.

> This right is necessarily limited to intervention [by a State] on behalf of its own nationals because, in the absence of a special agreement, it is the bond of nationality between the State and the individual which alone confers upon the State the right of diplomatic protection, and it is as a part of the function of diplomatic protection that the right to take up a claim and to ensure respect for the rules of international law must be envisaged. (Panevezys-Saldutiskis Railway, Judgment, 1939, P.C.I.J., Series A/B, No. 76, p. 16.)

It follows that the same question is determinant in respect of Spain's responsibility towards Belgium. Responsibility is the necessary corollary of a right. In the absence of any treaty on the subject between the Parties, this essential issue has to be decided in the light of the general rules of diplomatic protection.

* * *

46. It has also been contended that the measures complained of, although taken with respect to Barcelona Traction and causing it direct damage, constituted an unlawful act vis-à-vis Belgium, because they also, though indirectly, caused damage to the Belgian shareholders in Barcelona Traction. This again is merely a different way of presenting the distinction between injury in respect of a right and injury to a simple interest. But, as the Court has indicated, evidence that damage was suffered does not ipso facto justify a diplomatic claim. Persons suffer damage or harm in most varied circumstances. This in itself does not involve the obligation to make reparation. Not a mere interest affected, but solely a right infringed involves responsibility, so that an act directed against and infringing only the com-

pany's rights does not involve responsibility towards the shareholders, even if their interests are affected.

        *   *   *

50. In turning now to the international legal aspects of the
case, the Court must, as already indicated, start from the fact that
the present case essentially involves factors derived from municipal
law—the distinction and the community between the company and
the shareholder—which the Parties, however widely their interpretations may differ, each take as the point of departure of their reasoning. If the Court were to decide the case in disregard of the relevant
institutions of municipal law it would, without justification, invite
serious legal difficulties. It would lose touch with reality, for there
are no corresponding institutions of international law to which the
Court could resort. Thus the Court has, as indicated, not only to take
cognizance of municipal law but also to refer to it. It is to rules generally accepted by municipal legal systems which recognize the limited company whose capital is represented by shares, and not to the
municipal law of a particular State, that international law refers. In
referring to such rules, the Court cannot modify, still less deform
them.

51. On the international plane, the Belgian Government has advanced the proposition that it is inadmissible to deny the shareholders' national State a right of diplomatic protection merely on the
ground that another State possesses a corresponding right in respect
of the company itself. In strict logic and law this formulation of the
Belgian claim to jus standi assumes the existence of the very right
that requires demonstration. In fact the Belgian Government has repeatedly stressed that there exists no rule of international law which
would deny the national State of the shareholders the right of diplomatic protection for the purpose of seeking redress pursuant to unlawful acts committed by another State against the company in which
they hold shares. This, by emphasizing the absence of any express
denial of the right, conversely implies the admission that there is no
rule of international law which expressly confers such a right on the
shareholders' national State.

        *   *   *

        *   *   * [T]he process of lifting the veil, being an exceptional
one admitted by municipal law in respect of an institution of its own
making, is equally admissible to play a similar role in international
law. It follows that on the international plane also there may in
principle be special circumstances which justify the lifting of the veil
in the interest of shareholders.

        *   *   *

59. Before proceeding, however, to consider whether such circumstances exist in the present case, it will be advisable to refer to
two specific cases involving encroachment upon the legal entity, instances of which have been cited by the Parties. These are: first,
the treatment of enemy and allied property, during and after the

First and Second World Wars, in peace treaties and other international instruments; secondly, the treatment of foreign property consequent upon the nationalizations carried out in recent years by many States.

60.   With regard to the first, enemy-property legislation was an instrument of economic warfare, aimed at denying the enemy the advantages to be derived from the anonymity and separate personality of corporations.   Hence the lifting of the veil was regarded as justified ex necessitate and was extended to all entities which were tainted with enemy character, even the nationals of the State enacting the legislation.   The provisions of the peace treaties had a very specific function: to protect allied property, and to seize and pool enemy property with a view to covering reparation claims.   Such provisions are basically different in their rationale from those normally applicable.

61.   Also distinct are the various arrangements made in respect of compensation for the nationalization of foreign property.   Their rationale too, derived as it is from structural changes in a State's economy, differs from that of any normally applicable provisions. Specific agreements have been reached to meet specific situations, and the terms have varied from case to case.   Far from evidencing any norm as to the classes of beneficiaries of compensation, such arrangements are sui generis and provide no guide in the present case.

62.   Nevertheless, during the course of the proceedings both Parties relied on international instruments and judgments of international tribunals concerning these two specific areas.   It should be clear that the developments in question have to be viewed as distinctive processes, arising out of circumstances peculiar to the respective situations.   To seek to draw from them analogies or conclusions held to be valid in other fields is to ignore their specific character as lex specialis and hence to court error.

63.   The Parties have also relied on the general arbitral jurisprudence which has accumulated in the last half-century.   However, in most cases the decisions cited rested upon the terms of instruments establishing the jurisdiction of the tribunal or claims commission and determining what rights might enjoy protection; they cannot therefore give rise to generalization going beyond the special circumstances of each case.   Other decisions, allowing or disallowing claims by way of exception, are not, in view of the particular facts concerned, directly relevant to the present case.

*   *   *

85.   The Court will now examine the Belgian claim from a different point of view, disregarding municipal law and relying on the rule that in inter-State relations, whether claims are made on behalf of a State's national or on behalf of the State itself, they are always the claims of the State.   As the Permanent Court said,

"The question, therefore, whether the   *   *   *   dispute originates in an injury to a private interest, which in point of fact is the case in many international disputes, is irrelevant from this standpoint." (Mavrommatis Palestine Concessions, Judgment No. 2, 1924, P.C.I.J., Series A, No. 2, p. 12. See also Nottebohm, Second Phase, Judgment, I.C.J. Reports 1955, p. 24.)

86. Hence the Belgian Government would be entitled to bring a claim if it could show that one of its rights had been infringed and that the acts complained of involved the breach of an international obligation arising out of a treaty or a general rule of law. The opinion has been expressed that a claim can accordingly be made when investments by a State's nationals abroad are thus prejudicially affected, and that since such investments are part of a State's national economic resources, any prejudice to them directly involves the economic interest of the State.

* * *

89. Considering the important developments of the last half-century, the growth of foreign investments and the expansion of the international activities of corporations, in particular of holding companies, which are often multinational, and considering the way in which the economic interests of States have proliferated, it may at first sight appear surprising that the evolution of law has not gone further and that no generally accepted rules in the matter have crystallized on the international plane. Nevertheless, a more thorough examination of the facts shows that the law on the subject has been formed in a period characterized by an intense conflict of systems and interests. It is essentially bilateral relations which have been concerned, relations in which the rights of both the State exercising diplomatic protection and the State in respect of which protection is sought have had to be safeguarded. Here as elsewhere, a body of rules could only have developed with the consent of those concerned. The difficulties encountered have been reflected in the evolution of the law on the subject.

90. Thus, in the present state of the law, the protection of shareholders requires that recourse be had to treaty stipulations or special agreements directly concluded between the private investor and the State in which the investment is placed. States ever more frequently provide for such protection, in both bilateral and multilateral relations, either by means of special instruments or within the framework of wider economic arrangements. Indeed, whether in the form of multilateral or bilateral treaties between States, or in that of agreements between States and companies, there has since the Second World War been considerable development in the protection of foreign investments. The instruments in question contain provisions as to jurisdiction and procedure in case of disputes concerning the treatment of investing companies by the States in which they invest capital. Sometimes companies are themselves vested with a direct right to defend their interests against States through prescribed procedures. No such instrument is in force between the Parties to the present case.

* * *

92.   Since the general rule on the subject does not entitle the Belgian Government to put forward a claim in this case, the question remains to be considered whether nonetheless, as the Belgian Government has contended during the proceedings, considerations of equity do not require that it be held to possess a right of protection. It is quite true that it has been maintained that, for reasons of equity, a State should be able, in certain cases, to take up the protection of its nationals, shareholders in a company which has been the victim of a violation of international law. Thus a theory has been developed to the effect that the State of the shareholders has a right of diplomatic protection when the State whose responsibility is invoked is the national State of the company. Whatever the validity of this theory may be, it is certainly not applicable to the present case, since Spain is not the national State of Barcelona Traction.

93.   On the other hand, the Court considers that, in the field of diplomatic protection as in all other fields of international law, it is necessary that the law be applied reasonably. It has been suggested that if in a given case it is not possible to apply the general rule that the right of diplomatic protection of a company belongs to its national State, considerations of equity might call for the possibility of protection of the shareholders in question by their own national State. This hypothesis does not correspond to the circumstances of the present case.

94.   In view, however, of the discretionary nature of diplomatic protection, considerations of equity cannot require more than the possibility for some protector State to intervene, whether it be the national State of the company, by virtue of the general rule mentioned above, or, in a secondary capacity, the national State of the shareholders who claim protection. In this connection, account should also be taken of the practical effects of deducing from considerations of equity any broader right of protection for the national State of the shareholders. It must first of all be observed that it would be difficult on an equitable basis to make distinctions according to any quantitative test: it would seem that the owner of 1 per cent. and the owner of 90 per cent. of the share-capital should have the same possibility of enjoying the benefit of diplomatic protection. The protector State may, of course, be disinclined to take up the case of the single small shareholder, but it could scarcely be denied the right to do so in the name of equitable considerations. In that field, protection by the national State of the shareholders can hardly be graduated according to the absolute or relative size of the shareholding involved.

95.   The Belgian Government, it is true, has also contended that as high a proportion as 88 per cent. of the shares in Barcelona Traction belonged to natural or juristic persons of Belgian nationality, and it has used this as an argument for the purpose not only of determining the amount of the damages which it claims, but also of establishing its right of action on behalf of the Belgian shareholders. Nevertheless, this does not alter the Belgian Government's position, as expounded in the course of the proceedings, which implies, in the

last analysis, that it might be sufficient for one single share to belong to a national of a given State for the latter to be entitled to exercise its diplomatic protection.

96.   The Court considers that the adoption of the theory of diplomatic protection of shareholders as such, by opening the door to competing diplomatic claims, could create an atmosphere of confusion and insecurity in international economic relations. The danger would be all the greater inasmuch as the shares of companies whose activity is international are widely scattered and frequently change hands. It might perhaps be claimed that, if the right of protection belonging to the national States of the shareholders were considered as only secondary to that of the national State of the company, there would be less danger of difficulties of the kind contemplated. However, the Court must state that the essence of a secondary right is that it only comes into existence at the time when the original right ceases to exist. As the right of protection vested in the national State of the company cannot be regarded as extinguished because it is not exercised, it is not possible to accept the proposition that in case of its non-exercise the national States of the shareholders have a right of protection secondary to that of the national State of the company. Furthermore, study of factual situations in which this theory might possibly be applied gives rise to the following observations.

* * *

100.   In the present case, it is clear from what has been said above that Barcelona Traction was never reduced to a position of impotence such that it could not have approached its national State, Canada, to ask for its diplomatic protection, and that, as far as appeared to the Court, there was nothing to prevent Canada from continuing to grant its diplomatic protection to Barcelona Traction if it had considered that it should do so.

101.   For the above reasons, the Court is not of the opinion that, in the particular circumstances of the present case, jus standi is conferred on the Belgian Government by considerations of equity.

* * *

103.   Accordingly, The Court rejects the Belgian Government's claim by fifteen votes to one, twelve votes of the majority being based on the reasons set out in the present Judgment.

* * *

[Declarations, separate opinions and dissenting opinion omitted.]

REMEDIES FOR NATIONALIZATION

RESTATEMENT OF THE FOREIGN RELATIONS LAW OF THE UNITED STATES (1965)*

§ 185.   Comment *c*: *Taking and failure to pay compensation distinguished.* It is often stated that the taking of an alien's property is a violation of international law unless the state pays just compensation. Since payment is frequently delayed until some time after the taking, this would suggest that the legality of the taking may be determined ab initio by subsequent events. Such a theory has practical disadvantages from the point of view of international commerce as to the property taken. For example, if a state were to take property under a program providing for just compensation and otherwise consistent with the rule stated in this Section, the taking would appear to be lawful under international law at the time but might later turn out to be in violation of international law if the compensation were not forthcoming or did not constitute just compensation * * * The subsequent determination could present serious problems to third parties dealing in the property in the territory of states that do not apply the act of state doctrine * * * and treat a taking in violation of international law as ineffective in passing title. On the other hand, some writers have contended that a taking is never per se unlawful (assuming a public purpose and no violation of an international agreement) and that it is only the failure to pay compensation that constitutes a violation of international law. The rule stated in this Section treats a taking as unlawful on the ground of failure to pay just compensation only if it does not appear at the time of taking that just compensation will be provided. * * *

* * *

§ 185.   Reporters' Note 6: *Distinction between taking and failure to pay compensation.* The theory, rejected in Comment *c*, that a taking lawful when made becomes unlawful ab initio upon failure to pay just compensation is illustrated by the reasoning of the arbitrator in Goldenberg (Germany v. Rumania), 2 U.N.Rep.Int'l Arb.Awards 901, 909 (1928). For an exposition of the view that a taking is never per se unlawful (assuming a public purpose and no prohibition by international agreement), see Delson, Whether a Taking of an Alien's Property, Without Compensation, or in Derogation of the Terms of a Contract, is in Violation of Public International Law, Am.Branch, Int'l L.Ass'n, 1959–60 Proceedings 33.

* * *

§ 186.   Failure to Pay Just Compensation for Taking

Failure of a state to pay just compenstion for taking the property of an alien is wrongful under international law, regardless of whether the taking itself was wrongful under international law.

Comment:

a. General. * * * [C]ertain types of state conduct causing injury to the economic interests of aliens impose a duty to pay just compensation, even though the conduct is not itself wrongful under international law. The taking of an alien's property imposes such a duty. If the taking was wrongful under international law, the failure to pay constitutes a second violation of international law. If the taking was not wrongful under international law, international responsibility does not arise until the state fails to make the payment.

1. *Characterization of the theory of action against the taking state.* Some writers characterize a state that has violated international law (either in the taking itself or by failing to pay compensation) as having been guilty of tortious conduct. Others say that the theory of action is analogous to unjust enrichment, inasmuch as the taking state acquired property without paying for it. The first theory covers both injuries to aliens in their persons and their economic interests while the second does not. Historically, both types of injuries have given rise to international responsibilities, in some instances in the same case. The tort theory, therefore, has the utility of providing a conceptual basis for both situations. If the unjust enrichment theory is followed as to takings of economic interests, it requires further refinement as to situations covered by § 186 of the Restatement, above. That is, as to a taking that ab initio violates international law, is an unjust enrichment theory analytically convincing?

It should be borne in mind that both these characterizations draw heavily upon analogies to municipal legal systems, and that the analogies cannot be pushed very far beyond the fundamental concepts involved. As is well known, what is tort, with a whole array of sub-rules as to duty, proximate cause, damages, and the like, to a common law lawyer is not quite the same thing as civil responsibility to a civil law lawyer. And while legal systems agree that unjust enrichment should be redressed in some ways in some situations, the doctrines of quasi-contract and quantum meruit at common law are not of universal acceptance. Thus, it would seem inadmissible to derive conclusions about the remedies that international law provides for the taking of an alien's economic interest in violation of international law by logical deduction of explicit rules from these characterizations. If there is an international tort or an international cause of action for unjust enrichment it should be regarded as sui generis, rather than as a detailed transformation of national law into international law.

2. *The remedy of compensation.* There is common agreement that compensation ought to be sufficient in value to make the forcibly disinvested alien whole. The basic problem is *what value* of *what*. Valuation is an extremely difficult problem in domestic legal systems, and in such systems, too, there are questions as to what types of interests, expectations and prospects should be included. A fairly common problem in the international claims arena is as to the valuation of the interests of an oil company lost by the cancellation of its concession. Its physical installations raise only the problems of technique and criteria for fixing the value in money of what has been taken, not that these are simple. (Replacement value? Original cost depreciated? What kind of depreciation? etc.) But what of known but not extracted reserves of oil and gas in place? What of speculative value as to reserves not yet known? There is a natural tendency for claimants to put high valuations on what they have lost by nationalization and an equally natural tendency of the respondent state in any type of claims settlement proceeding to minimize the damage suffered.

Eventually some money value is going to have to be arrived at. On an individual case basis this may be done by party or diplomatic bargaining, a finding of the damages by an arbitral tribunal or a court (perhaps assisted by a fact-finding aide), or agreement of the parties to engage a professional and disinterested valuation expert to determine true value. In instances where a state has engaged in wholesale nationalization, as when Yugoslavia became socialist, a very great many claimants with many different types of losses exist. In such situations the settlement may take the form of the acceptance by the espousing state of a global or lump sum in complete satisfaction and waiver of all the claims included within the scope of the negotiation. The espousing state would, of course, find it necessary to analyze all the claims it had received as to amounts claimed, types of property involved, etc. and come to an overall negotiating figure that it would then use in bargaining with the other state concerned. (In a sense such an approach is not unlike the settlement out of court of a class action in the United States.)

In the Yugoslavian claims settlement negotiations of 1948–49, the United States Department of State received (as a result of published notice) the claims of United States citizens against Yugoslavia for the nationalization program carried on in that country. These submissions were then examined to determine espousibility by the United States and to estimate the degree of inflation or over-statement that might exist in particular claims. During the course of this operation, also, there were consultations with claimants and groups of claimants to explain the process and to seek general concurrence that a lump sum figure of such and such amount (to be divided ratably among the claimants in the proportion of total lump sum recovery to total eligible claims) would be acceptable. Eventually the United States decided that it could accept $17 million in gold in complete settlement and waiver of a total of espousible claims that, before analysis for overstatement of value, totaled $42 million. After the negotiation of an executive agreement with Yugoslavia for settlement along these lines, the Congress authorized the use of the value of the gold received for the benefit of the private claimants and set up an administrative body, now the Foreign Claims Settlement Commission, to pass upon the individual claims as to eligibility under the terms of the agreement and to award money recoveries.

As to lump sum settlements generally, see Lillich and Weston, International Claims: Their Settlement by Lump Sum Agreements (Parts I & II) (1975).

The remedy of compensation is adjectivally stated as having to be just, fair, appropriate, or in the classic United States formulation, "prompt, adequate and effective." The latter three adjectives are the subject of somewhat wishful further descriptions in standard sources for expression of United States viewpoints on what international law requires, such as Restatement Second: Foreign Relations Law of the United States (1965) §§ 187–190 and the various Department of

State digests of international law. As interpreted one of the American trilogy of adjectives, "effective," expresses a clear preference for compensation in freely convertible foreign exchange instead of compensation in inconvertible local currency. The effect of this requirement, if strictly adhered to, would be to prevent a state short of foreign exchange from nationalizing aliens' interests even under programs of social reform. But, of course, it is not adhered to in such cases, beyond a kind of discounted foreign exchange receipt in quittance under lump sum agreements to pay in convertible monetary assets. Payment over time, as by the issuance of government or government-guaranteed bonds, is in state practice prompt enough to be acceptable.

Finally, it should be noted that the nationalization of a going enterprise is a business disaster, and compensation under any criteria that the taking state would consider accepting is almost always below the real value of the economic loss. This reality properly justifies the classification of claims settlement as a species of salvage. It is important for lawyers to get salvage for their clients, but the law of salvage is hardly the best body of law to provide a secure and lasting basis for foreign investment that wants to stay in business.

3. *Restitution, invalidation of title and other specific recovery of property as remedies; cross-reference to Chapter 6.* The question whether customary international law has developed remedies for violations of an international minimum standard in addition to the remedy of fair compensation in state to state proceedings becomes pertinent at this point in consideration of what the injured private party's attorney can do. The cases bearing on the remedies of specific restitution, invalidation of the title derived from the nationalizing state, and other possible types of specific recovery of property have been dealt with in Chapter 6 as a necessary aspect of the act of state doctrine.

It will be recalled that in a few of the cases there arrayed, courts specifically held that a nationalizing state that did not abide by the international minimum standard would not be recognized in the courts of other states as having effectively acquired and transferred title to the property in question or its proceeds. In other instances the national courts upheld the defendant's title derived from the nationalizing state, either on the ground that the court could not make enquiry as to validity (act of state, United States version) or that the transactions complained of by the plaintiff did not raise issues of the fundamental public policy of the forum state (act of state, continental version). In the two decisions by the Second Circuit Court of Appeals in the Sabbatino case (one before and one after the second Hickenlooper amendment), it was seen that the court assumed that if the act of state doctrine did not apply, it followed without more under customary international law that the former owner did not lose title by the illicit nationalization. But a few commentators on Sabbatino and its progeny have brought out that the court may have leapt too far, from a problem comparable to forum non conveniens, political question, or other devices that prevent a court's having to decide on the merits, to a dubious conclusion about the opinio juris on remedies for legal wrongs by states. A tenable hunch for the practical lawyer at this writing is that the law of remedies for nationalization is in somewhat of a state of flux and that it might well make a big difference where suit is brought, both as between the International Court of Justice and municipal courts, and between the latter in various countries.

4. *Self-help by dispossessed owners of nationalized property: the pursuit into world markets of hot sugar, hot oil, hot copper and hot whatever.* In Chapter 6 you read the classic cases on the question whether national courts under their national ways of acting can reach the questions of (i) illegality of the taking under customary international law and (ii) invalidation of title as a remedy under customary international law. You are aware that even the most energetic proponents of the use of national courts to rule on these issues have always admitted that the claim of unaffected ownership (by an illegal nationalization) would not survive a sale to a bona fide purchaser. Even the statutory intervention provided by the Hickenlooper amendment in a limited way recognized that at the outer limits (irrevocable letters of credit on the shipment) the interests of free movement of goods in commerce outweigh the claim of invalidation of title as a remedy. Thus the question arises: Why all the effort, especially when the taking state has indicated that it would negotiate compensation? Probably at the time of the decision by the British magistrate at Aden (The Rosemary, see infra p. 415), invalidation was essentially a psychological alternative to a revival of gunboat diplomacy, the Labor Government having come in barely in time to put a stop to a Conservative intention in that direction. Certainly the Italian decision did not lend much encouragement to former owners pursuing "hot oil." Nonetheless, American lawyers continued the effort as to "hot sugar" (Sabbatino, Hickenlooper amendment, etc.), and as to the "hot copper ore" as well after the Kennecott Copper Company's minority shareholder and considerable creditor interests in copper mining and smelting in Chile were taken by the Allende regime in Chile, with an evasion of compensation. Recently, two major American oil multinationals considered themselves the beneficiaries of a sole arbitration against Libya (see pp. 1127 and 1139, this chapter) that found, by resort to certain writers and extrapolations from decisions of the old Permanent Court of International Justice (pp. 1106–1107 and 1104), that customary international law provides for the remedies of restitutio in integrum and of specific performance of oil concession contracts. Again, why? Such extreme positions, going beyond what any state would ever be willing to accept must be perceived as bearing at least one cost, that of driving the nationalizing country into "state of siege" intransigence. What are the benefits? Try to identify them. What weight do you give to the gratification of the egos of the corporate decision-makers? To effective *in terrorem* re-

sults? To admonition of third states? To the attainment of a just result? To other factors?

Is there always discernible, in the cases where self-help by pursuit of assets is resorted to, some element of outrage to the interests and the fundamental social values of the victims of the nationalization?

Could the assertion of these extreme positions by capital-exporting states have contributed to the polarization between the two worlds with respect to international minimum standards, as shown by the vote—see p. 1126 —on the Charter of Economic Rights and Duties of States?

5. *Two sole arbitrators differ.* The sole arbitrators in two claims by oil companies against the coupist government of Libya differed entirely on the question whether a nationalization that violates international law leaves in the claimant a title that may be followed into the hands of purchasers with notice. Compare the Dupuy award with that of Lagergren, cited at pp. 1127 and 1130. Refer, also, to the presentation in Chapter 6.

6. *Restitution of looted property distinguished from restitution as a remedy for nationalization of economic interests within the territory.* The Axis powers in World War II, particularly the German Reich, took by force or duress huge amounts of property of all kinds in territory occupied by them. These takings went far beyond the recognized requisitioning power of a military occupier. During the course of the war, on January 5, 1943, the Allied powers issued a declaration they they would do their utmost to defeat these Axis acts of dispossession, and after the surrender of the Axis powers various international agreements and governmental orders in occupied territories provided for the return to former owners of identifiable property looted from owners by force or duress. This Allied policy is the basis of the Department of State's letter to the court in the second Bernstein case, p. 376–377. It is generally accepted that the above restitution policy has no bearing on the question whether invalidation of the title taken or transferred by a state that nationalizes property within its territory in violation of international law is a commonly recognized remedy in international law, especially in peacetime. See 8 Whiteman, Digest of International Law (1967) 1202–03, for some of the looted property declarations.

7. *Investment insurance.* The Marshall Plan (1948) was not only the world's first major foreign assistance program; it also broke new ground in providing that qualified private sector investors (mainly United States companies) could, for fees of approximately ¾ to 1% of the principal per type of risk, receive the promise of the United States to reimburse them for certain types of non-business losses, such as from nationalization without adequate compensation, non-convertibility of earnings in soft currencies into dollars and damages resulting from hostilities. The investment guaranty, as it was then called, was designed to encourage the outflow of capital from

the United States' private sector to help rehabilitate the private sectors of the countries in Europe that were to benefit from the Marshall Plan. (The Soviet Union was included in the Marshall Plan's general invitation to participate, but it declined for itself and its dominated satellites.)

When, approximately a decade later, the United States began to engage for the first time in significant bilateral assistance to the world's poorer and developing countries, the investment guaranty program was extended to them, first for the above three risks, slightly expanded in the third instance (that of physical damage from hostilities, to include losses due to civil insurrection). By that time the writing of investment guaranties for developed countries had stopped. There had been no losses in Europe, but the amounts for which guaranties nonetheless were being sought were becoming too large to be prudently managed on the resource base Congress was willing to provide.

Certain types of all-risk guarantees were later developed, especially for Latin America, in the field of low cost housing; see 22 U. S.C. §§ 2181, 2182. Additionally, a government guarantee against loss was authorized for certain types of export credits financed by the Export-Import Bank of the United States, a wholly Government-owned corporation; 12 U.S.C. § 635j. Some other capital exporting states also have developed forms of insurance or guaranties as to exports, and there is even a slight use elsewhere of the insurance system for direct investments.

From the beginning it was accepted—and it still is—that the United States' contingent liabilities on investment guaranties are not funded with reserves to the same extent that true insurance underwriters generally are required to be. Thus, very heavy losses might require Congress to have to appropriate new money to cover them; but, in general, the investing community assumes that Congress would do this, as it has promised in 22 U.S.C. § 2197(c).

In 1969 Congress took the investment guaranty program out of the United States Foreign Assistance Administration (USAID) and turned it over to a wholly-owned government corporation, the Overseas Private Investment Corporation (OPIC); see 22 U.S.C.A. §§ 2191–2200a.

The investment insurance program simplifies the problem of the foreign investor as to getting compensation for new investment, provided the coverage is available. However, there is considerable hostility in Latin America to United States (and probably other foreign country) investment insurance. In part this resistance arose from the insistance of Congress in earlier years on a precondition that an investment-receiving country have entered into a bilateral agreement with the United States accepting the scheme and recognizing the right of the United States government to be subrogated to any covered claims it might discharge. Legislatures balked in a number of Latin countries as to contract subrogation and its implicit assertion of the international minimum standard. The Andean Investment Code binds the states members of the Andean Common Market (ANCOM) not to give foreign investors better than national treatment (Art. 50), and its Article 51 provides:

> In no instrument relating to investments or the transfer of technology shall there be clauses that remove possible conflicts from the national jurisdiction and competence of the recipient country or allow the subrogation by States to the rights and actions of their national investors.

These Latin strictures do not apply literally to investment guaranties or insurance by multipartite assistance agencies, such as the International Finance Corporation of the World Bank Group. For some time the staff of the latter has worked on a multipartite investment insurance plan. The Latin American states, on the whole, had been reserved even as to this approach.

The nationalizations without any actual compensation of foreign copper equity investments in Chile have threatened OPIC with very large claims, in excess, possibly, of the funds available for payment plus the continuation of meaningful programs elsewhere. The claimant copper companies and OPIC are now performing very much as insurance companies and insureds do in tight situations. They are bargaining hard and are prepared to litigate, if necessary.

OPIC's authority was extended to cover certain eastern bloc countries (but not the Soviet Union), and it has announced that it has made a true insurance arrangement with Lloyd's of London to re-insure its risks on conventional actuarial terms.

An early doubt about investment insurance (at the time of its first use in the Marshall Plan) was that it might change the nature of overseas investors from venture capitalists to timid dabblers in sure things. This does not seem to have happened. (Would it have been so bad if it had?) The main users of investment insurance, by far, have been well-established overseas investing corporations, many of whom have the alternative of income tax writeoffs where not covered by investment insurance.

---

4. REDUCTION OF TRANSNATIONAL INVESTMENT CONFLICT

The possibility of new foreign investment arrangements. The preceding material in Chapter 17, Section B, deals with the jural pathology of direct foreign investment in the present international legal system. Better treatment of investment diseases, as by better opportunity for authoritative and neutral settlement of investment disputes under existing international law, would help. Also, clarifications and substantive modifications in the rules themselves might reduce fears, suspicions and tensions in both capital exporting and capital importing states.

It is rather striking in this regard to note how little trouble creditor investments seem to give. Why? Is it because they are not very much protected by the international legal system, or is there some other reason? Would it help if for international purposes foreign equity investment should come to be regarded as limited rather than perpetual ownership, that is, to arrange the rules so that the foreign ownership investor is entitled to x times his total investment and then must get out?

Another factor that is coming more and more to planning attention in regard to direct foreign ownership investment, is that of the effect of development itself upon the stability of investment relationships. In general, investment disputes between the world's industrialized, rich countries are very few, except for the administration of prior restraints on entry in France and Japan and for some antitrust problems, especially with the United Kingdom and possibly other Commonwealth countries. It is between the private sector ownership investors of rich countries and the governments, politicians and publics of the less well-developed countries that most of the problems arise. To a considerable extent they seem to be related to differences in the levels of managerial skills of the foreign companies and the host country public administrators. But technological advances as host countries develop may tend toward the eventual tranquilization of the present general investment situation between the rich and poor halves of the planet and the evolution of more effective legal rules for the governance of relationships between capital exporting and capital receiving countries.

Codification efforts toward new rules for foreign investment have been made. Several proposed codes for foreign investment, to come into effect as law-making international agreements, have been made by groups within developed countries. In general these proposals have found little favor in developing countries. Why? Some developing countries individually have provided rules through legislation and administrative practice. These range from prior restraints and foreign ownership maxima to provisions designed actually to attract foreign investment, either generally or into lagging sectors of the national economies. The five countries in the Andean Group within the Latin American Free Trade Association (LAFTA) apply a complete system of regulation designed to put into effect nationally in each of them a uniform basic law on foreign investment. All of these efforts are parts of a quest for rules for foreign investment of greater precision and sophistication than provided by the vague principles of customary international law, which as we have seen sound more in salvage than in prevention.

TREATY OF FRIENDSHIP, ESTABLISHMENT AND NAVIGATION BETWEEN THE UNITED STATES AND BELGIUM OF FEBRUARY 21, 1961

14 U.S.T. 1284, 480 U.N.T.S. 149.

Article 4

(1) Property that nationals and companies of either Contracting Party own within the territories of the other Party shall enjoy constant security therein through full legal and judicial protection.

(2) Neither Party shall take unreasonable or discriminatory measures that would impair the acquired rights and interests within its territories of nationals and companies of the other Party in the enterprises which they have established, in their capital, or in the skills, arts or technology which they have supplied.

(3) Nationals and companies of either Party shall not be expropriated of their property within the territories of the other Party except for public benefit and with the prompt payment of just compensation. Such compensation shall be in an effectively realizable form and shall represent the full equivalent of the property taken. Furthermore, adequate provision shall have been made not later than the time of taking for the determination and payment thereof.

(4) Nationals and companies of either Party shall in no case be accorded, within the territories of the other Party, less than national treatment with respect to the matters set forth in paragraph 3 of the present Article and in paragraph 5 of Article 3. Moreover, enterprises in which nationals and companies of either Party have a substantial interest shall be accorded, within the territories of the other Party, not less than national treatment in all matters relating to the taking of privately owned enterprises into public ownership and to the placing of such enterprises under public control.

DRAFT CONVENTION ON THE PROTECTION OF FOREIGN PROPERTY

Council of the Office of Economic Cooperation and Development, 1967.
OECD Document, 1967.*

Article 3

Taking of Property

No Party shall take any measures depriving, directly or indirectly, of his property a national of another Party unless the following conditions are complied with:

(i) The measures are taken in the public interest and under due process of law;

---

* Draft convention prepared by the OECD. Reprinted with the permission of the OECD. Out of print.

(ii) The measures are not discriminatory; and

(iii) The measures are accompanied by provision for the payment of just compensation. Such compensation shall represent the genuine value of the property affected, shall be paid without undue delay, and shall be transferable to the extent necessary to make it effective for the national entitled thereto.

Article 7

Disputes

(a) Any dispute between Parties as to the interpretation or application of this Convention may be submitted by agreement between them either to an Arbitral Tribunal established in accordance with the provisions of the Annex to this Convention, which shall form an integral part thereof, or to any other international tribunal. If no agreement is reached for this purpose between the Parties within a period of sixty days from the date on which written notice of intention to institute proceedings is given, it is hereby agreed that an Arbitral Tribunal established in accordance with that Annex shall have jurisdiction.

(b) A national of a Party claiming that he has been injured by measures in breach of this Convention may, without prejudice to any right or obligation he may have to resort to another tribunal, national or international, institute proceedings against any other Party responsible for such measures before the Arbitral Tribunal referred to in paragraph (a), provided that:

(i) the Party against which the claim is made has accepted the jurisdiction of that Arbitral Tribunal by a declaration which covers that claim; and

(ii) the Party of which he is a national has indicated that it will not institute proceedings under paragraph (a) or, within six months of receiving a written request from its national for the institution of such proceedings, has not instituted them.

(c) The declaration referred to in paragraph (b)(i), whether general or particular, may be made or revoked at any time. In respect of claims arising out of or in connection with rights acquired during the period of the validity of such declaration, it shall continue to apply for a period of five years after its revocation.

(d) At any time after the expiry of the period of six months referred to in paragraph (b)(ii), the Party concerned may institute proceedings in accordance with paragraph (a). In this case proceedings instituted in accordance with paragraph (b) shall be suspended until the proceedings instituted in accordance with paragraph (a) are terminated.

CONVENTION ON SETTLEMENT OF INVESTMENT DISPUTES

International Bank for Reconstruction and Development, 1965.
8 Whiteman, Digest of International Law 805 (1967).

In 1965 the International Bank for Reconstruction and Development—after broad consultations with legal experts in some 86 countries and assistance in the actual drafting from specially designated representatives of 61 of its members—opened for signature a Convention on the Settlement of Investment Disputes between States and Nationals of Other States. In submitting the Convention for signature the Executive Directors made it clear that its purpose was the promotion of "an atmosphere of mutual confidence" and thus to stimulate "a larger flow of private international capital into those countries which wish to attract it." To that end, "It would provide facilities for conciliation and arbitration by specially qualified persons of independent judgment carried out according to rules known and accepted in advance by the parties concerned." The Convention (now in effect) [a] contemplates consent by parties to the dispute to conciliation or arbitration under the auspices of an International Centre for Settlement of Investment Disputes (which has its seat at the principal office of the Bank unless otherwise decided). Article 25 reads:

(1) The jurisdiction of the Centre shall extend to any legal dispute arising directly out of an investment, between a Contracting State (or any constituent subdivision or agency of a Contracting State designated to the Centre by that State) and a national of another Contracting State, which the parties to the dispute consent in writing to submit to the Centre. When the parties have given their consent, no party may withdraw its consent unilaterally.

(2) "National of another Contracting State" means:
* * *

(3) Consent by a constituent subdivision or agency of a Contracting State shall require the approval of that State unless that State notifies the Centre that no such approval is required.

(4) Any Contracting State may, at the time of ratification, acceptance or approval of this Convention or at any time thereafter, notify the Centre of the class or classes of disputes which it would or would not consider submitting to the jurisdiction of the Centre. The Secretary-General shall forthwith transmit such notification to all Contracting States. Such notification shall not constitute the consent required by paragraph (1).

On the subject of exhaustion of local remedies, the Executive Directors of the Bank explain in their Report on the Convention:

32. It may be presumed that when a State and an investor agree to have recourse to arbitration, and do not reserve the

a. 66 states were parties as of January 1, 1980.

right to have recourse to other remedies or require the prior exhaustion of other remedies, the intention of the parties is to have recourse to arbitration to the exclusion of any other remedy. This rule of interpretation is embodied in the first sentence of Article 26. In order to make clear that it was not intended thereby to modify the rules of international law regarding the exhaustion of local remedies, the second sentence explicitly recognizes the right of a State to require the prior exhaustion of local remedies.

Article 26 reads:

> Consent of the parties to arbitration under this Convention shall, unless otherwise stated, be deemed consent to such arbitration to the exclusion of any other remedy. A Contracting State may require the exhaustion of local administrative or judicial remedies as a condition of its consent to arbitration under this Convention.

As to "diplomatic protection", Article 27 expressly prohibits a Contracting State from giving diplomatic protection, or bringing an international claim, in respect of a dispute which one of its nationals and another Contracting State have consented to submit or shall have submitted to arbitration under the Convention, unless such other Contracting State shall have failed to abide by and comply with the award rendered in that dispute.

FRIEDMANN AND BEGUIN, JOINT INTERNATIONAL BUSINESS VENTURES IN DEVELOPING COUNTRIES 23 (1971)*

* * * [The joint venture] cannot be regarded as a panacea. It is a device to be adopted, rejected, or modified after a sober consideration of the many legal, psychological, and technical factors prevailing in a given situation. Confidence between the partners will overcome the most difficult obstacles; lack of confidence will destroy the most perfect devices. As a major negative factor, we mentioned disparity of outlook between the foreign and local partners:

> * * * In joint ventures between industrially developed countries, such as the United States, Britain, West Germany, the Netherlands, Italy, or Sweden, there is a certain community not only of tradition and of scientific, technical, and legal standards, but there has also been more experience with responsible investment practices and legal supervision, although such standards have often evolved only after disastrous experiences with unscrupulous speculators. In many of the less developed countries, this stage has not yet been reached in the business environment. Power and wealth are often concentrated in relatively few hands,

* Reprinted with the permission of the
Columbia University Press.

and they are not matched by a corresponding sense of responsibility. The partner from the industrialized country, usually a large corporation with worldwide interests and long experience, generally takes a long-term view of profits, placing the development of the enterprise before quick dividends. Tax considerations may provide an addditional incentive to reinvest in a developing foreign enterprise.

Inflationary conditions may produce the reverse situation: The local partner will want to leave his investment in the enterprise where it is relatively inflation-proof, while the foreign investor will be anxious to take out his earnings before devaluation decimates them.

A similar note is struck by Dr. Pieter Kuin, a member of the Board of Unilever and Chairman of the ICC Commission on International Investments and Economic Development, in his introduction to a report of that Commission on International Joint Business Ventures in Developing Countries:

* * * The rising tide of national independence and self-reliance in developing countries has created a desire for even more active participation by local people in this process. Shares in the capital and profits of foreign business have sometimes been claimed too readily, without much consideration for mutual performance. But gradually a more mature idea of partnership is taking shape, in which the partners share risks as well as benefits.

Joint ventures in production are one way of meeting this need for partnership. * * *

This is a sober and realistic appraisal of the place of the joint international business venture in contemporary conditions of economic development. It contrasts with the following expression, by Kenneth Weg, Senior Associate Editor of Business International, of a more negative point of view, as it was typical until a few years ago of many American business enterprises:

* * * Even though joint ventures may currently be in vogue, many firms with extensive international commitments are becoming increasingly dissatisfied with this approach to international business. The case against joint ventures in the less-developed countries rests on two major points: the presence of a local partner contributes to (1) day-to-day operational problems and policy conflicts, and (2) lack of managerial flexibility in adjusting to new market and investment requirements and opportunities.

Companies with a policy of establishing wholly owned subsidiaries whenever possible have been more fortunate in planning for rationalized operations in both industrialized and less-developed regions. For example, IBM World Trade Corp. has had a conscious policy of 100% ownership ever since it began moving into foreign markets. Today, IBM is an outstanding example of an international corporation in which full-line assembly plants tend to disappear in favor of a very few world production centers for a given product or component.

* * *

1. *Joint ventures between the private sector in market economy countries and socialist states.* The joint venture is being used increasingly as an alternative to licensing, exporting, and management-service contracts where the private sectors in market economy states and socialist states seek to do business with each other. In the normal (private sector to private sector) joint venture the foreigners and the locals jointly own a corporation. How do you suppose the joint venture is structured where in the host state private ownership of the means of production is forbidden?

2. *Multinational enterprises (MNEs).* In the last 20 years there has been great growth in the size and number of corporate families (parents and foreign subsidiaries) that carry on economic activity on multi-country, regional, or even global, bases. Even more growth, both as to the sizes and the numbers of families, is predicted, by all friends and by some foes of MNEs. Growth to date, however, has hardly matched the expansion of the wordage, in scientific, business and popular media, about MNEs. Aside from the influence of fashions in thought about business structure, why have the joint venture, earlier, and the MNE now, raised so many expectations as to preferred forms of direct foreign investment? It seems to us that in both instances new ideas for business structure have been or are seen as having utility in removing or reducing the brand of feeling of foreignness in host countries.

As is well known to experienced observers, the classic American parent wholly owned foreign subsidiary structure is very definitely tagged as very foreign in most host countries; and in socially volatile ones, such as the developing and highly nationalistic states of Latin America, the label can lead to very uncomfortable results. Thus, from the perspective of reducing or preventing transnational investment conflicts, the issue as to the MNE is one of credibility. Is the MNE really something new that does not deserve to be feared, controlled or discriminated against as both foreign and especially dangerous? Or is the MNE just a new name for an old and basically unchanged and increasingly controversial foreign investment structure?

With regard to this issue, the following viewpoints, culled from current discourses about MNEs, are of some conjectural relevance:

a. Whether the MNE can establish itself as something new depends upon the way the parent deals with the owned or controlled subsidiaries in various countries. If the parent runs each national subsidiary separately from all the others, instead of directing or permitting fairly free movement of capital, orders, personnel and technology between the various subsidiaries in different countries, the pattern does not vary enough from an old one to establish itself as something new and different. That is to say, if the old pattern was one of a very big developed-country corporation owning 95–100% of the shares in five, six or more rigorously controlled corporations in as many foreign states, with water-tight compartments between the subsidiaries themselves, and the same pattern is now called an MNE, nothing has really changed. The issue arises, the debate continues, because a widely-used definition of an MNE stresses only the transnational parent-subsidiary system, the centralization of decision-making with the parent and a rather vague common business policy. It will be noted that the counter-definition implicit above limits true MNEs to situations where economic movement throughout the system is free. Today there is only one such area, the European Economic Community. Hence, some argue, at the present time it is simply not possible to assert seriously that true MNEs can exist in, say South America, where free movement is not yet established.

b. The host state acceptability of MNEs vel non, need not turn on national preferences as to consigning particular economic activity to the private or to the public sector, because MNEs need not be limited to the private sector. Some observers aver that substantial interest, and some growth, exist in MNEs that combine private and state capital, even the state capital of socialist countries. Additionally, there is nothing to prevent wholly state-owned MNEs. On the other hand, it is asked: would a foreign state-dominated enterprise really be less objectionable in host countries?

c. In the private sector, is the MNE apt to be more or less vulnerable than ordinary foreign enterprises are to uncoordinated national controls in host states? Are MNEs seriously threatened by conflicting, overlapping, and, in the aggregate, crushing multinational regulation? Some enthusiasts who actually profess to see the MNE as the next great step beyond the national state in human societal evolution suggest, in taking this view, an undefined, statelike, invulnerability of MNEs to being nibbled or bitten to death. Others reject the notion that the corporate form would ever be acceptable for the governance of people and with it the implicit linking of the MNE to the status of a parastate. In another quarter the debate is over the question whether host countries might not come to see MNEs as so economically and socially effective, and so much a part of the conditions of good life in the host states themselves, that MNEs would be treated with scrupulous fairness in the national interest. A few cynics say that the only way an MNE can be sure that it will not be singled out for harsh control and taxation is for the MNE to be able to subvert the processes of governmental action in the host state, and they point to the redoubled vulnerability of an MNE when the fact of such subversion surfaces.

d. Another approach to the establishment of an effective and credible new economic structure—a truly true MNE—is to say that any sole or preponderant nationality factor must be eliminated in the ownership and management of the parent, in the complexion of the executive and labor forces of the corporate family, and in the degree of participation in decision-making by host state nationals, not only as to the national subsidiary, but in the whole arrangement. This type of MNE is, at this time only faintly perceptible in the world's structures for business enterprise.

e.   One difficulty the MNE image is apt to have, in developing countries at least, but possibly in others as well, is that some self-styled MNEs—and they fit the definition quoted above also—have been take-over conglomerates. Foreign take-over of the best indigenous enterprise is always politically unpopular in the host state. When to this there is added the controversies that swirl around the basic assumption in justification that undefined and largely still personalized asserted management skills make conglomerates economically and socially desirable, the damage that the asserted linkage can do to the general idea of MNEs is substantial. Another relationship that comes into play at this point is whether the worlds of today and tomorrow (short range) have put aside as no longer relevant the "Curse of Bigness" of late nineteenth century populism (and the late Louis D. Brandeis). MNEs are big; a little business MNE is almost unimaginable. Has business learned how to be big, yet agile, adaptive and efficient at the same time? Here new doctrines of management technology and earlier folk-doubts may face a moment of truth before long. Or, if not intellectual confrontations, then antitrust ones.

f.   In the United States at the present time, MNE parent corporations are not without their own problems. Organized labor complains that MNEs are largely responsible for "runaway plants" that take jobs away from American workers and bring in foreign made goods under freer trade auspices. Others complain that certain self-styled MNEs conspire against, and seek to involve the United States government in conspiring against certain foreign governments. Thus, Congress has to face what it will do about proposed legislation against imports here of goods made abroad by American-owned foreign companies, and in the Senate a sub-committee of the Foreign Relations Committee investigated the influence of MNEs on United States foreign policy. Some observers have seen in recent patterns of European Economic Community antitrust enforcement action a bias against certain large American companies with numerous subsidiaries (some of them by take-over) within the EEC. On the other hand, others say that the industrialized Europeans and the Japanese have enthusiastic ideas of their own about the further use of MNEs. It is sometimes added that more true MNEs are based in Europe—and have been for some time—than in the United States, because Europeans, more than the Americans, have found it expedient in past to share participations in capital at the top—and sometimes at lower—levels within the structure of a corporate family.

Student users of these materials—and some of their teachers—will in their professional lifetimes probably see how the foregoing issues and problems work themselves out. Will one straight line projection or its opposite occur? Or will evolution take a now unforeseen twist? Meanwhile, the profession of international lawyering is already considerably involved with the MNE as a new concept, a new rhetoric, or a new reality. More and more the term TNE (Transnational Enterprise) is used. Why?

OLIVER, THE ANDEAN FOREIGN INVESTMENT CODE: A NEW PHASE IN THE QUEST FOR NORMATIVE ORDER AS TO DIRECT FOREIGN INVESTMENT

66 American Journal of International Law 763 (1972).*

In the broad the Andean Investment Code does these things: (i) classifies equity (or ownership) investment in accordance with its degree of foreignness; (ii) imposes prior restraints upon the entry of new direct foreign investment; (iii) requires disinvestment by existing foreign elements down to minority levels, on pain of denial of the benefits of free movement of goods and services within a common market; (iv) closes certain sectors to foreign investment; (v) regulates repatriation of invested capital and the remittance of profits; (vi) limits the present opportunities of technology owner-transferrors through patents, trademarks and know-how to benefit collaterally from their industrial rights; (vii) makes or anticipates some important changes in corporation and tax law.

As promulgated the Code takes no position on the debated question, whether the *consentio juris* recognizes an international minimum standard as to the treatment of the economic interests of aliens. It was probably decided there was no need to re-affirm the traditional Latin American viewpoint on this issue, inasmuch as the Code does not at any point clash, *as law in books*, with whatever general international law is asserted to require by proponents of the international minimum standard. As is well known, prior restraints on entry are not illegal, except as they depart unilaterally from possible commercial treaty obligations. Detailed reporting by investors is merely an exercise of the police power. Disinvestment in most cases is not forced, only induced; and in any event, orderly sale of ownership "overage" to a governmental or private market is envisaged. Article 50, in a sense, approaches the "equality of treatment" viewpoint by the back door, providing that:

> Member countries shall not grant to foreign investors any treatment more favorable than that granted to national investors.

Foreign investors are not guaranteed national treatment. Under Article 50 they cannot have *more than* national treatment, which seems

* Reprinted by permission of the American Society of International Law.

inferentially to negate the notion of a substantive international minimum standard.

The Code definitely links the treatment of foreign investment to development goals, and it assumes that participation in a wider free market will be an incentive that outweighs the disincentives of regulation. In this respect the Code reflects optimism and expectation about the development process that is certainly commendable and reassuring * * *.

In its studies the Board, which formulated the Code that the Commission approved with relatively few alterations, acted upon the bases of technocratic conclusions that, as scientifically stated, mask the intensity of certain conditioning psycho-political attitudes about foreigners, foreignness, and foreign ownership investment in Latin America. * * * In a nutshell, the technocrats of the Code believed that (i) development and integration require continued and significant transfers of developed-country capital and technology; (ii) the Andean Group nations' interest in foreign private investment and know-how is to get it to help fill the gap caused by an insufficient supply of local capital and technology plus public sector development assistance; (iii) certain negative effects historically associated with the presence of foreign ownership investment should be regulated consistently with the recognized needs, stated above. These negative effects of (iii) cluster about too high costs, interference with the growth of a national private sector, and loss of effective national capacity to make and enforce national policies.

* * *

_____

Profile lowering devices. In the United States and in a number of other countries the legal profession, through practitioners specializing in international business transactions, is influential in the structuring of foreign investments. That clients prefer to be told how they can come somewhere near achieving their objectives, rather than to be told what they cannot do, is a reality here as in other sectors of practice involving prospective operations. Knowledge of the existing rules of the international legal system and of the lines along which these rules may evolve is highly important. It is also important that the lawyer be innovative, sensitive to the psycho-political setting in the potential host country and free of ideological prejudice. In particular, it is useful for him to consider ways in which the business venture itself can be organized and operated so as to avoid to the extent possible shifts for the worse in the investment climate after the client has become irrevocably committed to the venture, as by making a foreign investment in fixed assets. The fundamental principle of economics that such an investment is assuredly retrievable only for its scrap or salvage value should not be overlooked. Among the possibilities that modern foreign investors ought to be induced to consider, in particular circumstances, are

1. Management-service contracts as an alternative to ownership interests. Some countries have already limited the foreign investor to the former in the extractive industries and public utilities.

2. Joint ventures.

3. Wider offerings of stock in the host-country operating company to investors of that country, i. e. a departure from the pattern so often found in past of complete foreign stock ownership, except for qualifying shares, usually three percent or less of the total stock in that company. Such preponderance is not necessary for control.

4. Due regard to national and regional preferences that foreign investors not dominate particular sectors of the economy, such as defense-related industries, telecommunications, etc.

5. For the extractive industries, the possibility of negotiating the country-company sharing of the proceeds of the business at different ratios during the life of the concession, particularly if the term is a fairly long one. In many instances minerals concessions now giving the preponderant return to the country were originally contracted for on the basis of a far lower participation by the host, and as time went on pressures built up for changing the sharing that sometimes caused crises in the relationship, and even nationalizations under emotionally heated circumstances. It has been suggested that with the utilization of improved techniques of economic forecasting new concessions might be originally negotiated to provide for increasing the host share of the proceeds at successive stages in the life of the concession.

6. Acceptance of partial disinvestment down to substantial minority stock ownership. See Hirschman, How to Divest in Latin America, and Why, Princeton Essays in International Finance (No. 76, 1969). However, experience shows that foreign business capital will not flow if the foreign element does not have control through the period of 100% payout.

7. The multinationalization of the foreign ownership, thus reducing the association of the venture with any single foreign nationality. See Perlmutter, The Tortuous Evolution of the Multinational Corporation, 4 Columbia J. of World Business 9 (1969); Oliver, Speculations on Developing Country Reception of Multinational Enterprise, 11 Va.J. of Int'l Law 192 (1971).

Other possibilities involving legal structuring exist and still others will doubtless develop in the future. Outside the lawyer's sphere of specialization, but related, are managerial practices as to the use of nationals of the host country in executive suites as well as in the labor force, corporate good citizenship in the host country, maximum use of products of that country in the conduct of a manufacturing or sales business and the like.

Part VI

THEORIES ABOUT THE INTERNATIONAL LEGAL SYSTEM [a]

1. *Is theory influential on outcomes under international law and on its development?* If you have taken these materials in the order in which we have arranged them, your study of this chapter comes after you have had experience with many of the major aspects of law in the international system. You will have begun to form your own ideas about the similarities and differences between the law you have studied here and the public law you study in other courses. For example: putting to one side the difference between the United States Supreme Court and the International Court of Justice as to authorization to decide, do you find these courts acting similarly or in sharply different ways in types of cases that are similar, i. e. where the Supreme Court is sitting in judgment upon the conflicting interests of two or more states of the Union either in a suit in the original jurisdiction of the Supreme Court or in some other type of case?

We have put the theory material this far along for three reasons: (a) we wanted you to begin to grope toward theory on your own as you went along; (b) we wanted you to see from case study that so far as professional methodology and involvement go, international law calls upon the same range of skills as other systems of law do; (c) we wanted to avoid raising too many doubts and prospects before you had matured in the subject matter.

Although underdeveloped, the international legal system has been extensively theorized about. Why so much doctrine for so few rules and effective institutions to apply them? Is it because the scholars who have committed themselves to this field are creating theories and schools, casting their expectations and preferences as law simply because they have so little in the way of real law stuff to deal with? Do the materials which follow suggest that scholars are theorizing about reality or their dreams?

2. *Critical independence is indispensable.* International public law, more so than any other bodies of law, tends to be presented in discrete doctrinal packages. Schools abound. Learned men encourage disciples. Deviation becomes intellectual heresy. Those who do not agree are dolts. Also, international law is often appealed to by advocates in court or in print highly interested in particular outcomes. This is done either because international law is highly amorphous and hence susceptible to a wide range of assertion or because it

---

a. Suggested to one of us as the most fitting title for what we wished to try to do by the late Harold D. Las-swell, whose contributions to transnational legal science were many and great.

becomes an argument of last resort. Sometimes these groups of distorters, the didactic scholars and the argumentative activists, combine forces. As a result there is claimed for the international legal system a competence, a completeness and a virtue that it may not in fact possess. See, Oliver, On Saving International Law from its Friends (editorial), 52 Am.J.Int'l L. 498 (1958). In this field the rule of caveat emptor is quite important for would-be shoppers of doctrine.

In methodology, international public law is somewhat old-fashioned by the most modern techniques of some domestic systems. It is too often highly exegetic, rigorously logical (even when there are errors in the logic), antiseptic and remote. Quantification technique as to events, things and attitudes of social groups barely exists. Even the schools that claim for themselves the utmost in realistic modernity are hardly scientific in any sense of association with modern scientific and engineering technology. Major propositions are largely supported by secondary authorities. In large part, perhaps, the generally backward methodological standard reflects the reality that, after all, the international legal system exists by consensus, and the world does not yet have a consensus as to what law is and how it should be used.

3. *Basic jurisprudential problems.* International law shares with domestic law certain basic problems. These are the relationship of law and justice, the essential nature of law and the judicial process in relationship to other types of decision-making.

Beyond these, international law throws into issue other fundamental questions:

(1) Is international law law in terms of a general concept of law, whatever that concept is?

(2) If international law is law in some sense or other, what is its relationship to other congeries of law, such as natural law, national law, international organizations law, regional systems law?

Chapter 18

PERSPECTIVES ON THE JURISPRUDENTIAL PROBLEMS OF INTERNATIONAL LAW

---

1. *Jurisprudence, for what purpose considered?* What follows is intended to assist you in the development of your philosophic outlook about the legal element in the international system. This includes the development of cognition of both what international law is and what it ought to be or become. You will have been doing these cerebrations, subliminally perhaps, as you have gone through the preceding chapters. Chapter 1 ends with forward linkage to this chapter. Your instructor may have chosen to begin with this part or to go to it immediately after Chapter 1. Our preferences as to sequence are stated in the preface to the first edition, but we recognize that it is more traditional to begin with subject matter of the sort here dealt with.

The history, nature and sources of international law are sometimes coupled as parts of a single item of information. In this book sources are dealt with in Chapter 1 and elsewhere. History and nature are very closely linked by a number of thinkers about international law, especially those writing up to World War II. For others, mainly contemporary scholars, history is not seen as having much to do with nature.

2. *The origins of international law.* What a majority of modern writers regard as international law began to differentiate from a universalistic public law in the West about 600 years ago. Politically, after the Roman city-state that became an empire withered away, segments of the old imperium began to see themselves as entities, not as mere extentions of a king's domain. These discrete new entities, despite Louis XIV's famous statement of identity between himself and the state, were incorporeal and distinct from any monarch. Certainly by the time of Ferdinand and Isabella—and probably at least a 100 years earlier—the nation-state as we know it today (territory, population, government) was in being in the West.

These entities soon evolved standards of conduct toward each other beyond the rules of etiquette between monarchs. Some of these were and still are standards of political propriety, such as diplomatic protocol, principles of international relations and comity. Other standards of conduct—always minimum ones—came to be thought of as creating rights and obligations for states, analogous to the rules (or norms) that states themselves imposed on persons within their jurisdiction, not as whim or caprice but as law. Specifically, the part of Roman law that pertained in the hey-day of Roman authority to controversies between non-Romans, the jus gentium, became a term used yesterday, and in some measure still, to refer to "customary international law."

The international law of today does not show distinct linkages to ancient Oriental and African practices. Even the modern descendants of very old Oriental cultures accept international law as the product of Western evolution. Ignorance and neglect in the West of the history of law and related institutions in the East constitute the most likely explanation of this omission. Scholars in some of the modern states that have evolved from the Oriental historical matrix sometimes chide the West for this inattention and threaten (usually mildly) to set the matter aright sometime. New states in Africa sometimes are heard in similar vein. But nothing much seems to happen. Worldwide, the international order, political and legal, is based on Western prototypes.

This fact makes the existing international legal system somewhat vulnerable to attacks on its universality by states not present at its creation. More often, however, the states that are not satisfied with the existing order attack specific rules or principles, not the system. Classical, scholarly Marxists, and many realists who are non-Marxist, deprecate the system of customary international law because it seems to them unavoidably to state, as law, rules and principles fostering the interests of the power elites asserting them. The socialist states of the present Second World, however, have come in practice to accept the system and many of its most conventional rules and principles, while selectively seeking to deny status as law to other rules and principles because they are contradictory to national preferences including, but not limited to, ideological ones.

3. *Naturalists, positivists and eclectics.* In the West international law was systematized by more or less scholarly writers, publicists not power-wielding officials. The excerpt from Stone, a modern publicist, refers to some of these in the item at p. 1203. Vitoria (1480–1546) and Suarez (1548–1617) perceived that beyond states there was a community of states governed as to their interactions by international rules. These rules were to be found by rational derivation from basic moral principles of divine origin. These Spaniards' concepts developed into a school of natural law, paralleling for international law an even earlier jurisprudence about domestic secular law.

The school of scholastic naturalism was resisted by writers who recognized a legal community but said that its rules came either in whole or in part from state practice, not from God. Gentilis (1552–1608) seems to have been the first to dare say there was more earthliness than theology behind international law. Hugo Grotius (the latinized version of a Dutch name) was born in 1583, and if systematized international law has a single historical beginning it is in his De Jure Belli Ac Pacis, printed in 1625. Grotius served once as Sweden's ambassador, an interesting practice not long continued by states; and as a representative of fishing and sea-trading national interests he gave us, inter alia, the principle of the freedom of the seas as customary international law. Grotius is also type-cast as the first eclectic, because he accepted not only positive law—state practice—as a source of international law, but also natural law. But the natural law of Grotius was more secular than that of the Spanish scholastics, for it was based upon man's rationality—"the dictate of right reason"—rather than upon revelation, exegesis and deduction of God's will.

A second school of naturalism, secular and rationalist, evolved and had some influence on the early recognition and reception of international law by courts in the United States. Thus, in finding vessels engaged in the slave trade subject to seizure by American privateers, Justice Story, on Circuit, wrote:

> "* * * I think it may unequivocally be affirmed, that every doctrine that may be fairly deduced by correct reasoning from the rights and duties of nations, and the nature of moral obligation, may theoretically be said to exist in the law of nations; and unless it be relaxed or waived by the consent of nations, which may be evidenced by their general practice and customs, it may be enforced by a court of justice * * *." United States v. The Schooner La Jeune Eugenie, 2 Mason 409 (U.S. Cir.Ct., 1st Cir., 1822).

But at the Supreme Court the same commitment to positivism shown by Chief Justice Marshall in The Paquete Habana, Ch. 1, p. 7, prevailed in a philosophically indistinguishable slave trade situation. Marshall let the slavers keep their "property" [sic]: "* * * This, [slavery], which was the usage of all, could not be pronounced repugnant to the law of nations * * *." The Antelope, 23 U.S. (10 Wheat.) 66 (1825). Why? The "usage of all [States]" is otherwise and controls.

The divergence suggests that natural law, especially if of the second or rationalist variety, is a form of idealism about law. Positivism tends to emphasize conduct-phenomenology, e. g. how many states accept that "x" is law, just or unjust?

4. *The role of the writers.* Idealism tends to transform into law the decision-maker's preferences and down-grade the element of states' volition in accepting a rule or principle as one of law. There has long been in international law a pronounced emphasis on the distinction between the law that is and what ought to be the law. But in some legal philosophies about international law it may be harder to discern the line of difference than in others, especially if the publicist is an eclectic.

Some modern American writers, for example, devote themselves to telling us how to make better systems, stressing structural and procedural arrangements as if these were the basic need or problem. Others, self-characterized as American philosophic neo-realists, are really so idealistic as to assume that American values are common goal values on the planet and that law is not normative but an argumentative variable in the power process by which authorized decision-makers—lawyers, judges, diplomats, politicians—put these goal values into effect with authoritativeness. Still, perhaps at the central core are those who are essentially mild positivists—in the tradition of American pragmatism—who try to find out what the great weight of acceptance by states shows and to emphasize the norms stated in obligatory form in international agreements.

The writers—and now in the United States, the Restaters—have had, and continue to have, great influence on what judges—and even foreign offices—do in relationship to international law. In civil law countries, where doctrine, i. e. scholarly writing, is the primary influence on jurisprudence, i. e. case law, this is normal. In the common law world it is not normal for domestic law, but it is for international law. For today the judges' perceptions of customary international law are not their own but those of the writer or school they have chosen to follow, rejecting the others. And the writers, as we have seen, vary widely in what they perceive. This is the basis of their power and their responsibility. Advocacy in any arena, national or international, as to what the relevant international law rule is requires the advocate to be very familiar with the literature, both that which can help his cause and that which might destroy it.

5. *Some questions and issues for you to come back to.* With the above guide, and with questions in mind such as those that follow, evaluate the messages of the excerpts from writers that follow. Is the writer an idealist or is he reality-oriented? In the historic scheme of differentiation, what label do you give the writer? To your mind does the writer help or hurt the cause of legal order in the world community? Why?

What is international law to you now? Is its existence considered by you to be proved, disproved or not proved? Do you see an identity or a difference between international law and law in the international system? Is international law merely an aspect of a science of international relations? If not, where do you draw lines between principles of international relations and principles of international law? On which side of a line do these fall: self-determination of peoples, nonintervention, equality of states, use of economic force?

As to the existence or not of international law, should it suffice to note, as then Professor (later judge of the International Court of Justice) Jessup did in 1940, that foreign ministries have legal staffs, that diplomatic correspondence is full of assertion and counterassertion as to the international law rule involved in a controversy, that this has been true for at least three centuries, and that, by inference, there are jobs of international lawyering? See Jessup, The Reality of International Law, 18 Foreign Affairs 244 (1940).

1 AUSTIN, JURISPRUDENCE 177, 189 (1861)

* * * Speaking with greater precision, international law, or the law obtaining between nations, regards the conduct of sovereigns considered as related to one another.

And hence it inevitably follows, that the law obtaining between nations is not positive law: for every positive law is set by a given sovereign to a person or persons in a state of subjection to its author. As I have already intimated, the law obtaining between nations is law (improperly so called) set by general opinion. The duties which it imposes are enforced by moral sanctions: by fear on the part of nations, or by fear on the part of sovereigns, of provoking general hostility, and incurring its probable evils, in case they shall violate maxims generally received and respected.

* * *

* * * But if perfect or complete independence be of the essence of sovereign power, there is not in fact the human power to which the epithet sovereign will apply with propriety. Every government, let it be never so powerful, renders occasional obedience to commands of other governments. Every government defers frequently to those opinions and sentiments which are styled international law. And every government defers habitually to the opinions and sentiments of its own subjects. If it be not in a habit of obedience to the commands of a determinate party, a government has all the independence which a government can possibly enjoy.

PHILLIPSON, INTRODUCTION TO GENTILI, DE JURE BELLI LIBRI TRES (II TRANS., CARNEGIE ENDOWMENT, 1933) 22a *

* * *

5.   Conception of the Law of Nations—Society of States—Civil Basis —Membership of the Society

The law of nations, designated by Gentili ius gentium (the customary expression adapted from Roman Law) is that law which all nations or the greater part of them—"maior parsorbis"—agree upon. It is the law of the society or community of states, of the "Societas gentium". This is a concise and simple description, whereby the ambiguous Roman term is made to refer explicitly to international relations. It is not, of course, an exact definition, as it involves, though unavoidably, a tautologism. Indeed, no satisfactory definition had hitherto been formulated. Grotius adopts substantially the conception of Gentili, when he says that the law of nations (ius gentium) is that law which has received obligatory force from the will of all nations or of many; whilst Vattel, like Gentili, verges on tautology in

---

* Reprinted with the permission of the Carnegie Endowment for International Peace.

his statement that the law of nations (droit des gens) is the science of the rights and obligations which exist between nations. Some writers emphasize in their definitions the origin of the law of nations, others the nature of the subject-matter, and others again lay stress on those concerned in and bound by it. * * *

    * * *

    * * * Very frequently we find that Gentili appeals to the ius naturae in order to test the validity of a particular doctrine or the legitimacy of a certain practice; but usually he disregards the current vague metaphysico-legal significance of that term, and interprets it in the sense of humanity, justice, and the best common sense of mankind. And throughout his exposition he insists on the positive juridical sanction quite as much as on the considerations of ethics or on the behests of divine law, and he is careful to discriminate between the work and objects of theologians and the sphere and functions of jurists.

    The pioneer work of Gentili was in harmony with the larger movement of the sixteenth century which witnessed a transformation of society, the establishment of a new spirit and wider outlook, the decline of theocracy, and the rise of the modern State. The political conceptions of the Middle Ages, which identified civil and ecclesiastical authority, were derived on the one hand from Greek and Roman doctrines, and on the other from Hebrew and Christian teaching. Towards the end of the thirteenth century the temporal supremacy of the papacy began to be seriously opposed, especially in France, and its decline was further hastened on by the great schism. The conciliar movement of the fifteenth century spread the theory that sovereign power was of the nature of a trust. The Renaissance and the Reformation, two sides of the same great intellectual and moral awakening, revived humanism, scientific curiosity, established a spirit of independence, political as well as spiritual, and a desire to find a more rational basis than the arbitrary theocratic for human society, and substituted civil for clerical authority, a society of territorial States resting on law and juridical sanction for a theocratic confederation subject to canon law. * * *

JAMES, THE VARIETIES OF RELIGIOUS EXPERIENCE 516
(1902)

    [On the question: If God exists how do we know it?]

    God is the natural appellation * * * for the supreme reality * * *. I only translate into schematic language what I may call the instinctive belief of mankind: God is real since he produces real effects.

    Does similar reasoning lead to the conclusion that international law is real?

2 WOLFF, CLASSICS OF INTERNATIONAL LAW
CARNEGIE ENDOWMENT 11, 19 (1934) *

*   *   *

§ 7.—Of the society established by nature among nations. Nature herself has established society among all nations and binds them to preserve society. For nature herself has established society among men and binds them to preserve it. Therefore, since this obligation, as coming from the law of nature, is necessary and immutable, it cannot be changed for the reason that nations have united into a state. Therefore society, which nature has established among individuals, still exists among nations and consequently, after states have been established in accordance with the law of nature and nations have arisen thereby, nature herself also must be said to have established society among all nations and bound them to preserve society.

*   *   *

§ 25.—Of the positive law of nations. That is called the positive law of nations which takes its origin from the will of nations. Therefore since it is plainly evident that the voluntary, the stipulative, and the customary law of nations take their origin from the will of nations, all that law is the positive law of nations. And since furthermore it is plain that the voluntary law of nations rests on the presumed consent of nations, the stipulative upon the express consent, the customary upon the tacit consent, since moreover in no other way is it conceived that a certain law can spring from the will of nations, the positive law of nations is either voluntary or stipulative or customary.

*   *   *

§ 26.—General observation. We shall carefully distinguish the voluntary, the stipulative, and the customary law of nations from the natural or necessary law of nations, nevertheless we shall not teach the former separately from the latter *   *   *.

*   *   *

STONE, LEGAL CONTROLS OF INTERNATIONAL
CONFLICT liii (1954)*

*   *   * Is there an international law? In what sense, if any, are its rules binding? To whom are such rules (insofar they exist and bind) directed? Can international law be said to be the law of a society or a community? Nor have the new approaches yielded even substantially new answers to the old questions.

John Austin's denial of the *legal* force of international law lacked, no doubt, the temperateness of Professor Corbett or the pas-

* Reprinted with the permission of the Carnegie Endowment for International Peace.

* © Julius Stone 1954. Reprinted with the permission of Julius Stone and Wm. W. Gaunt & Sons, Inc., Holmes Beach, Fla.

sionate cynicism of a Lundstedt; but there is little now said that he did not foreshadow a century ago. Today, as centuries ago, those who champion the cause of international law as "law", find its source of validity either in natural law, as did Vitoria and Suàrez, or in positive enactment, as did Gentili and Zouche, or in a mixture of the two as in Grotius. Even Kelsen's reduction of the relations between international law and international society to the identity of *legal order* and *legal community*, while apparently resolving a traditional perplexity into a mere verbal illusion, has proved to be a new evasion rather than a new solution. Its identification of the international legal order with the international legal community is achieved only by excluding from the notion of "society" the very reference to the world of existence which was the essential source of the exorcised perplexity. Nor will the yearning, shared both by modern believers and modern sceptics, for a "real" world community, stir new emotions in students of the classical civitas maxima, since Dante's fourteenth century vision.

No doubt modern thought has exposed, within the classical field, novel shades and directions of interest, and modes of analysis. Yet for the international lawyer, the novelties of feelings, insights, or analysis of empiricist, phenomenologist, existentialist, or neo-Kantian formalist, have only that point which they can contribute to easing his perplexities.

It may be, for instance, of literary interest to assert with Dr. Schwarzenberger the basic role of force in the relations of States. Yet it adds little in itself to Hobbes' proposition that in politics clubs are trumps; or to that implicit in Austin's denial that international law is law. To produce fruitful novelty the notion of power involved must be carried to finer definition and deeper analysis.

So, too, it may be striking that modern theories as opposed in temper as those of Professors Lauterpacht, Lundstedt and Messner converge by different paths on the importance of recognising the role of the individual in international law. But these questions of the "Aye" or "No" of the international status of individuals are in themselves as old as the natural law of a Suàrez or a Grotius: and mere theory is unlikely to advance them further. What theory rather requires is a fuller understanding of the mediating, distorting or obstructing operation of State entities on human relations.

Such fuller new inquiries do not lend themselves to quick answers, nor at all to armchair answers. The need for long and arduous field research within the most inaccessible and dangerously controversial area of human relations is (it is believed) a basic reason for the modern stalemate in juristic thought concerning international law. If such needed inquiries are shunned, then theory is thrown back on such barren questions as whether the actual self-subordination of States to wider international association, functionally limited, warrants the use of the term "community" to describe such an international association. And since the degrees of such self-subordination are potentially infinite in number, ranging from the most transient association on the battlefield by way of a truce for burying the dead, through the intimate organic association (on paper) of a United Nations Organisation, to the intimacy in fact of a successful federation such as that of the United States or the Commonwealth of Australia, such inquiries are as interminable as they are barren.

Insofar, therefore, as we are concerned with a "living" or "operative" international law, with "law in action" as distinct from "the books", the continuance of armchair debate whether international law is "law", will not advance understanding. Nor does it really advance matters to interpret "law in action", as do Dr. Schwarzenberger and others, to mean the law enounced or applied by tribunals or competent State organs, as distinct from the writings of publicists. So far as concerns the effects of international law *on men*, and *of men on law*, the law of tribunals and State organs may still be "law in the books" rather than "law in action". Nor has Professor Corbett's search for international "law in action", despite its courage and vigour, really faced the preliminary question, what "international law in action" may mean. It is, in the present view, impossible to study "law in action" without relating the law not merely to the supposed interests and conduct of States, but also (and above all) to those of the men and women of particular times and places. And if this be so, then it becomes apparent that the task of assessing the effect on human interests and human conduct of the interposition of State entities between the great aggregations of mankind, is an inescapable preliminary.

Judge Alvarez's and Professor Northrop's calls for an international law based respectively on the "psychology of peoples" or on reconciled national cultures, which have committed the "international" aspect of their lives to international law, do, indeed, show a commendable tendency to transcend the traditional framework of inter-State relations. But despite their earnest efforts, the "psychological" or "inter-cultural" frameworks which they would respectively substitute are still but remotely related to the actual inter-play of State and human claims and conduct. Only because of that remoteness could such theories fail to take account of the grave crisis in human communications (already examined) between populations variously conditioned in the insulated chambers of the several States. That failure is, indeed, understandable in another sense, for the difficulties of taking account of it become almost beyond contemplation when we remember that the relation between each State and its citizens has unique features, forbidding easy generalisation. Yet, the fact remains that it is probably from here that the explanation is to be sought for the stubborn political frustration of the technological drive towards an integrated world community.

It is at least probable, that the magic circle of the unsolved classical problems will not be broken until we cease to assume that the categories, conceptions, and methods of municipal law are sufficient, or even necessarily relevant, either for testing the validity of international law or for understanding its actual operation. Certainly our plight seems to cry out for insights which the classical problems, even when clothed in twentieth century philosophical garb, fail to yield. Such an escape from the classical magic circle might also release intellectual energy for tasks more fruitful than those which now engage them.

KELSEN, THE PURE THEORY OF LAW

51 Law Quarterly Review 517 (1935).*

*   *   *

28. The law, or the legal order, is a system of legal norms. The first question we have to answer, therefore, is this: What constitutes the unity in diversity of legal norms? Why does a particular legal norm belong to a particular legal order? A multiplicity of norms constitutes a unity, a system, an order, when validity can be traced back to its final source in a single norm. This basic norm constitutes the unity in diversity of all the norms which make up the system. That a norm belongs to a particular order is only to be determined by tracing back its validity to the basic norm constituting the order. According to the nature of the basic norm, i. e. the sovereign principle of validity, we may distinguish two different kinds of orders, or normative systems. In the first such system the norms are valid by virtue of their content, which has a directly evident quality compelling recognition. *   *   *

29. With legal norms the case is different. These are not valid by virtue of their content. Any content whatsoever can be legal; there is no human behaviour which could not function as the content of a legal norm. A norm becomes a legal norm only because it has been constituted in a particular fashion, born of a definite procedure and a definite rule. Law is valid only as positive law, that is, statute (constituted) law. Therefore the basic norm of law can only be the fundamental rule, according to which the legal norms are to be produced; it is the fundamental condition of law-making. The individual norms of the legal system are not to be derived from the basic norm by a process of logical deduction. They must be constituted by an act of will, not deduced by an act of thought. If we trace back a single legal norm to its source in the basic norm, we do so by showing that the procedure by which it was set up conformed to the requirements of the basic norm. Thus, if we ask why a particular act of compulsion—the fact, for instance, that one man has deprived another of his freedom by imprisoning him—is an act of law and belongs to a particular legal order, the answer is, that this act was prescribed by a certain individual norm, a judicial decision. If we ask, further, why this individual norm is valid, the answer is, that it was constituted according to the penal statute book. If we inquire as to the va-

* Reprinted with the permission of Stevens & Sons, Ltd., London.

lidity of the penal statute book, we are confronted by the State's constitution, which has prescribed rules and procedure for the creation of the penal statute book by a competent authority. If, further, we ask as to the validity of the constitution, on which repose all the laws and the acts which they have sanctioned, we come probably to a still older constitution and finally to an historically original one, set up by some single usurper or by some kind of corporate body. It is the fundamental presupposition of our recognition of the legal order founded on this constitution that that which the original authors declared to be their will should be regarded as valid norm. Compulsion is to be exercised according to the method and conditions prescribed by the first constitutional authority, or its delegated power. This is the schematic formulation of the basic norm of a legal order.

30.   The Pure Theory of Law operates with this basic norm as with an hypothesis. Presupposed that it is valid, then the legal order which rests on it is valid also. Only under this presupposition can we systematize as law (i. e. arrange as a system of norms) the empirical material which presents itself for legal recognition. On the composition of this material (acts) will depend also the particular content of the basic norm. This norm is only an expression for the necessary presupposition of all positivistic constructions of legal material. In formulating the basic norm, the Pure Theory of Law in no way considers itself as inaugurating a new scientific method of jurisprudence. It is only trying to make conscious in the minds of jurists what they are doing when, in seeking to understand their subject, they reject a validity founded on natural law, yet affirm the positive law, not as a mere factual assembly of motives, but as a valid order, as Norm. With the theory of the basic norm, the Pure Theory of Law is only trying to elucidate, by an analysis of the actual procedure, the transcendental-logical conditions of the historic methods of positive legal knowledge.

31.   Just as the nature of law, and of the community which it constitutes, stands most clearly revealed when its very existence is threatened, so the significance of the basic norm emerges most clearly when the legal order undergoes not legal change, but revolution or substitution. In an hitherto monarchic State a number of men attempt to overthrow by force the legitimate monarchic government and to set up a republican form in its place. If in this they are successful, if, that is, the old government ceases and the new begins to be effective, in that the behaviour of the men and women, for whom the order claims to be valid, conforms in the main no longer to the old but to the new order, then this latter is operated as a legal order, the acts which it performs are declared legal, the conditions which it proscribes, illegal. A new basic norm is presupposed—no longer that which delegated legislative authority to the monarch, but one which delegates such authority to the revolutionary government. Had the attempt been a failure, had the new order, that is, remained ineffective, in that behaviour did not conform to it, then the acts of the new government become not constitutional but criminal (high treason),

not legislation but delict, and this on the ground of the validity of the old order, which presupposed a basic norm delegating legislative power to the monarch.

If we ask what, then, determines the content of the basic norm, we find, on analysing judicial decisions back to their first premiss, the following answer: The content of the basic norm is determined by the condition of fact out of which the order emerges, given that to the order there corresponds, amongst the human beings to whom it refers, a substantial measure of actual behaviour.

This gives us the content of a positive legal norm. (It is not, of course, a norm of a State's legal order, but a norm of international law, which, as a legal order superior to that of the individual States, legally determines their sphere of jurisdiction.) * * *

KELSEN, PRINCIPLES OF INTERNATIONAL LAW 6 (1ST ED. 1952)*

* * *

3. Legal Norm and Rule of Law: The "Ought"

A norm prescribes or permits a certain human behavior. A set of norms which form for some reason or another a unit we call a normative order. The law is a normative order, and since legal norms provide for coercive acts as sanctions, the law is a coercive order.

The statements by which the science of law describes its object, the law, as a system of legal norms are statements to the effect that under certain conditions (among which the delict plays an essential part) a certain consequence, namely a sanction, ought to take place. These statements are called rules of law in contradistinction to legal norms, described by the rules of law. Legal norms are issued by legal authorities, rules of law are statements made by the legal science, which is not a legal authority and hence not competent to issue legal norms prescribing or permitting human behavior.

The connection established by a legal norm between the delict as condition and the sanction as consequence, is not a relation between cause and effect, such as is indicated in the statement: If a metallic body is heated, it expands. This statement is a so-called law of nature. By the laws of nature natural science describes its object, nature, just as legal science describes its object, the law, by rules of law. In the rule of law the connection between condition and consequence is characterized by the term "ought," in order to emphasize that the rule of law has not the meaning of a law of nature. It does not express the idea of a necessary or probable connection between one fact and another. Its meaning is not: if a delict occurs, a sanction will—necessarily or probably—take place; but: if a delict is

* Reprinted with the permission of Maria Kelsen Feder and Holt, Rinehart, & Winston, Inc.

committed, a sanction ought to be applied, even if it is actually not applied. By the formula "ought to be applied" nothing else is expressed but the idea that if the delict is committed the application of the sanction is legal. The statement that a sanction ought to be applied if a delict has been committed does not necessarily mean that a certain individual is legally obliged to apply a sanction. He may be only authorized to apply the sanction. Whether the application of the sanction provided for by the law is or is not the content of an obligation is a question different from the question as to the meaning of the connection between condition and consequence in the rule of law.

DeVISSCHER, THEORY AND REALITY IN PUBLIC INTERNATIONAL LAW 404 (1968)*

CONCLUSION

It was doubtless inevitable that a long period of war on a world scale and of unexampled political tensions should have a profound influence on the direction of thought in the field of international law. The descriptive methods of voluntarist positivism in vogue at the beginning of the century, like those derived exclusively from formal logic, are everywhere in retreat. Contemporary legal thought is intensely alive to the need of a new set of values in the foundations of positive international law. From now on it refuses to see in that law merely a technical order without moral inspiration or teleological direction.

The legal thought of today seeks in the direct observation of international life a new field of study. This is not a matter, as there is a tendency to say, of reconstructing international law on a foundation of sociology, but of scrutinizing the *raison d'être* of norms, restoring the contract between the normative apparatus and the underlying realities, and thus sifting through a more broadly informed criticism the rules and practices of international law perceived in the living process of application. In this renewed study the man of law will confront without methodological prejudice realities which at times are ill-adapted to his formal categories. He will not forget, however, that the observation of international life, though it never consists in the mere collection of raw facts, provides only the data for legal elaboration; that legal elaboration has its proper function, which is to select from these data only those which are adapted to social ends and which a complex of characteristics (external prominence, generality, regularity) makes fit material for his particular technique. So understood, enquiries into international relations promise to be fruitful. Properly conducted, they will have a vivifying influence; they will re-establish international law in the plenitude of its ends and its efficacity.

* Translated by P. E. Corbett (copyright © 1968 by Princeton University Press). Reprinted with the permission of the translator and the Princeton University Press.

Even now this new orientation is apparent on the plane of doctrinal studies. We can find it again in the jurisprudence of the International Court of Justice, in the work of codification going on under the auspices of the United Nations, in the creative effort of international organizations. Everywhere is felt the need to reinvigorate legal technique, to free it from prefabricated categories by associating it more closely with the study of a social milieu in accelerated evolution.

From this realization flow new demands. One is fundamental and moral; in a crisis of human values it insists upon respect for these at the heart of every organized society. There are others, more contingent in character, because tied to the present forms of the distribution of power among nations: such is that demand of effectivity which we have so often encountered and which, in a still primitive order of relations, has a more prominent place than anywhere else.

The study of power, both in its distribution and in its action, has had a large part in our discussion. The reason is that, more than any other, it reveals the tensions and the convergences that characterize the present relations between the political fact and the law. Belonging as it does both to the internal and to the international order, the action of the State is at the center of international relations and is for the moment their most salient feature. It compels the man of law to penetrate beyond the formal manifestations of power into its intimate springs and to do his share towards endowing power with an organization adapted to the common international good.

The problem of the future is that of the transformations of power. There are many signs that the structure of international relations is on the eve of profound changes. Territory, which since the end of the middle ages has provided the firmest base for these relations and ensured their stability, has no longer the same significance. It is all too clear that the existence of atomic weapons, of long-range rockets of increasing accuracy, rob frontiers of their traditional role as bulwarks of power and security. It is not less evident that some of the pacific activities of States cannot go on without more or less serious repercussions in neighboring countries. Consequently some scientific and technological operations (nuclear experiments, diversion and pollution of waters) call for international regulation. Similarly, an economy of international dimensions can no longer conform to political and legal conceptions allied with a configuration of close-walled national units. Association, even integration, are the new forms of power-distribution that force themselves upon States in search of wider markets.

Some of these structural transformations are partially in effect and in course of development. Others are scarcely visible on the horizon. The man of law owes it to himself to watch them; he will go surety for them only in so far as they seem to him factors of progress. No more than any other form of organization do federal structures have value in themselves: like the others they may become the instrument of political or economic antagonisms that divide peoples. The redistribution of power can be efficacious only when based upon solid realities; it can be beneficent only if it guarantees order and peace.

———

1 O'CONNELL, INTERNATIONAL LAW 38 (2D ED. 1970)*

The Theory of the Relationship: Monism and Dualism

Almost every case in a municipal court in which a rule of international law is asserted to govern the decision raises the problem of the relationship of international law and municipal law; and in many cases before international tribunals it must also be disposed of when deciding the jurisdictional competence of a State to affect alien interests through its own internal legal order.

There are four possible attitudes towards the question:

(a) That international law has primacy over municipal law in both international and municipal decisions. This is the *monist* theory.

(b) That international law has primacy over municipal law in international decisions, and municipal law has primacy over international law in municipal decisions. This is the *dualist* theory.

(c) That municipal law has primacy over international law in both international and municipal decisions. This is a species of monism in reverse.

(d) That there should be no supposition of conflict between international law and municipal law.

Each of these four attitudes will be examined in turn.

(a) Monism

The monist position is an emanation of Kantian philosophy which favours a unitary conception of law. According to this view, since the capacities of States derive from the idea of law, the jurisdiction to exercise these capacities is granted by the law. It follows that the law to which jurisdictional reference must be made is independent of sovereignty and determinative of its limits. If a State exceeds the limits, its acts are invalid. This argument concedes to international law a broader and more fundamental competence than to municipal law. However, it tends to sidestep the point made by the dualists, namely, that a municipal court may be instructed to apply municipal law and not international law, and hence has no jurisdiction (using the term as descriptive of the capacity in municipal law to decide a case) to declare the relevant municipal law invalid. Hence, the characterisation of the jurisdictional excess as "invalid," or even merely "illegal" (if there is any difference between the

* Reprinted with the permission of
Sweet & Maxwell, Ltd., London.

terms), is of no meaning internally within the municipal law of the acting State. To this objection, the monist has only one answer, that this conflict of duties, owing to a defect in organisation, has been wrongly resolved.

* * *

(b) Dualism

The dualist position is associated with Hegelianism and has governed the judicial attitudes of States where this philosophy has prevailed. The common starting point is the proposition that law is an act of sovereign will, municipal law being differentiated from international law in that it is a manifestation of this will internally directed, as distinct from participation in a collective act of will by which the sovereign undertakes obligations with respect to other sovereigns. This results in a dualism of legal origin, of subjects and of subject matters. International law and municipal law are two quite different spheres of legal action, and theoretically there should be no point of conflict between them. Municipal law addresses itself to the subjects of sovereigns, international law to the sovereigns themselves. If the sovereign by an act of municipal law exceeds his competence in international law it does not follow that municipal law is void; it merely follows that the sovereign has violated international law. Anzilotti has explained the relationship between the dualist thesis and the alleged incapacity of the individual in international law as follows:

> A rule of international law is by its very nature absolutely unable to bind individuals, i. e., to confer upon them rights and duties. It is created by the collective will of States with the view of regulating their mutual relations; obviously it cannot therefore refer to an altogether different sphere of relations. If several States were to attempt the creation of rules regulating private relations, such an attempt, by the very nature of things, would not be a rule of international law, but a rule of uniform municipal law common to several States.

(c) Inverted monism

The theory that municipal law is in its nature superior to international law has never found favour in international tribunals, and is no more than an abstract possibility. It is associated with Bergbohm, whose almost pathological resentment against natural law led to an exaggerated emphasis on the State will. Unlike Austin, who would deny even the term "law" to international law and thereby avoid a potential collision of two systems, Bergbohm allows for international law as a manifestation of the "auto limitation" of the sovereign will. The State is superior to and antecedent to the international community, and remains the only law-making entity. Unlike Triepel, who would distinguish the State will as internally manifested from the State will as externally manifested, Bergbohm allows for only one manifestation, and international law is thus a derivation from municipal law.

(d) The theory of harmonisation

According to this view, neither the monist nor the dualist position can be accepted as sound. Each attempts to provide an answer, derived from a single theoretical premise, to two quite different questions. The first question is whether international law is "law" in the same sense as municipal law, i. e., whether both systems are concordant expressions of a unique metaphysical reality. The second question is whether a given tribunal is required by its constitution to apply a rule of international law or municipal law, or vice versa, or authorised to accord primacy to the one over the other. The resemblance between the two questions is only apparent; the lack of jurisdiction in a given tribunal to accord primacy to international law in the event of a conflict between it and municipal law has no relevance to the question whether municipal law does or does not derive its competence from the same basic juridical reality as international law. In some federal systems of law, a State court may be required to apply state legislation which a federal court would declare unconstitutional. The norms of reference are different but the systems are concordant.

The starting point in any legal order is man himself, considered in relation to his fellow man. Law, it has often been said, is life, and life is law. The individual does not live his life exclusively in the legal order of the State any more than he lives it exclusively in the international order. He falls within both jurisdictions because his life is lived in both. Here again, the comparison with a federal system is instructive. It follows that a monistic solution to the problem of the relationship of international law and municipal law fails because it would treat the one system as a derivation of the other, ignoring the physical, metaphysical and social realities which in fact detach them. The world has not yet reached that state of organisation where there is only one civitas maxima delegating specific jurisdiction to regional administrations.

But a dualist solution is equally deficient because it ignores the all-prevailing reality of the universum of human experience. States are the formal instruments of will for the crystallisation of law, but the impulse to the law derives from human behaviour and has a human goal. Positive international law is not pure whim, but an expression of needs and convictions. If it were otherwise, international law and municipal law would be competitive regimes ill-suited to the solution of human problems. The correct position is that international law and municipal law are concordant bodies of doctrine, each autonomous in the sense that it is directed to a specific, and, to some extent, an exclusive area of human conduct, but harmonious in that in their totality the several rules aim at a basic human good.

Questions about monism and dualism. What do you think about this: are these terms descriptive merely of what a particular state does with international law in its own courts and agencies, or do they have direct relevance to the fundamental question whether international law is law?

Review Chapters 1 and 16 and take a position as to whether the United States is properly classifiable as a monist or a dualist state.

If a federal state has in its constitution a provision that rules of customary international law prevail over state of the union law and constitutions, is that federal state necessarily monist?

If any state, federal or unitary, has in its constitution a provision that rules of customary international law prevail over any national law, is that state necessarily monist?

OLIVER, CONTEMPORARY PROBLEMS OF TREATY LAW

[1955] II Académie de Droit International, Recueil des Cours
421, 422, 433 (1955).

Traditional international law is, tragically at a very low level of effective application in today's world, and its development along traditional lines is not currently promising. For most areas development through codification has not come, despite dedicated and scholarly efforts over the years. The settlement of international disputes through the effective utilization of the judicial process has actually lost ground. Meanwhile, legal scholarship has tended more and more to detach itself from reality by (a) excluding from legal science the whole activity of relative valuation; or (b) by devoting meticulous attention to the study of a customary international public law which actually has developed very little, or (c) by claiming for legal methods a degree of effectiveness which legal institutions and the men of the law actually cannot supply.

While these discouraging things have been happening something else has been taking place: I suggest that the real international law of the present, and possibly of the very considerable future, may, * * * be found relatively unnoticed in the underbrush of international agreements, of foreign office practice, of national judicial and administrative actions, and of the ways of life of international organizations.

* * *

Although scholars in international law do not always face up to them, the facts are that international law grows mainly by international agreements; that international law is put into effect principally by foreign offices and by national courts, rather than by international tribunals; and that treaties very seldom, in contemporary times, at least, find their enforcement through international judicial organs.

Under this condition of international society it seems clear that national inhibitions on the negotiation of international agreements and national disinclinations to enforce treaties through municipal tribunals would have very direct and important effects, not only on the conduct of foreign relations, but also upon the viability of international law itself.

KAPLAN AND KATZENBACH, THE POLITICAL FOUNDATIONS OF INTERNATIONAL LAW 5 (1961)*

No one can observe the international political system without being aware of the fact that order does exist, and that this order is related in important ways to formal and authoritative rules, that is, to a body of law and to a process of law-government. These rules are sustained by the genuine interests which nations have in restraining certain forms of international conduct, even though these constraints must apply to their own conduct as well as to that of other states. To understand the substance and limits of such constraining rules, it is necessary to examine the interests which support them in the international system, the means by which they are made effective, and the functions they perform. * * *

* * *

International Law as "Law"

Sometimes international law is viewed as a rather strange breed of law to which the term "law" is applied only by courtesy if at all. A number of great legal philosophers—Hobbes, Pufendorf, Bentham, and Austin are examples—have all doubted the legal character of international law, and the charges and counter charges which pervade the international community today seem to provide empirical support for their view. Clearly some definitions of law would exclude international law. Disputes, for example, are not routinely decided by an international judiciary, and there exists no coercive agency of formal international status which can effectively enforce the law. Rules do not emanate from any single "sovereign." Indeed, the legal order is not primarily vertical, or hierarchical, as it normally is in domestic government. Rather it is structured horizontally, composed predominantly of formally equal centers of legal authority called "states." We have only the beginnings of supranational authority in the United Nations and in various regional organizations.

It is possible, of course, to define law in such a way as to require a hierarchical structure. Austin did this in his theory that rules become authoritative and binding because they are sovereign commands. If law is defined in this way, then it is accurate to say that there is little in the international community.

* * *

Now, in spite of the differences in terminology and the fact that a critic may get considerable political mileage from invoking the accusation that international law has been flouted, processes in the international and domestic arenas are in some respects comparable.

The particular decision disposes of the case and enters into the body of available precedent, whether that decision is persuasive or not. The focus of critical attention is to undercut its status as a norm to be invoked by others in similar circumstances, and it is to this end that some continue to call it a violation of international law. The more arbitrary it can be made to appear, the more radical the innovation, the more it can be related to selfish objectives of a particular state, and the more it offends widely shared and deeply felt values, the less persuasive it will be as precedent for others.

We cannot ignore the fact that in this process the same official may combine legislative and adjudicative functions, with emphasis, indeed, upon the former. Although national officials talk as if they were concerned only with what the law is, they are in fact equally concerned with promoting rules for the future which support policies they favor. * * *

* * *

Doubts about a law-system which lacks judge and sheriff have, we think misleadingly, been frequently expressed as a theory of international law which describes it as a "voluntary" system based on the "consent" of "sovereign" states. It does not require much insight into law-politics to see a parallel between this theory and the consent theory of domestic government. Whatever the moral appeal of the consent theory at both levels (it represents a dislike for coercion), states "consent" to international prescriptions in the same sense that individuals "consent" to existing laws. They recognize the general need for a system of order, they regard the bulk of existing regulation as either desirable or at least tolerable, and they accept what remains because they have to—because they lack the ability to change it. The more intolerable a regulation is, the more pressure there is to seek a change by any means possible.

The point is not, of course, that legal institutions in the international community are adequate to contemporary affairs. Obviously they are not. But these institutions, such as they are, exist and contribute to international order. They will continue until some political combination has the capability to create new institutions more consonant with order and, we can at least hope, with a decent regard for human values. This creative process is presently taking place, on both a universal scale (the United Nations complex) and, perhaps more successfully, in a variety of regional and functional organizations such as NATO and the European Communities.

The authors recognize the merits of criticisms that distinguished observers such as George Kennan have made regarding too great a reliance upon legal processes. American foreign policy has often been formulated without suffcient attention to the role of force and of national interests. We do not wish to encourage naiveté of the sort he describes as "legal idealism," a reliance upon abstract rules that are institutionally unsupported. We concede that nations often do act in partisan ways in support of immediate political objectives.

But we contend that much of international conduct is doctrinally consonant with normative standards, even though inconsistent with particular immediate interests, and that long-term self-interest can and does provide political support for internationally lawful conduct.

———

Question. At this stage of your study are you willing to accept international law as law? Why or why not? In retrospect, does Chapter 1 have a positive, negative, or neutral influence on your attitude? If you do not consider at this point that international law is law, what is the minimum required to make it law?

———

TUNKIN, FORTY YEARS OF CO-EXISTENCE AND INTERNATIONAL LAW

Soviet Yearbook of International Law 1958, at 42 (Moscow, 1959).

Bourgeois jurisprudence usually regards agreement between states as the result of the "concurrence of wills" of these states, expressing their "common will".

* * *

This coordination of wills of the states in the process of creating a norm of general international law does not signify their merging into some kind of "common will" or "single will". These wills cannot fuse because their class natures, expressed in the aims and tasks of the states concerned, are different and even contradictory (the wills of socialist and capitalist states), they are, however, coordinated and aimed at establishing a definite rule as a norm of law. A norm of general international law is an expression not of a "single will", but of "coordinated wills", i. e., wills equally directed towards a definite aim-recognition of the given rule as a norm of international law.

Agreement presupposes that the wills of states are not only "coordinated" in relation to recognition of the given rule, but are also mutually conditioned. Agreement between states includes "interconditionality" of wills, the substance of which is that the assent of one state to recognize a particular rule as a norm of international law is conditional on analogous assent by the other state. "Interconditionality" is the thread which links the wills of different states in the process of shaping or extending the sphere of operation of a norm of international law.

The norms of general international law, then express the "coordinated and mutually conditioned wills" of the states belonging to two co-existing social systems.

General international law reflects not only community of interests, as claimed by bourgeois international lawyers, but also the contradictions between them; not only co-operation, but also a struggle.
* * *

* * *

The rules of international law being borne in the process of struggle and co-operation between states, are the result of the clash and coordination of the wills of the ruling classes of different states. They are created by sovereign states. The wills of the ruling classes in the different countries, which clash in the process of creating these rules, are juridically equal. But it goes without saying that in moulding international law the actual influence exerted by these wills is not at all identical. It depends on the rôle played by the particular state in international relations and on the nature of the principles which it advances. Contemporary international law develops under the evergrowing influence of the socialist states and the other states pursuing the policy of peaceful co-existence in international relations, under the influence exerted by all the forces of peace.

* * *

As a result of the struggle waged by all the progressive forces, and primarily by the Soviet Union and the other socialist states, there have arisen in international law such important universally recognized principles as the principle of prohibition of the use of force in international relations (the principle of non-aggression), the principle of self-determination of nations, non-interference in internal affairs, equality, and others.

At the same time we see the continued development and strengthening of the old democratic principles and rules: respect for state sovereignty, non-interference in internal affairs, equality, and others.

The process of establishing new progressive principles and norms of international law is continuing. Vital significance should be attached to the formation of international-law rules concerning reduction of armaments and banning atomic and hydrogen weapons—use of which should be recognized as contrary to law in view of the generally recognized principles of international law—the efforts to secure a generally recognized definition of aggression, universal recognition of the rules banning war propaganda, etc.

* * *

* * * [W]e find in bourgeois international-law literature nowadays not a few pessimistic assessments concerning the importance of international law in international relations.

Particularly widespread at present in bourgeois international-law literature is the view that international law in its present state is embryonic, primitive law, and that only the establishment of a "world state" or the greatest possible approximation to it can make international law "real" law.

Were we to accept this view the prospects for international law would be gloomy indeed, since the idea of establishing a "world state", a "world government", and so on, as things are today, is not realistic—it is out of tune with the laws of social development in our times.

Concepts of world government in present conditions are not only utopian, they are reactionary. From these concepts it is but a step to affirming the hopelessness of any attempt to consolidate and develop general international law, to recognition of the rule of force in international relations.

Enhancing the rôle of international law in ensuring peaceful co-existence should be sought not by establishing a world state and abolishing the state sovereignty of the countries, by creating a new international law, etc., but primarily by consolidating, developing and consistently observing the generally accepted principles and norms of the international law now in operation, which to a large degree is inscribed in the Charter of the United Nations.

The basic condition for the effectiveness of contemporary general international law is a recognition by all states of the situation when capitalist and socialist states exist side by side, and rejection of any attempt to change this situation by force.

* * *

Question. Is not the Soviet academician's view of international law a rather limited one? Are the principles that he finds within the coordinated wills of bourgeois states and socialist states principles of international law or of international politics? Is there any difference to him?

The writer of the next excerpt is one of the most prodigious American workers of modern times in the vineyards of international order. His structure for studying, applying and developing world order has been stated by him several times; but we think this excerpt is the most useful one to present to you. Professor McDougal for many years collaborated with Professor Harold D. Lasswell in the formulation of the outlook sketched below. With other collaborators he has used this approach in making massive studies of particular topics, such as the law of the sea, interpretation of international agreements, use of nuclear weapons, a structure for order in the world community. Often inspiring and always provocative, his legal philosophy has been influential in this country—although often resisted as well—but still rather puzzling to scholars in other countries—unless they were his students. Why?

McDOUGAL, INTERNATIONAL LAW, POWER AND POLICY: A CONTEMPORARY CONCEPTION

[1953] I Académie de Droit International, Recueil des Cours, 137.

The Tasks of a Policy-Oriented Jurisprudence (Philosophy-Science of Law) in Our Time

* * *

2.   The great challenge to students of international law today, in this context of world social and power processes and growing threat to freedom, is, * * * to extend their aspirations beyond traditional exercises in technical formulae for determining what conduct is lawful and what unlawful to the much more urgent task of determining and recommending that international law, of the many possible systems of international law, which is best designed to promote a free world society.   The dilemma that confronts us in the world today offers alternatives not so much between non-law, or naked force, and law, as between different kinds of law, a law promoting human indignity or a law promoting human dignity.   In this dilemma, it is the over-riding moral responsibility of legal scholars, as the appropriate skilled specialists of society, to identify or invent and to recommend the prescriptions, organizations, and decisions that favor a law of human dignity.

To meet this challenge legal scholars will require a comprehensive guiding theory and intellectual techniques adequate to perform certain specific functions.   These functions the author and a colleague have elsewhere characterized as the elements of a "policy-oriented" approach to the study of law.   We emphasize policy purposes because we do not believe that a jurisprudence which purports to be "scientific" only is adequate to the crisis of our time.   Though it is imperative that a scholar should seek to minimize the degree to which his preferences distort the accuracy of his observation of events, a creative jurisprudence requires not only the ways of thinking and procedures of observation commonly called scientific but also other integrated and interrelated methods of thought and observation.   In briefest summary, the various functions indispensable to a policy-oriented approach to the study of international law and to the choice of an international law appropriate to a free world society may be indicated as follows:

(1) The clarification of goal values and the detailed relation of the flow of particular decisions that constitute the world power process to such goal values.

(2) The description of trends in decision, in terms of effects upon values, and the identification in the greatest degree possible of the variables, predispositional and environmental, that affect particular decisions.

(3) The critical projection of trends into the future, on the basis of historical and scientific knowledge, in attempt to predict what future decisions are likely to be.

(4) The appraisal of decisions in terms of their compatibility with goal values and the invention and evaluation of new alternatives of policy—prescriptions and institutions—designed for the better securing of such goal values.

3.   Each of these multiple functions of a creative jurisprudence—preferential, descriptive-scientific, predictive, and inventive—has been a principal focus or objective of varying conceptions of law in the past and each function is today performed, by legal scholars and others, consciously or unconsciously, with varying degrees of effectiveness. * * *

*   *   *

It is, fortunately, becoming increasingly recognized that "law" and "policy" are not distinct and that every application of general rules, customary or conventional or however derived, to specific cases in fact requires the making of policy choices.   From the perspective of a scientific observer, it is obvious that the behavior of decision-makers in the world power process is influenced by many variables, environmental and predispositional, other than legal rules, and that technical legal rules, divorced from the content of the policy perspectives of decision-makers and the groups with which they identify, are not competent to coerce or predict decisions or to prescribe what decisions ought to be or even adequately to describe what decisions have been.   This impotence of technical legal rules has seldom been better stated than by Professor Kelsen: [a reiteration of his "Pure Theory" doctrine, see p. 1206].

*   *   *

It should perhaps be added that we recognize that we draw from Professor Kelsen's observation a conclusion different from that drawn by Professor Kelsen himself.   Professor Kelsen considers it a "veritable usurpation of competence" for "jurists" to attempt "to determine the social ends to be attained" because "no matter how profound may be one's understanding of what the law is, this cannot cast light on what, because it is 'just', socially good, must be the content of law".   "This question," he insists, "is not juridical but specifically political.   It is the domain par excellence of the politician".   Where, with deference, we differ from Professor Kelsen is in this insistence that the task of the jurist, the peculiarly legal function, must stop when the jurist outlines for decision-makers the various alternatives that the legal forms afford.   Our suggestion is that, if an international law of human dignity is to be achieved, the jurist, as a responsible interpreter of the policy commitments embodied in legal prescriptions and procedures and as a skilled specialist with peculiarly intimate opportunity to observe such prescriptions and procedures in action, must extend his role beyond mere inquiry into and advice about legal syntactics, or the logical interrelations among legal propositions, to the further tasks of inquiry into and advice about the possible effects upon overall community values of the various alternatives that the legal forms afford.

II.   Over-emphasis on Naked Power as a Factor in Decision

At the opposite extreme from over-emphasis on technical rules, is an attitude increasingly common today which underestimates the rule of rules, and of legal processes in general, and over-emphasizes the importance of naked power. This attitude is sometimes referred to as the "pure theory of power" as contrasted with the "pure theory of law". In many of the manifestations of this attitude it seems to be assumed, though the assumption is not always made explicit, that the detailed application of legal rules is always a function of the immediate power interests, of a mere calculation of momentary expediencies without regard to long-term community interests of the decisionmaker and that legal rules—however clearly related to community policies, however sustained by balancing of power, and however sanctioned—are in some unchangeable nature of things irretrievably powerless to restrain the lawless behavior of absolutely and permanently sovereign nation-states.

＊　＊　＊

It is submitted that all the contemporary manifestations of the "pure power" theory ＊ ＊ ＊ both profoundly misconceive law and power and greatly underestimate both the role that law presently plays in the world power process and the role that, with a more effective balancing of power, it could be made to play in promoting and preserving the values of a free, peaceful, and abundant world society.
＊　＊　＊

III.   Failure to Achieve Comprehensive Description of the Participants in the World Power Process

It is common knowledge that in recent years the participants in the world power process have undergone and are continuing to undergo tremendous transformations. The traditional territorially organized bodies politic, known as "nation-states", are, on the one hand, being dwarfed by the emergence of huge new bi-polarized and other regional groupings and, on the other hand, being challenged by the rise of a host of new and powerful functional organizations—including international governmental organizations, transnational political parties, transnational pressure groups, and transnational private associations. Contemporary theory about international law, obsessed by a technical conception of the "subjects of international law", continues, however, greatly to over-estimate the role of the "nation-state" and to underestimate the role of all these other new participants.
＊　＊　＊

IV.   Failure to Achieve Comprehensive Description of the Techniques of Policy Formulation and Application in the World Power Process

The most casual observation of the flow of decisions in the world arena today reveals that policies are being formulated, recommended, prescribed, and reformulated and represcribed in multiplied thousands of agreements, conferences, resolutions, declarations, codifications, and customary practices of foreign office and other officials as well as by judicial and arbitral decision and that policies are being applied, appraised and terminated, in countless informal interactions in international and national arenas of all kinds. In much of the technical literature on international law, however, one still finds an over-concentration on "the court" as the principal instrument of law in world affairs and a supporting assumption that the principal function of a court, with its "given" rules, is the maintenance of opposition to change   *   *   *.

The inadequacies of contemporary theory about international law add up, accordingly, to failure effectively to perform the various functions indicated above as indispensable to a policy-oriented approach to the study of international law.

The question now is what framework of inquiry might permit the more effective performance of these functions and, in particular, assist the legal scholar in his distinctive task of clarifying the policies implicit in past and proposed systems of international law. It is reasonably obvious that such a framework must offer a comprehensive way of talking about the world social and power processes in which decisions occur, rational criteria for identifying the decisions regarded as law, and an organization of studies for examining the flow of specific decisions which will facilitate both the testing of specific decisions for compatibility with the goal values of a free society and scientific study of the variables which in fact affect decision. Many different systems of inquiry might of course be devised for achieving these purposes. The framework we propose seeks both a way of outlining the total context of world social and power processes and a way of keeping specific decisions constantly at the focus of attention, however various the participants, the arenas of interaction, the base values invoked, the instruments of policy applied, or outcomes achieved in any particular context. It must be recognized, however, that no intellectual tools can be devised which will cut the "big, blooming, buzzing confusion" which is the world about us with final and dogmatic precision. What we are attempting to do is, almost literally, slowly to turn a globe or sphere (the context of the world social and power processes) for the purpose of spotlighting, investigating, and relating to total context now one set of decisions, with all their goals and conditioning variables, and then another set. The performance of this task must inevitably be marked by over-laps, gaps, and imprecisions.

*   *   *

The comprehensive framework of theory that we propose for describing the world social process is indicated in skeletonized form in Chart I, which is set out below.

Chart I

Community Process

```
People
  with                           power
  perspectives                   respect
    identifications  using base values  enlightenment through institutions
    demands                      wealth
    expectations                 well-being
                                 rectitude
  myth  doctrine                 skill
        formula (legal rules)    affection
        miranda

                                 unprocessed
      organizational routines  on resources  land   to shape and distribute
            government                  processed    scope values
  technique  party                      land
             pressure groups            facilities
             private associations       human energy
        non-organizational
power
respect                          people
enlightenment     among          with
wealth                           perspectives
well-being                         identifications
rectitude                          demands
skill                              expectations
affection
```

The most general formulation upon which this Chart is based is: *people* strive to maximize *values* by applying *institutions* to *resources*.[2]

With respect to *people*, we would emphasize that the most relevant description must include not merely their numbers, spatial distribution, physical characteristics, value and institutional positions and so on, but also their perspectives (subjectivities, predispositions)— their demands for values, their identifications with others, and their factual expectations (beliefs) about past and future.

By the term *values*, we refer to major categories of desired events. For purposes of the present comprehensive analysis we recommend as convenient the following eight categories: power, respect, enlightenment, wealth, well-being, skill, affection, and rectitude. In brief, preliminary definition, *power* may be taken to refer to participation in the making of important decisions (decisions involving severe deprivations) ; *respect*, to access to other values on the basis of merit, without discrimination on grounds irrelevant to capacity; *enlightenment*, to access to the knowledge on which rational choice depends;

---

2. More detailed expositions of the general mode of analysis we recommend may be found in Lasswell and Kaplan, Power and Society (1950); Lasswell, Power and Personality (1948) and The World Revolution of our Time (1951); Lerner and Lasswell (eds.) The Policy Sciences (1951); Lasswell, Leites and Associates, Language of Politics (1949).

wealth, to control over economic goods and services; *well-being,* to the enjoyment of physical and psychic health; *skill,* to proficiency in the exercise of latent talent; *affection* to the enjoyment of congenial human relations; and *rectitude,* to the sharing of common standards of responsibility.

The term *institutions* is used to refer to the pattern of practices by which values are shaped and shared. Such patterns include, as may be seen from the Chart, both myth and technique, or both rules and operations.

Resources include the physical objects and materials and human energy that are employed in the shaping and sharing of values and their significance obviously varies greatly from value to value and context to context.

The postulate that people strive to maximize their values is introduced as a dynamic principle to account for individual and group choices. It is a postulate that has proved most fruitful in many branches of psychological and social science investigation.

Keeping in mind this brief explanation of terms and major postulate, we may now read Chart I as formulating a description of community or social process in terms of people, with varying perspectives, in varying situations, employing base values, by practices (myth and technique), to effect a redistribution among people of certain demanded or "scope" values. In any particular study of specific value processes, the people and their perspectives, the situations in which they demand values, the base values they employ, the practices by which they shape and share values, and the effects they obtain upon the distribution of values may be described in as much detail as the materials permit or as the particular problem of the investigator requires.

It may be emphasized that any particular value may be either employed as a means or sought as an end, may be either a base value or a scope value. The total world social process may, indeed, be usefully conceived as a series of interrelated value processes: a power process, a respect process, an enlightenment process, a wealth process, a well-being process, a skill process, an affection process, and a rectitude process. Any given interaction may be identified by examining in detail the demands and expectations of the people in the situation.

It is because of the interrelation of value processes, the point may bear further emphasis, that rational inquiry by jurists cannot be confined exclusively to power processes. Though we will presently recommend a conception of law in terms of a form of power (including both myth and technique, rules and operations), any realistic study of power processes requires the relation of such processes to the other value processes. The events which give rise to controversies and result in the invocation of power decisions occur, as already indicated, in every value process; power decisions may be in fact affected by considerations of any or all the other values; and, finally, such decisions may in turn affect any one or all of the values. In more abstract statement, the world process affects each of the other value processes and the other value processes in turn affect the world power process and each other. The jurist who would concern himself with causes and effects, conditions and consequences, must be prepared to extend his inquiries to the totality of value processes.

* * *

Some observations. Can it be denied that this is the most idealistic concept of law for world society presented in this chapter? Within the Department of State, how much of what a McDougal analysis would require in the way of inquiry and decision-making falls to the lawyers in the Legal Adviser's Office, as distinguished from other personnel, whether law trained or not, elsewhere within the department? Do lawyers as lawyers know enough to be the top users of the techniques sketched? Is not the view of the lawyer's power and responsibility very distinctly American? Who makes the big decisions at the World Bank or at the International Monetary Fund, lawyers or other types of experts?

Does McDougal reject the notion of law as a normative science? If so, is this desirable?

International law and international justice. In a narrow sense international justice involves fair and humane exercise of state power. Beyond denial of justice and controverted principles as to nationalization, however, customary international law has contributed little in this area. The various conventions on civil, political, economic and social rights, against genocide, slavery and discrimination based on race or sex attempt more.

Most American legal philosophers have no difficulties with treating both absolute and relative values as within their competence. European philosophers tend to differentiate more sharply between legal science and the advocacy of value choices, leaving the latter (more than American lawyers do) to the humanities, social science and politics. Kelsen is the most adamant in denying that value judgments are within the competence of the legal scientist.

What does McDougal's human dignity, the ultimate common goal value, include insofar as international justice is concerned? Which of these values is entitled to the higher priority: the dignity of the individual (protection against indignities) or the minimal subsistence and developmental needs of a developing country of thirty million people? Is it satisfactory in today's world to answer that the values are equal and that neither should be preferred over the other. If you believe that the first value is unquestionably entitled to the higher priority, are you sure there is no ethnocentrism in the position? If common goal values are to determine the ends of just law, how are they to be determined?

OLIVER, THE UNITED STATES OF AMERICA AND INTERNATIONAL PUBLIC LAW, 1900–1976

9 St. Mary's Law Journal 1, 3 (1977).

* * *

In describing and analyzing national attitudes toward the international legal order, one must be aware at all times that in some, but perhaps not most, states there are several acting groups other than the state itself. This * * * perspective is especially important in the case of the United States where significant communities of interest in the subject of international law exist entirely independent of the government and its attitudes toward international law. It would be seriously inaccurate, for example, to equate the American Society of International Law and its prestigious journal with any particular foreign affairs agency of the United States Government.

The community of American scholarly interest in international law is highly developed, generally independent of the American state, and divided into two interacting but distinct scholarly groups: the lawyers and the political scientists. In the socialist states, and in some nonideological authoritarian states, the degree of independence of the scholarly community as to international law is not nearly so definite as it is in the United States. In addition, there are very few states in which the scholarly sector of international legal studies is so generously supported by foundations and other nongovernmental sources.

The foregoing is not, of course, a denial of the existence in nongovernmental quarters of preferences as to what international law is —or should be—that reflect an "American" system of values, those embraced by various groups in a pluralistic, free society. Nor is it to be taken as denying that many American international law experts are drawn into public service for temporary duty. Finally, as to this particular, it is true in the United States, as elsewhere, that there exists a "grey zone" in which what a government or a scholarly community or an economic interest group wishes a rule of international law to be is asserted as being what the law is.[6]

Despite these linkages and interrelationships, however, the American role as to legal order must of necessity be viewed from distinctly governmental and nongovernmental standpoints. Generally, United States contributions to major affirmative developments of international law in the twentieth century have originated with the

---

6. The United States, for example, still officially insists on a customary international law rule concerning the duties of a nationalizing state when the investments of another's citizens are nationalized, that is not followed by a considerable numerical majority of states. On the other hand, the United States has recently given legal effect to its version of a 200 mile economic (fisheries) zone that it has previously resisted as illegal, even when authority was restricted to the regulation of fisheries. In these two instances the key preferences, cast as law, have been those of certain economic interests and their lawyers, including among the latter some recognized scholars who have functioned as advocates without making this role explicit.

nongovernmental sectors and have eventually attracted some degree of official support as U.S. foreign policy on the international legal order.

Finally, in viewing governmentally-supported principles of international law, one must bear in mind that as a member of a community of states, the United States has historically perceived international law in essentially the same way as have other major Western powers. The history of international legal order in the present century has been that of curbing—or seeking to curb—national state will to use its military power and other advantages in the pursuit of immediate or shorter-range national interest. In this grand development—still far from accomplished—the United States has played an ambivalent role, now that of just another national-interest-pursuing state among states in the world arena, and at other times that of an idealistically inclined nation, determined to bring about the legal and political ordering of freedom, justice, equality, and human dignity.

＊ ＊ ＊

Concluding question. Should or should not a scholar in international law be required by scholarly ethics to differentiate sharply between his/her preferences as to what the law should be and the process of determining what it is? Is such differentiation possible, psychologically?

Part VII

THE USE OF FORCE IN THE INTERNATIONAL SYSTEM

Throughout most of the life of the world's present state system, states have been regarded by international law as being permitted to use almost all of their advantages, political, economic and military, in pursuit of their national interests. Although minor military incursions on the territory of a neighboring state might be considered unlawful (unless justified, possibly, as an act of reprisal in response to some unlawful act of the neighbor), if the military actor chose to make war [a] upon its neighbor that state of affairs was not considered a violation of international law. Two qualifications must be made to this assertion, however. A state could, of course, be bound by treaty not to make war on a particular state. And as seen in Chapter 10, by international custom and conventions, states at war with each other were bound to wage it more or less humanely; that is, although the fact of war could not be prevented by law, it was hoped that the manner of waging it could be regulated.

In this part, we are concerned with modern efforts to outlaw war and other uses of military force. We shall also explore the extent to which international law seeks as well to control the way in which states pursue their national interests through forcing their will on other states by non-military means.

When states are forbidden to pursue their national interests by the use of armed force, an urgent need arises for other authorized sources of regulated force in the international system. In this part, we examine the extent to which the United Nations and regional organizations may use force for lawful ends when individual nation states or groups of states allied with each other are forbidden to use force in pursuit of their national interests.

a. In international jurisprudence in recent centuries, war has been a word of art. In popular usage it has meant the overt use of military force against another state. In law, however, it meant a legal relationship existing between states, created by intention of those states and generally but not always involving the use of armed force. Whether this legal relationship could be created (or lawfully created) without a declaration of war was a question entangled in inconsistent state practice and international convention. See, generally, Starke, An Introduction to International Law, Chapter 16 (5th ed., 1963).

Chapter 19

THE USE OF FORCE BY STATES

SECTION A. EVOLUTION OF LAW AGAINST USE OF FORCE BY STATES

The League of Nations. The Covenant of the League of Nations did not outlaw war as such. Instead, it sought to obligate states to resort to methods of peaceful settlement; in turn, members of the League agreed under certain circumstances not to resort to war. See in particular the following articles of the covenant: Article 12 ("* * * they agree in no case to resort to war until three months after the award by the arbitrators or the report by the Council."); Article 13 ("The Members of the League agree that they will carry out in full good faith any award that may be rendered, and that they will not resort to war against a Member of the League which complies therewith."); Article 15 ("If a report by the Council is unanimously agreed to by the Members thereof other than the representatives of one or more of the parties to the dispute, the Members of the League agree that they will not go to war with any party to the dispute which complies with the recommendations of the report.")

These qualified commitments against waging war should be contrasted to the language of the Peace Pact of Paris and of Article 2(4) of the United Nations Charter, set forth hereafter. Also to be contrasted with Article 2(4) of the charter is Article 10 of the covenant, in which members of the League undertook to "respect and preserve as against external aggression the territorial integrity and existing political independence of all members of the League." Was this article also a backhanded commitment not to commit such aggression?

The mechanisms for enforcing the ambiguous and qualified obligations not to wage war were contained in Article 10 of the covenant ("* * * the Council shall advise upon the means by which this obligation shall be fulfilled") and in Article 16 (the provisions for collective measures by the members of the League in the event a member of the League should "resort to war in disregard of its covenants under Articles 12, 13 or 15").

As is well known, the United States did not become a member of the League of Nations. The Covenant of the League was an integral part of the Treaty of Versailles. When it was submitted to the Senate for its advice and consent, Senator Henry Cabot Lodge led the Senate to the adoption of a number of reservations, notably one to Article 10, to the effect that the United States would not assume an obligation to preserve the territorial integrity or political independence of any country unless "in any particular case the Congress,

1230

which, under the Constitution, has the sole power to declare war or authorize the employment of the military or naval forces of the United States, shall by act or joint resolution so provide." Stone (ed.), Wilson and the League of Nations 98 (1967). President Wilson refused to accept the Lodge reservations. As a result, the treaty (with the covenant) was rejected by the Senate. Analyses of the rejection of the League from a variety of points of view are published in the Stone symposium.

As for the effect of the covenant on the unilateral use of force by states and the efforts of the League to restrain that force, it can only be stated that the results were dismal.

MORGENTHAU, POLITICS AMONG NATIONS 290 (4TH ED., 1967)*

* * * Collective measures of enforcement under Article 16 were applied in only one of the five cases in which undoubtedly a member of the League resorted to war in violation of the Covenant. With regard to the Sino-Japanese conflict that started in 1931, the Assembly of the League of Nations found unanimously that "without any declaration of war, part of the Chinese territory has been forcibly seized and occupied by the Japanese troops," and that far-flung hostilities, initiated by Japan, had taken place between troops of the Chinese and Japanese governments. Yet the Assembly found also that Japan had not resorted to war in violation of the Covenant and that, therefore, Article 16 did not apply.

In 1934, during the Chaco War of 1932–35, when Paraguay continued hostilities against Bolivia in violation of the Covenant, many members of the League limited the arms embargo, originally imposed upon both belligerents, to Paraguay. This was a discriminatory measure falling far short of the spirit and the letter of the first paragraph of Article 16. When Japan, which by then had resigned from the League, invaded China in 1937, the Assembly found that Japan had violated the Nine Power Treaty of 1922 and the Briand-Kellogg Pact, that Article 16 was applicable, and that the members of the League had the right to take enforcement measures individually under that provision. No such measures were ever taken. When the Soviet Union went to war with Finland in 1939, it was expelled from the League by virtue of Article 16, paragraph 4, but no collective action of enforcement was taken against it.

In contrast to these cases, the Assembly found in 1935 that the invasion of Ethiopia by Italy constituted resort to war within the meaning and in violation of the Covenant and that, therefore, Article 16, paragraph 1, was to apply. In consequence, collective economic sanctions against Italy were decided upon and applied. Yet the two measures, provided for by Article 16, paragraph 1, that offered the best chance of making international law prevail under the circumstances and that in all probability would have compelled Italy to desist from its attack upon Ethiopia—namely, an embargo on oil shipments to Italy and the closure of the Suez Canal—were not taken. "However," as Sir H. Lauterpacht puts it, "although the sanctions of Article 16, paragraph 1, were formally put into operation and although an elaborate machinery was set up with a view to their successive and gradual enforcement, the nature of the action taken was such as to suggest that the repressive measures were being adopted as a manifestation of moral reprobation rather than as an effective means of coercion."

One can, therefore, sum up the attempts at establishing a centralized system of law enforcement under Article 16 of the Covenant by saying that in most of the cases that would have justified the application of sanctions, sanctions were not applied at all. In the sole case in which they were applied, they were applied in such an ineffective fashion as virtually to assure both their failure and the success of the recalcitrant state.

TRAVAUX–PREPARATOIRES FOR THE PEACE PACT OF PARIS (THE KELLOGG–BRIAND PACT)

[1928] 1 Foreign Relations of the United States 32 (1942).

French Draft of Treaty for the Condemnation and Renunciation of War as an Instrument of National Policy

The President of the German Empire, the President of the United States of America, the President of the French Republic, His Majesty the King of England, Ireland and the British Dominions, Emperor of India, His Majesty the King of Italy, His Majesty the Emperor of Japan:

Equally desirous not only of perpetuating the happy relations of peace and friendship now existing among their peoples, but also of avoiding the danger of war between all other nations in the world,

Having agreed to consecrate in a solemn act their most formal and most definite resolution to condemn war as an instrument of national policy and to renounce it in favor of a peaceful settlement of international conflicts,

Expressing, finally, the hope that all the other nations of the world will be willing to join in this humane effort to bring about the association of the civilized peoples in a common renunciation of war as an instrument of national policy, have decided to conclude a treaty and to that end have designated as their respective plenipotentiaries:

The President of the German Empire:

The President of the United States of America:

The President of the French Republic:

His Majesty the King of Great Britain, Ireland and the British Dominions, Emperor of India:

His Majesty the King of Italy:

His Majesty the Emperor of Japan:

who, after exchanging their full powers found to be in good and due form have agreed on the following provisions:

Article One

The High Contracting Parties without any intention to infringe upon the exercise of their rights of legitimate self-defense within the framework of existing treaties, particularly when the violation of certain of the provisons of such treaties constitutes a hostile act, solemnly declare that they condemn recourse to war and renounce it as an instrument of national policy; that is to say, as an instrument of individual, spontaneous and independent political action taken on their own initiative and not action in respect of which they might become involved through the obligation of a treaty such as the covenant of the League of Nations or any other treaty registered with the League of Nations. They undertake on these conditions not to attack or invade one another.

Article Two

The settlement or solution of all disputes or conflicts of whatever nature or origin which might arise among the High Contracting Parties or between any two of them shall never be sought on either side except by pacific methods.

Article Three

In case one of the High Contracting Parties should contravene this treaty, the other Contracting Powers would ipso facto be released with respect to that Party from their obligations under this treaty.

Article Four

The provisions of this treaty in no wise affect the rights and obligations of the Contracting Parties resulting from prior international agreements to which they are parties.

Article Five

The present treaty will be offered for the accession of all Powers and will have no binding force until it has been generally accepted unless the signatory Powers in accord with those that may accede hereto shall agree to decide that it shall come into effect regardless of certain abstentions.

*   *   *

The Secretary of State to the Ambassador in France (Herrick)

WASHINGTON, April 23, 1928—5 p. m.

*   *   * In its present form the French draft treaty is wholly unacceptable to the United States since it cannot in any respect be regarded as an effective instrument for the promotion of world peace. It emphasizes war, not peace, and seems in effect to be a justification rather than a renunciation of the use of armed force. The United States will sign no treaty of the nature now under discussion which cannot reasonably be expected to lessen the danger of an outbreak of war and thus promote the cause of world peace. *   *   *

There seem to be six major considerations which the French Government has emphasized in its correspondence and in its draft treaty, namely, that the treaty must not (1) impair the right of legitimate self-defense; (2) violate the Covenant of the League of Nations; (3) violate the treaties of Locarno; (4) violate certain unspecified treaties guaranteeing neutrality; (5) bind the parties in respect of a state breaking the treaty; (6) come into effect until accepted by all or substantially all of the Powers of the world. The views of the United States on these six points are as follows:

(1) Self-defense. There is nothing in the American draft of an anti-war treaty which restricts or impairs in any way the right of self-defense. That right is inherent in every sovereign state and is implicit in every treaty. Every nation is free at all times and regardless of treaty provisions to defend its territory from attack or invasion and it alone is competent to decide whether circumstances require recourse to war in self-defense. If it has a good case, the world will applaud and not condemn its action. Express recognition by treaty of this inalienable right, however, gives rise to the same difficulty encountered in any effort to define aggression. It is the identical question approached from the other side. Inasmuch as no treaty provision can add to the natural right of self-defense, it is not in the interest of peace that a treaty should stipulate a juristic conception of self-defense since it is far too easy for the unscrupulous to mold events to accord with an agreed definition.

*   *   *

KELLOGG

GENERAL TREATY FOR RENUNCIATION OF WAR AS AN INSTRUMENT OF NATIONAL POLICY OF AUGUST 27, 1928

46 Stat. 2343, 94 L.N.T.S. 59 (1929).

Article I

The High Contracting Parties solemnly declare in the names of their respective peoples that they condemn recourse to war for the solution of international controversies, and renounce it as an instrument of national policy in their relations with one another.

Article II

The High Contracting Parties agree that the settlement or solution of all disputes or conflicts of whatever nature or of whatever origin they may be, which may arise among them, shall never be sought except by pacific means.

LIST OF PARTIES TO THE TREATY FOR THE RENUNCIATION OF WAR, AS OF JANUARY 1, 1980

Treaty providing for the renunciation of war as an instrument of national policy. Signed at Paris August 27, 1928; entered into force for the United States July 24, 1929.

46 Stat. 2343; TS 796; 2 Bevans 732; 94 LNTS 57.

States which are parties:

Afghanistan
Albania
Australia
Austria
Barbados
Belgium
Brazil
Bulgaria
Canada
Chile
China [1]
Colombia
Costa Rica
Cuba
Czechoslovakia
Denmark
Dominican Republic
Ecuador
Egypt
Estonia
Ethiopia
Fiji
Finland
France
Germany
Greece
Guatemala
Haiti
Honduras
Hungary
Iceland
India
Iran

Iraq
Ireland
Italy
Japan
Latvia
Liberia
Lithuania
Luxembourg
Mexico
Netherlands
New Zealand
Nicaragua
Norway
Panama
Paraguay
Peru
Poland, including
    Free City of Danzig
Portugal
Romania
Saudi Arabia
South Africa
Spain
Sweden
Switzerland
Thailand
Turkey
Union of Soviet
    Socialist Reps.
United Kingdom
United States
Venezuela
Yugoslavia

1. Pre 1949 convention, applicable only to Taiwan.

1. *Parties during World War II.* The Department of State's compilation of Treaties in Force on December 31, 1941, lists all of the above states except Austria, Barbados and Fiji as parties to the Pact of Paris (subject to a Special Note disclaiming the department's having passed upon the effect of war on any of the treaties in the compilation).

2. *Why was the Pact of Paris a futile bar to war?* Even before the outbreak of World War II, armed conflict had been carried on by Japan in China, by Germany, Italy and the USSR in Spain, and by Italy in Ethiopia.

BROWN, UNDECLARED WARS

33 American Journal of International Law 538, 540 (1939).*

We see, therefore, in the light of theory and practice, that the problem of the undeclared war remains largely an academic one which involves considerations more ethical than legal. And this is true also of the self-denying declaration embodied in the General Treaty of 1928 for the Renunciation of War, generally entitled the Kellogg Pact. This agreement, while purporting to renounce the use of war, really consecrated the vague and dangerous right of self-defence. The various signatories explicitly reserved the right to resort to war and to judge for themselves "whether circumstances require recourse to war in self-defence." Within four years of the signing of this Pact occurred three breaches of the Pact, namely, the aggression by Russia against China in 1929, the occupation of Manchuria by Japan in 1931, and the invasion of Colombia by Peru in 1932. The more recent instances of warlike acts by Japan, Germany, and Italy are too vividly in mind to require comment. It is necessary, however, to stress the lamentable and unforeseen consequence of the Kellogg Pact in encouraging aggressor nations hypocritically to avoid any formal declaration of war in order to elude the constraints of this pious declaration.

Still another most unexpected inducement to avoid a formal declaration of war, as revealed in the case of the conflict now going on between Japan and China, has been the natural desire to escape the disabilities of recent neutrality legislation of the United States, whereby the shipment of arms and munitions of war to belligerents is automatically forbidden. The question presents itself whether, in the absence of a formal declaration of war by either side, it should not be incumbent on neutral nations to brush all legal niceties aside and openly acknowledge a state of war where the laws of war and neutrality should apply. Nations intent on peace and determined to uphold the reign of law have a solemn duty to avoid any implied connivance in the evasion of international obligations. Neutrality is not merely to

* Reprinted with the permission of the American Society of International Law.

conserve national interests, but also to preserve an impartial rôle which may enable a nation to affirm with vigor the responsibilities and rights of peoples under international law.

The situation is certainly a most unhappy one. It is stultifying to discover that an idealistic agreement such as the Kellogg Pact, and neutrality legislation conceived for a generous purpose, should actually conduce to the fiction of the undeclared war.   *   *   *

CHARTER OF THE UNITED NATIONS

Article 2

The Organization and its Members, in pursuit of the Purposes stated in Article 1, shall act in accordance with the following Principles.

    *   *   *

4. All Members shall refrain in their international relations from the threat or use of force against the territorial integrity or political independence of any state, or in any other manner inconsistent with the Purposes of the United Nations.

    *   *   *

Article 39

The Security Council shall determine the existence of any threat to the peace, breach of the peace, or act of aggression and shall make recommendations, or decide what measures shall be taken in accordance with Articles 41 and 42, to maintain or restore international peace and security.

Article 41

The Security Council may decide what measures not involving the use of armed forces are to be employed to give effect to its decisions, and it may call upon the Members of the United Nations to apply such measures. These may include complete or partial interruption of economic relations and of rail, sea, air, postal, telegraphic, radio, and other means of communication, and the severance of diplomatic relations.

Article 42

Should the Security Council consider that measures provided for in Article 41 would be inadequate or have proved to be inadequate, it may take such action by air, sea, or land forces as may be necessary to maintain or restore international peace and security. Such action may include demonstrations, blockade, and other operations by air, sea, or land forces of Members of the United Nations.

Article 51

Nothing in the present Charter shall impair the inherent right of individual or collective self-defence if an armed attack occurs against a Member of the United Nations, until the Security Council has taken measures necessary to maintain international peace and security. Measures taken by Members in the exercise of this right of self-defence shall be immediately reported to the Security Council and shall not in any way affect the authority and responsibility of the Security Council under the present Charter to take at any time such action as it deems necessary in order to maintain or restore international peace and security.

Intervention in relation to the force prohibition of the Charter. The term "intervention" has factual, political and legal connotations. Common to all three meanings, in the context of international affairs, is the series of overriding or dominant influences of one state upon the will or capabilities of another state, particularly as to events and conditions in the latter. In the history of Latin American relations prior to the coming into being of the United Nations and the Organization of American States, the opposition by Latin America to the penchant of the United States to land the Marines to protect American lives and property, and for other purposes viewed as good by the United States, coalesced into a principle of non-intervention. While some writers of that period contended that this principle was one of general international law, others viewed it as a political principle without legal content that ought eventually to be stated as a rule of international law. Since the creation of the United Nations, legal discourse has, with increased frequency, engaged the term. Does it now have legal meaning; if so, what is its scope?

The Charter of the United Nations does not apply the term in describing the rights and duties of states with respect to the employment of physical force. As seen, Article 2(4) forbids the use of force directed against * * * "territorial integrity or political independence of any state, or in any manner inconsistent with the Purposes of the United Nations." The existence of an act of aggression (not intervention), if found by the Security Council, triggers certain permissible United Nations responses, but even aggression is not in terms forbidden to states. It is from Article 2(7) of the Charter of the United Nations that emanations have emerged forbidding intervention by states although, in its terms, that provision is directed toward the organization rather than its members: "Nothing contained in the present Charter shall authorize the United Nations to intervene in matters which are essentially within the domestic jurisdiction of any state * * *." This provision is buttressed in the charter by broadly stated principles: self-determination of peoples, Article 1(2); sovereign equality of states, Article 2(1).

By the twenty-fifth year of the United Nations, the General Assembly was able, in its Declaration of Principles of International Law

Concerning Friendly Relations and Co-operation Among States in Accordance with the Charter of the United States,[a] to proclaim the following:

> The principle concerning the duty not to intervene in matters within the domestic jurisdiction of any State, in accordance with the Charter.

In elucidation of this principle, the assembly declared: "No State or group of States has the right to intervene directly or indirectly, for any reason whatever in the internal or external affairs of any other State." And further: "Every State has an inalienable right to choose its political, economic, social and cultural systems, without interference in any form by another State."

Consider the following polar situations: (1) State A crosses the border into State B to conquer and annex that state. There is no doubt that Article 2(4) has been violated; the event would probably not be described by such a gentle term as "intervention."

(2) State A provides military aid to the government of State B at its request; that government is under threat from elements in its own country. Is State A using force against State B's "political independence"; i. e. is this an Article 2(4) violation? How do you define the state whose political independence is endangered? Surely not the established government; possibly the dissidents; or the people of the state as whole? If the latter, does Article 2(4) mean that they are free to (literally) fight their way to a resolution of diverse political goals without outside contributions of men and arms to any side in the fray? If that conclusion is not readily deducible from Article 2(4), has the emerging positive law of intervention and non-intervention brought the law to that point? Or does intervention by states remain, as it once was, a means of describing an international relations political objective?

Comparable problems of determining whether intervention is a term of legal significance or of political rhetoric arise in connection with attempts to exert pressure on the will of a state by means other than military, e. g., economic. See p, 1289.

           a. The complete text of the declaration is set forth in the Documentary Supplement.

SECTION B. THE PROBLEM OF SELF-DEFENSE

---

1. MISSILES IN CUBA

THE SOVIET THREAT TO THE AMERICAS, ADDRESS BY PRESIDENT KENNEDY

47 United States Department of State Bulletin 715 (1962).

* * *

Neither the United States of America nor the world community of nations can tolerate deliberate deception and offensive threats on the part of any nation, large or small. We no longer live in a world where only the actual firing of weapons represents a sufficient challenge to a nation's security to constitute maximum peril. Nuclear weapons are so destructive and ballistic missiles are so swift that any substantially increased possibility of their use or any sudden change in their deployment may well be regarded as a definite threat to peace.

For many years both the Soviet Union and the United States, recognizing this fact, have deployed strategic nuclear weapons with great care, never upsetting the precarious status quo which insured that these weapons would not be used in the absence of some vital challenge. Our own strategic missiles have never been transferred to the territory of any other nation under a cloak of secrecy and deception; and our history, unlike that of the Soviets since the end of World War II, demonstrates that we have no desire to dominate or conquer any other nation or impose our system upon its people. Nevertheless, American citizens have become adjusted to living daily on the bull's eye of Soviet missiles located inside the U.S.S.R. or in submarines.

In that sense missiles in Cuba add to an already clear and present danger—although it should be noted the nations of Latin America have never previously been subjected to a potential nuclear threat.

* * *

Acting, therefore, in the defense of our own security and of the entire Western Hemisphere, and under the authority entrusted to me by the Constitution as endorsed by the resolution of the Congress, I have directed that the following initial steps be taken immediately:

First: To halt this offensive buildup, a strict quarantine on all offensive military equipment under shipment to Cuba is being initiated. All ships of any kind bound for Cuba from whatever nation or port will, if found to contain cargoes of offensive weapons, be turned back. This quarantine will be extended, if needed, to other types of cargo and carriers. We are not at this time, however, denying the necessities of life as the Soviets attempted to do in their Berlin blockade of 1948.

Second: I have directed the continued and increased close surveillance of Cuba and its military buildup. The Foreign Ministers of the OAS [Organization of American States] in their communiqué of October 3 rejected secrecy on such matters in this hemisphere. Should these offensive military preparations continue, thus increasing the threat to the hemisphere, further action will be justified. I have directed the Armed Forces to prepare for any eventualities; and I trust that, in the interest of both the Cuban people and the Soviet technicians at the sites, the hazards to all concerned of continuing this threat will be recognized.

Third: It shall be the policy of this nation to regard any nuclear missile launched from Cuba against any nation in the Western Hemisphere as an attack by the Soviet Union on the United States, requiring a full retaliatory response upon the Soviet Union.

Fourth: As a necessary military precaution I have reinforced our base at Guantanamo, evacuated today the dependents of our personnel there, and ordered additional military units to be on a standby alert basis.

Fifth: We are calling tonight for an immediate meeting of the Organ of Consultation, under the Organization of American States, to consider this threat to hemispheric security and to invoke articles 6 and 8 of the Rio Treaty in support of all necessary action. The United Nations Charter allows for regional security arrangements—and the nations of this hemisphere decided long ago against the military presence of outside powers. Our other allies around the world have also been alerted.

Sixth: Under the Charter of the United Nations, we are asking tonight that an emergency meeting of the Security Council be convoked without delay to take action against this latest Soviet threat to world peace. Our resolution will call for the prompt dismantling and withdrawal of all offensive weapons in Cuba, under the supervision of U.N. observers, before the quarantine can be lifted.

Seventh and finally: I call upon Chairman Khrushchev to halt and eliminate this clandestine, reckless, and provocative threat to world peace and to stable relations between our two nations.
* * *

This nation is prepared to present its case against the Soviet threat to peace, and our own proposals for a peaceful world, at any time and in any forum—in the OAS, in the United Nations, or in any other meeting that could be useful—without limiting our freedom of action.

     * * *

INTER–AMERICAN TREATY OF RECIPROCAL ASSISTANCE OF SEPTEMBER 2, 1947

62 Stat. 1681, 21 U.N.T.S. 77.

Article 6.   If the inviolability or the integrity of the territory or the sovereignty or political independence of any American State should be affected by an aggression which is not an armed attack or by an extra-continental or intra-continental conflict, or by any other fact or situation that might endanger the peace of America, the Organ of Consultation shall meet immediately in order to agree on the measures which must be taken in case of aggression to assist the victim of the aggression or, in any case, the measures which should be taken for the common defense and for the maintenance of the peace and security of the Continent.

Article 7.   In the case of a conflict between two or more American States, without prejudice to the right of self-defense in conformity with Article 51 of the Charter of the United Nations, the High Contracting Parties, meeting in consultation shall call upon the contending States to suspend hostilities and restore matters to the statu quo ante bellum, and shall take in addition all other necessary measures to reestablish or maintain inter-American peace and security and for the solution of the conflict by peaceful means. The rejection of the pacifying action will be considered in the determination of the aggressor and in the application of the measures which the consultative meeting may agree upon.

Article 8.   For the purposes of this Treaty, the measures on which the Organ of Consultation may agree will comprise one or more of the following: recall of chiefs of diplomatic missions; breaking of diplomatic relations; breaking of consular relations; partial or complete interruption of economic relations or of rail, sea, air, postal, telegraphic, telephonic, and radiotelephonic or radiotelegraphic communications; and use of armed force.

Article 9.   In addition to other acts which the Organ of Consultation may characterize as aggression, the following shall be considered as such:

a.   Unprovoked armed attack by a State against the territory, the people, or the land, sea, or air forces of another State;

b.   Invasion, by the armed forces of a State, of the territory of an American State, through the trespassing of boundaries demarcated in accordance with a treaty, judicial decision, or arbitral award, or, in the absence of frontiers thus demarcated, invasion affecting a region which is under the effective jurisdiction of another State.

CHARTER OF THE ORGANIZATION OF AMERICAN STATES

2 U.S.T. 2394, 119 U.N.T.S. 3 ª

Article 15.   No State or group of States has the right to intervene, directly or indirectly, for any reason whatever, in the internal or external affairs of any other State.   The foregoing principle prohibits not only armed force but also any other form of interference or attempted threat against the personality of the State or against its political, economic and cultural elements.

Article 16.   No State may use or encourage the use of coercive measures of an economic or political character in order to force the sovereign will of another State and obtain from it advantages of any kind.

Article 17.   The territory of a State is inviolable; it may not be the object, even temporarily, of military occupation or of other measures of force taken by another State, directly or indirectly, on any grounds whatever.   No territorial acquisitions or special advantages obtained either by force or by other means of coercion shall be recognized.

Article 18.   The American States bind themselves in their international relations not to have recourse to the use of force, except in the case of self-defense in accordance with existing treaties or in fulfillment thereof.

Article 19.   Measures adopted for the maintenance of peace and security in accordance with existing treaties do not constitute a violation of the principles set forth in Articles 15 and 17.

RESOLUTION OF COUNCIL OF THE ORGANIZATION OF AMERICAN STATES, MEETING AS THE PROVISIONAL ORGAN OF CONSULTATION, OCTOBER 23, 1962

47 United States Department of State Bulletin 722 (1962).

Whereas,

The Inter-American Treaty of Reciprocal Assistance of 1947 (Rio Treaty) recognizes the obligation of the American Republics to "provide for effective reciprocal assistance to meet armed attacks against any American state and in order to deal with threats of aggression against any of them,"

*   *   *

a.   Subsequent to the time the Cuban missile crisis occurred, the Charter of the OAS was revised (Protocol of Buenos Aires, February 27, 1967, 21 UST 607).   Articles 15 through 19 were renumbered 18 through 22 in the revision.

The Council of the Organization of American States, Meeting as the Provisional Organ of Consultation, Resolves:

1.   To call for the immediate dismantling and withdrawal from Cuba of all missiles and other weapons with any offensive capability;

2.   To recommend that the member states, in accordance with Articles 6 and 8 of the Inter-American Treaty of Reciprocal Assistance, take all measures, individually and collectively, including the use of armed force, which they may deem necessary to ensure that the Government of Cuba cannot continue to receive from the Sino-Soviet powers military material and related supplies which may threaten the peace and security of the Continent and to prevent the missiles in Cuba with offensive capability from ever becoming an active threat to the peace and security of the Continent;

3.   To inform the Security Council of the United Nations of this resolution in accordance with Article 54 of the Charter of the United Nations and to express the hope that the Security Council will, in accordance with the draft resolution introduced by the United States, dispatch United Nations observers to Cuba at the earliest moment;

4.   To continue to serve provisionally as Organ of Consultation and to request the Member States to keep the Organ of Consultation duly informed of measures taken by them in accordance with paragraph two of this resolution.

UNITED STATES PROCLAMATION

INTERDICTION OF THE DELIVERY OF OFFENSIVE WEAPONS TO CUBA

47 United States Department of State Bulletin 717 (1962).

Whereas the peace of the world and the security of the United States and of all American States are endangered by reason of the establishment by the Sino-Soviet powers of an offensive military capability in Cuba, including bases for ballistic missiles with a potential range covering most of North and South America;

Whereas by a Joint Resolution passed by the Congress of the United States and approved on October 3, 1962, it was declared that the United States is determined to prevent by whatever means may be necessary, including the use of arms, the Marxist-Leninist regime in Cuba from extending, by force or the threat of force, its aggressive or subversive activities to any part of this hemisphere, and to prevent in Cuba the creation or use of an externally supported military capability endangering the security of the United States; and

Whereas the Organ of Consultation of the American Republics meeting in Washington on October 23, 1962, recommended that the Member States, in accordance with Articles 6 and 8 of the Inter-American Treaty of Reciprocal Assistance, take all measures, individually and collectively, including the use of armed force, which they may deem necessary to ensure that the Government of Cuba cannot continue to receive from the Sino-Soviet powers military material and related supplies which may threaten the peace and security of the Continent and to prevent the missiles in Cuba with offensive capability from ever becoming an active threat to the peace and security of the Continent:

Now, Therefore, I, John F. Kennedy, President of the United States of America, acting under and by virtue of the authority conferred upon me by the Constitution and statutes of the United States, in accordance with the aforementioned resolutions of the United States Congress and of the Organ of Consultation of the American Republics, and to defend the security of the United States, do hereby proclaim that the forces under my command are ordered, beginning at 2:00 p. m. Greenwich time October 24, 1962, to interdict, subject to the instructions herein contained, the delivery of offensive weapons and associated materiel to Cuba.

For the purposes of this Proclamation, the following are declared to be prohibited materiel:

Surface-to-surface missiles; bomber aircraft; bombs, air-to-surface rockets and guided missiles; warheads for any of the above weapons; mechanical or electronic equipment to support or operate the above items; and any other classes of materiel hereafter designated by the Secretary of Defense for the purpose of effectuating this Proclamation.

To enforce this order, the Secretary of Defense shall take appropriate measures to prevent the delivery of prohibited materiel to Cuba, employing the land, sea and air forces of the United States in cooperation with any forces that may be made available by other American States.

The Secretary of Defense may make such regulations and issue such directives as he deems necessary to ensure the effectiveness of this order, including the designation, within a reasonable distance of Cuba, of prohibited or restricted zones and of prescribed routes.

Any vessel or craft which may be proceeding toward Cuba may be intercepted and may be directed to identify itself, its cargo, equipment and stores and its ports of call, to stop, to lie to, to submit to visit and search, or to proceed as directed. Any vessel or craft which fails or refuses to respond to or comply with directions shall be subject to being taken into custody. Any vessel or craft which it is believed is en route to Cuba and may be carrying prohibited materiel or may itself constitute such materiel shall, whenever possible, be directed to proceed to another destination of its own choice and shall be taken into custody if it fails or refuses to obey such directions. All vessels or craft taken into custody shall be sent into a port of the United States for appropriate disposition.

In carrying out this order, force shall not be used except in case of failure or refusal to comply with directions, or with regulations or directives of the Secretary of Defense issued hereunder, after reasonable efforts have been made to communicate them to the vessel or craft, or in case of self-defense. In any case, force shall be used only to the extent necessary.

[The Proclamation was signed by President Kennedy at 7:06 P. M., October 23, 1962.]

MEEKER, DEFENSIVE QUARANTINE AND THE LAW

57 American Journal of International Law 515, 523 (1963.)*

Charter Limitation on the "Threat or Use of Force"

Before leaving the Charter of the United Nations it is relevant also to consider Article 2, paragraph 4, which provides:

> All Members shall refrain in their international relations from the threat or use of force against the territorial integrity or political independence of any state, or in any other manner inconsistent with the Purposes of the United Nations.

It was recognized that the defensive quarantine was dependent, ultimately, upon the use of naval forces for its effectiveness. Accordingly, there was acknowledged to be a threat, and potentially a use, of armed force. However, it did not follow that this must contravene Article 2, paragraph 4.

In considering the obligations imposed on Members by that article, it should be noted that not all threats or uses of force are prohibited; only those which are inconsistent with the purposes of the United Nations are covered by Article 2, paragraph 4. The presence of the word "other" in the concluding clause of the paragraph makes this clear. Even assuming that the measures taken could be considered to impinge upon the territorial integrity or political independence of some state or states, they would not be contrary to Article 2, paragraph 4, as long as they were not inconsistent with the purposes of the United Nations. The defensive quarantine, as indicated earlier, was considered to be in accordance with Chapter VIII of the Charter.

It is clear that collective action for peace and security which the Security Council may take under Chapter VII does not contravene Article 2, paragraph 4. It is also clear that individual or collective self-defense against armed attack, in accordance with Article 51, does not violate the Charter. Here it may be noted that the United States, in adopting the defensive quarantine of Cuba, did not seek to justify it as a measure required to meet an "armed attack" within the meaning of Article 51. Nor did the United States seek to sustain its action on the ground that Article 51 is not an all-inclusive statement of the right of self-defense and that the quarantine was a measure of self-defense open to any country to take individually for its own defense in a case other than "armed attack." Indeed, as shown by President Kennedy's television address of October 22 and by other statements of the Government, reliance was not placed on either contention, and the United States took no position on either of these issues.

The quarantine was based on a collective judgment and recommendation of the American Republics made under the Rio Treaty. It was considered not to contravene Article 2, paragraph 4, because it was a measure adopted by a regional organization in conformity with the provisions of Chapter VIII of the Charter.[a] The purposes of the Organization and its activities were considered to be consistent with the purposes and principles of the United Nations as provided in Article 52. This being the case, the quarantine would no more violate Article 2, paragraph 4, than measures voted by the Council under Chapter VII, by the General Assembly under Articles 10 and 11, or taken by United Nations Members in conformity with Article 51.

Finally, in relation to the Charter limitation on threat or use of force, it should be noted that the quarantine itself was a carefully limited measure proportionate to the threat and designed solely to prevent any further build-up of strategic missile bases in Cuba.

---

2.   PRESERVATION OF SOCIALISM IN CZECHOSLOVAKIA

KOVALEV, SOVEREIGNTY AND INTERNATIONAL DUTIES OF SOCIALIST COUNTRIES

Reprinted from Pravda.
The New York Times, Sept. 27, 1968, Sec. 1, at 3, col. 1.*

[In 1968, military forces of the USSR and other Warsaw Pact countries entered Czechoslovakia; the displacement of the existing "liberal" Communist government followed.]

In connection with the events in Czechoslovakia, the question of the correlation and interdependence of the national interests of the socialist countries and their international duties acquire particular topical and acute importance.

The measures taken by the Soviet Union, jointly with other socialist countries, in defending the socialist gains of the Czechoslovak people are of great significance for strengthening the socialist community, which is the main achievement of the international working class.

---

a. At p. 522, the author addresses the question of the conformity of the action of the regional organization to Article 53(1) of the Charter: "But no enforcement action shall be taken under regional arrangements or by regional agencies without the authorization of the Security Council * * *."

* © 1968 by the New York Times Company. Reprinted by permission.

We cannot ignore the assertions, held in some places, that the actions of the five socialist countries run counter to the Marxist-Leninist principle of sovereignty and the rights of nations to self-determination.

Abstract Approach Seen

The groundlessness of such reasoning consists primarily in that it is based on an abstract, nonclass approach to the question of sovereignty and the rights of nations to self-determination.

The peoples of the socialist countries and Communist parties certainly do have and should have freedom for determining the ways of advance of their respective countries.

However, none of their decisions should damage either socialism in their country or the fundamental interests of other socialist countries, and the whole working class movement, which is working for socialism.

This means that each Communist party is responsible not only to its own people, but also to all the socialist countries, to the entire Communist movement. Whoever forgets this, in stressing only the independence of the Communist party, becomes one-sided. He deviates from his international duty.

One-Sidedness Opposed

Marxist dialectics are opposed to one-sidedness. They demand that each phenomenon be examined concretely, in general connection with other phenomena, with other processes.

Just as, in Lenin's words, a man living in a society cannot be free from the society, one or another socialist state, staying in a system of other states composing the socialist community, cannot be free from the common interests of that community.

The sovereignty of each socialist country cannot be opposed to the interests of the world of socialism, of the world revolutionary movement. Lenin demanded that all Communists fight against small-nation narrow-mindedness, seclusion and isolation, consider the whole and the general, subordinate the particular to the general interest.

The socialist states respect the democratic norms of international law. They have proved this more than once in practice, by coming out resolutely against the attempts of imperialism to violate the sovereignty and independence of nations.

It is from these same positions that they reject the leftist, adventurist conception of "exporting revolution," of "bringing happiness" to other peoples.

However, from a Marxist point of view, the norms of law, including the norms of mutual relations of the socialist countries, cannot be interpreted narrowly, formally, and in isolation from the general context of class struggle in the modern world. The socialist countries resolutely come out against the exporting and importing of counter-revolution.

Opposing Systems Stressed

Each Communist party is free to apply the basic principles of Marxism-Leninism and of socialism in its country, but it cannot depart from these principles assuming, naturally, that it remains a Communist party.

Concretely, this means, first of all, that, in its activity, each Communist party cannot but take into account such a decisive fact of our time as the struggle between two opposing social systems—capitalism and socialism.

This is an objective struggle, a fact not depending on the will of the people, and stipulated by the world's being split into two opposite social systems. Lenin said: "Each man must choose between joining our side or the other side. Any attempt to avoid taking sides in this issue must end in fiasco."

It has got to be emphasized that when a socialist country seems to adopt a "non-affiliated" stand, it retains its national independence, in effect, precisely because of the might of the socialist community, and above all the Soviet Union as a central force, which also includes the might of its armed forces. The weakening of any of the links in the world system of socialism directly affects all the socialist countries, which cannot look indifferently upon this.

NATO Threat Seen

The antisocialist elements in Czechoslovakia actually covered up the demand for so-called neutrality and Czechoslovakia's withdrawal from the socialist community with talking about the right of nations to self-determination.

However, the implementation of such "self-determination," in other words, Czechoslovakia's detachment from the socialist community, would have come into conflict with its own vital interests and would have been detrimental to the other socialist states.

Such "self-determination," as a result of which NATO troops would have been able to come up to the Soviet border, while the community of European socialist countries would have been split, in effect encroaches upon the vital interests of the peoples of these countries and conflicts, as the very root of it, with the right of these people to socialist self-determination.

Discharging their internationalist duty toward the fraternal peoples of Czechoslovakia and defending their own socialist gains, the U.S.S.R. and the other socialist states had to act decisively and they did act against the antisocialist forces in Czechoslovakia.

Gomulka Is Quoted

Comrade W. Gomulka, First Secretary of the Central Committee of the Polish United Workers party, commented figuratively on this score when he said:

"We tell those friends and comrades of ours in the other countries who think they are upholding the righteous cause of socialism and the sovereignty of the peoples by condemning and protesting against the entry of our troops into Czechoslovakia: When the enemy mines our house, the community of socialist states, with dynamite, it is our patriotic, national and international duty to obstruct this by using the means that are necessary."

People who "disapprove" of the actions of the allied socialist states are ignoring the decisive fact that these countries are defending the interests of all of world socialism, of the entire world revolutionary movement.

The system of socialism exists in concrete form in some countries, which have their own definite state boundaries; this system is developing according to the specific conditions of each country. Furthermore, nobody interferes in the concrete measures taken to improve the socialist system in the different socialist countries.

However, the picture changes fundamentally when a danger arises to socialism itself in a particular country. As a social system, world socialism is the common gain of the working people of all lands; it is indivisible and its defense is the common cause of all Communists and all progressives in the world, in the first place, the working folk of the socialist Countries.

"Rightist" Aim Described

The Bratislava statement of the Communist and Workers' parties says of socialist gains that "support, consolidation and defense of these gains, won at the price of heroic effort and the self-sacrifice of each people, represents a common international duty and obligation for all the socialist countries."

What the right-wing antisocialist forces set out to achieve in recent months in Czechoslovakia did not refer to the specific features of socialist development or the application of the principle of Marxism-Leninism to the concrete conditions obtaining in that country, but constituted encroachment on the foundations of socialism, on the basic principles of Marxism-Leninism.

This is the nuance that people who have fallen for the hypocritical nonsense of the antisocialist and revisionist elements still cannot understand. Under the guise of "democratization" these elements were little by little shaking the socialist state, seeking to demoralize the Communist party and befog the minds of the masses, stealthily hatching a counterrevolutionary coup, and they were not duly rebuffed inside the country.

Could Not Stand Aside

Naturally the Communists of the fraternal countries could not allow the socialist states to be inactive in the name of an abstractly understood sovereignty, when they saw that the country stood in peril of antisocialist degeneration.

The actions in Czechoslovakia of the five allied socialist countries accords also with the vital interests of the people of the country themselves.

Socialism, by delivering a nation from the shackles of an exploiting regime, insures the solution of the fundamental problems of the national development of any country that has embarked upon the socialist road. On the other hand, by encroaching upon the mainstays of socialism, the counterrevolutionary elements in Czechoslovakia undermined the very foundations of the country's independence and sovereignty.

Formal observance of the freedom of self-determination of a nation in the concrete situation that arose in Czechoslovakia would mean freedom of "self-determination" not of the popular masses, the working people, but of their enemies.

The antisocialist path, "neutrality", to which the Czechoslovak people were pushed would bring it to the loss of its national independence.

World imperialism, on its part, supported the antisocialist forces in Czechoslovakia, tried to export counterrevolution to that country in this way.

The help to the working people of Czechoslovakia by other socialist countries, which prevented the export of counterrevolution from abroad, constitutes the actual sovereignty of the Czechoslovak socialist republic against those who would like to deprive it from its sovereignty and give up the country to imperialism.

Political Means Exhausted

The fraternal Communist parties of the socialist countries were for a long time taking measures, with maximum self-restraint and patience, to help the Czechoslovak people with political means to stop the onslaught of antisocialist forces in Czechoslovakia. And only when all such measures were exhausted did they bring armed forces into the country.

The soldiers of the allied socialist countries now in Czechoslovakia proved by their actions indeed that they have no other tasks than the tasks of defending socialist gains in that country.

They do not interfere in the internal affairs of the country, are fighting for the principle of self-determination of the peoples of Czechoslovakia not in words but in deeds, are fighting for their inalienable right to think out profoundly and decide their fate themselves, without intimidation on the part of counterrevolutionaries, without revisionists and nationalist demagogy.

Class Approach to Law

Those who speak about the "illegal actions" of the allied socialist countries in Czechoslovakia forget that in a class society there is not and there cannot be non-class laws.

Laws and legal norms are subjected to the laws of the class struggle, the laws of social development. These laws are clearly formulated in Marxist-Leninist teaching, in the documents jointly adopted by the Communist and Workers' parties.

Formally juridical reasoning must not overshadow a class approach to the matter. One who does it, thus losing the only correct class criterion in assessing legal norms, begins to measure events with a yardstick of bourgeois law.

Such an approach to the question of sovereignty means that, for example, the progressive forces of the world would not be able to come out against the revival of neo-Nazism in the Federal Republic of Germany, against the actions of butchers Franco and Salazar, against reactionary arbitrary actions of "black colonels" in Greece, because this is "the internal affair" of "sovereign" states.

Vietnam Example Cited

It is characteristic that both the Saigon puppets and their American protectors also regard the notion of sovereignty as prohibiting support for the struggle of progressive forces.

They proclaim at every crossroads that the socialist countries, which are rendering help to the Vietnamese people in their struggle for independence and freedom, are violating the sovereignty of Vietnam. Genuine revolutionaries, being internationalists, cannot but support progressive forces in all countries in their just struggle for national and social liberation.

The interests of the socialist community and of the whole revolutionary movement, the interests of socialism in Czechoslovakia demand complete exposure and political isolation of the reactionary forces in that country, consolidation of the working people and consistent implementation of the Moscow agreement between the Soviet and Czechoslovak leaders.

There is no doubt that the actions of the five allied socialist countries in Czechoslovakia directed to the defense of the vital interests or the socialist community, that the sovereignty of socialist Czechoslovakia first and foremost, will be increasingly supported by all those who have the interest of the present revolutionary movement, of peace and security of peoples, of democracy and socialism at heart.

3. THE CLAIM OF COLLECTIVE SELF-DEFENSE
IN SOUTH VIETNAM

THE LEGALITY OF UNITED STATES PARTICIPATION IN THE DEFENSE OF VIET-NAM, MEMORANDUM PREPARED BY THE LEGAL ADVISER OF THE DEPARTMENT OF STATE

54 United States Department of State Bulletin 474 (1966).

March 4, 1966

The United States and South Viet-Nam Have the Right Under International Law to Participate in the Collective Defense of South Viet-Nam Against Armed Attack.

In response to requests from the Government of South Viet-Nam, the United States has been assisting that country in defending itself against armed attack from the Communist North. This attack has taken the forms of externally supported subversion, clandestine supply of arms, infiltration of armed personnel, and most recently the sending of regular units of the North Vietnamese army into the South.

International law has long recognized the right of individual and collective self-defense against armed attack. South Viet-Nam and the United States are engaging in such collective defense consistently with international law and with United States obligations under the United Nations Charter.

A. South Viet-Nam Is Being Subjected to Armed Attack by Communist North Viet-Nam

The Geneva accords of 1954 established a demarcation line between North Viet-Nam and South Viet-Nam. They provided for withdrawals of military forces into the respective zones north and south of this line. The accords prohibited the use of either zone for the resumption of hostilities or to "further an aggressive policy."

During the 5 years following the Geneva conference of 1954, the Hanoi regime developed a covert political-military organization in South Viet-Nam based on Communist cadres it had ordered to stay in the South, contrary to the provisions of the Geneva accords. The activities of this covert organization were directed toward the kidnaping and assassination of civilian officials—acts of terrorism that were perpetrated in increasing numbers.

In the 3-year period from 1959 to 1961, the North Viet-Nam regime infiltrated an estimated 10,000 men into the South. It is estimated that 13,000 additional personnel were infiltrated in 1962, and, by the end of 1964, North Viet-Nam may well have moved over 40,000 armed and unarmed guerrillas into South Viet-Nam.

The International Control Commission reported in 1962 the findings of its Legal Committee:

> * * * [T]here is evidence to show that arms, armed and unarmed personnel, munitions and other supplies have been sent

from the Zone in the North to the Zone in the South with the objective of supporting, organizing and carrying out hostile activities, including armed attacks, directed against the Armed Forces and Administration of the Zone in the South.

    * * * [T]here is evidence that the PAVN [People's Army of Viet Nam] has allowed the Zone in the North to be used for inciting, encouraging and supporting hostile activities in the Zone in the South, aimed at the overthrow of the Administration in the South.

Beginning in 1964, the Communists apparently exhausted their reservoir of Southerners who had gone North. Since then the greater number of men infiltrated into the South have been native-born North Vietnamese. Most recently, Hanoi has begun to infiltrate elements of the North Vietnamese army in increasingly larger numbers. Today, there is evidence that nine regiments of regular North Vietnamese forces are fighting in organized units in the South.

    In the guerrilla war in Viet-Nam, the external aggression from the North is the critical military element of the insurgency, although it is unacknowledged by North Viet-Nam. In these circumstances, an "armed attack" is not as easily fixed by date and hour as in the case of traditional warfare. However, the infiltration of thousands of armed men clearly constitutes an "armed attack" under any reasonable definition. There may be some question as to the exact date at which North Viet-Nam's aggression grew into an "armed attack," but there can be no doubt that it had occurred before February 1965.

B. International Law Recognizes the Right of Individual and Collective Self-Defense Against Armed Attack

    International law has traditionally recognized the right of self-defense against armed attack. This proposition has been asserted by writers on international law through the several centuries in which the modern law of nations has developed. The proposition has been acted on numerous times by governments throughout modern history. Today the principle of self-defense against armed attack is universally recognized and accepted.

    The Charter of the United Nations, concluded at the end of World War II, imposed an important limitation on the use of force by United Nations members. Article 2, paragraph 4, provides:

    All Members shall refrain in their international relations from the threat or use of force against the territorial integrity or political independence of any state, or in any other manner inconsistent with the Purposes of the United Nations.

In addition, the charter embodied a system of international peacekeeping through the organs of the United Nations. Article 24 summarizes these structural arrangements in stating that the United Nations members:

    * * * confer on the Security Council primary responsibility for the maintenance of international peace and security, and agree that in carrying out its duties under this responsibility the Security Council acts on their behalf.

However, the charter expressly states in article 51 that the remaining provisions of the charter—including the limitation of article 2, paragraph 4 and the creation of United Nations machinery to keep the peace—in no way diminish the inherent right of self-defense against armed attack. Article 51 provides:

> Nothing in the present Charter shall impair the inherent right of individual or collective self-defense if an armed attack occurs against a Member of the United Nations, until the Security Council has taken the measures necessary to maintain international peace and security. Measures taken by Members in the exercise of this right of self-defense shall be immediately reported to the Security Council and shall not in any way affect the authority and responsibility of the Security Council under the present Charter to take at any time such action as it deems necessary in order to maintain or restore international peace and security.

Thus, article 51 restates and preserves, for member states in the situations covered by the article, a long-recognized principle of international law. The article is a "saving clause" designed to make clear that no other provision in the charter shall be interpreted to impair the inherent right of self-defense referred to in article 51.

Three principal objections have been raised against the availability of the right of individual and collective self-defense in the case of Viet-Nam: (1) that this right applies only in the case of an armed attack on a United Nations member; (2) that it does not apply in the case of South Viet-Nam because the latter is not an independent sovereign state; and (3) that collective self-defense may be undertaken only by a regional organization operating under chapter VIII of the United Nations Charter. These objections will now be considered in turn.

* * *

H.   Summary

The analysis set forth above shows that South Viet-Nam has the right in present circumstances to defend itself against armed attack from the North and to organize a collective self-defense with the participation of others. In response to requests from South Viet-Nam, the United States has been participating in that defense, both through military action within South Viet-Nam and actions taken directly against the aggressor in North Viet-Nam. This participation by the United States is in conformity with international law and is consistent with our obligations under the Charter of the United Nations.

* * *

WRIGHT, LEGAL ASPECTS OF THE VIET–NAM SITUATION

60 American Journal of International Law 750, 755 (1966).[a]

* * *

The legal issues, clarification of which might contribute to a judgment of the validity of the diverse images of the Viet-Nam situation, may be stated as follows:

1.   Are the hostilities between North and South Viet-Nam international hostilities or civil strife, i. e., is Viet-Nam two states or one?

2.   Was the requirement for an election in 1956 dependent on the development of conditions assuring that the election would be free and fair?

3.   Was the requirement concerning elections in the resolutions of the Geneva Conference such an integral part of the Cease-Fire Agreement between France and the Democratic Republic of Viet-Nam (Ho Chi Minh) as to permit suspension of the cease-fire when the elections were frustrated?

4.   If it is assumed that the cease-fire line continued in operation, was North Viet-Nam guilty of "armed attacks" upon South Viet-Nam justifying the United States bombing attacks north of the cease-fire line, which began in February, 1965, as measures of "collective self-defense"?

* * *

1.   The evidence suggests that Viet-Nam is one state and that the hostilities of Ho Chi Minh's government against the Saigon Government would be civil strife within its domestic jurisdiction unless forbidden by the cease-fire Agreement.

During the hostilities between the "Democratic Republic of Viet-Nam" under Ho Chi Minh and France, supporting the "Republic of Viet-Nam" under Bao Dai from 1946 to 1954 and during the Geneva Conference, both sides regarded Viet-Nam as one state, the legal issue being whether it was an independent state or a "Free State" within the French Community. When the hostilities ended with French defeat, large areas of the south were occupied by Ho Chi Minh's forces, the Viet-Minh, and areas in the north by forces of France and Bao Dai. The Cease-Fire Agreement of 1954 signed by representatives of France and the Democratic Republic of Viet-Nam provided for the withdrawal of these forces across the cease-fire line, substantially the 17th parallel, and very explicitly declared that this line was not an international boundary but a "provisional military demarcation line" and that the territories at each side were not states but "zones." The final resolutions of the Conference declared that "the independence, unity and territorial integrity" of Viet-Nam should

a. Reprinted with the permission of the American Society of International Law.

This article is reprinted at p. 271 in a symposium entitled The Vietnam War and International Law (R. Falk, ed., 1968).

be respected, and provided that elections "shall" be held in July, 1956, to determine the government of Viet-Nam. These resolutions did not constitute a formal treaty and were not signed by any of the delegates. They were, however, accepted by all of the delegates except those of the United States and Bao Dai's Republic of Viet-Nam, both of whom made statements "noted" by the Conference. In regard to the reservation by Bao Dai's representative, the Chairman at the final session of the Conference, Anthony Eden, said:

> We can not now amend our final act, which is the statement of the Conference as a whole, but the Declaration of the Representative of the State of Vietnam will be taken note of.

It seems clear that the Conference recognized Viet-Nam as one state and provided that it should be united by one government in 1956.

* * *

Questions. Article 51 of the Charter of the United Nations contemplates that a state can use force in individual or collective self-defense only until action is taken by the Security Council. The design of the charter apparently envisioned only temporary self-defense measures. But fighting in Vietnam continued for many years. Why did the Security Council not take action in this case?

In 1980 Iraq invaded Iran to vindicate territorial claims. No action was taken by, or even suggested in the Security Council. Why?

4. SOVIET TROOPS IN AFGHANISTAN

DRAFT RESOLUTION ON AFGHANISTAN IN THE SECURITY COUNCIL, JANUARY 7, 1980

United States Department of State Bulletin, January 1980, Special D.

The Security Council,

Having considered the letter dated 3 January 1980 addressed to the President of the Security Council (S/13724 and Add. 1 and 2),

Gravely concerned over recent developments in Afghanistan and their implications for international peace and security,

Reaffirming the right of all peoples to determine their own future free from outside interference, including their right to choose their own form of government,

Mindful of the obligations of Member States to refrain in their international relations from the threat or use of force against the territorial integrity or political independence of any State, or in any other manner inconsistent with the purposes of the United Nations,

1. Reaffirms anew its conviction that the preservation of sovereignty, territorial integrity and political independence of every

State is a fundamental principle of the Charter of the United Nations, any violation of which on any pretext whatsoever is contrary to its aims and purposes;

2.   Deeply deplores the recent armed intervention in Afghanistan, which is inconsistent with that principle;

3.   Affirms that the sovereignty, territorial integrity, political independence and nonaligned status of Afghanistan must be fully respected;

4.   Calls for the immediate and unconditional withdrawal of all foreign troops from Afghanistan in order to enable its people to determine their own form of government and choose their economic, political and social systems free from outside intervention, coercion or constraint of any kind whatsoever;

5.   Requests the Secretary-General to submit a report on progress towards the implementation of this resolution within two weeks;

6.   Decides to remain seized of this question.

[The draft resolution was not adopted, because of the Soviet veto. Bangladesh, China, France, Jamaica, Mexico, Niger, Norway, Philippines, Portugal, Tunisia, the United Kingdom, the United States and Zambia voted in favor of the resolution. The Soviet Union and the German Democratic Republic voted against it.]

EXCERPTS FROM THE DEBATES IN THE SECURITY COUNCIL ON THE DRAFT RESOLUTION CONCERNING AFGHANISTAN

United States Department of State Bulletin, Janury 1980, Special B.

U. S. Ambassador McHENRY, Jan. 6, 1980:

The Security Council meets today, at the request of more than 50 members of the United Nations from all parts of the world and of all political persuasions. We meet to consider a matter of fundamental importance to world peace and to the principles on which the United Nations was founded.

A member state of this world organization has been invaded by massive contingents of troops from another state. Its government has been overthrown. Its leaders have been killed. Its people have been silenced. Its territory has been occupied.

The United States has joined in the call for an urgent meeting of the Security Council to consider the Soviet Union's blatant act of aggression against the territory and people of Afghanistan. We have done so because the action of the Soviet Union not only breaches the peace and violates international law, but also threatens the viability of the fundamental principles that underlie the U.N. Charter.

Sequence of Events

The representative of the Soviet Union has offered us a wide and confusing range of rationales for the so-called "limited" but surely deadly assistance foisted on the people of Afghanistan. Let us look at the chilling sequence of events connected with the Soviet invasion of Afghanistan.

During the first weeks of December, the Soviet Union secured Bagram airfield, north of the Afghan capital of Kabul, by sending the equivalent of an airborne regiment there. It also landed troops and equipment at the Kabul airport and, at the same time, mobilized enormous forces in areas bordering Afghanistan.

On December 25 and 26, a massive Soviet airlift into Kabul took place. In over 200 flights, roughly 10,000 Soviet troops were transported into Afghanistan.

On the evening of December 27, a special Soviet assault unit surrounded the presidential palace in Kabul. Afghan soldiers defending the palace were attacked and overcome, and President Amin was summarily executed. Simultaneously, Soviet troops attacked Afghan forces guarding radio Afghanistan and other key government installations and took them under control.

The first announcement of the Soviet-engineered coup d'etat, and the replacement of President Amin by Babrak Karmal, who had been in exile in Eastern Europe, was made using frequencies purporting to be Radio Kabul. In fact, the transmitters from which these announcements were made were located in the Soviet Union. We know this because the real Radio Kabul continued normal transmissions for at least 1½ hours after these announcements were first heard. Nothing in these broadcasts from Kabul confirmed the content of the Soviet broadcast disseminated in Afghanistan's name.

Subsequently, Soviet troops captured all key civilian and military installations in the Kabul area and established a defense perimeter around Kabul. Afghan military forces have been disarmed.

Immediately after the coup, two Soviet motorized rifle divisions entered Afghanistan by land, one at Kushka and the other at Termez. Elements of the western division arrived at Herat, where fighting between Soviet and Afghan forces was reported. Much of the Termez division proceeded to the Kabul area.

The Soviet Union now has up to 50,000 troops in Afghanistan. There are indications that other Soviet divisions are moving into the Soviet-Afghan border. Soviet forces have moved out to secure other key towns.

The Soviet Union has claimed that the leadership of Afghanistan requested Soviet military assistance. Which leadership? It is beyond doubt that President Amin was still in office when the Soviet troops attacked the presidential palace and when he was executed. Are we to believe that President Amin invited Soviet troops to come into Afghanistan in order to oversee his own downfall and his own execution? Or was it the leadership of Babrak Karmal, President Amin's Soviet-appointed successor, a man who was not even in Afghanistan at the time of the Soviet intervention but was, rather, in the Soviet Union?

The Afghan people and Afghan army units have resisted this Soviet aggression, despite the overwhelming military superiority of the invader. Fighting continues in several areas of the country.

The facts of the situation are clear. Over a period of months, the Soviet Union carefully planned and prepared to invade Afghanistan, because it was dissatisfied with the degree of subservience of the Amin government and undoubtedly with its performance against Moslem insurgents in Afghanistan who long have been struggling for their rights. The Soviet Union then carried out its military operation—quickly and brutally. They offered no recourse whatsoever to the authorities then in power in Afghanistan. The Soviet Union overthrew the Amin government, which it had previously supported, and replaced it with a puppet regime.

U.N. Principles

The armed intervention of the Soviet Union in Afghanistan and the presence of an uninvited occupation force in that country is a gross and blatant violation of the most important principles of international law and of the U.N. Charter. What are those principles?

• That one state must not use force against the territorial integrity and political independence of another state;

• That a state must not intervene by force in the internal affairs of another state;

• That all states must respect the principle of equal rights and self-determination of peoples;

• That fundamental principles of human rights must be respected by all governments; and

• That states must settle international disputes by peaceful means.

The Soviet claim that it was acting in furtherance of collective self-defense under Article 51 of the Charter is a perversion of the Charter—an insult to the intelligence of the members of this Council. Article 51 can be invoked only "if an armed attack occurs against a Member of the United Nations." From whence came the armed attack on Afghanistan? The only armed attack on Afghanistan was the one launched by the Soviet Union. No one can believe the claim that the Soviet Union was requested by the Afghan Government to intervene in Afghanistan in the fashion in which it did, unless one also believes that President Amin invited the Soviet Union in to overthrow him. Article 51 of the Charter requires that measures taken by members in exercise of their right of self-defense "shall be immediately reported to the Security Council and shall not in any way affect the authority and responsibility of the Security Council under the * * * Charter to take at any time such action as it deems necessary in order to maintain or restore international peace and security." That neither the Soviet Union, nor the puppet regime it has installed in power in Kabul, has given the required notice to the Security Council under Article 51 is itself evidence of the hollowness of the Soviet Union's refuge behind the Charter.

Nor can one believe that the Soviet Union was requested by the Afghan Government to intervene in Afghanistan pursuant to the terms of the so-called Treaty of Friendship and Cooperation it entered into with that country in 1978. For the Soviet invasion of Afghanistan violates the Soviet Union's obligation, under the terms of the treaty, to respect Afghanistan's national sovereignty and to refrain from interfering in its internal affairs.

The U.N. Charter does not give the Soviet Union or any nation, the right to take military action in another country or to replace its government because it disagrees with the policies or performance of the existing government. The fact is that the Soviet Union has flouted international law and has violated regional and international peace and stability. That the Soviet Union has done so with cold calculation and advance planning, in an area of the world which is now experiencing particular instability and tension, makes its act even more egregious and irresponsible. That the Soviet Union is taking military action against a deeply religious and fiercely independent people, who are struggling for human and religious rights, underscores the brutality and illegality of its action.

The Need for U.N. Action

Accordingly, it remains for this Council to take action under the Charter to restore international peace and security.

A terrible miscalculation has been made by Soviet authorities. The ramifications of the Soviet intervention in Afghanistan are enormous. For no state will be safe against a larger and more powerful neighbor if the international community appears to condone the Soviet Union's armed intervention. This must be of particular concern to states whose territories lie near the Soviet borders.

It is, therefore, incumbent upon this Council and upon every nation that believes in the rule of law and opposes the use of force in international affairs to denounce this dangerous breach of peace and security. It is incumbent upon this Council to make the weight of world opinion felt.

We note that the Soviet Union has stated that it intends to withdraw its troops from Afghanistan at some point. We urge the Soviet Union to do so immediately and to allow the people of Afghanistan to conduct their own affairs, to choose their own system of government, to choose their own national leaders without outside pressure and interference. Only in this way can the grave threat to international peace and security created by the Soviet Union be diminished and this most serious challenge to the basic principles of the United Nations be removed.

No state, not even a great power, can be allowed to ignore with impunity the responsibilities, obligations, and commitments it assumed when it became a member of the United Nations. The United

States therefore calls on all members of the Council to act vigorously in discharge of their Charter obligations.

SOVIET SAYS AFGHAN MOVES ENRAGE U. S. BECAUSE IT SOUGHT BASES ITSELF

The New York Times, January 2, 1980, Sect. A, p. 1, col. 4.*

MOSCOW, Jan. 1—The Soviet Union said today that the United States was enraged by Moscow's intervention in Afghanistan because Washington had been plotting to turn the country into an American base to replace the loss of Iran.

The charge that the United States had hoped to exploit the Afghan tribal insurgency to acquire a springboard for potential aggression against the Soviet Union was made in an article in the Government newspaper, Izvestia.

It was the second authoritative exposition of the Soviet view of the crisis since the Communist Party's principal daily, Pravda, said two days ago that the Soviet Union had sent a contingent to Afghanistan to help repel "reactionary bands" armed, trained and directed by the United States and China.

Press Plays Down the Situation

Despite these charges, the Soviet press generally continued to play down the situation, limiting its foreign coverage mainly to expressions of support from Communist governments and publications and to statements attributed to the new Afghan Government.

The official press agency, Tass, distributed the text of a message from the new Afghan leader, Babrak Karmal, to Leonid I. Brezhnev thanking the Soviet leaders for their "very warm, fraternal congratulations in connection with my election to my party and government posts."

Mr. Karmal voiced conviction that, with Soviet aid, "we shall win and overcome all difficulties inherited from the past" and defend the "sovereignty, independence and national pride of Afghanistan."

The Izvestia article, signed by M. Mikhailov, elaborated on the Pravda account and seemed to broaden the scope of the accusations against the United States.

April 1978 Revolution Recalled

The new explanation placed the intervention against the background of the April 1978 revolution, in which the People's Democratic Party headed by the late Noor Mohammad Taraki toppled the republican Government headed by President Mohammad Daud.

According to Izvestia, the United States was unwilling to accept this reverse in a country where its commercial interests had only recently had an open field and launched a counteroffensive. Agents of the Central Intelligence Agency were said to have trained Afghan insurgents in Pakistan and fomented subversive activities inside Afghanistan.

Some of these activities, according to Izvestia, were carried out under the cover of a program against illegal traffic in narcotics; some took the guise of refugee aid. Egged on by the United States and Britain, Pakistan was said to have assigned army officers to command groups trained for action in Afghanistan; training was also provided by Chinese and Egyptian advisers, Izvestia said.

"Many members of these groups, after undergoing special training in China, were dropped on Afghan territory for acts of sabotage," the newspaper said. "These operations were financed by Washington and Peking."

Weapons, ammunition and equipment were shipped from the United States and China to depots in Peshawar, Pakistan, the paper said, and at least one insurgent chief was known to have visited the State Department in Washington.

"What were the motivating factors of Washington's anti-Afghan activities?" Izvestia asked. "Those motives are directly linked with the loss by the United States of its dominating influence in Iran. How the United States would have liked, at this point, to have forced Afghanistan to submit to its primarily anti-Soviet designs, to make the Afghan people abandon their revolutionary course!"

Reiterating the Soviet contention that the Afghan Government had made repeated requests for Soviet military assistance in 1978 and 1979 against the dangers it was facing, Izvestia said the Soviet Government had hesitated to respond, hoping that those supporting the rebellion would realize that the new course in Afghanistan was irreversible.

"At the same time," Izvestia said, "it should have been clear to all that we would not permit a neighboring country with a long common border to be turned into a base for the preparation of imperialist aggression against the Soviet state."

But, the paper said, intervention in Afghanistan continued, and power in Kabul was usurped by a "traitor to the ideas of the April revolution," Hafizullah Amin. The Afghan people and the People's Democratic Party were able to "render harmless the criminals and traitors who had established a regime of terror and violence," Izvestia said, adding that Mr. Amin was executed and Babrak Karmal called on the Afghans to rally behind him in a new National Front.

The Izvestia account, like the one in Pravda, was vague on the circumstances of the subsequent Afghan request for Soviet aid and the identity of those who made the request. Izvestia said the date of the request, "as reported by the Kabul radio," was Dec. 23. But that was after the Soviet troop airlift had begun and one day after fighting, in which Soviet troops participated, broke out in Kabul.

Today, Izvestia said, "the imperialists are enraged because their plots against the new Afghanistan have foundered."

As for the Western reaction to the Soviet move, the paper said, "there can be nothing but disdain for the noise raised in the bourgeois mass media about the 'occupation of Afghanistan' by Soviet troops, about 'Soviet intervention,' and other such nonsense."

A similar view was expressed in a statement attributed by Tass to Rahim Rafat, editor in chief of the newspaper New Times of Kabul. Mr. Rafat was quoted as having said, "The American press and the Voice of America are foaming at the mouth, trying to smear revolutionary Afghanistan and drive a wedge into Soviet-Afghan relations."

Ridiculing what he called Washington's attempt to pose as a champion of Afghan independence and of Islam, Mr. Rafat assailed American support for the Shah of Iran and said preparations for a military "quick reaction corps" were a threat to the Moslem countries in the Mideast.

SECTION C.   CHALLENGES TO THE PROHIBITION OF THE USE OF FORCE

---

1.   VITAL NATIONAL INTERESTS

President Nasser of Egypt nationalized the Universal Suez Canal Company in July, 1956. British and French concern about this assumption of control over access to oil from the Middle East was intense. Higgins concludes that "[s]ecret arrangements were proceeded with for an Anglo-French 'police' action following an Israeli attack upon Egypt. * * * There now seems ample evidence that a highly secret meeting took place at Sèvres on 23 October between the French, British, and Israelis, when plans for the Israeli attack, and the ensuing 'police action' were co-ordinated, and formally agreed upon. The United States was not informed." Higgins, United Nations Peacekeeping, 1946–1967, I. The Middle East 225 (1969).

On October 29, Israel attacked Egyptian fedayeen (Palestine army) bases in Sinai and advanced toward the Suez Canal. Britain and France served ultimatums on Israel and Egypt to cease hostilities and withdraw from the canal. When Egypt rejected the ultimatum, British and French aircraft launched attacks on Egyptian air bases, and troops from both countries entered Egyptian territory at Port Said, from the air and from the sea. A draft resolution calling upon Israel and Egypt to cease fire and calling upon all members to refrain from the use of force in any manner inconsistent with the purposes of the United Nations was vetoed by Britain and France in the Security Council and the matter was brought before the General Assembly at an emergency meeting.[a] The United Kingdom representative (Sir Pierson DIXON) gave the following explanation of the action of his country and France (Gen.Ass.Off.Rec., 1st Emergency Special Sess., 1956 Plenary, p. 5):

*   *   *

69. From all the information at our disposal, we had reason to judge that a major clash, whose consequences would have been incalculable, between Israel and its Arab neighbours was more imminent than at any time since the signing of the armistice agreements in 1949. The sudden Israel mobilization and incursion into Egypt made it imperative to take very speedy and effective measures to prevent a war between Israel and Egypt which could only lead to a general conflagration throughout the Middle East and which would, in its train, have involved prolonged disruption of free passage through the Suez Canal, the canal which is of such vital interest to so many nations.

*   *   *

74. With regret, I say that the Security Council, in our opinion, could have provided no effective remedy in time.

75. I need not here go into the reasons why those provisions of the Charter which were designed to provide the Council with a military arm have remained in abeyance. It is well known that it is because a permanent member of the Security Council, by a persistent misuse of the veto, has seen fit to thwart the intentions of the Charter. The result has been that the world has not been able to rely on the United Nations for the collective security which the Organization was designed to provide. Least of all, in view of the intransigence of the parties and the cynical misuse of its veto power by the Soviet Union, could we expect swift and effective action from the United Nations in an emergency in the Middle East.

76. It is hard to say these things, but I fear they are true. It is precisely because of this unhappy limitation in the effective powers of the Security Council to deal with such an emergency that the United Kingdom and French Governments were compelled to intervene at once, as they were fortunately in a position to do.

77. It was through no wish of ours that a situation arose in which we were compelled to act independently of the United Nations. Indeed, as soon as the news of the Israel action reached us here in New York, in the afternoon of 29 October, I took immediate steps, with the representatives of the United States and France, to make it clear that the Council should be seized of this situation at once.

a. The General Assembly's subsequent establishment of a peacekeeping force (UNEF) is discussed in Chapter 20.

78.   We did not, however, consider that the course of action proposed by the United States, without consultation with Her Majesty's Government, could effectively achieve the twin objectives of separating the belligerents at once and of safeguarding free passage through the Canal.

79.   It was in these circumstances that we were obliged to cast our negative votes in the Security Council.   The action which we and the French Government have taken is essentially of a temporary character, and, I repeat it, designed to deal with a unique emergency.   Our intervention was swift because the emergency brooked no delay.   It has been drastic because drastic action was evidently required.   It is an emergency police action. The situation is not dissimilar to that which obtained at the time of the North Korean invasion.   On that occasion the Member of the United Nations which had forces on hand and was in a position to intervene at once courageously did so.   By a happy chance—and I mean the absence of the Soviet representative from the Security Council on that occasion—the Council was able to endorse the United States action.   The same fortunate chance was not ours.   I cannot, however, believe that the United States would not, in any case, have acted, and rightly so, in the circumstances.

*   *   *

99.   Let me, at this stage, towards the end of my speech, briefly restate the objectives of the Anglo-French intervention. The overriding purposes are: the safeguarding of the Suez Canal and the restoration of peaceful conditions in the Middle East. Let me say with all the emphasis at my command that neither we nor the French Government have any desire whatever that the military action which we have taken should be more than temporary in its duration.   It will be terminated as soon as the emergency is over.   It is our intention that our action to protect the Canal, to terminate hostilities and to separate the combatants should be as short as possible in duration.

100.   The action taken by my Government and by the Government of France has been called an act of aggression against Egypt. This is a charge which we emphatically deny.   There is much debate about what constitutes aggression, but it is certainly not true to say that every armed action constitutes aggression. Every action must clearly be judged in the light of the circumstances in which it has taken place and the motives which have prompted it.

101.   The action of France and the United Kingdom is not aggression.   We do not seek the domination of Egypt or of any part of Egyptian territory.   Our purpose is peaceful, not warlike.   Our aim is to re-establish the rule of law, not to violate it; to protect, and not to destroy.   What we have undertaken is a temporary police action necessitated by the turn of events in the

Middle East and occasioned by the imperative need not only to protect the vital interests of my own and many other countries, but also to take immediate measures for the restoration of order.

102.   Our action is in no way aimed at the sovereignty of Egypt, and still less at its territorial integrity. It is not of our choice that the police action which we have been obliged to take is occurring on Egyptian territory. We have taken the only action which we could clearly see would be effective in holding the belligerents apart and which would give us a chance to re-establish peace in the area. By entering the Suez Canal area, we would only be seeking to protect a vital waterway, and it is also the only practicable line of division between the combatants.

---

2.   ANTICIPATORY SELF–DEFENSE

THE SIX DAY WAR

IV U.N. Monthly Chronicle, July 1967, p. 8.

Meeting of June 5

Following the outbreak of hostilities in the Middle East, the Security Council met in emergency session.

The Council had a letter from the representative of the United Arab Republic which stated that Israel had "committed a treacherous premeditated aggression" against his country that morning, launching attacks in the Gaza Strip, Sinai, and several airports in Cairo, the Suez Canal area, and other localities. Preliminary reports, it was stated, indicated that 23 Israeli planes had been shot down and several pilots captured. The letter went on to say that the United Arab Republic, "in repelling this aggression * * * had decided to defend itself by all means in accordance with Article 51 of the Charter of the United Nations".

The Secretary-General, U THANT, in his statement, said the United Nations had no means of ascertaining how the hostilities began. Reports coming in from the parties were conflicting, but all agreed that there was serious military action on land and in the air at a number of points which was spreading. The United Nations Emergency Force (UNEF), which was in the process of withdrawal, was no longer on the Line. Information from the UNEF Commander, General Indar Jit Rikhye, therefore, was necessarily general. He gave the Council the information he had received, including the report that three UNEF soldiers in the Indian contingent were killed and an undetermined number wounded when Israeli aircraft strafed a UNEF convoy. The authorities of the United Arab Republic reported large-scale air raids throughout the country, including Cairo, but Israel denied that Cairo had been raided. The authorities of the United Arab Republic also reported an Israeli attack on El Quiseima in Sinai and stated that its artillery in Gaza had started firing at Israel-controlled territory. General Odd Bull, Chief of Staff of the United Nations Truce Supervision Organization in Palestine (UNTSO), reported firing in Jerusalem. At his request, Israel and Jordan had accepted a ceasefire. Overflights by Syrian jet fighters and air battles over the Syrian-Israeli Armistice Line were reported.

The Secretary-General went on to say that the Israeli representative at ISMAC had informed the UNTSO officer at Tiberias that Israel considered itself at war with Syria. ISMAC reported that the Damascus airport had been attacked. The Secretary-General said that UNTSO headquarters had been occupied by Jordanian soldiers. Israeli troops, following heavy firing, had driven out the Jordanian soldiers and, ordering General Bull and his staff out of Government House, escorted them into Israel. The Secretary-General had requested Israel to restore the compound to exclusive United Nations control.

The Secretary-General also reported that Damascus airport and other locations in Syria were said to be under intermittent air attack, and that Israel claimed that Megiddo, Ailabum and a locality south of Akko had been attacked from the air. Firing was still going on in Jerusalem, and he supported the idea of declaring it an open city in order to protect its irreplaceable religious places.

Gopalaswami PARTHASARATHI (India) asked the Council to condemn Israel for the "wanton, irresponsible and brutal action" in which Indian soldiers were killed.

Mr. RAFAEL (Israel) told the Council that fighting had broken out on Israel's frontiers and that the Israeli Defence Forces were repelling the Egyptian Army and Air Force. He said that, in the early morning hours, Egyptian armoured columns had moved in an offensive thrust against Israel's borders and Egyptian planes had taken off from airfields in Sinai and struck out towards Israel. Egyptian artillery in the Gaza Strip had shelled the villages of Kissufim, Nahal-Oz and Ein Hashelosha in Israel. Israeli forces had engaged the Egyptians in the air and on land, and fighting continued.

Mr. Rafael said he was bringing this development to the attention of the Council in accordance with Article 51 of the Charter. The Israeli Minister of Defence, he added, had stated that Israel had no desire for conquest; it was simply defending itself.

Mohamed Awad EL KONY (United Arab Republic) said the attack on his country was so widespread that it had to be premeditated. The United Arab Republic, he said, had no choice but to defend itself in accordance with Article 51 of the Charter, and it would continue to do so. He asked that the Council condemn the aggression.

*   *   *

[At a subsequent meeting of the Security Council, the spokesman for Israel delivered the following explanation of Israel's military action. Security Council, Off.Rec. 1358th Meeting, 13 June 1967, S/PV. 1358, at p. 20.]

198. Let us look again at the events which preceded the outbreak of fighting on 5 June. On 18 May, the Government of the United Arab Republic demanded the eviction of the United Nations Emergency Force which was deployed along the Gaza Strip and the Sinai desert and at Sharm el Sheikh at the entrance to the Gulf of Aqaba, and on that day UNEF ceased to exist. Was this an act which promoted peace? Was this an act which demonstrated peaceful intent? It was not; it was preparation for aggression. The Emergency Force had to be gotten out of the way so that the aggression on Israel could be prepared and mounted.

199. On 23 May, the United Arab Republic declared that the Strait of Tiran would be closed to Israel shipping and to ships of other nations carrying what were described as strategic goods, that is to say, anything which the United Arab Republic chose to define as strategic goods, to Israel's southernmost port of Eilat. Was this act of blockade a peaceful act? Did this re-imposition of the blockade demonstrate peaceful intent? It did not. This was a clear act of hostility and the exercise of an internationally rejected claim to belligerency. A blockade is a classical act of war.

200. During this time, that is, the last week of May, Egypt started a massive build-up of forces in the Sinai desert. Some 80,000 men were assembled, with hundreds of assault aircraft, a thousand tanks. These huge forces were deployed in an offensive position along the Sinai frontier with Israel, along the Gaza Strip and at the approaches to Eilat. The deployment of these forces was accompanied by a mounting crescendo of warlike propaganda from Cairo. A holy war was proclaimed by the religious authorities in the Egyptian capital, and the Egyptian people were urged to march forward in a jehad to destroy Israel. The Egyptian President naturally was foremost in inciting his people for the coming war. This is what he said before the Central Council of Arab Trade Unions on 26 May 1967:

> The Arab people want to fight. We have been waiting for the suitable day when we shall be completely ready, since if we enter a battle with Israel we should be confident of victory and should take strong measures. We do not speak idly. We have lately felt that our strength is sufficient and that if we enter into battle with Israel we shall, with God's help, be victorious. Therefore, we have now decided to take real steps. The battle will be a full-scale one, and our basic aim will be to destroy Israel.

201. What were we in Israel and what was the Security Council expected to make of these words? A call for peace, or a call for war?

202. On 30 May, President Nasser signed a military agreement with King Hussein of Jordan, and Jordan began to mobilize. On 4 June, a similar agreement was signed with Iraq, and Iraqi detachments began arriving in Jordan and in Egypt. Was this evidence of peaceful intent? Were these agreements in keeping with the Charter of the United Nations? Were these aggressive movements of troops

in accordance with solemn agreements which Egypt and Jordan had entered into with Israel in 1949 with the object of preventing all hostile acts and serving as a transition to permanent peace? They were clear evidence of a preparation for aggression.

203.　While these military moves were going on in Egypt, Jordan and Iraq, Syria had also mobilized its forces to the last man, and 50,000 troops were poised aggressively on the heights which overlook Israel. We were surrounded. The armed ring was closed. All that the Arab forces were waiting for was the signal to start.

204.　That signal was given on 5 June, when Egyptian planes in accordance with the plans contained in battle order 6/67 of Air Force and Air Defence Headquarters of the Eastern Area in Sinai, dated 26 May 1967, took off for their assigned targets in Israel, while at the same time an artillery barrage on Israel farming villages was opened from the Gaza Strip. Shortly afterwards, Jordan guns sited amid the holy places of the Holy City of Jerusalem started shelling the Israel capital, causing heavy casualties, and the Syrian artillery joined the devil's chorus in the north. The aggression had begun.

205.　This is the record; this is what happened. Israel was designated to be the helpless victim of a massive assault. In accordance with its rights under Article 51 of the United Nations Charter, the victim defended itself, alone and successfully.

1.　*Territorial control.* Israel's success in the Six Day War resulted in her military occupation of substantial territory: Sinai, the Gaza Strip, parts of Jerusalem, portions of Jordan on the West Bank of the Jordan River and the Syrian Golan Heights.

2.　*Questions.* Was Israel's military action lawful under the Charter? Article 51 preserves "the inherent right of individual * * * self-defense if an armed attack occurs * * *." Was Israel's response to an attack that occurred or to a threatened attack? Was Israel acting in anticipatory self-defense? Is such action lawful under the Charter?

3.　*Views of certain writers.* Writing before there had been major tests of the meaning of the Charter, Stone observed in discussing Article 51: "Major troop concentrations on the border would presumably warrant anticipatory use of force * * *." Stone, Legal Controls of International Conflict 244, n. 8 (1954).

Following the Cuban missile crisis and prior to the events in the Middle East in 1967, the publicists in the United States were deeply divided on anticipatory self-defense, at least as an abstract concept. *Wright:*

Finally it has been argued that the quarantine and the O.A. S. resolution were justified as measures of "individual or collective self-defense" permitted by Article 51 of the Charter. It is suggested that the term "armed attack," which alone justified such defense without prior United Nations authority, must be interpreted to include a serious threat of armed attack.[53]   Reference has been made to the statement by Secretary of State Webster in the Caroline case, generally accepted prior to the Charter, that military defensive action was permissible in case of "an instant and overwhelming necessity," thus creating a limited right of preventive action; that such a construction is necessary in the nuclear age because to delay defensive action until an actual nuclear attack would be suicidal, and that the Charter supports this construction by forbidding "threat" as well as "use" of force in Article 2, paragraph 4.

These arguments are not convincing. It appears that the Charter intended to limit the traditional right of defense by states to actual armed attack, even though it forbade "threat of force" and authorized the Security Council to intervene to stop "threats to the peace." Professor, later judge, Philip Jessup wrote in 1948:

> This restriction in Article 51 very definitely narrows the freedom of action which states had under international law. A case could be made out for self-defense in the traditional law where the injury was threatened but no attack had yet taken place. Under the Charter, alarming military preparations by a neighboring state would justify a resort to the Security Council, but would not justify resort to anticipatory force by the state which believed itself threatened.[54]

The obligation of states to refrain from threats to the peace under Article 2, paragraph 4, and the competence of the United Nations to take action in case of a threat to the peace under Article 39, were not intended to give a unilateral right of military self-defense in case of such threats. For that reason, self-defense against threats was excluded in Article 51, and states were explicitly obliged to submit disputes or situations which they think threaten peace, to the United Nations and to refrain from unilateral use of force. * * * The Cuban Quarantine, 57 Am.J.Int'l L. 546, 559 (1963).

McDougal:

> The more important limitations imposed by the general community upon this customary right of self-defense have been, in conformity with the overriding policy it serves of minimizing coercion and violence across state lines, those of necessity and proportionality. The conditions of necessity required to be shown by the target state have never, however, been restricted to

---

53. The United States has not used this argument officially * * *.

54. Philip Jessup, A Modern Law of Nations 166 (New York, Macmillan, 1948). After an exhaustive discussion of "The Use of Force in Self-Defence," Ian Brownlie concludes that "the beginning of an armed attack is a condition precedent for resort to force in self-defence." 37 Brit.Yr.Bk. of Int.Law 266 (1962). * * *

"actual armed attack"; imminence of attack of such high degree as to preclude effective resort by the intended victim to non-violent modalities of response has always been regarded as sufficient justification, and it is now generally recognized that a determination of imminence requires an appraisal of the total impact of an initiating state's coercive activities upon the target state's expectations about the costs of preserving its territorial integrity and political independence. Even the highly restrictive language of Secretary of State Webster in the Caroline case, specifying a "necessity of self defense, instant, overwhelming, leaving no choice of means and no moment for deliberation," did not require "actual armed attack," [4] and the understanding is now widespread that a test formulated in the previous century for a controversy between two friendly states is hardly relevant to contemporary controversies, involving high expectations of violence, between nuclear-armed protagonists. The requirement of proportionality, in further expression of the policy of minimizing coercion, stipulates that the responding use of the military instrument by the target state be limited in intensity and magnitude to what is reasonably necessary promptly to secure the permissible objectives of self-defense under the established conditions of necessity.

* * *

* * * The apparent purpose of the inept language of Article 51, commonly ascribed to the late Senator Vandenburg, was only that of accommodating regional organizations, as specifically envisioned for the inter-American system by the Act of Chapultepec, with the more comprehensive centralized system of collective security projected by the Charter. Similarly, nothing in the "plain and natural meaning" of the words of the Charter requires an interpretation that Article 51 restricts the customary right of self-defense. The proponents of such an interpretation substitute for the words "if an armed attack occurs" the very different words "if, and only if, an armed attack occurs." The Soviet-Cuban Quarantine and Self-Defense, 57 Am.J.Int'l L. 597, 598 (1963).

Henkin:

* * * While there have been few challenges to Article 2, recurring crises, we have noted, have evoked suggestions for broader readings of the exception of Article 51. One that has been strongly urged is that in the day of nuclear weapons and the ever-present possibility of sudden devastation, nations cannot wait for an armed attack to occur. At least, it is urged, the Charter must now be read to permit "anticipatory self-defense" —the right to act in self-defense in anticipation of attack.

4. Mr. Webster to Mr. Fox, April 24, 1841, in 29 British and Foreign State Papers 1129, 1138 (1840–41). See also Jennings, "The Caroline and McLeod Cases," 32 A.J.I.L. 82 (1938).

The argument has specious appeal, but is fundamentally unpersuasive. If the Charter originally permitted force in self-defense only if an armed attack occurs, today's weapons hardly argue for extending the exception. The original reasons for barring "anticipatory self-defense" in regard to "old-fashioned war" apply even more to the new war. The logic of the deterrent and the balance of terror does not suggest that nations should be encouraged to preventive or even pre-emptive attack. The exception of Article 51 was limited to the situation "if an armed attack occurs," which is comparatively clear, objective, easy to prove, difficult to misinterpret or fabricate. To permit anticipation may virtually destroy the rule against the use of force, leaving it to every nation to claim anticipation and unlease the fury. Nations will not be prevented or deterred by the fear that later —if there is anyone left to judge—someone may determine that there had in fact been no threat of armed attack legitimately anticipated.

Proponents of anticipatory self-defense raise the specter of the all-out nuclear attack and of the obvious need to anticipate it. In fact, of course, for determining what the Charter means or should mean, the major nuclear attack and the pre-emptive strike are not the relevant concerns. A nation planning all-out attack will not be deterred by the Charter, though it may well talk "anticipatory self-defense" in its justification. Nor does one prescribe rules for the nation threatened with such an attack. If a nation is satisfied that another is about to obliterate it, it will not wait. But it has to make that decision on its own awesome responsibility. Anticipation in that case may have to be practiced; it need not be preached. The Charter need not make a principle of it; the law need not authorize or encourage it. But surely that extreme hypothetical case, beyond the realm of law, should not be used to justify new rules for situations that do not involve the impending mortal thrust. "Anticipatory self-defense" as a rule of law has meaning only in less extreme cases. There, anticipatory self-defense, it should be clear, becomes easily a euphemism for "preventive war." The United Nations Charter in the beginning did not authorize it. Attempts later, in relation to Suez and Sinai, to read the Charter as permitting anticipatory self-defense, were rejected. Nothing since, least of all the new weapons, suggests that international society would be better if the Charter were changed or read to authorize it. Force, Intervention and Neutrality in Contemporary International Law, Proceedings, Am.Soc.Int'l L. 147, 150 (1963).

4. *Israeli disaffection with the United Nations.* Are the following observations persuasive as to the lawfulness of the Israeli military action in the Six Day War?

It will be recalled that ever since 1948, the year of Israel's accession to statehood, the Arab states, including Lebanon, have regarded themselves as being in a state of war with her. This state of war has never been officially terminated; on the contrary, the Arab states have on numerous occasions asserted its continuing existence in seeking to justify various anti-Israel measures taken by them (such as the blocking of the Suez Canal and the Tiran Strait to Israeli navigation). Blum, The Beirut Raid and the International Double Standard, 64 Am.J.Int'l L. 73, 77 (1970). The author further states:

> * * * One of the most disturbing aspects of the Middle East conflict—disturbing as much to the cause of "world order" as to the cause of Israel—is the fact that on no single occasion over the past fifteen years has Israel been able to get satisfaction from the political organs of the United Nations on her complaints against neighboring Arab states. The Soviet veto that has been made available to the Arabs, to block any decision by the Security Council which the latter regarded as unfavorable to them, ensured that such a decision, even if it received the requisite number of votes in the Council, would not be adopted. This fact was naturally taken into account by other members of the Security Council more favorably disposed to Israel, and largely conditioned the very tone and formulation of many a watered-down draft resolution concerning Israeli complaints, since it was realized that the submission of a draft resolution giving satisfaction to Israel was bound to become an exercise in futility. This pattern, in turn, led to a growing conviction in Israel, which United Nations practice never effectively disproved, that it was difficult, if not impossible, for her rights to be recognized by the United Nations. (at 98)

---

3. NATIONAL LIBERATION MOVEMENTS

DECLARATION ON THE GRANTING OF INDEPENDENCE TO COLONIAL COUNTRIES AND PEOPLES [a]

General Assembly Resolution 1514 (XV) of Dec. 14, 1960. U.N.Gen.Ass. Off.Rec., 15th Sess., Supp. No. 16 (A/4684), p. 66.

1. The subjection of peoples to alien subjugation, domination and exploitation constitutes a denial of fundamental human rights, is contrary to the Charter of the United Nations and is an impediment to the promotion of world peace and co-operation.

2. All peoples have the right to self-determination; by virtue of that right they freely determine their political status and freely pursue their economic, social and cultural development.

4. All armed action or repressive measures of all kinds directed against dependent peoples shall cease in order to enable them to exercise peacefully and freely their right to complete independence, and the integrity of their national territory shall be respected.

> a. The complete text of the declaration is in the Documentary Supplement.

5.   Immediate steps shall be taken, in Trust and Non-Self-Governing Territories or all other territories which have not yet attained independence, to transfer all powers to the peoples of those territories, without any conditions or reservations, in accordance with their freely expressed will and desire, without any distinction as to race, creed or colour, in order to enable them to enjoy complete independence and freedom.

UNITED NATIONS, GENERAL ASSEMBLY RESOLUTION ADOPTED NOVEMBER 10, 1975

A/Res/3382 (XXX).

The General Assembly,

Recalling its resolutions 2955 (XXVII) of 12 December 1972, 3070 (XXVIII) of 30 November 1973 and 3246 (XXIX) of 29 November 1974,

Reaffirming the importance of the universal realization of the right of peoples to self-determination, to national sovereignty and territorial integrity and of the speedy granting of independence to colonial countries and peoples as imperatives for the enjoyment of human rights,

Welcoming whole-heartedly the independence of Mozambique, Sao Tome and Principe Cape Verde and Papua New Guinea,

Concerned about the current conflict in Angola,

Equally concerned about the maintenance of the independence and territorial integrity of the Comoros,

Confident in the hope that the nationalist movements will co-operate with the Fact-Finding Commission of Inquiry and Conciliation of the Organization of African Unity,

Indignant at the continued violations of the human rights of the peoples still under colonial and foreign domination and alien subjugation, the continuation of the illegal occupation of Namibia and the persistence of the racist minority regimes in Zimbabwe and South Africa,

1.   Reaffirms the legitimacy of the peoples' struggle for independence, territorial integrity and liberation from colonial and foreign domination and alien subjugation by all available means including armed struggle;

2.   Welcomes the efforts by the Fact-Finding Commission of Inquiry and Conciliation of the Organization of African Unity to resolve amicably the current conflict in Angola;

3.   Rejects any foreign interference in the internal affairs of Angola and of the Comoros;

4.   Condemns the policies of those members of the North Atlantic Treaty Organization and those countries whose military, economic, sporting or political relations with the racist régimes of southern Af-

rica and elsewhere encourage these régimes to persist in their suppression of the aspirations of peoples for self-determination and independence;

5.　Strongly condemns all Governments which do not recognize the right to self-determination and independence of peoples under colonial and foreign domination and alien subjugation, notably the peoples of Africa and the Palestinian people;

6.　Demands full respect for the basic human rights of all individuals detained or imprisoned as a result of their struggle for self-determination and independence, and strict respect for article 5 of the Universal Declaration of Human Rights under which no one shall be subjected to torture or to cruel, inhuman or degrading treatment, and their immediate release;

7.　Keenly awaits the conclusion of the following studies by the Sub-Commission on Prevention of Discrimination and Protection of Minorities:

(a) Adverse consequences for the enjoyment of human rights of political, military, economic and other forms of assistance given to colonial and racist régimes in southern Africa;

(b) Historical and current development of the right to self-determination on the basis of the Charter of the United Nations and other instruments adopted by United Nations organs, with particular reference to the promotion and protection of human rights and fundamental freedoms;

(c) Implementation of United Nations resolutions relating to the right of peoples under colonial and alien domination to self-determination;

8.　Notes with appreciation the material and other forms of assistance that peoples under colonial and alien régimes continue to receive from Governments, United Nations agencies and intergovernmental and non-governmental organizations and calls for a maximization of this assistance;

9.　Decides to remain seized of this item at its thirty-first session on the basis of reports that Governments, United Nations agencies and intergovernmental and non-governmental organizations are requested to submit concerning the strengthening of assistance to colonial Territories and peoples under alien domination and foreign subjugation.

> 2400th plenary meeting
> 10 November 1975

[The foregoing resolution was considered and approved in draft form by the third committee of the General Assembly and reported to the assembly, where it was adopted by a vote of 99 to 1, with 18 abstentions. Extracts from the committee debate appear below.]

UNITED NATIONS, GENERAL ASSEMBLY, EXCERPTS FROM DEBATE IN THE THIRD COMMITTEE

U. N. Gen. Ass. Off. Rec., 30th Sess., Third Committee, pp. 64–99, A/C.3/SR. 2111–2181.

6.   Mr. BAROODY (Saudi Arabia) said that, historically, what was now known as the right of peoples to self-determination had been referred to as the principle of self-determination.   The importance of that principle had been recognized at the signing of the Treaty of Versailles, on 28 June 1919, when President Wilson of the United States had stated that colonial peoples should be able to exercise their right to self-determination.   Unfortunately, however, the victors of the First World War had clung tenaciously to their colonies and had referred to self-determination as only a vague principle which should not be taken too seriously.   Wilson had been saddened by the attitude of the leaders of France and the United Kingdom because his own country had entered that war in order to bring about the liberation of peoples and make the world safe for democracy.   He had also been saddened by the results of the Treaty: the map of Europe had been redrawn without regard for the wishes of peoples or the principle of self-determination.   Thus, perhaps unwittingly, the leaders of the victorious countries had sown the seeds of the Second World War by creating hatred and bitterness in the hearts of the German people.

7.   Another example of disregard for the principle of self-determination could be found in the countries of the Fertile Crescent, which had been placed under United Kingdom and French mandates in 1922 and had experienced the rule of British and French High Commissioners, who had supposedly been appointed in order to train the people for self-government.   Such mandates had, however, only been a pretext for the maintenance of colonialism.

8.   Subsequently the Second World War had broken out, bringing with it slogans such as "freedom from want, freedom from fear, freedom of speech and freedom of belief".   The British and French mandates over Syria, Lebanon, Iraq and Palestine had been terminated as a result of that war, but the slogans rang hollow now because there was still want and fear in the world and colonialism still existed. The major Powers had learnt nothing from the Second World War. They had divided Korea, and the Korean War had broken out in 1950. They had partitioned Germany and Palestine; they had accepted South Africa's claim to sovereignty over what they called South West Africa and they had done nothing to promote the realization of the right to self-determination in Southern Rhodesia.

9.   He recalled that he had been the first to bring up the question of self-determination during the formulation of the Universal Declaration of Human Rights in 1948.   His request that the right to self-determination should be included in the Declaration had been challenged on the grounds that that right was a collective right, rather than an individual one, although in his view the Declaration concerned man as

a member of society. He had been overruled, with the result that there was no mention of the right to self-determination in the Declaration. He had then urged that that right should be included in the Covenants on Human Rights, and self-determination had been enshrined as a right in common article 1 of those instruments. He recalled that at that time the Latin American countries had supported him in his insistence that a reference to the right to self-determination should be included.

10.   He hoped to live to see the people in the remaining enclaves of colonialism, particularly Namibia, Southern Rhodesia and Palestine, gain their inalienable right to self-determination. It was not enough to pass resolutions mentioning the Namibian, Southern Rhodesian or Palestinian people; the United Nations must speak out so that all countries might be represented at the United Nations with dignity. It was not enough to call for sanctions against South Africa and Southern Rhodesia, because despite those sanctions the white minority régimes in those countries were thriving. The United Nations must therefore press for self-determination and campaign in every country so that the Africans in Namibia and Southern Rhodesia, and the Palestinians, might exercise that alienable right.

11.   His delegation would whole-heartedly support any resolution on the right to self-determination, and considered that there should be a target date for the realization of that right. The peoples who had once been under the colonialist yoke should set other peoples free and the United Nations should work as one people to that end.

*   *   *

1.   Mr. JANKOWITSCH (Austria) * * *.

*   *   *

4.   Austria considered that all available peaceful means should be employed in the pursuit of the goals set forth in the Declaration on the Granting of Independence to Colonial Countries and Peoples (General Assembly resolution 1514 (XV)). It would never approve of a policy of social and racial discrimination pursued by a small minority against the will of the vast majority of the population. Thus Austria faithfully carried out the sanctions imposed by the Security Council on Southern Rhodesia. His Government hoped that the authorities responsible for the continuation of colonial situations would realize the necessity and urgency of a fundamental change of policy.

5.   Austria was also convinced that the efforts of the colonial peoples to avail themselves of their right to self-determination should also be supported financially; it had made contributions to the United Nations Trust Fund for South Africa, the United Nations Educational and Training Programme for Southern Africa and the United Nations Fund for Namibia. Those financial contributions had been increased regularly and were considerably higher in 1975 than in 1974. In compliance with General Assembly resolution 3302 (XXIX), Austria had furthermore contributed to the training programme for inhabitants of Non-Self-Governing Territories by offering scholarships,

among them scholarships for participation in courses at the Diplomatic Academy in Vienna.

* * *

11.   Miss OLOWO (Uganda) said that her delegation too supported the draft resolution and wished to join in sponsoring it. It was in favour of the armed struggle of peoples still under colonial domination. She expressed her delegation's gratitude to Governments, United Nations bodies and intergovernmental and non-governmental organizations for their material and moral support of the cause of peoples still under colonial domination.

* * *

6.   Mrs. de BARISH (Costa Rica) said that her delegation had always maintained that one of the most fundamental rights of all peoples was that of self-determination and independence. It therefore supported the draft resolution under consideration. However, it expressed reservations with regard to operative paragraph 1, since, while it agreed with the objectives of the paragraph, it could not agree that they should be achieved through armed struggle. As her delegation had already pointed out, acts of violence could be carried out unscrupulously and thus involve innocent persons. Her delegation's position was also based on its desire for peace.

* * *

21.   Miss DUBRA (Uruguay) said that her delegation supported the draft resolution, but reserved its position with regard to operative paragraph 1 because the words "including armed struggle" were contrary to the provisions of the Charter which called for the peaceful settlement of disputes.

22.   Mr. MORENO MARTÍNEZ (Dominican Republic) said that, since his country had formerly been a colony, it naturally supported peoples in their struggle for independence and self-determination. His delegation therefore supported draft resolution A/C.3/L.2158, but wished to express a reservation concerning operative paragraph 1 because it considered that the use of armed struggle was contrary to those provisions of the Charter calling for the peaceful settlement of disputes. His delegation also wished to reserve its position with regard to operative paragraph 5, in particular, the words "and the Palestinian people". Although it agreed with the principle of the right of the Palestinian people to self-determination, it could not agree with the way that right was referred to in operative paragraph 5.

* * *

25.   Mr. DABO (Guinea) said that he had some difficulty in understanding the reservations expressed by Uruguay, Costa Rica and the Dominican Republic concerning operative paragraph 1 because those countries had achieved their independence through armed struggle and should therefore not oppose the use of that method by other countries still struggling for freedom.

26.   Mr. MORENO MARTÍNEZ (Dominican Republic) said that the Latin American countries had achieved their independence before the

United Nations had been established. Now, however, countries were able to achieve their independence peacefully and without armed struggle thanks to the existence of the United Nations.

* * *

30. Mr. ALFONSO (Cuba) said that his delegation fully supported the draft resolution because it embodied principles to which his country attached the greatest importance. Referring in particular to operative paragraph 1, he said that the use of the words "including armed struggle" was essential because the United Nations could not set any limitation on the way in which peoples achieved their independence. No such limitation had been set in the Charter and the Committee had always recognized the principle of the realization of the right to self-determination by any available means.

31. He, too, wished to request a separate vote on operative paragraph 4 and proposed that it should be taken by a roll-call vote. He also requested a separate roll-call vote on operative paragraph 5.

* * *

9. Mr. BROAD (United Kingdom) regretted that, on an issue as important as the right of peoples to self-determination, it had not been possible to arrive at a text which could be supported by the Committee as a whole. His delegation had a slight problem with regard to the second preambular paragraph: it could not accept, and in any case the Charter did not specify, that the realization or non-realization of the right to self-determination could in itself be regarded as synonymous with the enjoyment or non-enjoyment of human rights. The United Kingdom rejected the call to arms made in operative paragraph 1, and therefore interpreted paragraph 8 as referring solely to humanitarian assistance. He had voted against paragraph 4 and recalled in that respect that, in February 1975 the Secretary-General of NATO had told the Chairman of the Special Committee against Apartheid, while the latter was visiting Brussels, that NATO under its Charter had a well-defined geographical limit which did not include South Africa, and that it had no contact or political, military or technical understanding with South Africa which could give comfort to the latter in the implementation of its apartheid policy or lend it respectability. Lastly, paragraph 5 was unacceptable in its current form because it described an extremely complex matter in a simplistic way.

---

1. *Assistance to liberation movements.* Is lawful assistance to liberation movements limited to humanitarian aid? Is it lawful for states to provide military assistance (money and arms) to liberation movements? Is provision of such military assistance consistent with Article 2(4) of the charter? Or is there an exception from Article 2(4)'s prohibition in the case of wars of liberation waged against a colonial state by people in the colony? Does Article 1(2) of the charter, referring to self-determination of peoples, supply the answer to these questions?

2. *United Nations declaration.* Note the following provisions of the General Assembly's Declaration on Principles of International Law Concerning Friendly Relations and Cooperation Among States in Accordance with the Charter of the United Nations, adopted in 1970:

The principle of equal rights and self-determination of peoples

By virtue of the principle of equal rights and self-determination of peoples enshrined in the Charter of the United Nations, all peoples have the right freely to determine, without external interference, their political status and to pursue their economic, social and cultural development, and every State has the duty to respect this right in accordance with the provisions of the Charter.

Every State has the duty to promote, through joint and separate action, realization of the principle of equal rights and self-determination of peoples, in accordance with the provisions of the Charter, and to render assistance to the United Nations in carrying out the responsibilities entrusted to it by the Charter regarding the implementation of the principle, in order:

(a) To promote friendly relations and co-operation among States; and

(b) To bring a speedy end to colonialism, having due regard to the freely expressed will of the peoples concerned;

and bearing in mind that subjection of peoples to alien subjugation, domination and exploitation constitutes a violation of the principle, as well as a denial of fundamental human rights, and is contrary to the Charter.

Every State has the duty to promote through joint and separate action universal respect for and observance of human rights and fundamental freedoms in accordance with the Charter.

The establishment of a sovereign and independent State, the free association or integration with an independent State or the emergence into any other political status freely determined by a people constitute modes of implementing the right of self-determination by that people.

Every State has the duty to refrain from any forcible action which deprives peoples referred to above in the elaboration of the present principle of their right to self-determination and freedom and independence. In their actions against, and resistance to, such forcible action in pursuit of the exercise of their right to self-determination, such peoples are entitled to seek and to receive support in accordance with the purposes and principles of the Charter.

The territory of a colony or other Non-Self-Governing Territory has, under the Charter, a status separate and distinct from the territory of the State administering it; and such separate and distinct status under the Charter shall exist until the people of the colony or

Non-Self-Governing Territory have exercised their right of self-determination in accordance with the Charter, and particularly its purposes and principles.

Nothing in the foregoing paragraphs shall be construed as authorizing or encouraging any action which would dismember or impair, totally or in part, the territorial integrity or political unity of sovereign and independent States conducting themselves in compliance with the principle of equal rights and self-determination of peoples as described above and thus possessed of a government representing the whole people belonging to the territory without distinction as to race, creed or colour.

Every State shall refrain from any action aimed at the partial or total disruption of the national unity and territorial integrity of any other State or country.[a]

LEGITIMACY OF SELF–DETERMINATION

Buchheit, Secession: The Legitimacy of Self-Determination 216–218 (1978).*

From the preceding discussion we can draw several conclusions. First, secessionist activity is an irrepressible feature of the contemporary world scene, and the future, from all indications, will not see an abatement in the frequency of these claims. Second, many of these movements seek legal justification in the international doctrine of self-determination. Third, at the present time there is neither an international consensus regarding the status of secession within this doctrine nor (should it be conceded such a status) is there an accepted teaching regarding the nature of a legitimate secessionist movement. Fourth, by its present inability to distinguish legitimate from illegitimate claims to secessionist self-determination, the international community is seriously handicapped in its attempt to minimize instances of unwarranted third-party intervention in secessionist conflicts under the aegis of the "peremptory norm" of self-determination. Finally, aside from the immense cost of secessionist wars to the immediate parties, the danger of unrestrained intervention inevitably brings in its wake a possibility of escalation and the confrontation of major power blocs. One is left, therefore, with the disturbing result that situations involving a potentially serious threat to international world order, situations which are by their nature arguably unregulated by the general legal restrictions upon the international use of force, remain equally unfettered by any specific doctrines of international law.

There are several apparent solutions to this problem. It is possible for the world community to make an ex cathedra pronouncement that secession has no place within the doctrine of self-determination,

---

a. The full text of the declaration appears in the Documentary Supplement.

* Copyright 1978. Reprinted with the permission of Buchheit and Yale University Press.

thus embracing a limitation of this principle to cases of overseas co-lonization, interracial domination, or some other arbitrary category. This approach is, I believe, both dangerous and highly unrealistic. Such a transparently artificial restriction of the principle to the rela-tively "safe" context of European-style colonialism, when articulated by the very entities (independent States) liable to be inconvenienced by its further extension, is not likely to convince minority groups within established States that their claims have been adjudged illegit-imate by an impartial collective verdict. They will therefore tend to disregard all opinions coming from that body, whether concerning the outbreak, conduct, or settlement of separatist conflicts, as hopelessly self-protective. The international community would thus effectively cast itself in a role similar to that occupied by the Holy Alliance dur-ing the last century in its goal of guarding monarchic supremacy against "anarchic" nationalism; that is, the role of an entrenched power bloc flailing against threats to its dominance arising from the dissatisfactions of its own constituents. At the very least, the com-munity will have to abandon its fondness for decrying the evils per-petrated by colonial Powers unless it can discover a convincing meth-od of distinguishing, in principle, these evil policies from the equiva-lent deportment of "alien" governors occupying a contiguous land mass.

A second alternative is to leave the issue of the basic validity of secessionist self-determination to some future generation having greater wisdom, and concentrate upon the more immediate task of preserving the integrity of norms such as nonintervention and the proscription of the use of force. This might be attempted by an un-equivocal declaration saying that the "higher" principle of self-deter-mination may not be invoked to subvert these norms by States seek-ing to intervene in separatist conflicts on the basis of someone's right to self-determination. Overall, this approach has much to commend it and may by default be the least offensive course of action. It is marred by three difficulties: (1) the United Nations General Assem-bly has clearly *not* taken this position in the area of colonial self-de-termination; (2) any attempt to limit this declaration to cases of in-tra-State domination while affirming its direct opposite in the con-text of colonial domination will inevitably appear unconvincing; and (3) States continue to maintain their right to intervene on behalf of incumbent governments in this kind of conflict and therefore the question of the legitimacy of the separatists' claim will still arise in a roundabout fashion (not "Can I legally intervene on behalf of the claimants?" but "Can I legally aid those attempting to thwart the claim?").

A third solution, and the one that will be pursued here, seeks to maintain the underlying force of the self-determination principle and yet minimize the dangers to international peace and security by con-centrating upon a method of ascertaining *legitimate* claims of this kind. Acknowledging that self-determination (insofar as it derives its strength from an innate urge to self-government coupled with a

sense of the moral objections to alien domination resulting in exploitation, humiliation, and deprivation of human rights) is prima facie
applicable to some but not all groups within independent States, the
focus of attention ought to be on determining which groups are entitled to invoke the principle.   Inevitably, this will involve an inquiry
into the nature of the group, its situation within its governing State,
its prospects for an independent existence, and the effect of its separation on the remaining population and the world community in general.   Taken as a whole, these considerations would evolve standards
by which the international community could ascertain instances of legitimate claims to separatist self-determination.

The probable benefits of this approach are significant.   Most importantly, the international community would be given the chance to
adjust its posture with regard to a particular separatist demand by
virtue of its ability to distinguish the legal merits of the claim.   This
might permit a collective judgment, as was reached in the cases of
Rhodesia and South Africa, concerning the proper scope of outside
States' behavior toward the situation.   In addition, the norms of non-
intervention and proscription of force would again enjoy some protection under this scheme.   Unless specifically prohibited by an authoritative international decision, of course, intervention on behalf of the
"legitimate" party would still be possible and perhaps invited as enforcement of a community standard; but then, even in the halcyon
days before the emergence of self-determination as a peremptory
norm only a minority of jurists opposed *all* intervention.   Jurists
then purported to acknowledge that States interfere with the lives of
other States for a variety of reasons (by request, for humanitarian
purposes, as part of collective self-defense, and so on), not all of
which are legally objectionable.   The problem with permitting intervention on behalf of a people claiming a right of self-determination
was that it opened the door to a virtually unlimited freedom of intervention precisely because no one knew (within very broad limits)
when the claimants, and thus their would-be patrons, were legally entitled to invoke the principle.   With the resolution of this basic uncertainty, other primary norms of international behavior would no longer be endangered by unrestricted, subjective decisions of third-party
States regarding the legality of their actions as furthering the principle of self-determination   *   *   *.

4. RESCUE OF HOSTAGES

SUMMARY ACCOUNT OF ENTEBBE INCIDENT

McDowell, Introductory Note [a]
15 International Legal Materials 1224 (1976).[*]

An Air France airplane that left Israel for France with over 250 passengers and a crew of 12 aboard was hijacked by terrorists on June 28, 1976, after a stopover in Athens. The hijackers forced the plane to land first at Benghazi in Libya, and then at Entebbe Airport in Uganda. Acting for the Popular Front for the Liberation of Palestine, the hijackers demanded the release of some 153 terrorists jailed in Israel, West Germany, France, Switzerland, and Kenya. On June 30 the hijackers released 47 non-Israeli passengers, and the following day released an additional 100. The remaining 104 passengers and crew were held hostage in Uganda until rescued by an Israeli military commando unit on July 3 and taken to Israel. Reports indicated that in the rescue operation three of the hostages, one Israeli soldier, seven of the terrorists, and a number of Ugandan soldiers were killed. There were conflicting opinions on whether the Government of Uganda acted to protect the hostages and negotiate for their release, or was directly implicated in collaborating with the terrorists.

On July 9, the Security Council of the United Nations began consideration of a complaint by the Prime Minister of Mauritius, current chairman of the Organization of African Unity, which referred to the "act of aggression" by Israel against the Republic of Uganda. See U.N. Doc. S/12126. On July 12, two draft resolutions were introduced—one by the United Kingdom and the United States, the other by Tanzania, Libya, and Benin.

The U.K.–U.S. resolution, inter alia, condemned hijacking and called on states to prevent and punish all such terrorist acts, while reaffirming the need to respect the sovereignty and territorial integrity of all states.

The Tanzania-Libya-Benin draft condemned Israel's violation of Uganda's sovereignty and territorial integrity and demanded that Israel meet Uganda's claims for full compensation for damage and destruction.

When the Security Council voted on the U.K.–U.S. draft resolution on July 14, the resolution lacked the 9 affirmative votes required for adoption. The vote was 6 in favor (U.S., U.K., France, Italy, Japan, Sweden), with 2 abstentions (Panama, Romania), and 7 countries not participating in the vote (Benin, the People's Republic of China, Guyana, Libya, Pakistan, Tanzania, and the U.S.S.R.).

a. The note serves as an introduction to various United Nations materials concerning the incident.

* Reprinted with the permission of the American Society of International Law.

The Tanzania-Libya-Benin draft was not pressed to a vote, but in a statement by the Tanzanian delegate on July 14, the co-sponsors reserved the right to revive consideration of it "at an appropriate moment."

EXCERPTS FROM UNITED NATIONS SECURITY COUNCIL DEBATE ON THE ENTEBBE INCIDENT

XVII U. N. Monthly Chronicle, Aug.-Sept. 1976, p. 15.

In the debate, Kurt WALDHEIM, Secretary-General of the United Nations, said he had issued a statement on 8 July immediately after his return from Africa in which he had given a detailed account of the role he had played in efforts to secure the release of the hostages at Entebbe.

The case before the Council raised a number of complex issues because, in this instance, the response of one State to the results of an act of hijacking involved an action affecting another sovereign State. In reply to a specific question, he had said: "I have not got all the details, but it seems to be clear that Israeli aircraft have landed in Entebbe and this constitutes a serious violation of the sovereignty of a State Member of the United Nations." The Secretary-General said he felt it was his obligation to uphold the principle of the territorial integrity and sovereignty of every State.

However, that was not the only element involved in considering cases of the kind which the Council was discussing. That was particularly true when the world community was required to deal with unprecedented problems arising from acts of international terrorism, which Mr. Waldheim said he had consistently condemned and which raised many issues of a humanitarian, moral, legal and political character for which, at the present time, no commonly agreed rules or solutions existed.

It was hoped that the Council would find a way to point the world community in a constructive direction so that it might be spared a repetition of the human tragedies of the past and the type of conflict between States which the Council would now be considering.

*   *   *

Percy HAYNES (Guyana) said the action taken by Israel against Uganda was nothing but naked and brutal aggression. Guyana strongly condemned Israel for its aggression against the black African country of Uganda.

It was being argued that the principle of sovereignty was subordinate to the principle of human freedom and that Israel had the right, whenever it chose, to violate the sovereignty of other States in order to secure the freedom of its own citizens. That was nothing but a modern-day version of gun-boat diplomacy.

Those who, like Israel, sought to give legitimacy to the violation of the sovereignty of other States were making many small States, whose faith in and commitment to international law were unshakable, hostage to the dictates of naked power.

* * *

Kaj SUNDBERG (Sweden) said the drama was started by an abhorrent act of terrorism perpetrated by a group of extremist Palestinian Arabs and Europeans. There was no excuse for that criminal act.

The world must react vigorously against terrorist acts and take all possible protective measures. New efforts must be undertaken to achieve broad international agreement to combat terrorism, in the form of generally recognized standards of international conduct. The international community must work towards general recognition of the clear obligation resting on every State to do everything in its power, where necessary in collaboration with other States, to prevent acts of terrorism and, even more, to refrain from any action which might facilitate the perpetration of such acts.

Any State where hijackers landed with hostages must be prepared to shoulder the heavy responsibility of protecting all victims under circumstances which were bound to be difficult and delicate.

The Israeli action being considered involved an infringement of the national sovereignty and territorial integrity of Uganda. At the same time, Sweden was aware of the terrible pressures to which the Israeli Government and people were subjected, faced with this unprecedented act of international piracy and viewing the increasing threat to the lives of so many of their compatriots.

Sweden, although unable to reconcile the Israeli action with the strict rules of the Charter, did not find it possible to join in a condemnation in such a case.

* * *

Mr. SCRANTON (United States) said the United States reaffirmed the principle of territorial sovereignty in Africa. In addition to that principle, the United States was deeply concerned over the problem of air piracy and the callous and pernicious use of innocent people as hostages to promote political ends. The Council could not forget that the Israeli operation in Uganda would never have come about had the hijacking of the Air France flight from Athens not taken place.

Israel's action in rescuing the hostages necessarily involved a temporary breach of the territorial integrity of Uganda. Normally, such a breach would be impermissible under the Charter. However, there was a well established right to use limited force for the protection of one's own nationals from an imminent threat of injury or death in a situation where the State in whose territory they were located was either unwilling or unable to protect them. The right, flowing from the right of self-defence, was limited to such use of force as was necessary and appropriate to protect threatened nationals from injury.

The requirements of that right to protect nationals were clearly met in the Entebbe case. Israel had good reason to believe that at the time it acted Israeli nationals were in imminent danger of execution by the hijackers. In addition, there was substantial evidence that the Government of Uganda cooperated with and aided the hijackers. The ease and success of the Israeli effort to free the hostages suggested that the Ugandan authorities could have overpowered the hijackers and released the hostages if they had really had the desire to do so.

* * *

Under such circumstances, the Government of Israel invoked one of the most remarkable rescue missions in history, a combination of guts and brains that had seldom, if ever, been surpassed. It was justified because innocent decent people had a right to live and be rescued from terrorists who recognized no law and who were ready to kill if their demands were not met.

* * *

Mikhail KHARLAMOV (USSR) said that the flight carried out, the material destruction wrought, the substantial number of Ugandans killed were all regarded by Israel as a measure which was just or at least justified. But there existed no laws in the world, no moral or international laws, which could justify such action.

However much the representative of Israel might have tried to refute the irrefutable, the armed action against Uganda was an act of direct, flagrant aggression and an outright violation of the Charter, especially of Article 2, paragraph 4, which stated: "All Members shall refrain in their international relations from the threat or use of force against the territorial integrity or political independence of any State, or in any other manner inconsistent with the purposes of the United Nations."

The Soviet Union consistently opposed acts of terrorism, and was prepared to do its part in order to end that phenomenon. But one could not replace one matter with another. The Council was considering not the matter of international terrorism but an attack on Uganda, the killing of Ugandans, the destruction of Entebbe Airport, and other material destruction inflicted by the Israeli action against that State.

There was a gap between individual acts of terrorism and an attack by one State—in this case Israel—against another. Therefore a policy approved by a State could not be exceptional, even in the case in question.

The Council must condemn in the most vigorous manner the Israeli aggression against the sovereignty and territorial integrity of Uganda and compel Israel to recompense Uganda for the material damage done in connexion with the attack. In addition, the Council must extend a serious warning to Israel that such acts of aggression would not go unpunished in future.

* * *

Isao ABE (Japan) said international terrorism, whatever form it might take, constituted an abhorrent crime against mankind and must denounced in the strongest terms by the world community. The countries in the world must take effective measures to prevent and eliminate such a crime against humanity, and they were required to co-operate fully with each other in attaining that goal.

The Air France hijacking was terminated in an extraordinary circumstance—military action by a State within the territory of another State. Although the motives as well as the circumstances which led Israel to take such action were presented in detail, nevertheless there was an act of violation by Israel of the sovereignty of Uganda.

Japan reserved its opinion as to whether the Israeli military action had or had not met the conditions required for the exercise of the right of self-defence recognized under international law, as the Israeli representative contended.

SECTION D.   USE OF STATE COERCION SHORT OF MILITARY FORCE

Is non-military coercion subject to the law? Is a state free to impose its will on that of another so long as it refrains from the grosser violations of state personality that are encompassed in physical, military force? Does Article 2(4) of the charter proscribe only military force, or also coercions of different types? Is there an emerging law of non-intervention (or a developing body of general international law) that embraces such a proscription? For example, is an economically strong state guilty of illegal conduct if it uses its economic power to seek to force another state to do what it wishes: (a) as to internal non-economic matters, such as establishing honest and democratic governments; (b) as to alignment among power blocs in international relations; (c) as to economic conduct (i) of the same sort as that of the denial practiced by the powerful state (e. g., trade denial as a pressure for change in the trading policy of the pressured state) or (ii) of a different sort (e. g., denial of economic development assistance to induce settlement of a nationalization claim)?

CHARTER OF THE ORGANIZATION OF AMERICAN STATES

119 U.N.T.S. 3; 2 UST 2394; as amended February 27, 1967, 21 UST 607.

Article 19.   No State may use or encourage the use of coercive measures of an economic or political character in order to force the sovereign will of another State and obtain from it advantages of any kind.

JOVA, A REVIEW OF THE PROGRESS AND PROBLEMS OF THE ORGANIZATION OF AMERICAN STATES

65 United States Department of State Bulletin 284, 287 (1971).

* * *

An uncomfortable departure in our OAS affairs occurred in January of this year when Ecuador accused the United States of violating article 19 of the OAS Charter, which prohibits "use of coercive measures of an economic or political character in order to force the sovereign will of another State." Our dispute with Ecuador arose over the right of American vessels to fish off the coast of that country, in waters which Ecuador claims lie within its maritime sovereignty but which we maintain are high seas. After Ecuador had seized 14 American tuna boats in less than 2 weeks, the United States applied section 3(b) of the Foreign Military Sales Act suspending such sales to that country.

On the assertion that the United States move violated charter article 19, Ecuador called for a Meeting of Consultation of OAS Foreign Ministers, who happened to be in Washington anyway for the special General Assembly session. In their concurrent meeting on this new issue, there were severe criticisms of the United States laws which allegedly apply economic sanctions and impinge upon other nations' sovereignty. For its part, the United States defended its duty to protect the legitimate rights of its citizens in international waters. The outcome, however, was a resolution supported by both Ecuador and the United States, which merely stated the positions of the two disputing parties and called upon them to resolve their differences in accordance with charter principles and "abstain from the use of any kind of measure that may affect the sovereignty" of another state. This in itself involved a constructive effort on both sides to calm the situation, although the basic issue continues.

While the OAS action hardly constituted an indictment of the United States in its dispute with Ecuador, the implications of the issue for the future are of concern to us should there be future applications of U.S. legislation that might be deemed by OAS members to be "coercive" and in violation of charter article 19.

ANNEX TO UNITED NATIONS GENERAL ASSEMBLY RESOLUTION 2625 (XXV) OF OCTOBER 24, 1970

U.N. Gen. Ass. Off. Rec. Annexes, 25th Sess., Supp. No. 28 (A/8028), pp. 122, 123.

Declaration on Principles of International Law Concerning Friendly Relations and Co-operation Among States in Accordance with the Charter of the United Nations

* * *

The principle concerning the duty not to intervene in matters within the domestic jurisdiction of any State, in accordance with the Charter

No State or group of States has the right to intervene, directly or indirectly, for any reason whatever, in the internal or external affairs of any other State. Consequently, armed intervention and all other forms of interference or attempted threats against the personality of the State or against its political, economic and cultural elements, are in violation of international law.

No State may use or encourage the use of economic, political or any other type of measures to coerce another State in order to obtain from it the subordination of the exercise of its sovereign rights and to secure from it advantages of any kind. Also, no State shall organize, assist, foment, finance, incite or tolerate subversive, terrorist or armed activities directed towards the violent overthrow of the régime of another State, or interfere in civil strife in another State.

The use of force to deprive peoples of their national identity constitutes a violation of their inalienable rights and of the principle of non-intervention.

Every State has an inalienable right to choose its political, economic, social and cultural systems, without interference in any form by another State.

Nothing in the foregoing paragraphs shall be construed as affecting the relevant provisions of the Charter relating to the maintenance of international peace and security.

* * *

THE USE OF NONVIOLENT COERCION: A STUDY IN LEGALITY UNDER ARTICLE 2(4) OF THE CHARTER OF THE UNITED NATIONS

122 University of Pennsylvania Law Review 983 (1973).*

The partial oil embargo instituted by certain Arab nations in the wake of the 1973 Yom Kippur War in the Middle East suddenly in-

* Reprinted with the permission of the University of Pennsylvania Law Review and Fred B. Rothman & Co.

volved nearly every industrialized nation in the affairs of that troubled section of the globe. For all the shock and surprise voiced by the oil-dependent nations, the Arab move was within the tradition of international coercive policies. International law has long recognized and provided for the use of economic sanctions by one combatant against another during a time of war. Even the employment of economic measures against neutrals, which gained such wide currency during the Napoleonic Wars, has become an accepted part of our vocabulary of "total war."

The Arab policy of regulating the supply of crude oil in response to the customer nation's posture with regard to the Middle East situation was a predictable, but nonetheless important, expansion of this tradition. The embargo was directed at noncombatant nations, after the armed conflict had ostensibly ended. More importantly, there was no suggestion that the economic measures would improve the Arabs' military position. The sanctions were not aimed at influencing a military solution of the Middle East dispute, but rather were intended to alter the relative bargaining positions of the parties in some future political settlement. President Houari Boumediene of Algeria, following a meeting of Arab chiefs of state in November, 1973, is reported to have expressed satisfaction over "the economic, political and military weapons now in the hands of the Arabs."[2] A New York Times article appearing after the close of the conference reported that the participants had agreed "to exert continued economic pressure on outside countries by manipulating Arab oil exports according to 'the attitude of every country toward the Arab cause.' "[3]

The reaction of international jurists to this expansion of the use of economic coercion is as yet uncertain. This Comment will explore the legality of this type of coercion within the context of the body of international law that has developed around the United Nations Charter. A conclusion reached under Charter law does not, of course, preclude a separate judgment under either customary or other positive international law from being reached independently of the Charter.[4] But this Comment will consider legal sources outside the United Nations Charter only insofar as they may shed light upon its interpretation.

* * *

Should a state determine, either from lack of volition or lack of ability, to refrain from the use of direct or indirect military force, it is still not without tools to implement policy in the international sphere. At least two nonviolent modes of influence, the diplomatic (or political) and economic, are still available.

2. N.Y. Times, Nov. 29, 1973, at 1, col. 6.

3. Id.

4. For a consideration of economic coercion in the light of non-Charter international legal principles, particularly the principle of nonintervention, see Bowett, Economic Coercion and Reprisals by States, 13 Va.J.Int'l L. 1 (1972).

Diplomacy has always been a method, employed with varying degrees of success, of both conveying a nation's wishes to its neighbors and applying pressure toward achieving compliance with those wishes. * * *

* * *

Economic coercion may entail any or all of the traditional methods of economic compulsion. Although it is by no means novel, this weapon has assumed tremendous importance as the nations of the world have grown to depend upon one another for the requirements of everyday living. Countries relying on world markets for food or industrial raw materials are vulnerable to compulsive measures such as boycotts, embargoes, or attempts by rival nations to freeze the victim-state's assets or dry up its markets on a global scale.

* * *

Unless all means of coercion are considered illegitimate—a position unlikely to prevail in today's international atmosphere—to say that a particular coercive act is impermissible means that it was undertaken with unnecessary intensity, or for an improper purpose. However, there are no rigid categories of the "permissible" or "impermissible" into which a particular action may be placed without delicate sifting and balancing. Perhaps the strongest statement which can be made in a world which ostensibly has accepted the Charter of the United Nations is that the use of armed force, for any purpose not explicitly condoned by article 39 or article 51 of the Charter, is prima facie illegal regardless of intensity. Another weighty body of opinion would extend the prohibition of armed force to include indirect military and ideological coercion. But even the limitation on intermediate force is not explicitly authorized by the Charter, and many would argue that a blanket prohibition, without regard to the elements of intensity or purpose, would impose an undesirable rigidity on the affairs of nations. With regard to economic and political coercion, each with its wide range of intensity, the waters become even murkier. * * *

* * *

If article 2(4) is read to extend to economic and political coercion, difficulties will undoubtedly arise in separating legal from illegal uses of these forms of coercion. All states attempt to exercise some degree of influence in their normal acts of diplomacy and trade, and certainly not all such attempts should be branded as illegal. Determination of legality would necessarily involve a delicate balancing of such factors as the severity of the action, its objective and its place within a pattern of similarly unacceptable coercive actions. While the difficulty of making such determinations should not prevent us from reading article 2(4) to cover economic and political coercion if that reading is in other respects the preferable one, this difficulty must at least be acknowledged as a real factor militating against adoption of such an expansive reading.

Professor Louis Henkin has offered another argument against an expansive reading of article 2(4):

> For the present [1963], then, it may serve little purpose to insist that Article 2(4) goes farther than many nations will tolerate. It may be better to leave its authority clear and undisputed to cover at least cases of direct, overt aggression which are generally capable of objective and persuasive proof * * *. The battle of interventions, for the present, will have to be fought as political battles with little help from law.[47]

Although these remarks were directed to the scope of article 2(4) in the area of indirect aggression, whatever weight the argument commands in that context would seem to apply to the still more subtle devices of economic and political coercion. Henkin's argument rests either on the fear that the nations of the world are simply unwilling to accept any inhibitions on their use of nonviolent coercion, or on the fear that the inevitable balancing of motives which would characterize the application of article 2(4) to cases of economic and political coercion would be transferred to cases of military force, thereby weakening its effectiveness in the area of military force. In either case, the argument is that rather than turn article 2(4) into an unwieldy behavioral norm, it would be better to bring the full weight of the article to bear on the most conspicuous and dangerous problem —open, armed aggression.

* * *

The basic arguments for expanding the scope of article 2(4) to include some political and economic policies may be reduced to three. They are: that the inclusion of these coercions is legitimate within the textual confines of the Charter; that other international documents drafted since the Charter came into effect demonstrate a growing world sensitivity to the problem posed by the use of political and economic weapons; and that outlawing this genre of coercion can have only a salutary effect on international relations, and may well constitute a necessary step in the evolution of normative standards of international coercive conduct.

* * *

The question whether to include economic and political coercion within article 2(4)'s proscription must therefore turn on the felt necessity to develop among nations a commitment to refrain from these forms of force. That many nations seek such a commitment is demonstrated by the expanded notions of force included in the international documents described in the previous section. The probability that other nations will eventually accede to a ban on at least some economic and political weapons is perhaps best demonstrated by describing briefly several recent examples of alleged economic and political aggression, and the reactions of the alleged target nations.

47. Henkin, Force, Intervention, and Neutrality in Contemporary International Law, 57 Am.Soc'y Int'l L.Proc. 147, 158–59 (1963).

Egyptian interference with Israeli-connected ships passing through the Suez Canal was heavily debated in the Security Council in the 1950's. The Egyptian action was eventually condemned not as aggression, but rather as a violation of the armistice agreements between Israel and neighboring Arab states. The draft resolution, presented jointly by the delegations of France, the United Kingdom and the United States, contained the following provision:

> [T]he restrictions on the passage of goods through the Suez Canal to Israel ports are denying to nations at no time connected with the conflict in Palestine valuable supplies required for their economic reconstruction, and * * * these restrictions together with sanctions applied by Egypt to certain ships which have visited Israel ports represent unjustified interference with the rights of nations to navigate the seas and to trade freely with one another, including the Arab States and Israel * * *.

A Cuban accusation of economic aggression arose in 1960 in response to the United States' reduction of the Cuban sugar quota and decision to cease refining of Cuban crude oil. The Cuban delegate to the Security Council, after describing economic aggression as an "international crime" added:

> The accusations made and the punitive measures proposed [by the United States] have * * * ranged from the elimination of the sugar quota—economic aggression—to the landing of marines—military aggression. For over eighteen months the people of Cuba have been subjected to a policy of intimidation, coercion and threats * * *.

Ecuador voiced similar accusations of illegal economic and political force when the United States suspended sales of military material to Ecuador in response to that country's seizure of fourteen American tuna boats within its claimed territorial waters.

More recently, there have been claims that American economic policies effectively undermined the stability of the Marxist Allende government in Chile and eventually contributed to its downfall. An article published before the Chilean coup described the United States' measures as follows:

> Economic pressure on Chile has taken the form of cutting U.S. and "international" lines of credit to the Allende government. Two examples of this response present themselves. Chile's application for a small loan from the Export-Import Bank for the purchase of commercial passenger aircraft from Boeing (a U.S. firm) for the Chilean National Airlines was denied. As a result the United States has forced Chile to consider alternative European producers, perhaps a minor inconvenience. U.S. representatives within the Inter-American Development Bank reacting to threats to reduce or withhold U.S. funds to IDB because of its willingness to listen to Chilean requests for development loan funding have "delayed" Chilean requests (which has the same effect as an overt denial). U.S. AID funds

have not been either requested or suggested in the case of Chile since the end of the Frei regime.

* * *

The over-all purpose of U.S. policy is to create economic dislocation and provoke a domestic social crisis that could lead to either the overthrow of the Allende government by a civil-military coalition made up of the Army, the Christian Democrats, and the extreme right-wing National Party, or the discrediting of the government and its defeat in the 1973 congressional elections, thus undercutting the basis for future changes.

These alleged incidents of economic and political aggression demonstrate that economic and political weapons of coercion, like military weapons, can impair a nation's sovereignty and give rise to the resentment, humiliation and lasting damage that breed international tension. The anxiety of the coerced nation watching its economic life or political status be overwhelmed by the encroaching policies of another nation is understandable, as is the tendency of the victim to seek aid from its international friends—particularly members of the large power blocs.

As the recent Arab oil embargo demonstrates, the more powerful nations themselves are no longer immune to economic coercion. Indeed, the incident provides a striking preview of a possible future in which the industrialized nations gradually exhaust their domestic resources, and fall prey to manipulation by the nations to which they must look for substitutes. Nor are the tools of economic coercion available to the lesser developed nations and their industrialized neighbors limited to control of natural resources: concern has recently developed, for example, over the use of stockpiles of another nation's currency as a potential threat to its value.

Economic and political coercion pose genuine threats to international harmony, and the vulnerability of the militarily powerful industrialized nations compounds the dangers. In a lecture delivered at the Geneva Institute of International Relations in 1930, Professor Andre Seigfried spoke of the need to develop a "code of international economic morality." [93] In 1974, even more than in 1930, that need is a compelling one, and a step toward its fulfillment would be the inclusion of economic and political force within article 2(4)'s proscription.

* * *

To say that article 2(4) covers economic and political coercion as well as military force is not to say that every instance of economic or political influence is a violation of the Charter. The disputed actions described in the previous section all are colorably legitimate. If one were asked to render a legal opinion on actions of a similar nature between two competing merchants, the conclusion would be dictated

93. Seigfried, Economic Causes of War, Geneva Institute, Problems of Peace 97–98 (5th ser. 1930).

generally by the principle of freedom of contract: within the broad confines of "fair" business practices, American law offers no relief to the businessman victimized by intense, even predatory, competition. Similarly, international law, even the law of the Charter, does not presume to alter the essentially gladiatorial theory of survival that governs international trade, as long as the stakes remain commercial. It is only when a nation undertakes to use its economic power "against the territorial integrity or political independence of any State, or in any other manner inconsistent with the Purposes of the United Nations" that the norm of article 2(4) is violated.

This is admittedly a vague standard, and the difficulties involved in drawing lines between proper and improper forms of economic and political coercion are formidable. But these difficulties are not insurmountable. There has been some success in a similar search for the earmarks of "intermediate" coercion, and there is every reason to believe that, given time and thought, similar progress will be made in the area of economic and political coercion. Only a few preliminary remarks in this regard will be offered here.

The precise scope of a proscription on the use of economic and political force must turn on the legal and practical justifications for limiting the use of economic and political power in the international arena. The United Nations Charter proclaims the right of self-determination of peoples and "the sovereign equality of all its Members." It is this sovereignty that distinguishes a nation from an individual merchant within a particular nation. When the individual considers himself wronged but the courts deny him a remedy, it is because an acknowledged superior entity—the State—has determined that the alleged transgressor is in possession of a greater right. On the international plane, the principle of national sovereignty is superior to all others, and the Charter declares that it be subordinated to none.

There is also a serious practical difference between commercial and international disputes. The danger that a businessman victimized by competition will resort to forceful self-help in remedying the situation is minimized by the presence of the local police and courts which stand ready to punish any such violent retaliation. There are no effective international counterparts to these institutions. We must therefore contend with the increased probability that a victim nation will seek to redress, with armed force, an impairment of its sovereignty achieved by economic means. It is this possibility of military retaliation, always at least theoretically within the reach of an offended state, which justifies the imposition of legal restrictions on economic freedom.

In the final analysis, relatively few types of conduct would constitute violations of article 2(4). Not only must such economic or political coercion be undertaken for impermissible purposes; it also must be of sufficient intensity to pose a genuine threat to the sovereignty of the target state. If not of that intensity, the coercion would best be dealt with, in the words of one author, "not [as] an international crime, but [as] an international tort." [98]

Of course, the present state of Charter law, proscribing force only when it is used for the purposes listed in article 2(4), is not a necessary, or perhaps even a wise, limitation in the case of economic coercion. Even under the broad reading of article 2(4) urged in this Comment, international law would not pass judgment on economic polices not intended to impair the sovereignty of other nations, even if these policies otherwise forced the affected state into the direst of circumstances. The desire to interfere with the sovereignty of another state is not the only motive that can prompt hostile economic action: greed, or simple envy may provide an equivalent inducement.[99] As long as the resort to war remains an appealing response to destructive economic policies, whatever their motivation, the community of nations will need to continue refining its standards of economic behavior.

Conclusion

Examination of the language and historical background of article 2(4) provides no clear indication of its intended meaning. The vagueness of article 2(4)'s prohibition requires that its present scope be determined by reference to modern notions of what are permissible and impermissible forms of coercion, and it is in this respect that the argument for a broad reading of article 2(4) is most compelling. The nations of the world are growing to realize, as indeed they must, that economic and political coercion, like military coercion, can impair the target State's sovereignty and create the kinds of feelings of which international fear and tension are made. And as the events of this century have so clearly demonstrated, tension among nations is, like jealousy, a monster which "doth mock the meat it feeds upon."

98. Higgins, [The Legal Limits to the Use of Force by Sovereign States: United Nations Practice, 37 Brit.Y.B. Int'l L. 269, at 276 (1961)].

99. For example, the United States, which supplies Japan with vital soybeans, might choose instead to sell soybeans to a nation which offered a higher price. The motive would be purely greed—a desire to maximize profits—but the effect on Japan would be no different than if the motive were a desire to interfere with the policies of the Japanese government.

Chapter 20

THE USE OF FORCE BY THE UNITED NATIONS

LETTER FROM EDWARD R. STETTINIUS, SECRETARY OF STATE OF THE UNITED STATES, TO PRESIDENT HARRY TRUMAN

13 United States Department of State Bulletin 77, 80 (1945).

Summary of Report on Results of San Francisco Conference

*   *   *

It will be the duty of the Security Council, supported by the pledged participation, and backed by military contingents to be made available by the member states, to use its great prestige to bring about by peaceful means the adjustment or the settlement of international disputes. Should these means fail, it is its duty, as it has the power, to take whatever measures are necessary, including measures of force, to suppress acts of aggression or other breaches of the peace. It will be the duty of the Security Council, in other words, to make good the commitment of the United Nations to maintain international peace and security, turning that lofty purpose into practice. To that end the Council will be given the use and the support of diplomatic, economic and military tools and weapons in the control of the United Nations.

*   *   *

1. *The Grand Design.* As we have seen, the Charter of the United Nations forbade the use of force by states (Article 2(4)), save in the limited area of self-defense (Article 51). A near monopoly of force was reposed in the Security Council, under Chapter VII, [a] in which the Council was empowered to respond to the dramatic conditions of Article 39 ("any threat to the peace, breach of the peace, or act of aggression") by resort to the powerful measures of Articles 41 and 42, including armed forces at its disposal under the terms of Article 43, especially "immediately available national air-force contingents" (Article 45).

It was a vision of many in 1945 that the airborne strike forces of the United Nations Security Council would range forth, on call, to restrain and control anyone who dared disturb the peace that World War II had painfully produced.

2. *What went wrong?* The charter was grounded in a belief and a hope: the belief that only with the cooperation of the great

---

a. The monopoly was recognized also in Chapter VIII, in which Article 53 required Security Council authoriza- tion for enforcement action under regional arrangements.

powers could the United Nations succeed, and the hope that because they had cooperated in war they would continue to do so during the peace (hence, the veto). That cooperation was not forthcoming. An immediate effect of the fragmentation of great power policy was the failure of the powers to make the agreements called for in Article 43; the council thus did not have at its disposal the forces projected at the United Nation's founding. See Sohn, Basic Documents of the United Nations 89 (2nd ed. rev'd, 1968), especially Note at 98, detailing the United States and Soviet disagreements with respect to the size relationships of the various force contributions to be made by the permanent members of the force.

Indeed, in the one case in which the Security Council has acted in anything like the classic case of aggressive invasion envisioned at the founding (the case of Korea), the council was able to act only because the Soviet Union was not present to prevent its acting. See p. 750.

A further factor of significance in the appraisal of the charter provisions for dealing with threats to the peace is the fact that world tensions have taken new shapes since the days of World War II. The disintegration of old empires and the rise of the self-consciousness of formerly subject peoples and races have brought new demands on the organs of the United Nations, e. g., with respect to the question of apartheid.

3. *Scope of the chapter.* This chapter is concerned with two principal themes that have become significant because of the foregoing political factors: first, the ways in which the United Nations has accommodated to the fact that the Security Council's monopoly of force has not worked as it was designed; second, the development of the power of the United Nations to use force for assisting the drive of subject peoples toward self-determination.

SECTION A. UNITING FOR PEACE

When North Korean troops crossed the 38th parallel into South Korea (the Republic of Korea) in June, 1950, the Security Council of the United Nations was able immediately to adopt resolutions responding to this event. The council determined there had been a breach of the peace; it recommended that members of the United Nations furnish assistance to the Republic of Korea and that such assistance take the form of military forces available to a unified command under the United States and authorized to use the United Nations flag.

The Soviet Union's representative was not present in meetings of the council from January 1950 until August of that year. The resolutions of the Security Council dealing with the Korean case were adopted without veto.

After the representative of the USSR returned to the meetings of the Security Council, the General Assembly was urged by a group of states acting under the leadership of the United States to assert its own authority in cases in which the security council failed to act because of the veto. The Uniting for Peace Resolution was the form in which that assertion was cast. Resolution 337 (V) follows.

UNITING FOR PEACE, RESOLUTION 377(V)

U.N. Gen. Ass. Off. Rec., 5th Sess., Supp. No. 20 (A/1775), p. 10.

The General Assembly,

Recognizing that the first two stated Purposes of the United Nations are:

> To maintain international peace and security, and to that end: to take effective collective measures for the prevention and removal of threats to the peace, and for the suppression of acts of aggression or other breaches of the peace, and to bring about by peaceful means, and in conformity with the principles of justice and international law, adjustment or settlement of international disputes or situations which might lead to a breach of the peace, and

> To develop friendly relations among nations based on respect for the principle of equal rights and self-determination of peoples, and to take other appropriate measures to strengthen universal peace,

Reaffirming that it remains the primary duty of all Members of the United Nations, when involved in an international dispute, to seek settlement of such a dispute by peaceful means through the procedures laid down in Chapter VI of the Charter, and recalling the successful achievements of the United Nations in this regard on a number of previous occasions,

Finding that international tension exists on a dangerous scale,

Recalling its resolution 290(IV) entitled "Essentials of peace", which states that disregard of the Principles of the Charter of the United Nations is primarily responsible for the continuance of international tension, and desiring to contribute further to the objectives of that resolution,

Reaffirming the importance of the exercise by the Security Council of its primary responsibility for the maintenance of international peace and security, and the duty of the permanent members to seek unanimity and to exercise restraint in the use of the veto,

Reaffirming that the initiative in negotiating the agreements for armed forces provided for in Article 43 of the Charter belongs to the Security Council, and desiring to ensure that, pending the conclusion of such agreements, the United Nations has at its disposal means for maintaining international peace and security,

Conscious that failure of the Security Council to discharge its responsibilities on behalf of all the Member States, particularly those responsibilities referred to in the two preceding paragraphs, does not relieve Member States of their obligations or the United Nations of its responsibility under the Charter to maintain international peace and security,

Recognizing in particular that such failure does not deprive the General Assembly of its rights or relieve it of its responsibilities under the Charter in regard to the maintenance of international peace and security,

Recognizing that discharge by the General Assembly of its responsibilities in these respects calls for possibilities of observation which would ascertain the facts and expose aggressors; for the existence of armed forces which could be used collectively; and for the possibility of timely recommendation by the General Assembly to Members of the United Nations for collective action which, to be effective, should be prompt,

A

1.   Resolves that if the Security Council, because of lack of unanimity of the permanent members, fails to exercise its primary responsibility for the maintenance of international peace and security in any case where there appears to be a threat to the peace, breach of the peace, or act of aggression, the General Assembly shall consider the matter immediately with a view to making appropriate recommendations to Members for collective measures, *including in the case of a breach of the peace or act of aggression the use of armed force when necessary,* to maintain or restore international peace and security.   If not in session at the time, the General Assembly may meet in emergency special session within twenty-four hours of the request therefor.   Such emergency special session shall be called if requested by the Security Council on the vote of any seven Members, or by a majority of the Members of the United Nations; *   *   *   [Emphasis supplied.]

*   *   *

Authority under the Charter of the United Nations.   A major argument that the United Nations General Assembly does not have the authority under the charter to exercise the power it has asserted in operative paragraph 1 of the Uniting for Peace Resolution is that Article 11(2) of the charter provides: "Any such question on which *action* is necessary shall be referred to the Security Council by the General Assembly either before or after discussion."   [Emphasis supplied.]   How do you appraise this argument?

SECTION B.   THE UNITED NATIONS EMERGENCY FORCE IN EGYPT

SEYERSTED, UNITED NATIONS FORCES IN THE LAW OF PEACE AND WAR 46 (1966)*

[As recounted at p. 1264, in October 1956, Egypt was attacked first by Israel and thereafter by France and the United Kingdom, the latter two states purporting to be carrying on a police action to quell the Israeli–Egyptian fighting. The Security Council of the United Nations was called into session and a draft resolution calling for a cease-fire was vetoed by France and the United Kingdom.]

* * * The Security Council, being unable to act because of French and United Kingdom negative votes, called an emergency special session of the General Assembly, as provided in the Uniting for Peace Resolution, "in order to make appropriate recommendations". The Assembly adopted on 2 November 1956 Resolution 997 (ES–I) urging the parties to agree to an immediate cease-fire (par. 1) and promptly to "withdraw all forces behind the armistice lines, to desist from raids across the armistice lines into neighbouring territory and to observe scrupulously the provisions of the armistice agreements" (par. 2). The resolution also urged, generally, that "steps be taken to reopen the Suez Canal and restore secure freedom of navigation" (par. 4).

On the following day the Secretary-General reported to the Assembly that France and the United Kingdom had declared themselves willing to stop military action if, inter alia, both the Egyptian and the Israeli Governments agreed to accept a United Nations Force to keep the peace; and if the United Nations decided to constitute and maintain such a Force until an Arab-Israeli peace settlement was reached and until satisfactory arrangements had been agreed in regard to the Suez Canal, both agreements to be guaranteed by the United Nations.

By Resolutions 998 (ES–I) of 4 November, 1000 (ES–I) of 5 November and 1001 (ES–I) of 7 November 1956 the General Assembly thereupon without a negative vote established an emergency international United Nations Force—later referred to as the United Nations Emergency Force (UNEF). The purpose, organization, status, functioning and financing of the Force were defined (a) in the Assembly's resolutions of 5 and 7 November 1956, (b) in the Second and Final Report of the Secretary-General on the Plan for an Emergency International United Nations Force approved by General Assembly Resolution 1001; (c) in a number of subsequent General Assembly resolutions; (d) in an "Aide-memoire on the Basis for Presence and Functioning of UNEF in Egypt", approved by Egypt and

* Reprinted by permission of Sijt-hoff & Nordhoff International Pub-lishers b. v., P.O. Box 4, 2400 MA Al-phen aan den Rijn, The Netherlands.

the General Assembly in November 1956; (e) in another agreement concluded by the Secretary-General with Egypt on 8 February 1957 concerning the status of UNEF in Egypt; (f) in the "Regulations for the United Nations Emergency Force" enacted by the Secretary-General on 20 February 1957; and lastly, (g) in a letter dated 21 June 1957 from the Secretary-General to the States providing contingents. This letter of 21 June 1957 refers to or reproduces as annexes most of the documents cited above and constitutes, together with the replies of each "participating" State, the basic agreements between these States and the United Nations.

* * *

The Force is equipped with normal regimental weapons and with means of transportation and reconnaissance—including motor vehicles and aircraft—but not with heavy arms. The troops have a right to fire in self-defence. They are never to take the initiative in the use of arms, but may respond with force to an armed attack upon them, including attempts to use force to make them withdraw from positions which they occupy under orders from the Commander. It has been said that UNEF serves by being present and by acting as a plate-glass window—not capable of withstanding assault but nevertheless a lightly armed barrier that all see and tend to respect.

As we have seen, in Korea the United Nations had entrusted to one of its Member States the task of organizing the Force and directing its operations, and the Collective Measures Committee had also recommended this system for military action under the Uniting for Peace Resolution. In the case of UNEF, however, the Organization chose itself to assume these functions. The General Assembly appointed a *Commander* of the Force—as a regular United Nations official, responsible to the Organization and fully independent of the policies of any one nation—to organize the Force "in consultation with the Secretary-General as regards size and composition". He was entrusted with full command authority and operational responsibility for the performance of the functions assigned to the Force by the United Nations and for the deployment and assignment of troops placed at the disposal of the Force, though he was to exercise this authority and responsibility "in consultation with the Secretary-General".

* * *

The Force is a subsidiary organ of the United Nations and in particular of the General Assembly, and it enjoys the status, privileges and immunities of the Organization in accordance with the Convention on the Privileges and Immunities of the United Nations. This applies also to the property, funds and assets of "participating" Governments used in the host State. The Commander and the staff detailed from the United Nations Secretariat to serve with him are entitled to privileges and immunities under the Convention as officials of the United Nations; the military members of the UNEF Command are entitled to privileges and immunities as experts on mission for the United Nations. Personnel recruited locally enjoy only immunity in respect of official acts as provided in § 18(a) of the Convention, which is the most basic immunity of an international official. Members of national contingents are not covered by the Convention on the Privileges and Immunities of the United Nations, but are accorded largely corresponding privileges and immunities, including immunity in respect of official acts, in Egypt under the Status Agreement with that country. All members of the Force are entitled to the legal protection of the United Nations as agents of the Organization.

*   *   *

UNITED NATIONS GENERAL ASSEMBLY RESOLUTIONS ESTABLISHING THE EMERGENCY FORCE (UNEF)

U.N. Gen. Ass. Off. Rec., 1st Emergency Special Sess. (1956), Annexes, p. 33.

Resolution 997 (ES–I)

[Document A/RES/390]

The General Assembly,

Noting the disregard on many occasions by parties to the Israel-Arab armistice agreements of 1949 of the terms of such agreements, and that the armed forces of Israel have penetrated deeply into Egyptian territory in violation of the General Armistice Agreement between Egypt and Israel of 24 February 1949,

Noting that armed forces of France and the United Kingdom of Great Britain and Northern Ireland are conducting military operations against Egyptian territory,

Noting that traffic through the Suez Canal is now interrupted to the serious prejudice of many nations,

Expressing its grave concern over these developments,

1.   Urges as a matter of priority that all parties now involved in hostilities in the area agree to an immediate cease-fire and, as part thereof, halt the movement of military forces and arms into the area;

2.   Urges the parties to the armistice agreements promptly to withdraw all forces behind the armistice lines, to desist from raids across the armistice lines into neighbouring territory, and to observe scrupulously the provisions of the armistice agreements;

3.   Recommends that all Member States refrain from introducing military goods in the area of hostilities and in general refrain from any acts which would delay or prevent the implementation of the present resolution;

4.   Urges that, upon the cease-fire being effective steps be taken to reopen the Suez Canal and restore secure freedom of navigation;

5.   Requests the Secretary-General to observe and report promptly on the compliance with the present resolution to the Securi-

ty Council and to the General Assembly, for such further action as they may deem appropriate in accordance with the Charter;

6.   Decides to remain in emergency session pending compliance with the present resolution.

Resolution 998 (ES–I)

[Document A/RES/391]

The General Assembly,

Bearing in mind the urgent necessity of facilitating compliance with its resolution 997 (ES–I) of 2 November 1956,

Requests, as a matter of priority, the Secretary-General to submit to it within forty-eight hours a plan for the setting up, with the consent of the nations concerned, of an emergency international United Nations Force to secure and supervise the cessation of hostilities in accordance with all the terms of the aforementioned resolution.

Resolution 1000 (ES–I)

[Document A/RES/394]

The General Assembly,

Having requested the Secretary-General, in its resolution 998 (ES–I) of 4 November 1956, to submit to it a plan for an emergency international United Nations Force, for the purposes stated,

Noting with satisfaction the first report of the Secretary-General on the plan (A/3289), and having in mind particularly paragraph 4 of that report,

1.   Establishes a United Nations Command for an emergency international Force to secure and supervise the cessation of hostilities in accordance with all the terms of General Assembly resolution, 997 (ES–I) of 2 November 1956;

2.   Appoints, on an emergency basis, the Chief of Staff of the United Nations Truce Supervision Organization, Major-General E. L. M. Burns, as Chief of the Command;

3.   Authorizes the Chief of the Command immediately to recruit, from the observer corps of the United Nations Truce Supervision Organization, a limited number of officers who shall be nationals of countries other than those having permanent membership in the Security Council, and further authorizes him, in consultation with the Secretary-General, to undertake the recruitment directly, from various Member States other than the permanent members of the Security Council, of the additional number of officers needed;

4.   Invites the Secretary-General to take such administrative measures as may be necessary for the prompt execution of the actions envisaged in the present resolution.

Resolution 1002 (ES–I)

[Document A/RES/396]

The General Assembly,

Recalling its resolution 997 (ES–I) of 2 November 1956, 998 (ES–I) and 999 (ES–I) of 4 November 1956 and 1000 (ES–I) of 5 November 1956, adopted by overwhelming majorities,

Noting in particular that the General Assembly, by its resolution 1000 (ES–I), established a United Nations Command for an emergency international Force to secure and supervise the cessation of hostilities in accordance with all the terms of its resolution 997 (ES–I),

1.   Reaffirms the above-mentioned resolutions;

2.   Calls once again upon Israel immediately to withdraw all its forces behind the armistice lines established by the General Armistice Agreement between Egypt and Israel of 24 February 1949,

3.   Calls once again upon the United Kingdom and France immediately to withdraw all their forces from Egyptian territory, consistently with the above-mentioned resolutions;

4.   Urges the Secretary-General to communicate the present resolution to the parties concerned, and requests him promptly to report to the General Assembly on the compliance with this resolution.

––––––––––

1.   *Legal basis for the United Nations Emergency Force.* In establishing the Emergency Force, did the General Assembly of the United Nations avail itself of all of the power it had asserted in the Uniting for Peace Resolution? The force was not physically located on Israeli territory. Could it have lawfully entered Israeli territory to perform its function as a plate-glass window without the consent of the government of Israel?

2.   *Withdrawal of the Emergency Force.* At the request of the government of the United Arab Republic (Egypt), the Secretary-General of the United Nations (U Thant) withdrew the Emergency Force from the territory of the Republic in May and June 1967. (See the account of the Six Day War of June 1967 at p. 1267.) The action of the Secretary-General of the United Nations in acceding to this request at that particular time was highly controversial. He explained his action in detail in a report to the United Nations. Gen.Ass.Off.Rec., 5th Emergency Spec.Sess. (1967), Annexes (A/6730/Add. 3), p. 9.

SECTION C.   THE UNITED NATIONS IN THE CONGO

**SEYERSTED, UNITED NATIONS FORCES IN THE LAW
OF PEACE AND WAR 60 (1966)***

*   *   *

Shortly after the accession to independence of the Republic of the Congo on 30 June 1960, some units of the Congolese forces mutinied against their Belgian officers and committed acts of violence against members of the European population, in particular Belgians. The Belgian Government, acting against the wish of the Congolese Government, sent troops in order to maintain or restore order. This gave rise to bitterness and panic among the African population and to a new flight of Europeans and the consequent breakdown of many public services and important economic enterprises. In this situation the President and the Prime Minister of the Congo, by telegrams of 12 and 13 July 1960, requested the urgent dispatch of a United Nations Force composed of military units from neutral countries in order to protect Congolese territory against what they termed the Belgian "act of aggression".

On 14 July the Security Council, at the request of the Secretary-General and without a dissenting vote, adopted a resolution calling upon Belgium to withdraw its troops and authorizing the Secretary-General

> to take the necessary steps, in consultation with the Government of the Republic of the Congo, to provide the Government with such military assistance, as may be necessary, until, through the efforts of the Congolese Government with the technical assistance of the United Nations, the national security forces may be able, in the opinion of the Government, to meet fully their tasks.

The vote was 8–0–3. China, France and the United Kingdom abstained because they could not support Belgian troop withdrawal before the United Nations Force had taken over; they did, however, support the dispatch of the United Nations Force.

*   *   *

Despite its greater size and heavier tasks, the United Nations Force in the Congo was constituted on a much more modest formal basis than the UNEF. In view of the urgency of the matter and the difficulties involved in reaching agreement among its members, the Security Council did not lay down in its resolutions even the basic principles on which the Force should be organized, as the General Assembly had done in the case of UNEF. The organization of the Force, including the appointment of its Supreme Commander, was thus left to the Secretary-General, who, however, made detailed reports to the Council. In September 1960, when the Security Council

* Reprinted by permission of Sijthoff & Nordhoff International Publishers b. v., P.O. Box 4, 2400 MA Alphen aan den Rijn, The Netherlands.

was unable to agree on what action to take after the split between President Kasa-Vubu and Prime Minister Lumumba, the matter was referred to the General Assembly under the Uniting for Peace Resolution. However, the resolutions of the General Assembly did not concern themselves directly with the Force, except for the budgetary aspects.

*   *   *

The costs of the Force were covered by the United Nations in essentially the same manner as those of UNEF. In 1961 the expenses of ONUC averaged approximately $10 million per month, of which about 83 per cent were for direct expenses and about 17 per cent were for reimbursement to the Governments providing contingents. The budgets for 62–63 were of the same order. The sums were assessed upon Member States after deduction for voluntary contributions and for waiver of reimbursement by States providing airlift services. The General Assembly had expressly decided that the expenses were "expenses of the Organization" subject to legally binding assessment of Member States under Article 17 of the Charter, but that they were nevertheless to be kept separate as being essentially different in nature from the expenses under the regular budget. However, some Members refused to accept this decision and to pay the corresponding amounts assessed upon them in respect of UNEF and ONUC. Consequently, the General Assembly, by its Resolution 1731 (XVI), decided to submit the question to the International Court of Justice for an advisory opinion.[a]

*   *   *

The Congo Force had to perform a number of tasks throughout a vast territory in order to fulfil its mandate to assist in the maintenance of law and order and the protection of life and property, to prevent foreign intervention in the form of men, arms or military supplies, and to prevent civil war. Apart from a number of civilian activities, like maintenance of essential services, mediation and persuasion, the Force performed, inter alia, the following functions: patrolling areas threatened by disorders, establishing and guarding United Nations protected areas where people in danger of arbitrary arrest or other persecution could take refuge; guarding and defending the residences of Congolese political leaders and diplomatic representatives of foreign States to protect them against arbitrary arrest or violence; guarding government buildings; guarding, isolating and neutralizing the meeting place of the Congolese Parliament and ensuring the free passage through the Congo of its members; guarding, and in emergencies temporarily closing, ports and airfields to secure the supplies to and the movements of the United Nations Force and to prevent Congolese troop movements or external aid to the opposing sides in the civil war; arrest and eviction of foreign military personnel or mercenaries; disarming civilians and military groups which

a.   The advisory opinion of the International Court of Justice is set forth at p. 1314.

have broken loose from their commanders; rescuing civilians, wounded and dead out of areas affected by civil war. Last, but not least, the functions included occupying, patrolling and if necessary defending areas threatened by armed invasion, and establishing, guarding and defending road blocks or neutral zones between opposing Congolese forces, or removing road blocks or other obstacles and opposition to the United Nations movements and operations created by local military units; guarding and defending United Nations personnel and positions.

These and other activities could not avoid interfering with the plans of the various central and provincial authorities in the Congo
* * *.

Less violent, but more extensive military operations took place during the final phase of the United Nations action in Katanga in December 1962 and January 1963. After a six-day period of unanswered firing on United Nations positions and incidents involving seizure and detention of members of the United Nations Force by the Katangese gendarmerie, the United Nations on 28 December launched its final action against the forces of the provincial Katangese government. The United Nations Force first cleared the Katangese road blocks in Elisabethville and seized the key positions in that city. Subsequently, it advanced towards and occupied other cities in southern Katanga. This action cost 10 killed and 77 wounded on the United Nations side and nearly as many civilian casualties. One of the actions carried out during this phase—the advance on and occupation of Jadotville, which was carried out by the commanders in the field without consultation with headquarters at New York and Leopoldville —was termed by the Officer-in-Charge of the United Nations operation in the Congo as "the first experience of a strictly United Nations armed force under United Nations command with combat conditions in the field". By 21 January 1963 the United Nations Force had under control all important centres hitherto held by the Katangese, the Katangese airforce had been eliminated and the Katangese gendarmerie as an organised fighting force had ceased to exist. M. Tschombe ended the seccessionist activities and officials and security forces of the Central Government could gradually move into the Province, although these forces were, during the first period, placed under United Nations command (as a Congolese contingent of the United Nations Force).

This ended the major United Nations military operations in the Congo. The Force remained in the country for another year-and-a-half, but it was gradually reduced in strength, not merely because of the restoration of national unity, but also because of the lack of funds. The last United Nations troops left the Congo in the summer of 1964.

* * *

UNITED NATIONS SECURITY COUNCIL RESOLUTIONS ESTABLISHING THE OPERATIONS IN THE CONGO (ONUC)

Resolutions and Decisions of the Security Council 1960.
U.N. Sec. Council Off. Rec., 15th Year, p. 5.

143 (1960). Resolution of 14 July 1960

[S/4387]

The Security Council,

Considering the report of the Secretary-General on a request for United Nations action in relation to the Republic of the Congo,

Considering the request for military assistance addressed to the Secretary-General by the President and the Prime Minister of the Republic of the Congo,

1. Calls upon the Government of Belgium to withdraw its troops from the territory of the Republic of the Congo;

2. Decides to authorize the Secretary-General to take the necessary steps, in consultation with the Government of the Republic of the Congo, to provide the Government with such military assistance as may be necessary until, through the efforts of the Congolese Government with the technical assistance of the United Nations, the national security forces may be able, in the opinion of the Government, to meet fully their tasks;

3. Requests the Secretary-General to report to the Security Council as appropriate.

> Adopted at the 873rd meeting by 8 votes to none, with 3 abstentions (China, France, United Kingdom of Great Britain and Northern Ireland).

145 (1960). Resolution of 22 July 1960

[S/4405]

The Security Council,

Having considered the first report of the Secretary-General on the implementation of Security Council resolution 143 (1960) of 14 July 1960,

Appreciating the work of the Secretary-General and the support so readily and so speedily given to him by all Member States invited by him to give assistance,

Noting that, as stated by the Secretary-General, the arrival of the troops of the United Nations Force in Leopoldville has already had a salutary effect,

Recognizing that an urgent need still exists to continue and to increase such efforts,

Considering that the complete restoration of law and order in the Republic of the Congo would effectively contribute to the maintenance of international peace and security,

Recognizing that the Security Council recommended the admission of the Republic of the Congo to membership in the United Nations as a unit,

1.   Calls upon the Government of Belgium to implement speedily Security Council resolution 143 (1960) on the withdrawal of its troops and authorizes the Secretary-General to take all necessary action to this effect;

2.   Requests all states to refrain from any action which might tend to impede the restoration of law and order and the exercise by the Government of the Congo of its authority and also to refrain from any action which might undermine the territorial integrity and the political independence of the Republic of the Congo;

3.   Commends the Secretary-General for the prompt action he has taken to carry out resolution 143 (1960) and for his first report;

4.   Invites the specialized agencies of the United Nations to render to the Secretary-General such assistance as he may require;

5.   Requests the Secretary-General to report further to the Security Council as appropriate.

Adopted unanimously at the 879th meeting.

146 (1960).   Resolution of 9 August 1960

[S/4426]

The Security Council,

Recalling its resolution 145 (1960) of 22 July 1960, inter alia calling upon the Government of Belgium to implement speedily Security Council resolution 143 (1960) of 14 July 1960 on the withdrawal of its troops and authorizing the Secretary-General to take all necessary action to this effect,

Having noted the second report of the Secretary-General on the implementation of the aforesaid two resolutions and his statement before the Council,

Having considered the statements made by the representatives of Belgium and the Republic of the Congo to the Council at this meeting,

Noting with satisfaction the progress made by the United Nations in carrying out the Security Council resolutions in respect of the territory of the Republic of the Congo other than the province of Katanga,

Noting however that the United Nations had been prevented from implementing the aforesaid resolutions in the province of Katanga although it was ready, and in fact attempted, to do so,

Recognizing that the withdrawal of Belgian troops from the province of Katanga will be a positive contribution to and essential for the proper implementation of the Council's resolutions,

1.   Confirms the authority given to the Secretary-General by Security Council resolutions 143 (1960) and 145 (1960) and requests him to continue to carry out the responsibility placed on him thereby;

2.   Calls upon the Government of Belgium to withdraw immediately its troops from the province of Katanga under speedy modalities determined by the Secretary-General and to assist in every possible way the implementation of the Council's resolutions;

3.   Declares that the entry of the United Nations Force into the province of Katanga is necessary for the full implementation of the present resolution;

4.   Reaffirms that the United Nations Force in the Congo will not be a party to or in any way intervene in or be used to influence the outcome of any internal conflict, constitutional or otherwise;

5.   Calls upon all Member States, in accordance with Articles 25 and 49 of the Charter of the United Nations, to accept and carry out the decisions of the Security Council and to afford mutual assistance in carrying out measures decided upon by the Council;

6.   Requests the Secretary-General to implement the present resolution and to report further to the Security Council as appropriate.

> Adopted at the 886th meeting by 9 votes to none, with 2 abstentions (France, Italy).

157 (1960).   Resolution of 17 September 1960

[S/4526]

The Security Council,

Having considered the item on its agenda as contained in document S/Agenda/906,

Taking into account that the lack of unanimity of its permanent members at the 906th meeting of the Security Council has prevented it from exercising its primary responsibility for the maintenance of international peace and security,

Decides to call an emergency special session of the General Assembly, as provided in General Assembly resolution 377A(V) of 3 November 1950, in order to make appropriate recommendations.

> Adopted at the 906th meeting by 8 votes to 2 (Poland, Union of Soviet Socialist Republics), with 1 abstention (France).

1. *Legal basis for the United Nations operations in the Congo.* The Congolese action was authorized by the Security Council of the United Nations. Was the legality of the Congolese action more firmly based on the charter than the Emergency Force in the Middle East (which, as seen above, was authorized by the General Assembly)? Did the council act pursuant to Article 39? If so, what was the requisite threat to the peace, breach of the peace, or act of aggression? Was it the sending of troops by Belgium to maintain and restore order? The council never made a finding to that effect.

Can the council's action be grounded on the request of the Congolese government for aid? What is the charter basis for the council's response to such a request?

2. *Analysis of the legal basis for peacekeeping forces by the International Court of Justice.* The legal basis for both the Emergency Force and the Congolese operations was the subject of analysis by the International Court in the Certain Expenses case, which follows. The court was asked for an advisory opinion because certain members of the United Nations refused to pay amounts assessed against them as "expenses of the Organization" (Article 17). The members refusing claimed that the Middle East and Congolese operations did not qualify as such expenses. The case was significant because of its financial implications, since Article 19 of the charter prescribes a loss of the right to vote in the General Assembly in the case of certain financial delinquencies on the part of a member. But the advisory opinion of the court is also significant because of its analysis of the constitutional powers of the United Nations and its organs to employ or authorize military force.

CERTAIN EXPENSES OF THE UNITED NATIONS
(ADVISORY OPINION)

International Court of Justice, 1962.
[1962] I.C.J.Rep. 151, 153, 156, 162.

[The General Assembly of the United Nations requested an advisory opinion by Resolution 1731 (XVI), adopted on December 20, 1961. The request, as it appears below, has been edited by omitting designations, by number and date, of specific resolutions adopted by the Security Council and the General Assembly .]

The General Assembly.

Recognizing its need for authoritative legal guidance as to obligations of Member States under the Charter of the United Nations in the matter of financing the United Nations operations in the Congo and in the Middle East,

Decides to submit the following question to the International Court of Justice for an advisory opinion:

Do the expenditures authorized in General Assembly resolutions relating to the United Nations operations in the Congo and the expenditures authorized in General Assembly resolutions relating to the operations of the United Nations Emergency Force constitute "expenses of the Organization" within the meaning of Article 17, paragraph 2, of the Charter of the United Nations?

* * *

The question on which the Court is asked to give its opinion is whether certain expenditures which were authorized by the General Assembly to cover the costs of the United Nations operations in the Congo (hereinafter referred to as ONUC) and of the operations of the United Nations Emergency Force in the Middle East (hereinafter referred to as UNEF), "constitute 'expenses of the Organization' within the meaning of Article 17, paragraph 2, of the Charter of the United Nations".

* * *

The text of Article 17 is in part as follows:

    1.   The General Assembly shall consider and approve the budget of the Organization.

    2.   The expenses of the Organization shall be borne by the Members as apportioned by the General Assembly.

* * *

Article 17 is the only article in the Charter which refers to budgetary authority or to the power to apportion expenses, or otherwise to raise revenue, except for Articles 33 and 35, paragraph 3, of the Statute of the Court which have no bearing on the point here under discussion. Nevertheless, it has been argued before the Court that one type of expenses, namely those resulting from operations for the maintenance of international peace and security, are not "expenses of the Organization" within the meaning of Article 17, paragraph 2, of the Charter, inasmuch as they fall to be dealt with exclusively by the Security Council, and more especially through agreements negotiated in accordance with Article 43 of the Charter.

The argument rests in part upon the view that when the maintenance of international peace and security is involved, it is only the Security Council which is authorized to decide on any action relative thereto. It is argued further that since the General Assembly's power is limited to discussing, considering, studying and recommending, it cannot impose an obligation to pay the expenses which result from the implementation of its recommendations. This argument leads to an examination of the respective functions of the General Assembly and of the Security Council under the Charter, particularly with respect to the maintenance of international peace and security.

Article 24 of the Charter provides:

    In order to ensure prompt and effective action by the United Nations, its Members confer on the Security Council primary responsibility for the maintenance of international peace and security. * * *

The responsibility conferred is "primary", not exclusive. This primary responsibility is conferred upon the Security Council, as stated in Article 24, "in order to ensure prompt and effective action". To this end, it is the Security Council which is given a power to impose an explicit obligation of compliance if for example it issues an order or command to an aggressor under Chapter VII. It is only the Security Council which can require enforcement by coercive action against an aggressor.

The Charter makes it abundantly clear, however, that the General Assembly is also to be concerned with international peace and security. Article 14 authorizes the General Assembly to "recommend measures for the peaceful adjustment of any situation, regardless of origin, which it deems likely to impair the general welfare or friendly relations among nations, including situations resulting from a violation of the provisions of the present Charter setting forth the purposes and principles of the United Nations". The word "measures" implies some kind of action, and the only limitation which Article 14 imposes on the General Assembly is the restriction found in Article 12, namely, that the Assembly should not recommend measures while the Security Council is dealing with the same matter unless the Council requests it to do so. Thus while it is the Security Council which, exclusively, may order coercive action, the functions and powers conferred by the Charter on the General Assembly are not confined to discussion, consideration, the initiation of studies and the making of recommendations; they are not merely hortatory.

              *   *   *

The Court has considered the general problem of the interpretation of Article 17, paragraph 2 * * *. In determining whether the actual expenditures authorized constitute "expenses of the Organization within the meaning of Article 17, paragraph 2, of the Charter", the Court agrees that such expenditures must be tested by their relationship to the purposes of the United Nations in the sense that if an expenditure were made for a purpose which is not one of the purposes of the United Nations, it could not be considered an "expense of the Organization."

The purposes of the United Nations are set forth in Article 1 of the Charter. The first two purposes as stated in paragraphs 1 and 2, may be summarily described as pointing to the goal of international peace and security and friendly relations. The third purpose is the achievement of economic, social, cultural and humanitarian goals and respect for human rights. The fourth and last purpose is: "To be a center for harmonizing the actions of nations in the attainment of these common ends".

The primary place ascribed to international peace and security is natural, since the fulfilment of the other purposes will be dependent upon the attainment of that basic condition. These purposes are broad indeed, but neither they nor the powers conferred to effectuate them are unlimited. Save as they have entrusted the Organization with the attainment of these common ends, the Member States retain their freedom of action. But when the Organization takes action

which warrants the assertion that it was appropriate for the fulfilment of one of the stated purposes of the United Nations, the presumption is that such action is not ultra vires the Organization.

* * *

The expenditures enumerated in the request for an advisory
opinion may conveniently be examined first with reference to UNEF
and then to ONUC. In each case, attention will be paid first to the
operations and then to the financing of the operations.

In considering the operations in the Middle East, the Court must
analyze the functions of UNEF as set forth in resolutions of the General Assembly. Resolution 998 (ES–I) of 4 November 1956 requested the Secretary-General to submit a plan "for the setting up, with
the consent of the nations concerned, of an emergency international
United Nations Force to secure and supervise the cessation of hostilities in accordance with all the terms of" the General Assembly's previous resolution 997 (ES–I) of 2 November 1956. The verb "secure"
as applied to such matters as halting the movement of military forces
and arms into the area and the conclusion of a cease-fire, might suggest measures of enforcement, were it not that the Force was to be
set up "with the consent of the nations concerned".

In his first report on the plan for an emergency international
Force the Secretary-General used the language of resolution 998
(ES–I) in submitting his proposals. The same terms are used in
General Assembly resolution 1000 (ES–I) of 5 November in which
operative paragraph 1 reads:

> Establishes a United Nations Command for an emergency
> international Force to secure and supervise the cessation of hos-
> tilities in accordance with all the terms of General Assembly res-
> olution 997 (ES–I) of 2 November 1956.

This resolution was adopted without a dissenting vote. In his second
and final report on the plan for an emergency international Force of
6 November, the Secretary-General, in paragraphs 9 and 10 stated:

> While the General Assembly is enabled to establish the
> Force with the consent of those parties which contribute units to
> the Force, it could not request the Force to be stationed or oper-
> ate on the territory of a given country without the consent of the
> Government of that country. This does not exclude the possibili-
> ty that the Security Council could use such a Force within the
> wider margins provided under Chapter VII of the United Na-
> tions Charter. I would not for the present consider it necessary
> to elaborate this point further, since no use of the Force under
> Chapter VII, with the rights in relation to Member States that
> this would entail, has been envisaged.

> 10. The point just made permits the conclusion that the
> setting up of the Force should not be guided by the needs which
> would have existed had the measure been considered as part of
> an enforcement action directed against a Member country.
> There is an obvious difference between establishing the Force in

order to secure the cessation of hostilities, with a withdrawal of forces, and establishing such a Force with a view to enforcing a withdrawal of forces.

Paragraph 12 of the Report is particularly important because in resolution 1001 (ES–I) the General Assembly, again without a dissenting vote, "Concurs in the definition of the functions of the Force as stated in paragraph 12 of the Secretary-General's report". Paragraph 12 reads in part as follows:

> the functions of the United Nations Force would be, when a cease-fire is being established, to enter Egyptian territory with the consent of the Egyptian Government, in order to help maintain quiet during and after the withdrawal of non-Egyptian troops, and to secure compliance with the other terms established in the resolution of 2 November 1956. The Force obviously should have no rights other than those necessary for the execution of its functions, in co-operation with local authorities. It would be more than an observers' corps, but in no way a military force temporarily controlling the territory in which it is stationed; nor, moreover, should the Force have military functions exceeding those necessary to secure peaceful conditions on the assumption that the parties to the conflict take all necessary steps for compliance with the recommendations of the General Assembly.

It is not possible to find in this description of the functions of UNEF, as outlined by the Secretary-General and concurred in by the General Assembly without a dissenting vote, any evidence that the Force was to be used for purposes of enforcement. Nor can such evidence be found in the subsequent operations of the Force, operations which did not exceed the scope of the functions ascribed to it.

It could not therefore have been patent on the face of the resolution that the establishment of UNEF was in effect "enforcement action" under Chapter VII which, in accordance with the Charter, could be authorized only by the Security Council.

On the other hand, it is apparent that the operations were undertaken to fulfil a prime purpose of the United Nations, that is, to promote and to maintain a peaceful settlement of the situation. This being true, the Secretary-General properly exercised the authority given him to incur financial obligations of the Organization and expenses resulting from such obligations must be considered "expenses of the Organization within the meaning of Article 17, paragraph 2."

* * *

The operations in the Congo were initially authorized by the Security Council in the resolution of 14 July 1960 which was adopted without a dissenting vote. The resolution, in the light of the appeal from the Government of the Congo, the report of the Secretary-General and the debate in the Security Council, was clearly adopted with a view to maintaining international peace and security. However, it is argued that that resolution has been implemented, in violation of provisions of the Charter inasmuch as under the Charter it is the Security Council that determines which States are to participate in carrying out decisions involving the maintenance of international peace and security, whereas in the case of the Congo the Secretary-General himself determined which States were to participate with their armed forces or otherwise.

     *   *   *

The Security Council resolutions of 14 July, 22 July and 9 August 1960 were noted by the General Assembly in its resolution 1474 (ES–IV) of 20 September, adopted without a dissenting vote, in which it "fully supports" these resolutions. Again without a dissenting vote, on 21 February 1961 the Security Council reaffirmed its three previous resolutions "and the General Assembly resolution 1474 (ES–IV) of 20 September 1960" and reminded "all States of their obligations under these resolutions".

Again without a dissenting vote on 24 November 1961 the Security Council, once more recalling the previous resolutions, reaffirmed "the policies and purposes of the United Nations with respect to the Congo (Leopoldville) as set out" in those resolutions. Operative paragraphs 4 and 5 of this resolution renew the authority to the Secretary-General to continue the activities in the Congo.

In the light of such a record of reiterated consideration, confirmation, approval and ratification by the Security Council and by the General Assembly of the actions of the Secretary-General in implementing the resolution of 14 July 1960, it is impossible to reach the conclusion that the operations in question usurped or impinged upon the prerogatives conferred by the Charter on the Security Council. The Charter does not forbid the Security Council to act through instruments of its own choice: under Article 29 it "may establish such subsidiary organs as it deems necessary for the performance of its functions"; under Article 98 it may entrust "other functions" to the Secretary-General.

It is not necessary for the Court to express an opinion as to which article or articles of the Charter were the basis for the resolutions of the Security Council, but it can be said that the operations of ONUC did not include a use of armed force against a State which the Security Council, under Article 39, determined to have committed an act of aggression or to have breached the peace. The armed forces which were utilized in the Congo were not authorized to take military action against any State. The operation did not involve "preventive or enforcement measures" against any State under Chapter VII and therefore did not constitute "action" as that term is used in Article 11.

For the reasons stated, financial obligations which, in accordance with the clear and reiterated authority of both the Security Council and the General Assembly, the Secretary-General incurred on behalf of the United Nations, constitute obligations of the Organization for which the General Assembly was entitled to make provision under the authority of Article 17.

 *   *   *

For these reasons, The COURT is of opinion, by nine votes to five,

that the expenditures authorized in General Assembly resolutions * * * relating to the United Nations operations in the Congo * * * and the expenditures authorized in General Assembly resolutions * * * relating to the operations of the United Nations Emergency Force constitute "expenses of the Organization" within the meaning of Article 17, paragraph 2, of the Charter of the United Nations.

[A declaration, separate opinions and dissenting opinions omitted.]

———

Aftermath of Certain Expenses case.   Although the General Assembly of the United Nations subsequently adopted a resolution in which it accepted the advisory opinion of the International Court of Justice, members that had refused to recognize peacekeeping expenses as "expenses of the organization" (principally France and the Soviet Union) continued to refuse to accept the court's interpretation of the charter and became in arrears in their payments to the United Nations.   The United States determined to force the issue of Article 19, entailing the loss of vote by those members.   When the assembly met for the Nineteenth Session in December 1964, it was decided to avoid an immediate clash on the issue and the assembly proceeded to do such business as it could without taking any formal votes.   This working arrangement was almost shattered by Albania, however, which forced a formal vote over the question of returning to a normal voting procedure.   The significance of this vote was brushed aside by being denominated procedural, so as to avoid a sharp declaration that the delinquents had lost the right to have their votes counted.

Shortly before the opening of the next session of the assembly, the United States took the position that it would not press for the application of the vote deprivation provisions of Article 19 but that it would reserve its position on the law.   The assembly thus returned, in the fall of 1965, to its normal voting procedures, with no member deprived of a vote for failing to pay UNEF or ONUC assessments.

Years of continuing consideration of the problem in the United Nations have not resulted in a resolution of the constitutional issue of financing peacekeeping, except through practice.

SECTION D.   USE OF UNITED NATIONS AUTHORITY NOT INVOLVING MILITARY FORCE

1.   SOUTH AFRICA: APARTHEID

The racial situation in South Africa has concerned the United Nations since its founding. Numerous resolutions directed toward the abolition of the system of racial separation (apartheid) in that country produced no discernible effect. See, for example, the General Assembly resolution and debate at p. 575. In 1963, the members of the Security Council apparently decided that persuasion and exhortation were insufficient means to correct at least one aspect of that country's policies. Resolution 181 (1963), the text of which follows, was adopted to call upon states to impose an arms embargo. Note the concern of the United States representative with the question of the legal basis under the Charter for the council's action. The council imposed a mandatory embargo by its 1977 resolution, the text of which is on p. 1324. What was the legal basis for that action? Had the United States changed its position on the law, or on the facts? Note the legal position taken by South Africa with respect to the council's action.

SECURITY COUNCIL RESOLUTION 181 (1963) OF AUGUST 7, 1963

Resolutions and Decisions of the Security Council 1963.
U.N. Sec. Council Off. Rec. 18th year, p. 7.

The Security Council,

Having considered the question of race conflict in South Africa resulting from the policies of apartheid of the Government of the Republic of South Africa, as submitted by the thirty-two African Member States,

Recalling its resolution 134 (1960) of 1 April 1960,

Taking into account that world public opinion has been reflected in General Assembly resolution 1761 (XVII) of 6 November 1962, and particularly in its paragraphs 4 and 8,

Noting with appreciation the interim reports adopted on 6 May and 16 July 1963 by the Special Committee on the Policies of apartheid of the Government of the Republic of South Africa,

Noting with concern the recent arms build-up by the Government of South Africa, some of which arms are being used in furtherance of that Government's racial policies,

Regretting that some States are indirectly providing encouragement in various ways to the Government of South Africa to perpetuate, by force, its policy of apartheid,

Regretting the failure of the Government of South Africa to accept the invitation of the Security Council to delegate a representative to appear before it,

Being convinced that the situation in South Africa is seriously disturbing international peace and security,

1. Strongly deprecates the policies of South Africa in its perpetuation of racial discrimination as being inconsistent with the principles contained in the Charter of the United Nations and contrary to its obligations as a Member of the United Nations;

2. Calls upon the Government of South Africa to abandon the policies of apartheid and discrimination, as called for in Security Council resolution 134 (1960), and to liberate all persons imprisoned, interned or subjected to other restrictions for having opposed the policy of apartheid;

3. Solemnly calls upon all States to cease forthwith the sale and shipment of arms, ammunition of all types and military vehicles to South Africa;

4. Requests the Secretary-General to keep the situation in South Africa under observation and to report to the Security Council by 30 October 1963.

> Adopted at the 1056th meeting by 9 votes to none, with 2 abstentions (France, United Kingdom of Great Britain and Northern Ireland).

EXTRACTS FROM DEBATE ON THE ARMS EMBARGO RESOLUTION

U.N. Sec. Council Off. Rec., Plenary Meeting 1056, August 7, 1963.

* * *

3. Mr. FEDORENKO (Union of Soviet Socialist Republics) (translated from Russian): In the course of the Security Council's debate we have heard a number of deeply interesting and cogent speeches by representatives of the African continent, which revealed to the full the tragic situation of the many millions of people of African and Asian origin in the Republic of South Africa who are subjected by Verwoerd's criminal régime to savage racial discrimination, persecution and oppression.

4. It is quite clear that the Security Council is faced with a dangerous situation which is a source of serious international tension and constitutes a threat to peace and security not limited to the continent of Africa.

* * *

5. The Soviet delegation considered and still considers that the Security Council should condemn the racist régime of South Africa in

the strongest possible terms for its most flagrant violation of the elementary rights of the people and its flouting of United Nations decisions and institute immediate economic, political and other sanctions against the Republic of South Africa. It is precisely by this means that the South African racists can be forced to change their criminal and barbaric policies. It has long been time to pass from exhortation and persuasion, from the exercise of mere "moral influence" on the South African racists, as is proposed by the Western Powers, to positive action and decisive measures.

6. As regards the draft resolution submitted to the Security Council by the representatives of Ghana, Morocco and the Philippines [S/5384] it represents, as has already been noted, the very least that the Security Council should do in the present circumstances in order to put a stop to the wild excesses of racism in South Africa and eradicate a hotbed of international tension.

7. Confirmation of this is to be found also in the speech by the representative of Ghana, Mr. Quaison-Sackey, who remarked [1054th meeting] when introducing the draft resolution that "In fact, world opinion expects the Council to take measures which are far more stern that the present draft resolution would ask the Council to take". The same point was also made by the Ministers for Foreign Affairs of Sierra Leone and Tunisia, Mr. Karefa-Smart and Mr. Mongi Slim.

8. However, since the African countries have found it possible to confine themselves at this stage to the measures contained in the draft resolution by Ghana, Morocco and the Philippines, the Soviet delegation will support this draft and will vote for it. Needless to say, in so doing, the Soviet Union has not abandoned its deep conviction of the need to adopt more radical measures against the racist régime in the Republic of South Africa.

* * *

23. Mr. YOST (United States of America): My Government is able to support this resolution because it reflects the attitude of the United States toward the racial policies of the Republic of South Africa. We particularly appreciate the co-operation of the sponsors of the resolution which has facilitated our desire to vote in favour of it. We have, over a period of years, expressed our strong disapproval of the policy of racial discrimination being pursued in South Africa contrary to the obligations of the Republic's Government under Articles 55 and 56 of the Charter. Thus we wholeheartedly endorse the appeal to South Africa to abandon these policies and to liberate those persons who have been imprisoned, interned or subjected to other restrictions merely because they are opposed to the policy of apartheid. My delegation also supports the request that all Member States cease forthwith the sale and shipment of arms, ammunition and military vehicles. As you will recall, Ambassador Stevenson announced in this chamber [1052nd meeting] that the United States Government had taken another important step demonstrating its concern at the continued lack of progress in ending racial discrimination in South

Africa, by voluntarily deciding to end the sale of all military equipment to the Government of South Africa by the end of this year.

* * *

26.   With respect to the eighth preambular paragraph of the resolution, I wish to emphasize that the United States is most gratified that the sponsors have seen fit to change their original formulation from "is seriously endangering international peace and security" to "is seriously disturbing international peace and security". In making this change they clearly recognize that a number of Council members are not prepared to agree that the situation in South Africa is one which now calls for the kind of action appropriate in cases of threats to the peace or breaches of the peace under Chapter VII of the United Nations Charter. As members of the Council are aware, Chapter VII does not speak in terms of disturbances of the peace, even serious ones, but only of actual threats to the peace or breaches of the peace or acts of aggression. The resolution's preambular reference to disturbing the peace thus refers to those underlying elements of this certainly serious situation which, if continued, are likely to endanger the maintenance of international peace and security. This is quite different from finding a fully matured threat to, or breach of, the peace in the present situation. There are in this troubled world many disturbances of international peace and security, but even in those parts of the world where there is now sporadic fighting on international frontiers, this Organization has wisely been cautious about invoking the powers of the Security Council under Chapter VII.

27.   The change in wording to which I have referred has been of the greatest importance in determining the decision of the United States to vote for this resolution; in fact, it was a decisive factor. I might add that the fact that operative paragraphs 2 and 3 of the resolution as adopted call upon Member States to take certain action, does not of course give these paragraphs a mandatory character.

28.   The words "call upon" are found in Chapter VI as well as Chapter VII of the Charter. They have been repeatedly employed by the General Assembly as well as by the Security Council and in the customary practice of the United Nations they do not carry mandatory force.

SECURITY COUNCIL RESOLUTION 418 (1977) OF NOVEMBER 4, 1977

XIV U.N. Monthly Chronicle, December 1977, p. 11.

THE SECURITY COUNCIL,

Recalling its resolution 392 (1976), adopted on 19 June 1976, strongly condemning the racist régime of South Africa for its resort to massive violence against, and wanton killings of, the African people, including schoolchildren and students and others opposing racial discrimination, and calling upon the South African racist régime urgently to end violence against the African people and take urgent steps to eliminate apartheid and racial discrimination,

Recognizing that the military build-up and persistent acts of aggression by South Africa against the neighboring States seriously disturb the security of those States,

Further recognizing that the existing arms embargo must be strengthened and universally applied, without any reservations or qualifications whatsoever, in order to prevent a further aggravation of the grave situation in South Africa,

Taking note of the Lagos Declaration for Action against Apartheid (S/12426),

Gravely concerned that South Africa is at the threshold of producing nuclear weapons,

Strongly condemning the South African Government for its acts of repression, its defiant continuance of the system of apartheid and its attacks against neighbouring independent States,

Considering that the policies and acts of the South African Government are fraught with danger to international peace and security,

Recalling its resolution 181 (1963) and other resolutions concerning a voluntary arms embargo against South Africa,

Convinced that a mandatory arms embargo needs to be universally applied against South Africa in the first instance,

Acting therefore under Chapter VII of the Charter of the United Nations,

1.   Determines, having regard to the policies and acts of the South African Government, that the acquisition by South Africa of arms and related matériel constitutes a threat to the maintenance of international peace and security;

2.   Decides that all States shall cease forthwith any provision to South Africa of arms and related matériel of all types, including the sale or transfer of weapons and ammunition, military vehicles and equipment, paramilitary police equipment, and spare parts for the aforementioned, and shall cease as well the provision of all types of equipment and supplies, and grants of licensing arrangements, for the manufacture or maintenance of the aforementioned;

3.   Calls on all States to review, having regard to the objectives of this resolution, all existing contractual arrangements with and licenses granted to South Africa relating to the manufacture and maintenance of arms, ammunition of all types and military equipment and vehicles, with a view to terminating them;

4.   Further decides that all States shall refrain from any co-operation with South Africa in the manufacture and development of nuclear weapons;

5.   Calls upon all States, including States non-members of the United Nations, to act strictly in accordance with the provisions of this resolution;

6.   Requests the Secretary-General to report to the Council on the progress of the implementation of this resolution, the first report to be submitted not later than 1 May 1978;

7.   Decides to keep this item on its agenda for further action, as appropriate, in the light of developments.

EXTRACTS FROM DEBATE ON THE MANDATORY ARMS EMBARGO RESOLUTION

XIV U.N. Monthly Chronicle, December 1977, p. 8.

Mr. YOUNG (United States) said all could take satisfaction in the adoption of the resolution. It represented a genuine compromise in which Council members demonstrated a willingness to adjust their views to the necessity of reaching an agreement. Success in reaching a compromise through the excellent work of the Council Presidents for October and November demonstrated once again the viability of the Council as a means of corresponding to situations which threatened international peace and security.

*   *   *

It must be made clear to the South African Government that there was a desire for reconciliation, provided it was willing to begin progress towards ending apartheid and the full participation of all South Africans in the political and economic life of the country.

It was gratifying that the unanimous Council vote was accompanied by the vote of an overwhelming majority of 347 to 54 in the House of Representatives of the United States Congress, also expressing concern and condemnation of the acts in South Africa.

The United States looked forward to early South African adherence to the nuclear non-proliferation Treaty and a decision to put all its facilities under international safeguards. It also looked forward to the day when South Africa would no longer be an issue before the Council. It was hoped that resolution 418 (1977) would not mark the beginning of a process of increasing international sanctions against South Africa, but rather the end of a period of growing confrontation between South Africa and the rest of the world.

*   *   *

Mr. TROYANOVSKY (USSR) said the USSR had always taken the view that a mandatory and effective embargo on arms shipments to the South African racist régime, in accordance with the Charter, would help bring pressure to bear on the Pretoria régime, with a view to cutting off the endless chain of crimes committed by racism and apartheid.

That purpose would have been best served by the draft resolutions of the three African countries.[a]

---

a.   The reference here is to the draft resolutions that failed of adoption on October 31, 1977, by reason of the negative votes of France, the United Kingdom and the United States (i. e. vetoes). Canada and the Federal Re-

The resolution adopted by the Council bore the traces of compromise; thus it did not go as far as one might have wished. Nevertheless, the USSR found it possible to support it, since, by its adoption, the Council was in essence taking the first definite step forward in application to South Africa of mandatory sanctions in accordance with Chapter VII of the Charter.

It was the first instance in United Nations history where the Security Council had taken a decision on mandatory sanctions against a Member State on the basis of Chapter VII. That step was an important advance and a basis for further effective measures to be taken by the Council in the fight against racism and apartheid in South Africa.

Given goodwill from Council members, the decision could serve as a point of departure for application of effective economic and other mandatory sanctions against the Pretoria régime, and would become an important milestone on the road to the liberation of the peoples of southern Africa. It was essential that the resolution ordering the embargo on arms shipments to South Africa be strictly implemented.

By adopting the resolution, the Council had taken upon itself a great responsibility. It would have to discharge those obligations in full to the peoples of southern Africa and to the peoples of the whole African continent.

* * *

ELIAS NTLOEDIBE, PAC,[b] said although expectations were raised by the pronouncements of Western countries supporting a mandatory arms embargo, that support came late and fell short. Racist South Africa stated that an arms embargo would not hurt because it was self-sufficient.

While accepting the application of Chapter VII as supportive of the struggle, PAC would continue to be contemptuous of the manoeuvres to apply selectively certain provisions of Chapter VII in order to hijack the effective provisions. The PAC registered its strong disappointment over the negative votes cast on 31 October which killed three draft resolutions containing measures which could have completed the isolation of the fascist régime of Pretoria.

Mass killings were carried out because Western countries, Christian civilized nations, permanent Security Council members, had for the last 17 years assisted the racist régime to stockpile arms to use for oppression. If resolution 418 (1977) had been adopted in 1960, several thousand lives would have been saved and bitterness avoided. It was a symbolic gesture arriving 17 years too late. Western technicians were still in South Africa assisting completion of nuclear-weap-

public of Germany also voted against these resolutions, which would have imposed more drastic restrictions on South Africa, such as restrictions on loans and credits to that country and companies registered there.

b. Pan Africanist Congress of Azania, whose representative was among those invited by the Security Council to speak during the debate.

on capability and the licences granted for local weaponry production made the adoption of the resolution a mockery.

*   *   *

Mr. RICHARD (United Kingdom) said that the United Kingdom rejected totally the claim of the South African Government that it was a staunch defender of Western civilization.

The South African Government was withdrawing behind the barricades. It was deliberately, almost capriciously, cutting itself off from the majority of its own population. Extremism was growing on both sides and those in the middle who advocated at least a start to the dismantling of present barriers spoke with a lonely and muted voice.

The United Kingdom was ready to use the political and economic influence at its disposal to urge and encourage change within South Africa, but not to use it merely as a punitive measure. The United Kingdom's response would in each instance be carefully judged. For many years, Britain had observed a voluntary arms embargo against South Africa. It did not co-operate in the nuclear field. Three years ago, it sought the agreement of British companies operating in South Africa to observe a code of business conduct. The European Economic Community published its own code, one main purpose of which was to encourage the growth of free, non-discriminatory trade unionism and the equal treatment of workers, irrespective of their race.

The United Kingdom carefully considered its responsibilities in the light of recent events and came to the conclusion that acquisition by South Africa of arms and related material in the current situation did constitute a threat to maintenance of international peace and security. The United Kingdom would therefore accept and vote for a mandatory arms embargo under Chapter VII of the Charter. It expected, also, that States not members of the Organization would take immediate and similar action.

Many Members of the Organization would argue that South Africa should be totally ostracized. The problem that all had to face was that a sizable part of the white population of South Africa positively invited such ostracism. For historical reasons with which everyone was familiar, the United Kingdom was more aware than most of the attitudes of the South African white population. It did not want white South Africans to drive themselves into a mental fortress from which they would be unable to escape. Isolation bred further isolation and a mindless contempt for outside opinion. The United Kingdom believed that the South African Government and all South Africans should speak and be listened to.

SOUTH AFRICA SAYS IT IS NOT PREPARED TO BE HELD HOSTAGE TO SECURITY COUNCIL

XIV U.N. Monthly Chronicle, December 1977, p. 9.

In a letter to the United Nations Secretary-General, dated 4 November (S/12439), following the action taken by the Security Council, South Africa stated that the two resolutions adopted said more about the state of the world than about the state of South Africa and were "a supreme example of the hypocrisy" threatening the institutions of the international community.

It was "ludicrous" for the Security Council to pronounce on the freedom of expression in South Africa while, in more than half of its members, the concept hardly existed and, in some cases, was non-existent. No known system was perfect, the letter continued, and South Africa's system was a practical and adaptable system, "which is neither stagnant nor inflexible".

The South African Government was committed to solving its internal political problems by peaceful means, the letter stated. Those who framed the Charter provided that States should have sole responsibility for their own internal affairs. No State could accept the prescriptions of an international body as to how it should deal with its own affairs and no State could accept that its capacity to act in a given domestic situation was qualified by what an outside body might later have to say. South Africa was not prepared to be held hostage to the Security Council in that way.

It was the duty and responsibility of the South African Government, the letter said, to determine what constituted a threat to internal peace. It was not the responsibility of the Security Council, neither did the Council members suffer the consequences of failure to take the necessary steps to maintain internal law and order.

The resolution (418 (1977)) was adopted under Chapter VII of the Charter which required a prior determination that there was a threat to the peace. But the threat to the peace in southern Africa was the threat encouraged and stimulated from abroad. The South African Government did not pose a threat to the peace of any country of the region, stated the letter.

The resolution would serve to stiffen the resolve of South Africans to do what was necessary to defend their country, even if it should be more difficult and demand sacrifice: it would increase the resistance of South Africans to the dictates of outsiders about their own affairs.

The letter noted with particular regret the sponsorship and support of the resolutions by countries of the Western world from which, it stated, a greater sense of responsibility could have been expected. "We leave to their conscience the morality of such callous exploitation of a vulnerable situation which extends far beyond the confines of South Africa," the letter said.

It might well be asked whether they had considered the implications of their action and whether they were prepared to accept full responsibility for what could only be termed incitement to violence.

---

2. NAMIBIA (SOUTH WEST AFRICA)

At the conclusion of the First World War, the Covenant of the League of Nations provided, Article 22, for the establishment of a system of Mandates, whereby advanced nations would be entrusted with the tutelage of colonies and territories formerly belonging to defeated Germany and the Turkish Empire. The covenant adopted "the principle that the well-being and development of such peoples form a sacred trust of civilization."

The allies agreed to confer a Mandate for German South West Africa upon "His Britannic Majesty to be exercised on his behalf by the Government of the Union of South Africa to administer the territory * * *." Under the terms of the Mandate, as defined by the Council of the League, "The Mandatory shall promote to the utmost the material and moral well-being and the social progress of the inhabitants of the territory * * *." League of Nations, Off.Jour., 2nd year No. 1, 89 (1921). In addition, the Mandatory was required to make an annual report to the council indicating the measures taken to carry out its obligations under the terms of the Mandate.

Upon the demise of the League at the founding of the United Nations, a new system of trusteeships was established under Chapter XII of the charter. All states upon whom Mandates had been conferred, except South Africa, made agreements bringing the Mandates into the trusteeship system. The United Nations took the position that it had the legal right to assume the supervisory powers over the Mandate that had previously been exercised by the League; South Africa countered that it had no responsibility to the United Nations. A series of advisory opinions by the International Court of Justice defined the relationship between the United Nations and South Africa with respect to the Mandate; in 1966, a contentious case testing South Africa's performance of its obligations under the Mandate was dismissed by the International Court of Justice for what may be called lack of standing by the states initiating the proceeding, Liberia and Ethiopia.

The General Assembly's Resolution 2145 in October 1966 moved the question of South West Africa to a new level of discourse. The assembly's resolution was followed in 1970 by a Security Council resolution designed to put teeth into the assembly's prior action.

GENERAL ASSEMBLY RESOLUTION 2145 (XXI) OF OCTOBER 27, 1966

U.N. Gen. Ass. Off. Rec., 21st Sess., Supp. No. 16 (A/6316), p. 2.[a]

The General Assembly,

Reaffirming the inalienable right of the people of South West Africa to freedom and independence in accordance with the Charter of the United Nations, General Assembly resolution 1514 (XV) of 14 December 1960 and earlier Assembly resolutions concerning the Mandated Territory of South West Africa,

Recalling the advisory opinion of the International Court of Justice of 11 July 1950,[7] accepted by the General Assembly in its resolution 449 A (V) of 13 December 1950, and the advisory opinions of 7 June 1955 [8] and 1 June 1956 [9] as well as the judgment of 21 December 1962,[10] which have established the fact that South Africa continues to have obligations under the Mandate which was entrusted to it on 17 December 1920 and that the United Nations as the successor to the League of Nations has supervisory powers in respect of South West Africa,

Gravely concerned at the situation in the Mandated Territory, which has seriously deteriorated following the judgment of the International Court of Justice of 18 July 1966,[11]

Having studied the reports of the various committees which had been established to exercise the supervisory functions of the United Nations over the administration of the Mandated Territory of South West Africa,

Convinced that the administration of the Mandated Territory by South Africa has been conducted in a manner contrary to the Mandate, the Charter of the United Nations and the Universal Declaration of Human Rights,

Reaffirming its resolution 2074 (XX) of 17 December 1965, in particular paragraph 4 thereof which condemned the policies of apartheid and racial discrimination practised by the Government of South Africa in South West Africa as constituting a crime against humanity,

Emphasizing that the problem of South West Africa is an issue falling within the terms of General Assembly resolution 1514 (XV),

a. The footnotes in the text are those of the original.

7. International status of South West Africa, Advisory Opinion: I.C.J. Reports 1950, p. 128.

8. South West Africa—Voting procedure, Advisory Opinion of June 7th, 1955: I.C.J. Reports 1955, p. 67.

9. Admissibility of hearings of petitioners by the Committee on South West Africa, Advisory Opinion of June 1st, 1956: I.C.J. Reports 1956, p. 23.

10. South West Africa Cases (Ethiopia v. South Africa; Liberia v. South Africa), Preliminary Objections, Judgment of 21 December 1962: I.C.J. Reports 1962, p. 319.

11. South West Africa, Second Phase, Judgment, I.C.J. Reports 1966, p. 6.

Considering that all the efforts of the United Nations to induce the Government of South Africa to fulfil its obligations in respect of the administration of the Mandated Territory and to ensure the well-being and security of the indigenous inhabitants have been of no avail,

Mindful of the obligations of the United Nations towards the people of South West Africa,

Noting with deep concern the explosive situation which exists in the southern region of Africa,

Affirming its right to take appropriate action in the matter, including the right to revert to itself the administration of the Mandated Territory,

1. Reaffirms that the provisions of General Assembly resolution 1514 (XV) are fully applicable to the people of the Mandated Territory of South West Africa and that, therefore, the people of South West Africa have the inalienable right to self-determination, freedom and independence in accordance with the Charter of the United Nations;

2. Reaffirms further that South West Africa is a territory having international status and that it shall maintain this status until it achieves independence;

3. Declares that South Africa has failed to fulfil its obligations in respect of the administration of the Mandated Territory and to ensure the moral and material well-being and security of the indigenous inhabitants of South West Africa and has, in fact, disavowed the Mandate;

4. Decides that the Mandate conferred upon His Britannic Majesty to be exercised on his behalf by the Government of the Union of South Africa is therefore terminated, that South Africa has no other right to administer the Territory and that henceforth South West Africa comes under the direct responsibility of the United Nations;

5. Resolves that in these circumstances the United Nations must discharge those responsibilities with respect to South West Africa;

6. Establishes an Ad Hoc Committee for South West Africa—composed of fourteen Member States to be designated by the President of the General Assembly—to recommend practical means by which South West Africa should be administered, so as to enable the people of the Territory to exercise the right of self-determination and to achieve independence, and to report to the General Assembly at a special session as soon as possible and in any event not later than April 1967;

7. Calls upon the Government of South Africa forthwith to refrain and desist from any action, constitutional, administrative, political or otherwise, which will in any manner whatsoever alter or tend to alter the present international status of South West Africa;

8.   Calls the attention of the Security Council to the present resolution;

9.   Requests all States to extend their whole-hearted co-operation and to render assistance in the implementation of the present resolution;

10.   Requests the Secretary-General to provide all the assistance necessary to implement the present resolution and to enable the Ad Hoc Committee for South West Africa to perform its duties.

SECURITY COUNCIL RESOLUTION 276 (1970) OF JANUARY 30, 1970

Resolutions and Decisions of the Security Council 1970.
U.N. Sec. Council Off. Rec., 25th year, p. 1.

The Security Council,

Reaffirming the inalienable right of the people of Namibia to freedom and independence recognized in General Assembly resolution 1514 (XV) of 14 December 1960,

Reaffirming General Assembly resolution 2145 (XXI) of 27 October 1966, by which the United Nations decided that the Mandate for South West Africa was terminated and assumed direct responsibility for the Territory until its independence,

Reaffirming Security Council resolution 264 (1969) of 20 March 1969 in which the Council recognized the termination of the Mandate and called upon the Government of South Africa to withdraw immediately its administration from the Territory,

Reaffirming that the extension and enforcement of South African laws in the Territory together with the continued detentions, trials and subsequent sentencing of Namibians by the Government of South Africa constitute illegal acts and flagrant violations of the rights of the Namibians concerned, the Universal Declaration of Human Rights and the international status of the Territory, now under direct United Nations responsibility,

Recalling Security Council resolution 269 (1969) of 12 August 1969,

1.   Strongly condemns the refusal of the Government of South Africa to comply with the resolutions of the General Assembly and Security Council pertaining to Namibia;

2.   Declares that the continued presence of the South African authorities in Namibia is illegal and that consequently all acts taken by the Government of South Africa on behalf of or concerning Namibia after the termination of the Mandate are illegal and invalid;

3.   Declares further that the defiant attitude of the Government of South Africa towards the Council's decisions undermines the authority of the United Nations;

4. Considers that the continued occupation of Namibia by the Government of South Africa in defiance of the relevant United Nations resolutions and of the Charter of the United Nations has grave consequences for the rights and interests of the people of Namibia;

5. Calls upon all States, particularly those which have economic and other interests in Namibia, to refrain from any dealings with the Government of South Africa which are inconsistent with paragraph 2 of the present resolution;

6. Decides to establish, in accordance with rule 28 of its provisional rules of procedure, an Ad Hoc Sub-Committee of the Council to study, in consultation with the Secretary-General, ways and means by which the relevant resolutions of the Council, including the present resolution, can be effectively implemented in accordance with the appropriate provisions of the Charter, in the light of the flagrant refusal of South Africa to withdraw from Namibia, and to submit its recommendations by 30 April 1970;

7. Requests all States, as well as the specialized agencies and other relevant organs of the United Nations, to give the Sub-Committee all the information and other assistance it may require in pursuance of the present resolution;

8. Further requests the Secretary-General to give every assistance to the Sub-Committee in the performance of its task;

9. Decides to resume consideration of the question of Namibia as soon as the recommendations of the Sub-Committee have been made available.

> Adopted at the 1529th meeting by 13 votes to none, with 2 abstentions (France, United Kingdom of Great Britain and Northern Ireland).

ADVISORY OPINION ON THE CONTINUED PRESENCE OF SOUTH AFRICA IN NAMIBIA (SOUTH WEST AFRICA) [a]

International Court of Justice, 1971.
[1971] I.C.J.Rep. 16.

[The Security Council of the United Nations submitted the following question to the International Court of Justice for an advisory opinion:

What are the legal consequences for States of the continued presence of South Africa in Namibia, notwithstanding Security Council resolution 276 (1970)?

The International Court of Justice reviewed the history of the Mandate and its own prior advisory opinions. It concluded that the

---

a. The full name of the case is: Legal Consequences for States of the Continued Presence of South Africa in Namibia (South West Africa), notwithstanding Security Council Resolution 276 (1970), Advisory Opinion.

Mandate had survived the demise of the League, that South Africa's obligations continued unimpaired and that the General Assembly of the United Nations had the authority to exercise the supervisory functions formerly exercised by the Council of the League. In its summary of the events preceding the request for the advisory opinion, the court took note of South Africa's claim of a right to annex South West Africa.]

82. * * * In the present proceedings the representative of South Africa maintained on 15 March 1971:

> * * * if it is accepted that the Mandate has lapsed, the South African Government would have the right to administer the Territory by reason of a combination of factors, being (a) its original conquest; (b) its long occupation; (c) the continuation of the sacred trust basis agreed upon in 1920; and, finally (d) because its administration is to the benefit of the inhabitants of the Territory and is desired by them. In these circumstances the South African Government cannot accept that any State or organization can have a better title to the Territory.

83. These claims of title, which apart from other considerations are inadmissible in regard to a mandated territory, lead by South Africa's own admission to a situation which vitiates the object and purpose of the Mandate. Their significance in the context of the sacred trust has best been revealed by a statement made by the representative of South Africa in the present proceedings on 15 March 1971: "it is the view of the South African Government that no legal provision prevents its annexing South West Africa." As the Court pointed out in its Advisory Opinion on the International Status of South West Africa, "the principle of non-annexation" was "considered to be of paramount importance" when the future of South West Africa and other territories was the subject of decision after the First World War (I.C.J. Reports 1950, p. 131). What was in consequence excluded by Article 22 of the League Covenant is even less acceptable today.

84. Where the United Nations is concerned, the records show that, throughout a period of twenty years, the General Assembly, by virtue of the powers vested in it by the Charter, called upon the South African Government to perform its obligations arising out of the Mandate. * * *

85. Further fruitless negotiations were held from 1952 to 1959. In total, negotiations extended over a period of thirteen years, from 1946 to 1959. In practice the actual length of negotiations is no test of whether the possibilities of agreement have been exhausted; it may be sufficient to show that an early deadlock was reached and that one side adamantly refused compromise. In the case of Namibia (South West Africa) this stage had patently been reached long before the United Nations finally abandoned its efforts to reach agreement. Even so, for so long as South Africa was the mandatory Power the way was still open for it to seek an arrangement. But that chapter came to an end with the termination of the Mandate.

86.   To complete this brief summary of the events preceding the present request for advisory opinion, it must be recalled that in 1955 and 1956 the Court gave at the request of the General Assembly two further advisory opinions on matters concerning the Territory. Eventually the General Assembly adopted resolution 2145 (XXI) on the termination of the Mandate for South West Africa. Subsequently the Security Council adopted resolution 276 (1970), which declared the continued presence of South Africa in Namibia to be illegal and called upon States to act accordingly.

*   *   *

90.   As indicated earlier, with the entry into force of the Charter of the United Nations a relationship was established between all Members of the United Nations on the one side, and each mandatory Power on the other. The mandatory Powers while retaining their mandates assumed, under Article 80 of the Charter, vis-à-vis all United Nations Members, the obligation to keep intact and preserve, until trusteeship agreements were executed, the rights of other States and of the peoples of mandated territories, which resulted from the existing mandate agreements and related instruments, such as Article 22 of the Covenant and the League Council's resolution of 31 January 1923 concerning petitions. The mandatory Powers also bound themselves to exercise their functions of administration in conformity with the relevant obligations emanating from the United Nations Charter, which member States have undertaken to fulfil in good faith in all their international relations.

91.   One of the fundamental principles governing the international relationship thus established is that a party which disowns or does not fulfil its own obligations cannot be recognized as retaining the rights which it claims to derive from the relationship.

92.   The terms of the preamble and operative part of resolution 2145 (XXI) leave no doubt as to the character of the resolution. In the preamble the General Assembly declares itself "Convinced that the administration of the Mandated Territory by South Africa has been conducted in a manner contrary" to the two basic international instruments directly imposing obligations upon South Africa, the Mandate and the Charter of the United Nations, as well as to the Universal Declaration of Human Rights. In another paragraph of the preamble the conclusion is reached that, after having insisted with no avail upon performance for more than twenty years, the moment has arrived for the General Assembly to exercise the right to treat such violation as a ground for termination.

93.   In paragraph 3 of the operative part of the resolution the General Assembly "*Declares* that South Africa has failed to fulfil its obligations in respect of the administration of the Mandated Territory and to ensure the moral and material well-being and security of the indigenous inhabitants of South West Africa and has, in fact, disavowed the Mandate". In paragraph 4 the decision is reached, as a consequence of the previous declaration "that the Mandate conferred

upon His Britannic Majesty to be exercised on his behalf by the Government of the Union of South Africa is *therefore* terminated * * * ". (Emphasis added.) It is this part of the resolution which is relevant in the present proceedings.

94. In examining this action of the General Assembly it is appropriate to have regard to the general principles of international law regulating termination of a treaty relationship on account of breach. * * * The rules laid down by the Vienna Convention on the Law of Treaties concerning termination of a treaty relationship on account of breach (adopted without a dissenting vote) may in many respects be considered as a codification of existing customary law on the subject. In the light of these rules, only a material breach of a treaty justifies termination, such breach being defined as:

(a) a repudiation of the treaty not sanctioned by the present Convention; or

(b) the violation of a provision essential to the accomplishment of the object or purpose of the treaty (Art. 60, para. 3).

95. General Assembly resolution 2145 (XXI) determines that both forms of material breach had occurred in this case. By stressing that South Africa "has, in fact, disavowed the Mandate", the General Assembly declared in fact that it had repudiated it. The resolution in question is therefore to be viewed as the exercise of the right to terminate a relationship in case of a deliberate and persistent violation of obligations which destroys the very object and purpose of that relationship.

* * *

100. The revocability of a mandate was envisaged by the first proposal which was made concerning a mandates system:

> In case of any flagrant and prolonged abuse of this trust the population concerned should be able to appeal for redress to the League, who should in a proper case assert its authority to the full, even to the extent of removing the mandate and entrusting it to some other State if necessary. (J. C. Smuts, The League of Nations: A Practical Sugestion, 1918, pp. 21–22.)

Although this proposal referred to different territories, the principle remains the same. The possibility of revocation in the event of gross violation of the mandate was subsequently confirmed by authorities on international law and members of the Permanent Mandates Commission who interpreted and applied the mandates system under the League of Nations.

* * *

106. By resolution 2145 (XXI) the General Assembly terminated the Mandate. However, lacking the necessary powers to ensure the withdrawal of South Africa from the Territory, it enlisted the cooperation of the Security Council by calling the latter's attention to the resolution, thus acting in accordance with Article 11, paragraph 2, of the Charter.

* * *

108.   Resolution 276 (1970) of the Security Council, specifically mentioned in the text of the request, is the one essential for the purposes of the present advisory opinion.   *   *   *
*   *   *

110.   As to the legal basis of the resolution, Article 24 of the Charter vests in the Security Council the necessary authority to take action such as that taken in the present case.   The reference in paragraph 2 of this Article to specific powers of the Security Council under certain chapters of the Charter does not exclude the existence of general powers to discharge the responsibilities conferred in paragraph 1.   Reference may be made in this respect to the Secretary-General's Statement, presented to the Security Council on 10 January 1947, to the effect that "the powers of the Council under Article 24 are not restricted to the specific grants of authority contained in Chapters VI, VII, VIII and XII   *   *   *   the Members of the United Nations have conferred upon the Security Council powers commensurate with its responsibility for the maintenance of peace and security.   The only limitations are the fundamental principles and purposes found in Chapter I of the Charter."

111.   As to the effect to be attributed to the declaration contained in paragraph 2 of resolution 276 (1970), the Court considers that the qualification of a situation as illegal does not by itself put an end to it.   It can only be the first, necessary step in an endeavour to bring the illegal situation to an end.

112.   It would be an untenable interpretation to maintain that, once such a declaration had been made by the Security Council under Article 24 of the Charter, on behalf of all member States, those Members would be free to act in disregard of such illegality or even to recognize violations of law resulting from it.   When confronted with such an internationally unlawful situation, Members of the United Nations would be expected to act in consequence of the declaration made on their behalf.   The question therefore arises as to the effect of this decision of the Security Council for States Members of the United Nations in accordance with Article 25 of the Charter.

113.   It has been contended that Article 25 of the Charter applies only to enforcement measures adopted under Chapter VII of the Charter.   It is not possible to find in the Charter any support for this view.   Article 25 is not confined to decisions in regard to enforcement action but applies to "the decisions of the Security Council" adopted in accordance with the Charter.   Moreover, that Article is placed, not in Chapter VII, but immediately after Article 24 in that part of the Charter which deals with the functions and powers of the Security Council.   If Article 25 had reference solely to decisions of the Security Council concerning enforcement action under Articles 41 and 42 of the Charter, that is to say, if it were only such decisions which had binding effect, then Article 25 would be superfluous, since this effect is secured by Articles 48 and 49 of the Charter.

114.   It has also been contended that the relevant Security Council resolutions are couched in exhortatory rather than mandatory lan-

guage and that, therefore, they do not purport to impose any legal duty on any State nor to affect legally any right of any State. The language of a resolution of the Security Council should be carefully analysed before a conclusion can be made as to its binding effect. In view of the nature of the powers under Article 25, the question whether they have been in fact exercised is to be determined in each case, having regard to the terms of the resolution to be interpreted, the discussions leading to it, the Charter provisions invoked and, in general, all circumstances that might assist in determining the legal consequences of the resolution of the Security Council.

115. Applying these tests, the Court recalls that in the preamble of resolution 269 (1969), the Security Council was *"Mindful* of its responsibility to take necessary action to secure strict compliance with the obligations entered into by States Members of the United Nations under the provisions of Article 25 of the Charter of the United Nations". The Court has therefore reached the conclusion that the decisions made by the Security Council in paragraphs 2 and 5 of resolution 276 (1970), as related to paragraph 3 of resolution 264 (1969) and paragraph 5 of resolution 269 (1969), were adopted in conformity with the purposes and principles of the Charter and in accordance with its Articles 24 and 25. The decisions are consequently binding on all States Members of the United Nations, which are thus under obligation to accept and carry them out.

116. In pronouncing upon the binding nature of the Security Council decisions in question, the Court would recall the following passage in its Advisory Opinion of 11 April 1949 on Reparation for Injuries Suffered in the Service of the United Nations:

> The Charter has not been content to make the Organization created by it merely a centre "for harmonizing the actions of nations in the attainment of these common ends" (Article 1, para. 4). It has equipped that centre with organs, and has given it special tasks. It has defined the position of the Members in relation to the Organization by requiring them to give it every assistance in any action undertaken by it (Article 2, para. 5), and to accept and carry out the decisions of the Security Council. (I.C.J. Reports 1949, p. 178.)

Thus when the Security Council adopts a decision under Article 25 in accordance with the Charter, it is for member States to comply with that decision, including those members of the Security Council which voted against it and those Members of the United Nations who are not members of the Council. To hold otherwise would be to deprive this principal organ of its essential functions and powers under the Charter.

117. Having reached these conclusions, the Court will now address itself to the legal consequences arising for States from the continued presence of South Africa in Namibia, notwithstanding Security Council resolution 276 (1970). A binding determination made by a competent organ of the United Nations to the effect that a situation

is illegal cannot remain without consequence. Once the Court is faced with such a situation, it would be failing in the discharge of its judicial functions if it did not declare that there is an obligation, especially upon Members of the United Nations, to bring that situation to an end. As this Court has held, referring to one of its decisions declaring a situation as contrary to a rule of international law: "This decision entails a legal consequence, namely that of putting an end to an illegal situation" (I.C.J. Reports 1951, p. 82).

118. South Africa, being responsible for having created and maintained a situation which the Court has found to have been validly declared illegal, has the obligation to put an end to it. It is therefore under obligation to withdraw its administration from the Territory of Namibia. By maintaining the present illegal situation, and occupying the Territory without title, South Africa incurs international responsibilities arising from a continuing violation of an international obligation. It also remains accountable for any violations of its international obligations, or of the rights of the people of Namibia. The fact that South Africa no longer has any title to administer the Territory does not release it from its obligations and responsibilities under international law towards other States in respect of the exercise of its powers in relation to this Territory. Physical control of a territory, and not sovereignty or legitimacy of title, is the basis of State liability for acts affecting other States.

119. The member States of the United Nations are, for the reasons given in paragraph 115 above, under obligation to recognize the illegality and invalidity of South Africa's continued presence in Namibia. They are also under obligation to refrain from lending any support or any form of assistance to South Africa with reference to its occupation of Namibia, subject to paragraph 125 below.

120. The precise determination of the acts permitted or allowed —what measures are available and practicable, which of them should be selected, what scope they should be given and by whom they should be applied—is a matter which lies within the competence of the appropriate political organs of the United Nations acting within their authority under the Charter. Thus it is for the Security Council to determine any further measures consequent upon the decisions already taken by it on the question of Namibia. In this context the Court notes that at the same meeting of the Security Council in which the request for advisory opinion was made, the Security Council also adopted resolution 283 (1970) which defined some of the steps to be taken. The Court has not been called upon to advise on the legal effects of that resolution.

121. The Court will in consequence confine itself to giving advice on those dealings with the Government of South Africa which, under the Charter of the United Nations and general international law, should be considered as inconsistent with the declaration of illegality and invalidity made in paragraph 2 of resolution 276 (1970), because they may imply a recognition that South Africa's presence in Namibia is legal.

122. For the reasons given above, and subject to the observations contained in paragraph 125 below, member States are under obligation to abstain from entering into treaty relations with South Africa in all cases in which the Government of South Africa purports to act on behalf of or concerning Namibia. With respect to existing bilateral treaties, member States must abstain from invoking or applying those treaties or provisions of treaties concluded by South Africa on behalf of or concerning Namibia which involve active intergovernmental cooperation. With respect to multilateral treaties, however, the same rule cannot be applied to certain general conventions such as those of a humanitarian character, the non-performance of which may adversely affect the people of Namibia. It will be for the competent international organs to take specific measures in this respect.

123. Member States, in compliance with the duty of non-recognition imposed by paragraphs 2 and 5 of resolution 276 (1970), are under obligation to abstain from sending diplomatic or special missions to South Africa including in their jurisdiction the Territory of Namibia, to abstain from sending consular agents to Namibia, and to withdraw any such agents already there. They should also make it clear to the South African authorities that the maintenance of diplomatic or consular relations with South Africa does not imply any recognition of its authority with regard to Namibia.

124. The restraints which are implicit in the non-recognition of South Africa's presence in Namibia and the explicit provisions of paragraph 5 of resolution 276 (1970) impose upon member States the obligation to abstain from entering into economic and other forms of relationship or dealings with South Africa on behalf of or concerning Namibia which may entrench its authority over the Territory.

125. In general, the non-recognition of South Africa's administration of the Territory should not result in depriving the people of Namibia of any advantages derived from international co-operation. In particular, while official acts performed by the Government of South Africa on behalf of or concerning Namibia after the termination of the Mandate are illegal and invalid, this invalidity cannot be extended to those acts, such as, for instance, the registration of births, deaths and marriages, the effects of which can be ignored only to the detriment of the inhabitants of the Territory.

126. As to non-member States, although not bound by Articles 24 and 25 of the Charter, they have been called upon in paragraphs 2 and 5 of resolution 276 (1970) to give assistance in the action which has been taken by the United Nations with regard to Namibia. In the view of the Court, the termination of the Mandate and the declaration of the illegality of South Africa's presence in Namibia are opposable to all States in the sense of barring erga omnes the legality of a situation which is maintained in violation of international law: in particular, no State which enters into relations with South Africa concerning Namibia may expect the United Nations or its Members to recognize the validity or effects of such relationship, or of the consequences thereof. The Mandate having been terminated by decision

of the international organization in which the supervisory authority over its administration was vested, and South Africa's continued presence in Namibia having been declared illegal, it is for non-member States to act in accordance with those decisions.

127. As to the general consequences resulting from the illegal presence of South Africa in Namibia, all States should bear in mind that the injured entity is a people which must look to the international community for assistance in its progress towards the goals for which the sacred trust was instituted.ª

* * *

132. The Government of South Africa also submitted a request that a plebiscite should be held in the Territory of Namibia under the joint supervision of the Court and the Government of South Africa (para. 16 above). This proposal was presented in connection with the request to submit additional factual evidence and as a means of bringing evidence before the Court. The Court having concluded that no further evidence was required, that the Mandate was validly terminated and that in consequence South Africa's presence in Namibia is illegal and its acts on behalf of or concerning Namibia are illegal and invalid, it follows that it cannot entertain this proposal.

* * *

133. For these reasons,

The COURT is of Opinion, in reply to the question:

"What are the legal consequences for States of the continued presence of South Africa in Namibia, notwithstanding Security Council resolution 276 (1970) ?"

by 13 votes to 2,

(1) that, the continued presence of South Africa in Namibia being illegal, South Africa is under obligation to withdraw its administration from Namibia immediately and thus put an end to its occupation of the Territory;

by 11 votes to 4,

(2) that States Members of the United Nations are under obligation to recognize the illegality of South Africa's presence in Namibia and the invalidity of its acts on behalf of or concerning Namibia, and to refrain from any acts and in particular any dealings with the Government of South Africa implying recognition of the legality of, or lending support or assistance to, such presence and administration;

(3) that it is incumbent upon States which are not Members of the United Nations to give assistance, within the scope of subparagraph (2) above, in the action which has been taken by the United Nations with regard to Namibia.

[A declaration and separate and dissenting opinions omitted.]

a. Paragraphs 128 through 131 of the opinion are set forth at p. 585 in the context of the United Nations Charter obligations respecting human rights.

1. *Security Council action.* By Resolution 301 (1971) of October 20, 1971 (Resolutions and Decisions of the Security Council, 1971, Sec. Council Off. Rec., 26th year p. 7), the Security Council took note of the advisory opinion and stated that it agreed with its opinion as expressed in paragraph 133. It called upon South Africa to withdraw from the Territory of Namibia and further:

11.   Calls upon all States, in the discharge of their responsibilities towards the people of Namibia and subject to the exceptions set forth in paragraphs 122 and 125 of the advisory opinion of 21 June 1971:

(a) To abstain from entering into treaty relations with South Africa in all cases in which the Government of South Africa purports to act on behalf of or concerning Namibia;

(b) To abstain from invoking or applying those treaties or provisions of treaties concluded by South Africa on behalf of or concerning Namibia which involve active intergovernmental cooperation;

(c) To review their bilateral treaties with South Africa in order to ensure that they are not inconsistent with paragraphs 5 and 6 above;

(d) To abstain from sending diplomatic or special missions to South Africa that include the Territory of Namibia in their jurisdiction;

(e) To abstain from sending consular agents to Namibia and to withdraw any such agents already there;

(f) To abstain from entering into economic and other forms of relationship or dealings with South Africa on behalf of or concerning Namibia which may entrench its authority over the Territory;

12.   Declares that franchises, rights, titles or contracts relating to Namibia granted to individuals or companies by South Africa after the adoption of the General Assembly resolution 2145 (XXI) are not subject to protection or espousal by their States against claims of a future lawful Government of Namibia
*   *   *.

The resolution was adopted by a vote of 13 to none, with France and the United Kingdom abstaining.

2. *Legal basis for actions by the General Assembly and the Security Council of the United Nations.* Was the action of the assembly in terminating the Mandate legislative in character or can it be explained as merely the act of a party to an agreement declaring that, in its opinion, the agreement has been terminated by the other party's breach?

Is the court's view, in Paragraphs 110, 113 and 115, of the power of the Security Council to make legally binding decisions justified by the charter? If the Security Council is not limited to making binding decisions only in Chapter VII cases involving breaches of the peace, what are the limits now? Must it be acting in the "maintenance of international peace and security," under the first paragraph of Article 24? Or is it limited only by the "fundamental principles and purposes found in Chapter 1 of the Charter"? See Paragraph 110 of the court's opinion. If such an expansive reading is possible, then the limits are (a) formal, i. e. the existence of the veto, and (b) practical, i. e. the unwillingness of the council to exercise force to enforce even its legally binding resolutions.

3. *Efforts to secure withdrawal of South Africa from Namibia.* Although South Africa agreed to cooperate with a United Nations plan to lead the Territory of Namibia to independence (see XVI U.N. Monthly Chronicle, January 1979, p. 5), no significant movement in that direction had been made by December 1980. A number of resolutions were adopted by the General Assembly on December 12 condemning South Africa and calling for the Security Council to impose mandatory sanctions, to force compliance with United Nations resolutions. Members of the majority voting on one such resolution (125 in favor, to none against, with 17 abstentions) "strongly condemned the manoeuvres of South Africa to impose in Namibia a so-called internal settlement, designed to give a semblance of power to a puppet régime and a cover of legality to racist occupation, as an alternative to SWAPO, and reaffirmed that a just and durable settlement of the question of Namibia was possible only with the direct and full participation of SWAPO, the sole and authentic representative of the Namibian people." XVII U.N. Monthly Chronicle, January 1980, p. 20.

---

2. SOUTHERN RHODESIA

Although Southern Rhodesia was largely a self-governing territory rather than strictly a colony in the British system, it was not fully independent up until the 1960's. Because it was governed by a white majority, the United Kingdom was unwilling to grant it independence until satisfactory constitutional arrangements were arrived at in Rhodesia to provide improvements in the political powers of the black minority. Negotiations between the British and the governing regime in Southern Rhodesia having failed, Southern Rhodesia declared its independence on November 11, 1965 (an act referred to as Unilateral Declaration of Independence or UDI).

A series of resolutions in the Security Council of the United Nations condemned UDI, called on the United Kingdom to quell the rebellion and even specifically called on the United Kingdom to prevent, by force if necessary, the delivery of oil by tankers destined for Rhodesia. Security Council Resolutions 216 and 217 [a] (1965) of Novem-

a. Resolutions and Decisions of the Security Council 1965. U.N.Sec. Council Off.Rec., 20th Year, p. 8.

ber 12, 1965 and 221 [b] (1966) of April 9, 1966. Selective Sanctions were voted by the council in Resolution 232 [c] (1966) of December 16, 1966. Stating that it was acting in accordance with Articles 39 and 41 of the United Nations Charter, the council determined "that the present situation in Southern Rhodesia constitutes a threat to international peace and security." The council thereupon decided that all States Members of the United Nations shall prevent:

(a) the import into their territories of asbestos, iron ore, chrome, pig-iron, sugar, tobacco, copper, meat and meat products and hides, skins and leather originating in Southern Rhodesia and exported therefrom after the date of this resolution;

(b) any activities by their nationals or in their territories which promote or are calculated to promote the export of their commodities from Southern Rhodesia and any dealings by their nationals or in their territories in any of these commodities originating in Southern Rhodesia and exported therefrom after the date of this resolution, including in particular any transfer of funds to Southern Rhodesia for the purposes of such activities or dealings.

These measures having failed, the council adopted more comprehensive sanctions two years later.

SECURITY COUNCIL RESOLUTION 253 (1968)
OF MAY 29, 1968

Resolutions and Decisions of the Security Council 1968.
U.N. Sec. Council Off. Rec., 23rd year, p. 5.

The Security Council,

Recalling and reaffirming its resolutions 216 (1965) of 12 November 1965, 217 (1965) of 20 November 1965, 221 (1966) of 9 April 1966, and 232 (1966) of 16 December 1966,

Taking note of resolution 2262 (XXII) adopted by the General Assembly on 3 November 1967,

Noting with great concern that the measures taken so far have failed to bring the rebellion in Southern Rhodesia to an end,

* * *

Reaffirming its determination that the present situation in Southern Rhodesia constitutes a threat to international peace and security,

Acting under Chapter VII of the Charter of the United Nations,

* * *

3. Decides that, in furtherance of the objective of ending the rebellion, all States Members of the United Nations shall prevent:

b. Resolutions and Decisions of the Security Council 1966. U.N.Sec. Council Off.Rec., 21st Year, p. 5.

c. Resolutions and Decisions of the Security Council 1966. U.N.Sec. Council Off.Rec., 21st Year, p. 7.

(a) The import into their territories of all commodities and products originating in Southern Rhodesia and exported therefrom after the date of this resolution (whether or not the commodities or products are for consumption or processing in their territories, whether or not they are imported in bond and whether or not any special legal status with respect to the import of goods is enjoyed by the port or other place where they are imported or stored);

(b) Any activities by their nationals or in their territories which would promote or are calculated to promote the export of any commodities or products from Southern Rhodesia; and any dealings by their nationals or in their territories in any commodities or products originating in Southern Rhodesia and exported therefrom after the date of this resolution, including in particular any transfer of funds to Southern Rhodesia for the purposes of such activities or dealings;

(c) The shipment in vessels or aircraft of their registration or under charter to their nationals, or the carriage (whether or not, in bond) by land transport facilities across their territories of any commodities or products originating in Southern Rhodesia and exported therefrom after the date of this resolution;

(d) The sale or supply by their nationals or from their territories of any commodities or products (whether or not originating in their territories, but not including supplies intended strictly for medical purposes, educational equipment and material for use in schools and other educational institutions, publications, news material and, in special humanitarian circumstances, food-stuffs) to any person or body in Southern Rhodesia or to any other person or body for the purposes of any business carried on in or operated from Southern Rhodesia, and any activities, by their nationals or in their territories which promote or are calculated to promote such sale or supply;

(e) The shipment in vessels or aircraft of their registration, or under charter to their nationals, or the carriage (whether or not in bond) by land transport facilities across their territories of any such commodities or products which are consigned to any person or body in Southern Rhodesia, or to any other person or body for the purposes of any business carried on in or operated from Southern Rhodesia;

4.   Decides that all States Members of the United Nations shall not make available to the illegal régime in Southern Rhodesia or to any commercial, industrial or public utility undertaking, including tourist enterprises, in Southern Rhodesia any funds for investment or any other financial or economic resources and shall prevent their nationals and any persons within their territories from making available to the régime or to any such undertaking any such funds or resources and from remitting any other funds to persons or bodies within Southern Rhodesia, except payments exclusively for pensions or for strictly medical, humanitarian or educational purposes or for

the provision of news material and in special humanitarian circumstances, foodstuffs;

5.   Decides that all States Members of the United Nations shall:

(a) Prevent the entry into their territories, save on exceptional humanitarian grounds, of any person travelling on a Southern Rhodesian passport, regardless of its date of issue, or on a purported passport issued by or on behalf of the illegal régime in Southern Rhodesia;

(b) Take all possible measures to prevent the entry into their territories of persons whom they have reason to believe to be ordinarily resident in Southern Rhodesia and whom they have reason to believe to have furthered or encouraged, or to be likely to further or encourage, the unlawful actions of the illegal régime in Southern Rhodesia or any activities which are calculated to evade any measure decided upon in this resolution or resolution 232 (1966) of 16 December 1966;

6.   Decides that all States Members of the United Nations shall prevent airline companies constituted in their territories and aircraft of their registration or under charter to their nationals from operating to or from Southern Rhodesia and from linking up with any airline company constituted or aircraft registered in Southern Rhodesia;

7.   Decides that all States Members of the United Nations shall give effect to the decisions set out in operative paragraphs 3, 4, 5 and 6 of this resolution notwithstanding any contract entered into or licence granted before the date of this resolution;

*   *   *

11.   Calls upon all States Members of the United Nations to carry out these decisions of the Security Council in accordance with Article 25 of the Charter of the United Nations and reminds them that failure or refusal by any one of them to do so would constitute a violation of that Article;

*   *   *

Adopted unanimously at the 1428th meeting.

UNITED STATES EXTENDS PROGRAM BANNING TRADE WITH SOUTHERN RHODESIA

59 United States Department of State Bulletin 199 (1968).

The President on July 29 signed an Executive order implementing United Nations Security Council Resolution No. 253 of May 29, 1968, which extends the program of mandatory economic sanctions against Southern Rhodesia.

The President acted under the United Nations Participation Act of 1945, as amended. Section 5 of the act empowers the President to implement Security Council decisions adopted pursuant to article 41 of the United Nations Charter.

* * *

This Executive order prohibits these activities covered by the resolution, including transactions involving commodities and products exported from Southern Rhodesia after May 29 (the date of the resolution). The order delegates to the Secretaries of Commerce, the Treasury, and Transportation authority to promulgate regulations necessary to carry out the prohibitions. The Secretary of Commerce on July 16 acted under authority of the Export Control Act to impose the further restrictions on exports to Southern Rhodesia called for by the resolution. The further regulations required under the Executive order will be issued shortly and will be effective July 29. The prohibitions of Executive Order No. 11322 of January 5, 1967, implementing Security Council Resolution No. 232 of December 16, 1966, continue in effect.

It is a criminal offense to engage in the prohibited activities. Provision will be made in the regulations to deal with cases of undue hardship arising from transactions commenced before the date of the order.

In Resolution No. 253 the Security Council also decided that member states shall prevent the entry into their territory of persons traveling on Southern Rhodesian passports and take all possible measures to prevent the entry of individuals ordinarily resident in Southern Rhodesia who are likely to further or encourage the illegal regime or evade the economic sanctions. The Departments of State and Justice are implementing these provisions under the Immigration and Nationality Act.

The mandatory sanctions imposed by the Security Council's resolution of May 29 supplement the selective mandatory sanctions imposed in December 1966 and the earlier voluntary measures taken by a large majority of the members of the United Nations in response to the Council's appeal of November 20, 1965, just after the Smith regime in Southern Rhodesia had unilaterally declared its independence, that economic relations with Southern Rhodesia be broken. The United States is fully supporting the Security Council resolutions.

UNITED STATES DISCUSSES ENFORCEMENT OF SANCTIONS AGAINST RHODESIA

66 United States Department of State Bulletin 490 (1972).

[Statement by Ambassador Phillips, United States Representative in United Nations Security Council, February 28, 1972.]

The United States Government, both inside and outside of the U. N., has supported the right of self-determination and has opposed the odious practice of racial discrimination.

From the inception, the United States has voted for Security Council decisions imposing mandatory economic sanctions against the rebel regime in Rhodesia. I submit that the United States has been second to none in the vigorous enforcement of these sanctions. The effectiveness of the action of my government is documented in the reports of the Sanctions Committee.

Members of the Council are aware of a special situation affecting the United States enforcement of the sanctions on Rhodesia. I refer, of course, to the so-called Byrd provision of the military procurement bill, the provisions of which I am certain are well known to all around this table.

The considerations leading to the enactment into law of the Byrd provision emerged clearly in the statements and testimony on the legislation in our Congress. Among these was the concern of Congressmen that while the United States was becoming dependent on a single high-priced source of chrome ore, Rhodesian ore was being exported in quantity to other countries. Since the United States was scrupulously observing the sanctions, U. S. executive officials found it impossible to offer any persuasive refutation of this conclusion. The Congress felt that for compelling reasons of national security the United States should not be placed in a distinctly disadvantageous position with regard to the importation of strategic commodities.

It is an inescapable fact of life that this legislation, having been duly enacted according to our constitutional processes, is now the law of the land. However, as Ambassador Bush made clear both at Addis and in later statements in various African countries he was privileged to visit, the United States remains interested in seeing that sanctions work. I reaffirm that we stand ready to assist the Sanctions Committee in its efforts, and we pledge that we will continue our full participation in its activities.

However, Mr. President, we also believe that this Council should face squarely the true nature of the problem confronting the U. N. concerning the effectiveness of the sanctions program.

The United States continues to be committed to the sanctions program voted in Security Council Resolution 253 of 1968, but we also believe that the enforcement of these sanctions by other countries is patently inadequate. It seems to us that countries that are open with information about their imports are at a disadvantage visa-vis countries that are not open with such information. To put it more bluntly, there are widespread violations of the sanctions which are not being brought to light, while the light is being focused on relatively unimportant exceptions to the application of sanctions in the case of my country. Others have during this debate alluded to this aspect of the sanctions program.

Let us be blunt about the nature of the problem. The sanctions are not going to work if there is a double standard about compliance with them. There are countries around this very table that have consistently voted for the sanctions and that say they favor strengthening the machinery, yet which may be violators of the program.

The first and essential step is to acknowledge that sanctions, while they have had a measurable effect on the Rhodesian economy, have not been working very well with respect to a number of Rhodesian exports for a long period of time. Rhodesian exports continue at levels which appear to approximate, and in some cases exceed, presanctions levels. This can be explained only by a widespread pattern of violation of or indifference to the requirements of the sanctions effort.

There have been alleged violations which concern at least nine countries sitting in this Council, including most of the permanent members. In fairness both to the countries against which the allegations have been made and to the countries which have tried scrupulously to adhere to the sanctions, these allegations should be investigated.

The fourth report of the Sanctions Committee established that Rhodesian indirect exports to world markets through third countries rose from $8 million in 1966 to $215 million in 1970. It is common knowledge that in the last few years Rhodesia has been able to export the bulk of its mineral output. These exports must go somewhere—and they did not go to the United States.

It is notable that the fourth report of the Sanctions Committee points out that exports of chrome ore from South Africa to some major industrial countries more than doubled and in one case rose more than 10 times within the past 4 years. Many of the importing countries are members of this Security Council, and it is most difficult to escape the presumption that much of this increased purchase of ore did come from Rhodesia. As members of the Council are aware, we have been unable to obtain general agreement that where there is reasonable question as to the origin of imported minerals, those minerals be subject to the effective chemical tests that are available. And, as you know, only the United Kingdom, the United States, and Denmark have actually taken steps to prosecute firms found to be in violation of sanctions.

Mr. President, in 1965 Rhodesia exported $67 million in strategic materials.

All indications are that Rhodesia's exports of strategic commodities in 1970 were as high as or higher than the 1965 exports, and none of those commodities were imported into the United States. Somebody bought these goods. Somebody has been buying them each year since sanctions went into effect. And it was not the United States, which has scrupulously enforced the sanctions program. In short, the United States has not been the problem.

As a result of our recent legislation, the United States no longer prohibits the importation of strategic commodities from Rhodesia. But let us keep this in perspective. Prior to sanctions, however, United States imports of those commodities amounted to less than 2 percent of Rhodesia's total presanctions exports. The United States continues, therefore, to enforce scrupulously the embargo on commodities which constitute 98 percent of Rhodesia's presanctions exports. The Byrd provision therefore is only a very small part of the problem, and the United States is prepared to report all exceptions under it. In 1968, 1969, 1970, and 1971, all indications are that Rhodesian exports of strategic commodities were as high or higher than they were in 1965. In these 4 years, the United States took only one lot, which had been paid for before sanctions. That one lot represented 6 percent of 1 year's production of only one commodity and less than one-half of 1 percent of Rhodesia's total exports through third countries. I say again, the United States has not been the problem.

My government therefore suggests that this Council ask the Sanctions Committee to request from governments periodic reports on the importation of strategic minerals from all sources. The list of minerals should show worldwide trade in all those key commodities which are also produced in Rhodesia. The reports should also indicate sources of origin for each item or commodity. Reports of this nature should greatly assist the Sanctions Committee to obtain a fuller picture of on-going trade with Rhodesia. We could envisage that in case of questionable shipments, the committee would be able to request and obtain samples of such shipments and subject those samples to chemical analysis to determine their origin. My government would be prepared to cooperate fully in this effort.

* * *

DIGGS v. SHULTZ, SECRETARY OF TREASURY

United States Court of Appeals, District of Columbia, 1972.
470 F.2d 461.

McGOWAN, Circuit Judge: This is an appeal from the dismissal by the District Court of a complaint seeking declaratory and injunctive relief in respect of the importation of metallurgical chromite from Southern Rhodesia. The gravamen of this action was an asserted conflict between (1) the official authorization of such importation by the United States, and (2) the treaty obligations of the United States under the United Nations Charter. Plaintiff-appellants sought summary judgment, as did defendant-appellees alternatively to a motion to dismiss for failure to state a claim upon which relief could be given.

The District Court's ruling for appellees was grounded primarily upon lack of standing, but it encompassed as well a concept of the nonjusticiability of the issues raised. Although we believe there was standing upon the part of at least some of the appellants to pursue their cause of action judicially, we think that cause is not one in respect of which relief can be granted. Accordingly, we affirm the judgment of dismissal.

I

In 1966 the Security Council of the United Nations, with the affirmative vote of the United States, adopted Resolution 232 directing that all member states impose an embargo on trade with Southern Rhodesia—a step which was reaffirmed and enlarged in 1968. In compliance with this resolution, the President of the United States issued Executive Orders 11322 and 11419, 22 U.S.C. § 287c, establishing criminal sanctions for violation of the embargo. In 1971, however, Congress adopted the so-called Byrd Amendment to the Strategic and Critical Materials Stock Piling Act, 50 U.S.C. § 98–98h, which provides in part:

> Sec. 10. Notwithstanding any other provision of law * * *
> the President may not prohibit or regulate the importation into
> the United States of any material determined to be strategic and
> critical pursuant to the provisions of this Act, if such material is
> the product of any foreign country or area not listed as a Com-
> munist-dominated country or area * * * for so long as
> the importation into the United States of material of that kind
> which is the product of such Communist-dominated countries or
> areas is not prohibited by any provision of law.

Since Southern Rhodesia is not a Communist-controlled country, and inasmuch as the United States imports from Communist countries substantial quantities of metallurgical chromite and other materials available from Rhodesia, the Byrd Amendment contemplated the resumption of trade by this country with Southern Rhodesia. By direction of the President, the Office of Foreign Assets Control issued to the corporate appellees in this case a General License authorizing the importation of various materials from Southern Rhodesia, and they began importation.

Alleging that the Byrd Amendment did not and could not authorize issuance of such a license contrary to this country's treaty obligations, appellants sought to enjoin further importation, to require official seizure, and to restrain use, of materials already imported under the General License, and to declare the General License null and void.

II

The question of standing turns first on whether the party seeking relief has alleged a sufficient personal interest in the controversy to insure concrete adverseness in the presentation of the issues. Data Processing Service v. Camp, 397 U.S. 150, 152, 90 S.Ct. 827 (1969); Baker v. Carr, 369 U.S. 186, 204, 82 S.Ct. 691 (1962). Appellants allege various personal injuries, and we agree with the District Court that these allegations amply provide the injury in fact element of the standing requirement.[1]

---

1. We adopt the District Court's identification of those plaintiffs who meet
   the injury in fact requirement. Appellants M'Gabe and Zimbabive com-

Another requirement of standing is that the complainant be within the zone of interests sought to be protected by the law in question. Data Processing Service v. Camp, 397 U.S. 150, 153, 90 S.Ct. 827 (1969). United Nations Security Council Resolution 232 was— and is—an attempt by means of concerted international pressure to turn the Rhodesian Government away from the course of action which has resulted in the adverse circumstances experienced by appellants. They are unquestionably within the reach of its purpose and among its intended beneficiaries.

Finally, the concept of standing has been characterized as contemplating that there be a "logical nexus between the status asserted and the claim sought to be adjudicated," in order to insure that the litigant is the proper party to represent the interests involved. Flast v. Cohen, 392 U.S. 83, 102, 88 S.Ct. 1942, 1953 (1967).[2] The District Court found the causal relationship of appellants' claims to the challenged actions too attenuated to constitute such a nexus. That finding rested largely on the conclusion that appellants' quarrel was really with the Rhodesian Government rather than with appellees. But that view fails to focus on the exact nature of the grievance appearing in the complaint.

Appellants, along with many other persons, have suffered, and continue to suffer, tangible injuries at the hands of Southern Rhodesia. In an attempt to terminate the policies giving rise to those wrongs, the United Nations, with the United States as an assenting member, established the embargo. The precise injury of which appellants complain in this law suit is allegedly illegal present action by the United States which tends to limit the effectiveness of the embargo and thereby to deprive appellants of its potential benefits. That quarrel is directly and immediately with this government, and not with Southern Rhodesia.

Appellees suggest that the prospects of significant relief by means of the embargo are so slight that this relationship of intended benefit is too tenuous to support standing. But this strikes us as tantamount to saying that because the performance of the United Nations is not always equal to its promise, the commitments of a mem-

---

plain they are unable to return to their homeland, Rhodesia. Appellants Diggs, Conyers, Rangel, Stokes and Franck all alleged that they have been refused entry into Rhodesia; and the American Committee on Africa complains that its chairman has also been denied entry. The Council for Christian Social Action of the United Church of Christ alleges its missionaries have been arrested and deported from Rhodesia. Appellant Vidal asserts injury because sale of one of his books is banned in Rhodesia. None of the other plaintiffs have standing; and it is not contended in this court that they have.

2. It is far from clear that this formulation adds anything of substance to the two requirements just discussed. It states a proposition that can well be thought to be related to the merits of a claim rather than to the existence of standing to press it. The District Court, with some support in Supreme Court language, chose to pursue the question as an aspect of standing, although the rationale followed by it is relevant to its dismissal for failure to state a claim warranting relief.

ber may be disregarded without having to respond in court to a charge of treaty violation. It may be that the particular economic sanctions invoked against Southern Rhodesia in this instance will fall short of their goal, and that appellants will ultimately reap no benefit from them. But, to persons situated as are appellants, United Nations action constitutes the only hope; and they are personally aggrieved and injured by the dereliction of any member state which weakens the capacity of the world organization to make its policies meaningful.

Of course it is true that appellants' plight stems initially from acts done by Southern Rhodesia, and that their primary quarrel is with it. But this does not foreclose the existence of a judicially cognizable dispute between appellants, on the one hand, and appellees, on the other, who are said to be acting in derogation of the solemn treaty obligation of the United States to adhere to the embargo for so long as it is in being.[3]

III

The District Court, in its comments to the effect that non-justiciability would necessitate dismissal of the complaint even if standing be found, reasoned as follows: It is settled constitutional doctrine that Congress may nullify, in whole or in part, a treaty commitment. Congress, by the Byrd Amendment in 1971, acted to abrogate one aspect of our treaty obligations under the U.N. Charter, that is to say, our continued participation in the economic sanctions taken against Southern Rhodesia. The considerations underlying that step by Congress present issues of political policy which courts do not inquire into. Thus, appellants' quarrel is with Congress, and it is a cause which can be pursued only at the polls and not in the courts.

In this court appellants do not seriously contest the first of these propositions, namely, the constitutional power of Congress to set treaty obligations at naught.[4] They seek, rather, to show that, in the

---

3. The passage of the Byrd Amendment was the subject of widespread notice and comment within the United Nations, resulting in the reaffirmation by the Security Council on February 8, 1972 of the sanctions against Southern Rhodesia. The resolution to this end declared that any legislation passed by any member state "with a view to permitting, directly or indirectly, the importation from Southern Rhodesia of any commodity falling within the scope of obligations imposed (by the 1968 resolution), including chrome ore, would undermine sanctions and would be contrary to the obligations of States."

4. Moser v. United States, 341 U.S. 41, 45, 71 S.Ct. 553 (1951); Clark v. Al-

len, 331 U.S. 503, 508–9, 67 S.Ct. 1431 (1947); Pigeon River Co. v. Cox, 291 U.S. 138, 160, 54 S.Ct. 361 (1934); Edge v. Robertson, 112 U.S. 580, 597, 5 S.Ct. 247 (1884).

Although appellants concede that Congress has the power to override treaty obligations (Appellants' Br. at 23), they contend that our commitment to the U.N. has more force than an ordinary treaty. Appellants argue on the basis of their interpretation of the U.N. Charter that Congress could override Resolution 232 only by withdrawing from the U.N. entirely. There is, however, no evidence that this country's membership in that organization was intended to be on the all-or-nothing basis suggested by appellants.

Byrd Amendment, Congress did not really intend to compel the Executive to end United States observance of the Security Council's sanctions, and that, therefore, it is the Executive which is, without the essential shield of Congressional dispensation, violating a treaty engagement of this country. Appellants point out in this regard that the Byrd Amendment does not in terms require importation from Southern Rhodesia, but leaves open two alternative courses of action. The statute says the President may not ban importation from Rhodesia of materials classified as critical and strategic unless importation from Communist countries is also prohibited. Instead of permitting resumption of trade with Rhodesia, the President, so it is said, could (1) have banned importation of these materials from Communist nations as well as from Rhodesia, or (2) have taken steps to have these materials declassified, thereby taking them in either case out of the scope of the Byrd Amendment.

Citing the canon of construction that a statute should, if possible, be construed in a manner consistent with treaty obligations, appellants argue that the Byrd Amendment, although discretionary on its face, should be construed to compel the President to take one or the other of these two steps as a means of escape from the necessity of breaching the U.N. Charter. But these alternatives raise questions of foreign policy and national defense as sensitive as those involved in the decision to honor or abrogate our treaty obligations.[5] To attempt to decide whether the President chose properly among the three alternatives confronting him "would be not to decide a judicial controversy, but to assume a position of authority over the governmental acts of another and co-equal department, an authority which plainly we do not possess." Frothingham v. Mellon, 262 U.S. 447, 489, 43 S.Ct. 597, 601 (1923).

We think that there can be no blinking the purpose and effect of the Byrd Amendment. It was to detach this country from the U.N. boycott of Southern Rhodesia in blatant disregard of our treaty undertakings. The legislative record shows that no member of Congress voting on the measure was under any doubt about what was involved then; and no amount of statutory interpretation now can

---

5. Russia supplied 60 per cent of our metallurgical chromite in 1970 while the embargo was being observed by the United States, S.Rep.No.92–359, 92d Cong., 1st Sess., 121 (1971), and a decision to discontinue importation would be a serious step in a very delicate area. Similarly, the decision to remove certain materials from the critical and strategic list should be done in a manner consistent with the objectives of that act. 50 U.S.C.A. § 98. Appellants' view would require reclassification of materials without regard to whether they continue to be critical to national defense. Appellants argue that the apparent surplus in the stockpile indicates the materials are no longer critical. This confuses two distinct functions under the act. One is classification of materials as strategic or critical in order to encourage their development in this country and to avoid dangerous dependency upon other nations. The other is the acquisition of certain quantities of these materials to be stockpiled for use in an emergency. A surplus in the stockpile at a given moment does not mean that it is no longer necessary to be concerned about the dependency of this country on outside sources for the materials in question.

make the Byrd Amendment other than what it was as presented to the Congress, namely, a measure which would make—and was intended to make—the United States a certain treaty violator. The so-called options given to the President are, in reality, not options at all. In any event, they are in neither case alternatives which are appropriately to be forced upon him by a court.[6]

Under our constitutional scheme, Congress can denounce treaties if it sees fit to do so, and there is nothing the other branches of government can do about it. We consider that this is precisely what Congress has done in this case; and therefore the District Court was correct to the extent that it found the complaint to state no tenable claim in law.

Affirmed.

Wilbur K. MILLER, Senior Circuit Judge, concurs in the result.

Questions. Ambassador Phillips and the Court of Appeals assume without question that the United States is legally bound internationally to comply with the Security Council's directive to apply economic sanctions. Is it clear that the Security Council's directive is lawful under the Charter? The council purported to act under Articles 39 and 41. What was the factual basis for the finding that the "present situation in Southern Rhodesia constitutes a threat to international peace and security?" [a] Or is that question irrelevant? That is, can the following be said to be the law of the Charter? Once the Security Council has found under Article 39 that there is a threat to the peace it has the power to require member states to take whatever actions it deems appropriate under Article 41 and member states are obligated to comply with its directive by reason of Article 25, since the council's findings of fact under Article 39 are conclusive.

SECURITY COUNCIL RESOLUTION 320 (1972), OF SEPTEMBER 29, 1972

IX U.N. Monthly Chronicle, October 1972, p. 29.

The Security Council,

Recalling its resolution 253 (1968) of 29 May 1968 and subsequent resolutions in which all States are required to implement and

---

6. The Supreme Court in Baker v. Carr was at pains to point out that the so-called "political question doctrine" is an aspect of the separation of powers prescribed by the Federal Constitution; and that, in the intra-federal context, it continues to have meaningful vitality to restrain interference by one branch of the federal establishment with concerns committed to another. The case before us is a classic one for the careful appraisal by a court of the consequences of an exercise of jurisdiction it may technically be thought to have.

a. Compare Fenwick, When is There a Threat to the Peace?—Rhodesia, 61 Am.J.Int'l L. 753 (1967), with McDougal and Reisman, Rhodesia and the United Nations: The Lawfulness of International Concern, 62 Am.J. Int'l L. 1 (1968).

make effective the economic, political and other sanctions against Southern Rhodesia (Zimbabwe) decided upon by the Council in furtherance of the objective of ending the rebellion in that territory,

Taking into account its resolutions 314 (1972) of 28 February 1972 and 318 (1972) of 28 July 1972 concerning the co-operation and obligations of States and the measures necessary to ensure the scrupulous observance and strict implementation of sanctions,

Deeply concerned that, despite their obligations under Article 25 of the Charter, several States continue to violate sanctions covertly and overtly in contravention of the provisions of resolution 253 (1968),

Gravely concerned about the detrimental consequences which violations could cause to the effectiveness of sanctions and, in the wider sense, to the authority of the Council,

Deeply concerned by the report of the United States that it has authorized the importation of chrome ore and other minerals from Southern Rhodesia (Zimbabwe),

Condemning the refusal of South Africa and Portugal to co-operate with the United Nations in the observance and implementation of sanctions against Southern Rhodesia (Zimbabwe),

1. Reaffirms its decision that sanctions against Southern Rhodesia (Zimbabwe) shall remain fully in force until the aims and objectives set out in resolution 253 (1968) are completely achieved;

2. Calls upon all States to implement fully all Security Council resolutions establishing sanctions against Southern Rhodesia (Zimbabwe) in accordance with Article 25 and Article 2(6) of the Charter;

3. Urges the United States to co-operate fully with the United Nations in the effective implementation of sanctions;

4. Requests the Security Council Committee established in pursuance of resolution 253 (1968) concerning the Question of Southern Rhodesia to undertake, as a matter of urgency, consideration of the type of action which could be taken in view of the open and persistent refusal of South Africa and Portugal to implement sanctions against the illegal régime in Southern Rhodesia (Zimbabwe) and to report to the Council not later than 31 January 1973;

5. Further requests the Committee to examine and submit a report to the Security Council not later than 31 January 1973 on all proposals and suggestions made at the 1663rd to 1666th meetings of the Council for extending the scope and improving the effectiveness of sanctions against Southern Rhodesia (Zimbabwe).

PRESIDENT SIGNS BILL RESTORING EMBARGO ON RHODESIAN CHROME

76 United States Department of State Bulletin 333 (1977).

[Following is a statement by President Carter issued on March 18.]

I have today signed H.R. 1746 [Public Law 95–12], which restores executive authority to enforce sanctions against Rhodesian chrome.

This measure is a central element in our African policy. Members of my Administration have supported it with one voice. With it, we are bringing the United States back in line with the decisions of the Security Council and with our obligations under the United Nations Charter.

H.R. 1746 effectively reinstates an embargo against the importation of Rhodesian chrome and other minerals, as well as any steelmill product containing Rhodesian chromium. As a matter of equity, however, I am issuing an Executive order [No. 11978] which authorizes the Secretary of the Treasury to exempt shipments now in transit to the United States.

Our country is committed to the concept of rapid transition to majority rule in Rhodesia under nonviolent conditions. I view this measure today as an appropriate and positive step toward that goal. We have consistently stated our belief that a peaceful solution in Rhodesia depends upon negotiations that involve a full spectrum of opinion among its leaders, both black and white. With the enactment of this measure, there can be no mistake about our support for that principle.

I hope that the present Rhodesian authorities, as well as the black African nationalist leaders, will accurately assess the vote of the Congress and this Administration's stand on Rhodesia. The solution rests in their hands, not ours. Further delay in negotiations will invite more violence and increase the prospect of outside intervention —an outcome which every person of good will wishes to avoid.

With the cooperation of the Congress, we have taken a step of great importance in our southern African policy. I want to thank the leadership of both Houses for their initiative in bringing about this encouraging development.

SOUTHERN RHODESIA SETTLEMENT

United States Department of State Bulletin
February 1980, p. 11.

Department Statement, Dec. 15, 1979

With the arrival of the British Governor in Salisbury on December 12, the United Kingdom has assumed legal and constitutional authority in Rhodesia, and a process leading to impartial elections and independence has begun. The British Government has taken this action on the basis of proposals developed by the parties at the Lancaster House conference.

On the Governor's arrival, ordinances have come into effect which establish the powers of the Election Commissioner and make provision for the Election Council. All parties which agree to campaign peacefully will be able to do so freely. All parties which wish to participate in the elections have been invited to register. The British Government is taking the legislative action necessary to bring into force those parts of the independence constitution required for elections to be held.

It has been heartening that the two delegations led by Bishop Muzorewa and Messrs. Nkomo and Mugabe have accepted the basic principles of all the proposals elaborated by the British delegation in the Lancaster House negotiations. The remaining issues relate to some aspects of the implementation of the cease-fire. On December 11, British Foreign Secretary Lord Carrington presented detailed cease-fire proposals which we believe provide the assurances necessary for the Patriotic Front to have confidence in the conditions under which the elections will take place.

Having studied all the British proposals presented at Lancaster House for the constitution, the transitional arrangements, and the cease-fire, it is our judgment that they are fair and make possible an impartial election leading to a just settlement of the Rhodesian conflict.

In these circumstances, it seems clear that the aims and objectives of the U.N. sanctions as set forth in the relevant resolutions of the Security Council, have, in fact, been achieved.

President Carter, in explaining his November 14 decision to maintain sanctions against Rhodesia, stated that he would be prepared to lift sanctions when a British Governor assumes authority in Salisbury and a process leading to impartial elections has begun. These conditions have now been met, and the President has ordered, effective midnight the 16th of December, that U.S. sanctions against Rhodesia be lifted.

COUNCIL LIFTS SANCTIONS AGAINST SOUTHERN RHODESIA

XVII U.N. Chronicle, No. 1, January 1980, p. 13.

On 21 December [1979], the Security Council decided to call upon Member States of the United Nations "to terminate the measures taken against Southern Rhodesia under Chapter VII of the Charter pursuant to resolutions 232 (1966), 253 (1968) and subsequent related resolutions on the situation in Southern Rhodesia." The Council took this action having regard to the agreement reached at the Lancaster House Conference in London.

At the same time the Council called upon the administering Power, the United Kingdom, to ensure that no South African or other external forces, regular or mercenary, would remain in or enter Southern Rhodesia, except those forces provided for under the Lancaster House agreement. Resolution 460 (1979) was adopted by a vote of 13 in favour to none against with 2 abstentions (Czechoslovakia, USSR).

Under other provisions of the resolution, the Council called upon all Member States and the United Nations specialized agencies to provide urgent assistance to Southern Rhodesia and the front-line States (Angola, Botswana, Mozambique, United Republic of Tanzania, Zambia) for reconstruction purposes and to facilitate repatriation of all refugees or displaced persons to Southern Rhodesia.

The Council reaffirmed the inalienable right of the people of Zimbabwe to self-determination, freedom and independence and commended the Member States, particularly the front-line States, for their implementation of the Security Council resolutions on sanctions against Southern Rhodesia.

The Council called for strict adherence to the agreements reached, and for full and faithful implementation by the administering Power and all the parties concerned. It decided to dissolve its sanctions established under resolution 253 (1968). It decided to keep the situation in Southern Rhodesia under review until the Territory attained full independence.

In December 1966, under resolution 232 (1966), the Council, for the first time in the history of the United Nations, imposed selective mandatory sanctions against Southern Rhodesia. Those sanctions were imposed against certain exports from and imports to the Territory. The exports included certain minerals as well as certain animal and agricultural products. The imports were all military in nature. When that failed to bring about the desired result, the Council in May 1968, by resolution 253 (1968), decided to extend the sanctions to include all exports from and imports to Southern Rhodesia, except for medical and educational supplies and, in special circumstances, foodstuffs.

The Council had met at the request of the United Kingdom, contained in a letter of 21 December to the Council President (S/13698). The letter referred to an earlier letter of 12 December from the United Kingdom to the Council President (S/13688) in which it was stated that the assumption of full legislative and executive authority over Southern Rhodesia by a British Governor had been made on 3 December. His authority had been accepted by the commanders of the military and police forces and the leading civil authorities there and, accordingly, the state of rebellion in the Territory had been brought to an end.

The letter of 12 December also stated that the obligations of Member States under Article 25 of the United Nations Charter in relation to those measures were, in the view of the United Kingdom

Government, to be regarded as having been discharged. That being so, the United Kingdom was terminating the measures taken by it pursuant to the decisions adopted by the Council in regard to the then situation of illegality.

Secretary-General Sees Opportunity, Challenge

In a statement after the adoption of the resolution, the United Nations Secretary-General, Kurt Waldheim, said that the resumption of normal relations with Southern Rhodesia provided both an opportunity and a challenge for the international community and particularly for those neighbouring States whose economies were so closely linked to that country.

He said that the successful outcome of the Lancaster House Conference created a new situation for the countries of the region. In all cases, the economic and social structures had been seriously disrupted. There would, therefore, be an urgent requirement for international assistance on a massive scale to enable those countries to restore their economies and to take advantage of the opportunities which peace and security would provide.

The assistance required would involve rebuilding basic facilities which had been destroyed in the fighting, rehabilitating transport and communication networks, particularly railroads and ports. It would also take advantage of the new opportunities, for the revival of agriculture, industry and services in the region.

*

INDEX

The text of many of the documents indexed appears in the Documentary Supplement to this casebook.

References are to Pages

END OF VOLUME